S0-ARN-964

Immigration Law Library
U.S. Citizenship and Naturalization Handbook
2013-2014 Edition

by Daniel Levy

Update Editor

Charles Roth

under the auspices of the National Immigration Project
of the National Lawyers Guild

THOMSON REUTERS

For Customer Assistance Call 1-800-328-4880

Mat #41285175

ISBN: 978–0314–61170–3

In Memoriam

Daniel Levy died on September 14, 2001 in Los Angeles at the age of 48. A wonderful human being, a dedicated civil rights attorney, immigrant rights advocate, scholar, and computer wizard, Daniel was the recipient of the National Immigration Project's Carol King Award for 2001 and the American Immigration Lawyers Association's Edith Lowenstein Memorial Award. He also was a member of the legal team in several landmark immigration victories. See *Gorbach v. Reno,* 219 F.3d 1087 (9th Cir. 2000) (halting INS' attempts to denaturalize people administratively) *Walters v. Reno,* 145 F.3d 1032 (9th Cir 1998) (finding INS' procedures violated due process).

Daniel unselfishly shared his wisdom with countless practitioners, law students, and legal workers. A long-time National Lawyers Guild and National Immigration Project member, he leaves his wife, two children, and hundreds of devoted friends.

A fund has been set up to help Daniel Levy's family. Donations should be sent to:

"Raquel Ackerman, Custodian of Antonio Levy and Eva Levy"
c/o Bernard Wolfsdorf
17383 Sunset Boulevard, Suite 120
Pacific Palisades, CA 90272
e-mail: Bernard@Wolfsdorf.com

Acknowledgments

This handbook would have been impossible without the assistance of many persons. My first debt of gratitude is to the National Lawyers Guild, which invited me to write this book. Lynn Alvarez, Mary Ann Heimann, Dan Kesselbrenner, Steve Keogh, Karen Miksch, Larry Siems, and Alex Zisman reviewed and corrected several chapters of the first edition of this book. Their keen eye for detail has made this a much better book. Patricia Mariani and Juan Osuna of Federal Publications granted permission to reproduce material that had first appeared in Immigration Briefings and Interpreter Releases. Robert Mautino graciously agreed to allow the author to reproduce some of his materials, and Amy Novick granted permission to reproduce materials that appeared in AILA's 1998-99 Immigration and Nationality Law Handbook. The certificates and INS forms reproduced in this Handbook were specifically provided for that purpose by the Los Angeles District of the INS, and I hereby acknowledge its assistance. Charles Wheeler and Tomas Olmos granted me a leave of absence in order to write the first edition of this handbook. My deepest debt of gratitude is to my wife Raquel and to my children, Antonio and Eva. Not only did Raquel take over some of my parenting responsibilities during the production of the book, but the three of them stoically accepted my weekend absences while working on the book. This book was written and revised on time which by right was theirs. To them I dedicate the book.

Daniel Levy

Table of Contents

CHAPTER 1. OVERVIEW

CHAPTER 2. BIRTH IN THE U.S. AND ITS POSSESSIONS

CHAPTER 3.   NONCITIZEN NATIONALS

I.   UNINCORPORATED POSSESSIONS

II.   ACQUISITION OF NONCITIZEN NATIONALITY

VI.   PERSONS BORN ABROAD ON OR AFTER NOVEMBER 14, 1986

VII.   SPECIAL CASES

VIII.   PROOF OF CITIZENSHIP

CHAPTER 5. DERIVATION OF CITIZENSHIP AFTER BIRTH

I. INTRODUCTION

II. APPLICABLE PRINCIPLES

III. DERIVATIVE CITIZENSHIP PROVISIONS UNDER SPECIFIC LAWS

D. FAILURE TO PASS EXAMINATION

VIII. LEGAL COMPETENCE/CAPACITY TO TAKE OATH

IX. RACE AND NATIONAL ORIGIN

CHAPTER 8. REMOVABILITY AND REMOVAL PROCEEDINGS

I. INTRODUCTION

CHAPTER 9. NATURALIZATION PROCEDURE: APPLICATION AND EXAMINATION

I. INTRODUCTION

II. INITIAL APPLICATION

A. WHAT, WHERE AND WHEN TO FILE

B. WITHDRAWAL, AMENDMENT, AND TRANSFER OF APPLICATION

III. THE N-400

A. INTRODUCTION

B. QUESTION-BY-QUESTION ANALYSIS

C. ADDITIONAL DOCUMENTS AND FORMS

IV. FINGERPRINTING

CHAPTER 10. FEDERAL JUDICIAL REVIEW

§ 10:1   Overview of judicial review

I. JUDICIAL REVIEW OVER NATURALIZATION

II. JUDICIAL REVIEW OTHER CITIZENSHIP MATTERS

CHAPTER 11. NATURALIZATION OF SPECIAL CLASSES: SPOUSES, WIDOWS AND WIDOWERS, CHILDREN, AND OTHERS

CHAPTER 13.   PROOF OF CITIZENSHIP

I.   INTRODUCTION

II.   BIRTH CERTIFICATE

III.   U.S. PASSPORT

IV.   CONSULAR REPORT OF BIRTH

V.   CERTIFICATE OF CITIZENSHIP

VI.   SPECIAL PROVISIONS FOR PERSONS BORN BEFORE MAY 24, 1934, TO U.S. CITIZEN MOTHERS

VII.   U.S. CITIZENSHIP CARD FOR AMERICAN INDIANS AND MEMBERS OF COMMONWEALTH OF NORTHERN MARIANA

VIII.   CERTIFICATE OF NATURALIZATION

IX.   AMENDING AND REPLACING CITIZENSHIP-RELATED DOCUMENTS

X.   CANCELLATION OF DHS DOCUMENTS

XI.   OTHER RECORDS

CHAPTER 14.   REVOCATION OF NATURALIZATION

I.   INTRODUCTION

II.   BASES FOR DENATURALIZATION

A.   IN GENERAL

B.   FRAUD, CONCEALMENT AND WILLFUL MISREPRESENTATION

C. ILLEGAL PROCUREMENT

III. PROCEDURES IN JUDICIAL DENATURALIZATION PROCEEDINGS

IV. PRESUMPTIONS AND SPECIAL CASES

V. DENATURALIZATION ANCILLARY TO CRIMINAL CONVICTION FOR NATURALIZATION FRAUD

VI. ADMINISTRATIVE DENATURALIZATION

VII. CONSEQUENCES OF DENATURALIZATION

CHAPTER 15. RELINQUISHMENT OF CITIZENSHIP: EXPATRIATION STATUTES

I. GENERAL PRINCIPLES

II. STRUCTURE OF CURRENT LOSS OF CITIZENSHIP PROVISIONS

Chapter 1

Overview

I. OVERVIEW

Research References

West's Key Number Digest
Aliens, Immigration and Citizenship ⚷650 to 751

Westlaw Databases
Immigration Law Service (2d ed.) (IMMLS2D)
Steel on Immigration Law (STEEL)

Treatises and Practice Aids
Steel on Immigration Law, Ch 15

KeyCite®: Cases and other legal materials listed in KeyCite Scope can be researched through the KeyCite service on Westlaw®. Use KeyCite to check citations for form, parallel references, prior and later history, and comprehensive citator information, including citations to other decisions and secondary materials.

I. OVERVIEW

§ 1:1 Sources of U.S. citizenship; generally

Research References
Steel on Immigration Law §§ 15:1, 15:8

The Supreme Court has stated on occasion that there are "two sources of citizenship, and two only: birth and naturalization."[1] Perhaps this is so; but if so, the Supreme Court is using the word "naturalization" to mean considerably more than

---

[Section 1:1]

[1]United States v. Wong Kim Ark, 169 U. S. 649, 702 (1898); Miller v. Albright, 523 U.S. 420, 424 (1998).

its meaning under the statute.[2] The Supreme Court's formulation hides a truly dizzying array of legal issues and challenges.

For instance, Congress makes certain classes of persons not born in the United States citizens automatically, at birth. The Fourteenth Amendment specifically grants citizenship to "[a]ll persons born or naturalized in the United States and subject to the jurisdiction thereof."[3] Individuals acquiring citizenship though born abroad are not "in the United States" when they become citizens, and thus are not covered directly by the Fourteenth Amendment.[4] Congress has treated individuals acquiring citizenship at birth as "natural born citizens."[5] Are such individuals naturalized? The answer is not entirely clear.[6]

This is but an example of the odd and interesting world of citizenship law. The INA contains more than a dozen means of naturalization after birth, in addition to the "normal" route requiring five years after obtaining permanent resident status.[7] Individuals may obtain citizenship by treaty or by Congressional act when Congress makes a territory part of the United States.[8] Sometimes Congress may take away citizenship; sometimes it chooses thereafter to give it back.[9] This book seeks to cover all the rules and varieties of citizenship, whether simple or complex, which may confront the immigration practitioner.

§ 1:2 Sources of U.S. citizenship; generally—Vesting of U.S. citizenship

Research References

Steel on Immigration Law §§ 15:2, 15:4

U.S. citizenship vests upon almost all persons who are born inside the United States. The rights of citizenship attach to these individuals without any action on their part. Americans are so familiar with this principle that virtually no one born inside the United States would doubt his or her right to U.S. citizenship.

Some persons born to U.S. citizen parents abroad or in the outlying possessions of the U.S. may also be U.S. citizens at birth. As with being born inside the United States, the rights of citizenship attach to these persons automatically. However, the rules that determine who is a U.S. citizen at birth outside the United States are complex and depend on the person's date of birth.

Some children automatically derive U.S. citizenship when their parents become citizens. The rules governing derivative citizenship are similar to those governing U.S. citizenship at birth abroad in that they vary according to the date the relevant event occurred. However, the requirements for derivative citizenship have been more consistent throughout the years than the rules relating to birth abroad.

---

[2]8 U.S.C.A. § 1101(a)(23) (defining naturalization as "the conferring of nationality of a state upon a person after birth, by any means whatsoever").

[3]U.S. Const. amend. XIV, § 1.

[4]See, e.g., Rogers v. Bellei, 401 U.S. 815, 91 S.Ct. 1060, 28 L.Ed.2d 499 (1971) ("acquisition of citizenship by being born abroad of an American parent" is "not covered by the Fourteenth Amendment" but is instead "left to proper Congressional action").

[5]See § 1:7.

[6]Miller v. Albright, 523 U.S. 420, 480 (1998) (Breyer, J., dissenting) ("Congress does not believe that [acquisition] of citizenship involves 'naturalization.' ").

[7]See generally, Chs. 11, 12.

[8]See generally, §§ 2:1 et seq.

[9]See, e.g., §§ 11:12, 11:30, 12:2.

On October 30, 2000, President Clinton signed into law the Child Citizenship Act of 2000, which provides a new method for automatically becoming a U.S. citizen. Under this law, some children of U.S. citizens, who reside in the United States as lawful permanent residents, automatically become U.S. citizens in the United States if they are under the age of eighteen and under the legal and physical custody of their U.S. citizen parent.

Some persons who are born in territories controlled by the U.S. acquire an intermediate status between citizenship and alienage. They are considered noncitizen nationals. This special status provides some of the benefits of citizenship, such as not being considered a noncitizen for purposes of immigration laws. However, the political rights associated with citizenship are beyond the reach of these people.

Part I of this book presents all the ways in which citizenship and nationality can vest automatically. Ch 2 discusses birth inside the United States. It explores the changing definition of *United States* for purposes of citizenship at birth, and the exemption of certain persons from the rule that persons born inside the United States are citizens at birth. Ch 3 discusses noncitizen nationality and the rights of people who have such status. It also covers the process through which noncitizen nationals can become U.S. citizens. Ch 4 explores the vesting of citizenship upon children born to U.S. citizens abroad and in outlying possessions of the U.S. Ch 5 discusses the acquisition of U.S. citizenship upon the naturalization of a parent or parents.

§ 1:3 Sources of U.S. citizenship; generally—Naturalization

Most persons born outside the United States do not acquire U.S. citizenship automatically. If they wish to become citizens, they have to undergo an administrative process called naturalization. Before 1990, this process was almost exclusively the purview of the courts. However, the Immigration Act of 1990 transferred jurisdiction from the courts to the Immigration and Naturalization Service (INS). The INS was abolished in 2003, and the responsible agency is now the United States Citizenship and Immigration Services (USCIS) of the Department of Homeland Security (DHS).[1]

The requirements and the process of naturalization can vary tremendously according to the category under which the person naturalizes. There is one basic model of naturalization from which all the different naturalization procedures derive; this is the naturalization of lawful permanent residents who have resided continuously in the United States for five years. This model has then been altered and relaxed to fit the different conditions applicable to special groups, such as noncitizens serving in the U.S. armed forces or spouses of U.S. citizens.

Part II of this book discusses all the forms of naturalization. Chs 7 to 10 discuss the basic naturalization model. Ch 11 discusses the naturalization procedures avail-

---

[Section 1:3]

[1]Up until March 1, 2003, the agency primarily responsible for carrying out the immigration laws of the United States was the Immigration and Naturalization Service (INS). The Homeland Security Act of 2002, Pub. L. No. 107-296, 116 Stat. 2135 (2002), abolished the INS and transferred the majority of its functions to various bureaus within the Department of Homeland Securty (DHS). See §§ 1:9 to 1:11 for an overview of these changes. In this edition of this book, the legacy INS will be referred to with respect to past practices and policies. Current agency references will, wherever possible, be to the particular bureau within DHS designated to carry out the relevant function. Where there is one bureau or department that is responsible, the agency reference will simply be to DHS.

able to all special groups with the exception of military-based naturalization. Ch 12 discusses the special requirements and procedures available to members or former members of the armed or security forces.

§ 1:4   Evidence of citizenship

Persons who acquire citizenship automatically have that status independently from any act of the U.S. government. They can demand the U.S. government to provide evidence of their status. Naturalization requires the interested person or, in the case of minors, his or her parent or parents, to file an application or petition. The moment those persons become U.S. citizens, they receive a certificate attesting to their changed status. Ch 13 discusses the documents different agencies are required to accept as legal proof of citizenship and how to obtain them.

§ 1:5   Loss of citizenship

Research References
Steel on Immigration Law § 15:25

Citizenship acquired either by vesting or through naturalization may be lost through a process which used to be referred to as expatriation and now is simply called "loss of citizenship." The Supreme Court has held that U.S. citizenship may only be relinquished voluntarily. However, before the Supreme Court arrived at that formulation, many persons lost their citizenship through statutes designed to punish them or to accommodate the interests of the U.S. government. Ch 15 discusses the issues relating to loss of citizenship.

In addition, naturalized citizens may have their naturalization revoked either because it was obtained illegally or because it was obtained by fraud. Bases for revocation and revocation proceedings are discussed in Ch 14.

§ 1:6   Difference between immigration and nationality laws

Nationality law is unlike immigration law in many respects. One particularly notable difference for the practitioner is the fact that in nationality law, the applicable law is more often than not the law that was in effect at the time the relevant event took place. Thus, to determine whether a person was a citizen at birth or whether a person derived citizenship, the practitioner must know the applicable law at the time of the person's birth or at the time the last event of the derivation took place. A practical consequence of this principle is that the practitioner may not find the answer to a legal question by going to the current code and finding the relevant provisions. This book provides a clear and accurate description of all relevant provisions of prior laws, taking into account that the original materials may not always be easily found. In many cases, the original documents are attached as appendices to the relevant chapters.

Unlike automatic acquisition of citizenship, naturalization only requires knowledge of the current procedural and substantive requirements. In the process of naturalization, however, the possible shortcomings lie in the need to review the person's acquisition and continued existence of his or her lawful permanent status. This, in turn, may require the practitioner to be familiar with the provisions of law applicable at the time of acquisition of that status and with the various provisions of law governing deportability. The continuity of lawful permanent resident status is beyond the scope of this book. Several other treatises and manuals deal with exclusion and deportation of lawful permanent residents. Those books are referred to wherever relevant.

§ 1:7 Rights and liabilities of citizenship

Citizenship in the United States provides certain rights and privileges not available to noncitizens. These benefits include the right to vote,[1] the right to hold public office,[2] and eligibility for unlimited types of employment.[3] Citizens are able to confer immigration benefits upon their family members more easily and quickly than permanent resident noncitizens.[4]

Most importantly, perhaps, is the fact that naturalized citizens have not yet been subject to the rapid erosion of rights that lawful permanent residents have experienced since the 1996 Congress.[5] For example, the Personal Responsibility and Work Opportunity Reconciliation Act of 1996 restricted the eligibility of lawful permanent residents for public benefits but did not affect naturalized citizens.[6] At the most fundamental level, citizens are not subject to removal from the country (be it deportation or inadmissibility).[7]

Generally, there are no distinctions made between naturalized citizens and those who obtained citizenship at birth.[8] One exception is that the Constitution provides that only a "natural born Citizen" may serve as President or Vice President of the United States.[9] That clause is commonly believed to permit election of individuals who acquire citizenship at birth (Franklin Delano Roosevelt was born in Canada),

---

[Section 1:7]

[1]Generally, the qualifications for voting are fixed by individual states, subject to the provision against discrimination provided for in the Fifteenth Amendment, which states that "[t]he right of citizens of the United States to vote shall not be denied or abridged by the United States or by any State on account of race, color, or previous condition of servitude." U.S. Const. amend. XV, § 1.

[2]The Constitution of the United States requires citizenship for persons seeking election to the House of Representatives or the Senate, U.S. Const. art. 1, §§ 2, 3. The offices of President or Vice President of the United States are limited to natural born citizens. U.S. Const. art. 2, § 1.

[3]The federal government may preclude even lawful permanent resident noncitizens from certain types of employment. See Mow Sung Wong v. Campbell, 626 F.2d 739 (9th Cir. 1980), cert. denied, 450 U.S. 959 (1981); Vergara v. Hampton, 581 F.2d 1281 (7th Cir. 1978), cert. denied, 441 U.S. 905 (1979); cf. Hampton v. Mow Sung Wong, 426 U.S. 88, 96 S.Ct. 1895, 48 L.Ed.2d 495 (1976).

[4]Under the provisions of the Immigration and Nationality Act, citizenship provides the basis for immigration of immediate relatives without regard to the imposed numerical limitations. In addition, it provides first preference to unmarried children of United States citizens under the immigration preference system. See INA §§ 201(b), 203(a), 8 U.S.C.A. §§ 1151(b), 1153(a).

[5]See, e.g., Illegal Immigration Reform and Immigrant Responsibility Act of 1996 (IIRAIRA), Pub.L. 104-208, 110 Stat. 3009, (Sept. 30, 1996); Personal Responsibility and Work Opportunity Reconciliation Act of 1996 (PRWOR), Pub.L. 104-194, Title IV, 110 Stat. 2260 (Aug. 22, 1996); Antiterrorism and Effective Death Penalty Act of 1996, Pub. L. 104-132, Titles III–IV, 110 Stat. 1214 (Apr. 24, 1996).

[6]PRWOR, Title IV.

[7]See INA § 242(b)(5), (e)(2)(A), 8 U.S.C.A. § 1252(b)(5), (e)(2)(A) as amended by IIRAIRA § 306(a)(2).

[8]Knauer v. U.S., 328 U.S. 654, 658, 66 S.Ct. 1305, 1307, 90 L.Ed. 1500 (1946) (with minor exceptions, citizenship acquired by naturalization carries all the same rights and prerogatives as citizenship obtained by birth).

[9]See U.S. Const. Art. II § 1, cl. 4. The office of Vice President requires that "no person constitutionally ineligible to the office of President shall be eligible to that of Vice-President of the United States." U.S. Const. amend. XII.

but not individuals who naturalize after birth.[10] The issue, however, has not been tested in court, and indeed, may be a political question not susceptible to judicial resolution.[11] In addition, a court can revoke the citizenship of a naturalized person.[12] Citizens at birth can only lose their citizenship by committing a voluntary act with the intent to abandon their citizenship.[13]

Acquisition or loss of U.S. citizenship may have serious tax consequences. U.S. citizens are subject to federal income and gifts and estate taxes whether they live in the United States or abroad.[14] Attorneys and practitioners may wish to refer clients to a competent tax attorney to determine the tax liability of those who acquire or lose U.S. citizenship.[15]

On a related issue, some U.S. citizens voluntarily renounce their U.S. citizenship in order to avoid certain tax consequences. These former citizens are now subject to a new ground of inadmissibility, which permanently bars their admission to the United States.[16]

§ 1:8 Dual citizenship

Research References

Steel on Immigration Law § 15:7

Dual citizenship is where an individual is simultaneously a citizen of two different countries. The most common reason for dual citizenship is that a child is born a citizen of two different countries because of the intersection of the principles of nationality by descent (jus sanguinis), i.e. by being the child of a national, and nationality by birth within a certain territory (jus soli).[1] It is not uncommon for a person to obtain citizenship in one country because he or she was born there (jus soli) while deriving citizenship of another country under the principle of jus

---

[10]Weedin v. Chin Bow, 274 U.S. 657, 670 (1927), citing the minority opinion in U.S. v. Wong Kim Ark, 169 U.S. 649, 714 (1898) ("[A]t common law the children of our citizens born abroad were always natural born citizens from the standpoint of this Government . . . ."); see also, Charles Gordon, Who Can Be President of the United States: An Unresolved Enigma, 28 Md. L. Rev. 1, 5 (1968); Jill A. Pryor, The Natural-Born Citizen Clause and Presidential Eligibility: An Approach for Resolving Two Hundred Years of Uncertainty, 97 Yale L.J. 881, 899 (1988); Sarah Helene Duggin & Mary Beth Collins, "Natural Born" in the USA: The Striking Unfairness and Dangerous Ambiguity of the Constitution's Presidential Qualifications Clause and Why We Need to Fix It, 85 B.U. L. Rev. 53, 82–83 (2005). It should be noted that there is authority on both sides of the issue. See, Lawrence Friedman, An Idea Whose Time Has Come-The Curious History, Uncertain Effect, and Need for Amendment of the "Natural Born Citizen" Requirement for the Presidency, 52 St. Louis U. L.J. 137, 143 (2007).

[11]There were at least two legal challenges to John McCain's inclusion on the 2008 presidential ballot, by individuals alleging that his birth in the Panama Canal Zone to U.S. parents did not make him a "natural born Citizen"; those challenges were both dismissed for lack of standing. Robinson v. Bowen, 567 F.Supp.2d 1144, 1147 (N.D.Cal., 2008) (suggesting that the Twelfth Amendment — permitting objections in Congress to electoral votes — might be the only permissible way to challenge a candidate's eligibility); cf. Hollander v. McCain, 566 F.Supp.2d 63 (D.N.H., 2008) (no voter standing).

[12]See §§ 14:1 et seq.

[13]See §§ 15:1 et seq.

[14]See Rev. Rul. 92-109, 1992-52 IRB 5.

[15]See § 15:24.

[16]See § 15:2.

[Section 1:8]

[1]For a collection of laws concerning nationality, see U.N. Secretariat, Laws Concerning Nationality, U.N. Doc. ST/LEG/SER.B/4 (1954), supplemented by ST/LEG/SER.B/9 (1959).

sanguinis, as the child of a citizen of that country. Thus, a child born in the United States to Italian parents will be a U.S. citizen and perhaps a citizen of Italy.[2] Most children born abroad to U.S. citizen parents could be both U.S. citizens and citizens of the foreign country, depending upon the laws of that country.[3]

A second common reason for dual citizenship is when a person who naturalizes in the U.S. does not lose their citizenship abroad, in spite of the U.S. law requirement that they take an oath renouncing all foreign allegiances.[4] Many countries do not allow their citizens to renounce their nationality.[5] Other countries permit their nationals to regain their former citizenship without taking an oath of allegiance (which could have the effect of renouncing U.S. citizenship).[6] Therefore, persons who naturalize as U.S. citizens may continue to be citizens of the country of prior citizenship. Similarly, in some cases, U.S. citizens who naturalize in a foreign country may not lose their U.S. citizenship, and may also become dual citizens.[7] Dual citizenship is discussed in detail in Chapter 15.[8]

§ 1:9 Agency references in this text

Research References

Dizon and Wettstein, Immigration Law Service 2d §§ 1:108, 1:231

On November 25, 2002, Congress enacted the Homeland Security Act of 2002 (HSA), which radically reformed the governmental structure for carrying out the immigration laws.[1] This Act abolished the Immigration and Naturalization Service (INS) and transferred the majority of the immigration functions previously performed by the INS to the newly created Department of Homeland Security (DHS).[2] The Act transferred overall authority for administering the laws relating to visa issuance to the Department of Homeland Security.[3] The Executive Office of Immigration Review (EOIR), which includes both the offices of the immigration judges and the Board of Immigration Appeals (BIA), remains under the direction of the Attorney General in the Department of Justice.[4]

The INS previously performed the dual functions of enforcing the immigration laws and providing immigration services and benefits. The HSA assigned these dif-

---

[2]See Mandoli v. Acheson, 344 U.S. 133, 73 S. Ct. 135, 97 L. Ed. 146 (1952); Tomoya Kawakita v. U. S., 343 U.S. 717, 72 S. Ct. 950, 96 L. Ed. 1249 (1952).

[3]See Rogers v. Bellei, 401 U.S. 815, 91 S. Ct. 1060, 28 L. Ed. 2d 499 (1971).

[4]8 C.F.R. § 337.

[5]See §§ 15:17, 15:18.

[6]See §§ 15:17, 15:18. For constitutional reasons, U.S. citizenship may not be lost except by willful renunciation. See § 15:1.

[7]See §§ 15:6, 15:7.

[8]See §§ 15:17 to 15:19; see also App. 15-1.

[Section 1:9]

[1]The Homeland Security Act of 2002, Pub. L. No. 107-296, 116 Stat. 2135 (2002). Many of the provisions of this Act have been codified at 6 U.S.C.A. §§ 101, et seq.

[2]See, e.g., sections 441, 451 and 471 of the Homeland Security Act of 2002, Pub. L. No. 107-296, 116 Stat. 2135.

[3]Section 428 of the Homeland Security Act of 2002, Pub. L. No. 107-296, 116 Stat. 2135.

[4]Sections 1101 to 1103 of the Homeland Security Act of 2002, Pub. L. No. 107-296, 116 Stat. 2135.

ferent functions to independent entities within DHS, and prohibits the Executive Department from combining those entities or consolidating their functions.[5]

The United States Citizenship and Immigration Services (USCIS) took over the former INS functions related to naturalization, along with family and employment-based visa petitions, asylum and refugee processing, adjustment of status, and document issuance and renewal.[6] The Director of the USCIS is responsible for overseeing the administration of these programs and for establishing national immigration policies and procedures.[7] Other positions within the agency include a legal advisor, who is responsible, inter alia, for representing the USCIS in visa petition appeal procedures before EOIR.[8] The Act also creates the position of Chief of the Office of Citizenship, responsible for instruction and training on citizenship responsibilities for potential naturalization applicants.[9]

USCIS has taken over the service-related portions of the former INS Websites. Their Web site address is http://www.uscis.gov. Immigration forms and instructions are available at this Web site, as are decisions of the Administrative Appeals Office.[10]

---

[5]Sections 471(b) of the Homeland Security Act of 2002, Pub. L. No. 107-296, 116 Stat. 2135.

[6]Section 451 of the Homeland Security Act of 2002, Pub. L. No. 107-296, 116 Stat. 2135; see also http://www.uscis.gov/.

[7]Section 451(a)(3) of the Homeland Security Act of 2002, Pub. L. No. 107-296, 116 Stat. 2135.

[8]Section 451(a)(d) of the Homeland Security Act of 2002, Pub. L. No. 107-296, 116 Stat. 2135. See http://www.dhs.gov.

[9]Section 451(f) of the Homeland Security Act of 2002, Pub. L. No. 107-296, 116 Stat. 2135.

[10]See http://www.uscis.gov.

Chapter 2

Birth in the U.S. and Its Possessions

I. INTRODUCTION

II. DEFINITION OF "UNITED STATES"

A. CURRENT DEFINITION

B. CHANGING DEFINITION OF UNITED STATES

C. POSSESSIONS AND TERRITORIES THAT NEVER BECAME STATES OF UNITED STATES

III. UNDER THE JURISDICTION OF THE UNITED STATES

IV. PRESUMPTION AS TO FOUNDLINGS

§ 2:28 Generally

V. SUMMARY

§ 2:29 Generally

Research References

West's Key Number Digest

Aliens, Immigration and Citizenship ⚷650 to 685

Westlaw Databases

Immigration Law Service (2d ed.) (IMMLS2D)

Steel on Immigration Law (STEEL)

Treatises and Practice Aids

Steel on Immigration Law §§ 15:2, 15:3

KeyCite®: Cases and other legal materials listed in KeyCite Scope can be researched through the KeyCite service on Westlaw®. Use KeyCite to check citations for form, parallel references, prior and later history, and comprehensive citator information, including citations to other decisions and secondary materials.

I. INTRODUCTION

§ 2:1 Background

Research References

Steel on Immigration Law §§ 15:1, 15:2

The U.S. Constitution and federal statutes were originally silent as to who was a U.S. citizen.[1] Even though the very first Congress dealt with the status of a child

---

[Section 2:1]

[1]Rogers v. Bellei, 401 U.S. 815, 828–29, 91 S.Ct. 1060, 1068, 28 L.Ed.2d 499 (1971); 7 State Dept. Foreign Affairs Manual (FAM) 1111; Hackworth, 3 Digest of International Law 8.

born abroad to a U.S. citizen, it was not until 1866 that Congress enacted the first statute dealing with U.S. citizenship at birth within the United States.[2]

As a general rule, any person born inside the geographical boundaries of the United States is a U.S. citizen at birth, provided the person is not exempt from the laws of this country.[3] This rule derives from the common law principle of *jus soli*, which confers citizenship of a state upon persons born within its boundaries.[4] The principle of *jus soli* seems to have been incorporated into U.S. common law since the beginning of the republic.[5] In 1804, the Supreme Court already held that a person born in the territory of a state of the United States who remained there after the war of independence was a U.S. citizen until such person expatriated himself or herself.[6] This same view was upheld in subsequent decisions.[7] By 1856, however, the Supreme Court arrived at the conclusion that runaway slaves and free persons of African descent were not citizens of the U.S. because they were not understood as members of the community by the thirteen original states at the time the U.S. Constitution was framed.[8]

To correct this restrictive view of U.S. citizenship, Congress passed the Civil Rights Act of 1866, incorporating into federal statutory law the principle of *jus soli*, making any person born in the U.S. a citizen of the U.S.[9] Two years later this principle was enshrined in the Fourteenth Amendment to the U.S. Constitution, as a guarantee of equality of rights in the U.S.[10]

§ 2:2 Fourteenth Amendment; generally

Research References
Dizon and Wettstein, Immigration Law Service 2d § 14:14
Steel on Immigration Law § 15:2

---

[2]Civil Rights Act of April 9, 1866, 14 Stat. 27, codified as sec. 1992 of the Revised Statutes (first statute discussing citizenship by birth inside the United States); Act of March 26, 1790, 1 Stat. 103 reprinted as Appendix 4-1 to Ch 4 (first citizenship statute, dealt with naturalization, derivative citizenship, and U.S. citizens born abroad; but silent as to birth inside the United States).

[3]INA § 301(a), 8 U.S.C.A. § 1401(a).

[4]See U.S. v. Wong Kim Ark, 169 U.S. 649, 655–66, 18 S.Ct. 456, 459–63, 42 L.Ed. 890 (1898).

[5]For an interesting discussion of the fortunes of the common-law principle of *jus soli* since its adoption by the American Republic, see Jonathan C. Drimmer, The Nephews of Uncle Sam: The History, Evolution, and Application of Birthright Citizenship in the United States, 9 Georgetown Immigration Law Journal 667 (1995).

[6]Murray v. Schooner Charming Betsy, 6 U.S. (2 Cranch) 64, 119–120, 2 L.Ed. 208 (1804).

[7]McIlvaine v. Coxe's Lessee, 8 U.S. (4 Cranch) 209, 211, 2 L.Ed. 279 (1808); Inglis v. The Trustee of the Sailor's Snug Harbor, 28 U.S. (3 Pet.) 99, 120–21, 156, 7 L.Ed. 618 (1830). See generally U.S. v. Wong Kim Ark, 169 U.S. 649, 655-66, 18 S. Ct. 456, 459-63, 42 L. Ed. 890 (1898) (historical discussion of the incorporation of the principle of jus soli into U.S. jurisprudence).

[8]Dred Scott v. Sanford, 60 U.S. (19 How.) 393, 15 L.Ed. 691 (1856).

[9]14 Stat. 27, codified as sec. 1992 of the Revised Statutes. See also INS Interpretation 301.1(a)(1) (hereinafter INS Interp.). The INS Interpretations is reproduced in Gordon & Mailman, Immigration Law and Procedure, Volume 9 (rev. ed. 1993) [hereinafter Gordon & Mailman].

[10]U.S. Const. amend. XIV, § 1. See further, Children Born in the U.S. to Illegal Alien Parents: Hearings on H.R. 1363 Before the Subcomm. on Immigration and Claims and the Subcomm. on the Constitution of the Comm. of the Judiciary, 104th Congress, 1st Sess. (December 13, 1995) (statements of Gerald Neuman, Professor, Columbia University, and Walter Dellinger, Assistant Attorney General, Office of Legal Counsel—pointing out that the aim of this provision was to prevent the creation of castes whose members could be born in the United States for generations without ever achieving the rights of citizens).

The Fourteenth Amendment to the U.S. Constitution mandates that "all persons born . . . in the United States and subject to the jurisdiction thereof are citizens of the United States and of the State wherein they reside."[1] Acts of Congress or laws of the different states may not contradict the Constitution as supreme law of the land.[2] Whoever qualifies for citizenship under this definition must be accorded U.S. citizenship at birth.[3]

The constitutional rule allows for very few exceptions.[4] Under the Constitution, every person born in the United States is a citizen at birth except for children of foreign diplomats, Native Americans who are not taxed, and children of members of an armed force in hostile occupation of the United States.[5] Even when Congress decided that a certain racial or national group could not acquire U.S. citizenship through naturalization, the children of those persons were U.S. citizens if born inside the United States.[6] Similarly, the fact that a person would obtain dual citizenship by the application of both this constitutional principle and a foreign country's citizenship by descent rule does not prevent the person from being a U.S. citizen if born in the United States.[7] In addition, a person born in an area of land that was legally part of the United States is a U.S. citizen even when at the time of the birth the U.S. did not exercise governmental control over that area and did not resist foreign exercise of governmental control.[8] The few exceptions to this rule will be discussed in the section on who is subject to the jurisdiction of the U.S.[9]

§ 2:3 Fourteenth Amendment; generally—Statutory expansion

The principle of *jus soli* contained in the Fourteenth Amendment may, however, be expanded by Congress. Congress has the power to create a uniform law of naturalization, which includes the power to grant citizenship at birth to certain categories of persons not contemplated in the constitutional definition.[1] Indeed, Congress' first use of this power in 1790 provided U.S. citizenship at birth to chil-

---

[Section 2:2]

[1]U.S. Const. amend. XIV, § 1.

[2]See e.g. Matter of Cantu, 17 I. & N. Dec. 190, 194, n.7 (B.I.A. 1978) ("[no] statutory act could diminish, lawfully, the constitutional definition"). Cf. Dred Scott v. Sandford, 60 U.S. 393, 405, 19 How. 393, 15 L. Ed. 691 (1856) (States cannot naturalize persons as U.S. citizens because the Constitution provides that Congress shall make a uniform rule of naturalization).

[3]Congress has incorporated the constitutional definition into the INA. Thus, the INA also provides that "a person born in the United States, and subject to the jurisdiction thereof" is a citizen of the U.S. INA § 301(a), 8 U.S.C.A. § 1401(a).

[4]U.S. v. Wong Kim Ark, 169 U.S. 649, 18 S. Ct. 456, 42 L. Ed. 890 (1898).

[5]See §§ 2:24 to 2:27.

[6]Wong Kim Ark, 169 U.S. 649, 18 S.Ct. 456, 42 L.Ed. 890 (person of Chinese ancestry born in the United States); Morrison v. California, 291 U.S. 82, 85, 54 S.Ct. 281, 78 L.Ed. 664 (1934) (persons of Japanese descent are U.S. citizens if born in the United States or if they qualify as U.S. citizens born abroad).

[7]Perkins v. Elg, 307 U.S. 325, 329, 59 S.Ct. 884, 83 L.Ed. 1320 (1939).

[8]Matter of Cantu, 17 I&N Dec. 190.

[9]See §§ 2:24 to 2:27.

[Section 2:3]

[1]U.S. Const. art. 1 § 8, cl. 4.

dren born abroad to U.S. citizens.[2] Congress has also used this power to grant U.S. citizenship at birth to persons who, like some members of Native American nations were not subject to the jurisdiction of the U.S.[3] It has similarly used this power to grant U.S. citizenship to certain inhabitants of territories not incorporated into the U.S.[4]

Thus, citizenship at birth inside the geographical boundaries of the United States can have either a statutory or a constitutional basis. For all practical purposes, the source of a person's claim to U.S. citizenship at birth does not make any difference in terms of the rights that person enjoys. However, barring a constitutional amendment, no law may limit the access to U.S. citizenship of any person who satisfies the constitutional definition. Statutory citizenship at birth, on the other hand, may be restricted by conditions precedent or conditions subsequent or elimination altogether by Congress.[5]

This process of statutory and constitutional incorporation did not solve all the problems relating to birth inside the United States. Two important issues were left to be answered by case law: (1) what is considered the United States for purposes of this definition; and (2) who is subject to the jurisdiction of the United States and, therefore, not exempt from the application of this rule. This chapter will discuss both issues in detail.

II. DEFINITION OF "UNITED STATES"

A. CURRENT DEFINITION

§ 2:4 Applicability to U.S. territories; under Constitution

Research References

Steel on Immigration Law § 15(2)

The term *United States* has been the subject of controversy from the beginning of U.S. history.[1] The issue, as it relates to nationality law, affects the status of persons born in territories which are not states of the union but which are subject to the jurisdiction of the United States. The first such area was the United States territory northwest of the Ohio River, whose organic act predates the U.S. Constitution.[2] With the continued expansion of the United States, many new areas were acquired by the United States and were ruled as territories for a considerable period of time.[3]

The acquisition of new territories involves two separate processes: (1) the territory stops being part of a foreign country, and (2) it becomes part of the United States. Case law has had no problem with the cessation of allegiance to a former sovereign; when a territory was conquered by the United States or conveyed to it by

---

[2]Act of March 26, 1790, 1 Stat. 103 reprinted as Appendix 4-1 to Ch 4.

[3]See e.g, INA § 301(b), 8 U.S.C.A. § 1401(b).

[4]See Boyd v. Nebraska, 143 U.S. 135, 162, 12 S.Ct. 375, 36 L.Ed. 103 (1892). This process known as "collective naturalization" will be described in more detail below. See §§ 2:8 to 2:14

[5]See §§ 4:1 et seq.

[Section 2:4]

[1]See American Ins. Co. v. Canter, 26 U.S. (1 Pet.) 511, 7 L.Ed. 242 (1828) (discussing the relationship of the Territory of Florida to the United States).

[2]An Ordinance for the Government of the Territory of the United States North-West of the River Ohio, Act of July 13, 1787.

[3]See §§ 2:8 to 2:14 (short historical summary of U.S. expansion).

treaty, allegiance of the inhabitants to the former ruler ceased and passed to the United States.[4]

Up until the turn of the twentieth century, allegiance and citizenship appeared to be equivalent. It was only with the end of the Spanish-American war and the cession of the Spanish territories of the Philippines, Puerto Rico, and Guam that a new status was created conferring upon those subjects the obligations of allegiance to the U.S. but not the rights of citizenship.[5] The old sovereign conveys the allegiance of noncitizen nationals to the U.S. by the transfer of the territories, but the noncitizen nationals do not automatically become U.S. citizens. Even more importantly, birth in a territory subject to the jurisdiction of the United States was not by itself sufficient for acquisition of U.S. citizenship.[6]

In a series of decisions relating to the status of the territories acquired after the Spanish-American war, the U.S. Supreme Court held that under the scheme set up by the Constitution, Congress had the prerogative of making the U.S. Constitution applicable to newly acquired territories.[7] Justice Edward White, in his concurring opinion in *Downes v. Bidwell*, expressed this principle somewhat differently when he said that Congress has the power of incorporating the territory into the United States, thus granting the inhabitants the privileges of U.S. citizenship.[8] Once the Constitution is made applicable to a territory, it becomes embedded and cannot be withdrawn. As Justice White phrased it, neither Congress nor the executive has the power of divesting itself of a territory incorporated into the United States.[9]

The relationship between the inhabitants of a territory and the United States is defined by the duly ratified treaties conveying the territory and by the acts of Congress in relation to those territories.[10] For example, the Virgin Islands, which the U.S. purchased from Denmark in 1916, were not incorporated into the United States.[11] The Revised Organic Act of the Virgin Islands specifically provided which articles of the U.S. Constitution applied to the inhabitants of the islands.[12] The act

---

[4]American Ins. Co. v. 356 Bales of Cotton, 26 U.S. 511, 7 L. Ed. 242 (1828).

[5]See §§ 3:1 et seq.

[6]Downes v. Bidwell, 182 U.S. 244, 279–80, 21 S.Ct. 770, 784, 45 L.Ed. 1088 (1901).

[7]Downes v. Bidwell, 182 U.S. 244, 278-79, 21 S. Ct. 770, 783-84, 45 L. Ed. 1088 (1901). On the other hand, Congress does not have the power to legislate over the territories in a manner which the Constitution generally forbade it from doing (e.g. abridging the right to free speech). Downes v. Bidwell, 182 U.S. 244, 292, 21 S. Ct. 770, 789, 790, 45 L. Ed. 1088 (1901) (J. White, concurring) ("there are general prohibitions in the Constitution in favor of liberty and property of the citizen which are not mere regulations as to the form and manner in which a conceded power may be exercised, but which are an absolute denial of all authority under any circumstances . . . ").

[8]Downes v. Bidwell, 182 U.S. 244, 333, 21 S. Ct. 770, 805, 45 L. Ed. 1088 (1901). Justice White's opinion later became the settled law on the issue. Balzac v. Porto Rico, 258 U.S. 298, 305, 42 S.Ct. 343, 346, 66 L.Ed. 627 (1922).

[9]Downes v. Bidwell, 182 U.S. 244, 270, 21 S. Ct. 770, 780, 45 L. Ed. 1088 (1901).

[10]Even though the concept of noncitizen nationality did not arise until the beginning of the twentieth century, this problem was already a potential issue in the early Supreme Court decisions. See, e.g., American Ins. Co. v. 356 Bales of Cotton, 26 U.S. 511, 542, 7 L. Ed. 242, 255 (1828) ("the ceded territory becomes part of the nation to which it is annexed; either on the terms stipulated in the treaty of cession, or on such as its new master shall impose").

[11]48 U.S.C.A. § 1541(a); Treaty of August 4, 1916, Denmark and U.S., 39 Stat. 1715, TS 629, 3 Redmond 2558, 7 Bevans 56 reproduced as Appendix 2-7. U.S. law still provides that the Virgin Islands are an unincorporated territory of the U.S. 48 U.S.C.A. § 1541(a).

[12]48 U.S.C.A. § 1561.

did not make the citizenship clause applicable to them.[13] In spite of that, U.S. law has made Virgin Island natives U.S. citizens from birth since 1927.[14] Similarly, the U.S. acquired Puerto Rico after the Spanish-American War.[15] According to the terms of the treaty with Spain, the U.S. Supreme Court concluded that Puerto Rico had not been incorporated into the United States.[16] In 1900, Congress passed a law that granted Puerto Rican rather than U.S. citizenship to persons born in Puerto Rico.[17] It was only in 1917 that Congress granted U.S. citizenship to citizens of Puerto Rico.[18]

The continuing validity of *Downes v. Bidwell* was recently put to a test in relation to persons born in the Philippines while it was a territory of the United States. In a two-to-one decision, the Ninth Circuit held that during its territorial period, the Philippines was not part of the United States for purposes of the citizenship clause of the Fourteenth Amendment.[19] In his dissent, Justice Pregerson argued that the proper test to determine whether a territory was part of the United States for purposes of the citizenship clause is whether the territory was within the U.S. dominion. This translates into whether the U.S. exercised sovereignty or control over the islands, that is, whether the U.S. governed the territory or U.S. authority was exercised in the territory. There was no doubt that the Philippines were within the "dominion" of the U.S. during its territorial period.[20] This issue was once again raised in the Second Circuit where the court agreed with the majority in *Rabang*, holding that birth in the Philippines during the territorial period was not a basis for a claim of U.S. citizenship under the U.S. Constitution.[21] In 1998, the Third Circuit also upheld the decision in *Rabang*, stating that the petitioner did not derive citizenship from the petitioner's parents, who had been born in the Philippines when it was a U.S. territory.[22]

§2:5 Applicability to U.S. territories; under Constitution—Under statutes

The debate over the status of persons born in the territories of the U.S. has become less important because Congress granted U.S. citizenship at birth to persons born in most of the territories previously held to be unincorporated.[1] In addition, the Nationality Act of 1940 and the Immigration and Nationality Act of 1952 (INA)

---

[13]48 U.S.C.A. § 1561.

[14]See § 2:17.

[15]Art. 2, Treaty of Paris, United States and Spain., December 10, 1898 (proclaimed, April 11, 1899), 30 Stat. 1755, 2 Malloy 1690, 11 Bevans 615 reproduced as Appendix 2-4.

[16]Puerto Rico v. Shell Co., 302 U.S. 253, 58 S.Ct. 167, 82 L.Ed. 235 (1937); Balzac v. Porto Rico, 258 U.S. 298, 42 S. Ct. 343, 66 L. Ed. 627 (1922).

[17]Sec. 7, Act of April 12, 1900, 31 Stat. 77 reproduced as Appendix 2-5, part A.

[18]Sec. 5, Act of March 2, 1917 reproduced as Appendix 2-5, part A. It may be presumed that at that point Puerto Rico was incorporated into the United States in Justice White's terms.

[19]Rabang v. INS., 35 F.3d 1449 (9th Cir. 1994), cert. denied, 115 S. Ct. 2554 (1995).

[20]Rabang v. INS., 35 F.3d 1449 (9th Cir. 1994), cert. denied, 115 S. Ct. 2554 (1995).

[21]Valmonte v. INS, 136 F.3d 914 (2d Cir. 1998).

[22]Lacap v. INS, 138 F.3d 518 (3d Cir. 1998).

[Section 2:5]

[1]See e.g., 44 Stat. 1234 reproduced as Appendix 2-7, part A, as amended by 47 Stat. 336 reproduced as Appendix 2-7, part B, (1927 act awarding U.S. citizenship to persons born in the U.S. Virgin Islands). As demonstrated by the recent decisions regarding the Philippines, the issue refuses to die. See § 2:4.

define the geographical meaning of the United States for nationality at birth purposes.[2] Thus, there is no longer any question that persons born in what the statutes define as the United States are U.S. citizens at birth.

The present statutory definition of *United States* is in section 101(a)(38) of the INA.[3] It provides that in its geographical sense, the United States includes the continental United States, Alaska, Hawaii, Puerto Rico, Guam, the U.S. Virgin Islands and the Commonwealth of the Northern Mariana Islands.[4] Any person born in those areas is a citizen of the U.S. at birth.[5]

The Commonwealth of the Northern Marianas was recognized as part of the United States in the INA in 2009.[6] However, even prior to that statutory development, the Ninth Circuit had interpreted the treaty with the Northern Mariana Islands to provide that persons born in the Northern Mariana Islands after January 9, 1978, are U.S. citizens at birth.[7] The Department of State has now acquiesced in that interpretation.[8]

§ 2:6 Applicability to margins of U.S. territory

Another area of debate relates to persons who are born on the margins of a territory. It has historically been held that, for purposes of citizenship at birth in the United States, the ports, harbors, bays, enclosed arms of the sea along its coasts, and the territorial waters (then a three-mile marginal belt along the coasts of these territories) are part of the United States.[1] U.S. territorial waters were extended to twelve nautical miles by presidential proclamation in 1988.[2] Under the traditional understanding of these seas as U.S. territory, persons born on foreign commercial vessels within the twelve-mile territorial waters are U.S. citizens by birth in the U.S.[3] Note, however, that persons born on foreign public vessels such as warships are not U.S. citizens by birth in the U.S. because they are not subject to

---

[2]Sec. 101(d), Nationality Act of 1940, Pub.L. 76-853, 54 Sat. 1137 (October 14, 1940) reproduced as Appendix 4-12 to Ch 4; INA § 101(a)(38) Both acts also incorporate into the statute the text of the citizenship clause of the Fourteenth Amendment. Sec. 201(a), Nationality Act of 1940; INA § 301(a).

[3]8 U.S.C.A. § 1101(a)(38).

[4]INA § 101(a)(38), 8 U.S.C.A. § 1101(a)(38).

[5]INA §§ 101(a), 301(a), 8 U.S.C.A. §§ 1101(a), 1401(a).

[6]See INA § 101(a)(36), 8 U.S.C.A. § 1101(a)(36); INA § 101(a)(38), 8 U.S.C.A. § 1101(a)(38); the Consolidated Natural Resources Act of 2008 (CNRA), Pub. L. No. 110-229, 122 Stat. 754 (2008). That statute and its implementing regulation made federal immigration law applicable to the CNMI beginning on November 28, 2009. See 48 U.S.C.A. § 1806(a)(1); Eche v. Holder, 694 F.3d 1026 (9th Cir. 2012), cert. denied, 133 S.Ct. 2825 (2013).

[7]See Gordon & Mailman, § 92.04(9); Sabangan v. Powell, 375 F.3d 818, 819–820 (9th Cir. 2004).

[8]7 FAM 1126.3(c)(5) ("Although the Department (CA and L/CA) believed the decision was clearly erroneous, the Solicitor General's office did not seek Supreme Court review, and it is now final. In order to maintain a uniform application of the nationality laws and for operations reasons, the Department (CA) decided to apply the decision worldwide.").

[Section 2:6]

[1]Cunard S.S. Co., Ltd. v. Mellon, 262 U.S. 100, 122, 43 S.Ct. 504, 507, 67 L.Ed. 894 (1923); Matter of A-, 3 I&N Dec. 677 (Central Office 1949); INS Interp. 301.1(a)(2); 7 FAM 1113.1-2.

[2]Presidential Proclamation 5928 of Dec. 27, 1988, 54 Fed. Reg. 777 (Jan. 9, 1989). The INS Interpretations is somewhat confused about this issue. It seems to argue that citizenship is granted only within the three miles of the coast and yet it provides for exceptions to the rule that a person born within the territorial waters is a U.S. citizen. INS Interp. 301.1(a)(2), (5).

[3]See INS Interp. 301.1(a)(2); 7 FAM 1116.1-2

the jurisdiction of the U.S.[4] The same rule applies for birth in the U.S. territorial air space.[5]

This, at least, has been the government's view for many years. The current FAM states that new research has suggested that the issue is unsettled; it now deems the matter a "substantial legal question," and instructs State Department officers to submit any claims of U.S. citizenship in this category to the Department for adjudication.[6] The apparent issue is whether there is a distinction between the "territorial sea" (presumably in open waters) and "territorial waters" (which may include rivers and bays).[7] The legacy INS interpretation in 301.1(a)(7) continues to state that birth in the three-mile territorial waters is birth in the U.S.[8]

A related problem arises in relation to the legal definition of entry into the United States. The Fourteenth Amendment contemplates the United States in physical terms. A person's birth within the country makes the person a citizen unless he or she is not subject to the jurisdiction of the U.S. Thus, regardless of the legal fiction that while a noncitizen is applying for admission, the noncitizen is not "inside" the United States for immigration purposes, children born while their mothers are in DHS custody pending a determination of their admissibility are U.S. citizens under the Fourteenth Amendment.[9]

§ 2:7   Applicability to U.S. vessels and other extensions of U.S

Research References

Dizon and Wettstein, Immigration Law Service 2d § 14:15
Steel on Immigration Law § 15(2)

The United States does not extend beyond these limits. Birth in a United States vessel that is not within the territorial waters of the U.S. is not birth in the United States.[1] Even though a person born in a U.S. public vessel is born within the jurisdiction of the U.S., he or she is not born within the territory of the United States and is, therefore, not a U.S. citizen at birth.[2]

Birth in U.S. Naval stations abroad is not birth in the United States for purposes of the Fourteenth Amendment or the statutory equivalent.[3] The same applies for children born inside a U.S. consulate or embassy abroad.[4]

B.   CHANGING DEFINITION OF UNITED STATES

§ 2:8   In general

The current definition of the geographical extent of the United States is useful

---

[4]INS Interp. 301.1(a)(5). See §§ 2:24 to 2:27.

[5]7 FAM 1115.

[6]7 FAM 1114(c).

[7]7 FAM 1114(c).

[8]INS Interp. 301.1(a)(2).

[9]7 FAM 1113.2-1; Memorandum of the Office of the Solicitor for the Department of State, Feb. 6, 1930, MS. Dept. of State, file 130 Laszas, Ona quoted in 3 Hackworth, Digest of Int. Law 10.

[Section 2:7]

[1]Lam Mow v. Nagle, 24 F.2d 316 (9th Cir. 1928); Matter of A-, 3 I&N Dec. 677; 7 FAM 1113.1-4.

[2]Legal Opinion, Aleinikoff, INS General Counsel, Genco Opinion 94-27, File No CO 301-P (June 16, 1994).

[3]See 7 FAM 1113.1-4; 3 Hackworth, Digest of Intl. Law 9.

[4]7 FAM 1113.1-4. See generally, Gordon & Mailman, § 92.03[2][d].

only to determine which persons born at the present will be U.S. citizens by birth in the United States. To be able to determine whether a person born in the past was born inside the United States, one must consider whether the place where the person was born was part of the United States at the time of the birth. Clearly, if the place was part of the United States, the person is a U.S. citizen at birth.[1] Even if the territory was not part of the United States, however, the person may still be a U.S. citizen since Congress has passed several laws granting U.S. citizenship collectively to certain categories of residents living in some of the territories at the time of incorporation into the United States. This phenomenon is referred to as "collective naturalization" and also will be discussed in detail in this section.

§ 2:9 Citizenship by birth in original colonies

The inhabitants of the former colonies, who did not elect to continue to be British subjects after the individual state declared independence from Britain, became members of their respective states.[1] When the U.S. Constitution was adopted, any person who was a citizen of one of the original states became a citizen of the United States.[2] Persons who left the United States after the U.S. Constitution was adopted, who adhered to the British cause, and who never returned to the United States were deemed to have elected British citizenship, and those persons never became U.S. citizens.[3] Appendix 2-1 provides a list of the original states that ratified the U.S. Constitution.

§ 2:10 Mechanism for incorporation of new states

The U.S. Constitution provides a mechanism whereby other states may be admitted into the United States.[1] However, before admission, Congress must pass (1) an enabling act, specifying the conditions precedent to the admission and defining the political status of its inhabitants,[2] and (2) a resolution declaring the specific state admitted after the performance of the conditions.[3] Every enabling act that has been passed by Congress stipulated that the U.S. would admit the territory on an equal

---

[Section 2:8]

[1]Unless the person fell within the exception of not being subject to the jurisdiction of the United States. See §§ 2:24 to 2:27.

[Section 2:9]

[1]Inglis v. Sailors Snug Harbor, 28 U.S. (3 Pet.) at 121, 7 L.Ed. 617; Shanks v. Dupont, 28 U.S. (3 Pet.) 242, 7 L.Ed. 666 (1830); McIlvaine v. Coxe's Lessee, 8 U.S. 209, 2 L. Ed. 598 (1808). See generally, Gordon & Mailman, § 92.02[1].

[2]Boyd v. State of Nebraska, 143 U.S. 135, 159-60, 12 S. Ct. 375, 36 L. Ed. 103 (1892); Dred Scott v. Sandford, 60 U.S. 393, 406, 19 How. 393, 15 L. Ed. 691 (1856); Minor v. Happersett, 88 U.S. (21 Wall.) 162, 167, 22 L.Ed. 627 (1874); Cf. INS Interp. 301.1(a)(8)(i).

[3]Inglis v. Trustees of Sailor's Snug Harbor, 28 U.S. 99, 7 L. Ed. 617 (1830); Shanks v. Dupont, 28 U.S. 242, 245, 7 L. Ed. 666 (1830).

[Section 2:10]

[1]U.S. Const. art. 4 § 3, cl. 1. President Jefferson appears to have held the view that before that clause could be applied, the new territory had to have been incorporated into the United States. See Downes v. Bidwell, 182 U.S. 244, 329-30, 21 S. Ct. 770, 803, 45 L. Ed. 1088 (1901).

[2]Gordon & Mailman, § 92.02[2].

[3]Gordon & Mailman, § 92.02[2].

footing with the original thirteen states.[4] Admission on an equal footing involves equality of constitutional rights and power to its citizens.[5] Appendix 2-1 details the date of admission of the 37 states that have been admitted under this process.

When the United States admitted new territories as states, all U.S. citizens who had migrated to the territory retained U.S. citizenship.[6] Upon admission, Congress determined for each territory the citizenship and nationality status of all the other inhabitants of the territory, *i.e.* noncitizens living in the territory and people born in the territory while it was under U.S. jurisdiction.

After the passage of the Fourteenth Amendment, there should have been no doubt as to the status of persons born in the territories.[7] The question of status, however, has become more confusing because of the development around the turn of the twentieth century of the distinction between citizens and noncitizen nationals.

§2:11 Citizenship by birth in territories inside continental U.S

The Constitution granted Congress power to legislate over territories acquired by the U.S.[1] The U.S. governed, as territories prior to their admission, almost all states admitted after the U.S. Constitution became effective.[2] It is clear that U.S. citizens who had moved to the territories, or for some other reason resided in them, continued to be U.S. citizens.[3]

In contrast, there was controversy as to the citizenship status of noncitizens who took up residence in the territories before they became states.[4] Territories ceded by treaty usually made provision for the status of the inhabitants of the territory *vis-à-*

---

[4]Gordon & Mailman, § 92.02[2].

[5]Boyd v. State of Nebraska, 143 U.S. 135, 170, 12 S. Ct. 375, 385, 36 L. Ed. 103 (1892); Pollard's Lessee v. Hagan, 44 U.S. (3 How.) 212, 223 (1845).

[6]See Boyd v. State of Nebraska, 143 U.S. 135, 175, 12 S. Ct. 375, 387, 36 L. Ed. 103 (1892).

[7]See Loughborough v. Blake, 18 U.S. (5 Wheat.) 317, 319 (1820) (holding that for constitutional purposes the term United States extended to the full extent of the American Empire, including both States and territories. As it emphasizes, "[t]he district of Columbia, or the territory west of the Missouri, is not less within the United States, than Maryland or Pennsylvania."

[Section 2:11]

[1]U.S. Const. art. 4 § 3, cl. 2. In Dred Scott, Chief Justice Taney claimed that this section of the Constitution only applied to territory already held by the federal government at the time and not to future territories to be acquired by the Dred Scott v. Sandford, 60 U.S. 393, 435-37, 19 How. 393, 15 L. Ed. 691 (1856). Subsequent courts have held that in spite of the Dred Scott statement, there is no doubt that Congress has plenary power over territories acquired by the United States. See DeLima v. Bidwell, 182 U.S. 1, 196, 21 S.Ct. 743, 45 L.Ed. 1041 (1901) (pointing out that Chief Justice Taney's statement not only contradict an earlier holding of Chief Justice Marshall, but whatever its source, Congress has exercised this power in an uninterrupted fashion for over a century). See also Boyd v. State of Nebraska, 143 U.S. 135, 169-170, 12 S. Ct. 375,385, 36 L. Ed. 103 (1892) ("It is too late at this day to question the plenary power of Congress over the Territories"). This power has been held to derive either from the constitutional provision allowing Congress to legislate over the territory or from the general power of the federal government to acquire territory. Downes v. Bidwell, 182 U.S. 244, 290, 21 S. Ct. 770, 788, 45 L. Ed. 1088 (1901).

[2]Vermont, Kentucky, Maine, West Virginia, Texas, and California were never territories. Vermont was admitted as a state in 1791. Act of February 18, 1791, 1 Stat. 191. Kentucky was formed out of part of the state of Virginia. Act of February 4, 1791, 1 Stat. 189. Maine was formed out of part of the state of Massachusetts. Act of March 3, 1820, 1 Stat. 544. West Virginia, was also formed out of the state of Virginia. West Virginia Constitution, Art. 2, § 1.

[3]See generally, Gordon & Mailman, § 92.02[2].

[4]Compare State v. Primrose, 3 Ala. 546 (1842) and Boyd v. State of Nebraska, 143 U.S. 135, 169-70, 12 S. Ct. 375, 385, 36 L. Ed. 103 (1892).

vis the United States and may have achieved the granting of citizenship with the transfer of allegiance.[5] Even in the territories that were not acquired in this fashion, Congress provided resident noncitizens with such political rights as the right to vote in the affairs of the territories.[6] In addition, noncitizens residing in territories have always had the same right to naturalize as noncitizens who lived in the original states.[7] Once the territories became states of the U.S., Congress provided for some noncitizens in some of the states to become U.S. citizens automatically through the process of collective naturalization.[8] Some typical examples follow.

Louisiana was ceded by France in a treaty on October 21, 1803.[9] The treaty transferring sovereignty over the territory to the United States specifically provided that "the inhabitants shall be incorporated into the Union of the United States and admitted as soon as possible . . . to the enjoyment of all the rights, advantages and immunities of citizens of the United States."[10] Until its admission as a state of the United States in 1812, Louisiana was ruled as the territory of Orleans.[11] Some courts have considered that residents of the territory became U.S. citizens at the time of the cession of the territory to the United States.[12] At the time of Louisiana's admission as a state, U.S. citizenship also vested on noncitizens who had moved to the territory of Orleans after the cession.[13]

Spain transferred Florida to the United States in 1819 under a treaty that had substantially the same provision as the Louisiana treaty.[14] Justice Marshall found that the treaty, as the law of the land, admitted the inhabitants of the territory to U.S. citizenship.[15] They, however, would not share in the government until Florida became a state.[16] This view may have been somewhat simplistic, as it was not until

---

[5]See Downes v. Bidwell, 182 U.S. 244, 280, 21 S. Ct. 770, 784, 45 L. Ed. 1088 (1901).

[6]Boyd v. State of Nebraska, 143 U.S. 135, 169-70, 12 S. Ct. 375, 385, 36 L. Ed. 103 (1892). See generally, INS Interp. 301.1(a)(8)(iv).

[7]See Sec. 1, Act of January 29, 1795, 1 Stat. 414 reproduced as Appendix 4-2 to Ch 4 ("He shall, at the time of his application to be admitted, declare on oath or affirmation, before some on of the courts aforesaid, that he has resided within the United States, five years at least, and within the state or territory, where such court is at the time held, one year at least"); Sec. 1, Act of April 14, 1802, 2 Stat. 153 reproduced as Appendix 4-3 to Ch 4 ("That the court admitting such alien shall be satisfies that he has resided within the United States five years at least, and within the state or territory where such court is at the time held, one year at least").

[8]INS Interp. 301.1(a)(8)(iv). See general statement in Boyd v. State of Nebraska, 143 U.S. 135, 170, 12 S. Ct. 375, 385, 36 L. Ed. 103 (1892).

[9]State v. Primrose, 3 Ala. 546, 1842 WL 150 (1842).

[10]Downes v. Bidwell, 182 U.S. 244, 280, 21 S. Ct. 770, 784, 45 L. Ed. 1088 (1901).

[11]See INS Interp. 301.1(a)(8)(iv).

[12]State v. Primrose, 3 Ala. 546, 549, 1842 WL 150 (1842).

[13]In re Desbois, 2 Martin 185, 1812 WL 764 (La. 1812); United States v. Laverty, 26 Fed. Cas. 875 (No. 15,569) (D.La. 1812), 3 Martin 736 (La. 1813). Cf. State v. Primrose, 3 Ala. 546, 1842 WL 150 (1842) (limiting collective naturalization to those Louisiana citizens who were already residents of the territory at the time it was ceded to the United States).

[14]American Ins. Co. v. 356 Bales of Cotton, 26 U.S. 511, 7 L. Ed. 242 (1828) (citing the provision: "The inhabitants of the territories . . . shall be incorporated in the Union of the United States, as soon as may be consistent with the principles of the federal Constitution; and admitted to the enjoyment of the privileges, rights, and immunities of the citizens of the United States").

[15]American Ins. Co. v. 356 Bales of Cotton, 26 U.S. 511, 7 L. Ed. 242 (1828).

[16]American Ins. Co. v. 356 Bales of Cotton, 26 U.S. 511, 7 L. Ed. 242 (1828).

1822 that Congress passed an act conferring upon the inhabitants of Florida the rights of citizenship.[17] Florida did not become a state until 1845.[18]

The organic acts that ruled the territories of Montana, Nebraska, Washington, and Wyoming extended the right to vote in the internal affairs of the territories not only to U.S. citizens residing there but also to noncitizens who had made a declaration of intention of becoming U.S. citizens.[19] When these territories became states of the United States, declarant noncitizens became U.S. citizens.[20]

The territory of Dakota was ruled under the Organic Act of 1861[21] until the admission of North and South Dakota as states in 1889. The organic act granted the right to vote in the internal affairs of the territory to resident U.S. citizens and to noncitizens who resided in the territory, who had made a declaration of intention of becoming U.S. citizens, and who had taken the oath to support the U.S. Constitution.[22] At the time of admission of the territory, the voters became U.S. citizens.[23] In addition, the organic act made the U.S. Constitution fully applicable to the territory.[24] There should be no doubt that persons born in the territory while it was a territory were U.S. citizens at birth.

Unlike most other territories, the Enabling Act of the Territory of Utah conferred the right to vote only upon U.S. citizens residing there.[25] Noncitizen residents of the territory were not conferred these political rights. When the territory became a state, those resident noncitizens did not automatically become U.S. citizens even if they had filed declarations of intention of becoming U.S. citizens.[26]

The Organic Act of the Oklahoma territory granted the right to vote to U.S. citizens residing in the territory and to male noncitizens over twenty-one who, within the previous twelve months, had made a declaration of intention of becoming U.S. citizens.[27] However, the later Enabling Act did not adopt the noncitizens' right

---

[17]Downes v. Bidwell, 182 U.S. 244, 334, 21 S. Ct. 770, 805, 45 L. Ed. 1088 (1901) (J. White, concurring).

[18]See Appendix 2-1.

[19]INS Interp. 301.1(a)(8)(iv) citing In re Michael Daniel Maloney, Legal Branch, file 56018/423, March 18, 1940 (Montana); Boyd v. State of Nebraska, 143 U.S. 135, 175-76, 12 S. Ct. 375, 387, 36 L. Ed. 103 (1892) (Nebraska); In re William Albert Richards, Board of Review, file A-14527, July 14, 1939 (Washington); In re George Watson Wright, Legal Branch, file A-20025, February 3, 1941 (Washington); In re Alfred Bertrand Mac All-Whereat, Board of Review, file 23/30824, March 16, 1938 (Wyoming).

[20]INS Interp. 301.1(a)(8)(iv) citing In re Michael Daniel Maloney, Legal Branch, file 56018/423, March 18, 1940 (Montana); Boyd v. State of Nebraska, 143 U.S. 135, 175-76, 12 S. Ct. 375, 387, 36 L. Ed. 103 (1892) (Nebraska); In re William Albert Richards, Board of Review, file A-14527, July 14, 1939 (Washington); In re George Watson Wright, Legal Branch, file A-20025, February 3, 1941 (Washington); In re Alfred Bertrand Mac All-Whereat, Board of Review, file 23/30824, March 16, 1938 (Wyoming).

[21]Act of March 2, 1861, 12 Stat. 239; continued by the Organic Law of the Territory of Dakota of 1877 (Cf. 48 U.S.C.A. § 1460).

[22]Sec. 5, Act of March 2, 1861. The enabling statute incorporated the description of voters of the organic act. Sec. 3, Act of February 22, 1889, 25 Stat. 676.

[23]See Application of Brandt, A-13029807 (1966) cited in INS Interp. 301.1(a)(8)(iv).

[24]Sec. 16, Act of March 2, 1861.

[25]Sec. 2, Act of July 16, 1894, 28 Stat. 107.

[26]CO letters of August 9, 1938, December 23, 1940, and April 7, 1942 relating to files 23/35408, 23/53794, and 23/52924 respectively cited in INS Interp. 301.1(a)(8)(iv).

[27]Sec. 5, Act of May 2, 1890, 26 Stat. 81.

to vote.[28] Therefore, when the territory became a state, these residents did not automatically become U.S. citizens.[29] The organic act did, however, incorporate the U.S. Constitution to the territory of Oklahoma, so persons born there were U.S. citizens at birth.[30]

§ 2:12   States incorporated without prior status as territories

Unlike most other states admitted to the Union after the adoption of the U.S. Constitution, neither Texas nor California was a territory before becoming states. Texas was admitted into the U.S. on December 29, 1845, and California was admitted on September 9, 1850.[1] The courts have held that all persons who were citizens of Texas at the time of its admission to the U.S. became citizens of the United States.[2] It has been determined administratively that the same rule applies to California citizens.[3]

§ 2:13   Citizenship by birth in Alaska

Research References

Dizon and Wettstein, Immigration Law Service 2d § 14:22
Steel on Immigration Law § 15(3)

The U.S. purchased Alaska from Russia in 1867.[1] The treaty ceding the territory provided that all the inhabitants of the territory on that date, except for "uncivilized tribes," became U.S. citizens unless they elected to preserve their allegiance to Russia by returning to that country within three years.[2] Thus, they became citizens through collective naturalization. Members of Alaskan Native tribes who did not preserve their allegiance to Russia by returning within three years of the 1867 treaty became statutory citizens in 1924.[3]

Alaska was ruled as a territory until 1959, when it became a state of the United

---

[28]Sec. 2, Act of June 16, 1906, 34 Stat. 267.

[29]INS Interp. 301.1(a)(8)(iv), citing In re William J. Cassidy, Board of Review, file 23/29911, February 12, 1938; In re Gustaf Fridolfberg, file C-4449201 (1938).

[30]Sec. 28, Act of May 2, 1890.

[Section 2:12]

[1]INS Interp. 301.1(a)(8)(iii). The only other states that were never territories were Vermont, Kentucky, Maine, and West Virginia. Vermont was admitted as a state in 1791. Act of February 18, 1791, 1 Stat. 191. Kentucky was formed out of part of the state of Virginia. Act of February 4, 1791, 1 Stat. 189. Maine was formed out of part of the state of Massachusetts. Act of March 3, 1820, 1 Stat. 544. West Virginia, was also formed out of the state of Virginia. West Virginia Constitution, Art. 2, § 1.

[2]Contzen v. U.S., 179 U.S. 191, 193, 21 S.Ct. 98, 45 L.Ed. 148 (1900); see also McKinney v. Saviego, 59 U.S. (18 How.) 235 (1855); Boyd v. State of Nebraska, 143 U.S. 135, 169, 12 S. Ct. 375, 385, 36 L. Ed. 103 (1892).

[3]INS Interp. 301.1(a)(8)(iii).

[Section 2:13]

[1]Art. 3, Treaty of Cession of the Russian Possessions in North America, Russia and United States, March 30, 1856, 15 Stat. 539, TS 301, 18 Stat. (2) 671, 2 Malloy 1521, 11 Bevans 1216 reproduced as Appendix 2-3.

[2]Art. 3, Treaty of Cession of the Russian Possessions in North America, Russia and United States, March 30, 1856, 15 Stat. 539, TS 301, 18 Stat. (2) 671, 2 Malloy 1521, 11 Bevans 1216 reproduced as Appendix 2-3.

[3]See § 2:26.

States.[4] During the period in which Alaska was ruled as a territory, persons born inside that territory were considered to have been born inside the United States for Fourteenth Amendment purposes, because the Supreme Court ruled that the treaty of 1867 incorporated the territory into the United States.[5] The Nationality Act of 1940 and the INA included Alaska in their definitions of the United States.[6] These statutes, therefore, confirm the citizenship status for people born in Alaska after 1940. In addition, the INA included a declaratory statement that people born in Alaska on or after March 30, 1867 were U.S. citizens at birth.[7]

§ 2:14 Citizenship by birth in Hawaii

Research References

Dizon and Wettstein, Immigration Law Service 2d § 14:23
Steel on Immigration Law § 15(3)

Hawaii was acquired by the United States in 1898. The Hawaiian Islands had been a monarchy until a revolution in 1893 overthrew the government and established a republic.[1] After negotiations with the Republic of Hawaii, Congress passed a joint resolution accepting the cession of the Hawaiian Islands on July 7, 1898.[2] Even though the sovereignty over the Hawaiian Islands passed to the United States on August 12, 1898, the islands were not incorporated into this country until Congress passed the statute organizing the Territory of Hawaii on April 30, 1900.[3] Hawaii became a state on August 21, 1959.[4]

The April 30, 1900 Act collectively naturalized all persons who were citizens of the Republic of Hawaii on August 12, 1898.[5] It also provided that the U.S. Constitution had the same force and effect in Hawaii as elsewhere in the United States.[6] Therefore, the Fourteenth Amendment had full applicability to people born in Hawaii. Both the Nationality Act of 1940 and the INA confirmed that Hawaii is part of the United States for nationality purposes.[7] The INA also confirmed that persons who were citizens of the Republic of Hawaii as of August 12, 1898, and persons who

---

[4]Act of July 7, 1958, 72 Stat. 339, 48 U.S.C.A. ch. 2, note; Pres. Proc. 3269, 24 Fed. Reg. 81.

[5]Rassmussen v. U.S., 197 U.S. 516, 525, 25 S.Ct. 514, 517, 49 L.Ed. 862 (1905).

[6]Section 101(d), Nationality Act of 1940 reproduced as Appendix 4-12 to Ch 4; INA § 101(a)(38); 8 U.S.C.A. § 1001(a)(38).

[7]INA § 304, 8 U.S.C.A. § 1404. The statute granting statehood in 1959 did not affect section 304. See Sec. 24 of the Act of July 27, 1958, 72 Stat. 351.

[Section 2:14]

[1]Gordon & Mailman, § 92.04[3].

[2]Joint Resolution of Congress, July 7, 1898, 30 Stat. 750.

[3]Act of June 14, 1900, 31 Stat. 141; Hawaii v. Mankichi, 190 U.S. 197, 210–11, 23 S.Ct. 787, 788, 47 L.Ed. 1016 (1903).

[4]Act of March 18, 1959, 73 Stat. 4, 48 U.S.C.A., note preceding § 491; Pres. Proc. 3309, 24 Fed. Reg. 6868.

[5]Sec. 4, Act of April 30, 1900, 31 Stat. 141. For a description of who was a citizen of Hawaii at the time, see U.S. v. Lum, 88 F.2d 88 (9th Cir. 1937); 23 Op. Atty. Gen. 345 (1901) (this included Chinese persons born or naturalized in the Hawaiian Islands prior to the annexation by the U.S.—the racial bars do not apply to this collective naturalization); 3 Hackworth, Digest of Int. Law 119. See generally, Gordon & Mailman, § 92.04[3], n. 40.

[6]Sec. 5, Act of April 30, 1900, 31 Stat. 141.

[7]Sec. 101(d), Nationality Act of 1940 reproduced as Appendix 4-12 to Ch 4; INA § 101(a)(38), 8 U.S.C.A. § 1101(a)(38).

were born in Hawaii on that date and before April 30, 1900, became U.S. citizens on April 30, 1900.[8] Similarly, it confirmed that persons born in Hawaii on or after April 30, 1900 are citizens of the United States at birth.[9]

C. POSSESSIONS AND TERRITORIES THAT NEVER BECAME STATES OF UNITED STATES

§ 2:15   In general

Research References

Steel on Immigration Law § 15(3)

This section discusses the nationality and citizenship status of inhabitants of territories that are or were at one point subject to the jurisdiction of the United States. Three possible scenarios appear. The territories may have become part of the United States, in which case persons born in these territories are, at least statutorily, U.S. citizens by birth. Arguably, and in spite of congressional protests to the contrary in the Organic Acts, these territories may have become incorporated *sub silentio*, and the Fourteenth Amendment to the U.S. Constitution would be applicable to them. Second, the U.S. may treat the territories as unincorporated possessions, referred to as "outlying possessions" in the INA, in which case, natives of those possessions are noncitizen nationals of the United States. Third, the U.S. may view the territories as foreign countries for nationality purposes. In that case, persons born in those territories have no claim to U.S. nationality. The table in Appendix 2-2 describes the citizenship and nationality status of persons born in U.S. territories.

§ 2:16   Puerto Rico

Research References

Dizon and Wettstein, Immigration Law Service 2d § 14:19
Steel on Immigration Law § 15(3)

The treaty with Spain ceding Puerto Rico, the Philippines, and Guam provided that "the civil rights and political *status* of the native inhabitants . . . shall be determined by Congress."[1] Unlike Hawaii and Alaska, the treaty and congressional action that followed did not make these territories part of the United States.[2] Therefore, the citizenship clause of the Constitution did not apply to Puerto Rico's inhabitants when the U.S acquired it.

Different provisions have governed the citizenship status of Puerto Ricans since its annexation. The original treaty with Spain gave Spanish subjects born and residing in Puerto Rico the choice either to retain Spanish nationality by making a declaration at a court within one year of the ratification of the treaty or to be

---

[8]INA § 305, 8 U.S.C.A. § 1405.
[9]INA § 305, 8 U.S.C.A. § 1405.

[Section 2:16]

[1]Art. 9, Treaty of Paris reproduced as Appendix 2-4.
[2]Balzac v. Porto Rico, 258 U.S. 298, 304-05, 42 S. Ct. 343, 345, 66 L. Ed. 627 (1922).

granted U.S. nationality.[3] All other Spanish subjects who resided in Puerto Rico automatically became U.S. nationals on the date of ratification of the treaty.[4]

On April 12, 1900, Congress granted Puerto Rican citizenship (and U.S. noncitizen nationality) to all the former Spanish subjects who resided in Puerto Rico on the date of ratification of the treaty and continued to reside there on the date of enactment of the act.[5] Children born in Puerto Rico to these former Spanish subjects became Puerto Rican citizens and U.S. nationals on April 12, 1900, or if born after that date, at birth.[6] Those natives who elected to retain their allegiance to Spain continued to retain their Spanish nationality after this act, and their children did not become Puerto Rican citizens at birth even when they were born in Puerto Rico.[7]

On March 2, 1917, Congress granted U.S. citizenship to all Puerto Rican citizens unless, within six months, they elected to retain their current political status.[8] It also granted U.S. citizenship to those natives of Puerto Rico who had been absent from the island on April 11, 1899 but who were now residing on the island, unless they made a formal declaration within six months to retain their current nationality.[9] That act did not make Puerto Rico a part of the United States for purposes of the Fourteenth Amendment's citizenship clause.[10] Persons born in Puerto Rico after that date but before 1934 did not acquire U.S. citizenship at birth.[11]

In 1934, Congress granted U.S. citizenship to all persons born in Puerto Rico after April 11, 1899 who were not nationals of another country.[12] Persons born in Puerto Rico between June 27, 1934 and January 13, 1941 who did not acquire another nationality by descent were granted U.S. citizenship at birth.[13] Persons who acquired another nationality by descent during this period did not qualify for U.S. citizenship.[14]

Finally, in 1940, Congress provided that all persons born in Puerto Rico on or after April 11, 1899 who were not made U.S. citizens under any of the prior acts of Congress were declared to be U.S. citizens provided that on the effective date of the Act (January 13, 1941), they were residing in Puerto Rico or any other territory over which the U.S. had jurisdiction.[15]

The INA repeats this provision, stating that those people became U.S. citizens on

---

[3]Art. 9, Treaty of Paris reproduced as Appendix 2-4; INS Interp. 308.1(a).

[4]INS Interp. 308.1(a). Those subjects were not given the right to elect to retain their Spanish nationality under the treaty. See Art. 9, Treaty of Paris reproduced as Appendix 2-4.

[5]Sec. 7, Act of April 12, 1900, 31 Stat. 77 reproduced as Appendix 2-5, part A. Cf. Gonzalez v. Williams, 192 U.S. 1 (1904) (interpreting the act as making Puerto Ricans not noncitizens to the U.S.); 24 Op. Atty. Gen. 40, 43 (1902) (by referring to former Spanish subjects, Congress meant to exclude those inhabitants of Puerto Rico who were German, French, or Italian).

[6]Sec. 7, Act of April 12, 1900 reproduced as Appendix 2-5; INS Interp. 308.1(a).

[7]Matter of O-M-, 9 I. & N. Dec. 188 (B.I.A. 1961).

[8]Act of March 2, 1917, Pub.L. 64-368, 39 Stat. 951 reproduced as Appendix 2-5, part B.

[9]INS Interp. 302.1(a).

[10]See Balzac v. Porto Rico, 258 U.S. 298, 305-09, 42 S. Ct. 343, 346-47, 66 L. Ed. 627 (1922).

[11]See Conrad v. Dulles, 155 F.Supp. 542 (D.P.R. 1957); Matter of O-M-, 9 I&N Dec. 188; 3 Hackworth, Digest of Int. Law 144.

[12]Act of June 27, 1934, Pub.L. 73-477, 48 Stat. 1245 reproduced as Appendix 2-5, part C.

[13]INS Interp. 302.1(b); Gordon & Mailman, § 92.

[14]Sec. 3, INS General Order 213, Jan. 19, 1935, quoted in Matter of O--M--, 9 I. & N. Dec. 188, 205, 1960 WL 12079 (B.I.A. 1960). See generally Gordon & Mailman, § 92.04[4].

[15]Sec. 202, Nationality Act of 1940 reproduced as Appendix 4-12 to Ch 4.

January 13, 1941.[16] The INA also specifically provides that people born in Puerto Rico after January 13, 1941 are U.S. citizens at birth, provided they were subject to the jurisdiction of the U.S. at the date of birth.[17] In other words, the same rule applies to Puerto Ricans born on the island after January 13, 1941 that applies to any other person born within the United States. This repetition is probably superfluous since both the 1940 act and the INA include Puerto Rico in their definitions of the geographical scope of the United States for nationality at birth purposes.[18]

The residence in Puerto Rico required by these statutes does not refer to physical presence at the time, but to a broader concept of permanent residence.[19] Thus persons, who were absent on the date, even because they were temporarily residing in another country, but were *bona fide* inhabitants of the island at the time and had no intention of permanently abandoning the island, were considered to qualify for the provisions of the 1900 act.[20]

The term "residence" in the 1940 act had a statutorily defined meaning.[21] Under its terms, persons are considered to reside wherever they have their general place of abode.[22] Even though by statute this meaning was not extended to the clause governing the collective naturalization of Puerto Ricans, the courts have found that it is applicable to that provision.[23] Persons born in Puerto Rico after April 11, 1899, who were absent on January 13, 1941 even for an extended period surrounding that date, may still have resided in Puerto Rico for purposes of the collective naturalization of the 1940 act.[24]

Apparently generated by Congressional interest, a former INS General Counsel speculated as to the effect the independence of Puerto Rico would have on the transmission of U.S. citizenship upon Puerto Ricans nationals.[25] On an individual case, a Puerto Rican sued the U.S. State Department seeking to renounce his U.S. citizenship while remaining a Puerto Rican citizen.[26] The court agreed with the State Department's view that the fact that Mr. Colon returned to Puerto Rico without documenting himself as a noncitizen, evinced a desire not to relinquish his rights as

---

[16]INA § 302, 8 U.S.C.A. § 1402.

[17]INA § 302, 8 U.S.C.A. § 1402.

[18]Sec. 101(d), Nationality Act of 1940 reproduced as Appendix 4-12 to Ch 4; INA § 101(a)(38), 8 U.S.C.A. § 1101(a)(38). Prior to the 1940 Act, Puerto Rico has been repeatedly held not to have been incorporated into the People of Puerto Rico v. Shell Co., 302 U.S. 253, 58 S. Ct. 167, 82 L. Ed. 235 (1937); Balzac v. Porto Rico, 258 U.S. 298, 42 S. Ct. 343, 66 L. Ed. 627 (1922); Downes v. Bidwell, 182 U.S. 244, 280, 21 S. Ct. 770, 784, 45 L. Ed. 1088 (1901). These cases also established that the U.S. Constitution did not apply to Puerto Rico during this period.

[19]24 Op. Atty. Gen. 40; 3 Hackworth, Digest of Int. Law 142.

[20]24 Op. Atty. Gen. at 42 (Puerto Rican painter residing in France on April 11, 1899 qualified for Puerto Rican citizenship, being a native Puerto Rican who did permanently abandon the island).

[21]See generally, §§ 4:45 to 4:48.

[22]Sec. 104, Nationality Act of 1940 reproduced as Appendix 4-12 to Ch 4.

[23]Puig Jimenez v. Glover, 255 F.2d 54 (1st Cir. 1958).

[24]Puig Jimenez v. Glover, 255 F.2d 54, 58-59 (1st Cir. 1958) (went to Spain on a visit in 1936 and was prevented from returning to Puerto Rico until July 1941 by the Spanish civil war—was residing in Puerto Rico on January 13, 1941).

[25]Legal Opinion, Aleinikoff, INS General Counsel, Genco Opinion 95-6, File No. HQ 322-P (Mar. 10, 1995).

[26]Colon v. U.S. Dept. of State, 2 F.Supp.2d 43 (D.D.C. 1998) aff'd 170 F.3d 191 (D.C.Cir 1999).

a U.S. citizen.[27] It dismissed the writ of mandamus stating that the court was not the appropriate forum to present the question of the political status of Puerto Rico.[28]

§ 2:17 Virgin Islands

Research References

Dizon and Wettstein, Immigration Law Service 2d §§ 14:24, 14:25
Steel on Immigration Law § 15(3)

The United States purchased the U.S. Virgin Islands from Denmark in 1916.[1] The treaty ceding the islands stipulated that Danish nationals would be allowed to preserve their allegiance to Denmark by making a declaration before a court.[2] In the absence of such a declaration within one year of ratification of the treaty, Danish nationals became nationals of the U.S.[3] That same article provided that those who elected to retain Danish nationality who thereafter renounced that nationality would acquire U.S. national status in the same terms as those who chose not to retain it.[4] In 1927, Congress awarded U.S. citizenship to many of the residents.[5] The INA incorporated into the statute an amended version of this granting of U.S. citizenship to residents and nationals of the Virgin Islands.[6]

Under the INA, all persons born in the U.S. Virgin Islands subject to the jurisdiction of the U.S. between January 17, 1917 and February 25, 1927 became U.S. citizens on February 25, 1927.[7] All persons born in the U.S. Virgin Islands under the jurisdiction of the U.S. on or after that date became U.S. citizens at birth.[8]

Persons born before January 17, 1917 became U.S. citizens on February 25, 1927 if: (1) they were former Danish citizens who on January 17, 1917 resided in the U.S. Virgin Islands and who on February 25, 1927 resided in the United States, Puerto Rico or the U.S. Virgin Islands, provided they did not elect to become Danish citizens by making a declaration in a court of record, or if they did, renounced or would later renounce Danish citizenship in a court of record;[9] (2) they were natives of the U.S. Virgin Islands and on January 17, 1917 resided in the U.S. Virgin Islands and on

---

[27]Colon v. U.S. Dept. of State, 2 F.Supp.2d 43 (D.D.C. 1998) aff'd 170 F.3d 191 (D.C.Cir 1999).

[28]Colon v. U.S. Dept. of State, 2 F.Supp.2d 43 (D.D.C. 1998) aff'd 170 F.3d 191 (D.C.Cir 1999).

[Section 2:17]

[1]Gordon & Mailman, § 92.04[5].

[2]Art. 6, Treaty of August 4, 1916, Denmark and U.S., 39 Stat. 1715, TS 629, 3 Redmond 2558, 7 Bevans 56 reproduced as Appendix 2-6.

[3]Art. 6, Treaty of August 4, 1916, Denmark and U.S., 39 Stat. 1715, TS 629, 3 Redmond 2558, 7 Bevans 56 reproduced as Appendix 2-6.

[4]Art. 6, Treaty of August 4, 1916, Denmark and U.S., 39 Stat. 1715, TS 629, 3 Redmond 2558, 7 Bevans 56 reproduced as Appendix 2-6.

[5]Act of February 25, 1927, Pub.L. 69-640, 44 Stat. 1234 as amended by Act of June 28, 1932, Pub.L. 72-198, 47 Stat. 336, reproduced as Appendix 2-7.

[6]INA § 306, 8 U.S.C.A. § 1406. The INA made persons born in the Virgin Islands between January 17, 1917 and February 25, 1927 U.S. citizens on February 25, 1927, and those born thereafter citizens at birth. INA § 306(b), 8 U.S.C.A. § 1406(b). This was, no doubt, the intention of the Act of February 25, 1927. See sec. 3, Act of February 25, 1927, Pub.L. 69-640, 44 Stat. 1234 reproduced as Appendix 2-7.

[7]INA § 306(b), 8 U.S.C.A. § 1406(b).

[8]INA § 306(b), 8 U.S.C.A. § 1406(b).

[9]INA § 306(a)(1), 8 U.S.C.A. § 1406(a)(1). The State Department takes the position that Danish citizens who elected to retain Danish citizenship in the one-year period of 1917, could only renounce

February 25, 1927 resided in the U.S. Virgin Islands, the United States, or Puerto Rico, provided that on February 25, 1927 they were not citizens or subjects of any other country;[10] (3) they were natives of the U.S. Virgin Islands who on January 17, 1917 resided in the United States, and on February 25, 1927 were residing in the U.S. Virgin Islands, provided that on February 25, 1927 they were not citizens or subjects of any other country;[11] (4) they were natives of the U.S. Virgin Islands and on June 28, 1932 were residing in the Continental United States, Puerto Rico, the Panama Canal Zone, or any other insular possession or territory of the United States, provided that on June 28, 1932 they were not citizens or subjects of any other country.[12] Children born after January 17, 1917 to persons within any of these four categories also became U.S. citizens on February 25, 1927, regardless of the place of birth of the child.[13]

The statutory requirement of "residence" in these statutes does not mean "physical presence" but "domicile," in the sense that persons temporarily abroad who return within a reasonable time, and establish that even while absent they were *bona fide* residents of the islands.[14] The requirement that the person must not have acquired a foreign citizenship or nationality by 1932 refers to foreign citizenship preserved or acquired by affirmative acts and not to foreign nationality acquired through marriage or by descent through a parent.[15] This interpretation is more liberal than the one applied to Puerto Ricans.[16]

Both the Nationality Act of 1940 and the INA included the U.S. Virgin Islands as part of the definition of the United States for nationality purposes.[17] Therefore, the principle of *jus soli* also applies to natives after January 13, 1941.

The treaty and laws provided that Danish citizens who resided in the Virgin

---

the Danish citizenship after Congress defined the status of U.S. Virgin Islanders in 1927. See 3 Hackworth, Digest of Int. Law 151.

[10] INA § 306(a)(2), 8 U.S.C.A. § 1406(a)(2).

[11] INA § 306(a)(3), 8 U.S.C.A. § 1406(a)(3).

[12] INA § 306(a)(4), 8 U.S.C.A. § 1406(a)(4). To qualify under this provision it is irrelevant where they were residing in 1917. "[N]atives of the Virgin Islands who were absent from islands at the time of annexation by the United States in January 1917, but were residing in 'continental United States, the Virgin Islands of the United States, Puerto Rico, the Canal Zone, or . . . other insular possession or Territory of the United States' on June 28, 1932" acquired U.S. citizenship under the statute. 38 Op. Atty. Gen. 525 (1936). Apparently, the State Department originally read into this subsection a requirement that the person must not have been residing in the U.S. Virgin Islands on January 17, 1917. 3 Hackworth, Digest of Int. Law 151 (citing State Department decision denying U.S. citizenship to former Danish subject who obtained U.S. nationality on 1917, but who in 1927 was living in the Dominican Republic: he remained a noncitizen national of the U.S.). See generally, Gordon & Mailman, § 92.04[5]. The current Foreign Affairs Manual simply restates the INA's wording that for purposes of this provision, it is irrelevant where the person was residing on January 17, 1917. 7 FAM 1123.1(b), (f).

[13] INA § 306(a), 8 U.S.C.A. § 1406(a) (introductory paragraph). Children became U.S. citizens even if the parent's U.S. citizenship was acquired through other means, provided that parent qualified under one of the four subsections. See Matter of S-, 3 I. & N. Dec. 870 (Central Office 1950).

[14] Matter of L-, 6 I. & N. Dec. 226, 229 (B.I.A. 1949); INS Interp. 306.1(b). The State Department interprets the residence requirement as not being precluded by temporary absences from the Virgin Islands at the time of cession. It construed "residence" to mean a permanent dwelling place to which the person, when absent, intended to return. 7 FAM 1123.2-1(d).

[15] Matter of L-, 3 I. & N. Dec. 719 (Central Office 1949); INS Interp. 306.1(c).

[16] See § 2:16.

[17] Sec. 101(d), Nationality Act of 1940 reproduced as Appendix 4-12 to Ch 4; INA § 101(a)(38), 8 U.S.C.A. § 1101(a)(38).

Islands could choose to retain their Danish citizenship; but also that if they thereafter renounced their Danish citizenship, they would automatically become U.S. citizens, as if they had not retained their Danish citizenship.[18]

§ 2:18 Guam

Research References
Steel on Immigration Law § 15(3)
Dizon and Wettstein, Immigration Law Service 2d §§ 14:20, 14:21

Like Puerto Rico, Guam was ceded to the United States by Spain in 1898.[1] Under the terms of the treaty, Spanish subjects native to the Spanish peninsula were given one year to elect to retain Spanish allegiance.[2] Those who did not so elect became U.S. nationals.[3] The treaty also provided that Congress would determine the rights of native inhabitants.[4]

Congress did not pass legislation defining the nationality status of natives of Guam until 1950. However, natives of Guam, Spanish subjects not born in Guam, and Spanish subjects born in Guam who did not elect to retain Spanish allegiance became U.S. nationals at the time the island was transferred to the United States.[5] Persons born in Guam after it was ceded to the United States became U.S. nationals at birth, if their fathers were U.S. nationals.[6]

The Organic Act of Guam was enacted on August 1, 1950.[7] It specifically provides that Guam is an "unincorporated" territory of the United States.[8] It, however, also confers U.S. citizenship to most natives and many residents of Guam.[9] The INA not only reenacted the citizenship provisions of the Organic Act of Guam, but also included Guam in the definition of the United States, thus extending the principle of *jus soli* to Guam.[10]

Under these laws, the following are U.S. citizens: (1) all persons born in Guam subject to the jurisdiction of the U.S. after August 1, 1950;[11] (2) all persons born in Guam subject to the jurisdiction of the U.S. on or after April 11, 1899 and before August 1, 1950 who have not taken affirmative steps to acquire or preserve foreign nationality.[12] The requirement of having been under the jurisdiction of the U.S. applies to the time of birth and in no way imposes any type of additional residence

---

[18]See § 11:28.

[Section 2:18]

[1]Art. 2, Treaty of Paris reproduced as Appendix 2-4.

[2]Art. 9, Treaty of Paris reproduced as Appendix 2-4.

[3]INS Interp. 308.1(f)(1).

[4]See § 2:16.

[5]INS Interp. 308.1(f)(1).

[6]INS Interp. 308.1(f)(2).

[7]Act of August 1, 1950, Pub.L. 81-630, 64 Stat. 384 codified as 48 U.S.C.A. §§ 1421 et seq.

[8]48 U.S.C.A. § 1421a.

[9]Sec. 4, Act of Aug. 1, 1950, 64 Stat. 384, adding Sec. 206 of the Nationality Act of 1940.

[10]INA §§ 101(a)(38), 307, 8 U.S.C.A. §§ 1101(a)(38), 1407.

[11]INA § 307(b), 8 U.S.C.A. § 1407(b).

[12]INA § 307(b), 8 U.S.C.A. § 1407(b).

requirement for people born before August 1, 1950.[13] In addition, the following two groups were granted U.S. citizenship effective August 1, 1950: (3) all persons born on the island of Guam who resided on that island on April 11, 1899, who after that date continued to reside in Guam or other territory under U.S. jurisdiction, who took no affirmative steps to preserve or acquire a foreign nationality and who on August 1, 1950 were residing in Guam or other territory under U.S. jurisdiction; (4) all Spanish subjects who on April 11, 1899 were residing in Guam and thereafter continued to reside in Guam or other territory under U.S. jurisdiction, who took no affirmative steps to preserve or acquire a foreign nationality and who on August 1, 1950 were residing in Guam or other territory under U.S. jurisdiction.[14] Children born to members of the last two groups after April 11, 1899 were also granted U.S. citizenship effective August 1, 1950, provided they were also residing in a territory subject to U.S. jurisdiction on that date.[15]

Since this grant of citizenship covered persons who derived foreign citizenship or nationality without an affirmative act of their own, the act provided a mechanism whereby those people could elect not to become U.S. citizens; they were allowed to file a declaration prior to August 1, 1952 electing to retain their foreign allegiance.[16] If they so chose, they ceased to be U.S. nationals as of the filing of the declaration, and, presumably since they had taken an affirmative step to preserve a foreign nationality, did not become citizens of the U.S.[17]

§ 2:19   American Samoa and Swains Island

Research References
Steel on Immigration Law § 15(3)

The United States acquired the different islands composing what is now referred to as American Samoa in a process that originated with the tripartite treaty of the United States, Great Britain, and Germany on December 2, 1899 in which the two European powers renounced their claims to the islands in favor of the United States.[1] The United States takes the position that American Samoa was actually acquired by the United States on February 16, 1900, the date on which Congress ratified the treaty with Great Britain and Germany.[2] On March 4, 1925, Congress issued a joint resolution proclaiming U.S. sovereignty over the Swains Island and adding it to American Samoa.[3] On February 20, 1929, Congress issued a joint resolution confirm-

---

[13]INS Interp. 307.1.

[14]INA § 307(a), 8 U.S.C.A. § 1407(a).

[15]INA § 307(a), 8 U.S.C.A. § 1407(a) (introductory paragraph).

[16]INA § 307(c), 8 U.S.C.A. § 1407(c).

[17]INA § 307, 8 U.S.C.A. § 1407.

[Section 2:19]

[1]Treaty of December 2, 1899, United States, Germany, and United Kingdom, 31 Stat. 1878, 2 Malloy 1595, 1 Bevans 276. See generally, INS Interp. 308.1(g)(1), Gordon & Mailman, § 92.04[7].

[2]23 Op. Atty. Gen. 629 (1902) ("By recent events, including the making and executing of a treaty between Great Britain, Germany, and the United States, the island of Tuitila . . . has come under the control and into the possession of the United States"—therefore, it is not a foreign country); INS Interp. 308(g)(1).

[3]43 Stat. 1256, 48 U.S.C.A. § 1662.

ing an agreement with the chieftains of Tutuila and the other islands in which the chieftains accepted U.S. sovereignty over the islands.[4]

The territory of American Samoa has never been incorporated into the United States. The Nationality Act of 1940 declared Samoans noncitizen nationals of the U.S.[5] The INA provides that American Samoa and the Swains Island are the only outlying possessions of the United States.[6] At present, Samoans and Swains Islanders are the only groups recognized as noncitizen nationals of the U.S.[7] The status of noncitizen nationals is discussed in more detail in Ch 3.

§ 2:20 Northern Mariana Islands

Research References

Steel on Immigration Law § 15(3)

In 1947, the United Nations named the United States trustee over the Northern Mariana Islands, Micronesia, the Marshall Islands, and Palau.[1] Because of this arrangement, the United States did not have sovereignty over the islands.[2] Therefore, its inhabitants were not nationals of the U.S.[3]

In 1975, however, the Northern Mariana Islands entered into a covenant of political union with the United States. This covenant was ratified by the Mariana Islands District Legislature and by the people of the Marianas Islands in 1975; it was approved by joint resolution of Congress in 1976.[4]

Multiple portions of the covenant were relevant for citizenship purposes. Section 501(a) of the Covenant provided that "the following provisions of the Constitution of the United States will be applicable within the Northern Mariana Islands as if the Northern Mariana Islands were one of the several States: . . . Amendment 14, Section 1."[5] Section 501 took effect on January 9, 1978, pursuant to a Presidential proclamation.[6]

---

[4]45 Stat. 1253, 48 U.S.C.A. § 1661. Cf. Matter of W-, 2 I. & N. Dec. 778, 779–80 (B.I.A. 1947).

[5]Sec. 101(e), Nationality Act of 1940 reproduced as Appendix 4-12.

[6]INA § 101(a)(29), 8 U.S.C.A. § 1101(a)(29).

[7]See INA § 308, 8 U.S.C.A. § 1408 (identifying as noncitizen nationals persons born in the outlying possessions of the U.S. and their children); see also §§ 3:1 et seq.

[Section 2:20]

[1]48 U.S.C.A. Ch. 14, note. Guam, which is the only other island in the Marianas, was already a territory of the U.S. See § 2:18. Cf. 7 FAM 1127.1-1(a) (defining the Trust Territory of the Pacific Islands as including the Mariana Islands except for Guam). See also 48 U.S.C.A. § 1844 (providing for possible political union between Northern Mariana Islands and Guam).

[2]See Gordon & Mailman, § 92.03[9].

[3]U.S. v. Shiroma, 123 F.Supp. 145 (D.Hawaii 1954); 7 FAM 1127.1-2(a) (1984); 8 Whiteman, Digest of Int. Law 5.

[4]Act of March 24, 1976, Pub. L. 94-241, 90 Stat. 263, codified as amended 48 U.S.C.A. § 1801.

[5]Sec. 301, Covenant to Establish the Commonwealth of Northern Mariana Islands, Pub.L. 94-241, 90 Stat. 263 (Mar. 24, 1976) codified as amended 48 U.S.C.A. § 1801. Congress used similar language in the Organic Act of Puerto Rico, 61 Stat. 772, 48 U.S.C.A. § 737 (providing that "[t]he rights, privileges, and immunities of citizens of the United States shall be respected in Puerto Rico to the same extent as though Puerto Rico were a State of the Union and subject to the provisions of paragraph 1 of section 2 of article IV of the Constitution of the United States."); Mullaney v. Anderson, 342 U.S. 415, 420 n.2, 96 L.Ed. 458, 463 n.2, 72 S.Ct. 428, 431 n.2 (1952).

[6]See Proclamation No. 4534, 42 Fed. Reg. 56593 (1977).

Meanwhile, Section 301(a) of the Covenant took effect on November 4, 1986.[7] Section 301(a) provided that all persons domiciled in the Northern Mariana Islands on November 4, 1986, who did not already owe allegiance to the United States or to any other country on that date became U.S. citizens if they: (1) were born in the Northern Mariana Islands, (2) were citizens of the Trust Territory of the Pacific Islands on November 3, 1986, had been continuously domiciled in the Northern Mariana Islands for at least five years preceding that date, and, unless under age, had registered to vote prior to January 1, 1975, for the elections for the Mariana Islands District Legislature or for any municipal election of the Northern Mariana; or (3) were not citizens of the Trust Territory of the Pacific Islands but had been continuously domiciled in the Northern Mariana Islands since before January 1, 1974.[8]

People born in the Northern Mariana Islands who, on November 4, 1986, were residing in the United States or any of its territories or possessions also became U.S. citizens on that date.[9] These provisions allowed beneficiaries to elect to become noncitizen nationals rather than U.S. citizens, by making a declaration under oath in an appropriate court within six months of that date.[10] Children under eighteen of those who became citizens under these provisions, also became U.S. citizens if they did not owe allegiance to the United States or to any other country.[11] All persons born in the islands after that date are U.S. citizens at birth.[12] The DHS issues a special citizen card for U.S. citizens from the Northern Mariana Commonwealth.[13]

The USCIS and State Department initially took the position that individuals born in the Northern Mariana Islands before November 4, 1986, were U.S. citizens only if they fell within the provisions of § 301(a) of the Covenant.[14] However, the Ninth Circuit recently rejected that interpretation.[15] Interpreting § 501(a) of the Covenant, which made § 1 of the Fourteenth Amendment applicable to the Northern Marianas, the Ninth Circuit held that anyone born in the Northern Marianas after January 9, 1978, became a citizen pursuant to the Covenant.[16] The State Department has now acquiesced in the Ninth Circuit's interpretation.[17]

Those individuals who did not become U.S. citizens under the Covenant, but who were immediate relatives of U.S. citizens and who resided on the Commonwealth of Northern Mariana Islands on November 4, 1986, are presumed to be noncitizens lawfully admitted to permanent residence in the United States as of November 4,

---

[7]Sec. 2, Presidential Proclamation No. 5564, November 3, 1986, 51 Fed. Reg. 40399; Guerrero v. U.S., 691 F. Supp. 260 (D. N. Mar. I. 1988).

[8]Sec. 301, Covenant to Establish the Commonwealth of Northern Mariana Islands, Pub.L. 94-241, 90 Stat. 263 (Mar. 24, 1976) codified as amended 48 U.S.C.A. § 1801.

[9]Sec. 301(a), Covenant to Establish the Commonwealth of Northern Mariana Islands.

[10]Sec. 302, Covenant to Establish the Commonwealth of Northern Mariana Islands.

[11]Sec. 301, Covenant to Establish the Commonwealth of Northern Mariana Islands.

[12]Sec. 303, Covenant to Establish the Commonwealth of Northern Mariana Islands.

[13]See § 13:34.

[14]See, *2004 WL 540049* (Defendant-Appellee's Answering Brief (Jan. 12, 2004)

[15]Sabangan v. Powell, 375 F.3d 818 (9th Cir. 2004).

[16]Sabangan v. Powell, 375 F.3d 818, 819-20 (9th Cir. 2004).

[17]See 7 FAM 1126.3(c)(5) ("Although the Department (CA and L/CA) believed the decision was clearly erroneous, the Solicitor General's office did not seek Supreme Court review, and it is now final. In order to maintain a uniform application of the nationality laws and for operations reasons, the Department (CA) decided to apply the decision worldwide.").

1986.[18] This benefit is available to immediate relatives of persons who became U.S. citizens through the covenant.[19] There was a certification process established for this effect, whereby the government of Northern Mariana would certify both that the noncitizen was a lawful permanent resident of Northern Mariana as of that date and was also the immediate relative of a U.S. citizen as of that date.[20]

Until 2009, immigration into the Northern Marianas was an amalgam of some matters controlled by CNMI, and other aspects controlled by the federal government.[21] Since 2009, the INA has become applicable in the CNMI.[22] The Northern Marianas were incorporated into the definition of the United States, and the CNMI became treated as the 50 states, Puerto Rico, and the District of Columbia.[23]

One of the items clarified in statute was the status of lawful permanent residents who were residing in the Commonwealth of Northern Mariana. Before 2009, it appeared that only immediate relatives of U.S. citizens could reside there without jeopardizing their lawful permanent resident status.[24] The 2008 statute retroactively eliminated that risk, clarifying that for purposes of abandonment of residence, presence in the CNMI "shall be considered to be presence in the United States."[25]

At the same time, the new statute does not support the contention that residence in CNMI before 2009 counts for purposes of the five year residency requirement for naturalization.[26] The Ninth Circuit has held that it does not.[27]

§ 2:21 Micronesia, Marshall Islands, and Palau

Research References

Steel on Immigration Law § 15(3)

The other three groups of islands in the Trust Territory of the Pacific Islands signed Compacts of Free Association with the United States.[1] Two different compacts were signed. One provided for the association of the Federated States of Micronesia

---

[18]Legal Opinion, Virtue, INS Acting General Counsel, Genco Op. 94-10, File Nos. HQ 1432-P, HQ 245-P (Feb. 9, 1994).

[19]Legal Opinion, Virtue, INS Acting General Counsel, Genco Op. 94-10, File Nos. HQ 1432-P, HQ 245-P (Feb. 9, 1994).

[20]Legal Opinion, Virtue, INS Acting General Counsel, Genco Op. 94-10, File Nos. HQ 1432-P, HQ 245-P (Feb. 9, 1994).

[21]Legal Opinion, Virtue, INS Acting General Counsel, Genco Op. 94-10, File Nos. HQ 1432-P, HQ 245-P (Feb. 9, 1994).

[22]See the Consolidated Natural Resources Act of 2008 (CNRA), Pub. L. No. 110-229, 122 Stat. 754 (2008). That statute and its implementing regulation made federal immigration law applicable to the CNMI beginning on November 28, 2009. See 48 U.S.C.A. § 1806(a)(1); Eche v. Holder, 694 F.3d 1026 (9th Cir. 2012), petition for cert. filed, 81 U.S.L.W. 3475 (U.S. Feb. 8, 2013).

[23]See INA § 101(a)(36), 8 U.S.C.A. § 1101(a)(36); INA § 101(a)(38), 8 U.S.C.A. § 1101(a)(38).

[24]Legal Opinion, Virtue, INS Acting General Counsel, Genco Op. 94-10, File Nos. HQ 1432-P, HQ 245-P (Feb. 9, 1994).

[25]CNRA § 705(c), 122 Stat. at 867 (codified at 48 U.S.C.A. § 1806 note).

[26]CNRA § 705(c), 122 Stat. at 867 (codified at 48 U.S.C.A. § 1806 note).

[27]Eche v. Holder, 694 F.3d 1026 (9th Cir. 2012), cert. denied, 133 S.Ct. 2825 (2013).

[Section 2:21]

[1]48 U.S.C.A. Ch. 14, note.

and of the Marshall Islands with the United States.[2] A different compact was signed between the government of Palau and the United States.[3] The compact between the United States and the Republic of the Marshall Islands became effective on October 21, 1986.[4] The same compact became effective between the United States and the Federated States of Micronesia on November 3, 1986.[5] The compact between the United States and the Republic of Palau became effective on October 1, 1994.[6] The compacts between the United States and the Federated States of Micronesia and the Marshall Islands were both extended, with some amendments, in 2003.[7]

Unlike the covenant with the Northern Mariana Islands, the compacts with the other former trust territories do not provide for the collective naturalization of the natives of those islands.[8] Indeed, the covenants were careful to recite that the people of these territories "have and retain their sovereignty."[9] Presumably this means that even though these states have entered into compacts of free association with the U.S., the inhabitants do not owe allegiance to the U.S. and are therefore not to be considered noncitizen nationals of the U.S.[10]

Instead, both Compacts provide that the majority of citizens and nationals of these three island countries became eligible to enter, live, work, and be educated in the United States and its territories and possessions without regard to the documentation and labor certifications of the INA.[11] Both Compacts refer to this residence in the U.S. as "habitual residence," which they define as having "a place of general abode or a principal, actual dwelling place of a continuing or lasting nature."[12]

The Compacts also provide that reasonable restrictions can be placed upon habitual residence in U.S. territories and possessions, although no such limitations can

---

[2]48 U.S.C.A. § 1901.

[3]48 U.S.C.A. § 1931.

[4]48 U.S.C.A. Ch. 14, note.

[5]48 U.S.C.A. Ch. 14, note.

[6]48 U.S.C.A. Ch. 14, note.

[7]*See* Compact of Free Association with Micronesia and the Marshall Islands, Pub.L. 108-188, 117 Stat. 2720 (December 17, 2003). The compact with the government of Palau has not changed.

[8]Compact of Free Association, U.S. - Palau, Pub.L. 99-658, 100 Stat. 3672 (Nov. 14, 1986) codified as amended 48 U.S.C.A. § 1931; Compact of Free Association, U.S. - Micronesia & Marshall Islands, Pub.L. 99-239, 99 Stat. 1770 (Jan. 14, 1986) codified as amended 48 U.S.C.A. § 1901.

[9]Preamble, Compact of Free Association, U.S. - Palau, codified as amended 48 U.S.C.A. § 1931; Preamble, Compact of Free Association, U.S. - Micronesia & Marshall Islands, codified as amended 48 U.S.C.A. § 1901 (identical language in both compacts).

[10]See 7 FAM 1127.1-2(a) (1984) (the trust territory of the Pacific Islands [TTPI] is considered to be a foreign country for nationality purposes, and citizens of the TTPI are considered to be noncitizens under U.S. law).

[11]Sec. 141, Compact of Free Association, U.S.—Palau, *codified as amended* 48 U.S.C.A. § 1931, note; Sec. 141, Compacts of Free Association, U.S.—Micronesia and Marshall Islands, *codified as amended* 48 U.S.C.A. § 1901, note. The Compacts provide specifically for exemption from INA §§ 212(a)(5)(A) and 212(a)(7) (A), (B), formerly §§ 212(a) (14), (20), and (26). Despite the freedom from the INA's documentary requirements, both Compacts refer to the status of these individuals upon entry and residence in the U.S., its territories or possessions as "non-immigrant."

[12]Sec. 461(e), Compact of Free Associations, U.S.—Palau, *codified as amended* 48 U.S.C.A. § 1931, note; Sec. 461(g), Compact of Free Association, U.S.—Micronesia and Marshall Islands, *codified as amended* 48 U.S.C.A. § 1901, note (identical language in both Compacts).

be placed on residence anywhere else in the U.S.[13] Pursuant to a directive from Congress, the legacy INS in 2000 promulgated a new regulation to define the rights and limitations on habitual residence in the U.S. territories and possessions.[14] In particular, the regulation explains the grounds for the possible removal of a habitual resident from a U.S. territory or possession.[15]

The regulation only applies to citizens of the three countries who are living in U.S. territories and possessions to which the INA applies—which currently are Guam, Puerto Rico, and the Virgin Islands.[16] The regulation does not apply to citizens of the three countries living in American Samoa or the Northern Mariana Islands because the INA does not apply to them.[17] The regulation also does not apply to citizens of the three countries living in the fifty states or the District of Colombia, since the Compacts do no allow for any restrictions on such residence.

The regulation only applies to citizens of the three countries whose cumulative physical presence in the territory or possession is 365 days or more.[18] Excluded from the definition of a habitual resident are full-time students and dependents—as defined in the regulation—of a principal habitual resident.[19] The regulation also does not apply to anyone whose presence in the territory or possession is under an authority other than section 141(a) of the Compacts, such as certain members of the U.S. Armed Forces, legal permanent residents, or persons having nonimmigrant status under the authority of the INA.[20]

The regulation subjects a habitual resident of any of the three island countries to removal from the territory or possession if the individual is not self-supporting for a period of more than 60 consecutive days for reasons other than a lawful labor dispute; has received welfare benefits by fraud or misrepresentation; or is subject to removal pursuant to INA § 237, 8 U.S.C.A. § 1227, or any other provision of the INA.[21] The term self-supporting is specifically defined in the regulation.[22] A dependant of a habitual resident is removable if the principal habitual resident becomes subject to removal, unless the dependant can show that he or she has become a dependant on another habitual resident or has become self-supporting.[23] A dependant is also removable if he or she receives unauthorized public benefits by fraud or misrepresentation or if he or she is subject to removal under the INA.[24]

The amended compacts with the Federated States of Micronesia and the Marshall Islands (referred to as "Compacts") place some limitations on the ability of its citizens to benefit from the Compacts. First, they specify that the U.S. immigration-related benefits of the Compacts extend to certain naturalized citizens of the two

---

[13]Habitual Residence in the Territories and Possessions of the United States, 65 Fed. Reg. 56463 (September 19, 2000) (Supplementary Information citing to section 141(b) of the Compacts).

[14]Habitual Residence in the Territories and Possessions of the United States, 65 Fed. Reg. 56463 (September 19, 2000) *adopting new* 8 CFR § 214.7.

[15]65 Fed. Reg. 56464.

[16]65 Fed. Reg. 56464; 8 CFR § 214.7(b).

[17]65 Fed. Reg. 56464; 8 CFR § 214.7(b).

[18]8 CFR § 214.7(a)(4)(i)(A).

[19]8 CFR § 214.7(a)(4)(i)(B) and (C).

[20]8 CFR § 214.7(a)(4)(ii).

[21]8 CFR § 214.7(e)(1).

[22]8 CFR § 214.7(a)(7).

[23]8 CFR § 214.7(e)(2)(i).

[24]8 C.F.R. § 214.7(e)(2)(ii), (iii).

countries. The amended Compacts also state, however, that these benefits shall be deemed not to extend to any naturalized citizen with respect to whom a U.S. official can draw a reasonable inference that the individual naturalized primarily in order to obtain the right to enter and work in the United States under the Compacts.[25] The amended Compacts also exclude from their coverage any person who is coming to the United States pursuant to an adoption outside of the country or in order to be adopted within the United States. This provision applies to any person who was an applicant for admission to the United States on or after March 1, 2003, including anyone in removal proceedings on or after that date.[26] The Compacts also exclude from coverage any citizen who gained citizenship through investment, passport sale, or similar program.[27]

For citizens of these nations who are allowed admission, the amended Compact makes clear that they are subject to all grounds of inadmissibility or excludability, except INA §§ 212(a)(5) (relating to labor certifications and qualifications) and 212(a)(7)(B)(i)(II) (relating to documentary requirements for nonimmigrants). Moreover, the amended Compacts also state that the public charge ground of deportation, INA § 237(a)(5), shall be construed and applied as if the statutory section reads: "any alien who has been admitted under the Compact, or the Compact, as amended, who cannot show that he or she has sufficient means of support in the United States, is deportable."[28]

The Compacts have been further amended to eliminate the need for any citizen or national of these countries permitted to enter the United States to apply for an employment authorization document in order to work. A valid, non-expired passport from either country, coupled with the U.S. entry document, will be sufficient to demonstrate eligibility to work in the U.S.[29]

§ 2:22   Panama Canal Zone

Research References
Dizon and Wettstein, Immigration Law Service 2d §§ 14:20, 14:21
Steel on Immigration Law § 15(3)

The Panama Canal Zone was leased "in perpetuity" to the United States by a treaty ratified on February 26, 1904.[1] The treaty provided that the United States

---

[25]Compact of Free Association with Micronesia and the Marshall Islands, Pub.L. 108-188, 117 Stat. 2720 (December 17, 2003).

[26]Compact of Free Association with Micronesia and the Marshall Islands, Pub.L. 108-188, 117 Stat. 2720 (December 17, 2003).

[27]Compact of Free Association with Micronesia and the Marshall Islands, Pub.L. 108-188, 117 Stat. 2720 (December 17, 2003).

[28]Compact of Free Association with Micronesia and the Marshall Islands, Pub.L. 108-188, 117 Stat. 2720 (December 17, 2003).

[29]Compact of Free Association with Micronesia and the Marshall Islands, Pub.L. 108-188, 117 Stat. 2720 (December 17, 2003).

[Section 2:22]

[1]Isthmian Canal Convention, United States and Panama, November 18, 1903, proclaimed February 26, 1904, 33 Stat. 2234, TS 431, 2 Malloy 1349, 10 Bevans 663 reproduced as Appendix 2-8; INS Interp. 303.1(a).

would exercise sovereignty rights over the leased territory.[2] Panamanians who remained in the territory and who did not elect to retain their Panamanian allegiance became U.S. nationals.[3] Children of such persons born in the Canal Zone were also U.S. noncitizen nationals.[4] Congress, however, has generally treated the Canal Zone as a foreign country for nationality purposes. Neither the INA nor the 1940 Nationality Act incorporated it into the definition of the United States or the definition of U.S. outlying possessions.[5] Therefore, children born in the Canal Zone to persons who were neither U.S. citizens nor nationals did not acquire U.S. nationality. On October 1, 1979, sovereignty over the Canal Zone was transferred back to the Republic of Panama.[6] The noncitizen nationality status ceased to exist with the transfer of sovereignty.[7]

Congress has passed special legislation for children of U.S. citizens born in the Panama Canal Zone and the Republic of Panama. This legislation will be discussed in the chapter dealing with U.S. citizens through birth abroad.[8]

§ 2:23 Philippines

Research References

Steel on Immigration Law § 15(3)

Like Puerto Rico and Guam, the United States acquired the Philippines from Spain after the Spanish-American war.[1] The same treaty that settled the status of Puerto Rico and Guam settled the status of the Philippines. The treaty gave Spanish subjects born in the Philippines one year to file a declaration to retain Spanish allegiance.[2] The U.S. extended for an extra six months the time to file the declaration of retention of Spanish allegiance.[3] Spaniards born in the Philippines who failed to file such declarations and all other Spanish subjects who were residents of the Philippines on April 11, 1899 became U.S. noncitizen nationals on that date.[4]

---

[2]Art. 2, Isthmian Canal Convention, reproduced as Appendix 2-8; 26 Op. Atty. Gen. 376 (1907); Wilson v. Shaw, 204 U.S. 24, 32, 27 S.Ct. 233, 51 L.Ed. 351 (1907); Gordon & Mailman, § 92.04[8].

[3]26 Op. Atty. Gen. 376, 378 (1907) ("the words 'sovereign rights' 'within the zone' [in art. 3 of the Isthmian Canal Convention] mean, among other things, the right to the allegiance of the Zone's people"); INS Interp. 308.1(b).

[4]INS Interp. 308.1(b). For children born after January 13, 1941 there was the additional requirement that both parents must have resided in the U.S. before the child's birth in order for nationality to be transmitted by descent to the child born in the Canal Zone. INS Interp. 308.1(b).

[5]Sec. 101(d), (e), Nationality Act of 1940 reproduced as Appendix 4-12 to Ch 4; INA § 101(a)(29), (38), 8 U.S.C.A. § 1101(a)(29), (38).

[6]7 FAM 1121(b)(3); H.Rep. 96-98, Part 1, pages 33, 35, 39.

[7]See § 3:1; Matter of M-, 6 I. & N. Dec. 182 (BIA 1954).

[8]See §§ 4:67 to 4:69.

[Section 2:23]

[1]Art. 3, Treaty of Paris reproduced as Appendix 2-4.

[2]Art. 9, Treaty of Paris reproduced as Appendix 2-4.

[3]31 Stat. 1754.

[4]INS Interp. 308.1(d)(1).

Children born in the Philippines to these noncitizen nationals between April 11, 1899 and July 4, 1946 also became U.S. noncitizen nationals at birth.[5]

Early after the cession of the territory, Congress made persons born in the Philippines citizens of the Philippines.[6] The Philippines Islands were not incorporated into the United States,[7] and persons born in the Philippines did not acquire U.S. citizenship at birth.[8] The Philippines legislature was empowered on March 26, 1920 to extend Philippine citizenship to persons other than those designated by the earlier U.S. legislation.[9] People who became citizens of the Philippines under the statutes enacted by the legislature of the Philippines automatically became U.S. nationals.[10]

Not only were the Philippine citizens not considered U.S. citizens during this period, but also racial quotas barred Filipinos from obtaining judicial naturalization.[11] Even though Philippine citizens became noncitizen nationals of the U.S.,[12] they could not move freely to the continent between 1934 and the independence of the Philippines in 1946.[13]

In 1934, Congress passed the Philippine Independence Act, which provided for Philippine independence after a ten-year period of transition.[14] During this ten-year period, Filipinos would continue to owe allegiance to the United States.[15] Japan invaded the Philippines during this ten-year period, and the island did not attain independence until July 4, 1946.[16] When the U.S. relinquished its right of sovereignty over the islands, independence of the Philippines terminated U.S. noncitizen nationality of Philippine citizens.[17] Filipinos residing in the United States on July 4, 1946 also were regarded as noncitizens upon the independence of the Philippines.[18] Of course, independence of the Philippines did not affect the U.S. citizenship status of Filipinos who were U.S. citizens born abroad based on the parent's prior residence in the Philippines during the time it was an outlying possession of the United States.[19]

---

[5]Act of July 1, 1902, 32 Stat. 692, as amended by Act of March 23, 1912, 37 Stat. 77; and by Act of Aug. 29, 1916, 39 Stat. 545; INS Interp. 308.1(d)(1).

[6]Sec. 4 of the Act of July 1, 1902, 32 Stat. 692, as amended by Act of March 23, 1912, 37 Stat. 77; and by Act of Aug. 29, 1916, 39 Stat. 545.

[7]Dorr v. U.S., 195 U.S. 138, 24 S.Ct. 808, 49 L.Ed. 128 (1904).

[8]Matter of Hermoza, 14 I. & N. Dec. 447 (B.I.A. 1973).

[9]INS Interp. 308.1(d)(2).

[10]INS Interp. 308.1(d)(2).

[11]De La Ysla v. U.S., 77 F.2d 988, 989 (9th Cir. 1935) cert. denied, 296 U.S. 575 (1935); Matter of Hermoza, 14 I&N Dec. 447.

[12]Roque Espiritu De La Ysla v. U.S., 77 F.2d 988, 989 (C.C.A. 9th Cir. 1935); Application of Viloria, 84 F. Supp. 584, 585 (D. Haw. 1949); INS Interp. 308.1(d).

[13]See § 3:6.

[14]Tydings-McDuffie Act of March 24, 1934, 48 Stat. 456 effective on May 1, 1934 (after the Philippine legislature passed a concurrent resolution accepting the act). See INS Interp. 326.1.

[15]Sec. 2(a), Tydings-McDuffie Act.

[16]Pres. Proc. 2695, 60 Stat. 1352; Treaty of July 4, 1946, effective on October 22, 1946, 61 Stat. 1174, 1179, TIAS 1568, 11 Bevans 3, 11 Bevans 32.

[17]Rabang v. Boyd, 353 U.S. 427, 77 S.Ct. 985, 1 L.Ed.2d 956 (1957); Manlangit v. U.S. INS, 488 F.2d 1073, 1074 (4th Cir. 1973); Matter of M-, 6 I. & N. Dec. 182 (B.I.A. 1954).

[18]Rabang v. Boyd, 353 U.S. 427, 430-431, 77 S. Ct. 985, 987, 1 L. Ed. 2d 956 (1957).

[19]In Status Determination, 4 I&N Dec. 575 (Central Office 1951). See §§ 4:1 et seq.

III. UNDER THE JURISDICTION OF THE UNITED STATES

§ 2:24 Meaning of "subject to jurisdiction"; generally

The Fourteenth Amendment uses the phrasing that persons born in the United States and "subject to the jurisdiction thereof" are citizens of this country.[1] The phrase "subject to the jurisdiction of the United States" refers to the country's ability to make its laws obligatory within its territory.[2] A person subject to the jurisdiction of the United States is a person who has the obligation of following the laws of this country. This phrase was intended apparently to recognize and adopt a number of common law exceptions to the principle of *jus soli*.[3]

Under English common law, the rule regarding nationality at birth was that "every person born within the dominions of the crown, no matter whether of English or of foreign parents, and, in the latter case, whether the parents were settled or merely temporarily in the country, was an English subject; save only the children of foreign ambassadors (who were excepted because their parent carried their own nationality with them), or a child born to a foreigner during hostile occupation of any part of the territories of England."[4] This rule was adopted in the Fourteenth Amendment when it provided that "all persons born . . . in the United States and subject to the jurisdiction thereof are citizens of the United States and of the State wherein they reside."[5]

In general terms, a country has exclusive and absolute jurisdiction over its territory.[6] All restrictions upon this power derive from the implied or expressed consent of the sovereign.[7] Such exclusive and absolute jurisdiction has been waived for reasons of comity, for reasons of expedience, and, in the United States, because of the legal status granted to Native American communities. Under comity, there are the following exemptions: (1) when a foreign sovereign visits another country, he or she is not subject to the jurisdiction of that country; (2) foreign ministers and ambassadors of foreign sovereigns are not subject to such jurisdiction; (3) when a sovereign allows foreign troops to pass through the territory of his or her country, they are not under his or her jurisdiction; and (4) foreign armed ships that are allowed into the territory are considered not to be under the jurisdiction of the local sovereign.[8]

The exemption based on expediency covers exclusively children of foreign enemies during hostile occupation of the country's territory. This rule derives from the fact that during hostile occupation, the sovereign has been forced to suspend its sovereignty over its territory. This precise issue was raised during the British occupation of Castine, Maine, in the early 19th century. During the occupation:

The sovereignty of the United States over the territory was, of course, suspended, and

---

[Section 2:24]

[1]U.S. Const. amend. XIV, § 1.

[2]U.S. v. Wong Kim Ark, 169 U.S. 649, 683, 18 S. Ct. 456, 470, 42 L. Ed. 890 (1898).

[3]Matter of Cantu, 17 I&N Dec. 190.

[4]Cockburn, Nat. 7 quoted in U.S. v. Wong Kim Ark, 169 U.S. 649, 657, 706, 18 S. Ct. 456, 460, 42 L. Ed. 890 (1898) (quoted by both majority and the dissent).

[5]U.S. Const. amend. XIV, § 1.

[6]The The Schooner Exchange v. McFaddon, 11 U.S. 116, 136, 3 L. Ed. 287, 1812 WL 1310 (1812).

[7]U.S. v. Wong Kim Ark, 169 U.S. 649, 684-86, 18 S. Ct. 456, 470-71, 42 L. Ed. 890 (1898).

[8]The The Schooner Exchange v. McFaddon, 11 U.S. 116, 137-39, 147, 3 L. Ed. 287, 1812 WL 1310 (1812).

the laws of the United States could no longer be rightfully enforced there, or be obligatory upon inhabitants who remained and submitted to the conquerors. By the surrender, the inhabitants passed under a temporary allegiance to the British government, and were bound by such laws, and such only, as it chose to recognize and impose. From the nature of the case, no other laws could be obligatory upon them; for, where there is no protection or allegiance or sovereignty, there can be no claim to obedience.[9]

The foregoing exception is limited only to children of foreign enemies, and then only when the occupation is hostile. It does not cover children of other noncitizens who occupied territories over which the U.S. government had *de facto* failed to exercise its jurisdiction. This situation was brought to light in *Matter of Cantu*.[10] Shortly after the treaty with Mexico setting the Rio Grande as the border between the two countries, a private company in Texas illegally diverted the waters of the river to the north in order to use them for irrigation. As a consequence, an area of land, known as the Horcon tract, that used to be north of the river passed to the south of it. Both Mexico and the United States recognized the illegality of this action. However, during the period in which the river was so diverted, the Mexican town of Rio Rico, Tamaulipas, unknowingly expanded into this area. The town had such services as police and schools. In practical terms, during this time the U.S. government did not exercise governmental control over this territory and the Mexican government did. The U.S. Attorney General, however, held that children born in this territory during this time were U.S. citizens.

A third restriction peculiar to the United States covers the particular legal status of territories held by Native American nations recognized as such by the United States. As will be discussed more fully below, these nations are legally considered separate nations, though a "dependent power" of the United States.[11] The Civil Rights Act of April 9, 1866, which served as the basis for the Fourteenth Amendment provided that "[a]ll persons born in the United States . . . excluding Indians not taxed, are declared to be citizens of the United States."[12] Members of the Native American nations, however, have been granted statutory U.S. citizenship.[13]

§ 2:25   Meaning of "subject to jurisdiction"; generally—Diplomats

Research References

Dizon and Wettstein, Immigration Law Service 2d § 14:16
Steel on Immigration Law § 15(2)

Under the common-law rule, as adopted by the Fourteenth Amendment, children of foreign diplomats are exempt from jurisdiction of the United States and, therefore, do not acquire U.S. citizenship by birth in the United States.[1] However, not all representatives of foreign governments are exempt from the jurisdiction of the United States and, therefore, from the applicability of the Fourteenth Amendment.[2] Thus in *In re Baiz*, the Supreme Court pointed out that consuls, unlike ambas-

---

[9]U.S. v. Rice, 17 U.S. (3 Wheat.) 246, 254 (1819).

[10]Matter of Cantu, 17 I. & N. Dec. 190.

[11]For a discussion of the Indian Tribes regimes, see § 2:26.

[12]Gordon & Mailman, § 92.03[1][b].

[13]See § 2:26.

[Section 2:25]

[1]U.S. v. Wong Kim Ark, 169 U.S. 649, 682, 18 S. Ct. 456, 469, 42 L. Ed. 890 (1898).

[2]See 8 CFR § 101.3(b).

sadors, are not considered so entrusted with authority to represent their sovereign, or to vindicate its prerogatives, or entitled by the laws of nations to the privileges and immunities of ambassadors or public ministers, but are subject to the jurisdiction, civil and criminal, of the courts of the country in which they reside.[3]

Current law relies on this distinction. It excludes from the workings of the citizenship clause of the Fourteenth Amendment children of foreign heads of state on official visits and of those foreign diplomatic officers who as a matter of international law are not subject to the jurisdiction of the United States.[4] To be able to ascertain whether a child born to a representative of a foreign country is exempt from the workings of United States laws, the State Department publishes every three months in the Department's Diplomatic List, often called the "Blue List," the names of all foreign officials who are accredited to the United States and who have full diplomatic privileges and immunities.[5] These persons and their immediate dependents are completely exempt from the workings of the United States laws. For some reason, the Blue List includes the names of the spouses and adult daughters of diplomats who are residing with them, but does not include the names of their minor children or dependent adult sons attending school or college or residing with them.[6] All these relatives—spouses, minor children, and dependent adult sons and daughters who are either residing with the diplomat parent or attending school—are entitled to diplomatic immunity.[7] The categories of foreign officials listed in the Blue List include ambassadors, ministers, charges d' affairs, counselors, secretaries of embassies and legations, attaches, other employees of embassies or legations, and persons with comparable diplomatic status and immunity who are accredited to the United Nations.[8] The current blue list, as well as archives to earlier blue lists and a searchable database, can be found at: http://www.state.gov/s/cpr/rls/dpl/.

Children of other foreign officials, including consular officials and their staff, are not exempt from the workings of U.S. laws and are U.S. citizens at birth.[9] Every three months, the State Department publishes a list of Employees of Diplomatic Missions Not Printed in the Diplomatic List, which is known as the "White List."[10] This list gives the names of all official employees of diplomatic missions in Washington and the names of all servants of accredited diplomatic officers.[11] By law and custom, these persons are entitled to certain diplomatic privileges and immunities, but such immunities do not extend to their families.[12] Their children are born subject to the jurisdiction of the United States and acquire U.S. citizenship at birth.[13] The State Department also publishes a list of "Foreign Consular Officers in

---

[3]In re Baiz, 135 U.S. 403, 424, 10 S. Ct. 854, 34 L. Ed. 222 (1890) cited in U.S. v. Wong Kim Ark, 169 U.S. 649, 678, 18 S. Ct. 456, 468, 42 L. Ed. 890 (1898).

[4]INS Interp. 301.1(a)(4)(i). However, children born in the United States to foreign heads of state during nonofficial visits are U.S. citizens at birth. 7 FAM 1113-3.2-4(b).

[5]7 FAM 1113.2-2(b).

[6]7 FAM 1113.2-2(b).

[7]7 FAM 1113.2-2(b).

[8]8 CFR § 101.3(a)(2); INS Interp. 301.1(a)(4)(i); In re Thenault, 47 F.Supp. 952 (1942).

[9]8 CFR § 101.3(b); INS Interp. 301.1(a)(4)(ii).

[10]7 FAM 1113.2-2(c).

[11]7 FAM 1113.2-2(c).

[12]7 FAM 1113.2-2(c).

[13]7 FAM 1113.2-2(c); INS Interp. 301.1(a)(4)(ii).

the United States."[14] Their children are also born subject to the jurisdiction of the U.S.[15]

The Foreign Affairs Manual summarizes these rules as follows. Children born in the United States to the following foreign government representatives are U.S. citizens at birth: (1) employees of foreign missions accredited to the United States and included in the publication referred to as the "White List;" (2) foreign diplomats accredited to a country other than the United States; (3) foreign diplomats whose assignments in the United States have terminated or have not yet begun; (4) foreign diplomats married to U.S. citizens capable of transmitting U.S. citizenship to children born abroad; (5) consular officers and members of their staffs (some consular officers assigned to embassies have diplomatic titles and are included in the Diplomatic List).[16]

It appears that most courts accept as conclusive the State Department's determination as to diplomatic status, including whether an individual is appropriately on the Blue or White List.[17]

Foreign representatives to international organizations in the United States are treated in the same manner as foreign representatives to the U.S. Representatives of foreign governments to the United Nations have diplomatic rank and are exempt from the workings of the U.S. laws.[18] Their children born in the United States are, therefore, not U.S. citizens at birth.[19] On the other hand, since the agreement between the United Nations and the U.S. only provides for limited immunity for representatives of governments not recognized by the U.S., children born to them in the United States are U.S. citizens at birth.[20] Similarly, international employees of the United Nations, who do not represent their specific countries, are fully subject to the jurisdiction of the U.S.[21] Representatives to the North Atlantic Treaty Organization (NATO) and the Organization of American States (OAS) enjoy the same privileges as representatives of foreign governments to the United Nations.[22]

Procedurally, the Foreign Affairs Manual provides guidelines to U.S. consular posts abroad regarding the treatment of children born in the United States to representatives of foreign governments. It advises the posts not to rely on the recol-

---

[14]8 CFR § 101.3(b).

[15]8 CFR § 101.3(b)(2).

[16]8 CFR § 101.3(b); 7 FAM 1113.2-2(d); INS Interp. 301.1(a)(4)(ii).

[17]U.S. v. Al-Hamdi, 356 F.3d 564, 573, 1 A.L.R. Fed. 2d 695 (4th Cir. 2004) ("[T]he State Department's certification, which is based upon a reasonable interpretation of the Vienna Convention, is conclusive evidence as to the diplomatic status of an individual. Thus, we will not review the State Department's factual determination that, at the time of his arrest, Al-Hamdi fell outside the immunities of the Vienna Convention."); Carrera v. Carrera, 174 F.2d 496, 497 (D.C. Cir. 1949) ("[it] is enough that an ambassador has requested immunity, that the State Department has recognized that the person for whom it was requested is entitled to it, and that the Department's recognition has been communicated to the court"); Abdulaziz v. Metropolitan Dade County, 741 F.2d 1328, 1331, 40 Fed. R. Serv. 2d 110 (11th Cir. 1984) ("courts have generally accepted as conclusive the views of the State Department as to the fact of diplomatic status"). The Supreme Court's framing is more circumspect. In re Baiz, 135 U.S. 403, 421, 10 S. Ct. 854, 34 L. Ed. 222 (1890) ("the certificate of the secretary of state . . . is the best evidence to prove the diplomatic character of a person").

[18]7 FAM 1113.2-3(a).

[19]7 FAM 1113.2-3(b).

[20]See 7 FAM 1113.2-3(c).

[21]7 FAM 1113.2-3(f).

[22]7 FAM 1113.2-3(e).

lections of the parents or the children about the parents' diplomatic status at the time of the child's birth. Instead it requires a review of the Diplomatic Lists and other records dating from the time of the birth.[23] A post that receives an application from a first-time applicant born in the United States to a diplomat or an inquiry about the citizenship status of such a person is advised to send a telegram to the State Department requesting Washington to check the pertinent records.[24] The telegram must include the child's name and date and place of birth, the name of the parent who may have had diplomatic status at the time of the child's birth, and the name of the country represented.[25] The telegram should indicate whether the other parent was a U.S. citizen when the child was born.[26]

When the parent was a representative to the United Nations in the United States, the telegram must also indicate that the parent was assigned to the United Nations.[27] In such cases, the State Department will check the U.N. records and provide an opinion as to the child's claim to citizenship.[28] When the diplomat was a representative to NATO or the OAS, such a fact must be communicated to the State Department in the telegram. Even though there is no list of diplomats accredited to those organizations, the State Department will still make a determination whether the person had full diplomatic immunity at the time of the child's birth.[29]

Finally, it must be pointed out that even when one of the parents is a diplomat, the child may be a U.S. citizen if the other parent is a U.S. citizen. This is because the laws dealing with U.S. citizens born abroad have been interpreted to apply to children born inside the United States to one diplomat parent and one U.S. citizen parent.[30]

§ 2:26 Meaning of "subject to jurisdiction"; generally—Native Americans

Research References

Dizon and Wettstein, Immigration Law Service 2d § 14:15
Steel on Immigration Law § 15(2)

Native Americans are considered not to be subject to the jurisdiction of the United States for purposes of citizenship determination under the Fourteenth Amendment.[1] As expressed in *Wong Kim Ark*, "the Indian tribes, being within the territorial limits of the United States, were not, strictly speaking, foreign states, but were noncitizen nations, distinct political communities, the members of which owed immediate allegiance to their several tribes, and were not part of the people of the United States."[2] *Elk v. Williams* succinctly states the issue when it says that

---

[23]7 FAM 1113.2-2(e).

[24]7 FAM 1113.2-2(e).

[25]7 FAM 1113.2-2(e).

[26]7 FAM 1113.2-2(e).

[27]7 FAM 1113.2-3(d).

[28]7 FAM 1113.2-3(d) (a list of members of permanent missions to the United Nations who are entitled to diplomatic privileges and immunities is issued by the U.S. Mission to the United Nations).

[29]7 FAM 1113.2-3(e).

[30]7 FAM 1113.2-2(f). See § 4:16.

[Section 2:26]

[1]Elk v. Wilkins, 112 U.S. 94, 5 S.Ct. 41, 28 L.Ed. 643 (1884).

[2]U.S. v. Wong Kim Ark, 169 U.S. 649, 681, 18 S. Ct. 456, 469, 42 L. Ed. 890 (1898).

"Indians born within the territorial limits of the United States, members of, and owing immediate allegiance to, one of the Indian tribes (a noncitizen, though dependent, power), although in a geographical sense born in the United States, are no more 'born in the United States, and subject to the jurisdiction thereof,' within the meaning of the first section of the Fourteenth Amendment, than the children of subjects of any foreign government born within the domain of that government, or the children born within the United States of ambassadors or other public ministers of foreign nations."[3]

In 1924, Congress enacted a statute granting citizenship to all Native Americans born in the United States who had not previously acquired citizenship at birth.[4] Furthermore, since 1940 there has been a special provision in the citizenship laws dictating that any person born in the United States to a member of a Native American nation is a United States citizen at birth.[5]

§ 2:27 Meaning of "subject to jurisdiction"; generally—Children of noncitizens

The Supreme Court, in *U.S. v. Wong Kim Ark*,[1] recognized that the alienage status of the parents would not affect the citizenship of the children born in the United States. This is just the application of the principle of *jus soli*. Unless specifically exempted as foreign ambassadors, noncitizens are subject to the jurisdiction of the sovereign where they are. As was pointed out by Secretary of State Webster in the middle of last century, "[i]ndependently of a residence with intention to continue such residence; independently of any domiciliation; independently of the taking of any oath of allegiance, or of renouncing any former allegiance,—it is well known that by the public law a noncitizen or a stranger born, for so long a time as he continues within the dominions of a foreign government, owes obedience to the laws of that government, and may be punished for treason or other crimes as a native-born subject might be, unless his case is varied by some treaty stipulations."[2]

The fact that the parents are and have always been noncitizens will not prevent their children from becoming U.S. citizens.[3] Even if racial bars prevent the parents from becoming U.S. citizens through naturalization, their children will be U.S. citizens if born in the United States.[4] Also, the parents' temporary or illegal presence in the United States will not prevent their children from being citizens if born here.[5]

---

[3]Elk v. Wilkins, 112 U.S. 94, 99-103, 5 S. Ct. 41, 44-46, 28 L. Ed. 643 (1884).

[4]Act of June 2, 1924, 43 Stat. 253.

[5]Sec. 201(b), Nationality Act of 1940; INA § 301(b), 8 U.S.C.A. § 1401(b); INS Interp. 301.1(a)(6).

[Section 2:27]

[1]U.S. v. Wong Kim Ark, 169 U.S. 649, 18 S.Ct. 456, 42 L.Ed. 890 (1898).

[2]Webster, Report to the President on the Thrasher case quoted in U.S. v. Wong Kim Ark, 169 U.S. 649, 693-94, 18 S. Ct. 456, 474, 42 L. Ed. 890 (1898).

[3]Perkins v. Elg, 307 U.S. 325, 59 S. Ct. 884, 83 L. Ed. 1320 (1939); Von Schwerdtner v. Piper, 23 F.2d 862 (D.Md. 1928); Regan v. King, 134 F.2d 413 (9th Cir.), cert. denied, 319 U.S. 753 (1943).

[4]Morrison v. People of State of California, 291 U.S. 82, 54 S. Ct. 281, 78 L. Ed. 664 (1934); In re Sing, 21 Fed. 905 (D.Cal. 1894).

[5]U.S. v. Wong Kim Ark, 169 U.S. 649, 649, 18 S. Ct. 456, 42 L. Ed. 890 (1898); Lynch v. Clarke, 1 Sandf. Ch. 583 (NY 1844); INS Interp. 301.1(a)(3); 7 FAM 1113.2-1(b)(1); Gordon & Mailman, § 92.03[2][e].

IV. PRESUMPTION AS TO FOUNDLINGS

§ 2:28 Generally

Research References

Steel on Immigration Law § 15(2)

Children who are found in the U.S. at a young age are presumed to have been born in the United States and are thus considered U.S. citizens.[1] The Nationality Act of 1940 gave statutory expression to this presumption. It provided that a child of unknown parentage found in the U.S. will be presumed to have been born in the United States until it is established that the child was not in fact born in this country.[2] Under current law, if a child of unknown parentage is found in the U.S. while the child is less than five years of age, the child will be presumed conclusively to have been born in the United States unless the person's birth outside the United States is established before the child reaches majority.[3] The 1940 Act was in effect between January 1, 1941 and December 23, 1952. After that date, the INA provision would define the status of the found child.

V. SUMMARY

§ 2:29 Generally

Research References

Steel on Immigration Law §§ 15(1), 15(2)

Except for children of certain diplomats, persons born in the United States become U.S. citizens at birth.[1] The nationality, alienage status, or race of the parents will not affect the citizenship of a child born in the United States.[2] For purposes of U.S. citizenship at birth inside the U.S., the *United States* includes the 50 states, Puerto Rico, the U.S. Virgin Islands, and Guam.[3] Persons born in the Northern Marianas after January 9, 1978, are also United States citizens at birth.[4]

Persons born in the ports, harbors, and territorial waters of the United States are citizens of the United States.[5] Thus, persons born aboard foreign merchant vessels within the 12 miles of U.S. territorial waters or in U.S. ports are citizens of the

---

[Section 2:28]

[1]See Gorman v. Forty Second St. Ry. Co., 203 N.Y.S. 632, 208 App. 214 (1924); Atchley v. Verner, 134 Okla. 156 (1929); Jantzen v. Arizona Copper Co., 3 Ariz. 6 (1889).

[2]Sec. 201(f), Nationality Act of 1940. Cf. INS Interp. 301.1(a)(7) (citing administrative decisions regarding this section of the law).

[3]INA § 301(f), 8 U.S.C.A. § 1401(f).

[Section 2:29]

[1]INA § 301, 8 U.S.C.A. § 1401; INS Interpretation 301.1(a)(4).

[2]INS Interp. 301.1(a)(3).

[3]INA § 101(a)(38), 8 U.S.C.A. § 1101(a)(38); INS Interp. 301.1(a)(2).

[4]Sabangan v. Powell, 375 F.3d 818, 819-20 (9th Cir. 2004); see generally, § 2:20.

[5]INS Interp. 301.1(a)(2).

United States.[6] However, persons born aboard foreign public vessels, such as warships, do not obtain U.S. citizenship at birth.[7] The territory of the United States does not extend beyond these narrowly defined territorial limits. Thus, birth in a United States vessel that is not within the territorial waters of the U.S., as well as birth inside U.S. consulates or embassies abroad or on U.S. Naval Stations abroad, is not birth within the United States and does not by itself confer U.S. citizenship upon the child.[8]

A child of unknown parents who was found in the United States between January 12, 1941 and December 24, 1952 is presumed to have been born in the U.S. until proven otherwise.[9] After December 24, 1952, anyone whose parents are unknown and is found within the United States while under five years of age is conclusively presumed to be a native-born U.S. citizen unless his or her foreign birth is established before he or she turns 21 years of age.[10]

---

[6]Cunard S.S. Co. v. Mellon, 262 U.S. 100, 122, 43 S. Ct. 504, 507, 67 L. Ed. 894, 27 A.L.R. 1306 (1923); Presidential Proclamation 5928 of Dec. 27, 1988, 54 Fed. Reg. 777 (Jan. 9, 1989); Gordon & Mailman, § 92.03[2][c].

[7]INS Interp. 301.1(a)(5).

[8]See generally, Gordon & Mailman, § 92.03[2][c], [d].

[9]INS Interp. 301.1(a)(7).

[10]INA § 301(f), 8 U.S.C.A. § 1401(f); INS Interp. 301.1(a)(7).

APPENDIX 2-1

List of the States and Dates of Admission into the United States[1]

State	Date of Admission as a State to the U.S.	Date Originally Organized as Territory	Comments
Alabama	December 14, 1819	March 3, 1817	
Alaska	January 3, 1959	May 17, 1884	
Arizona	February 14, 1912	February 24, 1863	
Arkansas	June 15, 1836	March 2, 1819	
California	September 9, 1850		Never a territory
Colorado	August 1, 1876	February 28, 1861	
Connecticut	(March 4, 1789)		Original State
Delaware	(March 4, 1789)		Original State
Florida	March 3, 1845	March 30, 1822	
Georgia	(March 4, 1789)		Original State
Hawaii	August 21, 1959	April 30, 1900	
Idaho	July 3, 1890	March 3, 1863	
Illinois	December 3, 1818	January 11, 1805	Part of Indiana Territory before that date
Indiana	December 11, 1816	May 7, 1800	Part of North-West Territory before that date
Iowa	March 3, 1845	June 12, 1838	
Kansas	January 29, 1861	May 30, 1854	
Kentucky	June 1, 1792	May 26, 1790	Nominally part of Indiana Territory (South of River Ohio) for a short time
Louisiana	April 8, 1812	March 26, 1804	
Maine	March 15, 1820		Formed from part of the state of Massachusetts
Maryland	(March 4, 1789)		Original State
Massachusetts	(March 4, 1789)		Original State
Michigan	January 26, 1837	June 11, 1805	Part of Indiana Territory before that date
Minnesota	May 11, 1858	March 3, 1849	
Mississippi	December 10, 1817	April 7, 1798	
Missouri	August 10, 1821	June 4, 1812	Part of Louisiana Territory before that date
Montana	November 8, 1889	May 26, 1864	

[1]Dates of Admission derived from United States, Organic Acts for the Territories of the United States, 1900. List of Original States derived from Constitution, USCA, historical notes.

State	Date of Admission as a State to the U.S.	Date Originally Organized as Territory	Comments
Nebraska	February 9, 1867	May 30, 1854	
Nevada	October 13, 1864	March 2, 1861	
New Hampshire	(March 4, 1789)		Original State
New Jersey	(March 4, 1789)		Original State
New York	(March 4, 1789)		Original State
New Mexico	January 6, 1912	September 9, 1850	
North Carolina	(March 4, 1789)		Original State
North Dakota	November 2, 1889	March 2, 1861	Date of creation of Dakota territory
Ohio	November 29, 1802	July 13, 1787	
Oklahoma	November 16, 1907	May 2, 1890	
Oregon	February 14, 1859	August 14, 1848	
Pennsylvania	(March 4, 1789)		Original State
Rhode Island	(March 4, 1789)		Original State
South Carolina	(March 4, 1789)		Original State
South Dakota	November 2, 1889	March 2, 1861	Date of creation of Dakota territory
Tennessee	June 1, 1796	May 26, 1790	
Texas	December 29, 1845		Never a territory
Utah	July 16, 1894	September 9, 1850	
Vermont	March 4, 1791		Never a territory
Virginia	(March 4, 1789)		Original State
Washington	February 22, 1889	March 2, 1853	
West Virginia	June 19, 1863		Formed from part of the state of Virginia
Wisconsin	May 29, 1848	April 20, 1836	Originally part of the North-West territory
Wyoming	June 10, 1890	July 25, 1868	

APPENDIX 2-2

Status by Birth in Territories Incorporated into the United States

	Date of Acquisition of Territory by U.S.	Effect on Inhabitants at date of Acquisition	Collective Naturalizations & Date Subjects Became U.S. Citizens	U.S. Citizenship at Birth before incorporation to U.S.	Date Become Part of U.S. for Citizenship: U.S. Citizenship at birth
Puerto Rico (P.R.)	April 11, 1899	(1) Spanish subjects residents in P.R.[1] become U.S. nationals and P.R. citizens (2) Their children born after 4/11/1899 become U.S. nationals & P.R. citizens at birth or on 4/12/1900	3/2/17: (A) All P.R. citizens become U.S. citizens (B) Natives of P.R. not residents on 4/11/1899 but residents now become U.S. citizens 6/27/34: All persons born in P.R. after 4/11/1899 who are not nationals of another country become U.S. citizens	All persons born in P.R. after 6/27/34 and before 1/13/41 who did not acquire another nationality by descent are U.S. citizens at birth	January 13, 1941
U.S. Virgin Islands (U.S.V.I.)	January 17, 1917	(1) Danish nationals who resided in U.S.V.I. became U.S. nationals[11] (2) Danish nationals who resided in U.S.V.I. and elected to remain Danish nationals but later changed their minds became U.S. nationals	2/25/27: (A) All persons in the previous column who on 2/25/27 resided in the U.S., P.R., or U.S.V.I. (B) Natives of U.S.V.I. who on 1/17/17 and on 2/25/27 resided in the U.S., P.R., or U.S.V.I.[2] (C) Natives of U.S.V.I. who on 1/17/17 resided in the U.S. and on 2/25/27 resided in U.S.V.I.[12] (D) Natives of U.S.V.I. who on 6/28/32 resided in the Continental U.S., P.R., Panama Canal Zone, or Insular Possessions of the U.S.[13] (E) Children of the other groups in this column regardless of the place of birth	Persons born in U.S.V.I. under U.S. jurisdiction after 2/25/27	January 13, 1941
Panama Canal Zone	February 26, 1904	(1) Panamanians who remained in the territory became U.S. nationals[14] (2) Children born to the U.S. nationals in the Canal Zone	None	None[3]	Sovereignty returned to Panama on Sept. 27, 1979

	Date of Acquisition of Territory by U.S.	Effect on Inhabitants at date of Acquisition	Collective Naturalizations & Date Subjects Became U.S. Citizens	U.S. Citizenship at Birth before incorporation to U.S.	Date Become Part of U.S. for Citizenship: U.S. Citizenship at birth
Guam	April 11, 1899	(1) Spanish subjects residents in Guam [15] became U.S. nationals (2) Persons born after 4/11/1899 become U.S. nationals at birth	August 1, 1950 [4] (A) All Persons who resided in Guam on 4/11/1899 and were either (i) born in Guam, or (ii) were Spanish subjects [5] (B) All persons born in Guam after U.S. jurisdiction after 4/11/1899 and before 8/1/50 (C) All Children born to group (A) after 4/11/1899	All persons born in Guam after 8/1/50 subject to the jurisdiction to the U.S.	December 24, 1952
American Samoa and Swains Island	February 16, 1900 (American Samoa) March 4, 1925 (Swains Island)	(1) All inhabitants of the Islands became U.S. nationals (2) All persons born on the Islands after acquisition were granted U.S. nationality retroactively to birth by the INA [6] (3) Specific descent rules for children born outside the Islands to national parents [16]	None	None	Never
Philippines	April 11, 1899	(1) Spanish subjects residents in the Philippines [17] become U.S. nationals (2) Their children born after 4/11/1899 and before 7/4/46 became U.S. nationals at birth	None	None	Philippines was granted independence on 7/4/46. All Philippine nationals lost U.S. noncitizen nationality on that date.

	Date of Acquisition of Territory by U.S.	Effect on Inhabitants at date of Acquisition	Collective Naturalizations & Date Subjects Became U.S. Citizens	U.S. Citizenship at Birth before incorporation to U.S.	Date Become Part of U.S. for Citizenship: U.S. Citizenship at birth
Northern Mariana Islands	July 18, 1947	U.S. acquired trusteeship over the Marianas—inhabitants did not come noncitizen nationals	November 4, 1986 Persons who did not owe allegiance of the U.S. or any other country, became U.S. citizens [7] if: (A) born in N. Mariana and, on 11/4/86 domiciled in Northern Mariana, the U.S. or its possessions; or (B) citizens of the Trust Territory of the Pacific Islands on 11/3/86, and (i) on 11/4/84 were domiciled in Northern Mariana Islands, (ii) had been continuously domiciled there for 5 years prior to 11/4/86; and (iii) had registered to vote for Northern Mariana elections priore to 1/1/75; or (C) not citizens of Trust Territory of the Pacific Islands, but were domiciled there on 11/4/84, and had been continuously domiuciled in Northern Marianas since before 1/1/74; or (D) were children under 18 of (A) – (C).	None	January 7, 1978[8] November 28, 2009[9]
Micronesia, Marshall Islands, and Palau	July 18, 1947	U.S. acquired these Islands as a trustee—inhabitants did not become noncitizen nationals	None	None	In 1986 associated with the U.S. as free states. Special immigration privileges apply.

[1] Subjects who elected not to did not acquire the new status.

[2] Provided at the time they were not nationals of another country.

[3] Special Provisions for Children of U.S. citizens born there.

[4] Since this grant of citizenship covered persons who derived foreign nationalities without an affirmative act of their own, the U.S. allowed them to elect not to become U.S. citizens by filing a declaration prior to 8/1/52.

[5] Provided they did not take any affirmative steps to preserve their old nationality or acquire a new one.

[6] See §§ 3:1 et seq.

[7] Could elect to become U.S. national instead by making a declaration under oath in an appropriate court within 6 months from 11/4/86.

[8] This reflects the holding of the Ninth Circuit in Sabangan v. Powell, 375 F.3d 818, 819–20 (9th Cir. 2004). The State Department has decided to acquiesce in that decision and to apply it nationwide, though it says that it considers the decision erroneous. See 7 FAM 1126.3(c)(5).

[9] As of this date, the Northern Marianas were added to the definition of the United States found in the INA. The Consolidated Natural Resources Act of 2008 (CNRA), Pub. L. No. 110-229, 122 Stat. 754 (2008); see 48 U.S.C.A. § 1806(a)(1). As noted in the prior footnote, the

Ninth Circuit found that they had been incorporated previously into the territory of the United States in 1986.

APPENDIX 2-3

Excerpts of the Treaty of Ceding Alaska to the United States[1]

By the President of the United States of America, A Proclamation.

Whereas, a treaty between the United States of America and his Majesty the Emperor of all the Russias was concluded and signed by their respective plenipotentiaries at the city of Washington, on the thirtieth day of March, last, which treaty, being in the English and French languages, is, word for word as follows:

. . .

Article III.

The inhabitants of the ceded territory, according to their choice, reserving their natural allegiance, may return to Russia within three years; but if they should prefer to remain in the ceded territory, they, with the exception of uncivilized native tribes, shall be admitted to the enjoyment of all the rights, advantages, and immunities of citizens of the United States, and shall be maintained and protected in the free enjoyment of their liberty, property, and religion. The uncivilized tribes will be subject to such laws and regulations as the United States may, from time to time, adopt in regard to aboriginal tribes of that country.

. . . .

---

[1]Treaty Concerning the Cession of the Russian Possessions in North America, Russia and United States, concluded March 30, 1856, ratified by the United States May 28, 1867, exchanged June 20, 1867, proclaimed by the United States June 20, 1867, 15 Stat. 539, TS 301 18 Stat. (2) 671, 2 Malloy 1521, 11 Bevans 1216.

APPENDIX 2-4

Excerpts of the Treaty of Peace with Spain of April 11, 1899 (Treaty of Paris)[1]

By the President of the United States of America, A Proclamation.

Whereas, a Treaty of Peace between the United States of America and Her Majesty the Queen Regent of Spain, in the name of her August Son, Don Alfonso XIII, was concluded and signed by their respective plenipotentiaries at Paris on the tenth day of December, 1898, the original of which Convention being in the English and Spanish languages, is word for word as follows:

. . . .

Article II.

Spain cedes the United States the island of Porto Rico and other islands now under Spanish sovereignty in the West Indies, and the island of Guam in the Marianas or Ladrones.

Article III.

Spain cedes to the United States the archipelago known as the Philippine Islands, and comprehending the islands lying within the following line:

. . . .

Article IX

Spanish subjects, native of the Peninsula, residing in the territory over which Spain by the present treaty relinquishes or cedes her sovereignty, may remain in such territory or may remove therefrom, retaining in either event all their rights of property, including the right to sell or dispose of such property or of its proceeds; and they shall also have the right to carry on their industry, commerce and professions, being subject in respect thereof to such laws as are applicable to other foreigners. In case they remain in the territory they may preserve their allegiance to the Crown of Spain by making, before a court of record, within a year from the date of exchange of ratifications of this treaty, a declaration of their decision to preserve such allegiance; in default of which declaration they shall be held to have renounced it and to have adopted the nationality of the territory in which they may reside.

The civil rights and political status of the native inhabitants of the territories hereby ceded to the United States shall be determined by the Congress.

. . . .

---

[1]Treaty of Peace between United States of America and Spain. Signed at Paris, December 10, 1898; ratification advised by the Senate, February 6, 1899; ratified by the president, February 6, 1899; ratified by her Majesty the Queen Regent of Spain, March 19, 1899; ratification exchanged at Washington, April 11, 1899; proclaimed, Washington, April 11, 1899, 30 Stat. 1754, 2 Malloy 1690, 11 Bevans 615.

APPENDIX 2-5

Statutes Relating to the Citizenship of Puerto Ricans

A. Act of April 12, 1900, 31 Stat. 77

An Act Temporarily to provide revenues and a civil government for Porto Rico, and for other purposes.

Be it enacted by the Senate and House of Representatives of the United States of America in Congress assembled, That the provisions of this Act shall apply to the island of Porto Rico and to the adjacent islands . . .

. . .

Sec. 7. That all inhabitants continuing to reside therein who were Spanish subjects on the eleventh day of April, eighteen hundred and ninety-nine, and then resided in Porto Rico, and their children born subsequent thereto, shall be deemed and held to be citizens of Porto Rico, and as such entitled to the protection of the United States, except such as shall have elected to preserve their allegiance to the Crown of Spain on or before the eleventh day of April, nineteen hundred, in accordance with the provisions of the treaty of peace between the United States and Spain entered into on the eleventh day of April, eighteen hundred and ninety-nine; and they, together with such citizens of the United States as may reside in Porto Rico, shall constitute a body politic under the name of The People of Porto Rico, with governmental powers as hereinafter conferred, and with power to sue and be sued as such.

. . .

Sec. 14. That the statutory laws of the United States not locally inapplicable, except as hereinbefore or hereinafter otherwise provided, shall have the same force and effect in Porto Rico as in the United States, except the internal-revenue laws, which, in view of the provisions of section three, shall not have force and effect in Porto Rico.

. . .

B. Act of March 2, 1917, Pub.L. 64-368, 39 Stat. 951

An Act To provide a civil government for Porto Rico, and for other purposes.

Be it enacted by the Senate and House of Representatives of the United States of America in Congress assembled, That the provisions of this Act shall apply to the island of Porto Rico and to the adjacent islands belonging to the United States, and waters of those islands; and the name Porto Rico as used in this Act shall beheld to include not only the island of that name by all the adjacent islands as aforesaid.

. . .

Sec. 5. That all citizens of Porto Rico, as defined by section seven of the Act of April twelfth, nineteen hundred, "temporarily to provide revenues and a civil government of Porto Rico, and for other purposes," and all natives of Porto Rico who were temporarily absent from the island on April eleventh, eighteen hundred and ninety-nine, and have since returned and are permanently residing in that island, and are not citizens of any foreign country, are hereby declared, and shall be deemed and held to be, citizens of the United States; *Provided*, That any person herein before described may retain his present political status by making a declaration, under oath, of his decision to do so within six months of the taking effect of this Act before the district court in the district in which he resides, the declaration to be in form as follows:

"I, being duly sworn, hereby declare my intention not to become a citizen of the United States as provided in the Act of Congress conferring United States citizenship upon citizens of Porto Rico and certain natives permanently residing in said island."

In the case of any such person who may be absent from the island during said six months the term of this proviso may be availed of by transmitting a declaration, under oath, in the form herein provided within six months of the taking effect of this Act to the executive secretary of Porto Rico: *And further provided*, That any person who is born in Porto Rico of a noncitizen parent and is permanently residing in that island may, if of full age, within six months of the taking effect of this Act, or if a minor, upon reaching his majority or within one year thereafter, make a sworn declaration of allegiance to the United States before the United States District Court of Porto Rico, setting forth therein all the facts connected with his or her birth and residence in Porto Rico and accompanying due proof thereof, and from and after the making of such declaration shall be considered to be a citizen of the United States.

. . .

C. Act of June 27, 1934, Pub.L. 73-477, 48 Stat. 1245

An Act To amend the Act of March 2, 1917, entitled "An Act to provide a civil government for Puerto Rico, and for other purposes."

Be it enacted by the Senate and House of Representatives of the United States of America in Congress assembled, That a new section is hereby inserted between sections 5a and 6 of the Act entitled "An Act to provide a civil government for Puerto Rico, and for other purposes", approved March 2, 1917, as amended, as follows . . .

. . . "Sec. 5b. All persons born in Puerto Rico on or after April 11, 1899 (whether before or after the effective date of this Act) and not citizens, subjects, or nationals of any foreign power, are hereby declared to be citizens of the United States: *Provided*, That this Act shall not be construed as depriving any person, native of Puerto Rico, of his or her American citizenship heretofore otherwise lawfully acquired by such person; or to extend such citizenship to persons who shall have renounced or lost it under the treaties and/or laws of the United States or who are now residing permanently abroad and are citizens or subjects of a foreign country: *And provided further*, That any woman, native of Puerto Rico and permanently residing therein, who prior to March 2, 1917, had lost her American nationality by reason of her marriage to a noncitizen eligible to citizenship, or by reason of the loss of the United States citizenship by her husband, may be naturalized under the provisions of section 4 of the Act of September 22, 1922, entitled 'An Act relative to the naturalization and citizenship of married women', as amended."

APPENDIX 2-6

Excerpts of the Treaty of August 4, 1916 with Denmark, For the Cession of the Danish West Indies[1]

By the President of the United States of America, A Proclamation.

Whereas a Convention between the United States of America and Denmark providing for the cession to the United States of all territory asserted or claimed by Denmark in the West Indies, including the islands of St. Thomas, St. John and St. Croix, together with the adjacent islands and rocks, was concluded and signed by their respective Plenipotentiaries at the City of New York on the Fourth day of August, one thousand nine hundred and sixteen, the original of which Convention, being in the English and Danish languages, is word for word as follows:

. . . .

Article 6.

Danish citizens residing in said islands may remain therein or may remove therefrom at will, retaining in either event all their rights of property, including the right to sell or dispose of such property or its proceeds; in case they remain in the Islands, they shall continue until otherwise provided, to enjoy all the private, municipal and religious rights and liberties secured to them by the laws now in force. If the present laws are altered, the said inhabitants shall not thereby be placed in a less favorable position in respect to the above mentioned rights and liberties than they now enjoy. Those who remain in the islands may preserve their citizenship in Denmark by making before a court of record, within one year from the date of the exchange of ratifications of this convention, a declaration of their decision to preserve such citizenship; in default of which declaration they shall be held to have renounced it, and to have accepted citizenship in the United States; for children under eighteen years the said declaration may be made by their parents or guardians. Such election of Danish citizenship shall however not, after a lapse of the said term of one year, be a bar to their renunciation of their preserved Danish citizenship and their election of citizenship in the United States and admission to the nationality thereof on the same terms as may be provided according to the laws of the United States, for other inhabitants of the islands.

The civil rights and the political status of the inhabitants of the islands shall be determined by the Congress, subject to the stipulations contained in the present convention.

Danish citizens not residing in the islands but owning property therein at the time of the cession, shall retain their rights of property, being placed in this regard on the same basis as the Danish citizens residing in the islands and remaining therein or removing therefrom, to whom the first paragraph of this article relates.

---

[1]Treaty of August 4, 1916, Denmark and U.S., signed in New York, August 4, 1916; ratification advised by the Senate September 7, 1916; ratified by the President January 16, 1917; ratified by Denmark December 22, 1916; proclaimed January 25, 1917, 39 Stat. 1715, TS 629, 3 Redmond 2558, 7 Bevans 56.

APPENDIX 2-7

Statutes Relating to U.S. Citizenship for Inhabitants of the Virgin Islands

A. Act of February 25, 1927, Pub.L. 69-640, 44 Stat. 1234

An Act To confer United States citizenship upon certain inhabitants of the Virgin Islands and to extend the naturalization laws thereto.

Be it enacted by the Senate and House of Representatives of the United States of America in Congress assembled, That the following persons and their children born subsequent to January 17, 1917, are hereby declared to be citizens of the United States:

(a) All former Danish citizens who, on January 17, 1917, resided in the Virgin Islands of the United States, and are now residing in those islands or in the United States or Porto Rico, and who did not made the declaration required to preserve their Danish citizenship by article 6 of the treaty entered into on August 4, 1916 between the United States and Denmark, or who, having made such a declaration have heretofore renounced or may hereafter renounce it by a declaration before a court of record;

(b) All natives of the Virgin Islands of the United States who, on January 17, 1917, resided in those islands, and are now residing in those islands or in the United States or Porto Rico, and who are not citizens or subjects of any foreign country; and

(c) All natives of the Virgin Islands of the United States who on January 17, 1917, resided in the United States, and are now residing in the Virgin Islands of the United States, and who are not citizens or subjects of any foreign country.

Sec. 2. The following persons, if not ineligible to citizenship, may, upon petition filed within one year after the effective date of this Act, and upon full and complete compliance with all other provisions of the naturalization laws, be naturalized without making a declaration of intention:

(a) All natives of the Virgin Islands of the United States who, on January 17, 1917, resided in those islands or in the United States, and who are now residing in those islands or in the United States or Porto Rico, and who are citizens or subjects of any foreign country;

(b) All natives of the Virgin Islands of the United States who, on January 17, 1917, resided in the United States, and are now residing in the United States or Porto Rico, and who are not citizens or subjects of another country; and,

(c) Excepts as otherwise provided in this section or in section 1, all persons who, on January 17, 1917, resided in the Virgin Islands of the United States, and are now residing in those islands, and who are not citizens of the United States.

Sec. 3. All persons born in the Virgin Islands of the United States on or after January 17, 1917 (whether before or after the effective date of this Act), and subject to the jurisdiction of the United States, are hereby declared to be citizens of the United States.

Sec. 4. The district court of the Virgin Islands of the United States shall have jurisdiction for naturalization purposes (including jurisdiction for the purpose of setting aside and canceling certificates of citizenship under section 15 of the Act entitled "An Act to establish a Bureau of Immigration and Naturalization, and to provide a uniform rule for the naturalization of noncitizens throughout the United States," approved June 29, 1906, as amended); and for the purpose of the naturalization laws residence in the Virgin Islands of the United States shall be considered as residence in the United States.

Sec. 5. Section 4 of the Act entitled "An Act to provide temporary government for the West Indian Islands acquired by the United States from Denmark by the convention entered into between said countries on the 4th day of August, 1916, and ratified by the Senate of the United States on the 7th day of September, 1916, and for other purposes," approved March 3, 1917, is amended by striking figure "8" and inserting in lieu thereof the figure "6".

B. Act of June 28, 1932, Pub.L. 72-198, 47 Stat. 336

An Act Relating to the immigration and naturalization of certain natives of the Virgin Islands.

Be it enacted by the Senate and House of Representatives of the United States of America in Congress assembled, That a native of the Virgin Islands of the United States who is now residing in any foreign country shall for the purpose of the Immigration Act of 1924, as amended, be considered as a nonquota immigrant for the purposes of admission to the United States; but shall be subject to all the other provisions of that Act and of the immigration laws . . .

Sec. 5. Section 1 of the Act entitled "An Act to confer United States citizenship upon certain inhabitants of the Virgin Islands and to extend the naturalization laws thereto," approved February 25, 1927, is amended by adding at the end thereof the following:

"(d) All natives of the Virgin Islands of the United States who are, on the date of enactment of this subdivision, residing in continental United States, Puerto Rico, the Canal Zone, or any other insular possession or Territory of the United States, who are not citizens or subjects of any foreign country, regardless of their place of residence on January 17, 1917."

APPENDIX 2-8

Excerpts of the Isthmian Canal Convention[1]

By the President of the United States of America, A Proclamation.

Whereas a Convention between the United States of America and the Republic of Panama to insure the construction of a ship canal across the Isthmus of Panama to connect the Atlantic and Pacific Oceans, was concluded and signed by their respective Plenipotentiaries at the city of Washington, on the eighteenth day of November, one thousand nine hundred and three, the original of which Convention, being in the English language, is word for word as follows:

ISTHMIAN CANAL CONVENTION

. . . .

Article I.

The United States guarantees and will maintain the independence of the Republic of Panama,

Article II.

The Republic of Panama grants to the United States in perpetuity the use, occupation and control of a zone of land and land under water for the construction, maintenance, operation, sanitation and protection of said Canal of the width of ten miles extending to the distance of five miles on each side of the center line of the route of the Canal to be constructed; the said zone beginning in the Caribbean Sea three marine miles from mean low water mark and extending to and across the Isthmus of Panama into the Pacific ocean . . . The Republic of Panama further grants to the United States in perpetuity the use, occupation and control of any other lands and waters outside of the zone above described which may be necessary and convenient for the construction, maintenance, operation, sanitation and protection of the said Canal or of any auxiliary canals or other works necessary and convenient for the construction, maintenance, operation, sanitation and protection of the said enterprise.

The Republic of Panama further grants in like manner to the United States in perpetuity all islands within the limits of the zone above described and in addition thereto the group of small islands in the Bay of Panama, named Perico, Naos, Culebra and Flamenco.

Article III

The Republic of Panama grants to the United States all the rights, power and authority within the zone mentioned and described in Article II of this agreement and within the limits of all auxiliary lands and waters mentioned and described in said Article II which the United States would possess and exercise if it were the sovereign of the territory within which said lands and waters are located to the entire exclusion of the exercise by the Republic of Panama of any such sovereign rights, power or authority.

---

[1]Isthmian Canal Convention, United States and Panama, November 18, 1903, proclaimed February 26, 1904, 33 Stat. 2234, TS 431, 2 Malloy 1349, 10 Bevans 663.

. . .

Article V.

The Republic of Panama grants to the United States in perpetuity a monopoly for the construction, maintenance and operation of any system of communication by means of canal or railroad across its territory between the Caribbean Sea and the Pacific ocean.

. . .

Article XII.

The Government of the Republic of Panama shall permit the immigration and free access to the lands and workshops of the Canal and its auxiliary works of all employees and workmen of whatever nationality under contract to work upon or seeking employment upon or in any wise connected with the said Canal and its auxiliary works, with their respective families, and all such persons shall be free and exempt from the military service of the Republic of Panama.

. . .

APPENDIX 2-9

Excerpts of Covenant between the CNMI and the United States, Act of Mar. 24, 1976, Pub.L. No. 94-241, 90 Stat. 263, reprinted in 48 U.S.C.A. § 1801.

JOINT RESOLUTION

To approve the "Covenant To Establish a Commonwealth of the Northern Mariana Islands in Political Union with the United States of America", and for other purposes.

Whereas the United States is the administering authority of the Trust Territory of the Pacific Islands under the terms of the trusteeship agreement for the former Japanese-mandated islands entered into by the United States with the Security Council of the United Nations on April 2, 1947, and approved by the United States on July 18, 1947; and

Whereas the United States, in accordance with the trusteeship agreement and the Charter of the United Nations, has assumed the obligation to promote the development of the peoples of the trust territory toward self-government or independence as may be appropriate to the particular circumstances of the trust territory and its peoples and the freely expressed wishes of the peoples concerned; and

Whereas the United States, in response to the desires of the people of the Northern Mariana Islands clearly expressed over the past twenty years through public petition and referendum, and in response to its own obligations under the trusteeship agreement to promote self-determination, entered into political status negotiations with representatives of the people of the Northern Mariana Islands; and

Whereas, on February 15, 1975, a "Covenant to Establish A Commonwealth of the Northern Mariana Islands in Political Union with the United States of America" was signed by the Marianas Political Status Commission for the people of the Northern Mariana Islands and by the President's Personal Representative, Ambassador F. Haydn Williams for the United States of America, following which the covenant was approved by the unanimous vote of the Mariana Islands District Legislature on February 20, 1975 and by 78.8 per centum of the people of the Northern Mariana Islands voting in a plebiscite held on June 17, 1975: Now be it

Resolved by the Senate and House of Respresentatives of the United States of America in Congress assembled, That the Covenant to Establish a Commonwealth of the Northern Mariana Islands in Political Union with the United States of America, the text of which is as follows, is hereby approved.

"Covenant To Establish a Commonwealth of the Northern Mariana Islands in Political Union With the United States of America

"Whereas, the Charter of the United Nations and the Trusteeship Agreement between the Security Council of the United Nations and the United States of America guarantee to the people of the Northern Mariana Islands the right freely to express their wishes for self-government or independence; and

"Whereas, the United States supports the desire of the people of the Northern Mariana Islands to exercise their inalienable right of self-determination; and

"Whereas, the people of the Northern Mariana Islands and the people of the

United States share the goals and values found in the American system of government based upon the principles of government by the consent of the governed, individual freedom and democracy; and

"Whereas, for over twenty years, the people of the Northern Mariana Islands, through public petition and referendum, have clearly expressed their desire for political union with the United States;

"Now, therefore, the Marianas Political Status Commission, being the duly appointed representative of the people of the Northern Mariana Islands, and the Personal Representative of the President of the United States have entered into this Covenant in order to establish a self-governing commonwealth for the Northern Mariana Islands within the American political system and to define the future relationship between the Northern Mariana Islands and the United States. This Covenant will be mutually binding when it is approved by the United States, by the Mariana Islands District Legislature and by the people of the Northern Mariana Islands in a plebiscite, constituting on their part a sovereign act of self-determination.

ARTICLE I: POLITICAL RELATIONSHIP

Section 101. Northern Mariana Islands upon termination of the Trusteeship Agreement will become a self-governing commonwealth to be known as the ' Commonwealth of the Northern Mariana Islands', in political union with and under the sovereignty of the United States of America.

Section 102. The relations between the Northern Mariana Islands and the United States will be governed by this Covenant which, together with those provisions of the Constitution, treaties and laws of the United States applicable to the Northern Mariana Islands, will be the supreme law of the Northern Mariana Islands.

Section 103. The people of the Northern Mariana Islands will have the right of local self-government and will govern themselves with respect to internal affairs in accordance with a Constitution of their own adoption.

Section 104. The United States will have complete responsibility for and authority with respect to matters relating to foreign affairs and defense affecting the Northern Mariana Islands.

Section 105. The United States may enact legislation in accordance with its constitutional processes which will be applicable to the Northern Mariana Islands, but if such legislation cannot also be made applicable to the several States the Northern Mariana Islands must be specifically named therein for it to become effective in the Northern Mariana Islands. In order to respect the right of self-government guaranteed by this Covenant the United States agrees to limit the exercise of that authority so that the fundamental provisions of this Covenant, namely Articles, I II and III and Section 501 and 805, may be modified only with the consent of the Government of the United States and the Government of the Northern Mariana Islands.

. . . .

ARTICLE III: CITIZENSHIP AND NATIONALITY

Section 301. The following persons and their children under the age of 18 years on the effective date of this Section, who are not citizens or nationals of the United States under any other provision of laws, and who on that date do not owe allegiance to any foreign state, are declared to be citizens of the United States, except as otherwise provided in Section 302:

(a) all persons born in the Northern Mariana Islands who are citizens of the Trust Territory of the Pacific Islands on the day preceding the effective date of this Section, and who on that date are domiciled in the Northern Mariana Islands or in the United States or any territory or possession thereof;

(b) all persons who are citizens of the Trust Territory of the Pacific Islands on the day preceding the effective date of this Section, who have been domiciled continuously in the Northern Mariana Islands for at least five years immediately prior to that date, and who, unless under age, registered to vote in elections for the Marianas Islands District Legislature or for any municipal election in the Northern Mariana Islands prior to January 1, 1975; and

(c) all persons domiciled in the Northern Mariana Islands on the day preceding the effective date of this Section, who, although not citizens of the Trust Territory of the Pacific Islands, on that date have been domiciled continuously in the Northern Mariana Islands beginning prior to January 1, 1974.

Section 302. Any person who becomes a citizen of the United States solely by virtue of the provisions of Section 301 may within six months after the effective date of that Section or within six months after reaching the age of 18 years, whichever date is the later, become a national but not a citizen of the United States by making a declaration under oath before any court established by the Constitution or laws of the United States or any court of record in the commonwealth in the form as follows:

"'I —— being duly sworn, hereby declare my intention to be a national but not a citizen of the United States.'"

Section 303. All persons born in the Commonwealth on or after the effective date of this Section and subject to the jurisdiction of the United States will be citizens of the United States at birth.

Section 304. Citizens of the Northern Mariana Islands will be entitled to all privileges and immunities of citizens in the several States of the United States.

. . . .

ARTICLE V: APPLICABILITY OF LAWS

Section 501. (a) To the extent that they are not applicable of their own force, the following provisions of the Constitution of the United States will be applicable within the Northern Mariana Islands as if the Northern Mariana Islands were one of the several States: Article I, Section 9, Clauses 2, 3, and 8; Article I, Section 10, Clauses 1 and 3; Article IV, Section 1 and Section 2, Clauses 1 and 2; Amendments 1 through 9, inclusive; Amendment 13; Amendment 14, Section 1; Amendment 15; Amendment 19; and Amendment 26; provided, however, that neither trial by jury nor indictment by grand jury shall be required in any civil action or criminal prosecution based on local law, except where required by local law. Other provisions of or amendments to the Constitution of the United States, which do not apply of their own force within the Northern Mariana Islands, will be applicable within the Northern Mariana Islands only with approval of the Government of the Northern Mariana Islands and of the Government of the United States.

"(b) The applicability of certain provisions of the Constitution of the United States to the Northern Mariana Islands will be without prejudice to the validity of and the power of the Congress of the United States to consent to Sections 203, 506 and 805 and the proviso in Subsection (a) of this Section.

. . . .

Section 503. The following laws of the United States, presently inapplicable to the Trust Territory of the Pacific Islands, will not apply to the Northern Mariana Islands except in the manner and to the extent made applicable to them by the Congress by law after termination of the Trusteeship Agreement:

"(a) except as otherwise provided in Section 506, the immigration and naturalization laws of the United States;

"(b) except as otherwise provided in Subsection (b) of Section 502, the coastwise laws of the United States and any prohibition in the laws of the United States against foreign vessels landing fish or unfinished fish products in the United States; and

"(c) the minimum wage provisions of Section 6, Act of June 25, 1938, 52 Stat. 1062, as amended.

. . . .

Section 506. (a) Notwithstanding the provisions of Subsection 503(a), upon the effective date of this Section the Northern Mariana Islands will be deemed to be a part of the United States under the Immigration and Nationality Act, as amended for the following purposes only, and the said Act will apply to the Northern Mariana Islands to the extent indicated in each of the following Subsections of this Section.

(b) With respect to children born abroad to United States citizen or non-citizen national parents permanently residing in the Northern Mariana Islands the provisions of Sections 301 and 308 of the said Act will apply.

(c) With respect to aliens who are 'immediate relatives' (as defined in Subsection 201(b) of the said Act) of United States citizens who are permanently residing in the Northern Mariana Islands all the provisions of the said Act will apply, commencing when a claim is made to entitlement to 'immediate relative' status. A person who is certified by the Government of the Northern Mariana Islands both to have been a lawful permanent resident of the Northern Mariana Islands and to have had the 'immediate relative' relationship denoted herein on the effective date of this Section will be presumed to have been admitted to the United States for lawful permanent residence as of that date without the requirement of any of the usual procedures set forth in the said Act. the purposes of the requirement of judicial naturalization, the Northern Mariana Islands will be deemed to constitute a State as defined in Subsection 101(a) a paragraph (36) of the said Act. The Courts of record of the Northern Mariana Islands and the District Court for the Northern Mariana Islands will be included among the courts specified in Subsection 310(a) of the said Act and will have jurisdiction to naturalize persons who become eligible under this Section and who reside within their respective jurisdictions.

(d) With respect to persons who will become citizens or nationals of the United States under Article III of this Covenant or under this Section the loss of nationality provisions of the said Act will apply.

. . . .

ARTICLE X: APPROVAL, EFFECTIVE DATES, AND DEFINITIONS

Section 1001. (a) This Covenant will be submitted to the Mariana Islands District Legislature for its approval. After its approval by the Mariana Islands District Legislature, this Covenant will be submitted to the people of the Northern Mariana Islands for approval in a plebiscite to be called by the United States. Only persons who are domiciled exclusively in the Northern Mariana Islands and who meet such other qualifications, including timely registration, as are promulgated by the United States as administering authority will be eligible to vote in the plebiscite. Approval must be by a majority of at least 55% of the valid votes cast in the plebiscite. The results of the plebiscite will be certified to the President of the United States.

(b) This Covenant will be approved by the United States in accordance with its constitutional processes and will thereupon become law.

Section 1002. The President of the United States will issue a proclamation announcing the termination of the Trusteeship Agreement, or the date on which the Trusteeship Agreement will terminate, and the establishment of the Commonwealth in accordance with this Covenant. Any determination by the President that the Trusteeship Agreement has been terminated or will be terminated on a day certain will be final and will not be subject to review by any authority, judicial or otherwise, of the Trust Territory of the Pacific Islands, the Northern Mariana Islands or the United States.

Section 1003. The provisions of this Covenant will become effective as follows, unless otherwise specifically provided:

(a) Sections 105, 201—203, 503, 504, 606, 801, 903 and Article X will become effective on approval of this Covenant;

(b) Sections 102, 103, 204, 304, Article IV, Sections 501, 502, 505, 601— 605, 607, Article VII, Sections 802—805, 901 and 902 will become effective on a date to be determined and proclaimed by the President of the United States which will be not more than 180 days after this Covenant and the Constitution of the Northern Mariana Islands have both been approved; and

(c) The remainder of this Covenant will become effective upon the termination of the Trusteeship Agreement and the establishment of the Commonwealth of the Northern Mariana Islands.

Section 1004 (a) The application of any provision of the Constitution or laws of the United States which would otherwise apply to the Northern Mariana Islands may be suspended until termination of the Trusteeship Agreement if the President finds and declares that the application of such provision prior to termination would be inconsistent with the Trusteeship Agreement.

(b) The Constitution of the Northern Mariana Islands will become effective in accordance with its terms on the same day that the provisions of this Covenant specified in Subsection 1003(b) become effective, provided that if the President finds and declares that the effectiveness of any provision of the Constitution of the Northern Mariana Islands prior to termination of the Trusteeship Agreement would be inconsistent with the Trusteeship Agreement such provision will be ineffective until termination of the Trusteeship Agreement. Upon the establishment of the Commonwealth of the Northern Mariana Islands the Constitution will become effective in its entirety in accordance with its terms as the Constitution of the Commonwealth of the Northern Mariana Islands.

Chapter 3

Noncitizen Nationals

Research References

West's Key Number Digest
Aliens, Immigration and Citizenship ⚷654

Westlaw Databases
Steel on Immigration Law (STEEL)

Immigration Law Service (2d ed.) (IMMLS2D)

Treatises and Practice Aids

Dizon and Wettstein, Immigration Law Service 2d § 14:57
Steel on Immigration Law § 15:6

> **KeyCite®:** Cases and other legal materials listed in KeyCite Scope can be researched through the KeyCite service on Westlaw®. Use KeyCite to check citations for form, parallel references, prior and later history, and comprehensive citator information, including citations to other decisions and secondary materials.

I. UNINCORPORATED POSSESSIONS

§ 3:1 Noncitizen nationality

Research References

Dizon and Wettstein, Immigration Law Service 2d § 14:57

All citizens of the United States are also nationals of this country.[1] In addition, noncitizens who owe permanent allegiance to the United States are considered noncitizen nationals of this country.[2]

The status of noncitizen nationals developed from the U.S. acquisition of Puerto Rico, the Philippines, and Guam from Spain after the Spanish-American war.[3] The treaty with Spain provided for the transfer of the allegiance of the inhabitants of these islands to the U.S.[4] However, it left the determination of their status in the hands of the U.S. Congress.[5] Congress made them citizens of their own islands rather than of the U.S., and thus the concept of noncitizen nationals,[6] persons who owe allegiance to the U.S. but who are not citizens of this country, was born.[7]

Congress passed the first law directly addressing the immigration and citizenship rights of noncitizen nationals in 1906, allowing noncitizen nationals to naturalize.[8] Under prior law only *noncitizens* were allowed to naturalize.[9] Even though the provision was envisioned to apply specifically to Puerto Ricans and Filipinos, the courts held that the racial bars to naturalization applied to the naturalization of noncitizen

---

[Section 3:1]

[1]INA § 101(a)(22)(A), 8 U.S.C.A. § 1101(a)(22)(A).

[2]INA § 101(a)(22)(B), 8 U.S.C.A. § 1101(a)(22)(B).

[3]Cabede v. Acheson, 183 F.2d 795, 797–80 (9th Cir. 1950) ("[w]ith the cession of populated areas by the Crown of Spain to the United States . . . persons became nationalized but not naturalized . . . [a] hybrid status appeared, the so-called 'non-citizen national'"). Cf. U.S. v. Gonzales, 192 U.S. 1, 24 S.Ct. 177, 48 L.Ed. 317 (1904); In re Mallari, 239 F. 416, 417 (D.Mass. 1916); Hackworth, 3 Digest of International Law 1–2, 115–16.

[4]Gonzales v. Williams, 192 U.S. 1, 9, 24 S. Ct. 177, 178, 48 L. Ed. 317 (1904).

[5]Gonzales v. Williams, 192 U.S. 1, 9, 24 S. Ct. 177, 178, 48 L. Ed. 317 (1904).

[6]See U.S. v. Gonzales, 192 U.S. at 12–13 24 S.Ct. at 179, 48 L.Ed. 317 (a citizen of Puerto Rico was not a noncitizen of the U.S.).

[7]In re Mallari, 239 F. 416, 417 (D. Mass. 1916). Cf. §§ 2:15 to 2:23.

[8]In re Mallari, 239 F. 416, 417 (D. Mass. 1916).

[9]In re Mallari, 239 F. 416, 417 (D. Mass. 1916).

nationals.[10] This rendered these naturalization provisions almost inapplicable until the elimination of the racial bars in the late 1940s and early 1950s.[11]

Unlike citizenship, which requires an expatriating act in order to terminate it, noncitizen nationality is terminated automatically the moment the allegiance of the noncitizen national is transferred to another sovereign.[12] Thus when a former territory becomes independent from the U.S., all the noncitizen nationals, whether residing in the territory or in the United States, become noncitizens.[13]

§ 3:2 Current possessions

At the present time, there are only two groups that have the status of noncitizens U.S. nationals: (1) most Samoans and Swains Islanders, and (2) residents of the Northern Mariana Islands who do not elect to become United States citizens.[1]

Nationals are not aliens, and they may enter the United States without restrictions.[2] They are not subject to removal from the United States under the current removal provisions.[3]

II. ACQUISITION OF NONCITIZEN NATIONALITY

§ 3:3 Generally

Research References

Dizon and Wettstein, Immigration Law Service 2d §§ 14:58, 14:59

It has been consistently held that persons who resided in a territory at the time of the transfer acquired U.S. noncitizen nationality.[1] Some sovereigns have made a

---

[10]In re Rallos, 241 F. 686 (E.D.N.Y. 1917). Cf. In re Mallari, 239 F. 416, 417 (D. Mass. 1916) (discussing the legislative history of this provision).

[11]INS Interp. 325.1(a)(1). See § 7:105.

[12]Matter of M-, 6 I. & N. Dec. 182 (B.I.A. 1954).

[13]Matter of M-, 6 I. & N. Dec. 182, 183–84 (B.I.A. 1954).

[Section 3:2]

[1]INS Interp. 308.1(g). For a full discussion of the status of residents of the Northern Mariana Islands, *see* § 2:20. However, it also may be possible for an individual not belonging to one of these two groups to be a national of the U.S. See § 3:13.

[2]INS Interp. 325.1(a)(2). However, it must be pointed out that while Filipinos were noncitizen nationals, Congress imposed travel restrictions upon then, defining them as noncitizens for purposes of immigration. Among other things it set a quota limitation that no more than fifty could move to the United States in any given year. Sec. 8, Act of March 24, 1934, 48 Stat. 456. See Gordon & Mailman, § 91.05[1][b].

[3]See, e.g., INA § 237, 8 U.S.C.A. § 1227 (pertaining to grounds of deportation applicable to "aliens"); INA § 240, 8 U.S.C.A., § 1229a (pertaining to removal proceedings against "aliens"). The INA defines aliens as "any person who is not a citizen or a *national* of the United States." INA § 101(a)(3), 8 U.S.C.A. § 1101(a)(3) (emphasis added).

[Section 3:3]

[1]Matter of B-, 3 I. & N. Dec. 729, 731 (B.I.A. 1949) (there is no rule more firmly established in international law than the principle that on a transfer of a territory by one nation to another, the nationality of the inhabitants becomes that of the government under whose dominion they pass).

provision in the treaty of cession for their subjects to elect whether to retain their nationality or acquire the new nationality.[2]

The same is not the case for persons born in the territory *after* it was acquired by the United States.[3] The general rule until 1940 was that, unless specifically provided otherwise by Congress or in the treaty ceding the territory, persons born in the outlying possessions after the cession only acquired U.S. noncitizen nationality if their fathers were noncitizen nationals.[4] However, children born to U.S. noncitizen nationals outside the United States and its outlying possessions did not acquire U.S noncitizen nationality at birth.[5] Thus, in so far as noncitizen nationals were concerned, the U.S. applied nationality by descent when the children were born in an outlying possession, but not when they were born outside the possessions.[6]

The 1940 act modified this process statutorily by providing that children born in an outlying possession to either a father or mother who was a noncitizen national would acquire nationality upon birth.[7] It also provided that U.S. noncitizen nationality would descend to a child born outside the United States or its outlying possessions if both parents were noncitizen nationals of the United States and both had resided in the United States or its outlying possessions prior to the birth of the child.[8] The 1940 act was held to apply prospectively only.[9]

The INA once again modified this scheme by allowing the following (unless they are U.S. citizens) to be U.S. noncitizen nationals at birth:[10]

(1) A person born in an outlying possession of the United States on or after the date of formal acquisition of such possession;

(2) A person born outside the United States and its outlying possessions of parents both of whom are nationals, but not citizens of the United States, and have had a residence in the United States, or one of its outlying possessions prior to the birth of such person;

(3) A person of unknown parentage found in an outlying possession of the United States while under the age of five years, until shown, prior to his or her attaining the age of 21 years, not to have been born in such outlying possession; and

(4) A person born outside the United States and its outlying possessions of parents one of whom is a noncitizen, and the other a national, but not a citizen, of the United States who, prior to the birth of such person, was physically present in the United States, or its outlying possessions for a period or periods totaling not less than seven years in any continuous period of 10 years.

(A) during which the national parent was not outside the United States or its outlying possessions for a continuous period of more than one year, and

---

[2]See e.g. art. 9, Treaty of Paris, United States and Spain., December 10, 1898 (proclaimed, April 11, 1899), 30 Stat. 1755, 2 Malloy 1690, 11 Bevans 615 reproduced as Appendix 2-4 to Ch 2. See generally §§ 2:15 to 2:23.

[3]Matter of S-, 3 I. & N. Dec. 589, 593–94 (B.I.A. 1949) (the U.S. applies the principle of jus sanguinis and not jus soli to acquisition of nationality in an outlying possession).

[4]Matter of S-, 3 I. & N. Dec. 589, 593–95 (B.I.A. 1949).

[5]Matter of T-, 5 I. & N. Dec. 380 (B.I.A. 1953).

[6]Matter of T-, 5 I&N Dec. 380 appears inconsistent with Matter of S-, 3 I&N Dec. 589.

[7]Sec. 204(a), Nationality Act of 1940, Pub.L. 76-853, 54 Sat. 1137 (October 14, 1940) reproduced as Appendix 4-12 to Ch 4.

[8]Sec. 204(b), Nationality Act of 1940 reproduced as Appendix 4-12 to Ch 4.

[9]Matter of S-, 3 I. & N. Dec. 589, 594 (B.I.A. 1949).

[10]INA § 308, 8 U.S.C.A. § 1408.

(B) at least five years of which were after attaining the age of 14 years.[11]

Acquisition of U.S. noncitizen nationality under the INA is retroactive to birth after the acquisition of the outlying possession by the U.S.[12] Adopted children born outside the outlying possessions do not acquire U.S. noncitizen nationality through the adoption.[13]

Children born out-of-wedlock have always been considered U.S. nationals if their mother was a U.S. national. A child born out-of-wedlock before the enactment of the INA was a noncitizen national if the mother was a noncitizen national and had resided in the United States or one of its outlying possessions prior to the birth of the child.[14] After the date of enactment of the INA, there is an additional requirement that the mother must have resided in the United States or one of its outlying possessions for a continuous period of one year before the birth of the child in order for the child to acquire U.S. citizenship at birth.[15] Both laws apply whether the child was born in an outlying possession or anywhere else in the world.[16]

Acquisition of noncitizen nationality from a noncitizen national father requires legitimation in accordance with the rules applicable for transmission of citizenship by U.S. citizen fathers of out-of-wedlock children born abroad.[17] A similar gender distinction has been upheld against constitutional challenge.[18]

§ 3:4 American Samoa and Swains Island

Applying these principles to the case of American Samoa and the Swains Islands, the following principles result:

(1) All the inhabitants of American Samoa and the Swains Island became noncitizen nationals with the acquisition of those territories by the U.S.[1]

(2) Until December 24, 1952, any person, regardless of race, born to a United States national father in American Samoa on or after February 16, 1900, and in Swains Island on or after March 4, 1925, acquired U.S. nationality at birth.[2]

---

[11]Note also that a child born outside the United States or its outlying possessions to one noncitizen national and one citizen parent who resided continuously for one year in the U.S. or its possessions prior to the child's birth is a U.S. citizen. INA § 301(d), 8 U.S.C.A. § 1401(d). See §§ 4:1 et seq.

[12]Matter of A-, 5 I. & N. Dec. 144 (Special Inquiry Officer) approved (B.I.A. 1953); INS Interp. 308. 1(g)(3).

[13]Matter of Tuitasi, 15 I. & N. Dec. 102 (B.I.A. 1974).

[14]Sec. 205, Nationality Act of 1940 reproduced as Appendix 4-12 to Ch 4.

[15]INA § 309(c), 8 U.S.C.A. § 1409(c).

[16]Sec. 205, Nationality Act of 1940 reproduced as Appendix 4-12 to Ch 4; INA § 309(c), 8 U.S.C.A. § 1409(c). Of course, if a child is born inside the United States, the child is a U.S. citizen at birth. See Ch 2.

[17]Sec. 205, Nationality Act of 1940 reproduced as Appendix 4-12 to Ch 4; INA § 309(a), 8 U.S.C.A. § 1409(a). See §§ 4:1 et seq. (for adiscussion of the application of these rules).

[18]Tuan Anh Nguyen v. I.N.S., 121 S. Ct. 2053, 150 L. Ed. 2d 115 (U.S. 2001).

[Section 3:4]

[1]Matter of B-, 3 I. & N. Dec. 729, 731-32, 1949 WL 6531 (B.I.A. 1949); Matter of S-, 3 I. & N. Dec. 589, 603 (B.I.A. 1949); Matter of W-, 2 I. & N. Dec. 778, 780 (B.I.A. 1947). See §§ 4:1 et seq. (discussion of the acquisition of the islands by the U.S.).

[2]Matter of S-, 3 I. & N. Dec. 589, 603–604 (B.I.A. 1949); INS Interp. 308.1(g)(2).

(3) Persons born in either place to a U.S. national father or mother after January 13, 1941 became a national at birth.[3]

(4) However, as a result of the INA, and retroactive to the acquisition of American Samoa and the Swains Island by the U.S., any person born in the island regardless of the nationality of his or her parents, is a U.S. national at birth.[4]

(5) Children born outside the United States and its possessions after January 13, 1941 are U.S. noncitizen nationals if both parents were nationals.[5]

(6) Children born outside the United States and its possessions after December 24, 1952 to one national and one noncitizen parent are U.S. noncitizen nationals if the noncitizen parent had the required prior physical presence as described above.[6]

(7) Children born out-of-wedlock in American Samoa, or anywhere else in the world (except for the United States) will be U.S. noncitizen nationals if their mother was a U.S. noncitizen national at the time of the birth and, for births occurring before December 24, 1952, resided in the U.S. or one of its outlying possessions before the birth of the child, or, for births occurring on or after that date, was continuously physically present in the United States or one of its outlying possessions for a period of one year in the United States or one of its outlying possessions any time before the child's birth.[7]

III. LOSS OF NATIONALITY

§ 3:5 Generally

Just as the removal laws of the U.S. are inapplicable to nationals because they are written to apply to aliens, laws relating to expatriation are inapplicable to nationals because they are written in terms of citizenship rather than nationality.[1] Thus, a noncitizen national woman who married a noncitizen ineligible for citizenship after 1922 did not lose her U.S. nationality as a consequence.[2] On the other hand, noncitizen nationality is automatically lost when the territory ceases to be a possession of the U.S.[3]

IV. RIGHTS OF NATIONALS

A. IMMIGRATION RIGHTS

§ 3:6 Generally

Since nationals are not noncitizens, they are not subject to U.S. immigration laws

---

[3]Matter of S-, 3 I. & N. Dec. 589, 604 (B.I.A. 1949); INS Interp. 308.1(g)(2).

[4]Matter of A-, 5 I. & N. Dec. 144, 145, 1953 WL 7416 (B.I.A. 1953).

[5]INA § 308(2), 8 U.S.C.A. § 1408(2); Matter of S-, 3 I. & N. Dec. 589, 604 (B.I.A. 1949).

[6]See rules set forth in § 3:3; INA § 308(4), 8 U.S.C.A. § 1408(4).

[7]Sec. 205, Nationality Act of 1940 reproduced as Appendix 4-12 to Ch 4; INA § 309(c), 8 U.S.C.A. § 1409(c).

[Section 3:5]

[1]U.S. v. Gonzales, 192 U.S. at 13, 24 S.Ct. at 179, 48 L.Ed. 317 (exclusion laws not applicable because nationals are not noncitizens); Matter of W-, 2 I. & N. Dec. 778, 780 (B.I.A. 1947) (loss of citizenship law not applicable because it only applies to citizens).

[2]Matter of W-, 2 I. & N. Dec. 778, 780-81, 1947 WL 7021 (B.I.A. 1947).

[3]See, e.g., § 2:23 (example of the Philippines).

that impose restrictions on noncitizens.[1] Thus, they are not subject to numerical or categorical restrictions on entry, nor are they subject to deportation.[2]

This was not the case, however, with the Philippines. On March 24, 1934, Congress passed the Philippine Independence Act, which provided for full independence of the island after a ten-year transitional period.[3] This act became effective on May 1, 1934, when the Philippine legislature passed a concurrent resolution accepting the act.[4] Even though Philippine citizens continued to be noncitizen nationals of the U.S. until full independence of the Philippines in 1946, the 1934 act provided that "citizens of the Philippine Islands who are not citizens of the United States shall be considered as if they were aliens" for purposes of U.S. immigration law.[5] Only a few of these U.S. nationals would be admitted into the United States as lawful permanent residents each year.[6] After independence, Philippine citizens became noncitizens for all purposes.

Noncitizen nationals may provide U.S. immigration benefits to their family members. A family-based relative petition filed by a noncitizen national is treated the same way as a petition filed by a lawful permanent resident.[7]

Regarding immigration-related employment verification systems, the Illegal Immigration Reform and Immigrant Responsibility Act of 1996, specifically provided that under the pilot programs created by that act, U.S. nationals are treated as citizens for employment verification purposes.[8] Civil penalties are assessed for immigration-related employment of unauthorized *noncitizens*.[9]

B. CITIZENSHIP RIGHTS

§ 3:7 Children born abroad to one U.S. citizen and one noncitizen national parent

Children born abroad to one U.S. citizen and one noncitizen national parent have been considered U.S. citizens at birth since May 24, 1934.[1] Until the enactment of the INA, the only requirement was prior residence in the United States by the citi-

---

[Section 3:6]

[1]U.S. v. Gonzales, 192 U.S. at 13, 24 S.Ct. at 179, 48 L.Ed. 317.

[2]See INA Chapters 2, 4 as amended by IIRAIRA Title III-A (predicating visa requirements, inadmissibility, and deportation on "alienage").

[3]INS Interp. 326.1. Cf. Ch 2.

[4]Matter of E-, 6 I. & N. Dec. 429, 430 (B.I.A. 1954). Judicial decisions have set the date of effect of the act variously at May 14, 1935 (date of approval of the Philippine Constitution) and November 15, 1935 (date first president of the Philippines began serving). See Mangaoang v. Boyd, 205 F.2d 553 (9th Cir. 1953); Cabebe v. Acheson, 183 F.2d 795 (9th Cir. 1950); Del Guerico v. Gabot, 161 F.2d 559 (9th Cir. 1947).

[5]Matter of T-, 7 I. & N. Dec. 201, 302 (B.I.A. 1956) citing to section 8(a)(1), Philippine Independence Act of March 24, 1934.

[6]Matter of T-, 7 I. & N. Dec. 201. Cf. Matter of V-, 7 I. & N. Dec. 242 (B.I.A. 1956) (applicability of deportation clause to Filipino who arrived days after the effective date of the Philippine Independence Act).

[7]Matter of Ah San, 15 I. & N. Dec. 315 (B.I.A. 1975).

[8]IIRAIRA § 401(d)(6).

[9]INA § 274a(a), (b), (h)(3), 8 U.S.C.A. § 1324a(a), (b), (h)(3).

[Section 3:7]

[1]See §§ 4:1 et seq.

zen parent.[2] The 1940 statute provided that the prior residence may have been accomplished in an outlying possession of the U.S.[3] The INA only allowed the passing of U.S. citizenship to such a child if the U.S. citizen parent was continuously physically present in the United States or one of its outlying possessions for a period of one year at any time prior to the child's birth.[4]

§ 3:8 Children born to U.S. citizen in outlying possession

The 1940 act provided that children of one U.S. citizen parent born in an outlying possession were U.S. citizens at birth if the U.S. citizen parent had resided in the United States or one of its outlying possessions prior to the birth of the child.[1] The INA provided that such children would be U.S. citizens at birth if the U.S. citizen parent was continuously physically present in the United States or one of its outlying possessions for a period of one year at any time prior to the child's birth.[2]

C. DOCUMENTATION

§ 3:9 Generally

Noncitizen nationals are entitled to obtain U.S. passports.[1] Ch 13 discusses procedures for obtaining passports.[2]

V. SPECIAL RULES TO NATURALIZE

§ 3:10 Requirements

Research References

Steel on Immigration Law § 15:8

The INA includes a special provision for the naturalization of persons who are nationals but not citizens of the U.S.[1] The applicant has to comply with all the requirements and procedures applicable under the general naturalization rules, except that residence and physical presence in an outlying possession of the U.S. is deemed to be residence and physical presence in the United States.[2]

If the person is married to a U.S. citizen, the expedited naturalization proceedings available to spouses of U.S. citizens apply also to nationals with the caveat that the three-year residence and physical presence may have taken place in the outly-

---

[2]See §§ 4:1 et seq.

[3]See §§ 4:1 et seq.

[4]See §§ 4:1 et seq.

[Section 3:8]

[1]See §§ 4:1 et seq.

[2]See §§ 4:1 et seq.

[Section 3:9]

[1]22 C.F.R. §§ 51.1(d), 51.2(a)

[2]See §§ 13:3 to 13:14.

[Section 3:10]

[1]INA § 325, 8 U.S.C.A. § 1436.

[2]INA § 325, 8 U.S.C.A. § 1436; 8 CFR § 325.2. For a description of the general naturalization requirements and procedures see §§ 6:1 et seq. to 9:1 et seq.

ing possessions, i.e. American Samoa, Swains Island, and the Northern Mariana Islands.[3]

A noncitizen national must take up residence in a state of the U.S. before he or she may naturalize, and must comply with the state or USCIS district physical presence and residence requirements.[4] In the case of noncitizen nationals, the requirement of having the intention of establishing a residence in the United States after naturalization may be satisfied by intending to establish a residence in an outlying possession.[5]

§ 3:11 Procedures

Research References

Steel on Immigration Law § 15:19

The applicant is required to file the naturalization application INS Form N-400 with accompanying forms and documents according to the procedures set for the general naturalization process.[1] In addition, the applicant must submit: (1) a birth certificate or other evidence of national status; (2) proof of identity; and (3) evidence of residence in the state or USCIS district in which the application is filed for three months preceding the filing of the application, or three months preceding the INS examination if the application was filed early pursuant to the provisions of the INA that allow applications to be filed up to three months before complying with the residence and physical presence requirements.[2]

The requirement that applicants submit proof of residence developed because nationals are not noncitizens, and therefore, the DHS is not required to establish a record of their admission.[3] Such evidence as passport stamps of entries into the United States, or declaration records of the Bureau of Customs and Border Protection (BCBP), or records of transportation lines may help establish compliance with the state or USCIS district residence requirements.[4] The regulations, however, do not limit the type of evidence required, and generally any type of evidence, such as rent receipts or electric bills, may be submitted to establish the required residence.

§ 3:12 Special rule for certain former Filipino U.S. nationals

Philippine citizens lost U.S. nationality when the Philippines became independent in 1946.[1] After 1946, Philippine citizens who were residing in the United States

---

[3]8 CFR §§ 325.2(b), 325.3(a).

[4]INA § 325, 8 U.S.C.A. § 1436; 8 CFR §§ 325.2, 325.3(a); INS Interp. 325.1(a)(3)(residence in a state reduced from six to three months by IMMACT 90); Petition of Taulapapa, 282 F. Supp. 156 (D. Haw. 1968) (naturalization petitioner is required to reside six months in a state).

[5]8 CFR § 325.3(b). See Ch 7 for a discussion of all the residency requirements under the general naturalization provisions.

[Section 3:11]

[1]8 CFR §§ 316.4(a), 325.4(a).

[2]8 CFR § 325.4(b).

[3]See INS Interp. 325.1(a)(3)(i), (ii).

[4]INS Interp. 325.1(a)(3)(ii).

[Section 3:12]

[1]See §§ 2:1 et seq.

became noncitizens.[2] Those Philippine nationals who entered before 1934 and were residing permanently in the United States did not have a lawful admission for permanent residence and were thus ineligible to naturalize.[3] To remedy this situation when Congress amended the naturalization laws to remove the racial bar to the naturalization of Filipinos, it also provided that those Philippine citizens who entered the United States before May 1, 1934 and resided continuously in the United States since then, would be deemed to be lawful permanent residents for naturalization purposes.[4] A similar provision was enacted in the INA.[5] Thus those Philippine citizens may naturalize upon full compliance with all the naturalization requirements.[6]

VI. OTHER NATIONALS

§ 3:13 Other individuals owing permanent allegiance to the United States

Research References

Dizon and Wettstein, Immigration Law Service 2d § 14:57

The INA definition of the term "national" includes any "person who, though not a citizen of the United States, owes permanent allegiance to the United States."[1] There are arguments that a person may owe "permanent allegiance to the United States" (and thus acquire nationality) by means other than birth or naturalization. These arguments have been found persuasive by a few courts.[2]

Courts that have found that there are other means of meeting the INA requirement of permanent allegiance to the United States agree that long-term permanent residency alone is not enough.[3] Similarly, a subjective belief by the person that he or she owes allegiance to the United States is insufficient.[4] Some objective evidence of

---

[2]Rabang v. Boyd, 353 U.S. 427, 430–31, 77 S.Ct. 985, 987, 1 L.Ed.2d 956 (1957).

[3]INS Interp. 326.1. Those who entered after May 1, 1934 were treated as if they were noncitizens for immigration purposes and thus would have been admitted as lawful permanent residents if allowed to reside in the United States. See § 3:6.

[4]Act of July 2, 1946, 60 Stat. 416.

[5]INA § 326, 8 U.S.C.A. § 1436.

[6]See §§ 7:1 et seq. and 8:1 et seq. Congress also passed special rules permitting naturalization for Filipino veterans of World War II. See § 12:10.

[Section 3:13]

[1]INA § 101(a)(22), 8 U.S.C.A. § 1101(a)(22).

[2]Lee v. Ashcroft, 216 F. Supp. 2d 51 (E.D. N.Y. 2002), reinstated by 2003 WL 21310247 (E.D.N.Y. 2003) (holding that a long-term permanent resident originally from Hong Kong who had applied for citizenship was a national); Shittu v. Elwood, 204 F. Supp. 2d 876, 879-880 (E.D. Pa. 2002) (rejecting INS argument that only residents of outlying possessions of U.S. can be nationals); see, also, U.S. v. Morin, 80 F.3d 124, 126 (4th Cir. 1996) (murdered permanent resident who had applied for citizenship was "national" for purposes of statute criminalizing murder of a national; Asemani v. Islamic Republic of Iran, 266 F. Supp. 2d 24 (D.D.C. 2003) (Iranian who had applied for U.S. citizenship demonstrated sufficient permanent allegiance to the U.S. to make him a "national" within the meaning of the Foreign Sovereign Immunities Act).

[3]Lee v. Ashcroft, 216 F. Supp. 2d 51 (E.D. N.Y. 2002), reinstated by 2003 WL 21310247 (E.D.N.Y. 2003); Oliver v. U. S. Dept. of Justice, Immigration and Naturalization Service, 517 F.2d 426, 427 (2d Cir. 1975); Sierra-Reyes v. Immigration and Naturalization Service, 585 F.2d 762, 764 (5th Cir. 1978); Shittu v. Elwood, 204 F. Supp. 2d 876, 879-880 (E.D. Pa. 2002); Carreon-Hernandez v. Levi, 409 F. Supp. 1208, 1210 (D. Minn. 1976), judgment aff'd, 543 F.2d 637 (8th Cir. 1976).

[4]U.S. v. Sotelo, 109 F.3d 1446, 1448, 177 A.L.R. Fed. 783 (9th Cir. 1997).

permanent allegiance would be required.[5] Several courts have indicated that an application for citizenship by a long-term permanent resident may be proof of such allegiance.[6] Registration for the Selective Service or service in the USA Freedom Corps may also demonstrate permanent allegiance.[7] One court found that a long-term resident who had applied for naturalization and who had registered with the Selective Service was a national and therefore could not be removed for having committed an aggravated felony.[8] The court found that his application for citizenship combined with his previous registration for Selective Service was sufficient objective evidence to demonstrate his allegiance to the U.S.[9] The court also considered his strong ties to the U.S., including a U.S. citizen wife and U.S. citizen children; his lack of any ties to Hong Kong, which he had left as a child; and his relatively minor criminal offense.[10]

However, the vast majority of courts reject this entire argument. The First, Second, Third, Fifth, Eighth, Ninth, Tenth, and Eleventh Circuit Courts of Appeals have uniformly rejected this broad understanding of "national," and instead have held that birth and naturalization are the only means of acquiring United States nationality under the Immigration and Nationality Act[11] This is so, even with regard to oaths given in the military context.[12] Indeed, even the Fourth Circuit, which held to the minority view in a published decision in the criminal context, has now joined the majority of circuits in finding that a military oath does not manifest

---

[5]Shittu v. Elwood, 204 F. Supp. 2d 876, 880 (E.D. Pa. 2002).

[6]Lee v. Ashcroft, 216 F. Supp. 2d 51, 57 (E.D. N.Y. 2002), reinstated by 2003 WL 21310247 (E.D.N.Y. 2003) ("At a minimum, it appears that to qualify as a national, an individual must have demonstrated his or her allegiance by applying for citizenship"); Shittu v. Elwood, 204 F. Supp. 2d 876, 880 (E.D. Pa. 2002) (though not conclusive, an application for citizenship is one form of objective evidence of permanent allegiance); U.S. v. Morin, 80 F.3d 124, 126 (4th Cir. 1996) ("[A]n application for citizenship is the most compelling evidence of permanent allegiance to the United States short of citizenship itself.").

[7]Shittu v. Elwood, 204 F. Supp. 2d 876, 880 (E.D. Pa. 2002); Lee v. Ashcroft, 216 F. Supp. 2d 51, 58 (E.D. N.Y. 2002), reinstated by 2003 WL 21310247 (E.D.N.Y. 2003); but cf. Carreon-Hernandez v. Levi, 543 F.2d 637 (8th Cir. 1976) (rejecting petitioner's claim of "national" status although he had registered for Selective Service).

[8]Lee v. Ashcroft, 216 F. Supp. 2d 51, 58 (E.D. N.Y. 2002), reinstated by 2003 WL 21310247 (E.D.N.Y. 2003).

[9]Lee v. Ashcroft, 216 F. Supp. 2d 51, 58 (E.D. N.Y. 2002), reinstated by 2003 WL 21310247 (E.D.N.Y. 2003).

[10]Lee v. Ashcroft, 216 F. Supp. 2d 51, 58 (E.D. N.Y. 2002), reinstated by 2003 WL 21310247 (E.D.N.Y. 2003).

[11]See Abou-Haidar v. Gonzales, 437 F.3d 206 (1st Cir. 2006); Marquez-Almanzar v. I.N.S., 418 F.3d 210 (2d Cir. 2005); Salim v. Ashcroft, 350 F.3d 307, 5 A.L.R. Fed. 2d 759 (3d Cir. 2003) (finding that for a citizen of another country, nothing less than U.S. citizenship will show permanent allegiance to the U.S. to make the person a national); Alwan v. Ashcroft, 388 F.3d 507 (5th Cir. 2004); Carreon-Hernandez v. Levi, 543 F.2d 637, 638 (8th Cir. 1976); Perdomo-Padilla v. Ashcroft, 333 F.3d 964 (9th Cir. 2003) (finding that a naturalization applicant who had taken an oath of allegiance pursuant to the naturalization application was not a national); U.S. v. Jimenez-Alcala, 353 F.3d 858 (10th Cir. 2003) (finding that a national, for purposes of the offense of being in the U.S. without permission, refers only to those born in the U.S. territories); Sebastian-Soler v. U.S. Atty. Gen., 409 F.3d 1280 (11th Cir. 2005); Tovar-Alvarez v. U.S. Atty. Gen., 427 F.3d 1350 (11th Cir. 2005).

[12]Reyes-Alcarez v. Ashcroft, 363 F.3d 937 (9th Cir. 2004) (standard military oath for Army veteran not demonstration of permanent allegiance); Theagene v. Gonzales, 411 F.3d 1107 (9th Cir. 2005) (same for combat veteran).

a permanent allegiance to the United States, and thus does not make one a national.[13]

The Board has also rejected a broader definition of the term "national," and has specifically rejected the proposition that an individual can gain nationality status by taking an oath of allegiance in connection with an application for naturalization.[14] The Board also held that INA § 308 controls the determination of who is a national rather than the definition of nationality found in INA § 101(a)(22)(B); the latter section, according to the Board, "does not set forth the terms and conditions for acquiring nationality."[15]

VII.   EFFECT OF NATIONAL/CITIZEN DISTINCTION

§ 3:14   Claims to be citizen or national

Research References

Immigration Law Service (2d ed.) §§ 3:96, 14:57

When hiring someone, an employer is legally obligated to complete form I-9, and to undertake good faith efforts to verify an individual's legal right to accept employment.[1] As part of this process, an individual seeking employment must complete specific sections on the I-9, attesting under penalty of perjury that they are either: (1) a citizen or national; (2) a permanent resident; or (3) an alien authorized to accept employment.[2] For many years, the form only had one checkbox, asking whether the individual was a citizen or a national; it did not distinguish between the two.[3]

Where an individual has claimed, on the I-9 form, to be a citizen or national, it would seem that they could plausibly have been claiming to be a national, rather than to have been a citizen. Thus, the Ninth Circuit has held that checking the "citizen or national" box on the I-9 form is not a false claim to U.S. citizenship, for purposes of 8 U.S.C.A. § 1182(a)(6)(C)(ii).[4] By contrast, the Eighth Circuit has held that checking this box can nonetheless be a false claim to citizenship,[5] at least in

---

[13]Dragenice v. Gonzales, 470 F.3d 183 (4th Cir. 2006); Patel v. Napolitano, 706 F.3d 370 (4th Cir. 2013); cf. U.S. v. Morin, 80 F.3d 124 (4th Cir. 1996) (application for citizenship rendered permanent resident a "national" for purposes of protection under U.S. criminal laws).

[14]Matter of Moises Navas-Acosta, 23 I. & N. Dec. 586 (B.I.A. 2003).

[15]Matter of Moises Navas-Acosta, 23 I. & N. Dec. 586 (B.I.A. 2003).

[Section 3:14]

[1]8 U.S.C.A. § 1324a(b).

[2]8 U.S.C.A. § 1324a(b)(2).

[3]The current I-9 form can be found at http://www.uscis.gov/files/form/i-9.pdf.

[4]U.S. v. Karaouni, 379 F.3d 1139 (9th Cir. 2004).

[5]Ateka v. Ashcroft, 384 F.3d 954 (8th Cir. 2004) reh'g and reh'g en banc denied (Dec. 14, 2004). The Eighth Circuit treated the question in *Ateka* as relating to whether sufficient evidence of the false claim to citizenship had been presented, rather than whether checking the box was a per se claim to citizenship. In this vein, the Eighth Circuit pointed out that when Ateka testified, he did not know what nationality is. *Ateka v. Ashcroft, at 957.* It did not purport to establish a rule that checking that box on the I-9 is a per se false claim to citizenship. Moreover, as Judge Bright noted in his concurrence, *Ateka v. Ashcroft,. at 958,* the *Ateka* decision did not consider whether an I-9 representation would be considered to be for a purpose under the Act, which is necessary to trigger inadmissibility under 8 U.S.C.A. § 1182(a)(6)(C)(ii).

the absence of evidence that the individual thought they were claiming nationality. The Fifth and Tenth Circuits have agreed with this analysis.[6]

The issue is significant, because there is currently no waiver for inadmissibility under 8 U.S.C.A. § 1182(a)(6)(C)(ii), at least in the absence of evidence that the individual thought they were claiming nationality.[7]

However, the 2009 revisions to the I-9 form include separate boxes for individuals claiming to be a noncitizen national of the United States, and those claiming to be citizens.[8] Presumably, individuals who check the box for "nationals" will now have strong claims that they are not in fact claiming to be citizens; those individuals checking the "citizen" box will have weaker claims.

---

[6]Kechkar v. Gonzales, 500 F.3d 1080 (10th Cir. 2007); Theodros v. Gonzales, 490 F.3d 396 (5th Cir. 2007). The Board's analysis in Matter of Barcenas, 25 I. & N. Dec. 40, 43 (BIA 2009) ("the respondent never claimed to be a 'national'") also supports this view.

[7]But see 8 U.S.C.A. § 1182(a)(2)(C)(ii)(II) (creating an exception to inadmissibility for individuals who obtained permanent residence while under 16 years of age, and whose naturalized or adopted parents are both U.S. citizens).

[8]See http://www.uscis.gov/files/form/i-9.pdf.

Chapter 4

Citizenship through Birth Outside United States to Citizen Parent or Parents

I. GENERAL PRINCIPLES

II. PERSONS BORN ABROAD BEFORE MAY 24, 1934

III. PERSONS BORN ABROAD BETWEEN MAY 24, 1934 AND JANUARY 13, 1941

VIII. PROOF OF CITIZENSHIP

Research References

West's Key Number Digest

Aliens, Immigration and Citizenship ⚷650 to 685

Westlaw Databases

Steel on Immigration Law (STEEL)
Immigration Law Service (2d ed.) (IMMLS2D)

Treatises and Practice Aids

Steel on Immigration Law § 15:3

KeyCite®: Cases and other legal materials listed in KeyCite Scope can be researched through the KeyCite service on Westlaw®. Use KeyCite to check citations for form, parallel references, prior and later history, and comprehensive citator information, including citations to other decisions and secondary materials.

I. GENERAL PRINCIPLES

§ 4:1 Citizenship by descent and citizenship by birth in U.S

Research References

Dizon and Wettstein, Immigration Law Service 2d § 14:27

When the U.S. gained its independence from England, it inherited the common law principle of *jus soli*, which confers citizenship upon persons born inside the United States.[1] Children born abroad to U.S. citizens did not automatically acquire U.S. citizenship under the common law.[2]

In Europe, by contrast, the principle of citizenship by descent, also referred to as *jus sanguinis*, became the accepted norm after the French Revolution.[3] Under the principles of *jus sanguinis*, a child inherits the citizenship of the parent or parents rather than of the place where the child is born. By the turn of the twentieth century, this principle was so entrenched in Europe that Germany, Switzerland, Sweden, and Norway did not confer their citizenship upon children born within their territory unless the parents were nationals of those countries; and France, Belgium, Spain, Italy, Greece, and Russia only conferred their citizenship upon children born to non-national parents in their countries under specific circumstances.[4] In the U.S. the opposite development took place. The accepted common law principle of universal citizenship by birth inside the United States not only continued, but also was reaffirmed constitutionally.[5]

Citizenship by descent, however, was not unknown in the U.S. The U.S. Constitution conferred upon Congress the power to establish a "uniform Rule of

---

[Section 4:1]

[1]U.S. v. Wong Kim Ark, 169 U.S. 649, 655–66, 18 S.Ct. 456, 459–63, 42 L.Ed. 890 (1898). See generally §§ 2:1 et seq.

[2]U.S. v. Wong Kim Ark, 169 U.S. 649, 666–67, 18 S.Ct. 456, 463–64, 42 L.Ed. 890 (1898).

[3]U.S. v. Wong Kim Ark, 169 U.S. 649, 666–67, 18 S.Ct. 456, 463–64, 42 L.Ed. 890 (1898).

[4]U.S. v. Wong Kim Ark, 169 U.S. 649, 667, 18 S.Ct. 456, 464, 42 L.Ed. 890 (1898). Before the French Revolution, all European countries subscribed to the principle of jus soli. U.S. v. Wong Kim Ark, 169 U.S. 649, 666–67, 18 S.Ct. 456, 463–64, 42 L.Ed. 890 (1898).

[5]U.S. v. Wong Kim Ark, 169 U.S. 649, 674–75, 18 S.Ct. 456, 467, 42 L.Ed. 890 (1898).

Naturalization."[6] During the very first Congress, this power was used to confer U.S. citizenship upon children born abroad to U.S. citizen parents.[7] Congress has since enacted several statutes governing citizenship by birth abroad.[8] Since citizenship by descent is statutory in nature, the appropriate statute must be reviewed to determine whether a child born abroad acquired U.S. citizenship at birth.[9] As a general rule, the statute that governs the citizenship of the child is the one that was in effect at the time of the child's birth.

Citizenship at birth abroad vests without an individual having to file an application or take an oath. In most respects, U.S. citizens at birth who are born abroad are treated as native-born citizens. Persons who acquire U.S. citizenship at birth abroad may not be excluded or deported from the U.S.[10] In general, the executive does not have the power to deport U.S. citizens.[11] Therefore, unless it is established that the person is a noncitizen, the immigration courts lack jurisdiction to start removal proceedings against the person.[12] In removal proceedings, it is DHS that has the burden of proof to establish deportability, including establishing that the person is a noncitizen.[13] When a person is born abroad, there is a nonstatutory presumption that the person is a noncitizen.[14] Although the statutory burden of proof still remains with DHS to prove deportability by clear and convincing evidence, the Board has held that the alien must present a preponderance of evidence proving citizenship before the DHS will be forced to prove the alien a citizen.[15]

Since they are already citizens by right, there are several ways in which U.S. citizens born abroad may obtain evidence of their U.S. citizenship status. Among

---

[6]U.S. Const. art. 1 § 8, cl. 4.

[7]Sec. 1, Act of March 26, 1790, 1 Stat. 103 reproduced as Appendix 4-1.

[8]See § 4:17 et seq. for a discussion of specific statutes.

[9]Rogers v. Bellei, 401 U.S. 815, 830, 91 S.Ct. 1060, 1068–69, 28 L.Ed.2d 499 (1971) (no noncitizen has the slightest right to naturalization unless the statutory requirements are complied with-interpreting constitutionality of conditions subsequent imposed on children born abroad to U.S. citizens); Weedin v. Chin Bow, 274 U.S. 657, 660, 47 S.Ct. 772, 773, 47 L.Ed. 1284 (1927).

[10]See Weedin v. Chin Bow, 274 U.S. 657, 658, 47 S. Ct. 772, 71 L. Ed. 1284 (1927); D'Alessio v. Lehmann, 289 F.2d 317 (6th Cir. 1961).

[11]Ng Fung Ho v. White, 259 U.S. 276, 284, 42 S. Ct. 492, 495, 66 L. Ed. 938 (1922).

[12]See INA § 237(a), 8 U.S.C.A. § 1227(a) ("Any alien . . ."); Ng Fung Ho v. White, 259 U.S. 276, 284, 42 S. Ct. 492, 495, 66 L. Ed. 938 (1922); Matter of Benitez, 19 I. & N. Dec. 173, 175, 1984 WL 48602 (B.I.A. 1984) ("birth in the United States would almost certainly mean United States citizenship and no deportation for this respondent").

[13]Matter of Guevara, 20 I. & N. Dec. 238, 1990 WL 385763 (B.I.A. 1990).

[14]Matter of Benitez, 19 I. & N. Dec. 173, 176, 1984 WL 48602 (B.I.A. 1984); Matter of Tijerina-Villarreal, 13 I. & N. Dec. 327, 330, 1969 WL 16974 (B.I.A. 1969).

[15]See Matter of Tijerina-Villarreal, 13 I. & N. Dec. 327, 1969 WL 16974 (B.I.A. 1969) (discussing burden to overcome "presumption" of alienage); Matter of Baires-Larios, 24 I. & N. Dec. 467, 468, 2008 WL 643136 (B.I.A. 2008); Leal Santos v. Mukasey, 516 F.3d 1, 4 (1st Cir. 2008). While the Board finds that birth abroad triggers a requirement that the alleged alien show by a preponderance of the evidence that they are a citizen, one could argue that the Board has over-stated that level of proof. If Rule 301 of the Federal Rules of Evidence is applied, only "more than a scintilla" of evidence is necessary to shift the burden back onto the government. See generally, Charles Roth, "Burdens of Proof Issues in Removal Proceedings," in 2005 Immigration & Nationality Handbook 906-07 (Stephanie Browning, ed., 2005); cf. Matter of Vivas, 16 I. & N. Dec. 68, 70, 1977 WL 39219 (B.I.A. 1977) (discussing shift of burden of production in deportation hearings).

others, they may apply for a U.S. passport, file for a certificate of citizenship from USCIS, or if under 18, seek a Consular Report of Birth.[16]

§ 4:2 Continuing validity of previous citizenship acts

Although all prior citizenship at birth abroad statutes have been repealed, the citizenship rights acquired under them have been preserved.[1] On the one hand, the expatriation of a parent after his or her child is born does not change the child's U.S. citizenship.[2] On the other hand, revocation of naturalization of the parent after his or her child is born may have an effect on the child's citizenship rights.[3]

Thus, in order to determine whether the person is a U.S. citizen born abroad, recourse must be had to the laws in effect at the time of the birth of the child.[4] These laws are discussed in detail below.

Indeed, it might be possible to apply this reasoning even to a change in agency interpretation of law. As noted below, the BIA has now revised its view of whether all distinctions based on legitimation have been eliminated in Jamaica.[5] On remand from the Second Circuit in *Watson v. Holder*,[6] DHS took the position—a position the Board did not ultimately address in the subsequent unpublished decision—that any reinterpretation of foreign law would not be applied retroactively to an individual who would have automatically acquired citizenship under the then-reigning interpretation.[7]

§ 4:3 Citizenship at birth abroad and collective naturalization

Most of the statutes regarding citizenship at birth were meant to apply prospectively to children born after the enactment of the statute. The only exceptions were the acts prior to 1802 that conferred U.S. citizenship at birth abroad on children born before the enactment of the act.[1] Actually, the Act of 1802 has been

---

[16]See §§ 13:1 et seq. (discussing method of proving U.S. citizenship).

[Section 4:2]

[1]Sec. 504, Nationality Act of 1940; INA §§ 403, 405. (Reference to the INA without qualification means the INA as amended by the various amendments up to the present). Cf. § 14:33.

[2]Matter of M-, 6 I. & N. Dec. 70 (B.I.A. 1953) (parent's loss of U.S. citizenship prior to the child's birth deprives the child of U.S. citizenship); Matter of O-, 2 I. & N. Dec. 6, 7 (B.I.A. 1944) (expatriation occurring after child's birth does not affect the child's citizenship).

[3]INS Interp. 301.1(b)(1)(i).

[4]U.S. v. Viramontes-Alvarado, 149 F.3d 912, 915 (9th Cir.) cert. denied, 525 U.S. 976 (1998); Ablang v. Reno, 52 F.3d 801, 803 (9th Cir. 1995).

[5]See infra at 4:9; Matter of Clahar, 18 I. & N. Dec. 1, 1981 WL 158807 (B.I.A. 1981); Matter of Hines, 24 I. & N. Dec. 544, 2008 WL 2310959 (B.I.A. 2008).

[6]Watson v. Holder, 643 F.3d 367 (2d Cir. 2011).

[7]In re Davino Hopeton Watson, No. 046-633-823, DHS Brief on Remand, Nov. 25, 2011, at 11–23 (on file with author); cf. In re Davino Hopeton Watson, No. 046-633-823 (BIA Jan. 23, 2013) (unpublished).

[Section 4:3]

[1]Sec. 1, Act of March 26, 1790 reproduced as Appendix 4-1; sec. 3, Act of January 29, 1795 reproduced as Appendix 4-2; sec. 4, Act of April 14, 1802 reproduced as Appendix 4-3.

held to apply *only* to children born before its enactment.[2] This provision is in the nature of collective naturalization of those children already born abroad. Prospectivity was restored in 1855, when Congress passed an almost identical statute that applied to children to be born in the future as well as to those already born abroad.[3] The 1802 act was reenacted in 1874, once again collectively naturalizing those children born abroad to U.S. citizen parents before 1874 who did not become U.S. citizens at birth under the provisions of the 1855 act.[4]

§ 4:4 Requirements common to most birth abroad statutes

Laws governing citizenship at birth abroad have always imposed conditions that must be satisfied before the child is born for a child to be considered a U.S. citizen.[1] Common to all statutes is the requirement that at least one parent must be a citizen at the time of the child's birth and usually must have resided in the U.S. for a specified period before the birth.[2]

Some statutes have imposed different requirements depending on whether one or both of the parents are citizens at the time of the birth. In addition, different requirements usually apply to legitimate children and children born out-of-wedlock. Some of the laws also imposed conditions subsequent that the child must comply with before a certain age if the child is not to lose his or her U.S. citizenship. These conditions are called "retention requirements."

The parameters that affect U.S. citizenship at birth abroad are: (1) date of the child's birth; (2) U.S. citizenship of one as opposed to both of the parents at the time of the child's birth; (3) noncitizen nationality of the noncitizen parent; (4) child's legitimacy at birth; (5) length of residence of citizen parent in the U.S. prior to the birth of the child; and (6) child's compliance with conditions subsequent imposed by the law in effect at the time of the child's birth.

The principles applicable to each of the relevant periods governed by specific statutes are summarized in Appendix 4-24. That chart is divided into six columns. In the first column are the beginning and ending birth dates to which the row refers. The second column describes the prior residence and retention requirements applicable when both parents were U.S. citizens at the time of the child's birth. The third column provides the requirements when one parent was a citizen and the

---

[2]See Mock Gum Ying v. Cahill, 81 F.2d 940 (9th Cir. 1936) citing to dicta in Weedin v. Chin Bow, 274 U.S. 657, 663–64, 47 S. Ct. 772, 772–74, 71 L. Ed. 1284 (1927) and U.S. v. Wong Kim Ark, 169 U.S. 649, 674, 18 S. Ct. 456, 466, 42 L. Ed. 890 (1898).

[3]Act of February 10, 1855 reproduced as Appendix 4-4. The 1855 act, however, transformed a gender neutral statute into a gender specific one by making its provisions applicable to children of U.S. "fathers" rather than to children of "persons" who are citizens of the U.S. as provided in the 1802 act. Compare Act of February 10, 1855 reproduced as Appendix 4-4 with sec. 4, Act of April 14, 1802 reproduced as Appendix 4-3. Cf. Montana v. Kennedy, 366 U.S. 308, 310–12, 81 S.Ct. 1336, 1338–39, 6 L.Ed.2d 313 (1961) (regardless of whether the 1802 statute allowed children of U.S. women to be citizens at birth abroad, such statute has no prospective application).

[4]Act of June 22, 1874 incorporated as sec. 2172, Revised Statutes of the United States, 1878 reproduced as Appendix 4-5. Cf. §§ 4:17 to 4:21.

[Section 4:4]

[1]INS Interp. 301.1(b)(1)(i).

[2]See Weedin v. Chin Bow, 274 U.S. 657, 47 S. Ct. 772, 71 L. Ed. 1284 (1927) (even if the statute is silent on the issue, the parent's residence must have preceded the birth of the child). Residence may have been as a noncitizen provided that at the time of the child's birth, the parent is a citizen. INS Interp. 301.1(b)(1)(i).

other a noncitizen national of the U.S. at the time the child was born. The fourth column applies to children of one citizen and one noncitizen parent. The fifth column applies to out-of-wedlock children of U.S. citizen mothers. The last column deals with requirements for out-of-wedlock children of U.S. citizen fathers.

§ 4:5 Conditions precedent

Research References

Dizon and Wettstein, Immigration Law Service 2d § 14:29

Since the first statute granting citizenship at birth to children born abroad of a U.S. citizen parent, all statutes have required that before the birth of the child, the parent must have resided in the United States.[1] This condition precedent seems to have been designed to prevent the acquisition of U.S. citizenship by children whose family had no connection with this country for generations.[2]

Until 1940, all statutes had the same condition precedent for the acquisition of citizenship by descent: at least one of the citizen parents under whom citizenship is claimed must have resided in the United States prior to the birth of the child.[3] The 1940 act introduced a heightened condition precedent when one of the parents was a noncitizen.[4] Under that provision, a child born abroad will not be a U.S. citizen at birth unless prior to the birth of the child, the U.S. citizen parent has resided for ten years in the United States or its outlying possessions, at least five of which were after the parent attained the age of sixteen.[5] The Immigration and Nationality Act (INA) as originally enacted had a similar requirement but the five years started after the parent was fourteen rather than sixteen.[6] Finally, in 1986, the prior residence requirement was reduced to a total of five years, at least two of which must have been after the parent was 14.[7]

The statutes making these changes to the prior residence requirements made clear that these changed requirements apply prospectively only, to children born af-

---

[Section 4:5]

[1]See sec 1, Act of March 26, 1790 reproduced as Appendix 4-1; sec. 3, Act of January 29, 1795, 1 Stat. 414 reproduced as Appendix 4-2; sec. 4, Act of April 14, 1802, 2 Stat. 153 reproduced as Appendix 4-3; sec. 1, Act of February 10, 1855, 10 Stat. 604 reproduced as Appendix 4-4; sec. 1, Act of May 24, 1934, Pub. L. No. 73-250, 48 Stat. 797 reproduced as Appendix 4-10; sec. 201, Nationality Act of 1940, Pub.L. 76-853, 54 Sat. 1137 (October 14, 1940) reproduced as Appendix 4-12; INA § 301, 8 U.S.C.A. § 1401. Cf. Weedin v. Chin Bow, 274 U.S. 657, 666–67, 47 S. Ct. 772, 774–75, 71 L. Ed. 1284 (1927) (parent's residence in the United States must have occurred before the birth of the child).

[2]Weedin v. Chin Bow, 274 U.S. 657, 666–67, 47 S. Ct. 772, 774–75, 71 L. Ed. 1284 (1927).

[3]Sec 1, Act of March 26, 1790 reproduced as Appendix 4-1; sec. 3, Act of January 29, 1795 reproduced as Appendix 4-2; sec. 4, Act of April 14, 1802 reproduced as Appendix 4-3; sec. 1, Act of February 10, 1855 reproduced as Appendix 4-4; sec. 1, Act of May 24, 1934 reproduced as Appendix 4-10.

[4]Sec. 201(g), Nationality Act of 1940 reproduced as Appendix 4-12.

[5]See §§ 4:32 to 4:50.

[6]INA § 301(a)(7), 8 U.S.C.A. § 1401(a)(7) as originally enacted by Act of June 27, 1952, 66 Stat. 163 reproduced as Appendix 4-14.

[7]INA § 301(g), 8 U.S.C.A. § 1401(g) as amended by sec. 12, Act of November 14, 1986, Pub.L. 99-653, 100 Stat. 3655 reproduced as Appendix 4-19A.

ter the date of enactment of the respective acts.[8] Thus, for example, children born to one citizen parent and one noncitizen parent prior to January 14, 1941 acquired citizenship at birth abroad if their U.S. citizen parent resided in the United States prior to the birth of the child, regardless of the length of that residence.[9] The heightened requirement of the 1940 act did not apply to them.

Due to the differential treatment provided to children when one of the parents is not a citizen, and because, as will be discussed below, children of one noncitizen parent have at different times also been required to comply with conditions subsequent, the citizenship status of both parents is relevant in determining the requirements applicable for the vesting of U.S. citizenship upon children born abroad to U.S. citizens.

§ 4:6 Conditions subsequent

Research References

Dizon and Wettstein, Immigration Law Service 2d § 14:29

In 1934, Congress introduced a new concept in citizenship for children born abroad. For the first time, children born abroad would lose their U.S. citizenship if they failed to come to the United States by a certain age.[1] Throughout the history of U.S. nationality law applicable to U.S. citizens born abroad, conditions subsequent have only been imposed on children born to one citizen and one noncitizen parent. If neither parent was a noncitizen, i.e. if both parents were U.S. citizens or one parent was a citizen and the other was a noncitizen national, no conditions subsequent have ever been imposed on the child.

These conditions subsequent, also referred to as "retention requirements," originally applied prospectively, i.e. only children born after May 24, 1934 had to comply with them.[2] However, these requirements have subsequently been liberalized, and the more lenient provision made applicable to persons born before the date of enactment of the respective acts.[3] Furthermore, Congress passed an amendment to the INA in 1972 not only reducing the retention requirements, but also restoring U.S. citizenship upon those children who prior to the passing of the amendment had lost U.S. citizenship for failure to comply with the more stringent requirements ap-

---

[8]Secs. 504, 601, Nationality Act of 1940 reproduced as Appendix 4-12; INA §§ 403, 405; sec. 8(r) of the Immigration Technical Corrections Act of 1988, Pub.L. 100-525, 102 Stat. 2609 reproduced as Appendix 4-19B. Cf. Runnet v. Schultz, 901 F.2d 782, 783 (9th Cir. 1990); INS Interp. 301.1(b)(1)(i) (amendments to citizenship at birth abroad statutes are prospective only unless specifically made retroactive by the statute).

[9]January 14, 1941 is the date the 1940 act took effect. See sec. 601, Nationality Act of 1940 reproduced as Appendix 4-12.

[Section 4:6]

[1]Sec. 1, Act of May 24, 1934 reproduced as Appendix 4-10. The 1907 act had a similar provision but it was interpreted to mean that children would lose diplomatic protection, not their U.S. citizenship. See §§ 4:17 to 4:21.

[2]See §§ 4:22 to 4:31.

[3]Sec. 201(h), Nationality Act of 1940 reproduced as Appendix 4-12; INA § 301(c), 8 U.S.C.A. § 1401(c) as originally enacted by Act of June 27, 1952 (both acts made their liberalized provisions applicable to all children born after May 24, 1934).

plicable before the amendment.[4] Finally, in 1978, Congress removed the retention requirements altogether effective as of that date.[5] Thus, persons who had not lost their U.S. citizenship as of that date, including everybody who was born after October 10, 1952, did not have to comply with any retention requirements.[6]

Because of these successive amendments to the law, retention requirements apply only to persons born between May 24, 1934 and October 10, 1952.[7] Since their inception, retention requirements have only applied to children born to one U.S. citizen parent and one noncitizen parent.[8]

In 1994, Congress amended section 324 of the INA to allow for the resumption of citizenship by persons who lost their U.S. citizenship by failing to comply with the retention requirements.[9] This subsection took effect on March 1, 1995.[10] It allows the restoration of citizenship for all those who failed to meet the retention requirements, except for persons who would be barred from naturalizing because of the political grounds contained in INA § 313.[11] This restoration is not retroactive.[12] The procedures for the restoration of citizenship are discussed in detail below.[13]

§ 4:7 Establishing actual filiation

The State Department takes the blood metaphor quite seriously, specifically between the child and father. Under its guidelines, being born in wedlock is not sufficient to establish U.S. citizenship through a U.S. citizen father.[1] According to the Foreign Affairs Manual, the laws on acquisition of U.S. citizenship through a parent have always contemplated the existence of a blood relationship between the child and the parent(s) through whom citizenship is claimed.[2] For the State Department, it is not enough that the child is presumed to be the issue of the parents' marriage by the laws of the jurisdiction where the child was born.[3] Absent a blood relationship between the child and the parent on whose citizenship the child's own claim is based, the State Department will not recognize U.S. citizenship of the child.[4] The

---

[4]INA § 301(b), (c), 8 U.S.C.A. § 1401(b), (c) reproduced as Appendix 4-14, as amended by sec. 1, Act of October 27, 1972, Pub.L. 92-582, 86 Stat. 1289 reproduced as Appendix 4-17; INS Interp. 301. 1(b)(6)(vii). U.S. citizenship was not restored, however, if the person had not been in the U.S. long enough to comply with the post-amendment retention requirements. See §§ 4:24 to 4:28.

[5]Sec. 1, Act of October 10, 1978, Pub.L. 95-432, 92 Stat. 1046 reproduced as Appendix 4-18.

[6]See §§ 4:51 to 4:62.

[7]See §§ 4:24 to 4:28, 4:38 to 4:44.

[8]See §§ 4:24 to 4:28.

[9]Sec. 103(a), Immigration Nationality Technical Corrections Act of 1994 (INTCA), Pub.L. 103-416, 108 Stat. 4305 (Oct. 25, 1994) adding INA § 324(d), 8 U.S.C.A. § 1435(d), reproduced as Appendix 4-21.

[10]INTCA § 103(b) reproduced as Appendix 4-21.

[11]INA § 324(d), 8 U.S.C.A. § 1435(d).

[12]INA § 324(d), 8 U.S.C.A. § 1435(d).

[13]See § 11:30.

[Section 4:7]

[1]7 FAM 1131.4-1(a).

[2]7 FAM 1131.4-1(a).

[3]7 FAM 1131.4-1(a).

[4]7 FAM 1131.4-1(a).

Foreign Affairs Manual lists circumstances that should give rise to a reasonable doubt of paternity.[5]

The State Department has procedures in place for DNA testing as a means of establishing actual filiation.[6] The Foreign Affairs Manual provides a useful summary:

> [D]ue to the expense, complexity and logistical delays inherent in parentage testing, genetic testing should be used only if other credible proof does not establish to the satisfaction of the adjudicating officer that the relationship exists. When genetic testing appears warranted, the consular officer should advise the applicant that genetic testing may establish the validity of the relationship; that such testing is entirely voluntary; and that all costs of testing and related expenses must be borne by the applicant and paid to the laboratory in advance. In addition, the consular officer should caution the applicant that submitting to testing does not at all guarantee the subsequent issuance of a U.S. passport, and that the results of DNA testing may instead preclude issuance.[7]

Under the State Department procedures, the applicant is responsible for selecting an AABB-accredited organization, though a post panel physician should collect any necessary samples.[8]

For a child born out of wedlock, the current statute requires a "blood relationship" between a father and child for the child to acquire citizenship at birth.[9] But the statute does not explicitly answer other scenarios, such as where a child born within a marriage, but is biologically the child of only one of the spouses. The Ninth Circuit has held that a blood relationship is not necessary in that context, regardless of whether the biological parent was the husband or wife.[10] However, this exception to the blood requirement is a very limited one, and does not apply, for instance, to children adopted by U.S. citizens, neither of whom was the child's biological parent.[11]

The Board of Immigration Appeals has yet to address that argument directly. The Board has rejected potential derivation of citizenship after birth through adopted parents, but in reaching that decision the Board noted that derivation, unlike acquisition, turns on the definition of "child."[12]

§ 4:8 Children born out-of-wedlock

For children born out of wedlock to U.S. citizen fathers, the law has repeatedly

---

[5]7 FAM 1131.4-1(b) (listing (1) conception or birth of a child when either of the alleged natural parents was married to another, (2) naming on the birth certificate, as father, mother, or both, persons other than the alleged natural parents, (3) establishment of lack of access by evidence contrary to the statements of the alleged parents).

[6]See generally, 7 FAM 1110 App. A.

[7]See generally, 7 FAM 1110 App. A para. (f).

[8]See generally, 7 FAM 1120 App. A para. (a), (b).

[9]INA § 309(a) [8 U.S.C.A. § 1409(a)] (1986).

[10]Scales v. I.N.S., 232 F.3d 1159 (9th Cir. 2000) (husband was not biological father, but was married to biological mother at the time of birth); Solis-Espinoza v. Gonzales, 401 F.3d 1090 (9th Cir. 2005) (biological father was married at time of birth, and child was adopted by the wife of his biological father).

[11]Martinez-Madera v. Holder, 559 F.3d 937 (9th Cir. 2009); Marquez-Marquez v. Gonzales, 455 F.3d 548, 558 (5th Cir. 2006); Colaianni v. I.N.S., 490 F.3d 185, 187 (2d Cir. 2007); see also U.S. v. Marguet-Pillado, 560 F.3d 1078, 1082–84 (9th Cir. 2009) (finding no acquisition of citizenship where the biological parent was not a citizen, and the subsequent marriage with a U.S. citizen and her adoption of the child took place many years later).

[12]Matter of Guzman-Gomez, 24 I. & N. Dec. 824, 826 n.3 (BIA 2009) (rejecting derivation of citizenship through non-adoptive step-parent, but leaving open the possibility of adopting Scales).

changed, and must be analyzed based on the law in effect at the time of birth or legitimation. Even though the 1855 act stated that children born abroad to U.S. citizen fathers were U.S. citizens at birth, out-of-wedlock children born abroad to U.S. citizen fathers were not considered to be U.S. citizens at birth.[1] The rationale behind this exclusion is that out-of-wedlock children were not considered children of the father for certain purposes under common law.[2] However, if the child had been legitimated under the laws of the father's domicile, the child would be considered to have become legitimate as of the date of birth and would be entitled to U.S. citizenship by descent.[3] Appendix 4-25 summarizes the BIA's and State Department's interpretations of the legitimation laws of different countries and of the states of the United States.

The 1940 act required legitimation to take place before the child reached the age of maturity.[4] This limitation, however, only applies if the child was born after January 13, 1941.[5] The INA, as interpreted by the legacy INS, once again changed the requirements for legitimation adding the requirement that the child be unmarried.[6] In 1986, the acquisition of birth abroad from a natural U.S. citizen father was radically revised, adding, among other requirements, the need to obtain a written agreement from the father that he will support the child until the child reaches the age of eighteen.[7]

A special rule applies to children born out-of-wedlock in the Republic of Panama and the Panama Canal Zone which is unaffected by the changes brought about by the acts of 1940 and the INA.[8]

The law that deals with citizenship of out-of-wedlock children born to U.S. citizen mothers has also changed over the years. Originally, before May 24, 1934, children born out-of-wedlock to U.S. citizen mothers were not citizens at birth.[9] Congress amended the law in 1940 to confer U.S. citizenship at birth to out-of-wedlock children of U.S. citizen mothers who had previously resided in the United States or one of its outlying possessions, whether the child was born before or after the passage of the act.[10] Certain children born out-of-wedlock to U.S. citizen mothers could not take advantage of this 1940 amendment if they were legitimated by noncitizen fathers prior to reaching 16 years and such legitmation took place before January 14,

---

[Section 4:8]

[1]Sec. 1, Act of February 10, 1855 reproduced as Appendix 4-4; 23 Op. Atty. Gen. 162 (1920).

[2]32 Op. Atty. Gen. at 162. Cf. Ablang v. Reno, 52 F.3d 801, 803 (9th Cir. 1995) (legitimation is not a "condition subsequent"; rather, citizenship does not inhere unless and until paternity is established through legitimation).

[3]32 Op. Atty. Gen. at 164–65. The law applicable at this point is the law of the domicile of the father even when the legitimating act occurred somewhere else. 39 Op. Atty. Gen. 556, 558 (1937) (marriage of biological parents occurred in Paris but father was domiciled in New York-New York law applied).

[4]Sec. 205, Nationality Act of 1940 reproduced as Appendix 4-12. This requirement has been found to be constitutional. Ablang v. Reno, 52 F.3d 801, 806 (9th Cir. 1995).

[5]Matter of L-, 3 I. & N. Dec. 225, 226 (Central Office 1948).

[6]See § 4:63.

[7]See § 4:66.

[8]INS Interp. 309.1(b)(1). See §§ 4:67 to 4:69.

[9]39 Op. Atty. Gen. 397 (1939).

[10]Sec. 205, Nationality Act of 1940 reproduced as Appendix 4-12. Cf. 39 Op. Atty. Gen. 291 (1939) (calling attention to the need to enact remedial legislation to allow out-of-wedlock children born before 1934 to acquire U.S. citizenship at birth abroad).

1941.[11] Children born out-of-wedlock to U.S. citizen mothers after May 24, 1934, or who were legitimated by a noncitizen father after January 14, 1941, are citizens of the United States at birth.[12]

In 1952, Congress added a requirement that in order to pass on U.S. citizenship to her out-of-wedlock children born abroad, a U.S. citizen woman must have been continuously physically present in the United States for one year prior to the birth of the child.[13] This additional requirement is only applicable after the date of enactment of the INA.[14]

Laws of legitimation vary from state to state and from country to country. See Appendix 4-25 for a summary of the BIA and State Department interpretation of legitimation rules of the several states and countries.[15] A child born after a state or foreign country eliminates the distinction between legitimate and out-of-wedlock children is considered "legitimate" at birth.[16]

This can give rise to various possibilities. The Third Circuit has held that where an individual is born in a country which recognizes no distinction between legitimate and illegitmate children, that the individual was not "born out of wedlock."[17] The Third Circuit's logic does not seem to follow; the author sees no inconsistency between a child being born out of wedlock and the child being legitimated. Under Brandao, even where a child does not know who his father was, the child is not born out of wedlock and presumably cannot acquire or derive citizenship under the more liberal provisions pertaining to children born out of wedlock. The Ninth Circuit considered a claim that because El Salvador had abolished all distinctions based on legitimation, that the subsequent marriage of his mother and father did not "legitimate" him because he was already legitimated.[18] That argument, while creative, was rejected by the Court of Appeals.[19]

The INA applies different tests for an out-of-wedlock parent to transmit citizenship based on the gender of the parent.[20] The Supreme Court has upheld gender-based distinctions where they are found related to biological differences between

---

[11]Matter of M-, 4 I. & N. Dec. 440, 443–44 (Central Office 1951).

[12]Matter of M-D-, 3 I. & N. Dec. 485, 489 (Central Office 1949).

[13]INA § 309(c), 8 U.S.C.A. § 1409(c).

[14]INA § 309(c), 8 U.S.C.A. § 1409(c) ("a person born, after December 23, 1952 . . . "). On November 15, 1995, Congress enacted a law amending the definition of "child" for immigration purposes. Act of November 15, 1995, Pub.L. 104-51. This amendment does not affect the definition of child for nationality purposes. See Appendix 4-23 (introductory remarks).

[15]Matter of Cabrera, 21 I. & N. Dec. 589 (B.I.A. 1996); Matter of Goorahoo, 20 I. & N. Dec. 782 (B.I.A. 1994).

[16]In re Moraga, 23 I. & N. Dec. 195, 2001 WL 1513198 (B.I.A. 2001); Anderson v. Holder, 673 F.3d 1089 (9th Cir. 2012) (finding child legitimated based on domicile in Arizona, which has abolished distinctions between legitimate and illegitimate children).

[17]Brandao v. Attorney General of U.S., 654 F.3d 427 (3d Cir. 2011) (finding that because Cape Verde abolished the distinction between legitimate and illegitimate children, child was not born "out of wedlock" and could not derive citizenship through his mother).

[18]Romero-Mendoza v. Holder, 665 F.3d 1105, 1109 (9th Cir. 2011).

[19]Romero-Mendoza v. Holder, 665 F.3d 1105, 1109–10 (9th Cir. 2011).

[20]Compare INA § 309(c), 8 U.S.C.A. § 1409(c) (providing standard for mothers) with, INA § 309(a), 8 U.S.C.A. § 1409(a) (providing standard for fathers).

men and women.[21] However, gender-based distinctions that do not directly relate to biology might not fare so well; the Supreme Court split 4-4 in considering a statute requiring 10 years of physical presence for an unmarried father to convey citizenship, but only one year of continuous physical presence for an unmarried mother to do so.[22] Because the Court split 4-4, the issue has not been resolved.

§ 4:9 Legal principles governing legitimation

Although illegitimacy was treated as an immutable status in the common law,[1] all American jurisdictions now have statutes permitting some form of legitimation.[2] "Legitimation" is relevant for various purposes under the immigration laws.[3] The relevant legal question for citizenship purposes is whether a child has been legitimated "under the law of the child's residence or domicile, or under the law of the father's residence or domicile, whether in the United States or elsewhere."[4] Thus, the Board looks to the laws of the various American jurisdictions as well as foreign jurisdictions to determine whether a child was legitimate or legitimated. Laws of legitimation vary from state to state and from country to country. See Appendix 4-25 for a summary of the BIA and State Department interpretation of legitimation rules of the several states and countries.

The term "legitimate" was initially interpreted to apply only to children born in wedlock.[5] The term has since been held, however, to include children legitmated after birth. A "legitimated" child is one placed "in all respects upon the same footing as if begotten and born in wedlock...", is "invested with all the rights of a lawful child...", and his or her "civil and social status becomes that of a lawful child of the natural father, the child and father thereafter [standing] in their relations to each other as though the birth had been during wedlock."[6]

The most common form of legitimation is the subsequent marriage of a child's natural parents, but other methods of conferring the full status of a legitimate child are recognized in different jurisdictions. This includes legitimation by acknowledgement and by judicial decree.[7]

---

[21]Nguyen v. I.N.S., 533 U.S. 53, 121 S. Ct. 2053, 150 L. Ed. 2d 115 (U.S. 2001) (because male unmarried parents might not know of child or have connection to child, Court upheld additional requirements at INA § 309 for unmarried fathers).

[22]Flores-Villar v. U.S., 131 S.Ct. 2312 (2011).

[Section 4:9]

[1]See generally, Cleveland, Status in Common Law, 38 Harv.L.Rev. 1074 (1925).

[2]4 Vernier, American Family Laws (1936) § 242.

[3]See, e.g., INA § 101(c) [8 U.S.C.A. § 1101(c)].

[4]See, e.g., INA § 101(c) [8 U.S.C.A. § 1101(c)]; see generally, Matter of Cabrera, 21 I. & N. Dec. 589, 591 (BIA 1996).

[5]See Matter of Kubicka, 14 I & N. Dec. 303 (BIA 1972).

[6]Matter of Reyes, 17 I. & N. Dec. 512 (BIA 1980) (quoting Pfeifer v. Wright, 41 F.2d 464, 466 (10th Cir.1930), cert. denied, 283 U.S. 896 (1931)).

[7]See, Matter of Chambers, 17 I. & N. Dec. 117 (BIA 1979) (Maryland; legitimation by acknowledgment); Matter of Ramirez, 13 I & N. Dec. 666 (BIA 1971) (Louisiana; legitimation by acknowledgment); Matter of C--, 9 I & N. Dec. 268 (BIA 1961) (Michigan; legitimation by acknowledgment); Matter of Duncan, 15 I. & N. Dec. 272 (BIA 1975) (Liberia; legitimation by judicial decree).

Where a jurisdiction has truly eliminated all distinctions between legitimate and illegitimate children, that is held to effectuate a legitimation by act of law.[8]

However, it is not always clear whether a foreign country has actually eliminated all distinctions based on legitimacy. For instance, the Board initially held that Jamaica's 1976 "Jamaican Status of Children Act" did not eliminate all vestiges of differentiation between legitimate and illegitimate children.[9] It reversed itself only three years later, after receiving a memorandum from the Jamaican Minister of Justice and the American-British Law Division of the Library of Congress, finding that "a child within the scope of the Jamaican Status of Children Act may be included within the definition of a legitimate or legitimated 'child.' "[10] In 2009, the Board reversed course again, finding that the Jamaican statutes had not in fact equalized legitimate and illegitimate children.[11] While the 1976 law eliminated discrimination on the basis of legitimacy, and permitted acknowledgement of paternity by fathers, it did not actually overturn the earlier Jamaican Legitimation Act.

The Board's reversal as to Jamaican law was foretold by its similar reversal as to Guyanese law. The Board's 2006 decision in Matter of Rowe,[12] reversed its 1994 decision in Goorahoo,[13] which had found that the Guayanese "Children Born Out of Wedlock (Removal of Discrimination) Act" had equalized status between legitimate and illegitimate children. In essence, it held that "Guyana's statute relating to legitimation must take precedence over its antidiscrimination law with respect to questions of legitimacy arising under the immigration laws of the United States."[14]

According to the Library of Congress, "the existence of both a Legitimacy Act and a Status of Children Act is not unique in the West Indies."[15] Asked for an opinion as to legitimation laws in St. Christopher and Nevis, the library found those laws very similar to those in Jamaica.[16] It summed up the dilemma as follows: "[T]he Jamaican Status of Children Act did not repeal the Legitimation Act. This has created a situation in which persons who would benefit from the application of the older law argue that Jamaica still recognizes a legal distinction between legitimate and illegitimate children, and those who would benefit from the abolition of that distinction argue that the Status of Children did have that effect."[17] For individuals claiming citizenship through their mother, such as in Matter of Hines and Matter of Rowe, it

---

[8]See e.g., Matter of Pavlovic, 17 I. & N. Dec. 407 (BIA 1980) (Yugoslavia); Matter of Bautista, 17 I. & N. Dec. 122 (BIA 1979) (Puerto Rico); Matter of Wong, 16 I & N. Dec. 646 (BIA 1978) (Peoples' Republic of China); Matter of Patrick, 19 I. & N. Dec. 726 (BIA 1988) (Trinidad and Tobago); Matter of Moraga, 23 I. & N. Dec. 195 (B.I.A. 2001) (El Salvador).

[9]Matter of Clahar, 16 I. & N. Dec. 484 (BIA 1978).

[10]Matter of Clahar, 18 I. & N. Dec. 1 (BIA 1981).

[11]Matter of Hines, 24 I. & N. Dec. 544 (BIA 2008).

[12]Matter of Rowe, 23 I. & N. Dec. 962, 967 (BIA 2006).

[13]Matter of Goorahoo, 20 I. & N. Dec. 782 (BIA 1994) (reversing Matter of Gouveia, 13 I. & N. Dec. 604 (BIA 1970)).

[14]Matter of Hines, 24 I. & N. Dec. 544, 548 (BIA 2008).

[15]Law Library of Congress, Saint Christopher and Nevis, Legitimation, 2008-01411 (September 2008) (attached as exhibit in Douglas v. U.S., 2011 WL 2471516 (M.D.Fla., June 22, 2011) (NO. 8:09-CV-2145-T-33TBM)) (on file with author).

[16]Id. at *3.

[17]Id. at *4.

is advantageous not to be legitimate; for individuals claiming benefits through their father, such as in *Matter of Clahar*, legitimation is generally required.[18]

There is dicta in the Second and Seventh Circuits, adopting the Board's previous view that these laws eliminated all distinctions between legitimate and illegitimate children.[19] However, those decisions did not have the benefit of the Board's subsequent published case law, which may perhaps receive deference, and leaves the issue unclear even in those circuits.

A recent Second Circuit case—while not rejecting the Board's interpretation in *Rowe* and *Hines*—found it necessary to remand to the Board for further explanation of the Board's position.[20] The Court of Appeals specifically asked the Board to answer whether a legitimacy distinction is recognized where the "difference between legitimate and illegitimate that is purely formalistic . . . [or whether] some substantive discrimination in the law [is] necessary."[21] The Court also found itself "unclear as to the legal and/or logical basis for the BIA's interpretation."[22] The Second Circuit's remand will likely trigger further and potentially clarifying analysis in this area.

It is also worth noting that there may be a distinction between the meaning of legitimation in different parts of the statute. For instance, former INA § 309, as enacted by the INA, asked whether "paternity" had been "established . . . by legitimation."[23] Similarly, former INA § 321 allowed derivation through a U.S. citizen mother if "the paternity of the child has not been established by legitimation."[24] By contrast, INA 101(c)(1) asks, not whether *paternity* has been established, but whether the child has been "legitimated under the law of the child's residence or domicile, or under the law of the father's residence or domicile, whether in the United States or elsewhere."[25] Legitimation seems to play different roles in these statutes, particularly in that former 309 and 321 focus primarily on whether "paternity" has been established by legitimation, rather than focusing on whether legitimation itself occurred.

The ultimate outcome of this question is significant for thousands of people, many of whom have been held to be U.S. citizens for decades. It is unclear whether decisions such as *Hines* and *Rowe* could be applied retroactively to individuals who have previously been found to be citizens, or to family members who have obtained permanent residence status on the basis of that citizenship.[26] Even denaturalization might be an option — for instance, where an individual immigrated to the United States through a spousal petition filed by someone later found not to be a citizen.[27]

---

[18]*Cf.* Matter of Hines, 24 I. & N. Dec. 544, 547 (BIA 2008), Matter of Rowe, 23 I&N Dec. 962, 967 (BIA 2006), with Matter of Clahar, 18 I. & N. Dec. 1 (BIA 1981).

[19]Lewis v. Gonzales, 481 F.3d 125, 131 (2d Cir.2007); Wedderburn v. INS, 215 F.3d 795, 797, 802 (7th Cir.2000).

[20]Watson v. Holder, 643 F.3d 367 (2d Cir. 2011).

[21]Watson v. Holder, 643 F.3d 367, 370 (2d Cir. 2011).

[22]Watson v. Holder, 643 F.3d 367, 370 (2d Cir. 2011).

[23]INA § 309(a), 8 U.S.C.A. § 1409(a) (1952).

[24]INA § 321(a)(3), 8 U.S.C.A. § 1432(a)(3) (1952).

[25]INA § 101(c)(1), 8 U.S.C.A. § 1101(c)(1).

[26]See § 8:26 (rescission and removal proceedings).

[27]See generally, §§ 14:16 to 14:19.

The immigration authorities have discretion not to seek denaturalization or rescission,[28] and would not be likely to seek such relief absent other negative factors.

Finally, there may be some constitutional limit to the Board's treatment of legitimation issues. Laws making a distinction on the basis of legitimacy are not subject to heightened scrutiny as such, but numerous laws discriminating on the basis of legitimacy have been reversed by the Supreme Court.[29] Moreover, it may be relevant that under the Jamaican and Guyanese laws, only marriage between the parents (as opposed to acknowledgement or a judicial declaration) appears to suffice to legitimate a child. The degree of the barrier created by a legitimation requirement may be relevant to the courts' handling of that rule. An American court presumably could not find a foreign statute unconstitutional, but it might enjoin American courts from relying on irrational distinctions created by foreign courts as a result of the statutory requirement of legitimacy.

§ 4:10 Applicability to adopted children

Research References
Dizon and Wettstein, Immigration Law Service 2d § 14:31

As a general rule, adopted children cannot qualify for acquisition of citizenship under INA § 301. Although adopted children may qualify as children under INA § 101(c), INA § 301 only applies to children who are "born ... of" U.S. citizens.[1] Indeed, INA § 301 does not use the word "child," though it is possible that its use of the term "parent" could incorporate that term by reference.[2] Thus, most courts have held that adopted children cannot acquire under INA § 301.[3] Under this reading, Chapter 4 is simply inapplicable to adopted children, because no blood relation exists at the time of the child's birth.

That said, the Ninth Circuit has held "that a blood relationship between a child and a U.S. citizen was not required to establish citizenship under 8 U.S.C.A. § 1401(g), if the child in question was not born out of wedlock."[4] The origin of that doctrine was a case where a child was born within wedlock to a U.S. citizen father, but that man was not the biological father of the child; thus, the child was born within wedlock, but was not a biological child of the father. The Court held that the child did derive citizenship under INA § 301.[5] In *Marquez-Marquez*, the biological father was not a U.S. citizen, nor was the biological mother; but the biological father was married to a U.S. citizen woman. The biological mother abandoned the child, who was raised by the U.S. citizen woman, whose name even appeared on the birth certificate. Under California law, where a father acknowledges a child and

---

[28]See generally, Trimble v. Gordon, 430 U.S. 762, 766 n.11 (1977).

[29]See Labine v. Vincent, 401 U.S. 532, 539 (1971) (emphasizing the absence of any "insurmountable barrier" to the illegitimate child).

[Section 4:10]

[1]INA § 101(c) [8 U.S.C.A. § 1101(c)].

[2]See INA § 101(c)(2) [8 U.S.C.A. § 1101(c)(2)]; but compare with INA § 101(b)(2) [8 U.S.C.A. § 1101(b)(2)] (specifically defining "parent" in relation to the term "child," defined at (b)(1)).

[3]See, e.g., Marquez-Marquez v. Gonzales, 455 F.3d 548, 556-57 (5th Cir. 2006); Colaianni v. I.N.S., 490 F.3d 185 (2d Cir. 2007).

[4]Solis-Espinoza v. Gonzales, 401 F.3d 1090 (9th Cir. 2005) (citing Scales v. INS, 232 F.3d 1159, 1166 (9th Cir.2000)).

[5]Scales v. INS, 232 F.3d 1159, 1166 (9th Cir.2000).

takes it into the home, the child is considered as legitimate for all purposes. Therefore, the Court of Appeals concluded that the child was not illegitimate, and that the blood requirement therefore did not apply.[6]

The Ninth Circuit has refused to extend this rule to a situation where the unmarried noncitizen mother married a U.S. citizen seven years after the child's birth.[7] The Board of Immigration Appeals, without rejecting the Ninth Circuit's rule, has also found it inapplicable where the marriage forming the claimed basis for citizenship does not occur until after birth.[8] The Ninth Circuit's approach probably would not apply to adopted children, but situations of unclarity abound: for instance, a child born into wedlock, but thereafter orphaned and then adopted. Due to the Child Citizenship Act, the question may never arise, since adopted children now acquire citizenship automatically upon becoming permanent residents.[9]

§ 4:11   Limits on Congress; generally

Congress has great latitude in creating conditions under which a person born abroad may become a U.S. citizen. Congress, however, is not free to impose absolutely any condition it wants. Four areas have been affected by constitutional limitations on congressional power. The first is the constitutional limitations on the expatriation of the U.S. citizen parents prior to the birth of the child. The second limitation involves possible equal protection challenges to the sex-based distinction on citizenship by descent prior to 1934. The third involves constitutional challenges to the differential treatment of legitimate and out-of-wedlock children in U.S. citizenship at birth abroad statutes. The fourth area involves the unsuccessful challenges to the constitutionality of conditions imposed on the parents prior to the birth of the child and subsequent conditions imposed on the child.

§ 4:12   Limits on Congress; generally—Invalid loss of citizenship by parents

The general rule on citizenship by descent is that the parent must be a U.S. citizen at the time his or her child is born. If the parent lost U.S. citizenship through expatriation prior to the birth of the child, the child does not obtain U.S. citizenship at birth. However, the law of expatriation changed significantly in 1967.[1] Loss of citizenship prior to that time may have been illegal and the parent may still have been a U.S. citizen at the time of the birth of the child.

Thus, for example, as is discussed in the chapter on expatriation, under the laws in effect prior to 1922, women who married noncitizens automatically lost their U.S. citizenship.[2] The statutes providing for such loss have been held unconstitutional.[3] Even if the woman had been determined prior to 1967 to have lost her U.S. citizen-

---

[6]Solis-Espinoza v. Gonzales, 401 F.3d 1090, 1093-94 (9th Cir. 2005).

[7]Martinez-Madera v. Holder, 559 F.3d 937 (BIA 2009).

[8]Matter of Guzman-Gomez, 24 I. & N. Dec. 824 (BIA 2009).

[9]See generally, §§ 5:16 to 5:19.

[Section 4:12]

[1]See §§ 15:1 to 15:2.

[2]See § 15:16.

[3]Rocha v. I.N.S., 450 F.2d 947, 948 (1st Cir. 1971) (per curiam).

ship, her children born abroad may still qualify as U.S. citizens since her loss of U.S. citizenship was most likely illegal.[4]

§4:13 Limits on Congress; generally—Children of U.S. citizen women

In recent years there have been several constitutional challenges to the pre-1934 rule that citizenship abroad was only conferred upon children of U.S. citizen fathers. The Ninth Circuit has held that such a rule violated equal protection of the U.S. citizen mothers and found the two plaintiffs whose mothers had been U.S. citizens to themselves be citizens of the U.S.[1] The same result was reached at the district court level.[2] Most recently, the Third Circuit has joined the Ninth Circuit in finding the pre-1934 rule unconstitutional.[3] The Fifth Circuit, on the other hand, has found that such a statute is constitutional.[4] The Supreme Court has never ruled on this issue.[5] As a result, the State Department would only grant passports to children of U.S. citizen mothers born prior to 1934, if the person applies for a passport within the Third or Ninth Circuits.[6] On October 7, 1994, Congress passed legislation that would grant citizenship retroactively to children born abroad to U.S. citizen women before 1934.[7]

§4:14 Limits on Congress; generally—Constitutionality of gender-based distinctions

In the context of out-of-wedlock children, the immigration statutes have made distinctions based on the gender of the U.S. citizen parent. Under the pre-1934 law, illegitimate children could become citizens only through a U.S. citizen father, and not through a U.S. citizen mother.[1] Under subsequent statutes, the immigration laws have permitted easier transmission of citizenship through a U.S. citizen mother, requiring U.S. citizen fathers to comply with various requirements before citizenship would be transmitted.[2] These distinctions have appeared vulnerable to

---

[4]INS Interp. 301.1(b)(1)(ii). The legacy INS found that some loss of citizenship by marriage prior to 1922 is constitutional.

[Section 4:13]

[1]Wauchope v. Dept. of State, 985 F.2d 1407 (9th Cir. 1993).

[2]Aguayo v. Christopher, 865 F. Supp. 479 (N.D. Ill. 1994); Elias v. Dept. of State, 721 F.Supp. 243, 249 (N.D.Cal. 1989).

[3]Breyer v.Meissner, 214 F.3d 416, 426 (3d Cir. 2000), aff'd Breyer v. Ashcroft, 350 F.3d 327, 332 n.4 (3rd Cir. 2003) (declining to reconsider in light of Nguyen v. I.N.S., 533 U.S. 53 (2001), noting the difference between requiring a father to meet additional requirements to prove parentage and the issue in *Breyer*, which involved a U.S. citizen mother).

[4]Villanueva-Jurado v. Immigration and Naturalization Service, 482 F.2d 886 (5th Cir. 1973).

[5]Cf. Rogers v. Bellei, 401 U.S. 815, 91 S. Ct. 1060, 28 L. Ed. 2d 499 (1971) (holding retention requirements constitutional); Montana v. Kennedy, 366 U.S. 308, 310–12, 81 S. Ct. 1336, 1338–39, 6 L. Ed. 2d 313 (1961) (statutory interpretation of section 1993, rather than constitutional challenge).

[6]DiPlacido, Naturalization: Problem Clients, Dual Citizenship, Expatriation and Repatriation, 1994 AILA Annual Convention, Tape 14.

[7]INTCA § 101 reproduced as Appendix 4-21. See §§ 4:17 to 4:21.

[Section 4:14]

[1]See § 4:13.

[2]Cf., e.g., INA § 309(a) and § 309(c).

Equal Protection challenges, given case law rejecting distinctions based on legiti-macy[3] or gender.[4]

As noted in the previous section, discrimination against transmission of citizen-ship through a U.S. citizen mother has been rejected by several courts.[5] By contrast, the Supreme Court has upheld distinctions which condition transmission of citizen-ship through a U.S. citizen father on compliance with various requirements, includ-ing legitimation.[6] Applying intermediate scrutiny, the majority found that the stat-ute served important governmental objectives and that the distinction between U.S. citizen fathers and U.S. citizen mothers was substantially related to those ends; the statutory rule, said the Court, was "not marked by misconception and prejudice, nor does it show disrespect for either class."[7]

The majority in *Nguyen* noted the biological differences between men and women, which, it said, guaranteed some direct connection between mother and child (by virtue of birth), but not any connection with the father.[8]

Justice O'Connor's dissent in *Nguyen* criticized the majority for failing to scruti-nize the gender-based classifications more rigorously. Section 309(a)(4), Justice O'Connor explained, is "paradigmatic of a historic regime that left women with responsibility, and freed men from responsibility, for nonmarital children."[9] She found the "disparity between the majority's defense of the statue and the INS' prof-fered justification," to be "striking, to say the least."[10]

In a case subsequent to *Nguyen*, the Supreme Court considered whether it was permissible to permit unmarried citizen fathers to convey U.S. citizenship only if they could meet the difficult physical presence conditions of INA § 301, whereas unmarried citizen mothers may convey citizenship more easily under INA § 309(c). In *Flores-Villar v. U.S.*, the Supreme Court split 4-4 on the issue, with Justice Kagan recused due to her earlier involvement in the case as Solicitor General.[11] Because the Court split 4-4, it did not decide the issue.

Flores-Villar also raised, indirectly, a separate question: whether Congress might have exceeded its authority by imposing an age-based requirement. By statute, Flores-Villar's U.S. citizen father would have needed to have resided in the U.S. for five years after age 14 for him to have acquired citizenship; but his father was only 16 years of age at the time of birth.[12] The rules, in effect, prevented Flores-Villar's father from conveying citizenship until at least age 19. In Flores-Villar's case, this

---

[3]See, Trimble v. Gordon, 430 U.S. 762, 97 S.Ct. 1459, 52 L.Ed.2d 31 (1977).

[4]See, U.S. v. Virginia, 518 U.S. 515, 533, 116 S.Ct. 2264, 135 L.Ed.2d 735.

[5]Wauchope v. Dept. of State, 985 F.2d 1407 (9th Cir. 1993); Breyer v. Meissner, 214 F.3d 416, 426 (3d Cir. 2000), aff'd 350 F.3d 327, 332 n.4 (3rd Cir. 2003); Aguayo v. Christopher, 865 F. Supp. 479 (N.D. Ill. 1994); Elias v. Dept. of State, 721 F.Supp. 243, 249 (N.D.Cal. 1989); cf Villanueva-Jurado v. Immigration and Naturalization Service, 482 F.2d 886 (5th Cir. 1973).

[6]Tuan Anh Nguyen v. I.N.S., 533 U.S. 53, 121 S. Ct. 2053, 150 L. Ed. 2d 115 (U.S. 2001).

[7]Tuan Anh Nguyen v. I.N.S., 533 U.S. 53, 73, 121 S. Ct. 2053, 2066, 150 L. Ed. 2d 115 (U.S. 2001).

[8]Tuan Anh Nguyen v. I.N.S., 533 U.S. 53, 54-55, 121 S. Ct. 2053, 150 L. Ed. 2d 115, 178 A.L.R. Fed. 587 (2001).

[9]Tuan Anh Nguyen v. I.N.S., 533 U.S. 53, 121 S. Ct. 2053, 2066, 150 L. Ed. 2d 115, 178 A.L.R. Fed. 587 (2001) (O'Connor, J., dissenting).

[10]Tuan Anh Nguyen v. I.N.S., 533 U.S. 53, 121 S. Ct. 2053, 2066, 150 L. Ed. 2d 115, 178 A.L.R. Fed. 587 (2001) (O'Connor, J., dissenting).

[11]Flores-Villar v. U.S., 131 S.Ct. 2312 (2011).

[12]U.S. v. Flores-Villar, 536 F.3d 990, 994 (9th Cir. 2008)

appeared as a gender-based discrimination claim, but the age-related arguments can also be conceived of as an equal protection challenge to the rationality of the statute. The Sixth Circuit recently rejected such a challenge (where the U.S. citizen parent had been a mother who could not convey citizenship because the child was born in wedlock).[13]

§ 4:15 Limits on Congress; generally—Prior residence and retention requirements

The Supreme Court has held that imposition of conditions subsequent in order for U.S. citizens born abroad to retain their U.S. citizenship does not violate the Fourteenth or the Fifth Amendment.[1] According to the Supreme Court, the first sentence of the Fourteenth Amendment is not implicated at all since it only applies to persons born in the United States or naturalized inside the United States.[2] U.S. citizens born abroad are persons who are naturalized at birth *outside* the United States.[3] The court also found that conditions subsequent did not violate the Fifth Amendment to the U.S. Constitution, as they were not an unreasonable, arbitrary, or unlawful procedure to resolve the problem of dual citizenship and divided loyalties.[4] On the other hand, a lower court has found that differential retention requirements as applied to out-of-wedlock children are a violation of the equal protection clause.[5]

It has also been held that prior residence requirements are constitutional even when they apply to involuntary absences while the parent was a child.[6]

§ 4:16 Children born to foreign diplomats in U.S

It has been held administratively that the laws applicable to U.S. citizens born abroad also apply to children born in the U.S. to foreign diplomats (who are not "subject" to the jurisdiction of the laws of the United States and thus do not become citizens automatically under the Fourteenth Amendment). Thus, a child born in the United States to one U.S. citizen parent and one foreign diplomat parent will be a U.S. citizen at birth if he or she satisfies all the prerequisites imposed upon children born abroad to one U.S. citizen and one noncitizen parent at the time of the birth of the child.[1]

II. PERSONS BORN ABROAD BEFORE MAY 24, 1934

§ 4:17 Generally

Research References

Dizon and Wettstein, Immigration Law Service 2d § 14:31

---

[13]Guzman v. U.S. Dept. of Homeland Sec., 679 F.3d 425 (6th Cir. 2012).

[Section 4:15]

[1]Rogers v. Bellei, 401 U.S. 815, 91 S. Ct. 1060, 28 L. Ed. 2d 499 (1971).

[2]Rogers v. Bellei, 401 U.S. 815, 827, 91 S. Ct. 1060, 1067, 28 L. Ed. 2d 499 (1971)

[3]Rogers v. Bellei, 401 U.S. 815, 827, 91 S. Ct. 1060, 1067, 28 L. Ed. 2d 499 (1971).

[4]Rogers v. Bellei, 401 U.S. 815, 831–34, 91 S. Ct. 1060, 1069–70, 28 L. Ed. 2d 499 (1971).

[5]LeBrun v. Thornburgh, 777 F. Supp. 1204, 1212-13 (D.N.J. 1991).

[6]U. S. v. Trevino Garcia, 440 F.2d 368 (5th Cir. 1971).

[Section 4:16]

[1]7 FAM 1113.2-2(f), (g). Cf. In re Thenault, 47 F.Supp. 952, 953 (D.D.C. 1942) (reaching the same conclusion in the context of naturalization); INS Interp. 322.1(b) (same).

Between 1790 and 1934, there were four statutes that governed U.S. citizenship at birth abroad. The first two, the Acts of 1790 and 1795 lasted only a few years; the Act of 1790 was repealed in 1795, and the Act of 1795 was repealed in 1802.[1] Following these, the Acts of 1802 and 1855 governed citizenship at birth abroad until 1934.[2]

The Act of 1802 is of little relevance at present since it has been held only to apply retroactively to persons born before the dates of enactment and reenactment.[3] The main difference between the statutes of 1802 and 1855 is that the prior statute could be read to provide for the acquisition of U.S. citizenship by children born abroad to U.S. citizen mothers, even when the fathers were noncitizens.[4]

§ 4:18 Father or mother must be U.S. citizen at time of birth

Research References

Steel on Immigration Law § 11:16

The Act of 1855, which was incorporated into the revised statutes as section 1993, conferred U.S. citizenship on children born abroad to U.S. citizen fathers provided those fathers resided in the United States at one point in their lives.[1] Thus, for children born during this period, it was irrelevant whether the mother was a U.S. citizen or a noncitizen. If the father was a U.S. citizen at the time of the birth, so was the child.[2] Citizenship did not descend through the mother unless the child was out-of-wedlock.[3] This provision, however, was successfully challenged as violating equal protection of U.S. citizen mothers.[4]

On October 7, 1994, Congress passed a law granting citizenship retroactively to birth to children born abroad to a noncitizen father and a U.S. citizen mother before May 24, 1934.[5] Thus, Congress has corrected by statute the discriminatory treatment regarding the transmission of U.S. citizenship before 1934. To qualify for

---

[Section 4:17]

[1]See sec. 1, Act of March 26, 1790 reproduced as Appendix 4-1; sec. 3, 4, Act of January 29, 1795 reproduced as Appendix 4-2, sec. 5, Act of April 14, 1802 reproduced as Appendix 4-3.

[2]See sec. 4, Act of April 14, 1802 reproduced as Appendix 4-3; sec. 1, Act of February 10, 1855 reproduced as Appendix 4-4. The Act of 1855 was amended by sec. 6, Act of March 2, 1907, Pub.L. 59-193, 34 Stat. 1228 reproduced as Appendix 4-6, which required the child to file a declaration of intention with the consulate upon reaching the age of eighteen, and to take an oath upon reaching majority. However, failure to comply with those requirements did not result in the loss of citizenship by the child, but only in the loss of diplomatic protection. Rueff v. Brownell, 116 F.Supp. 298, 305 (D.N.J. 1953).

[3]Montana v. Kennedy, 366 U.S. 308, 310–12 81 S. Ct. 1336, 1338–39, 6 L. Ed. 2d 313 (1961). That act was reenacted in 1874; therefore, it applies to children born before that date. See § 4:10.

[4]See Montana v. Kennedy, 366 U.S. 308, 310–11, 81 S. Ct. 1336, 1338–39, 6 L. Ed. 2d 313 (1961).

[Section 4:18]

[1]Sec. 1, Act of February 10, 1855 reproduced as Appendix 4-4, incorporated as sec. 1993, Revised Statutes of the United States, 1878 reproduced as Appendix 4-5.

[2]The act of 1855 also provided for automatic naturalization of women who married U.S. citizens, provided they were eligible for naturalization. Sec. 2, Act of February 10, 1855 reproduced as Appendix 4-4.

[3]See Montana v. Kennedy, 366 U.S. 308, 312, 81 S. Ct. 1336, 1339, 6 L. Ed. 2d 313 (1961). Cf discussion of out-of-wedlock children.

[4]See §§ 4:14 to 4:15.

[5]INTCA § 101(a)(2) adding INA § 301(h), 8 U.S.C.A. § 1401(h) reproduced as Appendix 4-21.

citizenship under this provision, the U.S. citizen mother must have resided in the United States before the birth of the child.[6] This provision, which has been codified at INA § 301(h), 8 U.S.C.A. § 1401(h), is retroactive to birth.[7] There is one exception, however, to this retroactive grant of citizenship: persons who participated in persecution under the direction of the Nazi government or who have engaged in genocide are barred from obtaining the benefits of this section.[8] However, one court found that this exception violated the Constitution's equal protection clause because it continued the gender-based discrimination of the original statute.[9] The court went on to find, however, that the petitioner in that case committed expatriating acts when, as an adult, he voluntarily joined the Death's Head Battalion of the SS during a period in which Germany was at war with the United States. Because this act was wholly inconsistent with U.S. citizenship, the court found that the necessary intent for expatriation was present, despite the fact that at the time the petitioner committed the acts, he did not know he was a U.S. citizen.[10]

Since there were no retention requirements that applied to persons born before May 24, 1934, persons claiming citizenship under section 301(h) of the INA are not subject to retention requirements.[11] Congress specifically provided that persons claiming U.S. citizenship as descendants of a beneficiary of the 1994 law, will themselves not be subject to retention requirements.[12] However, Congress also specifically provided that these descendants would only acquire U.S. citizenship if their U.S. citizen parent or parents satisfied the prior residence or physical presence that was required for transmission of citizenship at the time of the descendant's birth.[13] The difference between the prior physical presence/residence (conditions precedent) and the retention requirements (conditions subsequent) is discussed elsewhere in this chapter.[14] Procedural regulations on how to obtain citizenship under the 1994 law are described in Ch 13.[15]

§ 4:19 Residence in U.S. prior to birth

For descent to occur under the original statute, the father must have resided in the United States prior to the child's birth.[1] Pursuant to INA § 301(h) these same

---

[6]INA § 301(h), 8 U.S.C.A. § 1401(h).

[7]INTCA § 101(c)(1) reproduced as Appendix 4-21.

[8]INTCA § 101(c)(2) reproduced as Appendix 4-21. These people may still be U.S. citizens in spite of the 1994 law because the pre-1934 law was found unconstitutional and, hence, they were born citizens. Unless they later lost their citizenship, they continue to be U.S. citizens.

[9]Breyer v. Meissner, 214 F.3d 416, 429 (3d Cir. 2000).

[10]Breyer v. Meissner, 214 F.3d 416, 431 (3d Cir. 2000).

[11]See § 4:6.

[12]INTCA § 101(b) reproduced as Appendix 4-21. In the supplementary information to the regulations implementing procedures for obtaining evidence of citizenship under section 301(h), the legacy INS erroneously read this section as waiving the retention requirement of the beneficiaries of section 301(h) themselves. See 62 Fed. Reg. 39926 (July 25, 1997) (Supplementary Information).

[13]INTCA § 101(d) reproduced as Appendix 4-21.

[14]See §§ 4:5, 4:6.

[15]See §§ 13:32 to 13:33.

[Section 4:19]

[1]Weedin v. Chin Bow, 274 U.S. 657, 666–67, 47 S. Ct. 772, 774–75, 71 L. Ed. 1284 (1927).

rules now apply to children of U.S. citizen mothers.[2] The prior residence must have taken place in a territory understood as the United States at the time of the residence.[3] The DHS, and to some extent the State Department, takes the position that residence in Alaska after March 29, 1867, Puerto Rico after April 10, 1899, or the Virgin Islands after January 16, 1917 qualifies as residence in the United States for purposes of citizenship at birth abroad.[4] In addition, by statute, residence in Hawaii even prior to its annexation by the U.S. is considered as residence in the United States for purposes of U.S. citizenship at birth abroad.[5] However, residence in the Philippines does not satisfy the prior residence requirement under section 1993 of the Revised Statutes.[6]

It has been determined administratively that physical presence alone was sufficient to satisfy the concept of "residence" under section 1993 of the Revised Statues.[7] Any temporary physical presence in the United States was sufficient to satisfy this requirement, even if the parent was a minor, or was here pending exclusion proceedings.[8] The only exception to this general rule was presence for a few hours while in transit through the U.S.[9] This definition of "residence" also applies to out-of-wedlock children born abroad to U.S. citizen mothers regardless of the fact that the provisions governing citizenship at birth for those people was introduced retroactively by the 1940 act.[10]

§ 4:20   Out-of-wedlock children and legitimation

Research References

Dizon and Wettstein, Immigration Law Service 2d § 14:53

Out-of-wedlock children acquired U.S. citizenship if their mothers were U.S. citizens who had resided in the U.S. prior to the birth of the child.[1] This provision was added by the 1940 act, but applies retroactively to persons born before the act

---

[2]INA § 301(h), 8 U.S.C.A. § 1401(h).

[3]See generally Ch 2 §§ 2:8 to 2:14.

[4]INS Interp. 301.1(b)(2); 7 FAM 1153.2-3. Those are the dates of the territories were effectively ceded to the United States. See §§ 2:1 et seq.

[5]Wong Kam Wo v. Dulles, 236 F.2d 622 (9th Cir. 1956) (holding that residence in Hawaii prior to the taking effect of the Organic Act of Hawaii is considered residence in the United States for purposes of U.S. citizens at birth abroad); Matter of L-G-J- and C-I-P-, 1 I. & N. Dec. 206 (B.I.A. 1948) (same); INS Interp. 301.1(b)(2); 7 FAM 1153.2-3(b), (c).

[6]Friend v. Reno, 172 F.3d 638 (9th Cir. 1999).

[7]Matter of V-, 6 I. & N. Dec. 1 (Att'y Gen. 1954) (two sojourns in the U.S. prior to the birth of the child; the first of two days, the second of a few hours); INS Interp. 301.1(b)(5)(i); 7 FAM 1135.2-2(c).

[8]INS Interp. 301.1(b)(5) citing to State ex. rel. Phelps v. Jackson, 79 Vt. 504 (1907); 7 FAM 1135. 2-2(c); Matter of E-, 9 I. & N. Dec. 479 (Reg. Comm'r) approved (Ass't Comm'r 1961) (visit of 2 days); Matter of V-, 6 I. & N. Dec. 1 (one two-day visit and another for few hours); Matter of Y-W-S-, 3 I. & N. Dec. 885 (Central Office 1950) (only residence of the father in the United States prior to the child's birth was while in exclusion proceedings).

[9]Matter of V-, 6 I. & N. Dec. 1, 7, 1953 WL 7389 (B.I.A. 1953).

[10]See Matter of E--, 9 I. & N. Dec. 479, 481, 1961 WL 12192 (B.I.A. 1961).

[Section 4:20]

[1]Sec. 205, Nationality Act of 1940 reproduced as Appendix 4-12 (granting U.S. citizenship at birth for children born before the date of enactment of the act).

was passed.[2] If a noncitizen father legitimated the child during the child's minority and prior to the January 13, 1941, the effective date of the 1940 act, the child did not acquire U.S. citizenship.[3] The reason for this peculiar situation is that the 1940 act only granted U.S. citizenship retroactively to children who had not been legitimated during minority.[4] On the other hand, if the child was not so legitimated, the retroactive citizenship vests at birth regardless of whether the person was already an adult on January 13, 1941.[5]

This provision may have been affected by the retroactive grant of citizenship to children of U.S. citizen women and noncitizen fathers.[6] Children who were legitimated while minors and before January 13, 1941 would now be able to acquire citizenship retroactively to birth because they would be children of a noncitizen father and a U.S. citizen mother. Their citizenship would not be based on their out-of-wedlock status, but on the right of U.S. citizen women to transmit citizenship to their children even though they were married to noncitizen men.

Prior to 1934, out-of-wedlock children could acquire U.S. citizenship at birth from their U.S. citizen fathers, if they were legitimated at any time under the laws of the father's domicile.[7] The law that governs is the law where the father was domiciled, even when the legitimating act occurred somewhere else.[8] Legitimation under foreign law is as effective as legitimation under the laws of a state of the United States.[9] The legitimation was effective in conferring U.S. citizenship at birth even if it occurred many years after the child had become an adult.[10] Legitimation that occurred after the passage of the 1940 act would also be effective, as the provisions of that act were designed to govern cases of children born *after* the date of enactment.[11]

The Supreme Court has upheld gender-based distinctions requiring legitimation, where they are found related to biological differences between men and women.[12] However, gender-based distinctions that do not directly relate to biology might not fare so well; the Supreme Court split 4-4 in considering a statute requiring 10 years of physical presence for an unmarried father to convey citizenship, but only one year of continuous physical presence for an unmarried mother to do so.[13] Because the Court split 4-4 in *Flores-Villar*, no decision was issued and the issue has not been resolved.

---

[2]Sec. 205, Nationality Act of 1940 reproduced as Appendix 4-12 (granting U.S. citizenship at birth for children born before the date of enactment of the act).

[3]Matter of M-, 4 I. & N. Dec. 440, 443–44, 1951 WL 7035 (B.I.A. 1951).

[4]See sec. 205, Nationality Act of 1940 reproduced as Appendix 4-12.

[5]Matter of M-, 4 I. & N. Dec. 440, 444, 1951 WL 7035 (B.I.A. 1951). For a summary of what the BIA considers to have been the valid legitimation laws of the different countries and the states of the U.S. at different points in time, see Appendix 4-26.

[6]INTCA § 101 reproduced as Appendix 4-21.

[7]Matter of P-, 4 I. & N. Dec. 354, 358 (Central Office 1951); 7 FAM 1135.3-1(a)(2).

[8]39 Op. Atty. Gen. at 558 (marriage of natural parents occurred in France but father was domiciled in New York-New York law governed).

[9]7 FAM 1135.3-1(a)(3).

[10]Matter of P-, 4 I. & N. Dec. 354, 358, 1951 WL 7014 (B.I.A. 1951) (child born in 1877, legitimate in 1913); 7 FAM 1135.3-1(b).

[11]Matter of L-, 3 I. & N. Dec. 225.

[12]Nguyen v. I.N.S., 533 U.S. 53, 121 S. Ct. 2053, 150 L. Ed. 2d 115 (U.S. 2001) (because male unmarried parents might not know of child or have connection to child, Court upheld additional requirements at INA § 309 for unmarried fathers).

[13]Flores-Villar v. U.S., 131 S.Ct. 2312 (2011).

§ 4:21   State Department summary of proof of claim for this period

Research References

Steel on Immigration Law § 15:5

The State Department, in light of the retroactive effect of INA 301(h), now provides that proof of a claim of U.S. citizenship for persons born abroad before May 24, 1934, should consist of: (1) a birth certificate or other evidence of the child's birth to a U.S. citizen mother, father, or both; (2) if applicable, the parents' marriage certificate or other evidence of the child's legitimacy or legitimation; (3) proof of at least one parent's U.S. citizenship; (4) evidence of that parent's residence in the United States at any time before the child's birth; and (5) for persons born to one citizen and one alien parent, proof that the person met or has been exempted from applicable retention requirements.[1]

III.   PERSONS BORN ABROAD BETWEEN MAY 24, 1934 AND JANUARY 13, 1941

§ 4:22   Generally

Research References

Dizon and Wettstein, Immigration Law Service 2d § 14:33

The Act of May 24, 1934 amended section 1993 of the Revised Statutes to allow U.S. citizenship to be conferred at birth to children born abroad to a U.S. citizen parent regardless of the parent's gender.[1] This amendment had prospective application only and governed U.S. citizenship at birth abroad from May 24, 1934 until its repeal on January 13, 1941.[2]

§ 4:23   Neither parent is noncitizen at time of birth

The law for persons born abroad between May 24, 1934 and January 13, 1941 provided that when both parents were U.S. citizens only one U.S. citizen parent was required to have resided in the United States prior to the birth of the child.[1] When one parent was a U.S. noncitizen national and the other was a U.S. citizen, the citizen parent had to reside in the United States prior to the birth of the child.[2] No specific period of residence was required in either case and the child acquired citizenship without any conditions subsequent attached.[3]

[Section 4:21]

   [1]7 FAM 1135.5; 7 FAM 1135.9.

[Section 4:22]

   [1]Sec. 1, Act of May 24, 1934 reproduced as Appendix 4-10.

   [2]Sec. 504, Nationality Act of 1940 reproduced as Appendix 4-12 (repealing sec. 1993, Revised Statutes, as amended).

[Section 4:23]

   [1]Sec. 1, Act of May 24, 1934 reproduced as Appendix 4-10.

   [2]Sec. 1, Act of May 24, 1934 reproduced as Appendix 4-10.; U.S. v. Gonzales, 192 U.S. 1, 13, 24 S.Ct. 177, 179, 48 L.Ed. 317 (1904) (providing that noncitizen nationals are not noncitizens). For a discussion of noncitizen nationals, see §§ 3:1 et seq.

   [3]Sec. 1, Act of May 24, 1934 reproduced as Appendix 4-10.

§ 4:24 One parent is a noncitizen at time of birth; generally

Even as the law was liberalized to allow transmission of U.S. citizenship through the mother, it was also restricted by imposing two conditions subsequent in order for children who had one noncitizen parent to retain U.S. citizenship.[1] Thus children of one U.S. citizen and one noncitizen parent would lose their U.S. citizenship unless the child (1) came to the United States and resided there for five years immediately preceding his or her eighteenth birthday, and (2) took an oath of allegiance to the U.S within six months of becoming twenty-one.[2]

A series of amendments have liberalized the nature of retention requirements as applicable to persons born during this time period. What follows summarizes the impact of those amendments. In addition, because of the retroactive effect of some of the amendments, in practical terms, the retention requirements applicable to persons born between January 14, 1941 and December 23, 1952 are virtually identical to those applicable to persons born between 1934 and 1940. The more detailed discussion of retention requirements in that section should also be consulted.[3]

§ 4:25 One parent is a noncitizen at time of birth; generally—Impact of the 1940 Act

The retention requirement applicable to persons born between May 24, 1934 and January 13, 1941 was retroactively liberalized by the 1940 act which provided that in order to avoid losing his or her citizenship, a child born abroad after May 24, 1934 to one citizen and one noncitizen parent had to reside in the United States or one of its outlying possessions for a period of five years between the ages of thirteen and twenty-one years.[1] These children were exempted from the retention requirements if their parents worked for the U.S. government or a specified American firm abroad.[2] Also exempt were out-of-wedlock children who were legitimated after the age in which they could have complied with the requirement.[3] Since children born after May 24, 1934 were at most seven years old at the time the 1940 act became effective, no child had yet lost his or her U.S. citizenship for failure to comply with the retention requirements of the 1934 act. Therefore, the 1940 act effectively repealed the retention requirements of the 1934 act.[4]

[Section 4:24]

[1]Sec. 1, Act of May 24, 1934 reproduced as Appendix 4-10; 38 Op. Atty. Gen. 10, 17–18 (1934) (child acquires U.S. citizenship at birth, subject to being divested if child thereafter fails to comply with the two conditions); INS Interp. 301.1(b)(6)(i) (the retention requirements were conditions subsequent, not precedent); 7 FAM 1135.6-3 (same).

[2]Sec. 1, Act of May 24, 1934 reproduced as Appendix 4-10.

[3]See §§ 4:35 to 4:44.

[Section 4:25]

[1]Sec. 201(g), (h), Nationality Act of 1940 reproduced as Appendix 4-12.

[2]Sec. 201(g), (h), Nationality Act of 1940 reproduced as Appendix 4-12; INS Interp. 301.1(b)(6)(i).

[3]See § 4:30.

[4]Lee Wing Hong v. Dulles, 214 F.2d 753, 758–59 (7th Cir. 1954); Matter of Farley, 11 I. & N. Dec. 51 (Dist. Dir.) approved (Ass't Comm'r 1965); Matter of Yanez-Carrillo, 10 I. & N. Dec. 366, 367 (B.I.A. 1963). See also sec. 504, Nationality Act of 1940 reproduced as Appendix 4-12 (it only prevents the restoration of U.S. citizenship for those who at the time of the repeal of the 1934 act had lawfully lost their citizenship under that act. Children who had not yet lost their U.S. citizenship because of failure

§ 4:26 One parent is a noncitizen at time of birth; generally—Impact of INA

The INA once again retroactively liberalized the retention requirement applicable to persons born to one U.S. citizen parent after May 24, 1934.[1] Those children could now retain their U.S. citizenship by complying with the retention requirements of the INA.[2] Thus the child would still be a U.S. citizen provided he or she entered the United States before attaining the age of 23 and was continuously physically present in the United States for five years between the ages of 14 and 28.[3] This liberalization is applicable to all children born after May 24, 1934, regardless of whether they had reached the age of sixteen before the INA was enacted.[4]

If the child had come to the United States before the age of sixteen and before December 24, 1952, the child could still comply with the retention requirements of the 1940 act.[5] The five-year residence requirement of the 1940 act could be completed after the date of enactment of the INA.[6] Even if the child took up residence after his or her sixteenth birthday, the child was held to have constructively complied with the requirement if the reason the child could not comply with it was a failure of the U.S. consular officer to provide the child with the necessary documentation to travel to the United States.[7]

§ 4:27 One parent is a noncitizen at time of birth; generally—Impact of 1972 amendment

Another liberalization took place in 1972.[1] Under the legacy INS' interpretation of that amendment, if before October 27, 1972, the person had enough physical presence in the United States at the appropriate ages to comply with the 1972 amendment then the person would be deemed to have satisfied the retention requirements

---

to comply with the retention requirements of the 1934 act were no longer subject to them after the repeal of that law).

[Section 4:26]

[1]INA § 301(b), 8 U.S.C.A. § 1401(b) as originally enacted by Act of June 27, 1952.

[2]INA § 301(c), 8 U.S.C.A. § 1401(c) as originally enacted by Act of June 27, 1952. The INS originally took the positions that children could take advantage of the INA provisions only if they had not lost their U.S. citizenship before December 24, 1952 by failing to come to the United States before becoming 16. Matter of V-V-, 7 I. & N. Dec. 122, 123 (B.I.A. 1956). This position was later changed holding that all children born after May 24, 1934 could take advantage of the INA provisions whether or not they had turned 16 before December 24, 1934. Matter of Navarrete, 12 I. & N. Dec. 138, 141 (B.I.A. 1967).

[3]INA § 301(b), 8 U.S.C.A. § 1401(b) as originally enacted by Act of June 27, 1952. See §§ 4:51 to 4:63.

[4]Lee You Fee v. Dulles, 355 U.S. 61, 78 S.Ct. 138 (1957) (per curiam) reversing 236 F.2d 885 (7th Cir. 1956) (Supreme Court reversed and remanded after the Solicitor General confessed error); Matter of Navarrete, 12 I. & N. Dec. 138, 141, 1967 WL 13979 (B.I.A. 1967).

[5]INA § 301(c), 8 U.S.C.A. § 1401(c) as originally enacted by Act of June 27, 1952; Matter of V- V-, 7 I. & N. Dec. 122, 123, 1956 WL 10235 (B.I.A. 1956).

[6]INA § 301(c), 8 U.S.C.A. § 1401(c) as originally enacted by Act of June 27, 1952.

[7]Matter of L-B-D-, 4 I. & N. Dec. 639, 643 (Att'y Gen. 1952) (when failure to comply with the retention requirements of the 1940 act was not the result of applicant's own inaction or lack of diligence, such failure will not divest applicant of applicant's U.S. citizenship). See §§ 4:32 to 4:50 (discussion of constructive residence).

[Section 4:27]

[1]See §§ 4:35 to 4:44.

and never to have lost his or her U.S. citizenship.[2] An alternative way of complying with this retention requirement was if the child took up residence in the United States and the noncitizen parent naturalized prior to the child turning 18.[3]

§4:28 One parent is a noncitizen at time of birth; generally—Impact of the 1994 Act

The 1994 Immigration and Nationality Technical Corrections Act amended section 324 of the INA to allow for the non-retroactive restoration of citizenship for persons who lost their U.S. citizenship because of failure to comply with the retention requirements in effect before October 10, 1978.[1] This provision does not confer any benefits on persons who would have been barred from naturalizing because of the political bars contained in INA §313.[2] The procedures governing resumption of citizenship under this section are discussed below.[3]

§4:29 Meaning of residence

Research References

Dizon and Wettstein, Immigration Law Service 2d §14:35

The parental residence required to satisfy the 1934 Act is the same as under prior statutes. The parent must establish some form of physical presence longer than just being a few hours in the United States while in transit to another country.[1] Since the retention requirements were retroactively liberalized by the 1940 Act and the INA, the child must comply with the residence and physical presence requirements as understood by those acts, to satisfy their respective retention requirements.[2] Residence under the 1940 Act is discussed below.[3] The INA worded its retention requirement in terms of continuous physical presence.[4] Children born after May 24, 1934 must comply with the physical presence requirement as defined by the INA in order to retain their citizenship under the INA provision.[5] The constructive physical presence requirements described below apply to all children who must comply with the physical presence requirements of the INA.[6]

§4:30 Out-of-wedlock children

Out-of-wedlock children born to a U.S. citizen mother between May 24, 1934 and

---

[2]INS Interp. 301.1(b)(6)(vii).

[3]See §§ 4:35 to 4:44 (retention requirements).

[Section 4:28]

[1]INA § 324(d)(1), 8 U.S.C.A. § 1435(d)(1).

[2]INA § 324(d)(1), 8 U.S.C.A. § 1435(d)(1). For a discussion of the political bars, See §§ 8:2 to 8:26.

[3]See § 11:30.

[Section 4:29]

[1]INS Interp. 301.1(b)(5)(i); 7 FAM 1135.2-2(c). See §§ 4:11 to 4:21.

[2]See sec. 201(g), (h), Nationality Act of 1940 reproduced as Appendix 4-12 (making the 1940 requirement applicable to children born after May 24,1934).

[3]See §§ 4:35 to 4:44.

[4]INA § 301(b), 8 U.S.C.A. § 1401(b) as originally enacted by Act of June 27, 1952.

[5]INA § 301(c), 8 U.S.C.A. § 1401(c) as originally enacted by Act of June 27, 1952. Cf, §§ 4:51 to 4:61 (discussing the physical presence requirement under the INA).

[6]See §§ 4:35 to 4:44.

January 13, 1941, acquired U.S. citizenship at birth through the general provision of the 1934 Act, which granted U.S. citizenship to children born abroad to a U.S. citizen parent.[1] Since the natural father in such cases is not considered the legal father, the retention requirement when one parent is a noncitizen does not apply.[2] The citizenship acquired under this provision is not affected by subsequent legitimation of the child.[3]

The same rules that applied to acquisition of U.S. citizenship by out-of-wedlock children of U.S. citizen fathers before 1934, applied as well during this period. Children acquired U.S. citizenship at birth from their U.S. citizen fathers if they were legitimated under the laws of the father's domicile.[4] Legitimation could occur at any time even after the child had become an adult,[5] and even after the passage of the 1940 Act.[6] If legitimation occurred while the child was in an age that he or she could comply with the retention requirements, then retention requirements were applicable.[7] However, if legitimation occurred after the retention requirement age, retention requirements were not applicable.[8]

The Supreme Court has found that gender-specific provisions distinguishing between children born out-of-wedlock to U.S. citizen men and those born to U.S. citizen women do not violate equal protection guarantees.[9]

§ 4:31   State Department summary of proof of claim for this period

Research References

Steel on Immigration Law § 15:5

According to the State Department, a person should submit the following evidence to establish citizenship acquired if born during this period: (1) a birth certificate or other proof of the child's birth to a U.S. citizen mother, father, or both; (2) if applicable, the parents' marriage certificate or other proof of the child's legitimacy or legitimation; (3) proof of at least one parent's U.S. citizenship; and (4) proof of that parent's residence in the United States at any time before the child's birth.[1] In

---

[Section 4:30]

[1]Sec. 1, Act of May 24, 1934 reproduced as Appendix 4-10.

[2]Matter of P-, 7 I. & N. Dec. 523, 524 (Reg. Comm'r) approved (Central Office 1957).

[3]Matter of P-, 7 I. & N. Dec. 523, 524 (Reg. Comm'r) approved (Central Office 1957); Matter of M-D-, 3 I. & N. Dec. 485, 489, 1949 WL 6481 (B.I.A. 1949).

[4]39 Op. Atty. Gen. at 558 (marriage of natural parents occurred in France but father was domiciled in New York-New York law governed); Matter of P-, 4 I. & N. Dec. 354, 358, 1951 WL 7014 (B.I.A. 1951). For a discussion of the BIA's interpretation of the legitimation laws of the different countries and states of the U.S. at different periods of time, see Appendix 4-25.

[5]Matter of P-, 4 I. & N. Dec. 354, 358, 1951 WL 7014 (B.I.A. 1951) (child born in 1877, legitimate in 1913).

[6]Matter of L-, 3 I. & N. Dec. 225.

[7]7 FAM 1135.7-1(b).

[8]7 FAM 1135.7-1(c).

[9]Tuan Anh Nguyen v. I.N.S., 121 S. Ct. 2053, 150 L. Ed. 2d 115 (U.S. 2001). See § 4:14.

[Section 4:31]

[1]7 FAM 1135.9(a).

addition, persons born to one citizen and one noncitizen parent must also prove that they met or have been exempted from applicable retention requirements.[2]

IV. PERSONS BORN ABROAD BETWEEN JANUARY 14, 1941 AND DECEMBER 23, 1952

§ 4:32 Generally

Research References

Dizon and Wettstein, Immigration Law Service 2d § 14:34

The Nationality Act of 1940 repealed section 1993 of the Revised Statutes.[1] Therefore, after January 14, 1941, the effective date of the 1940 act, children born abroad to U.S. citizens could no longer acquire citizenship at birth according to the 1934 statute.[2] Of course, the repeal of section 1993 did not affect the nationality status of persons who had already acquired U.S. citizenship under that section.[3]

§ 4:33 Both parents are U.S. citizens

The 1940 Act continued the rule that if both parents were U.S. citizens at the time of the birth of the child abroad, and one parent had resided previously in the United States, the child was a U.S. citizen at birth and no subsequent conditions were attached to this citizenship.[1]

§ 4:34 One parent is U.S. citizen and either the other is noncitizen national or child is born in an outlying possession of U.S

The statute also continued the rule, albeit this time explicitly, that if one of the parents is a U.S. citizen and the other is a U.S. noncitizen national, the child is a U.S. citizen at birth abroad if the U.S. citizen parent resided in the United States prior to the birth of the child.[1] A new provision was introduced by the 1940 act to take into account birth of a child in an outlying possession of the United States to a U.S. citizen parent.[2] In such a case, the child is a U.S. citizen at birth if the U.S. citizen parent resided in the United States or one of its outlying possessions prior to the birth of the child.[3]

---

[2]7 FAM 1135.9(b).

[Section 4:32]

[1]Sec. 504, Nationality Act of 1940 reproduced as Appendix 4-12.

[2]The effective date of the 1940 act was 90 days after date of approval of the 1940 act, i.e. October 14, 1940. See sec. 601, Nationality Act of 1940 reproduced as Appendix 4-12.

[3]Sec. 504, Nationality Act of 1940 reproduced as Appendix 4-12.

[Section 4:33]

[1]Sec. 201(c), Nationality Act of 1940 reproduced as Appendix 4-12.

[Section 4:34]

[1]Sec. 201(d), Nationality Act of 1940 reproduced as Appendix 4-12.

[2]Sec. 201(e), Nationality Act of 1940 reproduced as Appendix 4-12.

[3]Sec. 201(e), Nationality Act of 1940 reproduced as Appendix 4-12. See discussion of the meaning of United States for citizenship at birth abroad in the 1940 act.

§ 4:35 One parent is citizen and one parent is noncitizen; prior residence of parent

If one of the parents of the child was a noncitizen, the child could only be a U.S. citizen at birth abroad if the U.S. citizen parent had resided in the United States for 10 years prior to the birth of the child, and at least five of those years were after the parent had attained 16 years of age.[1]

The prior residence provision introduced by the Nationality Act of 1940 was quite harsh. It prevented U.S. citizenship at birth of children born abroad to a U.S. citizen parent and a noncitizen parent, if the citizen parent was under the age of 21 at the time of the birth of the child. Since the law required the parent to have resided in the U.S. for at least five years after the age of 16, U.S. citizen parents under age 21 could not meet the prior residence requirements.[2] This provision affected the citizenship rights of many children of U.S. armed forces personnel.

§ 4:36 One parent is citizen and one parent is noncitizen; prior residence of parent—Special provisions for service in armed forces

In 1946, Congress passed an amendment to remedy this situation.[1] The amendment added section 201(i) to the Nationality Act of 1940.[2] This section allowed parents who served honorably in the U.S. armed forces during World War II to transmit citizenship to their children if the parent resided ten years in the United States prior to the birth of the child and at least five of those years were after attaining the age of 12.[3] Thus, if the U.S. citizen parent was in the military, the child may be a citizen provided the parent resided in the United States until at least age 17. One of the key advantages of this provision is that children born out-of-wedlock could acquire U.S. citizenship through its provisions without being legitimated.[4]

This amendment was applied both retroactively to confer U.S. citizenship to children of qualifying parents born after January 14, 1941, but before July 31, 1946; as well as prospectively to children born from that date until the Nationality Act of 1940 was repealed in 1952.[5] This legislation is applicable even when the birth of the child occurred before the commencement of military service of the U.S. citizen parent.[6] However, children who qualified under the provisions of this section could not take advantage of the exemption from the retention requirements available to children of employees of the U.S. government and of American firms abroad, which are discussed below.[7]

In 1956, Congress enacted a retroactive provision that allowed children born abroad during the period of effectiveness of the 1940 act to acquire U.S. citizenship

---

[Section 4:35]

   [1]Sec. 201(g), Nationality Act of 1940 reproduced as Appendix 4-12.

   [2]Matter of S-F- and G-, 2 I. & N. Dec. 182 (B.I.A.) approved (Att'y Gen. 1944).

[Section 4:36]

   [1]Act of July 31, 1946, Pub.L. 79-571, 60 Stat. 721 reproduced as Appendix 4-13.

   [2]Act of July 31, 1946, Pub.L. 79-571, 60 Stat. 721 reproduced as Appendix 4-13.

   [3]INS Interp. 301.1(b)(3)(ii).

   [4]See § 4:30.

   [5]Matter of A-, 2 I. & N. Dec. 799, 812 (B.I.A. 1947).

   [6]Matter of A-, 2 I. & N. Dec. 799, 812–14 (B.I.A. 1947); INS Interp. 301.1(b)(3)(ii).

   [7]INS Interp. 301.1(b)(6)(i). See §§ 4:38 to 4:44.

retroactive to their birth if their U.S. citizen parent had served in the U.S. armed forces after December 31, 1946 and before December 24, 1952.[8] Thus, children born to parents who served in the U.S. armed forces *after* World War II were also provided for. Under this amendment, the child would be a U.S. citizen at birth if the parent was physically present in the United States prior to the birth of the child for periods totaling 10 years, five of which were after attaining the age of 14.[9] Time served in the armed forces abroad was counted as presence in the United States for purposes of the physical presence requirement.[10] Since the person had to comply with the requirements of the INA, physical presence has the meaning attached to it by the INA.[11] The DHS takes the position that this provision only applies if the parent served honorably during the required period.[12] In addition, only service in active duty will count towards physical presence in the United States.[13]

§4:37 One parent is citizen and one parent is noncitizen; prior residence of parent—Special provisions for children born out-of-wedlock to U.S. citizen fathers

Research References

Dizon and Wettstein, Immigration Law Service 2d § 14:50

Because of the interplay of remedial provisions, children born out-of-wedlock to U.S. citizen fathers have ended up in a slightly better position than children born to the marriage of one U.S. citizen and one noncitizen parent.[1] Section 309(b) of the Immigration and Nationality Act provides that

[e]xcept as otherwise provided in section 405, the provisions of section 301(a)(7) shall apply to a child born out-of-wedlock on or after January 13, 1941, and prior to the effective date of this Act, as of the date of birth, if the paternity of such child is established before or after the effective date of this Act while such child is under the age of twenty one years by legitimation.[2]

This means that children born out-of-wedlock to a U.S. citizen father abroad after January 13, 1941 and before December 23, 1952 can take advantage of the prior residence requirements applicable under the INA.[3] Just like the Nationality Act of 1940, the INA required ten years of prior residence for transmission of U.S. citizenship. However, under the INA, five of those years had to be after age 14,

---

[8]Act of Mar 16, 1956, Pub. L. 84-430, 70 Stat. 50 reproduced as Appendix 4-15; INS Interp. 301.1(b)(4)(iii) (interpreting the act to confer citizenship retroactively).

[9]Act of Mar 16, 1956 reproduced as Appendix 4-15; INS Interp. 301.1(b)(4)(iii) (interpreting the act to confer citizenship retroactively).

[10]Act of Mar 16, 1956 reproduced as Appendix 4-15; INS Interp. 301.1(b)(4)(iii) (interpreting the act to confer citizenship retroactively).

[11]See §§ 4:51 to 4:63.

[12]INS Interp. 301.1(b)(4)(iv).

[13]INS Interp. 301.1(b)(4)(ii).

[Section 4:37]

[1]See 7 FAM 1134.4-3. For the legitimation requirements of the Nationality Act of 1940, see § 4:30.

[2]INA §§ 309(b), 1409(b).

[3]7 FAM 1134.4-3.

rather than age 16 as required by the Nationality Act of 1940.[4] Thus, children born out-of-wedlock during the period of validity of the Nationality Act of 1940, would be U.S. citizens if their U.S. citizen parent either complied with the prior residence and legitimation requirements of the Nationality Act or if the U.S. citizen fathers complied with the prior residence requirements of the INA and the child was legitimated under the age of 21.[5] This applies regardless of whether the legitimation took place before or after December 24, 1952.[6]

By contrast, children born out-of-wedlock to U.S. citizen mothers between January 14, 1941, and December 23, 1952, are citizens if the U.S. citizen mother resided in the U.S. or its outlying possessions prior to the child's birth.[7] The Supreme Court has upheld a gender-based requirement that fathers legitimate and promise to support their children born abroad, requirements found related to biological differences between men and women.[8] However, gender-based distinctions that do not directly relate to biology might not fare so well; the Supreme Court split 4-4 in considering the constitutionality of provisions requiring 10 years of physical presence for an unmarried father to convey citizenship, but only one year of continuous physical presence for an unmarried mother to do so.[9] Because the Court split 4-4 in *Flores-Villar*, the issue has not been resolved.

§ 4:38   One parent is citizen and one parent is noncitizen; prior residence of parent—Retention requirements; generally

The 1940 act as originally enacted imposed upon children born abroad to one citizen and one noncitizen parent a condition subsequent requiring the child to reside in the United States for five years between the ages of 13 and 21.[1] If the child reached the age of 16 and had not resided in the United States, the child would lose his or her U.S. citizenship at that point since it would be impossible to reside five years in the United States before the age of 21.[2]

A special proviso was made for children whose parents were in the employment of the U.S. government or U.S. companies abroad, in which case, the children are exempt from the retention requirements.[3] In interpreting this provision, the State Department has held that a child born after the citizen parent's death cannot be exempted from the retention requirements under this exemption, because that par-

---

[4]See §§ 4:54 to 4:56.

[5]7 FAM 1134.4-3(d).

[6]7 FAM 1134.4-3(d).

[7]See § 4:49.

[8]Nguyen v. I.N.S., 533 U.S. 53, 121 S. Ct. 2053, 150 L. Ed. 2d 115 (U.S. 2001) (because male unmarried parents might not know of child or have connection to child, Court upheld additional requirements at INA § 309 for unmarried fathers).

[9]Flores-Villar v. U.S., 131 S.Ct. 2312 (2011).

[Section 4:38]

[1]Sec. 201(g), Nationality Act of 1940 reproduced as Appendix 4-12; Matter of V-V-, 7 I. & N. Dec. 122.

[2]Sec. 201(g), Nationality Act of 1940 reproduced as Appendix 4-12; Matter of N-J-Q-, 4 I. & N. Dec. 360 (Central Office 1951) (even though child arrived in New York two days after the sixteenth birthday, the plane had stopped en route on U.S. territory one day before the child's sixteenth birthday).

[3]Sec. 201(g), Nationality Act of 1940 reproduced as Appendix 4-12.

ent was not residing abroad or employed at the time of the child's birth.[4] On the other hand, the State Department holds that children of employees of companies founded by an association of American corporations to carry out a single business venture abroad for joint profit are exempt from the retention requirements of Section 201(g) INA provided that (1) such joint ventures are not separate legal entities for all purposes, and (2) all of the contracting organizations have their principal offices in the United States, even though the sole office and the place of business of the joint venture were in a foreign country.[5] The State Department requires cases in which it is not clear whether the retention requirements apply to be referred to the Washington, D.C.[6]

§ 4:39 One parent is citizen and one parent is noncitizen; prior residence of parent—Retention requirements; generally—Impact of INA

With the passage of the INA, Congress provided that children born during the period of validity of the 1940 Act could retain their U.S. citizenship by complying with the retention requirements of the INA.[1] Thus the child would still be a U.S. citizen provided he or she entered the United States before attaining the age of 23 and immediately following that entry was continuously physically present in the United States for five years between the ages of 14 and 28.[2] The person was therefore required to start the five-year of continuous residence sometime after his or her fourteenth birthday and before the twenty-third birthday.[3] However, in a number of different circumstances, the courts and agencies have found individuals to satisfy "constructive physical presence" and thus to remain citizens.[4]

§ 4:40 One parent is citizen and one parent is noncitizen; prior residence of parent—Retention requirements; generally—Impact of 1957 Amendment

In 1957, Congress amended this section to provide that the continuous physical presence required to comply with the retention requirement would not be broken by absences that added together total less than twelve months during the five years.[1]

---

[4]7 FAM 1134.5-2(a)(2).

[5]7 FAM 1134/5-2(b).

[6]7 FAM 1134.5-2(a)(2).

[Section 4:39]

[1]INA § 301(c), 8 U.S.C.A. § 1401(c) as originally enacted by Act of June 27, 1952 reproduced as Appendix 4-14.

[2]INA § 301(b), 8 U.S.C.A. § 1401(b) as originally enacted by Act of June 27, 1952 reproduced as Appendix 4-14. See §§ 4:51 to 4:63.

[3]INA § 301(b), 8 U.S.C.A. § 1401(b) as originally enacted by Act of June 27, 1952 reproduced as Appendix 4-14. See §§ 4:51 to 4:63.

[4]See § 4:48.

[Section 4:40]

[1]Sec. 16, Act of Sept. 11, 1957, Pub. L. 85-316, 71 Stat. 644, reproduced as Appendix 4-16.

§ 4:41 One parent is citizen and one parent is noncitizen; prior residence of parent—Retention requirements; generally—Impact of 1972 Amendment; reduction of retention requirement time

In 1972, Congress once again relaxed the conditions subsequent.[1] Under the 1972 provisions, children could comply with the retention requirements by being continuously present in the United States for a period of two years between the ages of 14 and 28.[2] According to the State Department interpretation the two years had to be completed before the twenty-eighth birthday.[3] Absences of less than 60 days would not break the continuity of the physical presence.[4]

Persons who came to the United States before October 27, 1972 were allowed by the amendment to choose either to comply with the two-year provision of the amendment, or to comply with the original five-year requirement immediately following the coming into the United States.[5] Special provision was made to allow those persons who were in the process of complying with the original five-year requirement to complete it after the date of enactment of the amendment.[6] Thus, persons who came to the United States prior to the date of enactment and had complied with the original retention requirements or were in the process of complying with them were not required to comply with the amended requirement.[7] Because the original retention requirement allowed absences of up to 12 months in the aggregate while the amended requirement only allowed for absences of up to 60 days, some persons who complied with the original requirement may have failed to comply with the amended one.[8]

In addition, persons who had lost U.S. citizenship before October 27, 1972 by failure to comply with the original five-year requirement had their citizenship restored if they satisfied the two-year retention requirement imposed by the amendments either prior to the 1972 amendment or after its enactment.[9]

§ 4:42 One parent is citizen and one parent is noncitizen; prior residence of parent—Retention requirements; generally—Impact of 1972 Amendment; reduction of retention requirement time—Special provision when noncitizen parent naturalizes

The 1972 amendment also had a provision making the retention requirement

---

[Section 4:41]

[1]INA § 301(b), 8 U.S.C.A. § 1401(b) as amended by sec 1, Act of Oct. 27, 1972 reproduced as Appendix 4-17.

[2]INA § 301(b), 8 U.S.C.A. § 1401(b) as amended by sec. 1, Act of Oct. 27, 1972 reproduced as Appendix 4-17, made applicable to children born after May 24,1934 by INA § 301(c), 8 U.S.C.A. § 1401(c) as originally enacted by Act of June 27, 1952; INS Interp. 301.1(b)(6)(vii).

[3]See 7 FAM 133.5-7(c) (persons who had not started residing in the United States before their twenty-sixth birthday are ineligible to comply with the requirement).

[4]INA § 301(b), 8 U.S.C.A. § 1401(b) as amended by sec. 1, Act of Oct. 27, 1972 reproduced as Appendix 4-17.

[5]INA § 301(d), 8 U.S.C.A. § 1401(d) as added by sec. 3, Act of Oct. 27, 1972 reproduced as Appendix 4-17; INS Interp. 301.1(b)(6)(x).

[6]INA § 301(d), 8 U.S.C.A. § 1401(d) as added by sec. 3, Act of Oct. 27, 1972 reproduced as Appendix 4-17.

[7]See INA § 301(d), 8 U.S.C.A. § 1401(d) as added by sec. 3, Act of Oct. 27, 1972 reproduced as Appendix 4-17.

[8]Cf. § 4:40.

[9]INS Interp. 301.1(b)(6)(vii).

inapplicable to the child if the noncitizen parent naturalized before the child turned eighteen and the child began to reside permanently in the United States before turning 18.[1]

The exemption from the retention requirements when the noncitizen parent naturalizes is one of the few INA provisions relating to U.S. citizens born abroad that require "residence" rather than physical presence in the U.S.[2] Thus mere presence will not satisfy this requirement.[3] There must be an intention to reside permanently in the United States as evinced by the facts and circumstances surrounding the child's presence in the United States.[4] Once the noncitizen parent naturalized and the child began to reside permanently in the United States before the age of 18, the U.S. citizenship of the child became absolute and the child did not lose it even if he or she abandoned permanent residence in the United States and moved to a foreign country.[5]

§ 4:43 One parent is citizen and one parent is noncitizen; prior residence of parent—Retention requirements; generally—Impact of 1978 Amendment

In 1978, Congress repealed the retention requirement.[1] Persons who were under the age of 26 on the date of enactment, and who could therefore still comply with the requirements, were altogether exempt.[2] Since the amendment was enacted on October 10, 1978, no person born after October 10, 1952 is subject to retention requirement.[3] The amendment, however, did not restore U.S. citizenship to those who had already lost it by failure to comply with the retention requirements prior to October 10, 1952.[4]

On the other hand, courts have applied equitable theories to excuse retention requirements in certain circumstances. These circumstances are discussed in detail below.[5]

§ 4:44 One parent is citizen and one parent is noncitizen; prior residence of parent—Retention requirements; generally—The 1994 Amendment

Even when citizenship was lost by failure to comply with the retention requirements, the person may still have his or her U.S. citizenship restored by taking an

---

[Section 4:42]

[1]INA § 301(b), 8 U.S.C.A. § 1401(b) as amended by sec. 1, Act of Oct. 27, 1972 reproduced as Appendix 4-17.

[2]Since the child is a U.S. citizen, there is no requirement of lawful admission to permanent residence as in the derivative citizenship provisions. See §§ 5:1 et seq.

[3]INS Interp. 301.1(b)(6)(ii).

[4]INS Interp. 301.1(b)(6)(ii).

[5]INS Interp. 301.1(b)(6)(ii).

[Section 4:43]

[1]INA § 301(d), 8 U.S.C.A. § 1401(d), as amended by sec. 1, Act of Oct. 10, 1978, Pub. L. 95-432, 92 Stat. 1046, reproduced as Appendix 4-18.

[2]See § 4:57.

[3]See § 4:57.

[4]See § 4:57.

[5]See § 4:48.

oath of allegiance.[1] The requirements and procedures for the oath are discussed below.[2]

In deciding whether to rely on equitable theories or to take the oath, the practitioner should take several issues into consideration, including possible taxation issues. In addition, one should consider the possibility of children deriving citizenship upon the reacquisition of citizenship upon the parent's oath.[3]

§ 4:45 Nature of residence requirements; residence in U.S. and its outlying possessions

Under the 1940 Act, a parent satisfied the prior residence requirement by residing in the United States *or* its outlying possession for the required period prior to the birth of the child.[1] Similarly, the child satisfied the retention requirements by residing for the required amount of time in the United States *or* in its outlying possessions.[2]

The principle that residence in an outlying possession counts toward prior residence of the parent applies even to determination of U.S. citizenship of children born in an outlying possession. Thus, if the U.S. citizen parent had resided in the United States *or* an outlying possession of the United States, the child would be a U.S. citizen at birth.[3] There are no retention requirements for children born in outlying possessions.[4]

The Act itself defined the term United States to include the continental United States, Alaska, Hawaii, Puerto Rico, and the Virgin Islands of the United States.[5] The term "outlying possession" was defined to include all territories over which the United States exercises sovereignty, except for the Panama Canal Zone.[6] The outlying possessions of the United States during this period were American Samoa, Swains Island, Guam, and, prior to July 4, 1946, the Philippines.[7] If the child was born after the independence of the Philippines but the U.S. citizen parent had completed his or her residence requirements in the Philippines before the independence, the residence would be counted as prior residence since it was completed while the Philippines were an outlying possession of the U.S.[8]

[Section 4:44]

[1]INA § 324(d), 8 U.S.C.A. § 1435(d).

[2]See § 11:30.

[3]See §§ 5:1 et seq.

[Section 4:45]

[1]Sec. 201(c), (d), (e), (g), Nationality Act of 1940 reproduced as Appendix 4-12.

[2]Sec. 201(g), Nationality Act of 1940 reproduced as Appendix 4-12.

[3]Sec. 201(e), Nationality Act of 1940 reproduced as Appendix 4-12.

[4]Sec. 201(e), Nationality Act of 1940 reproduced as Appendix 4-12.

[5]Sec. 101(d), Nationality Act of 1940 reproduced as Appendix 4-12.

[6]Sec. 101(g), Nationality Act of 1940 reproduced as Appendix 4-12.

[7]INS Interp. 301.1(b)(3)(iii). Cf. Chs 2 and 3 for a discussion of the territories of the United States.

[8]Matter of Y-, 7 I. & N. Dec. 667 (Reg. Comm'r) approved (Ass't Comm'r 1958).

§ 4:46 Nature of residence requirements; residence in U.S. and its outlying possessions—Definition of residence

Research References

Dizon and Wettstein, Immigration Law Service 2d § 14:35

The Nationality Act of 1940 also included a statutory definition of "residence" for purposes of U.S. citizenship at birth abroad.[1] It defined residence as the place of general abode.[2] The DHS interprets this by regulation to mean the principal dwelling place.[3] To satisfy this "residence" requirement, the person needed more than temporary residence.[4] Domicile was not sufficient if it was not the principal place of dwelling, unless coupled with some form of physical presence.[5] For example, the actual residence of the parent could not be imputed to the child.[6] The definition of residence required an objective fact and excluded subjective intent.[7] Thus, even when the person had the intention to return to the United States, the person did not satisfy the definition of residence.[8] However, the purpose of the person's presence in a specific place was relevant to determine whether that was the general place of abode.[9]

Temporary absences from the United States do not preclude the establishment of the necessary residence; the absences themselves are counted as residence in the United States, provided the United States is still the place of general abode during the absences.[10] As a result, one court has found that a U.S. citizen father who was physically present and working in the United States for nine months per year in eight out of a nine-year period, had established that his residence during this period was in the United States.[11] The court overturned the BIA's conclusion that, because the father's time in the U.S. was incidental to employment which was not to exceed

---

[Section 4:46]

[1]Sec. 104, Nationality Act of 1940 reproduced as Appendix 4-12.

[2]Sec. 104, Nationality Act of 1940 reproduced as Appendix 4-12.

[3]8 CFR § 301.8 (1949); INS Interp. 301.1(b)(5)(ii).

[4]Matter of M-, 4 I. & N. Dec. 418, 419 (B.I.A. 1951).

[5]Matter of B-, 4 I. & N. Dec. 424, 426–27, 432 (Central Office 1951); Matter of D-, 3 I. & N. Dec. 652 (Central Office 1949).

[6]Matter of B-, 4 I. & N. Dec. 424; Matter of D-, 3 I. & N. Dec. 652, 656, 1949 WL 6515 (B.I.A. 1949) (to determine whether the father of a U.S. citizen resided while he was a child, we look at his own residence, not the residence of his father).

[7]Savorgnan v. U.S., 338 U.S. 491, 70 S.Ct. 292, 94 L.Ed.2d 287 (1950); Rodrigues-Romero v. I.N.S., 434 F.2d 1022, 1024 (9th Cir. 1970) (per curiam); Alcarez-Garcia v. Ashcroft, 293 F.3d 1155, 1157 (9th Cir. 2002).

[8]See generally Ch 7 §§ 7:4 to 7:10.

[9]U.S. v. Karahalias, 205 F.2d 331 (2d Cir. 1953) (purpose of visit is relevant to determine abode); Acheson v. Yee King Gee, 184 F.2d 382, 384 (9th Cir. 1950) (same); Lee You v. Acheson, 109 F.Supp. 98 (S.D.Tex. 1952) (same); Toy Teung Kwong v. Acheson, 97 F.Supp. 745 (N.D.Cal. 1951) (purpose of the trip will determine what the principal place of residence is); Wong Gan Ghee v. Acheson, 95 F.Supp. 816 (N.D.Cal. 1951) (same).

[10]Acheson v. Yee King Gee, 184 F.2d 382, 384 (9th Cir. 1950) (visits abroad were for the purpose of visiting relative, therefore the U.S. was still place of general abode during the absences); Lee You v. Acheson, 109 F.Supp. 98 (S.D.Tex. 1952) (sold all his property and went abroad on business trip months before having ten years of residence in the U.S.-his place of general abode was still the U.S.).

[11]Alcarez-Garcia v. Ashcroft, 293 F.3d 1155, 1157-1158 (9th Cir. 2002).

a definite, fixed period, his residence was really with his family in Mexico.[12] The court found that this conclusion erroneously applied an "intent" or "domicile" definition to the word residence.[13]

Staying in the United States as a student has been held to be residence in the United States for purposes of the birth abroad provisions of the 1940 Act.[14] Protracted absences did not preclude a finding that the residence in the United States was the place of general abode during that time if the absence was occasioned by circumstances beyond the person's control.[15] Absence as a member of the U.S. armed forces did not preclude a finding of residence in the United States.[16] However, temporary visits of the parent to the United States were insufficient to establish principal place of abode in the United States.[17]

A 1948 opinion of the Legal Advisor of the Department of State concurred, holding that Section 201 of the 1940 Nationality Act did not require the parents to remain continuously and without interruption in the United States during the prescribed period, but required the parents to maintain their place of abode in the United States during any absences.[18] It further held that (1) residence was not terminated by visits abroad but was terminated by the establishment of a dwelling place abroad; (2) absence from the United States as a member of the U.S. armed forces was counted as residence in the United States, provided the service was honorably performed; 3) absences from the United States due to employment or schooling abroad could also be included as residence in the United States as long as the persons maintained their place of general abode in the United States.[19]

There is one exception to the rule that temporary visits to the United States were not sufficient to satisfy the residence requirements of the 1940 Act. Out-of-wedlock children born abroad to U.S. citizen mothers are not governed under the general provisions of children born abroad, but rather under a special provision.[20] The general definition of residence in the 1940 Act does not apply.[21] For out-of-wedlock children of U.S. citizen mothers, prior residence of the mother is satisfied under the

---

[12]Alcarez-Garcia v. Ashcroft, 293 F.3d 1155, 1156 (9th Cir. 2002).

[13]Alcarez-Garcia v. Ashcroft, 293 F.3d 1155, 1157-1158 (9th Cir. 2002).

[14]Matter of M-, 7 I. & N. Dec. 643 (Reg. Comm'r) approved (Ass't Comm'r 1958); Matter of V- V-, 7 I. & N. Dec. 122, 123, 1956 WL 10235 (B.I.A. 1956) (same for purposes of the retention requirement).

[15]Lee You v. Acheson, 109 F. Supp. 98 (S.D. Tex. 1952) (went abroad on business trip before World War II and could not return until 1946); Toy Teung Kwong v. Acheson, 97 F. Supp. 745 (N.D. Cal. 1951) (had to stay abroad for approximately three years because of illness of his mother and maritime strike); Wong Gan Chee v. Acheson, 95 F. Supp. 816 (N.D. Cal. 1951) (went to visit his mother and was forced to stay in China more than five years during the war). Cf. Puig Jimenez v. Glover, 255 F.2d 54, 58–59 (1st Cir. 1958) (went to Spain on a visit in 1936 and was prevented from returning to Puerto Rico until July 1941 by the Spanish Civil War-was residing in Puerto Rico on January 13, 1941).

[16]INS Interp. 301.1(b)(5)(ii).

[17]Matter of M-, 4 I. & N. Dec. 418. But see, Garlasco v. Dulles, 243 F.2d 679, 682 (2d Cir. 1957) (in the context of expatriation proceedings, residence in a New York hotel for two and a half months may have been principal place of abode for that period).

[18]7 FAM 1134.2-2(d).

[19]7 FAM 1134.2-2(d).

[20]Sec. 205, Nationality Act of 1940 reproduced as Appendix 4-12.

[21]Sec. 104, Nationality Act of 1940 reproduced as Appendix 4-12; Matter of E--, 9 I. & N. Dec. 479, 480, 481, 1961 WL 12192 (B.I.A. 1961).

principles applicable to births under the 1934 Act and prior statutes.[22] Temporary visits to the United States for a short duration prior to the birth of the child satisfy this requirement[23]

§ 4:47 Nature of residence requirements; residence in U.S. and its outlying possessions—Constructive residence

U.S. citizens who were erroneously prevented entry to the United States have been held to have been constructively continuously physically present in the United States for purposes of transmission of citizenship to their children.[1] Thus, a mother who prior to the birth of her children was prevented from entering the United States by the legacy INS' erroneous interpretation of the law regarding her nationality status was deemed to have been physically present for the period required for her transmission of U.S. citizenship to her children.[2] However, absent affirmative misadvice by U.S. government personnel, the courts have not found constructive residence so as to give a parent enough years of residence to convey citizenship to a child.[3] Constructive residence so as to convey citizenship to a child must be distinguished from constructive residence which permits someone to maintain citizenship in the face of the retention requirements; the Courts have been very willing to find constructive presence to satisfy those bars.[4] The Ninth Circuit has explained this phenomena by explaining that the loss of citizenship entailed by the retention is different in type from the residence which would be required to actually convey citizenship in the first instance, because of heightened solicitude towards potential loss of citizenship.[5]

However, constructive residence is less of an issue because the definition of residence does not require the parents to remain continuously and uninterruptedly in the United States during the prescribed period, but required the parents to maintain their place of abode in the United States during any absences.[6] While this requirement can be satisfied by short absences, extensive residence abroad without maintaining an abode in the United States will not be considered as "residence" in the United States.[7]

---

[22]Matter of E--, 9 I. & N. Dec. 479, 481, 1961 WL 12192 (B.I.A. 1961).

[23]Matter of E--, 9 I. & N. Dec. 479, 480, 1961 WL 12192 (B.I.A. 1961).

[Section 4:47]

[1]Matter of Navarrete, 12 I. & N. Dec. 138 (BIA 1967); Matter of S-, 8 I. & N. Dec. 221 (B.I.A. 1958); INS Interp. 301.1(b)(5)(iii).

[2]Matter of Navarrete, 12 I. & N. Dec. 138, 141–42, 1967 WL 13979 (B.I.A. 1967).

[3]Runnett v. Shultz, 901 F.2d 782, 783–785 (9th Cir. 1990); Drozd v. I.N.S., 155 F.3d 81, 85–88 (2d Cir. 1998) (prior physical presence case); Tullius v. Albright, 240 F.3d 1317 (11th Cir. 2001) (constructive physical presence case).

[4]See § 4:48.

[5]Runnett v. Shultz, 901 F.2d 782, 784 (9th Cir. 1990).

[6]7 FAM 1134.2-2(d). See § 4:47.

[7]Rodriguez-Romero v. Immigration and Naturalization Service, 434 F.2d 1022 (9th Cir. 1970) cert. denied 401 U.S. 976, 91 S.Ct. 1199, 28 L.Ed.2d 326 (1971). But see Puig Jimenez v. Glover, 255 F.2d 54 (1st Cir.1958) (in the context of collective naturalization of Puerto Ricans, person prevented from returning to Puerto Rico because of Spanish Civil War still had Puerto Rico as his place of general abode).

§ 4:48 Nature of residence requirements; residence in U.S. and its outlying possessions—Constructive physical presence

The concept of physical presence has some limited applicability to persons born abroad during this period, in the context of retention requirements. Unlike residence, the courts and the agency found the physical presence requirement could be satisfied "constructively" in the context of the retention requirements. Children who did not know they were U.S. citizens until it was too late to comply with the retention requirements do not forfeit their U.S. citizenship unless they fail to come to the United States as U.S. citizens within a reasonable period of time after learning of such claim to citizenship.[1] When constructive physical presence applies in relation to the five-year physical presence requirement of the INA, the person is deemed to have been physically present in the United States from a date immediately prior to his or her twenty-third birthday until the date of actually coming to the United States.[2] The person must comply with the remainder of the continuous physical presence requirement.[3] There is no additional physical presence requirement beyond the age of 28.[4] If the person did not learn of his or her U.S. citizenship until after the age of 28, no physical presence at all in the United States is required to retain citizenship.[5]

The Foreign Affairs Manual contains a lengthy analysis of arguments for constructive physical presence, which is worth consulting.[6]

As opposed to failure to know about their citizenship status, persons who knew they had acquired U.S. citizenship through one citizen and one noncitizen parent were not excused from satisfying the retention requirement by the fact that they ignored the existence of the retention requirement.[7]

Constructive physical presence in the United States is also applied when the person is serving honorably in the U.S. armed forces abroad.[8] The DHS takes the position that this constructive presence only applies to active duty. Members of a military reserve unit are regarded as having been physically present in the United States for retention purposes only during such periods of absence when they were

---

[Section 4:48]

[1]Matter of Navarrete, 12 I. & N. Dec. 138, 141, 1967 WL 13979 (B.I.A. 1967); Matter of Yanez-Carrillo, 10 I. & N. Dec. 366, 369, 1963 WL 12332 (B.I.A. 1963). Cf. Matter of C-S-, 9 I. & N. Dec. 670 (Att'y Gen. 1962) (holding that a person who voted in foreign elections without knowing that he was a U.S. citizen, did not expatriate himself with that action). The DHS takes contradictory positions regarding whether the lack of knowledge must be based on erroneous interpretation of the retention requirements applicable after the passage of the INA, or whether lack of knowledge of U.S. citizenship was enough for constructive compliance. See INS Interp. 301.1(b)(6)(iii), (viii).

[2]Matter of Farley, 11 I. & N. Dec. 51, 54, 1965 WL 12221 (B.I.A. 1965).

[3]Matter of Farley, 11 I. & N. Dec. 51, 54, 1965 WL 12221 (B.I.A. 1965); INS Interp. 301.1(b)(6)(iii).

[4]Matter of Farley, 11 I. & N. Dec. 51, 54, 1965 WL 12221 (B.I.A. 1965).

[5]Matter of Navarrete, 12 I. & N. Dec. 138, 141, 1967 WL 13979 (B.I.A. 1967); INS Interp. 301.1(b)(6)(iii).

[6]See 7 FAM 1100 Appendix K, Defenses of Unawareness, Impossibility of Performance, Constructive Compliance, and Official Misinformation.

[7]INS Interp. 301.1(b)(6)(ix).

[8]Matter of Szajlai, 10 I. & N. Dec. 103, 107 (Ass't Comm'r 1962). This constructive presence was necessitated because unlike the provision relating to prior presence of the parent, the statutory provision relating to retention requirement does not address service in the U.S. armed forces.

actually engaged in active military duty or related activity as members of the U.S. armed forces.[9]

§ 4:49 Children born out-of-wedlock

Research References

Dizon and Wettstein, Immigration Law Service 2d § 14:54

A child born out-of-wedlock between January 14, 1941 and December 23, 1952 to a U.S. citizen mother, was a U.S. citizen at birth if the mother had resided in the United States or one of its outlying possessions prior to the child's birth.[1] The U.S. citizenship so acquired is *not* divested by subsequent legitimation by a noncitizen father, even when such legitimation occurs during the child's minority.[2] Furthermore, subsequent legitimation by a noncitizen father does *not* impose retroactively the same prior residence and retention requirements that are imposed on children born abroad to one citizen and one noncitizen parent.[3]

A child born out-of-wedlock abroad to a U.S. citizen father and a noncitizen mother would acquire U.S. citizenship at birth if, before reaching the age of 21, the child was legitimated or if paternity was established through court proceedings.[4] The DHS takes the position that under the Nationality Act of 1940, legitimation must take place according to the laws of the father's domicile.[5] This issue is somewhat irrelevant as the provisions of the INA may also apply in these cases.[6]

Legitimation or court decrees are *not* necessary for transmission of citizenship if the child's U.S. citizenship was acquired under the special provision for U.S. armed forces personnel.[7] The rational for this decision is that when Congress amended section 201 of the Nationality Act to provide special treatment for children born

---

[9]INS Interp. 301.1(b)(6)(vi).

[Section 4:49]

[1]Sec. 205, Nationality Act of 1940 reproduced as Appendix 4-12.

[2]Matter of M-, 4 I. & N. Dec. 440, 444, 1951 WL 7035 (B.I.A. 1951).

[3]Matter of Villanueva, 16 I. & N. Dec. 84, 86 (B.I.A. 1976).

[4]Secs. 101(g), 205, Nationality Act of 1940 reproduced as Appendix 4-12; INS Interp. 309.1(b)(1) citing to unpublished decision where paternity was established by a court action in the Philippines which resulted in an award of child support and educational expenses of the child. In addition, the DHS now takes the position that legitimation according to the requirements of the 1940 Act is also effective in conferring U.S. citizenship at birth when the father complied with the reduced prior residence requirements applicable to persons in military service under the provisions of sec. 201(i) of the 1940 Act.

[5]INS Interp. 309(b)(1). It argues that by its terms sec. 102(h) of the 1940 Act which provides for legitimation under the law of the child's residence or domicile, applies only to chapter III of the 1940 Act and acquisition of citizenship at birth is in chapter I. See Nationality Act of 1940 reproduced as Appendix 4-12. For a discussion of the BIA's interpretation of the legitimation laws of the different countries and states of the U.S. at different periods of time, See Appendix 4-26.

[6]See § 4:63.

[7]Y.T. v. Bell, 478 F. Supp. 828 (W.D. Pa 1979); 7 FAM 1134.4-2(c). The DHS appears to take the position that legitimation according to the requirements of the 1940 Act was required in conferring U.S. citizenship at birth when the father complied with the reduced prior residence requirements applicable to persons in military service under the provisions of sec. 201(i) of the 1940 Act. INS Interp. 309.1(b)(1). For a discussion of the reduced residence requirements, see § 4:37.

abroad to U.S. servicemen, it did not amend section 205 to require legitimation or court order for acquisition by children born out-of-wedlock to the servicepersons.[8]

The Immigration and Nationality Act provided that a child born out-of-wedlock after January 13, 1941 who failed to acquire citizenship under the provisions of the Nationality Act of 1940, acquired U.S. citizenship if the U.S. citizen father complied with the prior residence applicable under the INA and the child was legitimated before his or her twenty-first birthday.[9] This provision applies whether legitimation occurred before or after December 24, 1952.[10]

The Supreme Court has found that gender-specific provisions distinguishing between children born out-of-wedlock to U.S. citizen men and those born to U.S. citizen women do not violate equal protection guarantees.[11]

The Supreme Court has upheld gender-based distinctions requiring legitimation, which it found related to biological differences between men and women.[12] Gender-based distinctions that do not directly relate to biology might not fare so well; the Supreme Court split 4-4 in considering the constitutionality of provisions requiring 10 years of physical presence for an unmarried father to convey citizenship, but only one year of continuous physical presence for an unmarried mother to do so.[13] At any rate, the legitimation requirements of this time period seem immune to constitutional challenge.

§ 4:50   State Department summary of proof of claim for this period

Research References
Steel on Immigration Law § 15:5

In order to prove a citizenship claim for this period, the State Department requires the following evidence: (1) a birth certificate or other proof of the child's birth to a U.S. citizen mother, father, or both; (2) if applicable, the parents' marriage certificate or other proof of the child's legitimacy or legitimation; (3) proof of at least one parent's U.S. citizenship; and (4) evidence of that parent's residence in the United States before the child's birth for the length of time required by the section of law under which the child is claiming U.S. citizenship.[1] In addition, sons and daughters of one U.S. and one noncitizen parent, must also prove that they have complied with or have been exempted from applicable retention requirements.[2]

---

[8]See 7 FAM 1134.4-2(c).

[9]INA § 309(b), 8 U.S.C.A. § 1409(b); 7 FAM 1134.4-3(b). For a discussion of the prior residence requirements of the INA, see §§ 4:57 to 4:58.

[10]7 FAM 1134.4-3.

[11]Tuan Anh Nguyen v. I.N.S., 121 S. Ct. 2053, 150 L. Ed. 2d 115 (U.S. 2001). See § 4:14.

[12]Nguyen v. I.N.S., 533 U.S. 53, 121 S. Ct. 2053, 150 L. Ed. 2d 115 (U.S. 2001) (because male unmarried parents might not know of child or have connection to child, Court upheld additional requirements at INA § 309 for unmarried fathers).

[13]Flores-Villar v. U.S., 131 S.Ct. 2312 (2011).

[Section 4:50]
[1]7 FAM 1134.6(a).
[2]7 FAM 1134.6(b).

V. PERSONS BORN ABROAD BETWEEN DECEMBER 24, 1952 AND NOVEMBER 13, 1986

§ 4:51 Generally

The Immigration and Nationality Act of 1952 repealed the Nationality Act of 1940.[1] It specifically provided that "repeal of any statute by this Act shall not terminate nationality lawfully acquired . . . under any law of the United States" or affect "any status . . . existing at the time" the INA took effect."[2] The provisions introduced by the INA to replace those of the 1940 Act were only minimally different from their predecessors. The citizenship at birth abroad provisions of the INA apply only to children born after December 24, 1952, unless otherwise specified by the INA or its amendments.[3]

§ 4:52 Both parents are U.S. citizens

Research References

Dizon and Wettstein, Immigration Law Service 2d § 14:38

The INA continues the same rule regarding children born abroad when both parents are U.S. citizens. It provides that "a person born outside of the United States and its outlying possessions of parents both of whom are citizens of the United States and one of whom has had a residence in the United States or one of its outlying possessions, prior to the birth of such person" is a U.S. citizen at birth.[1] The meaning of the term "residence" for the INA is discussed below.[2]

§ 4:53 One parent is U.S. citizen and either the other is noncitizen national or child is born in outlying possession of U.S

The INA also continued the rule that children born abroad to a U.S. citizen and to a noncitizen national were U.S. citizens at birth provided, however, the citizen parent had been physically present in the United States or one of its outlying possessions for a continuous period of one year prior to the birth of the child.[1] The INA also modified the rule applicable to birth in an outlying possession of a child of a U.S. citizen parent. Under the INA provision, the child would acquire U.S. citizenship at birth if the U.S. citizen parent had been physically present in the United

---

[Section 4:51]

[1]INA § 403(a)(42).

[2]INA § 405(a), (c), 8 U.S.C.A. § 1101, note.

[3]Wolf v. Brownell, 253 F.2d 141, 142 (9th Cir. 1957).

[Section 4:52]

[1]INA § 301(a)(3), 8 U.S.C.A. § 1401(a)(3) redesignated by sec. 3, Act of October 10, 1978, Pub.L. 95-432, 92 Stat. 1046 as INA § 301(a)(c), 8 U.S.C.A. § 1401(a)(c).

[2]See § 4:58.

[Section 4:53]

[1]INA § 301(a)(4), 8 U.S.C.A. § 1401(a)(4) redesignated by sec. 3, Act of October 10, 1978 as INA § 301(a), (d), 8 U.S.C.A. § 1401(a), (d).

States or one of its outlying possessions for a continuous period of one year at any time prior to the birth of the child.[2]

§ 4:54 One parent is U.S. citizen and other is noncitizen; prior physical presence of U.S. citizen parent

As originally enacted, the INA conferred U.S. citizenship at birth upon "a person born outside the geographical limits of the United States and its outlying possessions of parents one of whom is a noncitizen, and the other a citizen of the United States who, prior to the birth of such person, was physically present in the United States or its outlying possessions for a period or periods totaling not less than ten years, at least five of which were after attaining the age of fourteen years."[1]

Several recent cases have challenged the less favorable residence requirement for a U.S. citizen parent under this section, compared to that afforded a U.S. citizen mother of a child born out-of-wedlock under INA § 309(c), 8 U.S.C.A. § 1409(c).[2] In *Cervantes-Nava*, the Fifth Circuit refused to reach the constitutional issue, instead dismissing the case after finding that the possible remedies available to the plaintiff—severance of one or another of the residency sections or nullification of the entire INA—would not afford relief to the plaintiff because they would not result in his citizenship.[3] The Ninth Circuit reached the constitutional issue in *Flores-Villar*, and rejected the challenge. The Supreme Court granted certiorari regarding the issue, but split 4-4 on the issue, with Justice Kagan recused.[4] The Supreme Court's even split leaves the Ninth Circuit's case law in place, but suggests that a challenge along these lines might well succeed.

§ 4:55 One parent is U.S. citizen and other is noncitizen; prior physical presence of U.S. citizen parent—Service in armed forces exemption

Research References

A.L.R. Index, Immigration and Naturalization

Validity, Construction, and Application of 8 U.S.C.A. § 1401(c)-(g), Providing for American Citizenship in Certain Circumstances of Child Born Outside United States, or Found Within United States and of Unknown Parentage, and Predecessor Statutes, 175 A.L.R. Fed. 67

Dizon and Wettstein, Immigration Law Service 2d § 14:41

---

[2]INA § 301(a)(5), 8 U.S.C.A. § 1401(a)(5) redesignated by sec. 3, Act of October 10, 1978 as INA § 301(a), (e), 8 U.S.C.A. § 1401(a), (e).

[Section 4:54]

[1]INA § 301(a)(7), 8 U.S.C.A. § 1401(a)(7) as originally enacted by Act of June 27, 1952 reproduced as Appendix 4-14.

[2]U.S. v. Cervantes-Nava, 281 F.3d 501 (5th Cir. 2002), cert. denied, 122 S. Ct. 2379, 153 L. Ed. 2d 197 (U.S. 2002); U.S. v. Flores-Villar, 536 F.3d 990 (9th Cir. 2008).

[3]U.S. v. Cervantes-Nava, 281 F.3d 501, 504–06 (5th Cir. 2002).

[4]Flores-Villar v. U.S., 131 S.Ct. 2312 (2011).

Periods of honorable military service in the U.S. armed forces by the parent were considered as physical presence in the United States.[1] The DHS takes the position that only periods of active service in the armed forces may count as physical presence in the United States.[2] The DHS will only count members of a reserve unit as being physically present in the United States during those periods abroad when they are actually engaged in active duty or related activity as members of the armed forces of the United States.[3]

The State Department position is much more inclusive. Its very specific guidance is reproduced in full:[4]

(1) The Department holds that nothing in the phrase "any periods of honorable service in the Armed Forces of the United States" precludes a citizen from counting as qualifying physical presence all periods of honorable foreign service in the U.S. armed forces from the date of enlistment, whether the enlistment occurred in the United States or abroad.

(2) A naturalized U.S. citizen who, as an alien, served honorably abroad in the U.S. armed forces may count the overseas service as physical presence in the United States for purposes of transmitting citizenship.

(3) The Department and the Immigration and Naturalization Service hold that members of Reserve components of the U.S. armed forces may count as U.S. physical presence all time served abroad on active duty, except for training, provided the service was honorable. Other periods of foreign residence or travel while in the Reserves do not qualify (U.S.C. 2105d). Other members of uniformed services are considered U.S. government employees pursuant to 5 U.S.C. 2105(a).

(4) Only periods of honorable U.S. military service abroad count as periods of physical presence in the United States. However, some persons who have received other than honorable discharges may have some periods of honorable service that can be confirmed by the military authorities.

(5) In 1977, the General Counsel, Selective Service System, informed the Department that alternate service performed by conscientious objectors is not considered military service or employment by the U.S. government. Such persons receive no pay from the U.S. government, receive no government compensation if injured on the job, and are not entitled to veterans' benefits.

§4:56 One parent is U.S. citizen and other is noncitizen; prior physical presence of U.S. citizen parent—Government service abroad exemption

In the Immigration and Nationality Act as originally enacted, the only absences from the United States that could be counted toward the physical presence required to transmit U.S. citizenship were those due to assignments abroad in the U.S. armed forces.[1] It soon became clear that in a growing number of cases foreign service officers, other U.S. government employees who served abroad, U.S. representa-

---

[Section 4:55]

[1] INA § 301(a)(7), 8 U.S.C.A. § 1401(a)(7) as originally enacted by Act of June 27, 1952 reproduced as Appendix 4-14 ("any periods of honorable service in the Armed Forces of the United States by such citizen parent may be included in computing the physical presence requirements of this paragraph").

[2] INS Interp. 301.1(b)(4)(ii).

[3] INS Interp. 301.1(b)(4)(ii).

[4] 7 FAM 1133.3-4(d).

[Section 4:56]

[1] INA § 301(a)(7), 8 U.S.C.A. § 1401(a)(7) as originally enacted by Act of June 27, 1952 reproduced as Appendix 4-14.

tives to international organizations, all of whom might have spent much time outside the United States in connection with their official duties, and, in particular, the children of such persons or of military personnel who had spent their early lives accompanying their parents on foreign tours of duty were unable to transmit U.S. citizenship to their children.[2]

The proviso of section 301(a)(7) INA was amended in 1966 to read:

> That any periods of honorable service in the Armed Forces of the United States, or periods of employment with the United States Government or with an international organization as that term is defined in section 1 of the International Organizations Immunities Act (59 Stat. 669; 22 U.S.C. 288) by such citizen parent, or any periods during which such citizen parent is physically present abroad as the dependent unmarried son or daughter and a member of the household of a person (A) honorably serving with the Armed Forces of the United States, or (B) employed by the United States Government or an international organization as defined in section I of the International Organizations Immunities Act, may be included in order to satisfy the physical presence requirement of this paragraph. This proviso shall be applicable to persons born on or after December 24, 1952, to the same extent as if it had become effective in its present form on that date.[3]

The State Department holds that residence abroad in any capacity mentioned in the proviso can be substituted for all or part of the required 10 years of physical presence in the United States.[4] It, therefore, would be possible for a citizen who had never been in the United States to transmit citizenship if the citizen had worked abroad in qualifying employment for ten years, including five years after reaching age fourteen, or had, for a similar period, been the dependent, unmarried, son or daughter of a person so employed.[5]

§ 4:57 One parent is U.S. citizen and other is noncitizen—Retention requirements; generally

Research References

Dizon and Wettstein, Immigration Law Service 2d § 14:43

Retention requirements for persons born under the INA are only of historical interest. Because of repeated liberalization of the retention requirements, persons born after October 10, 1952 are not subject to retention requirements.

In 1978, Congress amended the INA by eliminating all retention requirements.[1] This amendment only applies prospectively, i.e., persons who lost their U.S. citizenship prior to October 10, 1978 by failure to comply with the retention requirements are not restored to U.S. citizenship by the amendment.[2] Persons who were under 26 on October 10, 1978, and therefore were still U.S. citizens were no longer required

---

[2]7 FAM 1133.3-4(c)(1).

[3]INA § 301(a)(7), 8 U.S.C.A. § 1401(a)(7) as amended by Act of November 6, 1966, 80 Stat. 1322.

[4]7 FAM 1133.3-4(c)(3).

[5]7 FAM 1133.3-4(c)(3).

[Section 4:57]

[1]INA § 301, 8 U.S.C.A. § 1401 as amended by sec. 1, Act of October 10, 1978, Pub. L. 95-432, 92 Stat. 1046, reproduced as Appendix 4-18.

[2]See Act of October 10, 1978, reproduced as Appendix 4-18; INS Interp. 301.1(b)(6)(xii).

to comply with any retention requirements.[3] Thus any child born to a U.S. citizen and a noncitizen parent after October 10, 1952, is exempt from the retention requirements.

§ 4:58 Residence under the INA

The definition of "residence" is of very limited value for the purposes of acquisition of U.S. citizenship at birth abroad during this period, since the only provisions framed in terms of "residence" are (1) the requirement imposed on children of two U.S. citizen parents, that one of them must have "resided" in the United States prior to the birth of the child, and (2) the exemption to the retention requirement introduced by the 1972 Act which required the child to have "[begun] to reside permanently in the United States while under the age of eighteen years."[1] In general, as it relates to acquisition of citizenship at birth, the issue will be "physical presence," not "residence."[2]

The INA defines "residence" as the "place of general abode."[3] The INA adds that "the place of general abode of a person means the principal, actual dwelling place without regard to intent," the same language used in the 1940 Act.[4]

§ 4:59 Physical presence under the INA

Research References

Dizon and Wettstein, Immigration Law Service 2d §§ 14:38, 14:39

Generally, the provisions in the INA relating to the length of time spent in the United States (including the archaic retention requirements) have always been phrased in terms of "physical presence."[1] Physical presence has its literal meaning, and is computed by the actual time spent in the United States.[2] The intent of the person at the time of his or her presence here is completely irrelevant to this determination.[3] Any time spent in the United States or its outlying possessions, even without maintaining a U.S. residence, is counted toward the required physical presence.[4]

Since physical presence is an objective concept, naturalized citizens may count as physical presence any time they spent in the United States or its outlying posses-

---

[3]INS Interp. 301.1(b)(6)(xii).

[Section 4:58]

[1]INA § 301(c) [8 U.S.C.A. § 1401(c)]; sec. 3, Act of Oct. 27, 1972 reproduced as Appendix 4-17, amending INA § 310(b) [8 U.S.C.A. § 1401(b)]. The derivative citizenship provisions of the INA are also worded in terms of residence rather than physical presence. See § 5:8.

[2]See generally § 4:59.

[3]INA § 101(a)(33) [8 U.S.C.A. § 1101(a)(33). For the definition under the 1940 Act, see §§ 4:35 to 4:47.

[4]INA § 101(a)(33) [8 U.S.C.A. § 1101(a)(33)]. For a discussion of the meaning of residence under the INA, see Ch 7.

[Section 4:59]

[1]INA § 301(d), (e), (g), 8 U.S.C.A. § 1401(d), (e), (g) as amended by sec. 3, Act of October 10, 1978; INA § 301(b), 8 U.S.C.A. § 1401(b) as originally enacted by Act of June 27, 1952.

[2]INS Interp. 301.1(b)(5)(iv), (6)(ii); 7 FAM 1133.3-4(a)(1) ("the Department holds that [physical presence] means actual bodily presence").

[3]Matter of Bustillos-Ruiz, 10 I. & N. Dec. 60 (B.I.A. 1962); INS Interp. 301.1(b)(6)(ii).

[4]7 FAM 1133.3-4(a)(1).

sions both before and after being naturalized, regardless of their status.[5] Time spent in the United States illegally is also counted as physical presence.[6] Residents of Canada and Mexico who commute daily to school or work in the United States may count the time they spend in the United States each day toward the physical presence requirement.[7] Conversely, absences, no matter how short, from the United States and its outlying possessions cannot be counted as U.S. physical presence even if a U.S. residence is maintained, unless the absence is required for U.S. military service, employment with the U.S. government or an international organization listed in 22 U.S.C.A. § 288, or, under certain circumstances, such service or employment by a parent.

§ 4:60 When physical presence is "continuous"

Several provisions of the INA — notably, provisions relating to children of a U.S. citizen and a noncitizen national and children of U.S. citizens born in outlying possessions, but also children of unwed mothers — require proof that physical presence was "continuous" at some point prior to the child's birth.[1] Continuous physical presence is also required by the retention requirements that apply to children of one citizen and one noncitizen parent, both as originally enacted and under the 1972 amendment.[2]

As originally interpreted, any absence was interpreted to break the continuity of the physical presence required under the INA.[3] However, after the BIA interpreted similar statutory language to permit brief, casual, and innocent departures, the then-INS amended its interpretation to provide that brief departures were not inconsistent with continuous physical presence.[4] However, in *INS v. Phinpathya*, the Supreme Court ultimately rejected the Board's interpretation of similar language in the Suspension statute.[5] The Board then held that the INS Interpretations had been effectively overruled.[6] Interestingly, Congress acted statutorily to overrule the Supreme Court's decision in *Phinpathya*;[7] but the text of its amendment was limited to the direct context in which the *Phinpathya* interpretation had been reached. While no court has ever held that this language expressed a more general will regarding the interpretation of the "continuity" of "physical presence," it is clear that Congress wished to abrogate *Phinpathya*,[8] and it would be somewhat odd to ap-

---

[5]7 FAM 1133.3-4(a)(2).

[6]7 FAM 1133.3-4(a)(2).

[7]7 FAM 1133.3-4(a)(3).

[Section 4:60]

[1]INA § 301(d), (e) [8 U.S.C.A. § 1401(d), (e)]; INA § 309(c) [8 U.S.C.A. § 1409].

[2]INA § 301(b) [8 U.S.C.A. § 1401(b)] as originally enacted by Act of June 27, 1952 reproduced as Appendix 4-14; Act of October 27, 1972 reproduced as Appendix 4-17.

[3]Matter of A-, 7 I. & N. Dec. 710 (Comm. 1958).

[4]INS Interp.316.1(c)(3).

[5]INS v. Phinpathya, 464 U.S. 183, 104 S. Ct. 584 (1984).

[6]See Matter of Copeland, 19 I. & N. Dec. 788 (Comm'r 1988); Matter of Graves, 19 I. & N. Dec. 337 (Comm'r 1985). Cf. Ch 7 §§ 7:7 to 7:9.

[7]Immigration Reform and Control Act ("the Act"), Pub.L. No. 99-603, 100 Stat. 3359 (1986), codified at INA § 244(b)(2) [8 U.S.C.A § 1254(b)(2)] (repealed).

[8]For legislative history, see H.R.Rep. No. 3810, 99th Cong., 2nd Sess. at 78, reprinted in 1986 U.S. Code Cong. & Admin. News 5649, 5682; see also 130 Cong. Rec. H16,348 (June 14, 1984) (Rep.

ply the Phinpathya holding in other portions of the INA where Congress had so clearly expressed its disagreement with that interpretation.

One statutory exception to the continuity requirements relates to the retention requirements. Congress amended the statute in 1957 to provide that absences of less than 12 months would not break the continuity of the physical presence requirement for purposes of the five-year retention requirement.[9] This amendment applies retroactively.[10] The 12 months of permissible absences are counted in the aggregate.[11] Thus, a commuter laborer who worked in the United States but slept in Mexico during part of the period for which the retention requirement applied was found to have satisfied the continuous physical presence requirement because adding up the hours of the days in which he was absent from the United States, they did not add up to 12 months.[12] Since the retention condition did not relate to "residence," the fact that he was domiciled in Mexico did not bar him from fulfilling the U.S. physical presence requirement.[13]

In computing the physical presence for purposes of the retention requirement, the DHS takes the position that permissible absences—i.e. absences that in the aggregate are less than twelve months—are counted as if the person were constructively present in the United States.[14] Thus, for example, to satisfy the five-year requirement, the person only needs to prove physical presence for four years and one day.[15] In addition, the period before the person learns that he or she has a claim to U.S. citizenship after turning 23 for purposes of the five-year requirement, or 26 for purposes of the two-year requirement, is also constructively counted as physical presence in the United States.[16]

§ 4:61 Residence and physical presence under INA—Residence and physical presence in Philippines, other possessions, and extensions of U.S. territory

Research References

Steel on Immigration Law §§ 14:40, 15:3

Residence and physical presence in the Philippines after April 10, 1899 and before July 4, 1946 may be used to satisfy the residence or physical presence require-

---

Roybal expressing "the intent of Congress that the requirement [of continuous physical presence] not be literally or strictly construed in light of the recent Supreme Court opinion that did so. The practical result of the Supreme Court's opinion is to nullify the suspension of deportation provision, a result Congress could not have intended."). The Ninth Circuit decided to apply the new statute retroactively, after examining Congressional intent and finding an intention of overruling the Supreme Court's decision. DeGurules v. I.N.S., 833 F.2d 861 (9th Cir. 1987).

[9]Sec. 16, Act of Sept. 11, 1957, Pub. L. 85-316, 71 Stat. 644 reproduced as Appendix 4-16, subsequently repealed by sec. 2, Act of Oct. 27, 1972 reproduced as Appendix 4-17.

[10]See Rogers v. Bellei, 401 U.S. 815, 825, 91 S. Ct. 1060, 1066, 28 L. Ed. 2d 499 (1971).

[11]Matter of Flores-Maldonado, 10 I. & N. Dec. 22, 26 (B.I.A. 1962).

[12]Matter of Flores-Maldonado, 10 I. & N. Dec. 22, 26 (B.I.A. 1962).

[13]Matter of Flores-Maldonado, 10 I. & N. Dec. 22, 24–25 (B.I.A. 1962); Matter of Bustillos-Ruiz, 10 I. & N. Dec. 60, 64, 1962 WL 12905 (B.I.A. 1962).

[14]INS Interp. 301.1(b)(6)(iv), (v).

[15]INS Interp. 301.1(b)(6)(iv).

[16]See §§ 4:32 to 4:50 (discussion of constructive physical presence).

ments of the INA.[1] Similarly, residence or physical presence in the other outlying possessions of the United States (except for the Panama Canal Zone) prior to December 24, 1952 may be used to satisfy the residence and physical presence of the INA.[2] However, the State Department considers that after December 24, 1952, only residence or physical presence in the continental United States, Alaska, Hawaii, Puerto Rico, Guam, and the Virgin Islands of the United States satisfies the physical presence and residence requirements.[3] The State Department specifically holds that time spent in the Trust Territories as not counting toward either requirement.[4] However, given the Ninth Circuit's decision in *Sabangan v. Powell*,[5] it would appear that residence in the Northern Marianas Islands would now likely be considered part of the United States, and therefore sufficient for residence and physical presence requirements in the statute.

Time spent in territorial waters within three nautical miles of the United States will be counted as physical presence in the United States; but time spent on a U.S.-registered ship outside U.S. waters cannot be counted as physical presence in the United States.[6]

§ 4:62 Residence and physical presence under INA—Constructive physical presence

The principles of constructive residence and physical presence described above also apply to the provisions of the INA.[1] Thus, in general, courts have refused to apply constructive physical presence to satisfy the period required of the parent prior to the birth of the child.[2] However, when the parent was prevented from entering the United States by a government official's erroneous interpretation of the law, constructive physical presence is applied.[3]

Constructive physical presence in the context of retention requirements is more loosely applied. Thus, persons who did not know they were U.S. citizens until they were over the age of 26 years were not divested of their citizenship until they had a

---

[Section 4:61]

[1]Matter of V-, 9 I. & N. Dec. 558 (Reg. Comm'r) approved (Ass't Comm'r 1962); Matter of Y-, 7 I. & N. Dec. 667; 7 FAM 1133.3-4(b)(1). However, such physical presence is not residence or physical presence in the United States for purposes of the special provisions of the INA, which required presence to be in the United States and not in its outlying possessions. Petition of Garces, 192 F.Supp. 439, 400 (N.D.Cal. 1961) (relating to naturalization under the provisions for service in the U.S. armed forces, see Ch 12).

[2]7 FAM 1133.3-4(b)(1). For a discussion of the meaning of the United States at different periods of U.S. history, see §§ 2:8 to 2:14.

[3]7 FAM 1133.3-4(b)(2).

[4]7 FAM 1133.3-4(c).

[5]Sabangan v. Powell, 375 F.3d 818 (9th Cir. 2004).

[6]7 FAM 1133.3-4(d), (e).

[Section 4:62]

[1]See §§ 4:32 to 4:50.

[2]See Drozd v. I.N.S., 155 F.3d 81, 85–88 (2d Cir.1998); Tullius v. Albright, 240 F.3d 1317 (11th Cir. 2001).

[3]Matter of Navarrete, 12 I. & N. Dec. 138.

reasonable opportunity to come to the United States after learning of their citizenship.[4]

The principle of constructive physical presence also applies to the provision governing birth abroad of children born out-of-wedlock to U.S. citizen mothers.[5]

§ 4:63 Children born out-of-wedlock

Research References

Dizon and Wettstein, Immigration Law Service 2d §§ 14:51, 14:55

Children born out-of-wedlock abroad to a U.S. citizen mother after December 24, 1952 are U.S. citizens at birth if the mother was continuously physically present in the United States or one of its outlying possessions for a period of one year at any time prior to the birth of the child.[1]

Children born out-of-wedlock abroad to U.S. citizen fathers during this period acquired U.S. citizenship at birth if paternity of the child was established by legitimation before the child turned 21.[2] There is somewhat of a contradiction between this requirement that the child must have been legitimated before the age of 21 and the requirement in the definition of child for purposes of nationality which mandates the child to be legitimated before the age of 16.[3] Apparently based on this contradiction, the DHS takes the position that the general definition of child does not apply to citizenship at birth to children born out-of-wedlock abroad.[4] Thus if the child is legitimated before 21, even though legitimated after the age of 16 and not in the legal custody of the legitimating father, the child will be recognized as U.S. citizen born abroad.[5]

The DHS will also require the child to have been legitimated under the law of the father's domicile.[6] This is significant because the general provision relating to children allows legitimation for citizenship purposes to occur under the laws of either the child's or the father's domicile.[7] However, the DHS applies the general definition of child for citizenship purposes to impose a requirement that children must be

---

[4]INS Interp. 301.1(b)(6)(ii). See §§ 4:32 to 4:50 (discussing constructive physical presence more fully).

[5]Matter of Navarrete, 12 I. & N. Dec. 138.

[Section 4:63]

[1]INA § 309(c), 8 U.S.C.A. § 1409(c).

[2]INA § 309(a), 8 U.S.C.A. § 1409(a) as originally enacted by Act of June 27, 1952 reproduced as Appendix 4-14. For a discussion of the BIA's interpretation of the legitimation laws of the different countries and states of the U.S. at different periods of time and the State Department's recent interpretation of state laws, See Appendix 4-25.

[3]Compare INA § 309(a), 8 U.S.C.A. § 1409(a) as originally enacted by Act of June 27, 1952 reproduced as Appendix 4-14 with INA § 101(c)(1), 8 U.S.C.A. § 1101(c)(1).

[4]INS Interp. 309.1(b)(2)(i).

[5]INS Interp. 309.1(b)(2)(i). The exemption from the legal custody requirement is less significant than it may, at first impression appear, as it has been interpreted that unless local law specifically divests the father of custody, all children are assumed to be in the custody of both natural parents. Matter of Rivers, 17 I. & N. Dec. 419, 421 (B.I.A. 1980).

[6]INS Interp. 309.1(b)(2)(i).

[7]INA § 101(c)(1), 8 U.S.C.A. § 1101(c)(1).

legitimated while unmarried to obtain the benefits of U.S. citizenship at birth abroad.[8]

As opposed to the DHS, the State Department correctly takes the position that legitimation can take place under the laws of either the father's or the child's place of residence.[9] In addition, the State Department considers adoption by the natural father to be legitimation regardless of the law of the jurisdiction.[10]

The requirements that applied to children born out-of-wedlock to U.S. citizen fathers were amended in 1986.[11] Those requirements are discussed in detail below.[12] Children who were under 18 on November 14, 1986 and who had not been legitimated before that date would only qualify as U.S. citizens born abroad if they fulfilled the new requirements of INA § 309 as amended.[13] An exception was made for children who on November 14, 1986 were between the ages of fifteen and eighteen. Those children could choose to have either the pre- or post-amendment provisions apply to them.[14]

The Supreme Court has upheld a gender-based requirement that citizen fathers cannot pass on citizenship unless they comply with a statute requiring them to legitimate and promise to support their children born abroad, while those children are under age 18.[15] The Supreme Court found those requirements related to biological differences between men and women.[16] However, gender-based distinctions that do not directly relate to biology might not fare so well; in 2011, the Supreme Court split 4-4 in considering the constitutionality of provisions requiring 10 years of physical presence for an unmarried father to convey citizenship, but only one year of continuous physical presence for an unmarried mother to do so.[17] Because the Court split 4-4 in *Flores-Villar*, with Justice Kagan recused, it issued no decision, and the issue has not been resolved. The Supreme Court's even split leaves the Ninth Circuit's case law in place, but suggests that a challenge along these lines might well succeed.

---

[8]INS Interp. 309.1(b)(i). The DHS also has an interpretation of the California law of legitimation that is contrary to that which has been established by the courts. Compare INS Interp. 309.1(b)(ii) with Kaliski v. District Director, 620 F.2d 214 (9th Cir. 1980). See generally, Levy, The Family in Immigration and Nationality Law: Part I, 92-9 Immigration Briefings 10 (1992).

[9]7 FAM 1133.4-3(a)(1). See also, Alexander v. I.N.S., 1997 WL 97114 (D. Me. 1997) (dicta).

[10]7 FAM 1133.4-3(c)(7)(b).

[11]Sec. 9(r), The Immigration Technical Corrections Act of 1988 reproduced as Appendix 4-19B (adding a new section 23(e) to the Immigration and Nationality Amendments of 1986); sec. 13(b), Act of November 14, 1986 reproduced as Appendix 4-19A amending INA § 309(a), 8 U.S.C.A. § 1409(a). For a discussion of the effective date of the 1988 Act, see § 4:66.

[12]See § 4:70.

[13]Sec. 23(e)(1), (2), Immigration and Nationality Amendments of 1986 as added by sec. 9(r), The Immigration Technical Corrections Act of 1988 reproduced as Appendix 4-19B.

[14]Sec. 23(e)(3), Immigration and Nationality Amendments of 1986 as added by sec. 9(r), The Immigration Technical Corrections Act of 1988 reproduced as Appendix 4-19B.

[15]Nguyen v. I.N.S., 533 U.S. 53, 121 S. Ct. 2053, 150 L. Ed. 2d 115 (U.S. 2001).

[16]Nguyen v. I.N.S., 533 U.S. 53, 121 S. Ct. 2053, 150 L. Ed. 2d 115 (U.S. 2001) (because male unmarried parents might not know of child or have connection to child, Court upheld additional requirements at INA § 309 for unmarried fathers).

[17]Flores-Villar v. U.S., 131 S.Ct. 2312 (2011).

VI. PERSONS BORN ABROAD ON OR AFTER NOVEMBER 14, 1986

§ 4:64 When neither parent is a noncitizen

The rules applicable to children born abroad when both parents are U.S. citizens or when one parent is a citizen and the other a noncitizen national have not been amended since the original enactment of the INA: (1) a child born abroad to two U.S. citizens acquires citizenship when one parent has resided in the U.S. and made the U.S. a place of general abode; (2) a child born to one citizen parent and one national is a citizen at birth if the citizen parent had been physically present in the United States or one of its outlying possessions for a continuous period of one year prior to the birth of the child; or (3) the same one year continuous physical presence rule applies to a child born in an outlying possession to a U.S. citizen.[1] There are no retention requirements applicable to any of these children.[2]

§ 4:65 Child has one noncitizen parent

A child born on or after November 14, 1986 to one citizen parent and one noncitizen parent acquires citizenship if the citizen parent was physically present in the U.S. for five years, at least two of which occurred after the citizen parent was 14 years of age.[1] There are no retention requirements for the child.[2]

§ 4:66 Children born out-of-wedlock

Research References

Dizon and Wettstein, Immigration Law Service 2d § 14:51

A significant legal change affects children who born after November 14, 1986.[1] The new provisions do not particularly affect children born out-of-wedlock to a U.S. citizen mother who was physically present in the U.S. for a continuous period of one year prior to the birth of the child; such children continue to acquire citizenship.[2]

However, the law of 1986 introduced drastic changes to the acquisition of citizenship at birth by children born to U.S. citizen fathers who were unmarried.[3] Under the current provisions, a child born out-of-wedlock acquires citizenship at birth if: (1) a blood relationship between the child and the father is established by clear and convincing evidence; (2) the father had the nationality of the United States at the

---

[Section 4:64]

[1]INA § 301(c), (d), (e), 8 U.S.C.A. § 1401(c), (d), (e) as redesignated by sec. 3, Act of October 10, 1978 reproduced as Appendix 4-18.

[2]INA § 301(c), (d), (e), 8 U.S.C.A. § 1401(c), (d), (e) as redesignated by sec. 3, Act of October 10, 1978 reproduced as Appendix 4-18.

[Section 4:65]

[1]INA § 301(g), 8 U.S.C.A. § 1401(g), limited by technical amendment Pub. L. 100-525 (1988).

[2]INA § 301, 8 U.S.C.A. § 1401 as amended by sec. 1, Act of October 10, 1978 reproduced as Appendix 4-18.

[Section 4:66]

[1]Sec. 9(r), The Immigration Technical Corrections Act of 1988, reproduced as Appendix 5-2 (adding a new section 23(d) to the Immigration and Nationality Amendments of 1986).

[2]INA § 301(c), 8 U.S.C.A. § 1401(c).

[3]See sec. 13(b), Act of November 14, 1986 reproduced as Appendix 4-19A amending INA § 309(a), 8 U.S.C.A. § 1409(a).

time of the child's birth; (3) the father unless deceased has agreed in writing to provide financial support until the child reaches the age of 18 years; and (4) while the child is under the age of 18 years, (a) the child is legitimated under the law of the child's residence or domicile; or (b) the father acknowledges paternity of the child in writing under oath; or (c) the paternity of the child is established by adjudication of a competent court.[4]

The new legitimation provisions are not retroactive. The provisions apply to children who had not attained 18 years as of November 14, 1986.[5] However, if the individual had been legitimated before the date of enactment even if the individual was under the age of 18, the old rule applied.[6] An individual who was at least fifteen years old but less than 18 on November 14, 1986, could elect whether to have the old or the new rule apply to him or her.[7]

There is some controversy as to whether the 1988 technical corrections provide that the effective date of the legitimation requirements introduced in 1986 is November 14, 1986 or October 24, 1988. The text of the 1988 technical corrections amends the 1986 Act to provide that the applicability of the amendments to section 309 of the INA will be effective for individuals under the age of 18 years on the "date of enactment of this Act" with a further provision that those between the ages of 15 and 18 at the time of enactment of the act could elect to have the old law apply to them.[8] In the 1988 technical corrections, the effective date of all the other provisions of the 1986 amendments is specifically designated as November 14, 1986.[9] By a cannon of statutory construction, if Congress meant November 14, 1986 when it referred to the "effective date of this Act," it would not have specifically designated that date on all the other subsections of the 1988 amendment. On the other hand, the dates in the 1988 technical corrections were included as an amendment to the 1986 Act, and both 8 U.S.C.A. and the Immigration and Nationality Act published by the U.S. printing office, interpret this to make the phrase "this Act" to refer to the 1986 amendments.[10] This handbook follows that interpretation with the caveat that there is a plausible argument that the effective date of the amendments to INA § 309 is October 24, 1988.

The Supreme Court has found that gender-specific provisions distinguishing between children born out-of-wedlock to U.S citizen men and those born to U.S. citizen women do not violate equal protection guarantees.[11]

---

[4]INA § 309(a), 8 U.S.C.A. § 1409(a).

[5]Sec. 9(r), The Immigration Technical Corrections Act of 1988 reproduced as Appendix 4-19B (adding a new section 23(e) to the Immigration and Nationality Amendments of 1986).

[6]Sec. 9(r), The Immigration Technical Corrections Act of 1988 reproduced as Appendix 4-19B (adding a new section 23(e) to the Immigration and Nationality Amendments of 1986).

[7]Sec. 9(r), The Immigration Technical Corrections Act of 1988 reproduced as Appendix 4-19B (adding a new section 23(e) to the Immigration and Nationality Amendments of 1986).

[8]Sec. 23(e) to the Immigration and Nationality Amendments of 1986 as added by sec. 9(r), The Immigration Technical Corrections Act of 1988 reproduced as Appendix 4-19B.

[9]See sec. 23(a), (b), (c), (d), (f), (g), (h) to the Immigration and Nationality Amendments of 1986 as added by sec. 9(r), The Immigration Technical Corrections Act of 1988 reproduced as Appendix 4-19B.

[10]Historical and Statutory Notes, Effective Date of 1988 Amendment; INA § 309, note.

[11]Tuan Anh Nguyen v. I.N.S., 121 S. Ct. 2053, 150 L. Ed. 2d 115 (U.S. 2001). See § 4:14.

VII. SPECIAL CASES

§ 4:67 Children born to U.S. citizens in Panama Canal Zone

Research References

Steel on Immigration Law § 15:3

The Republic of Panama leased the Canal Zone to the United States "in perpetuity" by the Isthmian Canal Convention of 1904.[1] On August 4, 1937, Congress passed an act declaring that children born to U.S. citizens on the Canal Zone on or after February 26, 1904 were U.S. citizens.[2] If the child was born before August 4, 1937, U.S. citizenship vested on August 4, 1937.[3] If the child was born after that date, citizenship vested at birth.[4] The Nationality Act of 1940 and the INA recodified the provisions of the 1937 Act.[5] Even though the INA was never amended, no child born after October 1, 1979 can take advantage of this provision because the Panama Canal Zone ceased to exist on that date.[6] Section 303(a) speaks only of "fathers," "mothers," and the "person" who is born; it does not refer to a "child," or contain any express requirement that the child have been legitimated by an unwed father in order for citizenship to pass. Thus, the Fourth Circuit has held that legitimation by a U.S. citizen father is not required under this section, agreeing with the Second Circuit with regard to similar language in 303(b).[7]

§ 4:68 Children born to U.S. citizens in Republic of Panama

Research References

Steel on Immigration Law § 15:3

Children born in the Republic of Panama to a U.S. citizen who was employed by the government of the United States, the Panama Railroad Company, or its successor in title had the same rights as a child born in the Canal Zone.[1] Unlike the provision relating to birth in the Canal Zone, this provision did not cease to be effective on October 1, 1979.[2] On the contrary, the 1979 treaty expanded the applicability of the provision relating to birth in the Republic of Panama, by including the area

---

[Section 4:67]

[1]Art 2, Isthmian Canal Convention, United States and Panama, November 18, 1903, proclaimed February 26, 1904, 33 Stat. 2234, TS 431, 2 Malloy 1349, 10 Bevans 663 reproduced as Appendix 2-8, to Ch 2.

[2]Act of August 4, 1937, Pub.L. 75-242, 50 Stat. 558 reproduced as Appendix 4-20.

[3]INS Interp. 303.1(a).

[4]INS Interp. 303.1(a).

[5]Sec. 203(a), Nationality Act of 1940 reproduced as Appendix 4-12; INA § 303(a), 8 U.S.C.A. § 1403(a).

[6]INS Interp. 303.1(a).

[7]U.S. v. Thompson-Riviere, 561 F.3d 345, 355–56 (4th Cir. 2009); United States v. Connolly, 552 F.3d 86, 90–91 (2nd Cir.2008) (interpreting INA § 303(b)).

[Section 4:68]

[1]Act of August 4, 1937, reproduced as Appendix 4-20; sec. 203(b), Nationality Act of 1940 reproduced as Appendix 4-12; INA § 303(b), 8 U.S.C.A. § 1403(b).

[2]INS Interp. 303.1(b)(1).

formerly known as the Canal Zone as part of the Republic of Panama.[3] The legacy INS further accepted that the current Panama Canal Commission is the successor in title to the Panama Railroad Company and the Panama Canal Company.[4] Section 303(b) speaks only of "fathers," "mothers," and the "person" who is born; it does not refer to a "child," or contain any express requirement that the child have been legitimated by an unwed father in order for citizenship to pass. Thus, the Second Circuit has held that legitimation by a U.S. citizen father is not required under this section; the Fourth Circuit has found that interpretation persuasive in interpreting § 303(a).[5]

§ 4:69   Children born out-of-wedlock in Republic of Panama or Canal Zone

Neither the Canal Zone nor the Republic of Panama provisions has ever had a restriction limiting citizenship by descent to legitimate children.[1] Furthermore, the provisions of the Act of 1940 and the INA restricting the rights of out-of-wedlock children were inapplicable to the sections regarding birth in the Canal Zone and the Republic of Panama.[2] In addition, the DHS takes the position that since the provisions relating to the Canal Zone and the Republic of Panama are expressed in terms of "fathers" and "persons," the general definition of "child" for purposes of nationality law of the INA is inapplicable to those provisions.[3]

The DHS argues that a child must have been legitimated under the law of the father's domicile, possibly even after the child's attainment of maturity, in order to obtain the benefits of acquisition of U.S. citizenship in the Canal Zone and the Republic of Panama.[4] The DHS relies on interpretations of citizenship by descent prior to the passage of the 1940 Act.[5] It is unclear whether the DHS will be allowed to impose such a restriction on a statutory scheme that is otherwise silent regarding legitimacy status of the child.

Complicating the situation even further, in 1946 the Constitution of the Republic of Panama eliminated the distinction between legitimate and out-of-wedlock children.[6] Thus, all children are born legitimate and have a right to be acknowledged by their fathers.[7] Contrary to the DHS position, acknowledgment by the fathers

---

[3]INS Interp. 303.1(b)(1) (the treaty transferred sovereignty over the Canal Zone back to the Republic of Panama).

[4]INS Interp. 303.1(b)(1).

[5]United States v. Connolly, 552 F.3d 86, 90–91 (2nd Cir.2008); U.S. v. Thompson-Riviere, 561 F.3d 345, 355–56 (4th Cir. 2009) (interpreting INA § 303(a)).

[Section 4:69]

[1]Act of August 4, 1937 reproduced as Appendix 4-20; sec. 203(b), Nationality Act of 1940 reproduced as Appendix 4-12; INA § 303(b), 8 U.S.C.A. § 1403(b).

[2]Sec. 102(h), Nationality Act of 1940 reproduced as Appendix 4-12 (applies only to Title III on the 1940 Act); INA § 309(a), 8 U.S.C.A. § 1409(a) (applies only to some provisions of sections 301 and 308 of the INA).

[3]INS Interp. 303.1(b)(2).

[4]INS Interp. 303.1(b)(2).

[5]INS Interp. 303.1(b)(2).

[6]INS Interp. 303.1(b)(3)(ii).

[7]Matter of Sinclair, 13 I. & N. Dec. 613, 614 n. 2 (B.I.A. 1970).

does not legitimate the children retroactive to birth.[8] Children in the Republic of Panama are *legitimate* from birth rather than being retroactively legitimated.[9]

Therefore, regardless of whether the DHS can succeed in convincing a court that the distinction between legitimate and out-of-wedlock children should be applied to the provisions relating to birth in Panama, the issue of legitimacy should not properly arise for any person born after March 2, 1946, the effective date of the legitimacy provision of the Panamanian Constitution.[10]

§4:70 Children born to U.S. citizens in outlying possessions of U.S

Since 1934, there has been differential treatment of children born abroad to one citizen parent and to those born to two citizen parents.[1] Between 1934 and 1940, children born to one citizen parent in one of the outlying possessions were not given special consideration under the law. These children had to comply with the retention requirements imposed by law on children born abroad to one U.S. citizen parent.[2]

The 1940 Act introduced a new provision, which in effect treated children born in an outlying possession of the U.S. to one U.S. citizen parent as if they were born to two citizen parents.[3] These children would be U.S. citizens at birth if the U.S. citizen parent resided in the United States or in any of its outlying possessions at any point prior to the birth of the child.[4]

The INA also included a special provision relating to children born in an outlying possession to a U.S. citizen. Under that provision, the child will be a U.S. citizen at birth if the U.S. citizen parent had been continuously physically present in the United States or one of its outlying possessions for a period of one year at any time prior to the child's birth.[5] This provision also governs birth in an outlying possession after November 14, 1986.[6]

§4:71 Surrogate mothers and in vitro fertilization

Advances in medical technology have led to various medical possibilities which for citizenship purposes must be fit within the existing law.

Where a foreign surrogate mother is also the biological mother (i.e., the source of

---

[8]See INS Interp. 303.1(b)(3)(ii) (also describing what it considers sufficient acknowledgment to establish legitimation under Panamanian law).

[9]See Matter of Sinclair, 13 I. & N. Dec. 613, 615, 1970 WL 18749 (B.I.A. 1970). Cf. Matter of Pavlovic, 17 I. & N. Dec. 407 (B.I.A. 1980) (under a similar provision in the Yugoslavian Constitution, the BIA held specifically that natural child is legitimate at birth, not legitimated; subsequent acknowledgment only establishes the identity of the father). On November 15, 1995, President Clinton signed into law a bill changing the definition of child for immigration purposes. Act of November 15, 1995, Pub.L. 104-51. Even though that law radically diminished the immigration rights of children born out-of-wedlock in countries that abolished the distinction between legitimate and out-of-wedlock children, it did not affect their nationality rights.

[10]Matter of Sinclair, 13 I. & N. Dec. 613, 615, 1970 WL 18749 (B.I.A. 1970).

[Section 4:70]

[1]See §§ 4:22 to 4:23.

[2]See §§ 4:22 to 4:31.

[3]Sec. 201(2), Nationality Act of 1940 reproduced as Appendix 4-12.

[4]Sec. 201(2), Nationality Act of 1940 reproduced as Appendix 4-12. See generally §§ 4:32 to 4:50.

[5]INA § 301(e), 8 U.S.C.A. § 1401(e). See generally § 4:63.

[6]See § 4:65.

the egg), the FAM would treat the birth as a birth out-of-wedlock to a citizen father.[1] The FAM calls for certification by medical authorities of the facts and circumstances surrounding the entire insemination procedure, including hospital records from the facility where the sperm donation was made, an affidavit from the doctor who performed the operation, and possibly blood tests.[2]

Where a foreign surrogate mother is not the biological mother (i.e., she was not the source of the egg), the FAM would treat the birth as an out-of-wedlock birth to the U.S. citizen mother or as the child of two U.S. citizen parents.[3] In keeping with the government's view of acquisition cases turning on biology, the FAM would find the status of the surrogate mother "immaterial."[4]

Of course, advanced reproductive techniques may also be used by individuals not in marital relationships. The rules appear straightforward when applied to a U.S. citizen woman who conceives through artificial insemination; such a child would be conceived out-of-wedlock, and the relaxed rules for acquisition of citizenship would apply.[5] Where a biological (sperm donor) father is an American male and the recipient of that insemination is a non-citizen female, the scenario appears more complicated; it appears that the child would be treated as the out-of-wedlock offspring of that U.S. citizen man.[6] That would trigger the enhanced requirements for out-of-wedlock children of U.S. citizen men, and in the anonymous donor context, it would be very unusual for the father to actually meet those requirements.[7]

In the in vitro context, it is possible for a child to be born well after the death of the father and /or the mother.[8] For purposes of the citizenship laws, Congress has defined "[t]he terms 'parent', 'father', and 'mother' [to] include in the case of a posthumous child a deceased parent, father, and mother."[9] While Congress likely did not enact this provision with in vitro fertilization in mind, the statute appears to freeze in place (no pun intended) parental status, no matter how long the parent is deceased before the birth of the child.[10]

Moreover, while Congress generally requires a father to agree in writing to provide

---

[Section 4:71]

[1]7 FAM 1131.4-2(a).

[2]7 FAM 1131.4-2(a).

[3]7 FAM 1131.4-2(b).

[4]7 FAM 1131.4-2(c).

[5]See generally § 4:63.

[6]7 FAM 1131.4-2(a).

[7]It is however not impossible to conceive of situations where acquisition would in fact occur. The first two criteria for an out-of-wedlock father (a blood relation and U.S. citizenship) would commonly be met in this scenario. INA § 309(a)(1) to (2), 8 U.S.C.A. § 1409(a)(1) to (2). Where a child is domiciled in a place which has abolished all distinctions between legitimacy and illegitimacy, that would function as legitimation of the child. INA § 309(a)(4), 8 U.S.C.A. § 1409(a)(4); see generally § 4:9. The only remaining requirement would be the promise to support the child until age 18; and the father is excused from that requirement if they are deceased. INA § 309(a)(3), 8 U.S.C.A. § 1409(a)(3).

[8]See, e.g., Astrue v. Capato ex rel. B.N.C., 132 S. Ct. 2021, 182 L. Ed. 2d 887, 179 Soc. Sec. Rep. Serv. 10, Unempl. Ins. Rep. (CCH) P 14965C (2012) (child conceived 18 months after father's death not eligible to inherit under Florida law).

[9]INA § 101(c)(2), 8 U.S.C.A. § 1101(c)(2).

[10]The INA's approach is different from that of many states in the wills and estates context, where many states impose a time limit on inheritance. See Cal. Prob.Code Ann. § 249.5(c) (West Supp.2012) (allowing inheritance if child is in utero within two years of parent's death); Colo.Rev.Stat. Ann. § 15-11-120(11) (2011) (child in utero within three years or born within 45 months); Iowa Code Ann.

for a child through age 18 in order for the child to acquire citizenship, that provision does not apply if the father is deceased.[11]

Note that for a child to acquire citizenship through the father, if born out-of-wedlock, a child born after 1986 would need to meet one of the requirements of INA § 309(d), i.e., they must be legitimated, paternity must be acknowledged in writing under oath, or paternity must be established by a court.[12] State legitimation laws in the in vitro context are not uniform; in many states, a child conceived in vitro is not considered the legitimate child of the biological father.[13]

VIII. PROOF OF CITIZENSHIP

§ 4:72 Generally

Research References
Steel on Immigration Law § 15:5

Foreign-born individuals who acquire citizenship at birth may obtain proof of their U.S. citizenship by either applying for a certificate of citizenship with the USCIS or by applying for a U.S. passport with the Department of State. Moreover, if the individual acquiring citizenship is abroad and under 18 years of age, she may also request a Consular Report of Birth. All of these application procedures are discussed more fully in Ch 13. By statute, an individual must take an oath of allegiance in order to be issued a certificate of citizenship (though not, it should be noted, a passport).[1]

§ 4:73 Generally—Citizenship upon application by citizen parent

Research References
West's Key Number Digest, Naturalization ⬯62
A.L.R. Index, Immigration and Naturalization
Validity, Construction, and Application of Child Citizenship Act, 194 A.L.R. Fed. 383
Dizon and Wettstein, Immigration Law Service 2d §§ 14:209, 14:211, 14:214
Steel on Immigration Law §§ 15:11, 15:16

This chapter has considered only the question of whether a child has automati-

---

§ 633.220A(1) (West Supp.2012) (child born within two years); La.Rev.Stat. Ann. § 9:391.1(A) (West 2008) (child born within three years); N.D. Cent.Code Ann. § 30.1-04-19(11) (Lexis 2001) (child in utero within three years or born within 45 months). See also Uniform Probate Code § 2-120(k), 8 U.L.A. 58 (Supp.2011) (treating a posthumously conceived child as "in gestation at the individual's death," but only if specified time limits are met). Other states do not treat posthumously conceived offspring as children. See, Fla. Stat. Ann. § 732.106 (West 2010) ("afterborn heirs" are "heirs of the decedent conceived before his or her death, but born thereafter"); Fla. Stat. Ann. § 742.17(4) (West 2010) (posthumously conceived child "shall not be eligible for a claim against the decedent's estate unless the child has been provided for by the decedent's will").

[11]INA § 309(a)(3), 8 U.S.C.A. § 1409(a)(3).

[12]See INA § 309(a)(4), 8 U.S.C.A. § 1409(a)(4).

[13]See, e.g., Cal. Fam.Code Ann. § 7613(b) (West Supp.2012) ("The donor of semen . . . for use in artificial insemination or in vitro fertilization of a woman other than the donor's wife is treated in law as if he were not the natural father of a child thereby conceived, unless otherwise agreed to in a writing signed by the donor and the woman prior to the conception of the child."); Mass. Gen. Laws, ch. 46, § 4B (West 2010) ("Any child born to a married woman as a result of artificial insemination with the consent of her husband, shall be considered the legitimate child of the mother and such husband.").

[Section 4:72]

[1]See INA § 341, 8 U.S.C.A. § 1452; 8 C.F.R. § 341.7.

cally become a citizen at birth. Where a child has not acquired citizenship at birth, the INA permits a citizen parent to apply for a Certificate of Citizenship.[1] These provisions, whose requirements are simpler in many respects, are discussed elsewhere in this book.[2]

[Section 4:73]

[1]See §§ 11:18 to 11:25. Prior to 2001, the terminology would have been different; under pre-2001 law, the U.S. citizen parent applied for naturalization for their child. See § 11:18.

[2]See §§ 11:18 to 11:25.

APPENDIX 4-1

Act of March 26, 1790, 1 Stat. 103

Chap. III.—*An Act to establish an uniform rule of Naturalization.*

Section 1. *Be it enacted by the Senate and House of Representatives of the United States of America in Congress assembled,* That any alien, being a free white person, who shall reside within the limits and under the jurisdiction of the United States for the term of two years, may be admitted to become a citizen thereof, on the application to any common law court of record, in any one of the states wherein he shall have resided for the term of one year at least, and making proof to the satisfaction of such court, that he is a person of good moral character and taking the oath or affirmation prescribed by law, to support the Constitution of the United States, which oath or affirmation such court shall administer; and the clerk of such court shall record such application, and the proceedings thereon; and thereupon such person shall be considered as a citizen of the United States. And the children of such person so naturalized, dwelling within the United States, being under the age of twenty-one years at the time of such naturalization, shall also be considered as citizens of the United States. And the children of citizens of the United States, that may be born beyond sea, or out of the limits of the United States, shall be considered as natural born citizens: *Provided,* That the right of citizenship shall not descend to persons whose fathers have never been resident in the United States: *Provided also,* That no person heretofore proscribed by any state shall be admitted a citizen as aforesaid, except by an act of the legislature of the state in which such person was proscribed.

APPENDIX 4-2

Act of January 29, 1795, 1 Stat. 414

Chap. XX—*An Act to establish a uniform rule of Naturalization; and to repeal the act heretofore passed on that subject.*

For carrying into complete effect, the power given by the Constitution, to establish an uniform rule of naturalization throughout the United States:

Section 1. *Be it enacted by the Senate and House of Representatives of the United States of America in Congress assembled,* That any alien, being a free white person, may be admitted to become a citizen of the United States, or any of them, on the following conditions, and not otherwise:—

First. He shall declare on oath or affirmation, before the supreme, superior, district or circuit court of the states, or of the territories northwest or south of the river Ohio, or a circuit or district of the United States, three years, at least, before his admission, that it was bona fide, his intention to become a citizen of the United States, and to renounce forever all allegiance and fidelity to any foreign prince, potentate, state or sovereignty whatever, and particularly, by name, the prince, potentate, state or sovereignty whereof such alien may, at the time, be a citizen or subject.

Secondly. He shall, at the time of his application to be admitted, declare on oath or affirmation, before some on of the courts aforesaid, that he has resided within the United States, five years at least, and within the state or territory, where such court is at the time held, one year at least; that he will support the Constitution of the United States; and that he doth absolutely and entirely renounce and abjure all allegiance and fidelity to every foreign prince, potentate, state or sovereignty whatever, and particularly by name, the prince, potentate, state or sovereignty, whereof he was before a citizen or subject; which proceedings shall be recorded by the clerk of the court.

Thirdly. The court admitting such alien, shall be satisfied that he has resided within the limits and under the jurisdiction of the United States five years; and it shall further appear to their satisfaction, that during that time, he has behaved as a man of good moral character, attached to the principles of the Constitution of the United States, and well disposed to the good order and happiness of the same.

Forthly. In case the alien applying to be admitted to citizenship shall have borned any hereditary title, or been of any of the orders of nobility, in the kingdom or state from which he came, he shall, in addition to the above requisites, make an express renunciation of his title or order of nobility, in the court to which his application shall be made; which renunciation shall be recorded in the said court.

Sec. 2. *Provided always, and be it further enacted,* That any alien now residing within the limits and under the jurisdiction of the United States, may be admitted to become a citizen, on his declaring on oath or affirmation, in some one of the courts aforesaid, that he has resided two years, at least, within and under the jurisdiction of the same, and one year, at least, within the state or territory where such court is at the time held; that he will support the Constitution of the United States; and that he doth absolutely and entirely renounce and abjure all allegiance and fidelity to any foreign prince, potentate, state or sovereignty whatever, and particularly by name, the prince, potentate, state or sovereignty, whereof he was before a citizen or subject; and moreover on its appearing to the satisfaction of the court, that during the said term of two years, he has behaved as a man of good moral character, attached to the Constitution of the United States, and well disposed to the good order and happiness of the same; and, where the alien applying for admission to citizenship, shall have borned any hereditary title, or been of any of the orders of nobility in the kingdom or state from which he came, on his moreover making in the court an express renunciation of his title or order of nobility, before he shall be entitled to such admission; all of which proceedings, require in this proviso to be performed in the court, shall be recorded by the clerk thereof.

Sec. 3. *And be it further enacted*, That the children of persons duly naturalized dwelling within the United States, and being under the age of twenty-one years, at the time of such naturalization; and the children of citizens of the United States, born out of the limits and jurisdiction of the United States, shall be considered as citizens of the United States: *Provided*, That the right of citizenship shall not descend to persons, whose fathers have never been resident in the United States: *Provided also*, That no person heretofore proscribed by any state, or who has been legally convicted of having joined the army of Great Britain, during the late war, shall be admitted a citizen as aforesaid, without the consent of the legislature of the state, in which such person was proscribed.

Sec. 4. *And be it further enacted*, That the act intituled "An act to establish an uniform rule of naturalization," passed the twenty-sixth day of March, one thousand seven hundred and ninety, be, and the same is hereby repealed.

APPENDIX 4-3

Act of April 14, 1802, 2 Stat. 153[1]

Chap. XXVIII.—*An Act to establish an uniform rule of Naturalization, and to repeal the acts heretofore passed on that Subject.*

Be it enacted by the Senate and House of Representatives of the United States of America in Congress assembled, That any alien, being a free white person, may be admitted to become a citizen of the Untied States or any of time, on the following conditions, and not otherwise:—

First, That he shall have declared, on oath or affirmation, before the supreme, superior, district or circuit courts of some one of the states, or of the territorial district of the United States, or a circuit or district court of the United States, three years at least, before his admission, that it was, bona fide, his intention to become a citizen of the United States, and to renounce for ever all allegiance and fidelity to any foreign prince, potentate, state or sovereignty whatever, and particularly, by name, the prince, potentate, state or sovereignty whereof such alien may, at the time, be a citizen or subject.

Secondly, That he shall, at the time of his application to be admitted, declare on oath or affirmation, before some one of the courts aforesaid, that he will support the Constitution of the United States, and that the doth absolutely and entirely renounce and abjure all allegiance and fidelity to every foreign prince, potentate, state or sovereignty whatever, and particularly, by name, the prince, potentate, state, or sovereignty whereof he was before a citizen or subject; which proceedings shall be recorded by the clerk of the court.

Thirdly, That the court admitting such alien shall be satisfies that he has resided within the United States five years at least, and within the sate or territory where such court is at the time held, one year at least; and it shall further appear to their satisfaction, that during that time, he has behaved as a man of a good moral character, attached to the principles of the Constitution of the United States, and well disposed to the good order and happiness of the same: *Provided*, that the oath of the applicant shall, in no case, be allowed to prove his residence.

Fourthly, That in case the alien, applying to be admitted to citizenship, shall have borne any hereditary title, or been of any of the orders of nobility in the kingdom or state from which he came, he shall, in addition to the above requisites, make an express renunciation of his title or order of nobility in the court to which his application shall be made, which renunciation shall be recorded in the said court:

---

[1]Amended by Act of March 26, 1804, 2 Stat. 292 (providing a special procedure for persons who had resided in U.S. between 1795 and 1802); Act of July 30, 1813, 3 Stat. 53 (special savings clause for those who had not made a declaration by 1812); Act of March 22, 1816, 3 Stat. 258 (requiring the certificate that the person has been in the United States of the 1802 Act to be presented at the naturalization proceedings and to be recited verbatim in the record of naturalization proceedings); Act of May 26, 1824, 4 Stat. 69 (exempting noncitizens who arrived in the U.S. before they were 18 and who have resided since age 18 in the U.S. from the requirement of declaration of intent to become a U.S. citizen; also generally relaxing the formal requirements of the declaration); Act of May 24, 1828, 4 Stat. 310 (repealing the 1816 Amendment—evidence no longer required); reenacted and incorporated into Revised Statutes of 1878 as sec. 2172.

Provided, that no alien who shall be a native citizen, denizen or subject of any country, state or sovereign, with whom the United States shall be at war, at the time of his application, shall be then admitted to be a citizen of the United States: *Provided also*, that any alien who was residing within the limits, and under the jurisdiction of the United States, before the twenty-ninth of January, one thousand seven hundred and ninety-five, maybe admitted to become a citizen, on due proof made to someone of the courts aforesaid, that he has resided two years, at least, within and under the jurisdiction of the United States, and one year, at least, immediately preceding his application, within the state or territory where such court is at the time held; and on his declaring on oath or affirmation, that he will support the Constitution of the United States, and that he doth absolutely and entirely renounce and abjure all allegiance and fidelity to every foreign prince, potentate, state or sovereignty whatever, and particularly, by name, the prince, potentate, state, or sovereignty whereof he was before a citizen or subject: and moreover, on its appearing to the satisfaction of the court, that during the said term of two years, he has behaved as a man of good moral character, attached to the Constitution of the United States, and well disposed to the good order and happiness of the same; and where the alien, applying for admission to citizenship, shall have borne any hereditary title, or been of any of the orders of nobility in the kingdom or state from which he came, on his moreover making in the court an express renunciation of his title or order of nobility, before he shall be entitled to such admission; all of which proceedings shall be recorded by the clerk thereof: and provided also, that any alien who was residing within the limits, and under the jurisdiction of the United States at any time between the said twenty-ninth day of January, one thousand seven hundred and ninety-five, and the eighteenth day of June, one thousand and ninety-eight, may, within two years after the passing of this act, be admitted to become a citizen, without a compliance with the first condition above specified.

Sec. 2, *Provided also, and be it further enacted*, That in addition to the directions aforesaid, all free white persons, being aliens, who may arrive in the United States after the passing of this act, shall, in order to become citizens of the United States, make registry, and obtain certificates, in the following manner, to wit: every person desirous of being naturalized shall, f of the age of twenty-one years, make report of himself; or if under the age of twenty-one years, or held in service, shall be reported by his parent, guardian, master or mistress, to the clerk of the district court of the district where such alien or aliens shall arrive or to some other court of record of the United States, or of either of the territorial districts of the same, or of a particular state; and such report shall ascertain the name, birthplace, age, nation and allegiance of each such alien, together with the country whence he or she migrated, and the place of his or her intended settlement: and it shall be the duty of such clerk, on receiving such report, to record the same in his office, and to grant to the person making such report, and to each individual concerned therein, whenever he shall be required, a certificate under his hand and seal of office of such report and registry; and for receiving and registering each record of an individual family, he shall receive fifty cents; and for each certificate granted pursuant to this act, to an individual or family, fifty cents; and such certificate shall be exhibited to the court by every alien who may arrive in the United States, after the passing of this act, on his application to be naturalized, as evidence of the time of his arrival within the United States.

Sec. 3. *And whereas*, Doubts have arisen whether certain courts of record in some of the states, are included within the description of district or circuit courts: *Be it further enacted*, that every court of record in any individual state, having common law jurisdiction, and a seal and clerk or prothonotary, shall be considered as a district court within the meaning of this act; and every alien who may have been naturalized in any such court, shall enjoy, from and after the passing of the act, the same rights and privileges, as if he had been naturalized in a district or circuit court of the United States.

Sec. 4. *And be it further enacted*, That the children of persons duly naturalized under any of the laws of the United States, or who, previous to the passing of any law on that subject, by the government of the United States, may have become citizens of any one of the said states, under the laws thereof, being under the age of twenty-one years, at the time of their parents being so naturalized or admitted to the rights of citizenship, shall, if dwelling in the United States, be considered as citizens of the United States, and the children of persons who now are, or have been citizens of the United States, shall, though born out of the limits and jurisdiction of the United States, be considered as citizens of the United States: *Provided*, that the right of citizenship shall not descend to persons whose fathers have never resided within the United States: *Provided also*, that no person heretofore proscribed by any state, or who has been legally convicted of having joined the army of Great Britain, during the late war, shall be admitted a citizen, as aforesaid, without the consent of the legislature of the state in which such person was proscribed.

Sec. 5. *And be it further enacted*, That all acts heretofore passed respecting naturalization, be, and the same are hereby repealed.

APPENDIX 4-4

Act of February 10, 1855, 10 Stat. 604

Chap. LXXI.—*An act to secure the Right of Citizenship to Children of Citizens of the United States born out of the Limits thereof.*

Be it enacted by the Senate and House of Representatives of the United States of America in Congress assembled, That persons heretofore born, or hereafter to be born, out of the limits and jurisdiction of the United States, whose fathers were or shall be at the time of their birth citizens of the United States, shall be deemed and considered and are hereby declared to be citizens of the United States: *Provided, however,* That the rights of citizenship shall not descend to persons whose fathers never resided in the United States.

Sec. 2. *And be it further enacted,* That any woman who might lawfully be naturalized under the existing laws, married, or who shall be married to a citizen of the United States, shall be deemed and taken to be a citizen.

APPENDIX 4-5

Revised Statutes of the United States, 1878, Sections 1992–2001, 2165–2174

REVISED STATUTES

OF

THE UNITED STATES,

PASSED AT THE

FIRST SESSION OF THE FORTY-THIRD CONGRESS,

1873-'74;

EMBRACING THE STATUTES OF THE UNITED STATES, GENERAL AND PERMANENT IN
THEIR NATURE, IN FORCE ON THE FIRST DAY OF DECEMBER, ONE THOUSAND
EIGHT HUNDRED AND SEVENTY-THREE, AS REVISED AND CONSOLIDATED
BY COMMISSIONERS APPOINTED UNDER AN ACT OF CONGRESS; AND AS
REPRINTED, WITH AMENDMENTS, UNDER AUTHORITY OF AN ACT OF
CONGRESS APPROVED THE SECOND DAY OF MARCH, IN THE YEAR
ONE THOUSAND EIGHT HUNDRED AND SEVENTY-SEVEN,

WITH

AN APPENDIX.

EDITED, PRINTED, AND PUBLISHED UNDER THE AUTHORITY OF AN ACT OF CONGRESS,
AND UNDER THE DIRECTION OF THE SECRETARY OF STATE.

WASHINGTON:
GOVERNMENT PRINTING OFFICE.
1878.

TITLE XXV.

CITIZENSHIP.

Who are citizens.

9 April, 1866, c. 31, s. 1, v. 14, p. 27.

SEC. 1992. All persons born in the United States and not subject to any foreign power, excluding Indians not taxed, are declared to be citizens of the United States.

Planters' Bank *v.* St. John, 1 Woods, 585; McKay *r.* Campbell, 2 Saw., 118.

Citizenship of children of citizens born abroad.

14 April, 1802, c. 28, s. 4, v. 2, p. 155.
10 Feb., 1855, c. 71, s. 1, v. 10, p. 604.

SEC. 1993. All children heretofore born or hereafter born out of the limits and jurisdiction of the United States, whose fathers were or may be at the time of their birth citizens thereof, are declared to be citizens of the United States; but the rights of citizenship shall not descend to children whose fathers never resided in the United States.

Citizenship of married women.

10 Feb., 1855, c. 71, s. 2, v. 10, p. 604.

SEC. 1994. Any woman who is now or may hereafter be married to a citizen of the United States, and who might herself be lawfully naturalized, shall be deemed a citizen.

—Kelly *v.* Owen, 7 Wall., 496.

Of persons born in Oregon.

18 May, 1872, c. 172, s. 3, v. 17, p. 134.

SEC. 1995. All persons born in the district of country formerly known as the Territory of Oregon, and subject to the jurisdiction of the United States on the 18th May, 1872, are citizens in the same manner as if born elsewhere in the United States.

Rights as citizens forfeited for desertion, &c.

3 Mar., 1865, c. 79, s. 21, v. 13, p. 490.

SEC. 1996. All persons who deserted the military or naval service of the United States and did not return thereto or report themselves to a provost-marshal within sixty days after the issuance of the proclamation by the President, dated the 11th day of March, 1865, are deemed to have voluntarily relinquished and forfeited their rights of citizenship, as well as their right to become citizens; and such deserters shall be forever incapable of holding any office of trust or profit under the United States, or of exercising any rights of citizens thereof.

Certain soldiers and sailors not to incur the forfeitures of the last section.

19 July, 1867, c. 28, v. 15, p. 14.

SEC. 1997. No soldier or sailor, however, who faithfully served according to his enlistment until the 19th day of April, 1865, and who, without proper authority or leave first obtained, quit his command or refused to serve after that date, shall be held to be a deserter from the Army or Navy; but this section shall be construed solely as a removal of any disability such soldier or sailor may have incurred, under the preceding section, by the loss of citizenship and of the right to hold office, in consequence of his desertion.

Avoiding the draft.

3 Mar., 1865, c. 79, s. 21, v. 13, p. 490.

SEC. 1998. Every person who hereafter deserts the military or naval service of the United States, or who, being duly enrolled, departs the jurisdiction of the district in which he is enrolled, or goes beyond the limits of the United States, with intent to avoid any draft into the military or naval service, lawfully ordered, shall be liable to all the penalties and forfeitures of section nineteen hundred and ninety-six.

Right of expatriation declared.

27 July, 1868, c. 249, s. 1, v. 15, p. 223.

SEC. 1999. Whereas the right of expatriation is a natural and inherent right of all people, indispensable to the enjoyment of the rights of life, liberty, and the pursuit of happiness; and whereas in the recognition of this principle this Government has freely received emigrants from all nations, and invested them with the rights of citizenship; and whereas it is claimed that such American citizens, with their descendants, are subjects of foreign states, owing allegiance to the governments thereof; and whereas it is necessary to the maintenance of public peace that this claim of foreign allegiance should be promptly and finally disavowed: Therefore any declaration, instru tion, opinion, order, or decision of any officer of the United States which denies, restricts, impairs, or questions the right of expatriation, is declared inconsistent with the fundamental principles of the Republic.

SEC. 2000. All naturalized citizens of the United States, while in foreign countries, are entitled to and shall receive from this Government the same protection of persons and property which is accorded to native-born citizens.

Protection to naturalized citizens in foreign states.

27 July, 1868, c. 249, s. 2, v. 15, p. 224.

SEC. 2001. Whenever it is made known to the President that any citizen of the United States has been unjustly deprived of his liberty by or under the authority of any foreign government, it shall be the duty of the President forthwith to demand of that government the reasons of such imprisonment; and if it appears to be wrongful and in violation of the rights of American citizenship, the President shall forthwith demand the release of such citizen, and if the release so demanded is unreasonably delayed or refused, the President shall use such means, not amounting to acts of war, as he may think necessary and proper to obtain or effectuate the release; and all the facts and proceedings relative thereto shall as soon as practicable be communicated by the President to Congress.

Release of citizens imprisoned by foreign governments to be demanded.

27 July, 1868, c. 249, s. 3, v. 15, p. 224.

TITLE XXX.

NATURALIZATION.

Aliens, how naturalized.

Declaration of intention.

14 April, 1802, c. 28, ss. 1, 3, v. 2, pp. 153, 155.
26 May, 1824, c. 186, s. 4, v. 4, p. 69.
1 Feb., 1876, c. 5, v. 19, p. 2.—Campbell r. Gordon, 6 Cr., 176; Stark v. Chesapeake Ins. Co., 7 Cr., 420; Chirack r. Chirack, 2 Wh., 259; Osborn r. United States Bank, 9 Wh., 827; Spratt r. Spratt, 4 Pet., 393.

Oath to support the Constitution of the United States.

14 April, 1802, c. 28, s. 1, v. 2, p. 153.

Residence in United States, or States, and good moral character.

Titles of nobility to be renounced.

Persons residing in the United States before 29 January, 1795.

SEC. 2165. An alien may be admitted to become a citizen of the United States in the following manner, and not otherwise:

First. He shall declare on oath, before a circuit or district court of the United States, or a district or supreme court of the Territories, or a court of record of any of the States having common-law jurisdiction, and a seal and clerk, two years, at least, prior to his admission, that it is bona fide his intention to become a citizen of the United States, and to renounce forever all allegiance and fidelity to any foreign prince, potentate, state, or sovereignty, and, particularly, by name, to the prince, potentate, state, or sovereignty of which the alien may be at the time a citizen or subject.

Second. He shall, at the time of his application to be admitted, declare, on oath, before some one of the courts above specified, that he will support the Constitution of the United States, and that he absolutely and entirely renounces and abjures all allegiance and fidelity to every foreign prince, potentate, state, or sovereignty; and, particularly, by name, to the prince, potentate, state, or sovereignty of which he was before a citizen or subject; which proceedings shall be recorded by the clerk of the court.

Third. It shall be made to appear to the satisfaction of the court admitting such alien that he has resided within the United States five years at least, and within the State or Territory where such court is at the time held, one year at least; and that during that time he has behaved as a man of a good moral character, attached to the principles of the Constitution of the United States, and well disposed to the good order and happiness of the same; but the oath of the applicant shall in no case be allowed to prove his residence.

Fourth. In case the alien applying to be admitted to citizenship has borne any hereditary title, or been of any of the orders of nobility in the kingdom or state from which he came, he shall, in addition to the above requisites, make an express renunciation of his title or order of nobility in the court to which his application is made, and his renunciation shall be recorded in the court.

Fifth. Any alien who was residing within the limits and under the jurisdiction of the United States before the twenty-ninth day of January, one thousand seven hundred and ninety-five, may be admitted to become a citizen, on due proof made to some one of the courts above specified, that he has resided two years, at least, within the jurisdiction of the United States, and one year, at least, immediately preceding his application, within the State or Territory where such court is at the time held; and on his declaring on oath that he will support the Constitution of the United States, and that he absolutely and entirely renounces and abjures all allegiance and fidelity to any foreign prince, potentate, state, or sovereignty, and, particularly, by name, to the prince, potentate, state, or sovereignty whereof he was before a citizen or subject; and, also, on its appearing to the satisfaction of the court, that during such term of two years he has behaved as a man of good moral character, attached to the Constitution of the United States, and well disposed to the good order and happiness of the same; and where the alien, applying for admission to citizenship, has borne any hereditary title, or been of any of the orders of nobility in the kingdom or state from which he came, on his, moreover, making in the court an express renunciation of his title or order of nobility. All of the proceedings, required in this condition to be performed in the court, shall be recorded by the clerk thereof.

Sixth. Any alien who was residing within the limits and under the jurisdiction of the United States, between the eighteenth day of June, one thousand seven hundred and ninety-eight, and the eighteenth day of June, one thousand eight hundred and twelve, and who has continued to reside within the same, may be admitted to become a citizen of the United States without having made any previous declaration of his intention to become such; but whenever any person, without a certificate of such declaration of intention, makes application to be admitted a citizen, it must be proved to the satisfaction of the court, that the applicant was residing within the limits and under the jurisdiction of the United States before the eighteenth day of June, one thousand eight hundred and twelve, and has continued to reside within the same; and the residence of the applicant within the limits and under the jurisdiction of the United States, for at least five years immediately preceding the time of such application, must be proved by the oath of citizens of the United States, which citizens shall be named in the record as witnesses; and such continued residence within the limits and under the jurisdiction of the United States, when satisfactorily proved, and the place where the applicant has resided for at least five years, shall be stated and set forth, together with the names of such citizens, in the record of the court admitting the applicant; otherwise the same shall not entitle him to be considered and deemed a citizen of the United States. [Be it enacted by the Senate and House of Representatives of the United States of America in Congress assembled, That the declaration of intention to become a citizen of the United States, required by section two thousand one hundred and sixty five of the Revised Statutes of the United States, may be made by an alien before the clerk of any of the courts named in said section two thousand one hundred and sixty five; and all such declarations heretofore made before any such clerk are hereby declared as legal and valid as if made before one of the courts named in said section.]

SEC. 2166. Any alien, of the age of twenty-one years and upward, who has enlisted, or may enlist, in the armies of the United States, either the regular or the volunteer forces, and has been, or may be hereafter, honorably discharged, shall be admitted to become a citizen of the United States, upon his petition, without any previous declaration of his intention to become such; and he shall not be required to prove more than one year's residence within the United States previous to his application to become such citizen; and the court admitting such alien shall, in addition to such proof of residence and good moral character, as now provided by law, be satisfied by competent proof of such person's having been honorably discharged from the service of the United States.

SEC. 2167. Any alien, being under the age of twenty-one years, who has resided in the United States three years next preceding his arriving at that age, and who has continued to reside therein to the time he may make application to be admitted a citizen thereof, may, after he arrives at the age of twenty-one years, and after he has resided five years within the United States, including the three years of his minority, be admitted a citizen of the United States, without having made the declaration required in the first condition of section twenty-one hundred and sixty-five; but such alien shall make the declaration required therein at the time of his admission; and shall further declare, on oath, and prove to the satisfaction of the court, that, for two years next preceding, it has been his bona-fide intention to become a citizen of the United States:

Sidenotes (right margin):

Persons residing between 18 June, 1798, and 18 June, 1812.

22 Mar., 1816, c. 31, s. 2, v. 3, p. 259. 24 May, 1828, c. 116, s.2, v.4, p. 310.

Declaration for naturalization, how made.

1 Feb., 1876, c.5, r. 19, p. 2.

Aliens honorably discharged from military service.

17 July, 18 2, c. 200, s. 21, v. 12, p. 597.

Minor residents.

26 May, 1824, c. 186, s. 1, v. 4. p. 69.

and he shall in all other respects comply with the laws in regard to naturalization.

Widow and children of declarants.

26 Mar., 1804, c. 47, s. 2, v. 2, p. 293.

SEC. 2168. When any alien, who has complied with the first condition specified in section twenty-one hundred and sixty-five, dies before he is actually naturalized, the widow and the children of such alien shall be considered as citizens of the United States, and shall be entitled to all rights and privileges as such, upon taking the oaths proscribed (*) by law.

Aliens of African nativity and descent.

14 July, 1870, c. 254, s. 7, v. 16, p. 256.   18 *Feb.*, 1875, *c.* 80, *v.* 18, *p.* 318.

SEC. 2169. The provisions of this Title shall apply to aliens [being free white persons, and to aliens] of African nativity and to persons of African descent.

Residence of five years in United States.

3 Mar., 1813, c. 42, s. 12, v. 2, p. 811.

SEC. 2170. No alien shall be admitted to become a citizen who has not for the continued term of five years next preceding his admission resided within the United States.

Alien enemies not admitted.

14 April, 1802, c. 28, s. 1, v. 2, p. 153.
30 July, 1813, c. 36, v. 3, p. 53.

SEC. 2171. No alien who is a native citizen or subject, or a denizen of any country, state, or sovereignty with which the United States are at war, at the time of his application, shall be then admitted to become a citizen of the United States; but persons resident within the United States, or the Territories thereof, on the eighteenth day of June, in the year one thousand eight hundred and twelve, who had before that day made a declaration, according to law, of their intention to become citizens of the United States, or who were on that day entitled to become citizens without making such declaration, may be admitted to become citizens thereof, notwithstanding they were alien enemies at the time and in the manner prescribed by the laws heretofore passed on that subject; nor shall anything herein contained be taken or construed to interfere with or prevent the apprehension and removal, agreeably to law, of any alien enemy at any time previous to the actual naturalization of such alien.

Children of persons naturalized under certain laws to be citizens.

14 April, 1802, c. 28, s. 4, v. 2, p. 155.

Campbell *v.* Gordon, 6 Cr., 176.
U. S. *v.* Hirshfield, 13 Blatch., 330.

SEC. 2172. The children of persons who have been duly naturalized under any law of the United States, or who, previous to the passing of any law on that subject, by the Government of the United States, may have become citizens of any one of the States, under the laws thereof, being under the age of twenty-one years at the time of the naturalization of their parents, shall, if dwelling in the United States, be considered as citizens thereof; and the children of persons who now are, or have been, citizens of the United States, shall, though born out of the limits and jurisdiction of the United States, be considered as citizens thereof; but no person heretofore proscribed by any State, or who has been legally convicted of having joined the army of Great Britain during the Revolutionary War, shall be admitted to become a citizen without the consent of the legislature of the State in which such person was proscribed.

Police court of District of Columbia has no power to naturalize foreigners.

17 June, 1870, c. 133, s. 5, v. 16, p. 154.

SEC. 2173. The police court of the District of Columbia shall have no power to naturalize foreigners.

Naturalization of seamen.

7 June, 1872, c. 322, s. 29, v. 17, p. 268.

SEC. 2174. Every seaman, being a foreigner, who declares his intention of becoming a citizen of the United States in any competent court, and shall have served three years on board of a merchant-vessel of the United States subsequent to the date of such declaration, may, on his application to any competent court, and the production of his certificate of discharge and good conduct during that time, together with the certificate of his declaration of intention to become a citizen, be admitted a citizen of the United States; and every seaman, being a foreigner, shall, after his declaration of intention to become a citizen of the United States, and after he shall have served such three years, be deemed a citizen of the United States for the purpose of manning and serving on board any merchant-vessel of the United States, anything to the contrary in any act of Congress notwithstanding; but such seaman shall, for all purposes of protection as an American citizen, be deemed such, after the filing of his declaration of intention to become such citizen.

(*) Error in the Roll; should be *prescribed*.

APPENDIX 4-6

Act of March 2, 1907, Pub. L. 59-193, 34 Stat. 1228

Chap. 2534.—An Act In reference to the expatriation of citizens and their protection abroad.

Be it enacted by the Senate and House of Representatives of the United States of America in Congress assembled, That the Secretary of the Sate shall be authorized, in his discretion, to issue passports to persons not citizens of the United States as follows: Where any person has made a declaration of intention to become such a citizen as provided by law and has resided in the United States for three years a passport may be issued to him entitling him to the protection of the Government in any foreign country: *Provided*, That such passport shall not be valid for more than six months and shall not be renewed, and that such passport shall not entitle the holder to the protection of this Government in the country of which he was a citizen prior to making such declaration of intention.

Sec. 2. That any American citizen shall be deemed to have expatriated himself when he has been naturalized in any foreign state in conformity with its laws, or when he has taken an oath of allegiance to any foreign state.

When any naturalized citizen shall have resided for two years in the foreign state from which he came, or for five years in any other foreign state it shall be presumed that he has ceased to be an American citizen, and the place of his general abode shall be deemed his place of residence during said years: *Provided, however*, That such presumption may be overcome on the presentation of satisfactory evidence to a diplomatic or consular officer of the United States, under such rules and regulations as the Department of State may prescribe: *And provided also*, That no American citizen shall be allowed to expatriate himself when this country is at war.

Sec. 3. That any American woman who marries a foreigner shall take the nationality of her husband. At the termination of the marital relation she may resume her American citizenship, if abroad, by registering as an American citizen within one year with a consul of the United States, or by returning to reside in the United States, or, if residing in the United States at the termination of the marital relation, by continuing to reside therein.

Sec. 4. That any foreign woman who acquires American citizenship by marriage to an American shall be assumed to retain the same after the termination of the marital relation if she continue to reside in the United States, unless she makes formal renunciation thereof before a court having jurisdiction to naturalize aliens, or if she resides abroad she may retain her citizenship by registering as such before a United States consul within one year after the termination of such marital relation.

Sec. 5. That a child born without the United States of alien parents shall be deemed a citizen of the United States by virtue of the naturalization of or resumption of American citizenship by the parent: *Provided*, That such naturalization or resumption takes place during the minority of such child: *And provided further*, That the citizenship of such minor child shall begin at the time such minor child begins to reside permanently in the United States.

Sec. 6. That all children born outside the limits of the United States who are citizens thereof in accordance with the provisions of section nineteen hundred and ninety-three of the Revised Statutes of the United States and who continue to reside outside the United States shall, in order to receive the protection of this Government, be required upon reaching the age of eighteen years to record at an American consulate their intention to become residents and remain citizens of the United States and shall be further required to take the oath of allegiance to the United States upon attaining their majority.

Sec. 7. That duplicates of any evidence, registration, or other acts required by this Act shall be field with the Department of State for record.

APPENDIX 4-7

Revised Statutes of 1907

TITLE XXV, CITIZENSHIP

Sec. 1993. Citizenship of children of citizens born abroad.

Further provisions relating to the protection of children born outside the limits of the United States who are citizens in accordance with the provisions of this section, set forth in Comp. St. 1901, p. 1268 are contained in Act March 2, 1907, c. 2534, § 6, set forth post under Rev. St. § 2000.

Sec. 1994. Citizenship of married women

Further provisions relating to the retention of the American citizenship of a foreign woman acquired by marriage to a citizen, as provided by his section, set forth in Comp. St. 1901, p. 1268, are contained in Act March 2, 1907, c. 2534, § 4, set forth post, under Rev. St. § 2000.

Sec. 1999. Right of expatriation declared.

Provisions relating to expatriation of American citizens are contained in Act March 2, 1907, c. 2534, § 2, set forth post, under Rev. St. § 2000.

Sec. 2000. Protection to naturalized citizens in foreign states.

Besides the provisions of this section and of Rev. St. § 2001, set forth in Comp. St. 1901, p. 1270, for protection of naturalized citizens in foreign countries, provisions for the issue of passports to and protection of persons who have made declaration of intention to become citizens, and as to when naturalized citizens residing abroad shall be presumed to have ceased to be American citizens, are contained in Act March 2, 1907, c. 2534, set forth below.

[March 2, 1907, c. 2534 is omitted here as it was reproduced as Appendix 4-6.]

APPENDIX 4-8

Act of September 22, 1922, Pub. L. 67-346, 42 Stat. 1021

An Act Relative to the naturalization and citizenship of married women.

Be it enacted by the Senate and House of Representatives of the United States of America in Congress assembled, That the right of any woman to become a naturalized citizen of the United States shall not be denied or abridged because of her sex or because she is a married woman.

Sec. 2. That any woman who married a citizen of the United States after the passage of this Act, or any woman whose husband is naturalized after the passage of this Act, shall not become a citizen of the United States by reason of such marriage of naturalization; but, if eligible to citizenship, she may be naturalized upon full and complete compliance with all requirements of naturalization laws, with the following exceptions:

(a) No declaration of intention shall be required;

(b) In lieu of the five-year period of residence within the United States and the one-year period of residence within the State or Territory where the naturalization court is held, she shall have resided continuously in the United States, Hawaii, Alaska, or Porto Rico for at least one year immediately preceding the filing of the petition.

Sec. 3. That a woman citizen of the United States shall not cease to be a citizen of the United States by reason of her marriage after the passage of this Act, unless she makes a formal renunciation of her citizenship before a court having jurisdiction over naturalization of aliens: *Provided*, That any woman citizen who marries an alien ineligible to citizenship shall cease to be a citizen of the United States. If at the termination of the marital status she is a citizen of the United States she shall retain her citizenship regardless of her residence. If during the continuance of the marital status she resides continuously for two years in a foreign State of which her husband is a citizen or subject, or for five years continuously outside the United States, she shall thereafter be subject to the same presumption as is a naturalized citizen of the United States under the second paragraph of section 2 of the Act entitled "An Act in reference to the expatriation of citizens and their protection abroad," approved March 2, 1907. Nothing herein shall be construed to repeal or amend the provisions of Revised Statutes 1999 or of section 2 of the Expatriation Act of 1907 with reference to expatriation.

Sec. 4. That a woman who, before the passage of this Act, has lost her United States citizenship by reason of her marriage to an alien eligible for citizenship, may be naturalized as provided by section 2 of this Act: *Provided*, That no certificate of arrival shall be required to be filed with her petition if during the continuance of the marital status she shall have resided within the United States. After her naturalization she shall have the same citizenship status as if her marriage had taken place after the passage of this Act.

Sec. 5. That no woman whose husband is not eligible to citizenship shall be naturalized during the continuance of the marital status.

Sec. 6. That section 1994 of the Revised Statutes and section 4 of the Expatriation Act of 1907 are repealed. Such repeal shall not terminate citizenship acquired or retained under either of such sections nor restore citizenship lost under section 4 of the Expatriation Act of 1907.

Sec. 7. That section 3 of the Expatriation Act of 1907 is repealed. Such repeal shall not restore citizenship lost under such section nor terminate citizenship resumed under such section. A woman who has resumed under such section citizenship lost by marriage shall, upon the passage of this Act, have for all purposes the same citizenship status as immediately preceding her marriage.

APPENDIX 4-9

Excerpts From the Act of March 3, 1931, Pub. L. 71-829, 46 Stat. 1511

An Act To amend the naturalization laws in respect of posting notices of petitions, and for other purposes.

Be it enacted by the Senate and House of Representatives of the United States of America in Congress assembled, That . . .

. . .

Sec. 3.

(a) Any person, born in the United States, who had established permanent residence in a foreign country prior to January 1, 1917, and who has heretofore lost his United States citizenship by becoming naturalized under the laws of such foreign country, may, if eligible to citizenship and if, prior to the enactment of this Act, he has been admitted to the United States for permanent residence, be naturalized upon the full and complete compliance with all of the requirements of the naturalization laws, with the following exceptions:

   (1) The five-year period of residence within the United States shall not be required;

   (2) The declaration of intention may be made at any time after admission to the United States, and the petition may be filed at any time after the expiration of sic months following the declaration of intention;

   (3) If there is attached to the petition, at the time of filing, a certificate from a naturalization examiner stating that the petitioner has appeared before him for examination, the petition may be heard at any time after filing.

(b) After naturalization such person shall have the same citizenship status as immediately preceding the loss of United States citizenship.

Sec. 4.

(a) Section 3 of the Act entitled "An Act relative to the naturalization and citizenship of married women," approved September 22, 1922, as amended, is amended to read as follows:

"Sec. 3.

(a) A woman citizen of the United States shall not cease to be a citizen of the United States by reason of her marriage after this section, as amended, takes effect, unless she makes a formal renunciation of her citizenship before a court having jurisdiction over naturalization of aliens.

(b) Any woman who before this section, as amended, takes effect, has lost her United States citizenship by residence abroad after marriage to an alien or by marriage to an alien ineligible to citizenship, if she has not acquired any other nationality by affirmative act, be naturalized in the manner prescribed in section 4 of this Act, as amended. Any woman who was a citizen of the United States at birth shall not be denied naturalization under section 4 on account of her race.

(c) No woman shall be entitled to naturalization under section 4 of this Act, as amended, if her United States citizenship originated solely by reason of her marriage to a citizen of the United States or by reason of the acquisition of United States citizenship by her husband."

(b)   Section 5 of such Act of September 22, 1922, is repealed.

APPENDIX 4-10

Act of May 24, 1934, Pub. L. 73-250, 48 Stat. 797

An Act To Amend the law relative to citizenship and naturalization, and for other purposes.

Be it enacted by the Senate and House of Representatives of the United States of America in Congress assembled, That section 1993 of the Revised Statutes[1] is amended to read as follows:

"Sec. 1993. Any child hereafter born out of the limits and jurisdiction of the United States, whose father or mother or both at the time of the birth of such child is a citizen of the United States, is declared to be a citizen of the United States; but the rights of citizenship shall not descend to any such child unless the citizen father or citizen mother, as the case may be, has resided in the United States previous to the birth of such child. In cases where one of the parents is an alien, the right of citizenship shall not descend unless the child comes to the United States and resides therein for at least five years continuously immediately previous to his eighteenth birthday, and unless, within six months after the child's twenty-first birthday, he or she shall take an oath of allegiance to the United States of America as prescribed by the Bureau of Naturalization."

Sec. 2. Section 5 of the Act entitled "An Act in reference to the expatriation of citizens and their protection abroad",[2] approved March 2, 1907, as amended, is amended to read as follows:

"Sec. 5. That a child born without the United States of alien parents shall be deemed a citizen of the United States by virtue of the naturalization of or resumption of American citizenship by the father or mother: *Provided*, That such naturalization or resumption shall take place during the minority of such child: *And provided further*, That the citizenship of such minor child shall begin five years after the time such minor child begins to reside permanently in the United States."

Sec. 3. A citizen of the United States may upon marriage to a foreigner make a formal renunciation of his or her United States citizenship before a court having jurisdiction over naturalization of aliens, but no citizen may make such renunciation in time of war, and if war shall be declared within one year after such renunciation then such renunciation shall be void.

Sec. 4. Section 2 of the Act entitled "An Act relative to the naturalization and citizenship of married women", approved September 22, 1922, is amended to read as follows:

"Sec. 2. That an alien who marries a citizen of the United States, after the passage of this Act, as here amended, or an alien whose husband or wide is naturalized after the passage of this Act, as here amended, shall not become a citizen of the United States by reason of such marriage or naturalization; but, if eligible to citizenship, he or she may be naturalized upon full and complete compliance with all requirements of the naturalization laws, with the following exceptions"

---

[1]Reproduced as Appendix 4-5.

[2]Reproduced as Appendix 4-6.

"(a) No declaration of intention shall be required.

"(b) In lieu of the five-year period of residence within the United States and the on-year period of residence within the State or Territory where the naturalization court is held, he or she shall have resided continuously in the United States, Hawaii, Alaska, or Porto Rico for at least three years immediately preceding the filing of the petition."

Sec. 5. The Following Acts and parts of Acts, respectively, are repealed: The Act entitled "An Act providing for the naturalization of the wise and minor children of insane aliens, making homestead entries under the land laws of the United States", approved February 24, 1911; subdivision "Sixth" of section 4 of the act entitled "An Act to establish a Bureau of Immigration and Naturalization, and to provide for a uniform rule for the naturalization of aliens throughout the United States", approved June 29, 1906; and section 8 of the act entitled "An Act relative to the naturalization and citizenship of married women", approved September 22m 1922, as said section was added y the Act approved July 3, 1930, entitled "An Act to amend an Act entitled 'An Act relative to naturalization and citizenship of married women,' approved September 22, 1922."

The repeal herein made of Acts and parts of Acts shall not affect any right or privilege or terminate any citizenship acquired under such Acts and parts of Acts before such repeal.

APPENDIX 4-11

Act of June 25, 1936, Pub. L. 74-793, 49 Stat. 1917

An Act to repatriate native-born women who have heretofore lost their citizenship by marriage to an alien, and for other purposes.

Be it enacted by the Senate and House of Representatives of the United States of America in Congress assembled, That hereafter a woman, being a native-born citizen, who has or is believed to have lost her United States Citizenship solely by reason of her marriage prior to September 22, 1922, to an alien, and whose marital status with such alien has or shall have terminated [or who has resided continuously in the United States since the date of such marriage][1], shall be deemed to be a citizen of the United States until she shall have duly taken the oath of allegiance as prescribed in section 4 of the Act approved June 29, 1906 (34 Stat. 596; U.S.C., title 8, sec. 381), at any place within or under the jurisdiction of the United States before a court exercising naturalization jurisdiction thereunder or, outside of the jurisdiction of the United States, before a secretary of embassy or legation or a consular officer as prescribed in section 1750 of the Revised Statutes of the United States (U.S.C., title 22, sec. 131); and such officer before whom such oath of allegiance shall be taken shall make entry thereof in the records of his office or in the naturalization records of the court, as the case may be, and shall deliver to such person taking such oath, upon demand, a certified copy of the proceedings had, including a copy of the oath administered, under the seal of his office or of such court, at a cost not exceeding $1, which shall be evidence of the facts stated therein before any court of record or judicial tribunal and in any department of the United States.

---

[1]Text in brackets added by the Act of July 2, 1940, Pub. L. 76-704, 54 Stat. 715.

APPENDIX 4-12

Excerpts from the Nationality Act of 1940, Pub. L. 76-853, 54 Stat. 1137 (October 14, 1940)

. . .

Sec. 101. For the purposes of this Act—

(a) The term "national" means a person owing permanent allegiance to a state.

(b) The term "national of the United States" means (1) a citizen of the United States, or (2) a person who, though not a citizen of the United States, owes permanent allegiance to the United States. It does not include an alien.

(c) The term "naturalization" means the conferring of nationality of a state upon a person after birth.

(d) The term "United States" when used in a geographical sense means the continental United States, Alaska, Hawaii, Puerto Rico, and the Virgin Islands of the United States.

(e) The term "outlying possessions" means all territory, other than as specified in subsection d, over which the United States exercises rights of sovereignty, except the Canal Zone.

(f) The tern "parent" includes in the case of a posthumous child a deceased parent.

(g) The Term "minor" means a person under twenty-one years of age.

Sec. 102. For the purposes of chapter III of this Act—

. . .

(h) The term "child" includes a child legitimated under the law of the child's residence or domicile, whether in the United States or elsewhere; also a child adopted in the United States, provided such legitimation or adoption takes place before the child reached the age of sixteen years and the child is in the legal custody of the legitimating or adopting parent or parents.

. . .

Sec. 104. For the purposes of sections 201, 307(b), 403, 404, 405, 406, and 407 of this Act the place of general abode shall be deemed the place of residence.

CHAPTER II—NATIONALITY AT BIRTH

Sec. 201. The following shall be nationals and citizens of the United States at birth:

. . .

(c) A person born outside of the United States and its outlying possessions of parents both of whom are citizens of the United States and one of whom has resided in the United States or one of its outlying possessions prior to the birth of such person;

(d) A person born outside of the United States and its outlying possessions of parents one of whom is a citizen of the United States who resided in the United States or one of its outlying possessions prior to the birth of such person, and the other of whom is a national, but not a citizen of the United States;

(e)   A person born in an outlying possessions of the United States of parents one
      of whom is a citizen of the United States who resided in the United States
      or one of its outlying possessions prior to the birth of such person;

. . .

(g)   A person born outside of the United States and its outlying possessions of
      parents one of whom is a citizen of the United States who, prior to the birth
      of such person, has had ten years' residence in the United States or one of
      its outlying possessions, at least five of which were after attaining the age of
      sixteen years, the other being an alien: *Provided*, That, in order to retain
      such citizenship, the child must reside in the United States or its outlying
      possessions for a period or periods totaling five years between the ages of
      thirteen and twenty-one years: *Provided further*, That, if the child has not
      taken up a residence in the United States or its outlying possessions by the
      time he reached the age of sixteen years, or if he resides abroad for such a
      time that it becomes impossible for him to complete the five years' residence
      in the United States or its outlying possessions before reaching the age of
      twenty-one years, his American citizenship shall thereupon cease.

The preceding provisos shall not apply to a child born abroad whose American
parent is at the time of the child's birth residing abroad solely or principally in
the employment of the Government of the United States or a bona fide American,
educational, scientific, philanthropic, religious, commercial, or financial organization, having its principal office or place of business in the United States, or an
international agency of an official character in which the United States
participates, for which he receives a substantial compensation;

(h)   The foregoing provisions of subsection (g) concerning retention of citizenship
      shall apply to a child born abroad subsequent to May 24, 1934.

Sec. 202. All persons born in Puerto Rico on or after April 11, 1899, subject to the
jurisdiction of the United States, residing on the effective date of this Act in Puerto
Rico or other territory over which the United States exercises rights of sovereignty
and not citizens of the United States under any other Act, are hereby declared to be
citizens of the United States.

Sec. 203.

(a)   Any persons born in the Canal Zone on or after February 26, 1904, and
      whether before or after the effective date of this Act, whose father or mother
      or both at the time of the birth of such person was or is citizen of the United
      States employed by the Government of the United States or by the Panama
      Railroad Company, is declared to be a citizen of the United States.

(b)   Any person born in the Republic of Panama on or after February 26, 1904,
      and whether before or after the effective date of this Act, whose father or
      mother or both at the time of the birth of such person was or is a citizen of
      the United States employed by the Government of the United States or by
      the Panama Railroad Company, is declared to be a citizen of the United
      States.

Sec. 204. Unless otherwise provided in section 201, the following shall be nationals, but not citizens of the United States at birth:

(a)   A person born in an outlying possession of the United States of parents one
      of whom are nationals, but not a citizen, of the United States;

(b)   A person born outside the United States and its outlying possessions of
      parents both of whom are nationals, but not citizens, of the United States,
      and have resided in the United States or one of its outlying possessions prior
      to the birth of such person;

(c)   A child of unknown parentage found in an outlying possession of the United States, until shown not to have been born in such outlying possession.

Sec. 205. The provisions of section 201, subsections (c), (d), (e), and (g), and section 204, subsections (a) and (b), hereof apply, as of the date of birth, to a child born out-of-wedlock, provide the paternity is established during minority, by legitimation, or adjudication of a competent court.

In absence of such legitimation or adjudication, the child, whether born before or after the effective date of this Act, if the mother had the nationality of the United States at the time of the child's birth, and had previously resided in the United States or one of its outlying possessions, shall be held to have acquired at birth her nationality status.

CHAPTER III—NATIONALITY THOUGH NATURALIZATION

. . .

Sec. 303. The right to become a naturalized citizen under the provisions of this Act shall extend only to white persons, persons of African nativity or descent, and descendants of races indigenous to the Western Hemisphere: *Provided*, That nothing in this section shall prevent the naturalization of native-born Filipinos having the honorable service in the United States Army, Navy, Marine Corps, or Coast Guard as specified in section 324, nor of former citizens of the United States who are otherwise eligible to naturalization under the provisions of section 317.

. . .

Sec. 313. A child born outside of the United States, one of whose parents at the time of the child's birth was an alien and the other of whose parents then was and never thereafter ceased to be a citizen of the United States, shall, if such alien parent is naturalized, be deemed a citizen of the United States, when—

(a)   Such naturalization takes place while such child is under the age of eighteen years; and

(b)   Such child is residing in the United States at the time of naturalization or thereafter and begins to reside permanently in the United States while under the age of eighteen years.

Sec. 314. A child born outside of the United States of alien parents, or of an alien parent and a citizen parent who has subsequently lost citizenship of the United States, becomes a citizen of the United States upon fulfillment of the following conditions:

(a)   The naturalization of both parents; or

(b)   The naturalization of the surviving parent if one of the parents is decease; or

(c)   The naturalization of the parent having legal custody of the child when there has been a legal separation of the parents; and if—

(d)   Such naturalization takes place while such child is under the age of eighteen years; and

(e)   Such child is residing in the United States at the time of the naturalization of the parent last naturalized under section (a) of this section, or the parent naturalized under subsection (b) or (c) of this section, or thereafter begins to reside permanently in the United States while under the age of eighteen years,

. . .

Sec. 317.

(a)   A person who was a citizen of the United States and who prior to September

22, 1922, lost United States citizenship by marriage to an alien or by the spouse's loss of United States citizenship, and any person who lost United States citizenship on or after September 22, 1922, by marriage to an alien ineligible to citizenship, may if no other nationality was acquired by affirmative act other than such marriage, be naturalized upon compliance with all requirements of the naturalization laws with the following exceptions:

. . .

(b)

    (1) From and after the effective date of this Act, a woman, who was a citizen of the United States at birth, and who has or is believed to have lost her United States citizenship solely by reason of her marriage prior to September 22, 1922, to an alien, and whose marital status with such alien has or shall have terminated, if no other nationality was acquired by affirmative act other than such marriage, shall, from and after the taking of the oath of allegiance prescribed by subsection (b) of section 335 of this Act, be deemed to be a citizen of the United States to the same extent as though her marriage to said alien had taken place on or after September 22, 1922.

    (2) Such oath of allegiance may be taken abroad before a diplomatic or consular officer of the United States, or in the United States before a judge or clerk of a naturalization court.

    (3) Such oath of allegiance shall be entered in the records of the appropriate embassy or legation or consulate or naturalization court, and upon demand, a certified copy of the proceedings, including a cop of the oath administered, under the seal of the embassy or legation or consulate or naturalization court, shall be delivered to such woman at a cost not exceeding $1, which certified copy shall be evidence of the facts stated therein before any court of record or judicial tribunal and in any department of the United States.

. . .

CHAPTER V—MISCELLANEOUS

. . .

Sec. 504. The following Acts or parts of Acts are hereby repealed;

Section 1992, Revised Statutes (U.S.C., title 8, sec. 1);

Section 1993, Revised Statutes, as amended by section 1, Act of May 24, 1934 (48 Stat. 797; U.S.C., title 8, sec. 6);

. . .

Section 2172, Revised Statutes (U.S.C., title 8, sec. 7);

. . .

Sections 2, 5, 6, and 7, Act of March 2, 1907 (34 Stat. 1228, 1229), as amended by section 2, Act of May 24, 1934 (48 Stat. 797, U.S.C., title 8, sec. 8, 16, and 17);

. . .

Sections 1, 2, 3, and 4, Act of September 22, 1922 (42 Stat,. 1021–1022); as amended by sections 1 and 2, Act of July 3, 1930 (46 Stat. 854); section 4 Act of March 3, 1931 (46 Stat. 1511–1512); and section 4, Act of May 24, 1934 (48 Stat. 797; U.S.C., title 8, secs. 367, 368, 368a, 369, and 369a);

. . .

Sections 1, 2, 3, and 4, Act of May 24, 1934 (48 Stat. 797, U.S.C., title 8, secs. 6, 8, 17a, and 368) . . .

. . .

Act of June 25, 1936, chapter 801 (49 Stat. 1917);

. . .

The repeal herein provided shall not terminate nationality heretofore lawfully acquired, nor restore nationality heretofore lost under any law of the United States or any treaty to which the United States may have been a party.

. . .

TITLE II

Sec. 601. This Act shall take effect from and after ninety days from the date of its approval.

APPENDIX 4-13

Act of July 31, 1946, Pub. L. 79-571, 60 Stat. 721

An Act To amend section 201 (g) of the Nationality Act of 1940 (54 Stat. 1138–1139; 8 U.S.C.A. 601).

Be it enacted by the Senate and House of Representatives of the United States of America in Congress assembled, That section 201 of the Nationality Act of 1940 (54 Stat. 1138–1139; 8 U.S.C.A. 601) is hereby amended by adding the following subsection to be known as subsection (i):

"(i) A person born outside the United States and its outlying possessions of parents one of whom is a citizen of the United States who has served or shall serve honorably in the armed forces of the United States after December 7, 1941, and before the date of termination of hostilities in the present war as proclaimed by the President or determined by a joint resolution by the Congress and who, prior to the birth of such person, has had ten years' residence in the United States or one of its outlying possessions, at least five of which were after attaining the age of twelve years, the other being an alien: *Provided*, That in order to retain such citizenship, the child must reside in the United States or its outlying possessions for a period or periods totaling five years between the ages of thirteen and twenty-one years: *Provided further*, That, if the child has not taken up a residence in the United States or its outlying possessions by the time he reaches the age of sixteen, or if he resides abroad for such a time that it becomes impossible for him to complete the five years' residence in the United States or its outlying possessions before reaching the age of twenty-one years, his American citizenship shall thereupon cease."

APPENDIX 4-14

Excerpts from the Immigration and Nationality Act, as originally enacted by the Act of June 27, 1952, Pub. L. 82-414, 66 Stat. 163

. . . .

TITLE III - NATIONALITY AND NATURALIZATION

Chapter 1—Nationality at Birth and By Collective Naturalization
Sec. 301.

(a)   The following shall be nationals and citizens of the United States at birth:

. . .

(7)   a person born outside the geographical limits of the United States and its outlying possessions of parents one of whom is an alien, and the other a citizen of the United States who, prior to the birth of such person, was physically present in the United States or its outlying possessions for a period or periods totaling not less than ten years, at least five of which were after attaining the age of fourteen years: *Provided*, That any periods of honorable service in the Armed Forces of the United States by such citizen parent may be included in computing the physical presence requirements of this paragraph.

(b)   Any person who is a national and citizen of the United States at birth under paragraph (7) of subsection (a), shall lose his nationality and citizenship unless he shall come to the United States prior to attaining the age of twenty-three years and shall immediately following such coming be continuously physically present in the United States for at least five years: *Provided*, That such physical presence follows the attainment of the age of fourteen years and precedes the age of twenty-eight years.

(c)   Subsection (b) shall apply to a person born abroad subsequent to May 24, 1934: *Provided, however*, That nothing contained in this subsection shall be construed to alter or affect the citizenship of any person born abroad subsequent to May 24, 1934, who, prior to the effective date of this Act, has taken up a residence in the United States before attaining the age of sixteen years, and thereafter, whether before or after the effective date of this Act, complies or shall comply with the residence requirements for retention of citizenship specified in subsections (g) and (h) of section 201 of the Nationality Act of 1940, as amended.

. . .

CHILDREN BORN OUT-OF-WEDLOCK
Sec. 309

(a)   The provisions of paragraphs (3), (4), (5), and (7) of section 301 (a), and of the paragraph (2) of section 308, of this title shall apply as of the date of birth to a child out-of-wedlock on or after the effective date of this Act, if the paternity of such child is established while such child is under the age of twenty-one years by legitimation.

(b)   Except as otherwise provided in section 405, the provisions of section 301 (a) (7) shall apply to a child born out-of-wedlock on or after January 13, 1941, and prior to the effective date of this Act, as of the date of birth, if the paternity of such child is established before the effective date of this Act and while such child is under the age of twenty-one years by legitimation.

(c)   Notwithstanding the provision of subsection (a) of this section, a person born, on or after the effective date of this Act, outside the United States out-of-wedlock shall be held to have acquired at birth the nationality status of his mother, if the mother had the nationality of the United States at the time of such person's birth, and if the mother had previously been physically present in the United States or one of its outlying possessions for a continuous period of one year.

. . .

APPENDIX 4-15

Act of March 16, 1956, Pub. L. 84-430, 70 Stat. 50

An Act Granting the benefits of section 301(a)(7) of the Immigration and Nationality Act to certain children of United States citizens.

Be it enacted by the Senate and House of Representatives of the United States of America in Congress assembled, That section 301(a)(7) of the Immigration and Nationality Act shall be considered to have been and to be applicable to a child born outside of the United States and its outlying possessions after January 12, 1941, and before December 24, 1952, of parents one of whom is a citizen of the United States who has served in the Armed Forces of the United States after December 31, 1946, and before December 24, 1952, and whose case does not come within the provisions of section 201(g) or (i) of the Nationality Act of 1940.

APPENDIX 4-16

Act of September 11, 1957, Pub. L. 85-316, 71 Stat. 639

An Act To amend the Immigration and Nationality Act, and for other purposes.

Be it enacted by the Senate and House of Representatives of the United States of America in Congress assembled, That . . . .

Sec. 16. In the Administration of section 301 (b) of the Immigration and Nationality Act, absences from the United States of less than twelve months in the aggregate, during the period for which continuous physical presence in the United States is required, shall not be considered to break the continuity of such physical presence.

APPENDIX 4-17

Act of October 27, 1972, Pub. L. 92-582, 86 Stat. 1289

An Act To amend section 301 of the Immigration and Nationality Act.

Be it enacted by the Senate and House of Representatives of the United States of America in Congress assembled, That section 301(b) of the Immigration and Nationality Act (8 U.S.C.A. 1401) is amended to read as follows:

"(b) Any person who is a national and citizen of the United States under paragraph (7) of subsection (a) shall lose his nationality and citizenship unless—(1) he shall come to the United States and be continuously present therein for a period of not less than two years between the ages of fourteen years and twenty-eight years; or (2) the alien parent is naturalized while the child begins to reside permanently in the United States while under the age of eighteen years. In the administration of this subsection absences from the United States of less than sixty days in the aggregate during the period for which continuous physical presence in the United States is required shall not break the continuity of such physical presence."

Sec. 2. Section 16 of the Act of September 11, 1957, is hereby repealed.

Sec. 3. Section 301 of the Immigration and Nationality Act is amended by adding at the end thereof a new subsection (d) to read as follows:

"(d) Nothing contained in subsection (b), as amended, shall be construed to alter or affect the citizenship of any person who has come to the United States prior to the effective date of this subsection and who, whether before or after the effective date of this subsection, immediately following such coming complies or shall comply with the physical presence requirements for retention of citizenship specified in subsection (b) prior to its amendment and the repeal of the Act of September 11, 1957."

APPENDIX 4-18

Act of October 10, 1978, Pub. L. 95-432, 92 Stat. 1046

An Act To repeal certain sections of title III of the Immigration and Nationality Act, and for other purposes.

Be it enacted by the Senate and House of Representatives of the United States of America in Congress assembled, That subsections (b), (c), and (d) of section 301 and section 350 of the Immigration and Nationality Act are hereby repealed, effective as of the date of enactment of this Act.

Sec. 2. Paragraphs (5) and (8) of section 349 and sections 352, 353, 354, and 355 of the Immigration and Nationality Act are hereby repealed.

Sec. 3. Section 301 of the Immigration and Nationality Act is amended by striking out "(a) after "Sec. 301," and by redesignating paragraphs (1) through (7) as subsections (a) through (g) respectively.

Sec. 4. Section 349 of the Immigration and Nationality Act is amended by inserting "(a)" after "Sec. 349", and by renumbering paragraphs (6), (7), and (9) as paragraphs (5), (6), and (7), respectively.

APPENDIX 4-19

Excerpts from Act of November 14, 1986, Pub. L. 99-653, 100 Stat. 3655

A. Excerpts from Act of November 14, 1986, Pub.L. 99-653, 100 Stat. 3655

An Act To amend the Immigration and Nationality Act, and for other purposes.

Be it enacted by the Senate and House of Representatives of the United States of America in Congress assembled, That this Act may be cited as the "Immigration and Nationality Act Amendments of 1986".

. . .

Sec. 12. Section 301(g) (8 U.S.C.A. 1401(g)) is amended by striking out "ten years, at least five" and inserting in lieu thereof "five years, at least two".

Sec. 13. Subsection (a) of section 309 (8 U.S.C.A. 1409) is amended—

(a)   by striking out "paragraphs (3), (4), (5), and (7) of section 301(a)" and inserting in lieu thereof "paragraphs (c), (d), (e), and (g) of section 301"; and

(b)   by striking out all after "wedlock", and inserting in lieu thereof "if blood relationship between the child and the father is established by clear and convincing evidence, provide the father had the nationality of the United States the time of the child's birth, the father unless deceased has agreed in writing to provide financial support for the child until such child reaches the age of eighteen years and if, while such child is under the age of eighteen years, (1) such child is legitimated under the law of the child's residence or domicile, or (2) the father acknowledges paternity of the child in writing under oath, or (3) paternity of the child is established by adjudication of a competent court.".

Sec. 14. Section 320(a) (8 U.S.C.A. 1431(a)) is amended by inserting "unmarried and" after "(1) such naturalization takes place while such child is".

Sec. 15. Section 321(a) (8 U.S.C.A. 1432(a)) is amended by inserting "unmarried and" after "(4) Such naturalization takes place while such child is".

Sec. 16. Section 322(a) (8 U.S.C.A. 1433(a)) is amended by inserting "unmarried and" after "may be naturalized if".

Sec. 17. Subsection (d) of section 340 (8 U.S.C.A. 1451) is amended by striking out "within five years after such naturalization" and inserting in lieu thereof "within one year after such naturalization".

Sec. 18. Subsection (a) of section 349 (8 U.S.C.A. 1481) is amended—

(a)   by inserting "voluntarily performing any of the following acts with the intention of relinquishing United States nationality:" after "shall lose his nationality by";

(b)   by striking out ", upon application filed in his behalf by a parent, guardian or duly authorized agent, or through the naturalization of a parent having legal custody of such person" and all that follows through "section 101(a)(27)(E)" in paragraph (1) and inserting in lieu thereof "or upon an application filed by a duly authorized agent, after having attained the age of eighteen years";

(c) by inserting ", after having attained the age of eighteen years" in paragraph (2) after "thereof";

(d) by striking out "unless, prior to such entry" and all that follows in paragraph (3) and inserting in lieu thereof "if (a) such armed forces are engaged in hostilities against the United States, or (b) such persons serve as a commissioned or noncommissioned officer; or"; and

(e) by inserting "after attaining the age of eighteen years" after "foreign state or political subdivision thereof" in subparagraph (4)(A);

(f) by inserting "after attaining the age of eighteen years" after "foreign state or political subdivision thereof" in subparagraph (4)(B);

Sec. 19. Section 349 (8 U.S.C.A. 1481) is further amended by striking subsection (b).

Sec. 20. Subsection (b) of section 351 (8 U.S.C.A. 1483) is amended by striking "paragraphs (2), (4)," and inserting in lieu thereof "paragraph (3)".

Sec. 21. Section 2 of chapter 24 of the Act of April 14, 1792, amended by the Act of July 12, 1940 (22 U.S.C.A. 4195), is amended by striking "article by article,".

. . .

B. Excerpts from The Immigration Technical Corrections Act of 1988, Pub.L. 100-525, 102 Stat. 2609

. . .

Sec. 8. Immigration and Nationality Act Amendments of 1986 (Pub.L. 99-653).

. . . .

(r) Effective Dates.—INAA is further mended by adding at the end the following new section:

"Effective Dates

"Sec. 23 . . .

"(d) The amendment made by section 12 shall apply to persons born on or after November 14, 1986.

"(e)

(1) Except as provided in paragraph (2)(B), the new section 309(a) (as defined in paragraph 4(A)) shall apply to persons who have not attained 18 years of age as of the date of the enactment of this Act.

"(2) The old section 309(a) shall apply—

"(A) to any individual who has attained 18 years of age as of the date of the enactment of this Act, and

"(B) and individual with respect to whom paternity was established by legitimation before such date.

"(3) An individual who is at least 15 years of age, but under 18 years of age, as of the date of the enactment of this Act, may elect to have old section 309(a) apply to the individual instead of the new section 309(a).

"(4) In this subsection:

"(A) The term 'new section 309(a)' means section 309(a) of the Immigration and Nationality Act, as amended by section 13 of this Act and as in effect after the date of enactment of this Act.

"(B) The term 'old section 309(a)' means section 309(a) of the Immigration and Nationality Act, as in effect before the date of enactment of this Act.

"(f) The amendment made by section 17 shall not apply to individuals who have taken up permanent residence outside the United States before November 14, 1986.

"(g) The amendments made by sections 18, 19, and 20 shall apply to actions taken before, on, or after November 14, 1986.

"(h) The amendment made by section 21 shall not apply to individuals who die on or after November 14, 1986.".

. . .

APPENDIX 4-20

Act of August 4, 1937, Pub. L. 75-242, 50 Stat. 558

An Act Relating to the citizenship of certain classes of persons born in the Canal Zone or the Republic of Panama.

Be it enacted by the Senate and House of Representatives of the United States of America in Congress assembled, That any person born in the Canal Zone on or after February 26, 1904, and whether before or after the effective date of this Act, whose father or mother or both at the time of the birth of such person was or is a citizen of the United States declared to be a citizen of the United States.

Sec. 2. Any person born in the Republic of Panama on or after February 26, 1904, and whether before or after the effective date of this Act, whose father or mother or both at the time of the birth of such person was or is a citizen of the United States employed by the Government of the United States or by the Panama Railroad Company, is declared to be a citizen of the United States.

APPENDIX 4-21

The Immigration and Nationality Technical Corrections Act of 1994 (INTCA), Pub. L. 103-416, Title I, 108 Stat. 4305 (Oct. 25, 1994)

TITLE I—NATIONALITY AND NATURALIZATION

SEC. 101. EQUAL TREATMENT OF WOMEN IN CONFERRING CITIZENSHIP TO CHILDREN BORN ABROAD.

(a) IN GENERAL- Section 301 of the Immigration and Nationality Act (8 U.S.C.A. 1401) is amended—

(1) by striking the period at the end of paragraph (g) and inserting "; and", and

(2) by adding at the end the following new paragraph:

"(h) a person born before noon (Eastern Standard Time) May 24, 1934, outside the limits and jurisdiction of the United States of an alien father and a mother who is a citizen of the United States who, prior to the birth of such person, had resided in the United States.".

(b) WAIVER OF RETENTION REQUIREMENTS- Any provision of law (including section 301(b) of the Immigration and Nationality Act (as in effect before October 10, 1978), and the provisions of section 201(g) of the Nationality Act of 1940) that provided for a person's loss of citizenship or nationality if the person failed to come to, or reside or be physically present in, the United States shall not apply in the case of a person claiming United States citizenship based on such person's descent from an individual described in section 301(h) of the Immigration and Nationality Act (as added by subsection (a)).

(c) RETROACTIVE APPLICATION-

(1) Except as provided in paragraph (2), the immigration and nationality laws of the United States shall be applied (to persons born before, on, or after the date of the enactment of this Act) as though the amendment made by subsection (a), and subsection (b), had been in effect as of the date of their birth, except that the retroactive application of the amendment and that subsection shall not affect the validity of citizenship of anyone who has obtained citizenship under section 1993 of the Revised Statutes (as in effect before the enactment of the Act of May 24, 1934 (48 Stat. 797)).

(2) The retroactive application of the amendment made by subsection (a), and subsection (b), shall not confer citizenship on, or affect the validity of any denaturalization, deportation, or exclusion action against, any person who is or was excludable from the United States under section 212(a)(3) (E) of the Immigration and Nationality Act (8 U.S.C.A. 1182(a)(3)(E)) (or predecessor provision) or who was excluded from, or who would not have been eligible for admission to, the United States under the Displaced Persons Act of 1948 or under section 14 of the Refugee Relief Act of 1953.

(d) APPLICATION TO TRANSMISSION OF CITIZENSHIP- This section, the amendments made by this section, and any retroactive application of such amendments shall not effect any residency or other retention requirements for citizenship as in effect before October 10, 1978, with respect to the transmission of citizenship.[1]

SEC. 102. NATURALIZATION OF CHILDREN ON APPLICATION OF CITIZEN PARENT.

(a) IN GENERAL- Section 322 of the Immigration and Nationality Act (8 U.S.C.A. 1433) is amended to read as follows:

> "CHILD BORN OUTSIDE THE UNITED STATES; APPLICATION FOR CERTIFICATE OF CITIZENSHIP REQUIREMENTS
>
> "SEC. 322.
>
> (a) A parent who is a citizen of the United States may apply to the Attorney General for a certificate of citizenship on behalf of a child born outside the United States. The Attorney General shall issue such a certificate of citizenship upon proof to the satisfaction of the Attorney General that the following conditions have been fulfilled:
>
> > "(1) At least one parent is a citizen of the United States, whether by birth or naturalization.
> >
> > "(2) The child is physically present in the United States pursuant to a lawful admission.
> >
> > "(3) The child is under the age of 18 years and in the legal custody of the citizen parent.
> >
> > "(4) If the citizen parent is an adoptive parent of the child, the child was adopted by the citizen parent before the child reached the age of 16 years and the child meets the requirements for being a child under subparagraph (E) or (F) of section 101(b)(1).
> >
> > "(5) If the citizen parent has not been physically present in the United States or its outlying possessions for a period or periods totaling not less than five years, at least two of which were after attaining the age of fourteen years—
> >
> > > "(A) the child is residing permanently in the United States with the citizen parent, pursuant to a lawful admission for permanent residence, or
> > >
> > > "(B) a citizen parent of the citizen parent has been physically present in the United States or its outlying possessions for a period or periods totaling not less than five years, at least two of which were after attaining the age of fourteen years.
> >
> > "(b) Upon approval of the application (which may be filed abroad) and, except as provided in the last sentence of section 337(a), upon taking and subscribing before an officer of the Service within the United States to the oath of allegiance required by this Act of an applicant for naturalization, the child shall become a citizen of the

---

[1] IIRAIRA § 671(b)(1) amended this paragraph to read: "(d) ~~APPLICATION TO TRANSMISSION OF CITIZENSHIP~~ *Applicability of Transmission Requirements*-This section, the amendments made by this section, and any retroactive application of such amendments shall not effect ~~any residency or other retention requirements for~~ the application of any provision of law relating to residence or physical presence in the United States for purposes of transmitting United States citizenship ~~as in effect before October 10, 1978, with respect to the transmission of citizenship~~ *to any person whose claim is based on the amendment made by subsection (a) or through whom such a claim is derived.*" [deleted text is stricken through, added text is italicized]. IIRAIRA § 671(b) amendments are reproduced as Appendix 4-22.

United States and shall be furnished by the Attorney General with a certificate of citizenship.

"(c) Subsection (a) of this section shall apply to the adopted child of a United States citizen adoptive parent if the conditions specified in such subsection have been fulfilled."

(b) CONFORMING AMENDMENT- Subsection (c) of section 341 of such Act (8 U.S.C.A. 1452) is repealed.

(c) CLERICAL AMENDMENT- The item in the table of contents of such Act relating to section 322 is amended to read as follows:

"Sec. 322. Child born outside the United States; application for certificate of citizenship requirements."

(d) EFFECTIVE DATE- The amendments made by this section shall take effect on the first day of the first month beginning more than 120 days after the date of the enactment of this Act.[2]

SEC. 103. FORMER CITIZENS OF UNITED STATES REGAINING UNITED STATES CITIZENSHIP.

(a) IN GENERAL- Section 324 of the Immigration and Nationality Act (8 U.S.C.A. 1435) is amended by adding at the end the following new subsection:

"(d)

(1) A person who was a citizen of the United States at birth and lost such citizenship for failure to meet the physical presence retention requirements under section 301(b) (as in effect before October 10, 1978), shall, from and after taking the oath of allegiance required by section 337 be a citizen of the United States and have the status of a citizen of the United States by birth, without filing an application for naturalization, and notwithstanding any of the other provisions of this title except the provisions of section 313. Nothing in this subsection or any other provision of law shall be construed as conferring United States citizenship retroactively upon such person during any period in which such person was not a citizen.

"(2) The provisions of paragraphs (2) and (3) of subsection (c) shall apply to a person regaining citizenship under paragraph (1) in the same manner as they apply under subsection (c)(1)."

(b) EFFECTIVE DATE- The amendment made by subsection (a) shall take effect on the first day of the first month beginning more than 120 days after the date of the enactment of this Act.

SEC. 104. INTENT TO RESIDE PERMANENTLY IN THE UNITED STATES AFTER NATURALIZATION.

(a) IN GENERAL- Section 338 of the Immigration and Nationality Act (8 U.S.C.A. 1449) is amended by striking "intends to reside permanently in the United States, except in cases falling within the provisions of section 324(a) of this title,".

(b) CONFORMING REPEAL- Section 340(d) of such Act (8 U.S.C.A. 1451(d)) is repealed.

(c) CONFORMING REDESIGNATION- Section 340 of such Act (8 U.S.C.A. 1451) is amended—

---

[2]IIRAIRA § 671 amended the INTCA by adding a transitional rule as § 102(e), which reads as follows: "(e) Transition.—In applying the amendment made by subsection (a) to children born before November 14, 1986, any reference in the matter inserted by such amendment to 'five years, at least two of which' is deemed a reference to '10 years, at least 5 of which'."

(1) by redesignating subsections (e), (f), (g), (h), and (i) as subsections (d), (e), (f), (g), and (h), respectively; and

(2) in subsection (d) (as redesignated), by striking "subsections (c) or (d)" and inserting "subsection (c)".

(d) CONFORMING AMENDMENT- Section 405 of the Immigration Act of 1990 is amended by striking subsection (b).

(e) EFFECTIVE DATE- The amendment made by subsection (a) shall apply to persons admitted to citizenship on or after the date of enactment of this Act.

SEC. 105. TERMINOLOGY RELATING TO EXPATRIATION.

(a) IN GENERAL- Section 351 of the Immigration and Nationality Act (8 U.S.C.A. 1483) is amended—

(1) in the heading, by striking "EXPATRIATION" and inserting "LOSS OF NATIONALITY ";

(2) in subsection (a)—

(A) by striking "expatriate himself, or be expatriated" and inserting "lose United States nationality ", and

(B) by striking "expatriation" and inserting "loss of nationality"; and

(3) in subsection (b), by striking "expatriated himself" and inserting "lost United States nationality ".

(b) CLERICAL AMENDMENT- The item in the table of contents of such Act relating to section 351 is amended to read as follows:

"Sec. 351. Restrictions on loss of nationality."

SEC. 106. ADMINISTRATIVE AND JUDICIAL DETERMINATIONS RELATING TO LOSS OF CITIZENSHIP.

Section 358 of the Immigration and Nationality Act (8 U.S.C.A. 1501) is amended by adding at the end the following new sentence: "Approval by the Secretary of State of a certificate under this section shall constitute a final administrative determination of loss of United States nationality under this Act, subject to such procedures for administrative appeal as the Secretary may prescribe by regulation, and also shall constitute a denial of a right or privilege of United States nationality for purposes of section 360."

SEC. 107. CANCELLATION OF UNITED STATES PASSPORTS AND CONSULAR REPORTS OF BIRTH.

(a) IN GENERAL- Title III of the Immigration and Nationality Act is amended by adding at the end the following new section:

"CANCELLATION OF UNITED STATES PASSPORTS AND CONSULAR REPORTS OF BIRTH

"SEC. 361.

(a) The Secretary of State is authorized to cancel any United States passport or Consular Report of Birth, or certified copy thereof, if it appears that such document was illegally, fraudulently, or erroneously obtained from, or was created through illegality or fraud practiced upon, the Secretary. The person for or to whom such document has been issued or made shall be given, at such person's last known address, written notice of the cancellation of such document, together with the procedures for seeking a prompt post-cancellation hearing. The cancellation under this section of any document purporting to show the citizenship status of the person to whom it was issued shall affect only the document and not the citizenship status of the person in whose name the document was issued.

"(b) For purposes of this section, the term "Consular Report of Birth' refers to the report, designated as a "Report of Birth Abroad of a Citizen of the United States", issued by a consular officer to document a citizen born abroad."

(b) CLERICAL AMENDMENT- The table of contents is amended by inserting after the item relating to section 360 the following new item:

"Sec. 361. Cancellation of United States passports and Consular Reports of Birth.".SEC. 108. EXPANDING WAIVER OF THE GOVERNMENT KNOWLEDGE, UNITED STATES HISTORY, AND ENGLISH LANGUAGE REQUIREMENTS FOR NATURALIZATION.

(a) IN GENERAL- Section 312 of the Immigration and Nationality Act (8 U.S.C.A. 1423) is amended—

(1) by inserting "(a)" after "312."

(2) by striking "this requirement" and all that follows through "That",

(3) by striking "this section" and inserting "this paragraph", and

(4) by adding at the end the following new subsection:

"(b)

(1) The requirements of subsection (a) shall not apply to any person who is unable because of physical or developmental disability or mental impairment to comply therewith.

"(2) The requirement of subsection (a)(1) shall not apply to any person who, on the date of the filing of the person's application for naturalization as provided in section 334, either—

"(A) is over fifty years of age and has been living in the United States for periods totaling at least twenty years subsequent to a lawful admission for permanent residence, or

"(B) is over fifty-five years of age and has been living in the United States for periods totaling at least fifteen years subsequent to a lawful admission for permanent residence.

"(3) The Attorney General, pursuant to regulations, shall provide for special consideration, as determined by the Attorney General, concerning the requirement of subsection (a)(2) with respect to any person who, on the date of the filing of the person's application for naturalization as provided in section 334, is over sixty-five years of age and has been living in the United States for periods totaling at least twenty years subsequent to a lawful admission for permanent residence."

(b) CONFORMING AMENDMENTS- Section 245A(b)(1)(D) of such Act (8 U.S.C.A. 1254a(b)(1)(D)) is amended by striking "312" each place it appears and inserting "312(a)".

(c) EFFECTIVE DATE- The amendments made by subsection (a) shall take effect on the date of the enactment of this Act and shall apply to applications for naturalization filed on or after such date and to such applications pending on such date.

(d) REGULATIONS- Not later than 120 days after the date of enactment of this Act, the Attorney General shall promulgate regulations to carry out section 312(b)(3) of the Immigration and Nationality Act (as amended by subsection (a)).

SEC. 109. REPORT ON CITIZENSHIP OF CERTAIN LEGALIZED ALIENS.

Not later than June 30, 1996, the Commissioner of the Immigration and Naturalization Service shall prepare and submit to the Congress a report concerning the citizenship status of aliens legalized under section 245A and section 210 of the Immigration and Nationality Act. Such report shall include the following information by district office for each national origin group:

(1) The number of applications for citizenship filed.

(2) The number of applications approved.

(3) The number of applications denied.

(4) The number of applications pending.

APPENDIX 4-22

Illegal Immigration Reform and Immigrant Responsibility Act of 1996 (IIRAIRA), Pub. L. 104-208, §§ 643, 671(b), 110 Stat. 3009 (Sept. 30, 1996)

. . .

SEC. 643. REGULATIONS REGARDING HABITUAL RESIDENCE.

Not later than 6 months after the date of the enactment of this Act, the Commissioner of Immigration and Naturalization shall issue regulations governing rights of "habitual residence" in the United States under the terms of the following:

(1) The Compact of Free Association between the Government of the United States and the Governments of the Marshall Islands and the Federated States of Micronesia (48 U.S.C.A. 1901 note).

(2) The Compact of Free Association between the Government of the United States and the Government of Palau (48 U.S.C.A. 1931 note).

. . . . . .

SEC. 671. MISCELLANEOUS TECHNICAL CORRECTIONS.

. . . .

(b) Amendments Relating to Immigration and Nationality Technical Corrections Act of 1994.—

 (1) Section 101(d) of the Immigration and Nationality Technical Corrections Act of 1994 (Public Law 103-416) (in this subsection referred to as "INTCA") is amended—

  (A) by striking "Application" and all that follows through "This" and inserting "Applicability of Transmission Requirements.—This";

  (B) by striking "any residency or other retention requirements for" and inserting "the application of any provision of law relating to residence or physical presence in the United States for purposes of transmitting United States"; and

  (C) by striking "as in effect" and all that follows through the end and inserting "to any person whose claim is based on the amendment made by subsection (a) or through whom such a claim is derived."

 (2) Section 102 of INTCA is amended by adding at the end the following:

"(e) Transition.—In applying the amendment made by subsection (a) to children born before November 14, 1986, any reference in the matter inserted by such amendment to 'five years, at least two of which' is deemed a reference to '10 years, at least 5 of which'."

 (3) Section 351(a) (8 U.S.C.A. 1483(a)), as amended by section 105(a)(2)(A) of INTCA, is amended by striking the comma after "nationality".

 (4) Section 207(2) of INTCA is amended by inserting a comma after "specified".

 (5) Section 101(a)(43) (8 U.S.C.A. 1101(a)(43)) is amended in subparagraph (K)(ii), by striking the comma after "1588".

 (6) Section 273(b) (8 U.S.C.A. 1323(b)), as amended by section 209(a) of INTCA, is amended by striking "remain" and inserting "remains".

(7) Section 209(a)(1) of INTCA is amended by striking "$3000" and inserting "$3,000".

(8) Section 209(b) of INTCA is amended by striking "subsection" and inserting "section".

(9) Section 219(cc) of INTCA is amended by striking "'year 1993 the first place it appears' " and inserting " 'year 1993' the first place it appears".

(10) Section 219(ee) of INTCA is amended by adding at the end the following: "(3) The amendments made by this subsection shall take effect on the date of the enactment of this Act."

(11) Paragraphs (4) and (6) of section 286(r) (8 U.S.C.A. 1356(r)) are amended by inserting "the" before "Fund" each place it appears.

(12) Section 221 of INTCA is amended—

   (A) by striking each semicolon and inserting a comma,

   (B) by striking "disasters." and inserting "disasters,"; and

   (C) by striking "The official" and inserting "the official".

(13) Section 242A (8 U.S.C.A. 1252a), as added by section 224(a) of INTCA and before redesignation as section 238 by section 308(b)(5) of this division, is amended by redesignating subsection (d) as subsection (c).

(14) Except as otherwise provided in this subsection, the amendments made by this subsection shall take effect as if included in the enactment of INTCA.

APPENDIX 4-23

Act of August 8, 1997, Pub. L. 105-38

One Hundred Fifth Congress

of the

United States of America

AT THE FIRST SESSION

Begun and held at the City of Washington on Tuesday,
the seventh day of January, one thousand nine hundred and ninety-seven
An Act

To amend the Immigration and Nationality Technical Corrections Act of 1994 to eliminate the special transition rule for issuance of a certificate of citizenship for certain children born outside the United States.

Be it enacted by the Senate and House of Representatives of the United States of America in Congress assembled,

SECTION 1. ELIMINATION OF CERTIFICATE OF CITIZENSHIP TRANSITION RULE APPLICABLE TO CERTAIN CHILDREN.

  (a) IN GENERAL—Section 102 of the Immigration and Nationality Technical Corrections Act of 1994 (Public Law 103-416; 108 Stat. 4307) (as amended by section 671(b) of the Illegal Immigration Reform and Immigrant Responsibility Act of 1996 (Public Law 104-208; 110 Stat. 3009-1856)) is amended by striking subsection (e).

  (b) EFFECTIVE DATE—The amendment made by subsection (a) shall take effect as if included in the enactment of the Immigration and Nationality Technical Corrections Act of 1994.

APPENDIX 4-24

Chart Summarizing Requirements To Acquire Citizenship at Birth Abroad Under Relevant Statutes

Date of Birth	Both Parents U.S. Citizens	One Parent Citizen/One National	One Parent Citizen/One Noncitizen	Illegitimate Children of U.S. Citizen Women	Illegitimate Children of U.S Citizen Men
Before 5/24/34	Citizenship Transmitted by Either Parent: Prior Residence: Must have been present in the U.S. at any time prior to the child's birth. Retention Requirements: None	[Same as when both parents are U.S. citizens]	[Same as when both parents are U.S. citizens]	U.S. citizen mother must have been present in the U.S. at any time prior to child's birth.[1]	• Must comply with all requirements for descent of citizenship through U.S. citizen father • In addition, must be legitimated at any time according to the laws of father's domicile
Between 5/24/34 and 1/13/41	Prior Residence: One of the parents must have been present in the U.S. at any time prior to the child's birth. Retention Requirements: None	Prior Residence: U.S. citizen parent must have been present in the U.S. at any time prior to the child's birth. Retention Requirements: None	Prior Residence: U.S. citizen parent must have been present in the U.S. at any time prior to the child's birth. Retention Requirements:[2] (1) 5 years continuous physical presence in the U.S. between ages of 14 and 28 or (2) 2 years continuous physical presence in the U.S. between ages 14 and 28.[3]	U.S. citizen mother must have been present in the U.S. at any time prior to child's birth.	• Must comply with all requirements for descent of citizenship through U.S. citizen father • In addition, must be legitimated at any time according to the laws of father's domicile

Date of Birth	Both Parents U.S. Citizens	One Parent Citizen/One National	One Parent Citizen/One Noncitizen	Illegitimate Children of U.S. Citizen Women	Illegitimate Children of U.S Citizen Men
Between 1/13/41 and 12/24/52	*Prior Residence:* One of the parents must have resided in the U.S. or Possessions at any time prior to the child's birth. *Retention Requirements:* None	*Prior Residence:* Citizen parent must have resided in the U.S. or Possessions at any time prior to the child's birth. *Retention Requirements:* None	Birth Outside U.S. and Possessions: *Prior Residence:* Citizen parent must have resided in the U.S. or possessions for 10 years prior to the child's birth, at least 5 of which must have been after the age of 16.[4] *Retention Requirements:* Either (1) 5 years continuous physical presence in the U.S. between ages of 14 and 28 or (2) 2 years continuous physical presence in the U.S. between ages 14 and 28.[5] Birth in Possessions of the U.S.: *Prior Residence:* Citizen parent must have resided in the U.S. or possessions at any time prior to the child's birth. *Retention Requirements:* None	U.S. citizen mother must have resided in the U.S. at any time prior to child's birth.	● Must comply with all requirements for descent of citizenship through U.S. citizen father ● In addition, before child reaches 21 years of age must have been legitimated[6] or paternity must have been established through court proceedings. ● If legitimated before age 21, prior residence requirements of the INA will apply if US citizen father failed to comply with prior residence requirements of the Nationality Act of 1940.

Date of Birth	Both Parents U.S. Citizens	One Parent Citizen/One National	One Parent Citizen/One Noncitizen	Illegitimate Children of U.S. Citizen Women	Illegitimate Children of U.S Citizen Men
Between 12/24/52 and 11/13/86	Prior Residence: One of the parents must have resided in the U.S. or possessions at any time prior to the child's birth. Retention Requirements: None	Prior Residence: U.S. citizen parent must have been *physically present* in the U.S. or possessions for a continuous period of one year at any time prior to the child's birth. Retention Requirements: None	A) Child Born Abroad — *Prior Residence:* U.S. citizen parent must have been *physically present* in the U.S. or possessions for 10 years prior to the child's birth, at least 5 of which after parent turned 14.[7] *Retention Requirements:* None (B) Child Born in Outlying U.S. Possession — *Prior Residence:* U.S. citizen parent must have been *physically present* in the U.S. or possessions for a continuous period of one year at any time prior to the child's birth. *Retention Requirement:* None	U.S. citizen mother must have been *physically present* in the U.S. or possessions for a continuous period of one year at any time prior to the child's birth.	● Must comply with all requirements for descent of citizenship through U.S. citizen father. ● In addition, before child attains the age of 21, must be legitimated.[8] If child born after 11/14/68, same acknowledgment/ legitimation requirements as children born after 11/14/86 may apply.[9]

Date of Birth	Both Parents U.S. Citizens	One Parent Citizen/One National	One Parent Citizen/One Noncitizen	Illegitimate Children of U.S. Citizen Women	Illegitimate Children of U.S Citizen Men
After 11/14/86	Prior Residence: One of the parents must have resided in the U.S. or possessions at any time prior to the child's birth. Retention Requirements: None	Prior Residence: U.S. citizen parent must have been *physically present* in the U.S. or possessions for a continuous period of one year at any time prior to the child's birth. Retention Requirements: None	A) Child Born Abroad — *Prior Residence*: U.S. citizen parent must have been *physically present* in the U.S. or possessions for 5 years prior to the child's birth, at least 2 of which after the parent turned 14.[10] *Retention Requirements*: None (B) Child Born in Outlying U.S. Possession — *Prior Residence*: U.S. citizen parent must have been *physically present* in the U.S. or possessions for a continuous period of one year at any time prior to the child's birth. Retention Requirement: None	U.S. citizen mother must have been *physically present* in the U.S. or possessions for a continuous period of one year at any time prior to the child's birth.	• Must comply with all requirements for descent of citizenship through father • In addition: (A) before child attains 18, (i) child is legitimated, or (ii) father acknowledges paternity in writing under oath, or (iii) paternity is established by competent court; AND (B) father must have agreed in writing to support child financially until age 18.[11]

[1] Before the passage of INTCA, if the illegitimate child of a U.S. citizen woman was legitimated by noncitizen parent prior to 1/13/41 and before child turned 21, child never acquired U.S. citizenship. As a consequence of INTCA, this requirement no longer exists.

[2] Children born before December 24, 1936 who entered the U.S. prior to December 24, 1952 could also satisfy this requirement by having a domicile of five years between the ages of 13 and 21.

[3] 5 years continuous physical presence allows for absences aggregating to only 60 days. To be able to comply with the 5 year requirement rather than the 2 year one, the person must have arrived in the U.S., and have started complying with the requirement, prior to October 27, 1972. Persons born after October 10, 1952 are exempted from all retention requirements. Noncitizens who failed to comply with these retention requirements lost their citizenship, but may have it restored by taking an oath of allegiance.

[4] Because of the definition of *residence* periods of stay abroad are considered part of residence in the U.S., provided the person's general place of abode continued to be the United States. There are ameliorating provisions relating to service in the U.S. armed forces and to children born out of wedlock.

[5] 5 years continuous physical presence allows for absences from the U.S. totaling 1 year for the entire period; 2 years continuous presence allows for absences aggregating to only 60 days. To be able to comply with the 5 year requirement rather then the 2 year one, the person must

have arrived in the U.S., and have started complying with the requirement, prior to October 27, 1972. Persons born after October 10, 1952 are exempted from all retention requirements. Noncitizens who failed to comply with these retention requirements lost their citizenship, but may have it restored by taking an oath of allegiance.

[6] USCIS takes the position that legitimation must occur according to the laws of the father's domicile.

[7] Because of the definition of *residence* periods of stay abroad are considered part of residence in the U.S., provided the person's general place of abode continued to be the United States. There are ameliorating provisions relating to service in the U.S. armed forces and to children born out of wedlock.

[8] USCIS adds two requirements: (1) child must have been legitimated according to the laws of the father's domicile, and (2) the child must be unmarried at the time of legitimation.

[9] Even if the child did not acquire citizenship at birth, one should also consider whether a child may also have become a citizen derivatively under the Child Citizenship Act, which applies to children born after February 27, 1983. See §§ 5:16 to 5:19.

[10] Because of the definition of *residence* periods of stay abroad are considered part of residence in the U.S., provided the person's general place of abode continued to be the United States. There are ameliorating provisions relating to service in the U.S. armed forces and to children born out of wedlock.

[11] The new legitimation provisions only apply to persons who were under 18 and had not yet become citizens as of November 14, 1986. Persons who were between 15 and 18 on November 14, 1986 could elect to have the legitimation rule in effect prior to the 1986 amendment apply to them. There is controversy whether the effective date of the 1986 amendment is November 14, 1986 or October 24, 1988.

APPENDIX 4-25

Legitimation Laws by Foreign Country and States of the United States—As Interpreted by the BIA and the FAM[1]

This appendix contains the cites and a summary of the decisions of the Board of Immigration Appeals (B.I.A.) and of the interpretation of the Foreign Affairs Manual (FAM) regarding the applicable legitimation law of the different jurisdictions of the U.S. and foreign countries. There are two important caveats. First, the interpretations of the BIA, the FAM, and the author, are not set in stone; over the past decades, numerous states have amended their legitimation rules, including abolishing the distinction between legitimate and illegitimate children. Moreover, the chart of U.S. state and territorial legitimation laws is derived from the FAM, which purports to be updated only through 1993.

Second, the family laws of the different jurisdictions are issues of fact for both the BIA and the State Department. The BIA and the State Department arrive at conclusions based on the information provided to them. These factual determinations are subject to correction if more accurate information is provided. In addition, there is no guarantee that both agencies will interpret these facts in the same manner. Therefore, this table should be taken as a beginning point for research rather than as the ultimate statement on the laws of the different jurisdictions.

In 1995, Congress amended the definition of child for immigration purposes.[2] The immigration rights of children born out-of-wedlock are greatly affected by that amendment. However, Congress did not amend the definition of child for nationality purposes. The distinction between legitimacy and illegitimacy continues to play a central role in nationality law. Therefore, the BIA and FAM discussion of the rights of legitimate and out-of-wedlock children continue to be applicable in full force in the nationality area.

1. Foreign Countries:

Austria: Matter of B-, 6 I. & N. Dec. 161 (B.I.A. 1954) (adoption and legitimation in Austria); Matter of Mandewirth, 12 I. & N. Dec. 199 (B.I.A. 1967) (acknowledgment of paternity and agreement to support is not legitimation under Austrian law).

Barbados: Matter of Clarke, 18 I. & N. Dec. 369 (B.I.A. 1983) (Barbados law abolished distinction between legitimate and out-of-wedlock children in 1979; out-of-wedlock children born before that date are legitimated as of that date).

Bolivia: Matter of Espinoza, 17 I. & N. Dec. 522 (B.I.A. 1980) (Bolivian Constitution of 1967 eliminated the distinction between legitimate and out-of-wedlock children; children born out-of-wedlock after that date are legitimate for immigration purposes; those born before that date become legitimated as of that date for immigration purposes).

---

[1]An earlier version of this appendix was originally published as Appendix 4, "Immigration Decisions Regarding Legitimation—By Foreign Country and State of the United States," in Daniel Levy, "The Family in Immigration and Nationality Law: Part I," 92-9 Immigration Briefings (September 1992). Used with permission of Immigration Briefings. Copyright © 1992 Federal Publications, Inc.

[2]Act of November 15, 1995, Pub.L. 104-51.

British Guiana: Matter of J-, 9 I. & N. Dec. 246 (B.I.A. 1961) (acknowledgment of paternity and legitimation).

British Honduras: Matter of Adam and Augustine, 13 I. & N. Dec. 177 (B.I.A. 1969) (legitimation of child born out-of-wedlock only through subsequent marriage of natural parents).

China: Matter of B- S-, 6 I. & N. Dec. 305 (Att'y Gen. 1955) (child born out-of-wedlock is deemed legitimate to the mother); Matter of Wong, 10 I. & N. Dec. 288 (B.I.A. 1963) (acknowledgment of paternity and legitimation); Matter of Lo, 14 I. & N. Dec. 379 (B.I.A. 1973) (legitimation by establishment of paternity before and after the Communist takeover); Lau v. Kiley, 563 F.2d 543 (9th Cir. 1977) (acknowledgment without formal proceeding is sufficient to legitimate child in the People's Republic of China).

Cuba: Matter of Martinez, 18 I. & N. Dec. 399 (B.I.A. 1983) (a law in 1975 abolished the distinction between legitimate and out-of-wedlock children; those born after that date are legitimate regardless of parent's marital status).

Curacao, Netherlands Antilles: Matter of Mourillon, 18 I. & N. Dec. 122 (B.I.A. 1981) (legitimate only by marriage of natural parents with a contemporaneous acknowledgment of paternity).

Dominica, British West Indies: Matter of James, 15 I. & N. Dec. 544 (B.I.A. 1975) (subsequent marriage of parents is only procedure for legitimation).

Dominican Republic: Matter of Doble-Pena, 13 I. & N. Dec. 366 (B.I.A. 1969) (marriage of parents is the only way to legitimate child); Matter of Reyes, 17 I. & N. Dec. 512 (B.I.A. 1980) (acknowledgment of paternity does not constitute legitimation, since it does not confer full rights of a legitimate child; this case has been overruled, see Matter of Cabrera); Matter of Cabrera, Interim Decision # 3296 (B.I.A. 1996) (a child born out-of-wedlock in the Dominican Republic is placed in the same legal position as one born in wedlock once the child has been acknowledged by the father in accordance with Dominican law; Matter of Reyes overruled); Matter of Martinez, Interim Decision # 3329 (B.I.A. 1997) (In order to qualify as a legitimated child, a child residing or domiciled in the Dominican Republic must have been under the age of 18 at the time the new law regarding legitimation took effect and must have been acknowledged by his or her father prior to her 18th birthday, unless he or she was legitimated under the former laws of that country); Los Santos v. I.N.S., 690 F.2d 56 (2d Cir. 1982) (natural filiation does not establish legitimation since such children enjoy property rights less than those of legitimate children).

Ecuador: Matter of Campuzano, 18 I. & N. Dec. 390 (B.I.A. 1983) (1970 statute gave equal rights to children born out-of-wedlock; children previously born must have been both under 18 in 1970 and acknowledged by one parent to derive immigration benefits).

El Salvador: Matter of Ramirez, 16 I. & N. Dec. 222 (B.I.A. 1977) (legitimation occurs by marriage of natural parents after child has been acknowledged by both natural parents; memorandum on Salvadoran law attached). Modified by Matter of Moraga, 23 I. & N. Dec. 195 (B.I.A. 2001) (a child born out-of-wedlock on or after December 16, 1965, is legitimated once the child's paternity is established).

Germany: Matter of Lauer, 12 I. & N. Dec. 210 (B.I.A. 1967) (legitimation in Germany requires either marriage of natural parents or a court or state order declaring the child legitimate issued upon application by the natural father).

Greece: Matter of Anastasiadis, 12 I. & N. Dec. 99 (B.I.A. 1967) (recognition by natural father is not legitimation; legitimation occurs either by subsequent marriage of parents or by court decree).

Grenada: Matter of Bullen, 16 I. & N. Dec. 378 (B.I.A. 1977) (marriage of parents is a way to legitimate child, but date of legitimation is either the date of marriage or the date of passage of the Legitimation Ordinance, whichever happened last; otherwise legitimation requires a decree from the Supreme Court of Grenada declaring the person legitimate).

Guadeloupe, French West Indies: Matter of Julianus, 14 I. & N. Dec. 435 (B.I.A. 1973) (legitimation is accomplished by subsequent marriage of parents).

Guatemala: Matter of Hernandez, 17 I. & N. Dec. 7 (B.I.A. 1979) (1963 law and 1965 Constitution give equal rights to all children; acknowledgment in birth records may be effected upon personal appearance of parent).

Guyana: In re Rowe, 23 I. & N. Dec. 962, 2006 WL 1794486 (B.I.A. 2006); see also, Gorsira v. Chertoff, 364 F. Supp. 2d 230 (D. Conn. 2005); Matter of Gouveia, 13 I. & N. Dec. 604 (B.I.A. 1970) (acknowledgment of paternity is not legitimation; it requires marriage of natural parents); Gorsira v. Loy, 357 F.Supp.2d 453 (D.Conn. 2005).

Haiti: Matter of Remy, 14 I. & N. Dec. 183 (B.I.A. 1972) (marriage of parents is the only way to legitimize child; overruled by Matter of Richard); Matter of Levy, 17 I. & N. Dec. 539 (B.I.A. 1980) (remanded to investigate effect of abolition of distinction between legitimate and out-of-wedlock children in Haiti); Matter of Richard, 18 I. & N. Dec. 208 (B.I.A. 1982) (child born out-of-wedlock after Jan. 27, 1959 is legitimate upon acknowledgment by natural father); Matter of Mesias, 18 I. & N. Dec. 298 (B.I.A. 1982) (legitimated by father's formal acknowledgment before child's 18th birthday and after change in law of Haiti); Matter of Cherismo, 19 I. & N. Dec. 25 (B.I.A. 1984) (acknowledgment is valid manner of legitimation even when it occurred before the change of law in Haiti; legitimation occurs as of the date of the 1959 decree).

Honduras: Matter of Sanchez, 16 I. & N. Dec. 671 (B.I.A. 1979) (all legal distinctions between legitimate and out-of-wedlock children eliminated in 1957; previously born children were legitimated).

Hungary: Matter of G-, 9 I. & N. Dec. 518 (B.I.A. 1961) (Hungary abolished all distinctions between legitimate and out-of-wedlock children in 1947, except for the terminology of "child born out-of-wedlock;" this terminology was later abolished in 1953 which effectively erased all trace of distinctions).

Indonesia: Matter of The, 10 I. & N. Dec. 744 (B.I.A. 1964) (acknowledgment of paternity is not legitimation; Indonesia law requires a declaration by the Governor-General (now the President of the Republic of Indonesia) after consultation with the Supreme Court, for the legitimation of a legally acknowledged child).

Italy: Matter of D-, 7 I. & N. Dec. 438 (B.I.A. 1957) (acknowledgment not legitimation; only subsequent marriage or royal or presidential decrees provide legitimation); Matter of C-, 9 I. & N. Dec. 268 (B.I.A. 1961) (acknowledgment is not legitimation).

Japan: Matter of Monma, 12 I. & N. Dec. 265 (B.I.A. 1967) (acknowledgment of paternity, plus subsequent marriage of parents, and entry of both in the official family register constitutes legitimation).

Jamaica: Matter of W-, 7 I. & N. Dec. 373 (B.I.A. 1956) (custody of out-of-wedlock children); Matter of Clahar, 16 I. & N. Dec. 484 (B.I.A. 1978) (modified by later decision in the same case); Matter of Clahar, 18 I. & N. Dec. 1 (B.I.A. 1981) (1976 statute eliminated distinction; those born before were legitimated as of that date) (overruled by *Matter of Hines*); Matter of Hines, 24 I&N Dec. 544 (BIA 2008) (1976 statute did not effect legitimation of children, only way to legitimize children in

Jamaica is through marriage); Lewis v. Gonzales, 481 F.3d 125, 131 (2d Cir.2007); Wedderburn v. INS, 215 F.3d 795, 797, 802 (7th Cir.2000); Watson v. Holder, 643 F.3d 367 (2d Cir. 2011).

Korea: Matter of Kim, 14 I. & N. Dec. 561 (B.I.A. 1974) (marriage of parents and recognition of child by registration in Korean Family Registry accomplishes legitimation); Matter of Lee, 16 I. & N. Dec. 305 (B.I.A. 1977) (recognition by registration in Family Registry creates the same legal relationship between a natural father and a natural child as that of legitimate child; legitimation is therefore accomplished by registration in the Family Registry).

Liberia: Matter of Duncan, 15 I. & N. Dec. 272 (B.I.A. 1975) (legitimation by court decree).

Montserrat, West Indies: Matter of Greer, 14 I. & N. Dec. 16 (B.I.A. 1972) (acknowledgment is not legitimation).

Netherlands: Matter of Van Pamelen, 12 I. & N. Dec. 11 (B.I.A. 1966) (no legitimation by acknowledgment without subsequent marriage of parents).

Nigeria: Matter of Cocker, 14 I. & N. Dec. 521 (B.I.A. 1974) (either marriage of parents or father's acknowledgment is sufficient to legitimate child).

Panama: Matter of Sinclair, 13 I. & N. Dec. 613 (B.I.A. 1970) (all distinctions between legitimate and out-of-wedlock children were abolished in 1946; acknowledgment by natural father makes the child legitimate as of that date).

Peru: Matter of Quispe, 16 I. & N. Dec. 174 (B.I.A. 1977) (acknowledgment of paternity does not achieve legitimation; legitimation requires either subsequent marriage of parents or judicial declaration upon application by legitimating parent); Matter of Breninzon, 19 I. & N. Dec. 40 (B.I.A. 1984) (legitimation only by marriage of parent or by judicial declaration upon petition of the legitimating parent; reaffirms Matter of Quispe); Matter of Torres, Int. Dec. 3347 (B.I.A. 1988) (Children under 18 years of age on November 14, 1984 were legitimated by change in Peruvian law obliterating the distinction between legitimate and out-of-wedlock children; those born after that date were legitimated as of date of birth; *Breninzon* and *Quispe* modified).

Philippines: Matter of Maungca, 11 I. & N. Dec. 885 (B.I.A. 1966) (acknowledgment of natural parent is only one step in legitimation; parents must also marry); Matter of Blancaflor, 14 I. & N. Dec. 427 (B.I.A. 1973) (legitimation only if child born to parents free to marry, acknowledgment by parents, and subsequent marriage of natural parents); Matter of Espiritu, 16 I. & N. Dec. 426 (B.I.A. 1977) (legitimation only by marriage of parents who were free to marry when child conceived and recognition or acknowledgment of child by parents).

Poland: Matter of K-, 8 I. & N. Dec. 73 (B.I.A. 1958) (child legitimated when acknowledged by father); Matter of Chojnowski, 11 I. & N. Dec. 287 (B.I.A. 1965) (registration of birth certificate including natural father's name with the Vital Statistics Bureau constitutes acknowledgment of paternity; acknowledgment under Polish law is legitimation); Matter of Kubicka, 14 I. & N. Dec. 303 (B.I.A. 1972) (child born of a bigamous marriage was legitimated by the act of recognition of the child by the father in a report of the child's birth to the Civil Registry Office).

Portugal: Matter of F-, 7 I. & N. Dec. 448 (B.I.A. 1957) (child legitimated only by marriage of the parents, provided there had been "recognition" or "affiliation" of the child); Matter of C-, 9 I. & N. Dec. 242 (B.I.A. 1961) (acknowledgment of paternity is neither legitimation nor adoption).

Spain: Matter of C-, 9 I. & N. Dec. 597 (B.I.A. 1962) (parents must marry to legitimate child, recognition of paternity is not sufficient). Saint Christopher and Nevis:

Douglas v. U.S., 2011 WL 2471516 (M.D.Fla., June 22, 2011) (NO. 8:09-CV-2145-T-33TBM) (citing Library of Congress report).

Surinam: Matter of W-, 9 I. & N. Dec. 223 (B.I.A. 1961) (formal acknowledgment or recognition not enough; legitimation requires marriage of parents).

Trinidad and Tobago: Matter of Archer, 10 I. & N. Dec. 92 (B.I.A. 1962) (in Trinidad marriage of parents is only way to legitimate child).

Yugoslavia: Matter of Jancar, 11 I. & N. Dec. 365 (B.I.A. 1965) (acknowledgment of paternity is sufficient for legitimation); Matter of Pavlovic, 17 I. & N. Dec. 407 (B.I.A. 1980) (natural child is legitimate at birth; subsequent acknowledgment establishes the identity of father).

Legitimation by State

	Is child legitimated by subsequent marriage of parents?	Is issue of a void marriage legitimate?	Can a child be legitimated in a manner not involving marriage of natural parents?
Alabama	Yes, if child is recognized by natural father. Section 26-11-1 of Alabama Code. (1993)	Yes. Section 26-17-3 & 5 of Alabama Code. (1993)	Yes, by the father (1) making a declaration in writing (2) attested to by 2 witnesses (3) setting forth the name, sex, supposed age, and name of the mother and (4) recognizing that it is his child. Section 26-11-2 of Alabama Code or if the father admits a paternity complaint or is found to be the father. (1993)
Alaska	Yes. Section 25.20.050 of Alaska Statutes (1993)	Yes. Section 25.05.050 and 25.05.051 Alaska Statutes. (1992)	Yes, if putative parent acknowledges being a parent of the child in writing. Section 25.20.050(a)(2) of Alaska Statutes. (1993)
Arizona	Yes. Section 8-601 of Arizona Revised Statutes. (1992)	Yes. Section 8-601 of Arizona Revised Statutes. (1992)	Yes, Arizona law states that every child is the legitimate child of its natural parents and entitled as such to support and education as if born in lawful wedlock. Thus, if satisfied as to paternity, the child may be regarded as a legitimate child of the natural father under Arizona law. Section 8-601 of Arizona Statutes. (1992)
Arkansas	Yes. Section 28-9-209 of the Arkansas Statutes. (1992)	Yes. Section 28-9-209 of Arkansas Statutes (1992)	No. Section 28-9-209 of Arkansas Statutes.
California[1]	Yes, if in addition to the marriage the father: (1) Consents to being named as the father on the child's birth certificate or (2) Is obligated to support the child under a voluntary written promise or by court order. Section 7004(a)(3) of California Civil Code. (1992)	Yes. Section 7001 and 7004 of California Civil Code. (1992)	Yes, if father receives the child into his home as well as openly holds it out as his own. Section 7004(a)(4) of California Civil Code. (1992)

---

[1] Matter of De F-, 6 I. & N. Dec. 325 (B.I.A. 1954) (legitimation under § 230 of the California Civil Code is valid for immigration purposes; it requires public acknowledgment and receipt into the family); Matter of Wong, 10 I. & N. Dec. 288 (B.I.A. 1963) (acknowledgment of a child without bringing the child into the

	Is child legitimated by subsequent marriage of parents?	Is issue of a void marriage legitimate?	Can a child be legitimated in a manner not involving marriage of natural parents?
Colorado	Yes. Section 19-4-103 and 19-4-105 of Colorado Revised Statutes.(1992)	Yes. Section 19-4-103 and 19-4-105 of Colorado Revised Statutes. (1992)	Yes, if while the child is a minor, the father receives the child into his home and openly holds the child as his natural child. Section 19-4-105 of Colorado Revised Statutes. (1992)
Connecticut	Yes. Section 45a-438(b)(1) of Connecticut General Statutes. (1992)	Yes. Section 46b-60 of Connecticut Statutes. (1993)	Yes, by written affirmation of paternity by father; or by court decree. Section 45(a)-438 of Connecticut Code. (1993)
Delaware	Yes. Section 1301 of Title 13 of Delaware Code. (1988)	Yes. Title 13, Section 105of Delaware Code. (1992)	Yes, by acknowledgement of parentage in writing by either parent and filed in Prothonotary's office in any county in the State. Title 13, Sec. 1301 of Delaware Code. (1988)
District of Columbia	Yes. Sections 16-907 and 16-908 Code of District of Columbia. (1993)	Yes. A child born in or out of wedlock is the legitimate child of mother and father and is legitimate relative of their relatives by blood or adoption. 16-908 of the D.C. Code. (1993)	Yes. Sections 16-907 and 16-908 Code of District of Columbia, as amended on April 7, 1977. (1993)
Florida	Yes. Section 742.091 of Florida Statutes. (1992)	Yes. Section 732.108(2)(a) of Florida Statutes. (1992)	Yes. Paternity may be acknowledged in writing thereby legitimizing a child born out-of-wedlock. Section 732-108 of Florida Statutes. (1992)

---

family is not sufficient to establish legitimation in California); Matter of Palacio, 11 I. & N. Dec. 132 (B.I.A. 1965) (California judgment of legitimation must be issued before the child turns 18 to obtain immigration benefits); Matter of Pableo, 12 I. & N. Dec. 503 (Dist. Dir. 1967) (public acknowledgment and receiving into the family are sufficient for legitimation in California even when events occurred outside the state and before the natural father settled in California); Matter of Garcia, 12 I. & N. Dec. 628 (B.I.A. 1968) (child legitimated as soon as acknowledgment and taking into the family occurred regardless of whether the petitioner resided in California at the time and regardless of the fact that the "family" consisted of unmarried natural parents); Matter of Singh, 15 I. & N. Dec. 370 (B.I.A. 1974) (either petitioner or beneficiary must have resided in California before the beneficiary turned 18 for the legitimation by acknowledgment and taking into the family to create immigration benefits; Ninth Circuit disagrees, see Kaliski v. District Director, 620 F.2d 214 (9th Cir. 1980); also seems to conflict with BIA precedents); Kaliski v. District Director, 620 F.2d 214 (9th Cir. 1980) (relied on California law because it was the current domicile of the father even though the father domiciled in state after legitimation took place); Matter of Martinez, 18 I. & N. Dec. 399 (B.I.A. 1983) (legitimation requires marriage of natural parents);

	Is child legitimated by subsequent marriage of parents?	Is issue of a void marriage legitimate?	Can a child be legitimated in a manner not involving marriage of natural parents?
Georgia	Yes, if the father recognizes the child as his. Section 19-7-20 of Code of Georgia. (1993)	Yes. Section 19-5-15 of the Code of Georgia. (1993)	Yes, if father does so by petitioning superior court in county of his residence setting forth child's name, age, sex and the name of the mother. Section 19-7-22 of the Code of Georgia. (1993)
Hawaii[2]	Yes. Sections 338-21 and 584-2 of Hawaii Revised Statutes. (1991)	Yes. Section 580-27 of Hawaii Revised Statutes. (1991)	Yes, if father and mother acknowledges paternity in writing. Sections 584-2 and 338-21(a)(2) of Hawaii Revised Statutes. (1991)
Idaho	Yes. Section 32-1006 of Idaho Code. (1992)	Yes, if marriage is void for any reason other than for fraud whereby the wife is pregnant with the child of a man other than her husband. Section 32-503 of Idaho Code. (1992)	Yes, if father (1) acknowledges child as his and (2) receives it into his family as such, with the consent of his wife if he is married. Section 16-1510 of Idaho Code. (1992)
Illinois	Yes. Chapter 40, Sections 2502 and 2505 of Illinois Revised Statutes. (1993)	Yes. Chapter 40, Section 303 of Illinois Revised Statutes. (1992)	Yes. Parent child relationship is not dependent on marriage. Chapter 40, Sections 2502 and 2503 of Illinois Revised Statutes. (1992)
Indiana	Yes, if putative father marries the mother of the child and acknowledges the child to be his own. Section 29-1-2-7 of the Indiana Statutes. (1992)	Yes, Sections 31-7-8-5 of Indiana Statutes. (1992)	Yes, if paternity of child has been established by law during father's life-time. Section 29-1-2-7 of the Indiana Statutes. (1992)
Iowa	Yes. Section 595.18 of Code of Iowa. (1993)	Yes. Section 598.31 of Code of Iowa. (1993)	Yes, by adoption. Sections 600.4 and 600.13 of Code of Iowa. (1993)

[2] Matter of Espiritu, 16 I. & N. Dec. 426 (B.I.A. 1977) (three methods to establish legitimation: marriage of parents, or their free acknowledgment of paternity, or establishment of parent/child relationship under the Uniform Parenting Act; under that statute receiving child into parent's home before child attains majority is one method of establishing legitimation).

	Is child legitimated by subsequent marriage of parents?	Is issue of a void marriage legitimate?	Can a child be legitimated in a manner not involving marriage of natural parents?
Kansas	Yes. Sections 38-1112 and 38-1114 of Kansas Revised Statutes. (1990)	Yes. Section 38-1113 and 38-1114 of Kansas Statutes Annotated. (1990)	Yes, if the father notoriously or in writing recognizes his paternity of the child. Section 38-1114 (4) of Kansas Statutes Annotated. (1990)
Kentucky	Yes, if the natural parents participated in a marriage ceremony before or after the birth of the child, even though the attempted marriage is void. Section 391.105 of Kentucky Revised Statutes. (1989)	Yes. Section 391.100 of Kentucky Revised Statutes. (1989)	Yes. A child adopted by a natural father is considered the natural child of the adopting parents the same as if born of their bodies. Sections 199.470 and 199.520 of Kentucky Revised Statutes. (1989)
Louisiana[3]	Yes, when the child has been formally or informally acknowledged by both parents, whether before or after the marriage. Article 198 of Louisiana Civil Code. (1992)	Yes, except in cases of incest. Article 198 of Louisiana Civil Code. (1992)	Yes, a child may be legitimated by notarial act. Art. 200 of Louisiana Civil Code. (1992)
Maine[4]	Yes. Title 18-A Section 2-109(2)(1) of Maine Revised Statutes. (1992)	Yes. Title 19, Section 633 of Maine Revised Statutes. (1992)	Yes, if (1) the father adopts the child into his family. Under Title 18-A Section 2-109(ii) of Maine Revised Statutes or (2) the father acknowledges that he is the father of the child before a notary public or justice of the peace or (3) there is an adjudication to this effect before a court or (4) by a court after the father's death on the basis of clear and convincing evidence. Title 18-A Section 2-109(2) (iii) of Maine Revised Statutes. (1992)

---

[3] Matter of Ramirez, 13 I. & N. Dec. 666 (B.I.A. 1971) (a parent cannot legitimate a child by notarial act of acknowledgment when there exist on the part of such parent legitimate ascendants or descendants).

[4] Alexander v. I.N.S., 1997 WL 97114 (D. Me. 1997) (under Maine law in effect in 1955, "if the father of a child born out-of-wedlock adopts him or her into his

	Is child legitimated by subsequent marriage of parents?	Is issue of a void marriage legitimate?	Can a child be legitimated in a manner not involving marriage of natural parents?
Maryland[5]	Yes, if the father has acknowledged himself, orally or in writing, to be the father. Section 1-208 of Estates and Trusts Code of Maryland. (1993)	Yes. Section 1-206 of Estates and Trusts Code of Maryland. (1993)	Yes, if father (1) has acknowledged himself to be father in writing or (2) has openly and notoriously recognized the child as his or (3) has been found to be the father after judicial paternity proceedings. Section 1-208 of Estates & Trusts Code of Maryland (several Maryland court decisions have said this constitutes legitimation for all purposes.) (1993)
Massa-chusetts[6]	Yes, if acknowledged by father or ordered by court. Chapter 190, Section 7 of Massachusetts General Laws. (1992)	Yes. Chapter 207, Sections 14-17. Annotated Laws of Massachusetts. (1992)	No. An illegitmate child can be acknowledged but this does not legitimate. Chapter 190 Sec. 7 of Annotated Laws of Massachusetts. (1992)
Michigan[7]	Yes. Sections 27.5111 and 25.107 of Michigan Compiled Laws Annotated. (1991)	Yes, Section 25.108 and 25.109 of Michigan Statutes Annotated. (1991)	Yes. Section 25.107 of Michigan Compiled Laws Annotated. (1991)
Minnesota	Yes. Section 257.55 and 257.52 of Minnesota Statutes. (1992)	Yes. Section 257.54 and 257.54 of Minnesota Statutes. (1992)	Yes, if while the child is a minor the father receives the child into his home and openly holds out the child as his own. Section 257.52 and 257.55 of Minnesota Statutes. (1992)

family, or in writing acknowledges before some justice of the peace or notary public that he is the father, such child is . . . the heir and legitimate child of his or her father'').

[5] Matter of Chambers, 17 I. & N. Dec. 117 (B.I.A. 1979) (legitimation accomplished by: (1) adjudication in paternity proceedings; or (2) acknowledgment in writing; or (3) open or notorious recognition of paternity; or (4) marriage to mother and either written or oral acknowledgment of paternity).

[6] Matter of C-, 9 I. & N. Dec. 242 (B.I.A. 1962) (adoption decree is not legitimation); Matter of Oduro, 18 I. & N. Dec. 421 (B.I.A. 1983) (legitimation only by marriage of natural parents and formal acknowledgment of paternity, or judicial declaration of paternity).

[7] Matter of Cortez, 16 I. & N. Dec. 289 (B.I.A. 1977) (subsequent marriage of parents legitimates child, but no immigration benefits as child legitimated when he was over 18).

	Is child legitimated by subsequent marriage of parents?	Is issue of a void marriage legitimate?	Can a child be legitimated in a manner not involving marriage of natural parents?
Mississippi	Yes. An illegitimate child is legitimated if the natural father marries the natural mother and acknowledges the child. Section 93-17-1 of Mississippi Code. (1991)	Yes. See Section 93-7-5 of Mississippi Code. (1992)	Yes, but only by specific decree of Chancery Court. Section 93-17-1 of Mississippi Code. (1991)
Missouri	Yes. If father acknowledges that child is his. Section 474.070 of Missouri Revised Statutes. (1992)	Yes. Section 474.080 of Missouri Statutes. (1992)	Yes, when paternity is established and the father has openly treated the child as his and has not refused to support the child. Section 474.060 of Missouri Statutes. (1992)
Montana	Yes. Section 40-6-203 of Montana Code. (1989)	Yes. Sections 40-6-104 and 40-6-105 of Montana Code Annotated. (1989)	Yes, if (1) the father while the child is a minor receives the child into his home and openly holds it out as his own or (2) acknowledges the child in a writing filed with the department of health provided the child's mother does not dispute the acknowledgement within a reasonable time. Sections 40-6-102 and 40-6-105 of Montana Code Annotated. (1989)
Nebraska	Yes. Section 43.1409 of Revised Statutes of Nebraska. (1991)	Yes. Section 42-377 of Revised Statutes of Nebraska. (1991)	No. Although a child's paternity can be acknowledged in writing or by providing support, paternity does not appear to be tantamount to legitimacy. Section 13-1409 of Revised Statutes of Nebraska. (1991)
Nevada	Yes. Section 122.140 of Nevada Revised Statutes. (1992)	Yes. Section 125.410 of Nevada Revised Statutes. (1992)	Yes, if the father (1) while the child is a minor receives it into his home and openly holds it out as his own or (2) acknowledges the child in a writing filed with the registrar of vital statistics. Sections 126.031 and 126.051 of Nevada Revised Statutes. (1992)
New Hampshire	Yes. Section 457.42 of New Hampshire Revised Statutes Annotated. (1989)	Yes, child considered legitimate unless court explicitly states otherwise. Section 458.23 of New Hampshire Revised Statutes Annotated. (1989)	Yes, but only if a court in New Hampshire where the father resides grants a petition legitimating the child in all respects. Section 460.29 of New Hampshire Revised Statutes Annotated. (1989)

	Is child legitimated by subsequent marriage of parents?	Is issue of a void marriage legitimate?	Can a child be legitimated in a manner not involving marriage of natural parents?
New Jersey[8]	Yes. Sections 9:17-39, 9:17-40 and 9:17-43 of Revised Statues of New Jersey (1992)	Yes. Section 9:17-40 of Revised Statutes of New Jersey. (1992)	Yes, by judicial proceedings to establish paternity; under laws of probate; or by a court of competent jurisdiction in another state. Section 9:17 et seq. of Revised Statutes of New Jersey. (1992)
New Mexico	Yes. Section 45-2-109 of New Mexico Statutes. (1992)	Yes. Section 45-2-109(B)(1) of New Mexico Statutes. (1992)	Yes, if the father has signed an instrument in writing which on its face is for the purpose of recognizing the child as his heir and such writing is accompanied by proof of "general and notorious recognition" by the father. See 45-2-109 B. (2) of New Mexico Statutes Annotated. (1992)
New York[9]	Yes. Article 3, Section 24 of Consolidated Laws of New York. (1992)	Yes. Article 3, Section 24, Note 6 of Consolidated Laws of New York. (1992)	Yes, if father files acknowledgment of paternity instrument with the New York Department of Social Services, Putative Father Registry. Section 4-1.2 of the New York Estates, Powers and Trusts Law (1992)
North Carolina	Yes. Section 49-12 General Statues of North Carolina. (1989)	Yes. Section 50-11.1 of North Carolina General Statutes. (1989)	Yes, if done by father's filing a petition so requesting in the Superior Court in North Carolina. Section 49-10 and 49-11 of General Statutes of North Carolina. (1989)
North Dakota	Yes. Section 14-09-02 of North Dakota Century Code. (1989)	Yes. Section 14-04-03 of North Dakota Code. (1989)	Yes, if father receives the child into his home while the child is a minor and openly holds out the child as his own. Section 14-17-04(d) of the North Dakota Century Code. (1989)
Ohio[10]	Yes. Section 3111.03 of Ohio Revised Code. (1992)	Yes. Sections 3111.02 and 3111.03 of Ohio Revised Code. (1992)	Yes, if (1) such acknowledgement is applied for in the probate court of the county where the father or child resides and (2) the mother consents and (3) the court accepts the application, then the child is legitimate for all purposes. Section 2105.18 of Ohio Revised Code. (1992)
Oklahoma	Yes. Title 10 Section 2 of Oklahoma Statutes Annotated. (1992)	Yes. Title 10 Section 1.2 of Oklahoma Statutes. (1992)	Yes. All children born in Oklahoma are legitimate after July 1, 1974. Title 10 Section 1.2 of Oklahoma Statutes. (1992)

---

[8] Matter of Garcia, 19 I. & N. Dec. 416 (B.I.A. 1986) (parentage act of 1983 made all children equal regardless of marital status of parents).

[9] Matter of Archer, 10 I. & N. Dec. 92 (B.I.A. 1962) (marriage of natural parents is the only way to legitimate child); Matter of Bullen, 16 I. & N. Dec. 378 (B.I.A. 1977) (marriage of parents only way to legitimate child); Matter of Reyes, 16 I. & N. Dec. 475 (B.I.A. 1978) (natural parents must marry); Matter of Levy, 17 I. & N. Dec. 539 (B.I.A. 1980) (marriage of natural parents is required).

[10] Matter of W-, 7 I. & N. Dec. 373 (B.I.A. 1956) (legitimation by court decree).

	Is child legitimated by subsequent marriage of parents?	Is issue of a void marriage legitimate?	Can a child be legitimated in a manner not involving marriage of natural parents?
Oregon	Yes. Section 109.070(3) to be read in combination with Section 109.060 of Oregon Revised Statutes. (1991)	Yes. Sections 106.190 and 106.210 of Oregon Revised Statutes. (1991)	Yes. See section 109.060 of Oregon Revised Statutes. (1991)
Pennsyl-vania	Yes. Pa.C.S.A. 20 Sec. 2107 and 23 Pa.C.S.A.Sec. 5101 of Purdon's Pennsylvania Statutes Annotated. (1992)	Yes. Section 23 Pa.C.S.A., section 5102 of Purdon's Pennsylvania Statutes Annotated.(1992)	Yes, (a) if during the lifetime of the child, the father openly holds out the child to be his own and either (1) receives it into his home or (2) provides support for the child. (b) If there is clear and convincing evidence that the man was the father of the child, which may include a prior court determination of paternity. 20 Pa C.S.A. Sec. 2107 and 23 PaC.S.A. Sec. 5102. Pennsylvania Statutes Annotated. (1992)
Rhode Island	Yes. Section 33-1-8 of General Laws of Rhode Island. (1992)	Yes. Section 15-8-3 of General Laws of Rhode Island. (1992)	Yes, by adoption. Sections 15-7-5 and 15-7-14 of General Laws of Rhode Island. (1992)
South Carolina	Yes. Section 20-1-60 of Code of Laws of South Carolina. (1990)	Yes. Section 20-1-80 and 20-1-90 of Code of Laws of South Carolina.	Yes, an unmarried father may adopt his own illegitimate child. Section 15-45-30 of Code Laws of South Carolina. (1990)
South Dakota	Yes. Section 29-1-15.1 of South Dakota Codified Laws. (1992)	Yes. Section 25-3-3 of South Dakota Codified Laws. (1992)	Yes, by adoption. Section 25-6-1 of South Dakota Codified Laws. (1992)
Tennessee[11]	Yes. Section 36-2-207 of Tennessee Code Annotated. (1992)	Yes, if the father recognizes the child as his. Section 36-2-207 of Tennessee Code Annotated. (1992)	Yes, (a) An application to legitimate a child born outof-wedlock is made by petition, in writing, signed by the person wishing to legitimate such child, and setting forth the reasons therefor and the state and date of the child's birth. (b) A father may establish paternity of a child born out-of-wedlock by executing a prescribed acknowledgement of paternity before a notary public. The father's name will be entered on the birth certificate and forwarded to the juvenile court for entry of an order of legitimation. Section 36-2-202 of Tennessee Code Annotated. (1992).

---

[11] Matter of J- and Y-, 3 I. & N. Dec. 657 (B.I.A. 1949) (Tennessee court decree legitimates child).

	Is child legitimated by subsequent marriage of parents?	Is issue of a void marriage legitimate?	Can a child be legitimated in a manner not involving marriage of natural parents?
Texas[12]	Yes. Title 2, Section 12.01 and 12.02 of Texas Code Annotated. (1992)	Yes. Title 2, Section 12.01 and 12.02 of Texas Code Annotated. (1992)	Yes, if the father consents in writing to be named as the child's father on the child's birth certificate, or before the child reaches the age of majority, the father receives the child into his home and openly holds the child out as his. Title 2, Section 12.01 and 12.02. (1992)
Utah	Yes. Section 75-2-109(2)(a) of Utah Code Annotated. (1992)	Yes. Section 30-1-17.2 of Utah Code Annotated. (1992)	Yes, if he publicly acknowledges the child as his own, and receives it into his home (with the consent of his wife, if he is married) and otherwise treats it as his own legitimate child. Section 78-30-12 of Utah Code Annotated. (1992)
Vermont	Yes, if the child is recognized by the father. Title 14 Section 554 of Vermont Statutes Annotated. (1993)	Yes. Title 15, Section 520 of Vermont Statutes Annotated. (1993)	No. Vermont Statutes Annotated. (1993)
Virginia	Yes. Section 20-31.1 of Code of Virginia (1992)	Yes. Section 20-31.1 of Code of Virginia. (1992)	No. Although a child can inherit property if certain circumstances occur, this does not appear to constitute legitimation. Section 64.1-5.2 of Code of Virginia. (1992)
Washington[13]	Yes. Section 26.26.040(c) of the Revised Code of Washington. (1992)	Yes. Section 26.26.030 and 26.26.040. (1992)	Yes, if while the child is a minor, the father receives the child into his home openly holds out the child as his own. Section 26.26.040(d) of Revised Code of Washington. (1992)
West Virginia	Yes. Section 42-1-6 of Michie's West Virginia Code. (1989)	Yes. Section 42-1-7 of West Virginia Code. (1992)	Yes. The father of a natural child may file an application to establish paternity in circuit court which establishes parent child relationship as though "born in lawful wedlock". Section 48A-6-6 of West Virginia Statutes. (1989)
Wisconsin	Yes. Section 767.60 of Wisconsin Statutes (1992)	Yes. Section 767.60 of Wisconsin Statutes. (1992)	Yes. Natural father can adopt his child born out-of-wedlock thereby establishing parent and child relationship with all the rights, duties and other legal consequences. (1993)

[12] Matter of A- E-, 4 I. & N. Dec. 405 (B.I.A. 1951) (common-law marriage with recognition of paternity by father legitimates child).
[13] Burgess v. Meese, 802 F.2d 338 (9th Cir. 1986) (nationality case; a man is presumed to be a minor child's natural father if he receives the child into his home and openly holds the child as his own; law to be applied is the law of the current domicile of either the child or the father).

	Is child legitimated by subsequent marriage of parents?	Is issue of a void marriage legitimate?	Can a child be legitimated in a manner not involving marriage of natural parents?
Wyoming	Yes, if in addition to the marriage, the father is obligated to support the child under a written voluntary promise or by court. Section 14-2-102 and 14-2-101 Wyoming Statutes. (1993)	Yes. Sections 14-2-101 and 14-2-102 of Wyoming Statutes. (1989)	Yes, if while the child is a minor the father receives the child into his home and holds the child out as his own. Section 14-2-102(iv) of Wyoming Statutes. (1989)
Guam	Yes. Title II, Chapter 1, Section 215. Guam Civil Code. (1970)	Yes. Article I, Section 84 of Guam Civil Code. (1970)	Yes. The father of an illegitimate child, by publicly acknowledging it as his own, receiving it as such with the consent of his wife, if he is married, into his family, and otherwise treating it as if it were a legitimate child, thereby adopts it as such; and such child is thereupon deemed for all purposes legitimate from the time of its birth. Chapter II, Section 230 of the Guam Civil Code. (1970)
Puerto Rico[14]	Yes. Title 31, Section 442, Puerto Rico Civil Code. (1988)	Yes. Title 31, Section 412a. Puerto Rico Civil Code. (1988)	Yes. By adoption. An adoptee, for all legal purposes, be considered as a legitimate child of the adopter. Title 31, Sections 532 and 533 of the Puerto Rico Civil Code. (1988)
Virgin Islands[15]	Yes. Title 16, Section 461 of Virgin Islands Code Annotated. (1993)	Yes. Title 16, Section 461 of Virgin Islands Code Annotated. (1993)	Yes. The father of an illegitimate by publicly acknowledging it as his own, receiving it as such, with the consent of his wife, if he is married, into his family, and otherwise treating it as if it were a legitimate child, thereby adopts it as such; and such child is thereupon deemed for all purposes legitimate from the time of its birth. Title 16, Section 462 of Virgin Islands Code Annotated. (1993)

[14] Matter of Doble-Pena, 13 I. & N. Dec. 366 (B.I.A. 1969) (marriage of parents is the only way to legitimate child); Matter of Bautista, 17 I. & N. Dec. 122 (B.I.A. 1979) (acknowledgment of paternity legitimates child in Puerto Rico); Petition of Fraga, 429 F.Supp. 549 (D.P.R. 1974) (nationality case; paternity acknowledged in Venezuelan birth certificate legitimates child in Puerto Rico); Rios v. Civiletti, 571 F.Supp. 218 (D.P.R. 1983) (nationality case; acknowledgment of paternity in birth certificate in Mexico is basis of legitimation under Puerto Rico law).

[15] Matter of Peters, 11 I. & N. Dec. 691 (B.I.A. 1966) (legitimation occurs through adoption by natural father and his wife, since it constitutes public acknowledgment of paternity with the consent of his wife and a taking into the family of the natural child); Matter of Obando, 16 I. & N. Dec. 278 (B.I.A. 1977) (legitimation when over 18; no immigration benefits as a child even though legitimation decree stated it was retroactive to date of birth).

Chapter 5

Derivation of Citizenship after Birth

Research References

West's Key Number Digest

Aliens, Immigration and Citizenship ☜650 to 685

Westlaw Databases

Steel on Immigration Law (STEEL)

Immigration Law Service (2d ed.) (IMMLS2D)

Treatises and Practice Aids

Dizon and Wettstein, Immigration Law Service 2d §§ 14:206 to 14:210
Steel on Immigration Law § 15:4

> **KeyCite®:** Cases and other legal materials listed in KeyCite Scope can be researched through the KeyCite service on Westlaw®. Use KeyCite to check citations for form, parallel references, prior and later history, and comprehensive citator information, including citations to other decisions and secondary materials.

I. INTRODUCTION

§ 5:1 Overview

Research References

Steel on Immigration Law § 15:4

In addition to acquiring United States citizenship at birth through a parent, a person may derive citizenship from a U.S. citizen parent after birth. This is referred to as derivative citizenship. The importance of derivative citizenship is that, like all other forms of acquisition of citizenship, it confers upon the person all the benefits of U.S. citizenship. Most importantly, a person who derives citizenship is not subject to deportation.[1]

Until October 30, 2000, the main vehicle for automatic derivation of U.S. citizenship after birth was the naturalization of the parent or parents of the noncitizen child.[2] In the year 2000, Congress amended the nationality provisions, to allow derivation of citizenship, not based on the naturalization of the parent, but on a combination of factors, including U.S. citizenship of one parent and acquisition of lawful permanent residence by the child.[3]

This new provision must be distinguished from acquisition of citizenship at birth, and also from the provision allowing for naturalization of children upon application by a U.S. citizen parent.[4] If the child did not acquire U.S. citizenship at the time of birth abroad, be it because the parent was not a U.S. citizen at the time or because of failure to comply with the various residence and retention requirements, the child may have derived U.S. citizenship at a later date either through the naturalization of the parent or under the new provision. In addition, children who did not derive citizenship automatically, either at birth or later, are still eligible for naturalization upon application by a U.S. citizen parent.[5]

[Section 5:1]

[1]Matter of P-, 1 I. & N. Dec. 127, 136 (B.I.A.) approved (Att'y Gen. 1941).

[2]Between 1855 and 1922, noncitizen women who married U.S. citizen men also derived U.S. citizenship. Sec. 2 of Act of Feb. 10, 1855, 10 Stat. 604 reproduced as Appendix 4-4 to Ch 4. This law was repealed by the Cable Act of 1922, Pub. L. No. 67-3466, §§ 2, 3, 6, 7, 42 Stat. 1021 (Sept. 22, 1922) reproduced as Appendix 4-8 to Ch 4. For a discussion of rules relating to citizenship and naturalization of noncitizen women, see §§ 11:2 to 11:16.

[3]Child Citizenship Act of 2000, Pub. L. No. 106-395, 114 Stat. 1631 (Oct. 30, 2000) reproduced as Appendix 5-2.

[4]See §§ 4:1 et seq. and §§ 11:18 to 11:25.

[5]See §§ 11:18 to 11:25. The new provision will tend to limit the usefulness of the naturalization procedures described in Ch 11. Some situations, however, will still call for those procedures.

II. APPLICABLE PRINCIPLES

§ 5:2 Automatic vesting: Lack of knowledge by citizen

Research References

Dizon and Wettstein, Immigration Law Service 2d § 14:206
Steel on Immigration Law § 15:4

Derivative citizenship is a form of naturalization that occurs automatically. Children who become citizens under these provisions do not need to meet any of the substantive requirements of naturalization.[1] They do not need to file an application or submit any other paperwork to become citizens. Nor are they required to follow any designated procedures. Derivative citizenship statutes have always been written so that they vest automatically upon the occurrence of all relevant conditions.[2] Therefore, derivative citizens may be unaware of the fact that they are U.S. citizens.

Thus, for example, section 320 of the Immigration and Nationality Act now provides that "[a] child born outside of the United States *automatically becomes* a citizen of the United States *when* all of the following conditions have been fulfilled . . ."[3]

This provision is noteworthy for three reasons. First, it mandates the transformation without any decision of the USCIS. Thus, it provides that the child *automatically* becomes a citizen upon certain events occurring. Second, it refers to the transformation as *becoming a citizen* rather than being naturalized. Third, the transformation happens when a certain condition is met, rather than as a result of an application.

[Section 5:2]

[1]See INA § 320, 8 U.S.C.A. § 1431 *as amended by* Child Citizenship Act of 2000 *reproduced* as Appendix 5-2.

[2]Sec. 1, Act of March 26, 1790, 1 Stat. 103 reproduced as Appendix 4-1 to Ch 4 (the children of such person so naturalized . . . shall also be considered as citizens of the United States); Sec. 3, Act of Jan. 29, 1795, 1 Stat. 414 reproduced as Appendix 4-2 to Ch 4 (almost identical language); Sec. 4, Act of April 14, 1802, 2 Stat. 153 reproduced as Appendix 4-3 to Ch 4 ("the children of persons duly naturalized . . . shall, if dwelling in the United States, be considered as citizens of the United States"); Sec. 2172, Revised Statutes of 1878 reproduced as Appendix 4-5 to Ch 4; Sec. 5, Act of March 2, 1907, Pub.L. No. 59-193, 34 Stat. 1228 reproduced as Appendix 4-6 to Ch 4 ("a child born without the United States of noncitizen parents shall be deemed a citizen of the United States by virtue of the naturalization of or resumption of American citizenship by the parent"); Sec. 2, Act of May 24, 1934, Pub.L. 73-250, 48 Stat. 797 reproduced as Appendix 4-10 to Ch 4 (same); Secs. 313, 314, Nationality Act of 1940, Pub.L. 76-853, 54 Stat. 1137 reproduced as Appendix 4-12 to Ch 4 (section 313 is worded "is deemed a citizen", section 314 is worded "becomes a citizen upon."); Sections 320 and 321 of the Immigration Nationality Act, Pub.L. 82-414, §§ 321, 322, 66 Stat. 245 (June 27, 1952), as amended by Act of Oct. 5, 1978, Pub. L. 95-417, §§ 4, 5, 92 Stat. 917; Act of Dec. 29, 1981, Pub. L. 97-116, § 18(m), 95 Stat. 1620; Act of Nov. 14, 1986, Pub. L. 99-653, §§ 14, 15, 100 Stat. 3657; Act of Oct. 24, 1988, Pub. L.100-525, §§ 8(l), 9 (w), 102 Stat. 2618 reproduced as Appendix 4-24 to Ch 4; INA § 320, 8 U.S.C.A. § 1431; INS Interp. 320.1 (under all statutes, derivation was complete and citizenship vested upon the realization of the last essential element in a required combination). See e.g., Zartarian v. Billings, 204 U.S. 170, 174, 27 S.Ct. 182, 183, 51 L.Ed. 428 (1907).

[3]INA § 320(a), 8 U.S.C.A. § 1431(a) as amended by Child Citizenship Act of 2000 *reproduced* as Appendix 5-2 (emphasis added).

Since they are already citizens, persons who derive citizenship may obtain proof of their U.S. citizenship status by filing for a certificate of citizenship with the USCIS or for a passport with the passport office of the State Department.[4]

§ 5:3 Applicable law and common requirements

Research References

A.L.R. Index, Immigration and Naturalization
Validity, Construction, and Application of Child Citizenship Act, 194 A.L.R. Fed. 383
Dizon and Wettstein, Immigration Law Service 2d §§ 14:206, 14:209

Derivative citizenship statutes go back to the beginning of the republic. During the second session of the first Congress, the first act to establish a uniform law of naturalization included a derivative citizenship provision.[1] Throughout the history of the U.S., different laws have imposed different requirements in order to derive U.S. citizenship through the naturalization of the parents.[2] In general, every subsequent statute repealed in whole or in part the equivalent provisions of the prior statute.[3] Judicial and administrative interpretations have found the citizenship statutes to confer benefits prospectively.[4]

In general, statutes governing the derivation of U.S. citizenship have always required a combination of qualifying events to take place before the child turns a certain age. The law that determines which requirements apply to a person is the law that was in effect at the time the "last qualifying act" took place, i.e. when the last material prerequisite was met.[5]

The minimum requirements shared by all derivative citizenship statutes up to the year 2000 were the naturalization of one parent and the acquisition of lawful permanent residence by the child.[6] The Child Citizenship Act of 2000 removed the

---

[4]See §§ 13:1 et seq.

[Section 5:3]

[1]Act of March 26, 1790 reproduced as Appendix 4-1 to Ch 4.

[2]Between 1855 and 1922, women who married U.S. citizens also derived U.S. citizenship from their husbands. Sec. 2, Act of February 10, 1855, 10 Stat. 604 reproduced as Appendix 4-4 to Ch 4, codified as sec. 1994, Revised Statutes of 1878, reproduced as Appendix 4-5 to Ch 4. That provision was repealed in 1922 and was replaced by relaxed procedures for the naturalization of wives of U.S. citizens. Secs. 2, 6, Act of September 22, 1922, Pub.L. 67-346, 42 Stat. 1021 reproduced as Appendix 4-8 to Ch 4. This section was finally amended to provide the same benefits for noncitizen men who married U.S. citizen women. Sec. 4, Act of May 24, 1934 reproduced as Appendix 4-10 to Ch 4. See §§ 11:2 to 11:16.

[3]The relevant statutes are reproduced as appendices to Ch 4. The Act of 1907 only repealed part of the derivative citizenship provisions of the Act of 1802. See § 5:12.

[4]Zartarian v. Billings, 204 U.S. 170, 174, 27 S. Ct. 182, 183, 51 L. Ed. 428 (1907) (interpreting Act of 1802); Bertoldi v. McGrath, 178 F.2d 977, 978 (D.C. Cir. 1949) (interpreting the Nationality Act of 1940); Matter of L-, 8 I. & N. Dec. 272, 273–74 (B.I.A. 1959) (interpreting the INA); Matter of L-, 7 I. & N. Dec. 512, 513 (Reg. Comm'r 1957) (same). See also Buffalino v. Irvine, 103 F.2d 830 (10th Cir. 1939) (dicta finding lack of retroactivity for the 1934 act).

[5]Matter of Sepulveda, 14 I. & N. Dec. 616, 618 (B.I.A. 1974); INS Interp. 320.1(a).

[6]Before 1907, statutes required the parent to naturalize and the child to be "dwelling" in the U.S. See Sec. 1, Act of March 26, 1790 reproduced as Appendix 4-1 to Ch 4; Sec. 3, Act of Jan. 29, 1795 reproduced as Appendix 4-2 to Ch 4; Sec. 4, Act of April 14, 1802 reproduced as Appendix 4-3 to Ch 4; Revised Statutes 2172. reproduced as Appendix 4-5 to Ch 4. After 1907, the statutes require the child to be "residing permanently" in the U.S. Sec. 5, Act of March 2, 1907 reproduced as Appendix 4-6 to Ch 4; Sec. 2, Act of May 24, 1934 reproduced as Appendix 4-10 to Ch 4; Secs. 313, 314, Nationality Act of

requirement of the naturalization of the parent, expanding derivation to those children of a U.S. citizen parent (whether native born or naturalized) if the children commenced residence in the United States by a certain age.[7]

The order in which the events required for derivation took place is generally immaterial, provided they all took place before the child turned a certain age.[8] Thus, children who become lawful permanent residents after the naturalization of their parents could derive citizenship to the same extent as those who become lawful permanent residents before their parents' naturalization[9]

It should be noted, however, that for derivative citizenship claims predicated upon parents who are legally separated, the order of events may nevertheless be relevant. The Third Circuit has twice held that a child cannot derive citizenship through a naturalized parent having legal custody over the child unless the parent naturalizes after the legal separation occurs.[10] It is not clear whether the briefing in those cases advised the Third Circuit of the Agency's interpretation of this point, but that holding is the law of the Third Circuit.

The Board of Immigration Appeals has rejected the Third Circuit's interpretation in *Jordon* and *Bagot*, finding that a child derives citizenship even if their naturalizing parent separates after naturalization, but before the child turns 18.[11]

The Board of Immigration Appeals held that the Child Citizenship Act of 2000 is not retroactive for persons who meet all of the requirements but who were eighteen

---

1940 reproduced as Appendix 4-12 to Ch 4 (relevant portions of these statutes have been reproduced as appendices to Ch 4); INA §§ 320, 321 prior to amendment by Child Citizenship Act of 2000 reproduced as Appendix 4-24 to Ch 4. Only the INA specifically provided that the permanent residence of the child must have been pursuant to lawful admission. INA §§ 320, 321, 8 U.S.C.A. §§ 1431, 1432 prior to Child Citizenship Act of 2000. However, the courts have read a requirement of lawful residence upon both the requirement of "dwelling" and the requirement of "residing permanently" U.S. ex rel. Patton v. Tod, 297 F. 385, 394 (2d Cir. 1924) appeal dismissed 267 U.S. 607 (1925); Matter of M-, 3 I. & N. Dec. 815, 816 (Central Office 1949). Cf. Matter of P-, 1 I. & N. Dec. 127, 135, 1941 WL 7928 (B.I.A. 1941); Matter of M-, 3 I. & N. Dec. 815, 816 (Central Office 1949). Cf. Matter of P-, 1 I. & N. Dec. 127, 135, 1941 WL 7928 (B.I.A. 1941). Cf. Matter of P-, 1 I. & N. Dec. 127, 135, 1941 WL 7928 (B.I.A. 1941) (using interchangeably coming to the United States for permanent residence in the text and being lawfully admitted for permanent residence in finding of fact No. 6).

[7]Child Citizenship Act of 2000, Public Law 106-395, § 1, 114 Stat. 1631 (Oct. 30, 2000) *amending* INA § 320, 8 U.S.C.A. § 1431 *reproduced* as Appendix 5-2.

[8]INS Interp. 320.1(a).

[9]In addition, the argument could be made that a close reading of the INA as it existed prior to the Child Citizenship Act of 2000 amendment supported the view that if the child begins to reside permanently after the parent naturalizes, that residence does not need to be as a lawful permanent resident in order for the child to derive citizenship. INA §§ 320, 321, 8 U.S.C.A. §§ 1431, 1432 prior to Child Citizenship Act of 2000 reproduced as Appendix 5–2. Both sections provided as a condition for derivation that the child be "residing in the United States pursuant to a lawful admission for permanent residence" at the time of the naturalization of the parent, or thereafter begin to "reside permanently in the United States while under the age" of eighteen. INA §§ 320(a)(2), 321(a)(5), 8 U.S.C.A. §§ 1431(a)(2), 1432(a)(5) prior to Child Citizenship Act of 2000. Before the 1978 amendment, the child required age for derivation was sixteen, but the relevant wording for the residence requirement was the same. INA §§ 320(a)(2), 321(a)(5), 8 U.S.C.A. §§ 1431(a)(2), 1432(a)(5) as originally enacted by Act of June 27, 1952, 66 Stat. 163. This view is further supported by the fact that Congress decided to explicitly include in the INA the requirement of lawful admission to permanent residence for children who were present in the United States before their parents naturalized. INS Interp. 320. 1(a). But see § 5:8.

[10]See Bagot v. Ashcroft, 398 F.3d 252, 257 (3d Cir.2005); Jordon v. Attorney General, 424 F.3d 320 (3d Cir. 2005).

[11]Matter of Baires-Larios, 24 I. & N. Dec. 467 (BIA 2008).

years or older on February 27, 2001, the effective date of the act.[12] Several courts have now held that the Child Citizenship Act does not confer citizenship retroactively.[13]

§ 5:4 Children born out-of-wedlock and adopted children

Research References

A.L.R. Index, Immigration and Naturalization
Validity, Construction, and Application of Child Citizenship Act, 194 A.L.R. Fed. 383
Who Is "Stepchild" for Purposes of § 101(b)(1)(b) of Immigration and Nationality Act (8 U.S.C.A. § 1101(b)(1)(b)), 54 A.L.R. Fed. 182
Dizon and Wettstein, Immigration Law Service 2d §§ 14:207 to 14:209
Steel on Immigration Law § 15:4

For purposes of derivative citizenship, children born out-of-wedlock to a naturalized mother were treated as if both parents had naturalized.[1] The only exception was for children whose mothers naturalized between January 13, 1941 and December 23, 1952. Those children did not derive U.S. citizenship at the time of naturalization of their mother. However, if on December 24, 1952 they were under the age of sixteen, still permanent residents, and their mothers were still U.S. citizens, they automatically derived U.S. citizenship on that date.[2]

Prior to the Child Citizenship Act of 2000 amendments, children born out-of-wedlock to a naturalizing father have only been able to derive citizenship if they were legitimated according to the requirements of the nationality statute in effect at the time the last prerequisite for derivation was met.[3] However, all the other requirements of the specific act must be met. This includes the naturalization of both parents when the statute so requires.[4]

Legitimation is based on municipal law and may take many forms, including the abolition of the distinction between legitimate and out-of-wedlock children.[5] Appendix 4-25 to Ch 4, summarizes the BIA's interpretation of the legitimation laws of foreign countries and of the different states of the U.S. at different points in time. It also summarizes a State Department interpretation of the legitimation laws of the states of the U.S.

The Child Citizenship Act of 2000 is silent as to the "legitimation" requirement.[6] However, the general definition of "child" for citizenship purposes continues to

---

[12]Matter of Rodriguez-Tejedor, 23 I. & N. Dec. 153 (B.I.A. 2001).

[13]Nehme v. I.N.S., 252 F.3d 415 (5th Cir. 2001); Hughes v. Ashcroft, 255 F.3d 752 (9th Cir. 2001); U.S. v. Arbelo, 288 F.3d 1262 (11th Cir. 2002); Drakes v. Ashcroft, 323 F.3d 189 (2nd Cir. 2003); Gomez-Diaz v. Ashcroft, 324 F.3d 913 (7th Cir. 2003); U.S. v. Hodulik, 2002 WL 1396904, *4 (6th Cir. 2002) (unpublished decision).

[Section 5:4]

[1]INS Interp. 320.1(c).

[2]INS Interp. 320.1(c).

[3]For specific requirements, see discussion under each statute.

[4]See INS Interp. 320.1(b).

[5]See generally, § 4:9. For an in depth discussion of legitimation, see Levy, The Family in Immigration and Nationality Law: Part I, 92-9 Immigration Briefings 10–11 (Sept. 1992).

[6]Child Citizenship Act of 2000, § 101 reproduced as Appendix 5-2.

distinguish between children who are legitimated and those who are not.[7] The only statutory requirement is for the child to be in the physical and legal custody of the U.S. citizen parent.[8] The interim rule issued by the legacy INS specifies that, in the case of a child born out-of-wedlock, the child must be legitimated and currently residing with the biological parent.[9] However, USCIS has since modified its position and made clear that there is no legitimation requirement under this provision when the mother of a child born out of wedlock naturalizes.[10] Thus, where a child born out of wedlock meets all other requirements of INA § 320, the child is eligible for derivative citizenship through the naturalization of the mother even if the child was never legitimated.[11] USCIS has instructed that this policy interpretation is to be applied to all cases pending on or filed after September 26, 2003, the date of the memorandum advising of the new interpretation. Additionally, USCIS has instructed that the memorandum should be considered a sufficient basis to grant an otherwise untimely motion to reopen or reconsider a previous decision, if the child is otherwise still eligible.[12]

The Supreme Court has held that the distinction between children born out-of-wedlock to U.S. citizen fathers and U.S. citizen mothers is not a violation of the equal protection guarantee.[13]

Before 1978, adopted children could not derive citizenship at the time of their adoptive parent's naturalization.[14] They could, before and after 1978, derive naturalization upon the naturalization of their *natural* parents, if all other requirements were met.[15] Similarly they could derive from their adoptive parents if the adoptive parent was the biological father and adoption resulted in the legitimation of the child.[16]

After October 5, 1978, the law was changed and adopted children could also derive naturalization from their adoptive parents,[17] but the statute required that the adopted child be "residing in the United States at the time of naturalization. . . in

---

[7]INA § 101(b)(1), 8 U.S.C.A. § 1101(b)(1).

[8]INA § 320(a)(3), 8 U.S.C.A. § 1431(a)(3) as amended by Child Citizenship Act of 2000, § 101 reproduced as Appendix 5-2.

[9]66 Fed. Reg. 32138 (Jun. 13, 2001), adding 8 C.F.R. § 320.1(1)(iii).

[10]Memorandum of William Yates, Acting Assoc. Dir., CIS, HQ 70/34.2-P (Sept. 26, 2003), entitled "Eligibility of Children Born out of Wedlock for Derivative Citizenship," *posted on* AILA InfoNet at Doc. No. 03100241.

[11]Memorandum of William Yates, Acting Assoc. Dir., CIS, HQ 70/34.2-P (Sept. 26, 2003), entitled "Eligibility of Children Born out of Wedlock for Derivative Citizenship," *posted on* AILA InfoNet at Doc. No. 03100241.

[12]Memorandum of William Yates, Acting Assoc. Dir., CIS, HQ 70/34.2-P (Sept. 26, 2003), entitled "Eligibility of Children Born out of Wedlock for Derivative Citizenship," *posted on* AILA InfoNet at Doc. No. 03100241.

[13]Tuan Anh Nguyen v. I.N.S., 121 S. Ct. 2053, 150 L. Ed. 2d 115 (U.S. 2001). See § 4:14.

[14]INS Interp. 320.1(d)(1). But see § 5:13. For additional requirements imposed on adoption by nationality law, see INA § 101(c)(1), 8 U.S.C.A. § 1101(c)(1). For case law interpreting some of these requirements, see Levy, The Family in Immigration and Nationality Law: Part I, 92-9 Immigration Briefings 11–13 (Sept. 1992).

[15]INS Interp. 320.1(d)(1).

[16]INS Interp. 320.1(d)(1).

[17]INA § 101(c)(1), 8 U.S.C.A. § 1101(c)(1).

the custody of his adoptive parent or parents."[18] It is not sufficient to be adopted and to be a permanent resident in the custody of the naturalized parent or parents after their naturalization. The Second Circuit has upheld this requirement against an Equal Protection challenge, under rational basis scrutiny.[19]

The Child Citizenship Act of 2000 also makes provisions for adopted children. They can derive citizenship "if the child satisfies the requirements applicable to adopted children under section 101(b)(1)."[20] This includes satisfying either the definition of adopted or orphan child in subsection 101(b)(1).[21]

Nationality law does not treat stepchildren as "children," and stepchildren may not derive naturalization from their stepparents.[22] The Board of Immigration Appeals has now agreed with DHS that a U.S. citizen cannot obtain citizenship for a stepchild unless that parent legally adopts the child.[23] Stepchildren do not qualify as children under INA § 101(c)(1).

§ 5:5 Marital status of child

Research References

Dizon and Wettstein, Immigration Law Service 2d § 14:209

Before December 24, 1952, a child could derive citizenship through the naturalization of his or her parent even when the child was married.[1] This rule applied even when a female child was married to a noncitizen during the time period when marriage to noncitizens expatriated women.[2] The INA introduced a requirement that the child be unmarried for derivation to occur.[3]

§ 5:6 Meaning of "naturalization" of parent for purposes of derivative citizenship

Research References

Steel on Immigration Law § 15:4

Under the pre-Child Citizenship Act case law, any form of naturalization, be it by the Agency, a court, or by operation of law under treaty or statute, could be the basis for derivative citizenship.[1] This includes both the vesting of citizenship upon women when they married U.S. citizens, and collective naturalization when a terri-

---

[18]Former INA § 322(b) (repealed).

[19]Smart v. Ashcroft, 401 F.3d 119 (2d Cir. 2005).

[20]INA § 320(b), 8 U.S.C.A. § 1431(b) as amended by Child Citizenship Act of 2000.

[21]INA § 101(b)(1)(E), (F), 8 U.S.C.A. § 1101(b)(1)(E), (F). For a detailed discussion of the adoption provisions under the current law, see §§ 5:18, 5:19.

[22]See INA § 101(c)(1); *former* 8 C.F.R. § 322.2(b)(2)(i) *prior to amendment by* 66 Fed. Reg. 32138 (2001); INS Interp 320.1(d)(1).

[23]See Matter of Guzman-Gomez, 24 I&N Dec. 824 (BIA 2009); INS Interp. 320.1(d)(1).

[Section 5:5]

[1]INS Interp. 320.1(a)(5); 7 FAM 1153.4-3(d).

[2]INS Interp. 320.1(a)(5); 7 FAM 1153.4-3(d).

[3]INA § 101(c)(1), 8 U.S.C.A. § 1101(c)(1); INS Interp. 320.1(a)(5).

[Section 5:6]

[1]INS Interp. 320.1(e)(1).

tory became a state.[2] Resumption of citizenship, even when such resumption has not been perfected by the taking of the oath when required, works as "naturalization" for purposes of derivative citizenship statutes.[3] Naturalization of a noncitizen national is also the basis for derivation of citizenship, even under those statutes where derivative citizenship was worded in terms of naturalization of noncitizens.[4]

Until 1941, derivative citizenship could also be based on what, for want of a better phrase, will be referred to as constructive resumption of citizenship. Under the Act of 1907, and under common law, U.S. citizen women who married foreigners automatically expatriated themselves.[5] U.S. citizen women who divorced noncitizens were deemed to be "resuming" U.S. citizenship for derivative citizenship purposes.[6] This, of course, was a basis for derivation.[7]

In 1922, however, Congress repealed that expatriating provision of the 1907 act and thereafter women who married a foreigner no longer forfeited their U.S. citizenship.[8] As a consequence, when those women returned to the United States, they no longer "resumed" their U.S. citizenship, since they had not lost it. Children born abroad to those women were not U.S. citizens at birth because before 1934, only children born abroad to U.S. citizen fathers and children born out-of-wedlock acquired U.S. citizenship at birth abroad.[9] According to a literal interpretation of the law, children of women who married noncitizens after 1922 would not acquire U.S. citizenship upon their return to the U.S. since their mothers never lost their U.S. citizenship and thus were not "resuming" citizenship upon their return to the United States.[10] The Attorney General in the case of Fernando de Coll y Picard expressed the view that there was no basis for distinguishing women who had been expatriated from those who had not in terms of conferring benefits upon their children.[11] Therefore, women who returned to the United States after divorcing a noncitizen were deemed to be resuming U.S. citizenship for purposes of their children's right to derive citizenship, even when such women married after 1922 and never expatriated themselves. This is known as the "De Coll" doctrine and it was in effect until 1941.

Fernando de Coll was a child born in Spain to a U.S. citizen woman who married

---

[2]INS Interp. 320.1(e)(1), citing to In re Bishop, 27 F.2d at 149 (child could derive citizenship even when naturalization vested upon the marriage to a U.S. citizen); Application of Brand, A-13029807 (1966) (unpublished decision); 7 FAM 1153.4-1(e)(1). For a discussion of collective naturalization, see Ch 2.

[3]INS Interp. 320.1(e)(1) citing to Petition of Drysdale, 20 F.2d 957 (E.D. Mich. 1927) (resumption of citizenship by woman who expatriated by marriage to foreigner before 1922); Matter of P-, 1 I. & N. Dec. 127, 129–32, 1941 WL 7928 (B.I.A. 1941) (child could derive citizenship when the 1936 Act deemed his mother a U.S. citizen because of her divorce even before she perfected her resumption of citizenship by taking the oath); Matter of B-, 1 I. & N. Dec. 283, 285 (B.I.A. 1942).

[4]INS Interp. 320.1(e)(3).

[5]Sec. 3, Act of March 2, 1907 reproduced as Appendix 4-7, to Ch 4; Mackensie v. Hare, 239 U.S. 299, 36 S.Ct. 106, 60 L.Ed. 297 (1917); Petition of Drysdale, 20 F.2d 957 (E.D. Mich. 1927); Petition of Drysdale, 20 F.2d 957 (E.D. Mich. 1927). For a discussion of special naturalization provisions relating to marriage, see Ch 11.

[6]See INS Interp. 320.1(a)(4).

[7]See Petition of Drysdale, 20 F.2d 957 (E.D. Mich. 1927).

[8]Sec. 3, Act of Sept. 22, 1922, 42 Stat. 1021 reproduced as Appendix 4-9, to Ch 4.

[9]See §§ 4:10 to 4:21.

[10]Until 1934, children born to U.S. citizen mother and a noncitizen father did not acquire U.S. citizenship at birth. See §§ 4:1 et seq.

[11]37 Op. Atty. Gen. 90.

a Spanish citizen in 1923. She returned to the United States with her minor child and secured a divorce in 1931.[12] The Attorney General determined in this case that the child had derived U.S. citizenship under the 1907 Act because he saw "no good reason for supposing the Congress intended to decline to grant citizenship to the minor child merely because its mother never lost American citizenship, having married after the effective date of the Act of 1922."[13] The "De Coll doctrine" applies to any child whose mother divorced before January 12, 1941, because the wording of the 1940 act precludes such interpretation.[14] This theory provides that divorce of a U.S. citizen woman from a noncitizen is treated as naturalization of the woman for derivation of citizenship purposes.[15]

§ 5:7 Derivation from naturalization of noncitizen national parents

Research References

Steel on Immigration Law § 15:4

Since 1907, the statutes have required the naturalizing parent to be an "alien" parent for derivation to occur.[1] This has raised the question whether the naturalization of a noncitizen national would affect derivative citizenship upon the child.[2] The USCIS takes the position that in spite of the wording, these statutes also effect derivation upon the naturalization of a noncitizen national parent.[3]

§ 5:8 Required residence of child

Research References

Dizon and Wettstein, Immigration Law Service 2d § 14:208

Before 1907, the statutes provided for the derivation of citizenship on condition that the child be "dwelling" within the United States.[1] Between 1907 and 1952 the statutes required the child to have been residing permanently in the United States

---

[12]Petition of Donsky, 77 F. Supp. 832, 833 (S.D. N.Y. 1948).

[13]37 Op. Atty. Gen. 90 quoted in Petition of Donsky, 77 F. Supp. 832, 833 (S.D. N.Y. 1948).

[14]INS Interp. 320.1(a)(4).

[15]INS Interp. 320.1(a)(4).

[Section 5:7]

[1]Sec. 5, Act of March 2, 1907 reproduced as Appendix 4-6 to Ch 4; Sec. 2, Act of May 24, 1934 reproduced as Appendix 4-10 to Ch 4; Sec. 313, Nationality Act of 1940 reproduced as Appendix 4-12 to Ch 4; INA § 321.

[2]INS Interp. 320.1(e)(3).

[3]INS Interp. 320.1(e)(3).

[Section 5:8]

[1]Sec. 1, Act of March 26, 1790 reproduced as Appendix 4-1 to Ch 4; Sec. 3, Act of Jan. 29, 1795 reproduced as Appendix 4-2 to Ch 4; Sec. 4, Act of April 14, 1802 reproduced as Appendix 4-3 to Ch 4; Sec. 2172, Revised Statutes of 1878 reproduced as Appendix 4-5 to Ch 4.

to derive citizenship.[2] Only the INA specifically provided that the permanent residence of the child must have been pursuant to lawful admission.[3]

All statutes regarding derivative naturalization, however, have been interpreted to require a lawful admission before the child would be considered to have been "dwelling" or "residing lawfully" in the United States.[4] Originally, this requirement developed from the view that persons who had been paroled into the country had never "entered" the United States and thus were not dwelling therein.[5] That reasoning should not have been applicable to persons who actually were residing in the United States after entering without inspection or by fraud, as those people *are* considered legally to have entered the country.[6] However, the position that lawful admission to permanent residence is required has subsequently been clearly established, at least for the purposes of the post-1907 statutes.[7] Thus, for example, a person who acquired permanent residence by fraud was held never to have derived citizenship when the person's mother naturalized, even though the person was a minor and in the United States at the time.[8] A person does not derive citizenship even when at the time of his or her original entry, he or she was eligible for lawful permanent residence and failed to obtain it through no fault of his or her own.[9] Even where there was no fraud in the admission process, if the applicant was in fact ineligible for permanent resident status, the courts have found that there was no "lawful admission."[10]

Several of the relevant statutes include language which might appear as if it could be satisfied by something less than lawful permanent residence. For instance, former INA § 321 required that the child be present "pursuant to a lawful admission for permanent residence at the time of the naturalization of the parent last natural-

---

[2]Sec. 5, Act of March 2, 1907 reproduced as Appendix 4-6 to Ch 4; Sec. 2, Act of May 24, 1934 reproduced as Appendix 4-10 to Ch 4; Secs. 313, 314, Nationality Act of 1940 reproduced as Appendix 4-12 to Ch 4.

[3]INA § 320, 8 U.S.C.A. § 1431 (2002); see also former INA § 321, 8 U.S.C.A. § 1432 prior to Child Citizenship Act of 2000.

[4]Kaplan v. Tod, 267 U.S. 228, 45 S.Ct. 257, 69 L.Ed. 585 (1925); Zartarian v. Billings, 204 U.S. 170, 27 S. Ct. 182, 51 L. Ed. 428 (1907); Zartarian v. Billings, 204 U.S. 170, 27 S. Ct. 182, 51 L. Ed. 428 (1907).

[5]Kaplan v. Tod, 267 U.S. 228, 230, 45 S. Ct. 257, 69 L. Ed. 585 (1925); Zartarian v. Billings, 204 U.S. 170, 175, 27 S. Ct. 182, 184, 51 L. Ed. 428 (1907) (in both cases the person was in the custody of the immigration authorities and was transferred to a designated organization on land for the person's safety pending).

[6]See Matter of Ching & Chen, 19 I. & N. Dec. 203 (B.I.A. 1984); Matter of Lin, 18 I. & N. Dec. 219 (B.I.A. 1982).

[7]U.S. ex re. Garos v. Reimer, 24 F.Supp. 869, 879 (S.D.N.Y. 1938); Matter of M-, 3 I. & N. Dec. 815, 816, 1949 WL 6550 (B.I.A. 1949); Matter of M-, 3 I. & N. Dec. 815, 816, 1949 WL 6550 (B.I.A. 1949); Matter of P-, 1 I. & N. Dec. 127, 135, 1941 WL 7928 (B.I.A. 1941) (using interchangeably coming to the United States for permanent residence in the text and being lawfully admitted for permanent residence in finding of fact No. 6). Cf. Patton, 385 F. at 394 (stating that 1907 Act requires lawfully begun permanent residence, while the 1802 statute requires the dwelling to have had a lawful inception and existence).

[8]U.S. ex rel. Garos v. Reimer, 24 F. Supp. 869, 870 (S.D. N.Y. 1938), order aff'd, 97 F.2d 1019 (C.C.A. 2d Cir. 1938).

[9]Schneider v. U.S.I.N.S., 65 F.Supp. 377 (W.D.Wash. 1946) aff'd 161 F.2d 1022 (9th Cir. 1947). Contra, Ted Albin Lundbergh v. I.N.S., A-11957007 (N.D.Cal. 1965) (unreported); Sarah Katherine Rodin v. Mitchell, et al., A-14232029 (N.D.Cal. 1969) (unreported) cited in INS Interp. 320.1(f).

[10]See Walker v. Holder, 589 F.3d 12, 19-21 (1st Cir. 2009) (citing Matter of Koloamatangi, 23 I. & N. Dec. 548 (B.I.A.2003)); see generally, § 7:11.

ized under clause (1) of this subsection . . . or thereafter begins to reside permanently in the United States while under the age of eighteen years." The latter provision does not on its face require permanent residency. However, the Board of Immigration Appeals, as well as the Ninth and Eleventh Circuits, have read it to do so.[11] The Board reasoned that a non-permanent resident could have no true expectation of being able to remain indefinitely in an unlawful status.[12] The Second Circuit has reasoned that while a mere subjective intent to remain is insufficient, "some lesser official objective manifestation" than permanent residence could suffice; that Court's analysis is probably dicta, but it would be fairly persuasive dicta in that circuit.[13]

Children born in the United States to diplomats are considered lawful permanent residents from birth.[14] Upon the naturalization of their parents, they become U.S. citizens if they comply with all the other requirements of derivative citizenship.[15] This rule is applied irrespective of the law governing derivative citizenship at the time of the naturalization of the parent.[16]

A person who abandons an established residence in the U.S. before the naturalization of the parent will not derive citizenship.[17] On the other hand, a temporary absence, even if it is of extensive duration, will not constitute an abandonment of residence depriving the person of the benefits of derivative citizenship.[18] A lawful permanent resident child who is temporarily absent at the time of the naturalization will be treated as constructively present in the United States during the absence, and citizenship will be derived as of the date of the parent's naturalization.[19]

§ 5:9 Legal separation: Last qualifying event between January 13, 1941, and February 27, 2001

The 1940 Act introduced the concept of "legal separation" to immigration law; under the 1940 Act, naturalization of one parent would grant automatic citizenship to a child where the parents were legally separated and the child was in custody of the naturalizing parent.[1] The rule regarding legal separation was a consistent feature of the law of derivative citizenship, until the passage of the Child Citizenship Act in 2000 altered the rules.[2]

As the U.S. Citizenship and Immigration Service (USCIS) and the Board of Immigration Appeals (BIA) have understood it, a legal separation is established by

---

[11]Matter of Nwozuzu, 24 I. & N. Dec. 609 (BIA 2008); Romero-Ruiz v. Mukasey, 538 F.3d 1057 (9th Cir. 2008); United States v. Forey-Quintero, 626 F.3d 1323 (11th Cir. 2010).

[12]Matter of Nwozuzu, 24 I. & N. Dec. 609, 613 (BIA 2008).

[13]Ashton v. Gonzales, 431 F.3d 95 (2d Cir. 2005).

[14]8 CFR § 101.3(a)(1).

[15]INS Interp. 320.1(f).

[16]INS Interp. 320.1(f).

[17]INS Interp. 320.1(f). citing to U.S. ex rel. Betty v. Day, 23 F.2d 489, 490 (2d Cir.), cert. denied, 277 U.S. 598 (1928).

[18]INS Interp. 320.1(f) citing to Matter of D-N-, 4 I. & N. Dec. 692 (B.I.A. 1952) (period of absence was over two years).

[19]INS Interp. 320.1(f); Matter of D- N-, 4 I. & N. Dec. 692, 693–94, 1952 WL 7300 (B.I.A. 1952).

[Section 5:9]

[1]§ 314(c), Nationality Act of 1940 reproduced as Appendix 4-12 to Chapter 4.

[2]See App. 5-2.

judicial proceedings and includes proceedings which terminate the marriage, as in absolute divorce, as well as proceedings which only separate the parties without destroying the marital union.[3] Once citizenship has vested under either statute as a result of such separation, it is not destroyed by the parents' subsequent resumption of the marital relationship.[4] However, all the requirements must have been met before the parties reunite in order for the child to derive.[5] The same analysis follows if a custodial order was entered by a court lacking jurisdiction.[6] As to a nunc pro tunc court order purporting to change custodial arrangements, the Fifth Circuit has examined the "correctness" of the state court order, and declined to give it effect.[7]

However, there are some important nuances to this understanding. Courts have held that "a legal separation . . . occurs only upon a formal governmental action, such as a decree issued by a court of competent jurisdiction that, under the laws of a state or nation having jurisdiction over the marriage, alters the marital relationship of the parties."[8] Informal separation is not sufficient.[9] Some courts of appeals, such as the Fifth Circuit, require a judicial decree in order for there to be a legal separation.[10] Similarly, the Fourth Circuit held that a separation agreement between the husband and wife, which was subsequently incorporated by a state court into the divorce decree, did not constitute a "legal separation" so as to render the child eligible for derivative naturalization.[11] The Second Circuit has agreed, giving no effect to a decree issued in the Dominican Republic where that court lacked jurisdiction.[12]

However, other courts, such as the Second and Ninth Circuits, would recognize forms of legal separation other than judicial orders.[13] The Ninth Circuit has found that where a state court enters a legal finding recognizing a separation years after the fact, this can have the effect of rendering the parents legally separated as of the earlier point.[14] The Ninth Circuit found that deference to the state law required this

---

[3]Matter of H-, 3 I. & N. Dec. 742, 1949 WL 6533 (B.I.A. 1949); 7 FAM 1153.4- 3(e)(3); INS Interp. 320.1(a)(6). For BIA discussion of the meaning of legal separation in other contexts, see Matter of Lenning, 17 I & N Dec. 476, 1980 WL 121921 (B.I.A. 1980); Matter of Miraldo, 14 I. & N. Dec. 704, 1974 WL 30171 (B.I.A. 1974).

[4]INS Interp. 320.1(a)(6) citing to In re Harvey Robert Hale, Adjud. Off. file 1415-673, Oct. 23, 1946 (copy of decision placed in CO 320-P, January 1972).

[5]INS Interp. 320.1(a)(6), n. 28a citing to Applications of Ui Koo Kim, A-17893530, and Ui Joon Kim, A-17893531 (1972).

[6]See, Garcia v. USICE (Dept. of Homeland Sec.), 669 F.3d 91, 97 (2d Cir. 2011).

[7]U.S. v. Esparza, 678 F.3d 389, 394 (5th Cir. 2012), cert. denied, 133 S. Ct. 1455, 185 L. Ed. 2d 367 (2013) (finding the timing "highly suspect" and questioning whether there was a "legitimate state reason" for entering the decree).

[8]Morgan v. Attorney General of U.S., 432 F.3d 226 (3d Cir. 2005).

[9]Brissett v. Ashcroft, 363 F.3d 130 (2d Cir. 2004).

[10]Nehme v. I.N.S., 252 F.3d 415 (5th Cir. 2001).

[11]Afeta v. Gonzales, 467 F.3d 402 (4th Cir. 2006).

[12]Garcia v. USICE (Dept. of Homeland Sec.), 669 F.3d 91, 96–97 (2d Cir. 2011).

[13]Brissett v. Ashcroft, 363 F.3d 130 (2d Cir. 2004) (requiring a "formal act which, under the laws of the state or nation having jurisdiction of the marriage, alters the marital relationship"); Minasyan v. Gonzales, 401 F.3d 1069 (9th Cir. 2005).

[14]Minasyan v. Gonzales, 401 F.3d 1069 (9th Cir. 2005).

conclusion because an order of legal separation had significant non-immigration-related legal effects under state law.[15]

In order for the parents to become legally separated by an act of divorce, it is necessary for the state or country entering the divorce or separation order to have jurisdiction. The Board of Immigration Appeals applies a two-step test to determining jurisdiction. First, if the parents subsequently married in a different state, the Board asks whether the earlier divorce would be given legal effect by the state where one or both subsequently marry.[16] Second, if the parents do not remarry, the Board will apply a two-part test to determine the divorce's validity: (a) the divorce must be valid in the place where it occurs, and (b) it must be worthy of recognition, which usually turns on factors such as whether at least one of the spouses were citizens of the place where one or both divorced, whether one or both lived in that place, whether both had notice and appeared or consented to the divorce, and whether the divorce occurs in the place of the marriage.[17] Under this second prong, the Board basically requires that at least one of the spouses have been domiciled in that state or country where the divorce occurs, before it will be given effect.[18] The Fourth Circuit has upheld this test.[19]

The Immigration and Naturalization Service (INS) interpretations point out that if the parents were never lawfully married, then there can be no "legal separation" as such and an award of custody to a naturalized parent under such circumstances does not result in derivation even though other requisite conditions are satisfied.[20] The Ninth Circuit has recently joined the Fifth Circuit in this interpretation.[21]

The author is unaware of any case where a court has applied Bustamonte-Barrera and Casasola in the context of the Child Citizenship Act (CCA). Whatever sense a sole custody requirement makes in the pre-CCA context — where, in most cases, both parents had to become citizens for the child to derive citizenship — a sole custody requirement would make little sense under the CCA. If that rule were applied to the CCA, so long as there were no legal separation, the naturalization of either parent would suffice to convey citizenship; but if the parents were legally separated, not even the naturalization of both parents would suffice, if the parents had joint custody over the child (since under the Bustamonte-Barrera theory, only a parent with sole custody could convey citizenship).

§ 5:10 Agency deference and citizenship

In general, the federal courts defer to agency interpretations of ambiguous statutory provisions when the agency is given authority to interpret that statute.[1] The strongest form of deference is known as "Chevron deference," after a landmark case

---

[15]Minasyan v. Gonzales, 401 F.3d 1069 (9th Cir. 2005) ("a separation by virtue of law entails important legal consequences under state law").

[16]See Matter of Hosseinian, 19 I. & N. Dec. 453 (BIA 1987).

[17]Matter of Ma, 15 I. & N. Dec. 70, 71-72 (BIA 1974).

[18]Matter of Ma, 15 I. & N. Dec. at 72.

[19]Jahed v. Acri, 468 F.3d 230 (4th Cir. 2006).

[20]Matter of H-, 3 I. & N. Dec. 742, 1949 WL 6533 (B.I.A. 1949); INS Interp. 320.1(a)(6).

[21]U.S. v. Casasola, 670 F.3d 1023, 1026 (9th Cir. 2012).

[Section 5:10]

[1]Chevron, U.S.A., Inc. v. Natural Resources Defense Council, Inc., 467 U.S. 837 (1984).

by that name.[2] Chevron deference applies where the agency has issued a formal, binding interpretation, either by regulation or by precedential decision of e.g., the Board of Immigration Appeals.[3] Where Chevron applies, it consists of two steps: (1) determining whether the statute has a plain meaning, and if so, applying that meaning; and (2) if the statute is ambiguous, deferring to a reasonable agency interpretation of those provisions.[4] The question of whether Chevron applies in the first instance is often referred to in academia as "step zero."[5] There are significant questions in the context of citizenship of whether Congress has authorized USCIS or the BIA to authoritatively interpret the provisions regarding acquisition or derivation of citizenship, and of the naturalization laws. It is often considered relevant that Congress has placed de novo review authority in the federal courts as to potential citizenship claims.[6]

The Ninth, Fifth, and Eleventh Circuits have found at "step zero" that no Chevron deference is appropriate in the context of determining whether an individual is a citizen, because the courts have been entrusted with that important task.[7] The Fourth Circuit disagrees.[8] It is worth noting that similar issues (and disagreements) exist in the naturalization context.[9]

§ 5:11 Legal custody under CCA and pre-CCA

Under both pre-CCA and post-CCA law, in order for a child to have derived citizenship through a naturalizing parent, that parent must have had legal custody over the child. There are significant differences between the law during those time periods; under the pre-CCA law, it was necessary to show both a legal separation and legal custody; under the CCA, it is necessary to show both legal and physical custody. Nevertheless, the issue of custody is a common thread running through all recent versions of the immigration laws.

Custody is determined according to the judicial or statutory decree. In the absence of judicial determination or judicial or statutory grant of custody in the case of a legal separation of the parents of a person claiming citizenship under section 314(c), the parent having actual uncontested custody is to be regarded as having "legal custody" of the person concerned for the purpose of determining that person's status

---

[2]Chevron, U.S.A., Inc. v. Natural Resources Defense Council, Inc., 467 U.S. 837 (1984).

[3]Rotimi v. Gonzales, 473 F.3d 55, 57–58 (2d Cir.2007) (per curiam); Arobelidze v. Holder, 653 F.3d 513, 519–20 (7th Cir.2011); Garcia-Quintero v. Gonzales, 455 F.3d 1006, 1013–14 (9th Cir.2006); Carpio v. Holder, 592 F.3d 1091, 1097 (10th Cir.2010); Quinchia v. U.S. Att'y Gen., 552 F.3d 1255, 1258 (11th Cir.2008); see also, United States v. Mead Corp., 533 U.S. 218 (2001).

[4]Chevron, U.S.A., Inc. v. Natural Resources Defense Council, Inc., 467 U.S. 837, 842–43 (1984).

[5]See, Cass R. Sunstein, Chevron Step Zero, 92 Va. L.Rev. 187, 191 (2006); Thomas W. Merrill & Kristin E. Hickman, Chevron's Domain, 89 Geo. L.J. 833, 836 (2001).

[6]8 U.S.C. § 1252(b)(5); see also 8 U.S.C. § 1421(c) (granting de novo authority over naturalization appeals).

[7]See, Hughes v. Ashcroft, 255 F.3d 752 (9th Cir. 2001); Sebastian-Soler v. U.S. Attorney Gen., 409 F.3d 1280, 1283 (11th Cir. 2005)(per curiam); Alwan v. Ashcroft, 388 F.3d 507 (5th Cir. 2004); but see Marquez-Marquez v. Gonzales, 455 F.3d 548, 554 n. 12 (5th Cir. 2006) (suggesting that enactment of 8 U.S.C. § 1252(a)(2)(D) might affect the deference question). The Tenth Circuit appears to agree with this analysis. Shepherd v. Holder, 678 F.3d 1171 (10th Cir. 2012).

[8]Fernandez v. Keisler, 502 F.3d 337, 342 (4th Cir. 2007).

[9]Cf. O'Sullivan v. U.S. Citizenship and Immigration Services, 453 F.3d 809, 811–12 (7th Cir. 2006) (granting no Chevron deference to naturalization eligibility question) with Boatswain v. Gonzales, 414 F.3d 413 (2d Cir.2005) (granting Chevron deference to same question).

under section 314(c).[1] Evidence showing that the person was living with the naturalizing parent will tend to establish this "actual uncontested custody."[2]

If there has been an actual judicial determination of custody for one of the parents, absent proof of mistake or that the decision was entered contrary to law, a nunc pro tunc order awarding custody to the other parent will not satisfy the requirement of "legal custody" if the order was entered after the child reached the age of eighteen years.[3] However, the Third Circuit ruled in one case that because the New York Court which awarded custody of a child to the non-U.S. citizen parent was in fact acting without jurisdiction, that no effect would be given to the custody order.[4] Because the child had, in fact, resided with the U.S. citizen parent, this was sufficient for him to derive citizenship under the rule in *Matter of M-*.[5]

A second issue that arises is the order of custody. The Third Circuit held, in two cases, that a child had to have been in the custody of the naturalizing parent before that parent naturalized, in order to derive citizenship.[6] The Board of Immigration Appeals thereafter reached the opposite conclusion in a published decision. In *Matter of Baires*,[7] the Board held to derive citizenship through the custody of a U.S. citizen who had already naturalized, one "must show only that she was in the legal custody of her father before she reached the age of 18 years, rather than on the date her father naturalized."[8] While the Baires decision technically applies everywhere but the Third Circuit, it is significantly possible that the Third Circuit will feel constrained by the Supreme Court's Brand X decision[9] to extend deference to the Board's decision in this area of legislative ambiguity.

Another, third issue that has arisen is the question of sole custody. The BIA and USCIS have not required that legal custody be sole or exclusive custody.[10] As traditionally understood, if the parents have joint custody, then both parents have legal custody.[11] Naturalization of either parent has satisfied the requirement for derivation.[12]

Unfortunately, a recent Fifth Circuit decision throws this somewhat into question. In *Bustamante-Barrera v. Gonzales*, the Fifth Circuit interpreted former INA § 321 to preclude derivation of citizenship unless the naturalizing parent had sole custody

---

[Section 5:11]

[1]7 FAM 1153.4-3(e)(1) citing to Matter of M-, 3 I. & N. Dec. 850, 1950 WL 6650 (B.I.A. 1950). The BIA subsequently reaffirmed this position. Matter of Yoon, File No. A39 764 548 (BIA Dec. 30, 1999) (unpublished).

[2]See Matter of Yoon, File No. A39 764 548 (BIA Dec. 30, 1999) (unpublished).

[3]Fierro v. Reno, 217 F.3d 1 (1st Cir. 2000).

[4]Bagot v. Ashcroft, 398 F.3d 252 (3d Cir. 2005).

[5]Bagot v. Ashcroft, 398 F.3d 252 (3d Cir. 2005).

[6]See Jordon v. Att'y Gen. of U.S., 424 F.3d 320, 330 (3d Cir. 2005); Bagot v. Ashcroft, 398 F.3d 252, 257 (3d Cir. 2005).

[7]Matter of Baires, 24 I&N Dec. 467 (BIA 2008).

[8]Matter of Baires, 24 I&N Dec. 467, 470 (BIA 2008).

[9]Nat'l Cable & Telecomms. Ass'n v. Brand X Internet Servs., 545 U.S. 967, 974–75, 125 S.Ct. 2688, 162 L.Ed.2d 820 (2005).

[10]Passport Bulletin 96-18 (Nov. 6, 1996) (interpreting the provision of the INA) cited in Matter of Yoon, File No. A39 764 548 (BIA Dec. 30, 1999) (unpublished).

[11]Passport Bulletin 96-18 (Nov. 6, 1996) (interpreting the provision of the INA).

[12]Passport Bulletin 96-18 (Nov. 6, 1996) (interpreting the provision of the INA).

of the child.[13] That Court, focusing on the language in former INA § 321(a)(3) referring to "the naturalization of **the** parent having legal custody," held that Congress had used the "singular form" of parent, signifying its clear intent that the statute apply only where the naturalizing parent had sole custody.[14] The Court distinguished this language from the "parent or parents" language of INA § 101(c)(1), which, it said, evinced an intention to include either parent.[15] The *Bustamante-Barrera* Court's analysis is questionable; it ignored (or was not informed of) authority holding the contrary of its conclusion, and by reading § 321(a)(3) in contrast to, rather than in conjunction with, § 101(c)(1), it would seem likely to do violence to clear Congressional intent, particularly in the Child Citizenship Act context. An alternate interpretation would have applied the principle of noscitur a sociis to reconcile INA § 101(c)(1) and former § 321(a)(3) in a harmonious manner. Still, as the Court of Appeals case most on point, *Bustamante-Barrera* is a prominent case which will have to be addressed in any subsequent similar case.

III. DERIVATIVE CITIZENSHIP PROVISIONS UNDER SPECIFIC LAWS

§ 5:12   Last qualifying event before May 24, 1934

Research References

A.L.R. Index, Immigration and Naturalization
Who Is "Stepchild" for Purposes of § 101(b)(1)(b) of Immigration and Nationality Act (8 U.S.C.A. § 1101(b)(1)(b)), 54 A.L.R. Fed. 182
Dizon and Wettstein, Immigration Law Service 2d §§ 14:209, 14:210
Steel on Immigration Law § 15:4

The first naturalization law of the U.S. had a provision granting U.S. citizenship to "the children of [a person] naturalized, dwelling within the United States, being under the age of twenty-one years at the time of such naturalization."[1] This same provision, as worded by the Act of 1802 governed the derivative citizenship of children of naturalizing parents until May 24, 1934, and indeed continued in effect until 1941.[2]

Under this provision, any child who was residing in the United States at the time of the father's naturalization became a U.S. citizen.[3] The child would also derive citizenship at the time of the mother's naturalization.[4] After 1907, derivative citizenship could be transmitted by the naturalization of the mother even when she was

---

[13]Bustamante-Barrera v. Gonzales, 447 F.3d 388 (5th Cir. 2006).

[14]Bustamante-Barrera v. Gonzales, 447 F.3d 388 (5th Cir. 2006).

[15]Bustamante-Barrera v. Gonzales, 447 F.3d 388 (5th Cir. 2006).

[Section 5:12]

[1]Sec. 1, Act of March 26, 1790 reproduced as Appendix 4-1 to Ch 4.

[2]See Sec. 3, Act of January 29, 1795 reproduced as Appendix 4-2 to Ch 4; Sec. 4, Act of April 14, 1802 reproduced as Appendix 4-3 to Ch 4 reenacted and incorporated into Sec. 2172, Revised Statutes of 1878 reproduced as Appendix 4-5 to Ch 4. The Act of 1802 provides that "the children of persons duly naturalized under any of the laws of the United States, . . . being under the age of twenty-one years, at the time of their parents being so naturalized . . . shall, if dwelling in the United States, be considered as citizens of the United States."

[3]See Zartarian v. Billings, 204 U.S. 170, 174, 27 S. Ct. 182, 183, 51 L. Ed. 428 (1907); Campbell v. Gordon, 2 U.S. (6 Cranch) 176, 183, 3 L.Ed. 190, 192–93 (1810).

[4]U.S. ex rel. Guest v. Perkins, 17 F.Supp. 177, 180–81 (D.D.C. 1936).

not divorced or widowed.[5] Before 1907, there was a requirement that the mother be divorced or widowed for her children to derive citizenship through her naturalization.[6]

Naturalization, during this and subsequent periods, refers to a number of different manners in which a noncitizen can acquire U.S. citizenship. The meaning of naturalization for derivative citizenship is discussed in detail above.[7]

The majority of court decisions hold that the child acquired citizenship even if he or she was not residing in the United States at the time of the parent's naturalization, but commenced to reside after the naturalization of the parents.[8] The legacy INS also subscribed to this position.[9] However, the INS would limit naturalization in these cases to those children whose permanent residence in the United States started before they turned twenty-one.[10] The courts, on the other hand, take the position that the child would derive citizenship even if he or she started residing in the United States after turning twenty-one years of age.[11] They read the statute as only requiring the child to have been under the age of twenty-one at the time of the parent's naturalization.[12]

To clarify that a child who started to reside in the United States after the parent naturalized also derived citizenship, Congress passed a law in 1907 specifically providing that if the parent naturalizes before the child turns twenty-one, the child will derive citizenship at the time he or she begins to reside permanently in the United States, provided he or she is still a minor.[13]

The 1907 act repealed the Act of 1802 only in so far as it applied to persons arriving in the United States after the naturalization of their parents. The 1907 act only applies to children who came to the United States after the naturalization of the parent.[14] If the child came before the naturalization of the parent, the Act of 1802 applied (as incorporated into section 2172 of the Revised Statutes).[15]

Prior to the 1907 act, a person derived citizenship when the parent naturalized

---

[5]U.S. ex rel. Guest v. Perkins, 17 F. Supp. 177, 180 (D. D.C. 1936). The State Department follows an earlier decision of the Attorney General holding otherwise. See 7 FAM 1153.4-1(e)(2) citing 36 Op. Atty. Gen. 197 (1929). See also § 5:6, for a discussion of derivative citizenship of the child upon the mother's resuming U.S. citizenship after having been expatriated by marriage to a foreigner. See § 5:12, for a discussion of the requirement's that the mother be divorced or widowed for the child to derive citizenship.

[6]See § 5:12.

[7]See § 5:6.

[8]See U.S. v. Tod, 297 F. 385, 389–392 (C.C.A. 2d Cir. 1924), cert. granted, 264 U.S. 580, 44 S. Ct. 454, 68 L. Ed. 859 (1924) and petition dismissed, 267 U.S. 607, 45 S. Ct. 229, 69 L. Ed. 811 (1925) (interpreting the wording of the 1802 Act).

[9]INS Interp. 320.1(a)(2).

[10]INS Interp. 320.1(a)(2).

[11]U.S. v. Tod, 297 F. 385, 391–92 (C.C.A. 2d Cir. 1924), cert. granted, 264 U.S. 580, 44 S. Ct. 454, 68 L. Ed. 859 (1924) and petition dismissed, 267 U.S. 607, 45 S. Ct. 229, 69 L. Ed. 811 (1925).

[12]See wording of the statute.

[13]Sec. 5, Act of March 2, 1907 reproduced as Appendix 4-7 to Ch 4 (the statute is worded in terms of the child's minority which at the time was under the age of twenty-one). See also, U.S. v. Tod, 297 F. 385, 391–92 (C.C.A. 2d Cir. 1924), cert. granted, 264 U.S. 580, 44 S. Ct. 454, 68 L. Ed. 859 (1924) and petition dismissed, 267 U.S. 607, 45 S. Ct. 229, 69 L. Ed. 811 (1925).

[14]U.S. v. Tod, 297 F. 385, 392–93 (C.C.A. 2d Cir. 1924), cert. granted, 264 U.S. 580, 44 S. Ct. 454, 68 L. Ed. 859 (1924) and petition dismissed, 267 U.S. 607, 45 S. Ct. 229, 69 L. Ed. 811 (1925).

[15]U.S. v. Tod, 297 F. 385, 393 (C.C.A. 2d Cir. 1924), cert. granted, 264 U.S. 580, 44 S. Ct. 454, 68 L. Ed. 859 (1924) and petition dismissed, 267 U.S. 607, 45 S. Ct. 229, 69 L. Ed. 811 (1925).

before the child turned twenty-one even when the child did not begin to reside in the United States until after he or she became twenty-one.[16] Once the child came to the United States, he or she had to be treated as a U.S. citizen.[17] After 1907, the child's residence and the parent's naturalization must both have occurred before the child turned twenty-one for the child to derive U.S. citizenship.[18] Both before and after 1907, the child could only derive citizenship if the child's residence in the U.S. was lawful.[19]

An out-of-wedlock child could only derive citizenship through the mother's naturalization, unless properly legitimated by the father according to the laws of the father's domicile.[20] Since the statutes before 1940 did not have a restriction regarding when the legitimation must have taken place, legitimation could have happened after the child turned twenty-one and the child would still have derived citizenship since legitimation is retrospective to the time of the child's birth.[21] If the parent naturalized before the child turned twenty-one, and the child was at one point a permanent resident, the child would derive citizenship even if he or she were legitimated after attaining maturity.[22] Under the statutes applicable prior to 1907, the child would derive citizenship even when he or she started residing in the United States after turning twenty-one years of age.[23]

For legitimated children, derivative citizenship is considered to have vested either at the time the father naturalized or when the child was admitted as a lawful permanent resident, whichever occurred last.[24] In addition, if both the naturalization of the father and the child's lawful permanent residence occurred before 1934, the law that applied was the derivation of citizenship law in effect at the time the last of these two acts took place, regardless of the fact that legitimation may have occurred after 1934, or indeed after 1940.[25]

Adopted children could not derive citizenship upon the naturalization of their adoptive parents.[26] Of course, if the adopting parent is the biological parent of the child and adoption results in legitimation of the child, then the rules of legitimation apply and the child would derive citizenship.[27] An adopted child may derive citizen-

---

[16]U.S. v. Tod, 297 F. 385, 391–92 (C.C.A. 2d Cir. 1924), cert. granted, 264 U.S. 580, 44 S. Ct. 454, 68 L. Ed. 859 (1924) and petition dismissed, 267 U.S. 607, 45 S. Ct. 229, 69 L. Ed. 811 (1925).

[17]U.S. v. Tod, 297 F. 385, 391 (C.C.A. 2d Cir. 1924), cert. granted, 264 U.S. 580, 44 S. Ct. 454, 68 L. Ed. 859 (1924) and petition dismissed, 267 U.S. 607, 45 S. Ct. 229, 69 L. Ed. 811 (1925).

[18]INS Interp. 329.1(a)(2).

[19]U.S. v. Tod, 297 F. 385, 394 (C.C.A. 2d Cir. 1924), cert. granted, 264 U.S. 580, 44 S. Ct. 454, 68 L. Ed. 859 (1924) and petition dismissed, 267 U.S. 607, 45 S. Ct. 229, 69 L. Ed. 811 (1925).

[20]INS Interp. 320.1(b), [c].

[21]INS Interp. 320.1(b) citing to 39 Op. Atty. Gen. 556 (1937).

[22]INS Interp. 320.1(b).

[23]See § 5:12.

[24]INS Interp. 320.1(b).

[25]INS Interp. 320.1(b). For a summary of BIA interpretation of the legitimation laws of foreign countries and states of the U.S. at different periods of time, and for a recent State Department interpretation of the legitimation laws of the states of the U.S., see Appendix 4-26 to Ch 4.

[26]INS Interp. 320.1(d)(1) citing to 38 Op. Atty. Gen. 217 (1935); Zimmerman v. Lehman, 339 F.2d 943, 946 (7th Cir.), cert. denied, 381 U.S. 925 (1965).

[27]See INS Interp. 320.1(d)(1).

ship from the naturalization of the biological parent if all the other requirements are met.[28]

Stepchildren cannot derive citizenship from their stepparent.[29] On the other hand, at least between 1855 and 1922, women who married U.S. citizens automatically acquired U.S. citizenship and their children could derive citizenship through this "naturalization."[30]

Married children had the same right to derive citizenship during this period, as did unmarried ones.[31]

§ 5:13 Last qualifying event between May 24, 1934 and January 13, 1941

Research References

Dizon and Wettstein, Immigration Law Service 2d § 14:208
Steel on Immigration Law § 15:4

Provisions allowing for derivation of citizenship if a parent was naturalized between May 24, 1934 and January 13, 1941 are almost identical to the provisions of the 1907 act.[1] However, under the 1934 law, citizenship does not vest until five years after the child begins to reside permanently in the United States.[2]

The Act of 1934 did not repeal the derivative citizenship provisions of the Act of 1802.[3] However, in adapting the 1802 statute to the twentieth century, courts have held that the Act of 1802 applied only in two circumstances. First, it applied when both parents naturalized. Second, it also applied when one parent naturalized, but only if the other parent was: (1) dead, (2) a U.S. citizen, or (3) the parents had divorced and the naturalizing parent had custody over the child.[4] In these circumstances a child became a U.S. citizen upon the latter of the parents' naturalization or the child becoming a lawful permanent resident, provided both events occured before the child turned twenty-one.[5]

When only one parent naturalized in other circumstances, the Act of 1934 applied and citizenship of the child would only begin five years after obtaining permanent residence.[6] The period of lawful permanent residence could have started before or

---

[28]INS Interp. 320.1(d)(1). citing to 38 Op. Atty. Gen. 397 (1936). Agree 7 FAM 1153.4-1(h)(1).

[29]INS Interp. 320.1(d)(1) citing to In re Bishop, 26 F. 2d 148, 148–49 (W.D.Wash. 1927).

[30]In re Bishop, 26 F.2d at 149. See § 11:2.

[31]See § 5:5.

[Section 5:13]

[1]Compare Sec. 2, Act of May 24, 1934 reproduced as Appendix 4-1 to Ch 4 with Sec. 5, Act of March 2, 1907 reproduced as Appendix 4-6 to Ch 4.

[2]Sec. 2, Act of May 24, 1934 reproduced as Appendix 4-10 to Ch 4. The only other difference between the statutes is that the Act of 1934 made explicit that derivation could occur through either father or mother. Compare sec. 2, Act of May 24, 1934 ("by virtue of the naturalization of or resumption of American citizenship by the father or mother) with sec. 5, Act of 1907 ('by virtue of the naturalization or resumption of American citizenship by the parent) (emphasis added), reproduced as Appendix 4-6, 4-10 to Ch 4.

[3]Petition of Donsky, 77 F. Supp. 832, 834 (S.D. N.Y. 1948).

[4]Petition of Donsky, 77 F. Supp. 832, 834–35 (S.D. N.Y. 1948).

[5]INS Interp. 320.1(a)(3) citing to Matter of M-, 3 I. & N. Dec. 815; Matter of P-, 1 I. & N. Dec. 127.

[6]INS Interp. 320.1(a)(3).

after the parent naturalized.[7] If lawful permanent residence began more than five years prior to the parent's naturalization, the child became a U.S. citizen on the date of the parent's naturalization.[8]

Although the child must have entered as a lawful permanent resident before age twenty-one, the five-year period of residence could have been completed after attaining age twenty-one.[9] The five years could also be completed subsequent to repeal of the 1934 act in January 12, 1941.[10] However, the five-year period must have started before January 12, 1941.[11]

The principles governing derivative citizenship of out-of-wedlock, legitimated, adopted, stepchildren and married children during this period are the same principles that apply for children whose derivative citizenship vested before 1934.[12]

§ 5:14 Last qualifying event between January 13, 1941 and December 23, 1952

Research References

A.L.R. Index, Immigration and Naturalization
Validity, Construction, and Application of Child Citizenship Act, 194 A.L.R. Fed. 383
Dizon and Wettstein, Immigration Law Service 2d §§ 14:208 to 14:210
Steel on Immigration Law § 15:4

Unlike the Acts of 1907 and 1934, the Nationality Act of 1940 repealed all the derivative citizenship provisions of the prior acts.[1] The 1940 act, however, specified that citizenship acquired under the prior statutes was not affected.[2] The Nationality Act of 1940 substantially reenacted the provisions of the Act of 1802 as they had come to be interpreted after the Act of 1934.[3] A significant difference, however, was that the child would not derive citizenship unless both the naturalization of the parent or parents and the child's lawful permanent residence occurred before the child turned eighteen years of age, rather than twenty-one as was the case under the previous laws.[4] This rule governed the vesting of derivative citizenship between January 13, 1941 and December 23, 1952.

The 1940 act provided that a child born outside of the United States derived U.S. citizenship if, between January 13, 1941 and December 23, 1952, the child complied with the requirements of being under eighteen years of age and being admitted for

---

[7]INS Interp. 320.1(a)(3).

[8]Matter of R-, 3 I. & N. Dec. 470 (Central Office 1949).

[9]Acheson v. Albert, 195 F.2d 573 (D.C. Cir. 1952).

[10]Bertoldi v. McGrath, 178 F.2d 977 (D.C. Cir. 1949); Petition of Pellegrini, 126 F. Supp. 742 (S.D. N.Y. 1954) (distinguishing Aberasturi); INS Interp. 320.1(a)(3). Contra U.S. ex rel. Aberasturi v. Cain, 147 F.2d 449 (2d Cir. 1945) (five years must be completed before Jan. 13, 1941); Matter of M-, 3 I. & N. Dec. 645 (B.I.A. 1950) (includes a footnote by the INS after the decision, that the INS follows Bertoldi and not Aberasturi).

[11]INS Interp. 320.1(a)(3).

[12]INS Interp. 320.1(b)–(d). See § 5:12.

[Section 5:14]

[1]Sec. 504, Nationality Act of 1940 reproduced as Appendix 4-12 to Ch 4.

[2]Sec. 504, Nationality Act of 1940 reproduced as Appendix 4-12 to Ch 4; INS Interp. 320.1(a)(4).

[3]See secs. 313, 314, Nationality Act of 1940 reproduced as Appendix 4-12 to Ch 4.

[4]Cf. §§ 5:12, 5:13.

permanent residence in the United States, and *both* parents naturalized.[5] A child could derive citizenship from the naturalization of only *one* parent if that parent was widowed, divorced, or legally separated or the other parent was already a U.S. citizen at the time of the naturalization.[6]

As in prior law, the fact that the child was married at the time of derivation did not prevent derivation of U.S. citizenship.[7]

The 1940 act did not contain the 1934 provision that allowed derivative citizenship of the child upon the naturalization of only one parent—the other remaining a noncitizen—after the child had been a lawful permanent resident for five years.[8] On the other hand, it introduced new wording relating to naturalization of one parent when the parents had *legally separated*.[9] Where the parents were legally separated, and one parent naturalized, a child derived naturalization if in the custody of the naturalizing parent.[10] For a full analysis of these provisions, please see § 5:9.

Under the Nationality Act of 1940, an out-of-wedlock child could no longer derive citizenship through the mother's naturalization. However, if on December 24, 1952 the child was under the age of sixteen, still a permanent resident, and his or her mother was still a U.S. citizen, he or she automatically derived U.S. citizenship on that date.[11] The 1940 act allowed for derivation of citizenship for a child who was properly legitimated according to the laws of the child's place of domicile and in the custody of the legitimating father, provided such legitimation occurred while the child was under the age of sixteen.[12] The Foreign Affairs Manual takes the position that administrative adjudication has established that legitimation under the laws of the father's domicile was also effective during this period.[13]

Both the USCIS and the State Department take the position that adopted children during this period could not derive citizenship.[14] This seems to contradict the wording of the statute, which provides that for purposes of naturalization, including derivative citizenship, the term "child" includes children adopted before reaching the age of sixteen.[15] Unlike the INA, adopted children were not specifically excluded from the derivative citizenship provisions.[16] The Nationality Act of 1940 had a special provision relating to adopted children which included more stringent requirements, but that provision only applied to naturalization petitions filed by adoptive

---

[5]Sec. 314, Nationality Act of 1940 reproduced as Appendix 4-12 to Ch 4.

[6]Secs. 313, 314, Nationality Act of 1940 reproduced as Appendix 4-12 to Ch 4.

[7]7 FAM 1153.4-3(d); INS Interp. 320.1(a)(5).

[8]Cf. § 5:12.

[9]Sec. 314(c), Nationality Act of 1940 reproduced as Appendix 4-12 to Ch 4.

[10]See App. 4-12, § 314(e).

[11]INS Interp. 320.1(c).

[12]Sec. 102(h), Nationality Act of 1940 reproduced as Appendix 4-12 to Ch 4.

[13]7 FAM 1153.4-3(b). Agree Gordon & Mailman, § 98.03[3][d][iii].

[14]INS Interp. 320.1(d) citing to 38 Op. Atty. Gen. 217 (1935); Zimmerman v. Lehmann, 339 F.2d 943 (7th Cir. 1965); Hein v. U.S.I.N.S., 456 F.2d 1239 (5th Cir. 1972). The references cited by the INS interpret statutes different from the Nationality Act of 1940. 7 FAM 1153.4-3(f)(2) (no citations).

[15]Sec. 102(h), Nationality Act of 1940 reproduced as Appendix 4-12 to Ch 4.

[16]INA § 101(c)(1), 8 U.S.C.A. § 1101(c)(1) (the term child includes adopted child "Except as otherwise provided in sections 320, 321, 322, and 323 of title III") Cf. INA §§ 320(b), 321 (b), 8 U.S.C.A. §§ 1431.(b), 1432(b) as originally enacted by Pub.L. 82-414, 66 Stat. 163 (derivative citizenship provisions do not apply to adopted children). See § 5:15.

parents on behalf of their adopted children.[17] A similar provision used to exist in the INA, but was repealed in 1978, because its coverage was incorporated into the general provision for naturalization of children upon petition by the U.S. citizen parent.[18]

As in prior laws, stepchildren could not derive citizenship.[19] Married children, on the other hand, were not barred from deriving citizenship.[20]

§ 5:15 Last qualifying event between December 24, 1952 and February 26, 2001

Research References

Dizon and Wettstein, Immigration Law Service 2d §§ 14:209, 14:210
Steel on Immigration Law § 15:4

The Immigration and Nationality Act repealed the Nationality Act of 1940 in its entirety.[1] It enacted derivative citizenship provisions that were patterned after the same provisions of the Nationality Act of 1940.[2] The most significant difference used to be that under the provision of the 1952 act, both the parent's naturalization and the beginning of the child's permanent residence must have occurred before the child reached the age of sixteen, rather than eighteen as under the previous law.[3] This is no longer the case.

In 1978, Congress amended these provisions to raise from sixteen to eighteen the age upon which the last relevant act must have occurred for derivative citizenship to vest.[4] Originally, the State Department took the position that the 1978 law did not benefit the children who had complied with all the requirements for derivation (i.e. both parents had naturalized and they had already become lawful permanent residents) before October 5, 1978.[5] In other words, persons who on October 5, 1978 were between the ages of sixteen and eighteen, and who had already complied with all substantial requirements for derivation would not derive U.S. citizenship. This position contradicted *Matter of L-*, a similar case involving the change of the law in 1952.[6] Eventually, both the legacy INS and the State Department retreated from that position.[7]

---

[17]Sec. 316, Nationality Act of 1940.

[18]INA § 323, 8 U.S.C.A. § 1434 as originally enacted by Pub.L. 82-414, 66 Stat. 163 repealed by Sec. 7, Act of Oct. 5, 1978, Pub.L. No. 95-417, 92 Stat. 917. Cf. Sec. 6, Act of Oct. 5, 1978 (authorizing naturalization of adopted children under the general naturalization of children provision of INA § 322).

[19]INS Interp. 320.1(d).

[20]See § 5:5.

[Section 5:15]

[1]INA § 403(a)(42).

[2]Compare INA §§ 320, 321, 8 U.S.C.A. §§ 1431, 1432 as originally enacted by Pub.L. 82-414, 66 Stat. 163 with secs. 313, 314, Nationality Act of 1940 reproduced as Appendix 4-12 to Ch 4.

[3]INA §§ 320, 321, 8 U.S.C.A. §§ 1431, 1432 as originally enacted by Pub.L. 82-414, 66 Stat. 163. Unlike prior statutes the relevant sections of the INA support the argument that if the child started residing in the United States after the parent's naturalization, the child would derive citizenship even if his or her residence was unlawful. Cf. § 5:3.

[4]INA §§ 320, 321, 8 U.S.C.A. §§ 1431, 1432 as amended by Secs. 4 and 5, Act of Oct. 5, 1978, Pub. L. 95-417, 92 Stat. 917.

[5]7 FAM 1153.4-4(c)(2).

[6]See Matter of L-, 8 I. & N. Dec. 272 (B.I.A. 1956) (out-of-wedlock child who had fulfilled all the requirements for derivation before the effective date of the 1952 Act, benefited from the INA in so far

In April 1997, the Board of Immigration Appeals held that the 1978 amendment was retroactive to the enactment of the INA.[8] Even before the BIA pronouncement, both the State Department and the INS had come around to that position.[9] Thus, at present, the BIA, State Department, and the USCIS agree that persons who were under eighteen years of age at both (1) the time of the naturalization of their parent or parents, and (2) the time they became lawful permanent residents, derived U.S. citizenship automatically if either event occurred after December 24, 1952 and they otherwise complied with the other requirements of the INA. It must also be noted that with this interpretation, the maximum age for derivation is the same under both the INA and the Nationality Act of 1940.[10] Thus, automatic derivation applies to persons who complied with all the requirements for derivation under the age of eighteen between January 1, 1941 and the present.

In one interesting case, an individual's mother naturalized on his 18th birthday, naturalizing in the morning while he had been born in the evening; the Second Circuit found that in light of the importance of citizenship, he was still "under the age of 18" on those facts.[11]

Just as in prior statutes, "naturalization" includes the panoply of process through which a person becomes a U.S. citizen.[12] This issue may become particularly relevant when dealing with U.S. citizen parents who reacquire U.S. citizenship at birth abroad through the taking of an administrative oath.[13]

Until enactment of the Child Citizenship Act of 2000, the statute provided for derivation upon the naturalization of the parent having legal custody of the child "when there has been a legal separation of the parents."[14] This provision continued from the 1940 act provision unchanged.[15] For a full analysis of the provisions relating to legal separation and custody, please see § 5:11.

The Immigration and Nationality Act of 1952 provided for derivative citizenship of an out-of-wedlock child through the naturalization of the mother.[16] The actual language of the statute refers to a child born out-of-wedlock whose paternity "has not been established by legitimation."[17] On the one hand, the Foreign Affairs Manual interprets this provision as requiring that the child must never have been

---

as on the date of enactment he was still within the age to comply with derivation requirements—the fact that the requirements had been complied with before the date of enactment was irrelevant). The position taken originally by the State Department also seems counter to the policy applied to changes in retention requirements for children born abroad to U.S. citizens. See § 4:57.

[7]See e.g. INS' Motion to Terminate Proceedings, Matter of Rudolf Kairuz, File No. A36-134-092 (filed Sept. 26, 1995) (where it reversed its original position after consultation with the State Department and argued that at least persons who were between sixteen and eighteen years of age on October 5, 1978 and complied with all the other requirements automatically became U.S. citizens).

[8]Matter of Fuentes-Martinez, 21 I. & N. Dec. 893 (B.I.A. 1997).

[9]Department of State, Passport Bulletin 96-18 (Nov, 6, 1996) superseding and canceling Passport Bulletin 93-2 (January 8, 1993); O'Reilly, Acting Assistant Commissioner, INS cable No. HQ 321 (Feb. 18, 1997).

[10]See § 5:14.

[11]Duarte-Ceri v. Holder, 630 F. 3d 83 (2d Cir. 2010).

[12]See § 5:6.

[13]See § 11:31.

[14]*Former* INA § 321(a), 8 U.S.C.A. § 1432(a) *prior to* Child Citizenship Act of 2000.

[15]See § 5:14.

[16]See INA § 321(a)(3), 8 U.S.C.A. § 1432(a)(3); INS Interp. 320.1(c).

[17]INA § 321(a)(3), 8 U.S.C.A. § 1432(a)(3).

legitimated before deriving citizenship.[18] On the other hand, legitimation by the father after citizenship has been derived, does not deprive the child of his or her U.S. citizenship.[19] To derive citizenship from the father, a child born out-of-wedlock must have been properly legitimated before reaching age sixteen and be in the custody of the legitimating parent at the time of legitimation.[20] Legitimation could take place under the laws of either the parent's or the child's domicile.[21] However, the naturalization of the father may not be enough to effect derivation under the statute as it existed prior to the Child Citizenship Act of 2000, as that earlier statute required the naturalization of both parents unless one of the specific exceptions applied.[22]

In 1978, Congress amended the Immigration and Nationality Act to allow adopted children to derive citizenship.[23] This amendment applies to citizenship that vests after October 5, 1978.[24] Originally, the legislation provided that the adoption must have taken place before the child turned sixteen, but this requirement was repealed in 1981.[25] Thus, after December 29, 1981 and before February 27, 2001, a child could derive citizenship regardless of the date of adoption.[26] It should be pointed out, however, that the subsections extending benefits to adopted children may be interpreted as requiring that the child be adopted at the time of vesting of the naturalization. This would limit the maximum age of adoption of the child to age eighteen, since all the other requirements must be fulfilled by that age for citizenship to vest.[27] This is the interpretation given to the statute by the State Department.[28] Thus, according to the State Department, an adopted child will derive citizenship if all the requirements for derivation, including adoption, are met before reaching the age of eighteen, regardless of the order in which the requirements are met.[29]

After December 24, 1952, married children could no longer derive citizenship through the naturalization of their parents. The INA definition of child for naturalization purposes specifically requires the child to be unmarried.[30]

---

[18]7 FAM 1153.4-4(b)(1)(d).

[19]7 FAM 1153.4-4(b)(1)(d).

[20]See INA § 101(c)(1), 8 U.S.C.A. § 1101(c)(1); INS Interp. 320.1(b).

[21]INS Interp. 320.1(b). For a summary of BIA interpretation of the legitimation laws of foreign countries and states of the U.S. at different periods of time, and for a recent State Department interpretation of the legitimation laws of the states of the U.S., see Appendix 4-26 to Ch 4.

[22]Former INA § 320(a), 8 U.S.C.A. § 1432(a), prior to the Child Custody Act of 2000.

[23]Secs. 4, 5, Act of Oct. 5, 1978, Pub.L. No. 95-417, 92 Stat. 917; INS Interp. 320.1(d)(2).

[24]INS Interp. 320.1(d)(2).

[25]INS Interp. 320.1(d)(3) citing to Act of Dec. 29, 1981, 95 Stat. 1611.

[26]INS Interp. 320.1(d)(3). Cf. INA § 101(c)(1), 8 U.S.C.A. § 1101(c)(1) (child must be adopted before age sixteen to obtain nationality benefits as a child, except as otherwise provided by the derivative citizenship sections which do not impose any age requirement). For the requirements imposed since February 27, 2001, by the Child Citizenship Act of 2000, see § 5:15.

[27]See INA §§ 320(b), 321(b), 8 U.S.C.A. §§ 1431(b), 1432(b), prior to Child Citizenship Act of 2000 (both sections provide that subsection (a) of each section would apply to an "adopted" child residing with the adoptive parents in the custody of the adoptive parents).

[28]7 FAM 1153.4-4(d)(3).

[29]See 7 FAM 1153.4-4(d)(3).

[30]INA § 101(c)(1), 8 U.S.C.A. § 1101(c)(1).

IV. CHILD CITIZENSHIP ACT (CHILDREN BORN AFTER FEBRUARY 27, 1983)

§ 5:16 Child Citizenship Act, generally

Research References

A.L.R. Index, Immigration and Naturalization
Validity, Construction, and Application of Child Citizenship Act, 194 A.L.R. Fed. 383
Dizon and Wettstein, Immigration Law Service 2d §§ 14:208 to 14:210
Steel on Immigration Law § 15:4

On October 30, 2000, President Clinton signed into law the Child Citizenship Act of 2000. The amendments to nationality law took effect on February 27, 2001.[1] The legacy INS published an interim rule on June 13, 2001, implementing Title I of the act.[2] The rule took effect upon publication.

This law radically changed the provisions for derivation of citizenship after birth. First, it consolidated sections 320 and 321 of the INA into one section.[3] Second, it removed the requirement of naturalization of a parent for derivation of citizenship to take place.[4] Thus, it made derivation after birth available to children of native born U.S. citizens. Third, it required that the child be residing in the United States as a lawful permanent resident in the legal and physical custody of a U.S. citizen parent.[5] Fourth, it retained the requirement that all qualifying events must have occurred before the child turns eighteen years of age.[6] Finally, it allows adopted children to derive to the same extent as biological children, provided they fit under the immigration definition of "child".[7]

The new INA § 320 has three basic requirements: (1) U.S. citizenship of the parent; (2) age of the child; and (3) residence of the child.[8] As to citizenship of the parent, it requires that for automatic derivation to occur, the child must have at least one U.S. citizen parent.[9] It is irrelevant whether the parent is native-born or naturalized, provided the parent is a U.S. citizen before the child's eighteenth birthday.[10]

The second requirement is that the child be under the age of eighteen years at the

---

[Section 5:16]

[1]Child Citizenship Act of 2000, § 104 reproduced as Appendix 5-2 ("The amendments made by this title shall take effect 120 days after the date of the enactment of this Act." The act was enacted on October 10, 2000).

[2]66 Fed. Reg. 32138–47 (June 13, 2001).

[3]Child Citizenship Act of 2000, § 103 reproduced as Appendix 5-2.

[4]INA § 320(a)(1), 8 U.S.C.A. § 1431(a)(1) as amended by Child Citizenship Act of 2000, § 101 reproduced as Appendix 5-2.

[5]INA § 320(a)(3), 8 U.S.C.A. § 1431(a)(3) as amended by Child Citizenship Act of 2000, § 101 reproduced as Appendix 5-2.

[6]INA § 320(a)(2), 8 U.S.C.A. § 1431(a)(2) as amended by Child Citizenship Act of 2000, § 101 reproduced as Appendix 5-2.

[7]INA § 320(b), 8 U.S.C.A. § 1431(b) as amended by Child Citizenship Act of 2000, § 101 reproduced as Appendix 5-2.

[8]INA § 320(a), 8 U.S.C.A. § 1431(a) as amended by Child Citizenship Act of 2000, § 101 reproduced as Appendix 5-2.

[9]INA § 320(a)(1), 8 U.S.C.A. § 1431(a)(1) as amended by Child Citizenship Act of 2000, § 101 reproduced as Appendix 5-2.

[10]INA § 320(a)(1), 8 U.S.C.A. § 1431(a)(1) as amended by Child Citizenship Act of 2000, § 101 reproduced as Appendix 5-2.

time derivation occurs.[11] The effective date provisions of the Child Citizenship Act of 2000 and legislative history make it clear that qualifying children who were under eighteen years on February 27, 2001 derive citizenship automatically on that date.[12] The law specifically provides that the amendments "shall apply to individuals who satisfy the requirements of section 320 . . . of the Immigration and Nationality Act, as in effect on [the date the amendments take effect]."[13] Legislative history confirms this. Representative Smith, in introducing the motion to suspend the rules and pass the bill, pointed out that "H.R. 2883's grant of citizenship will also apply to qualifying children who arrived in the United States prior to its enactment and have not yet obtained citizenship pursuant to the Immigration and Nationality Act (as it existed before enactment)."[14]

Third, the child must be "residing in the United States in the legal and physical custody of the citizen parent pursuant to a lawful admission for permanent residence."[15] In reality, there are two requirements in this provision. First, the child must be a lawful permanent resident at the time of the derivation; this likely requires that the permanent residence status must have been lawfully obtained, precluding both fraudulent admissions and erroneous admissions where the applicant was not in fact eligible for permanent resident status.[16] Second, the child must be in the legal and physical custody of the U.S. citizen parent at the time of the derivation.

The requirement of "custody" has been interpreted in several other contexts. Before the repeal by the Child Citizenship Act of 2000, the INA § 321 provided for derivation upon the "naturalization of the parent having legal custody of the child when there has been a legal separation of the parents."[17] That provision had been inherited unchanged from the Nationality Act of 1940.[18] This interpretation is discussed above, and may be useful in interpreting the Child Citizenship Act; but it should be noted that the Child Citizenship Act has no legal separation provisions. The only issue for CCA purposes is whether the child is in the custody of the citizen parent.[19] Of particular concern is the holding of the Fifth Circuit in *Bustamante-Barrera v. Gonzales*, where the Fifth Circuit interpreted similar language in former INA § 321(a)(3) to require that the naturalizing parent had sole custody of the child

---

[11]INA § 320(a)(2), 8 U.S.C.A. § 1431(a)(2) as amended by Child Citizenship Act of 2000, § 101 reproduced as Appendix 5-2.

[12]Child Citizenship Act of 2000, § 104 reproduced as Appendix 5-2; 146 Cong. Rec. H7776 (daily ed. Sept. 19, 2000.

[13]Child Citizenship Act of 2000, § 104 reproduced as Appendix 5-2.

[14]146 Cong. Rec. H7776 (daily ed. Sept. 19, 2000).

[15]INA § 320(a)(3), 8 U.S.C.A. § 1431(a)(3) as amended by Child Citizenship Act of 2000, § 101 reproduced as Appendix 5-2.

[16]See generally, § 5:8; Walker v. Holder, 589 F.3d 12, 19-21 (1st Cir. 2009) (citing Matter of Koloamatangi, 23 I. & N. Dec. 548 (B.I.A.2003)).

[17]INA § 321(a)(3), 8 U.S.C.A. § 1432(a)(3) as originally enacted by Pub.L. 82-414, 66 Stat. 245 (June 27, 1952), and amended by Act of Oct. 5, 1978, Pub. L. 95-417, §§ 4, 5, 92 Stat. 917; Act of Dec. 29, 1981, Pub. L. 97-116, § 18(m), 95 Stat. 1620; Act of Nov. 14, 1986, Pub. L. 99-653, §§ 14, 15, 100 Stat. 3657; Act of Oct. 24, 1988, Pub. L. 100-525, §§ 8(l), 9 (w), 102 Stat. 2618 reproduced as Appendix 5-2.

[18]Nationality Act of 1940, § 314(c) reproduced as Appendix 4-12 to Ch 4.

[19]For a full analysis of the provisions relating to custody, please see § 5:9.

in order for the child to derive citizenship.[20] However, the *Bustamonte-Barrera* holding might make more sense in the context of former § 321(a)(3)—where naturalization of only one parent could convey citizenship only if the parents were separated—as opposed to the CCA context, where the citizenship of either parent would suffice.

§ 5:17   Out-of-wedlock children under the CCA

The new INA § 320 is silent as to legitimation.[1] Nevertheless, the regulations interpreting INA § 320 specify that a child born out-of-wedlock must be legitimated by and residing with the U.S. citizen parent.[2] These regulations also specifically define the term "child" as one who meets the requirement for a child in INA § 101(c)(1), 8 U.S.C.A. § 1101(c)(1).[3] INA § 101(c)(1) includes certain legitimated children within its definition, and this is presumably the basis for the legitimation requirement in the regulations interpreting INA § 320.[4]

Under the general definition of a child found in INA § 101(c)(1), a legitimation must take place according to the laws of either the father's or the child's residence or domicile.[5] Additionally, the statutory definition of a child requires that the legitimation take place while the child is under the age of sixteen and while he or she is in the legal custody of the legitimating parent.[6] The regulations implementing the Child Citizenship Act track INA § 101(c)(1) in that they specifically require proof of legitimation according to the child's or the father's residence or domicile.[7] UnlikeINA § 101(c)(1), however, they are silent regarding proof that the legitimation took place before the child was sixteen. It remains to be seen whether a legitimation that takes place while the child is between the ages of sixteen and eighteen will satisfy the requirements of the Child Citizenship Act.

§ 5:18   Adopted children under the CCA

The amended section 320 applies to adopted as well as biological children.[1] The law actually provides that section 320 "shall apply to a child adopted by a United States citizen parent if the child satisfies the requirements applicable to adopted children under section 101(b)(1)."[2] Indeed, section 101(b)(1) contains two provisions

---

[20]Bustamante-Barrera v. Gonzales, 447 F.3d 388 (5th Cir. 2006).

[Section 5:17]

[1]INA § 320, 8 U.S.C.A. § 1431 *as amended by* Child Citizenship Act of 2000 *reproduced* as Appendix 5-2.

[2]8 CFR § 320.1.

[3]8 CFR § 320.1.

[4]INA § 101(c)(1), 8 U.S.C.A. § 1101(c)(1); see also § 5:4.

[5]INA § 101(c)(1), 8 U.S.C.A. § 1101(c)(1).

[6]INA § 101(c)(1), 8 U.S.C.A. § 1101(c)(1).

[7]8 CFR § 320.3(b)(1)(v).

[Section 5:18]

[1]INA § 320(b), 8 U.S.C.A. § 1431(b) as amended by Child Citizenship Act of 2000, § 101 reproduced as Appendix 5-2.

[2]INA § 320(b), 8 U.S.C.A. § 1431(b) as amended by Child Citizenship Act of 2000, § 101 reproduced as Appendix 5-2.

relating to "adopted" children. One literally refers to "adopted" children.[3] The second refers to orphan children who are "released for emigration and adoption."[4] The new derivative citizenship provision applies to both understandings of the definition of "adopted".[5]

Prior to the amendment, derivative naturalization was also available to adopted children regardless of whether they immigrated as orphans or under the general adoption provision.[6] The amendment, however, introduces a reference to subsection 101(b) of the INA to introduce additional requirements to qualify for the benefits of derivative citizenship.[7] First, under section 101(b), both adopted children provisions generally require the child to have been adopted while under the age of sixteen.[8] There is only a limited exception for siblings of adopted children being adopted by the same adoptive parents.[9] In those cases, the adoption must have taken place before the child reaches the age of eighteen.[10]

Second, there are specific requirements applicable to the general adoption and the orphan provisions. For example, under the general adoption provision, the child must have been in the legal custody and resided with the adopting parent for two years prior to immigration.[11] In order to qualify for derivation, adopted children must satisfy all the other statutory requirements for immigration of adopted children under either section 101(b)(1)(E) or (F) of the INA.[12]

Additionally, the regulations require that the adoption be "full, final and complete."[13] Where a foreign adoption was not complete or was defective, or where the unmarried U.S. citizen parent or the married U.S. citizen parent and spouse did not see the child in person before the adoption was completed, the child will not be considered to be fully and finally adopted.[14] In that case, the child will need to be

---

[3]INA § 101(b)(1)(E), 8 U.S.C.A. § 1101(b)(1)(E).

[4]INA § 101(b)(1)(F), 8 U.S.C.A. § 1101(b)(1)(F).

[5]See H. Rep. 852, 106th Cong., 2d Sess.8 (discussing new subsection 320(b) as applying to adopted children who satisfy the requirements of either INA § 101(b)(1)(E) or (F)); Cong. Rec. H7774–78 (daily ed. Sept. 19, 2000) (virtually all examples used to support the legislation refer to children who immigrated under the orphan provisions); 8 CFR § 320.1.

[6]See INA §§ 320(b), 321(b), 8 U.S.C.A. §§ 1431(b), 1432(b) as originally enacted by Pub.L. 82-414, 66 Stat. 245 (June 27, 1952), and amended by Act of Oct. 5, 1978, Pub. L. 95-417, §§ 4, 5, 92 Stat. 917; Act of Dec. 29, 1981, Pub. L. 97-116, § 18(m), 95 Stat. 1620; Act of Nov. 14, 1986, Pub. L. 99-653, §§ 14, 15, 100 Stat. 3657; Act of Oct. 24, 1988, Pub. L. 100-525, §§ 8(l), 9 (w), 102 Stat. 2618 reproduced as Appendix 5–2.

[7]INA § 320(b), 8 U.S.C.A. § 1431(b) as amended by Child Citizenship Act of 2000, § 101 reproduced as Appendix 5-2.

[8]INA § 101(b)(1)(E), (F), 8 U.S.C.A. § 1101(b)(1)(E), (F).

[9]INA § 101(b)(1)(E)(ii), (F)(ii), (c)(1), 8 U.S.C.A. § 1101(b)(1)(E)(ii), (F)(ii), (c)(1) as amended by Act of December 7, 1999, Pub.L. 106-139, § 1(a), (b), 113 Stat. 1696.

[10]INA § 101(b)(1)(E)(ii), (F)(ii), 8 U.S.C.A. § 1101(b)(1)(E)(ii), (F)(ii) as amended by Act of December 7, 1999, Pub.L. 106-139, § 1(a), 113 Stat. 1696.

[11]INA § 101(b)(1)(E)(i), 8 U.S.C.A. § 1101(b)(1)(E)(i).

[12]INA § 320(b), 8 U.S.C.A. § 1431(b) as amended by Child Citizenship Act of 2000, § 101 reproduced as Appendix 5-2.

[13]8 CFR § 320.1.

[14]8 CFR § 320.1.

readopted in the U.S., although a waiver can be granted if the state law where the parent resides recognizes the adoption as full and complete.[15]

§ 5:19 Stepchildren under the CCA

As under previous statutes, stepchildren are not children for purposes of citizenship, and may not derive citizenship through the naturalization of a step-parent.[1] Of course, to the extent that stepchildren are also adopted children, their status as stepchildren does not preclude derivation.

---

[15]8 CFR § 320.1.

[Section 5:19]

[1]See Matter of Guzman-Gomez, 24 I&N Dec. 824 (BIA 2009); INS Interp. 320.1(d)(1).

APPENDIX 5-1

Derivative Citizenship Statutes and their Applicability

Derivative Citizenship Statutes and their Applicability

Statute	Effective Date	Prerequisites		Additional Requirements for Special Situations				Special Provisions
		Naturalization of Both Parent	Naturalization of One Parent	Illegitimate Child	Legitimated Child	Adopted Child	Stepchild	
Act of 1802, as supplemented by Act of 1907	4/14/1802 to 5/24/1934	Not required	• Child under 21 at date of parent's naturalization • Child could take up residence in the U.S. after parent's naturalization • Child could take up residence in the U.S. after turning 21 years of age (only before 1907) • Residence in the U.S. must be lawful	Can only derive from mother	• Must be legitimated according to the laws of the father's domicile • Legitimation could take place after child turns 21 • Vests upon naturalization of parent or child taking up residence in the U.S.	Cannot derive citizenship (unless adopting parent is biological parent and adoption works to legitimate child)	Cannot derive citizenship	• Before 1907, Mother could only transmit if divorced or widowed • After 1907, child must take up residence before turning 21 to derive
Act of 1934	5/24/34 – 1/13/41	Child must be under 21 when: (1) both parents naturalize, and (2) begins lawful permanent residence in the U.S.	• If other parent is dead, a U.S. citizen, or divorced and naturalizing parent has custody, same as if both parents naturalized • Otherwise, child's U.S. citizenship commences 5 years after child became lawful permanent resident	Can only derive from mother, in which case the child is treated as if both parents had naturalized	Same as under prior law	Same as under prior law	Same as under prior law	The 5-year period when only one parent naturalizes, can commence before or after the naturalization and can last until after child turns 21 and until after 1941.

Statute	Effective Date	Prerequisites		Additional Requirements for Special Situations				Special Provisions
		Naturalization of Both Parent	Naturalization of One Parent	Illegitimate Child	Legitimated Child	Adopted Child	Stepchild	
Nationality Act of 1940	1/13/41 – 12/23/52	Child must be under 18 when: (1) both parents naturalize, and (2) child begins lawful permanent residence in the U.S.	Child can only derive from one parent if the other one is dead, a U.S. citizen, or they are legally separated and naturalizing parent has custody	• Illegitimate children could not derive • Remedial provision: See special provisions	Must be legitimated under the law of the child's place of domicile before turning 16, and in the custody of legitimating father. Also requires naturalization of mother, unless dead, or U.S. citizen.	Arguably children who are adopted before turning 16 and are in the custody of the adopting parent(s) may derive	Cannot derive citizenship	If on 12/24/52 illegitimate child was under 16, still a lawful permanent resident, and mother still a U.S. citizen, child derived on that date
INA[1]	12/23/52 – 10/5/78	Child must be under 18 when: (1) both parents naturalize, and (2) begins lawful permanent residence in the U.S.[2]	Child can only derive from one parent if the other one is dead, a U.S. citizen, or they are legally separated and naturalizing parent has custody	Can only derive from mother. [Father's nationality is irrelevant— but if father legitimated child before derivation, both parents must be naturalized.]	Must be legitimated under the law of the parent's or child's place of domicile before turning 16. May also require naturalization of mother, unless dead or U.S. citizen.	May not derive, unless adopted by biological parent and adopting effects legitimation	Cannot derive citizenship	Married children cannot derive citizenship

Statute	Effective Date	Prerequisites		Additional Requirements for Special Situations				Special Provisions
		Naturalization of Both Parent	Naturalization of One Parent	Illegitimate Child	Legitimated Child	Adopted Child	Stepchild	
	10/5/78 – 2/26/01	Same as prior law	Same as prior law	Same as prior law	Same as prior law	May derive if adoption occurred before child turned 18	Cannot derive citizenship	• Married children cannot derive citizenship • Between 10/5/78 and 12/29/81, citizenship vested on adopted children only if adoption occurred before child turned 16
	2/27/01 - Present	Child under 18 (1) parent a citizen (2) child lawful permanent resident (3) child in physical and legal custody of USC parent (4) No naturalization of parent Required. Parent can be either native born or naturalized U.S. citizen	Same as if both parents citizens	Definition of child requires child legitimation under the laws of either the father's or the child's residence or domicile. Legitimation must occur while child is under the age of 16 years.	Section only requires child to be in physical and legal custody of USC parent. Under definition of child, legitimation must occur while child is under the age of 16 years.	May derive if adoption occurred before child turned 16 (18 if immigrated as adopted sibling) and satisfies all other requirements of INA 101(b)(1)	Cannot derive citizenship	Married children cannot derive citizenship

[1] If child does not qualify for derivation under this section, the U.S. citizen parent may be able to petition under section 322 of the INA. See §§ 11:17 to 11:25.

[2] The statute supports an argument that if the child started to reside in the United States after the parent's naturalization, such residence does not need to be pursuant to lawful admission to permanent residence.

APPENDIX 5-2

Sections 320 to 322 of Immigration and Nationality Act, as in effect in 1999, prior to the enactment of the Child Citizenship Act

320. Children born outside United States of one alien and one citizen parent; conditions for automatic citizenship

(a) A child born outside of the United States, one of whose parents at the time of the child's birth was an alien and the other of whose parents then was and never thereafter ceased to be a citizen of the United States, shall, if such alien parent is naturalized, become a citizen of the United States, when-

   (1) such naturalization takes place while such child is under the age of eighteen years; and

   (2) such child is residing in the United States pursuant to a lawful admission for permanent residence at the time of naturalization or thereafter and begins to reside permanently in the United States while under the age of eighteen years.

(b) Subsection (a) of this section shall apply to an adopted child only if the child is residing in the United States at the time of naturalization of such adoptive parent, in the custody of his adoptive parents, pursuant to a lawful admission for permanent residence.

321. Children born outside United States of alien parents; conditions for automatic citizenship

(a) A child born outside of the United States of alien parents, or of an alien parent and a citizen parent who has subsequently lost citizenship of the United States, becomes a citizen of the United States upon fulfillment of the following conditions:

   (1) The naturalization of both parents; or

   (2) The naturalization of the surviving parent if one of the parents is deceased; or

   (3) The naturalization of the parent having legal custody of the child when there has been a legal separation of the parents or the naturalization of the mother if the child was born out-of-wedlock and the paternity of the child has not been established by legitimation; and if

   (4) Such naturalization takes place while such child is unmarried and under the age of eighteen years; and

   (5) Such child is residing in the United States pursuant to a lawful admission for permanent residence at the time of the naturalization of the parent last naturalized under clause (1) of this subsection, or the parent naturalized under clause (2) or (3) of this subsection, or thereafter begins to reside permanently in the United States while under the age of eighteen years.

(b) Subsection (a) of this section shall apply to an adopted child only if the child is residing in the United States at the time of naturalization of such adoptive parent or parents, in the custody of his adoptive parent or parents, pursuant to a lawful admission for permanent residence.

322. Child born outside United States; application for certificate of citizenship requirements

(a) Application of citizen parents; requirements

A parent who is a citizen of the United States may apply to the Attorney General for a certificate of citizenship on behalf of a child born outside the United States. The Attorney General shall issue such a certificate of citizenship upon proof to the satisfaction of the Attorney General that the following conditions have been fulfilled:

(1) At least one parent is a citizen of the United States, whether by birth or naturalization.

(2) The child is physically present in the United States pursuant to a lawful admission.

(3) The child is under the age of 18 years and in the legal custody of the citizen parent.

(4) If the citizen parent is an adoptive parent of the child, the child was adopted by the citizen parent before the child reached the age of 16 years (except to the extent that the child is described in clause (ii) of subparagraph (E) or (F) of section 1101(b)(1) of this title) and the child meets the requirements for being a child under either of such subparagraphs.

(5) If the citizen parent has not been physically present in the United States or its outlying possessions for a period or periods totaling not less than five years, at least two of which were after attaining the age of fourteen years-

    (A) the child is residing permanently in the United States with the citizen parent, pursuant to a lawful admission for permanent residence, or

    (B) a citizen parent of the citizen parent has been physically present in the United States or its outlying possessions for a period or periods totaling not less than five years, at least two of which were after attaining the age of fourteen years.

(b) Attainment of citizenship status; receipt of certificate

Upon approval of the application (which may be filed abroad) and, except as provided in the last sentence of section 1448(a) of this title, upon taking and subscribing before an officer of the Service within the United States to the oath of allegiance required by this chapter of an applicant for naturalization, the child shall become a citizen of the United States and shall be furnished by the Attorney General with a certificate of citizenship.

(c) Adopted children

Subsection (a) of this section shall apply to the adopted child of a United States citizen adoptive parent if the conditions specified in such subsection have been fulfilled.

APPENDIX 5-3

Child Citizenship Act of 2000, Public Law 106-395, 114 Stat. 1631 (Oct. 30, 2000)

One Hundred Sixth Congress

of the

United States of America

AT THE SECOND SESSION

Begun and held at the City of Washington on Monday, the twenty-fourth day of January, two thousand

An Act

To amend the Immigration and Nationality Act to modify the provisions governing acquisition of citizenship by children born outside of the United States, and for other purposes.

Be it enacted by the Senate and House of Representatives of the United States of America in Congress assembled,

SECTION 1. SHORT TITLE.

This Act may be cited as the 'Child Citizenship Act of 2000'.

TITLE I—CITIZENSHIP FOR CERTAIN CHILDREN BORN OUTSIDE THE UNITED STATES

SEC. 101. AUTOMATIC ACQUISITION OF CITIZENSHIP FOR CERTAIN CHILDREN BORN OUTSIDE THE UNITED STATES.

(a) IN GENERAL- Section 320 of the Immigration and Nationality Act (8 U.S.C.A. 1431) is amended to read as follows:

'children born outside the united states and residing permanently in the united states; conditions under which citizenship automatically acquired 'SEC. 320.

(a) A child born outside of the United States automatically becomes a citizen of the United States when all of the following conditions have been fulfilled:

'(1) At least one parent of the child is a citizen of the United States, whether by birth or naturalization.

'(2) The child is under the age of eighteen years.

'(3) The child is residing in the United States in the legal and physical custody of the citizen parent pursuant to a lawful admission for permanent residence.

'(b) Subsection (a) shall apply to a child adopted by a United States citizen parent if the child satisfies the requirements applicable to adopted children under section 101(b)(1).'

(b)   CLERICAL AMENDMENT- The table of sections of such Act is amended by striking the item relating to section 320 and inserting the following:

'Sec. 320. Children born outside the United States and residing permanently in the United States; conditions under which citizenship automatically acquired.'

SEC. 102. ACQUISITION OF CERTIFICATE OF CITIZENSHIP FOR CERTAIN CHILDREN BORN OUTSIDE THE UNITED STATES.

(a)   IN GENERAL- Section 322 of the Immigration and Nationality Act (8 U.S.C.A. 1433) is amended to read as follows:

'children born and residing outside the united states; conditions for acquiring certificate of citizenship

'SEC. 322.

(a) A parent who is a citizen of the United States may apply for naturalization on behalf of a child born outside of the United States who has not acquired citizenship automatically under section 320. The Attorney General shall issue a certificate of citizenship to such parent upon proof, to the satisfaction of the Attorney General, that the following conditions have been fulfilled:

'(1) At least one parent is a citizen of the United States, whether by birth or naturalization.

'(2) The United States citizen parent—

'(A) has been physically present in the United States or its outlying possessions for a period or periods totaling not less than five years, at least two of which were after attaining the age of fourteen years; or

'(B) has a citizen parent who has been physically present in the United States or its outlying possessions for a period or periods totaling not less than five years, at least two of which were after attaining the age of fourteen years.

'(3) The child is under the age of eighteen years.

'(4) The child is residing outside of the United States in the legal and physical custody of the citizen parent, is temporarily present in the United States pursuant to a lawful admission, and is maintaining such lawful status.

'(b) Upon approval of the application (which may be filed from abroad) and, except as provided in the last sentence of section 337(a), upon taking and subscribing before an officer of the Service within the United States to the oath of allegiance required by this Act of an applicant for naturalization, the child shall become a citizen of the United States and shall be furnished by the Attorney General with a certificate of citizenship.

'(c) Subsections (a) and (b) shall apply to a child adopted by a United States citizen parent if the child satisfies the requirements applicable to adopted children under section 101(b)(1).'

(b)   CLERICAL AMENDMENT- The table of sections of such Act is amended by striking the item relating to section 322 and inserting the following:

'Sec. 322. Children born and residing outside the United States; conditions for acquiring certificate of citizenship.'

SEC. 103. CONFORMING AMENDMENT.

(a)   IN GENERAL- Section 321 of the Immigration and Nationality Act (8 U.S.C.A. 1432) is repealed.

(b)   CLERICAL AMENDMENT- The table of sections of such Act is amended by striking the item relating to section 321.

SEC. 104. EFFECTIVE DATE.

The amendments made by this title shall take effect 120 days after the date of the enactment of this Act and shall apply to individuals who satisfy the requirements of section 320 or 322 of the Immigration and Nationality Act, as in effect on such effective date.

Speaker of the House of Representatives.

Vice President of the United States and

President of the Senate.

Chapter 6

Overview of Naturalization

Research References

West's Key Number Digest
Aliens, Immigration and Citizenship ⊕689 to 751

Westlaw Databases
Steel on Immigration Law (STEEL)
Immigration Law Service (2d ed.) (IMMLS2D)

Treatises and Practice Aids
Steel on Immigration Law §§ 15:8 to 15:24

KeyCite®: Cases and other legal materials listed in KeyCite Scope can be researched through the KeyCite service on Westlaw®. Use KeyCite to check citations for form, parallel references, prior and later history, and comprehensive citator information, including citations to other decisions and secondary materials.

---

§ 6:1 Naturalization and citizenship

Research References
Dizon and Wettstein, Immigration Law Service 2d § 14:100
Steel on Immigration Law § 15:8

Part II of this book deals with the process of naturalization, an administrative procedure whereby a person acquires U.S. citizenship after complying with specific substantive and procedural requirements. Even though naturalization is commonly understood to be limited to this process, both the Immigration and Nationality Act and the Constitution define naturalization more broadly. For the INA, naturalization means "the conferring of nationality of a state upon a person *after* birth, by any means whatsoever."[1] The constitutional meaning of the term "naturalization" might include even or derivation at birth, as some courts have described every type of citizenship other than birth inside the U.S. as naturalization; though this is a

---

[Section 6:1]

[1]INA § 101(a)(23), 8 U.S.C.A. § 1101(a)(23) (emphasis added).

contested and complicated matter.[2] At any rate, Part II of this book discusses naturalization in the limited sense. All references to naturalization are also so limited.

The main difference between acquisition of citizenship and naturalization is that the former types of laws vest citizenship automatically, and the latter involves an application process to obtain citizenship. Unlike the statutes dealt with in part I, naturalization statutes require a government authority to determine that the person is eligible and has complied with all the requirements of naturalization *before* the person is admitted to citizenship. Generally, a person who dies before a final oath ceremony does not become a citizen.[3] For this reason, except for denaturalization proceedings, prior naturalization statutes are mainly of historical interest only, since all persons naturalized under them have been determined already to be eligible for the citizenship status they now have.[4]

Part II of this book refers to persons who apply for naturalization as applicants. However, before the 1990 amendments, naturalization generally was granted upon the filing of a petition in a court. Both state and federal courts had jurisdiction to naturalize, applying federal naturalization law.[5] Persons seeking naturalization under those proceedings were known as petitioners. Thus, within the same paragraph in this part, the reader will find that the person seeking naturalization will be called applicant, if naturalization is sought under the current procedures, and petitioner, if reporting on a case under the old procedures.

§ 6:2 Structure of INA

The naturalization provisions are all in chapter 2 of title III of the INA. The INA builds a basic structure of requirements and procedures that apply to the naturalization of all noncitizens. This book will refer to that structure as the "general naturalization" process. The naturalization requirements are described in sections

---

[2]Compare United States v. Wong Kim Ark, 169 U.S. 649, 702-03 (1898) ("The fourteenth amendment of the constitution, in the declaration that 'all persons born or naturalized in the United States, and subject to the jurisdiction thereof, are citizens of the United States and of the state wherein they reside,' contemplates two sources of citizenship, and two only,-birth and naturalization"); with Schneider v. Rusk, 377 U.S. 163, 168-69 (1964) (Unlike "naturalization," "acquisition of citizenship by being born abroad of an American parent" is "not covered by the Fourteenth Amendment" but is instead "left to proper Congressional action"); see also, Miller v. Albright, 523 U.S. 420, 480 (1998) (Breyer, J.,dissenting).

[3]Wiedersperg v. I.N.S., Case No. 98-15410, 1999 U.S. App. LEXIS 16952 (9th Cir. 1999) (unpublished decision). A limited exception to this rule allows for posthumous naturalization of certain victims of any of the four hijackings that occurred on September 11, 2001. See §§ 11:1 et seq.

[4]There are some exceptions to this general rule. When the INA was passed it provided for the continuing eligibility for naturalization of those who had already qualified under prior statutes. This is called the savings provision and is contained in INA § 405(a), (b), 8 U.S.C.A. § 1101(a), (b). Similarly, prior naturalization statutes are also relevant for denaturalization proceedings since those proceedings are based on the qualification of the applicant at the time of application. See §§ 14:1 et seq.

[5]See, e.g., sec. 1, Act of March 26, 1790, 1 Stat. 103 reproduced as Appendix 4-1 to Ch 4. See generally, INS Interp. 310.1(a). Cf. Holmgren v. U.S., 217 U.S. 509, 516–17, 30 S.Ct. 588, 589, 54 L.Ed. 861 (1910) (Congress can constitutionally delegate to state courts the power to naturalize).

310 through 318 of the INA.[1] All naturalization applicants must follow the procedures described in sections 332 through 339 of the INA.[2]

That basic structure has been statutorily altered for specific categories of people to take into account their special circumstances or other policy considerations. The INA describes the requirements for those classes as variations or exemptions to the requirements for general naturalization. Thus, for example, widows or widowers of U.S. citizens who died during active-duty service in the U.S. armed forces are allowed to naturalize if they comply with all the requirements and procedures for general naturalization except for the residency requirement, which is waived.[3] Sections 319 through 331 of the INA describe the variations for specific classes.[4]

§6:3 Declaration of intention to naturalize

In 1795, Congress passed a law mandating all persons who wanted to naturalize to file a "declaration of intention to naturalize"[1] a specific number of years before the naturalization petition.[2] The INA dispensed with this requirement in 1952.[3]

Even though the declaration is no longer a requirement to naturalize, the INA allows persons to file declarations of intention to naturalize if they wish.[4] Some state statutes require proof of U.S. citizenship or of having filed a declaration of intention to become a U.S. citizen in order to engage in certain occupations or professions and to obtain various licenses.[5]

Any lawful permanent resident over the age of 18 who is present in the United States at the time of the filing may file the declaration of intention to become a U.S. citizen.[6] The applicant may file Form N-300, reproduced in Appendix 6-1,[7] with the USCIS office having jurisdiction over the applicant's place of residence in the U.S.[8] Upon approval, USCIS will send the applicant the duplicate page of the Form N-300.[9] If USCIS denies the application, USCIS will advise the applicant of its deci-

---

[Section 6:2]

[1] 8 U.S.C.A. §§ 1421 to 1429.

[2] 8 U.S.C.A. §§ 1443 to 1450.

[3] INA § 319(d), 8 U.S.C.A. § 1430(d) (providing that such persons may be naturalized "upon compliance with all the requirements of [the Nationality and Naturalization Title of the INA] except that no prior residence or specified physical presence within the United States, or within a State or a district of the Service in the United States shall be required"). See §§ 12:1 et seq.

[4] 8 U.S.C.A. §§ 1430–1442.

[Section 6:3]

[1] Sec. 1, Act of January 29, 1795, 1 Stat. 414 reproduced as Appendix 4-2 to Ch 4.

[2] See e.g., sec. 1, Act of January 29, 1795 reproduced as Appendix 4-2 to Ch 4 (declaration must be filed 3 years before naturalization); sec. 2, Act of April 14, 1802, 2 Stat. 153 reproduced as Appendix 4-3 to Ch 4 (same); sec. 2165 Revised Statutes of the United States, 1878 reproduced as Appendix 4-5 to Ch 4 (declaration must be filed two years before naturalization); secs. 331, 332(a) Nationality Act of 1940.

[3] INA § 334(f), 8 U.S.C.A. § 1445(f); INS Interp. 334.2(e).

[4] INA § 334(f), 8 U.S.C.A. § 1445(f).

[5] INS Interp. 334.2(e)(1).

[6] INA § 334(f), 8 U.S.C.A. § 1445(f); 8 CFR § 334.11(a).

[7] See Appendix 6-1. Also available for download at http://uscis.gov/graphics/index.htm.

[8] 8 CFR § 334.11(a).

[9] 8 CFR § 334.11(b).

sion in writing.[10] There is no appeal from the denial of the filing of the declaration.[11] The current fee for filing the N-300 is $115.[12]

Each USCIS district office is required to maintain in chronological order a list of all declarations of intention, as well as a list of all naturalization applications, filed with that office.[13]

§ 6:4 Naturalization requirements and procedures

Research References

A.L.R. Index, Immigration and Naturalization

Kurtis A. Kemper, J.D., What Constitutes "Aggravated Felony" for Which Alien Can Be Deported or Removed Under § 237(a)(2)(a)(iii) of Immigration and Nationality Act (8 U.S.C.A. § 1227(a)), 168 A.L.R. Fed. 575

Dizon and Wettstein, Immigration Law Service 2d §§ 14:102, 14:103, 14:112, 14:143, 14:162, 14:169, 14:173

Steel on Immigration Law §§ 15:9, 15:10, 15:13, 15:15

Unless an applicant falls within one of the special naturalization categories, the applicant must comply with all the requirements of naturalization. These requirements include: (1) minimum age of 18 years to file an application for naturalization;[1] (2) five years of continuous residence after becoming a lawful permanent resident, at least two and a half years of which must have been physical presence in the United States; (3) three months residence in the state or USCIS district where the application is filed; (4) being attached to the principles of the U.S. Constitution; and (5) having basic English language skills and knowledge of the history and government of the U.S. These requirements are described in detail in Ch 7.

In addition, there are several bars or impediments to naturalization. Past criminal history will render naturalization impossible for some, and a naturalization application unwise for others. Good moral character is required for naturalization, and many crimes (particularly aggravated felonies) will preclude a showing of moral character. But more importantly, if a permanent resident has committed crimes or other acts which render him or her removable from the United States, USCIS will generally begin removal proceedings rather than adjudicating the naturalization application. There are still bars to naturalization based on political ideology and military activities; until 1952, there were still bars to the naturalization of certain races and nationalities. All these bars are discussed in Ch 8.

Chs 9 and 10 describe naturalization procedures. Ch 9 describes the application and examination of the applicant and includes a line-by-line description of the naturalization application form. Ch 10 describes administrative and judicial review of naturalization denials. Failed naturalization applications could result in removal proceedings.[2] Ch 10 also covers basic defenses to deportation.

---

[10]8 CFR § 334.11(c).

[11]8 CFR § 334.11(c).

[12]8 CFR § 103.7(b)(1); *see also* http://uscis.gov/graphics/index.htm.

[13]INA § 339(b), 8 U.S.C.A. § 1450(b).

[Section 6:4]

[1]U.S. citizen parents may file naturalization applications on behalf of their children. See §§ 11:1 et seq.

[2]See § 6:6.

§ 6:5 Relaxed procedures

Research References

A.L.R. Index, Immigration and Naturalization
James Lockhart, J.D., Construction and Application of (8 U.S.C.A. § 1440), Permitting Naturalization Through Active Duty Service in Armed Forces During Certain Periods of Military Hostilities, 196 A.L.R. Fed. 365
Steel on Immigration Law § 15:17

The INA exempts some applicants from fulfilling all the substantive eligibility requirements of naturalization. Following considerations of fairness and national policy, Congress has enacted legislation that relaxes some of these requirements for particular classes of persons.

Relaxed procedures may be based on family relationship. Thus, special procedures are available for spouses and children of U.S. citizens. They may also be based on historical accident, as some former Danish citizens of the Virgin Islands are still allowed to naturalize based on the treaty which transferred those islands to the U.S. Special procedures may be based on the perceived inequity of some of the prior U.S. expatriation laws. Thus, some former U.S. citizens are allowed to naturalize upon fulfillment of minimal requirements. Ch 11 discusses the special substantive requirements and relaxed procedures applicable to these classes.

National defense provides a second source of special naturalization legislation. Thus, noncitizens who serve in the U.S. armed forces are naturalized under special provisions. Secret service agents are also, to a limited extent, allowed to naturalize under special procedures. But national defense not only provides an avenue for naturalization, it also provides a bar. Nationals of countries at war with the U.S. may only naturalize upon compliance with special procedures to ensure their loyalty. Similarly, service in foreign armed forces has been the basis for expatriation in the past, and the INA provides for the naturalization of certain U.S. citizens who lost their citizenship through those provisions. Ch 12 covers the special forms of naturalization that are based on national defense.

§ 6:6 Potential adverse consequences: Deportation

Research References

A.L.R. Index, Immigration and Naturalization
Kurtis A. Kemper, J.D., What Constitutes "Aggravated Felony" for Which Alien Can Be Deported or Removed Under § 237(a)(2)(a)(iii) of Immigration and Nationality Act (8 U.S.C.A. § 1227(a)), 168 A.L.R. Fed. 575
Dizon and Wettstein, Immigration Law Service 2d § 14:110

The INA requires that only persons lawfully admitted to permanent residence in accordance with the provisions of the INA may naturalize.[1] The INA further provides that the term lawful admission for permanent residence requires the person to continue to be lawfully in the United States.[2] As a consequence, when an application for naturalization is filed, the Department of Homeland Security (DHS) will not only investigate whether the person's acquisition of permanent residence was lawful at its inception, but also whether the person has become subject to removal since

---

[Section 6:6]

[1]INA § 318, 8 U.S.C.A. § 1429.

[2]INA § 101(a)(20), 8 U.S.C.A. § 1101(a)(20).

becoming a permanent resident.[3] The *INS Operations Instructions* specifically require naturalization examiners to refer all cases where the person may have become deportable for consideration of whether to start removal proceedings.[4]

Of particular concern are those grounds of removal that do not bar the applicant from having good moral character. For example, a felony crime involving moral turpitude will not bar an applicant from showing good moral character, so long as the crime was outside the five-year period preceding the naturalization application.[5] However, if the crime occurred within five years of admission, or if the applicant committed another moral turpitude crime at some point, the applicant would be removable from the United States.[6]

Other particularly relevant grounds of deportation involve unlawful voting and false claims to citizenship.[7] Ch 9 discusses these grounds of deportation in more detail.[8]

The DHS will consider whether to start removal proceedings in each case of potential deportability, even when the person is eligible for naturalization.[9]

---

[3]See §§ 7:11 to 7:13, 8:2 to 8:25.

[4]Operations Instructions of the Immigration and Naturalization Service 318.1 (hereinafter "INS OI").

[5]INA § 101(f).

[6]INA § 237(a)(2)(A)(i) (felony moral turpitude offense within five years of admission); INA § 237(a)(2)(A)(ii) (multiple moral turpitude offenses not arising from the same scheme of criminal misconduct).

[7]See INA § 237(a)(3)(D), (6), 8 U.S.C.A. § 1227(a)(3)(D), (6).

[8]See §§ 9:58 to 9:62.

[9]See §§ 7:13 to 7:17.

APPENDIX 6-1

Form N-300

OMB No. 1615-0078; Expires 03/31/2016

Department of Homeland Security
U.S. Citizenship and Immigration Services

**Instructions for Form N-300, Application
to File Declaration of Intention**

The Purpose of Form N-300

This form enables you, a permanent resident, to notify U.S. Citizenship and Immigration Services (USCIS) that you intend to become a citizen of the United States. **USCIS does not require** that this form be filed to become eligible for naturalization.

Some states request that this form be submitted if the applicant is doing business with the state. Check with the state where you reside, or are doing business, to determine whether you are required to file this form.

Who Should File This Form

You should file this form if:

1. You are a permanent resident over 18 years of age; **and**

2. You are currently residing in the United States.

Required Evidence

Copy of Permanent Resident Card. Submit a copy of the front and back of your Form I-551 (Permanent Resident Card). USCIS must be able to read information on the photocopy.

Photographs. You must submit two identical color passport-style photographs of yourself taken within 30 days of filing Form N-300. The photos must have a white to off-white background, be printed on thin paper with a glossy finish, and be unmounted and unretouched. If a digital photo is submitted, it must to be taken from a camera with at least 3.5 mega pixels of resolution.

Passport-style photos must be 2" x 2". The photos must be in color with full face, frontal view on a white to off-white background. Head height should measure 1" to 1 3/8" from top of hair to bottom of chin, and eye height is between 1 1/8" to 1 3/8" from bottom of photo. Your head must be bare unless you are wearing a headdress as required by a religious denomination of which you are a member; however, your face must be visible. Using pencil or felt pen, lightly print your name and Alien Registration Number (A-Number) on the back of the photo.

General Instructions

1. **Type or print clearly using black ink.** Keep all information within the area provided.

If extra space is needed to answer any question, attach an additional sheet(s) of paper. You must provide the following information on the top of each sheet of paper:

A. Your A-Number;

B. The date;

C. Question number; **and**

D. Your signature.

2. **Answer all questions fully and accurately.** Write "N/A" if an item is not applicable. Write "None" if the answer is none.

3. **Avoid highlighting, crossing out, or writing outside the area provided for a response.**

If you must make substantial corrections to your Form N-300, USCIS recommends that you begin with a new Form N-300 rather than using correction tape or fluid to white out information. USCIS scanners may see through the white correction tape or fluid. This may lead to incorrect information being captured in USCIS systems which may cause processing delays or a rejection of your Form N-300.

Ensure that you are using the correct edition of the Form N-300. The correct edition is available on the USCIS Web site at **www.uscis.gov**.

4. **Provide your A-Number on the top right corner of each page.** Your A-Number is located on your Permanent Resident Card (formerly known as the Alien Registration or "Green" Card). The A-Number on your card consists of seven to nine numbers, depending on when your record was created. If the A-Number on your card has fewer than nine numbers, place enough zeros before the first number to make a *total of nine numbers* on Form N-300. For example, write number A1234567 as A001234567, or write number A12345678 as A012345678. **You must provide your A-Number. USCIS may reject your application if you do not write your A-Number.**

Copies. You may submit copies of documents unless USCIS requests original documents. Original documents submitted when not required may remain a part of the record.

Translations. You must provide a full English translation for any document written in a foreign language you submit to USCIS. The translator must certify that the translation is complete and accurate and that he or she is competent to translate from the foreign language into English.

Specific Form Instructions

This form is divided into five parts.

Part 1. Information About You, the Naturalization Applicant

1. **Current Legal Name.** Your current legal name is the name on your birth certificate unless it has been changed after birth by a legal action such as a marriage or court order. **Do not provide a nickname.**

2. **U.S. Social Security Number.** Print your U.S. Social Security Number. Write "N/A" if you do not have one.

3. **Date of Birth.** Always use eight numbers to show your date of birth. Write the date in this order: Month, Day, Year. For example, write May 1, 1958, as 05/01/1958.

4. **Country of Birth.** Provide the name of the country where you were born. Write the name of the country even if the country's name has since changed or the country no longer exists.

5. **Date You Became a Permanent Resident.** Provide the official date when your permanent residence began, as shown on your Permanent Resident Card. Write the date in this order: Month, Day, Year. For example, write August 9, 1988, as 08/09/1988. **USCIS will reject your application if you do not provide the information.**

6. **Country of Nationality.** Provide the name of the country(ies) where you are currently a citizen or national.

   A. If the country no longer exists or you are stateless, write the name of the country where you were last a citizen or national.

   B. If you are a citizen or national of more than one country, write the name of the country that issued your last passport.

7. **Home Address.** Provide the address where you now reside. Do **not** write a Post Office (P.O.) Box number here unless it is your **ONLY** address.

8. **Mailing Address.** Provide your mailing address even if it is the same as your home address. Provide "*in care of name*" information, if applicable. You must write something in every box, except an apartment number or "C/O" if you do not have one, within "Mailing Address."

NOTE: USCIS may not be able to contact you if you do not provide a complete and valid address. In addition, if USCIS does reject your application, USCIS may not be able to return the fee paid in connection with your Form N-300 to you if you do not provide a complete and valid address. If USCIS cannot return the fee, USCIS will cash your check.

9. **Telephone Numbers.** Provide your current telephone numbers. If the answer is none, write "None." If you are hearing impaired and use a TTY telephone connection, please indicate this by writing "TTY" after the telephone number.

10. **E-Mail Address.** Provide your current E-mail address. If you do not have an e-mail address, write "None."

Part 2. Your Signature

Sign the Form N-300 as you normally sign your name. You may place an "X" mark instead of a signature if you are unable to write in any language.

NOTE: USCIS will reject your Form N-300 if it is not signed.

Part 3. Signature of Person Who Prepared This Form N-300 For You *(if applicable)*

If you prepared this application by yourself, leave this section blank. If someone filled out this application for you, he or she must complete this section.

Part 4. Declaration of Intent

You are required to complete and sign this part. Refer to **Part. 1** (Information About You) for instructions to assist you.

USCIS will return page 3 of your Form N-300 if it is approved.

USCIS will retain a copy of page 3 of your Form N-300.

Processing Information

Any Form N-300 that is not signed or accompanied by the correct fee, except those accompanied by a fee waiver request (Form I-912, Request for a Fee Waiver), will be rejected. A Form N-300 that is not completed according to these instructions, is missing pages or otherwise not executed in its entirety, or is not accompanied by the required initial evidence may be rejected or delayed. If USCIS rejects your Form N-300 for any of the reasons above, the form and any fees will be returned to you if you provide a complete and valid mailing address. You will be notified why the form is considered deficient. You may correct the deficiency and refile a Form N-300. An application or petition is not considered properly filed until accepted by USCIS.

Requests for More Information or Interview

USCIS may request more information or evidence. USCIS may also request that you submit originals of any copies that you previously provided to USCIS for your Form N-300. In addition, USCIS may request that you appear for an interview.

Decision

The decision on Form N-300 involves a determination of whether you have established eligibility for the requested benefit. If you do not establish a basis for eligibility, USCIS will deny your Form N-300. You will be notified of the decision in writing.

What Is the Filing Fee

The fee for filing Form N-300 is **$250.**

Use the following guidelines when you prepare your check or money order for your Form N-300 fee:

1. The check or money order must be drawn on a bank or other financial institution located in the Unites States and must be payable in U.S. currency; **and**

2. Make the check or money order payable to **U.S. Department of Homeland Security.**

NOTE: Spell out U.S. Department of Homeland Security; do not use the initials "USDHS" or "DHS."

Notice to Those Making Payment by Check

USCIS will make a copy and convert your original check into an electronic funds transfer (EFT). This means USCIS will use the account information on your check to electronically debit your account for the check amount. This debit usually takes 24 hours and should show up on your regular account statement.

USCIS will not return your original check. USCIS will destroy it and keep a copy with your file. If the EFT cannot be processed due to technical reasons, you authorize USCIS to process the copy of the check. If the EFT cannot be completed because of insufficient funds, USCIS may try the EFT up to two times.

If you receive an insufficient funds notice, USCIS will send you instructions on how to submit your penalty fee. **Do not** send a check for the penalty fee to the address where you filed your Form N-300. It will be returned to you.

How To Check If the Fees Are Correct

The fee on Form N-300 is current as of the edition date appearing in the lower right corner of this page. However, because USCIS fees change periodically, you can verify if the fees are correct by following one of the steps below:

1. Visit the USCIS Web site at **www.uscis.gov**, select "**FORMS**," and check the "filing fee" column for the form you are filing; **or**

2. Telephone the USCIS National Customer Service Center at **1-800-375-5283** and ask for the fee information. For TDD (hearing impaired) call: **1-800-767-1833.**

Fee Waiver Request

Individuals may request a fee waiver based on an inability to pay. Form I-912 provides a standard means for submitting fee waiver requests. The instructions provide applicants with guidance on properly completing Form I-912 and submitting supporting documentation. The instructions also provide information on how USCIS makes a decision on a fee waiver request. To download a copy of Form I-912, including the instructions, click on the "**FORMS**" link on the USCIS Web site at **www.uscis.gov**.

Re-Filing Form N-300

If USCIS denied your previously filed Form N-300 and you are filing a new Form N-300, you must pay the full amount. **Otherwise, USCIS will not accept your Form N-300. USCIS cannot apply a previously submitted filing fee to a newly filed Form N-300.**

Where To File

Mail your completed Form N-300, and accompanying documentation, to the USCIS Dallas Lockbox facility at the following address:

> **USCIS**
> **P.O. Box 650809**
> **Dallas, TX 75265**

For Express Mail or courier deliveries, use the following address:

> **USCIS**
> **Attn: Form N-300**
> **2501 S. State Hwy. 121 Business**
> **Suite 400**
> **Lewisville, TX 75067**

E-Notification

If you are filing your Form N-300 at one of the USCIS Lockbox facilities, you may elect to receive an e-mail and/or text message notifying you that your Form N-300 has been accepted. You must complete Form G-1145, E-Notification of Application/Petition Acceptance, and attach it to the first page of your Form N-300. To download a copy of Form G-1145, including the instructions, click on the "**FORMS**" link on the USCIS Web site at **www.uscis.gov**.

Form Revision Date and Filing Addresses

The filing addresses provided on this form reflect the most current information as of the date this form was last printed. If you are filing Form N-300 more than 30 days after the latest edition date shown in the lower right corner, visit the USCIS Web site at www.uscis.gov before you file, and check the "**FORMS**" page to confirm the correct filing address and version currently in use. Check the edition date located at the lower right corner of the form. If the edition date on your Form N-300 matches the edition date listed for Form N-300 on the online "**FORMS**" page, your version is current. If the edition date on the online version is more recent, download a copy and use it. If you do not have Internet access, call the USCIS National Customer Service Center at **1-800-375-5283** to verify the current filing address and edition date. **USCIS will reject forms with the wrong revision date and the return the fee with instructions to resubmit the entire filing using the current form.**

Address Changes

If you have changed your address, you must inform USCIS of your new address. For information on filing a change of address go to the USCIS Web site at www.uscis.gov/addresschange or contact the National Customer Service Center at **1-800-375-5283**. For TDD (hearing impaired) call: **1-800-767-1833**.

NOTE: Do not submit a change of address request to the USCIS Lockbox facilities because the USCIS Lockbox facilities do not process change of address requests.

USCIS Forms and Information

To ensure you are using the latest version of this form, visit the USCIS Web site at **www.uscis.gov** where you can obtain the latest USCIS forms and immigration-related information. If you do not have internet access, you may order USCIS forms by calling our toll-free number at **1-800-870-3676**. You may also obtain forms and information by telephoning our USCIS National Customer Service Center at **1-800-375-5283**. For TDD (hearing impaired) call: **1-800-767-1833**.

You can schedule an appointment to meet with a USCIS representative at your local USCIS office through the USCIS Internet-based system, **InfoPass**. To access the system, visit the USCIS Web site. Use the **InfoPass** appointment scheduler and follow the screen prompts to set up your appointment. **InfoPass** generates an electronic appointment notice that appears on the screen.

Attorney or Representative

You may be represented, at no expense to the U.S. Government, by an attorney or other duly accredited representative. Your representative must submit Form G-28, Notice of Entry of Appearance as Attorney or Representative, with your Form N-300. If USCIS requests you to appear for an interview, your representative may also submit the Form G-28 at that time. Form G-28 can be obtained by visiting the USCIS Web site at **www.uscis.gov**, calling the USCIS forms line number at **1-800-870-3676**, or by contacting the USCIS National Customer Service Center at **1-800-375-5283**. For TDD (hearing impaired) call: **1-800-767-1833**.

Penalties

If you knowingly and willfully falsify or conceal a material fact or submit a false document with this Form N-300, USCIS will deny your Form N-300 and may deny any other immigration benefit. In addition, you may be subject to criminal prosecution and penalties provided by law.

USCIS Privacy Act Statement

AUTHORITIES: The information requested on this form, and the associated evidence, is collected under the Immigration and Nationality Act, section 101, et seq.

PURPOSE: The primary purpose for providing the requested information on this form is to determine if you have established eligibility for the immigration benefit for which you are filing. The information you provide will be used to grant or deny the benefit sought.

DISCLOSURE: The information you provide is voluntary. However, failure to provide the requested information, and any requested evidence, may delay a final decision or result in denial of your form.

ROUTINE USES: The information you provide on this form may be shared with other Federal, State, local, and foreign government agencies and authorized organizations following approved routine uses described in the associated published system of records notices [DHS-USCIS-007 - Benefits Information System and DHS-USCIS-001 - Alien File (A-File) and Central Index System (CIS), which can be found at **www.dhs.gov/privacy**]. The information may also be made available, as appropriate, for law enforcement purposes or in the interest of national security.

Paperwork Reduction Act

An agency may not conduct or sponsor information collection, and a person is not required to respond to a collection of information, unless Form N-300 displays a currently valid OMB control number. The public reporting burden for this collection of information is estimated at 45 minutes per response. This includes the time to review the instructions, as well as complete and submit your Form N-300. Send comments regarding this burden estimate or any other aspect of this collection of information, including suggestions for reducing this burden, to: U.S. Citizenship and Immigration Services, Regulatory Coordination Division, Office of the Policy & Strategy, 20 Massachusetts Avenue, NW, Washington, DC 20529-2140; OMB No. 1615-0078. **Do not mail your completed Form N-300 to this address**.

OMB No. 1615-0078; Expires 03/31/2016

Department of Homeland Security
U. S. Citizenship and Immigration Services

**Form N-300, Application to File
Declaration of Intention**

Print or type all your answers fully and accurately in black ink. Write "N/A" if an item is not applicable. Write "None" if the answer is none. Failure to answer all of the questions may delay your Form N-300.

NOTE: You must complete all portions of the form (four pages).

Part 1. Information About You

1. Current Legal Name *(do **not** provide a nickname)*

Family Name *(last name)*

Given Name *(first name)*

Middle Name *(if applicable)*

Your A-Number:

A _____ - _____ - _____

For USCIS Use Only

Bar Code	Date Stamp
	Remarks

2. U.S. Social Security Number *(if any)*   **3. Date of Birth** *(mm/dd/yyyy)*

4. Country of Birth

5. Date You Became a Permanent Resident *(mm/dd/yyyy)*

Since you were admitted to the United States as a permanent resident, have you been absent for a period of six months or longer?

☐ No   ☐ Yes   Attach a list of departure/arrival dates of all absences.

6. Country of Nationality

7. Home Address
Street Number and Name *(do **not** provide a P.O. Box in this space unless it is your **ONLY** address.)*

Apartment Number   City

County   State

ZIP Code

Action

8. Mailing Address

C/O *(in care of name)*

Street Number and Name

Apartment Number	City	State	ZIP Code

Form N-300 (03/21/13) N

Part 1. Information About You *(Continued)*

A ____ - ____ - ____

9. Daytime Phone Number

( )

Work Phone Number *(if any)*

( )

Evening Phone Number

( )

Mobile Phone Number *(if any)*

( )

10. E-Mail Address *(if any)*

Part 2. Your Signature *(USCIS will reject your Form N-300 if it is not signed.)*

Read the information on penalties in the instructions before completing this section. You must be in the United States when you file this application. You must sign your name below as well as in **Part 4 and Part 5**.

I desire to declare my intention to become a citizen of the United States. I certify, under penalty of perjury under the laws of the United States of America, that this application and the evidence submitted with it is all true and correct. I authorize release of any information from my records that U.S. Citizenship and Immigration Services needs to determine eligibility for the benefit I am seeking.

Your Signature

Date *(mm/dd/yyyy)*

Part 3. Signature of Person Who Prepared This Form for You *(if applicable)*

I declare under penalty of perjury that I prepared this form at the request of the above person, and it is based on all information of which I have any knowledge.

Preparer's Printed Name

Preparer's Signature

Date *(mm/dd/yyyy)*

Preparer's Firm or Organization Name *(if applicable)*

Preparer's Daytime Phone Number

( )

Preparer's Address
Street Number and Name

City

County

State

ZIP Code

Preparer's E-Mail Address *(if any)*

Preparer's Fax Number

( )

Part 4. Declaration of Intent	A _____ - _____ - _____

1. Current Legal Name (*do not* *provide a nickname*)

Family Name (*last name*)

Given Name (*first name*)

Middle Name (*if applicable*)

Affix

Photograph

Here

Not valid unless DHS Seal
applied below.

2. U.S. Social Security Number (*if any*)   **3. Date of Birth** (*mm/dd/yyyy*)

4. Country of Birth

5. Date You Became a Permanent Resident (*mm/dd/yyyy*)

6. Country of Nationality

7. Home Address

Street Number and Name (*do not provide a P.O. Box in this space*)   Apartment Number

City   County   State   ZIP Code

8. Mailing Address

C/O (*in care of name*)   Apartment Number

Street Number and Name

City   State   ZIP Code

9. Daytime Phone Number   **Work Phone Number** (*if any*)   **Evening Phone Number**
(   )   (   )   (   )

Mobile Phone Number (*if any*)   **10. E-Mail Address** (*if any*)
(   )

I am over the age of 18 years, have been lawfully admitted to the United States as a permanent resident, and am now residing in the United States based on such admission.

I hereby declare my intention in good faith to become a citizen of the United States and I certify that the photographs affixed to the original and duplicate hereof are a likeness of me and were signed by me.

I do swear (or affirm) that the statements I have made and the intentions I have expressed in this declaration of intention subscribed by me are true to the best of my knowledge and belief.

Your Signature (*USCIS will reject your Form N-300 if it is not signed*)   **Date** (*mm/dd/yyyy*)

USCIS Officer's Signature   **Date** (*mm/dd/yyyy*)

Form N-300 (03/21/13) N Page 3

Original Mailed to Applicant/Copy to File

Chapter 7

Naturalization Requirements*

I. REQUIREMENTS TO NATURALIZE

II. AGE

III. RESIDENCY AND LAWFUL PERMANENT RESIDENT STATUS

A. THE SEVERAL RESIDENCY REQUIREMENTS

B. FIVE-YEAR CONTINUOUS RESIDENCE REQUIREMENT

C. RESIDENCE MUST BE AFTER LAWFUL ADMISSION TO PERMANENT RESIDENCE

D. PHYSICAL PRESENCE REQUIREMENT

E. CONTINUOUS RESIDENCE AFTER FILING OF APPLICATION

F. STATE RESIDENCE REQUIREMENT

---

*This chapter includes materials previously published in D. Levy, "Exclusion Grounds Under the Immigration Act of 1990: Parts 1 & II," 91-8 & 91-9 Immigration Briefings (August & September 1991). Used with permission of Immigration Briefings. Copyright © 1991 Federal Publications, Inc.

Research References

West's Key Number Digest

Aliens, Immigration and Citizenship ⬤⟳689 to 751

Westlaw Databases

Steel on Immigration Law (STEEL)
Immigration Law Service (2d ed.) (IMMLS2D)

Treatises and Practice Aids

Dizon and Wettstein, Immigration Law Service 2d § 14:102
Fragomen Shannon, and Montalvo, Immigration Procedures Handbook, Ch 22
Steel on Immigration Law §§ 15:8 to 15:14

> **KeyCite®:** Cases and other legal materials listed in KeyCite Scope can be researched through the KeyCite service on Westlaw®. Use KeyCite to check citations for form, parallel references, prior and later history, and comprehensive citator information, including citations to other decisions and secondary materials.

I. REQUIREMENTS TO NATURALIZE

§ 7:1   In general

Research References

Dizon and Wettstein, Immigration Law Service 2d § 14:102

The INA imposes substantive requirements that a person must satisfy in order to naturalize. In addition to satisfying these requirements, the applicant must prove that he or she is not ineligible on various grounds, such as desertion, lack of good moral character, membership in totalitarian organizations, and membership in the Communist Party. Many of these bars developed because the general naturalization requirements did not prevent the naturalization of certain classes of people Congress intended to keep from naturalizing. This chapter will discuss the current interpretation of each of the substantive requirements and what an applicant must do to fulfill those requirements.

In 1790, the first naturalization law established three substantive requirements: that the applicant reside for a specific period of time in the United States and in the state where the applicant filed for naturalization; that he or she be a person of good moral character; and that he or she take the oath to support the Constitution.[1] By 1795, the period of prior residence in the United States was fixed at five years; the text of the oath included the oath to support the Constitution of the United States and the renunciation of "allegiance and fidelity to every foreign prince, potentate, state or sovereignty whatever;" and the court admitting the person to citizenship had to make a finding that the applicant had behaved during the five-year residence as a person "of good moral character, attached to the principles of the Constitution of the United States, and well disposed to the good order and happiness of the same."[2] In over 200 years of statutory development, the requirements for naturalization have changed very little.

II. AGE

§ 7:2   In general

Research References

Dizon and Wettstein, Immigration Law Service 2d § 14:103

The statute provides that no person under eighteen years of age may file an application for naturalization.[1] Persons who naturalize under the provisions for active duty service in times of war are exempt from the minimum age requirement.[2] In general, children under age eighteen may only become U.S. citizens under special provisions of the INA, such as the derivative naturalization provisions.[3]

Closely related to the age requirement is the fact that the person be alive at the time of naturalization. There is no posthumous naturalization except in the case of a specific type of military naturalization and for certain victims of the September 11, 2001 terrorist attacks.[4]

III. RESIDENCY AND LAWFUL PERMANENT RESIDENT STATUS

A. THE SEVERAL RESIDENCY REQUIREMENTS

§ 7:3 In general

Research References

Dizon and Wettstein, Immigration Law Service 2d § 14:112
Steel on Immigration Law § 15:10

[Section 7:1]

[1]Sec. 1, Act of March 26, 1790, 1 Stat. 103 reproduced as Appendix 4-1 to Ch 4.

[2]Sec. 1, Act of January 29, 1795, 1 Stat. 414 reproduced as Appendix 4-2 to Ch 4. In 1798, the period or prior residence required for naturalization was increased to fourteen years. Act of June 18, 1798, 1 Stat. 566. However in 1802, it was reduced again to five years and has been so ever since. Act of April 14, 1802 reproduced as Appendix 4-3 to Ch 4.

[Section 7:2]

[1]INA § 334(b), 8 U.S.C.A. § 1445(b).

[2]INA § 329(b)(1), 8 U.S.C.§ 1440(b)(1). For a description of the requirements for naturalization at time of war, see §§ 12:6 to 12:9.

[3]See §§ 5:1 et seq. and 11:1 et seq.

[4]Wiedersperg v. I.N.S., 189 F.3d 476 (9th Cir. 1999) (unpublished decision). For a description of posthumous naturalization in the military context, see Ch 12. For a description of posthumous citizenship for victims of the terrorist attacks, see §§ 11:33 to 11:35.

The INA provides that, unless otherwise specified, no person may be naturalized unless the applicant

(1) immediately preceding the date of filing for his [or her] application for naturalization has resided continuously, after being lawfully admitted for permanent residence, within the United States for at least five years and during the five years preceding the date of filing his [or her] application has been physically present therein for periods totaling at least half of that time, and who has resided within the State or within the district of the Service in the United States in which the applicant filed the application for at least three months, (2) has resided continuously within the United States from the date of application up to the time of admission to citizenship . . .[1]

This provision incorporates almost all of the different residency requirements for naturalization. First, it requires five years of residence. Second, it requires that this residence be continuous. Third, it requires that the continuous residence take place after the applicant was lawfully admitted for permanent residence. Fourth, it requires the applicant to be physically present in the United States for periods totaling at least two and a half years. Fifth, it requires residence in the state or in the USCIS district where the application was filed for at least three months prior to the application. Sixth, it requires the applicant to reside continuously in the U.S. from the date of the application to the date of admission to citizenship.

Until 1994, the applicant, at the time of application, was also required to have the intention of residing permanently in the U.S.[2] The Immigration and Nationality Technical Corrections Act of 1994 amendment eliminated this requirement for persons admitted to citizenship after the enactment of that law.[3]

Each of these aspects of the residency requirement is discussed separately below. Some sections of the INA relating to specific categories of people, such as spouses and children of U.S. citizens, provide exceptions to the different residency requirements. These exceptions are discussed in the sections dealing with those specific categories.[4]

B. FIVE-YEAR CONTINUOUS RESIDENCE REQUIREMENT

§ 7:4 Meaning of residence

Research References

Dizon and Wettstein, Immigration Law Service 2d §§ 14:112, 14:113, 14:115
Steel on Immigration Law § 15:10

The INA defines residency specifically as the place of general abode, that is, "the principal, actual dwelling place in fact, without regard to intent."[1] This definition was drafted specifically to exclude "intent" from the definition of residence for naturalization purposes. The regulations attempt to expand on this definition by explaining that a person's residence for naturalization purposes is the same as that

---

[Section 7:3]

[1]INA § 316(a), 8 U.S.C.A. § 1427(a).

[2]See INA §§ 338, 340(d), 8 U.S.C.A. §§ 1449, 1451(d).

[3]Sec. 104(e), Immigration Nationality Technical Corrections Act of 1994 (INTCA), Pub.L. 103-416, 108 Stat. 4305 (Oct. 25, 1994) reproduced as Appendix 4-21 to Ch 4.

[4]See also Chs 3, 11, and 12 discussing special procedures for noncitizen nationals; spouses and children of U.S. citizens; and military-related naturalization.

[Section 7:4]

[1]INA § 101(a)(33), 8 U.S.C.A. § 1101(a)(33).

person's domicile or principal actual dwelling place, without regard to intent.[2] The duration of that person's residence in that particular place is measured from the moment the person first established residence there.[3]

The Supreme Court has interpreted the statutory test as an objective one that does not involve the intention of the applicant: the USCIS must determine which is the principal dwelling place of the person.[4] Under this definition, a person who did not intend to leave the U.S., but who resided in Rome between 1941 and 1945, had a principal dwelling place in Rome rather than the U.S.[5] In another case, a district court held that a naturalization applicant failed to show proof of his actual residence because he did not indicate how long he had resided at his current address in New Mexico and did not include any other information regarding his physical residence in his application.[6] A person who moved permanently to another country one month prior to the person's naturalization hearing was not considered to be residing in the U.S. for purposes of naturalization.[7] Even though the court found that the petitioner failed to satisfy the naturalization residency requirement, the case could also have been resolved by a finding of abandonment of lawful permanent residence or intention to reside permanently in the U.S.[8]

There is a serious problem in defining residence in completely objective terms. As Judge Learned Hand noted, one may not always be able to determine a person's "permanent place of abode" by the person's external conduct alone without recourse to the purpose of a person's presence in that place.[9] Several lower courts have struggled with this problem in the context of U.S. citizenship at birth abroad.[10]

Persons in "commuter" noncitizen status afford a clear example where lack of "residence" in the U.S. will be found even when there have been no absences that would statutorily break the continuity of the residence. Commuter noncitizens are lawful permanent residents who work in the U.S. but reside in a foreign contiguous territory.[11] According to the regulations, they cannot satisfy the residency requirements for purposes of naturalization until they have taken up residence in the U.S.[12]

A situation peculiar to beneficiaries of the tax treaty between the U.S. and France

---

[2]8 CFR § 316.1(a).

[3]8 CFR § 316.1(a).

[4]Savorgnan v. U.S., 338 U.S. 491, 505, 70 S.Ct. 292, 299 (1950) (interpreting the wording of the 1940 act which did not refer to intent).

[5]Savorgnan v. U. S., 338 U.S. 491, 506, 70 S. Ct. 292, 300, 94 L. Ed. 287, 15 A.L.R.2d 538 (1950). Cf. U.S. v. Karahalias, 205 F.2d 331, 335 (2d Cir. 1953) (the purpose of the visit helps determine which is the principal place of residence); Acheson v. Yee King Gee, 184 F.2d 382, 384 (9th Cir. 1950) (same); Lee You v. Acheson, 109 F.Supp. 98 (S.D.Tex. 1952) (same); Toy Teung Kwong v. Acheson, 97 F.Supp. 745 (N.D.Cal. 1951) (same); Wong Gan Ghee v. Acheson, 95 F.Supp. 816 (N.D.Cal. 1951) (same).

[6]Alvear v. Kirk, 87 F. Supp. 2d 1241 (D.N.M. 2000); see § 7:5.

[7]In re Naturalization of Bartkiw, 199 F.Supp. 762, 765–66 (E.D.Pa. 1961).

[8]For a discussion of those requirements, see § 8:24.

[9]U.S. v. Karahalias, 205 F.2d 331, 335 (2d Cir. 1953).

[10]U.S. v. Karahalias, 205 F.2d 331 (2d Cir. 1953) (purpose of visit is relevant to determine abode); Acheson v. Yee King Gee, 184 F.2d 382, 384 (9th Cir. 1950) (same); Lee You v. Acheson, 109 F. Supp. 98 (S.D. Tex. 1952) (same); Toy Teung Kwong v. Acheson, 97 F. Supp. 745 (N.D. Cal. 1951) (purpose of the trip will determine what the principal place of residence is); Wong Gan Chee v. Acheson, 95 F. Supp. 816 (N.D. Cal. 1951) (same). See generally §§ 4:45 to 4:47.

[11]8 CFR § 211.5(a).

[12]8 CFR §§ 211.5(c), 316.5(b)(3).

will also affect residence for naturalization purposes. A lawful permanent resident who claims benefits under articles 16 or 25 of the treaty cannot count his or her residence during the calendar year for which such benefit was claimed for purposes of either the residency or the physical presence requirements of naturalization.[13] In addition, there are some situations when lawful permanent residents, regardless of treaties, may elect to claim nonresident status for tax purposes in the United States. This will not necessarily break their continuous residency for purposes of naturalization but may terminate their lawful permanent resident status making them ineligible for naturalization.[14]

Residence in the United States presumably includes residence in those territories of the U.S. that have been incorporated into the U.S.[15] Thus, presence in the Midway Islands was considered to be presence in the U.S. for purposes of naturalization since the Midway Islands were part of Hawaii until Hawaii became a state on August 21, 1959.[16] After Hawaii became a state and Congress decided not to include the Midway Islands in the grant of statehood to Hawaii, residence in the Midway Islands would not count as residence in the U.S. for purposes of the continuous residence requirement of naturalization.[17] Currently, residence in any of the territories that have been included as part of the INA definition of the United States will count for naturalization purposes.[18]

In addition, for persons who have served in the armed forces of the U.S. for periods aggregating up to three years or more, any time during which the person was serving in the military within the five years immediately preceding the application for naturalization is considered as both residence and physical presence in the United States.[19]

§ 7:5 Residence must be continuous

Research References
Dizon and Wettstein, Immigration Law Service 2d §§ 14:119 to 14:126
Steel on Immigration Law § 15:11

The presumptions associated with the second residence requirement may help determine where the person has his or her principal domicile. To satisfy this second naturalization requirement, the five-year residence prior to naturalization must be continuous.[1] Certain absences from the United States will not break continuity of residence.

First, only absences that are within the statutory period of required continuous residence may break continuity.[2] Thus for example, if a person was admitted to law-

---

[13]INS Interp. 316.1(b)(2)(iii).

[14]8 CFR § 316.5(c)(2). Cf. requirement of maintenance of lawful permanent residence.

[15]For a discussion of the notion of incorporation, see § 2:4, §§ 3:1 to 3:2.

[16]INS Interp. 316.1(b)(2)(i).

[17]INS Interp. 316.1(b)(2)(i).

[18]INA § 101(a)(38), 8 U.S.C.A. § 1101(a)(38) (defining the geographical scope of the United States for the purposes of the INA).

[19]INA § 328(d), 8 U.S.C.A. § 1439(d).

[Section 7:5]

[1]INA § 316(a), 8 U.S.C.A. § 1427(a).

[2]INS Interp. 316.1(b)(4).

ful permanent residence in 1953, and in February 1961 that person petitioned for naturalization; that person's absence from the United States from 1954 until January 1957 will not break the five years of continuous residence because the starting point for the calculation of the five years would have been February 1956, and between February 1956 and January 1957, the petitioner was absent for less than one year.[3] The applicant would still have to prove that he or she did not abandon lawful permanent residence between 1954 and 1957.[4]

Second, the statute by implication provides that absences of less than six months are unimportant for purposes of the five years of continuous residence prior to naturalization.[5] Any absence between six months and one year presumptively breaks the continuity of residence.[6] The applicant, however, can overcome the presumption with evidence that he or she did not intend to abandon residence in the U.S. during the absence.[7]

Third, as noted above, absences between six months and one year may break the continuity of residence, even when there is no concomitant abandonment of lawful permanent residence by the person.[8] The regulations suggest that proof of the following may document that the applicant did not abandon his or her residence: (1) the applicant did not terminate his or her employment in the United States during this absence; (2) the applicant's immediate family remained in the United States; (3) the applicant retained full access to his or her United States abode; or (4) the applicant did not obtain employment abroad.[9]

Fourth, absences of more than one year from the United States (whether before or after the filing of the naturalization application) will automatically break the continuity of the residence for naturalization purposes, unless the person falls into one of the categories of individuals eligible to file form N-470, and does actually file the form before having been abroad for a year.[10] Again the break of continuity is automatic and is not related to retention of lawful permanent residence.[11] The issue for abandonment of lawful permanent residence is whether the person intended to abandon his or her status when departing on a temporary visit abroad, while the issue for naturalization is whether the person was continuously absent for more than one year.[12] Thus, an Iranian national who went to Iran for the funeral of his mother and was prevented from returning to the U.S. for approximately two years by the hostage crisis was considered to have broken the five years continuous residence

---

[3]INS Interp. 316.1(b)(4).

[4]See § 8:24.

[5]INA § 316(b), 8 U.S.C.A. § 1427(b) (absences between six months and a year may break the continuity of residence); *but cf.* In re Romalez-Alcaide, 23 I. & N. Dec. 423, 2002 WL 1189034 (B.I.A. 2002) (considering similar language in the cancellation of removal statute).

[6]INA § 316(b), 8 U.S.C.A. § 1427(b) (absences between six months and a year may break the continuity of residence).

[7]See INA § 316(b), 8 U.S.C.A. § 1427(b) (absences between six months and a year may break the continuity of residence); 8 CFR § 316.5(c)(1)(i); Petition of Turner, 51 F.2d 1062 (S.D. Tex. 1931).

[8]8 CFR § 316.5(c)(1)(i).

[9]8 CFR § 316.5(c)(1)(i).

[10]INA § 316(b) [8 U.S.C.A. § 1427(b)]. For a discussion of who is eligible to preserve their residence in this way, see §§ 7:6 to 7:10.

[11]In re Naturalization of Vafaei-Makhsoos, 597 F.Supp. 499, 501 (D.Minn. 1984).

[12]In re Naturalization of Vafaei-Makhsoos, 597 F. Supp. 499, 501 (D. Minn. 1984).

even though he never abandoned his lawful permanent residence.[13] The fact that he originally intended only to remain a short time in Iran and was prevented from returning by reasons beyond his control was irrelevant to the break of his continuous residence for naturalization purposes.[14]

A person who does not intend to depart the United States will not break the continuity for naturalization purposes even if the person is absent for more than one year.[15] Thus a lawful permanent resident taken prisoner by the Japanese on American territory during World War II and interned in a prisoner of war camp for the duration of the war did not break the five years of continuous residence for naturalization purposes.[16] This situation is different from a person who leaves voluntarily and is prevented from returning. In the case of *involuntary* departure, the person is deemed never to have left the United States.[17]

An applicant may also avail himself or herself of another exception to the one-year requirement. An absence longer than one year will not interrupt the continuous residence if the applicant was abroad for a period longer than one year on reliance of misinformation provided by the DHS, or, as the *INS Interpretations* puts it, on reliance on incomplete, misleading, or erroneous advice from a government official whose duty it is to furnish full and accurate information on the subject matter involved.[18] The person is held not to be bound by the consequences of his or her actions but to have been constructively present in the United States.[19]

Similarly, a person who serves in the U.S. armed forces and is sent abroad pursuant to military orders is deemed not to have left the U.S. for purposes of the five-year residence requirement.[20]

Akin to the armed forces provision is the constructive residence available to some lawful permanent residents who serve on U.S. ships.[21] Those persons are deemed to be residing and physically present in the United States for the period they are serving on those ships if such service occurred within five years prior to the filing of the naturalization application.[22] To qualify, the person must have served honorably or with good conduct either (1) on board of a vessel operated by the U.S., or (2) on board a vessel whose home port is in the United States, (a) which is registered under the laws of the U.S., or (b) of which the full legal and equitable title of which is in a citizen of the U.S., or a corporation organized under the laws of a state of the

---

[13]In re Naturalization of Vafaei-Makhsoos, 597 F. Supp. 499, 501–01 (D. Minn. 1984).

[14]In re Naturalization of Vafaei-Makhsoos, 597 F. Supp. 499, 500 (D. Minn. 1984). There is an argument that his general place of abode may have remained the United States. See § 7:4. In spite of this, the statutory provision is clear that absences longer than one year will break continuity of residence for naturalization purposes.

[15]In re Yarina, 73 F.Supp. 688, 689 (N.D.Ohio 1947); INS Interp. 316.1(b)(4).

[16]In re Yarina, 73 F. Supp. 688, 688–89 (N.D. Ohio 1947).

[17]In re Yarina, 73 F. Supp. 688, 689 (N.D. Ohio 1947); INS Interp. 316.1(b)(4).

[18]In Re Petition of LaVoie, 349 F.Supp. 68 (D.C.V.I. 1972); INS Interp. 316.1(b)(4).

[19]INS Interp. 316.1(b)(4).

[20]INS Interp. 316.1(b)(4), (d)(2) citing to Matter of J-M-D-, 7 I. & N. Dec. 105 (B.I.A. 1956) (physical presence for purposes of suspension of deportation); Matter of Bauer, 10 I. & N. Dec. 304 (B.I.A. 1963) (no entry for purposes of grounds of exclusion because constructively never left the United States).

[21]INA § 330, 8 U.S.C.A. § 1441.

[22]INA § 330, 8 U.S.C.A. § 1441.

U.S.[23] This provision is not available to members of the armed forces of the U.S., and there are very specific requirements of proof.[24]

§ 7:6 Preserving residence for naturalization purposes; generally

Research References
Steel on Immigration Law § 15:12

In addition to the exceptions that prevent the break of continuous residence requirement, the INA provides a statutory mechanism that under certain circumstances allows some persons who are absent for more than one year to preserve their residence in the United States for naturalization purposes.[1] Note, however, that the granting of applications to preserve residence will not relieve the applicant from the physical presence requirement unless he or she is an employee or contractor of the U.S. government.[2]

Both of the following provisions for the preservation of residence are only available if the person that will engage in the qualifying employment is the naturalization applicant himself or herself. There is no provision that allows a person to preserve residence simply because his or her spouse or parent is engaged in qualifying employment abroad. However, except for the preservation available to religious practitioners, spouses and children may *derive* the benefits of preservation of residence extended to the principal if they live in the household of the principal noncitizen abroad.[3] If the person going abroad is the U.S. citizen spouse of a lawful permanent resident, the noncitizen spouse may be eligible for a form of expedited naturalization that disposes of the residency requirement altogether.[4]

§ 7:7 Preserving residence for naturalization purposes; generally— Requirements

Research References
Steel on Immigration Law § 15:12

There are two provisions in the INA that provide for the preservation of residence for naturalization purposes. One relates to the preservation of residence for employees and contractors of the U.S. government, certain corporations, and public international organizations.[1] The other provides for the preservation of residence of persons performing specific religious duties.[2]

---

[23]INA § 330, 8 U.S.C.A. § 1441.

[24]INA § 330, 8 U.S.C.A. § 1441. For further discussion of the applicability of this section and specific requirements, see 8 CFR § 330; INS Interp. 330.

[Section 7:6]

[1]INA § 316(b), 8 U.S.C.A. § 1427(b).

[2]INA § 316(c), 8 U.S.C.A. § 1427(c). For a description of the physical presence requirement, see § 7:19.

[3]INA § 316(b), 8 U.S.C.A. § 1427(b).

[4]See §§ 11:7 to 11:10.

[Section 7:7]

[1]INA § 316(b), 8 U.S.C.A. § 1427(b).

[2]INA § 317, 8 U.S.C.A. § 1428.

§7:8 Preserving residence for naturalization purposes; generally—Requirements—Employees and contractors of U.S. government, certain corporations, and public international organizations

Research References

Dizon and Wettstein, Immigration Law Service 2d §§ 14:134, 14:135

To qualify for preservation of residence for naturalization purposes, the person must:

(1) have been physically present in the United States for an uninterrupted period of at least one year after being lawfully admitted for permanent residence;

(2) be employed by or under contract with

a. the government of the U.S.,

b. an American institution of research recognized as such by the Attorney General,

c. an American firm or corporation engaged in whole or in part in the development of foreign trade or commerce of the U.S.,

d. a subsidiary of such American firm or corporation whose stock is fifty percent or more owned by an American firm or corporation, or

e. a public international organization of which the U.S. is a member by treaty or statute and by which the noncitizen was not employed until after being lawfully admitted to permanent residence;

(3) establish to the [DHS] prior to beginning such employment—whether before or after departing the United States, but in either case before being absent one year from the United States—that his or her absence from the United States will be:

a. on behalf of the U.S. government, or

b. for the purpose of carrying on scientific research on behalf of the qualifying research institution, or

c. to engage in the development of foreign trade and commerce on behalf of the qualifying firm or corporation or subsidiary thereof, or

d. residence abroad necessary to protect the property rights in such countries of the qualifying U.S. firm or corporation or subsidiary thereof which is engaging in the development of foreign trade and commerce, or

e. to be employed by the qualifying public international organization;

(4) prove to the [DHS] that, in effect, his or her absence from the United States for such period was for the described purposes.[1]

The spouse and unmarried sons or daughters of a person allowed to preserve residence through this mechanism are themselves also allowed to preserve such residence during the period they reside abroad as dependent members of the household of such a person.[2]

The list of American institutions of research and public international organizations (including designations under the International Immunities Act) has been reproduced in Appendix 7-1. It must be pointed out, however, that such a list may change and the practitioner should consult with the appropriate regulations where it is officially reproduced.[3]

The requirement of one-year continuous physical presence after admission to law-

---

[Section 7:8]

[1]INA § 316(b), 8 U.S.C.A. § 1427(b).

[2]INA § 316(b), 8 U.S.C.A. § 1427(b).

[3]8 CFR § 316.20.

ful permanent residence has come full circle to mean once again that any absence will interrupt that physical presence. This was the original position taken by the INS and the courts, which provided that any absence, no matter how brief, would interrupt continuous physical presence.[4] For some time, however, the INS changed its position holding that brief, casual, and innocent absences did not break the continuity of the physical presence.[5] This position was based on the *Fleuti* doctrine, which provides that lawful permanent residents who go abroad on brief, casual, and innocent visits have not made an entry for immigration purposes.[6] However, that doctrine did not directly involve physical presence requirements and, in 1984, the Supreme Court decided, in the context of a suspension of deportation application, that any absences, no matter how brief, interrupted the continuous physical presence requirement.[7] After *Phinpathya*, the INS reverted to the position that any absence will interrupt the preservation of residence one-year physical presence requirement.[8]

Statutorily, the requirement of one-year physical presence after admission to lawful residence has been relaxed for employees and contractors of the Central Intelligence Agency (CIA) who may satisfy that requirement at any time before the filing of the application for naturalization.[9] The INA also authorizes the naturalization of up to five persons each year under another provision of law upon the determination of the director of the CIA, the Attorney General, and the DHS that those persons have made an extraordinary contribution to national security.[10] That provision does not preclude other employees or contractors of the CIA from naturalizing under the general naturalization procedures.

The INS previously issued interpretations of the requirement of employment in a firm or corporation engaged in the development of foreign trade or commerce of the U.S. The sole owner of a firm who goes abroad to represent that firm may not obtain the benefits of preservation of residence.[11] However, a person other than the sole owner who is employed abroad representing a sole proprietorship doing business under a trade name is eligible for preservation of residence.[12] A person who is not an employee of an American firm, but rather goes abroad voluntarily for the purpose of soliciting business for that firm to be paid solely on a commission basis, is not entitled to the benefits of preserving residence because such a person is not considered an employee but an independent contractor.[13]

---

[4]Matter of A-, 7 I. & N. Dec. 710 (Att'y Gen. 1958); Petition of Pinner, 161 F. Supp. 337 (N.D. Cal. 1958); Petition of Pinner, 161 F. Supp. 337 (N.D. Cal. 1958).

[5]INS Interp. 316.1(c)(3)(i).

[6]See INS Interp. 316.1(c)(3)(i).

[7]Phinpathya v. I.N.S., 464 U.S. 183, 104 S.Ct. 584, 78 L.Ed.2d 401 (1984).

[8]Matter of Copeland, 19 I. & N. Dec. 788 (Comm'r 1988); Matter of Graves, 19 I. & N. Dec. 337 (Comm'r 1985). Cf. Letter, Martin, General Counsel, INS, File No. HQ 316a.1-P (Sept. 1, 1995) reprinted in 72 Interpreter Releases 1251 (reaffirming this position).

[9]INA § 316(c), 8 U.S.C.A. § 1427(c).

[10]INA § 316(f), 8 U.S.C.A. § 1427(f). See also § 12:15.

[11]INS Interp. 316.1(c)(4)(i).

[12]INS Interp. 316.1(c)(4)(i).

[13]INS Interp. 316.1(c)(4)(ii).

Persons who are employed abroad on a part-time basis may not receive these benefits unless they devote a substantial portion of time to this employment.[14] This means that such employment must not be incidental to other activities in which the person engages abroad.[15] If such is the case, the person is not prevented from preserving residence even when the motive for going abroad was other than the employment.[16]

For the purposes of this section, subsidiaries of U.S. firms or corporations are considered to include foreign firms owned by a U.S. firm or corporation through a third corporation.[17] A foreign corporation engaged in the development of trade and commerce with the U.S., whose stock was virtually completely owned by another foreign corporation, which, in turn, was solely owned by a U.S. corporation, was held to qualify as a subsidiary "more than fifty per centum of whose stock is owned by an American firm or corporation."[18] However, one U.S. firm or corporation must own more than fifty percent of the foreign firm or corporation; this section will not apply to employment in a foreign firm that is wholly owned by several U.S. firms, none of which owns more than fifty percent of the stock.[19] The nationality of a corporation for purposes of this section is determined by the nationality of the persons or corporations who own more than fifty percent of the stock of that firm and not by the place of incorporation; a subsidiary of a foreign corporation is not an American firm or corporation for purpose of this section even when incorporated in the U.S.[20]

Indeed, an INS General Counsel opinion takes this approach to its ultimate conclusions.[21] In that case, the employer was incorporated in New York. A second corporation, incorporated in Delaware, wholly owned that corporation. The Delaware corporation was wholly owned by a third corporation, which in turn was owned by a fourth corporation. Both the third and fourth corporations were also incorporated in Delaware. The fourth corporation was wholly owned by a fifth corporation, incorporated in New York, which in turn was owned by a Sixth corporation, which was a wholly owned subsidiary of a foreign corporation. Foreign nationals owned more than fifty percent of the stock of the foreign corporation. The General Counsel concluded that because foreign nationals ultimately owned more than fifty percent of the stock, the employer was not an American corporation for purposes of this provision.[22]

---

[14]INS Interp. 316.1(c)(4)(ii).

[15]Matter of P-, 5 I. & N. Dec. 332, 335 (Central Office 1953) (person worked as a language instructor for the Navy in Italy, and had a full course of language studies in the University of Naples Oriental Institute).

[16]Matter of P-, 5 I. & N. Dec. 332, 335, 1953 WL 7460 (B.I.A. 1953) (originally left for the sole purpose of studying languages at the Oriental Institute of the University of Naples).

[17]INS Interp. 316.1(c)(4)(iii).

[18]INS Interp. 316.1(c)(4)(iii).

[19]INS Interp. 316.1(c)(4)(iii).

[20]Matter of Warrach, 17 I. & N. Dec. 285 (Reg. Comm'r 1979).

[21]Legal Opinion, David Martin, INS General Counsel, File No. HQ 319-P (Sept. 14, 1995) reprinted in 73 Interpreter Releases 449.

[22]Legal Opinion, David Martin, INS General Counsel, File No. HQ 319-P (Sept. 14, 1995) reprinted in 73 Interpreter Releases 449.

However, the AAO has recently clarified that a publicly-held corporation which trades its stock only on U.S. markets is a U.S. corporation for purposes of § 316(b).[23] In such a situation, the applicant need not demonstrate the nationality of the corporation by establishing the nationality of those persons who own more than 51% of the stock of that firm.[24]

Development of foreign trade and commerce has been interpreted broadly enough to include the work done by refugee relief agencies and other nonprofit organizations. The basis of this interpretation is that these nonprofit organizations purchase relief supplies in the United States, pay ocean freight to U.S. shipholding companies to transport the supplies, pay U.S. shipping companies to transport refugees into the United States.[25] Thus, the activities of United HIAS Services, Inc., American Jewish Joint Distribution Committee, Inc., Catholic Relief Services, and CARE have been held to meet the essential elements of American corporations or firms engaged in part in the development of foreign trade and commerce of the U.S.[26]

Development of foreign trade has also been interpreted to include trading in services and technology, including working in a company that engages in management of artists.[27] On the other hand, it has been determined that "development of trade and commerce" is not broad enough to encompass teaching in an American school whose primary purpose is educating the dependents of the American business, military, embassy, and missionary community in a foreign country.[28]

There has also been interpretation of the meaning of employment or contract with the U.S. government. A person studying abroad under a grant of the HEW was held to have been employed under contract of the U.S. government for purposes of this section.[29] Similarly, a person employed abroad by the Near East Foundation, an American corporation wholly financed by the International Cooperation Administration (ICA), was considered to be employed or under contract for the U.S. government, even though the employment was financed under a contract between the ICA and a foreign government.[30] Employment by the University of Maryland to conduct classes for the U.S. military and government personnel and their dependents abroad was considered under contract with the U.S.[31] In general, when an American firm or corporation is under contract with the U.S. government, a person employed abroad by that firm or corporation who is engaged directly or indirectly in carrying out the terms of the contract is considered to be "employed or under contract with the U.S. government" for purposes of this section.[32]

---

[23]Matter of Chawathe, 25 I. & N. Dec. 369 (AAO 2010).

[24]Matter of Chawathe, 25 I. & N. Dec. 369 (AAO 2010).

[25]INS Interp. 316.5(c)(6).

[26]INS Interp. 316.5(c)(6).

[27]Memorandum, Rees, General Counsel, File No. HQ 319-C (Feb. 23, 1993) reprinted in 72 Interpreter Releases 1178.

[28]In Re Fang Lan Dankowski, 478 F.Supp. 1203 (D.Guam 1979).

[29]INS Interp. 316.1(c)(5).

[30]INS Interp. 316.1(c)(5).

[31]INS Interp. 316.1(c)(5).

[32]INS Interp. 316.1(c)(5).

§7:9 Preserving residence for naturalization purposes; generally— Requirements—Persons performing religious duties

A person will be considered to have been physically present and residing in the United States if the person

(1), (a) is authorized to perform the ministerial and priestly functions of a religious denomination having a *bona fide* organization within the United States; or

(b) is engaged solely by a religious denomination or by an interdenominational mission organization having a *bona fide* organization with the United States as a missionary, brother, nun, or sister;

(2) has been lawfully admitted to permanent residence in the United States;

(3) at any time [after lawful admission to permanent residence] and before the filing of naturalization application [has] been physically present and residing within the United States for an uninterrupted period of at least one year; and

(4) before or after the filing of the application to preserve residence, has been [or will be] absent temporarily from the United States in connection with or for the purpose of performing the ministerial or priestly functions of such religious denomination, or serving as a missionary, brother, nun, or sister;

(5) has been [absent] solely for the purpose of performing the ministerial or priestly functions of such religious denomination, or of serving as a missionary, brother, nun, or sister.[1]

Under the provisions of this section, while missionaries, brothers, nuns, and sisters need to establish that they are engaged by a religious organization in order to serve abroad in their respective capacities, persons who are authorized to perform ministerial or priestly functions need only establish that they are abroad for that sole purpose, whether engaged by a religious organization or not.[2] Thus a rabbi who was sent abroad by a private corporation which was not a religious organization could take advantage of this provision because he was authorized to perform ministerial functions, being an ordained rabbi, and he was abroad to perform a ministerial function, the teaching of religion to rabbinical students.[3]

Both groups must establish that the denomination to which they belong has a *bona fide* organization in the United States.[4] It has been determined that the Jewish religion, the Salvation Army, and the Salecian Society of the Catholic Church are religious denominations which qualify.[5]

Just like the requirement applicable to employees and contractors of the U.S. government, certain corporations, and international public organizations, religious applicants must also establish they have been physically present and resided in the United States for an uninterrupted period of at least one year after admission to

---

[Section 7:9]

[1]INA § 317, 8 U.S.C. § 1428 (the paragraph has been subdivided to facilitate its understanding).

[2]INS Interp. 317.1(b)(1).

[3]Matter of F-, 8 I. & N. Dec. 533, 534 (Ass't Comm'r 1960).

[4]Matter of F-, 8 I. & N. Dec. 533, 534, 1960 WL 12114 (B.I.A. 1960).

[5]INS Interp. 317.1(b) citing to Matter of N-, 5 I. & N. Dec. 173 (Central Office 1953); Matter of Z-, 5 I. & N. Dec. 700 (Central Office 1954); Matter of F-----, 8 I. & N. Dec. 533, 534, 1960 WL 12114 (B.I.A. 1960); Matter of Z-, 5 I. & N. Dec. 700 (Central Office 1954); Matter of F-----, 8 I. & N. Dec. 533, 534, 1960 WL 12114 (B.I.A. 1960); Matter of F-----, 8 I. & N. Dec. 533, 534, 1960 WL 12114 (B.I.A. 1960).

lawful permanent residence.[6] That physical presence and residence may occur before or after the application for preservation of residence with the DHS, provided it is completed prior to the filing of the naturalization application.[7]

Furthermore, persons who qualify under this section need not file an application to preserve residence if they remain abroad less than one year. In such cases they are deemed not to have in fact abandoned their residency for purposes of naturalization.[8]

Religious practitioners who are granted the benefits of this section must still establish the three-month state or DHS district residence requirement.[9] If after the absence the person returns to the same state or DHS district where he or she resided prior to the departure abroad, then the residence requirement will be satisfied provided the person had previously resided there for three months.[10] On the other hand, if upon return the person resumes residence in a state or DHS district other than the one he or she was residing in at the time of departure, then the person must comply anew with the state or DHS district residence requirement.[11] Similarly, a grant of the benefits of section 317 does not exempt the person from establishing that he or she has not abandoned his or her lawful permanent residence.[12]

§ 7:10   Preserving residence for naturalization purposes; generally— Application to preserve residence for naturalization purposes

Applications to preserve residence for purposes of naturalization are submitted on Form N-470 (see Appendix 7-2).[1] The fee for filing such application is $305.

If the application is filed by an employee or contractor of the U.S. government, qualifying corporation, or qualifying public international organization, the application must be filed before the beginning of the specific employment and before the applicant has been abroad for one year.[2] The DHS interprets the statutory language to require the filing of the application before the applicant had been abroad more than one year.[3]

Under certain circumstances, the DHS will consider applications as constructively filed even though they were received by DHS after the applicant had been abroad more than one year. Thus, the DHS will consider applications as constructively filed within the one year if: (1) when the qualifying company or employer, before the person had been abroad more than one year, files a letter requesting the preserva-

---

[6]INA § 317(2), 8 U.S.C.A. § 1428(2).

[7]INS Interp. 317.1(b)(2).

[8]INS Interp. 317.1(b)(2). See § 7:5.

[9]INS Interp. 317.1(b)(3).

[10]INS Interp. 316.1(c)(8).

[11]INS Interp. 316.1(c)(8).

[12]INS Interp. 317.1(b)(4). See § 8:24.

[Section 7:10]

[1]8 CFR § 316.5(d)(1). Also available for download at http://uscis.gov/graphics/index.htm.

[2]INA § 316(b)(1), 8 U.S.C.A. § 1427(b)(1); 8 CFR § 316.5(d)(1). The regulations do not require filing before the beginning of employment. Indeed, they specifically provide for filing "before or after the applicant's employment commences." 8 CFR § 316.5(d)(1)(i). Cautious practice suggests the attorney to file before the beginning of the employment as the statute overrides the regulations.

[3]8 CFR § 316.5(d)(1).

tion and includes the information that the applicant was employed by them abroad, the DHS considers the N-470 timely filed even though the application form itself did not arrive until after the person had been abroad more than one year;[4] (2) when the employer sends an application to the wrong DHS address and it is clearly established that the application was sent before the expiration of the one-year abroad, the DHS does not impute the employer's negligence to the employee, and accepts the filing as constructively effective even though it did not receive the copy of the application until after the one year was over;[5] or (3) when the applicant fails to file a timely application to preserve residence in reliance on erroneous information provided by DHS.[6] In addition, when the DHS erroneously approves an application to preserve residence that should have been denied, the DHS is estopped from claiming a break in the continuity of the residence.[7]

When the organization of research has not yet been granted recognition for purposes of this section, the *INS Operations Instructions* require the DHS officer to conduct what amounts to a "political correctness" review.[8] The officer is required to check the records branch of the FBI and the CIA for information regarding this organization. No check is necessary if "(1) the institution is a recognized and well-known school, institute, college, university, committee, commission, foundation, society, organization, business concern, or corporation, or (2) the activities of the institution are connected with a program or project of the United States Government; [but] even in such an instance, when there is any indication that the nature and activities of the institution may possibly involve a security question, such as propagandizing, the check shall be made."[9] The DHS district director makes the initial determination of eligibility of the organization for purposes of INA § 316(b), be it as an American institution of research or as a public international organization of which the U.S. is a member.[10] The regional commissioner must approve this determination before it becomes effective.[11] A copy of the memorandum approving the organization is forwarded to the USCIS assistant commissioner for naturalization.[12]

Applications on behalf of persons performing religious functions in accordance with section 317 of the INA may be filed either before or after the applicant's absence, as well as either before or after the performance of the religious duties specified in that section.[13]

The application must identify the applicant's spouse and dependent unmarried sons and daughters who are residing abroad. The notice of approval Form N-472 (Appendix 7-3) will identify all the family members covered by the grant of preservation of residence.[14] Note, however, that even though the law provides for the preservation of residence for relatives of employees and contractors of the U.S. govern-

---

[4]INS Interp. 316.1(c)(2)(ii).

[5]INS Interp. 316.1(c)(2)(iii).

[6]INS Interp. 316.1(c)(2)(iv).

[7]INS Interp. 316.1(c)(2)(v).

[8]See OI 316a.1.

[9]OI 316a.1.

[10]OI 316a.4.

[11]OI 316a.4.

[12]OI 316a.4.

[13]8 CFR § 316.5(d)(2).

[14]8 CFR § 316.5(d)(1)(ii).

ment, qualifying corporations, and qualifying public international organizations, the law is silent about the relatives of persons performing religious duties.[15] The benefits to spouses and children of employees and contractors were added by amendment to section 316(b) in 1981.[16]

Granting of the preservation does not insulate the recipient from the presumption of abandonment of lawful permanent residence if the recipient claims nonresident status for tax purposes.[17] This presumption also extends to all the family members who received the grant of preservation of residence with the principal.[18]

The applicant is notified of the USCIS' decision on Form N-472.[19] If the application is denied, the USCIS must inform the applicant of the reasons for the denial and of the applicant's right to seek review by the INS Administrative Appellate Unit (AAU).[20] The appeal is filed on Form I-290B (see Appendix 7-4) with a fee of $585.[21]

The appeal is filed with the USCIS office that made the original decision.[22] The USCIS officer who made the unfavorable decision will review the file on appeal and has the authority to reopen his or her decision and grant the application.[23] Attorneys and representatives must include a new Form G-28 with their appeal to the AAU.[24] Form G-28 is available for download in PDF format from the USCIS site at http://uscis.gov/graphics/index.htm.

C. RESIDENCE MUST BE AFTER LAWFUL ADMISSION TO PERMANENT RESIDENCE

§ 7:11 Residence must be pursuant to lawful admission to permanent residence

Research References

A.L.R. Index, Immigration and Naturalization
Steel on Immigration Law 2d § 15:9

The five years of continuous residence must be after admission to permanent residence and the status of permanent resident must not have been terminated.[1] This means that the individual must have validly obtained their permanent residence;[2] individuals who obtained residence through fraud or despite ineligibility cannot

---

[15]Compare INA § 316(b), 8 U.S.C.A. § 1427(b) with INA § 317, 8 U.S.C.A. § 1428.

[16]Immigration and Nationality Act Amendments of 1981, Pub.L. 97-116, 95 Stat. 1611 (Dec. 29, 1981); INS Interp. 316.1(c)(1)(i).

[17]8 CFR § 316.5(d)(1)(iii). See § 8:22.

[18]8 CFR § 316.5(d)(1)(iii).

[19]8 CFR § 316.5(d)(3).

[20]8 CFR §§ 103.1(f)(3)(iii)(O), 103.3(a)(1)(ii), (iv), 316.5(d)(3).

[21]8 CFR § 103.7(b). Also available for download at http://uscis.gov/graphics/index.htm.

[22]8 CFR § 103.3(a)(2).

[23]8 CFR § 103.3(a)(2)(ii), (iii).

[24]8 CFR § 103.3(a)(2)(v)(A)(2).

[Section 7:11]

[1]INA §§ 101(a)(20), 316(a), 318, 8 U.S.C.A. §§ 1101(a)(20), 1427(a), 1429.

[2]See §§ 8:23 to 8:24; INA § 318, 8 U.S.C.A. § 1429 (the applicant may not be granted naturalization unless he or she was lawfully admitted to permanent residence according to the provisions of the statute); Fedorenko v. U.S., 449 U.S. 490, 514-15, 101 S.Ct. 737, 751, 66 L.Ed.2d. 689 (1981).

naturalize.[3] Further, if an individual ever abandoned his or her residence in the United States, they lost their permanent residence at that point; they cannot naturalize absent a re-grant of permanent residence and another five year period of residence.[4] These subjects are discussed at some depth in Ch 8.

There are some groups which benefit from special counting rules for their period of residence. Filipinos who entered the U.S. before May 1, 1934 and have resided in the U.S. continuously are deemed to be lawful permanent residents for naturalization purposes and thus are not barred from naturalizing by this provision.[5] A similar rule applies to certain inhabitants of the Bonin Islands who entered the United States prior to July 11, 1972.[6] Similarly, noncitizens who were immediate relatives of U.S. citizens and who were residing lawfully on the Northern Mariana Islands on November 4, 1986, are considered lawful permanent residents of the United States as of that date.[7] Refugees are considered permanent residents as of the date of entry as refugees provided they have adjusted to lawful permanent residence.[8] Asylees are deemed to be lawful permanent residents as of one year before the date of approval of their application for adjustment to lawful permanent residents, provided asylum was granted more than one year before the approval of their adjustment to permanent residence.[9] Persons who become lawful permanent residents under the Cuban Adjustment Act of 1966 are granted retroactive residency to thirty months before the date of application or the last date of arrival into the United States, whichever is latest.[10]

§ 7:12 Removability issues

Most grounds of removability are not themselves bars to naturalization; however, the statute provides that once removal proceedings have been started, the agency

---

[3]Eng v. I.N.S., 464 F.2d 1265 (2d Cir. 1972) (excludable for misrepresentation, lawful permanent residence only started on date in which he was granted registry); Brymer v. U.S., 83 F.2d 276 (9th Cir. 1936) (reentry after conviction for crime of moral turpitude); Fedorenko v. U. S., 449 U.S. 490, 515, 101 S. Ct. 737, 751, 66 L. Ed. 2d 686 (1981); see also In re Koloamatangi, 23 I. & N. Dec. 548 (B.I.A. 2003) (person who obtained permanent residency through fraud or misrepresentation has never been "lawfully admitted for permanent residence" and is ineligible for cancellation of removal under INA § 240A(a)); INS Interp. 318.3; 318.5. See generally §§ 8:25, 8:26.

[4]See § 8:24.

[5]INA § 326, 8 U.S.C.A. § 1437 added by Immigration Act of 1990 ("IA90"), Act of Nov. 29, 1990, Pub. L. No. 101-649, § 407(c), 104 Stat. 4978. That provision applies to any person who (1) was a citizen of the Philippines on July 2, 1946, (2) entered the U.S. prior to May 1, 1934, and (3) has, since that entry, resided continuously in the United States and is deemed to have been lawfully admitted to permanent residence for purposes of applying for naturalization. See Chapter 3, for a discussion of the rationale of that provision.

[6]INS Interp. 318.1(g).

[7]Legal Opinion, Virtue, INS Acting General Counsel, Genco Opinion 94-10, File Nos. HQ 1432-P, 245-P (Feb. 9, 1994). See § 2:20.

[8]INA § 209(a)(2), 8 U.S.C.A. § 1159(a)(2).

[9]INA § 209(b), 8 U.S.C.A. § 1159(b); see also 8 CFR § 209.2(f).

[10]Act of November 2, 1966, Pub.L. No. 89-732, § 1, 80 Stat. 1161; Matter of Diaz-Chambrot, 19 I. & N. Dec. 674 (B.I.A. 1988).

cannot proceed forward on the naturalization application.[1] Removability issues are discussed at length in chapter 8.[2]

§ 7:13 Continuity of lawful permanent residence

Naturalization applicants are required to have been lawful permanent residents during the entire five-year period prior to the naturalization application.[1] Thus, any departure from the U.S. under an order of deportation breaks the continuity of the period even when the applicant returns to this country with a new immigrant visa.[2] On the other hand, a person who is readmitted after a deferred inspection or an exclusion hearing, has not broken his or her five years continuous residence.[3]

D. PHYSICAL PRESENCE REQUIREMENT

§ 7:14 In general

An applicant must have been physically present in the United States for at least thirty months during the five-year period of continuous residence.[1] These thirty months do not need to be continuous and are computed by adding up all the time when the person was in the U.S. during those five years.[2] Just as in the case of the continuous residence requirement, service abroad pursuant to military orders while in the U.S. army, service as a sailor on U.S.-based ships, and service as a religious minister, priest, missionary, nun, or sister abroad, also count as physical presence in the U.S.[3] In addition, persons who are employed for or under a contract from the U.S. government abroad, may count their period abroad as physical presence in the U.S.[4]

E. CONTINUOUS RESIDENCE AFTER FILING OF APPLICATION

§ 7:15 In general

Research References

A.L.R. Index, Immigration and Naturalization

A naturalization applicant must reside continuously in the United States from the time of filing the naturalization application until the time of admission to

---

[Section 7:12]

[1]INA § 318, 8 U.S.C.A. § 1429; INS Interp. 318.2(c)(1)(iii).

[2]See §§ 8:1 to 8:17.

[Section 7:13]

[1]See INA § 101(a)(20), 8 U.S.C.A. § 1101(a)(20) (the term "lawfully admitted to permanent residence" means the status of having been lawfully accorded the privilege of residing permanently in the United States as an immigrant in accordance with the immigration laws, such status not having changed).

[2]See 8 CFR § 316.5(c)(3).

[3]8 CFR § 316.5(c)(4).

[Section 7:14]

[1]INA § 316(a), 8 U.S.C.A. § 1427(a).

[2]INA § 316(a), 8 U.S.C.A. § 1427(a).

[3]INA §§ 317, 330, 8 U.S.C.A. §§ 1441, 1428; INS Interp. 316.1(d)(2).

[4]INA § 316(c), 8 U.S.C.A. § 1427(c), INS Interp. 316.1(d)(2).

citizenship.[1] The same principles that apply to absences prior to the filing of the naturalization application, apply to absences between the time of filing of the application and the admission to citizenship: (1) absences of less than six months between the filing of the application and the date of admission to citizenship do not interrupt continuous residence; (2) absences between six months and one year presumably break continuity; and (3) absences of more than one year break continuity unless the applicant's departure was involuntary or permitted under the statute.[2]

F. STATE RESIDENCE REQUIREMENT

§ 7:16 In general

The applicant must reside for at least three months in the state or the DHS district in which the naturalization application is to be filed.[1] The Immigration Act of 1990 liberalized this requirement.[2] Before that amendment, applicants where required to have resided for six months in the state where the application was to be filed.[3] In addition, the IA90 also introduced an amendment that allowed applicants to file for naturalization ninety days before the completion of the continuous residence requirement.[4] The Regulations interpret the state residence requirement in those circumstances to be fulfilled if the applicant has resided in the state or USCIS district for the three-month period immediately preceding the *examination* of the applicant.[5]

The regulations provide guidance in terms of where this residence may be in four specific situations. First, in the case of a student who is attending an educational institution in a state or USCIS district other than his or her home residence, the applicant may apply for naturalization either where the institution is located; or when the applicant can establish that he or she is financially dependent upon his or her parents at the time the application is filed and during the naturalization process, in the state of the applicant's home residence.[6]

Second, an applicant who resides in more than one state, is deemed for naturalization purposes to reside in the location where the annual federal income tax returns have been or are being filed.[7]

Third, applicants who have absences from the United States for less than one year are deemed to continue to reside in the state or USCIS district where they resided immediately prior to their departure.[8] Thus, if the applicant returns to the same state or USCIS district after the absence, the three months residence requirement starts from the date the applicant first started to reside in that state or

---

[Section 7:15]

   [1]INA § 316(a)(2), 8 U.S.C.A. § 1427(a)(2).

   [2]INA § 316(b), 8 U.S.C.A. § 1427(b); 8 CFR § 316.5(c)(1).

[Section 7:16]

   [1]INA § 316(a)(1), 8 U.S.C.A. § 1427(a)(1).

   [2]IA90 § 402.

   [3]Former INA § 316(a)(1), 8 U.S.C.A. § 1427(a)(1) (1989).

   [4]INA § 334(a), 8 U.S.C.A. § 1445(a), as amended by IA90 § 401(b).

   [5]8 CFR §§ 316.2(a)(5), 319.1(a)(5).

   [6]8 CFR § 316.5(b)(2).

   [7]8 CFR § 316.5(b)(4).

   [8]8 CFR § 316.5(b)(5)(i).

USCIS district and includes any period in which the applicant was absent.[9] However, if the applicant establishes residence in a new state or USCIS district after the absence, then the three months state/USCIS district residence requirement starts from the moment the applicant took up residence in the new state or USCIS district.[10]

Fourth, applicants who are serving in the armed forces of the U.S. but who do not qualify for naturalization under the provisions for military-related naturalization are considered to reside: (1) in the state or USCIS district where the applicant is physically present for at least three months prior to the filing of the application for naturalization; (2) at the location of the residence of the applicant's spouse or minor children; or (3) at the applicant's home of record as declared to the armed forces at the time of enlistment and as currently reflected in the applicant's military personnel file.[11]

G. INTENTION TO RESIDE PERMANENTLY IN U.S. AFTER NATURALIZATION

§ 7:17 In general

Before the passage of the INTCA, the applicant was also required to have the intent to reside permanently in the United States after naturalization.[1] The INA required the INS to make a finding that this was the intention of the applicant and to state such on the certificate of naturalization.[2] If a naturalized citizen established a permanent foreign residence within one year of obtaining citizenship, there was a presumption of fraud and the individual could be subject to denaturalization.[3] The INTCA amended both sections of the INA to provide that the agency is no longer required to make a finding that the applicant intends to reside permanently in the United States after naturalization and, concomitantly, repealed the presumption of fraud related to taking up foreign residence.[4]

IV. GOOD MORAL CHARACTER

A. NATURE OF REQUIREMENT

§ 7:18 In general

Research References
A.L.R. Index, Immigration and Naturalization
Dizon and Wettstein, Immigration Law Service 2d §§ 14:143, 14:144
Steel on Immigration Law § 15:13

---

[9]8 CFR § 316.5(b)(5)(ii).
[10]8 CFR § 316.5(b)(5)(ii).
[11]8 CFR § 316.5(b)(1).

[Section 7:17]
[1]Petition of Petcheff, 114 F. Supp. 764, 765 (S.D. N.Y. 1953).
[2]Former INA § 338, 8 U.S.C.A. § 1449.
[3]Former INA § 340(d), 8 U.S.C.A. § 1451(d).
[4]INTCA § 104.

Naturalization requires that an applicant be of good moral character for the period of the required continuous residence in the U.S.[1] Unless the applicant belongs to one of the specified classes, the statutory period of good moral character is five years immediately preceding the filing of the petition and from the date of the filing of the petition until citizenship is granted.[2] This includes the period between the examination and the administration of the oath of allegiance.[3]

For those special classes where there is no required statutory period of continuous residence, the person must prove he or she is a person of good moral character at the present.[4] To determine this, the USCIS will look at the moral character of the person for a reasonable period immediately preceding the application and during the period between the date of filing of the petition and the final hearing.[5] What the USCIS will consider a "reasonable time" depends on the acts committed. The greater the gravity of the misconduct, the more time the USCIS requires to have passed before it will consider the person as presently having good moral character.[6] In addition, persons who have engaged in conduct specifically mentioned as a statutory bar to good moral character may be required to present compelling evidence that their character has changed since that conduct.[7] Persons convicted of murder at any time or of aggravated felonies after November 29, 1990 are barred from establishing good moral character even under these provisions.[8]

By regulation, the USCIS will look at the moral character during the period of one year preceding the application in cases of naturalization for honorable service in time of war.[9] Several courts have now upheld this regulation and found it to have the force of law.[10]

The inquiry regarding good moral character centers primarily on acts committed during the statutory period for which good moral character is required. There are two exceptions to this rule. First, aggravated felony convictions that occurred after November 29, 1990 render the person ineligible to establish good moral character even when the conviction was before the statutory period.[11] The aggravated felony definition used to have very precise and limited contours, but Congress has repeat-

---

[Section 7:18]

[1]INA § 316(a)(3), 8 U.S.C.A. § 1427(a)(3).

[2]INA § 316(a)(1), 8 U.S.C.A. § 1427(a)(1).

[3]8 CFR § 316.10(a)(1).

[4]Matter of Sanchez-Linn, 20 I. & N. Dec. 362, 364–65 (B.I.A. 1991).

[5]INS Interp. 316.1(f)(3); Matter of Sanchez-Linn, 20 I. & N. Dec. 362, 365, 1991 WL 353523 (B.I.A. 1991). The rationale for looking at the conduct during a reasonable period prior to the filing of the application is clearly captured by INS Interp. 329.1(c)(6), where adjudicators are admonished that if they find conduct establishing lack of good moral character during a reasonable period prior to the application, they should predicate their denial of naturalization upon the conclusion that the petitioner has failed to establish that he or she is a person of good moral character at present, rather than he or she has failed to establish good moral character during a reasonable period immediately preceding the filing of the application.

[6]Matter of Sanchez-Linn, 20 I. & N. Dec. 362, 365, 1991 WL 353523 (B.I.A. 1991).

[7]Matter of Sanchez-Linn, 20 I. & N. Dec. 362, 365, 1991 WL 353523 (B.I.A. 1991).

[8]See Castiglia v. I.N.S., 108 F.3d 1101 (9th Cir. 1997).

[9]8 CFR § 329.2(d). See § 12:7.

[10]Santamaria-Ames v. I.N.S., 104 F.3d 1127 (9th Cir. 1996); O'Sullivan v. U.S. Citizenship and Immigration Services, 453 F.3d 809 (7th Cir. 2006).

[11]See INA § 101(f)(8), 8 U.S.C.A. § 1101(f)(8) ("one who at any time has been convicted of an aggravated felony"). See §§ 8:11 to 8:17.

edly expanded the definition of "aggravated felonies" resulting in a permanent bar from naturalization for a great variety of offenses.[12] Convictions of murder, even if they occurred before November 29, 1990, render the person permanently ineligible to establish good moral character.[13] Thus, an applicant who has been convicted of murder is ineligible for naturalization even under those provisions that require only good moral character at present.[14]

Second, the USCIS is not precluded from looking into events that occurred outside the statutory period for good moral character,[15] though some courts have held that a denial may not be based solely on events occurring outside the statutory period.[16] The relevance of behavior that precedes the statutory period is discussed in more detail below.[17]

B. STATUTORY DEFINITION

§ 7:19 In general

Research References

Dizon and Wettstein, Immigration Law Service 2d § 14:146
Steel on Immigration Law § 15:13

The INA introduced a definition of "good moral character" into immigration law for the first time.[1] Before 1952, good moral character was solely evaluated according to the facts of each case applying the standard of the average person in the community.[2] The INA introduced specific grounds that bar certain classes of persons from proving good moral character.[3] It also preserved the USCIS' ability to find a person as lacking good moral character for other reasons.[4]

The statutory provisions do not allow for a balanced test. If the person falls within the provision, the person is precluded from showing good moral character during the required period.[5] Conversely, if the person is not precluded by the INA from establishing good moral character, the USCIS must evaluate each application on a case-by-case basis.[6] This test will be described below.[7]

For purposes of naturalization, a person may not normally be found to lack good

---

[12]See §§ 8:11 to 8:17.

[13]Sec. 306(a)(7) of the Miscellaneous and Technical Immigration and Naturalization Amendments of 1991, Act of Dec. 12, 1991, Pub. L. No. 102-232, 105 Stat. 1733 (amending IA90 § 509(b)); Castiglia v. I.N.S., 108 F.3d 1101 (9th Cir. 1997); 8 C.F.R. § 316.10(b)(1)(i).

[14]Castiglia v. I.N.S., 108 F.3d 1101 (9th Cir. 1997).

[15]INA § 316(e) [8 U.S.C.A. § 1427(e)]; 8 C.F.R. § 316.10(a)(2).

[16]See Santamaria-Ames v. I.N.S., 104 F.3d 1127 (9th Cir. 1996); U.S. v. Hovsepian, 422 F.3d 883 (9th Cir. 2005); see particularly § 7:40.

[17]See §§ 7:40 to 7:46.

[Section 7:19]

[1]Matter of Gantus-Bobadilla, 13 I. & N. Dec. 777, 778 (B.I.A. 1971).

[2]Matter of Gantus-Bobadilla, 13 I. & N. Dec. 777, 778 (B.I.A. 1971).

[3]INA § 101(f), 8 U.S.C.A. § 1101(f). This is the same definition that is used in exclusion and deportation and is discussed further in Ch 4.

[4]INA § 101(f), 8 U.S.C.A. § 1101(f) (last sentence).

[5]Posusta v. U.S., 285 F.2d 533 (2d Cir. 1961); In Re Petition of Naniatakis, 376 F.2d 728 (3d Cir. 1967). Cf. 8 CFR § 316.10(b)(1) (requiring denial if applicant falls within the statutory grounds of INA § 101(f)).

[6]8 CFR § 316.10(a)(2).

moral character based on a state statute that criminalizes behavior, which is not criminalized in other states.[8] This standard developed out of the old preclusion for persons who had committed adultery and for the applicability of the crime of moral turpitude ground of inadmissibility for convictions for homosexual acts.[9] The rationale for this restriction is based on the constitutional mandate that Congress must establish a *uniform* rule of naturalization.[10] If not all states criminalize a certain behavior, only when the law criminalizes acts which are harmful to the public—as opposed to offensive to individual morality—may a person be barred from establishing good moral character based on conviction or admission of the elements of the crime.[11] Even though Congress repealed the adultery bar to good moral character in 1981,[12] the principle of uniformity continues to be relevant since, at the very least, it guides USCIS' interpretation of when homosexual acts may constitute a lack of good moral character.[13]

This section first discusses the statutory bars to good moral character and then the test used to determine good moral character under the residual category contained in the last sentence of INA § 101. The INA includes seven numbered categories that preclude a finding of good moral character.[14] These categories are presented in the order in which they appear in the INA.

§ 7:20 Habitual drunkard

Research References

Dizon and Wettstein, Immigration Law Service 2d § 14:146

The INA establishes that habitual drunkards are barred from establishing good moral character.[1] A "habitual drunkard" is akin to a chronic alcoholic.[2]

§ 7:21 Subject-specific grounds of inadmissibility; generally

The definition of good moral character incorporates by reference certain grounds of inadmissibility. These grounds are INA § 212(a)(2)(A), (B), (C), (D), (6)(E), and (10)(A) with the exception that a person who is inadmissible because of a single of-

---

[7]See §§ 7:40 to 7:46.

[8]Nemetz v. I.N.S., 647 F.2d 432, 435–36 (4th Cir. 1981).

[9]Nemetz v. Immigration and Naturalization Service, 647 F.2d 432 (4th Cir. 1981) (admission of a crime of moral turpitude); Petition of Schroers, 336 F.Supp. 1348 (S.D.N.Y. 1971).

[10]Nemetz v. Immigration and Naturalization Service, 647 F.2d 432, 435 (4th Cir. 1981); In re Schroers, 336 F. Supp. 1348, 1349–50 (S.D. N.Y. 1971).

[11]Nemetz v. Immigration and Naturalization Service, 647 F.2d 432, 436 (4th Cir. 1981); INS Interp. 316.1(f)(7). Cf. §§ 7:25, 7:26. See also, §§ 7:40 to 7:46.

[12]Sec. 2(b), Immigration and Nationality Act Amendments of 1981, Pub.L. 97-116, 95 Stat. 1611 (Dec. 29, 1981) repealing INA § 101(f)(2).

[13]See INS Interp. 316.1(f)(7). Cf. §§ 7:40 to 7:46. It should be noted that the Supreme Court's decision in Lawrence v. Texas, 539 U.S. 558, 123 S. Ct. 2472, 156 L. Ed. 2d 508 (2003), struck down all laws prohibiting homosexual sodomy on Due Process grounds, which renders the sexual orientation-based rules relating to homosexuality of dubious constitutionality.

[14]INA § 101(f), 8 U.S.C.A. § 1101(f). Subparagraph (2) was repealed by sec. 2(c)(1), Immigration and Nationality Act Amendments of 1981.

[Section 7:20]

[1]INA § 101(f)(1), 8 U.S.C.A. § 1101(f)(1).

[2]See Matter of H-, 6 I. & N. Dec. 614, 616 (B.I.A. 1955).

fense of simple possession of 30 grams or less of marijuana is not precluded from establishing good moral character.[1] These grounds of inadmissibility refer to conviction or admission of the essential elements of crimes of moral turpitude,[2] conviction or admission of essential elements of controlled substance violations,[3] multiple criminal violations,[4] trafficking in controlled substance,[5] prostitution and commercialized vice,[6] smugglers of "aliens,"[7] and practicing polygamists.[8]

These grounds of inadmissibility are not only relevant to see if the person is barred from establishing good moral character, but with the exception of the grounds relating to practicing polygamists and reason to believe that the person is a drug trafficker, they all have an equivalent ground of deportation.[9] In addition, the person is also deportable if the person was inadmissible under these grounds at the time the person entered the U.S. or adjusted status to permanent residence.[10] A naturalization applicant who is deportable will be placed in removal proceedings unless the case falls within the set of cases where the district director may exercise prosecutorial discretion.[11] Naturalization applicants placed in removal proceedings will forfeit their permanent residence unless found not to be deportable or granted a waiver by an immigration judge. Once a deportation based removal proceeding has commenced, the USCIS is barred from considering the naturalization application.[12] Noncitizens who have been lawful permanent residents for more than seven years may be able to obtain sections 212(h) and 240A(a) waivers of deportability, and individuals with pre-1997 convictions may still be eligible for relief under former INA § 212(c).[13]

§ 7:22 Subject-specific grounds of inadmissibility; generally—Convictions and admissions of crimes

Research References

A.L.R. Index, Immigration and Naturalization
Dizon and Wettstein, Immigration Law Service 2d § 14:147

Most of the criminal grounds of inadmissibility require either a conviction or an

---

[Section 7:21]

[1]INA § 101(f)(3), 8 U.S.C.A. § 1101(f)(3). Apparently, the reference to INA § 212(a)(9)(A), 8 U.S.C.A. § 1182(a)(9)(A) was not corrected when the IIRAIRA § 301(b)(1) redesignated that paragraph as INA § 212(a)(10)(A), 8 U.S.C.A. § 1182(a)(10)(A).

[2]INA § 212(a)(2)(A), 8 U.S.C.A. § 1182(a)(2)(A).

[3]INA § 212(a)(2)(A), 8 U.S.C.A. § 1182(a)(2)(A).

[4]INA § 212(a)(2)(B), 8 U.S.C.A. § 1182(a)(2)(B).

[5]INA § 212(a)(2)(C), 8 U.S.C.A. § 1182(a)(2)(C).

[6]INA § 212(a)(2)(D), 8 U.S.C.A. § 1182(a)(2)(D).

[7]INA § 212(a)(6)(E), 8 U.S.C.A. § 1182(a)(6)(E).

[8]INA § 212(a)(10)(A), 8 U.S.C.A. § 1182(a)(10)(A) as redesignated by IIRAIRA § 301(b)(1).

[9]Compare INA § 212(a)(2)(A), (B), (C), (D), (6)(E), (10)(A), 8 U.S.C.A. § 1182(a)(2)(A), (B), (C), (D), (6)(E), (10)(A) with INA § 237(a)(1)(E), (2)(A)(i), (ii), (B)(i), 8 U.S.C.A. § 1227(a)(1)(E), (2)(A)(i), (ii), (B)(i) as redesignated by IIRAIRA § 305(a)(2).

[10]INA § 237(a)(1)(A), 8 U.S.C.A. § 1227(a)(1)(A) as redesignated by IIRAIRA § 305(a)(2).

[11]OI 318.1; see generally §§ 8:1 to 8:26.

[12]INA § 318, 8 U.S.C.A. § 1429; see § 8:29.

[13]INA § 212(c), 8 U.S.C.A. § 1182(c) was repealed by IIRAIRA § 304(b), but the Supreme Court has found the repeal not to be retroactive. I.N.S. v. St. Cyr, 533 U.S. 289, 121 S. Ct. 2271, 150 L. Ed. 2d 347 (2001).

admission of the essential elements of the crime. If the ground of inadmissibility requires a conviction, the statutory bar to good moral character is not applicable unless the person was convicted of the violation.[1] The INA now contains a definition of "conviction."[2] Under INA § 101(a)(48), a conviction is established if: "(i) a judge or jury has found the alien guilty or the alien has entered a plea of guilty or *nolo contendere* or has admitted sufficient facts to warrant a finding of guilt, and (ii) the judge has ordered some form of punishment, penalty, or restraint on the alien's liberty to be imposed."[3]

Chapter 8 contains an in-depth discussion of criminal convictions in the context of removability.[4] The reader should consult that section for detailed information about each of the following points:

(1) a "term of imprisonment" includes any confinement ordered by a court, regardless of any suspension of the execution or imposition of the sentence;[5]

(2) juvenile dispositions are not criminal convictions;[6]

(3) state rehabilitative statutes permitting expungement of crimes will generally not be given effect, although post-conviction relief based on non-rehabilitative grounds will still be permitted, sentencing changes will be given effect, and executive pardons are effective for most purposes.[7]

§ 7:23 Subject-specific grounds of inadmissibility; generally—Convictions and admissions of crimes—Admissions of crimes

In some circumstances, the admission to having committed the essential elements of a crime is sufficient to render the individual removable, even without a conviction.[1] However, not all admissions of having committed the elements of a crime are valid for immigration purposes. For an admission to be valid, the DHS must establish that: (1) the act is considered a crime under the law where the act occurred; (2) the noncitizen was advised in a clear manner of the essential elements of the alleged crime; (3) the noncitizen has clearly admitted conduct constituting all the essential elements of the crime; and (4) the admission was made in a free and voluntary

---

[Section 7:22]

[1]See Matter of Grullon, 20 I. & N. Dec. 12, 15 (B.I.A. 1989).

[2]INA § 101(a)(48)(A), 8 U.S.C.A. § 1101(a)(48)(A).

[3]INA § 101(a)(48)(A), 8 U.S.C.A. § 1101(a)(48)(A). What was left out of this definition is the requirement that there is no conviction unless a judgment or adjudication of guilt may be entered without availability of further proceedings regarding his or her guilt or innocence of the original charge, if the person violates the terms of his or her probation or fails to comply with the requirements of the court's order. See Matter of Ozkok, 19 I. & N. Dec. 546, 1988 WL 235459 (B.I.A. 1988).

[4]See generally §§ 8:3 to 8:21.

[5]INA § 101(a)(48)(B), 8 U.S.C.A. § 1101(a)(48)(B); see generally, § 8:5.

[6]Matter of Devison, 22 I. & N. Dec. 1362 (B.I.A. 2000); see generally § 8:4.

[7]See discussion at §§ 8:6 to 8:10.

[Section 7:23]

[1]See, e.g., Pazcoguin v. Radcliffe, 292 F.3d 1209 (9th Cir. 2002) (admission made to a physician sufficient to prove petitioner committed a drug possession offense); Fernandez-Bernal v. Attorney General of U.S., 257 F.3d 1304 (11th Cir. 2001) (admission to conduct constituting a controlled substance offense).

manner.[2] A noncitizen cannot admit the essential elements of a delinquency adjudication even after she or he reaches adulthood because admitting to delinquency is not admitting to criminal conduct.[3] A person cannot retract a valid admission.[4] However, admissions obtained by misrepresentation or as a result of coercion are not valid.[5]

Guilty pleas are considered admissions for immigration purposes.[6] However, guilty pleas will not be given greater effect than court adjudications.[7] An admission made as a guilty plea, or even outside the courtroom, will not be valid if the person was not convicted of the crime.[8] However, failure to convict will only insulate the defendant from an admission if the court ruled on the specific crime that serves as the basis for the ground of inadmissibility.[9]

§ 7:24 Subject-specific grounds of inadmissibility; generally—Post conviction relief; expungements—Judicial recommendations against deportation

Judicial Recommendations Against Deportation (JRAD) was a statutory vehicle that existed prior to the Immigration Act of 1990.[1] The JRAD provisions allowed criminal courts to issue an order recommending that the noncitizen not be deported.[2] If the proper procedures were followed, JRADs were effective in overcoming deportability, excludability, and the bars to good moral character.[3]

The INS interpreted the abolition of the JRAD provision as having only *prospective* effect.[4] JRADs are not effective against a charge of deportability if they were granted on or after November 29, 1990 or if they were granted for deportability for

---

[2]Matter of K-, 7 I. & N. Dec. 594 (B.I.A. 1957), Matter of J-, 2 I. & N. Dec. 285, 287–88 (B.I.A. 1945). But see, Matter of W-, 5 I. & N. Dec. 578, 580 (B.I.A. 1953) (admission held valid even when the elements were not precisely explained by the INS because of the "indelicacy" of the subject matter).

[3]Matter of F, 4 I. & N. Dec. 726 (B.I.A. 1952); *but cf.* DeLuca v. Ashcroft, 203 F. Supp. 2d 1276 (M.D. Ala. 2002) (written confession of a shoplifting charge evidenced lack of good moral character even though criminal case was never tried because defendant was adjudicated a youthful offender).

[4]Matter of I-, 4 I. & N. Dec. 159 (Att'y Gen. 1950); Matter of R-, 1 I. & N. Dec. 359 (B.I.A. 1942).

[5]Gomes v. Tillinghast, 37 F.2d 935, 937 (D.Mass. 1930); Matter of M-C-, 3 I. & N. Dec. 76, 80 (B.I.A. 1947).

[6]Matter of Seda, 17 I. & N. Dec. 550, 554 (B.I.A. 1980) modified on other grounds, Matter of Ozkok, 19 I. & N. Dec. 546 (B.I.A. 1988); Matter of A-, 1 I. & N. Dec. 571 (B.I.A. 1943).

[7]Matter of Winter, 12 I. & N. Dec. 638, 642 (B.I.A. 1968).

[8]Matter of Seda, 17 I. & N. Dec. 550, 554, 1980 WL 121936 (B.I.A. 1980) (overruled in part by, Matter of Ozkok, 19 I. & N. Dec. 546, 1988 WL 235459 (B.I.A. 1988)) and (overruled as stated in, Paredes-Urrestarazu v. U.S. I.N.S., 36 F.3d 801 (9th Cir. 1994); Matter of Winter, 12 I. & N. Dec. 638; Matter of C-Y-C-, 3 I. & N. Dec. 623, 629 (B.I.A. 1950).

[9]Matter of I-, 4 I. & N. Dec. 159.

[Section 7:24]

[1]INA § 241(b), 8 U.S.C.A. § 1251(b) abolished by IA90 § 602(b).

[2]INA § 241(b), 8 U.S.C.A. § 1251(b) abolished by IA90 § 602(b).

[3]Santarelli v. Hughes, 116 F.2d 613 (3d Cir. 1940)(deportability); U.S. v. Castro, 26 F.3d 557, 558 n.2 (5th Cir. 1994)(Excludability); Giambanco v. I.N.S., 531 F.2d 141 (3d Cir. 1976)(good moral character).

[4]McNary, Commissioner, ImmAct90 Wire No.5 (Nov. 28,1990).

a drug offense under the former INA § 241(a)(11).[5] The cut-off is related to the date the JRAD was issued rather than to the date of the commission of the crime.[6]

§ 7:25 Subject-specific grounds of inadmissibility; generally—Crimes of moral turpitude; generally

Research References

A.L.R. Index, Immigration and Naturalization

A person who has been convicted of a crime of moral turpitude, or who admits committing the crime or acts that constitute the essential elements of the crime, is inadmissible.[1] A person who is inadmissible under this ground is also barred from proving good moral character. An extended discussion of what constitutes a crime involving moral turpitude is found in Chapter 8.[2]

Of course, crimes involving moral turpitude which also qualify as aggravated felonies are even more problematic, and for any post-1990 offense, would bar the applicant from ever showing good moral character.[3]

§ 7:26 Subject-specific grounds of inadmissibility—Crimes of moral turpitude; categorical approach

For decades, when analyzing whether a particular offense was for a crime involving moral turpitude, one needed to look only to the face of the statute under which the individual was convicted.[1] Under the categorical test, the BIA was precluded from looking behind the fact of conviction to the true facts at issue.[2] The BIA was obligated to ask whether the least reprehensible conduct prohibited by statute was turpitudinous,[3] though some courts referred alternately to the "general nature of the crime."[4] Where the statute defining the offense is divisible, reference was made to the record of conviction to determine which section of the statute was implicated

---

[5]8 CFR § 240.10(d).

[6]See U.S. v. Koziel, 954 F.2d 831 (2d Cir. 1992); U.S. v. Bodre, 948 F.2d 28 (1st Cir.) cert. denied 112 S.Ct. 1487 (1992) (ex post facto clause does not apply to crimes committed before the abolition of JRADs, where JRAD is sought after effective date of IA90 provision).

[Section 7:25]

[1]INA § 212(a)(2)(A), 8 U.S.C.A. § 1182(a)(2)(A).

[2]See § 8:20.

[3]See §§ 8:11 to 8:17.

[Section 7:26]

[1]Matter of Torres-Varela, 23 I. & N. Dec. 78, 84 (BIA 2001).

[2]Rodriguez-Castro v. Gonzales, 427 F.3d 316, 320–21 (5th Cir. 2005); Rodriquez-Herrera v. INS, 52 F.3d 238 (9th Cir. 1995).

[3]Amouzadeh v. Winfrey, 467 F.3d 451, 455 (5th Cir. 2006) (analyzing the "minimum criminal conduct necessary to sustain a conviction under the statute"); Partyka v. Att'y Gen., 417 F.3d 408, 411 (3d Cir. 2005) (considering whether the "least culpable conduct" covered by the criminal statute in issue would necessarily involve moral turpitude); see also, e.g., Quintero-Salazar v. Keisler, 506 F.3d 688, 692 (9th Cir. 2007) (analyzing "whether the full range of conduct encompassed by the statute" involves moral turpitude).

[4]See, e.g., Marciano v. INS, 450 F.2d 1022, 1025 (8th Cir. 1971); Nicanor-Romero v. Mukasey, 523 F.3d 992, 1004–05 (9th Cir. 2008).

by the conviction.[5] But under all variations, the analysis focused on the offense as defined in the statute; not the underlying facts.

A recent Attorney General decision appears to have significantly changed that approach. In *Matter of Silva-Trevino*, the Attorney General held that where the categorical approach was insufficient to determine whether an offense involves moral turpitude, that the immigration judges could look to the facts underlying the conviction.[6] Under the *Silva-Trevino* approach, there appears to be a three-step test. First, the courts will look to see if the categorical test can resolve the issue; if it can be said that all conduct reasonably likely to have been criminalized by the criminal statute is turpitudinous, then the analysis ends there.[7] Likewise, if "none of the circumstances in which there is a realistic probability of conviction involves moral turpitude," the crime categorically does not involve moral turpitude.[8]

Second, if the first step does not achieve clarity, one must look to the Record of Conviction, which would include any indictment or complaint, the judgment of conviction, jury instructions or signed guilty plea, and the plea transcript.[9] This will generally establish which section of a divisible statute was implicated. Analysis under this second step is often referred to as the "modified categorical approach."

Finally, held the Attorney General, if the categorical approach does not "resolve" the issue, extrinsic evidence may be considered to decide whether a particular conviction involved moral turpitude.[10] For instance, in *Silva-Trevino*, the Attorney General considered it dispositive whether *Silva-Trevino* "knew or reasonably should have known" that a female with whom me made "sexual contact" was a child under the age of 16.[11] Because the criminal statute penalized such sexual contact regardless of whether the defendant knew or should have known the victim's age (thus punishing criminally conduct which does not involve moral turpitude), the Attorney General found that an immigration judge ought to hold a factual hearing to consider whether Mr. Silva-Trevino could have reasonably believed his victim to be 16 or older.[12]

Although the *Silva-Trevino* decision purports to permit the use of the categorical test to categorically exclude certain crimes from the possibility of moral turpitude, that exception only applies if there is no "realistic possibility" that the circumstances giving rise to a conviction would be turpitudinous.[13] That exception does not appear to be very robust. For instance, possession of false documents has been held not to be turpitudinous, but use of false documents likely is.[14] It seems "realistically possible" for someone to possess false documents while using them (indeed, that is likely the reason why people commonly possess false document; thus, the Silva-Trevino test would appear to permit the introduction of extrinsic evidence to establish the use (as opposed to the mere possession) of the false documents.

---

[5]*Nicanor-Romero, 523 F.3d at 1007; Amouzadeh, 467 F.3d at 455.*

[6]Matter of Silva-Trevino, 24 I. & N. Dec. 687 (A.G. 2008).

[7]Matter of Silva-Trevino, 24 I. & N. Dec. 687, 698–99 (A.G. 2008).

[8]Matter of Silva-Trevino, 24 I. & N. Dec. 687, 699 n.2 (A.G. 2008).

[9]Matter of Silva-Trevino, 24 I. & N. Dec. 687, 704 (A.G. 2008).

[10]Matter of Silva-Trevino, 24 I. & N. Dec. 687, 704 (A.G. 2008).

[11]Matter of Silva-Trevino, 24 I. & N. Dec. 687, 706–08 (A.G. 2008).

[12]Matter of Silva-Trevino, 24 I. & N. Dec. 687, 708–09 (A.G. 2008).

[13]Matter of Silva-Trevino, 24 I. & N. Dec. 687, 699, n.2 (A.G. 2008).

[14]Matter of Serna, 20 I. & N. Dec. 579, 585–86 (B.I.A. 1992) (holding that mere possession of illegal documents, without intent to use said documents fraudulently or unlawfully, is not a crime involving moral turpitude).

It is possible to say that some crimes categorically are crimes involving moral turpitude,[15] but it is very difficult to say the converse. Under the *Silva-Trevino* test, few convictions would be safe from the possibility of extrinsic evidence being required. The one exception is where the record of conviction includes some specific statement about the offense. For instance, in *Matter of Ahortalejo-Guzman*, the judgment and sentence specifically stated that the offense did not involve family violence.[16] That statement was considered dispositive, notwithstanding police reports that indicated family violence as well as the respondent's own testimony.[17] The Board found that approach appropriate to "preserv[e] the results of a plea bargain."[18] Absent that level of strategic lawyering (which would have been unusual before *Silva-Trevino*), it appears difficult to exclude extrinsic evidence.

Applicants for citizenship have the burden of proving their good moral character, and bear a burden of proving by a preponderance of the evidence that any offenses within the required period of good moral character (generally five years prior to the filing of the application) did not involve turpitude.[19] Under *Silva-Trevino*, that seems likely to require the submission of extrinsic evidence in some cases. At this point, it does not appear that USCIS has implemented guidance with regard to *Silva-Trevino*.

The Board has held that it will apply *Silva-Trevino* even in circuits which previously required the categorical test, unless that Court of Appeals rejects *Silva-Trevino* explicitly.[20] Thus, *Silva-Trevino* binds adjudicators except where specifically rejected by the Court of Appeals.

As of the publication of this book, the Third, Fourth, Ninth, and Eleventh Circuits have rejected the third step of *Silva-Trevino*, which permits adjudicators to look beyond the record of conviction and examine the specific facts of the offense at issue.[21] Those courts generally found the Board's approach to go against the plain meaning of the statute; but the procedural oddities of Silva-Trevino have also been noted.[22] Challenges are pending in other circuits as well. The Seventh and Eighth Circuits have adopted Silva-Trevino's third prong.[23]

---

[15]See e.g., Matter of Louissaint, 24 I. & N. Dec. 754 (BIA 2009) (burglary is categorically a turpitudinous act under *Silva-Trevino*).

[16]25 I. & N. Dec. 465 (BIA 2011).

[17]*Matter of Ahortalejo-Guzman, 25 I.& N. Dec. at 468.*

[18]Id.

[19]8 C.F.R. §§ 316.2(a)(7), 316.2(b).

[20]Matter of Guevara Alfaro, 25 I. & N. Dec. 417, 421 (BIA 2011).

[21]Prudencio v. Holder, 669 F.3d 472, 480–84 (4th Cir. 2012); Fajardo v. U.S. Att'y Gen., 659 F.3d 1303, 1307–10 (11th Cir. 2011); Jean-Louis v. Att'y Gen. of U.S., 582 F.3d 462, 470–80 (3d Cir. 2009); Olivas-Motta v. Holder, 716 F.3d 1199 (9th Cir. 2013). The Eighth Circuit had appeared to reject Silva-Trevino, Guardado-Garcia v. Holder, 615 F.3d 900, 902 (8th Cir. 2010), but later deferred to it. Bobadilla v. Holder, 679 F.3d 1052 (8th Cir. 2012).

[22]For a useful exposition of these arguments, see Memorandum of Law of Amici Curiae American Immigration Lawyers Association, Florence Immigrant and Refugee Rights Project, Immigrant Defense Project of the New York State Defenders Association, Immigrant Legal Resource Center, National Immigration Project of the National Lawyers Guild, National Immigrant Justice Center, Refugio del Rio Grande, Inc., and Washington Defenders Association Immigration Project in Support of Reconsideration, led Dec. 5, 2008, available at http://www.immigrantdefenseproject.org/docs/08SilvaTrevinoAmicus Brief.pdf.

[23]Mata-Guerrero v. Holder, 627 F.3d 256, 260–61 (7th Cir. 2010); Bobadilla v. Holder, ___ F.3d ___, 679 F.3d 1052 (8th Cir. 2012).

The recent Supreme Court decision in *Moncrieffe v. Holder*,[24] does not directly address crimes of moral turpitude, but does criticize the possibility of minitrials as impractical and unfair.[25] Held the Supreme Court, the categorical approach "promotes judicial and administrative efficiency by precluding the relitigation of past convictions in minitrials conducted long after the fact."[26]

§ 7:27 Subject-specific grounds of inadmissibility; generally—Crimes of moral turpitude; generally—Exemptions

There are two exceptions to the moral turpitude ground of inadmissibility, and thus, to the bar to good moral character. The first involves crimes that were committed while the noncitizen was under the age of 18. The second involves "petty offenses."[1] Applicants who fall within these exemptions are not statutorily barred from establishing good moral character.[2] On the other hand, the conduct included in these exemptions will be taken into account under the general residual good moral character category.[3]

The law provides that if the crime was committed while the noncitizen was under the age of eighteen and the noncitizen was released from prison more than five years before the application for a visa, for other documentation or for admissions to the U.S., then the noncitizen is not inadmissible.[4] Note, however, that this provision is different from the rule that findings of juvenile delinquency are not considered convictions for purposes of immigration law. If the noncitizen had his or her acts adjudicated under juvenile proceedings, or if the foreign proceedings are interpreted as falling within federal juvenile type of proceedings, then this provision is unnecessary. In such a case, the noncitizen would not have been convicted of any crime and would not be inadmissible.[5] On the other hand, if the minor was convicted as if he or she were an adult, or in the case of foreign convictions, if the minor's conviction does not fall within the type of proceedings that federal law considers necessarily as juvenile proceedings, then this exception comes into play.[6]

The second exception is known as the "petty offense" exemption. It has two parts. First, the applicant only qualifies for this exemption if the crime of moral turpitude under which he or she was convicted, or to which he or she admitted, had a maximum possible penalty of one year of imprisonment.[7] Second, people who would be inadmissible because of a conviction must establish that they were sentenced to a term of imprisonment of no more than six months, regardless of how long they actu-

---

[24]Moncrieffe v. Holder, 133 S. Ct. 1678 (2013).

[25]Moncrieffe v. Holder, 133 S. Ct. 1678, 1690–92 (2013).

[26]Moncrieffe v. Holder, 133 S. Ct. 1678, 1690 (2013).

[Section 7:27]

[1]INA § 212(a)(2)(A)(ii), 8 U.S.C.A. § 1182(a)(2)(A)(ii).

[2]Lafarga v. I.N.S., 170 F.3d 1213 modified 1999 WL 181824 (9th Cir., 1999); Matter of Castro, 19 I. & N. Dec. 692, 696 (B.I.A. 1988); Matter of Turcotte, 12 I. & N. Dec. 206, 208 (B.I.A. 1964).

[3]Matter of Turcotte, 12 I. & N. Dec. 206, 208, 1967 WL 13995 (B.I.A. 1967).

[4]INA § 212(a)(2)(A)(ii)(I), 8 U.S.C.A. § 1182(a)(2)(A)(ii)(I).

[5]Matter of Ramirez-Rivero, 18 I. & N. Dec. 135.

[6]Matter of De La Nues, 18 I. & N. Dec. 140, 145, 1981 WL 158837 (B.I.A. 1981).

[7]INA § 212(a)(2)(A)(ii)(II), 8 U.S.C.A. § 1182(a)(2)(A)(ii)(II).

ally served.[8] Noncitizens who have committed more than one crime of moral turpitude, however, cannot claim either of the exemptions.[9] The BIA has now confirmed that the one crime limitation refers only to a crime involving moral turpitude.[10] Thus, an individual who has been convicted of two crimes will remain eligible for the petty offense exception if the second crime is not one involving moral turpitude.[11]

At least one court has held that when the original conviction could either be a felony or a misdemeanor, a later reduction by the court to a misdemeanor, makes the subject eligible for the petty offense exemption.[12] Similarly, where a statute provides that an offense can be treated as either a misdemeanor or a felony, but the state court declares that the offense is a misdemeanor, that declaration is binding on the subsequent immigration proceedings.[13] The Board of Immigration Appeals decision in *Matter of Almanza* seemed to call that into question, by treating a misdemeanor "wobbler statute" conviction as if it were a felony.[14] However, the decision in *Almanza* was unclear, since it did not cite any of the pertinent case law on this subject, and did not appear to limit its breadth to wobbler statutes.[15] The Board has since "clarified" *Almanza*, and has expressly held that a conviction under a turpitudinous wobbler statute does not bar cancellation, so long as the offense is in fact treated as a misdemeanor, and the person is otherwise eligible.[16]

For a crime to fit within the petty offense exception, the crime cannot have resulted in a sentence of imprisonment of more than six months.[17] Prior to the statutory amendments in 1996, the Board did not count time as a sentence of imprisonment where the execution of the sentence was suspended;[18] that case law has been abrogated by statutory changes to the petty offense language, and that statutory overruling has been recognized by the Board.[19]

§ 7:28 Subject-specific grounds of inadmissibility; generally—Multiple criminal convictions with five year sentence

Another of the grounds that makes the person statutorily barred from establishing good moral character is inadmissibility under the multiple criminal convictions

[8]INA § 212(a)(2)(A)(ii)(II), 8 U.S.C.A. § 1182(a)(2)(A)(ii)(II).

[9]INA § 212(a)(2)(A)(ii), 8 U.S.C.A. § 1182(a)(2)(A)(ii).

[10]In re Garcia-Hernandez, 23 I. & N. Dec. 590 (B.I.A. 2003); see also In re Deanda-Romo, 23 I. & N. Dec. 597 (B.I.A. 2003).

[11]In re Garcia-Hernandez, 23 I. & N. Dec. 590 (B.I.A. 2003); see also In re Deanda-Romo, 23 I. & N. Dec. 597 (B.I.A. 2003).

[12]Lafarga v. I.N.S., 170 F.3d 1213 modified 1999 WL 181824 (9th Cir., 1999); Matter of Castro, 19 I. & N. Dec. 692, 696 (B.I.A. 1988); Matter of Turcotte, 12 I. & N. Dec. 206, 208 (B.I.A. 1964).

[13]Garcia-Lopez v. Ashcroft, 334 F.3d 840 (9th Cir. 2003).

[14]Matter of Almanza-Arenas, 24 I. & N. Dec. 771 (BIA 2009).

[15]Cf. Matter of Almanza-Arenas, 24 I. & N. Dec. 771, 774–75 (BIA 2009).

[16]Matter of Pedroza, 25 I. & N. Dec. 312, 314–15 (BIA 2010). However, the Board simultaneously held that where a misdemeanor is punishable by 365 days, it falls within the ambit of INA § 237(a)(2)(A)(i)(II), because it is "a crime for which a sentence of one year or longer may be imposed," thus barring the applicant from eligibility for Cancellation of Removal for non-permanent residents. Matter of Cortez, 25 I. & N. Dec. 301, 307–08 (BIA 2010).

[17]INA § 212(a)(2)(A)(ii)(II), [8 U.S.C.A. § 1182(a)(2)(A)(ii)(II)].

[18]Matter of Castro, 19 I. & N. Dec. 692 (BIA 1988).

[19]Matter of Batista-Hernandez, 21 I. & N. Dec. 955, 1997 WL 398681 (B.I.A. 1997).

ground of inadmissibility.[1] To be inadmissible under this provision: (1) a noncitizen must have been convicted of two or more crimes (other than purely political offenses), and (2) the aggregate periods to which the noncitizen was sentenced to confinement (whether or not any part was suspended) must have been five years or more.[2] Under this ground it is *irrelevant* whether the convictions occurred in a single trial, whether the offenses arose from a single scheme of misconduct, or whether the offenses involved moral turpitude.[3]

In 1996, Congress amended this ground to remove the requirement that the five years be for sentences actually imposed.[4] Under the new formulation, suspended sentences count for their full term toward the calculation of the five years.[5]

This ground of inadmissibility is different from the analogous deportation provision.[6] For purposes of inadmissibility, the multiple offenses may arise from a single scheme of misconduct and need not involve moral turpitude. However, the aggregate sentences to confinement must have been five years or more. By contrast, for purposes of deportation, the multiple offenses must involve moral turpitude, must not arise out of a single scheme of criminal conduct, and both the length of sentence and the question of confinement are irrelevant. The statutory bar to good moral character is based on the ground of *inadmissibility* rather than deportability: a noncitizen who is deportable but not inadmissible because of multiple criminal convictions is *not* barred from establishing good moral character. Of course, such a noncitizen may face deportation, if he or she is bold enough to apply for naturalization.

§ 7:29 Subject-specific grounds of inadmissibility; generally—Controlled substance violations; generally

Research References

Dizon and Wettstein, Immigration Law Service 2d § 14:146

Inadmissibility under the two criminal provisions relating to controlled substances also bar the person from establishing good moral character. These two grounds of inadmissibility relate to persons who (1) have been convicted of or admit to commission of drug-related crimes, and (2) persons whom the DHS has reason to believe are drug traffickers,[1] or have knowingly profited from being the relative of a drug trafficker.[2] The only exception is that a person who has been convicted of a

---

[Section 7:28]

[1]INA § 212(a)(2)(B), 8 U.S.C.A. § 1182(a)(2)(B).

[2]INA § 212(a)(2)(B), 8 U.S.C.A. § 1182(a)(2)(B) as amended by IIRAIRA § 322(a)(2)(B); INA § 101(a)(48)(B), 8 U.S.C.A. § 1101(a)(48)(B).

[3]INA § 212(a)(2)(B), 8 U.S.C.A. § 1182(a)(2)(B).

[4]IIRAIRA § 322(a)(2)(B); INA § 101(a)(48)(B), 8 U.S.C.A. § 1101(a)(48)(B).

[5]State Department Cable No. 96-State-225256 (Oct. 29, 1996) reproduced in 73 Interpreter Releases 1585 (Nov. 11, 1996).

[6]INA § 237(a)(2)(A)(ii), 8 U.S.C.A. § 1227(a)(2)(A)(ii) as redesignated by IIRAIRA § 305(a)(2).

[Section 7:29]

[1]INA § 212(a)(2)(A)(i)(II), (C), 8 U.S.C.A. § 1182(a)(2)(A)(i)(II), (C).

[2]INA § 212 (a)(2)(C)(ii), 8 U.S.C.A. § 1182(a)(2)(C)(ii), as amended by Pub. Law 106-120 (Dec. 3, 1999). This provision is not discussed below; there is little case law and little known about how the government will apply this provision.

single offense of simple possession of thirty grams or less of marijuana is not statutorily barred from establishing good moral character.[3]

Conviction of most drug offenses also renders the person an aggravated felon and would therefore bar him or her from ever establishing good moral character.[4]

§ 7:30 Subject-specific grounds of inadmissibility; generally—Controlled substance violations; generally—Conviction and admission of elements of drug-related offense

Research References

A.L.R. Index, Immigration and Naturalization

The first of these provisions relates to persons who are convicted of or admit to the essential elements of a drug trafficking crime.[1] This applies to a violation or conspiracy to violate "any law or regulation of a State, the United States, or a foreign country relating to a controlled substance (as defined in [section 202 of the Controlled Substances Act])."[2] This ground is very inclusive. It covers virtually every type of drug.

The words "any law or regulation . . . relating to a controlled substance" have been interpreted as being broad enough to encompass convictions for being under the influence of drugs,[3] facilitation of the unlawful sale of cocaine,[4] attempted illicit possession,[5] possession of drug paraphernalia,[6] possession of lookalike substances,[7] and solicitation to possess drugs.[8] Violations of the Travel Act have also been interpreted to be violations of laws or regulations relating to controlled substances.[9]

On the other hand, courts have not accepted the BIA's position that all inchoate crimes are part of the main offense. The Ninth Circuit has held that *solicitation* to possess a controlled substance is not a crime related to a controlled substance.[10] It held that the plain language of the statute only refers to conspiracy and attempt and not to solicitation.[11] Under the prior statute, both misprision of a felony and il-

---

[3]INA § 101(f)(3), 8 U.S.C.A. § 1101(f)(3).

[4]See §§ 8:11 to 8:17.

[Section 7:30]

[1]INA § 212(a)(2)(A)(i)(II), 8 U.S.C.A. § 1182(a)(2)(A)(i)(II).

[2]INA § 212(a)(2)(A)(i)(II), 8 U.S.C.A. § 1182(a)(2)(A)(i)(II).

[3]Matter of Esqueda, 20 I. & N. Dec. 850 (B.I.A. 1994); Matter of Hernandez-Ponce, 19 I. & N. Dec. 613 (B.I.A. 1988).

[4]Matter of Del Risco, 20 I. & N. Dec. 109 (B.I.A. 1989).

[5]Abudu v. I.N.S., 802 F.2d 1096, 1099 (9th Cir. 1986), reversed on other grounds, 108 S.Ct. 904 (1988).

[6]Escobar Barraza v. Mukasey, 519 F.3d 388 (7th Cir. 2008); Alvarez Acosta v. U.S. Atty. Gen., 524 F.3d 1191, 1196 (11th Cir. Apr. 16, 2008).

[7]Desai v. Mukasey, 520 F.3d 762 (7th Cir. 2008).

[8]Matter of Beltran, 20 I. & N. Dec. 521 (B.I.A. 1992).

[9]Johnson v. I.N.S., 971 F.2d 340, 342–43 (9th Cir. 1992).

[10]Coronado-Durazo v. I.N.S., 123 F.3d 1322 (9th Cir.1997).

[11]Coronado-Durazo v. I.N.S., 123 F.3d 1322 (9th Cir.1997).

legally carrying a firearm during commission of a felony have been held not to be drug related crimes.[12]

In addition, even though the BIA holds that convictions for solicitation, facilitation, or accessory *before* the crimes are convictions of a law relating to a controlled substance, a conviction for accessory to a drug related crime *after* the fact is not.[13] Such a conviction, however, may be an aggravated felony under the heading of obstruction of justice if the sentence imposed was at least one year.[14]

The State Department recognizes that applicants should not be ineligible for a visa based upon an admission or conviction relating to simple possession or use of a controlled substance if the acts occurred while they were under the age of 18.[15] Neither the BIA nor the USCIS has explicitly recognized such an exception.

§ 7:31 Subject-specific grounds of inadmissibility; generally—Controlled substance violations; generally—Reason to believe person is trafficker

No conviction or even a valid admission is necessary to bar the admission of people believed to be drug traffickers. This ground applies to "[a]ny alien who the consular or immigration officer knows or has reason to believe is or has been an illicit trafficker in any . . . controlled substance."[1] It also applies to knowing assisters, abettors, conspirators, and those who collude with others.[2]

This section uses the words "such controlled substance" to specify its coverage.[3] The use of these words may seem anomalous since there is no prior reference for the word "such." However, it is there because this section was taken almost verbatim from the former law where it used to be a subsection of the same ground of inadmissibility that referred to controlled substance convictions.[4] By referring to the former law, it is clear that "such controlled substance" refers to controlled substances as defined in section 202 of the Controlled Substances Act.[5] As noted above, this definition is very broad and includes virtually any type of drug.

This ground does not require a conviction or even a valid admission. It is sufficient for the DHS or a consular officer to have "reason to believe" that the noncitizen was an illicit trafficker. This standard is much lower than that required

---

[12]Castaneda de Esper v. I.N.S., 557 F.2d 79 (6th Cir. 1977); Matter of Carrillo, 16 I. & N. Dec. 625 (B.I.A. 1978).

[13]Matter of Batista-Hernandez, 21 I. & N. Dec. 955 (B.I.A. 1997) (however, accessory after the fact is an obstruction of justice offense and if the sentence actually imposed in one year or more, it is an aggravated felony).

[14]See § 8:16.

[15]9 FAM 40.21(b) N.2.1.

[Section 7:31]

[1]INA § 212(a)(2)(C), 8 U.S.C.A. § 1182(a)(2)(C).

[2]INA § 212(a)(2)(C), 8 U.S.C.A. § 1182(a)(2)(C).

[3]INA § 212(a)(2)(C), 8 U.S.C.A. § 1182(a)(2)(C).

[4]INA § 212(a)(23)(A), (B), 8 U.S.C.A. § 1182(a)(23)(A), (B) (1989) as enacted by Act of June 27, 1952, 66 Stat. 163, as amended by Pub.L. 100-204.

[5]INA § 212(a)(23)(A), (B), 8 U.S.C.A. § 1182(a)(23)(A), (B) (1989) as enacted by Act of June 27, 1952, 66 Stat. 163, as amended by Pub.L. 100-204.

for valid admissions.[6] Further, this ground of inadmissibility is not negated because criminal charges were dropped in relation to the incident that gave the DHS "reason to believe" that noncitizen was an illicit trafficker.[7] Nor is it negated when the person, based on these underlying facts, is actually convicted for a different offense not involving drugs.[8] A detailed affidavit from a consular employee providing sufficient information may be sufficient to provide DHS with "reason to believe" the noncitizen is a drug trafficker even when criminal authorities have refused to prosecute the noncitizen.[9] On the other hand, however, there must be some evidence that the person knew the drugs were in his or her possession and was consciously acting as a conduit to transfer drugs.[10]

The State Department explains the standard of "reason to believe" in the following fashion:[11]

'Reason to believe' might be established by a conviction, an admission, a long record of arrests with an unexplained failure to prosecute by the local government, or several reliable and corroborative reports. The essence of the standard is that the consular officer must have more than a mere suspicion-there must exist a probability, supported by evidence, that the alien is or has been engaged in trafficking. The consular officer is required to assess independently evidence relating to a finding of ineligibility . . . . This evidence might include conclusions of other evaluators. Such conclusions, no matter how trustworthy, cannot alone support a finding of ineligibility.

This ground only applies if the officer actually knew, or had reason to believe the person to be a trafficker.[12] Thus, even if the person turned out to have been a drug trafficker at the time of entry, the person was not inadmissible if the DHS officers inspecting him or her did not have any reason to believe the person to be a drug trafficker at the time.[13] The BIA reached this conclusion in the context of deportation proceedings.[14] The application of this conclusion to the good moral character bar remains uncertain. It appears probable that if the DHS now has reason to believe the person is a drug trafficker, or has been a drug trafficker during the statutory period of good moral character, the person would be barred from establishing good moral character.[15]

The term "illicit trafficker" has also been very broadly interpreted. It requires "a knowing conscious participant or conduit in an attempt to smuggle" the controlled

---

[6]See Matter of Rico, 16 I. & N. Dec. 181, 185–86 (B.I.A. 1977); see also Lopez-Molina v. Ashcroft, 368 F.3d 1206 (9th Cir. 2004) (finding substantial evidence supported immigration officer's claim of "reason to believe" the individual was a drug trafficker).

[7]Matter of Rico, 16 I. & N. Dec. 181, 185–86, 1977 WL 39246 (B.I.A. 1977). Even before Ozkok, a noncitizen was also statutorily precluded from establishing good moral character because of his or her arrest and probation for transporting one pound of marijuana even though there was no conviction under Texas law. The court held that the INS had reason to believe the person was a trafficker. Nunez-Payan v. I.N.S., 811 F.2d 264 (5th Cir.), reh'g denied 815 F.2d 384 (1987).

[8]Matter of Favela, 16 I. & N. Dec. 753, 756 (B.I.A. 1979).

[9]See Hamid v. I.N.S., 538 F.2d 1389 (9th Cir. 1976).

[10]Pichardo v. I.N.S., 216 F.3d 1198 (9th Cir. 2000).

[11]9 FAM note 2 to 22 CFR § 40.23.

[12]See Matter of Rocha, 20 I. & N. Dec. 944, 947 (B.I.A. 1994).

[13]Matter of Rocha, 20 I. & N. Dec. 944, 946, 1995 WL 24858 (B.I.A. 1995).

[14]Matter of Rocha, 20 I. & N. Dec. 944, 1995 WL 24858 (B.I.A. 1995).

[15]The good moral character ground of inadmissibility bars entry of those for whom there is reason to believe they are or have been drug traffickers. INA § 212(a)(2)(C), 8 U.S.C.A. § 1182(a)(2)(C).

substance.[16] This definition does not apply only to persons who smuggle or attempt to smuggle drugs into the U.S. It also encompasses people who serve as a conduit for transfers within the U.S.[17] A person can be an illicit trafficker even if he or she has committed only one transgression, provided a sufficient amount of controlled substance is involved.[18] Profit is also not a requirement for a finding of illicit trafficking. A person who gives away drugs for free may be barred from admission under this ground.[19]

§ 7:32 Subject-specific grounds of inadmissibility; generally—Prostitution and commercialized vice

Research References

Dizon and Wettstein, Immigration Law Service 2d § 14:146

This is strictly speaking not a "criminal" ground of inadmissibility. It applies to persons who come from countries where prostitution is legal,[1] and presumably also if the person is living in a state of the U.S. where prostitution is legal. This ground of inadmissibility has three subsections. It renders inadmissible: (1) people who are coming to the U.S. to engage in prostitution or who have engaged in prostitution within ten years of the date of application for visa, adjustment of status, or entry into the U.S.;[2] (2) people who are procurers of prostitutes, attempt to procure, or receive the proceeds of prostitution, or who have done any of these activities within ten years of the date of application for visa, adjustment of status, or entry into the U.S.;[3] and (3) people who are coming to the U.S. to engage in unlawful commercialized vice, whether or not related to prostitution.[4]

The term "engage in prostitution" requires that the person must have engaged in this type of conduct over a period of time. Having been convicted of a single act of prostitution does not make the person subject to this ground of inadmissibility.[5] The person may however also be inadmissible because of a conviction for a crime of moral turpitude, unless the person qualifies for the petty offense exemption.[6]

Similarly "procuring a person for the purpose of prostitution" requires the procuring of another person "for the purpose of having her offer her body to *indiscriminate intercourse* with men."[7]

---

[16]Matter of Rico, 16 I. & N. Dec. 181, 1977 WL 39246 (B.I.A. 1977).

[17]Matter of R-H-, 7 I. & N. Dec. 675 (B.I.A. 1958).

[18]Matter of Favela, 16 I. & N. Dec. 753, 755, 1979 WL 44443 (B.I.A. 1979) (case involved one kilogram of marijuana); Matter of Rico, 16 I. & N. Dec. 181, 186, 1977 WL 39246 (B.I.A. 1977) (162 pounds of marijuana).

[19]Matter of R- H-, 7 I. & N. Dec. 675, 677, 1958 WL 9843 (B.I.A. 1958).

[Section 7:32]

[1]Matter of G-, 5 I. & N. Dec. 559 (B.I.A. 1953).

[2]INA § 212(a)(2)(D)(i), 8 U.S.C.A. § 1182(a)(2)(D)(i).

[3]INA § 212(a)(2)(D)(ii), 8 U.S.C.A. § 1182(a)(2)(D)(ii).

[4]INA § 212(a)(2)(D)(iii), 8 U.S.C.A. § 1182(a)(2)(D)(iii).

[5]Matter of T-, 6 I. & N. Dec. 474 (B.I.A. 1955); 9 FAM, note 1.1 to 22 CFR § 40.24.

[6]See §§ 7:25 to 7:27.

[7]Matter of R-, 6 I. & N. Dec. 444, 457 (B.I.A. 1954).

Activities covered under this ground of inadmissibility include transporting males for the purpose of sexual intercourse with prostitutes.[8] On the other hand, the statute would not bar the admission of medical personnel who routinely work at houses of prostitution and are paid by the owners of those houses if their work is in furtherance of the foreign country's health regulations.[9]

Criminal conviction of some prostitution management and transportation offenses renders the person an aggravated felon and would therefore bar him or her from ever establishing good moral character.[10]

§ 7:33 Subject-specific grounds of inadmissibility; generally—Smugglers and encouragers of unlawful entry

Research References

A.L.R. Index, Immigration and Naturalization
Dizon and Wettstein, Immigration Law Service 2d § 14:146

This ground of inadmissibility is likely to have a very serious effect on many naturalization applicants. After 1990, this ground of inadmissibility applies to any noncitizen who at any time knowingly encouraged, induced, assisted, abetted or aided any other noncitizen to enter the U.S. illegally.[1] Prior law required smuggling to be for gain in order to be actionable.[2] This amendment has made thousands of people inadmissible and deportable because many noncitizens probably have encouraged close family members to enter the U.S. illegally.

This is not a criminally related ground of inadmissibility. Thus, having engaged in the conduct is sufficient for the person to be inadmissible; no conviction or admission is required. However, a person who has a conviction for "alien" smuggling under 8 U.S.C.A. § 1324(a)(1),[3] is likely to be inadmissible under this section.[4] On the other hand, it has been held that "alien" smuggling is not a crime of moral turpitude for admission or deportation purposes.[5]

For a finding of inadmissibility under this section, there is no requirement that the "smuggler" must have accompanied the other noncitizens into the country.[6] Aiding and abetting another noncitizen to attempt to enter in violation of law also

---

[8]Matter of R-M-, 7 I. & N. Dec. 392 (B.I.A. 1957).

[9]Matter of C-, 7 I. & N. Dec. 432 (B.I.A. 1957).

[10]See §§ 8:11 to 8:17.

[Section 7:33]

[1]INA § 212(a)(6)(E), 8 U.S.C.A. § 1182(a)(6)(E).

[2]INA § 212(a)(31), 8 U.S.C.A. § 1182(a)(31) as originally enacted by Act of June 27, 1952.

[3]INA § 274(a)(1).

[4]Matter of Farias, 21 I. & N. Dec. 269 (B.I.A. 1996). This amends the decision in Matter of Tiwari, 19 I. & N. Dec. 875, 877 (B.I.A. 1989), motion to reconsider denied 20 I. & N. Dec. 254 (B.I.A. 1991) (holding that under the prior law a conviction for "alien" smuggling materially lessened the government's burden of proof but did not constitute prima facie evidence of excludability or deportability because the criminal statute did not require smuggling to be for gain.) In 1990, Congress amended the grounds of exclusion and deportation and removed the requirement "for gain." Thereafter conviction under the criminal statute, in so far as it relates to smuggling, is prima facie evidence of inadmissibility and deportability.

[5]Matter of Tiwari, 19 I. & N. Dec. 875, 880–81, 1989 WL 247508 (B.I.A. 1989).

[6]Matter of Vargas-Banuelos, 13 I. & N. Dec. 810 (B.I.A. 1971).

makes a person inadmissible under this ground.[7] Transporting within the U.S. noncitizens known to be illegally here does not necessarily render inadmissible the person providing the transportation.[8] For such transportation within the U.S. to render the person inadmissible, it must amount to aiding and abetting entry, such as when the transporter knew the noncitizens before they entered the U.S., or contacted them while they were still abroad, or knew a go-between who was arranging their entry and there was some prior arrangement before the noncitizens' entry.[9]

An exemption exists for persons who qualify for Family Unity under the 1990 act and who are either applying for Family Unity or for an immigrant visa under the immediate relative or the second preference family visa provisions of the INA.[10] Although such individuals might not be removable,[11] the Ninth Circuit has found that smugglers of family members would be barred nonetheless from showing good moral character.[12]

Like most of the other admission-related statutory bars to good moral character, this provision may lead to the loss of permanent residence for the naturalization applicant. In addition to the cancellation of removal waiver available to lawful permanent residents who resided lawfully in the U.S. for more than seven years,[13] there is a special waiver of deportation available to lawful permanent residents who smuggled their spouse, parent, son, or daughter.[14]

A criminal conviction for smuggling precludes the applicant from demonstrating good moral character because it constitutes an aggravated felony.[15] Such a conviction is also a statutory bar to cancellation of removal.[16]

§ 7:34 Subject-specific grounds of inadmissibility; generally—Practicing polygamists

Research References

Dizon and Wettstein, Immigration Law Service 2d § 14:146

This is a somewhat limited ground of inadmissibility. It provides that a noncitizen seeking permanent residence who is coming to the U.S. to practice polygamy is inadmissible.[1] It is clear that advocating polygamy or even having practiced polyg-

---

[7]Matter of Vargas-Banuelos, 13 I. & N. Dec. 810, 811–12, 1971 WL 24385 (B.I.A. 1971).

[8]Matter of I-M-, 7 I. & N. Dec. 389 (B.I.A. 1957).

[9]Matter of I- M-, 7 I. & N. Dec. 389, 391, 1957 WL 10529 (B.I.A. 1957).

[10]INA § 212(a)(6)(E), 8 U.S.C.A. § 1182(a)(6)(E). Family Unity is a special program available to spouses and children of legalized noncitizens who entered the U.S. before May 5, 1988. IA90 § 301.

[11]INA § 237(a)(1)(E)(ii), 8 U.S.C.A. § 1227(a)(1)(E)(ii) as redesignated by IIRAIRA § 305(a)(2). This protection is only limited to those relatives who were eligible for Family Unity and who became lawful permanent residents under the immediate relative or second family-based preference provisions. INA § 212(a)(6)(E), 8 U.S.C.A. § 1182(a)(6)(E). Family Unity is a special program available to spouses and children of legalized noncitizens who entered the U.S. before May 5, 1988. IA90 § 301.

[12]See Sanchez v. Holder, 560 F.3d 1028, 1031–33 (9th Cir. 2009) (en banc).

[13]INA § 240A(a), 8 U.S.C.A. § 1229b(a).

[14]INA § 237(a)(1)(E)(iii), 8 U.S.C.A. § 1227(a)(1)(E)(iii) as redesignated by IIRAIRA § 305(a)(2).

[15]INA § 101(a)(43)(N), 8 U.S.C.A. § 1101(a)(43)(N). See also §§ 8:11 to 8:17.

[16]INA § 240A(a)(3), 8 U.S.C.A. § 1229b(a)(3).

[Section 7:34]

[1]INA § 212(a)(10)(A), 8 U.S.C.A. § 1182(a)(10)(A).

amy abroad is not a ground of inadmissibility.[2] In addition, case law has established that the fact that a person is bigamous because of having remarried without obtaining a divorce from a former marriage does not bring the person within the coverage of this ground of inadmissibility.[3] The USCIS takes the position that persons who have practiced polygamy in the past are also barred from establishing good moral character.[4] Given the wording of the ground of inadmissibility, it is unlikely that a court would sustain a finding of lack of good moral character when the applicant had practiced polygamy abroad before entering the U.S. and did not come to the U.S. to practice polygamy.

§ 7:35 Income derived principally from illegal gambling activities

Research References

Dizon and Wettstein, Immigration Law Service 2d § 14:146

The INA bars those "whose income is derived principally from illegal gambling activities" from establishing good moral character.[1] Deriving income under this provision includes three things: (1) a noncitizen's financial interest in a gambling establishment, (2) the gambling activities of the noncitizen himself or herself, and (3) being an employee in a gambling establishment where the employment has some proximate relationship to the gambling activities.[2]

Thus a noncitizen who received salary for six months as the dealer or an operator of a gaming table was held to have derived income principally from illegal gambling activities.[3] A gaming establishment will still be held to be illegal even when the municipal authorities officially tolerate it, provided the activity is forbidden by an applicable statute.[4] The term "principally" does not require the illegal gambling activity to have been the main source of income during the entire period for which good moral character is required. Rather, it is sufficient that the illegal gambling activities must have been the principal source of income at any time during this period.[5]

Conviction for some gambling related violations would render the person an aggravated felon and would therefore bar him or her from ever establishing good moral character.[6]

§ 7:36 Convicted of two or more gambling offenses

Research References

Dizon and Wettstein, Immigration Law Service 2d § 14:146

A person who has been convicted of two or more gambling offenses committed

---

[2]Compare INA § 212(a)(10)(A), 8 U.S.C.A. § 1182(a)(10)(A) with INA § 212(a)(11), 8 U.S.C.A. § 1182(a)(11) as originally enacted by Act of June 27, 1952.

[3]Matter of G-, 6 I. & N. Dec. 9 (1953).

[4]8 CFR § 316.10(b)(2)(ix).

[Section 7:35]

[1]INA § 101(f)(4), 8 U.S.C.A. § 1101(f)(4).

[2]Matter of S-K-C-, 8 I. & N. Dec. 185, 187 (B.I.A. 1958).

[3]Matter of S-K-C-, 8 I. & N. Dec. 185, 187–88, 1958 WL 9888 (B.I.A. 1958).

[4]Matter of S-K-C-, 8 I. & N. Dec. 185, 188, 1958 WL 9888 (B.I.A. 1958).

[5]Matter of S-K-C-, 8 I. & N. Dec. 185, 188–89, 1958 WL 9888 (B.I.A. 1958).

[6]See §§ 8:11 to 8:17.

during the relevant statutory period for which good moral character is required will be barred from establishing good moral character.[1] A person who has been convicted for "lottery" and "bookmaking and pool selling" has been convicted of two gambling offenses.[2]

Conviction of some gambling offenses renders the person an aggravated felon and would therefore bar him or her from ever establishing good moral character.[3]

§ 7:37 Giving false testimony for purpose of obtaining a benefit under INA

Research References

A.L.R. Index, Immigration and Naturalization
Dizon and Wettstein, Immigration Law Service 2d §§ 14:146, 14:150 to 14:153

A person "who has given false testimony for the purpose of obtaining any benefits under this act" is barred from establishing good moral character.[1]

This bar to establishing good moral character must not be confused with the visa fraud ground of inadmissibility, as there are significant differences between them. The first difference is that this bar to moral character applies only to *oral* testimony.[2] Furthermore, these oral utterances must be made under oath.[3] Thus false statements on written applications, be they under oath or not do not bring the applicant within the purview of this statutory bar.[4] However, this type of fraud will certainly be considered in evaluating the applicant under the general good moral character provision contained in the residual category.[5]

Oral testimony given under oath gives rise to this statutory bar. It is clear that this includes false testimony given under oath in the context of a deportation hearing.[6] Oral utterances given under oath in an inquisitorial setting, however, have also been held to qualify as testimony-there is no requirement that testimony be given in an adversarial setting.[7] Thus, misrepresentations given through oral utterances sworn under oath in a question-and-answer statement before a DHS officer in connection with the replacement of a lost certificate of citizenship, or the process-

---

[Section 7:36]

[1]INA § 101(f)(5), 8 U.S.C.A. § 1101(f)(5).

[2]Matter of A-, 6 I. & N. Dec. 242, 245 (B.I.A. 1954).

[3]See §§ 8:11 to 8:17.

[Section 7:37]

[1]INA § 101(f)(6), 8 U.S.C.A. § 1101(f)(6).

[2]Matter of L-D-E-, 8 I. & N. Dec. 399 (B.I.A. 1959); Matter of Ngan, 10 I. & N. Dec. 725 (B.I.A. 1964) ("His oral sworn statements taken in connection therewith, after investigation had disclosed reason to doubt the bona fides of the status of the respondent as a citizen of the United States, constitute testimony as that term is used in section 101(f)(6) (8 U.S.C.A. 1101(g)(6)) since it was not written but oral and thus not within the restriction of *Sharaiha v. Hoy*").

[3]Matter of L-D-E-, 8 I. & N. Dec. 399 (B.I.A. 1959); Matter of G-L-T-, 8 I. & N. Dec. 403, 404 (B.I.A. 1959); Matter of G-, 6 I. & N. Dec. 208 (B.I.A. 1954) (not barred from establishing good moral character because statements were not required to be made under oath).

[4]Matter of L-D-E-, 8 I. & N. Dec. 399 (B.I.A. 1959).

[5]Matter of L-D-E-, 8 I. & N. Dec. 399 (B.I.A. 1959); see also DeLuca v. Ashcroft, 203 F. Supp. 2d 1276 (M.D. Ala. 2002) (considering misrepresentations on the naturalization application, but finding no intent to deceive or bad faith).

[6]Matter of Barcenas, 19 I. & N. Dec. 609, 612 (B.I.A. 1988).

[7]Matter of Ngan, 10 I. & N. Dec. 725, 729 (B.I.A. 1964).

ing of a visa petition for spouse and children, both qualify to bar the applicant from establishing good moral character.[8] Also, statements given under oath to an asylum officer as part of a political asylum application could bar the applicant from establishing good moral character.[9] Even statements given in a setting that is not quasi-judicial will bar the applicant from establishing good moral character provided they were given under oath.[10] Thus oral statement given under oath to a border patrol agent as part of a routine question-and-answer interview will trigger this statutory bar to good moral character.[11]

The requirement of a finding of lack of good moral character for noncitizens who have given false testimony is also different from the visa fraud ground of inadmissibility in that there is no materiality requirement in the good moral character provision.[12] Therefore, noncitizens may be barred from establishing good moral character because of misrepresentation which may have been completely irrelevant to their case.[13]

It is sufficient for the noncitizen to have misrepresented a fact and to have intended to obtain an immigration benefit through that misrepresentation.[14] If the person has told even the most immaterial of lies with the subjective intent of obtaining an immigration benefit, the person lacks good moral character, as 101(f)(6) does not distinguish between material and immaterial lies.[15]

That said, the link with the benefit is important, however, as the DHS must establish that the lie was told in order to obtain a benefit.[16] When a lie is not material, subjective intent becomes harder to prove; for the Supreme Court specifically noted that "[w]illful misrepresentations made for other reasons, such as embarrassment, fear, or a desire for privacy," are not done with subjective intent to obtain the immigration benefit, and are thus not covered by the false testimony bar.[17] Thus, where an individual lied in an asylum interview about his address, using his lawyer's address instead of his own, the Fifth Circuit held that there was no subjective intent to obtain a benefit.[18] Likewise, a federal court reversed the INS' denial of a petitioner's application for naturalization despite false statements concerning the petitioner's prior marriages and arrest because the court determined that the petitioner did not make the statements with the intention of obtaining immigration

---

[8]Matter of G-L-T-, 8 I. & N. Dec. 403 (B.I.A. 1959) (certificate of citizenship); Matter of Ngan, 10 I. & N. Dec. 725 (B.I.A. 1964) (visa petition).

[9]In re R-S-J, 22 I. & N. Dec. 863, 1999 WL 374555 (B.I.A. 1999); see also, Gonzalez-Maldonado v. Gonzales, 2007 WL 1518661 (5th Cir. May 25, 2007).

[10]Matter of Namio, 14 I. & N. Dec. 412, 414 (B.I.A. 1973).

[11]Matter of Namio, 14 I. & N. Dec. 412, 413–414, 1973 WL 29467 (B.I.A. 1973).

[12]Kungys v. I.N.S., 485 U.S. 759, 779, 108 S.Ct. 1537, 1551, 99 L.Ed.2d 839 (1988) (plurality opinion). The INS has incorporated this decision into its regulations, see 8 CFR § 316.10(b)(2)(vi).

[13]Linawag v. I.N.S., 872 F.2d 685, 689 (5th Cir. 1989).

[14]Kungys v. U.S., 485 U.S. 759, 779, 108 S. Ct. 1537, 1551, 99 L. Ed. 2d 839 (1988).

[15]Kungys v. U.S., 485 U.S. 759, 108 S. Ct. 1537, 99 L. Ed. 2d 839 (1988).

[16]Kungys v. U.S., 485 U.S. 759, 108 S. Ct. 1537, 99 L. Ed. 2d 839 (1988).

[17]Kungys v. U.S., 485 U.S. 759, 780, 108 S. Ct. 1537, 99 L. Ed. 2d 839 (1988).

[18]Gonzalez-Maldonado v. Gonzales, 487 F.3d 975 (5th Cir. 2007).

benefits.[19] However, the Second Circuit held that where a visa applicant represented herself as the wife of a wealthy Nigerian man was "capable of influencing" the consulate's decision to issue a visitor's visa, and was sufficient to raise a presumption that she obtained the visa thanks to her misrepresentation.[20]

The requirement of the testimony being linked to obtaining a benefit under the act has been held to include false testimony in order to avoid losing an immigration benefit.[21] Giving testimony under oath in the context of a visa petition is also giving testimony in order to obtain a benefit under the act since petitioners desire a personal benefit: to have their spouse or other family member join them.[22]

A testimony must be false for the applicant to be barred from establishing good moral character. For the ground of inadmissibility, there must be a willful misrepresentation or fraud, which means that the speaker must know that what he or she says is untrue.[23] Similarly, there is no bar to good moral character unless the person knew the statement to be false.[24]

Nevertheless, even when not clearly lying, applicants may still be found to lack good moral character under the general residual category of good moral character when through the combination of demeanor and the cumulative effect of contradictory and confusing testimony, it is established that the statements the witness later classified as "mistakes" were not in fact innocent.[25] Furthermore, if the applicant is seeking relief that relies on the exercise of discretion, the applicant will not be likely to obtain favorable exercise of discretion if the testimony was replete with half-truths, incomplete answers, misleading responses, suppressions, equivocations, and quibbling.[26]

Voluntary and timely retraction of the false testimony will make this bar to good moral character inapplicable.[27] The recantation, however, must be voluntary and without delay.[28] A recantation that is made a year after the statements were originally made and not until it appeared that the disclosure of the falsity of the statement was imminent, is neither timely nor voluntary.[29] A retraction will not be

---

[19]Chan v. I.N.S., 2001 WL 521706 (E.D.N.Y. 2001) see also Plewa v. I.N.S., 77 F. Supp. 2d 905 (N.D. Ill. 1999) (failure to tell naturalization examiner of an arrest did not evidence lack of good moral character when based upon a misunderstanding and incorrect advice from an immigration counselor).

[20]Emokah v. Mukasey, 523 F.3d 110 (2d Cir. 2008).

[21]Liwanag v. I.N.S., 872 F.2d 685, 689 (5th Cir. 1989).

[22]Matter of Ngan, 10 I. & N. Dec. 725; Matter of W-J-W-, 7 I. & N. Dec. 706, 707 (B.I.A. 1958).

[23]Matter of Healey and Goodchild, 17 I. & N. Dec. 22 (B.I.A. 1979).

[24]Rodriguez-Gutierrez V. INS, 59 F.3d 504 (5th Cir. 1995) ("False testimony means knowingly giving false information with an intent to deceive").

[25]See Matter of Bufalino, 11 I. & N. Dec. 351, 360–61 (B.I.A. 1965).

[26]Matter of Bufalino, 12 I. & N. Dec. 277, 280 (B.I.A. 1967). See also, Gambino v. I.N.S., 419 F.2d 1355 (2d Cir. 1970) (when the applicant has a long history of convictions, questions about his activities and associations, as well as his current sources of income are relevant to the establishing good moral character and the INS was correct in refusing to exercise discretion favorably when no answers were forthcoming).

[27]Matter of M-, 9 I. & N. Dec. 118 (B.I.A. 1960).

[28]Matter of Namio, 14 I. & N. Dec. 412, 414, 1973 WL 29467 (B.I.A. 1973).

[29]Matter of Namio, 14 I. & N. Dec. 412, 414, 1973 WL 29467 (B.I.A. 1973). See also Matter of Ngan, 10 I. & N. Dec. 725, 727, 1964 WL 12125 (B.I.A. 1964) (recantation made three years after the original misrepresentation is not timely).

effective even if it is given during the same examination, if the correction is due to the fact that the witness realizes that the false testimony would not deceive.[30]

§ 7:38 Confined to penal institution for 180 days or more as result of conviction

Research References

Dizon and Wettstein, Immigration Law Service 2d § 14:146

The INA bars a person from establishing good moral character if, during the relevant statutory period, the person "has been confined, as a result of conviction, to a penal institution for an aggregate period of one hundred and eighty days or more, regardless of whether the offense, or offenses, for which he [or she] has been confined were committed within or without such period."[1]

In order to be barred under this statutory provision, the noncitizen must have been confined to a penal institution for more than 180 days as a result of a conviction. This provision must be distinguished from the criminal grounds of inadmissibility. The applicant will be barred under this provision even when the person is not inadmissible.[2] Furthermore, there is no requirement that the person be a noncitizen while confined for more than 180 days. Thus a naturalized citizen who was confined as a result of a conviction while a U.S. citizen but who was later denaturalized for other reasons, will not be able to prove good moral character because of the confinement while a citizen.[3]

Confinement, however, must be as a result of a conviction.[4] Conviction for these purposes has the same meaning it has for grounds of inadmissibility or deportation.[5] The definition of "conviction" is discussed below.[6] Even when adjudication of guilt has been withheld, the person may be barred from establishing good moral character if the outcome of the proceedings satisfies the definition of conviction under the INA and the person is confined to more than 180 days as a result.[7]

Pre-sentence confinement also counts toward the 180 days if the confinement is credited to determine the date of release from custody after confinement.[8] Even though the time served actually occurs before the conviction, it will count if it is later incorporated into the conviction confinement in order to determine which por-

---

[30]See Llanos-Snarillos v. U.S., 77 F.2d 164, 165–66 (9th Cir. 1949) (the witness's withdrawal of the testimony needs to be of his or her own volition and without delay).

[Section 7:38]

[1]INA § 101(f)(7), 8 U.S.C.A. § 1101(f)(7).

[2]See Matter of Zangwill, 18 I. & N. Dec. 22 (B.I.A. 1981).

[3]Matter of B-, 7 I. & N. Dec. 405 (B.I.A. 1957).

[4]INA § 101(f)(7), 8 U.S.C.A. § 1101(f)(7).

[5]Matter of Ozkok, 19 I. & N. Dec. 546 modifying Matter of Zangwill, 18 I. & N. Dec. 22; Matter of Seda, 17 I. & N. Dec. 550.

[6]§§ 8:3 to 8:10.

[7]Matter of Zangwill, 18 I. & N. Dec. 22 as modified by Matter of Ozkok, 19 I. & N. Dec. at 552 and the IIRAIRA amendment to the definition of conviction. See INA § 101(a)(48)(A), 8 U.S.C.A. § 1101(a)(48)(A).

[8]Matter of Valdovinos, 18 I. & N. Dec. 343, 344 (B.I.A. 1982).

tion of the sentence the individual must actually serve and whether the individual should be credited this time for purposes of early release for good behavior.[9]

Probation is not a sufficient restraint on a person's liberty to be equivalent to confinement in a penal institution.[10] Thus a person who is sentenced to probation is not barred from establishing good moral character under this provision.[11] However, if the person is incarcerated as a result of probation violation, the time served for such incarceration counts toward the 180 days to bar the person from establishing good moral character.[12] Furthermore, it is irrelevant that the original crime occurred outside the statutory period of good moral character. If the person was confined during such period, the confinement counts.[13] Even if the person is not confined, a person's probation may be considered in evaluating whether a person is otherwise of good moral character under the general test.[14]

Confinement as a result of a conviction may occur in any type of penal facility. Thus, even when the person has been incarcerated in a minimal security area with work furlough facility, the time spent in that facility will count towards the 180 days.[15] In some states, confinement in a hospital for purposes of psychiatric or other type of medical rehabilitation will probably not be sufficient to count towards the 180 days, provided the confinement is not punitive.[16] House arrest has also been held to constitute a term of imprisonment.[17]

A pardon granted for the offense for which the person was confined for more than 180 days eradicates the bar for purposes of good moral character.[18] A pardoned offense may be considered for purposes of evaluating whether the person is a person of good moral character under the general residual category.[19]

§ 7:39   Has ever been convicted of aggravated felony—Date of conviction and applicability of bar

Research References

A.L.R. Index, Immigration and Naturalization
Dizon and Wettstein, Immigration Law Service 2d §§ 14:146, 14:154

Any person, who at any time has been convicted of an aggravated felony as defined

---

[9]Matter of Valdovinos, 18 I. & N. Dec. 343, 344–45, 1982 WL 190702 (B.I.A. 1982).

[10]Matter of Gantus-Bobadilla, 13 I. & N. Dec. 777, 778, 780, 1971 WL 24423 (B.I.A. 1971) (overruled by, Matter of Franklin, 20 I. & N. Dec. 867, 1994 WL 520990 (B.I.A. 1994)).

[11]Matter of Gantus-Bobadilla, 13 I. & N. Dec. 777.

[12]Matter of Piroglu, 17 I. & N. Dec. 578, 580 (B.I.A. 1980).

[13]Matter of Piroglu, 17 I. & N. Dec. 580 (stated in the head notes but not discussed in the text).

[14]Matter of Gantus-Bobadilla, 13 I. & N. Dec. 777, 780, 1971 WL 24423 (B.I.A. 1971) (overruled by, Matter of Franklin, 20 I. & N. Dec. 867, 1994 WL 520990 (B.I.A. 1994)).

[15]Matter of Valdovinos, 18 I. & N. Dec. 343, 345, 1982 WL 190702 (B.I.A. 1982).

[16]See Holzapfel v. Wyrsch, 250 F.2d 890 (3d Cir. 1958) (confinement in a hospital for psychiatric treatment will not support deportation under the crime of moral turpitude ground of deportation which requires confinement for one year). Whereas California's non-punitive commitment of an addict to California Rehabilitation Center will probably not constitute confinement, transfer of mentally ill prisoners to state hospitals would still count. Brady, California Criminal Law and Immigration 4–6.

[17]Ilchuk v. Attorney General of U.S., 434 F.3d 618, 623–24 (3d Cir. 2006)

[18]Matter of H-, 7 I. & N. Dec. 249 (B.I.A. 1956).

[19]Matter of Gonzalez, 16 I. & N. Dec. 134 (B.I.A. 1977). But see, Giambanco v. I.N.S., 531 F.2d 141 (3d Cir. 1976) (pardon eliminates consideration of offense for all purposes).

by the INA § 101(a) (43), is barred forever from establishing good moral character.[1] This bar was introduced by the Immigration Act of 1990 and is only applicable to convictions occurring on or after November 29, 1990, the effective date of the amendment.[2] Prior to this amendment, only people who were convicted of murder were permanently barred from establishing good moral character.[3] People convicted of murder, be it prior to November 29, 1990 or after that date, continue to be permanently barred from establishing good moral character.[4]

The IIRAIRA amendment to the effective date of the aggravated felony definition, does not affect the requirement that only post-November 29, 1990 aggravated felony convictions permanently bar the person from establishing good moral character.[5] This interpretation has been confirmed in an unpublished BIA decision[6] and by a legal opinion by the legacy INS general counsel.[7] It also continues to be enshrined in the regulations.[8]

The general counsel correctly warned, however, that a conviction for an aggravated felony entered prior to November 29, 1990 will be considered in evaluating the person's moral character under the residual category of the good moral character definition.[9]

The aggravated felony bar continues to preclude a showing of good moral character, even if a non-citizen has obtained a waiver of their inadmissibility under former INA § 212(c).[10]

More importantly, however, the DHS will make efforts to deport (remove) applicants who have been convicted of aggravated felonies, regardless of the date of the conviction.[11] This is because persons who are not barred from establishing good moral character by an aggravated felony conviction that pre-dates November 29, 1990 may still be deportable as aggravated felons. It has been clear for some time that persons convicted of an aggravated felony after November 18, 1988 are

---

[Section 7:39]

[1] INA § 101(f)(8), 8 U.S.C.A. § 1101(f)(8); Matter of Reyes, 20 I. & N. Dec. 789, 792 (B.I.A. 1994).

[2] IA90 § 509; Reyes, 20 I. & N. Dec. at 792; 8 CFR § 316.10(b)(1)(ii).

[3] INA § 101(f)(8), 8 U.S.C.A. § 1101(f)(8) as originally enacted by Act of June 27, 1952. IA90 § 509(a) replaced the words "the crime of murder" in subsection (f)(8) of the good moral character definition by inserting instead the phrase "an aggravated felony (as defined in subsection (a)(43)".

[4] Sec. 306(a)(7) of the Miscellaneous and Technical Immigration and Naturalization Amendments of 1991, Act of Dec. 12, 1991, Pub. L. No. 102-232, 105 Stat. 1733 (amending IA90 § 509(b)); Castiglia v. I.N.S., 108 F.3d 1101 (9th Cir. 1997); 8 CFR § 316.10(b)(1)(i).

[5] See Matter of Reyes, 20 I. & N. Dec. 789, 1994 WL 193367 (B.I.A. 1994) (pre-IIRAIRA holding that those aggravated felonies between the enactment of the 1988 definition of aggravated felony and the enactment of the 1990 act did not permanently bar the subjects from proving good moral character).

[6] Matter of Ortiz, Case No. A73 996 367 (B.I.A., August 12, 1997) (unpublished decision) ("We do not concur with the Immigration Judge's finding that the lead respondent is statutorily ineligible for voluntary departure, and we will grant such relief. We note that due to the date of the respondent's aggravated felony conviction for which he was imprisoned from 1986 to 1988, he is not precluded from establishing the requisite good moral character under section 101(f)(8) or section 244(e) of the Act").

[7] Legal Opinion, Martin, INS General Counsel, File No. Genco Opinion 96-16 (Dec. 3, 1996) reprinted in 74 Interpreter Releases 1530 (Oct. 6, 1997).

[8] 8 CFR § 316.10(b)(1)(ii).

[9] Legal Opinion, Martin (Oct. 6, 1997). See also §§ 7:40 to 7:46.

[10] Alocozy v. U.S. Citizenship and Immigration Services, 704 F.3d 795 (9th Cir. 2012).

[11] See Martin, Legal Opinion (Oct. 6, 1997).

deportable.[12] The BIA has extended this finding, concluding that a conviction that fits the definition of aggravated felonies makes the person deportable regardless of the date of the conviction.[13] Thus, under the Board's interpretation, convictions entered prior to November 18, 1988 also make the noncitizen deportable.[14] The Board's interpretation has been upheld in several circuits under varying reasoning, but has been rejected in the Ninth Circuit.[15] In addition, even if not deportable as an aggravated felon, the applicant may be deportable on other criminal grounds.[16]

There is an extended discussion of aggravated felonies in Chapter 8.[17]

C. THE RESIDUAL CLAUSE: OTHER BASES FOR DETERMINING LACK OF GOOD MORAL CHARACTER

§ 7:40 In general

In addition to the statutory grounds, the statute itself provides that a person may be found to lack good moral character even if the person does not fit within any of the seven numbered categories.[1] This residual category should not be construed as an afterthought by Congress. Even though the requirement of good moral character has existed in the naturalization context since 1790,[2] prior to 1952 there was no statutory definition of good moral character.[3] Good moral character determinations were made according to the facts of each case applying the standard of the average person in the community.[4] In determining whether an applicant possessed good moral character under the general category, the applicant was not required to prove outstanding moral character but simply that his or her behavior measured up to the standards of the average citizen in the community.[5]

The USCIS has adopted this standard in its determinations of good moral character under this residual category.[6] Each applicant's good moral character must be evaluated on a case-by-case basis.[7] If the applicant is not precluded from establishing good moral character by statute, the USCIS applies the standard of the

---

[12]Matter of A-A-, 20 I. & N. Dec. 492 (B.I.A. 1992).

[13]In re Lettman, 22 I. & N. Dec. 365, 1998 WL 811588 (B.I.A. 1998).

[14]In re Lettman, 22 I. & N. Dec. 365, 1998 WL 811588 (B.I.A. 1998).

[15]Compare Lettman v. Reno, 207 F.3d 1368, 1370-72 (11th Cir.2000) (deferring to Board's interpretation); Lewis v. INS, 194 F.3d 539, 545-46 (4th Cir.1999) (same), with Bell v. Reno, 218 F.3d 86 (2d Cir.2000) (rejecting Board's analysis but reaching same ultimate conclusion by different line of reasoning); cf. Ledezma-Galicia v. Holder, 599 F.3d 1055 (9th Cir. 2010) (rejecting the Board's analysis).

[16]See INA § 237(a)(2), 8 U.S.C.A. § 1227(a)(2). See § 6:6, discussing of grounds of deportability that do not bar good moral character.

[17]See §§ 8:11 to 8:17.

[Section 7:40]

[1]INA § 101(f), 8 U.S.C.A. § 1101(f).

[2]See sec. 1, Act of March 26, 1790, reproduced as Appendix 4-1 to Ch 4.

[3]Matter of Gantus-Bobadilla, 13 I. & N. Dec. 777, 778, 1971 WL 24423 (B.I.A. 1971) (overruled by, Matter of Franklin, 20 I. & N. Dec. 867, 1994 WL 520990 (B.I.A. 1994)).

[4]Matter of Gantus-Bobadilla, 13 I. & N. Dec. 777, 778, 1971 WL 24423 (B.I.A. 1971) (overruled by, Matter of Franklin, 20 I. & N. Dec. 867, 1994 WL 520990 (B.I.A. 1994)).

[5]Matter of T-, 1 I. & N. Dec. 158, 159 (B.I.A. 1941); Matter of B-, 1 I. & N. Dec. 611, 612 (B.I.A. 1943).

[6]8 CFR § 316.10(a)(2); INS Interp. 316.1(e)(1).

[7]8 CFR § 316.10(a)(2).

average citizen in the community of residence to determine whether the applicant complies with the good moral character requirement.[8]

The evaluation of present good moral character allows for the examination of bad conduct in the past, even when it predates the statutory period of required good moral character.[9] In some cases, a person's conduct throughout his or her life may be relevant.[10] In making such a determination under this category, the BIA is required to consider all the relevant factors before arriving at a conclusion of whether the person has established good moral character.[11] A single lapse of conduct, even within the statutorily required period of good moral character, will not necessarily bar the person from establishing good moral character.[12] The BIA holds, however, that the more serious the past misconduct of the person, the longer the period of intervening good conduct of the applicant needs to be to establish good moral character.[13]

This BIA position may not pass muster with reviewing courts however. Several courts have held that the applicant's conduct prior to the statutory period may not be the sole basis for denial of naturalization.[14] Even when an applicant has a long history of criminal violations, if he or she is not statutorily precluded from establishing good moral character, the USCIS may not deny an application without allowing the applicant to establish good moral character through "exemplary conduct with every evidence of reformation and subsequent good moral character" from the beginning of the statutory period of good moral character.[15] The longer and more serious the history of criminal violations, the harder it would be to establish good moral character. This does not necessarily translate into a long period of good moral character, however. If the applicant is able to carry this burden, naturalization must be granted.

In some instances, such as when the form of relief only requires demonstration of good moral character at present, the statutory bars contained in section 101(f) will

---

[8]8 CFR § 316.10(a)(2).

[9]INA § 316(e), 8 U.S.C.A. § 1427(e); 8 CFR § 316.10(a)(2); Matter of Sanchez-Linn, 20 I. & N. Dec. 362, 365, 1991 WL 353523 (B.I.A. 1991).

[10]Matter of Sanchez-Linn, 20 I. & N. Dec. 362, 365, 1991 WL 353523 (B.I.A. 1991).

[11]Torres-Guzman v. I.N.S., 804 F.2d 531, 533 (9th Cir. 1986); Gonzalez-Ruano v. I.N.S., Case No. 96-70616 (9th Cir., April 21, 1997) (unpublished decision).

[12]Matter of Gantus-Bobadilla, 13 I. & N. Dec. 777, 778, 1971 WL 24423 (B.I.A. 1971) (overruled by, Matter of Franklin, 20 I. & N. Dec. 867, 1994 WL 520990 (B.I.A. 1994)); Matter of T-, 1 I. & N. Dec. 158, 159, 1941 WL 7934 (B.I.A. 1941); Matter of B-, 1 I. & N. Dec. 611, 612, 1943 WL 6344 (B.I.A. 1943).

[13]Matter of Sanchez-Linn, 20 I. & N. Dec. 362, 365, 1991 WL 353523 (B.I.A. 1991).

[14]See Santamaria-Ames v. I.N.S., 104 F.3d 1127 (9th Cir. 1996) citing to Marcantonio v. U.S., 185 F.2d 934, 937 (4th Cir. 1950) (under predecessor to 8 U.S.C.A. § 1427, naturalization cannot be denied solely based on crimes committed prior to statutory period); Tan v, INS, 931 F.Supp. 725, 729–732 (D.Haw. 1996) (under 8 CFR § 329.2(d) and 8 U.S.C.A. § 1440, courts cannot use events outside the one-year regulatory period in denying naturalization application); Suey Chin, 173 F.Supp. 510, 512 (S.D.N.Y. 1959) (petitioner's conduct prior to statutory period may not be sole basis for denial of naturalization under 8 U.S.C.A. § 1440). But see, Nyari v. Napolitano, 562 F.3d 916, 923 (8th Cir. 2009) ("The district court could find that Nyari is not a person of good moral character if it determines that he sexually abused his daughters and that his 'conduct . . . during the statutory period does not reflect that there has been reform of character' "); Molsen v. Young, 182 F.2d 480, 483 (5th Cir. 1950) (under predecessor to 8 U.S.C.A. § 1427, statutory period is the minimum period in which good moral character must be demonstrated because the statutory period is "at least" five years), vacated on other grounds, 340 U.S. 880, 71 S.Ct. 195, 95 L.Ed.2d 639 (1950).

[15]Santamaria-Ames v. I.N.S., 104 F.3d 1127, 1132 (9th Cir. 1996).

not be directly applicable. Applicants who have engaged in conduct within the scope of the statutory bars included in section 101(f) may still be found to lack good moral character under the residual category unless they present compelling evidence that their character has changed.[16] Similarly, even though expungements, pardons, and the petty offense exemption negate some convictions for purposes of the statutory bars to good moral character, the conduct underlying those convictions will be considered in evaluating the good moral character of the individual under the residual category.[17] As the Ninth Circuit has explained, the fact that a conviction was expunged does not mean that the individual did not commit the crime or engage in the in the underlying behavior, all of which would be relevant to determination of the individual's moral character.[18] Even when the DHS has reached the conclusion that the person is not deportable under the INA, the person may still be found to lack good moral character.[19]

§ 7:41 Negative factors considered in regulations

Research References
Dizon and Wettstein, Immigration Law Service 2d § 14:156

The USCIS has singled out in its regulations certain circumstances that would preclude a finding of good moral character in naturalization cases unless the applicant establishes extenuating circumstances.[1] These are not automatic, however, and must involve a weighing of all relevant factors, as the USCIS is not allowed to add to the *per se* statutory categories.[2]

These circumstances are (1) willfully failing or refusing to support dependents; (2) having an extramarital affair which tended to destroy an existing marriage; and (3) committing unlawful acts that reflect adversely upon the applicant's moral character even though those acts do not statutorily bar the applicant from establishing good moral character.[3] These regulatory grounds derive from long standing positions of the former INS that are described in more detail in the *INS Interpretations*.[4]

Finding of lack of good moral character based on refusal to support dependents has a long history in judicial naturalization.[5] However, courts did not use this as an automatic rule. Petitioners were found to be eligible for naturalization even when

---

[16]See Matter of Sanchez-Linn, 20 I. & N. Dec. 362, 366, 1991 WL 353523 (B.I.A. 1991); *see also* Rico v. I.N.S., 262 F. Supp. 2d 6 (E.D.N.Y. 2003) (finding lack of good moral character for individual with five DUI's, only one of which was during the statutory period, where applicant failed to accept responsibility for past crimes, failed to show rehabilitation and exhibited a lack of candor during testimony).

[17]See § 8:6, § 8:7, and § 7:27.

[18]U.S. v. Hovsepian, 359 F.3d 1144 (9th Cir. 2004) (en banc).

[19]INA § 316(d), 8 U.S.C.A. § 1427(d).

[Section 7:41]

[1]8 CFR § 316.10(b)(3).

[2]See Torres-Guzman v. I.N.S., 804 F.2d 531, 534 (9th Cir. 1986).

[3]8 CFR § 316.10(b)(3).

[4]See INS Interp. 316.1(f)(5), (6), (g)(2)(vi).

[5]See In re Halas, 274 F.Supp. 604 (D.Pa. 1967); Petition of Spak, 164 F. Supp. 257 (E.D. Pa. 1958); Petition of Spak, 164 F. Supp. 257 (E.D. Pa. 1958); U.S. v. Konevitch, 67 F.Supp. 250 (M.D.Pa. 1946).

they had willfully stopped payment of child support, provided the surrounding circumstances failed to indicate lack of good moral character.[6]

Income tax fraud is presumably one example of an unlawful act that reflects negatively on the person's moral character.[7] On the one hand, a factfinder could determine that the applicant lacks good moral character even when a court dismissed the criminal tax fraud proceedings.[8] On the other hand, it has been held that an applicant's unpaid debts owed to individuals, even when subject to a civil court order, are not by themselves sufficient to establish lack of good moral character.[9]

The new N-400 includes questions designed to uncover an applicant's failure to pay child support.[10]

§ 7:42 Special circumstances—Sexual orientation

Research References

Dizon and Wettstein, Immigration Law Service 2d §§ 14:157 to 14:159, 14:161

The *INS Interpretations* discuss other considerations that have not been directly adopted by the regulations. First, the *Interpretations* point out that the fact that the applicant has been a practicing homosexual during the relevant statutory period will not bar the applicant from being a person of good moral character unless the homosexual acts (1) involved minors; (2) involved the use of threat or fraud; (3) involved the taking or giving of money or anything of value; (4) took place in public or involved solicitation in a public place; or (5) violated a marital vow.[1]

The INS Interpretation was adopted long before the Supreme Court's decision in *Lawrence v. Texas*[2] which struck down all laws prohibiting homosexual sodomy on Due Process grounds. Given that the INS Interpretation applies, on its face, only to homosexual conduct, it might appear to be a sexual orientation-based discriminatory rule, and is of dubious constitutionality. That said, the interpretation was designed to meet the interests of uniformity in the immigration laws, at a time when many states did not criminalize homosexuality; if the USCIS argues that these five considerations would render heterosexual conduct equally offensive, the interpretation may well be upheld by the courts, if and when it is challenged.

§ 7:43 Special circumstances—Receipt of public benefits

The *Interpretations* also discuss when receipt of public welfare may be considered as affecting good moral character. Such receipt of public benefits will only affect good moral character when it amounts to affirmative misconduct resembling fraud. The good moral character of a petitioner will be considered when the petitioner,

---

[6]In re Valad, 465 F.Supp. 120 (D.Va., 1979).

[7]Matter of Locicero, 11 I. & N. Dec. 805 (B.I.A. 1966).

[8]Matter of Locicero, 11 I. & N. Dec. 805 (B.I.A. 1966).

[9]Puciaty v. U.S. Dept. of Justice, I.N.S., 125 F. Supp. 2d 1035 (D. Haw. 2000).

[10]See 60 Fed. Reg. 31325 (June 14, 1995) (Draft Supplement A to Form N-400, question 5).

[Section 7:42]

[1]INS Interp. 316.1(f)(7). This position derives from the requirement of uniformity in naturalization cases as explained in Nemetz v. Immigration and Naturalization Service, 647 F.2d 432, 435–36 (4th Cir. 1981).

[2]Lawrence v. Texas, 539 U.S. 558, 123 S. Ct. 2472, 156 L. Ed. 2d 508 (2003).

during the statutory period, obtained benefits while (1) failing to fully disclose to the authorities his or her assets and income and support payments from his or her former spouse, (2) failing to disclose his or her true marital status, and (3) contending that he or she acted in good faith in believing that he or she earned less than the amount required to be reported.[1] Indigence, in and of itself, is not a bar to naturalization.[2]

§ 7:44 Special circumstances—Immigration violations

Repeated immigration violations by themselves do not necessarily establish lack of good moral character.[1] However, an immigration violation will be considered as establishing lack of good moral character when it includes circumstances tending to establish immigration fraud.[2]

§ 7:45 Special circumstances—Selective service

Research References

Dizon and Wettstein, Immigration Law Service 2d § 14:160

The legacy INS originally took the position that if an applicant willfully failed to register for the selective service when required to do so within the statutory period of good moral character, the applicant will be found to lack good moral character.[1] More recently, it has added the interpretation that "it is [agency] policy that refusal to or knowing and willful failure to register for selective service during the period for which an applicant is required to prove his compliance with § 316(a)(3) supports a finding that the applicant is not eligible for naturalization because he has failed to establish his willingness to bear arms when required and his disposition to the good order and happiness of the United States."[2]

All men between the ages of 18 and 26 must register for military service.[3] Male applicants for naturalization over the age of 26 will be required to establish that while they were between the ages of 18 and 26, they either were exempt from the

---

[Section 7:43]

[1] INS Interp. 316.1(f)(8).

[2] INS Interp. 316.1(f)(8). citing Weber v. U.S., 119 F.2d 932 (1941), aff'd 315 U.S. 787, reh'g denied 316 U.S. 710. An advocate has pointed out that the San Francisco offices of INS reiterated this position when it approved the case of a naturalization applicant who had received refugee assistance and AFDC over a span of 15 years. Letter, Susan Bowyer, ILRC (Jan. 12, 1995).

[Section 7:44]

[1] Matter of Lee, 17 I. & N. Dec. 275, 277–78 (Commissioner 1978) (several instances of entry without inspection for which granted voluntary departure and one deportation); Matter of Carbajal, 17 I. & N. Dec. 272, 273–74 (Commissioner 1978) (sailor who made repeated attempts to desert his ship in the U.S. and was finally successful on his fifth attempt); Matter of T-, 1 I. & N. Dec. 158 (three deportations and two convictions for reentry after deportation).

[2] Matter of Pimentel, 17 I. & N. Dec. 482 (B.I.A. 1980).

[Section 7:45]

[1] See Letter from R. Michael Miller, INS Deputy Assistant Commissioner, to Robert F. Belluscio, Esq. (Oct. 19, 1987), reprinted in 64 Interpreter Releases 1330 (Nov. 23, 1987).

[2] Virtue, General Counsel, INS, Legal Opinion, File No. HQCOU 90/15-P, HQCOU 70/33-P (no date), reproduced in 76 Interpreter Releases 573 (April 12, 1999); Yates, Deputy Executive Assoc. Comm'r, Field Operations, Memorandum, June 18, 1999 reproduced in AILA InfoNet.

[3] 50 App. U.S.C.A. § 4531.

registration requirements, they fulfilled the requirements, or their failure to register was not knowing or willful. Inability to satisfy this requirement does not result in an automatic denial of naturalization, but it bears upon the applicant's good moral character and attachment to the principles of the Constitution.[4]

Persons can inquire about their selective service number or obtain proof of registration by calling (847) 688-6888 or (847) 688-2576 between 7:30 a.m. and 3:30 p.m. central time.[5] The inquirer must provide a date of birth and social security number.[6] Written inquiries may be sent to: Registration Information Office, Selective Service System, Data Management Center, P.O. Box 94638, Palatine, IL 60094-4638.[7] This is also the address and telephone number an applicant will use to inquire for "status information" even when he did not register before reaching age 26.[8] Public and congressional inquiries may be addressed to: Public and Congressional Affairs, Selective Service System, 1515 Wilson Blvd., Arlington, Virginia 22209-2425; telephone: (703) 605-4100; facsimile: (703) 605-4106.[9]

Since applicants have until age 26 to register for the selective service, they cannot be found to have willfully failed to register until they are over that age. If general naturalization male applicants between the ages of 26 and 31 fail to provide evidence that they registered for the selective service, the INS will require them to fill out a questionnaire and send it to the selective service.[10] In response, the selective service will send the applicant a letter stating that their records show no registration on his part. Recent selective service letters have also added that in absence of evidence to the contrary, the selective service will assume that such failure to register was knowing and willful. Obviously, such letters do *not* establish willful failure to register for the selective service. Applicants who receive such letters from the selective service will be well advised, when filing the letter with the USCIS, to attach a declaration regarding their lack of knowledge of the requirement to register for the selective service or any other circumstance tending to establish that failure to register was not willful.

USCIS offices vary greatly as to the amount of evidence they will require to overcome the "willfulness" threshold. It has been reported that some suboffices have even issued blanket denials without considering the "willfulness" of the failure to register.[11] This is obviously illegal and should be challenged. Federal law specifically states that a person *may not* be denied any right, privilege or benefit under federal law if the person shows by *preponderance of the evidence* that the failure was not knowing and willful.[12] Indeed, the Office of Field Operations of the legacy INS has issued a memorandum advising officers that they "must consider all persuasive evi-

---

[4]Letter from R. Michael Miller, Oct. 19, 1987.

[5]Selective Service System Web Page, http://www.sss.gov/contact.htm.

[6]Selective Service System Web Page, http://www.sss.gov/contact.htm.

[7]Selective Service System Web Page, http://www.sss.gov/contact.htm.

[8]Selective Service System Web Page, http://www.sss.gov/men26.htm.

[9]Selective Service System Web Page, http://www.sss.gov/contact.htm.

[10]Naturalization applicants under the provision relating to spouses of U.S. citizens are only required to prove good moral character for a period of three years preceding naturalization. See §§ 11:2 to 11:5. Thus, in these cases only male applicants between the ages of 26 and 29 will be required to fill out this questionnaire.

[11]See Immigrant Legal Resources Center (ILRC), Naturalization Guide, 1997 Update to Chapter 6.

[12]50 App. U.S.C.A. § 462(g) ("A person may not be denied a right, privilege, or benefit under Federal law by reason of failure to present himself for and submit registration under section 3 if (1)

dence presented by the applicant relating to his failure to register" and that at a minimum, they must "take a statement under oath from an applicant in order to determine whether or not failure to register was knowing and willful."[13]

The Selective Service General Counsel has issued a generic letter to present to the USCIS, explaining that an applicant may *not* be denied a federal benefit if he can demonstrate that his failure to register was not knowing or willful.[14] It points out that the "[USCIS] has the duty to determine whether you have shown 'by the preponderance of the evidence'" that failure to register was not knowing and willful.[15] If the USCIS makes the determination that the applicant made the required showing, then the USCIS is prohibited from denying naturalization on this basis.[16] The letter is reproduced as Appendix 7-15.

When failure to register was willful, the general naturalization applicant will either have to wait until reaching the age of thirty-one, or will have to convince the USCIS that weighing the rest of his behavior during the required period, the applicant is a person of good moral character. Apparently to prevent this possibility, the USCIS has instructed regional and district directors to "state explicitly that the [USCIS] has found that [the applicant's] willful failure to register with selective service means he cannot show that, during the requisite period before filing his application, he was not well disposed to the good order and happiness of the United States."[17] It then instructs them to cite to INA § 316(a)(3).[18]

Failure to register must be distinguished from desertion and obtaining relief from service on the basis of alienage which are both bars to naturalization.[19] Indeed, the DHS has been warned not to analogize failure to register to those bars.[20]

§ 7:46 Special circumstances—Probation

Research References

Dizon and Wettstein, Immigration Law Service 2d § 14:148

On the one hand, having been on probation for part of the statutory period required for good moral character will not prevent a person from naturalizing.[1] On the other hand, the USCIS takes the position that it will not grant a naturalization

---

the requirement for the person to so register has terminated or become inapplicable to the person; and (2) the person shows by a preponderance of the evidence that the failure of the person to register was not a knowing and willful failure to register") cited in ILRC, Naturalization Guide, 1997 Update to Chapter 6. This same standard is reflected in the advice to the men who failed to register before reaching twenty-six posted on the Selective Service web site. See http://www.sss.gov/men26.htm.

[13]Yates, Memorandum, June 18, 1999.

[14]Williams, General Counsel, Selective Service System, Undated Letter attached as Appendix 7-11.

[15]Williams, General Counsel, Selective Service System, Undated Letter attached as Appendix 7-11.

[16]Williams, General Counsel, Selective Service System, Undated Letter attached as Appendix 7-11.

[17]Yates, Memorandum, June 18, 1999.

[18]Yates, Memorandum, June 18, 1999.

[19]See §§ 7:77 to 7:83.

[20]Virtue, Legal Opinion reproduced in 76 Interpreter Releases 562, 573 (April 12, 1999).

[Section 7:46]

[1]8 CFR § 316.10(c)(1).

application while a person is still on probation.[2] At least two courts have upheld the regulation barring naturalization while an individual is on probation.[3]

V. ATTACHMENT TO THE PRINCIPLES OF THE U.S. CONSTITUTION

A. GENERAL RULES

§ 7:47 In general

Research References

Dizon and Wettstein, Immigration Law Service 2d §§ 14:162, 14:163
Steel on Immigration Law § 15:14

There are three requirements which go to the "political acceptability" of the applicant seeking to be naturalized: (1) attachment to the principles of the U.S. Constitution; (2) the bar against the naturalization of members of certain political parties and advocates of certain political positions; and (3) the mental attitude required in taking the naturalization oath. The bar to naturalization for people espousing particular political beliefs is discussed below dealing with bars to naturalization.[1] The mental attitude required at the naturalization oath will be discussed in the naturalization procedures chapter.[2]

The requirement that the naturalization applicant be "attached to the principles of the Constitution of the United States, and well disposed to the good order and happiness of the same" has existed since the Naturalization Act of 1795.[3] The current statute has an identical provision.[4] Just provided by the 1795 statute, under the current statute, this "attachment" and "disposition" must have been present during the whole statutorily-required period of residence for naturalization.[5]

§ 7:48 Test for political beliefs

Research References

Dizon and Wettstein, Immigration Law Service 2d § 14:163
Steel on Immigration Law § 15:14

In essence, whether a person is attached to the Constitution of the U.S. and well disposed to its good order and happiness is a political test. But this test must be

---

[2]8 CFR § 316.10(c)(1).

[3]Jimenez v. Eddy, 153 F. Supp. 2d 1105 (D. Alaska 2001); U.S. v. Kiang, 175 F. Supp. 2d 942 (E.D. Mich. 2001).

[Section 7:47]

[1]See §§ 7:52 to 7:76.

[2]See §§ 9:61 to 9:65.

[3]Sec. 1, Act of January 29, 1795 reproduced as Appendix 4-2 to Ch 4. The naturalization statutes up to 1940 required the applicant to "behave" as a person attached to the principles of the Constitution and well disposed to the good order, rather than to be attached to those principles. The courts have interpreted the two requirements as being the same, namely that even before 1940, the person must have been attached to the principles of the Constitution and not only behaved as such a person. Schneiderman v. U.S., 320 U.S. 118, 133 n.12, 135, 63 S.Ct. 1333, 1340 n.12, 1341, 87 L.Ed. 1796 (1943).

[4]INA § 316(a), 8 U.S.C.A. § 1427(a).

[5]INA § 316(a), 8 U.S.C.A. § 1427(a); sec. 1, Act of January 29, 1795 reproduced as Appendix 4-2 to Ch 4.

interpreted in accordance with the political tolerance espoused by the Constitution.[1] Unlike the bars to naturalization written into the INA, membership in a party is not by itself sufficient to support a finding of lack of attachment.[2]

The regulations define the requirement of attachment to the Constitution as implying a "depth of conviction which would lead to active support of the Constitution."[3] The test searches the "mental attitude" of the applicant to prevent the naturalization of those who are "hostile to the basic form of government of the United States, or who disbelieve in the principles of the Constitution."[4]

Even when phrased in such a positivistic form, the main issue still remains. What is the "basic form of government" of the U.S., and which are the "principles of the Constitution" which the person must disbelieve in order to lack attachment to the Constitution?[5] The Supreme Court tried to tackle these issues in *Schneiderman v. U.S.*, and found these concepts to be elusive as the Constitution itself provides for changing virtually any part of it through the amendment process.[6] As was later pointed out by the Supreme Court, the U.S. Constitution "was made for an undefined and expanding future . . . [it creates] a being the development of which could not have been foreseen completely by the most gifted of its begetters."[7] The main principle the Supreme Court found to be basic to the constitutional scheme was that of freedom of thought; which meant "not free thought for those who agree with us but freedom for the thought we hate."[8]

The regulations outline the minimum requirements to prove attachment to the Constitution. The applicant is required to demonstrate "an acceptance of the democratic, representative process established by the Constitution, a willingness to obey the laws which may result from that process, and an understanding of the means of change which are prescribed by the Constitution."[9] This definition is a variation on one that was originally formulated by the Southern District of New York and adopted by the Northern District of Illinois. It provided that "[a]ttachment to the principles of the Constitution means an acceptance of the fundamental political habits and attitudes which prevail in the United States and a willingness to

---

[Section 7:48]

[1]Schneiderman v. U.S., 320 U.S. 118, 135, 63 S. Ct. 1333, 1341, 87 L. Ed. 1796 (1943) ("'the behavior requirement is a general phrase which should be construed, not in opposition to, but in accord with, the theory and practice of our government in relation to freedom of conscience'") quoting U.S. v. MacIntosh, 283 U.S. 605, 635, 51 S.Ct. 570, 579, 75 L.Ed. 1302 (Hughes, C.J., dissenting).

[2]See Petition of Yee Wing Toon, 148 F. Supp. 657 (S.D. N.Y. 1957). See generally, Schneiderman v. U.S., 320 U.S. 118, 63 S. Ct. 1333, 87 L. Ed. 1796 (1943). Mere membership is not sufficient even under the Communist party membership bar. See § 7:68 (discussion of Meaningful Association in "Membership in the Communist Party or a Totalitarian Organization").

[3]8 CFR § 316.11(a).

[4]8 CFR § 316.11(a).

[5]As was pointed out by the Ninth Circuit, "[a]ttachment to the Constitution is an especially nebulous concept, not easy of definition." Tauchen v. Barber, 183 F.2d 266, 268 (9th Cir. 1950).

[6]Schneiderman v. U.S., 320 U.S. 118, 137, 63 S. Ct. 1333, 1343, 87 L. Ed. 1796 (1943).

[7]Baumgartner v. U.S., 322 U.S. 665, 673, 64 S.Ct. 1240, 1244, 88 L.Ed. 1525 (1944) (citations omitted).

[8]Schneiderman v. U.S., 320 U.S. 118, 138, 63 S. Ct. 1333, 1343, 87 L. Ed. 1796 (1943) quoting U.S. v. Schwimmer, 279 U.S. 644, 49 S.Ct. 448, 73 L.Ed. 889 (Holmes, J., dissenting).

[9]8 CFR § 316.11(b).

obey the laws which may result from them."[10] Neither of these tests requires an affection for the democratic process, or even approval of it; acceptance and willingness to obey the laws are sufficient.[11]

It is not clear, however, that even the core elements of the structure of the U.S. government identified by the USCIS in its regulations would pass the statutory test set up by the Supreme Court. The Supreme Court has found a person attached to the U.S. Constitution in spite of his or her advocacy of such deep-rooted changes in the structure of the U.S. government as the abolition of the Senate, the Supreme Court, and the veto power of the President, and the replacement of congressional districts with "councils of workers" which would have both legislative and executive functions, did not constitute sufficient changes to evince that the person was not attached to the principles of the Constitution.[12]

§ 7:49 Problem of advocacy of political change

According to the regulations, working for political change in the U.S. is not contradictory with attachment to the Constitution "if the changes advocated would not abrogate the current Government and establish an entirely different form of government."[1] This definition begs the question since, as pointed out by the Supreme Court, given the structural changes allowed by Article V of the Constitution, it is difficult to envision what an "entirely different form of government" would mean.[2]

Some courts have taken the position that advocacy of political change, even when it involves a complete transformation of the U.S. government, will not disqualify the applicant from naturalization provided the applicant believes this change should take place in a nonviolent form.[3] This seems to be the logical conclusion from the Supreme Court position in *Schneiderman*.[4] On the other hand, other courts take the position that persons will not be found to be attached to the principles of the Constitution if they advocate the suppression of the principles of free speech and freedom of thought, even when they envision arriving to such state of affairs through peaceful means.[5]

The requirement that advocacy of change must be limited to nonviolent change is only applicable to change in the U.S. government. Advocacy, and even direct action, in attempting to overthrow a foreign government by force does not prevent a finding of attachment to the U.S. Constitution.[6] Note, however, that such action—or association with an organization that carries out such action—could be a ground of

---

[10]In re Burke, 335 F.Supp. 563, 565 (N.D.Ill, 1971) citing to In re Sittler's Petition, 197 F.Supp. 278, 280 (S.D.N.Y. 1961) aff'd 316 F.2d 312 (2d Cir. 1963), cert. denied, 376 U.S. 932, 84 S.Ct. 702, 11 L.Ed.2d 652 (1964). Cf. Stasiukevich v. Nicolls, 168 F.2d 474, 478 (1st Cir. 1948) (adopting a test similar to that of the INS regulations).

[11]In re Naturalization of Arbesu, 347 F.Supp. 1014, 1016 (E.D.La, 1972) citing to U.S. v. Rossler, 144 F.2d 463 (2d Cir. 1944); U.S. v. Siegel, 59 F.Supp. 183 (D.Conn. 1945) aff'd 152 F.2d 614 (2d Cir. 1945), cert. denied, 328 U.S. 868, 66 S.Ct. 1361, 90 L.Ed. 1639 (1946).

[12]Schneiderman v. U.S., 320 U.S. 118, 143, 63 S. Ct. 1333, 1345, 87 L. Ed. 1796 (1943).

[Section 7:49]

[1]8 CFR § 316.11(b).

[2]See § 7:48.

[3]U.S. v. Rossler, 114 F.2d at 465 (L. Hand, J.).

[4]See § 7:48.

[5]Stasiukevich v. Nicolls, 168 F.2d 474, 477–78 (C.C.A. 1st Cir. 1948).

[6]In re Arbesu, 347 F. Supp. 1014 (E.D. La. 1972); In re Pruna, 286 F.Supp. 861 (D.P.R. 1968).

inadmissibility and/or deportability if the action falls within the INA definition of terrorist activity.[7]

§ 7:50 Refusing to comply with certain political acts

Unwillingness to bear arms because of religious or philosophical reasons does not necessarily mean the applicant is not attached to the principles of the Constitution or well disposed toward good order and happiness of the United States.[1] The INA specifically allows modification of the oath of allegiance to take into consideration conscientious objectors.[2] Similarly, unwillingness to vote, serve in a jury, or otherwise participate in government because of religious belief does not necessarily evince lack of attachment or favorable disposition.[3] Even refusal to testify before the House Un-American Activities Committee has been held not to prove lack of attachment to the U.S. Constitution.[4]

The legacy INS espoused the position that willful failure to register for Selective Service is a sufficient basis to find that the person is not well disposed to the good order and happiness of the United States.[5] This position and other issues relating to failure to register for Selective Service are discussed in more detail in the section on good moral character.[6]

§ 7:51 Evidentiary issues

An applicant is required to disclose all organizations to which he or she has belonged.[1] Membership in some political organizations, such as the Communist party, even though not necessarily evincing lack of attachment to the U.S. Constitution, will bar the applicant from naturalizing.[2] Association with an organization that engages in terrorist activity, as this phrase is defined in the INA, could be both a bar to naturalization and a ground of deportability.[3] Furthermore, the INA provides that joining a Communist, anarchist, or subversive organization within five years after naturalization is *prima facie* proof that the person was not attached to

---

[7]*See* INA §§ 212(a)(3)(B) and (F), 8 U.S.C.A. §§ 1182(a)(3)(B) and (F); see also, §§ 7:59, 7:72.

[Section 7:50]

[1]Girouard v. U.S., 328 U.S. 61, 66 S.Ct. 826, 90 L.Ed. 1084 (1946). Cf. U.S. v. Seeger, 380 U.S. 163, 85 S.Ct. 850, 13 L.Ed.2d 733 (1965); Welsh v. U.S., 398 U.S. 333, 90 S.Ct. 1792, 26 L.Ed.2d 308 (1970) (expanding conscientious objector exemption under the Military Training and Service Act to include deeply held moral or ethical beliefs).

[2]INA § 337(a), 8 U.S.C.A. § 1448(a). See generally, Gordon & Mailman, § 96.08[2].

[3]INS Interp. 316.1(h)(3)(iv).

[4]In re Burke, 335 F.Supp. 563 (N.D.Ill. 1971).

[5]Yates, Memorandum, June 18, 1999, Virtue, General Counsel, INS, Legal Opinion, April 27, 1998 reproduced on AILA InfoNet at http://www.aila.org.

[6]See § 7:45.

[Section 7:51]

[1]Price v. U.S. INS, 941 F.2d 878 (9th Cir. 1991); *see also* U.S. v. Hovsepian, 359 F.3d 1144 (9th Cir. 2004) (en banc) (finding that district court erred in failing to consider naturalization applicant's refusal to answer questions about current affiliations with terrorist groups).

[2]See § 7:67.

[3]See INA §§ 237(a)(4)(B) [8 U.S.C.A. § 1227(a)(4)(B)]; see also, § 7:72.

the Constitution of the United States and was not well disposed to the good order and happiness of the United States at the time of naturalization.[4]

B. COMMUNISM, TOTALITARIANISM, AND TERRORISM

1. In General

§ 7:52 Statutory history

These politico-ideological bars developed as a supplement to the requirement of attachment to the Constitution of the United States. Legislation barring the naturalization of anarchists was introduced in 1903.[1] This legislation was not changed until 1940, when the Nationality Act of 1940 expanded the bar to include persons who advocate the overthrow of the U.S. Government by force.[2] The Subversive Activities Control Act of 1950 amended the 1940 act to provide a broad-ranging bar against members of Communist and Communist-related organizations.[3] An amended version of these provisions was adopted by the INA.[4]

The politico-ideological bars to naturalization must also be viewed in relation to the requirement of attachment to the U.S. Constitution. Even when the person is not directly barred from obtaining citizenship under these bars, the person may lack the necessary attachment to the principles of the Constitution and therefore be ineligible for naturalization.[5]

§ 7:53 Overview of statutory provisions

Research References

Immigration Law Service 2d § 14:271

The INA prohibits the naturalization of certain persons because of their political beliefs and associations.[1] The INA prohibits the naturalization of persons who:[2]

(1) advocate or teach, or are members of or affiliated with any organization that advocates or teaches, opposition to all organized government;

(2) are members of or affiliated with:

(A) the Communist party of the United States;

(B) any other totalitarian party of the United States;

(C) the Communist Political Association;

(D) the Communist or other totalitarian party of any State of the United States, of any foreign state, or of any political or geographical subdivision of any foreign state;

(E) any section, subsidiary, branch, affiliate, or subdivision of any such association or party; or

---

[4]INA § 340(c), 8 U.S.C.A. § 1451(c).

[Section 7:52]

[1]Sec. 39, Act of March 3, 1903, Pub.L. 57-162, 32 Stat. 1213.

[2]Sec. 305, Nationality Act of 1940, Pub.L. 76-853, 54 Stat. 1137 (Oct. 14, 1940).

[3]Sec. 25, Subversive Activities Act of 1950, Pub.L. 81-831, 64 Stat. 987 (Sept. 23, 1950).

[4]See §§ 7:52 to 7:76.

[5]See §§ 7:47 to 7:51.

[Section 7:53]

[1]8 U.S.C.A. § 1424.

[2]INA § 313(a), 8 U.S.C.A. § 1424(a)(the text of the law has been pluralized to facilitate its understanding).

(F) the direct predecessors or successors of any such association or party, regardless of what name such group or organization may have used, may now bear, or may hereafter adopt, unless such noncitizens establish that they did not have knowledge or reason to believe at the time they became members of or affiliated with such an organization (and did not thereafter and prior to the date upon which such organization was so registered or so required to be registered have such knowledge or reason to believe) that such organization was a Communist-front organization;

(3) although not within any of the other provision of this section, advocate the economic, international, and governmental doctrines of world communism or the establishment in the United States of a totalitarian dictatorship, or who are members of or affiliated with an organization that advocates the economic, international, and governmental doctrines of world communism or the establishment in the United States of a totalitarian dictatorship, either through its own utterances or through any written or printed publications issued or published by or with the permission or consent of or under authority of such organizations or paid for by the funds of such organizations;

(4) advocate or teach or are members of or affiliated with any organization that advocates or teaches:

(A) the overthrow by force or violence or other unconstitutional means of the Government of the United States or of all forms of law;

(B) the duty, necessity, or propriety of the unlawful assaulting or killing of any officer or officers (either of specific individuals or of officers generally) of the Government of the United States or of any other organized government because of the applicants' or the government's official character;

(C) the unlawful damage, injury, or destruction of property; or

(D) sabotage;

(5) write or publish or cause to be written or published, or who knowingly circulate, distribute, print, or display, or knowingly cause to be circulated, distributed, printed, published, or displayed or knowingly have in their possession for the purpose of circulation, publication, distribution, or display, any written or printed matter, advocating or teaching opposition to all organized government, or advocating

(A) the overthrow by force, violence, or other unconstitutional means of the Government of the United States or of all forms of law;

(B) the duty, necessity, or propriety of the unlawful assaulting or killing of any officer or officers (either of specific individuals or of officers generally) of the Government of the United States or of any other organized government, because of the applicants' or the government's official character;

(C) the unlawful damage, injury, or destruction of property;

(D) sabotage; or

(E) the economic, international, and governmental doctrines of world communism or the establishment in the United States of a totalitarian dictatorship; or

(6) are members of or affiliated with any organization, that writes, circulates, distributes, prints, publishes, or displays, or causes to be written, circulated, distributed, printed, published, or displayed, or that has in its possession for the purpose of circulation, distribution, publication, issue, or display, any written or printed matter of the character described in 8 U.S.C.A. § 1424(a) (5).

The bar is not only applicable to persons who are within these categories at the time of naturalization, but to anybody who within ten years immediately preceding the filing of the application for naturalization, or after the filing and before taking the oath was within any such class.[3]

2. Analysis of the Bar

§ 7:54 Statutory and regulatory definitions—Generally

The basic definitions of terms related to this bar are contained in the INA and are elaborated upon by the agency regulations.[1] In addition, courts have further interpreted these terms.

§ 7:55 Statutory and regulatory definitions—Prohibited behavior—To advocate

Research References

Gallagher, Immigration Law Service 2d § 14:271

The statute defines the verb to "advocate" to include, but not be limited to, advising, recommending, furthering by an overt act, and admitting belief in.[1] In addition, the INA provides that for the purposes of the INA, "[t]he giving, loaning, or promising of support or of money or any other thing of value to be used for advocating any doctrine shall constitute the advocating of such doctrine; but [this is not] an exclusive definition of advocating."[2] The regulations simply reiterate this general definition.[3]

§ 7:56 Statutory and regulatory definitions—Prohibited behavior—To circulate

The regulations define the term "circulate" to include circulating, distributing, or displaying a work.[1]

§ 7:57 Statutory and regulatory definitions—Prohibited behavior—To publish

According to the regulations, the publication or publishing of a work includes writing or printing a work; permitting, authorizing, or consenting to the writing or printing of a work; and paying for the writing or printing of a work.[1]

---

[3]INA § 313(c), 8 U.S.C.A. § 1424(c).

[Section 7:54]

[1]*See, generally,* INA § 101(a), 8 U.S.C.A. § 1101(a); 8 CFR § 313.1.

[Section 7:55]

[1]INA § 101(a)(2), 8 U.S.C.A. § 1101(a)(2).

[2]INA § 101(e)(1), 8 U.S.C.A. § 1101(e)(1).

[3]8 CFR § 313.1.

[Section 7:56]

[1]8 CFR § 313.1.

[Section 7:57]

[1]8 CFR § 313.1.

§ 7:58 Statutory and regulatory definitions—Prohibited behavior—Affiliation

The INA includes a presumption within the definition of affiliation:[1]

The giving, loaning, or promising of support or of money or any other thing of value for any purpose to any organization shall be presumed to constitute affiliation therewith; but nothing in this paragraph shall be construed as an exclusive definition of affiliation.

The Supreme Court has interpreted the term "affiliation" in relation to a prior statute.[2] It has held that cooperation, even long-term cooperation, was not sufficient to establish affiliation with the organization.[3] In addition, a "meaningful association" with the proscribed organization is required before this bar may be applied.[4]

§ 7:59 Statutory and regulatory definitions—Prohibited behavior—Membership—Meaningful association

Probably the most important development in relation to this bar to naturalization is the court-established requirement that a person may not be barred from naturalizing unless membership or affiliation was "meaningful association" with the proscribed organization. Originally, the bars to naturalization had a virtually identical counterpart in the grounds of exclusion and deportation.[1] The Supreme Court elaborated that those grounds of exclusion and deportation would not apply unless the person's membership in the proscribed organization was "meaningful."[2] This same test applies to naturalization proceedings.[3]

The "meaningful association" test requires proof that the applicant's membership in the proscribed organization was more than the "voluntary listing of a person's name on the Party rolls."[4] There must be substantial proof that "an alien committed himself [or herself] to the Communist Party in consciousness that he was 'joining an organization known as The Communist Party which operates as a distinct and active political organization . . .'"[5] This requires establishing that the dominating impulse to the "affiliation" with the Communist party must have political

---

[Section 7:58]

[1]INA § 101(e)(2), 8 U.S.C.A. § 1101(e)(2). Cf. 8 CFR § 313.1 (adopting the same definition without further elaboration).

[2]See Bridges v. Wixon, 326 U.S. 135, 141-49, 65 S.Ct. 1443, 1446-50, 89 L.Ed. 2103 (1945).

[3]Bridges v. Wixon, 326 U.S. 135, 141-49, 65 S. Ct. 1443, 1446-50, 89 L. Ed. 2103 (1945).

[4]See Rowoldt v. Perfetto, 355 U.S. 115, 120, 78 S.Ct. 180, 183, 2 L.Ed.2d 140 (1957) ("the dominant impulse to his 'affiliation' with the Communist Party may well have been wholly devoid of any 'political' implications"). Cf. § 7:76.

[Section 7:59]

[1]INA §§ 212(a)(28), (29), 241(a)(6), (7), 8 U.S.C.A. §§ 1182(a)(28), (29), 1251(a)(6), (7) as originally enacted by Act of June 27, 1952, 66 Stat. 163.

[2]Rowoldt v. Perfetto, 355 U.S. 115, 78 S. Ct. 180, 2 L. Ed. 2d 140 (1957); Galvan v. Press, 347 U.S. 737, 527, 74 S.Ct. 737, 740-41, 98 L.Ed. 911 (1954).

[3]See Polites v. U.S., 364 U.S. 426, 436, 81 S.Ct. 202, 208, 5 L.Ed.2d 173 (1960). The USCIS has accepted that the same standard applies to naturalization applications, and unless it can be established that the person had a meaningful association with the proscribed organization, the person would not be barred from naturalizing. INS Interp. 313.2(b).

[4]Gastelnum-Quinones v. Kennedy, 374 U.S. 469, 474, 83 S.Ct. 1819, 1820, 1822, 10 L.Ed.2d 1013 (1963) quoting Scales v. U.S., 367 U.S. 203, 222, 81 S.Ct. 1469, 1483, 6 L.Ed.2d 782 (1961).

[5]Rowoldt v. Perfetto, 355 U.S. 115, 78 S. Ct. 180, 2 L. Ed. 2d 140 (1957).

implications.[6] There must be a showing that the person was "during the time of his or her membership, sensible to the Party's nature as a political organization, or [a showing] that he [or she] engaged in Party activities to a degree substantially supporting an inference of his awareness of the Party's political aspect."[7]

Thus, a person who was a member of the Communist party, ran the party's bookstore, paid his or her dues, attended meetings, and remained a member for approximately one year until detained and placed in deportation proceedings, was not considered to have had a meaningful association with the party.[8] Similarly, a person who for a period of approximately two years paid his or her dues, and attended several meetings of a club of the Communist party in Los Angeles, and attended at least on Communist party convention in Los Angeles, was not found to have had a meaningful association with the Communist party.[9]

At its most extreme, of course, are the cases of persons who join political movements or trade unions without knowing these organizations were dominated by the Communist party.[10] In such cases, there can be no "meaningful association" on the petitioner's part.[11] This applies even when the person was a local officer in a trade union, which was later found to be a Communist front organization.[12] In addition, when the identity of the organization and the Communist party is not clear to the person joining the organization, the separate issue of whether the movement or organization is an affiliate of the Communist party within the meaning of the INA should also be explored.[13]

This issue has become more complicated, however, with respect to organizations that fall within the INA definition of a terrorist organization.[14] There is some overlap between the bar to naturalization found in INA § 313(a)(4) and the grounds of inadmissibility and deportability based upon engagement in terrorist activity.[15] Thus, an individual who is a member of or affiliated with a terrorist organization could be both barred from naturalizing under INA §§ 313(a)(4), (5) or (6) (relating to political assaults and assassinations, sabotage, and the destruction of property) and also inadmissible or deportable. Significantly, however, due to recent expansion of the terrorism-related grounds of inadmissibility and deportability, conduct that might not bar an individual from naturalizing could nevertheless be a ground of inadmissibility or deportability. Thus, it is important for naturalization applicants

[6]Rowoldt v. Perfetto, 355 U.S. 115, 78 S. Ct. 180, 2 L. Ed. 2d 140 (1957).

[7]Gastelum-Quinones v. Kennedy, 374 U.S. 469, 477, 83 S. Ct. 1819, 1823, 10 L. Ed. 2d 1013 (1963). However, there is no requirement that the applicant support, or even demonstrate knowledge of, the Communist Party's advocacy of violence. Galvan v. Press, 347 U.S. 522, 528, 74 S. Ct. 737, 741, 98 L. Ed. 911 (1954).

[8]Rowoldt, 355 U.S. 115, 78 S.Ct. 180, 2 L.Ed.2d 140 (1957).

[9]Gastelnum-Quinones, 374 U.S. 469, 83 S.Ct. 1819, 10 L.Ed.2d 1013 (1963).

[10]In re Pruna, 286 F.Supp. 861 (D.P.R. 1968) (joined a movement which advocated a representative and democratic government); Matter of C-, 6 I. & N. Dec. 20, 54 (Att'y Gen. 1955) (person not deportable where he did not know of the relationship between his trade union, of which he was a local officer, and the Communist party).

[11]In re Pruna, 286 F. Supp. 861, 863 (D.P.R. 1968).

[12]Matter of C-, 6 I. & N. Dec. 20, 54, 1953 WL 7392 (B.I.A. 1953).

[13]See § 7:63.

[14]INA § 212(a)(3)(B)(vi), 8 U.S.C.A. § 1182(a)(3)(B)(vi).

[15]Cf. INA § 313(a)(4), 8 U.S.C.A. § 1424(a)(4) *with* INA § 212(a)(3)(B), 8 U.S.C.A. § 1182(a)(3)(B) and INA § 237(a)(4)(B), 8 U.S.C.A. § 1227(a)(4)(B).

to consider whether their organizational memberships or associations could subject them to removal proceedings.[16]

In the USA Patriot Act of 2001, Congress expanded the grounds of inadmissibility related to terrorist activity, including the addition of grounds of inadmissibility relating to "association" or "membership" with terrorist organizations.[17] In 2005, the REAL ID Act made this a ground of removability, as well as adding a provision to include those who "endorse[] or espouse[] terrorist activity,"[18]

Under the new provisions, a noncitizen is both inadmissible and removable if the Secretary of State or the Attorney General determine that the individual has been associated with a terrorist organization and intends while in the United States to engage solely, principally or incidentally in activities which could endanger the welfare, safety or security of the United States.[19] The USA Patriot Act defines a terrorist organization as including both organizations that have been officially designated as such, and any group of two or more individuals, whether organized or not, that commits or incites to commit terrorist activity, plans a terrorist activity, or gathers information on potential targets for terrorist activity.[20]

The USA Patriot Act also broadened the definition of engaging in terrorist activity to include associational type of activities, such as fundraising.[21] According to the former INS Commissioner, the USA Patriot Act amended the definition of engaging in terrorist activity in two principal ways. First, it clarified that a noncitizen's solicitation of funds or members for a terrorist organization constitutes engaging in terrorist activity, even if the noncitizen did not intend to further terrorist activity and/or did not know that the organization was a terrorist organization.[22] Second, it also included within the definition any acts that the noncitizen knows, or reasonably should know, would provide material support to a terrorist organization, even if the noncitizen did not specifically intend to support terrorist activity, and did not know (and should not reasonably have known) that the organization was a terrorist organization.[23] However, the Act does create an exception to both the solicitation of funds or members and the provision of material support. These activities will not be considered engaging in terrorist activities if (1) the organization was not designated as a terrorist organization at the time and (2) the noncitizen can demonstrate that

---

[16]The naturalization application specifically asks about an applicant's association with a terrorist organization. See Chapter 9 (The N-400: Question by Question Analysis: Part 10, Ineligibility Factors; Affiliations).

[17]Uniting and Strengthening America by Providing Appropriate Tools Required to Intercept and Obstruct Terrorism Act of 2001 (USA Patriot Act), Pub. L. No. 107-56 § 411(a)(2), 115 Stat. 272 (October 26, 2001) creating INA § 212(a)(3)(F), 8 U.S.C.A. § 1182(a)(3)(F).

[18]The REAL ID Act of 2005, Pub. L. 109-13, § 105(a)(1), 119 Stat. 309 (May 11, 2005), codified at INA § 237(a)(4)(B); 8 U.S.C.A. § 1227(a)(4)(B).

[19]INA § 212(a)(3)(F), 8 U.S.C.A. § 1182(a)(3)(F); INA § 237(a)(4)(B); 8 U.S.C.A. § 1227(a)(4)(B).

[20]USA Patriot Act, Pub. L. No. 107-56 § 411(a)(1)(G) creating INA § 212(a)(3)(B)(vi), 8 U.S.C.A. § 1182(a)(3)(B)(vi).

[21]USA Patriot Act, Pub. L. No. 107-56 § 411(a)(1)(F) amending INA § 212(a)(3)(B)(iv), 8 U.S.C.A. § 1182(a)(3)(B)(iv).

[22]Zigler, Commissioner, INS, Memorandum, October 31, 2001 attached as Appendix 7-14; see also, generally, Parlak v. Holder, 578 F.3d 457 (6th Cir. 2009); Holder v. Humanitarian Law Project, 130 S.Ct. 2705, 2725 (2010) ("Money is fungible").

[23]Zigler, Commissioner, INS, Memorandum, October 31, 2001 attached as Appendix 7-14.

he or she did not know, and should not reasonably have known, that the activity would further the organization's terrorist activity.[24]

A noncitizen need not actually have engaged in these or other terrorist activities to be inadmissible or removable. A person will fall within those grounds if a consular officer, the Attorney General, or the Secretary of Homeland Security knows or has a reasonable ground to believe that the individual is likely to engage in such activity after entry.[25] Additionally, a noncitizen will be inadmissible or removable if he or she is a member of a foreign terrorist organization that has been officially designated by the U.S. or which the individual knows or should have known is a terrorist organization.[26] Finally, with limited exceptions, the spouse or child of an individual who is inadmissible under this section, will also be inadmissible.[27]

It is particularly important to consider the potential removal consequence of association with any group that might fall within this definition in light of the reach of the USA Patriot Act and the REAL ID Act. Both acts include broad retroactivity provisions, such that past activity is likely to render the individual either removable or deportable.[28]

§ 7:60 Statutory and regulatory definitions—Objects of prohibition—Doctrine

The term "doctrine" is defined statutorily as including, but not being limited to, policies, practices, aims, or procedures.[1]

§ 7:61 Statutory and regulatory definitions—Objects of prohibition—Organization

The term "organization" is defined by the INA to mean, but not to be limited to, an organization, corporation, company, partnership, association, trust, foundation or fund; and includes a group of persons, whether or not incorporated, permanently or temporarily associated together with joint action on any subject or subjects.[1]

§ 7:62 Statutory and regulatory definitions—Objects of prohibition—Totalitarian party

The term "totalitarian party" is defined to mean:[1]

an organization which advocates the establishment in the United States of a totalitarian

---

[24]Zigler, Commissioner, INS, Memorandum, October 31, 2001 attached as Appendix 7-14; see also INA §§ 212(a)(3)(B)(iv)(IV)(cc), (V)(cc) and (VI)(dd), 8 U.S.C.A. §§ 1182(a)(3)(B)(iv)(IV)(cc), (V)(cc) and (VI)(dd).

[25]INA § 212(a)(3)(B)(i)(II), 8 U.S.C.A. § 1182(a)(3)(B)(i)(II).

[26]INA § 212(a)(3)(B)(i)(V), 8 U.S.C.A. § 1182(a)(3)(B)(i)(V).

[27]INA § 212(a)(3)(B)(i)(VII), 8 U.S.C.A. § 1182(a)(3)(B)(i)(VII).

[28]USA Patriot Act, Pub. L. No. 107-56 § 411(c)(1); Pub. L. 109-13, § 105(a)(2), 119 Stat. 309 (May 11, 2005).

[Section 7:60]

[1]INA § 101(a)(12), 8 U.S.C.A. § 1101(a)(12).

[Section 7:61]

[1]INA § 101(a)(28), 8 U.S.C.A. § 1101(a)(28).

[Section 7:62]

[1]INA § 101(a)(37), 8 U.S.C.A. § 1101(a)(37).

dictatorship or totalitarianism. The terms "totalitarian dictatorship" and "totalitarianism" mean and refer to systems of government not representative in fact, characterized by (A) the existence of a single political party, organized on a dictatorial basis, with so close an identity between such party and its policies and the governmental policies of the country in which it exists, that the party and the government constitute an indistinguishable unit, and (B) the forcible suppression of opposition to such a party.

The regulations add to the definition of "Totalitarian party" as follows:

Totalitarian party includes: (1) Any party in the United States which advocated totalitarianism; (2) Any party in any State of the United States, in any foreign state, or in any political or geographical subdivision of any foreign state which advocates or practices totalitarianism; (3) Any section, subsidiary, branch, affiliate, or subdivision of any such association or party; and (4) The direct predecessors or successors of any such association or party, regardless of what name such group or organization may have used, may now bear, or may hereafter adopt.[2]

§ 7:63   Statutory and regulatory definitions—Objects of prohibition— Communist Party

Research References

Gallagher, Immigration Law Service 2d § 14:272

The regulations define the "Communist Party" to include: (1) The Communist Party of the United States; (2) The Communist Political Association; (3) The Communist party of any state of the United States, of any foreign state, or of any political or geographical subdivision of any foreign state; (4) any section, subsidiary, branch, affiliate, or subdivision of any such association or party; (5) the direct predecessors or successors of any such association or party, regardless of what name such group or organization may have used, may now bear, or may hereafter adopt; and (6) any Communist-action or Communist front organization that is registered or is required to be registered under section 786 of title 50 of the United States Code, provided that the applicant knew or had reason to believe, while he or she was a member, that such organization was a Communist-front organization.[1]

Judicial interpretation has discussed affiliate organizations of the Communist party as not including Communist-controlled organizations that are not an integral part of the Communist Party.[2] The meaning of "affiliate" in this sense is restricted to "a subdivision or branch so affiliated that it is in essence part of the Communist Party itself."[3]

§ 7:64   Statutory and regulatory definitions—Objects of prohibition— World communism

Research References

Gallagher, Immigration Law Service 2d § 14:271

The term "world communism" is defined statutorily to mean a revolutionary movement, the purpose of which is to establish eventually a Communist totalitarian

---

[2]8 CFR § 313.1.

[Section 7:63]

[1]8 CFR § 313.1.

[2]Petition of Klajic, 260 F.Supp. 807, 810 (C.D.Cal. 1966).

[3]In re Klajic, 260 F. Supp. 807, 810 (C.D. Cal. 1966).

dictatorship in any or all the countries of the world through the medium of an internationally-coordinated Communist political movement.[1]

§ 7:65 Statutory and regulatory definitions—Objects of prohibition— Subversive

Regulations define subversive as any individual who advocates or teaches: (1) opposition to all organized government; (2) the overthrow, by force or violence or other unconstitutional means, of the Government of the United States or of all forms of law; (3) the duty, necessity, or propriety of the unlawful assaulting or killing, either individually or by position, of any other officer or officers of the United States or of any other organized government, because of their official character; (4) the unlawful damage, injury, or destruction of property; or (5) sabotage.[1]

§ 7:66 Statutory and regulatory definitions—Objects of prohibition— Advocating doctrines of world communism

Research References

Gallagher, Immigration Law Service 2d § 14:271

For the purposes of the INA "[a]dvocating the economic, international, and governmental doctrines of world communism means advocating the establishment of a totalitarian Communist dictatorship in any or all of the countries of the world through the medium of an internationally-coordinated Communist movement."[1] The DHS regulations adopt the content of this definition for the more general term of "advocating communism."[2]

§ 7:67 Persons barred from naturalizing—Generally

The ideological bars can be classified into the four categories that they affect: Communists, anarchists, fascists, and advocates of sabotage. These bars are very uneven. As will be explained below, for example, supporters of the Republican side in the Spanish civil war would probably be barred from becoming U.S. citizens, while members of the Nazi Party of Germany or Mussolini's Fascist party would not.[1]

These bars only apply to persons who were members of these organizations or espoused these views within 10 years prior to the filing of the application for naturalization.[2] The USCIS does not have authority to deny the application if the

---

[Section 7:64]

[1]INA § 101(a)(40), 8 U.S.C.A. § 1101(a)(40).

[Section 7:65]

[1]8 CFR § 313.1.

[Section 7:66]

[1]INA § 101(e)(3), 8 U.S.C.A. § 1101(e)(3).

[2]8 CFR § 313.1.

[Section 7:67]

[1]See § 7:70.

[2]INA § 313(c), 8 U.S.C.A. § 1424(c); In re Garstka, 295 F.Supp. 833, 835 (W.D.Mich. 1969).

persons was within one of the barred classes more than ten years before the filing of the application.[3]

§ 7:68 Persons barred from naturalizing—Communists

Research References

Gallagher, Immigration Law Service 2d § 14:271

The first category covers bars directed to members and affiliates of the Communist party. The activities that are barred are: (1) membership or affiliation; (2) advocacy of Communist doctrines; (3) membership in an organization that advocates Communist doctrines; (4) publication, writing, or distribution of Communist doctrines; and (5) membership in an organization that publishes or distributes Communist writings or possesses such publications for distribution.[1]

The statute is at once very specific and very far-reaching in its bar of Communist parties. The bar includes not only the official Communist Party of the United States, but also the Communist Political Association, the Communist party of any state of the U.S. or any foreign country, sections, subdivisions, branches, affiliates, or subdivisions or such parties, and direct predecessors or successors of such organizations.[2] The meaning of an affiliate organization of the Communist party is discussed above.[3]

In addition, this section previously included any organization that was required to be registered as a Communist-action organization or a Communist-front organization under the Subversive Activities Control Act of 1950.[4] The Immigration Technical Corrections Act of 1991 eliminated these provisions, recognizing that the registry of the Subversive Activities Control Act of 1950 ceased to exist in 1968.[5] The regulations, however, continue to include the ban on naturalization of members or affiliates of Communist-front and Communist-action organizations that were required to be registered under the Subversive Activities Act of 1950.[6]

Only "meaningful association" counts as membership or affiliation with a Communist organization for purposes of the bar to naturalization.[7] In addition, certain

---

[3]U.S. v. Wakowski, 158 F.2d 962, 963 (7th Cir. 1947) (interpreting virtually identical language in the 1940 Nationality Act).

[Section 7:68]

[1]INA § 313(a)(2), (3), (5), (6), 8 U.S.C.A. § 1424(a)(2), (3), (5), (6); 8 CFR § 313.2(a), (b), (c), (e), (f), (g).

[2]INA § 313(a)(2), 8 U.S.C.A. § 1424(a)(2).

[3]See § 7:63.

[4]INA § 313(a)(2)(G), (H), 8 U.S.C.A. § 1424(a)(2)(G), (H) as originally enacted by Act of June 27, 1952, 66 Stat. 163.

[5]Immigration Technical Corrections Act of 1991 § 309(b)(13), Pub.L. 102-232, 105 Stat. 1743 (Dec. 12, 1991). Cf. Committee of the Judiciary, Section-by-Section Description of H.R. 2670, section 9 (c), House Report 102-383 at 10, 1991 U.S. Code Congressional and Administrative News 1381 ("makes . . . technical corrections in the Immigration and Nationality Act . . . to delete obsolete references and provisions"). The law requiring registration of Communist-front and Communist-action organizations was repealed by sec. 5, Act of January 2, 1968, Pub.L. 90-237, 81 Stat. 766.

[6]8 CFR § 313.1 (subsection 6 of the definition of "Communist Party").

[7]See § 7:63.

types of membership in a Communist party that are due to duress or workings of law are statutorily exempted from the bar.[8]

§ 7:69 Persons barred from naturalizing—Anarchists

Second, the bar applies to anarchists in so far as they: (1) advocate or teach anarchism; (2) are members or affiliated with an anarchist organization; (3) write, publish, distribute, or possess for distribution anarchist materials; (4) are members of an organization that publishes, distributes, or possesses for distribution anarchist materials.[1]

§ 7:70 Persons barred from naturalizing—Totalitarian parties

Research References

Gallagher, Immigration Law Service 2d § 14:271

Third, the bar as it relates to totalitarian parties forbids naturalization of those who: (1) are members or affiliates of totalitarian parties; (2) advocate the establishment *in the United States* of a totalitarian dictatorship; (3) are members of an organization that advocates the establishment *in the United States* of a totalitarian dictatorship; (4) write, publish, distribute, or possess for distribution materials advocating the establishment *in the United States* of a totalitarian dictatorship; (5) are members of an organization that publishes, distributes, or possesses for publication materials advocating the establishment *in the United States* of a totalitarian dictatorship.[1]

Unlike the bar on Communists, the bar relating to advocacy of totalitarian ideologies is limited to advocating the establishment *in the United States* of a totalitarian dictatorship. Lest it be believed that this difference is accidental, it must be pointed out that the 1940 Nationality Act as amended by the Internal Security Act of 1950 did not include such limitation.[2] In addition, the term "totalitarian party" was defined by Congress to mean the establishment *in the United States* of a totalitarian dictatorship.[3] Thus, membership in the Nazi Party of Germany is not within the scope of this bar.[4]

§ 7:71 Persons barred from naturalizing—Saboteurs

Research References

Gallagher, Immigration Law Service 2d § 14:271

---

[8]See § 7:74.

[Section 7:69]

[1]INA § 313(a)(1), (4), (5), (6), 8 U.S.C.A. § 1424(a)(1), (4), (5), (6); 8 CFR § 313.2(d), (e), (f), (g).

[Section 7:70]

[1]INA § 313(a)(2), (3), (5), (6), 8 U.S.C.A. § 1424(a)(2), (3), (5), (6); 8 CFR § 313.2(a), (b), (c).

[2]INS Interp. 313.1(c), (d).

[3]INA § 101(a)(37), 8 U.S.C.A. § 1101(a)(37) (emphasis added).

[4]Matter of B-, 5 I. & N. Dec. 255, 256 (B.I.A. 1953).

Fourth, advocates of sabotage and political assassination in general, and of *coup d'tat* in the United States are also barred from becoming U.S. citizens.[1] The actions barred are: (1) advocacy; (2) writing, publishing, distributing, or possessing for distribution materials which do such advocacy; and (3) membership in an organization which publishes, distributes, or possesses for distribution such materials.[2] For a discussion of how this bar relates to the grounds of inadmissibility and deportability for terrorist-related activity.[3]

§ 7:72 Persons barred from naturalizing—Terrorism supporters

Oddly enough, there are currently no specific provision in the INA which bar the naturalization of terrorists or supporters of terrorism. However, terrorists or those who support the goals of Al Qaeda or similar groups would likely be precluded from naturalizing on a number of grounds.

First, support for terrorism is a ground of both removability and inadmissibility.[1] The USCIS has a policy of referring individuals whom it perceives as security risks to ICE for issuance of a Notice to Appear.[2]

Second, groups like Al Qaeda proclaim an intention to establish an Islamic caliphate throughout the world; goals like this would bring many organizations within the prohibition of naturalization to those who seek to overthrow the U.S. government by force, or who support the establishment in the United States of a totalitarian government.[3] If the goals of an organization fit within that rubric, naturalization would also be barred to those creating or distributing literature supporting those ends, or becoming affiliated with an organization supporting those ends.[4]

That said, because there is no per se terrorism bar to naturalization, it is possible that individuals who have engaged in terrorist acts may be naturalized. Particularly where the terrorism was not directed against the United States, and where it was not motivated by fascism, communism, or anarchism, there would appear to be no provision precluding naturalization. Indeed, the Ninth Circuit upheld the naturalization of an individual who supported terrorist acts on behalf of Armenian separatists against Turkey, who had established that he was otherwise eligible.[5]

§ 7:73 Constitutional limitations

A substantially similar provision was sustained by the Supreme Court against a constitutional challenge in the context of deportation proceedings in the early

---

[Section 7:71]

[1]INA § 313(a)(4), 8 U.S.C.A. § 1424(a)(4).

[2]INA § 313(a)(4), (5), (6), 8 U.S.C.A. § 1424(a)(4), (5), (6); 8 CFR § 313.2(d), (e), (f), (g).

[3]See § 7:72.

[Section 7:72]

[1]See INA § 212(a)(3)(B), (F) [8 U.S.C.A. § 1182(a)(3)(B), (F)]; INA § 237(a)(4)(B) [8 U.S.C.A § 1227(a)(4)(B)].

[2]See App 8-5.

[3]See INA § 313(a)(3), (4) [8 U.S.C.A. § 1424(a)(3), (4)].

[4]See INA § 313(a)(5), (6) [8 U.S.C.A. § 1424(a)(5), (6)].

[5]U.S. v. Hovsepian, 422 F.3d 883 (9th Cir. 2005).

1950s.[1] In 1991, however, that same provision was challenged again on First Amendment grounds in the context of deportation proceedings and was held to be unconstitutional by a federal district court.[2] The district court decision was later vacated by the court of appeals because of lack of ripeness.[3]

The arguments espoused by the district court in *American Arab Anti-Discrimination Committee* apply with at least equal force to naturalization applicants, as not only are they within the borders of the United States but they are attempting to become part of the political community of this country.[4] As was pointed out by the Supreme Court, "once an alien gains admission and begins to develop the ties that go with permanent residence his [or her] constitutional status changes accordingly."[5] One circuit court, however, has given deference to the regulations and process for naturalization, holding that the agency's practice of requiring applicants to list all organizational membership does not violate the First Amendment.[6]

§ 7:74 Exemptions from bar—General exemptions

Research References

Gallagher, Immigration Law Service 2d §§ 14:274, 14:276 to 14:280

The statute exempts an individual from this bar on naturalization if any one of the following applies: the individual's membership (1) was involuntary; (2) was without awareness of the nature or aims of the organization and was discontinued if the applicant became aware of the nature or aims of the organization; (3) occurred and was terminated prior to the applicant attaining sixteen years of age; (4) occurred more than ten years prior to the filing of the application; (5) was by operation of law; or (6) was for the purpose of obtaining employment, food rations, or other essentials of living and was necessary for such purpose.[1] The regulations place the burden of proving the exemptions on the applicant.[2]

The regulations amplify some of the specific exemptions. For example, the lack of awareness exemption is only available to "an applicant whose participation in the activities of [one of the covered organizations] was minimal in nature, and who establishes that he or she was unaware of the nature of the organization while a

---

[Section 7:73]

[1]Harisiades v. Shaughnessy, 342 U.S. 580, 72 S.Ct. 512, 96 L.Ed. 586 (1952).

[2]American Arab Anti-Discrimination Committee v. Meese, 714 F.Supp. 1060, 1081-84 (C.D.Cal. 1989) vacated 940 F.2d 445 (9th Cir. 1991).

[3]American-Arab Anti-Discrimination Committee v. Thornburgh, 940 F.2d 445, 453-54 (9th Cir. 1991), opinion amended and superseded on denial of reh'g, 970 F.2d 501 (9th Cir. 1991).

[4]Johnson v. Eisentrager, 339 U.S. 763, 771, 70 S.Ct. 936, 940, 94 L.Ed. 1225 (1950) ("Mere lawful presence in the country creates an implied assurance of safe conduct and gives [the noncitizen] certain rights; they become more extensive and secure when he makes [a] preliminary declaration of intention to become a citizen, and they expand to those of full citizenship upon naturalization"); Fong Yue Ting v. U.S., 149 U.S. 698, 724, 13 S.Ct. 1016, 1026, 37 L.Ed. 905 (1893) ("having taken no steps towards becoming citizens [they] remain subject to the power of Congress to expel them").

[5]Landon v. Placencia, 459 U.S. 21, 32, 103 S.Ct. 321, 329, 74 L.Ed.2d 21 (1982).

[6]Price v. I.N.S., 962 F.2d 836, 842-44 (9th Cir. 1992).

[Section 7:74]

[1]INA §§ 313(a)(2)(F), (c) and (d), 8 U.S.C.A. §§ 1424(a)(2)(F), (c) and (d); 8 CFR § 313.3; INS Interp. No. 313.2(d).

[2]8 CFR § 313.3(a).

member of the organization."[3] Under the same rationale, if the person was a functionary of one of the covered organizations, he or she may not claim the exemptions that membership was by operation of law or that it was necessary for the purpose of obtaining employment, or other necessities of life.[4]

According to the regulations, in order to obtain an exemption under the "necessities of living" clause, the applicant must establish that membership in the covered organization was necessary to obtain the essentials of living like food, shelter, clothing, employment, and an education, which were routinely available to the rest of the population. For purposes of this exemption, higher education will qualify as an essential of living only if the applicant can establish the existence of special circumstances, which convert the need for higher education into a need as basic as the need for food or employment. The applicant must establish also that he or she participated only to the minimal extent necessary to receive the essential of living.[5]

The courts have found that higher education is an "essential of living" when the applicant finds himself or herself unable to obtain employment unless he or she obtains a college education.[6] Obtaining a high school education has been found to be an essential of living without any further qualification.[7]

Joining the Communist party for employment-related reasons is analyzed differently depending on whether membership occurred in a Communist or a noncommunist country. Joining the Communist party to obtain or maintain employment in a noncommunist country is not within the exemptions to the bar to naturalization unless it is demonstrated that such employment was necessary for survival and that unless the person joined the Communist party the person would have been unable to find alternative employment in the country.[8] On the other hand, a person who, as part of his or her employment, is forced to join a Communist trade union in a Communist country is contemplated within the exemptions to the bar.[9] A similar result is reached when joining the party in a Communist country represents an income increase substantial enough to make the difference between survival and starvation.[10]

Failure to terminate membership in the party more than twenty years prior to the filing of the naturalization application because of fear of reprisals rendered membership "involuntary" during the statutory period even when the person had originally voluntarily joined the party.[11]

In addition to the specific statutory exemptions discussed here, court interpretation has established that only meaningful membership in the proscribed organization prevents naturalization.[12] The USCIS takes the position that it is the burden of

---

[3]8 CFR § 313.3(c)(1).

[4]8 CFR § 313.3(c)(2).

[5]8 CFR § 313.3(d)(1).

[6]Grzymala-Siedlecki v. U.S., 285 F.2d 836, 839, 840 (5th Cir. 1961); In re Klajic, 260 F. Supp. 807, 811-12 (C.D. Cal. 1966); In re Klajic, 260 F. Supp. 807, 811-12 (C.D. Cal. 1966).

[7]Matter of Post, 11 I. & N. Dec. 228, 233 (B.I.A. 1965).

[8]Matter of D-, 4 I. & N. Dec. 675 (B.I.A. 1952).

[9]Matter of A-, 4 I. & N. Dec. 334 (B.I.A. 1951).

[10]Matter of V-, 8 I. & N. Dec. 554, 557 (B.I.A. 1960) (a sailor's salary for nonparty members was $10 per month while party members receive $14 a month and increased ration stamps).

[11]Petition of Bartok, No. 248011 (S.D.Cal. 1964) cited in INS Interp. 313.2(d)(2).

[12]See § 7:59.

the applicant to establish that membership in the organization was not meaningful or that one of the statutory exceptions applies.[13]

§ 7:75 Exemptions from bar—Exemption for contribution to national security or national intelligence mission

In 1999, Congress created an additional exemption for individuals who the director of Intelligence, in consultation with the Secretary of Defense and with the concurrence of the Attorney General, determines have made a contribution to the national security or to the national intelligence mission of the United States.[1] This exemption is applicable if, in addition to the above determination, all of the following apply: the individual (1) is otherwise eligible to naturalize; (2) is barred solely because of past membership or affiliation with one of the organizations listed in INA § 313(a)(2); and (3) does not fall within any of the other classes described in INA § 313.[2]

3.   Special Procedures

§ 7:76 In general

In all cases where the applicant claims membership or affiliation in an organization that would make him or her subject to this bar, the applicant must attach to the naturalization application a detailed written statement describing such membership or affiliation, including the periods of membership or affiliation, whether the applicant held any officer position in the organization, and whether membership or affiliation was voluntary or involuntary.[1] If the applicant alleges that membership was involuntary, or that one of the exemptions apply, the applicant must set forth the basis for such a claim.[2]

The burden of proof that they fall within the statutory exemptions is on the applicants.[3] However, applicants can sustain their burden even when "some reasonable doubts plague the trier of fact."[4]

The *INS Operations Instructions* have a special subsection relating to membership in organizations, but that subsection is not available to the public.[5]

Two presumptions assist the DHS in obtaining information and prosecuting naturalization fraud relating to the politico-ideological bar to naturalization and to lack of attachment to the U.S. Constitution. First, if within ten years of naturalization, a naturalized citizen is convicted of contempt for refusal to testify before a Congressional committee about his or her subversive activities, such refusal constitutes a ground for revocation of naturalization on the basis that the naturalization

---

[13]INS Interp. 313.2(c).

[Section 7:75]

[1]Section 306, Intelligence Authorization Act for Fiscal Year 2000, Pub.L. No. 106-1201, 113 Stat. 1606 (Dec. 3, 1999) *creating new* INA § 313(e), 8 U.S.C.A. § 1424(e).

[2]INA § 313(e), 8 U.S.C.A. § 1424(e).

[Section 7:76]

[1]8 CFR § 313.4.

[2]8 CFR § 313.4.

[3]In re Ferenci's Petition, 217 F.Supp. 714, 716 (E.D.Pa. 1963).

[4]In re Ferenci, 217 F. Supp. 714, 717 (E.D. Pa. 1963).

[5]OI 313.1.

was procured by concealment of a material fact or willful misrepresentation.[6] Second, when a person joins a Communist party within five years of becoming a U.S. citizen, the INA deems the person as not attached to the principles of the U.S. Constitution.[7] These presumptions are discussed in more detail in the chapter dealing with denaturalization.[8]

VI.   MILITARY-RELATED BARS

§ 7:77   In general

There have been military-related bars to naturalization since the Act of March 3, 1865.[1] Under the 1865 act, all noncitizens who deserted the armed forces or fled the jurisdiction in order to avoid serving in the armed forces were barred from becoming U.S. citizens.[2] Substantially similar provisions have governed the eligibility of deserters and draft evaders up to the present.[3] The current provisions relating to deserters and draft evaders are located in INA § 314.[4]

In addition, under all prior naturalization laws, noncitizens wishing to naturalize were required to make a declaration of intention to naturalize.[5] Starting in World War I, noncitizens who had made these declarations were required to serve in the armed forces of the United States.[6] Noncitizens from neutral countries who withdrew these declarations were relieved from service, but were subsequently barred from becoming citizens of the United States.[7] The patterns started by this procedure have been continued until the present, even though declarations of intent to become a U.S. citizen are no longer a requirement of naturalization.[8] Under the current statute noncitizens who obtain exemption from military service based on alienage are barred from naturalizing.[9]

§ 7:78   Deserters and draft evaders

Research References

Gallagher, Immigration Law Service 2d §§ 14:227, 14:228

The INA permanently bars the naturalization of any person who, "at any time

---

[6]INA § 340(a), 8 U.S.C.A. § 1451(a).

[7]INA § 340(c), 8 U.S.C.A. § 1451(c).

[8]See § § 14:25, 14:26.

[Section 7:77]

[1]Act of March 3, 1865, 13 Stat. 487 reproduced in Appendix 12-1C to Chapter 12 incorporated into sects. 1996, 1998, Revised Statutes reproduced as Appendix 4-5 to Chapter 4. Cf. Chapter 12 (discussing special military-related naturalization legislation).

[2]Sec. 21, Act of March 3, 1865 reproduced in Appendix 12-1C to Chapter 12.

[3]Compare sec. 21, Act of March 3, 1865 reproduced in Appendix 12-1C to § 12:1 with INA § 314, 8 U.S.C.A. § 1425.

[4]8 U.S.C.A. § 1426.

[5]INS Interp. 334.2(a).

[6]INS Interp. 315.1. Noncitizens from enemy countries were not required or allowed to serve in the U.S. armed forces. INS Interp. 334.2(a).

[7]INS Interp. 315.2(a).

[8]See INS Interp. 334.2(e).

[9]INA § 315, 8 U.S.C.A. § 1426. See §§ 7:78 to 7:83 (for a more detailed discussion of the requirements of this bar).

during which the United States has been or shall be at war, deserted or shall desert the military, air, or naval forces of the United States, or who, having been duly enrolled, departed, or shall depart from the jurisdiction of the district in which enrolled."[1] That same section also bars persons who "at any time during which the United States has been or shall be at war, . . . whether or not having been duly enrolled, went or shall go beyond the limits of the United States, with intent to avoid any draft in the military, air, or naval service, lawfully ordered."[2]

However, *no* bar to naturalization exists unless a court martial or a court of competent jurisdiction has duly convicted the person.[3] Nothing short of a conviction will suffice to make the person ineligible for naturalization. Thus, an admission of desertion, or a finding of desertion by a civil court, or a listing of the person on official military records as a deserter will *not* preclude the naturalization of the person.[4]

This bar is not applicable unless the United States was at war at the time of the desertion or draft evasion.[5] Whether the United States was at war at the time is a mixed issue of fact and law.[6]

Deserters who are unconditionally pardoned by the President are relieved from this bar and may be naturalized.[7] General amnesties have been declared by the President for all persons who deserted the U.S. armed forces after November 11, 1918—the date the actual hostilities ended in World War I—and before July 2, 1921—the date on which the war formally ended.[8] A similar amnesty was declared by the president for all persons who deserted the U.S. armed forces on or after August 14, 1945—the date hostilities terminated in World War II—and before June 25, 1950—the date of the Korean invasion.[9] Both these pardons relieve the covered persons from ineligibility for naturalization.[10]

§ 7:79   Exemption from training or service—Bar to citizenship based on claim of exemption or discharge from service

Research References

Gallagher, Immigration Law Service 2d § 14:229

The INA provides that "any alien who applies or has applied for exemption or discharge from training or service in the Armed Forces or in the National Security Training Corps of the United States on the ground that he [or she] is an alien, and

---

[Section 7:78]

[1]INA § 314, 8 U.S.C.A. § 1425.

[2]INA § 314, 8 U.S.C.A. § 1425.

[3]INA § 314, 8 U.S.C.A. § 1425.

[4]INS Interp. 314.1 citing to State v. Symonds, 57 Me. 148 (1869); Holt v. Holt, 59 Me. 464 (1871); McCafferty v. Gruyer, 59 Pa. 109 (1868).

[5]Polanski v. I.N.S., 2000 WL 869487 (SDNY 2000).

[6]Polanski v. I.N.S., 2000 WL 869487 (SDNY 2000).

[7]31 Op. Atty. Gen. 225 (1918); INS Interp. 314.2.

[8]Presidential Proclamation, March 5, 1924, 43 Stat. 1940 cited in INS Interp. 314.2.

[9]Presidential Proclamation 3001, December 24, 1952, 24 Stat. c24.

[10]INS Interp. 314.2.

is or was so relieved or discharged from such training or service on such ground, shall be permanently ineligible to become a citizen of the United States."[1]

This section applies to any naturalization proceedings and forbids the naturalization of noncitizens who were exempted or discharged from the armed services on the basis of alienage regardless of when the discharge or exemption occurred.[2] Unlike the previous section, no criminal action is involved here. Rather, this provision relates to the lawful claim of exemption under certain military service statutes and treaties of the United States. At present, there is no compulsory military service in the U.S., so this section applies only to persons who were exempted or discharge from service in the past.

§ 7:80 Exemption from training or service—Which noncitizens could claim exemption or discharge

Research References

Gallagher, Immigration Law Service 2d § 14:234

Since 1917, there have been some provisions in the U.S. military service acts allowing certain noncitizens to claim exemption or discharge from service based on alienage.[1] Until 1948, exemptions from military service based on alienage were limited to nationals of neutral countries that requested such exemptions.[2] After 1951, only noncitizens who were in the United States on status other than permanent residence could claim exemption based on alienage.[3] In 1971, the Military Service Act was amended deleting the statutory authority to grant exemptions from service based on alienage altogether.[4] On the other hand, nonimmigrants who continued to maintain nonimmigrant status were automatically exempted from registering with the military.[5] As a consequence of these changes, persons who were exempt as nonimmigrants after this date were no longer ineligible for citizenship, since they never requested exemption.[6]

Throughout this period and up to the present, certain countries have signed treaties with the U.S. allowing each other's nationals to be exempted from military service.[7] Nationals of those treaty countries could claim exemption or discharge from military service based on those treaties.[8] However, persons taking advantage of these treaties became ineligible for citizenship to the same extent as nationals of other countries who claimed exemptions or discharge based on U.S. statutory law

---

[Section 7:79]

[1]INA § 315(a), 8 U.S.C.A. § 1426(a).

[2]Petition for Naturalization of Bronkovitch, 172 F.Supp. 319, 320 (D.Md. 1959); In re Carvajal, 154 F.Supp. 525, 528 (N.D.Cal. 1957).

[Section 7:80]

[1]INS Interp. 315.2.

[2]INS Interp. 315.2, 315.3.

[3]INS Interp. 315.3(b)(1).

[4]INS Interp. 315.3(c)(2).

[5]INS Interp. 315.3(c)(2).

[6]See § 7:79.

[7]The INS regulations provide a listing of which countries have treaties with the U.S. mutually allowing each other's nationals to be exempted from military services. See next paragraph.

[8]See INS Interp. 315.5.

allowing certain resident noncitizens to request exemption from military service based on their alienage.[9] After 1951, the only permanent resident noncitizens who have been able to claim exemption from military service have been nationals of treaty countries.[10] Therefore, the ineligibility to citizenship provision has been closely identified with treaty nationals. In 1990, Congress provided limited relief to certain treaty nationals allowing them to become U.S. citizens if they had served in the armies of their countries prior to claiming the exemption in the U.S.[11]

The regulations list the following countries as currently having effective treaties providing reciprocal exemption of noncitizens from military service: Argentina (Art. X, 10 Stat. 1005, 1009, effective 1853), Austria (Art. VI, 47 Stat. 1876, 1880, effective 1928), China (Art. XIV, 63 Stat. 1299, 1311, effective 1946), Costa Rica (Art. IX, 10 Stat. 916, 921, effective 1851), Estonia (Art. VI, 44 Stat. 2379, 2381, effective 1925), Honduras (Art. VI, 45 Stat. 2618, 2622, effective 1927), Ireland (Art. III, 1 US 785, 789, effective 1950), Italy (Art. XIII, 63 Stat. 2255, 2272, effective 1948), Latvia (Art. VI, 45 Stat. 2641, 2643, effective 1928), Liberia (Art. VI, 54 Stat. 1739, 1742, effective 1938), Norway (Art. VI, 47 Stat. 2135, 2139, effective 1928) Paraguay (Art. XI, 12 Stat. 1091, 1096, effective 1859), Spain (Art. V, 33 Stat. 2105, 2108, effective 1902), Switzerland (Art. II, 11 Stat. 587, 589, effective 1850), Yugoslavia (Serbia) (Art. IV, 22 Stat. 963, 964, effective 1881).[12] The following countries previously had treaties providing for reciprocal exemption of noncitizens from military service: El Salvador (Art. VI, 46 Stat. 2817, 2821, effective 1926 to February 8, 1958), Germany (Art. VI, 44 Stat. 2132, 2136, effective 1923 to June 2, 1954), Hungary (Art. VI, 44 Stat, 2441, 2445, effective 1925 to July 5, 1952), Thailand (Siam) (Art. 1, 53 Stat. 1731, 1732, effective 1937 to June 8, 1968).[13]

§ 7:81 Exemption from training or service—Which claims of exemption or discharge bar noncitizen from citizenship

Research References

Gallagher, Immigration Law Service 2d § 14:231

Not all noncitizens who have received exemptions or discharge from military service are covered by this section. The statute itself provides specific requirements that must be satisfied before the noncitizen would be barred from citizenship.[1]

First, the noncitizen must have applied for the exemption.[2] The bar does not cover a person who is granted an exemption without applying for it.[3] Thus, a noncitizen who was discharged from service under a general directive of the Secretary of War that nationals of countries with which the U.S. was at war be discharged from service if they so desired was not sufficient to make the person ineligible for citizenship

---

[9]Gramaglia v. U.S., 766 F.2d 88, 92 (2d Cir. 1985).

[10]See generally INS Interp. 315.5(b).

[11]See § 7:83.

[12]8 CFR § 315.4(a).

[13]8 CFR § 315.4(b).

[Section 7:81]

[1]See INA § 315(a), 8 U.S.C.A. § 1426(a).

[2]Astrup v. I.N.S., 402 U.S. 509, 512-13, 91 S.Ct. 1583, 1585, 29 L.Ed.2d 68 (1971).

[3]8 CFR § 315.2(b)(2).

since there was no record that he or she actually applied for the exemption or discharge.[4]

Second, the bar is inapplicable if the basis for the noncitizen's application for the exemption or discharge is anything other than his or her alienage.[5] The choice between exemption on the basis of alienage and U.S. citizenship must be a clear one for the noncitizen; it must be clear to the individual that he or she is giving up U.S. citizenship by requesting the exemption.[6] Thus, the regulations exempt from this ground of ineligibility any person who "did not knowingly and intentionally waive the person's eligibility for naturalization because he or she was misled by advice from a competent United States government authority, or from a competent authority of his or her country of nationality," regarding the consequences of applying for an exemption from military service.[7]

Third, if the noncitizen was actually denied the exemption or discharge or was granted the exemption or discharge on another ground, no ineligibility attaches even if the noncitizen requested the exemption or discharge on the basis of alienage.[8] Thus, a person who applied for relief from military service on the basis of being a noncitizen but who in fact was relieved from service because he or she failed the medical examination was not ineligible for citizenship.[9] Similarly, a person who was ultimately exempted from service, on the ground that he or she was a person engaged in an activity in support of the national health, safety, or interest, was not barred from naturalizing, even though the person had originally been relieved on the basis of alienage as a national of a neutral country, but had to be reclassified because his or her country became cobelligerent with the U.S.[10] The exemption based on alienage is codified as 4-C in the selective service records.[11]

A person who is only relieved *temporarily* from service on the ground of alienage, but who is later forced to serve does not become ineligible for citizenship.[12] The exemption must be total and permanent to make the noncitizen ineligible.[13] On the other hand, once a person has received a permanent exemption or discharge from military service, the person will remain ineligible for naturalization even if he or she changes his or her mind and volunteers for military service at a later date.[14]

A person who was not liable for military service at the time he or she applied for exemption does not become ineligible for naturalization.[15] Thus, a person who was above the maximum age to serve in the military did not become ineligible to become a citizen by the mere fact that he [or she] requested exemption from service based

---

[4]Petition of Bronkovitch, 172 F. Supp. 319, 320 (D. Md. 1959).

[5]INA § 315(a), 8 U.S.C.A. § 1426(a).

[6]Moser v. U.S., 341 U.S. 41, 71 S.Ct. 553, 95 L.Ed. 729 (1951).

[7]8 CFR § 315.2(b)(4).

[8]8 CFR § 315.2(b)(3); Astrup v. Immigration and Naturalization Service, 402 U.S. 509, 514, 91 S. Ct. 1583, 1586, (1971).

[9]Astrup, 402 U.S. 509, 91 S.Ct. 1583 (1971).

[10]Villamar v. U.S., 651 F.2d 116 (2d Cir. 1981).

[11]See OI 315.1(b).

[12]Astrup v. Immigration and Naturalization Service, 402 U.S. 509, 513, 91 S. Ct. 1583, 1585, 29 L. Ed. 2d 68 (1971); Villamar v. U.S., 651 F.2d 116; U.S. v. Hoellger, 273 F.2d 760 (2d Cir. 1960).

[13]Matter of Carrelli, 466 F.Supp. 272, 275 (E.D.N.Y. 1979).

[14]8 CFR § 315.2(b)(5); U.S. v. Kenny, 247 F.2d 139 (2d Cir. 1957).

[15]8 CFR § 315.2(b)(1).

on alienage.[16] Likewise, the Ninth Circuit has held that where an individual volunteered for service when there was no draft in effect–as part of the "war on terrorism"–that where the alien subsequently obtained discharge on grounds of alienage, it did not render the individual "ineligible to citizenship."[17] The Ninth Circuit held that the "ineligible to citizenship" provisions only apply where there is a military draft.[18]

§ 7:82 Exemption from training or service—Proof issues

Research References
Gallagher, Immigration Law Service 2d § 14:237

To establish whether the noncitizen was relieved or discharged from the service on the basis of alienage, the records of the Selective Service or of the Department of Defense provide conclusive proof.[1] Thus when the Selective Service records do not show that the person was relieved from service because of alienage, then the person is not ineligible for citizenship.[2] A person who is given *de facto* exemption from military service does not thereby become ineligible for citizenship; the service records must state that relief from service was based on alienage.[3] In addition, the regulations provide that the regulations of the Selective Service administration and its predecessors are controlling regarding who was liable to register and to serve in the military.[4]

The USCIS will use Form N-422 to obtain the evidence from the military records.[5] Even when the applicant exhibits a Selective Service Registration Card with this exemption, he or she may not be disqualified because of cases of erroneous or automatic exemptions.[6] The USCIS examiner must inquire whether the name is on any of the Consolidated Lists, and whether there is any written request for exemption on the applicant's military file.[7] Written requests for exemptions should have been filed on Forms SSS-130, DDS-130, DDS-130, Local Board Form C-294 or simply by making the request in writing.[8] If no such form is found, the name of the applicant does not appear in the Consolidated Lists, and the USCIS examiner is satisfied the applicant did not request an exemption, the naturalization application will be approved even when the Selective Service Registration Card shows an exemption.[9]

§ 7:83 Statutory exemption for treaty nationals

The 1990 act added one statutory exemption to the ineligibility for citizenship

---

[16]In re Wendt, 300 F.Supp. 725, 726-27 (N.D.Ill. 1969). But see conclusive effect of selective service records.

[17]Gallarde v. I.N.S., 486 F.3d 1136 (9th Cir. 2007).

[18]Gallarde v. I.N.S., 486 F.3d 1136, 1148–49 (9th Cir. 2007).

[Section 7:82]

[1]INA § 315(b), 8 U.S.C.A. § 1426(b); 8 CFR § 315.3(a).

[2]In re Naturalization of Mirzoeff, 196 F.Supp. 230, 234 n. 1 (S.D.N.Y. 1961).

[3]See *Carrelli*, 272 F.2d at 275.

[4]8 CFR § 315.3(b).

[5]OI 315.1(a).

[6]OI 315.1(b).

[7]OI 315.1(b).

[8]OI 315.1(b).

[9]OI 315.1(b).

under this section.[1] A noncitizen who would otherwise be ineligible to U.S. citizenship because he or she exercised his or her rights under a treaty to be exempt from military service in the U.S., becomes eligible for naturalization if, before exercising those rights, the noncitizen had served in the Armed Forces of a foreign country of which the noncitizen was a national.[2] The regulations add a requirement that the person must have served specified minimum periods in the armed forces of the other country to be eligible under this provision.[3]

VII. ENGLISH LITERACY AND KNOWLEDGE OF U.S. HISTORY AND GOVERNMENT

A. INTRODUCTION

§ 7:84 Overview

Research References

Dizon and Wettstein, Immigration Law Service 2d §§ 14:169, 14:173
Steel on Immigration Law § 15:15

The INA imposes two separate educational requirements on naturalization applicants. The first relates to knowledge of the English language.[1] The second relates to the knowledge of history and the form of government of the U.S.[2] This second section is also known as the civics section. Until the passage of the INTCA, applicants could only be exempt from the English language requirement, i.e. *all* applicants had to comply with the history and government requirement.[3] In 1994, the INTCA expanded the exemptions and subdivided them into two classes: (1) those who were physically unable to comply, including developmentally disabled, would be exempted from both the English language and the history and government requirements, and (2) certain long term residents would only be exempted from the English language requirement but would still have to comply with the history and government requirement.[4] Congress has recently added a new exemption that benefits certain Hmong guerrilla fighters and other Hmong armed forces.[5] The new law exempts these people from the English language requirement and requires a simplified history and government examination instead of the standard civics test.[6]

The statute specifically limits the application of the English and the history and government requirements to a person who naturalizes *"upon his [or her] own*

[Section 7:83]

[1]Immigration Act of 1990 § 404, Pub.L. 101-649, 104 Stat. 5039 (Nov. 29, 1990) adding INA § 315(c).

[2]INA § 315(c), 8 U.S.C.A. § 1426(c).

[3]8 CFR § 315.2(b)(6).

[Section 7:84]

[1]INA § 312(a)(1), 8 U.S.C.A. § 1423(a)(1).

[2]INA § 312(a)(2), 8 U.S.C.A. § 1423(a)(2).

[3]INA § 312, 8 U.S.C.A. § 1423 as amended by Pub.L. 95-579, 92 Stat. 2474 (Nov. 2, 1978) and sec 403, Pub.L. 101-649, 104 Stat. 4978 (Nov. 29, 1990); 8 CFR § 312.2(a).

[4]INA § 312(b), 8 U.S.C.A. § 1423(b).

[5]Hmong Veterans' Naturalization Act of 2000, Pub.L. 106-207, 114 Stat. 316 (May 26, 2000) reproduced as Appendix 7-12.

[6]Hmong Veterans' Naturalization Act of 2000, §§ 2, 3 reproduced as Appendix 7-12.

application."[7] Since children under eighteen are naturalized upon application of their citizen parents, they have not been required to satisfy these requirements.[8]

B. KNOWLEDGE OF ENGLISH LANGUAGE

§ 7:85 Requirement

Research References

Dizon and Wettstein, Immigration Law Service 2d §§ 14:169, 14:170
Steel on Immigration Law § 15:15

The INA forbids the naturalization of an applicant unless he or she demonstrates "an understanding of the English language, including an ability to read, write, and speak words in ordinary usage in the English language."[1] The scope of the test is determined by the statute itself, which provides that the requirement to read and write English "shall be met if the applicant can read and write simple words and phrases."[2] It requires a "reasonable test of literacy" and that "no extraordinary or unreasonable conditions shall be imposed on the applicant."[3] A list of vocabulary words for the new test can be found at App 7-6.

The portion of the English language requirement dealing with oral understanding and ability to speak is always determined by a USCIS examiner from the answers provided by the applicant to questions normally asked at the interview.[4]

In the past, the legacy INS had allowed the written portion of the test to be satisfied by evidence of having passed one of the approved standardized tests provided by a non-governmental organization.[5] The INS discontinued this practice effective midnight Eastern Daylight Time August 30, 1998.[6] For a discussion of continuing validity of already taken tests see the section on civics exams.[7]

At present, the English test may only be satisfied at the naturalization interview.[8] The examiner will use excerpts from the Federal Textbooks on Citizenship.[9]

People who fail the English or civics requirement at the naturalization interview will be given a second opportunity to pass the exam within ninety days of the first interview.[10] Applicants who fail to show up for the second interview are deemed to have failed that second exam and will be denied naturalization.[11]

Once the ability to speak and understand English has been established, interpret-

---

[7]INA § 312(a), 8 U.S.C.A. § 1423(a) (emphasis added). The regulations also include that limitation. 8 CFR §§ 312.1(a), 312.2(a).

[8]See §§ 11:18 to 11:25.

[Section 7:85]

[1]INA § 312(a)(1), 8 U.S.C.A. § 1423(a)(1).

[2]INA § 312(a)(1), 8 U.S.C.A. § 1423(a)(1).

[3]INA § 312(a)(1), 8 U.S.C.A. § 1423(a)(1).

[4]8 CFR § 312.1(c)(1).

[5]See 63 Federal Register 25080 (May 6, 1998) (Supplementary Information).

[6]8 CFR § 312.3(a)(1).

[7]See § 7:102.

[8]8 CFR §§ 312.1(c)(2), 312.3.

[9]8 CFR § 312.1(c)(2). These textbooks are INS publications M-289 and M-291 and are available from the Superintendent of Documents, Government Printing Office, Washington, DC 20402.

[10]8 CFR § 312.5(a).

[11]8 CFR § 312.5(b).

ers may be used, even for applicants who are not exempt from the English language requirement, if the naturalization examiner needs to dwell on issues which are complex in nature and which may not be couched in simple language.[12]

§ 7:86 The new test for speaking, reading, and writing English

After several years of testing,[1] the USCIS has unveiled a new naturalization test. The goals of the new test are a test that is "uniform, fair, and meaningful."[2]

The new standards for English speaking, reading, and writing are found at App 7-6. They are not significantly different from the standards which were in place previously. The only intended difference is that the reading and writing portions of the test are intended to be related to the civics content, rather than focusing on everyday English.[3]

The new test went into effect on October 1, 2008, and as of October 1, 2009, all applicants must take the new test unless qualified to take some modified version.

§ 7:87 Exemptions—Generally

Research References

Steel on Immigration Law § 15:15

Several groups of people are exempted from the English language requirement. The first group includes persons who are physically unable to comply, developmentally disabled, or mentally impaired.[1] These persons are also exempted from the history and government requirement.[2] Two other groups are based on age and length of lawful permanent residence: (1) persons who are over fifty years of age and have been lawful permanent residents for more than twenty years, and (2) persons who are over fifty-five years of age and who have been lawful permanent residents for more than fifteen years.[3] They are only exempted from the English examination and are still required to comply with the civics requirement.[4] However, the statute grants the USCIS discretion to decide by regulation whether the history and government requirement should be relaxed for persons who are over the age of sixty-five and have been lawful permanent residents for more than twenty years.[5] Finally, Congress has exempted two other groups in statutes that are not included within the INA. These are certain Hmong veterans[6] and naturalization applicants killed as a result of the September 11, 2001 plane hijackings who are eligible to receive post-

---

[12]8 CFR § 312.2(c)(1)(ii); INS Interp. 312.1(a)(3). See generally § 9:91.

[Section 7:86]

[1]See generally, App. 7-18.

[2]App. 7-18.

[3]App. 7-18.

[Section 7:87]

[1]INA § 312(b)(1), 8 U.S.C.A. § 1423(b)(1).

[2]INA § 312(b)(1), 8 U.S.C.A. § 1423(b)(1).

[3]INA § 312(b)(2), 8 U.S.C.A. § 1423(b)(2).

[4]INA § 312(b)(2), 8 U.S.C.A. § 1423(b)(2).

[5]INA § 312(b)(3), 8 U.S.C.A. § 1423(b)(3).

[6]Hmong Veteran's Naturalization Act of 2000, Pub.L. 106-207, as amended by Pub.L. 106-415 and Pub.L. 107-77.

humous naturalization.[7] This latter group is also exempted from the civics and history requirements.

Individuals who do not qualify for exemptions from the requirement to take the test in English may nonetheless qualify for an accommodation or modification of the test, if they suffer from a disability.[8] These might include questions in plain language, written tests for people with hearing difficulties, or tests in large print (or even oral examinations) for people with vision problems.[9]

§ 7:88 Exemptions—Physically unable to comply; traditional position and Congressional action

Research References
Dizon and Wettstein, Immigration Law Service 2d § 14:171
Steel on Immigration Law § 15:15

The INA provides that the English and civics requirements "shall not apply to any person who is unable because of physical or developmental disability or mental impairment to comply therewith."[1]

Before the INTCA, the statute only exempted persons who were "physically unable to comply" and this exemption was only applicable to the English requirement.[2] The legacy INS had interpreted this exemption in a particularly restrictive manner.[3] It took the position that a physical disability would only exempt a person from that part of the English test with which the disability directly interfered.[4] Thus, it was the INS' original position that blind people were only exempted from the reading and writing parts of the English examination, and were required to be examined on oral understanding and spoken English.[5] After adverse decisions by the federal courts, the INS changed its position to allow exemption of all the portions of the English language test for persons who were blind or legally blind under state or federal statutes.[6] The INS also accepted the position that a person who suffered from complete bilateral deafness was exempted from all the portions of the English language test.[7]

On the other hand, during this period, the INS did not regard a person who had a general incapacity to learn because of developmental disability or advanced age to be physically unable to comply.[8] Even though the refusal to exempt the elderly could be justified legally, the lack of exemption for developmental disability had less of a

---

[7]Section 114(d)(2) of the Department of Justice Appropriations Act of 2002, Pub.L. 107-77. See also Ch 11 (Posthumous Naturalization of Victims of September 11, 2001).

[8]See Appendix 7-15.

[9]See Appendix 7-9.

[Section 7:88]

[1]INA § 312(b)(1), 8 U.S.C.A. § 1423(b)(1).

[2]INA § 312(1), 8 U.S.C.A. § 1423(1) as originally enacted by Act of June 27, 1952, Pub.L. 82-414, 66 Stat. 166.

[3]See INS Interp. 312.1(a)(2)(iii).

[4]INS Interp. 312.1(a)(2)(iii).

[5]INS Interp. 312.1(a)(2)(iii).

[6]INS Interp. 312.1(a)(2)(iii). citing to In re Petition of Sandolo, 307 F.Supp. 221 (D.Conn. 1969); In re Petition of Stefanatos, D.N.J. Apr. 19, 1974 (unpublished decision).

[7]INS Interp. 312.1(a)(2)(iii) citing to In re Petition of Vazquez, 327 F.Supp. 935 (S.D.N.Y. 1971).

[8]8 CFR § 312.1(b)(3); INS Interp. 312.1(a)(2)(iii).

legal basis. By specifically exempting developmentally disabled and mentally impaired from both the requirements of English and history and government, the INTCA was designed to compel the INS to change its approach to these exemptions.[9]

In its *Interpretations*, the legacy INS discusses other factors that interfere with the ability to learn which the courts may or may not accept as the basis for a "physical inability to comply" exemption. Citing a case of an Armenian who developed an emotional block against learning after being subjected to great mental anguish during the Armenian massacres, the court concluded that such a person did not qualify for the exemption because there was some medical evidence that the inability to learn might have been caused by the mere process of aging.[10] However, a court found a fifty-two year old petitioner exempt from the writing portion of the English exam when she presented ample medical evidence that she had suffered from a serious illness, resulting in neural and emotional strain, which interfered with her ability to learn to write the English language.[11] In that case, the petitioner proved an ability to speak and read English and was naturalized.[12]

§ 7:89 Exemptions—Physically unable to comply; traditional position and Congressional action—Current regulations

Research References

Steel on Immigration Law § 15:15

On March 19, 1997 the legacy INS issued regulations implementing the INTCA amendment regarding applicants who are physically unable to comply with the English and civics tests.[1]

As amended by the 1994 law, the Immigration and Nationality Act only provides that the English language and history and government requirements "shall not apply to any person who is unable because of physical or developmental disability or mental impairment to comply therewith."[2]

The regulations treat the English language and the civics requirements separately. However, the content of both regulatory sections is virtually identical.[3] Accordingly, the requirements to satisfy them will be discussed together in this section. However, since the requirements are treated separately in the regulations, the medical evidence provided to satisfy these requirements should address both of them separately.

The regulations exempt from the English and civics requirements those persons who, "because of a medically determinable physical or mental impairment or

---

[9]INTCA § 108(a)(4) amending INA § 312, 8 U.S.C.A. § 1423 reproduced as Appendix 4-21 to Ch 4.

[10]INS Interp. 312.1(b)(2)(iii) citing to Petition of Siranough Markarian, File A-11706612 (E.D.Mich., 1970) (unreported); Petition of Kalyopi Zhonga, No. 2270-837013 (S.D.N.Y. Dec. 20, 1976).

[11]INS Interp. 312.1(b)(2)(iii) citing to In re Petition of Adibe Amin, No. 20610 (D.Ohio 1977) (unreported).

[12]INS Interp. 312.1(b)(2)(iii) citing to In re Petition of Adibe Amin, No. 20610 (D.Ohio 1977) (unreported).

[Section 7:89]

[1]62 Fed. Reg. 12915 (March 19, 1997) (The rule amends 8 CFR §§ 312.1, 312.2, dealing with the English language and civics requirements respectively and 8 CFR §§ 299.5, 499, to create a new nationality form).

[2]INA § 312(b)(1), 8 U.S.C.A. § 1423(b)(1).

[3]8 CFR §§ 312.1(b)(3), 312.2(b).

combination of impairments which has lasted or is expected to last at least 12 months," are unable to demonstrate an understanding of the English language and/or a knowledge and understanding of the fundamentals of history, and of the principles of and form of government of the United States.[4]

Thus, the regulations interpret the law to require the impairment (1) to be medically determinable, and (2) to have lasted or be expected to last at least twelve months.

§7:90 Exemptions—Physically unable to comply; traditional position and Congressional action—Medically determinable impairments

Research References

Dizon and Wettstein, Immigration Law Service 2d §14:171
Steel on Immigration Law §15:15

The term "medically determinable" used by the regulations is borrowed from the Social Security Administration regulations.[1]

As included in the regulations, a "medically determinable impairment" is defined as: (a) an impairment; (b) that results from anatomical, physiological, or psychological abnormalities; (c) which can be shown by medically acceptable clinical or laboratory diagnostic techniques; (d) to have resulted in functioning so impaired; (e) as to render an individual unable to demonstrate an understanding of the English language or the knowledge of civics required by the regulations; or (f) that renders the individual unable to fulfill the requirements for English proficiency or to participate in the testing procedures for naturalization, even with reasonable modifications to the methods of determining English proficiency outlined by the regulations.[2]

The supplementary information to the regulations explains that the disability must be of such an extent as to preclude complying with the English and civics requirements. The burden is on the applicant to explain, via the medical certification, how the disability prevents the applicant from learning the information required by section 312.[3] The instructions on the medical certification form emphasize the agency's limited understanding of the exemption by providing that "if reasonable modifications and/or accommodations will allow [the applicant] to demonstrate knowledge of basic English and U.S. history and civics, [the] medical certification form is not required."[4] The USCIS understands such modifications to include, though not be limited to, Braille test forms, sign language interpreters, and off site testing.[5]

Medical practitioners are instructed to evaluate whether the applicant has the ability to learn sufficient English and civics to pass the DHS' citizenship test.[6] The medical certification form explains that this test requires an ability to speak and write basic English and the ability to answer basic questions about the history and

---

[4]8 CFR §§ 312.1(b)(3), 312.2(b)(1).

[Section 7:90]

[1]62 Fed. Reg. at 12917 (Supplementary Information, Definitions of the Disabilities).

[2]8 CFR. §§ 312.1(b)(3), 312.2(b)(1) as amended by 62 Fed. Reg. 12915 and 64 Fed. Reg. 7990.

[3]62 Fed. Reg. at 12917 (Supplementary Information: Definitions of Disability).

[4]Form N-648, instructions.

[5]Form N-648, instructions.

[6]Form N-648, instructions.

civics of the United States.[7] When filling out the medical form, the medical practitioner must address separately the English and civics exemptions.[8]

The regulations contemplate the granting of the English and civics exemption not only when inability to comply is based on an impairment, but also when it is based on a combination of impairments.[9] This specific reference was added to address situations where applicants suffer from several conditions, any one of which is not sufficient to prevent them from complying with the requirements, but the combination of which has such an effect.[10] Apparently because of a drafting mistake, the regulation dealing with knowledge of history and government failed to include the reference to the combination of impairments.[11]

§ 7:91 Exemptions—Physically unable to comply; traditional position and Congressional action—Regulatory refusal to exempt

The regulations provide that loss of cognitive skills based on the direct effect of the illegal use of drugs, will not be considered in determining an exemption.[1] This seems to contradict the language of the statute, which requires an exemption when the applicant is unable to comply "because of physical or developmental disability or mental impairment."[2] The language of the law is very broad and does not exclude impairments based on specific causes.[3] In addition, the Attorney General is given no discretion regarding the implementation of this section.[4] Rather than strictly adhering to the text of the law, the legacy INS believed that the intent of Congress justified this exclusion.[5] As opposed to the rest of the definition of "impairment", the legacy INS made a conscious decision that in this issue the regulations would *not* follow the Social Security Administration's regulatory language.[6]

§ 7:92 Exemptions—Physically unable to comply; traditional position and Congressional action—Medical evidence

Research References

Dizon and Wettstein, Immigration Law Service 2d § 14:175

The regulations require all persons seeking an exemption from the English language requirement based on an inability to comply to present medical evidence

---

[7]Form N-648, instructions.

[8]62 Fed. Reg. at 12921 (Supplementary Information: A Single Test and Single Determination).

[9]8 CFR § 312.1(b)(3).

[10]62 Fed. Reg. at 12917 (Supplementary Information: Definitions of the Disabilities).

[11]8 CFR § 312.2(b)(1).

[Section 7:91]

[1]8 CFR §§ 312.1(b)(3).

[2]INA § 312(b)(1), 8 U.S.C.A. § 1423(b)(1).

[3]INA § 312(b)(1), 8 U.S.C.A. § 1423(b)(1).

[4]INA § 312(b)(1), 8 U.S.C.A. § 1423(b)(1).

[5]62 Fed. Reg. at 12916 (Supplementary Information: Definitions of the Disabilities) citing to H.R. No. 103-387.

[6]62 Fed. Reg. at 12916.

to support their claim.[1] Thus, this procedure must be followed when the inability to comply is based on physical disability, as well as when it is based on developmental disability or mental impairment.

In order to claim the exemption, applicants are required to have a physician, osteopathic doctor, or licensed clinical psychologist fill out INS Form N-648.[2] In 1999, the legacy INS made some changes to Form N-648.[3] The current version is available for download from the USCIS website at http://uscis.gov/graphics/index. htm.

These professionals do not need to be specifically designated civil surgeons.[4] Any medical doctor licensed to practice medicine in the United States—including doctors licensed to practice in Guam, Puerto Rico, or the Virgin Islands—may fill out this form.[5] Alternatively, clinical psychologists licensed to practice psychology in the United States may fill out the form.[6] Finally, in 1999, the INS added licensed osteopathic doctors, to those practitioners who can fill out form N-648.[7] Affidavits by the applicant, parent, or guardian are not sufficient to satisfy this requirement.[8] Similarly unavailing is a certification of disability from another government agency.[9]

The physician, osteopathy doctor, or psychologist who fills out this form must be "experienced in diagnosing those with physical or mental medically determinable impairments," and must be able to attest to the origin, nature, and extent of the medical condition as it relates to the disability exceptions to naturalization.[10]

When adopting the regulations, the legacy INS attempted to ensure the integrity of the application system through a combination of civil and criminal penalties, and by reserving the right to review the medical records and to refer the applicant to another licensed practitioner for a supplemental determination.[11]

By signing the form, the applicant authorizes the doctor to release all relevant physical and mental health information to the USCIS.[12] On the form, the physician, osteopathic doctor, or psychologist also agrees to the release of all medical records relating to the applicant that may be requested by the USCIS, certifies under penalty to having answered all questions truthfully, and attests to his or her

---

[Section 7:92]

[1] 8 CFR § 312.2(b)(2).

[2] 8 CFR § 312.2(b)(2). See Form N-648 reproduced as Appendix 7-9. Part I of the Form N-648 is filled out by the applicant and Part II is filled out and signed by the doctor or licensed clinical psychologist. Form N-648, instructions.

[3] 64 Fed. Reg. 7990 (Feb. 18, 1999).

[4] 62 Fed. Reg. at 12918 (Supplementary Information: Disability Determinations: Use of the Civil Surgeons and Creation of a Form).

[5] 8 CFR § 312.2(b)(2).

[6] 8 CFR § 312.2(b)(2).

[7] 8 CFR § 312.2(b)(2).

[8] 8 CFR § 312.2(b)(2).

[9] 62 Fed. Reg. at 12919 (Supplementary Information: Acceptance of Disability Certifications from Other Government Agencies).

[10] 8 CFR § 312.2(b)(2).

[11] 62 Fed. Reg. at 12918 (Supplementary Information: Disability Determinations: Use of the Civil Surgeons and Creation of a Form).

[12] Form N-648, Part I. The INS provides the same accommodation in signing Form N-648 as they do in the signature of Form N-400. See Ch 9 (The N-400: Question by Question Analysis: Parts 11 and 12 - Signature).

understanding that false or misleading statements may be subject to civil penalties.[13] Surprisingly, the applicant is also required to verify under penalty of perjury that the information on the form is true.[14]

Doctors and psychologists are instructed to fill in all the questions.[15] If an answer does not apply, the practitioner is required to indicate it with "N/A."[16] When the space to answer is insufficient, the practitioner may attach additional pages, including the item number, which it is supplementing, and placing the applicant's first, middle and last name and "A" number on top of each page, as well as, the medical practitioner's first, middle and last name, with his or her title.[17] Additional medical reports may also be included but they must be limited to no more than two pages, and have the name of the applicant, "A" number, and the practitioner's signature on each page.[18] Medical records may also be submitted, but will not be accepted as replacements for the answers on the certification form.[19]

In filling out this form, doctors and psychologists must remember that they have to address separately the ability of the applicant to take both the English and the civics tests.[20]

Form N-648 must be filed within six months from the date of its completion and signed by the medical practitioner.[21]

In addition to all the other safeguards against fraud, when the USCIS has "credible doubts" about the veracity of the medical certification, it may refer the applicant to another medical practitioner for a supplemental determination of the disability.[22] USCIS has recently issued guidance to the field regarding disability waivers, which is reproduced as App. 7-17.

§ 7:93 Exemptions—Physically unable to comply; traditional position and Congressional action—Applicable standards

The legacy INS was sued in the Southern District of Florida on the basis that the INS' adjudications of disability waiver applications were arbitrary and idiosyncratically capricious.[1] The court refused to grant the INS motion to dismiss, finding that relief could be granted for all but one of the plaintiffs' claims against the INS.[2]

In response, the INS Office of Field Operations issued a memorandum in 1999 providing more detailed guidance for adjudicating disability waivers. The memorandum is reproduced as Appendix 7-17.

---

[13]8 CFR § 312.2(b)(2); Form N-648, Part II. To make its point plain, the instructions to the form also include a statement regarding criminal and civil penalties for providing false information in the form. Form N-648, instructions.

[14]Form N-648, Part I.

[15]Form N-648, instructions.

[16]Form N-648, instructions.

[17]Form N-648, instructions.

[18]Form N-648, instructions.

[19]Form N-648, instructions.

[20]62 Fed. Reg. at 12921 (Supplementary Information: A Single Test and Single Determination).

[21]62 Fed. Reg. at 12921 (Supplementary Information: A Single Test and Single Determination).

[22]8 CFR § 312.2(b)(2).

[Section 7:93]

[1]Campos v. I.N.S., 32 F.Supp.2d 1337 (S.D. Fla. 1998).

[2]Campos v. I.N.S., 32 F.Supp.2d 1337 (S.D. Fla. 1998).

This memorandum replaces all the prior field guidance on disability waivers, seeking to provide a comprehensive guidance on disability adjudication.[3]

The guidance starts by restating the proof that must be established by the physician. According to the memorandum, the doctor must establish that the applicant has "a physical or mental abnormality that has impaired an individual's functioning so severely that the individual is unable to learn or demonstrate knowledge of English and/or U.S. history and government."[4]

First, it reminds the adjudicators that doctors must attest that their medical specialty or their experience and other qualifications permit them to make a disability assessment.[5] The type of doctor filling out the form is not important, and the guidelines emphasize that mental impairment assessments made by general practitioners are acceptable if the form fulfills the other requirements for reliability.[6]

There is no time limit to these evaluations. The only requirement is that they be filed with the USCIS within six months of being completed and signed by the medical practitioner.[7] Thus even if the interview takes place several months after the filing, the medical evaluation continues to be valid indefinitely.[8] In the past, some INS officers were under the erroneous impression that these certifications were only valid for one year. This is not the case.[9]

In addition, if the USCIS requests an amended or new Form N-648, it will be valid indefinitely, provided it was completed and signed after the first interview and submitted before the time specified by the Form N-14.[10]

Form N-648 must be fully filled out when submitted at the interview.[11] The applicant, however, will be allowed to correct minor deficiencies, such as filling in such missing identifying information as his or her "alien" registration number.[12] The adjudicating officer will first make sure that all the questions are fully and legibly answered before continuing.[13] If the officer finds the form incomplete or insufficient, he or she will continue the case and request additional information.[14] However, if the officer is already reviewing a second or amended Form N-648, then the officer may reject the form as insufficient and proceed with the interview.[15]

In reviewing Form N-648, adjudicating officers are instructed to pay particular attention to Part II, Question 3.[16] This question asks the doctors to describe "any findings of a physical or mental disability or impairment" which, in their professional medical opinion, would prevent the applicant from demonstrating knowledge of En-

---

[3]Pearson, Exec. Assoc. Comm'r, Office of Field Operations, Memorandum No. HQ 70/33-P (Apr. 7, 1999) reproduced as Appendix 7-10.

[4]Pearson, Memorandum (Apr. 7, 1999) reproduced as Appendix 7-10.

[5]Pearson, Memorandum (Apr. 7, 1999) reproduced as Appendix 7-10.

[6]Pearson, Memorandum (Apr. 7, 1999) reproduced as Appendix 7-10.

[7]Pearson, Memorandum (Apr. 7, 1999) reproduced as Appendix 7-10.

[8]Pearson, Memorandum (Apr. 7, 1999) reproduced as Appendix 7-10.

[9]Pearson, Memorandum (Apr. 7, 1999) reproduced as Appendix 7-10.

[10]Pearson, Memorandum (Apr. 7, 1999) reproduced as Appendix 7-10.

[11]Pearson, Memorandum (Apr. 7, 1999) reproduced as Appendix 7-10.

[12]Pearson, Memorandum (Apr. 7, 1999) reproduced as Appendix 7-10.

[13]Pearson, Memorandum (Apr. 7, 1999) reproduced as Appendix 7-10.

[14]Pearson, Memorandum (Apr. 7, 1999) reproduced as Appendix 7-10.

[15]Pearson, Memorandum (Apr. 7, 1999) reproduced as Appendix 7-10.

[16]Pearson, Memorandum (Apr. 7, 1999) reproduced as Appendix 7-10.

glish and/or U.S. history and government.[17] The response must be based on the examination of the applicant and must list a Diagnostic Statistical Manual (DSM) code if appropriate.[18]

The INS previously wavered between requiring the doctors to provide a detailed explanation of how they reached their diagnosis and not requiring it.[19] At present, the USCIS policy is to accept the N-648 without such an explanation.

On the other hand, the USCIS still requires a detailed explanation on how the diagnosed condition has impaired the functioning of the applicant so severely that the applicant is unable to learn or demonstrate knowledge of English and/or U.S. history and government.[20] USCIS adjudicators have been instructed to center their review on the nexus between the disability, or impairments, and the applicant's ability to learn or demonstrate knowledge of English and/or U.S. history and government.[21] They are advised not to look for specific phraseology but to determine from all the information provided in Question 3 whether the applicant "has met the burden of showing that the anatomical, physiological, or psychological abnormality described has so impaired the applicant's functioning that he [or she] is unable to learn or demonstrate knowledge of English and/or U.S. history and government."[22] The USCIS provides examples of what it considers to be sufficient and insufficient answers.[23]

Finally, the doctors must express their conclusion whether the applicant is able to learn or demonstrate knowledge of English and/or U.S. history and government.[24]

The USCIS guidelines dedicate a special section to the issue of old age.[25] The fact that impairment is solely the result of old age does not disqualify it from serving as the basis of the waiver.[26] The guidelines specifically mention Alzheimer's, Parkinson's disease, and senile dementia as examples of such diseases.[27] The adjudicators are instructed to do a functional analysis and focus on whether the doctor has provided a sufficient nexus between the condition and the inability to learn or demonstrate knowledge.[28] Similarly, the adjudicators are instructed to treat "depression" in the same manner and perform the required analysis of the nexus provided by the doctor.[29]

The USCIS guidelines provide detailed procedural instructions for waiver-related actions to be taken at every step of the naturalization process.[30]

---

[17]Pearson, Memorandum (Apr.7, 1999) reproduced as Appendix 7-10.

[18]Pearson, Memorandum (Apr.7, 1999) reproduced as Appendix 7-10.

[19]Pearson, Memorandum (Apr.7, 1999) reproduced as Appendix 7-10.

[20]Pearson, Memorandum (Apr.7, 1999) reproduced as Appendix 7-10.

[21]Pearson, Memorandum (Apr.7, 1999) reproduced as Appendix 7-10.

[22]Pearson, Memorandum (Apr.7, 1999) reproduced as Appendix 7-10.

[23]See attachment A to Appendix 7-10.

[24]Pearson, Memorandum (Apr.7, 1999) reproduced as Appendix 7-10.

[25]Pearson, Memorandum (Apr.7, 1999) reproduced as Appendix 7-10.

[26]Pearson, Memorandum (Apr.7, 1999) reproduced as Appendix 7-10.

[27]Pearson, Memorandum (Apr.7, 1999) reproduced as Appendix 7-10.

[28]Pearson, Memorandum (Apr.7, 1999) reproduced as Appendix 7-10.

[29]Pearson, Memorandum (Apr.7, 1999) reproduced as Appendix 7-10.

[30]Pearson, Memorandum (Apr.7, 1999) reproduced as Appendix 7-10.

§7:94 Exemptions—Long time lawful permanent residents who are over certain age

Research References

Dizon and Wettstein, Immigration Law Service 2d §14:172

Some longtime residents are exempt from the English language tests. To qualify, the person must, on the date of the filing of the application for naturalization, be (1) over 50 years of age and have been living in the United States as a lawful permanent resident for periods totaling at least 20 years, or (2) over 55 years of age and have been living in the United States for periods totaling at least 15 years subsequent to becoming a lawful permanent resident.[1] It must be emphasized that eligibility is determined by the age and length of residence on the date of filing of the application for naturalization.[2] The USCIS refers to these exemptions as the 50/20 and 55/15 rules.

The required period of residence for these exemptions starts on the date the applicant became a lawful permanent resident.[3] Before 1978, applicants who had "lived" in the United States for periods totaling 20 years and were over 50 years of age on the effective date of the INA were exempted from the English test.[4] To qualify, the person had to comply with both the age and length of permanent residence requirements on or before December 24, 1952, the effective date of the INA.[5] In 1978, Congress passed an amendment updating the one-time compliance date of December 24, 1952, to the date of filing of each naturalization petition.[6] On the other hand, it added the requirement that the 20 years of residence in the United States must have been after admission to lawful permanent residence.[7]

Under the current law, for time-based exemptions to apply, the applicant must have achieved the required age and period of lawful permanent residence by the date of filing of the application.[8] The old N-400 instructions erroneously advise applicants that they are eligible for the exemption if they satisfy the requirement at the time of interview.[9] Starting in July 8, 1997, the INS distributed either an addendum to the instructions or a *Guide to Naturalization* explaining the correct requirements for the exemption.[10] Because of this confusion, many applicants filed prematurely in reliance on the erroneous instructions.[11] To ease the hardship created by its instructions, the INS issued a memorandum instructing adjudicators to allow applicants who filed prematurely to replace the N-400 at the time of the

---

[Section 7:94]

[1]INA §312(b)(2)(A), 8 U.S.C.A. §1423(b)(2)(A); 8 CFR §312.1(b)(1), (2).

[2]INA §312(b)(2)(B), 8 U.S.C.A. §1423(b)(2)(B); 8 CFR §312.1(b)(1), (2).

[3]INA §312(b)(2), 8 U.S.C.A. §1423(b)(2).

[4]INA §312(1), 8 U.S.C.A. §1423(1) as originally enacted by Act of June 27, 1952.

[5]INA §312(1), 8 U.S.C.A. §1423(1). as originally enacted by Act of June 27, 1952.

[6]Sec. 3, Act of November 2, 1978, Pub.L. 95-579, 92 Stat. 2474.

[7]Sec. 3, Act of November 2, 1978, Pub.L. 95-579, 92 Stat. 2474.

[8]INA §312(b)(2)(B), 8 U.S.C.A. §1423(b)(2)(B); 8 CFR §312.1(b)(1), (2).

[9]Yates, Deputy Exec. Assoc. Comm'r, Field Operations, Memorandum, June 29, 1999.

[10]Yates, Deputy Exec. Assoc. Comm'r, Field Operations, Memorandum, June 29, 1999.

[11]Yates, Deputy Exec. Assoc. Comm'r, Field Operations, Memorandum, June 29, 1999.

interview.[12] This policy applies to applications that were filed prior to June 29, 1999—the date of the memorandum—and where applicants are eligible for the exemption at the time of the interview.[13] The memorandum contains important procedural steps that must be followed in order to benefit from the policy.

The legacy INS corrected the instructions for the 2001 version of Form N-400. It is available for download at http://uscis.gov/graphics/index.htm.

§ 7:95 Exemptions—Hmong veterans

From 2000-2003, the Hmong Veterans' Naturalization Act permitted Hmong guerrilla fighters and members of the irregular armed forces of Laos to naturalize without meeting the English language requirements. Individuals who did not apply by 2003 are no longer able to take advantage of these provisions. The provisions of the Hmong Veterans' Naturalization Act have now expired, but the Act is reproduced for purposes of historical interest at App 7-14.

§ 7:96 Exemptions—Victims of September 11, 2001

Following the attacks on September 11, 2001, Congress enacted a special provision allowing for the posthumous naturalization of eligible non-citizens killed as a result of the attacks who had naturalization applications pending on September 11, 2001.[1] Under these provisions, family members or next of kin are able to complete the naturalization process for their deceased relative. While in general the deceased applicant must have satisfied the naturalization requirements, an exception is made for the English, history and civics requirements. Congress specified that demonstration of an understanding of English, history or civics is not necessary for a posthumous naturalization under this provision.[2] Moreover, the legacy INS instructed its examiners that this exemption applies to all cases without regard to whether or not there had been an initial examination prior to September 11, 2001, and without regard to whether or not the applicant demonstrated the INA § 312 requirements at a first or second examination.[3] The requirements and procedures for posthumous naturalization under this provision are discussed fully in Ch 11.

C. KNOWLEDGE OF HISTORY AND GOVERNMENT

§ 7:97 In general

Research References
Dizon and Wettstein, Immigration Law Service 2d § 14:173
Steel on Immigration Law § 15:15

The second requirement of the statute is that the applicant must demonstrate "a knowledge and understanding of the fundamentals of the history, and of the

---

[12]Yates, Deputy Exec. Assoc. Comm'r, Field Operations, Memorandum, June 29, 1999.

[13]Yates, Deputy Exec. Assoc. Comm'r, Field Operations, Memorandum, June 29, 1999.

[Section 7:96]

[1]Section 114 of the Department of Justice Appropriations Act of 2002, Pub.L. 107-77. See also Ch 11 (Posthumous Naturalization of Victims of September 11, 2001).

[2]Section 114(d)(2) of the Department of Justice Appropriations Act of 2002, Pub.L. 107-77. *See also,* Ch 11 (Posthumous Naturalization of Victims of September 11, 2001).

[3]Implementation Instructions for Section 114 of Public Law 107-77, "Department of Commerce, Justice, State, the Judiciary, and Related Agencies Appropriations Act, 2002," 115 Stat. 748 (November 28, 2001) *reproduced* as Appendix 11-3.

principles and form of government, of the United States."[1] Before the passage of the INTCA, no naturalization applicant was exempt from this requirement.[2] The INTCA added two exemptions to this requirement. First, it exempted those who were physically unable to comply, developmentally disabled, and mentally impaired.[3] Secondly, it granted the Attorney General the power to develop regulations to relax this requirement in relation to persons who are over sixty-five years of age and who have been lawful permanent residents for more than twenty years.[4] Recently, Congress has extended the relaxed treatment of the elderly to apply also to Hmong veterans.[5] Congress also exempted eligible victims of the September 11, 2001 attacks from this requirement entirely.[6] Unless, the applicant falls within these exemptions, he or she must comply with the history and civics requirements even when exempted from the English language requirement.[7]

That said, an individual who does not qualify for an exemption from the requirement to show knowledge of history and government may nonetheless qualify for an accommodation or modification of the test, if she suffers from a disability.[8] Accommodations might include being questioned in plain language, taking a written test if one suffers from hearing difficulties, or being given tests in large print (or even oral examinations) if one has a vision problem.[9]

This requirement may be satisfied by any one of the following: (1) taking an examination during the naturalization interview, (2) having taken the standardized citizenship test while they were available and within one year of filing the application for naturalization, or (3) having satisfied the English language and history and government requirements as part of adjustment to lawful permanent residence under the legalization program.[10]

§ 7:98 Test at USCIS interview

Research References

Dizon and Wettstein, Immigration Law Service 2d §§ 14:177, 14:178

If the test is taken at the interview, it will generally be conducted in English and will be given in oral form.[1] For those applicants who are exempt from the English language requirements, the examination may be conducted in the native language

---

[Section 7:97]

[1]INA § 312(a)(2), 8 U.S.C.A. § 1423(a)(2).

[2]8 CFR § 312.2(a).

[3]INA § 312(b)(1), 8 U.S.C.A. § 1423(b)(1). See § 7:103.

[4]INA § 312(b)(3), 8 U.S.C.A. § 1423(b)(3).

[5]Hmong Veterans' Naturalization Act of 2000, § 3 reproduced as Appendix 7-12.

[6]Section 114(d)(2) of the Department of Justice Appropriations Act of 2002, Pub.L. 107-77. *See also,* Ch 11 (Posthumous Naturalization of Victims of September 11, 2001).

[7]INA § 312(b)(2), 8 U.S.C.A. § 1423(b)(2); OI 312.3(b).

[8]See Appendix 7-15.

[9]See Appendix 7-21.

[10]8 CFR §§ 312.2(b)(1), 312.3(a), (b). The INS discontinued use of standardized tests provided by non-govermental organizations effective August 30, 1998. See § 7:97.

[Section 7:98]

[1]8 CFR § 312.2(b)(1).

of the applicant with the assistance of an interpreter.[2] The regulations, however, only allows this option if the command of the English language of the applicant is insufficient.[3] Even if the applicant is not exempt from the English language requirement, he or she may still be examined through the use of an interpreter if the USCIS officer conducting the examination determines that an inaccurate or incomplete record of the examination would result if the examination on these technical matters be conducted in English.[4]

The scope of examination is limited to subject matters covered in the Federal Textbooks on Citizenship.[5] The regulations require that in choosing the subject matter, in phrasing the questions, and in evaluating the responses, due consideration must be given to the applicant's "education, background, age, length of residence in the United States, opportunities available and efforts made to acquire the requisite knowledge, and any other elements or factors relevant to an appraisal of the adequacy of the applicant's knowledge and understanding."[6]

At the interview, the USCIS will normally test the applicant's knowledge of history and government of the U.S. from a standard list of 100 questions. The list of standard questions is attached as Appendix 7-5. The number of questions varies from district to district and from examiner to examiner, but normally the applicant is asked between six and ten questions. The examiner must be satisfied that the applicant possesses the adequate knowledge. In the Los Angeles district, this translated to answering at least half of the questions correctly. In other districts, examiners refused to give a percentage of correct answers that would satisfy the examiner.[7]

§ 7:99   Civics test for elderly applicants and Hmong Veterans

Congress has provided for "special consideration" in the naturalization exam to those who are over 65 years of age and who have been lawful permanent residents for more than 20 years are given a different civics test. The INS initially wavered on its position regarding the meaning of special consideration. Soon after the passage of the INTCA, the INS issued a cable to all its offices advising them that these applicants would not be tested.[1] Apparently due to political pressure, the INS was forced to require some form of testing of these applicants. Accordingly, on March 24, 1995, the INS issued another cable changing its position and establishing that applicants aged 65 years or older, who have been lawful permanent residents for 20 years or more will be tested from a set of 10 questions.[2] To pass the test, the ap-

---

[2]8 CFR § 312.2(b)(1)(i).

[3]8 CFR § 312.2(b)(1)(i).

[4]8 CFR § 312.2(b)(1)(ii).

[5]8 CFR § 312.2(b)(2).

[6]8 CFR § 312.2(b)(2).

[7]See Immigrant Legal Resource Center, Naturalization: a Guide for Legal Practitioners and Other Community Advocates, at 7-4 (1994).

[Section 7:99]

[1]INS Cable No. HQ 312-C (Feb. 6, 1995) reproduced in 72 Interpreter Releases 206 (Feb. 6, 1995).

[2]INS Cable No. HQ 312-P (Mar. 24, 1995) reproduced in 72 Interpreter Releases 503. 12INS Cable No. HQ 312-P (Mar. 24, 1995) reproduced in 72 Interpreter Releases 503.

plicant had to respond correctly to six of the 10 questions.[3] At the end of 1995, the former INS once again changed its interpretation of the "special consideration" provision of this section.[4]

The former INS consulted with current members of Congress as to the scope of the prior Congress' "special consideration" provision.[5] It then issued a list of 25 questions on U.S. history and government.[6] From these questions applicants will be asked 10 questions and must have at least six correct answers to pass the test. The 25 questions are reproduced below as Appendix 7-6. Since these applicants by definition are over the age of 55 and have been lawful permanent residents for more than 15 years, they are exempt from the English language requirements and are entitled to take the history and government exam in their native languages.[7] Spanish, Armenian, Chinese, Japanese, and Korean translations of the 25 questions are reproduced in Appendix 7-10.

A similar provision is now available for Hmong Veterans who qualify under the Hmong Veterans' Naturalization Act of 2000.[8] The same test used under the special rule for 65 years and over, is used for Hmong Veterans.[9]

§ 7:100   The new civics test

Beginning on October 1, 2008, the USCIS began administering the new civics test.[1] The new questions follow roughly the same format as the old test. The applicant will be asked 10 questions, and must answer six correctly in order to pass the test.[2] All applicants (who are not otherwise exempt) are now required to pass the new naturalization exam, rather than the prior naturalization exam.

§ 7:101   Lawful permanent residents who legalized their status under § 245A of INA; requirements under legalization program

In 1986, Congress passed several legalization programs, including the Special Agricultural Worker Program, the Cuban-Haitian Entrant Program, and the legaliza-

---

[3]Crocetti, Assoc. Comm'r, Examinations, Memorandum No. CO 70/33 2-P (Dec. 22, 1995) reproduced in 73 Interpreter Releases 86 (Jan. 16, 1996).

[4]See Crocetti, Assoc. Comm'r, Examinations, Memorandum No. CO 70/33 2-P (Dec. 22, 1995) reproduced in 73 Interpreter Releases 86 (Jan. 16, 1996).

[5]Crocetti, Assoc. Comm'r, Examinations, Memorandum No. CO 70/33 2-P (Dec. 22, 1995) reproduced in 73 Interpreter Releases 86 (Jan. 16, 1996).

[6]Crocetti, Assoc. Comm'r, Examinations, Memorandum No. CO 70/33 2-P (Dec. 22, 1995) reproduced in 73 Interpreter Releases 86 (Jan. 16, 1996).

[7]See § 7:94.

[8]Hmong Veterans' Naturalization Act of 2000, § 3 reproduced as Appendix 7-12.

[9]INS Fact Sheet, The Hmong Veterans' Naturalization Act of 2000 (Aug. 21, 2000) available at http://uscis.gov/graphics/index.htm.

[Section 7:100]

[1]See USCIS website, at www.uscis.gov/newtest (last accessed August 23, 2010).

[2]See Appendix 7-21.

tion program for noncitizens who had resided continuously in an unlawful status in the United States since before 1982, known as section 245A legalization.[1]

Applicants under the provisions of section 245A were barred from obtaining lawful permanent residence unless they demonstrated either (1) that they met the English and history and government requirements of naturalization, or (2) that they were pursuing a course of study to achieve such an understanding.[2] Under that legalization program, the law exempted individuals who were 65 years or older and developmentally disabled individuals from this requirement.[3] In addition, the INS exempted from this requirement those individuals who were over 50 years of age and had resided in the United States for more than 20 years.[4] The regulations also incorporated the naturalization exemption for persons who were physically unable to comply with the English language requirement.[5]

Under the section 245A regulations, the English literacy and history and government requirements could be satisfied either by taking a test during the interview with an INS officer or by taking a standardized test offered at the time by Educational Testing Services (ETS) and the Comprehensive Adult Student Assessment System (CASAS).[6] Since these applicants could not be granted permanent residence under the legalization program unless they also demonstrated an ability to speak and understand basic English, such an ability must have been demonstrated during the legalization interview.[7] Actually the test of such an ability was mandated by the regulations governing the English language and U.S. history and government tests during the INS interviews.[8] Persons who failed to demonstrate the required knowledge and understanding at the interview were provided additional time to present either the results of the standardized tests or proof that they were "pursuing a course of study" to achieve the required knowledge.[9]

The second alternative to obtaining permanent residence under section 245A was to establish that the applicant was "satisfactorily pursuing a course of study (recognized by the Attorney General) to achieve . . . an understanding of English and . . . knowledge and understanding of the history and government of the United States."[10] The INS regulations provided that the term "satisfactorily pursuing" meant one of the following alternative possibilities: (1) attending at least 40 hours out of a 60-hour course; (2) presenting a high school diploma or general equivalency diploma; (3) having attended one academic year at a recognized state institution

---

[Section 7:101]

[1] INA §§ 210, 245A, 8 U.S.C.A. §§ 1160, 1255a; sec. 202, Immigration Reform and Control Act of 1986 (IRCA), Pub.L. 99-603, 100 Stat. 3359. The legalization for recipients of extended voluntary departure was introduced by sec. 902, Foreign Relations Authorization Act, Fiscal Years 1988 and 1989, Pub.L. 100-204, 101 Stat. 1331.

[2] INA § 245A(b)(1)(D)(i), 8 U.S.C.A. § 1255a(b)(1)(D)(i), 8 CFR § 245a.3(b)(4)(i). No such bar existed under the provisions of the other legalization programs.

[3] INA § 245A(b)(1)(D)(ii), 8 U.S.C.A. § 1255a(b)(1)(D)(ii).

[4] 8 CFR § 245a.3(b)(4)(ii)(C).

[5] 8 CFR § 245a.3(b)(4)(ii)(E).

[6] 8 CFR § 245a.3(b)(4)(iii)(A).

[7] See INA § 245A(b)(1)(D)(i)(I), 8 U.S.C.A. § 1255a(b)(1)(D)(i)(I); 8 CFR § 245a.3(b)(4)(iii)(A).

[8] 8 CFR § 245a.(b)(4)(iii)(A)(1).

[9] 8 CFR § 245a.3(b)(4)(iii)(B).

[10] INA § 245A(b)(1)(D)(i)(II), 8 U.S.C.A. § 1255a(b)(1)(D)(i)(II).

which included certain required courses; and (4) having attended other INS-certified courses conducted by employers, social, community, or private organizations.[11]

In addition, the applicants were also allowed to demonstrate satisfactory pursuit by attesting they had studied for at least forty hours at home and had taken a standard test called IRCA Test for Permanent Residency.[12] The INS, some state departments of education, and some qualified designated entities gave this test.[13] Taking such an exam did not establish that the applicant met the requirements of English and history and government, but was rather another manner of demonstrating satisfactory pursuit of a course of study.[14] This test must be distinguished from the ETS and CASAS tests that were regulatorily authorized as proof of satisfying the requirements of English and history and government.[15]

§ 7:102 Lawful permanent residents who legalized their status under § 245A of INA; requirements under legalization program— Satisfaction of citizenship exams by proof of satisfaction of legalization tests

Section 245A of the INA provided that persons who demonstrated that they met the English language and history and government requirements would be exempt from those requirements when they naturalized.[1] On the other hand, obtaining permanent residence by proving satisfactory pursuit of a course of study did *not* satisfy the naturalization requirements.[2]

In addition, among the people who were exempted from the educational requirements during the legalization period, only those who are physically unable to comply are exempt from the English test at the naturalization stage.[3] Developmentally disabled persons and individuals who were over 65 years old who were exempt by law at the legalization stage are not exempted as such for naturalization.[4] People who had resided in the United States for over 20 years and were over 55 years of age will only be exempted from the naturalization test if the 20 years of residence in the United States occurred *after* becoming lawful permanent residents.[5]

The naturalization regulations incorporate the legalization provisions by mandating that if an applicant demonstrated English proficiency in reading and writing and knowledge of history and government of the U.S. by taking the naturalization test during the permanent residence interview with agency, or by taking one of the standardized tests which proved understanding of English language and knowledge of U.S. history and government, then the applicant is not required to take the En-

---

[11]8 CFR § 245a.1(s)(1)–(4). The requirements of recognition and certification of satisfactory attendance were regulated by 8 CFR § 245a.3(b)(4)(iv).

[12]8 CFR § 245a.1(s)(5).

[13]8 CFR § 245a.1(s)(5).

[14]See 8 CFR § 245a.3(b)(4)(iv) ("[s]uch applicants shall not the be required to demonstrate that they satisfy the requirements of § 245a.3(b)(4)(i)(A)").

[15]8 CFR § 245a.3(b)(4)(iii)(A)(2). See this section.

[Section 7:102]

[1]INA § 245A(b)(1)(D)(iii), 8 U.S.C.A. § 1255a(b)(1)(D)(iii).

[2]INA § 245A(b)(1)(D)(iii), 8 U.S.C.A. § 1255a(b)(1)(D)(iii).

[3]See §§ 7:88 to 7:94.

[4]INA § 245A(b)(1)(D)(iii), 8 U.S.C.A. § 1255a(b)(1)(D)(iii); 8 CFR § 245.3(b)(4)(ii).

[5]Compare 8 CFR § 312.1(b)(1), (2) with 8 CFR § 245a.3(b)(4)(ii)(C).

glish language reading and writing examination or the examination regarding knowledge of U.S. history and government.[6] The applicant, however, must still demonstrate his or her ability to speak English through testimony in the English language at the naturalization interview.[7]

D. FAILURE TO PASS EXAMINATION

§ 7:103 In general

Applicants who fail the English and U.S. history and government tests during the first examination must be provided a second opportunity to pass the test or tests within 90 days from the first examination.[1] Applicants who receive notice of the second examination and fail to appear without good cause will be deemed to have failed the second examination.[2] The USCIS will consider postponing a second examination, but only if the applicant agrees in writing to waive the requirement that the USCIS make a decision on the naturalization application within 120 days from the initial interview, and to permit the USCIS to render its decision within 120 days from the second interview.[3]

VIII. LEGAL COMPETENCE/CAPACITY TO TAKE OATH

§ 7:104 Legal competence/capacity to take oath

Even though the INA does not have a mental capacity requirement, under pre-2000 law, the legacy INS previously took the position that a person cannot comply with the naturalization requirements unless he or she were legally competent.[1] This bar apparently derived from the principle that a person who is legally incompetent lacks the capacity to comprehend the nature of the obligations of citizenship and to take the oath of allegiance.[2]

This non-statutory requirement came to the fore after Congress exempted developmentally disabled and mentally incapacitated persons from taking the English and civics exams.[3] When Congress provided for the exemption, it did not originally amend the requirement of taking the naturalization oath.[4] Although the exemption was specifically intended to permit developmentally disabled and mentally impaired individuals to naturalize, the requirement of having mental capacity to take the oath frustrated that end, and generated a bitter dispute within

---

[6]8 CFR § 312.3.

[7]8 CFR § 312.3.

[Section 7:103]

[1]8 CFR § 312.5(a).

[2]8 CFR § 312.5(b).

[3]8 CFR § 312.5(b). See § 9:55.

[Section 7:104]

[1]8 CFR § 316.12(a), INS Interp. 334.1(e).

[2]See McCampbell v. McCampbell, 13 F.Supp. 847 (W.D.Ky. 1936). See generally, Gordon & Mailman, § 95.03[3].

[3]See §§ 7:88 to 7:94.

[4]See INTCA, Title I reproduced as Appendix 4-23 to Chapter 4.

and without the INS.[5] In final regulations issued in 1997, the INS took the position that developmentally disabled and mentally incapacitated applicants had to establish that they had the capacity to take the oath.[6] Indeed, it refused to accept the suggestion that these oaths may be taken by proxy, through a relative, legal guardian, or court appointed trustee.[7] One federal district court disagreed finding that denial of naturalization to a severely developmentally disabled individual solely because of lack of capacity to take the oath violates the Rehabilitation Act of 1973.[8] Finally on November 6, 2000, President Clinton signed into law a waiver of the requirement of the oath for physically or developmentally disabled and mentally impaired persons.[9]

The new statute permitting an oath waiver for physically and developmentally disabled and mentally impaired persons has hopefully solved this.[10] The statute now exempts from the oath requirement any disabled individual who, in the opinion of the Secretary of DHS, is unable to understand or communicate an understanding of the meaning of the oath due to a physical or mental impairment.[11] Where the oath requirement is waived in this way, the individual "shall be considered to have met the requirements of [8 U.S.C.A. § 1427(a)(3)] with respect to attachment to the principles of the Constitution and well disposition to the good order and happiness of the United States."[12]

The new legislation is applicable to applications filed before, on, or after November 6, 2000.[13]

According to a 2003 memorandum from USCIS, to be eligible for an oath waiver, an individual must have a developmental or physical disability or mental impairment that prevents him or her from being able to understand the meaning of the oath or to communicate an understanding of the meaning of the oath requirement. The oath waiver is intended for individuals who are so severely impaired that they cannot, in any fashion or by any means, either demonstrate an understanding of the oath requirement or communicate that understanding.[14] The memo explains that the oath waiver is not for an individual who, because of a disability, needs assistance communicating his or her responses but who nevertheless can understand the meaning of the oath. The memo indicates that there are various methods by which a

---

[5]See 62 Fed. Reg. 12915, 12919 (Supplementary Information: Other Naturalization Requirements).

[6]62 Fed. Reg. 12915, 12919.

[7]62 Fed. Reg. 12915, 12919.

[8]Galvez-Letona v. Kirkpatrick, 54 F. Supp. 2d 1218 (D. Utah 1999), aff'd on other grounds, 3 Fed. Appx. 829 (10th Cir. 2001).

[9]Act of November 6, 2000, Pub.L. 106-448, *amending* 8 U.S.C.A. § 1448, reproduced as Appendix 7-13.

[10]Act of November 6, 2000, Pub.L. 106-448 reproduced as Appendix 7-13.

[11]8 U.S.C.A. § 1448(a).

[12]8 U.S.C.A. § 1448(a).

[13]See Act of November 6, 2000, § 2 reproduced as Appendix 7-13.

[14]Memorandum of William Yates, Acting Assoc. Director, CIS, HQ 70/33 (June 30, 2003), entitled "Procedures for Implementing the Waiving of the Oath of Renunciation and Allegiance for the Naturalization of Aliens having Certain Disabilities," reproduced as Appendix 7-16.

USCIS examiner can assess whether an individual understands the oath requirement.[15]

The USCIS decided not to develop a specific application form for the oath waiver because it believes that the waiver will apply to a "very small class of individuals."[16] Instead, an individual can apply for the waiver by annotating Part 3, section 1 of the N-400 or by submitting a letter requesting the waiver at the time of filing the N-400. This early filing requirement is not mandatory, however, because the agency recognizes that an impairment may get progressively worse while the application is pending, thereby justifying a later filed waiver request. Thus, USCIS will accept a waiver request any time up until the administration of the oath ceremony.[17]

The memo also discusses the medical documentary evidence that will be necessary to support a waiver request as well as the process for designating a representative for the applicant. Finally, it discusses procedures for handling the N-400 application for qualified waiver applicants.[18]

The regulations have not been altered to reflect the change in law. The regulations still provide that legal incompetence at the time of the naturalization interview or at the time of taking the oath of allegiance bars the applicant from naturalizing.[19] Under the former approach, where the applicant was declared legally incompetent prior to either event, the applicant had the burden of proving that legal competence was timely restored.[20] The *INS Interpretations* provide that if an applicant has been declared insane, or has been committed to, or has been a voluntary patient in, a mental institution, the laws of the State in which the proceedings of institutional care took place govern his or her legal competency.[21] Presumably, these rules would apply only where a waiver has not been granted as to the oath.

There may be situations where the individual committed acts that would reflect on his moral character, if the individual were sane. The regulations provide that an applicant has the burden of proving that any crimes were committed while the applicant was legally incompetent.[22]

In a separate development which may assist individuals with mental disabilities, the Office of Legal Counsel of the Department of Justice has issued a memorandum the effect of the Rehabilitation Act of 1973 on naturalization applications.[23] The memorandum concludes that the agency is required to allow a legal guardian or

---

[15]Memorandum of William Yates, Acting Assoc. Director, CIS, HQ 70/33 (June 30, 2003), entitled "Procedures for Implementing the Waiving of the Oath of Renunciation and Allegiance for the Naturalization of Aliens having Certain Disabilities," reproduced as Appendix 7-16.

[16]Memorandum of William Yates, Acting Assoc. Director, CIS, HQ 70/33 (June 30, 2003), entitled "Procedures for Implementing the Waiving of the Oath of Renunciation and Allegiance for the Naturalization of Aliens having Certain Disabilities," reproduced as Appendix 7-16.

[17]Memorandum of William Yates, Acting Assoc. Director, CIS, HQ 70/33 (June 30, 2003), entitled "Procedures for Implementing the Waiving of the Oath of Renunciation and Allegiance for the Naturalization of Aliens having Certain Disabilities," reproduced as Appendix 7-16.

[18]Memorandum of William Yates, Acting Assoc. Director, CIS, HQ 70/33 (June 30, 2003), entitled "Procedures for Implementing the Waiving of the Oath of Renunciation and Allegiance for the Naturalization of Aliens having Certain Disabilities," reproduced as Appendix 7-16.

[19]8 CFR § 316.12(a).

[20]8 CFR § 316.12(b)(2).

[21]INS Interp. 334.1(e).

[22]See 8 CFR § 316.12(b)(3).

[23]See Appendix 9-8, "Role of Legal Guardians or Proxies in Naturalization Proceedings" (March 13, 2002).

proxy assist a mentally disabled applicant who is unable to file the application or participate in the interview.[24]

IX. RACE AND NATIONAL ORIGIN

§ 7:105 Racial bars to naturalization

From the very first naturalization statute, Congress restricted the right to naturalize to free white persons.[1] In 1870, these categories were expanded to allow naturalization of not only free white persons but also of noncitizens of African nativity or descent.[2] The naturalization act of 1882, on the other hand, specifically barred Chinese from naturalizing.[3]

The "racial" bar has been held to apply regardless of the color of the skin, provided the person was not of "Caucasian race."[4] Even within the "Caucasian" race, it was restricted to Europeans and did not include high caste Hindus, or other people from the Asiatic exclusion zone imposed by the immigration act of 1917.[5] Thus, the following groups have been barred from naturalizing under these provisions: Burmese, Filipinos, Japanese, Koreans, Malayans, Polynesians, Samoans, and Siamese.[6] On the other hand, court decisions found the following as not being barred from naturalization by the racial and national origin bar: Afghanis, Arabs, Armenians, Egyptians, Kalmuks of Southeast European Russia, Persians, Syrians, Tartars of East Russia, Turks, and Mexican Indians.[7]

The bar applied regardless of the cultural background of the person. Thus, its reach extended to a person who had resided in the United States for over twenty years, studied high school and college in this country, spoke English at home, had educated his or her children in the United States, and went to U.S. churches.[8]

This attempt at national racial purity, however, was undermined by the fact that even when these persons were not allowed to naturalize, their children, if born inside the United States were U.S. citizens at birth.[9] It was also contradicted by the provisions for the collective naturalization of Hawaiians that included all citizens of

---

[24]See Appendix 9-8, "Role of Legal Guardians or Proxies in Naturalization Proceedings" (March 13, 2002).

[Section 7:105]

[1]See, e.g., sec. 1, Act of March 26, 1790, 1 Stat. 103 reproduced as Appendix 4-1 to Chapter 4; sec. 1, Act of January 29, 1795 reproduced as Appendix 4-2 to Chapter 4; sec. 1, Act of April 14, 1802 reproduced as Appendix 4-3 to Chapter 4.

[2]See In re Mallari, 239 F. 416, 417 (D.Mass. 1916). Cf. Revised Statutes § 2169 reproduced as Appendix 4-5 to Chapter 4.

[3]Sec. 14, Act of May 6, 1882, 22 Stat. 58.

[4]See Ozawa v. U.S., 260 U.S. 178, 197, 43 S.Ct. 65, 68-69, 67 L.Ed. 199 (1922) ("the test afforded by mere color of the skin is impracticable, as that differs greatly among persons of the same race, even among Anglo-Saxons . . . the words "white person" were meant to indicate only a person of what is popularly known as the Caucasian race").

[5]U.S. v. Bhagat Singh Thind, 261 U.S. 204, 43 S.Ct. 338, 67 L.Ed. 616 (1923); INS Interp. 311.1.

[6]INS Interp. 311.1. See also, Toyota v. U.S., 268 U.S. 402, 410, 45 S.Ct. 563, 565, 96 L.Ed. 1016, 1019 (1925) (holding Filipinos are not white).

[7]INS Interp. 311.1. See also, Toyota v. U.S., 268 U.S. 402, 410, 45 S.Ct. 563, 565, 96 L.Ed. 1016, 1019 (1925); In re Rodriguez, 81 F. 337 (W.D.Tex. 1897).

[8]Ozawa v. U.S., 260 U.S. at 189, 43 S.Ct. at 66, 67 L.Ed. 199 (1922).

[9]U.S. v. Wong Kim Ark, 169 U.S. 649, 18 S.Ct. 456, 42 L.Ed. 890 (1898). See generally § 2:1.

Hawaii, even those that would have been barred by the racial laws from naturalizing individually in the U.S.[10]

However, the search to exclude from the national project those noncitizens deemed racially and culturally unfit, appears to have been instrumental in the development of the notion of noncitizen nationals of the U.S.[11] Not surprisingly, the racial bar was held also to be applicable to the individual naturalization of noncitizen nationals.[12]

The racial bars began to break down in the 1940s. The 1940 act provided that the right to naturalize "shall extend only to white persons, persons of African nativity or descent, and descendants of races indigenous to the Western Hemisphere."[13] However, it also provided that Filipinos who served honorably in the armed forces were not barred from naturalizing under the military-related provision because of their race.[14] Nor were former U.S. citizens who had lost their citizenship barred from regaining their citizenship because of the racial bar.[15]

The Act of 1940 was amended in 1943, to allow naturalization of Chinese and persons of Chinese descent.[16] In 1947, it was once more amended to allow naturalization of Filipinos, and East Indians.[17] In 1950, Guamanians were permitted to naturalize.[18] Finally, the INA included a provision that the "right of a person to become a naturalized citizen of the United States shall not be denied or abridged because of race or sex or because such a person is married."[19]

---

[10]23 Op. Atty. Gen. 345 (1901) (the grant of collective naturalization to citizens of Hawaii included Chinese persons born or naturalized in the Hawaiian Islands prior to the annexation by the U.S.—the racial bars do not apply to this collective naturalization). See § 2:14.

[11]See Gordon & Mailman, § 92.04[1][a]. Cf. § 2:23, § 3:1.

[12]In re Rallos, 241 F. 686 (E.D.N.Y. 1917). Contra, In re Mallari, 239 F. 416, 418 (D. Mass. 1916). Contra, In re Mallari, 239 F. 416, 418 (D. Mass. 1916).

[13]Sec. 303, Nationality Act of 1940, reproduced as Appendix 4-12 to Chapter 4.

[14]Sec. 303, Nationality Act of 1940, reproduced as Appendix 4-12 to Chapter 4.

[15]Sec. 303, Nationality Act of 1940, reproduced as Appendix 4-12 to Chapter 4.

[16]Sec. 3, Act of December 17, 1943, Pub.L. 78-199, 57 Stat. 600.

[17]Act of July 2, 1946, Pub.L. 79-483, 60 Stat. 416.

[18]Sec. 4(b), Organic Act of Guam, Act of August 1, 1950, Pub.L. 81-630, 54 Stat. 384.

[19]INA § 311, 8 U.S.C.A. § 1422. Cf. § 15:16.

APPENDIX 7-1

List of American Institutions of Research, Public International Organizations, and Designations under the International Immunities Act[1]

A. AMERICAN INSTITUTIONS OF RESEARCH

African Medical and Research Foundation (AMREF-USA).

Albert Einstein College of Medicine of Yeshiva University (only in relationship to its research programs).

American Friends of the Middle East, Inc.

American Institutes of Research in the Behavioral Sciences (only in relationship to research projects abroad).

American Universities Field Staff, Inc.

American University, The, Cairo, Egypt.

American University of Beirut (Near East College Associations).

Arctic Institute of North America, Inc.

Armour Research Foundation of Illinois Institute of Technology.

Asia Foundation, The (formerly Committee for a Free Asia, Inc.).

Association of Universities for Research in Astronomy (AURA, Inc.), Tucson, AZ.

Atomic Bomb Casualty Commission.

Beirut University College.

Bermuda Biological Station for Research, Inc.

Bernice P. Bishop Museum of Polynesian Antiquities, Ethnology and Natural History at Honolulu, HI.

Brookhaven National Laboratory, Associated Universities, Inc.

Brown University (Department of Engineering), Providence, RI.

Buffalo Eye Bank and Research Society, Inc.

Burma Office of Robert N. Nathan Associates, Inc.

California State University at Long Beach, Department of Geological Sciences.

Carleton College (Department of Sociology and Anthropology), Northfield, MN.

Center of Alcohol Studies, Laboratory of Applied Biodynamics of Yale University.

Central Registry of Jewish Losses in Egypt.

College of Engineering, University of Wisconsin.

College of Medicine, State University of New York.

Colorado State University (Research Foundation), Fort Collins, CO.

Colorado University (International Economic Studies Center), Boulder, CO.

Columbia University (Parker School of Foreign and Comparative Law) and (Faculty of Pure Science), New York, NY.

---

[1]Reproduced from 8 CFR § 316.20.

Cornell University (International Agricultural Development, University of the Philippines-Cornell University Graduate Education Program).

Dartmouth Medical School.

Department of French, Department of Scandinavian Languages, and Department of Near Eastern Languages of the University of California, Berkeley, CA.

Duke University.

Environmental Research Laboratory of the University of Arizona.

Fletcher School of Law and Diplomacy, Medford, MA.

Ford Foundation, 477 Madison Avenue, New York, NY.

Free Europe, Inc. (formerly Free Europe Committee, Inc.; National Committee for a Free Europe (including Radio Free Europe)).

Georgetown University.

George Williams Hooper Foundation, San Francisco Medical Center, University of California, San Francisco, CA.

Gorgas Memorial Institute of Tropical and Preventive Medicine, Inc., and its operating unit, the Gorgas Memorial Laboratory.

Graduate Faculty of Political and Social Science Division of the New School for Social Research, New York, NY.

Harvard Institute for International Development.

Harvard-Yenching Institute.

Humboldt State University, School of Natural Resources, Wildlife Management Department.

Institute for Development Anthropology, Inc.

Institute of International Education, Inc.

Institute of International Studies, University of California, Berkeley, CA.

International Center for Social Research, New York, NY.

International Development Foundation, Inc.

International Development Services, Inc.

International Research Associates, Inc.

Inter-University Program for Chinese Language Studies (formerly Stanford Center for Chinese Studies) in Taipei, Taiwan.

Iowa State University.

Iran Foundation, Inc., The.

Kossuth Foundation, Inc., The, New York, NY.

Louisiana State University.

Massachusetts Institute of Technology.

Michigan State University, East Lansing, MI.

Missouri Botanical Garden (research and educational programs only)

Natural Science Foundation, Philadelphia, PA.

New York Zoological Society.

Paderewski Foundation, Inc.

Peabody Museum of Natural History of Yale University.

People to People Health Foundation, Inc., The (only in relationship to the scientific research activities that will be carried on abroad by the medical staff of the SS "Hope").

Pierce College (in relationship to research by an instructor, Department of

Psychology), Athens, Greece.

Population Council, The, New York, NY.

Radio Liberty Committee, Inc. (formerly American Committee for Liberation, Inc.; American Committee for Liberation of the Peoples of

Russia, Inc.; American Committee for Liberation from Bolshevism, Inc.).

Rockefeller Foundation.

School of International Relations of the University of Southern California.

SIRIMAR (Societa Internazionale Recerche Marine) Division, Office of the Vice President for Research, Pennsylvania State University.

Social Science Research Council.

Solar Energy Research Institute (SERI).

Stanford Electronic Laboratories, Department of Electrical Engineering, School of Engineering, Stanford University, Stanford, CA.

Stanford Research Institute, Menlo Park, CA.

Stanford University (the George Vanderbilt Foundation), Stanford, CA.

Syracuse University.

Tulane University Graduate School.

Tulane University Medical School.

University of Alabama.

University of Alabama Medical Center.

University of Chicago (as a participant in the International Cooperation Administration Program No. W-74 only).

University of Colorado (Department of History), Boulder, CO.

University of Connecticut, College of Liberal Arts and Science (Department of Germanic and Slavic Languages).

University of Hawaii, Honolulu, HI.

University of Illinois at Urbana-Champaign, Austria-Illinois Exchange Program.

University of Kansas, Office of International Programs.

University of La Verne (La Verne College of Athens)

University of Michigan (School of Natural Resources), Ann Arbor, MI.

University of Minnesota, Department of Plant Pathology (in relationship to research project abroad).

University of Nebraska Mission in Colombia, South America.

University of North Carolina at Chapel Hill.

University of Notre Dame, Notre Dame, IN.

University of Puerto Rico.

University of Washington (Department of Marketing, Transportation, and International Business) and (The School of Public Health and Community Medicine), Seattle, WA.

Wayne State University, Detroit, MI.

Wenner-Gren Foundation for Anthropological Research, Inc.

Williams College, Economic Department, Williamstown, MA.

B. PUBLIC INTERNATIONAL ORGANIZATIONS OF WHICH THE UNITED STATES IS A MEMBER BY TREATY OR STATUTE

1. Public International Organizations of Which the U.S. is a Member

The North Atlantic Treaty Organization.

United Nations and all agencies and organizations which are a part thereof.

2. Public International Organizations that Enjoy the Privileges, Exemptions, and Immunities Provided by Statute and are Considered Public International Organizations of Which the U.S. is a Member for Purposes of INA § 316(b)

African Development Bank.

African Development Fund.

Asian Development Bank.

Caribbean Organization.

Criminal Police Organization.

Customs Cooperation Council.

European Space Research Organization.

Food and Agriculture Organization.

Great Lakes Fishery, Commission.

Inter-American Defense Board.

Inter-American Development Bank.

Inter-American Institute for Cooperation in Agriculture.

Inter-American Statistical Institute.

Inter-American Tropical Tuna Commission.

Intergovernmental Committee for European Migration (formerly the Provisional Intergovernmental Committee for the Movements of Migrants from Europe).

Intergovernmental Maritime Consultative Organization.

International Atomic Energy Agency.

International Bank for Reconstruction and Development.

International Center for Settlement of Investment Disputes.

International Civil Aviation Organization.

International Coffee Organization.

International Cotton Advisory Committee.

International Development Association.

International Fertilizer Development Center.

International Finance Corporation.

International Food Policy Research Institute.

International Hydrographic Bureau.

International Institute for Cotton.

International Joint Commission—United States and Canada.

International Labor Organization, The (functions through staff known as the International Labor Office).

International Maritime Satellite Organization.

International Monetary Fund.

International Pacific Halibut Commission.

International Secretariat for Volunteer Services.

International Telecommunications Union.

International Telecommunications Satellite Organization.

International Wheat Advisory Committee.

Multinational Force and Observers.

Organization for European Economic Cooperation (Now known as Organization for Economic Cooperation and Development).

Organization of African Unity (OAU).

Organization of American States (includes Pan American Union).

Pan American Health Organization (includes Pan American Sanitary Bureau).

Preparatory Commission of the International Atomic Energy Agency.

Preparatory Commission for the International Refugee Organization and its successor, the International Refugee Organization.

South Pacific Commission.

United International Bureau for the Protection of Intellectual Property (BIRPI).

United Nations, The.

United Nations Educational, Scientific, and Cultural Organizations.

Universal Postal Union.

World Health Organization.

World Intellectual Property Organization.

World Meteorological Organization.

APPENDIX 7-2

Form N-470

OMB No. 1615-0056; Expires 01/31/2016

Department of Homeland Security
U.S. Citizenship and Immigration Services

**Instructions for Form N-470, Application to
Preserve Residence for Naturalization Purposes**

The Purpose of Form N-470

This form is for a permanent resident alien who must leave the United States for certain employment purposes and wishes to preserve his or her continuous residence to pursue naturalization.

You may be able to preserve continuous residency (previously accumulated for naturalization purposes) even though you may be residing outside the United States for longer than 1 year. The time spent abroad may be counted toward your residency requirement if you file a Form N-470.

Who Should File This Form

You should file this form if you meet **all** of the requirements below:

1. You must have been physically present and residing in the United States for an uninterrupted period, **without any absences,** for at least 1 year after your admission as a permanent resident (except religious workers);

2. You will be absent from the United States for 1 year or more;

3. You have qualifying employment in a specific job with the U.S. Government, private sector, or religious organization; **and**

4. You want to preserve your continuous residence for naturalization purposes.

If USCIS approves your Form N-470, your spouse and dependent unmarried son(s) or daughter(s) will receive the same benefit. All of them must be members of the same household and reside with you while you reside abroad.

NOTE: **You must still apply for a reentry permit in advance of trips outside the United States that you expect to last for 1 year or more. Approval of Form N-470 does not exempt applicants from the physical presence requirements for naturalization unless they are employed by, or under contract with the U.S. Government.**

Continuous residency requirements for Form N-400

Generally, applicants who file a Form N-400 must reside in the United States for **5** years immediately preceding the date of filing. Additionally, USCIS requires applicants to have been physically present in the United States for at least 30 months of those 5 years.

NOTE: Qualifying spouses of U.S. citizens who file Form N-400 must reside in the United States for **3** years immediately preceding the date of filing. Those spouses are required to have been physically present in the United States for at least 18 months of those 3 years.

Permanent residents who remain outside the United States for more than 1 uninterrupted year will disrupt their residency requirement unless they are the beneficiaries of an approved Form N-470.

Exception for spouse of U.S. Citizen employed by the U.S. Government, American institution of research, or an American firm engaged in development of foreign trade with the United States

A spouse of a U.S. citizen who is eligible for naturalization under Section 319(b) of the Immigration and Nationality Act (INA) is not required to file Form N-470 to preserve continuous residence, as such spouses are exempted from establishing the naturalization residency and physical presence requirements.

General Instructions

1. **Type or print clearly using black ink.** Keep all information within the area provided.

   If extra space is needed to answer any question, attach an additional sheet(s) of paper. You must provide the following information on the top of each sheet of paper:

   A. Your Alien Registration Number (A-Number);

   B. The date;

   C. Question number; **and**

   D. Your signature.

2. **Answer all questions fully and accurately.** Write "N/A" if an item is not applicable. Write "None" if the answer is none.

3. **Avoid highlighting, crossing out, or writing outside the area provided for a response.**

   If you must make substantial corrections to your Form N-470, USCIS recommends that you begin with a new Form N-470 rather than using correction tape or fluid to white out information. USCIS scanners may see through the white correction tape or fluid. This may lead to incorrect information being captured in USCIS systems which may cause processing delays or a rejection of your Form N-470.

Ensure that you are using the correct edition of the Form N-470. The correct edition is available on the USCIS Web site at **www.uscis.gov.**

4. **Provide your A-Number on the top right corner of each page.** Your A-Number is located on your Permanent Resident Card (formerly known as the Alien Registration or "Green" Card). The A-Number on your card consists of seven to nine numbers, depending on when your record was created. If the A-Number on your card has fewer than nine numbers, place enough zeros before the first number to make a *total of nine numbers* on the Form N-470. For example, write number A1234567 as A001234567 or write number A12345678 as A012345678. **You must provide your A-Number. USCIS may reject your application if you do not provide your A-Number.**

Translations. You must provide a full English translation for any document written in a foreign language you submit to USCIS. The translator must certify that the translation is complete and accurate and that he or she is competent to translate from the foreign language into English.

Copies. You may submit copies of documents unless USCIS requests original documents. Original documents submitted when not required may remain a part of the record.

Specific Form Instructions

This form is divided into five parts.

Part 1. Information About Your Eligibility

Check the box that shows why you are eligible to apply to preserve residence for naturalization purposes.

Part 2. Information About You

1. **Current Legal Name.** Your current legal name is the name on your birth certificate unless it has been changed after birth by a legal action such as a marriage or court order. **Do not provide a nickname**.

2. **Your name exactly as it appears on your Permanent Resident Card** (*if different from above*). Write your name exactly as it appears on your card even if it is misspelled.

3. **U.S. Social Security Number**. Print your U.S. Social Security Number. Write "N/A" if you do not have one.

4. **Date of Birth.** Always use eight numbers to show your date of birth. Write the date in this order: Month, Day, Year. For example, write May 1, 1958, as 05/01/1958.

5. **Country of Birth.** Provide the name of the country where you were born. Write the name of the country even if the country's name has since changed or the country no longer exists.

6. **Country of Nationality.** Provide the name of the country(ies) where you are currently a citizen or national.

   A. If the country no longer exists or you are stateless, write the name of the country where you were last a citizen or national.

   B. If you are a citizen or national of more than one country, write the name of the country that issued your last passport that you currently use to travel.

7. **Home address.** Provide the address where you now reside. Do **not** write your Post Office (P.O.) Box number here unless it is your **ONLY** address.

   If you reside outside the United States

   If you do not have a State or Province, enter the name of your city again in that box. If you do not have a ZIP or Postal Code, enter 00000 in the ZIP or Postal Code box.

8. **Mailing Address.** Provide your mailing address even if it is the same as your home address. Provide "*in care of name*" information, if applicable. You must write something in every box, except an apartment number or "C/O" if you do not have one, within "Mailing Address."

   NOTE: USCIS may not be able to contact you if you do not provide a complete and valid address. If USCIS rejects your application, USCIS may not be able to return the fee for the Form N-470 to you if you do not write a complete and valid address. If USCIS cannot return the fee, USCIS will cash your check.

9. **Telephone Numbers.** Provide your current telephone numbers. If the answer is none, write "None." If you are hearing impaired and use a TTY telephone connection, please indicate this by writing "TTY" after the telephone number.

10. **E-Mail Address.** Provide your current e-mail address. If you do not have one, write "None."

11. **Date You Became a Permanent Resident.** Provide the official date when your permanent residence began, as shown on your Permanent Resident Card. Write the date in this order: Month, Day, Year. For example, write August 9, 1988, as 08/09/1988. **USCIS may reject your application if you do not provide the information**.

12. **Uninterrupted Residence in the United States.** Check the box to indicate if you have, or have not, resided in and been physically present in the United States for an uninterrupted period of at least 1 year **since your admission as a permanent resident**.

13. Time Outside the United States. List below all the trips of 24 hours or more that you have taken outside the United States **since you became a permanent resident. Include trips to Canada, Mexico, and the Caribbean.** Begin with your most recent trip. If you need more space, use an additional sheet(s) of paper.

14. Employment Position and Length of Employment. Provide an explanation of your employment position requiring you to be absent from the United States. Also state the intended length of time you will be employed when absent from the United States. If you are a religious worker filing the N-470 after your return to the United States from abroad, please provide the entire length of time of your employment outside the United States in said capacity.

15. Income Tax. Check the box to indicate if you have, or have not, ever filed an income tax return as a nonresident or otherwise claimed or received benefits as a nonresident alien under U.S. Federal, State, or local income tax laws **since you became a permanent resident.**

Part 3. Information About Family Members Who Reside With You

1. Residence With You Inside the United States. Check the box to indicate whether you have permanent resident family members who reside with you inside the United States.

2. Residence With You Outside the United States. Check the box to indicate whether those permanent resident family members will reside with you outside the United States.

If you check "Yes," provide information for your spouse and **all** of your children who will reside with you outside the United States.

Part 4. Your Signature

Sign the Form N-470 as you normally sign your name. You may place an "X" mark instead of a signature if you are unable to write in any language.

NOTE: USCIS will reject your Form N-470 if it is not signed.

Part 5. Signature of Person Who Prepared Form N-470 for You *(if applicable)*

If you prepared this application by yourself, leave this section blank. If someone filled out this application for you, he or she must complete this section.

Processing Information

Any Form N-470 that is not signed or accompanied by the correct fee, except those accompanied by a fee waiver request (Form I-912, Request for Fee Waiver), will be rejected. A Form N-470 that is not completed according to these instructions, is missing pages or otherwise not executed in its entirety, or is not accompanied by the required initial evidence may be rejected or delayed. If USCIS rejects your Form N-470 for any of the reasons above, the form and any fees will be returned to you if you provided a complete and valid mailing address. You will be notified why the form is considered deficient. You may correct the deficiency and refile Form N-470. An application or petition is not considered properly filed until accepted by USCIS.

Requests for More Information or Interview

USCIS may request more information or evidence. USCIS may also request that you submit the originals of any copies you previously provided to USCIS with your Form N-470. In addition, USCIS may request that you appear for an interview.

Decision

The decision on Form N-470 involves a determination of whether you have established eligibility for the requested benefit. If you do not establish a basis for eligibility, USCIS will deny your Form N-470. You will be notified of the decision in writing.

When To File

1. Generally, you must have been physically present and residing in the United States for an uninterrupted period, **without any absences,** for at least 1 year after your admission as a permanent resident before you can file Form N-470.

2. You do not have to be in the United States to file Form N-470, but you must file it before you have been absent from the United States for a continuous period of 1 year.

Religious Workers Exception to the 1 Year Absence Requirement

Religious workers may apply:

1. Before departing from the United States;

2. After departing from the United States; **or**

3. After returning to the United States.

Religious workers are not required to have lived in the United States for a specific period of time prior to filing Form N-470.

What Is the Filing Fee

The filing fee for Form N-470 is **$330**.

Use the following guidelines when you prepare your check or money order for your Form N-470 fee:

1. The check or money order must be drawn on a bank or other financial institution located in the Unites States and must be payable in U.S. currency; **and**

2. Make the check or money order payable to **U.S. Department of Homeland Security.**

NOTE: Spell out U.S. Department of Homeland Security; do not write the initials "USDHS" or "DHS."

3. If you live outside the United States, contact the nearest U.S. Embassy or consulate for instructions on the method of payment.

Notice To Those Making Payment by Check

USCIS will make a copy and convert your original check into an electronic funds transfer (EFT). This means USCIS will use the account information on your check to electronically debit your account for the check amount. This debit usually takes 24 hours and should show up on your regular account statement.

USCIS will not return your original check. USCIS will destroy it and keep a copy with your file. If the EFT cannot be processed due to technical reasons, you authorize USCIS to process the copy of the check. If the EFT cannot be completed because of insufficient funds, USCIS may try the EFT up to two times.

If you receive an insufficient funds notice, USCIS will send you instructions on how to submit your penalty fee. **Do not** send a check for the penalty fee to the address where you filed your Form N-470. It will be returned to you.

How To Check If the Fees Are Correct

The fee on Form N-470 is current as of the edition date appearing in the lower right corner of this page. However, because USCIS fees change periodically, you can verify if the fees are correct by following one of the steps below.

1. Visit our Web site at **www.uscis.gov**, select "FORMS," and check the appropriate fee;

2. Telephone the USCIS National Customer Service Center at **1-800-375-5283** and ask for the fee information. For TDD (hearing impaired) call: **1-800-767-1833**.

Fee Waiver Request

Individuals may request a fee waiver based on an inability to pay. Form I-912 provides a standard means for submitting fee waiver requests. The instructions provide applicants with guidance on properly completing Form I-912 and submitting supporting documentation. The instructions also give information on how USCIS makes a decision on a fee waiver request. To download a copy of Form I-912, including the instructions, click on the "FORMS" link on the USCIS Web site at **www.uscis.gov**.

Re-filing Form N-470

If USCIS denied your previously filed Form N-470 and you are filing a new Form N-470, you must pay the full amount. **Otherwise, USCIS will not accept your Form N-470. USCIS cannot apply a previously submitted filing fee amount to a newly filed Form N-470.**

Where To File

Mail your completed Form N-470 and accompanying documentation to the USCIS Phoenix Lockbox facility at the following address:

**USCIS
PO Box 650809
Dallas, TX, 75265**

For Express Mail or commercial courier deliveries, use the following address:

**USCIS
Attn: Form N-470
2501 S. State Highway, 121 Business
Suite 400
Lewisville, TX, 75067**

E-Notification

If you are filing your Form N-470 at one of the USCIS Lockbox facilities, you may elect to receive an e-mail and/or text message notifying you that your Form N-470 has been accepted. You must complete Form G-1145, E-Notification of Application/Petition Acceptance, and attach it to the first page of your Form N-470. To download a copy of Form G-1145, including the instructions, click on the "FORMS" link on the USCIS Web site at **www.uscis.gov**.

Form Revision and Filing Addresses

The filing addresses provided on this form reflect the most current information as of the date this form was last printed. If you are filing Form N-470 more than 30 days after the latest edition date shown in the lower right corner, please visit the USCIS Web site at www.uscis.gov before you file, and check the "**FORMS**" page to confirm the correct filing address and version currently in use. Check the edition date located at the lower right corner of the form. If the edition date on your Form N-470 matches the edition date listed for Form N-470 on the online "**FORMS**" page, your version is current. If the edition date on the online version is more recent, download a copy and use it. If you do not have Internet access, call the USCIS National Customer Service Center at **1-800-375-5283** to verify the current filing address and edition date. For TDD (hearing impaired) call: **1-800-767-1833**. **USCIS will reject forms with the wrong revision date and return the fee with instructions to resubmit the entire filing using the current form.**

Address Changes

If you have changed your address, you must inform USCIS of your new address. For information on filing a change of address go to the USCIS Web site at www.uscis.gov/addresschange or contact the National Customer Service Center at 1-800-375-5283. For TDD (hearing impaired) call: **1-800-767-1833**.

NOTE: Do not submit a change of address request to the USCIS Lockbox facilities because the USCIS Lockbox facilities do not process change of address requests.

USCIS Forms and Information

To ensure you are using the latest version of this form, visit the USCIS Web site at www.uscis.gov where you can obtain the latest USCIS forms and immigration-related information. If you do not have internet access, you may order USCIS forms by calling our toll-free number at **1-800-870-3676**. You may also obtain forms and information by telephoning our USCIS National Customer Service Center at **1-800-375-5283**. For TDD (hearing impaired) call: **1-800-767-1833**.

You can schedule an appointment to meet with a USCIS representative at your local USCIS office through the USCIS Internet-based system, **InfoPass**. To access the system, visit the USCIS Web site. Use the **InfoPass** appointment scheduler and follow the screen prompts to set up your appointment. **InfoPass** generates an electronic appointment notice that appears on the screen.

Attorney or Representative

You may be represented, at no expense to the U.S. Government, by an attorney or other duly accredited representative. Your representative must submit Form G-28, Notice of Entry of Appearance as Attorney or Representative, with your Form N-470. If USCIS requests you to appear for an interview, your representative may also submit the Form G-28 at that time. Form G-28 can be obtained by visiting the USCIS Web site at www.uscis.gov, calling the USCIS forms line number at **1-800-870-3676**, or by contacting the USCIS National Customer Service Center at **1-800-375-5283**. For TDD (hearing impaired) call: **1-800-767-1833**.

Penalties

If you knowingly and willfully falsify or conceal a material fact or submit a false document with this Form N-470, USCIS will deny your Form N-470 and may deny any other immigration benefit. In addition, you may be subject to criminal prosecution and penalties provided by law.

USCIS Privacy Act Statement

AUTHORITIES: The information requested on this form, and the associated evidence, is collected under the Immigration and Nationality Act, section 101, et seq.

PURPOSE: The primary purpose for providing the requested information on this form is to determine if you have established eligibility for the immigration benefit for which you are filing. The information you provide will be used to grant or deny the benefit sought.

DISCLOSURE: The information you provide is voluntary. However, failure to provide the requested information, and any requested evidence, may delay a final decision or result in denial of your form.

ROUTINE USES: The information you provide on this form may be shared with other Federal, State, local, and foreign government agencies and authorized organizations following approved routine uses described in the associated published system of records notices [DHS-USCIS-007 - Benefits Information System and DHS-USCIS-001 - Alien File, Index, and National Filed Tracking System of Records, which can be found at www.dhs.gov/privacy]. The information may also be made available, as appropriate, for law enforcement purposes or in the interest of national security.

Paperwork Reduction Act

An agency may not conduct or sponsor an information collection, and a person is not required to respond to a collection of information unless it displays a currently valid OMB control number. The public reporting burden for this collection of information is estimated at 36 minutes per response, including the time for reviewing instructions and completing and submitting the form. Send comments regarding this burden estimate or any other aspect of this collection of information, including suggestions for reducing this burden to: U.S. Citizenship and Immigration Services, Regulatory Coordination Division, Office of Policy and Strategy, 20 Massachusetts Ave NW, Washington, DC 20529-2140; OMB No 1615-0056. **Do not mail your completed Form N-470 to this address.**

OMB No. 1615-0056; Expires 01/31/2016

Department of Homeland Security
U.S. Citizenship and Immigration Services

Form N-470, Application to Preserve
Residence for Naturalization Purposes

Print or type all your answers fully and accurately in black ink. Write "N/A" if an item is not applicable. Write "None" if the answer is none. Failure to answer all of the questions may delay your Form N-470.

Part 1. Information About Your Eligibility (*check only one*)

My absence from the United States is on behalf of:

1. ☐ The U.S. Government (*employed by, or are under contract with, the U.S. Government*).

2. ☐ An American institution of research to perform scientific research.

3. ☐ An American firm or corporation, or a subsidiary thereof, to engage in the development of foreign trade and commerce of the United States.

4. ☐ An American firm or corporation to protect the property rights outside the United States of that American firm or corporation engaged in the development of foreign trade and commerce of the United States.

5. ☐ A public international organization of which the United States is a member. (*Your employment must have started after your admission as a permanent resident*)

6. ☐ A denomination or mission having a bona fide organization in the United States in which I perform ministerial or priestly functions or my sole capacity is of a clergyman or clergywoman, missionary, brother, nun or sister.

Your A-Number:

A ____ - ____ - ____

For USCIS Use Only

Bar Code	Date Stamp
	Remarks
Action	

Part 2. Information About You

1. **Current Legal Name** (*do **not** provide a nickname*)

   Family Name (*last name*)

   Given Name (*first name*)

   Middle Name (*if applicable*)

2. **Your name exactly as it appears on your Permanent Resident Card**

   Family Name (*last name*)

   Given Name (*first name*)

   Middle Name (*if applicable*)

3. **U.S. Social Security Number** (*if any*)

4. **Date of Birth** (*mm/dd/yyyy*)

5. **Country of Birth**

6. **Country of Nationality**

7. **Home Address**

   Street Number and Name (*do not write a P.O. Box in this space unless it is your ONLY address.*)   Apartment Number

   City   County   State   ZIP Code

   Province (*foreign address only*)   Country (*foreign address only*)   Postal Code (*foreign address only*)

Form N-470 01/03/13 N Page 1

Part 2. Information About You *(Continued)*

A _____ - _____ - _____

8. Mailing Address

C/O *(in care of name)*

Street Number and Name   Apartment Number

City   State   ZIP Code

Province *(foreign address only)*   Country *(foreign address only)*   Postal Code *(foreign address only)*

9. Daytime Phone Number   **Work Phone Number** *(if any)*   **Evening Phone Number**

(   )   (   )   (   )

Mobile Phone Number *(if any)*   **10. E-Mail Address** *(if any)*

(   )

11. Date you became a Permanent Resident *(mm/dd/yyyy)*

12. Have you resided in and been physically present in the United States for an uninterrupted period of at least 1 year **since your admission as a permanent resident**? *(If you answer "No" you must provide an explanation on a separate sheet(s) of paper.)*   ☐ Yes ☐ No

13. Time Outside the United States *(include trips to Canada, Mexico, and the Caribbean)*

List below all the trips of 24 hours or more that you have taken outside the United States **since you became a permanent resident**. Begin with your most recent trip. **If you need more space, use an additional sheet(s) of paper.**

Date You Left the United States *(mm/dd/yyyy)*	Date You Returned to the United States *(mm/dd/yyyy)*	Did Trip Last 6 Months or More?	Countries You Traveled To	Total Days Outside the United States
		☐ Yes ☐ No		
		☐ Yes ☐ No		
		☐ Yes ☐ No		
		☐ Yes ☐ No		
		☐ Yes ☐ No		

14. Explain your employment position requiring your absence from the United States and the intended length of employment.

15. Have you ever filed an income tax return as a nonresident or otherwise claimed or received benefits as a nonresident alien under U.S. Federal, State or local income tax laws **since you became a permanent resident**?   ☐ Yes ☐ No

Part 3. Information About Family Members Who Reside With You

A _____ - _____ - _____

1. Do you have permanent resident family members who reside with you inside the United States? ☐ Yes ☐ No

2. Will those family members reside with you outside the United States? ☐ Yes ☐ No

If you answered "Yes," provide the information below for each permanent resident family member who will be residing with you outside the United States. **If you need more space, use an additional sheet(s) of paper.**

A. Family Name *(last name)* | Given Name *(first name)* | Middle Name *(if applicable)*

Date of Birth *(mm/dd/yyyy)* | Relationship to You | A-Number

B. Family Name *(last name)* | Given Name *(first name)* | Middle Name *(if applicable)*

Date of Birth *(mm/dd/yyyy)* | Relationship to You | A-Number

C. Family Name *(last name)* | Given Name *(first name)* | Middle Name *(if applicable)*

Date of Birth *(mm/dd/yyyy)* | Relationship to You | A-Number

Instructions if you are completing your Form N-470 electronically: To list additional family members, click the "Add Family Members" button and then click the "Go to Continuation Page" button.

[Add Family Members]   [Go To Continuation Page]

Part 4. Your Signature *(USCIS will reject your Form N-470 if it is not signed.)*

I certify, under penalty of perjury under the laws of the United States of America, that this application and the evidence submitted with it is all true and correct. I authorize the release of any information from my records that U.S. Citizenship and Immigration Services needs to determine eligibility for the benefit sought.

Your Signature | **Date** *(mm/dd/yyyy)*

Part 5. Signature of Person Who Prepared This Form N-470 for You *(if applicable)*

I declare **under the penalty of perjury** that I prepared this application at the request of the above person.

Preparer's Printed Name | **Preparer's Signature** | **Date** *(mm/dd/yyyy)*

Preparer's Firm or Organization Name *(if applicable)* | Preparer's Daytime Phone Number
(   )

Preparer's Address

Street Number and Name

City | County | State | ZIP Code

Province *(foreign address only)* | Country *(foreign address only)* | Postal Code *(foreign address only)*

Preparer's E-Mail Address *(if any)* | Preparer's Fax Number
(   )

Form N-470 01/03/13 N Page 3

Continuation Page

If you answered "Yes," provide the information below for each permanent resident family member who will be residing with you outside the United States. **If you need more space, use an additional sheet(s) of paper.**

D. Family Name *(last name)*　　　Given Name *(first name)*　　　Middle Name *(if applicable)*

Date of Birth *(mm/dd/yyyy)*　　　Relationship to You　　　A-Number

E. Family Name *(last name)*　　　Given Name *(first name)*　　　Middle Name *(if applicable)*

Date of Birth *(mm/dd/yyyy)*　　　Relationship to You　　　A-Number

F. Family Name *(last name)*　　　Given Name *(first name)*　　　Middle Name *(if applicable)*

Date of Birth *(mm/dd/yyyy)*　　　Relationship to You　　　A-Number

G. Family Name *(last name)*　　　Given Name *(first name)*　　　Middle Name *(if applicable)*

Date of Birth *(mm/dd/yyyy)*　　　Relationship to You　　　A-Number

H. Family Name *(last name)*　　　Given Name *(first name)*　　　Middle Name *(if applicable)*

Date of Birth *(mm/dd/yyyy)*　　　Relationship to You　　　A-Number

I. Family Name *(last name)*　　　Given Name *(first name)*　　　Middle Name *(if applicable)*

Date of Birth *(mm/dd/yyyy)*　　　Relationship to You　　　A-Number

J. Family Name *(last name)*　　　Given Name *(first name)*　　　Middle Name *(if applicable)*

Date of Birth *(mm/dd/yyyy)*　　　Relationship to You　　　A-Number

K. Family Name *(last name)*　　　Given Name *(first name)*　　　Middle Name *(if applicable)*

Date of Birth *(mm/dd/yyyy)*　　　Relationship to You　　　A-Number

L. Family Name *(last name)*　　　Given Name *(first name)*　　　Middle Name *(if applicable)*

Date of Birth *(mm/dd/yyyy)*　　　Relationship to You　　　A-Number

APPENDIX 7-3

Form N-472

[prescribed edition date: 5/05/82 (8 CFR § 499.1, *as amended by* 59 Fed. Reg. 25561 (May 17, 1994)]

_____   File No.:_____

                                    Date:_____

Your application to preserve residence for naturalization purposes has been approved to cover your absence from the United States from _____ , 19___ , to an indefinite date thereafter, for as long as you remain absent on behalf of _____

_____ .

At such time as you apply for naturalization, you will be required to prove to the naturalization court that your absence from the United States was for the purpose of being employed or engaged as alleged in your application. This approval does not relieve you of the requirement to present a valid document for reentry into the United States.

The block checked below explains the effect of the approval of your application:

☐ The approval of your application allows you to count the period of your absence toward <u>residence</u> in the United States for naturalization purposes, but not toward physical presence. Therefore, when you apply to file your petition for naturalization, you will have to show that, during the 5-year period just before the filing of your petition in court, you were physically present in the United States for a period or periods totaling at least 30 months; or, if at that time you are married to and have been living with a United States citizen for 3 years or more, you will have to show that, during the 3-year period just before the filing of your petition in court, you were physically present in the United States for a period or periods totaling 18 months.

☐ The approval of your application allows you to count the period of your absence toward the residence and physical presence requirements for naturalization.

☐ The approval of your application will permit you to count the period of your absence toward both the residence and physical presence requirements for naturalization, provided that, since becoming a permanent resident of the United States and before you apply for naturalization, you have completed an uninterrupted period of one year of physical presence in the United States.

                              Sincerely,

Form N-472 (Rev. 4-28-72) N

APPENDIX 7-4

Form I-290B

OMB No. 1615-0095; Expires 11/30/2014

Department of Homeland Security
U.S. Citizenship and Immigration Services

**Instructions for Form I-290B, Notice
of Appeal or Motion**

When Should I Use Form I-290B?

Form I-290B, Notice of Appeal or Motion, is used to file an appeal or motion on any decision under the immigration laws in any type of proceeding over which the Board of Immigration Appeals (BIA) does not have appellate jurisdiction. The appeal or motion must be filed with U.S. Citizenship and Immigration Services (USCIS) in accordance with the regulations at 8 C.F.R. § 103.3 and § 103.5.

Form I-290B must be filed within 30 calendar days after service of the decision. If the decision is mailed, the form must be filed within 33 days. If the appeal relates to a revocation of an immigrant petition approval, the appeal must be filed within 15 calendar days after service of the decision, 18 days if the decision was mailed. The date of service is normally the date of the decision.

Late filed appeals and motions may be rejected.

Form I-290B may be used in the following circumstances:

1. To file an appeal with the Administrative Appeals Office (AAO);

2. To file a motion to reconsider a decision of USCIS (either the AAO or a field office);

3. To file a motion to reopen a decision of USCIS (either the AAO or a field office); or

4. To file a motion to reopen a decision of USCIS under the Northwest Immigrant Rights Project (NWIRP) Settlement.

5. To file a motion to reopen a decision of USCIS under the Special Immigrant Juvenile (SIJ) *Perez-Olano* Settlement Agreement (POSA).

When a decision on a petition is appealed or a request for a motion is made, the petitioner, an authorized official of a petitioning employer, or the petitioner's attorney or representative must sign Form I-290B. (In the case of self-petitioners and applicants for certain waivers, the self-petitioner or waiver applicant must sign the form.)

Who May Not File Form I-290B?

If you are the beneficiary of a visa petition or the beneficiary's attorney or representative, you may not file an appeal or motion.

General Instructions

Fill Out Form I-290B

1. Type or print legibly in black ink.

2. If extra space is needed to complete any item, attach a continuation sheet, indicate the name and Alien Registration Number (A-Number) of the petitioner/applicant, the item number, and date and sign each sheet.

3. Answer all questions fully and accurately. State that an item is not applicable with "N/A." If the answer is none, write "None."

Form I-290B is divided into **Parts 1** through **4**. The following information should help you fill out the form.

Part 1. Information About Petitioner/Applicant
*(Individual/Business/Organization/Attorney/
Representative filing appeal or motion)*

1. **Family Name** (Last name) - Give your legal name. If you have two last names, include both and use a hyphen (-) between the names, if appropriate.

2. **Name of Business or Organization** - Give the complete name, without abbreviations.

3. **Mailing Address** - Give your complete mailing address.

4. **Daytime Phone Number** - Give a phone number with area code where you can be reached during the day.

5. **Fax Number** - Give a fax number with area code.

6. **E-mail Address** - If you have an E-mail address please provide it.

If you are acting as an attorney or representative - check the box provided and complete the rest of **Part 1** as follows:

1. **Family Name** (Last name) - Give your legal name. If you have two last names, include both and use a hyphen (-) between the names, if appropriate.

2. **Business/Organization/School Name** - Give the complete name, without abbreviations, if the party for whom you are filing is other than an individual.

3. **A-Number** - This is the USCIS (INS) file number. It begins with an "A" and can be found on a Permanent Resident Card or on correspondence that has been received from the Department of Homeland Security (DHS) or USCIS. If you do not have an A-Number, leave this blank.

Part 2 - Information About the Appeal or Motion

You must clearly indicate if you are filing an appeal or a motion. The adverse decision will indicate whether you may file an appeal or a motion. The requirements for motions to reopen and motions to reconsider are located at 8 C.F.R. § 103.5.

Part 3 - Basis for the Appeal or Motion

Your appeal or motion will be dismissed if you do not complete Part 3. If additional space is needed, attach a separate sheet of paper.

Part 4 - Signature of Person Filing the Appeal/Motion or His or Her Authorized Representative

You or your legal representative must sign and submit Form I-290B. Form G-28, Notice of Entry of Appearance as Attorney or Representative, must be attached if signed by a legal representative.

General Requirements

Your appeal or motion must include the following items.

Your signed and completed Form I-290B

NOTE: If you wish, you may be represented at no expense to the U.S. Government by an attorney or other duly authorized representative. Your attorney or representative must submit Form G-28 with the appeal or motion. If the appeal or motion is filed by an attorney or representative without a properly executed Form G-28, it will be dismissed or rejected.

Appeals

1. Brief

You do not need to submit a brief in support of your appeal, but you may submit one if you so choose. You may also submit additional evidence. Any brief and/or additional evidence must specifically reference the appeal for which it is being submitted. If an affected party has filed multiple appeals with the AAO, separate copies of the brief and/or evidence must be provided for each individual appeal. Failure to do so may result in the return of the brief or evidence to the individual or entity that submitted it and preclude such material from consideration.

You may submit a brief and evidence with Form I-290B. Or you may send these materials to the AAO within 30 days of filing the appeal. You must send any materials you submit after filing the appeal to:

USCIS Administrative Appeals Office
U.S. Citizenship and Immigration Services
20 Massachusetts Avenue, N.W., MS2090
Washington, DC 20529-2090

If you need more than 30 days, you must explain why in a separate letter attached to Form I-290B. The AAO may grant more time **only** for good cause.

2. Oral Argument

You may request oral argument before the AAO in Washington, D.C. in a separate letter attached to Form I-290B. The letter must explain specifically why an oral argument is necessary, i.e., why your argument cannot be adequately addressed in writing.

If your request is granted, the AAO will contact you about setting the date and time. The U.S. Government does not furnish interpreters for oral argument.

Motions

Although a petitioner may be permitted additional time to submit a brief and/or evidence to support an appeal, no such provision applies to motions. Any additional evidence must be submitted with the motion.

Translations

Any document containing a foreign language submitted to USCIS shall be accompanied by a full English language translation which the translator has certified as complete and accurate, and by the translator's certification that he or she is competent to translate from the foreign language into English.

What Is the Filing Fee?

The filing fee for Form I-290B is **$630.**

NOTE: The fee will be the same when an appeal or motion is taken from the denial of a petition with one or multiple beneficiaries, provided that they are all covered by the same petition, and therefore, the same decision.

The fee for Form I-290B may be waived, if the applicant can show an inability to pay and the appeal or motion is from denial of an immigration benefit request where the applicant or petitioner was not required to pay a fee, or the fee for the underlying application or petition could have been waived.

No fee is required when Form I-290B is filed to appeal a denial of a petition for a special immigrant visa by a Special Immigrant Iraqi or Afghan national who worked for or on behalf of the U.S. Government in Iraq or Afghanistan.

The fee will not be refunded, regardless of the action taken in your case.

For additional information on fees, fee waivers, and refunds visit our Web site at **www.uscis.gov**.

Use the following guidelines when you prepare your check or money order for the Form I-290B fee:

1. The check or money order must be drawn on a bank or other financial institution located in the United States and must be payable in U.S. currency; and

2. Make the check or money order payable to U.S. Department of Homeland Security.

3. If you live outside the United States, Guam, or the U.S. Virgin Islands, contact the nearest U.S. consulate or embassy for instructions on the method of payment.

   NOTE: Spell out U.S. Department of Homeland Security; do not use the initials "USDHS" or "DHS."

Notice to Those Making Payment by Check

If you send us a check, it will be converted into an electronic funds transfer (EFT). This means we will copy your check and use the account information on it to electronically debit your account for the amount of the check. The debit from your account will usually take 24 hours, and will be shown on your regular account statement.

You will not receive your original check back. We will destroy your original check, but we will keep a copy of it. If the EFT cannot be processed for technical reasons, you authorize us to process the copy in place of your original check. If the EFT cannot be completed because of insufficient funds, we may try to make the transfer up to 2 times.

How to Check If the Fees Are Correct

The form fee is current as of the edition date appearing in the lower right corner of Form I-290B. However, because USCIS fees change periodically, you can verify if the fees are correct by following one of the steps below:

1. Visit our Web site at **www.uscis.gov**, select "Check Filing Fees" and check the appropriate fee;

2. Telephone our National Customer Service Center at 1-800-375-5283 and ask for the fee information.

Where To File?

You must file your appeal or motion within 30 calendar days after service of the decision (33 days if your decision was mailed). If you are appealing the revocation of an immigrant petition approval, you must file the appeal within 15 days of the revocation decision (18 days if the decision was mailed). The date of service is normally the date of the decision.

Do **not** send your appeal or motion directly to the Administrative Appeals Office (AAO). Submit an original appeal or motion only. Additional copies are not required.

You must file your Notice of Appeal or Motion at the **USCIS Vermont Service Center** for unfavorable decisions made on:

1. A VAWA (self-petitioning spouse or child of an abusive U.S. Citizen or Lawful Permanent Resident) related Form I-360 to include work authorization (Form I-765);

2. Any T Visa related application/petition to include application for T nonimmigrant status (Form I-914/ I-914A), application for adjustment of status (Form I-485), work authorization (Form I-765) or advanced parole (Form I-131); or

3. Any U Visa related application/petition to include petition for U nonimmigrant status (Form I-918/I-918A), application for adjustment of status (Form I-485), work authorization (Form I-765), advanced parole (Form I-131), application to extend U nonimmigrant status (Form I-539) and petition to request immigration benefits on behalf of a family member who never held U nonimmigrant (Form I-929).

Mail your Form I-290B to:

USCIS Vermont Service Center
75 Lower Welden St.
St. Albans, VT 05479-0001

If you are filing a Notice of Appeal or Motion of any other decision made by a USCIS Service Center, mail your Form I-290B to the **USCIS Phoenix Lockbox** facility at:

For U.S. Postal Service deliveries, use the following address:

USCIS 290B
P.O. Box 21100
Phoenix, AZ 85036

For Express Mail or commercial courier deliveries, use the following address:

USCIS
Attn: 290B
1820 E. Skyharbor Cir S Ste 100
Phoenix, AZ 85034

If you are filing a motion to reopen a decision of USCIS under the Special Immigrant Juvenile (SIJ) *PEREZ-OLANO* **Agreement Settlement (POSA)**, mail the motion to the **USCIS Chicago Lockbox** facility at:

For U.S. Postal Service deliveries, use the following address:

> **USCIS**
> **P.O. Box 5510**
> **Chicago, IL 60680-5510**

For commercial courier deliveries, use the following address:

> **USCIS**
> **Attn: POSA**
> **131 South Dearborn - 3rd Floor**
> **Chicago, IL 60603-5517**

If you are filing a motion to reopen a decision made by a USCIS on Form N-470, Application to Preserve Residence for Naturalization Purposes or Form N-565, Application for Replacement Naturalization/Citizenship Document, you must file with the **USCIS Field Office** that made the unfavorable decision.

If you are filing a motion to reopen any other decision made by a USCIS Field Office, mail the motion to the **USCIS Chicago Lockbox** facility at:

For U.S. Postal Service deliveries, use the following address:

> **USCIS**
> **P.O. Box 805887**
> **Chicago, IL 60680-4120**

For commercial courier deliveries, use the following address:

> **USCIS**
> **ATTN: FBAS**
> **131 S. Dearborn, 3rd Floor**
> **Chicago, IL 60603-5517**

Because USCIS mailing address change periodically, you may verify that the addresses for your appeal are correct by following one of the steps below:

1. Visit our Web site at **www.uscis.gov**, select "FORMS," then "I-290B," and read the "Where to File" on the opening page; or

2. Telephone our National Customer Service Center at **1-800-375-5283** and ask for the mailing information.

Address Changes

While your **appeal** is pending, if you change your address, send a written notice of your change of address to the AAO.

Include the type of case that was denied and any available tracking number (receipt number and/or A-Number). Mail the notice to:

> **USCIS Administrative Appeals Office**
> **U.S. Citizenship and Immigration Services**
> **20 Massachusetts Avenue, N.W., MS2090**
> **Washington, DC 20529-2090**

If you change your address after you file a **motion**, where you send your notice depends on where your motion is pending. If your motion has been forwarded to the AAO, send a written notice of your change of address to the above address. If your motion has remained with the office where you submitted it, send the notice to that office. Include the type of case that was denied and any available tracking number (receipt number and/or A-Number).

Processing Information

An appeal or motion that is not signed or is not accompanied by the proper fee **will be dismissed or rejected** with a notice that the appeal is deficient. If completed timely, you may correct the deficiency and resubmit the appeal. However, an appeal or motion is not considered properly filed until it is accepted by USCIS.

Once the appeal or motion is accepted, it will be reviewed. If you do not have any standing to file the appeal or motion, or the decision is not appealable or filed timely, the appeal or motion will be dismissed or rejected without further review.

Decision. You will be notified in writing of any action taken on your appeal or motion.

USCIS Forms and Information

You can get USCIS forms and immigration-related information on the USCIS Internet Web site at **www.uscis.gov.** You may also obtain forms and information by telephoning our National Customer Service Center at **1-800-375-5283**.

As an alternative to waiting in line for assistance at your local USCIS office, you can now schedule an appointment through our Internet-based system, **InfoPass**. To access the system, visit our Web site. Use the **InfoPass** appointment scheduler and follow the screen prompts to set up your appointment. **InfoPass** generates an electronic appointment notice that appears on the screen.

Form I-290B Instructions 11/01/12 Y Page 4

Penalties

If you knowingly and willfully falsify or conceal a material fact or submit a false document with Form I-290B, we will deny the Form I-290B and may deny any other immigration benefit.

In addition, you will face severe penalties provided by law and may be subject to criminal prosecution.

Privacy Act Notice

We ask for the information on this form, and associated evidence, to determine if you have established eligibility for the immigration benefit for which you are filing. Our legal right to ask for this information can be found in the Immigration and Nationality Act, as amended. We may provide this information to other government agencies. Failure to provide this information, and any requested evidence, may delay a final decision or result in denial of your Form I-290B.

Paperwork Reduction Act

An agency may not conduct or sponsor an information collection and a person is not required to respond to a collection of information unless it displays a currently valid OMB control number. The public reporting burden for this collection of information is estimated at 90 minutes per response, including the time for reviewing instructions and completing and submitting the form. Send comments regarding this burden estimate or any other aspect of this collection of information, including suggestions for reducing this burden, to: U.S. Citizenship and Immigration Services, Regulatory Coordination Division, Office of Policy and Strategy, 20 Massachusetts Ave NW, Washington, DC 20529-2140; OMB No. 1615-0095. **Do not mail your application to this address.**

OMB No. 1615-0095; Expires 11/30/2014

Department of Homeland Security
U.S. Citizenship and Immigration Services

Form I-290B, Notice
of Appeal or Motion

In the Matter of:	File Number: A -

START HERE - Please Type or Print (Use black ink)

For USCIS Use Only

			Returned	Receipt

Part 1. Information About Petitioner/Applicant *(Individual/Business/*
Organization/Attorney/Representative filing appeal or motion)

Family Name	Given Name	Middle Name	Date

Name of Business/Organization *(if applicable)*

	Date
	Resubmitted

Mailing Address - Street Number and Name   Apt. #

	Date

C/O *(in care of)*:

	Date
	Reloc Sent

City	State or Province	Zip/Postal Code	Date

Country	Daytime Phone # *(Area/Country Code)*	Date
	( )	Reloc Rec'd

Fax # *(Area/Country Code)*	E-Mail Address *(if any)*	Date
( )		

☐ I am an attorney or representative. If you check this box, you must provide the
following information about the person or organization for whom you are
appearing. (**NOTE:** You must attach a Form G-28, Notice of Entry of Appearance
as Attorney or Representative.)

Date

Remarks

Family Name	Given Name	Middle Name

Complete Name of Business/Organization/School *(if applicable)*

A # *(if any)*	Daytime Phone # *(Area/Country Code)*
	( )

Fax # *(Area/Country Code)*	E-mail Address *(if any)*
( )	

Part 2. Information About the Appeal or Motion *(Check one box below that best describes your request)*

NOTE: If you indicate that you are filing an appeal, it may be considered by USCIS as a motion before it is forwarded to the AAO.

A. ☐ I am filing an appeal. My brief and/or additional evidence is attached.

B. ☐ I am filing an appeal. My brief and/or additional evidence will be submitted to the AAO within 30 days.

C. ☐ I am filing an appeal. No supplemental brief and/or additional evidence will be submitted.

D. ☐ I am filing a motion to reopen a decision. My brief and/or additional evidence is attached.

E. ☐ I am filing a motion to reconsider a decision. My brief is attached.

F. ☐ I am filing a motion to reopen and a motion to reconsider a decision. My brief and/or additional evidence is attached.

Form I-290B (Rev. 11/01/12) Y

In the Matter of:	File Number: A -

Part 2. Information About the Appeal or Motion   *(Continued)*

Information on the relating application/petition.

Application/Petition Form #	Receipt #	Date of Denial *(mm/dd/yyyy)*	USCIS Office Where Decision Issued

Part 3. Basis for the Appeal or Motion

Motion to Reopen: The motion must state new facts and must be supported by affidavits and/or documentary evidence.

Motion to Reconsider: The motion must be supported by citations to appropriate statutes, regulations, or precedent decisions.

Appeal: Provide a statement explaining any erroneous conclusion of law or fact in the decision being appealed.

Part 4. Signature of Person Filing the Appeal/Motion or His or Her Authorized Representative

Signature	Printed Name	Date *(mm/dd/yyyy)*

Make sure your appeal or motion is complete before filing.

Form I-290B (Rev. 11/01/12) Y Page 2

APPENDIX 7-5

List of 100 Sample Naturalization Questions

(rev. 03/11)

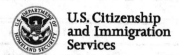 **U.S. Citizenship and Immigration Services**

Civics (History and Government) Questions for the Naturalization Test

The 100 civics (history and government) questions and answers for the naturalization test are listed below. The civics test is an oral test and the USCIS Officer will ask the applicant up to 10 of the 100 civics questions. An applicant must answer 6 out of 10 questions correctly to pass the civics portion of the naturalization test.

On the naturalization test, some answers may change because of elections or appointments. As you study for the test, make sure that you know the most current answers to these questions. Answer these questions with the name of the official who is serving at the time of your eligibility interview with USCIS. The USCIS Officer will not accept an incorrect answer.

Although USCIS is aware that there may be additional correct answers to the 100 civics questions, applicants are encouraged to respond to the civics questions using the answers provided below.

AMERICAN GOVERNMENT

A: Principles of American Democracy

1. **What is the supreme law of the land?**
    - *the Constitution*

2. **What does the Constitution do?**
    - *sets up the government*
    - *defines the government*
    - *protects basic rights of Americans*

3. **The idea of self-government is in the first three words of the Constitution. What are these words?**
    - *We the People*

4. **What is an amendment?**
    - *a change (to the Constitution)*
    - *an addition (to the Constitution)*

5. **What do we call the first ten amendments to the Constitution?**
    - *the Bill of Rights*

6. **What is <u>one</u> right or freedom from the First Amendment?***
    - *speech*
    - *religion*
    - *assembly*
    - *press*
    - *petition the government*

7. **How many amendments does the Constitution have?**
    - *twenty-seven (27)*

* If you are 65 years old or older and have been a legal permanent resident of the United States for 20 or more years, you may study just the questions that have been marked with an asterisk.

-1-
www.uscis.gov

394

8. **What did the Declaration of Independence do?**
   - *announced our independence (from Great Britain)*
   - *declared our independence (from Great Britain)*
   - *said that the United States is free (from Great Britain)*

9. **What are <u>two</u> rights in the Declaration of Independence?**
   - *life*
   - *liberty*
   - *pursuit of happiness*

10. **What is freedom of religion?**
    - *You can practice any religion, or not practice a religion.*

11. **What is the economic system in the United States?***
    - *capitalist economy*
    - *market economy*

12. **What is the "rule of law"?**
    - *Everyone must follow the law.*
    - *Leaders must obey the law.*
    - *Government must obey the law.*
    - *No one is above the law.*

B: System of Government

13. **Name <u>one</u> branch or part of the government.***
    - *Congress*
    - *legislative*
    - *President*
    - *executive*
    - *the courts*
    - *judicial*

14. **What stops <u>one</u> branch of government from becoming too powerful?**
    - *checks and balances*
    - *separation of powers*

15. **Who is in charge of the executive branch?**
    - *the President*

16. **Who makes federal laws?**
    - *Congress*
    - *Senate and House (of Representatives)*
    - *(U.S. or national) legislature*

17. **What are the <u>two</u> parts of the U.S. Congress?***
    - *the Senate and House (of Representatives)*

18. **How many U.S. Senators are there?**
    - *one hundred (100)*

* If you are 65 years old or older and have been a legal permanent resident of the United States for 20 or more years, you may study just the questions that have been marked with an asterisk.

www.uscis.gov

19. **We elect a U.S. Senator for how many years?**
    - *six (6)*

20. **Who is <u>one</u> of your state's U.S. Senators now?***
    - *Answers will vary. [District of Columbia residents and residents of U.S. territories should answer that D.C. (or the territory where the applicant lives) has no U.S. Senators.]*

21. **The House of Representatives has how many voting members?**
    - *four hundred thirty-five (435)*

22. **We elect a U.S. Representative for how many years?**
    - *two (2)*

23. **Name your U.S. Representative.**
    - *Answers will vary. [Residents of territories with nonvoting Delegates or Resident Commissioners may provide the name of that Delegate or Commissioner. Also acceptable is any statement that the territory has no (voting) Representatives in Congress.]*

24. **Who does a U.S. Senator represent?**
    - *all people of the state*

25. **Why do some states have more Representatives than other states?**
    - *(because of) the state's population*
    - *(because) they have more people*
    - *(because) some states have more people*

26. **We elect a President for how many years?**
    - *four (4)*

27. **In what month do we vote for President?***
    - *November*

28. **What is the name of the President of the United States now?***
    - *Barack Obama*
    - *Obama*

29. **What is the name of the Vice President of the United States now?**
    - *Joseph R. Biden, Jr.*
    - *Joe Biden*
    - *Biden*

30. **If the President can no longer serve, who becomes President?**
    - *the Vice President*

31. **If both the President and the Vice President can no longer serve, who becomes President?**
    - *the Speaker of the House*

32. **Who is the Commander in Chief of the military?**
    - *the President*

33. **Who signs bills to become laws?**
    - *the President*

34. **Who vetoes bills?**
    - *the President*

---

* If you are 65 years old or older and have been a legal permanent resident of the United States for 20 or more years, you may study just the questions that have been marked with an asterisk.

35.   **What does the President's Cabinet do?**
- *advises the President*

36.   **What are <u>two</u> Cabinet-level positions?**
- *Secretary of Agriculture*
- *Secretary of Commerce*
- *Secretary of Defense*
- *Secretary of Education*
- *Secretary of Energy*
- *Secretary of Health and Human Services*
- *Secretary of Homeland Security*
- *Secretary of Housing and Urban Development*
- *Secretary of the Interior*
- *Secretary of Labor*
- *Secretary of State*
- *Secretary of Transportation*
- *Secretary of the Treasury*
- *Secretary of Veterans Affairs*
- *Attorney General*
- *Vice President*

37.   **What does the judicial branch do?**
- *reviews laws*
- *explains laws*
- *resolves disputes (disagreements)*
- *decides if a law goes against the Constitution*

38.   **What is the highest court in the United States?**
- *the Supreme Court*

39.   **How many justices are on the Supreme Court?**
- *nine (9)*

40.   **Who is the Chief Justice of the United States now?**
- *John Roberts (John G. Roberts, Jr.)*

41.   **Under our Constitution, some powers belong to the federal government. What is <u>one</u> power of the federal government?**
- *to print money*
- *to declare war*
- *to create an army*
- *to make treaties*

42.   **Under our Constitution, some powers belong to the states. What is <u>one</u> power of the states?**
- *provide schooling and education*
- *provide protection (police)*
- *provide safety (fire departments)*
- *give a driver's license*
- *approve zoning and land use*

---

* If you are 65 years old or older and have been a legal permanent resident of the United States for 20 or more years, you may study just the questions that have been marked with an asterisk.

43. Who is the Governor of your state now?
- *Answers will vary. [District of Columbia residents should answer that D.C. does not have a Governor.]*

44. What is the capital of your state?*
- *Answers will vary. [District of Columbia residents should answer that D.C. is not a state and does not have a capital. Residents of U.S. territories should name the capital of the territory.]*

45. What are the <u>two</u> major political parties in the United States?*
- *Democratic and Republican*

46. What is the political party of the President now?
- *Democratic (Party)*

47. What is the name of the Speaker of the House of Representatives now?
- *(John) Boehner*

C: Rights and Responsibilities

48. There are four amendments to the Constitution about who can vote. Describe <u>one</u> of them.
- *Citizens eighteen (18) and older (can vote).*
- *You don't have to pay (a poll tax) to vote.*
- *Any citizen can vote. (Women and men can vote.)*
- *A male citizen of any race (can vote).*

49. What is <u>one</u> responsibility that is only for United States citizens?*
- *serve on a jury*
- *vote in a federal election*

50. Name <u>one</u> right only for United States citizens.
- *vote in a federal election*
- *run for federal office*

51. What are <u>two</u> rights of everyone living in the United States?
- *freedom of expression*
- *freedom of speech*
- *freedom of assembly*
- *freedom to petition the government*
- *freedom of worship*
- *the right to bear arms*

52. What do we show loyalty to when we say the Pledge of Allegiance?
- *the United States*
- *the flag*

53. What is <u>one</u> promise you make when you become a United States citizen?
- *give up loyalty to other countries*
- *defend the Constitution and laws of the United States*
- *obey the laws of the United States*
- *serve in the U.S. military (if needed)*
- *serve (do important work for) the nation (if needed)*
- *be loyal to the United States*

* If you are 65 years old or older and have been a legal permanent resident of the United States for 20 or more years, you may study just the questions that have been marked with an asterisk.

www.uscis.gov

54. **How old do citizens have to be to vote for President?***
    - *eighteen (18) and older*

55. **What are <u>two</u> ways that Americans can participate in their democracy?**
    - *vote*
    - *join a political party*
    - *help with a campaign*
    - *join a civic group*
    - *join a community group*
    - *give an elected official your opinion on an issue*
    - *call Senators and Representatives*
    - *publicly support or oppose an issue or policy*
    - *run for office*
    - *write to a newspaper*

56. **When is the last day you can send in federal income tax forms?***
    - *April 15*

57. **When must all men register for the Selective Service?**
    - *at age eighteen (18)*
    - *between eighteen (18) and twenty-six (26)*

AMERICAN HISTORY

A: Colonial Period and Independence

58. **What is <u>one</u> reason colonists came to America?**
    - *freedom*
    - *political liberty*
    - *religious freedom*
    - *economic opportunity*
    - *practice their religion*
    - *escape persecution*

59. **Who lived in America before the Europeans arrived?**
    - *American Indians*
    - *Native Americans*

60. **What group of people was taken to America and sold as slaves?**
    - *Africans*
    - *people from Africa*

61. **Why did the colonists fight the British?**
    - *because of high taxes (taxation without representation)*
    - *because the British army stayed in their houses (boarding, quartering)*
    - *because they didn't have self-government*

62. **Who wrote the Declaration of Independence?**
    - *(Thomas) Jefferson*

* If you are 65 years old or older and have been a legal permanent resident of the United States for 20 or more years, you may study just the questions that have been marked with an asterisk.

63. **When was the Declaration of Independence adopted?**
- *July 4, 1776*

64. **There were 13 original states. Name three.**
- *New Hampshire*
- *Massachusetts*
- *Rhode Island*
- *Connecticut*
- *New York*
- *New Jersey*
- *Pennsylvania*
- *Delaware*
- *Maryland*
- *Virginia*
- *North Carolina*
- *South Carolina*
- *Georgia*

65. **What happened at the Constitutional Convention?**
- *The Constitution was written.*
- *The Founding Fathers wrote the Constitution.*

66. **When was the Constitution written?**
- *1787*

67. **The Federalist Papers supported the passage of the U.S. Constitution. Name one of the writers.**
- *(James) Madison*
- *(Alexander) Hamilton*
- *(John) Jay*
- *Publius*

68. **What is one thing Benjamin Franklin is famous for?**
- *U.S. diplomat*
- *oldest member of the Constitutional Convention*
- *first Postmaster General of the United States*
- *writer of "Poor Richard's Almanac"*
- *started the first free libraries*

69. **Who is the "Father of Our Country"?**
- *(George) Washington*

70. **Who was the first President?***
- *(George) Washington*

B: 1800s

71. **What territory did the United States buy from France in 1803?**
- *the Louisiana Territory*
- *Louisiana*

* If you are 65 years old or older and have been a legal permanent resident of the United States for 20 or more years, you may study just the questions that have been marked with an asterisk.

72. **Name <u>one</u> war fought by the United States in the 1800s.**
    - *War of 1812*
    - *Mexican-American War*
    - *Civil War*
    - *Spanish-American War*

73. **Name the U.S. war between the North and the South.**
    - *the Civil War*
    - *the War between the States*

74. **Name <u>one</u> problem that led to the Civil War.**
    - *slavery*
    - *economic reasons*
    - *states' rights*

75. **What was <u>one</u> important thing that Abraham Lincoln did?***
    - *freed the slaves (Emancipation Proclamation)*
    - *saved (or preserved) the Union*
    - *led the United States during the Civil War*

76. **What did the Emancipation Proclamation do?**
    - *freed the slaves*
    - *freed slaves in the Confederacy*
    - *freed slaves in the Confederate states*
    - *freed slaves in most Southern states*

77. **What did Susan B. Anthony do?**
    - *fought for women's rights*
    - *fought for civil rights*

C: Recent American History and Other Important Historical Information

78. **Name <u>one</u> war fought by the United States in the 1900s.***
    - *World War I*
    - *World War II*
    - *Korean War*
    - *Vietnam War*
    - *(Persian) Gulf War*

79. **Who was President during World War I?**
    - *(Woodrow) Wilson*

80. **Who was President during the Great Depression and World War II?**
    - *(Franklin) Roosevelt*

81. **Who did the United States fight in World War II?**
    - *Japan, Germany, and Italy*

82. **Before he was President, Eisenhower was a general. What war was he in?**
    - *World War II*

---

* If you are 65 years old or older and have been a legal permanent resident of the United States for 20 or more years, you may study just the questions that have been marked with an asterisk.

         www.uscis.gov

83. **During the Cold War, what was the main concern of the United States?**
   - *Communism*

84. **What movement tried to end racial discrimination?**
   - *civil rights (movement)*

85. **What did Martin Luther King, Jr. do?***
   - *fought for civil rights*
   - *worked for equality for all Americans*

86. **What major event happened on September 11, 2001, in the United States?**
   - *Terrorists attacked the United States.*

87. **Name <u>one</u> American Indian tribe in the United States.**
   [USCIS Officers will be supplied with a list of federally recognized American Indian tribes.]
   - *Cherokee*
   - *Navajo*
   - *Sioux*
   - *Chippewa*
   - *Choctaw*
   - *Pueblo*
   - *Apache*
   - *Iroquois*
   - *Creek*
   - *Blackfeet*
   - *Seminole*
   - *Cheyenne*
   - *Arawak*
   - *Shawnee*
   - *Mohegan*
   - *Huron*
   - *Oneida*
   - *Lakota*
   - *Crow*
   - *Teton*
   - *Hopi*
   - *Inuit*

INTEGRATED CIVICS

A: Geography

88. **Name <u>one</u> of the two longest rivers in the United States.**
   - *Missouri (River)*
   - *Mississippi (River)*

89. **What ocean is on the West Coast of the United States?**
   - *Pacific (Ocean)*

* If you are 65 years old or older and have been a legal permanent resident of the United States for 20 or more years, you may study just the questions that have been marked with an asterisk.

www.uscis.gov

90. **What ocean is on the East Coast of the United States?**
   - *Atlantic (Ocean)*

91. **Name <u>one</u> U.S. territory.**
   - *Puerto Rico*
   - *U.S. Virgin Islands*
   - *American Samoa*
   - *Northern Mariana Islands*
   - *Guam*

92. **Name <u>one</u> state that borders Canada.**
   - *Maine*
   - *New Hampshire*
   - *Vermont*
   - *New York*
   - *Pennsylvania*
   - *Ohio*
   - *Michigan*
   - *Minnesota*
   - *North Dakota*
   - *Montana*
   - *Idaho*
   - *Washington*
   - *Alaska*

93. **Name <u>one</u> state that borders Mexico.**
   - *California*
   - *Arizona*
   - *New Mexico*
   - *Texas*

94. **What is the capital of the United States?***
   - *Washington, D.C.*

95. **Where is the Statue of Liberty?***
   - *New York (Harbor)*
   - *Liberty Island*
   - *[Also acceptable are New Jersey, near New York City, and on the Hudson (River).]*

B: Symbols

96. **Why does the flag have 13 stripes?**
   - *because there were 13 original colonies*
   - *because the stripes represent the original colonies*

97. **Why does the flag have 50 stars?***
   - *because there is one star for each state*
   - *because each star represents a state*
   - *because there are 50 states*

* If you are 65 years old or older and have been a legal permanent resident of the United States for 20 or more years, you may study just the questions that have been marked with an asterisk.

98.   **What is the name of the national anthem?**
   - *The Star-Spangled Banner*

C: Holidays

99.   **When do we celebrate Independence Day?***
   - *July 4*

100. **Name <u>two</u> national U.S. holidays.**
   - *New Year's Day*
   - *Martin Luther King, Jr. Day*
   - *Presidents' Day*
   - *Memorial Day*
   - *Independence Day*
   - *Labor Day*
   - *Columbus Day*
   - *Veterans Day*
   - *Thanksgiving*
   - *Christmas*

* If you are 65 years old or older and have been a legal permanent resident of the United States for 20 or more years, you may study just the questions that have been marked with an asterisk.

(rev. 03/11)

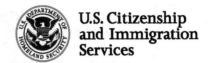
U.S. Citizenship
and Immigration
Services

公民（歷史與政府）歸化試題

以下所列爲公民（歷史與政府的）歸化的 100 道試題與答案。公民測驗是口試，由 USCIS 主考官向申請人提問 100 道公民試題中的 10 道。申請人必須從 10 道中正確回答 6 道才能通過入籍歸化的公民測驗部分。

在公民入籍考試中，有些問題的答案會因選舉或任命結果而改變。當您學習考題時，請務必確定您知道該類試題的最新答案。當您到美國公民及移民服務局（USCIS）接受公民入籍面試時，您需要回答當時在位任職的政府官員之姓名。美國公民及移民服務局的面試官將不會認可錯誤的答案。

USCIS瞭解這 100 道試題可能有額外的正確答案，但是我們建議申請人回答公民測驗試題時用以下提供的答案。

美國政府

A: 美國民主原則

1. 美國的最高法律是什麼？
   - *憲法*

2. 憲法的作用是什麼？
   - *建立政府體制*
   - *定義政府*
   - *保護美國人的基本權利*

3. 憲法的前三個字說明自治的概念。這三個字是什麼？
   - *我們人民*

4. 什麼是修正案？
   - *（憲法的）更正*
   - *（憲法的）補充*

5. 憲法的前十項修正案稱爲什麼？
   - *權利法案*

6. 列舉憲法第一條修正案中的一項權利或自由。*
   - *言論自由*
   - *宗教自由*
   - *集會結社的自由*
   - *出版自由*
   - *向政府請願的自由*

7. 憲法有幾條修正案？
   - *二十七 (27) 條*

* 如果您年滿 65 歲或以上，持綠卡（美國合法的永久居民）20 年以上，則只需學習標有星號的試題。

8. 「獨立宣言」的作用是什麼？
- *宣佈美國（脫離英國而）獨立*
- *宣告美國（脫離英國而）獨立*
- *表示美國（脫離英國而）獨立*

9. 列舉「獨立宣言」中的<u>兩項</u>權利。
- *生命（的權利）*
- *自由（的權利）*
- *追求幸福（的權利）*

10. 什麼是宗教自由？
- *你可以信仰任何宗教，也可以不信仰任何宗教。*

11. 美國的經濟制度是什麼？*
- *資本主義經濟*
- *市場經濟*

12. 「法治」是什麼？
- *人人都應遵守法律。*
- *領導人必須遵守法律。*
- *政府必須遵守法律。*
- *沒有任何人在法律之上。*

B: 政治體制

13. 列舉政府體制的<u>一個</u>分支或部門。*
- *國會*
- *立法部門*
- *總統*
- *行政部門*
- *法院*
- *司法部門*

14. 什麼防止一個政府分支變得過於強大？
- *制衡*
- *權力分立*

15. 誰負責行政部門？
- *總統*

16. 誰制定聯邦法律？
- *國會*
- *參議院及眾議院*
- *（美國或國家）立法部門*

17. 美國國會由哪<u>兩個</u>部分組成？*
- *參議院與眾議院*

18. 美國參議員有幾位？
- *一百(100)位*

* 如果您年滿 65 歲或以上，持綠卡（美國合法的永久居民）20 年以上，則只需學習標有星號的試題。

19. 我們選出的美國參議員任職多少年？
   - 六 *(6)* 年

20. 您所在州的現任一位美國參議員的名字是什麼？*
   - 答案依所在州不同而異。〔住在哥倫比亞特區和美國領土的居民可答:哥倫比亞特區當地（或應試居民所在領地）沒有美國參議員。〕

21. 眾議院中有投票權的眾議員有幾位？
   - 四百三十五 *(435)* 位

22. 我們選出的美國眾議員任職多少年？
   - 兩 *(2)* 年

23. 列舉您所在選區的美國眾議員的名字。
   - 答案依所在州不同而異。〔住在沒有投票權的美國領地當地代表或專員之應試者可以說明當地代表或專員的姓名。說明自己選區沒有國會（投票）代表也是可接受的答案。〕

24. 美國參議員代表何人？
   - 其所在州的所有人民

25. 為什麼有些州的眾議員人數比其他州多？
   - （由於）該州的人口
   - （由於）該州有更多人口
   - （由於）該州的人口比其他州多

26. 我們選出的總統任職多少年？
   - 四 *(4)* 年

27. 我們在哪一個月選總統？*
   - 十一月

28. 現任美國總統的名字是什麼？*
   - *Barack Obama*
   - *Obama*

29. 現任美國副總統的名字是什麼？
   - *Joseph R. Biden, Jr.*
   - *Joe Biden*
   - *Biden*

30. 如果總統不能視事，則由誰成為總統？
   - *副總統*

31. 如果總統和副總統都不能視事，則由誰成為總統？
   - *眾議院議長*

32. 誰是三軍統帥？
   - *總統*

33. 誰簽署法案使之成為法律？
   - *總統*

34. 誰否決法案？
   - *總統*

＊如果您年滿 65 歲或以上，持綠卡（美國合法的永久居民）20 年以上，則只需學習標有星號的試題。

35. 總統的內閣做什麼事？
    - *向總統提出建議*

36. <u>兩個</u>內閣級別的職位是什麼？
    - *農業部長*
    - *商務部長*
    - *國防部長*
    - *教育部長*
    - *能源部長*
    - *健康與人類服務部長*
    - *國土安全部長*
    - *住宅與都市發展部長*
    - *內政部長*
    - *勞工部長*
    - *國務卿*
    - *交通部長*
    - *財政部長*
    - *退伍軍人事務部長*
    - *司法部長*
    - *副總統*

37. 司法部門做什麼？
    - *審查法律*
    - *解釋法律*
    - *解決爭議（意見不一致）*
    - *決定某一法律是否牴觸憲法*

38. 美國最高法院是什麼？
    - *聯邦最高法院*

39. 最高法院有幾位大法官？
    - *九 (9) 位*

40. 現任聯邦首席大法官是誰？
    - *約翰‧羅伯茲（小約翰 G. 羅伯茲）*

41. 根據我國憲法，有些權力屬於聯邦政府。聯邦政府的<u>一項</u>權力是什麼？
    - *印製鈔票*
    - *宣戰*
    - *創立軍隊*
    - *簽訂條約*

42. 根據我國憲法，有些權力屬於州政府。州政府的<u>一項</u>權力是什麼？
    - *提供教育*
    - *提供保護（警員）*
    - *提供安全（消防局）*
    - *提供駕駛執照*
    - *批准區劃與土地使用*

* 如果您年滿 65 歲或以上，持綠卡（美國合法的永久居民）20 年以上，則只需學習標有星號的
試題。

43. 您居住州的現任州長是誰？
   - *答案依居住州不同而異。〔哥倫比亞特區的居民應回答：「我們沒有州長。」〕*

44. 您居住州的首府是哪裡？*
   - *答案依居住州不同而異。〔哥倫比亞特區居民應回答哥倫比亞特區不是一個州，沒有首府。美國領地居民應回答居住領地的首府。〕*

45. 美國當今兩大政黨為何？*
   - *民主黨與共和黨*

46. 現任總統屬於哪個政黨？
   - *民主黨*

47. 現任國會眾議院議長的名字是什麼？
   - *（約翰）博納*

C: 權利與責任

48. 憲法中有四個關於誰可以投票的修正案。試舉一個。
   - *十八 (18) 歲以上的公民（可以投票）。*
   - *您投票不必繳錢（繳投票稅）。*
   - *任何公民都可以投票（男性與女性都可以投票）。*
   - *任何種族的男性公民（都可以投票）。*

49. 列舉一項美國公民才有的責任？*
   - *當陪審員*
   - *在聯邦選舉中投票*

50. 列舉一項美國公民才享有的權利。
   - *在聯邦選舉中投票的權利*
   - *競選公職的權利*

51. 每一個住在美國的人享有的兩項權利是什麼？
   - *表達自由*
   - *言論自由*
   - *集會結社的自由*
   - *向政府請願的自由*
   - *宗教崇拜的自由*
   - *持有武器的自由*

52. 當我們宣誓效忠時，是向什麼表達忠誠？
   - *美利堅合眾國*
   - *國旗*

53. 當您成為美國公民時做出的一項承諾是什麼？
   - *放棄效忠其他國家*
   - *護衛美國的憲法及法律*
   - *遵守美國的法律*
   - *（必要時）加入美國軍隊*
   - *（必要時）為國效勞（為國做重要工作）*
   - *效忠美國*

* 如果您年滿 65 歲或以上，持綠卡（美國合法的永久居民）20 年以上，則只需學習標有星號的試題。

54. 美國公民必須幾歲才能投票選舉總統？*
- *十八 (18) 歲以上*

55. 美國人參與民主政治的**兩種**方法是什麼？
- *投票*
- *加入政黨*
- *協助競選活動*
- *加入公民團體*
- *加入社區團體*
- *向民選官員提供自己對某項議題的意見*
- *撥電給參議員和眾議員*
- *公開支持或反對某個議題或政策*
- *競選公職*
- *向報社投函*

56. 寄送聯邦所得稅表的截止日期是哪一天？*
- *（每年的）4 月 15 日*

57. 所有男性到了哪個年齡必須註冊「兵役登記」？
- *十八 (18) 歲*
- *十八 (18) 歲至二十六 (26) 歲之間*

美國歷史

A: 殖民期與獨立

58. 殖民者當初到美國的**一項**理由是什麼？
- *自由*
- *政治自由*
- *宗教自由*
- *經濟機會*
- *從事宗教活動*
- *逃避迫害*

59. 歐洲人抵達美國之前，誰已經居住在美國？
- *美國印地安人*
- *美國原住民*

60. 哪一群人被帶到美國並被販賣爲奴？
- *非洲人*
- *來自非洲的人*

61. 殖民者爲何與英國作戰？
- *因爲高額捐稅（只繳稅，沒有代表權）*
- *因爲英國軍隊住在他們的住宅內（寄宿、宿營）*
- *因爲他們沒有自治權*

62. 「獨立宣言」是誰寫的？
- *（湯瑪士）傑佛遜*

*如果您年滿 65 歲或以上，持綠卡（美國合法的永久居民）20 年以上，則只需學習標有星號的試題。

63. 「獨立宣言」是何時通過採用的？
   - *1776 年 7 月 4 日*

64. 美國原先有 13 個州。請列舉其中<u>三個州</u>。
   - *新罕布夏*
   - *麻薩諸塞*
   - *羅德島*
   - *康乃狄克*
   - *紐約*
   - *紐澤西*
   - *賓夕法尼亞*
   - *德拉瓦*
   - *馬裏蘭*
   - *維吉尼亞*
   - *北卡羅萊納*
   - *南卡羅萊納*
   - *喬治亞*

65. 制憲會議達成了什麼事？
   - *擬定憲法。*
   - *開國諸賢擬定了憲法。*

66. 憲法是何時擬定的？
   - *1787 年*

67. 《聯邦論》支持美國憲法的通過。請列舉<u>一名</u>《聯邦論》的作者。
   - *（詹姆士）麥迪森*
   - *（亞歷山大）漢米爾頓*
   - *（約翰）傑伊*
   - *普布利烏斯*

68. 班哲明・富蘭克林著稱的<u>一項</u>事蹟是什麼？
   - *美國外交官*
   - *制憲會議年紀最長的成員*
   - *美國第一任郵政總局局長*
   - *《窮人理查年鑑》的作者*
   - *開辦第一個免費圖書館*

69. 誰是「美國國父」？
   - *（喬治）華盛頓*

70. 誰是第一任總統？*
   - *（喬治）華盛頓*

B: 1800 *年代*

71. 美國在 1803 年向法國購買哪塊領地？
   - *路易士安納領地*
   - *路易士安納*

* 如果您年滿 65 歲或以上，持綠卡（美國合法的永久居民）20 年以上，則只需學習標有星號的試題。

72. 列舉<u>一場</u>美國在 1800 年代參與的戰爭。
   - *1812年戰爭*
   - *美墨戰爭*
   - *內戰*
   - *美國與西班牙戰爭*

73. 請說出美國南方與北方之間戰爭的名稱。
   - *內戰*
   - *州際戰爭*

74. 列舉<u>一項</u>導致內戰的問題。
   - *奴隸制度*
   - *經濟原因*
   - *各州的權利*

75. 亞伯拉罕 · 林肯的<u>一項</u>重要事蹟是什麼？*
   - *解放奴隸（《解放宣言》）*
   - *拯救（保留）聯盟*
   - *在內戰期間引領美國*

76. 《解放宣言》達成了什麼？
   - *解放了奴隸*
   - *解放了聯邦制下的奴隸*
   - *解放了聯邦各州的奴隸*
   - *解放了南方大部分州的奴隸*

77. 蘇珊 B. 安東尼的事蹟是什麼？
   - *為女權奮鬥*
   - *為民權奮鬥*

C: 美國近代史與其他重要的歷史資料

78. 列舉<u>一場</u>美國在 1900 年代參與的戰爭。*
   - *第一次世界大戰*
   - *第二次世界大戰*
   - *朝鮮戰爭*
   - *越戰*
   - *（波斯灣）海灣戰爭*

79. 第一次世界大戰期間的美國總統是誰？
   - *（伍德羅）威爾遜*

80. 美國經濟大蕭條和第二次世界大戰期間的總統是誰？
   - *（富蘭克林）羅斯福*

81. 美國在第二次世界大戰與哪些國家作戰？
   - *日本、德國、義大利*

82. 艾森豪在當總統以前是將軍。他曾參加哪一場戰爭？
   - *第二次世界大戰*

* 如果您年滿 65 歲或以上，持綠卡（美國合法的永久居民）20 年以上，則只需學習標有星號的
試題。

83.　在冷戰期間，美國的主要顧慮是什麼？
　　　▪ *共產主義*

84.　哪項運動試圖結束種族歧視？
　　　▪ *民權（運動）*

85.　小馬丁・路德・金的事蹟是什麼？ *
　　　▪ *為民權奮鬥*
　　　▪ *為所有美國人爭取平等*

86.　美國在2001年9月11日發生了什麼重大事件？
　　　▪ *恐怖份子攻擊美國。*

87.　列舉一個美國印地安人部族。
　　　〔USCIS主考官將有聯邦承認的美國印地安人部族清單。〕
　　　▪ *切洛基*
　　　▪ *納瓦荷*
　　　▪ *蘇*
　　　▪ *齊普瓦*
　　　▪ *喬克陶*
　　　▪ *布耶布洛*
　　　▪ *阿帕契*
　　　▪ *伊洛奎斯*
　　　▪ *庫瑞克*
　　　▪ *佈雷克非特*
　　　▪ *賽米諾利*
　　　▪ *夏安*
　　　▪ *阿拉瓦克*
　　　▪ *蕭尼*
　　　▪ *莫希根*
　　　▪ *休倫*
　　　▪ *歐尼達*
　　　▪ *拉科塔*
　　　▪ *克洛*
　　　▪ *泰頓*
　　　▪ *賀皮*
　　　▪ *伊努特*

綜合公民（歸化試題）

A: 地理

88.　列舉美國最長的兩條河中的一條。
　　　▪ *密蘇裏（河）*
　　　▪ *密西西比（河）*

* 如果您年滿65歲或以上，持綠卡（美國合法的永久居民）20年以上，則只需學習標有星號的
試題。

89. 美國西岸瀕臨什麼海洋？
    ▪ 太平洋

90. 美國東岸瀕臨什麼海洋？
    ▪ 大西洋

91. 列舉一個美國領地。
    ▪ 波多黎各
    ▪ 美屬維京群島
    ▪ 美屬薩摩亞
    ▪ 北馬裏亞納群島
    ▪ 關島

92. 列舉一個與加拿大毗連的州。
    ▪ 緬因
    ▪ 新罕布夏
    ▪ 佛蒙特
    ▪ 紐約
    ▪ 賓夕法尼亞
    ▪ 俄亥俄
    ▪ 密西根
    ▪ 明尼蘇達
    ▪ 北達科他
    ▪ 蒙大拿
    ▪ 愛達荷
    ▪ 華盛頓
    ▪ 阿拉斯加

93. 列舉一個與墨西哥毗連的州。
    ▪ 加利福尼亞
    ▪ 亞利桑那
    ▪ 新墨西哥
    ▪ 德克薩斯

94. 美國的首都在哪裡？*
    ▪ 華盛頓哥倫比亞特區

95. 自由女神像在哪裡？*
    ▪ 紐約（港）
    ▪ 自由島
    〔回答紐澤西、紐約市附近、哈德遜河上也可以接受〕

B: 標誌

96. 國旗上為什麼有十三個條紋？
    ▪ 因為當初有十三個殖民地
    ▪ 因為條紋代表當初的殖民地

* 如果您年滿 65 歲或以上，持綠卡（美國合法的永久居民）20 年以上，則只需學習標有星號的
  試題。

97. 國旗上爲什麼有五十顆星星？*
   - *因爲一個州有一顆星*
   - *因爲一顆星代表一個州*
   - *因爲有五十個州*

98. 美國國歌的名稱是什麼？
   - *星條旗之歌*

C: 國定假日

99. 我們在哪一天慶祝獨立紀念日？*
   - *7月4日*

100. 列舉兩個美國的國定假日。
   - *新年*
   - *馬丁路德金的生日*
   - *總統日*
   - *國殤日*
   - *美國國慶日*
   - *勞動節*
   - *哥倫布日*
   - *退伍軍人節*
   - *感恩節*
   - *聖誕節*

*如果您年滿 65 歲或以上，持綠卡（美國合法的永久居民）20 年以上，則只需學習標有星號的
試題。

(rev. 04/12)

U.S. Citizenship and Immigration Services

Preguntas de educación cívica del Examen de Naturalización

A continuación encontrara 100 preguntas y respuestas de educación cívica (historia y gobierno) del Examen de Naturalización. El examen de educación cívica es un examen oral durante el cual el oficial de USCIS le hará 10 de estas 100 preguntas. El solicitante debe contestar correctamente 6 de las 10 preguntas para aprobar la sección de educación cívica del Examen de Naturalización.

Examen de Naturalización, algunas respuestas varían y pueden cambiar por motivo de elecciones o nombramientos. Los solicitantes deben tener conocimiento de las respuestas actuales a estas preguntas. Los solicitantes deben contestar estas preguntas con el nombre del oficial o funcionario que ha sido nombrado y que está sirviendo en el puesto al momento de su entrevista con USCIS. El oficial de USCIS no aceptará una respuesta equivocada.

Aunque USCIS reconoce que podría haber otras respuestas correctas a las 100 preguntas sobre educación cívica, se le recomienda al solicitante responder usando las respuestas que aquí se presentan.

GOBIERNO AMERICANO

A: Principios de la democracia americana

1. **¿Cuál es la ley suprema de la nación?**
   - *la Constitución*

2. **¿Qué hace la Constitución?**
   - *establece el gobierno*
   - *define el gobierno*
   - *protege los derechos básicos de los ciudadanos*

3. **Las primeras tres palabras de la Constitución contienen la idea de la autodeterminación (de que el pueblo se gobierna a sí mismo). ¿Cuáles son estas palabras?**
   - *Nosotros el Pueblo*

4. **¿Qué es una enmienda?**
   - *un cambio (a la Constitución)*
   - *una adición (a la Constitución)*

5. **¿Con qué nombre se conocen las primeras diez enmiendas a la Constitución?**
   - *la Carta de Derechos*

Si usted tiene 65 años o más y ha sido residente permanente legal de los Estados Unidos por 20 años o más, usted sólo necesita estudiar las preguntas marcadas con un asterisco (*).

416

6. **¿Cuál es <u>un</u> derecho o libertad que la Primera Enmienda garantiza?***
   - *expresión*
   - *religión*
   - *reunión*
   - *prensa*
   - *peticionar al gobierno*

7. **¿Cuántas enmiendas tiene la Constitución?**
   - *veintisiete (27)*

8. **¿Qué hizo la Declaración de Independencia?**
   - *anunció nuestra independencia (de Gran Bretaña)*
   - *declaró nuestra independencia (de Gran Bretaña)*
   - *dijo que los Estados Unidos se independizó (de Gran Bretaña)*

9. **¿Cuáles son <u>dos</u> derechos en la Declaración de la Independencia?**
   - *la vida*
   - *la libertad*
   - *la búsqueda de la felicidad*

10. **¿En qué consiste la libertad de religión?**
    - *Se puede practicar cualquier religión o no tener ninguna.*

11. **¿Cuál es el sistema económico de los Estados Unidos?***
    - *economía capitalista*
    - *economía del mercado*

12. **¿En qué consiste el "estado de derecho" (ley y orden)?**
    - *Todos deben obedecer la ley.*
    - *Los líderes deben obedecer la ley.*
    - *El gobierno debe obedecer la ley.*
    - *Nadie está por encima de la ley.*

B: Sistema de gobierno

13. **Nombre <u>una</u> rama o parte del gobierno.***
    - *Congreso*
    - *Poder legislativo*
    - *Presidente*
    - *Poder ejecutivo*
    - *los tribunales*
    - *Poder judicial*

14. **¿Qué es lo que hace que <u>una</u> rama del gobierno no se vuelva demasiado poderosa?**
    - *pesos y contrapesos*
    - *separación de poderes*

15. **¿Quién está a cargo de la rama ejecutiva?**
    - *el Presidente*

Si usted tiene 65 años o más y ha sido residente permanente legal de los Estados Unidos por 20 años o más, usted sólo necesita estudiar las preguntas marcadas con un asterisco (*).

16. **¿Quién crea las leyes federales?**
    - *el Congreso*
    - *el Senado y la Cámara (de Representantes)*
    - *la legislatura (nacional o de los Estados Unidos)*

17. **¿Cuáles son las <u>dos</u> partes que integran el Congreso de los Estados Unidos?***
    - *el Senado y la Cámara (de Representantes)*

18. **¿Cuántos senadores de los Estados Unidos hay?**
    - *cien (100)*

19. **¿De cuántos años es el término de elección de un senador de los Estados Unidos?**
    - *seis (6)*

20. **Nombre a <u>uno</u> de los senadores actuales del estado donde usted vive.***
    - *Las respuestas variarán. [Los residentes del Distrito de Columbia y los territorios de los Estados Unidos deberán contestar que el D.C. (o territorio en donde vive el solicitante) no cuenta con Senadores a nivel nacional.]*

21. **¿Cuántos miembros votantes tiene la Cámara de Representantes?**
    - *cuatrocientos treinta y cinco (435)*

22. **¿De cuántos años es el término de elección de un representante de los Estados Unidos?**
    - *dos (2)*

23. **Dé el nombre de su representante a nivel nacional.**
    - *Las respuestas variarán. [Los residentes de territorios con delegados no votantes o los comisionados residentes pueden decir el nombre de dicho delegado o comisionado. Una respuesta que indica que el territorio no tiene representantes votantes en el Congreso también es aceptable.]*

24. **¿A quiénes representa un senador de los Estados Unidos?**
    - *todas las personas del estado*

25. **¿Por qué tienen algunos estados más representantes que otros?**
    - *(debido a) la población del estado*
    - *(debido a que) tienen más gente*
    - *(debido a que) algunos estados tienen más gente*

26. **¿De cuántos años es el término de elección de un presidente?**
    - *cuatro (4)*

27. **¿En qué mes votamos por un nuevo presidente?***
    - *Noviembre*

28. **¿Cómo se llama el actual Presidente de los Estados Unidos?***
    - *Barack Obama*
    - *Obama*

29. **¿Cómo se llama el actual Vicepresidente de los Estados Unidos?**
    - *Joseph R. Biden, Jr.*
    - *Joe Biden*
    - *Biden*

Si usted tiene 65 años o más y ha sido residente permanente legal de los Estados Unidos por 20 años o más, usted sólo necesita estudiar las preguntas marcadas con un asterisco (*).

30. **Si el Presidente ya no puede cumplir sus funciones, ¿quién se vuelve Presidente?**
    - *el Vicepresidente*

31. **Si tanto el Presidente como el Vicepresidente ya no pueden cumplir sus funciones, ¿quién se vuelve Presidente?**
    - *el Presidente de la Cámara de Representantes*

32. **¿Quién es el Comandante en Jefe de las Fuerzas Armadas?**
    - *el Presidente*

33. **¿Quién firma los proyectos de ley para convertirlos en ley?**
    - *el Presidente*

34. **¿Quién veta los proyectos de ley?**
    - *el Presidente*

35. **¿Qué hace el Gabinete del Presidente?**
    - *asesora al Presidente*

36. **¿Cuáles son <u>dos</u> puestos a nivel de gabinete?**
    - *Secretario de Agricultura*
    - *Secretario de Comercio*
    - *Secretario de Defensa*
    - *Secretario de Educación*
    - *Secretario de Energía*
    - *Secretario de Salud y Servicios Humanos*
    - *Secretario de Seguridad Nacional*
    - *Secretario de Vivienda y Desarrollo Urbano*
    - *Secretario del Interior*
    - *Secretario del Trabajo*
    - *Secretario de Estado*
    - *Secretario de Transporte*
    - *Secretario del Tesoro*
    - *Secretario de Asuntos de Veteranos*
    - *Procurador General*
    - *Vicepresidente*

37. **¿Qué hace la rama judicial?**
    - *revisa las leyes*
    - *explica las leyes*
    - *resuelve disputas (desacuerdos)*
    - *decide si una ley va en contra de la Constitución*

38. **¿Cuál es el tribunal más alto de los Estados Unidos?**
    - *la Corte Suprema de Justicia*

39. **¿Cuántos jueces hay en la Corte Suprema de Justicia?**
    - *nueve (9)*

Si usted tiene 65 años o más y ha sido residente permanente legal de los Estados Unidos por 20 años o más, usted sólo necesita estudiar las preguntas marcadas con un asterisco (*).

40. **¿Quién es el Presidente actual de la Corte Suprema de Justicia de los Estados Unidos?**
    - *John Roberts (John G. Roberts, Jr.)*

41. **De acuerdo a nuestra Constitución, algunos poderes pertenecen al gobierno federal. ¿Cuál es <u>un</u> poder del gobierno federal?**
    - *imprimir dinero*
    - *declarar la guerra*
    - *crear un ejército*
    - *suscribir tratados*

42. **De acuerdo a nuestra Constitución, algunos poderes pertenecen a los estados. ¿Cuál es <u>un</u> poder de los estados?**
    - *proveer escuelas y educación*
    - *proveer protección (policía)*
    - *proveer seguridad (cuerpos de bomberos)*
    - *conceder licencias de conducir*
    - *aprobar la zonificación y uso de la tierra*

43. **¿Quién es el gobernador actual de su estado?**
    - *Las respuestas variarán. [Los residentes del Distrito de Columbia deben decir "no tenemos gobernador".]*

44. **¿Cuál es la capital de su estado?***
    - *Las respuestas variarán. [Los residentes del Distrito de Columbia deben contestar que el D.C. no es estado y que no tiene capital. Los residentes de los territorios de los Estados Unidos deben dar el nombre de la capital del territorio.]*

45. **¿Cuáles son los <u>dos</u> principales partidos políticos de los Estados Unidos?***
    - *Demócrata y Republicano*

46. **¿Cuál es el partido político del Presidente actual?**
    - *(Partido) Demócrata*

47. **¿Cómo se llama el Presidente actual de la Cámara de Representantes?**
    - *(John) Boehner*

C: Derechos y responsabilidades

48. **Existen cuatro enmiendas a la Constitución sobre quién puede votar. Describa <u>una</u> de ellas.**
    - *Ciudadanos de dieciocho (18) años en adelante (pueden votar).*
    - *No se exige pagar un impuesto para votar (el impuesto para acudir a las urnas o "poll tax" en inglés).*
    - *Cualquier ciudadano puede votar. (Tanto las mujeres como los hombres pueden votar.)*
    - *Un hombre ciudadano de cualquier raza (puede votar).*

49. **¿Cuál es <u>una</u> responsabilidad que corresponde sólo a los ciudadanos de los Estados Unidos?***
    - *prestar servicio en un jurado*
    - *votar en una elección federal*

50. **¿Cuál es <u>un</u> derecho que pueden ejercer sólo los ciudadanos de los Estados Unidos?**
    - *votar en una elección federal*
    - *postularse a un cargo político federal*

Si usted tiene 65 años o más y ha sido residente permanente legal de los Estados Unidos por 20 años o más, usted sólo necesita estudiar las preguntas marcadas con un asterisco (*).

51. ¿Cuáles son <u>dos</u> derechos que pueden ejercer todas las personas que viven en los Estados Unidos?
    - *libertad de expresión*
    - *libertad de la palabra*
    - *libertad de reunión*
    - *libertad para peticionar al gobierno*
    - *libertad de culto*
    - *el derecho a portar armas*

52. ¿Ante qué demostramos nuestra lealtad cuando decimos el Juramento de Lealtad (Pledge of Allegiance)?
    - *los Estados Unidos*
    - *la bandera*

53. ¿Cuál es <u>una</u> promesa que usted hace cuando se convierte en ciudadano de los Estados Unidos?
    - *renunciar la lealtad a otros países*
    - *defender la Constitución y las leyes de los Estados Unidos*
    - *obedecer las leyes de los Estados Unidos*
    - *prestar servicio en las Fuerzas Armadas de los Estados Unidos (de ser necesario)*
    - *prestar servicio a (realizar trabajo importante para) la nación (de ser necesario)*
    - *ser leal a los Estados Unidos*

54. ¿Cuántos años tienen que tener los ciudadanos para votar por el Presidente?*
    - *dieciocho (18) años en adelante*

55. ¿Cuáles son <u>dos</u> maneras mediante las cuales los ciudadanos americanos pueden participar en su democracia?
    - *votar*
    - *afiliarse a un partido político*
    - *ayudar en una campaña*
    - *unirse a un grupo cívico*
    - *unirse a un grupo comunitario*
    - *presentar su opinión sobre un asunto a un oficial elegido*
    - *llamar a los senadores y representantes*
    - *apoyar u oponerse públicamente a un asunto o política*
    - *postularse a un cargo político*
    - *enviar una carta o mensaje a un periódico*

56. ¿Cuál es la fecha límite para enviar la declaración federal de impuesto sobre el ingreso?*
    - *el 15 de abril*

57. ¿Cuándo deben inscribirse todos los hombres en el Servicio Selectivo?
    - *a la edad de dieciocho (18) años*
    - *entre los dieciocho (18) y veintiséis (26) años de edad*

Si usted tiene 65 años o más y ha sido residente permanente legal de los Estados Unidos por 20 años o más, usted sólo necesita estudiar las preguntas marcadas con un asterisco (*).

www.uscis.gov

HISTORIA AMERICANA

A: Época colonial e independencia

58. **¿Cuál es <u>una</u> razón por la que los colonos vinieron a los Estados Unidos?**
    - *libertad*
    - *libertad política*
    - *libertad religiosa*
    - *oportunidad económica*
    - *para practicar su religión*
    - *para huir de la persecución*

59. **¿Quiénes vivían en los Estados Unidos antes de la llegada de los europeos?**
    - *Indios americanos*
    - *Nativos americanos*

60. **¿Qué pueblo fue traído a los Estados Unidos y vendido como esclavos?**
    - *Africanos*
    - *gente de África*

61. **¿Por qué lucharon los colonos contra los británicos?**
    - *debido a los impuestos altos (impuestos sin representación)*
    - *el ejército británico se quedó en sus casas (alojamiento, acuartelamiento)*
    - *no tenían autodeterminación*

62. **¿Quién escribió la Declaración de Independencia?**
    - *(Thomas) Jefferson*

63. **¿Cuándo fue adoptada la Declaración de Independencia?**
    - *el 4 de julio de 1776*

64. **Había 13 estados originales. Nombre <u>tres</u>.**
    - *Nueva Hampshire*
    - *Massachusetts*
    - *Rhode Island*
    - *Connecticut*
    - *Nueva York*
    - *Nueva Jersey*
    - *Pennsylvania*
    - *Delaware*
    - *Maryland*
    - *Virginia*
    - *Carolina del Norte*
    - *Carolina del Sur*
    - *Georgia*

Si usted tiene 65 años o más y ha sido residente permanente legal de los Estados Unidos por 20 años o más, usted sólo necesita estudiar las preguntas marcadas con un asterisco (*).

65. **¿Qué ocurrió en la Convención Constitucional?**
    - *Se redactó la Constitución.*
    - *Los Padres Fundadores redactaron la Constitución.*

66. **¿Cuándo fue escrita la Constitución?**
    - *1787*

67. **Los ensayos conocidos como "Los Federalistas" respaldaron la aprobación de la Constitución de los Estados Unidos. Nombre <u>uno</u> de los autores.**
    - *(James) Madison*
    - *(Alexander) Hamilton*
    - *(John) Jay*
    - *Publius*

68. **Mencione <u>una</u> razón por la que es famoso Benjamin Franklin.**
    - *diplomático americano*
    - *el miembro de mayor edad de la Convención Constitucional*
    - *primer Director General de Correos de los Estados Unidos*
    - *autor de "Poor Richard's Almanac" (Almanaque del Pobre Richard)*
    - *fundó las primeras bibliotecas gratuitas*

69. **¿Quién se conoce como el "Padre de Nuestra Nación"?**
    - *(George) Washington*

70. **¿Quién fue el primer Presidente?***
    - *(George) Washington*

B: Los años 1800

71. **¿Qué territorio compró los Estados Unidos de Francia en 1803?**
    - *el territorio de Louisiana*
    - *Louisiana*

72. **Mencione <u>una</u> guerra durante los años 1800 en la que peleó los Estados Unidos.**
    - *la Guerra de 1812*
    - *la Guerra entre México y los Estados Unidos*
    - *la Guerra Civil*
    - *la Guerra Hispanoamericana*

73. **Dé el nombre de la guerra entre el Norte y el Sur de los Estados Unidos.**
    - *la Guerra Civil*
    - *la Guerra entre los Estados*

74. **Mencione <u>un</u> problema que condujo a la Guerra Civil.**
    - *esclavitud*
    - *razones económicas*
    - *derechos de los estados*

Si usted tiene 65 años o más y ha sido residente permanente legal de los Estados Unidos por 20 años o más, usted sólo necesita estudiar las preguntas marcadas con un asterisco (*).

www.uscis.gov

75. **¿Qué fue <u>una</u> cosa importante que hizo Abraham Lincoln?***
    - *liberó a los esclavos (Proclamación de la Emancipación)*
    - *salvó (o preservó) la Unión*
    - *presidió los Estados Unidos durante la Guerra Civil*

76. **¿Qué hizo la Proclamación de la Emancipación?**
    - *liberó a los esclavos*
    - *liberó a los esclavos de la Confederación*
    - *liberó a los esclavos en los estados de la Confederación*
    - *liberó a los esclavos en la mayoría de los estados del Sur*

77. **¿Qué hizo Susan B. Anthony?**
    - *luchó por los derechos de la mujer*
    - *luchó por los derechos civiles*

C: Historia americana reciente y otra información histórica importante

78. **Mencione <u>una</u> guerra durante los años 1900 en la que peleó los Estados Unidos.***
    - *la Primera Guerra Mundial*
    - *la Segunda Guerra Mundial*
    - *la Guerra de Corea*
    - *la Guerra de Vietnam*
    - *la Guerra del Golfo (Persa)*

79. **¿Quién era presidente durante la Primera Guerra Mundial?**
    - *(Woodrow) Wilson*

80. **¿Quién era presidente durante la Gran Depresión y la Segunda Guerra Mundial?**
    - *(Franklin) Roosevelt*

81. **¿Contra qué países peleó los Estados Unidos en la Segunda Guerra Mundial?**
    - *Japón, Alemania e Italia*

82. **Antes de ser presidente, Eisenhower era general. ¿En qué guerra participó?**
    - *Segunda Guerra Mundial*

83. **Durante la Guerra Fría, ¿cuál era la principal preocupación de los Estados Unidos?**
    - *Comunismo*

84. **¿Qué movimiento trató de poner fin a la discriminación racial?**
    - *(el movimiento en pro de los) derechos civiles*

85. **¿Qué hizo Martin Luther King, Jr.?***
    - *luchó por los derechos civiles*
    - *trabajó por la igualdad de todos los ciudadanos americanos*

86. **¿Qué suceso de gran magnitud ocurrió el 11 de septiembre de 2001 en los Estados Unidos?**
    - *Los terroristas atacaron los Estados Unidos.*

Si usted tiene 65 años o más y ha sido residente permanente legal de los Estados Unidos por 20 años o más, usted sólo necesita estudiar las preguntas marcadas con un asterisco (*).

87. **Mencione <u>una</u> tribu de indios americanos de los Estados Unidos.**
    [A los oficiales del USCIS se les dará una lista de tribus amerindias reconocidas a nivel federal.]
    - *Cherokee*
    - *Navajo*
    - *Sioux*
    - *Chippewa*
    - *Choctaw*
    - *Pueblo*
    - *Apache*
    - *Iroquois*
    - *Creek*
    - *Blackfeet*
    - *Seminole*
    - *Cheyenne*
    - *Arawak*
    - *Shawnee*
    - *Mohegan*
    - *Huron*
    - *Oneida*
    - *Lakota*
    - *Crow*
    - *Teton*
    - *Hopi*
    - *Inuit*

CIVISMO INTEGRADO

A: Geografía

88. **Mencione <u>uno</u> de los dos ríos más largos en los Estados Unidos.**
    - *(el río) Missouri*
    - *(el río) Mississippi*

89. **¿Qué océano está en la costa oeste de los Estados Unidos?**
    - *(el océano) Pacífico*

90. **¿Qué océano está en la costa este de los Estados Unidos?**
    - *(el océano) Atlántico*

91. **Dé el nombre de <u>un</u> territorio de los Estados Unidos.**
    - *Puerto Rico*
    - *Islas Vírgenes de los Estados Unidos*
    - *Samoa Americana*
    - *Islas Marianas del Norte*
    - *Guam*

Si usted tiene 65 años o más y ha sido residente permanente legal de los Estados Unidos por 20 años o más, usted sólo necesita estudiar las preguntas marcadas con un asterisco (*).

92. **Mencione <u>un</u> estado que tiene frontera con Canadá.**
    - *Maine*
    - *Nueva Hampshire*
    - *Vermont*
    - *Nueva York*
    - *Pennsylvania*
    - *Ohio*
    - *Michigan*
    - *Minnesota*
    - *Dakota del Norte*
    - *Montana*
    - *Idaho*
    - *Washington*
    - *Alaska*

93. **Mencione <u>un</u> estado que tiene frontera con México.**
    - *California*
    - *Arizona*
    - *Nuevo México*
    - *Texas*

94. **¿Cuál es la capital de los Estados Unidos?***
    - *Washington, D.C.*

95. **¿Dónde está la Estatua de la Libertad?***
    - *(el puerto de) Nueva York*
    - *Liberty Island*

    [Otras respuestas aceptables son Nueva Jersey, cerca de la Ciudad de Nueva York y (el río) Hudson.]

B: Símbolos

96. **¿Por qué hay 13 franjas en la bandera?**
    - *porque representan las 13 colonias originales*
    - *porque las franjas representan las colonias originales*

97. **¿Por qué hay 50 estrellas en la bandera?***
    - *porque hay una estrella por cada estado*
    - *porque cada estrella representa un estado*
    - *porque hay 50 estados*

98. **¿Cómo se llama el himno nacional?**
    - *The Star-Spangled Banner*

C: Días feriados

99. **¿Cuándo celebramos el Día de la Independencia?***
    - *el 4 de julio*

Si usted tiene 65 años o más y ha sido residente permanente legal de los Estados Unidos por 20 años o más, usted sólo necesita estudiar las preguntas marcadas con un asterisco (*).

100. Mencione <u>dos</u> días feriados nacionales de los Estados Unidos.

- *el Día de Año Nuevo*
- *el Día de Martin Luther King, Jr.*
- *el Día de los Presidentes*
- *el Día de la Recordación*
- *el Día de la Independencia*
- *el Día del Trabajo*
- *el Día de la Raza (Cristóbal Colón)*
- *el Día de los Veteranos*
- *el Día de Acción de Gracias*
- *el Día de Navidad*

Si usted tiene 65 años o más y ha sido residente permanente legal de los Estados Unidos por 20 años o más, usted sólo necesita estudiar las preguntas marcadas con un asterisco (*).

www.uscis.gov

(rev. 03/11)

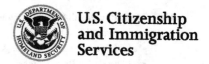

**U.S. Citizenship
and Immigration
Services**

Mga Katanungan sa Sibika (Kasaysayan at Pamahalaan) para sa Iksamen para sa Naturalisasyon

Ang 100 katanungan sa sibika (kasaysayan at pamahalaan) at mga sagot para sa iksamen para sa naturalisasyon ay nakalista sa ibaba. Ang iksamen sa sibika ay isang pasalitang iksamen at ang USCIS Officer ay magtatanong sa aplikante ng hanggang 10 ng 100 katanungan sa sibika. Ang isang aplikante ay dapat sumagot nang tama sa 6 mula sa 10 katanungan upang pumasa sa bahagi ng sibika ng iksamen sa naturalisasyon.

Sa iksamen o pagsusulit sa naturalisasyon, ang ilang mga sagot ay maaaring magbago dahil sa mga halalan o paghirang. Habang nag-aaral ka para sa pagsusulit, tiyakin na alam mo ang mga kasalukuyang sagot sa mga tanong na ito. Sagutin ang mga tanong na ito ng pangalan ng opisyal na naglilingkod sa panahon ng iyong panayam para sa pagiging karapat-dapat sa USCIS. Ang Opisyal ng USCIS ay hindi tatanggap ng maling sagot.

Bagaman alam ng USCIS na maaaring may mga karagdagang tamang sagot sa 100 katanungan sa sibika, ang mga aplikante ay hinihimok na sumagot sa mga katanungan sa sibika na ginagamit ang mga sagot na nasa ibaba.

PAMAHALAAN NG AMERIKA

A: Mga Prinsipyo ng Demokrasyang Amerikano

1. **Ano ang pinakamataas na batas ng bansa?**
   - *ang Konstitusyon*

2. **Ano ang Ginagawa ng Konstitusyon?**
   - *itinatatag ang pamahalaan*
   - *binibigyan ng kahulugan ang pamahalaan*
   - *nagpoprotekta sa mga basikong karapatan ng mga Amerikano*

3. **Ang ideya ng sariling-pamamahala ay nasa unang tatlong salita ng Konstitusyon. Ano ang mga salitang ito?**
   - *Tayong mga Tao*

4. **Ano ang isang susog?**
   - *isang pagbabago (sa Konstitusyon)*
   - *bilang karagdagan (sa Konstitusyon)*

5. **Ano ang tinatawag na unang sampung susog sa Kontistusyon?**
   - *ang Batas sa mga Karapatan*

---

* Kung ikaw ay 65 taong gulang o mas matanda at naging legal na permanenteng residente ng Estados Unidos ng 20 o higit na taon, maaari mong pag-aralan ang mga katanungan lamang na minarkahan ng asterisk.

6. **Ano ang <u>isang</u> karapatan o kalayaan mula sa Unang Susog?***
   - *pagsasalita*
   - *relihiyon*
   - *pagtitipon*
   - *pamamahayag*
   - *magpetisyon sa pamahalaan*

7. **Ilang susog mayroon ang Konstitusyon?**
   - *dalawampu't-pito (27)*

8. **Ano ang ginagawa ng Deklarasyon ng Kalayaan?**
   - *ipinahayag ang ating kalayaan (mula sa Great Britain)*
   - *idineklara ang ating kalayaan (mula sa Great Britain)*
   - *sinabi na ang Estados Unidos ay malaya (mula sa Great Britain)*

9. **Ano ang <u>dalawang</u> karapatan sa Deklarasyon sa Kalayaan?**
   - *buhay*
   - *kalayaan*
   - *la paghahangad ng kaligayahan*

10. **Ano ang kalayaan sa relihiyon?**
    - *Maaari kang magpraktis ng anumang relihiyon, o hindi magpraktis ng relihiyon.*

11. **Ano ang sistema ng ekonomiya sa Estados Unidos?***
    - *kapitalistang ekonomiya*
    - *ekonomiya ng pamiliha*

12. **Ano ang "pamamayani ng batas"?**
    - *Ang bawat isa ay dapat sumunod ng batas.*
    - *Ang mga lider ay dapat sumunod sa batas.*
    - *Ang pamahalaan ay dapat sumunod sa batas.*
    - *Walang hindi sakop ng batas.*

B: Sistema ng Pamahalaan

13. **Sabihin ang <u>isang</u> sangay o bahagi ng pamahalaan.***
    - *Kongreso*
    - *pambatasan*
    - *Pangulo*
    - *ehekutibo*
    - *mga korte*
    - *panghukuman*

14. **Ano ang pumipigil sa <u>isang</u> sangay ng pamahalaan na maging masyadong makapangyarihan?**
    - *mga pagsusuri at pagbalanse*
    - *paghihiwalay ng mga kapangyarihan*

15. **Sino ang namamahala sa sangay na ehekutibo?**
    - *ang Pangulo*

---

* Kung ikaw ay 65 taong gulang o mas matanda at naging legal na permanenteng residente ng Estados Unidos ng 20 o higit na taon, maaari mong pag-aralan ang mga katanungan lamang na minarkahan ng asterisk.

16. **Sino ang gumagawa ng mga pederal na batas?**
    - *Kongreso*
    - *Senado at Kapulungan (ng mga Kinatawan)*
    - *(Estados Unidos o pambansang) lehislatura*

17. **Ano ang <u>dalawang</u> bahagi ng Kongreso ng Estados Unidos?***
    - *the Senado at Kapulungan (ng mga Kinatawan)*

18. **Ilang Senador ng Estados Unidos ay mayroon?**
    - *isang daan (100)*

19. **Inihahalal natin ang isang Senador ng Estados Unidos para sa ilang taon?**
    - *anim (6)*

20. **Sino ang <u>isa</u> sa mga Senador ng inyong estado ngayon?***
    - *Ang mga sagot ay magkakaiba. [Ang mga residente ng District of Columbia at mga residente ng mga teritoryo ng Estados Unidos ay dapat sumagot na ang D.C. (o ang teritoryo kung saan nakatira ang aplikante) ay walang mga Senador ng Estados Unidos.]*

21. **Ang Kapulungan ng mga Kinatawan ay may ilang bumobotong miyembro?**
    - *apat na raan tatlumpu't-lima (435)*

22. **Naghahalal tayo ng Kinatawan ng Estados Unidos para sa ilang taon?**
    - *dalawa (2)*

23. **Sabihin kung sino ang inyong Kinatawan ng Estados Unidos.**
    - *Ang mga sagot ay magkakaiba. [Ang mga residente ng mga teritoryong may mga hindi bumobotong Delegado o Residenteng Komisyoner ay maaaring magbigay ng pangalan ng Delegado o Komisyoner. Katanggap-tanggap din sa anumang pahayag na ang teritoryo ay walang (bumobotong) mga Kinatawan sa Kongreso.]*

24. **Sino ang kumakatawan ng Senador ng Estados Unidos?**
    - *lahat ng mga tao ng estado*

25. **Bakit ang ilang estado ay may mas maraming Kinatawan kaysa ibang mga estado?**
    - *(dahil sa) populasyon ng estado*
    - *(dahil) maraming tao sa kanila*
    - *(dahil) mas maraming tao sa ilang estado*

26. **Naghahalal tayo ng Pangulo para sa ilang taon?**
    - *apat (4)*

27. **Sa anong buwan tayo bumoboto para sa Pangulo?***
    - *Nobyembre*

28. **Ano ang pangalan ng Pangulo ng Estados Unidos ngayon?***
    - *Barack Obama*
    - *Obama*

29. **Ano ang pangalan ng Pangalawang Pangulo ng Estados Unidos ngayon?**
    - *Joseph R. Biden, Jr.*
    - *Joe Biden*
    - *Biden*

* Kung ikaw ay 65 taong gulang o mas matanda at naging legal na permanenteng residente ng Estados Unidos ng 20 o higit na taon, maaari mong pag-aralan ang mga katanungan lamang na minarkahan ng asterisk.

30. **Kung ang Pangulo ay hindi na nakakapaglingkod, sino ang nagiging Pangulo?**
    - *ang Pangalawang Pangulo*

31. **Kung ang Pangulo at ang Pangalawang Pangulo ay hindi na nakakapaglingkod, sino ang nagiging Pangulo?**
    - *ang Ispiker ng Kapulungan*

32. **Sino ang Punong Kumander ng militar?**
    - *ang Pangulo*

33. **Sino ang pumipirma ng mga panukalang-batas upang maging mga batas?**
    - *ang Pangulo*

34. **Sino ang nagbebeto sa mga panukalang-batas?**
    - *ang Pangulo*

35. **Ano ang ginagawa ng Gabinete ng Pangulo?**
    - *nagpapayo sa Pangulo*

36. **Ano ang <u>dalawang</u> posisyon na nasa antas ng Gabinete?**
    - *Kalihim ng Agrikultura*
    - *Kalihim ng Komersiyo*
    - *Kalihim ng Depensa*
    - *Kalihim ng Edukasyon*
    - *Kalihim ng Enerhiya*
    - *Kalihim ng mga Palingkurang Pangkalusugan at Pantao*
    - *Kalihim ng Kapanatagan ng Bansa (Homeland Security)*
    - *Kalihim ng Pabahay at Pagpapaunlad ng Lunsod*
    - *Kalihim ng Interyor*
    - *Kalihim ng Paggawa*
    - *Kalihim ng Estado*
    - *Kalihim ng Transportasyon*
    - *Kalihim ng Tesorerya*
    - *Kalihim ng mga Gawain ng mga Beterano*
    - *Abugado Heneral*
    - *Pangalawang Pangulo*

37. **Ano ang ginagawa ng sangay na panghukuman?**
    - *nirerepaso ang mga batas*
    - *ipinaliliwanag ang mga batas*
    - *nilulutas ang mga pagtatalo (hindi pagkakasundo)*
    - *ipinapasiya kung ang isang batas ay labag sa Konstitusyon*

38. **Ano ang pinakamataas na hukuman sa Estados Unidos?**
    - *ang Korte Suprema*

39. **Ilan ang mga mahistrado sa Korte Supreme?**
    - *siyam (9)*

40. **Sino ang Punong Mahistrado ng Estados Unidos ngayon?**
    - *John Roberts (John G. Roberts, Jr.)*

* Kung ikaw ay 65 taong gulang o mas matanda at naging legal na permanenteng residente ng Estados Unidos ng 20 o higit na taon, maaari mong pag-aralan ang mga katanungan lamang na minarkahan ng asterisk.

41. **Sa ilalim ng ating Konstitusyo, ang ilang kapangyarihan ay nasa pederal na pamahalaan. Ano ang isang kapagyarihan ng pederal na pamahalaan?**
    - *maglimbag ng pera*
    - *magdeklara ng digmaan*
    - *bumuo ng isang armi*
    - *gumawa ng mga kasunduan*

42. **Sa ilalim ng ating Konstitusyon, ang ilang kapangyarihan ay nasa mga estado. Ano ang isang kapangyarihan ng mga estado?**
    - *magkaloob ng pag-aaral at edukasyon*
    - *magkaloob ng proteksiyon (pulisya)*
    - *magkaloob ng kaligtasan (mga kagawaran ng bumbero)*
    - *magbigay ng lisensiya para sa pagmamaneho*
    - *mag-aproba ng pagsosona at paggamit ng lupa*

43. **Sino ang Gobernador na iyong estado ngayon?**
    - *Ang mga sagot ay magkakaiba. [Ang mga residente ng District of Columbia ay dapat sumagot na ang D.C. ay walang Gobernador.]*

44. **Ano ang kapital ng iyong estado?***
    - *Ang mga sagot ay magkakaiba. [Ang mga residente ng District of Columbia ay dapat sumagot na ang D.C. ay hindi isang estado at walang kapital. Ang mga residente ng mga teritoryo ng Estados Unidos ay dapat sabihin ang kapital ng teritoryo.]*

45. **Ano ang dalawang pangunahing partidong pampulitika sa Estados Unidos?***
    - *Democratic at Republican*

46. **Ano ang partidong pampulitika ng Pangulo ngayon?**
    - *Democratic (Party)*

47. **Ano ang pangalan ng Ispiker ng Kapulungan ng mga Kinatawan?**
    - *(John) Boehner*

C: Mga Karapatan at Responsibilidad

48. **May apat na susog sa Konstitusyon tungkol sa kung sino ang makakaboto. Ilarawan ang isa sa mga ito.**
    - *Mga mamamayang labingwalong (18) taong gulang at mas matanda (ay makakaboto).*
    - *Hindi mo kailangang magbayad (ng isang poll tax) upang makaboto.*
    - *Sinumang mamamayan ay makakaboto. (Ang mga babae at mga lalaki ay makakaboto.)*
    - *Isang lalaking mamamayan ng anumang lahi (ay makakaboto).*

49. **Ano ang isang responsibilidad na para lamang sa mga mamamayan ng Estados Unidos?***
    - *magsilbi sa isang hurado*
    - *bumoto sa isang pederal na halalan*

* Kung ikaw ay 65 taong gulang o mas matanda at naging legal na permanenteng residente ng Estados Unidos ng 20 o higit na taon, maaari mong pag-aralan ang mga katanungan lamang na minarkahan ng asterisk.

50. **Sabihin ang <u>isang</u> karapatan na para lamang sa mga mamamayan ng Estados Unidos.**
    - *bumoto sa isang pederal na halalan*
    - *kumandidato para sa pederal na katungkulan*

51. **Ano ang <u>dalawang</u> karapatan ng bawat isang naninirahan sa Estados Unidos?**
    - *kalayaang magpahayag*
    - *kalayaang magsalita*
    - *kalayaang magtipun-tipon*
    - *kalayaang magpetisyon sa pamahalaan*
    - *kalayaang sumamba*
    - *karapatang magdala ng armas*

52. **Katapatan sa ano ang ipinapakita kapag sinasabi natin ang Pledge of Allegiance?**
    - *sa Estados Unidos*
    - *sa bandera*

53. **Ano ang <u>isang</u> pangako na ginagawa mo kapag ikaw ay naging mamamayan ng Estados Unidos?**
    - *isuko ang katapatan sa ibang mga bansa*
    - *ipagtanggol ang Konstitusyon at mga batas ng Estados Unidos*
    - *sundin ang mga batas ng Estados Unidos*
    - *maglingkod sa militar ng Estados Unidos (kung kailangan)*
    - *maglingkod (gumawa ng mahalagang trabaho para sa bansa (kung kailangan)*
    - *maging matapat sa Estados Unidos*

54. **Ilang taon kailangan ang mga mamamayan upang makaboto para sa Pangulo?***
    - *labingwalong (18) taong gulang at mas matanda*

55. **Ano ang <u>dalawang</u> paraan na ang mga Amerikano ay maaaring lumahok sa kanilang demokrasya?**
    - *bumoto*
    - *sumapi sa isang partidong pampulitika*
    - *tumulong sa isang kampanya*
    - *sumapi sa isang sibikong grupo*
    - *sumapi sa isang grupong pangkomunidad*
    - *bigyan ang isang inihalal na opisyal ng iyong opinyon sa isang isyu*
    - *tawagan ang mga Senador at Kinatawan*
    - *pampublikong suportahan o salungatin ang isang isyu o patakaran*
    - *kumandidato para sa katungkulan*
    - *sumulat sa isang pahayagan*

56. **Ano ang huling araw na maaari mong ipadala ang pederal na income tax forms?***
    - *Abril 15*

57. **Kailangan dapat magparehistro ang lahat ng mga lalaki sa Selective Service?**
    - *sa edad na labingwalo (18)*
    - *sa pagitan ng labingwalo (18) at dalawamp't-anim (26)*

---

* Kung ikaw ay 65 taong gulang o mas matanda at naging legal na permanenteng residente ng Estados Unidos ng 20 o higit na taon, maaari mong pag-aralan ang mga katanungan lamang na minarkahan ng asterisk.

KASAYSAYAN NG AMERIKA

A: Panahong Kolonyal at Kalayaan

58. **Ano ang <u>isang</u> dahilan kung bakit pumunta sa Amerika ang mga colonist?**
 - *kalayaan*
 - *kalayaang pampulitika*
 - *kalayaan sa relihiyon*
 - *pagkakataong pangkabuhayan*
 - *ipraktis ang kanilang relihiyon*
 - *tumakas sa pag-uusig*

59. **Sino ang nanirahan sa Amerika bago dumating ang mga Europeo?**
 - *Mga Amerikanong Indiyan*
 - *Mga Katutubong Amerikano*

60. **Anong grupo ng mga tao ang dinala sa Amerika at ipinagbili bilang mga alipin?**
 - *Mga Aprikano*
 - *mga tao mula sa Aprika*

61. **Bakit nilabanan ng mga colonist ang British?**
 - *dahil sa mga matataas na buwis (pagbubuwis nang walang pagkatawan)*
 - *dahil ang armi ng British ay tumigil sa kanilang mga bahay (kumakain, naninirahan)*
 - *dahil wala silang sariling pamahalaan*

62. **Sino ang sumulat ng Deklarasyon ng Kalayaan?**
 - *(Thomas) Jefferson*

63. **Kailan ipinagtibay ang Deklarasyon ng Kalayaan?**
 - *Hulyo 4, 1776*

64. **May 13 orihinal na estado. Magsabi ng <u>tatlo</u>.**
 - *New Hampshire*
 - *Massachusetts*
 - *Rhode Island*
 - *Connecticut*
 - *New York*
 - *New Jersey*
 - *Pennsylvania*
 - *Delaware*
 - *Maryland*
 - *Virginia*
 - *North Carolina*
 - *South Carolina*
 - *Georgia*

* Kung ikaw ay 65 taong gulang o mas matanda at naging legal na permanenteng residente ng Estados Unidos ng 20 o higit na taon, maaari mong pag-aralan ang mga katanungan lamang na minarkahan ng asterisk.

65. **Ano ang nangyari sa Kombensiyon para sa Konstitusyon?**
    - *Ang Konstitusyon ay isinulat.*
    - *Isinulat ng mga Tagapagtatag na Ama ang Konstitusyon.*

66. **Kailan isinulat ang Konstitusyon?**
    - *1787*

67. **Ang mga Pederalistang Papel ay sumuporta sa pagpasa ng Konstitusyon. Tukuyin ang isa sa mga sumulat.**
    - *(James) Madison*
    - *(Alexander) Hamilton*
    - *(John) Jay*
    - *Publius*

68. **Ano ang isang bagay na sikat si Benjamin Franklin?**
    - *diplomat ng Estados Unidos*
    - *pinakamatandang miyembro ng Kombensiyon para sa Konstitusyon*
    - *unang Postmaster General ng Estados Unidos*
    - *sumulat ng "Poor Richard's Almanac"*
    - *sinimulan ang mga unang libreng aklatan*

69. **Sino ang "Ama ng Ating Bansa"?**
    - *(George) Washington*

70. **Sino ang unang Pangulo?***
    - *(George) Washington*

B: Mga Taon ng 1800

71. **Anong teritoryo ang binili ng Estados Unidos mula sa France noong 1803?**
    - *ang Louisiana Territory*
    - *Louisiana*

72. **Magsabi ng isang digmaan na nakipaglaban ang Estados Unidos noong mga taon ng 1800.**
    - *Digmaan ng 1812*
    - *Digmaang Meksikano-Amerikano*
    - *Digmaang Sibil*
    - *Digmang Espanyol-Amerikano*

73. **Tukuyin ang digmaan ng Estados sa pagitan ng Hilaga at Timog.**
    - *ang Digmaang Sibil*
    - *ang Digmaan sa pagitan ng mga Estado*

74. **Sabihin ang isang problema na humantong sa Digmaang Sibil.**
    - *pang-aalipin*
    - *mga dahilang pangkabuhayan*
    - *mga karapatan ng estado*

* Kung ikaw ay 65 taong gulang o mas matanda at naging legal na permanenteng residente ng Estados Unidos ng 20 o higit na taon, maaari mong pag-aralan ang mga katanungan lamang na minarkahan ng asterisk.

75. **Ano ang <u>isang</u> mahalagang bagay na ginawa ni Abraham Lincoln?***
    - *pinalaya ang mga alipin (Proklamasyon ng Paglaya)*
    - *iniligtas(o pinangalagaan) ang Union*
    - *pinamunuan ang Estados Unidos sa Digmaang Sibil*

76. **Ano ang ginawa ng Proklamasyon ng Paglaya?**
    - *pinalaya ang mga alipin*
    - *pinalaya ang mga alipin sa Confederacy*
    - *pinalaya ang mga alipin sa mga estadong Confederate*
    - *pinalaya ang alipin sa karamihan ng mga estado sa Timog*

77. **Ano ang ginawa ni Susan B. Anthony?**
    - *nakipaglaban para sa mga karapatan ng mga babae*
    - *nakipaglaban para sa mga karapatang sibil*

C: Huling Kasaysayan ng Amerika at Ibang Mahalagang Impormasyong Pangkasaysayan

78. **Sabihin ang <u>isang</u> digmaan na nakipaglaban ang Estados Unidos noong 1900s.***
    - *Unang Digmaang Pandaigdig*
    - *Ikalawang Digmaang Pandaigdig*
    - *Digmaan sa Korea*
    - *Digmaan sa Vietnam*
    - *Digmaan sa (Persian) Gulf*

79. **Sino ang Pangulo noong Unang Digmaang Pandaigdig?**
    - *(Woodrow) Wilson*

80. **Sino ang Pangulo sa panahon ng Great Depression at Ikalawang Digmaang Pandaigdig?**
    - *(Franklin) Roosevelt*

81. **Sino ang nakalaban ng Estados Unidos noong Ikalawang Digmaang Pandaigdig?**
    - *Japan, Germany, at Italy*

82. **Bago siya naging Pangulo, si Eisenhower ay isang heneral. Sa anong digmaan siya nakipaglaban?**
    - *Ikalawang Digmaang Pandaigdig*

83. **Sa panahon ng Cold War, ano ang pangunahing inaalala ng Estados Unidos?**
    - *Komunismo*

84. **Anong kilusan ang nagtangkang tapusin ang diskriminasyon sa lahi?**
    - *mga karapatang sibil (kilusan)*

85. **Ano ang ginawa ni Martin Luther King, Jr.?***
    - *nakipaglaban para sa mga karapatang sibil*
    - *kumilos para sa pagkakapantay-pantay para sa lahat ng mga Amerikano*

86. **Anong malaking pangyayari ang nangyari noong Setyembre 11, 2001, sa Estados Unidos?**
    - *Inatake ng mga terorista ang Estados Unidos.*

* Kung ikaw ay 65 taong gulang o mas matanda at naging legal na permanenteng residente ng Estados Unidos ng 20 o higit na taon, maaari mong pag-aralan ang mga katanungan lamang na minarkahan ng asterisk.

87. **Magsabi ng <u>isang</u> tribo ng Amerikanong Indiyan sa Estados Unidos.**
[Ang mga Opisyal USCIS ay bibigyan ng isang listahan ng mga tribo ng Amerikanong Indiyan na kinikilala ng pederal na pamahalaan.]
- *Cherokee*
- *Navajo*
- *Sioux*
- *Chippewa*
- *Choctaw*
- *Pueblo*
- *Apache*
- *Iroquois*
- *Creek*
- *Blackfeet*
- *Seminole*
- *Cheyenne*
- *Arawak*
- *Shawnee*
- *Mohegan*
- *Huron*
- *Oneida*
- *Lakota*
- *Crow*
- *Teton*
- *Hopi*
- *Inuit*

PINAGSAMANG SIBIKA

A: Heograpiya

88. **Magsabi ng <u>isa</u> sa dalawang pinakamahabang ilog sa Estados Unidos.**
- *Missouri (River)*
- *Mississippi (River)*

89. **Anong karagatan ang nasa West Coast ng Estados Unidos?**
- *Pacific (Ocean)*

90. **Anong karagatan ang nasa East Coast ng Estados Unidos?**
- *Atlantic (Ocean)*

91. **Magsabi ng <u>isang</u> teritoryo ng Estados Unidos.**
- *Puerto Rico*
- *U.S. Virgin Islands*
- *American Samoa*
- *Northern Mariana Islands*
- *Guam*

* Kung ikaw ay 65 taong gulang o mas matanda at naging legal na permanenteng residente ng Estados Unidos ng 20 o higit na taon, maaari mong pag-aralan ang mga katanungan lamang na minarkahan ng asterisk.

92. **Magsabi ng <u>isang</u> estado na naghahangga sa Canada.**
    - *Maine*
    - *New Hampshire*
    - *Vermont*
    - *New York*
    - *Pennsylvania*
    - *Ohio*
    - *Michigan*
    - *Minnesota*
    - *North Dakota*
    - *Montana*
    - *Idaho*
    - *Washington*
    - *Alaska*

93. **Magsabi ng <u>isang</u> estado na naghahangga sa Mexico.**
    - *California*
    - *Arizona*
    - *New Mexico*
    - *Texas*

94. **Ano ang kapital ng Estados Unidos?***
    - *Washington, D.C.*

95. **Nasaan ang Istatwa ng Kalayaan?***
    - *New York (Harbor)*
    - *Liberty Island*

    [Tinatanggap din ang New Jersey, malapit sa New York City, at nasa Hudson (River).]

B: Mga Simbolo

96. **Bakit may 13 guhit ang bandera?**
    - *dahil may 13 orihinal na colony*
    - *dahil ang mga guhit ay kumakatawan sa mga orihinal na colony*

97. **Bakit may 50 bituin ang bandera?***
    - *dahil may isang bituin para sa bawat estado*
    - *dahil ang bawat bituin ay kumakatawan sa isang estado*
    - *dahil may 50 estado*

98. **Ano ang tawag sa pambansang awit?**
    - *The Star-Spangled Banner*

C: Mga Piyesta Opisyal

99. **Kailan tayo nagdiriwang ng Araw ng Kalayaan?***
    - *Hulyo 4*

* Kung ikaw ay 65 taong gulang o mas matanda at naging legal na permanenteng residente ng Estados Unidos ng 20 o higit na taon, maaari mong pag-aralan ang mga katanungan lamang na minarkahan ng asterisk.

100. **Magsabi ng <u>dalawang</u> pambansang Piyesta Opisyal ng Estados Unidos.**
- *Bagong Taon*
- *Kaarawan ni Martin Luther King, Jr.*
- *Presidents' Day*
- *Memorial Day*
- *Araw ng Kalayaan*
- *Araw ng Manggagawa*
- *Columbus Day*
- *Araw ng mga Beterano*
- *Araw ng Pasasalamat*
- *Pasko*

* Kung ikaw ay 65 taong gulang o mas matanda at naging legal na permanenteng residente ng Estados Unidos ng 20 o higit na taon, maaari mong pag-aralan ang mga katanungan lamang na minarkahan ng asterisk.

(rev. 03/11)

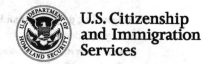

Các Câu Hỏi về Công Dân (Lịch Sử và Tổ Chức Công Quyền) cho Trắc Nghiệm Nhập Tịch

100 câu hỏi về công dân (Lịch Sử và Tổ Chức Công Quyền) cùng các giải đáp cho trắc nghiệm nhập tịch ghi dưới đây. Trắc nghiệm công dân được hỏi miệng và giám khảo của Cơ Quan Quốc Tịch Và Di Trú (USCIS) sẽ hỏi ứng viên nhập tịch tới 10 trong số 100 câu. Ứng viên phải trả lời đúng 6 trên 10 câu hỏi để được đậu phần nhập tịch này.

Trong bài trắc nghiệm nhập tịch, một vài câu giải đáp có thể đã thay đổi vì các cuộc bầu cử hoặc công cử. Khi học thi, bạn cần tìm hiểu để có các câu giải đáp cập nhật nhất. Vào lúc thi phỏng vấn với USCIS (Cơ Quan Quốc Tịch và Di Trú), bạn nhớ trả lời các câu hỏi này cho đúng với tên các giới chức đang phục vụ. Giám khảo USCIS sẽ không chấp nhận câu trả lời sai.

Mặc dù USCIS biết là có thể có những câu trả lời đúng khác, ngoài 100 câu trả lời mẫu, tuy vậy các ứng viên được khuyến khích trả lời các câu hỏi theo như các câu trả lời mẫu đã cho.

CÔNG QUYỀN HOA KỲ

A: Các Nguyên Tắc Của Dân Chủ Hoa Kỳ

1. **Luật cao nhất của quốc gia là gì?**
   - *Hiến Pháp*

2. **Hiến Pháp có mục đích gì?**
   - *thiết lập chánh phủ*
   - *mô tả tổ chức chánh phủ*
   - *bảo vệ các quyền căn bản của người dân Hoa Kỳ*

3. **Ý tưởng tự quản trị nằm trong ba chữ đầu tiên của Hiến Pháp. Các chữ này là những chữ nào?**
   - *Chúng tôi người dân (We the People)*

4. **Tu chính án là gì?**
   - *một sự thay đổi (trong Hiến Pháp)*
   - *một sự thêm (vào Hiến Pháp)*

5. **Ta gọi mười tu chính đầu tiên vào Hiến Pháp là gì?**
   - *Luật Dân Quyền*

6. **Kể ra <u>Một</u> quyền hoặc một tự do trong Tu Chính Án Đầu Tiên (First Amendment)?***
   - *tự do ngôn luận*
   - *tự do tôn giáo*
   - *tự do hội họp*
   - *tự do báo chí*
   - *tự do thinh nguyện chánh phủ*

---

* Nếu bạn 65 tuổi hoặc hơn và đã là thường-trú-nhân tại Hoa Kỳ được 20 năm hay hơn, bạn có thể chỉ cần học các câu hỏi có dấu hình sao (*) mà thôi.

7. **Hiến Pháp có bao nhiêu tu chính án?**
   - *hai mươi bảy (27)*

8. **Bản Tuyên Ngôn Độc Lập có ý nghĩa gì?**
   - *thông báo nền độc lập của chúng ta (khỏi Anh Quốc)*
   - *tuyên cáo nền độc lập của chúng ta (khỏi Anh Quốc)*
   - *cho biết Hoa Kỳ đã tự do (khỏi Anh Quốc)*

9. **Kể ra <u>Hai</u> quyền trong bản Bản Tuyên Ngôn Độc Lập?**
   - *quyền sống*
   - *quyền tự do*
   - *quyền theo đuổi hạnh phúc*

10. **Tự do tôn giáo là gì?**
    - *Bạn có thể theo bất cứ tôn giáo nào, hoặc không theo tôn giáo nào.*

11. **Hệ thống kinh tế của Hoa Kỳ gọi là gì?***
    - *kinh tế tư bản*
    - *kinh tế thị trường*

12. **"Thượng tôn luật pháp" là gì?**
    - *Mọi người đều phải tuân theo luật pháp.*
    - *Cả các người lãnh đạo đều phải tuân theo luật pháp.*
    - *Nhà cầm quyền phải tuân theo luật pháp.*
    - *Không ai được ở trên pháp luật cả.*

B: Hệ Thống Công Quyền

13. **Cho biết <u>một</u> ngành hay phần của công quyền.***
    - *Quốc Hội*
    - *lập pháp*
    - *Tổng Thống*
    - *hành pháp*
    - *các tòa án*
    - *tư pháp*

14. **Cách nào ngăn cản <u>một</u> ngành công quyền trở thành quá mạnh?**
    - *kiểm soát lẫn nhau*
    - *phân quyền*

15. **Ai phụ trách hành pháp?**
    - *Tổng Thống*

16. **Ai làm luật liên bang?**
    - *Quốc Hội*
    - *Thượng và Hạ Nghị Viện*
    - *Ngành Lập Pháp (của Liên Bang hay Quốc Gia)*

17. **<u>Hai</u> phần của Quốc Hội Hoa Kỳ là gì?***
    - *Thượng và Hạ Nghị Viện*

---

* Nếu bạn 65 tuổi hoặc hơn và đã là thường-trú-nhân tại Hoa Kỳ được 20 năm hay hơn, bạn có thể chỉ cần học các câu hỏi có dấu hình sao (*) mà thôi.

www.uscis.gov

18. **Có bao nhiêu Thượng Nghị Sĩ Liên Bang?**
    - *một trăm (100)*

19. **Chúng ta bầu Thượng Nghị Sĩ cho bao nhiêu năm?**
    - *sáu (6)*

20. **Ai là một trong những Thượng Nghị Sĩ Liên Bang của bạn?***
    - *Câu trả lời thay đổi tùy tiểu bang. [Cư dân ở thủ đô Washington, D.C. và cư dân ở các lãnh thổ Hoa Kỳ trả lời là DC hoặc lãnh thổ mình ở không có thượng-nghị-sĩ.]*

21. **Hạ-Nghị-Viện có bao nhiêu dân biểu?**
    - *bốn trăm ba mươi lăm (435)*

22. **Chúng ta bầu dân biểu cho mấy năm?**
    - *hai năm (2)*

23. **Cho biết tên dân biểu của bạn.**
    - *Câu trả lời sẽ thay đổi tùy nơi. [Cư dân ở các nơi có Đại Biểu "không có quyền biểu quyết" hoặc Đại Biểu Thường Trú có thể nói tên người đó. Cũng có thể trả lời là vùng đó không có đại diện có quyền biểu quyết tại Quốc Hội.]*

24. **Thượng-nghị-sĩ đại diện ai?**
    - *Tất cả người dân trong tiểu bang*

25. **Tại sao có những tiểu bang có nhiều đại biểu hơn các tiểu bang khác?**
    - *(Vì) dân số tiểu bang đó*
    - *(Vì) tiểu bang đó đông dân hơn*
    - *(Vì) một số tiểu bang đông dân hơn tiểu bang khác*

26. **Nhiệm kỳ Tổng Thống là mấy năm?**
    - *Bốn (4) năm*

27. **Bầu Tổng Thống vào tháng nào?***
    - *Tháng Mười Một*

28. **Hiện nay tên Tổng Thống Hoa Kỳ là gì?***
    - *Barack Obama*
    - *Obama*

29. **Hiện nay tên Phó Tổng Thống Hoa Kỳ là gì?**
    - *Joseph R. Biden, Jr.*
    - *Joe Biden*
    - *Biden*

30. **Nếu Tổng Thống không còn làm việc được nữa, ai sẽ thay thế làm Tổng Thống?**
    - *Phó Tổng Thống*

31. **Nếu cả Tổng Thống và Phó Tổng Thống không còn làm việc được nữa, ai sẽ thay thế?**
    - *Chủ Tịch Hạ Nghị Viện*

32. **Ai là Tổng Tư Lệnh quân đội?**
    - *Tổng Thống*

33. **Ai sẽ ký dự thảo luật thành luật?**
    - *Tổng Thống*

* Nếu bạn 65 tuổi hoặc hơn và đã là thường-trú-nhân tại Hoa Kỳ được 20 năm hay hơn, bạn có thể chỉ cần học các câu hỏi có dấu hình sao (*) mà thôi.

34. **Ai có quyền phủ quyết các dự luật?**
    - *Tổng Thống*

35. **Nội các của Tổng Thống làm gì?**
    - *Cố vấn cho Tổng Thống*

36. **Kể ra <u>Hai</u> chức vụ trong hàng nội các.**
    - *Bộ Trưởng Canh Nông*
    - *Bộ Trưởng Thương Mại*
    - *Bộ Trưởng Quốc Phòng*
    - *Bộ Trưởng Giáo Dục*
    - *Bộ Trưởng Năng Lượng*
    - *Bộ Trưởng Y Tế và Phục Vụ Nhân Sinh*
    - *Bộ Trưởng Nội An*
    - *Bộ Trưởng Gia Cư và Phát Triển Đô Thị*
    - *Bộ Trưởng Nội Vụ*
    - *Bộ Trưởng Lao Động*
    - *Bộ Trưởng Ngoại Giao*
    - *Bộ Trưởng Giao Thông*
    - *Bộ Trưởng Ngân Khố hay Tài Chính*
    - *Bộ Trưởng Cựu Chiến Binh*
    - *Bộ Trưởng Tư Pháp*
    - *Phó Tổng Thống*

37. **Ngành tư pháp làm gì?**
    - *duyệt lại luật lệ*
    - *cắt nghĩa luật lệ*
    - *giải quyết tranh cãi (bất hòa)*
    - *quyết định xem luật có đi ngược lại hiến pháp không*

38. **Tòa án cao nhất ở Hoa Kỳ là gì?**
    - *Tối Cao Pháp Viện*

39. **Có bao nhiêu thẩm phán ở Tối Cao Pháp Viện?**
    - *Chín (9)*

40. **Ai đang là Chủ Tịch Tối Cao Pháp Viện?**
    - *John Roberts (John G. Roberts, Jr.)*

41. **Theo Hiến Pháp, chánh phủ liên bang có một số quyền. <u>Một</u> trong các quyền của chánh phủ liên bang là?**
    - *in tiền*
    - *tuyên chiến*
    - *lập quân đội*
    - *ký các hòa ước*

42. **Theo Hiến Pháp, các tiểu bang có một số quyền. <u>Một</u> trong những quyền này là gì?**
    - *cung cấp trường học và giáo dục*
    - *bảo vệ dân chúng (cảnh sát)*
    - *bảo vệ an toàn (các sở cứu hỏa)*
    - *cấp bằng lái xe*
    - *chia vùng và chấp thuận cách xử dụng đất đai*

* Nếu bạn 65 tuổi hoặc hơn và đã là thường-trú-nhân tại Hoa Kỳ được 20 năm hay hơn, bạn có thể chỉ cần học các câu hỏi có dấu hình sao (*) mà thôi.

43. **Thống Đốc tiểu bang của bạn tên gì?**
   - *Câu trả lời tùy tiểu bang. [Cư dân vùng thủ đô Washington, D.C. phải trả lời là vùng thủ đô DC không có Thống Đốc.]*

44. **Thủ phủ của tiểu bang bạn tên gì?***
   - *Câu trả lời tùy theo tiểu bang. [Cư dân vùng thủ đô Washington, D.C. phải trả lời là vùng DC không phải là một tiểu bang và không có thủ phủ. Cư dân các lãnh thổ hải ngoại của Hoa Kỳ phải cho biết thủ phủ của vùng lãnh thổ hải ngoại này.]*

45. **Hai đảng <u>chính</u> của Hoa Kỳ là gì?***
   - *Dân Chủ và Cộng Hòa*

46. **Đảng của Tổng Thống hiện tại là đảng nào?**
   - *Đảng Dân Chủ*

47. **Chủ Tịch Hạ Viện hiện thời tên gì?**
   - *(John) Boehner*

C: Quyền Hạn và Bổn Phận

48. **Có bốn tu chính án Hiến Pháp về việc ai có quyền bầu cử. Kể ra <u>Một</u> trong các thứ đó.**
   - *Công dân mười tám (18) tuổi và hơn (được đi bầu).*
   - *Không phải trả (thuế bầu cử) để được bầu.*
   - *Bất cứ công dân nào cũng được bầu (phụ nữ và nam giới đều được bầu).*
   - *Nam giới của bất cứ chủng tộc nào (cũng đều được bầu).*

49. **<u>Một</u> trong các bổn phận chỉ dành riêng cho công dân Hoa Kỳ là gì?***
   - *phục vụ trong bồi thẩm đoàn*
   - *đi bầu trong bầu cử liên bang*

50. **Cho biết <u>một</u> quyền của riêng công dân Hoa Kỳ.**
   - *tham gia bầu cử cấp liên bang*
   - *ứng cử chức vụ liên bang*

51. **Cho biết <u>hai</u> quyền của mỗi người sống ở Hoa Kỳ?**
   - *tự do phát biểu ý kiến*
   - *tự do ngôn luận*
   - *tự do hội họp*
   - *tự do thỉnh nguyện chính quyền*
   - *tự do thờ phượng*
   - *quyền mang vũ khí tự vệ*

52. **Khi nói Lời Tuyên Thệ Trung Thành (Pledge of Allegiance), chúng ta chứng tỏ sự trung thành với cái gì?**
   - *Hoa Kỳ*
   - *Lá cờ*

---

* Nếu bạn 65 tuổi hoặc hơn và đã là thường-trú-nhân tại Hoa Kỳ được 20 năm hay hơn, bạn có thể chỉ cần học các câu hỏi có dấu hình sao (*) mà thôi.

53. Khi trở thành công dân Hoa Kỳ, <u>một</u> trong những lời hứa của bạn là gì?
- *từ bỏ sự trung thành với các quốc gia khác*
- *bảo vệ Hiến Pháp và luật lệ Hoa Kỳ*
- *tuân hành luật lệ của Hoa Kỳ*
- *phục vụ trong quân đội Hoa Kỳ (nếu cần)*
- *phục vụ (công việc quan trọng cho) Hoa Kỳ (nếu cần)*
- *trung thành với quốc gia Hoa Kỳ*

54. Công dân phải bao nhiêu tuổi mới được bầu Tổng Thống?*
- *Mười Tám (18) và hơn*

55. Có <u>hai</u> cách công dân Hoa Kỳ có thể tham dự vào nền dân chủ là các cách nào?
- *bầu cử*
- *tham gia một đảng phái chính trị*
- *tham dự vào một cuộc vận động tranh cử*
- *tham dự vào một nhóm hoạt động công dân*
- *tham dự vào một nhóm hoạt động cộng đồng*
- *phát biểu ý kiến về một vấn đề với một vị dân cử*
- *gọi điện thoại cho nghị sĩ và dân biểu*
- *công khai ủng hộ hoặc phản đối một vấn đề hay chính sách nào đó*
- *tranh cử*
- *góp ý kiến trên một tờ báo*

56. Ngày cuối cùng có thể nạp mẫu khai thuế cho liên bang là?*
- *15 Tháng Tư*

57. Khi nào tất cả nam giới phải ghi tên cho Sở Quân Vụ (Selective Service)?
- *ở tuổi mười tám (18)*
- *ở giữa tuổi mười tám (18) và hai mươi sáu (26)*

LỊCH SỬ HOA KỲ

A: Thời kỳ Thuộc Địa và Độc Lập

58. <u>Một</u> trong những lý do khiến người di dân thời thuộc địa tới Mỹ Châu là gì?
- *tự do*
- *tự do chính trị*
- *tự do tôn giáo*
- *cơ hội kinh tế*
- *hành xử tôn giáo của mình*
- *tránh sự áp bức*

59. Những ai sống tại Mỹ trước khi người Âu Châu tới?
- *người da đỏ Mỹ Châu*
- *thổ dân Mỹ Châu*

---

* Nếu bạn 65 tuổi hoặc hơn và đã là thường-trú-nhân tại Hoa Kỳ được 20 năm hay hơn, bạn có thể chỉ cần học các câu hỏi có dấu hình sao (*) mà thôi.

60. **Nhóm người nào được mang tới Mỹ Châu và bán làm nô lệ?**
    - *người Phi Châu*
    - *người từ Phi Châu*

61. **Tại sao những người di dân thời thuộc địa chống lại người Anh?**
    - *vì thuế má cao quá (phải đóng thuế mà không có người đại diện)*
    - *vì quân đội Anh đồn trú trong nhà của họ (ở trọ, làm trại binh)*
    - *vì người di dân thời thuộc địa không có chính quyền tự quản*

62. **Ai viết Bản Tuyên Ngôn Độc Lập?**
    - *(Thomas) Jefferson*

63. **Bản Tuyên Ngôn Độc Lập được chấp nhận lúc nào?**
    - *4 Tháng Bảy 1776*

64. **Có 13 tiểu bang nguyên thủy. Cho biết <u>ba</u> tiểu bang.**
    - *New Hampshire*
    - *Massachusetts*
    - *Rhode Island*
    - *Connecticut*
    - *New York*
    - *New Jersey*
    - *Pennsylvania*
    - *Delaware*
    - *Maryland*
    - *Virginia*
    - *North Carolina*
    - *South Carolina*
    - *Georgia*

65. **Việc gì xảy ra tại Đại Hội Lập Hiến (Constitutional Convention)?**
    - *Soạn thảo Hiến Pháp.*
    - *Các nhà lập quốc soạn thảo Hiến Pháp.*

66. **Hiến Pháp được soạn thảo khi nào?**
    - *1787*

67. **Các bài tham luận gọi là Federalist Papers có mục đích hỗ trợ việc thông qua Hiến Pháp Hoa Kỳ. Kể tên <u>một</u> trong những người viết tham luận.**
    - *(James) Madison*
    - *(Alexander) Hamilton*
    - *(John) Jay*
    - *Publius*

68. **<u>Một</u> việc gì làm Benjamin Franklin nổi tiếng?**
    - *nhà ngoại giao Hoa Kỳ*
    - *thành viên già nhất của Đại Hội Lập Hiến*
    - *Tổng Giám Đốc Bưu Điện đầu tiên của Hoa Kỳ*
    - *người viết cuốn lịch "Poor Richard's Almanac"*
    - *khởi công xây các thư viện miễn phí đầu tiên của Hoa Kỳ*

---

* Nếu bạn 65 tuổi hoặc hơn và đã là thường-trú-nhân tại Hoa Kỳ được 20 năm hay hơn, bạn có thể chỉ cần học các câu hỏi có dấu hình sao (*) mà thôi.

69. **Ai được gọi là cha đẻ của nước Mỹ?**
   - *(George) Washington*

70. **Ai là Tổng Thống đầu tiên?***
   - *(George) Washington*

B: Thời Kỳ 1800

71. **Hoa Kỳ mua lãnh thổ nào của Pháp vào năm 1803?**
   - *Lãnh Thổ Louisiana*
   - *Louisiana*

72. **Nói tên <u>một</u> trong những cuộc chiến Hoa Kỳ tham dự thời 1800.**
   - *Chiến tranh 1812*
   - *Chiến tranh Hoa Kỳ-Mễ-Tây-Cơ (Mexico)*
   - *Nội chiến*
   - *Chiến tranh Hoa Kỳ-Tây-Ban-Nha*

73. **Tên gọi của cuộc chiến trên đất Hoa Kỳ giữa miền Bắc và miền Nam là gì.**
   - *Nội chiến*
   - *Chiến tranh giữa các Tiểu Bang*

74. **Cho biết <u>một</u> vấn đề đưa tới cuộc nội chiến.**
   - *vấn đề nô lệ*
   - *các vấn đề kinh tế*
   - *quyền của các tiểu bang*

75. **<u>Một</u> điều quan trọng mà Abraham Lincoln làm là gì?***
   - *giải phóng nô lệ (Tuyên Ngôn Giải Phóng)*
   - *giữ gìn (hoặc bảo tồn) đoàn kết Quốc Gia*
   - *lãnh đạo Hoa Kỳ trong Cuộc Nội Chiến*

76. **Tuyên Ngôn Giải Phóng làm gì?**
   - *giải phóng nô lệ*
   - *giải phóng nô lệ thuộc tập hợp (nhóm) các tiểu bang ly khai miền Nam*
   - *giải phóng nô lệ ở các tiểu bang miền Nam*
   - *giải phóng nô lệ ở đa số các tiểu bang miền Nam*

77. **Bà Susan B. Anthony làm gì?**
   - *tranh đấu cho quyền phụ nữ*
   - *tranh đấu cho dân quyền*

C: Lịch Sử Cận Đại Hoa Kỳ và Các Thông Tin Lịch Sử Quan Trọng Khác

78. **Cho biết <u>một</u> cuộc chiến mà Hoa Kỳ tham dự vào thập niên 1900.***
   - *Thế Chiến Thứ Nhất*
   - *Thế Chiến Thứ Hai*
   - *Chiến Tranh Cao Ly (Triều Tiên)*
   - *Chiến Tranh Việt Nam*
   - *Chiến tranh Vùng Vịnh (Ba Tư)*

* Nếu bạn 65 tuổi hoặc hơn và đã là thường-trú-nhân tại Hoa Kỳ được 20 năm hay hơn, bạn có thể chỉ cần học các câu hỏi có dấu hình sao (*) mà thôi.

79. **Ai là Tổng Thống trong Thế Chiến Thứ Nhất?**
    - *(Woodrow) Wilson*

80. **Ai là Tổng Thống trong thời kỳ Khủng Hoảng Kinh Tế và Thế Chiến Thứ Hai?**
    - *(Franklin) Roosevelt*

81. **Trong Thế Chiến Thứ Hai, Hoa Kỳ chiến đấu chống các nước nào?**
    - *Nhật Bản, Đức và Ý*

82. **Trước khi trở thành Tổng Thống, Eisenhower là tướng lãnh. Ông ta đánh trận nào?**
    - *Thế Chiến Thứ Hai*

83. **Trong thời kỳ Chiến Tranh Lạnh, quan tâm chính của Hoa Kỳ là gì?**
    - *Chủ Nghĩa Cộng Sản*

84. **Phong trào nào tìm cách chấm dứt sự phân biệt chủng tộc?**
    - *(phong trào) dân quyền*

85. **Martin Luther King, Jr. đã làm gì?***
    - *tranh đấu cho dân quyền*
    - *hoạt động nhằm mang lại bình đẳng cho mọi người Mỹ*

86. **Biến cố lớn lao nào xảy ra vào ngày 11 tháng 9 năm 2001 tại Hoa Kỳ?**
    - *Bọn khủng bố tấn công Hoa Kỳ.*

87. **Kể tên một bộ lạc da đỏ tại Mỹ.**
    [Phỏng vấn viên USCIS sẽ được cung cấp một danh sách các bộ lạc da đỏ được liên bang công nhận.]
    - *Cherokee*
    - *Navajo*
    - *Sioux*
    - *Chippewa*
    - *Choctaw*
    - *Pueblo*
    - *Apache*
    - *Iroquois*
    - *Creek*
    - *Blackfeet*
    - *Seminole*
    - *Cheyenne*
    - *Arawak*
    - *Shawnee*
    - *Mohegan*
    - *Huron*
    - *Oneida*
    - *Lakota*
    - *Crow*
    - *Teton*
    - *Hopi*
    - *Inuit*

* Nếu bạn 65 tuổi hoặc hơn và đã là thường-trú-nhân tại Hoa Kỳ được 20 năm hay hơn, bạn có thể chỉ cần học các câu hỏi có dấu hình sao (*) mà thôi.

TỔNG HỢP VỀ KIẾN THỨC CÔNG DÂN

A: Địa Dư

88. **Cho biết <u>một</u> trong hai con sông dài nhất ở Hoa Kỳ.**
    - *(Sông) Missouri*
    - *(Sông) Mississippi*

89. **Biển nào ở bờ biển phía Tây Hoa Kỳ?**
    - *Thái-Bình-Dương*

90. **Biển nào ở bờ biển phía Đông Hoa Kỳ?**
    - *Đại-Tây-Dương*

91. **Cho biết <u>một</u> lãnh thổ hải ngoại của Hoa Kỳ.**
    - *Puerto Rico*
    - *Quần Đảo Virgin*
    - *Đảo Samoa*
    - *Quần Đảo Bắc Mariana*
    - *Đảo Guam*

92. **Cho biết <u>một</u> trong những tiểu bang ráp ranh Gia-Nã-Đại.**
    - *Maine*
    - *New Hampshire*
    - *Vermont*
    - *New York*
    - *Pennsylvania*
    - *Ohio*
    - *Michigan*
    - *Minnesota*
    - *North Dakota*
    - *Montana*
    - *Idaho*
    - *Washington*
    - *Alaska*

93. **Cho biết <u>một</u> trong những tiểu bang ráp ranh Mễ-Tây-Cơ.**
    - *California*
    - *Arizona*
    - *New Mexico*
    - *Texas*

94. **Thủ đô của Hoa Kỳ tên gì?***
    - *Washington, D.C.*

95. **Tượng Nữ Thần Tự Do ở đâu?***
    - *(Hải Cảng) Nữu Ước*
    - *Đảo Liberty*
    - *[Cũng chấp nhận nếu trả lời là New Jersey, gần thành phố New York và trên sông Hudson.]*

---

* Nếu bạn 65 tuổi hoặc hơn và đã là thường-trú-nhân tại Hoa Kỳ được 20 năm hay hơn, bạn có thể chỉ cần học các câu hỏi có dấu hình sao (*) mà thôi.

B: Các Biểu Tượng

96. **Tại sao lá cờ Hoa Kỳ có 13 lằn gạch?**
    - *bởi vì đã có 13 thuộc địa nguyên thủy*
    - *bởi vì các lằn này tượng trưng cho 13 thuộc địa nguyên thủy*

97. **Tại sao lá cờ Hoa Kỳ có 50 ngôi sao?***
    - *bởi vì mỗi tiểu bang có một ngôi sao*
    - *bởi vì mỗi ngôi sao tượng trưng cho một tiểu bang*
    - *bởi vì có 50 tiểu bang*

98. **Tựa của bài quốc ca Hoa Kỳ là gì?**
    - *The Star-Spangled Banner*

C: Các Ngày Lễ

99. **Ngày nào là ngày Lễ Độc Lập?***
    - *4 Tháng Bảy*

100. **Cho biết hai ngày lễ quốc gia của Hoa Kỳ.**
    - *Tết Tây*
    - *Ngày Sinh của Martin Luther King, Jr.*
    - *Ngày Các Tổng Thống*
    - *Lễ Chiến Sĩ Trận Vong (Memorial Day)*
    - *Lễ Độc Lập (Independence Day)*
    - *Lễ Lao Động (Labor Day)*
    - *Ngày Tưởng Niệm Columbus*
    - *Ngày Cựu Chiến Binh (Veterans Day)*
    - *Lễ Tạ Ơn (Thanksgiving)*
    - *Lễ Giáng Sinh*

* Nếu bạn 65 tuổi hoặc hơn và đã là thường-trú-nhân tại Hoa Kỳ được 20 năm hay hơn, bạn có thể chỉ cần học các câu hỏi có dấu hình sao (*) mà thôi.

APPENDIX 7-6

Vocabulary Lists for New Reading, Writing Tests

U.S. Citizenship
and Immigration
Services

Reading Vocabulary for the Redesigned (New) Naturalization Test

(rev. 08/08)

PEOPLE	CIVICS	PLACES	HOLIDAYS	QUESTION WORDS	VERBS	OTHER (FUNCTION)	OTHER (CONTENT)
Abraham Lincoln	American flag	America	Presidents' Day	How	can	a	colors
George Washington	Bill of Rights	U.S.	Memorial Day	What	come	for	dollar bill
	capital	United States	Flag Day	When	do/does	here	first
	citizen		Independence Day	Where	elects	in	largest
	city		Labor Day	Who	have/has	of	many
	Congress		Columbus Day	Why	is/are/was/be	on	most
	country		Thanksgiving		lives/lived	the	north
	Father of Our Country				meet	to	one
	government				name	we	people
	President				pay		second
	right				vote		south
	Senators				want		
	state/states						
	White House						

451

U.S. Citizenship and Immigration Services

Writing Vocabulary for the Redesigned (New) Naturalization Test

PEOPLE	CIVICS	PLACES	MONTHS	HOLIDAYS	VERBS	OTHER (FUNCTION)	OTHER (CONTENT)
Adams	American Indians	Alaska	February	Presidents' Day	can	and	blue
Lincoln	capital	California	May	Memorial Day	come	during	dollar bill
Washington	citizens	Canada	June	Flag Day	elect	for	fifty/50
	Civil War	Delaware	July	Independence Day	have/has	here	first
	Congress	Mexico	September	Labor Day	is/was/be	in	largest
	Father of Our Country	New York City	October	Columbus Day	lives/lived	of	most
	flag	United States	November	Thanksgiving	meets	on	north
	free	Washington			pay	the	one
	freedom of speech	Washington, D.C.			vote	to	one hundred/100
	President				want	we	people
	right						red
	Senators						second
	state/states						south
	White House						taxes
							white

(rev. 08/08)

APPENDIX 7-7

Scoring Guidelines for the English Portion of the Naturalization Test

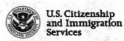
U.S. Citizenship and Immigration Services

U.S. NATURALIZATION TEST
SCORING GUIDELINES FOR THE ENGLISH TEST

Section 312 of the Immigration and Nationality Act (INA) provides that most applicants for naturalization demonstrate an understanding of the English language, including an ability to read, write, and speak words in ordinary usage in the English language, as well as a knowledge of U.S. government and history (civics).[1] This document provides a general description of how the English portion of the U.S. Naturalization Test is evaluated and scored by Officers of the U.S. Citizenship and Immigration Services (USCIS). These evaluation and scoring guidelines will not change with the implementation of the redesigned naturalization test.[2]

SPEAKING: An applicant's verbal skills are determined by the applicant's answers to questions normally asked by USCIS Officers during the naturalization eligibility interview. USCIS Officers are required to repeat and rephrase questions until the Officer is satisfied that the applicant either fully understands the question or does not understand English. If the applicant generally understands and can respond meaningfully to questions relevant to the determination of eligibility, the applicant has demonstrated the ability to speak English.

READING: To sufficiently demonstrate the ability to read in English, applicants must read one sentence, out of three sentences, in a manner suggesting to the USCIS Officer that the applicant appears to understand the meaning of the sentence. Applicants shall not be failed because of their accent when speaking English. A general description of how the reading test is scored follows:

Pass:
- Reads one sentence without extended pauses
- Reads all content words but may omit short words that do not interfere with meaning
- May make pronunciation or intonation errors that do not interfere with meaning

Fail:
- Does not read the sentence
- Omits a content word or substitutes another word for a content word
- Pauses for extended periods of time while reading the sentence
- Makes pronunciation or intonation errors that interfere with meaning

WRITING: To sufficiently demonstrate the ability to write in English, the applicant must write one sentence, out of three sentences, in a manner that would be understandable as written to the USCIS Officer. An applicant shall not be failed because of spelling, capitalization, or punctuation errors unless the errors would prevent understanding the meaning of the sentence. A general description of how the writing portion is scored follows:

Pass:
- Has the same general meaning as the dictated sentence
- May contain some grammatical, spelling, punctuation, or capitalization errors that do not interfere with meaning
- May omit short words that do not interfere with meaning
- Numbers may be spelled out or written as digits

Fail:
- Writes nothing or only one or two isolated words
- Is completely illegible
- Writes a different sentence or words
- Written sentence does not communicate the meaning of the dictated sentence

According to regulation, applicants who fail the English literacy and/or civics test during their first examination will be rescheduled to appear for a second opportunity to take the test (8 CFR 312.5).

---

[1] The English language requirement may be waived for an applicant, who on the date of filing the Application for Naturalization, Form N-400, was over 50 years old and has been a permanent resident for at least 20 years, or was over 55 years old and has been a permanent resident for at least 15 years. If either exemption applies, the applicant is not tested in English and may take the civics examination in the applicant's language of choice. An applicant, who on the date of filing the application, was over 65 years old and has been a permanent resident for 20 years, is not tested in English and qualifies to take a simpler version of the civics test in the applicant's language of choice. Also, both the English language and civics requirements for naturalization are waived for applicants who are unable to comply with these requirements because of a medical or physical impairment.

To achieve a passing score on the civics test, applicants are required to answer 6 out of 10 questions correctly.

[2] See www.uscis.gov/newtest for information regarding the redesigned naturalization test.

Learn About the United States: Quick Civics Lessons for the Naturalization Test

Learn About the United States

Quick Civics Lessons
for the Naturalization Test

U.S. Citizenship
and Immigration
Services

M-638 (rev. 07/11)

Learn About the United States: Quick Civics Lessons

Thank you for your interest in becoming a citizen of the United States of America. Your decision to apply for U.S. citizenship is a very meaningful demonstration of your commitment to this country and we applaud your efforts.

As you prepare for U.S. citizenship, *Learn About the United States: Quick Civics Lessons* will help you study for the civics and English portions of the naturalization interview. There are 100 civics (history and government) questions on the naturalization test. During your naturalization interview, you will be asked up to 10 questions from the list of 100 questions. You must answer correctly at least six (6) of the 10 questions to pass the civics test.

Applicants who are age 65 or older and have been a permanent resident for at least 20 years at the time of filing the *Application for Naturalization, Form N-400* are only required to study 20 of the 100 civics test questions for the naturalization test. These questions are flagged with an asterisk (*) in this booklet.

Learn About the United States contains short lessons based on each of the 100 civics (history and government) questions. This additional information will help you learn more about important concepts in American history and government. **During your naturalization interview, you will not be tested on the additional information in the short lessons.**

There are three components to the English portion of the test: speaking, reading, and writing. Your ability to speak English is determined by the USCIS Officer based on your answers to questions normally asked during the eligibility interview on the *Application for Naturalization, Form N-400*.

For the reading test, you must read one (1) out of three (3) sentences correctly to demonstrate an ability to read in English. There is a reading vocabulary list with all the words found in the English reading portion of the naturalization test included in the back of this booklet.

For the writing test, you must write one (1) out of three (3) sentences correctly to demonstrate an ability to write in English. There is a writing vocabulary list with all the words found in the English writing portion of the naturalization test included in the back of this booklet.

★★★

IMPORTANT NOTE: On the naturalization test, some answers may change because of elections or appointments. As you study for the test, make sure that you know the most current answers to these questions. Answer these questions with the name of the official who is serving at the time of your eligibility interview with USCIS. The USCIS Officer will not accept an incorrect answer.

★★★

Another Option to Help You Study: Civics Flash Cards

The USCIS Civics Flash Cards are a useful study tool to help you prepare for the naturalization test. These easy-to-use cards include each of the 100 civics (history and government) questions and answers on the naturalization test. With historical photos and informative captions, the Civics Flash Cards are an additional option to help you prepare for U.S. citizenship.

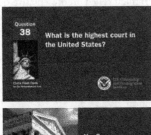

The Civics Flash Cards are available for free online at www.uscis.gov/citizenship. Hard copies are available for purchase from the U.S. Government Printing Office (GPO) by calling 1-866-512-1800 (toll-free) or by visiting http://bookstore.gpo.gov and searching for "Civics Flash Cards."

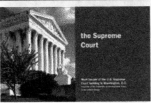

Learn About the United States

Civics Test

★★

AMERICAN GOVERNMENT

In the United States, the government gets its power to govern from the people. We have a government of the people, by the people, and for the people. Citizens in the United States shape their government and its policies, so they must learn about important public issues and get involved in their communities. Learning about American government helps you understand your rights and responsibilities and allows you to fully participate in the American political process. The Founders of this country decided that the United States should be a representative democracy. They wanted a nation ruled by laws, not by men. In a representative democracy, the people choose officials to make laws and represent their views and concerns in government. The following section will help you understand the principles of American democracy, the U.S. system of government, and the important rights and responsibilities of U.S. citizenship.

★★

A: Principles of American Democracy

1. **What is the supreme law of the land?**
   ★ **the Constitution**

The Founding Fathers of the United States wrote the Constitution in 1787. The Constitution is the "supreme law of the land." The U.S. Constitution has lasted longer than any other country's constitution. It establishes the basic principles of the United States government. The Constitution establishes a system of government called "representative democracy." In a representative democracy, citizens choose representatives to make the laws. U.S. citizens also choose a president to lead the executive branch of government. The Constitution lists fundamental rights for all citizens and other people living in the United States. Laws made in the United States must follow the Constitution.

2. **What does the Constitution do?**
   ★ **sets up the government**
   ★ **defines the government**
   ★ **protects basic rights of Americans**

The Constitution of the United States divides government power between the national government and state governments. The name for this division of power is "federalism." Federalism is an important idea in the Constitution. We call the Founding Fathers who wrote the Constitution the "Framers" of the Constitution. The Framers wanted to limit the powers of the government, so they separated the powers into three branches: executive, legislative, and judicial. The Constitution explains the power of each branch. The Constitution also includes changes and additions, called "amendments." The first 10 amendments are called the "Bill of Rights." The Bill of Rights established the individual rights and liberties of all Americans.

3. **The idea of self-government is in the first three words of the Constitution. What are these words?**
   ★ **We the People**

The Constitution says:

"We the People of the United States, in Order to form a more perfect Union, establish Justice, insure domestic Tranquility, provide for the common defence, promote the general Welfare, and secure the Blessings of Liberty to ourselves and our Posterity, do ordain and establish this Constitution for the United States of America."

★★

1

LEARN ABOUT THE UNITED STATES

With the words "We the People," the Constitution states that the people set up the government. The government works for the people and protects the rights of people. In the United States, the power to govern comes from the people, who are the highest power. This is called "popular sovereignty." The people elect representatives to make laws.

4. What is an amendment?

★ *a change (to the Constitution)*

★ *an addition (to the Constitution)*

An amendment is a change or addition to the Constitution. The Framers of the Constitution knew that laws can change as a country grows. They did not want to make it too easy to modify the Constitution, the supreme law of the land. The Framers also did not want the Constitution to lose its meaning. For this reason, the Framers decided that Congress could pass amendments in only two ways: by a two-thirds vote in the U.S. Senate and the House of Representatives or by a special convention. A special convention has to be requested by two-thirds of the states. After an amendment has passed in Congress or by a special convention, the amendment must then be ratified (accepted) by the legislatures of three-fourths of the states. The amendment can also be ratified by a special convention in three-fourths of the states. Not all proposed amendments are ratified. Six times in U.S. history amendments have passed in Congress but were not approved by enough states to be ratified.

5. What do we call the first ten amendments to the Constitution?

★ *the Bill of Rights*

The Bill of Rights is the first 10 amendments to the Constitution. When the Framers wrote the Constitution, they did not focus on individual rights. They focused on creating the system and structure of government. Many Americans believed that the Constitution should guarantee the rights of the people, and they wanted a list of all the things a government could not do. They were afraid that a strong government would take away the rights people won in the Revolutionary War. James Madison, one of the Framers of the Constitution, wrote a list of

individual rights and limits on the government. These rights appear in the first 10 amendments, called the Bill of Rights. Some of these rights include freedom of expression, the right to bear arms, freedom from search without warrant, freedom not to be tried twice for the same crime, the right to not testify against yourself, the right to a trial by a jury of your peers, the right to an attorney, and protection against excessive fines and unusual punishments. The Bill of Rights was ratified in 1791.

6. What is <u>one</u> right or freedom from the First Amendment?*

★ *speech*

★ *religion*

★ *assembly*

★ *press*

★ *petition the government*

The First Amendment of the Bill of Rights protects a person's right to freedom of expression. Freedom of expression allows open discussion and debate on public issues. Open discussion and debate are important to democracy. The First Amendment also protects freedom of religion and free speech. This amendment says that Congress may not pass laws that establish an official religion and may not limit religious expression. Congress may not pass laws that limit freedom of the press or the right of people to meet peacefully. The First Amendment also gives people the right to petition the government to change laws or acts that are not fair. Congress may not take away these rights. The First Amendment of the Constitution guarantees and protects these rights.

7. How many amendments does the Constitution have?

★ *twenty-seven (27)*

The first 10 amendments to the Constitution are called the Bill of Rights. They were added in 1791. Since then, 17 more amendments have been added. The Constitution currently has 27 amendments. The 27th Amendment was added in 1992. It explains how senators and representatives are paid. Interestingly, Congress first discussed this amendment back in 1789 as one of the original amendments considered for the Bill of Rights.

****

*If you are 65 or older and have been a permanent resident of the United States for 20 or more years, you may study just the questions marked with an asterisk.

2

8. **What did the Declaration of Independence do?**
   * ★ *announced our independence (from Great Britain)*
   * ★ *declared our independence (from Great Britain)*
   * ★ *said that the United States is free (from Great Britain)*

The Declaration of Independence contains important ideas about the American system of government. The Declaration of Independence states that all people are created equal and have "certain unalienable rights." These are rights that no government can change or take away. The author of the Declaration, Thomas Jefferson, wrote that the American colonies should be independent because Great Britain did not respect the basic rights of people in the colonies. Jefferson believed that a government exists only if the people think it should. He believed in the idea that the people create their own government and consent, or agree, to follow laws their government makes. This idea is called "consent of the governed." If the government creates laws that are fair and protect people, then people will agree to follow those laws. In the Declaration of Independence, Jefferson wrote a list of complaints the colonists had against the King of England. Jefferson ended the Declaration with the statement that the colonies are, and should be, free and independent states. The Second Continental Congress voted to accept the Declaration on July 4, 1776.

9. **What are <u>two</u> rights in the Declaration of Independence?**
   * ★ *life*
   * ★ *liberty*
   * ★ *pursuit of happiness*

The Declaration of Independence lists three rights that the Founding Fathers considered to be natural and "unalienable." They are the right to life, liberty, and the pursuit of happiness. These ideas about freedom and individual rights were the basis for declaring America's independence. Thomas Jefferson and the other Founding Fathers believed that people are born with natural rights that no government can take away. Government exists to protect these rights. Because the people voluntarily give up power to a government, they can take that power back. The British government was not protecting the rights of the colonists, so the colonies took back their power and separated from Great Britain.

Benjamin Franklin, John Adams, and Thomas Jefferson in "Writing the Declaration of Independence, 1776," by Jean Leon Gerome Ferris.
Courtesy of the Library of Congress, LC-USZC4-9904.

10. **What is freedom of religion?**
    * ★ *You can practice any religion, or not practice a religion.*

Colonists from Spain, France, Holland, England, and other countries came to America for many different reasons. One of the reasons was religious freedom. The rulers of many of these countries told their citizens that they must go to a certain church and worship in a certain way. Some people had different religious beliefs than their rulers and wanted to have their own churches. In 1620, the Pilgrims were the first group that came to America seeking religious freedom. Religious freedom was also important to the Framers. For this reason, freedom of religion was included in the Constitution as part of the Bill of Rights. The First Amendment to the Constitution guarantees freedom of religion. The First Amendment states, "Congress shall make no law respecting an establishment of religion, or prohibiting the free exercise thereof." The First Amendment also prohibits Congress from setting up an official U.S. religion, and protects citizens' rights to hold any religious belief, or none at all.

11. **What is the economic system in the United States?***
    * ★ *capitalist economy*
    * ★ *market economy*

The economic system of the United States is capitalism. In the American economy, most businesses are privately owned. Competition and profit motivate businesses. Businesses and consumers interact in the marketplace, where prices can be negotiated. This is

★★

Learn About the United States

called a "market economy." In a market economy, businesses decide what to produce, how much to produce, and what to charge. Consumers decide what, when, and where they will buy goods or services. In a market economy, competition, supply, and demand influence the decisions of businesses and consumers.

12. What is the "rule of law"?

★ Everyone must follow the law.

★ Leaders must obey the law.

★ Government must obey the law.

★ No one is above the law.

John Adams was one of the Founding Fathers and the second president of the United States. He wrote that our country is, "a government of laws, and not of men." No person or group is above the law. The rule of law means that everyone (citizens and leaders) must obey the laws. In the United States, the U.S. Constitution is the foundation for the rule of law. The United States is a "constitutional democracy" (a democracy with a constitution). In constitutional democracies, people are willing to obey the laws because the laws are made by the people through their elected representatives. If all people are governed by the same laws, the individual rights and liberties of each person are better protected. The rule of law helps to make sure that government protects all people equally and does not violate the rights of certain people.

B: System of Government

13. Name one branch or part of the government.*

★ Congress

★ legislative

★ President

★ executive

★ the courts

★ judicial

The Constitution establishes three branches of government: legislative, executive, and judicial. Article I of the Constitution establishes the legislative branch. Article I explains that Congress makes laws. Congress (the Senate and the House of Representatives) is the legislative branch of the U.S. government. Article II of the Constitution establishes the executive branch.

The executive branch enforces the laws that Congress passes. The executive branch makes sure all the people follow the laws of the United States. The president is the head of the executive branch. The vice president and members of the president's cabinet are also part of the executive branch. Article III of the Constitution establishes the judicial branch. The judicial branch places the highest judicial power in the Supreme Court. One responsibility of the judicial branch is to decide if government laws and actions follow the Constitution. This is a very important responsibility.

14. What stops one branch of government from becoming too powerful?

★ checks and balances

★ separation of powers

The Constitution separates the government's power into three branches to prevent one person or group from having too much power. The separation of government into three branches creates a system of checks and balances. This means that each branch can block, or threaten to block, the actions of the other branches. Here are some examples: the Senate (part of the legislative branch) can block a treaty signed by the president (the executive branch). In this example, the legislative branch is "checking" the executive. The U.S. Supreme Court (the judicial branch) can reject a law passed by Congress (the legislative branch). In this example, the judicial branch is "checking" the legislative branch. This separation of powers limits the power of the government and prevents the government from violating the rights of the people.

15. Who is in charge of the executive branch?

★ the President

The job of the executive branch is to carry out, or execute, federal laws and enforce laws passed by Congress. The head of the executive branch is the president. The president is both the head of state and the head of government. The president's powers include the ability to sign treaties with other countries and to select ambassadors to represent the United States around the world. The president also sets national policies and proposes laws to Congress. The president names the top leaders of the federal departments. When there is a vacancy on the Supreme

---

*If you are 65 or older and have been a permanent resident of the United States for 20 or more years, you may study just the questions marked with an asterisk.

Court, the president names a new member. However, the Senate has the power to reject the president's choices. This limit on the power of the president is an example of checks and balances.

16. Who makes federal laws?

★ **Congress**

★ **Senate and House (of Representatives)**

★ **(U.S. or national) legislature**

Congress makes federal laws. A federal law usually applies to all states and all people in the United States. Either side of Congress—the Senate or the House of Representatives—can propose a bill to address an issue. When the Senate proposes a bill, it sends the bill to a Senate committee. The Senate committee studies the issue and the bill. When the House of Representatives proposes a bill, it sends the bill to a House of Representatives committee. The committee studies the bill and sometimes makes changes to it. Then the bill goes to the full House or Senate for consideration. When each chamber passes its own version of the bill, it often goes to a "conference committee." The conference committee has members from both the House and the Senate. This committee discusses the bill, tries to resolve the differences, and writes a report with the final version of the bill. Then the committee sends the final version of the bill back to both houses for approval. If both houses approve the bill, it is considered "enrolled." An enrolled bill goes to the president to be signed into law. If the president signs the bill, it becomes a federal law.

17. What are the <u>two</u> parts of the U.S. Congress?*

★ **the Senate and House (of Representatives)**

Congress is divided into two parts—the Senate and the House of Representatives. Because it has two "chambers," the U.S. Congress is known as a "bicameral" legislature. The system of checks and balances works in Congress. Specific powers are assigned to each of these chambers. For example, only the Senate has the power to reject a treaty signed by the president or a person the president chooses to serve on the Supreme Court. Only the House of Representatives has the power to introduce a bill that requires Americans to pay taxes.

The Rotunda of the U.S. Capitol.
Courtesy of the Architect of the Capitol.

18. How many U.S. Senators are there?

★ **one hundred (100)**

There are 100 senators in Congress, two from each state. All states have equal power in the Senate because each state has the same number of senators. States with a very small population have the same number of senators as states with very large populations. The Framers of the Constitution made sure that the Senate would be small. This would keep it more orderly than the larger House of Representatives. As James Madison wrote in *Federalist Paper #63*, the Senate should be a "temperate and respectable body of citizens" that operates in a "cool and deliberate" way.

19. We elect a U.S. Senator for how many years?

★ **six (6)**

The Framers of the Constitution wanted senators to be independent from public opinion. They thought a fairly long, six-year term would give them this protection. They also wanted longer Senate terms to balance the shorter two-year terms of the members of the House, who would more closely follow public opinion. The Constitution puts no limit on the number of terms a senator may serve. Elections for U.S. senators take place on even-numbered years. Every two years, one-third of the senators are up for election.

★★

5

LEARN ABOUT THE UNITED STATES

20. Who is one of your state's U.S. Senators now?*

★ *Answers will vary. [District of Columbia residents and residents of U.S. territories should answer that D.C. (or the territory where the applicant lives) has no U.S. Senators.]*

For a complete list of U.S. senators and the states they represent, go to www.senate.gov.

21. The House of Representatives has how many voting members?

★ *four hundred thirty-five (435)*

The House of Representatives is the larger chamber of Congress. Since 1912, the House of Representatives has had 435 voting members. However, the distribution of members among the states has changed over the years. Each state must have at least one representative in the House. Beyond that, the number of representatives from each state depends on the population of the state. The Constitution says that the government will conduct a census of the population every 10 years to count the number of people in each state. The results of the census are used to recalculate the number of representatives each state should have. For example, if one state gains many residents that state could get one or more new representatives. If another state loses residents, that state could lose one or more. But the total number of voting U.S. representatives does not change.

22. We elect a U.S. Representative for how many years?

★ *two (2)*

People who live in a representative's district are called "constituents." Representatives tend to reflect the views of their constituents. If representatives do not do this, they may be voted out of office. The Framers of the Constitution believed that short two-year terms and frequent elections would keep representatives close to their constituents, public opinion, and more aware of local and community concerns. The Constitution puts no limit on the number of terms a representative may serve. All representatives are up for election every two years.

23. Name your U.S. Representative.

★ *Answers will vary. [Residents of territories with nonvoting Delegates or Resident Commissioners may provide the name of that Delegate or Commissioner. Also acceptable is any statement that the territory has no (voting) Representatives in Congress.]*

For a complete list of U.S. representatives and the districts they represent, go to www.house.gov.

24. Who does a U.S. Senator represent?

★ *all people of the state*

Senators are elected to serve the people of their state for six years. Each of the two senators represents the entire state. Before the 17th Amendment to the Constitution was ratified in 1913, the state legislatures elected the U.S. senators to represent their state. Now, all the voters in a state elect their two U.S. senators directly.

25. Why do some states have more Representatives than other states?

★ *(because of) the state's population*

★ *(because) they have more people*

★ *(because) some states have more people*

The Founding Fathers wanted people in all states to be represented fairly. In the House of Representatives, a state's population determines the number of representatives it has. In this way, states with many people have a stronger voice in the House. In the Senate, every state has the same number of senators. This means that states with few people still have a strong voice in the national government.

26. We elect a President for how many years?

★ *four (4)*

Early American leaders thought that the head of the British government, the king, had too much power. Because of this, they limited the powers of the head of the new U.S. government. They decided that the people would elect the president every four years. The president is the only official elected by the entire

---

*If you are 65 or older and have been a permanent resident of the United States for 20 or more years, you may study just the questions marked with an asterisk.

country through the Electoral College. The Electoral College is a process that was designed by the writers of the Constitution to select presidents. It came from a compromise between the president being elected directly by the people and the president being chosen by Congress. Citizens vote for electors, who then choose the president. Before 1951, there was no limit on the number of terms a president could serve. With the 22nd Amendment to the Constitution, the president can only be elected to two terms (four years each) for a total of eight years.

27. In what month do we vote for President?*

★ *November*

The Constitution did not set a national election day. In the past, elections for federal office took place on different days in different states. In 1845, Congress passed legislation to designate a single day for all Americans to vote. It made Election Day the Tuesday after the first Monday in November. Congress chose November because the United States was mostly rural. By November, farmers had completed their harvests and were available to vote. Another reason for this date was the weather. People were able to travel because it was not yet winter. They chose Tuesday for Election Day so that voters had a full day after Sunday to travel to the polls.

28. What is the name of the President of the United States now?*

★ *Barack Obama*

★ *Obama*

Barack Obama is the 44th president of the United States. He won the presidential election of 2008 and became the first African American president of the United States. As president, he is the head of the executive branch. As commander in chief, he is also in charge of the military. Obama was born in Hawaii on August 4, 1961. He graduated from Columbia University in New York. Obama also studied law and graduated from Harvard University in Massachusetts. He served as a U.S. senator for the state of Illinois before being elected president. President Obama's wife, called "the First Lady," is Michelle Obama.

The inauguration of President Theodore Roosevelt on March 4, 1905.
Courtesy of the Library of Congress, LC-USZ62-231.

29. What is the name of the Vice President of the United States now?

★ *Joseph R. Biden, Jr.*

★ *Joe Biden*

★ *Biden*

Joseph (Joe) R. Biden, Jr. is the 47th vice president of the United States. Biden was born November 20, 1942 in Pennsylvania. Later, his family moved to Delaware. He graduated from the University of Delaware in 1965. In 1968, he graduated from law school at Syracuse University in New York. From 1972-2009, Biden served as a U.S. senator for the state of Delaware. As vice president, Biden is president of the U.S. Senate and a top advisor to the president. Vice President Biden is married to Jill Biden.

30. If the President can no longer serve, who becomes President?

★ *the Vice President*

If the president dies, resigns, or cannot work while still in office, the vice president becomes president. For this reason, the qualifications for vice president and president are the same. A vice president became

★★★

7

president nine times in U.S. history when the president died or left office. William Henry Harrison died in office in 1841. Zachary Taylor died in office in 1850. Abraham Lincoln was killed in office in 1865. James Garfield was killed in office in 1881. William McKinley was killed in office in 1901. Warren Harding died in office in 1923. Franklin Roosevelt died in office in 1945. John F. Kennedy was killed in office in 1963. Richard Nixon resigned from office in 1974. No one other than the vice president has ever succeeded to the presidency.

31. If both the President and the Vice President can no longer serve, who becomes President?
★ **the Speaker of the House**

If both the president and vice president cannot serve, the next person in line is the speaker of the House of Representatives. This has not always been the procedure. Soon after the country was founded, a law was passed that made the Senate president pro tempore the next in line after the president and vice president. The president pro tempore presides over the Senate when the vice president is not there. Later in U.S. history, the secretary of state was third in line. With the Presidential Succession Act of 1947, Congress returned to the original idea of having a congressional leader next in line. In 1967, the 25th Amendment was ratified. It established procedures for presidential and vice presidential succession.

32. Who is the Commander in Chief of the military?
★ **the President**

The Founding Fathers strongly believed in republican ideals. A republic is a government where a country's political power comes from the citizens, not the rulers, and is put into use by representatives elected by the citizens. That is why they made the president the commander in chief. They wanted a civilian selected by the people. They did not want a professional military leader. The president commands the armed forces, but Congress has the power to pay for the armed forces and declare war. In 1973, many members of Congress believed that the president was misusing or abusing his powers as commander in chief. They thought that the president was ignoring the legislative branch and not allowing the system of checks and balances to work. In response, Congress passed the War Powers Act. The War Powers Act

gave Congress a stronger voice in decisions about the use of U.S. troops. President Richard Nixon vetoed this bill, but Congress overrode his veto. Because we have a system of checks and balances, one branch of government is able to check the other branches.

33. Who signs bills to become laws?
★ **the President**

Every law begins as a proposal made by a member of Congress, either a senator (member of the Senate) or representative (member of the House of Representatives). When the Senate or House begins to debate the proposal, it is called a "bill." After debate in both houses of Congress, if a majority of both the Senate and House vote to pass the bill, it goes to the president. If the president wants the bill to become law, he signs it. If the president does not want the bill to become law, he vetoes it. The president cannot introduce a bill. If he has an idea for a bill, he must ask a member of Congress to introduce it.

34. Who vetoes bills?
★ **the President**

The president has veto power. This means that the president can reject a bill passed by Congress. If the president vetoes a bill, he prevents it from becoming a law. The president can send the bill back to Congress unsigned. Often he will list reasons why he rejects it. The president has 10 days to evaluate the bill. If the president does not sign the bill after 10 days and Congress is in session, the bill automatically becomes a law. If the president does nothing with the bill and Congress adjourns within the 10-day period, the bill does not become law—this is called a "pocket veto." If two-thirds of the House and two-thirds of the Senate vote to pass the bill again, the bill becomes a law, even though the president did not sign it. This process is called "overriding the president's veto." It is not easy to do.

35. What does the President's Cabinet do?
★ **advises the President**

The Constitution says that the leaders of the executive departments should advise the president. These department leaders, most of them called "secretaries," make up the cabinet. The president nominates the

*If you are 65 or older and have been a permanent resident of the United States for 20 or more years, you may study just the questions marked with an asterisk.

cabinet members to be his advisors. For a nominee to be confirmed, a majority of the Senate must approve the nominee. Throughout history, presidents have been able to change who makes up the cabinet or add departments to the cabinet. For example, when the Department of Homeland Security was created, President George W. Bush added the leader of this department to his cabinet.

36. What are two Cabinet-level positions?

★ Secretary of Agriculture
★ Secretary of Commerce
★ Secretary of Defense
★ Secretary of Education
★ Secretary of Energy
★ Secretary of Health and Human Services
★ Secretary of Homeland Security
★ Secretary of Housing and Urban Development
★ Secretary of the Interior
★ Secretary of Labor
★ Secretary of State
★ Secretary of Transportation
★ Secretary of the Treasury
★ Secretary of Veterans Affairs
★ Attorney General
★ Vice President

The Contemplation of Justice statue outside the U.S. Supreme Court building in Washington, D.C.
Courtesy of the Collection of the Supreme Court of the United States.

The people on the president's cabinet are the vice president and the heads of the 15 executive departments. The president may appoint other government officials to the cabinet. When George Washington was president, there were only four cabinet members: the secretary of state, secretary of the treasury, secretary of war, and attorney general. The government established the other executive departments later.

37. What does the judicial branch do?

★ reviews laws
★ explains laws
★ resolves disputes (disagreements)
★ decides if a law goes against the Constitution

The judicial branch is one of the three branches of government. The Constitution established the judicial

branch of government with the creation of the Supreme Court. Congress created the other federal courts. All these courts together make up the judicial branch. The courts review and explain the laws, and they resolve disagreements about the meaning of the law. The U.S. Supreme Court makes sure that laws are consistent with the Constitution. If a law is not consistent with the Constitution, the Court can declare it unconstitutional. In this case, the Court rejects the law. The Supreme Court makes the final decision about all cases that have to do with federal laws and treaties. It also rules on other cases, such as disagreements between states.

38. What is the highest court in the United States?

★ the Supreme Court

The U.S. Supreme Court has complete authority over all federal courts. Its rulings have a significant effect. A Supreme Court ruling can affect the outcome of many cases in the lower courts. The Supreme Court's interpretations of federal laws and of the Constitution are final. The Supreme Court is limited in its power over the states. It cannot make decisions about state

9

law or state constitutions. The Court can decide that a state law or action conflicts with federal law or with the U.S. Constitution. If this happens, the state law becomes invalid. The Supreme Court case ruling *Marbury v. Madison* established this power, known as "judicial review." The Supreme Court also rules on cases about significant social and public policy issues that affect all Americans. The Supreme Court ruled on the court case *Brown v. the Board of Education of Topeka*, which ended racial segregation in schools.

39. How many justices are on the Supreme Court?

★ *nine (9)*

The Constitution does not establish the number of justices on the Supreme Court. In the past, there have been as many as 10 and as few as six justices. Now, there are nine justices on the Supreme Court: eight associate justices and one chief justice. The Constitution gives the president the power to nominate justices to the Supreme Court. The nominee must then be confirmed by the Senate. Justices serve on the court for life or until they retire. For more information on the Supreme Court, go to www.supremecourt.gov.

40. Who is the Chief Justice of the United States now?

★ *John Roberts (John G. Roberts, Jr.)*

John G. Roberts, Jr. is the 17th chief justice of the United States. After the death of former chief justice William Rehnquist in September 2005, President George W. Bush nominated Roberts for this position. Judge Roberts became chief justice when he was 50. He is the youngest chief justice since 1801, when John Marshall became chief justice at the age of 45. Before he became chief justice, Judge Roberts served on the U.S. Court of Appeals for the District of Columbia Circuit. Although the chief justice of the United States is the highest official in the judicial branch, his vote on the Supreme Court carries the same weight as the other justices.

41. Under our Constitution, some powers belong to the federal government. What is <u>one</u> power of the federal government?

★ *to print money*

★ *to declare war*

★ *to create an army*

★ *to make treaties*

The powers of government are divided between the federal government and the state governments. The federal government is known as a limited government. Its powers are restricted to those described in the U.S. Constitution. The Constitution gives the federal government the power to print money, declare war, create an army, and make treaties with other nations. Most other powers that are not given to the federal government in the Constitution belong to the states.

42. Under our Constitution, some powers belong to the states. What is <u>one</u> power of the states?

★ *provide schooling and education*

★ *provide protection (police)*

★ *provide safety (fire departments)*

★ *give a driver's license*

★ *approve zoning and land use*

In the United States, the federal and state governments both hold power. Before the Constitution, the 13 colonies governed themselves individually much like state governments. It was not until the Articles of Confederation and then the Constitution that a national or federal government was established. Today, although each state has its own constitution, these state constitutions cannot conflict with the U.S. Constitution. The U.S. Constitution is the supreme law of the land. The state governments hold powers not given to the federal government in the U.S. Constitution. Some powers of the state government are the power to create traffic regulations and marriage requirements, and to issue driver's licenses. The Constitution also provides a list of powers that the states do not have. For example, states cannot coin (create) money. The state and federal governments also share some powers, such as the ability to tax people.

*If you are 65 or older and have been a permanent resident of the United States for 20 or more years, you may study just the questions marked with an asterisk.

43. Who is the Governor of your state now?

★ *Answers will vary. [District of Columbia residents should answer that D.C. does not have a Governor.]*

To learn the name of the governor of your state or territory, go to www.usa.gov. Similar to the federal government, most states have three branches of government. The branches are executive, legislative, and judicial. The governor is the chief executive of the state. The governor's job in a state government is similar to the president's job in the federal government. However, the state laws that a governor carries out are different from the federal laws that the president carries out. The Constitution says that certain issues are covered by federal, not state, laws. All other issues are covered by state laws. The governor's duties and powers vary from state to state. The number of years that a governor is elected to serve—called a "term"—is four years. The exceptions are New Hampshire and Vermont, where governors serve for two years.

44. What is the capital of your state?*

★ *Answers will vary. [District of Columbia residents should answer that D.C. is not a state and does not have a capital. Residents of U.S. territories should name the capital of the territory.]*

To learn the capital of your state or territory, go to www.usa.gov. Each state or territory has its own capital. The state capital is where the state government conducts its business. It is similar to the nation's capital, Washington, D.C., where the federal government conducts its business. Some state capitals have moved from one city to another over the years, but the state capitals have not changed since 1910. Usually, the governor lives in the state's capital city.

45. What are the <u>two</u> major political parties in the United States?*

★ *Democratic and Republican*

The Constitution did not establish political parties. President George Washington specifically warned against them. But early in U.S. history, two political

Map of the United States including state capitals.
Courtesy of the National Atlas of the United States, March 5, 2003, http://nationalatlas.gov.

groups developed. They were the Democratic-Republicans and the Federalists. Today, the two major political parties are the Democratic Party and the Republican Party. President Andrew Jackson created the Democratic Party from the Democratic-Republicans. The Republican Party took over from the Whigs as a major party in the 1860s. The first Republican president was Abraham Lincoln. Throughout U.S. history, there have been other parties. These parties have included the Know-Nothing (also called American Party), Bull-Moose (also called Progressive), Reform, and Green parties. They have played various roles in American politics. Political party membership in the United States is voluntary. Parties are made up of people who organize to promote their candidates for election and to promote their views about public policies.

46. What is the political party of the President now?

★ *Democratic (Party)*

The two major political parties in the United States today are the Democratic and Republican parties. The current president, Barack Obama, is a member of the Democratic Party. Other notable Democratic presidents include Woodrow Wilson, Franklin D. Roosevelt, Harry Truman, John F. Kennedy, Lyndon B. Johnson, Jimmy Carter, and William "Bill" Clinton. Notable Republican presidents include Abraham Lincoln, Theodore Roosevelt, Warren Harding, Herbert Hoover, Dwight Eisenhower, Ronald Reagan, and George H. W. Bush. Since the middle of the 19th

11

century, the symbol of the Republican Party has been the elephant. The Republican Party is also known as the "Grand Old Party" or the "GOP." The symbol of the Democratic Party is the donkey.

47. What is the name of the Speaker of the House of Representatives now?

★ (John) Boehner

The current speaker of the House of Representatives is John Boehner. He has represented Ohio's Eighth District in the House of Representatives since 1991. As speaker, he presides over the House of Representatives and leads the majority political party in the House, the Republican Party. The speaker is second in line to the succession of the presidency after the vice president.

C: Rights and Responsibilities

48. There are four amendments to the Constitution about who can vote. Describe one of them.

★ Citizens eighteen (18) and older (can vote).

★ You don't have to pay (a poll tax) to vote.

★ Any citizen can vote. (Women and men can vote.)

★ A male citizen of any race (can vote).

Voting is one of the most important civic responsibilities of citizens in the United States. In a democratic society, the people choose the leaders who will represent them. There are four amendments to the Constitution about voting. The 15th Amendment permits American men of all races to vote. It was written after the Civil War and the end of slavery. The 19th Amendment gave women the right to vote. It resulted from the women's suffrage movement (the women's rights movement). After the 15th Amendment was passed, some leaders of the southern states were upset that African Americans could vote. These leaders designed fees called poll taxes to stop them from voting. The 24th Amendment made these poll taxes illegal. The 26th Amendment lowered the voting age from 21 to 18.

49. What is one responsibility that is only for United States citizens?*

★ serve on a jury

★ vote in a federal election

Two responsibilities of U.S. citizens are to serve on a jury and vote in federal elections. The Constitution gives citizens the right to a trial by a jury. The jury is made up of U.S. citizens. Participation of citizens on a jury helps ensure a fair trial. Another important responsibility of citizens is voting. The law does not require citizens to vote, but voting is a very important part of any democracy. By voting, citizens are participating in the democratic process. Citizens vote for leaders to represent them and their ideas, and the leaders support the citizens' interests.

50. Name one right only for United States citizens.

★ vote in a federal election

★ run for federal office

U.S. citizens have the right to vote in federal elections. Permanent residents can vote in local or state elections that do not require voters to be U.S. citizens. Only U.S. citizens can vote in federal elections. U.S. citizens can also run for federal office. Qualifications to run for the Senate or House of Representatives include being a U.S. citizen for a certain number of years. A candidate for Senate must be a U.S. citizen for at least 9 years. A candidate for the House must be a U.S. citizen for at least 7 years. To run for president of the United States, a candidate must be a native-born (not naturalized) citizen. In addition to the benefits of citizenship, U.S. citizens have certain responsibilities—to respect the law, stay informed on issues, participate in the democratic process, and pay their taxes.

51. What are two rights of everyone living in the United States?

★ freedom of expression

★ freedom of speech

★ freedom of assembly

★ freedom to petition the government

★ freedom of worship

★ the right to bear arms

Thomas Jefferson said, "[The] best principles [of our republic] secure to all its citizens a perfect equality of

*If you are 65 or older and have been a permanent resident of the United States for 20 or more years, you may study just the questions marked with an asterisk.

rights." Millions of immigrants have come to America to have these rights. The Constitution and the Bill of Rights give many of these rights to all people living in the United States. These rights include the freedom of expression, of religion, of speech, and the right to bear arms. All people living in the United States also have many of the same duties as citizens, such as paying taxes and obeying the laws.

52. What do we show loyalty to when we say the Pledge of Allegiance?

★ *the United States*

★ *the flag*

The flag is an important symbol of the United States. The Pledge of Allegiance to the flag states, "I pledge allegiance to the Flag of the United States of America and to the Republic for which it stands, one Nation, under God, indivisible, with liberty and justice for all." When we say the Pledge of Allegiance, we usually stand facing the flag with the right hand over the heart. Francis Bellamy wrote the pledge. It was first published in *The Youth's Companion* magazine in 1892 for children to say on the anniversary of Columbus's discovery of America. Congress officially recognized the pledge on June 22, 1942. Two changes have been made since it was written in 1892. "I pledge allegiance to my flag" was changed to "I pledge allegiance to the Flag of the United States of America." Congress added the phrase "under God" on June 14, 1954.

53. What is <u>one</u> promise you make when you become a United States citizen?

★ *give up loyalty to other countries*

★ *defend the Constitution and laws of the United States*

★ *obey the laws of the United States*

★ *serve in the U.S. military (if needed)*

★ *serve (do important work for) the nation (if needed)*

★ *be loyal to the United States*

When the United States became an independent country, the Constitution gave Congress the power to establish a uniform rule of naturalization. Congress made rules about how immigrants could become citizens. Many of these requirements are still valid today, such as the requirements to live in the United States for a specific period of time, to be of good

The American flag is an important symbol of the United States.

moral character, and to understand and support the principles of the Constitution. After an immigrant fulfills all of the requirements to become a U.S. citizen, the final step is to take an Oath of Allegiance at a naturalization ceremony. The Oath of Allegiance states, "I hereby declare, on oath, that I absolutely and entirely renounce and abjure all allegiance and fidelity to any foreign prince, potentate, state, or sovereignty of whom or which I have heretofore been a subject or citizen; that I will support and defend the Constitution and laws of the United States of America against all enemies, foreign and domestic; that I will bear true faith and allegiance to the same; that I will bear arms on behalf of the United States when required by the law; that I will perform noncombatant service in the Armed Forces of the United States when required by the law; that I will perform work of national importance under civilian direction when required by the law; and that I take this obligation freely without any mental reservation or purpose of evasion; so help me God."

54. How old do citizens have to be to vote for President?*

★ *eighteen (18) and older*

For most of U.S. history, Americans had to be at least 21 years old to vote. At the time of the Vietnam War, during the 1960s and 1970s, many people thought that people who were old enough to fight in a war should also be old enough to vote. In 1971, the 26th

LEARN ABOUT THE UNITED STATES

Amendment changed the minimum voting age from 21 to 18 for all federal, state, and local elections. The National Voter Registration Act of 1993 made it easier for people to register to vote. Now they can register to vote by mail, at public assistance offices, or when they apply for or renew their driver's license.

55. What are two ways that Americans can participate in their democracy?

- ★ vote
- ★ join a political party
- ★ help with a campaign
- ★ join a civic group
- ★ join a community group
- ★ give an elected official your opinion on an issue
- ★ call Senators and Representatives
- ★ publicly support or oppose an issue or policy
- ★ run for office
- ★ write to a newspaper

Citizens play an active part in their communities. When Americans engage in the political process, democracy stays alive and strong. There are many ways for people to be involved. They can volunteer to help new immigrants learn English and civics, join the Parent Teacher Association (PTA) of their child's school, run for a position on the local school board, or volunteer to help at a polling station. People can also vote, help with a political campaign, join a civic or community organization, or call their senator or representative about an issue that is important to them.

56. When is the last day you can send in federal income tax forms?*

- ★ April 15

The last day to send in your federal income tax to the Internal Revenue Service is April 15 of each year. The Constitution gave the federal government the power to collect taxes. The federal government needs money to pay the nation's debts and to defend and provide for the needs of the country. When the country was young, it was difficult to raise money from the 13

original states. The government began collecting income tax for the first time through the Revenue Act of 1861. This was only temporary. In 1894, a flat-rate federal income tax was enacted, but the Supreme Court said this was unconstitutional. Finally, in 1913, the 16th Amendment was ratified. It gave Congress the power to collect income taxes. Today, "taxable income" is money that is earned from wages, self-employment, tips, and the sale of property. The government uses these taxes to keep our country safe and secure. It also tries to cure and prevent diseases through research. In addition, the government protects our money in banks by insuring it, educates children and adults, and builds and repairs our roads and highways. Taxes are used to do these things and many more.

57. When must all men register for the Selective Service?

- ★ at age eighteen (18)
- ★ between eighteen (18) and twenty-six (26)

President Lincoln tried to draft men to fight during the Civil War, but many people became angry and rioted. In 1917, Congress passed the Selective Service Act. This act gave President Woodrow Wilson the power to temporarily increase the U.S. military during World War I. In 1940, President Franklin Roosevelt signed the Selective Training and Service Act, which created the first draft during peacetime. This was the beginning of the Selective Service System in the United States today. The draft was needed again for the Korean and Vietnam Wars. Today, there is no draft, but all men between 18 and 26 years old must register with the Selective Service System. When a man registers, he tells the government that he is available to serve in the U.S. Armed Forces. He can register at a United States post office or on the Internet. To register for Selective Service on the Internet, visit the Selective Service website at www.sss.gov.

---

14   *If you are 65 or older and have been a permanent resident of the United States for 20 or more years, you may study just the questions marked with an asterisk.

★★

AMERICAN HISTORY

For more than 200 years, the United States has strived to become a "more perfect union." Its history has been one of expansive citizenship for all Americans. By learning about our shared history, you will be able to understand our nation's traditions, milestones, and common civic values. Our country is independent because of the strength, unity, and determination of our forefathers. It is important for future Americans to know this story. We are people working toward great ideals and principles guided by equality and fairness. This is important to keep our country free. As Americans, we have been committed to each other and our country throughout our history. The following section will help you understand American history from the colonial period and independence to the Civil War and other important events during the 1800s, 1900s, and today.

★★

A: Colonial Period and Independence

58. What is <u>one</u> reason colonists came to America?

★ freedom

★ political liberty

★ religious freedom

★ economic opportunity

★ practice their religion

★ escape persecution

In the 1600s and 1700s, colonists from England and other European countries sailed across the Atlantic Ocean to the American colonies. Some left Europe to escape religious restrictions or persecution, to practice their religion freely. Many came for political freedom, and some came for economic opportunity. These freedoms and opportunities often did not exist in the colonists' home countries. For these settlers, the American colonies were a chance for freedom and a new life. Today, many people come to the United States for these same reasons.

59. Who lived in America before the Europeans arrived?

★ American Indians

★ Native Americans

Great American Indian tribes such as the Navajo, Sioux, Cherokee, and Iroquois lived in America at the time the Pilgrims arrived. The Pilgrims settled in an area where a tribe called the Wampanoag lived. The Wampanoag taught the Pilgrims important skills, such as how to farm with different methods and how to grow crops such as corn, beans, and squash. Relations with some American Indian tribes became tense and confrontational as more Europeans moved to America and migrated west. Eventually, after much violence, the settlers defeated those American Indian tribes and took much of their land.

60. What group of people was taken to America and sold as slaves?

★ Africans

★ people from Africa

Slavery existed in many countries long before America was founded. By 1700, many Africans were being brought to the American colonies as slaves. Men, women, and children were brought against their will. They were often separated from their families when they were sold as slaves. Slaves worked without payment and without basic rights. Most worked in agriculture, but slaves did many other kinds of work in the colonies, too. Slavery created a challenge for a nation founded on individual freedoms and democratic beliefs. It was one of the major causes of the American Civil War.

61. Why did the colonists fight the British?

★ because of high taxes (taxation without representation)

★ because the British army stayed in their houses (boarding, quartering)

★ because they didn't have self-government

The American colonists' anger had been growing for years before the Revolutionary War began in 1775. The decision to separate from the British was not an easy choice for many colonists. However, Great

★★

Britain's "repeated injuries" against the Americans, as noted in the Declaration of Independence, convinced many to join the rebellion. The British taxed the colonists without their consent, and the colonists had nobody to represent their needs and ideas to the British government. They were also angry because ordinary colonists were forced to let British soldiers sleep and eat in their homes. The colonists believed the British did not respect their basic rights. The British governed the colonists without their consent, denying them self-government.

62. Who wrote the Declaration of Independence?

★ (Thomas) Jefferson

Thomas Jefferson wrote the Declaration of Independence in 1776. He was a very important political leader and thinker. Some of the most important ideas about the American government are found in the Declaration of Independence, such as the idea that all people are created equal. Another important idea is that people are born with certain rights including life, liberty, and the pursuit of happiness. Jefferson was the third president of the United States, serving from 1801 to 1809. Before becoming president, Jefferson was governor of Virginia and the first U.S. secretary of state. He strongly supported individual rights, especially freedom of religion. Jefferson wanted to protect these rights. For this reason, he did not want a strong national government.

63. When was the Declaration of Independence adopted?

★ July 4, 1776

In 1774, representatives from 12 of the 13 colonies met in Philadelphia, Pennsylvania, for the First Continental Congress. Of the 13 colonies, only Georgia was absent. These representatives were angry about British laws that treated them unfairly. They began to organize an army. The Second Continental Congress met in 1775 after fighting began between the colonists and the British Army. This Congress asked Thomas Jefferson and others to write the Declaration of Independence. When Thomas Jefferson finished his draft of the Declaration of Independence, he took

it to John Adams, Benjamin Franklin, and the others on the committee to review it. After changes were made by the committee, the Declaration was read to the members of the entire Congress. The purpose of the Declaration was to announce the separation of the colonies from England. The Declaration of Independence stated that if a government does not protect the rights of the people, the people can create a new government. For this reason, the colonists separated from their British rulers. On July 4, 1776, the Second Continental Congress adopted the Declaration of Independence.

64. There were 13 original states. Name three.

★ New Hampshire	★ Delaware
★ Massachusetts	★ Maryland
★ Rhode Island	★ Virginia
★ Connecticut	★ North Carolina
★ New York	★ South Carolina
★ New Jersey	★ Georgia
★ Pennsylvania	

The 13 original states were all former British colonies. Representatives from these colonies came together and declared independence from Great Britain in 1776. After the Revolutionary War, the colonies became free and independent states. When the 13 colonies became states, each state set up its own government. They wrote state constitutions. Eventually, the people in these states created a new form of national government that would unite all the states into a single nation under the U.S. Constitution. The first three colonies to become states were Delaware, Pennsylvania, and New Jersey. This happened in 1787. Eight colonies became states in 1788. These were Georgia, Connecticut, Massachusetts, Maryland, South Carolina, New Hampshire, Virginia, and New York. North Carolina became a state in 1789. Rhode Island became a state in 1790. Although the colonies were recognized as states after the Declaration of Independence, the date of statehood is based on when they ratified (accepted) the U.S. Constitution. Today, the United States has 50 states.

16   *If you are 65 or older and have been a permanent resident of the United States for 20 or more years, you may study just the questions marked with an asterisk.

65. What happened at the Constitutional Convention?

★ *The Constitution was written.*

★ *The Founding Fathers wrote the Constitution.*

The Constitutional Convention was held in Philadelphia, Pennsylvania, from May to September 1787. Fifty-five delegates from 12 of the original 13 states (except for Rhode Island) met to write amendments to the Articles of Confederation. The delegates met because many American leaders did not like the Articles. The national government under the Articles of Confederation was not strong enough. Instead of changing the Articles of Confederation, the delegates decided to create a new governing document with a stronger national government—the Constitution. Each state sent delegates, who worked for four months in secret to allow for free and open discussion as they wrote the new document. The delegates who attended the Constitutional Convention are called "the Framers." On September 17, 1787, 39 of the delegates signed the new Constitution.

66. When was the Constitution written?

★ 1787

The Constitution, written in 1787, created a new system of U.S. government—the same system we have today. James Madison was the main writer of the Constitution. He became the fourth president of the United States. The U.S. Constitution is short, but it defines the principles of government and the rights of citizens in the United States. The document has a preamble and seven articles. Since its adoption, the Constitution has been amended (changed) 27 times. Three-fourths of the states (9 of the original 13) were required to ratify (approve) the Constitution. Delaware was the first state to ratify the Constitution on December 7, 1787. In 1788, New Hampshire was the ninth state to ratify the Constitution. On March 4, 1789, the Constitution took effect and Congress met for the first time. George Washington was inaugurated as president the same year. By 1790, all 13 states had ratified the Constitution.

The Constitution of the United States.
Courtesy of the National Archives.

67. The Federalist Papers supported the passage of the U.S. Constitution. Name <u>one</u> of the writers.

★ *(James) Madison*

★ *(Alexander) Hamilton*

★ *(John) Jay*

★ *Publius*

The Federalist Papers were 85 essays that were printed in New York newspapers while New York State was deciding whether or not to support the U.S. Constitution. The essays were written in 1787 and 1788 by Alexander Hamilton, John Jay, and James Madison under the pen name "Publius." The essays explained why the state should ratify the Constitution. Other newspapers outside New York also published the essays as other states were deciding to ratify the Constitution. In 1788, the papers were published together in a book called *The Federalist.* Today, people still read the Federalist Papers to help them understand the Constitution.

★★★

17

68. What is <u>one</u> thing Benjamin Franklin is famous for?

★ *U.S. diplomat*

★ *oldest member of the Constitutional Convention*

★ *first Postmaster General of the United States*

★ *writer of "Poor Richard's Almanac"*

★ *started the first free libraries*

Benjamin Franklin was one of the most influential Founding Fathers of the United States. He was the oldest delegate to the Constitutional Convention and one of the signers of the U.S. Constitution. He was a printer, author, politician, diplomat, and inventor. By his mid-20s, he was an accomplished printer, and he began writing books and papers. Franklin's most famous publication was *Poor Richard's Almanac*. He also organized America's first library. Its members loaned books to one another. He was very active in colonial politics. He also visited England and France many times as a U.S. diplomat. In 1775, the Second Continental Congress appointed Franklin the first postmaster general.

69. Who is the "Father of Our Country"?

★ *(George) Washington*

George Washington is called the Father of Our Country. He was the first American president. Before that, he was a brave general who led the Continental Army to victory over Great Britain during the American Revolutionary War. After his victory over the British Army, Washington retired to his farm in Virginia named Mount Vernon. He left retirement to help create the new country's system of government. He presided over the Constitutional Convention in Philadelphia in 1787.

70. Who was the first President?*

★ *(George) Washington*

George Washington was the first president of the United States. He began his first term in 1789. He served for a second term beginning in 1793. Washington played an important role in forming the new nation and encouraged Americans to unite. He also helped define the American presidency. He voluntarily resigned from the presidency after two terms. He set an example for future leaders in his own country and the world by voluntarily giving up power. The tradition of a president serving no more than two terms continued in the United States until Franklin D. Roosevelt, who was elected to office four times (1933–1945). The 22nd Amendment to the Constitution, passed in 1947, now limits presidents to two terms.

B: 1800s

71. What territory did the United States buy from France in 1803?

★ *the Louisiana Territory*

★ *Louisiana*

The Louisiana Territory was a large area west of the Mississippi River. It was 828,000 square miles. In 1803, the United States bought the Louisiana Territory from France for $15 million. The Louisiana Purchase Treaty was signed in Paris on April 30, 1803. It was the largest acquisition of land in American history. Farmers could now ship their farm products down the Mississippi River without permission from other countries. This was important because the city of New Orleans was a major shipping port. The Louisiana Purchase doubled the size of the United States and expanded it westward. Meriwether Lewis and William Clark led an expedition to map the Louisiana Territory.

72. Name <u>one</u> war fought by the United States in the 1800s.

★ **War of 1812**

★ **Mexican-American War**

★ **Civil War**

★ **Spanish-American War**

The United States fought four major wars in the 1800s—the War of 1812, the Mexican-American War, the Civil War, and the Spanish-American War.

The War of 1812 lasted from 1812 through 1815. President James Madison asked Congress to declare war on Great Britain. The British were stopping and seizing American ships. They were also arming American Indians to fight against the Americans. As a result of this war, the nation's trade was disrupted and the U.S.

****

Capitol was burned. The Americans won the war. This was the first time after the Revolutionary War that America had to fight a foreign country to protect its independence.

The Mexican-American War was a conflict between Mexico and America. The war began in Texas in 1846. President James Polk ordered General Zachary Taylor and his forces to occupy land claimed by both the United States and Mexico. President Polk believed westward expansion was important for the United States to grow. When Mexico attacked, the United States went to war with Mexico. When the war ended in February 1848, the United States and Mexico signed the Treaty of Guadalupe Hidalgo. This treaty gave Texas to the United States and extended the boundaries of the United States west to the Pacific Ocean.

In the Civil War, the people of the United States fought against each other. Americans in the northern states fought to support the federal government ("the Union") against Americans from the southern states. The southern states were trying to separate themselves to form a new nation, the Confederate States of America ("the Confederacy"). The war lasted from 1861 to 1865, when the Confederate army surrendered to the Union army. Many lives were lost in the American Civil War.

In 1898, the United States fought Spain in the Spanish-American War. The United States wanted to help Cuba become independent from Spain because the United States had economic interests in Cuba. The war began when a U.S. battleship was sunk near Cuba. Many Americans believed it was the Spanish who attacked the ship. For this reason, America went to war with Spain. By the end of 1898, the war was over with a victory for the United States. Cuba had its independence, and Guam, Puerto Rico, and the Philippines became territories of the United States.

73. Name the U.S. war between the North and the South.

★ *the Civil War*

★ *the War between the States*

The American Civil War is also known as the War between the States. It was a war between the people in the northern states and those in the southern

Civil War soldiers with cannon and caisson, Fort C.F. Smith, Co. L, 2d New York Artillery.
Courtesy of the Library of Congress, LC-USZ62-115177.

states. The Civil War was fought in many places across the United States, but most battles were fought in the southern states. The first battle was at Fort Sumter, South Carolina. The first major battle between the northern (Union) army and the southern (Confederate) army took place at Bull Run, in Manassas, Virginia, in July 1861. The Union expected the war to end quickly. After its defeat at the Battle of Bull Run, the Union realized that the war would be long and difficult. In 1865, the Civil War ended with the capture of the Confederate capital in Richmond, Virginia. Confederate General Robert E. Lee surrendered to Lt. General Ulysses S. Grant of the Union army at Appomattox Courthouse in central Virginia. Over the four-year period, more than 3 million Americans fought in the Civil War and more than 600,000 people died.

74. Name one problem that led to the Civil War.

★ *slavery*

★ *economic reasons*

★ *states' rights*

The Civil War began when 11 southern states voted to secede (separate) from the United States to form their own country, the Confederate States of America. These southern states believed that the federal government of the United States threatened their right to make their own decisions. They wanted states' rights with each state making their own decisions about their government. If the national government contradicted the state, they did not want to follow the national government. The North and South had very

LEARN ABOUT THE UNITED STATES

different economic systems. The South's agriculture-based economy depended heavily on slave labor. The southern states feared that the United States government would end slavery. The southern states believed that this would hurt their economic and political independence. The economy of the northern states was more industrial and did not depend on slavery. The northern states fought to keep all the United States together in "the Union." They tried to stop the southern states from separating into a new Confederate nation. There were also many people in the North who wanted to end slavery. These differences led to the American Civil War, which lasted from 1861 until 1865.

75. **What was <u>one</u> important thing that Abraham Lincoln did?***

★ *freed the slaves (Emancipation Proclamation)*

★ *saved (or preserved) the Union*

★ *led the United States during the Civil War*

Abraham Lincoln was president of the United States from 1861 to 1865, and led the nation during the Civil War. Lincoln thought the separation of the southern (Confederate) states was unconstitutional, and he wanted to preserve the Union. In 1863, during the Civil War, he issued the Emancipation Proclamation. It declared that the slaves who lived in the rebelling Confederate states were forever free. Lincoln is also famous for his "Gettysburg Address." He gave that speech at Gettysburg, Pennsylvania, in November 1863. Earlier that year, at the Battle of Gettysburg, the northern (Union) army had won a major battle to stop the Confederate army from invading the North. To honor the many who died in this battle, the governor of Pennsylvania established the Soldiers' National Cemetery at Gettysburg. Lincoln spoke at the dedication ceremony and praised those who fought and died in battle. He asked those still living to rededicate themselves to saving the Union so that "government of the people, by the people, for the people shall not perish from the earth." On April 14, 1865, soon after taking office for his second term, Abraham Lincoln was killed by a southern supporter, John Wilkes Booth, at Ford's Theatre in Washington, D.C.

76. **What did the Emancipation Proclamation do?**

★ *freed the slaves*

★ *freed slaves in the Confederacy*

★ *freed slaves in the Confederate states*

★ *freed slaves in most Southern states*

In 1863, in the middle of the Civil War, President Abraham Lincoln issued the Emancipation Proclamation. The Emancipation Proclamation declared that slaves living in the southern or Confederate states were free. Many slaves joined the Union army. In 1865, the Civil War ended and the southern slaves kept their right to be free. The Emancipation Proclamation led to the 13th Amendment to the Constitution, which ended slavery in all of the United States.

77. **What did Susan B. Anthony do?**

★ *fought for women's rights*

★ *fought for civil rights*

Susan B. Anthony was born in Massachusetts on February 15, 1820. She is known for campaigning for the right of women to vote. She spoke out publicly against slavery and for equal treatment of women in the workplace. In 1920, the 19th Amendment to the Constitution gave women the right to vote. Susan B. Anthony died 14 years before the adoption of the 19th Amendment, but it was still widely known as the Susan B. Anthony Amendment. In 1979, she became the first woman whose image appeared on a circulating U.S. coin. The coin is called the Susan B. Anthony dollar and is worth one dollar.

C: Recent American History and Other Important Historical Information

78. **Name <u>one</u> war fought by the United States in the 1900s.***

★ *World War I*

★ *World War II*

★ *Korean War*

★ *Vietnam War*

★ *(Persian) Gulf War*

The United States fought five wars in the 1900s: World War I, World War II, the Korean War, the Vietnam War, and the (Persian) Gulf War.

20

*If you are 65 or older and have been a permanent resident of the United States for 20 or more years, you may study just the questions marked with an asterisk.

World War I began in 1914. It was a long and bloody struggle. The United States entered the war in 1917 after German submarines attacked British and U.S. ships, and the Germans contacted Mexico about starting a war against the United States. The war ended in 1918 when the Allied Powers (led by Britain, France, and the United States) defeated the Central Powers (led by Germany, Austria-Hungary, and the Ottoman Empire). The Treaty of Versailles officially ended the war in 1919. World War I was called "the war to end all wars."

World War II began in 1939 when Germany invaded Poland. France and Great Britain then declared war on Germany. Germany had alliances with Italy and Japan, and together they formed the Axis powers. The United States entered World War II in 1941, after the Japanese attacked Pearl Harbor, Hawaii. The United States joined France and Great Britain as the Allied powers and led the 1944 invasion of France known as D-Day. The liberation of Europe from German power was completed by May 1945. World War II did not end until Japan surrendered in August 1945.

The Korean War began in 1950 when the North Korean Army moved across the 38th parallel into South Korea. The 38th parallel was a boundary established after World War II. This boundary separated the northern area of Korea, which was under communist influence, from the southern area of Korea, which was allied with the United States. At the time, the United States was providing support to establish a democratic South Korean government. The United States provided military support to stop the advance of the North Korean Army. In the Korean conflict, democratic governments directly confronted communist governments. The fighting ended in 1953, with the establishment of the countries of North Korea and South Korea.

From 1959 to 1975, United States Armed Forces and the South Vietnamese Army fought against the North Vietnamese in the Vietnam War. The United States supported the democratic government in the south of the country to help it resist pressure from the communist north. The war ended in 1975 with the temporary separation of the country into communist North Vietnam and democratic South Vietnam. In 1976, Vietnam was under total communist control.

"Raising the Flag on Iwo Jima," photographed by Joe Rosenthal, Associated Press, 1945.
Courtesy of the National Archives, 80-G-413988.

Almost 60,000 American men and women in the military died or were missing as a result of the Vietnam War.

On August 2, 1990, the Persian Gulf War began when Iraq invaded Kuwait. This invasion put the Iraqi Army closer to Saudi Arabia and its oil reserves, which supplied much of the world with oil. The United States and many other countries wanted to drive the Iraqi Army out of Kuwait and prevent it from invading other nearby countries. In January 1991, the United States led an international coalition of forces authorized by the United Nations into battle against the Iraqi Army. Within a month, the coalition had driven the Iraqis from Kuwait. The coalition declared a cease-fire on February 28, 1991.

79. Who was President during World War I?

★ *(Woodrow) Wilson*

Woodrow Wilson was the 28th president of the United States. President Wilson served two terms from 1913 to 1921. During his first term, he was able to keep the United States out of World War I. By 1917, Wilson knew this was no longer possible, and he asked

21

476

LEARN ABOUT THE UNITED STATES

Congress to declare war on Germany. On January 8, 1918, he made a speech to Congress outlining "Fourteen Points" that justified the war and called for a plan to maintain peace after the war. President Wilson said, "We entered this war because violations of right had occurred which touched us to the quick and made the life of our own people impossible unless they were corrected and the world secure once for all against their recurrence." The war ended that year and Wilson traveled to Paris to work out the details of the surrender by Germany.

80. Who was President during the Great Depression and World War II?

★ *(Franklin) Roosevelt*

Franklin Delano Roosevelt (FDR) was president of the United States from 1933 until 1945. He was elected during the Great Depression, which was a period of economic crisis after the stock market crash of 1929. His program for handling the crisis was called "the New Deal." It included programs to create jobs and provided benefits and financial security for workers across the country. Under his leadership, the Social Security Administration (SSA) was established in 1935. Roosevelt led the nation into World War II after Japan's attack on Pearl Harbor in December 1941. He gave the country a sense of hope and strength during a time of great struggle. Roosevelt was elected to office four times. He died in 1945, early in his fourth term as president. His wife, Eleanor Roosevelt, was a human rights leader throughout her lifetime.

81. Who did the United States fight in World War II?

★ *Japan, Germany, and Italy*

The Japanese bombed U.S. naval bases in a surprise attack on Pearl Harbor, Hawaii, on December 7, 1941. The next day, President Franklin D. Roosevelt, as commander in chief of the military, obtained an official declaration of war from Congress. Japan's partners in the Axis, Italy and Germany, then declared war on the United States. The Allies fought against the German Nazis, the Italian Fascists, and Japan's military empire. This was truly a world war, with battles fought in Europe, Africa, Asia, and the Pacific Ocean.

82. Before he was President, Eisenhower was a general. What war was he in?

★ *World War II*

Before becoming the 34th president of the United States in 1953, Dwight D. Eisenhower served as a major general in World War II. As commander of U.S. forces and supreme commander of the Allies in Europe, he led the successful D-Day invasion of Normandy, France, on June 6, 1944. In 1952, he retired from active service in the military. He was elected president of the United States later that year. As president, he established the interstate highway system and in 1953, the Department of Health, Education, and Welfare (now known as Health and Human Services) was created. He oversaw the end of the Korean War. Eisenhower left the White House in 1961, after serving two terms as president.

83. During the Cold War, what was the main concern of the United States?

★ *Communism*

The main concern of the United States during the Cold War was the spread of communism. The Soviet Union (Union of Soviet Socialist Republics, or USSR) was a powerful nation that operated under the principles of communism. The United States and its allies believed that a democratic government and a capitalist economy were the best ways to preserve individual rights and freedoms. The United States and its allies feared the expansion of communism to countries outside the Soviet Union. The Cold War began shortly after the end of World War II and lasted for more than 40 years. It ended with the fall of the Berlin Wall in 1989, the reunification of East and West Germany in 1990, and the breakup of the USSR in 1991.

84. What movement tried to end racial discrimination?

★ *civil rights (movement)*

The modern civil rights movement in the United States began in 1954 when the Supreme Court ruled that racial segregation in public schools was unconstitutional. The goal of the civil rights movement was to end racial discrimination against

*If you are 65 or older and have been a permanent resident of the United States for 20 or more years, you may study just the questions marked with an asterisk.

African Americans and to gain full and equal rights for Americans of all races. Using nonviolent strategies such as bus boycotts, sit-ins, and marches, people came together to demand social change. As a result, Congress passed the Civil Rights Act of 1964 and the Voting Rights Act of 1965. The Civil Rights Act made segregation in public facilities and racial discrimination in employment and education illegal. The law protects African Americans, women, and others from discrimination. The Voting Rights Act banned literacy tests and other special requirements that had been used to stop African Americans from registering to vote.

85. What did Martin Luther King, Jr. do?*

★ **fought for civil rights**

★ **worked for equality for all Americans**

Martin Luther King, Jr. was a Baptist minister and civil rights leader. He worked hard to make America a more fair, tolerant, and equal nation. He was the main leader of the civil rights movement of the 1950s and 1960s. Because of this movement, civil rights laws were passed to protect voting rights and end racial segregation. King believed in the ideals of the Declaration of Independence—that every citizen deserves America's promise of equality and justice. In 1963, King delivered his famous "I Have a Dream" speech, which imagines an America in which people of all races exist together equally. He was only 35 years old when he received the Nobel Peace Prize in 1964 for his civil rights work. King was killed on April 4, 1968.

86. What major event happened on September 11, 2001, in the United States?

★ **Terrorists attacked the United States.**

On September 11, 2001, four airplanes flying out of U.S. airports were taken over by terrorists from the Al-Qaeda network of Islamic extremists. Two of the planes crashed into the World Trade Center's Twin Towers in New York City, destroying both buildings. One of the planes crashed into the Pentagon in Arlington, Virginia. The fourth plane, originally aimed at Washington, D.C., crashed in a field in Pennsylvania. Almost 3,000 people died in these attacks, most of them civilians. This was the worst attack on American soil in the history of the nation.

American Indian woman and her baby in 1899.
Courtesy of the Library of Congress, LC-USZ62-94927.

87. Name <u>one</u> American Indian tribe in the United States.

[USCIS Officers will be supplied with a list of federally recognized American Indian tribes.]

★ **Cherokee**	★ **Cheyenne**
★ **Navajo**	★ **Arawak**
★ **Sioux**	★ **Shawnee**
★ **Chippewa**	★ **Mohegan**
★ **Choctaw**	★ **Huron**
★ **Pueblo**	★ **Oneida**
★ **Apache**	★ **Lakota**
★ **Iroquois**	★ **Crow**
★ **Creek**	★ **Teton**
★ **Blackfeet**	★ **Hopi**
★ **Seminole**	★ **Inuit**

American Indians lived in North America for thousands of years before the European settlers arrived. Today there are more than 500 federally recognized tribes in the United States. Each tribe has its own social and political system. American Indian cultures are different from one tribe to another, with different languages, beliefs, stories, music, and foods. Earlier in their history, some tribes settled in villages and farmed the land for food. Other tribes moved frequently as they hunted and gathered food and resources. The federal government signed treaties with American Indian tribes to move the tribes to reservations. These reservations are recognized as domestic, dependent nations.

★★

23

478

★★★

INTEGRATED CIVICS

An understanding of America's geography, symbols, and holidays is important. They provide background and more meaning to historical events and other landmark moments in U.S. history. The following section offers short lessons on our country's geography, national symbols, and national holidays. The geography of the United States is unusual because of the size of the country and the fact that it is bordered by two oceans that create natural boundaries to the east and west. Through visual symbols such as our flag and the Statue of Liberty, the values and history of the United States are often expressed. Finally, you will also learn about our national holidays and why we celebrate them. Most of our holidays honor people who have contributed to our history and to the development of our nation. By learning this information, you will develop a deeper understanding of the United States and its geographical boundaries, principles, and freedoms.

★★★

A: Geography

88. Name <u>one</u> of the two longest rivers in the United States.

★ Missouri (River)

★ Mississippi (River)

The Mississippi River is one of America's longest rivers. It runs through 10 U.S. states. The Mississippi River was used by American Indians for trade, food, and water before Europeans came to America. It is nicknamed the "Father of Waters." Today, the Mississippi River is a major shipping route and a source of drinking water for millions of people. The Missouri River is also one of the longest rivers in the United States. The Missouri River is actually longer than the Mississippi River. It starts in Montana and flows into the Mississippi River. In 1673, the French explorers Jolliet and Marquette were the first Europeans to find the Missouri River. It is nicknamed "Big Muddy" because of its high silt content.

89. What ocean is on the West Coast of the United States?

★ Pacific (Ocean)

The Pacific Ocean is on the West Coast of the United States. It is the largest ocean on Earth and covers one-third of the Earth's surface. The Pacific Ocean is important to the U.S. economy because of its many natural resources such as fish. Europeans first learned about the Pacific Ocean in the 16th century. Spanish explorer Vasco Núñez de Balboa reached the ocean in 1514 when he crossed the Isthmus of Panama. Later, Ferdinand Magellan sailed across the Pacific as he traveled around the Earth in search of spices. "Pacific" means "peaceful." Magellan named the Pacific Ocean the "peaceful sea," because there were no storms on his trip from Spain to the spice world. The U.S. states that border the Pacific Ocean are Alaska, Washington, Oregon, California, and Hawaii.

90. What ocean is on the East Coast of the United States?

★ Atlantic (Ocean)

The Atlantic Ocean is on the East Coast of the United States. The ocean was named after the giant Atlas from Greek mythology. It is the second largest ocean in the world. The Atlantic Ocean is a major sea route for ships. It is one of the most frequently traveled oceans in the world. The Atlantic Ocean is also a source of many natural resources. The Atlantic Ocean was formed by the separation of the North American and European continents millions of years ago. The ocean covers about one-fifth of the Earth's surface. In the middle of the ocean is the Mid-Atlantic Ridge, an immense underwater mountain range that extends the length of the Atlantic and is a source of volcanic activity. The U.S. states that border the Atlantic Ocean are Connecticut, Delaware, Florida, Georgia, Maine, Maryland, Massachusetts, New Hampshire, New Jersey, New York, North Carolina, Rhode Island, South Carolina, and Virginia.

★★★

24   ***If you are 65 or older and have been a permanent resident of the United States for 20 or more years, you may study just the questions marked with an asterisk.**

91. Name <u>one</u> U.S. territory.

★ Puerto Rico

★ U.S. Virgin Islands

★ American Samoa

★ Northern Mariana Islands

★ Guam

There are five major U.S. territories: American Samoa, Guam, the Northern Mariana Islands, Puerto Rico, and the U.S. Virgin Islands. A U.S. territory is a partially self-governing piece of land under the authority of the U.S. government. U.S. territories are not states, but they do have representation in Congress. Each territory is allowed to send a delegate to the House of Representatives. The people who live in American Samoa are considered U.S. nationals; the people in the other four territories are U.S. citizens. Citizens of the territories can vote in primary elections for president, but they cannot vote in the general elections for president.

92. Name <u>one</u> state that borders Canada.

★ Maine	★ Minnesota
★ New Hampshire	★ North Dakota
★ Vermont	★ Montana
★ New York	★ Idaho
★ Pennsylvania	★ Washington
★ Ohio	★ Alaska
★ Michigan	

The northern border of the United States stretches more than 5,000 miles from Maine in the East to Alaska in the West. There are 13 states on the border with Canada. The Treaty of Paris of 1783 established the official boundary between Canada and the United States after the Revolutionary War. Since that time, there have been land disputes, but they have been resolved through treaties. The International Boundary Commission, which is headed by two commissioners, one American and one Canadian, is responsible for maintaining the boundary.

Old Spanish Bridge in Umatac, Guam.
Courtesy of the Office of U.S. Representative Madeleine Z. Bordallo.

93. Name <u>one</u> state that borders Mexico.

★ California

★ Arizona

★ New Mexico

★ Texas

The border between the United States and Mexico is about 1,900 miles long and spans four U.S. states—Arizona, California, New Mexico, and Texas. The United States established the border with Mexico after the Mexican-American War and the Gadsden Purchase in 1853. The Gadsden Purchase helped the United States get the land it needed to expand the southern railroad. The United States bought this land for $10 million. The land bought through the Gadsden Purchase is now part of the states of Arizona and New Mexico. The U.S. border with Mexico is one of the busiest international borders in the world.

94. What is the capital of the United States?*

★ Washington, D.C.

When the Constitution established our nation in 1789, the capital of the United States was in New York City. Congress soon began discussing the location of a permanent capital city. In Congress, representatives of northern states argued with representatives of southern states. Each side wanted the capital to be in its own region. As part of the Compromise of 1790, the capital would be located in the South. In return, the North did not have to pay the debt it owed from the Revolutionary War. George Washington chose a location for the capital along the Potomac River between Maryland and Virginia. As part of the compromise, Philadelphia, Pennsylvania, became the temporary new location for the capital. In 1800, after 10 years, the capital was moved to its current location of Washington, D.C.

95. Where is the Statue of Liberty?*
- ★ New York (Harbor)
- ★ Liberty Island

[Also acceptable are New Jersey, near New York City, and on the Hudson (River).]

The Statue of Liberty is on Liberty Island, a 12-acre island in the New York harbor. France gave the statue to the United States as a gift of friendship. French artist Frederic-Auguste Bartholdi made the statue. It shows a woman escaping the chains of tyranny and holding a torch symbolizing liberty. The Statue of Liberty was dedicated on October 28, 1886, 110 years after the signing of the Declaration of Independence. President Grover Cleveland accepted the gift for the American people. The Statue of Liberty is a well-known symbol of the United States and of freedom and democracy. The Statue of Liberty became a symbol of immigration because it was located next to Ellis Island, which was the first entry point for many immigrants during the great waves of immigration. The Statue of Liberty was the first thing new immigrants saw as they approached New York harbor.

B: Symbols

96. Why does the flag have 13 stripes?
- ★ because there were 13 original colonies
- ★ because the stripes represent the original colonies

There are 13 stripes on the flag because there were 13 original colonies. We call the American flag "the Stars and Stripes." For 18 years after the United States became an independent country, the flag had only 13 stripes. In 1794, Kentucky and Vermont joined the United States, and two stripes were added to the flag. In 1818, Congress decided that the number of stripes on the flag should always be 13. This would honor the original states that were colonies of Great Britain before America's independence.

97. Why does the flag have 50 stars?*
- ★ because there is one star for each state
- ★ because each star represents a state
- ★ because there are 50 states

Each star on the flag represents a state. This is why the number of stars has changed over the years from 13 to 50. The number of stars reached 50 in 1959, when Hawaii joined the United States as the 50th state. In 1777, the Second Continental Congress passed the first Flag Act, stating, "Resolved, That the flag of the United States be made of thirteen stripes, alternate red and white; that the union be thirteen stars, white in a blue field, representing a new Constellation."

98. What is the name of the national anthem?
- ★ The Star-Spangled Banner

During the War of 1812, British soldiers invaded the United States. On the night of September 13, 1814, British warships bombed Fort McHenry. This fort protected the city of Baltimore, Maryland. An American named Francis Scott Key watched the bombing and thought that the fort would fall. As the sun rose the next morning, Key looked toward the fort. He saw that the flag above the fort was still flying. This let him know that the British had not defeated the Americans. Key immediately wrote the words to a poem he called the "Defence of Fort M'Henry." The words of the poem became "The Star-Spangled Banner." Congress passed a law in 1931 naming "The Star-Spangled Banner" the official national anthem. Here are the words to the first verse of the national anthem:

The Star-Spangled Banner

Oh, say, can you see, by the dawn's early light,

What so proudly we hailed at the twilight's last gleaming?

Whose broad stripes and bright stars, thro' the perilous fight;

O'er the ramparts we watched, were so gallantly streaming.

And the rockets red glare, the bombs bursting in air,

Gave proof through the night that our flag was still there.

Oh, say, does that star-spangled banner yet wave

O'er the land of the free and the home of the brave?

C: Holidays

99. When do we celebrate Independence Day?*

★ July 4

In the United States, we celebrate Independence Day on July 4 to mark the anniversary of the adoption of the Declaration of Independence. After signing the Declaration of Independence, John Adams wrote to his wife, "I am apt to believe that it will be celebrated, by succeeding Generations, as the great anniversary Festival." The Declaration of Independence, written by Thomas Jefferson, explained why the colonies had decided to separate from Great Britain. Americans celebrate the Fourth of July as the birthday of America, with parades, fireworks, patriotic songs, and readings of the Declaration of Independence.

In "The Star-Spangled Banner," by Percy Moran, Francis Scott Key reaches toward the flag flying over Fort McHenry.
Courtesy of the Library of Congress, LC-USZC4-6200.

100.   Name <u>two</u> national U.S. holidays.

★ New Year's Day

★ Martin Luther King, Jr. Day

★ Presidents' Day

★ Memorial Day

★ Independence Day

★ Labor Day

★ Columbus Day

★ Veterans Day

★ Thanksgiving

★ Christmas

Many Americans celebrate national or federal holidays. These holidays often honor people or events in our American heritage. These holidays are "national" in a legal sense only for federal institutions and in the District of Columbia. Typically, federal offices are closed on these holidays. Each state can decide whether or not to celebrate the holiday. Businesses, schools, and commercial establishments may choose whether or not to close on these days. Since 1971, federal holidays are observed on Mondays except for New Year's Day, Independence Day, Veterans Day, Thanksgiving, and Christmas.

★★

27

English Test

There are three components of the English test: speaking, reading, and writing. According to the law, an applicant must demonstrate: *"an understanding of the English language, including an ability to read, write, and speak...simple words and phrases...in ordinary usage in the English language...."* This means that to be eligible for naturalization, you must be able to read, write, and speak basic English.

You are required to pass each of the three components of the English test with the exception of applicants who qualify as: 50 years of age or older AND a permanent resident for at least 20 years at the time of filing the *Application for Naturalization, Form N-400*; 55 years of age or older AND a permanent resident for at least 15 years at the time of filing the *Application for Naturalization, Form N-400*; or, any person who is unable to demonstrate an understanding of English because of a medically determinable physical and/or medical impairment as determined by an approved *Medical Certification for Disability Exceptions, Form N-648*.

Speaking Portion

Your ability to speak English will be determined by the USCIS Officer from your answers to questions normally asked during the eligibility interview on the *Application for Naturalization, Form N-400*.

Reading Portion

Each reading test administered to you will contain no more than three (3) sentences. You must read one (1) out of three (3) sentences correctly to demonstrate an ability to read in English. To help you prepare, USCIS released a reading vocabulary list found below containing all the words found in the English reading portion of the naturalization test. The content focuses on civics and history topics.

PEOPLE
- ★ Abraham Lincoln
- ★ George Washington

CIVICS
- ★ American flag
- ★ Bill of Rights
- ★ capital
- ★ citizen
- ★ city
- ★ Congress
- ★ country
- ★ Father of Our Country
- ★ government
- ★ President
- ★ right
- ★ Senators
- ★ state/states
- ★ White House

PLACES
- ★ America
- ★ United States
- ★ U.S.

HOLIDAYS
- ★ Presidents' Day
- ★ Memorial Day
- ★ Flag Day
- ★ Independence Day
- ★ Labor Day
- ★ Columbus Day
- ★ Thanksgiving

QUESTION WORDS
- ★ How
- ★ What
- ★ When
- ★ Where
- ★ Who
- ★ Why

VERBS
- ★ can
- ★ come
- ★ do/does
- ★ elects
- ★ have/has
- ★ is/are/was/be
- ★ lives/lived
- ★ meet
- ★ name
- ★ pay
- ★ vote
- ★ want

OTHER (FUNCTION)
- ★ a
- ★ for
- ★ here
- ★ in
- ★ of
- ★ on
- ★ the
- ★ to
- ★ we

OTHER (CONTENT)
- ★ colors
- ★ dollar bill
- ★ first
- ★ largest
- ★ many
- ★ most
- ★ north
- ★ one
- ★ people
- ★ second
- ★ south

★★

ENGLISH TEST

Writing Portion

Each writing test administered to you will contain no more than three (3) sentences. You must write one (1) out of three (3) sentences correctly in order to demonstrate an ability to write in English. To help you prepare, USCIS released a writing vocabulary list found below containing all the words found in the English writing portion of the naturalization test. The content focuses on civics and history topics.

PEOPLE
- ★ Adams
- ★ Lincoln
- ★ Washington

CIVICS
- ★ American Indians
- ★ capital
- ★ citizens
- ★ Civil War
- ★ Congress
- ★ Father of Our Country
- ★ flag
- ★ free
- ★ freedom of speech
- ★ President
- ★ right
- ★ Senators
- ★ state/states
- ★ White House

PLACES
- ★ Alaska
- ★ California
- ★ Canada
- ★ Delaware
- ★ Mexico
- ★ New York City
- ★ United States
- ★ Washington
- ★ Washington, D.C.

MONTHS
- ★ February
- ★ May
- ★ June
- ★ July
- ★ September
- ★ October
- ★ November

HOLIDAYS
- ★ Presidents' Day
- ★ Memorial Day
- ★ Flag Day
- ★ Independence Day
- ★ Labor Day
- ★ Columbus Day
- ★ Thanksgiving

VERBS
- ★ can
- ★ come
- ★ elect
- ★ have/has
- ★ is/was/be
- ★ lives/lived
- ★ meets
- ★ pay
- ★ vote
- ★ want

OTHER (FUNCTION)
- ★ and
- ★ during
- ★ for
- ★ here
- ★ in
- ★ of
- ★ on
- ★ the
- ★ to
- ★ we

OTHER (CONTENT)
- ★ blue
- ★ dollar bill
- ★ fifty/50
- ★ first
- ★ largest
- ★ most
- ★ north
- ★ one
- ★ one hundred/100
- ★ people
- ★ red
- ★ second
- ★ south
- ★ taxes
- ★ white

To find this and other educational materials for permanent residents, please visit www.uscis.gov/citizenship.

For more information on the U.S. naturalization test, please visit www.uscis.gov/citizenshiptest.

Note: Some of the content in this publication may change due to elections and appointments. U.S. Citizenship and Immigration Services (USCIS) will make every effort to update this publication in a timely manner. As of July 2011, all information in this publication is current.

★★★

29

U.S. Government Official Edition Notice

Use of ISBN

This is the Official U.S. Government edition of this publication and is herein identified to certify its authenticity. Use of the ISBN 978-0-16-087265-5 is for U.S. Government Printing Office Official Editions only. The Superintendent of Documents of the U.S. Government Printing Office requests that any reprinted edition clearly be labeled as a copy of the authentic work with a new ISBN.

The information presented in *Learn About the United States: Quick Civics Lessons for the Naturalization Test* is considered public information and may be distributed or copied without alteration unless otherwise specified. The citation should be:

U.S. Department of Homeland Security, U.S. Citizenship and Immigration Services, Office of Citizenship, *Learn About the United States: Quick Civics Lessons for the Naturalization Test*, Washington, DC, 2011.

U.S. Citizenship and Immigration Services (USCIS) has purchased the right to use many of the images in *Learn About the United States: Quick Civics Lessons for the Naturalization Test*. USCIS is licensed to use these images on a non-exclusive and non-transferable basis. All other rights to the images, including without limitation and copyright, are retained by the owner of the images. These images are not in the public domain and may not be used except as they appear as part of this publication.

For sale by the Superintendent of Documents, U.S. Government Printing Office
Internet: bookstore.gpo.gov Phone: toll free (866) 512-1800; DC area (202) 512-1800
Fax: (202) 512-2104 Mail: Stop IDCC, Washington, DC 20402-0001

ISBN 978-0-16-087265-5

An audio CD of the 100 civics (history and government) questions and answers for the naturalization test accompanies this booklet. Use this CD as you prepare for the civics portion of the naturalization test. After you become familiar with the content, shuffle or randomly play the questions in your CD player or computer to help test your knowledge.

The audio CD has 99 individual tracks. Questions 1-98 are included consecutively in tracks 1-98 and track 99 contains the questions and answers for both question 99 and 100.

U.S. Citizenship and Immigration Services would like to acknowledge the National Endowment for the Humanities for their assistance in the development of this product. For more information on the Endowment, please visit www.neh.gov.

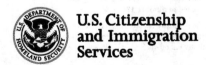

U.S. Citizenship
and Immigration
Services

www.uscis.gov

ISBN 978-0-16-087265-5

90000

9 780160 872655

APPENDIX 7-9

Form N-648

OMB No. 1615-0060; Expires 12/31/2014

Department of Homeland Security
U.S. Citizenship and Immigration Services

Instructions for Form N-648, Medical Certification for Disability Exceptions

What Is the Purpose of This Form?

In general, applicants for naturalization must demonstrate an understanding of the English language, including an ability to read, write, and speak words in ordinary usage. They must also demonstrate a knowledge and understanding of the fundamentals of the history and principles and form of government of the United States. Together, these are known as the English and civics requirements for naturalization. This form is intended for applicants who seek an exception to the English and/or civics requirements due to a physical or developmental disability or mental impairment that has lasted, or is expected to last, 12 months or more.

Who Should Submit This Form and When?

An applicant for naturalization seeking an exception to the English and/or civics requirements for naturalization because of a physical or developmental disability or mental impairment(s) should submit this form at the time he or she files an N-400, Application for Naturalization, with USCIS. Per Immigration and Nationality Act (INA) 312(b)(1), applicants are not required to fulfill the English **and/or** civics requirements if the person is unable to do so because of physical or developmental disability or mental impairment(s).

NOTE: Failure to submit Form N-648 with Form N-400 may delay the time for the adjudication of Form N-400.

Who Should Not Submit This Form?

An applicant who can satisfy the English and civics requirements for naturalization with reasonable accommodations provided under the Rehabilitation Act of 1973 does not need to submit this form. Reasonable accommodations include, but are not limited to, sign language interpreters, extended time for testing and off-site testing. An applicant requesting an accommodation should so indicate on Part 3 of his or her completed Form N-400. Illiteracy alone is not a valid reason to seek an exception to the English and civics requirement by submitting this form.

Who Is Authorized to Certify This Form?

Only medical doctors, doctors of osteopathy, or clinical psychologists licensed to practice in the United States (including the U.S. territories of CNMI, Guam, Puerto Rico, and the Virgin Islands) are authorized to certify the form. While staff of the medical practice associated with the medical professional certifying the form may assist in its completion, the medical professional is responsible for the accuracy of the form's content.

How to Complete This Form?

All parts of Form N-648 except the "Applicant Attestation" and "INTERPRETER'S CERTIFICATION", must be certified by a licensed medical professional. Before certifying Form N-648, the medical professional must have conducted an in-person examination of the applicant.

All questions or items must be answered fully and accurately. USCIS will not accept an incomplete Form N-648. Responses should use common terminology, without abbreviations, that a person without medical training can understand. If completed in writing, all responses must be legible and appear in blue or black ink. USCIS recommends that the certifying medical professional use the electronic Form N-648 located in the "FORMS" section at **www.uscis.gov.**

Failure to provide all information requested on the form may result in USCIS determination that the form is insufficient. In addition to providing a detailed assessment of the applicant's physical or developmental disability or mental impairment as requested on the form, a medical professional completing the form may attach supporting medical diagnostic reports or records. However, these attachments may not take the place of written responses to each question or item on Form N-648.

The following are examples of sufficient responses to some of the items on **Part III** of Form N-648:

1. **Provide the clinical diagnosis and DSM IV code (if applicable) of the applicant's disability and/or impairment(s) that form the basis for seeking an exception to the English and/or civics requirements. If you cannot provide a DSM IV code, write "N/A" and explain why you cannot provide a DSM IV code.**

   "DSM-IV 318.0 Down syndrome."

2. **Provide a basic description of the disability and/or impairment(s).**

   "Down syndrome is a genetic disorder that causes lifelong intellectual disability (also referred to as mental retardation), developmental delays, and other problems."

8. **What caused the applicant's medical disability and/or impairment(s) listed in number 1?**

   "Down syndrome is usually caused by an error in cell division occurring *in utero.* The cause of such errors in cell division is currently unknown."

9. **What clinical methods did you use to diagnose the applicant's medical disability and/or impairment(s) listed in number 1?**

"The patient was diagnosed *in utero* through a Chorionic Villus Sampling (CVS). CVS is a test done during early pregnancy that can identify certain genetic disorders or chromosomal birth defects, such as Down syndrome."

10. **Clearly describe how the applicant's disability and/or impairment(s), affect his or her ability to demonstrate a knowledge and understanding of English and/or civics.**

"The patient's condition is a global, lifelong impairment that severely affects cognition, language, and motor skills. While many individuals with mild to moderate forms of Down syndrome are capable of daily tasks and working in the community, this patient suffers from a particularly severe form. Because of this impairment, his memory is deficient, he cannot learn new skills, and he is not capable of reasoning but only of performing simple daily activities. The patient's severe intellectual disability (mental retardation) makes him incapable of learning a new language (even basic words) and demonstrating the required knowledge of U.S. history and government."

What Are the Penalties for Making False Representations?

Both the applicant and the medical professional are required to attest to the contents of this form **under penalty of perjury**. Title 18, United States Code, Section 1546, provides that:

Whoever knowingly makes under oath, or as permitted under penalty of perjury under Section 1746 of Title 28, United States Code, knowingly subscribes as true, any false statement with respect to a material fact in any application, affidavit, or other document required by the immigration laws or regulations prescribed thereunder, or knowingly presents any such application, affidavit, or other document containing any such false statement, shall be fined in accordance with this title or imprisoned not more than 10 years, or both.

If either the applicant or the medical professional includes in this form any information that the party knows to be false, that person may be liable for criminal prosecution under U.S. laws. In addition to the criminal penalties under Title 18 of the United States Code, Section 274C of the Immigration and Nationality Act and 8 U.S.C. 1324c provides for civil penalties.

General Instructions

USCIS recommends that the certifying medical professional complete and print the fillable electronic Form N-648 located in the "FORMS" section at www.uscis.gov.

1. Type or print clearly using black ink. Keep all information within the area provided. If you require additional space to complete the answer to any item, the information fields in the fillable electronic form will expand to accommodate the additional information. If you are not completing an electronic version of the form and you continue to need extra space to complete any item, write the applicant's name and Alien Registration Number (A-Number) at the top of each continuation sheet and indicate the part and number of the item to which the answer refers. You must sign and date each continuation sheet.

2. All questions must be answered fully and accurately. If an item is not applicable, indicate it with "N/A." If the answer is none, write "None."

3. The medical professional must provide the completed form to the applicant.

Privacy Act Notice

Authority for the collection of the information requested on this form is contained in 8 U.S.C. 1103, 1423, and 1427. USCIS will use the information principally to support an individual's application for naturalization. Submission of the information is voluntary. However, failure to provide the necessary information may result in the denial of a request for a waiver of the English language and U.S. history and civic requirements for naturalization. USCIS may also, as a matter of routine use, set forth in USCIS System of Records Notices published in the Federal Register, disclose the information collected on this form, to other Federal, State, local, and foreign law enforcement and regulatory agencies.

USCIS Forms and Information

You can get USCIS forms and immigration-related information on the USCIS Internet Web site at **www.uscis.gov.** You may order USCIS forms by calling our toll-free number at **1-800-870-3676.** You may also obtain forms and information by telephoning our National Customer Service Center at **1-800-375-5283.**

As an alternative to waiting in line for assistance at your local USCIS office, you can now schedule an appointment through our Internet-based system, **InfoPass.** To access the system, visit our Web site. Use the **InfoPass** appointment scheduler and follow the screen prompts to set up your appointment. **InfoPass** generates an electronic appointment notice that appears on the screen.

Paperwork Reduction Act

An agency may not conduct or sponsor an information collection and a person is not required to respond to a collection of information unless it displays a currently valid OMB control number. The public reporting burden for this collection of information is estimated at 120 minutes per response, including the time for reviewing instructions and completing and submitting the form. Send comments regarding this burden estimate or any other aspect of this collection of information, including suggestions for reducing this burden, to: U.S. Citizenship and Immigration Services, Regulatory Coordination Division, Office of Policy and Strategy, 20 Massachusetts Ave NW, Washington, DC 20529-2140. OMB No. 1615-0060. **Do not mail your completed Form N-648 to this address.**

OMB No. 1615-0060; Expires 12/31/2014

Form N-648, Medical Certification for Disability Exceptions

Department of Homeland Security
U.S. Citizenship and Immigration Services

ALL parts of this form, except the "APPLICANT ATTESTATION" and "INTERPRETER'S CERTIFICATION" must be certified by a licensed medical professional as provided in the instructions for Form N-648. Before certifying this form, the medical professional must conduct an in-person examination of the applicant. (See instructions for Form N-648 for additional information which is also located in the "FORMS" section at www.uscis.gov.)

Reminder About Eligibility Requirements

This form is intended for an applicant who seeks an exception to the English and/or civics requirements due to a physical or developmental disability or mental impairment that has lasted, or is expected to last, 12 months or more. An applicant who with reasonable accommodations provided under the Rehabilitation Act of 1973 can satisfy the English and civics requirements does not need to submit this form. Reasonable accommodations include, but are not limited to, sign language interpreters, extended time for testing, and off-site testing.

Completing and Certifying This Form

All questions or items must be answered fully and accurately. Responses should utilize common terminology, without abbreviations, that a person without medical training can understand. U.S. Citizenship and Immigration Services (USCIS) recommends that the certifying medical professional use the electronic Form N-648 located in the "FORMS" section www.uscis.gov. If the medical professional completes the form by hand, then responses must be legible and appear in black ink.

Type or print clearly in black ink.

Part I. APPLICANT INFORMATION				USCIS USE ONLY
I certify that I have examined:				This N-648 is:
Last Name	First Name	Middle Name	USCIS A-Number A-	☐ Sufficient ☐ Insufficient ☐ Continued/RFE
Address (Street Number and Name)			U.S. Social Security Number	Reviewer
City		State or Province	Zip Code or Postal Code	Location & Date
Telephone Number	E-Mail Address (if any)	Date of Birth	Gender ☐ Male ☐ Female	

Part II. MEDICAL PROFESSIONAL INFORMATION

Type or print clearly in black ink. If you need more space to complete an answer, use a separate sheet of paper. Write the applicant's name and Alien Registration Number (A-Number), at the top of each sheet of paper and indicate the part and number of the item to which the answer refers. You must sign and date each continuation sheet. You must answer and complete each question since USCIS will not accept an incomplete Form N-648. You may, but are not required to, attach to this completed form supportive medical diagnostic reports or records regarding the applicant.

NOTE: Only medical doctors, doctors of osteopathy, or clinical psychologists licensed to practice in the United States (including the U.S. territories of Guam, Puerto Rico, and the Virgin Islands) are authorized to certify the form. While staff of the medical practice associated with the medical professional certifying the form may assist in its completion, the medical professional is responsible for the accuracy of the form's content.

Last Name	First Name		Middle Name		
Business Address (Street Number and Name)	City	State or Province	Zip Code or Postal Code	Telephone Number
License Number	Licensing State	E-Mail Address (if any)		

1. Currently licensed as a *(Check all that apply):*   ☐ Medical Doctor   ☐ Doctor of Osteopathy   ☐ Clinical Psychologist

2. Medical practice type: _____

Applicant's Name	USCIS A-Number A-

Part III. INFORMATION ABOUT DISABILITY and/or IMPAIRMENT(S)

1. Provide the clinical diagnosis and DSM IV code (*if applicable*) of the applicant's disability and/or impairment(s) that form the basis for seeking an exception to the English and/or civics requirements; e.g., *"DSM-IV 318.0 Down syndrome"*. If you cannot provide a DSM IV code, write "N/A" and explain why you cannot provide a DSM IV code.

_____
_____
_____
_____
_____
_____
_____
_____
_____
_____
_____
_____

2. Provide a basic description of the disability and/or impairment(s), e.g., "Down syndrome is a genetic disorder that causes lifelong intellectual disability (also referred to as mental retardation), developmental delays, and other problems."

_____
_____
_____
_____
_____
_____
_____
_____
_____
_____
_____
_____
_____
_____

3. Date you first examined the applicant regarding the condition(s) listed in number 1.

Date *(mm/dd/yyyy)*	Location (if different from business address on Page 1; otherwise write "same as business address")

4. Date you last examined the applicant regarding the condition(s) listed in number 1, if different from above.

Date *(mm/dd/yyyy)*	Location (if different from business address on Page 1; otherwise write "same as business address")

5. Are you the medical professional regularly treating this applicant for the condition(s) listed in Item Number 1?

☐ Yes *(If "Yes," indicate duration of treatment.)*   Years _____   Months _____

☐ No *(If "No," provide the name of the applicant's regularly treating medical professional on the next page and explain why you are certifying this form instead of the regularly treating medical professional.)*

Applicant's Name	USCIS A-Number A-

Name of Regularly Treating Medical Professional and Address.

Last Name	First Name	Middle Name		
Business Address (Street Number and Name)	City	State or Province	Zip Code or Postal Code	Telephone Number

Explanation

_____
_____
_____
_____
_____
_____
_____
_____
_____
_____
_____

6. **Has the applicant's disability and/or impairment(s) lasted, or do you expect it to last, 12 months or more?**

   ☐ Yes *(If "Yes,"continue to complete this form.)*

   ☐ No *(If "No," the applicant is not eligible for this exception and you need not complete the remainder of the questions. Please go directly to the "Medical Professional's Certification.")*

7. **Is the applicant's disability and/or impairment(s) the result of the applicant's illegal use of drugs?**

   ☐ Yes *(If "Yes," the applicant is not eligible for this exception and you need not complete the remainder of the questions. Please go directly to the "Medical Professional's Certification.")*

   ☐ No *(If "No," continue to complete this form.)*

8. **What caused this applicant's medical disability and/or impairment(s) listed in number 1, if known?**

_____
_____
_____
_____
_____
_____
_____
_____
_____
_____
_____

Applicant's Name	USCIS A-Number **A-**

9. What clinical methods did you use to diagnose the applicant's medical disability and/or impairment(s) listed in number 1?

_____
_____
_____
_____
_____
_____
_____
_____
_____
_____
_____
_____
_____

10. Clearly describe how the applicant's disability and/or impairment(s) affect his or her ability to demonstrate knowledge and understanding of English and/or civics.

_____
_____
_____
_____
_____
_____
_____
_____
_____
_____
_____
_____
_____
_____

11. In your professional medical opinion, does the applicant's disability or impairment(s) prevent him or her from demonstrating the following requirements? *(Check all that apply. If none applies, the applicant is not eligible for this exception.)*

The ability to:

☐ Read English

☐ Write English

☐ Speak English

☐ Answer questions regarding United States history and civics, even in a language the applicant understands.

Applicant's Name	USCIS A-Number
	A-

12. Was an interpreter used during your examination of the applicant?

☐ Yes *(If "Yes," the interpreter must complete the "Interpreter Certification" section.)*

☐ No

Additional Comments *(Optional)*

_____
_____
_____
_____
_____
_____
_____
_____
_____
_____
_____
_____
_____
_____
_____
_____

MEDICAL PROFESSIONAL' S CERTIFICATION

Complete the following if an interpreter was not used during your examination of the applicant between the applicant and medical professional pertaining to the examination(s) that form the basis of this Form N-648 certification.

I am fluent in English and _____ , the language spoken by this patient. Therefore, an interpreter was not used during my examination(s) of this applicant.

All medical professionals **must** complete the certification below.

I certify that this applicant's identity has been verified through the following United States or State government-issued photographic identity document:

☐ Permanent Resident Card   ☐ State ID Number: _____

☐ Other Identification (State type and ID Number): _____

I certify, under penalty of perjury under the laws of the United States of America, that the information on this form and any evidence submitted with it are all true and correct. I will furnish relevant medical records to USCIS, if requested to do so by USCIS, based on the applicant's consent. I am aware that the knowing placement of false information on Form N-648 and related documents may also subject me to criminal penalties including under Title 18, U.S.C. Section 1546, civil penalties under Title 18, U.S.C. Section 247c of the Immigration and Nationality Act, and civil license suspension or revocation by the appropriate authorities.

Licensed Medical Professional Signature   **Date** *(mm/dd/yyyy)*

_____   _____

Applicant's Name	USCIS A-Number **A-**

INTERPRETER'S CERTIFICATION

An interpreter must complete, and certify, the section below if an interpreter translated communications between the applicant and medical professional on the day of the examination that formed the basis of this Form N-648 certification.

Interpreter Information

Last Name	First Name	Middle Name

Address (Street Number and Name)	City	State or Province	Zip Code or Postal Code

Was a phone interpreter used?

☐ Yes *(If yes, the interpreter is not required to complete the information below.)*

☐ No *(If no, the interpreter is required to complete the information below.)*

Interpreter Certification

I am fluent As the interpreter, I certify that I am fluent in English and the following language: _____ .
I further certify that I have accurately and completely translated all communications between the medical professional and the applicant that

occurred on _____ , the date(s) of the examination(s) that form the basis of this certification.

Interpreter Signature   **Date** *(mm/dd/yyyy)*

_____

APPLICANT (PATIENT) ATTESTATION/RELEASE OF INFORMATION

I, _____ , authorize _____
　　　　　　　(Applicant's Name)　　　　　　　　　　　(Licensed medical doctor, doctor of osteopathy, or clinical psychologist)

to release to U.S. Citizenship and Immigration Services all relevant physical and mental health information related to my medical status for the purpose of applying for an exception from the English language and U.S. civics requirements for naturalization. I certify under penalty of perjury, pursuant to Title 28, U.S.C. Section 1746, that the information I provided to the medical professional is true and correct. I am aware that the knowing placement of false information on Form N-648 and related documents may also subject me to civil penalties under Title 8, U.S.C. Section 1324c. I understand that if this form is not completely filled out or if I fail to submit any required documentation, I may not be found eligible for the requested disability exception.

Applicant or Applicant's Authorized Representative Signature   **Date** *(mm/dd/yyyy)*

_____

APPENDIX 7-10

25 Questions for Elderly Applicants

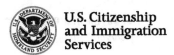

U.S. Citizenship and Immigration Services

Civics Questions for the 65/20 Exemption

The Immigration and Nationality Act provides for special consideration of the civics test for applicants who, at the time of filing their Form N-400, Application for Naturalization, are over 65 years old and have been a permanent resident for at least 20 years. These applicants qualify to take the civics test in the language of their choice. They are also given special consideration as they are only required to study 20 of the 100 civics test questions for the naturalization test.

1. **What is <u>one</u> right or freedom from the First Amendment?***
   - *speech*
   - *religion*
   - *assembly*
   - *press*
   - *petition the government*

2. **What is the economic system in the United States?***
   - *capitalist economy*
   - *market economy*

3. **Name <u>one</u> branch or part of the government.***
   - *Congress*
   - *legislative*
   - *President*
   - *executive*
   - *the courts*
   - *judicial*

4. **What are the <u>two</u> parts of the U.S. Congress?***
   - *the Senate and House (of Representatives)*

5. **Who is <u>one</u> of your state's U.S. Senators now?***
   - *Answers will vary. [District of Columbia residents and residents of U.S. territories should answer that D.C. (or the territory where the applicant lives) has no U.S. Senators.]*

6. **In what month do we vote for President?***
   - *November*

7. **What is the name of the President of the United States now?***
   - *Barack Obama*
   - *Obama*

8. **What is the capital of your state?***
   - *Answers will vary. [District of Columbia residents should answer that D.C. is not a state and does not have a capital. Residents of U.S. territories should name the capital of the territory.]*

9. **What are the <u>two</u> major political parties in the United States?***
   - *Democratic and Republican*

10. **What is <u>one</u> responsibility that is only for United States citizens?***
   - *serve on a jury*
   - *vote in a federal election*

11. **How old do citizens have to be to vote for President?***
   - *eighteen (18) and older*

12. **When is the last day you can send in federal income tax forms?***
   - *April 15*

13. **Who was the first President?***
   - *(George) Washington*

14. **What was <u>one</u> important thing that Abraham Lincoln did?***
   - *freed the slaves (Emancipation Proclamation)*
   - *saved (or preserved) the Union*
   - *led the United States during the Civil War*

15. **Name <u>one</u> war fought by the United States in the 1900s.***
   - *World War I*
   - *World War II*
   - *Korean War*
   - *Vietnam War*
   - *(Persian) Gulf War*

16. **What did Martin Luther King, Jr. do?***
   - *fought for civil rights*
   - *worked for equality for all Americans*

17. **What is the capital of the United States?***
   - *Washington, D.C.*

18. **Where is the Statue of Liberty?***
   - *New York (Harbor)*
   - *Liberty Island*
   [Also acceptable are New Jersey, near New York City, and on the Hudson (River).]

19. **Why does the flag have 50 stars?***
   - *because there is one star for each state*
   - *because each star represents a state*
   - *because there are 50 states*

20. **When do we celebrate Independence Day?***
   - *July 4*

(rev. 05/12)

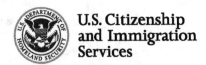

公民測試問題的65/20豁免

『美國移民和國籍法案』規定給予那些在填寫入籍申請表格N-400時年齡在65歲以上，並已成為永久居民至少20年的申請人在公民測試時特殊考慮。這些申請人有資格用自己選擇的語言進行公民測試。同時他們會獲得只需 要學習100題中20道題目的特別優待。

1. 列舉憲法第一條修正案中的一項權利或自由。*
   - *言論自由*
   - *宗教自由*
   - *集會結社的自由*
   - *出版自由*
   - *向政府請願的自由*

2. 美國的經濟制度是什麼？*
   - *資本主義經濟*
   - *市場經濟*

3. 列舉政府體制的一個分支或部門。*
   - *國會*
   - *立法部門*
   - *總統*
   - *行政部門*
   - *法院*
   - *司法部門*

4. 美國國會由哪兩個部分組成？*
   - *參議院與眾議院*

5. 您所在州的現任一位美國參議員的名字是什麼？*
   - *答案依所在州不同而異。[住在哥倫比亞特區和美國領土的居民可答:哥倫比亞特區當地（ 或應試居民所在領地）沒有美國參議員。]*

6. 我們在哪一個月選總統？*
   - *十一月*

7. 現任美國總統的名字是什麼？*
   - *Barack Obama*
   - *Obama*

8. 您居住州的首府是哪裡？*
   - *答案依居住州不同而異。[哥倫比亞特區居民應回答哥倫比亞特區不是一個州，沒有首府。美國領地居民應回答居住領地的首府。]*

9. 美國當今兩大政黨為何？*
   - *民主黨與共和黨*

10. 列舉一項美國公民才有的責任？*
    - *當陪審員*
    - *在聯邦選舉中投票*

11. 美國公民必須幾歲才能投票選舉總統？*
    - *十八 (18) 歲以上*

12. 寄送聯邦所得稅表的截止日期是哪一天？*
    - *（每年的）4 月 15 日*

13. 誰是第一任總統？*
    - *（喬治）華盛頓*

14. 亞伯拉罕·林肯的一項重要事蹟是什麼？*
    - *解放奴隸（《解放宣言》）*
    - *拯救（保留）聯盟*
    - *在內戰期間引領美國*

15. 列舉一場美國在 1900 年代參與的戰爭。*
    - *第一次世界大戰*
    - *第二次世界大戰*
    - *朝鮮戰爭*
    - *越戰*
    - *（波斯灣）海灣戰爭*

16. 小馬丁·路德·金的事蹟是什麼？*
    - *為民權奮鬥*
    - *為所有美國人爭取平等*

17. 美國的首都在哪裡？*
    - *華盛頓哥倫比亞特區*

18. 自由女神像在哪裡？*
    - *紐約（港）*
    - *自由島*
    - *[回答紐澤西、紐約市附近、哈德遜河上也可以接受]*

19. 國旗上為什麼有五十顆星星？*
    - *因為一個州有一顆星*
    - *因為一顆星代表一個州*
    - *因為有五十個州*

20. 我們在哪一天慶祝獨立紀念日？*
    - *7 月 4 日*

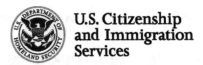

Educación Cívica (Historia y Gobierno): Preguntas para la Exención 65/20

El Servicio de Ciudadanía e Inmigración de los Estados Unidos provee una consideración especial en la prueba de civismo a los solicitantes que tengan 65 años de edad o más al momento de presentar su Solicitud de Naturalización (Formulario N-400) y hayan sido residentes permanentes de los Estados Unidos por un mínimo de 20 años. Estos solicitantes son elegibles para tomar el examen de civismo en el idioma de su elección. También se les concede el beneficio de tener que estudiar sólo 20 de las 100 preguntas de civismo que se utilizan para administrar la prueba de Naturalización.

1. **¿Cuál es un derecho o libertad que la Primera Enmienda garantiza?***
   - *expresión*
   - *religión*
   - *reunión*
   - *prensa*
   - *peticionar al gobierno*

2. **¿Cuál es el sistema económico de los Estados Unidos?***
   - *economía capitalista*
   - *economía del mercado*

3. **Nombre una rama o parte del gobierno.***
   - *Congreso*
   - *Poder legislativo*
   - *Presidente*
   - *Poder ejecutivo*
   - *los tribunales*
   - *Poder judicial*

4. **¿Cuáles son las dos partes que integran el Congreso de los Estados Unidos?***
   - *el Senado y la Cámara (de Representantes)*

5. **Nombre a uno de los senadores actuales del estado donde usted vive.***
   - *Las respuestas variarán. [Los residentes del Distrito de Columbia y los territorios de los Estados Unidos deberán contestar que el D.C. (o territorio en donde vive el solicitante) no cuenta con Senadores a nivel nacional.]*

6. **¿En qué mes votamos por un nuevo presidente?***
   - *Noviembre*

7. **¿Cómo se llama el actual Presidente de los Estados Unidos?***
   - *Barack Obama*
   - *Obama*

8. **¿Cuál es la capital de su estado?***
   - *Las respuestas variarán. [Los residentes del Distrito de Columbia deben contestar que el D.C. no es estado y que no tiene capital. Los residentes de los territorios de los Estados Unidos deben dar el nombre de la capital del territorio.]*

www.uscis.gov

9. **¿Cuáles son los <u>dos</u> principales partidos políticos de los Estados Unidos?***
   - *Demócrata y Republicano*

10. **¿Cuál es <u>una</u> responsabilidad que corresponde sólo a los ciudadanos de los Estados Unidos?***
    - *prestar servicio en un jurado*
    - *votar en una elección federal*

11. **¿Cuántos años tienen que tener los ciudadanos para votar por el Presidente?***
    - *dieciocho (18) años en adelante*

12. **¿Cuál es la fecha límite para enviar la declaración federal de impuesto sobre el ingreso?***
    - *el 15 de abril*

13. **¿Quién fue el primer Presidente?***
    - *(George) Washington*

14. **¿Qué fue <u>una</u> cosa importante que hizo Abraham Lincoln?***
    - *liberó a los esclavos (Proclamación de la Emancipación)*
    - *salvó (o preservó) la Unión*
    - *presidió los Estados Unidos durante la Guerra Civil*

15. **Mencione <u>una</u> guerra durante los años 1900 en la que peleó los Estados Unidos.***
    - *la Primera Guerra Mundial*
    - *la Segunda Guerra Mundial*
    - *la Guerra de Corea*
    - *la Guerra de Vietnam*
    - *la Guerra del Golfo (Persa)*

16. **¿Qué hizo Martin Luther King, Jr.?***
    - *luchó por los derechos civiles*
    - *trabajó por la igualdad de todos los ciudadanos americanos*

17. **¿Cuál es la capital de los Estados Unidos?***
    - *Washington, D.C.*

18. **¿Dónde está la Estatua de la Libertad?***
    - *(el puerto de) Nueva York*
    - *Liberty Island*
    [Otras respuestas aceptables son Nueva Jersey, cerca de la Ciudad de Nueva York y (el río) Hudson.]

19. **¿Por qué hay 50 estrellas en la bandera?***
    - *porque hay una estrella por cada estado*
    - *porque cada estrella representa un estado*
    - *porque hay 50 estados*

20. **¿Cuándo celebramos el Día de la Independencia?***
    - *el 4 de julio*

(rev. 05/12)

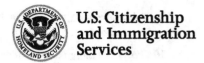

U.S. Citizenship and Immigration Services

Mga Tanong Tungkol sa Sibika para sa Pagkalibreng 65/20

Ang Immigration and Nationality Act ay nagbibigay ng pagsasaalang-alang na hindi pangkaraniwang examen sa sibika para sa mga aplikante na, sa panahon ng pagharap ng kanilang Form N-400, Application for Naturalization (Aplikasyon para sa Naturalisasyon), ay higit sila ng 65 taong gulang, at sila ay residente permanente na hindi kukulangin ng 20 taon. Itong mga aplikante ay maaaring kumuha ng examen ng sibika sa wikang pinili nila. Binibigyan din sila ng hindi pangkaraniwang pagsasaalang-alang dahil sa kinakailangan lamang silang mag-aral ng 20 sa 100 tanong tungkol sa examen sa sibika para sa examen ng pagkamamamayan.

1. **Ano ang <u>isang</u> karapatan o kalayaan mula sa Unang Susog?***
    - *pagsasalita*
    - *relihiyon*
    - *pagtitipon*
    - *pamamahayag*
    - *magpetisyon sa pamahalaan*

2. **Ano ang sistema ng ekonomiya sa Estados Unidos?***
    - *kapitalistang ekonomiya*
    - *ekonomiya ng pamiliha*

3. **Sabihin ang <u>isang</u> sangay o bahagi ng pamahalaan.***
    - *Kongreso*
    - *pambatasan*
    - *Pangulo*
    - *ehekutibo*
    - *mga korte*
    - *panghukuman*

4. **Ano ang <u>dalawang</u> bahagi ng Kongreso ng Estados Unidos?***
    - *the Senado at Kapulungan (ng mga Kinatawan)*

5. **Sino ang <u>isa</u> sa mga Senador ng inyong estado ngayon?***
    - *Ang mga sagot ay magkakaiba. [Ang mga residente ng District of Columbia at mga residente ng mga teritoryo ng Estados Unidos ay dapat sumagot na ang D.C. (o ang teritoryo kung saan nakatira ang aplikante) ay walang mga Senador ng Estados Unidos.]*

6. **Sa anong buwan tayo bumoboto para sa Pangulo?***
    - *Nobyembre*

7. **Ano ang pangalan ng Pangulo ng Estados Unidos ngayon?***
    - *Barack Obama*
    - *Obama*

8. **Ano ang kapital ng iyong estado?***
    - *Ang mga sagot ay magkakaiba. [Ang mga residente ng District of Columbia ay dapat sumagot na ang D.C. ay hindi isang estado at walang kapital. Ang mga residente ng mga teritoryo ng Estados Unidos ay dapat sabihin ang kapital ng teritoryo.]*

9.   **Ano ang <u>dalawang</u> pangunahing partidong pampulitika sa Estados Unidos?***
   - *Democratic at Republican*

10.   **Ano ang <u>isang</u> responsibilidad na para lamang sa mga mamamayan ng Estados Unidos?***
    - *magsilbi sa isang hurado*
    - *bumoto sa isang pederal na halalan*

11.   **Ilang taon kailangan ang mga mamamayan upang makaboto para sa Pangulo?***
    - *labingwalong (18) taong gulang at mas matanda*

12.   **Ano ang huling araw na maaari mong ipadala ang pederal na income tax forms?***
    - *Abril 15*

13.   **Sino ang unang Pangulo?***
    - *(George) Washington*

14.   **Ano ang <u>isang</u> mahalagang bagay na ginawa ni Abraham Lincoln?***
    - *pinalaya ang mga alipin (Proklamasyon ng Paglaya)*
    - *iniligtas(o pinangalagaan) ang Union*
    - *pinamunuan ang Estados Unidos sa Digmaang Sibil*

15.   **Sabihin ang <u>isang</u> digmaan na nakipaglaban ang Estados Unidos noong 1900s.***
    - *Unang Digmaang Pandaigdig*
    - *Ikalawang Digmaang Pandaigdig*
    - *Digmaan sa Korea*
    - *Digmaan sa Vietnam*
    - *Digmaan sa (Persian) Gulf*

16.   **Ano ang ginawa ni Martin Luther King, Jr.?***
    - *nakipaglaban para sa mga karapatang sibil*
    - *kumilos para sa pagkakapantay-pantay para sa lahat ng mga Amerikano*

17.   **Ano ang kapital ng Estados Unidos?***
    - *Washington, D.C.*

18.   **Nasaan ang Istatwa ng Kalayaan?***
    - *New York (Harbor)*
    - *Liberty Island*
    - *[Tinatanggap din ang New Jersey, malapit sa New York City, at nasa Hudson (River).]*

19.   **Bakit may 50 bituin ang bandera?***
    - *dahil may isang bituin para sa bawat estado*
    - *dahil ang bawat bituin ay kumakatawan sa isang estado*
    - *dahil may 50 estado*

20.   **Kailan tayo nagdiriwang ng Araw ng Kalayaan?***
    - *Hulyo 4*

(rev. 05/12)

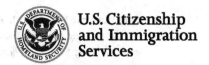

U.S. Citizenship and Immigration Services

Các Câu Hỏi Được Gọi là Điều Khoản Miễn Trừ 65/20

Đạo luật Di Trú và Quốc Tịch có điều khoản đặc biệt ưu đãi khi thi quốc tịch dành cho các ứng viên nào mà vào lúc nộp Đơn Xin Nhập Tịch, mẫu N-400, đã trên 65 tuổi và là thường trú nhân từ ít nhất 20 năm. Những ứng viên này có đủ điều kiện thi quốc tịch bằng thứ tiếng mà họ chọn. Họ cũng được ưu đãi đặc biệt vì chỉ phải học 20 trong số 100 câu hỏi lịch sử.

1. **Kể ra __Một__ quyền hoặc một tự do trong Tu Chính Án Đầu Tiên (First Amendment)?***
   - *tự do ngôn luận*
   - *tự do tôn giáo*
   - *tự do hội họp*
   - *tự do báo chí*
   - *tự do thỉnh nguyện chánh phủ*

2. **Hệ thống kinh tế của Hoa Kỳ gọi là gì?***
   - *kinh tế tư bản*
   - *kinh tế thị trường*

3. **Cho biết __một__ ngành hay phần của công quyền.***
   - *Quốc Hội*
   - *lập pháp*
   - *Tổng Thống*
   - *hành pháp*
   - *các tòa án*
   - *tư pháp*

4. **__Hai__ phần của Quốc Hội Hoa Kỳ là gì?***
   - *Thượng và Hạ Nghị Viện*

5. **Ai là __một__ trong những Thượng Nghị Sĩ Liên Bang của bạn?***
   - *Câu trả lời thay đổi tùy tiểu bang. [Cư dân ở thủ đô Washington, D.C. và cư dân ở các lãnh thổ Hoa Kỳ trả lời là DC hoặc lãnh thổ mình ở không có thượng-nghị-sĩ.]*

6. **Bầu Tổng Thống vào tháng nào?***
   - *Tháng Mười Một*

7. **Hiện nay tên Tổng Thống Hoa Kỳ là gì?***
   - *Barack Obama*
   - *Obama*

8. **Thủ phủ của tiểu bang bạn tên gì?***
   - *Câu trả lời tùy theo tiểu bang. [Cư dân vùng thủ đô Washington, D.C. phải trả lời là vùng DC không phải là một tiểu bang và không có thủ phủ. Cư dân các lãnh thổ hải ngoại của Hoa Kỳ phải cho biết thủ phủ của vùng lãnh thổ hải ngoại này.]*

9. **Hai đảng __chính__ của Hoa Kỳ là gì?***
   - *Dân Chủ và Cộng Hòa*

10. **Một** trong các bổn phận chỉ dành riêng cho công dân Hoa Kỳ là gì?*
   - *phục vụ trong bồi thẩm đoàn*
   - *đi bầu trong bầu cử liên bang*

11. **Công dân phải bao nhiêu tuổi mới được bầu Tổng Thống?***
   - *Mười Tám (18) và hơn*

12. **Ngày cuối cùng có thể nạp mẫu khai thuế cho liên bang là?***
   - *15 Tháng Tư*

13. **Ai là Tổng Thống đầu tiên?***
   - *(George) Washington*

14. **Một** điều quan trọng mà Abraham Lincoln làm là gì?*
   - *giải phóng nô lệ (Tuyên Ngôn Giải Phóng)*
   - *giữ gìn (hoặc bảo tồn) đoàn kết Quốc Gia*
   - *lãnh đạo Hoa Kỳ trong Cuộc Nội Chiến*

15. **Cho biết một cuộc chiến mà Hoa Kỳ tham dự vào thập niên 1900.***
   - *Thế Chiến Thứ Nhất*
   - *Thế Chiến Thứ Hai*
   - *Chiến Tranh Cao Ly (Triều Tiên)*
   - *Chiến Tranh Việt Nam*
   - *Chiến tranh Vùng Vịnh (Ba Tư)*

16. **Martin Luther King, Jr. đã làm gì?***
   - *tranh đấu cho dân quyền*
   - *hoạt động nhằm mang lại bình đẳng cho mọi người Mỹ*

17. **Thủ đô của Hoa Kỳ tên gì?***
   - *Washington, D.C.*

18. **Tượng Nữ Thần Tự Do ở đâu?***
   - *(Hải Cảng) Nữu Ước*
   - *Đảo Liberty*
   [Cũng chấp nhận nếu trả lời là New Jersey, gần thành phố New York và trên sông Hudson.]

19. **Tại sao lá cờ Hoa Kỳ có 50 ngôi sao?***
   - *bởi vì mỗi tiểu bang có một ngôi sao*
   - *bởi vì mỗi ngôi sao tượng trưng cho một tiểu bang*
   - *bởi vì có 50 tiểu bang*

20. **Ngày nào là ngày Lễ Độc Lập?***
   - *4 Tháng Bảy*

APPENDIX 7-11

Selective Service General Counsel Letter

Selective Service System

National Headquarters / Arlington, Virginia 22209-2425

Dear Mr.

You were required to register with the Selective Service System, but you did not register. You cannot register after attaining age 26 years.

Section 12(g) of the Military Selective Service Act (50 App. U.S.C. 462(g)) reads as follows:

(g)   A person may not be denied a right, privilege, or benefit under Federal law by reason of failure to present himself for and submit to registration under section 3 [of the Military Selective Service Act] if -
(1)   the requirement for the person to so register has terminated or become inapplicable to the person; and
(2)   the person shows by a preponderance of the evidence that the failure of the person to register was not a knowing and willful failure to register.

[The purpose of this provision is to] clarify that a non-registrant is not to be denied any Federal benefit if he can demonstrate that his failure to register was not knowing or willful. The conferees added this provision in order not to penalize an individual with an obvious disqualifying handicap, such as total paralysis of the limbs or an individual who has been honorably discharged from the armed services. Under the law, such an individual is required to register but the conferees did not believe it would be fair to extend this provision to an individual who honestly believed he did not have an obligation to register because of such a handicap or because he was a member of the armed forces. At the same time, the conferees do not intend for this provision in any way to provide an option for self-classification. For example, the conferees do not intend that a person who knowingly failed to register because he viewed himself as a conscientious objector would meet the standards of the conference provision as someone whose failure to register was not knowing or willful. Established procedures for classification, which follows

507

registration, are the only means for determining conscientious objector status. Total paralysis or the existence of an honorable discharge certificate, on the other hand, are objective factors that could lead one to believe, albeit erroneously, that he was not required to register. (House Conference Report No. 99-1001 (1986) p. 546)

You should present this letter to the INS examiner handling your file and explain to the examiner the reasons for your failure to complete a Selective Service Registration Card and give it to a postal employee or another authorized to receive it. INS has the duty to determine whether you have shown "by a preponderance of the evidence that [your] ...failure... to [complete and file a Registration Card] was not a knowing and willful failure to..." do so. If the INS officer determines that you made the required showing, the above quoted statutory language prohibits the denial of a recommendation by INS for your naturalization because of your failure to register with Selective Service. If that officer determines that you have not made the required showing, you will be denied the desired recommendation. An INS officer's decision that you did not make the required showing may be appealed within the INS.

Sincerely,

Henry N. Williams
General Counsel

APPENDIX 7-12

Hmong Veterans' Naturalization Act of 2000

A. Hmong Veterans' Naturalization Act of 2000, Public Law 106-207, 114 Stat. 316 (May 26, 2000)

An Act

To facilitate the naturalization of aliens who served with special guerrilla units or irregular forces in Laos.

Be it enacted by the Senate and House of Representatives of the United States of America in Congress assembled,

SECTION 1. SHORT TITLE.

This Act may be cited as the "Hmong Veterans' Naturalization Act of 2000".

SEC. 2. EXEMPTION FROM ENGLISH LANGUAGE REQUIREMENT FOR CERTAIN ALIENS WHO SERVED WITH SPECIAL GUER-RILLA UNITS OR IRREGULAR FORCES IN LAOS.

The requirement of paragraph (1) of section 312(a) of the Immigration and Nationality Act (8 U.S.C.A. 1423(a)(1)) shall not apply to the naturalization of any person—

  (1) who—

    (A) was admitted into the United States as a refugee from Laos pursuant to section 207 of the Immigration and Nationality Act (8 U.S.C.A. 1157); and

    (B) served with a special guerrilla unit, or irregular forces, operating from a base in Laos in support of the United States military at any time during the period beginning February 28, 1961, and ending September 18, 1978;

or

  (2) who—

    (A) satisfies the requirement of paragraph (1)(A); and

    (B) was the spouse of a person described in paragraph (1) on the day on which such described person applied for admission into the United States as a refugee.

SEC. 3. SPECIAL CONSIDERATION CONCERNING CIVICS REQUIRE-MENT FOR CERTAIN ALIENS WHO SERVED WITH SPECIAL GUERRILLA UNITS OR IRREGULAR FORCES IN LAOS.

The Attorney General shall provide for special consideration, as determined by the Attorney General, concerning the requirement of paragraph (2) of section 312(a) of the Immigration and Nationality Act (8 U.S.C.A. 1423(a)(2)) with respect to the naturalization of any person described in paragraph (1) or (2) of section 2 of this Act.

SEC. 4. DOCUMENTATION OF QUALIFYING SERVICE.

A person seeking an exemption under section 2 or special consideration under section 3 shall submit to the Attorney General documentation of their, or their spouse's, service with a special guerrilla unit, or irregular forces, described in section 2(1)(B), in the form of—

(1) original documents;

(2) an affidavit of the serving person's superior officer;

(3) two affidavits from other individuals who also were serving with such a special guerrilla unit, or irregular forces, and who personally knew of the person's service; or

(4) other appropriate proof.

SEC. 5. DETERMINATION OF ELIGIBILITY FOR EXEMPTION AND SPECIAL CONSIDERATION.

(a) In determining a person's eligibility for an exemption under section 2 or special consideration under section 3, the Attorney General—

(1) shall review the refugee processing documentation for the person, or, in an appropriate case, for the person and the person's spouse, to verify that the requirements of section 2 relating to refugee applications and admissions have been satisfied;

(2) shall consider the documentation submitted by the person under section 4;

(3) may request an advisory opinion from the Secretary of Defense regarding the person's, or their spouse's, service in a special guerrilla unit, or irregular forces, described in section 2(1)(B); and

(4) may consider any documentation provided by organizations maintaining records with respect to Hmong veterans or their families.

(b) The Secretary of Defense shall provide any opinion requested under paragraph (3) to the extent practicable, and the Attorney General shall take into account any opinion that the Secretary of Defense is able to provide.

SEC. 6. DEADLINE FOR APPLICATION AND PAYMENT OF FEES.

This Act shall apply to a person only if the person's application for naturalization is filed, as provided in section 334 of the Immigration and Nationality Act (8 U.S.C.A. 1445), with appropriate fees not later than 18 months after the date of the enactment of this Act.

SEC. 7. LIMITATION ON NUMBER OF BENEFICIARIES.

Notwithstanding any other provision of this Act, the total number of aliens who may be granted an exemption under section 2 or special consideration under section 3, or both, may not exceed 45,000.

Approved May 26, 2000.

B. Act of November 1, 2000, Pub. L. 106-415 (enrolled bill)

One Hundred Sixth Congress

of the

United States of America

AT THE SECOND SESSION

Begun and held at the City of Washington on Monday, the twenty-fourth day of January, two thousand

An Act,

To amend the Hmong Veterans' Naturalization Act of 2000 to extend the applicability of that Act to certain former spouses of deceased Hmong veterans.

Be it enacted by the Senate and House of Representatives of the United States of America in Congress assembled,

SECTION 1. EXTENSION OF HMONG VETERANS' NATURALIZATION ACT OF 2000 TO CERTAIN FORMER SPOUSES OF DECEASED HMONG VETERANS.

(a) IN GENERAL- Section 2 of the Hmong Veterans' Naturalization Act of 2000 (Public Law 106-207; 114 Stat. 316; 8 U.S.C.A. 1423 note) is amended—

(1) in paragraph (1), by striking 'or' at the end;

(2) in paragraph (2), by striking the period at the end and inserting '; or'; and

(3) by adding at the end the following new paragraph:

'(3) who—

'(A) satisfies the requirement of paragraph (1)(A); and

'(B) is the surviving spouse of a person described in paragraph (1)(B) which described person was killed or died in Laos, Thailand, or Vietnam.'

(b) CONFORMING AMENDMENT- Section 3 of such Act is amended by striking 'or (2)' and inserting ', (2), or (3)'.

SEC. 2. DEADLINE FOR APPLICATION.

Section 6 of such Act is amended by adding at the end the following new sentence: 'In the case of a person described in section 2(3), the application referred to in the preceding sentence, and appropriate fees, shall be filed not later than 18 months after the date of the enactment of this sentence.'

Speaker of the House of Representatives.

Vice President of the United States and

President of the Senate.

APPENDIX 7-13

Enrolled Version of the Act of November 6, 2000, Public Law 106-448

S. 2812

One Hundred Sixth Congress

of the

United States of America

AT THE SECOND SESSION

Begun and held at the City of Washington on Monday, the twenty-fourth day of January, two thousand

An Act

To amend the Immigration and Nationality Act to provide a waiver of the oath of renunciation and allegiance for naturalization of aliens having certain disabilities.

Be it enacted by the Senate and House of Representatives of the United States of America in Congress assembled,

SECTION 1. WAIVER OF OATH OF RENUNCIATION AND ALLEGIANCE FOR NATURALIZATION OF ALIENS HAVING CERTAIN DISABILITIES.

Section 337(a) of the Immigration and Nationality Act (8 U.S.C.A. 1448(a)) is amended by adding at the end the following: 'The Attorney General may waive the taking of the oath by a person if in the opinion of the Attorney General the person is unable to understand, or to communicate an understanding of, its meaning because of a physical or developmental disability or mental impairment. If the Attorney General waives the taking of the oath by a person under the preceding sentence, the person shall be considered to have met the requirements of section 316(a)(3) with respect to attachment to the principles of the Constitution and well disposition to the good order and happiness of the United States.'

SEC. 2. EFFECTIVE DATE.

The amendment made by section 1 shall apply to persons applying for naturalization before, on, or after the date of the enactment of this Act.

Speaker of the House of Representatives.

Vice President of the United States and

President of the Senate.

APPENDIX 7-14

INS Commissioner Zigler's October 31, 2002 Memorandum

U.S. Department of Justice
Immigration and Naturalization Service
INS Policy and Procedural Memoranda
MEMORANDUM FOR Regional Directors

Regional Counsel

SUBJECT: New Anti-Terrorism Legislation

FROM:
James W. Ziglar
Commissioner

October 31, 2001

On October 26, 2001, the President signed the Uniting and Strengthening America by Providing Appropriate Tools Required to Intercept and Obstruct Terrorism (USA PATRIOT) Act of 2001 (Act). The Act contains a broad package of budgetary and statutory amendments to enable the government to combat more effectively the threat of terrorism. The Act contains a number of significant immigration provisions. This memorandum lists the substantive new provisions and discusses in further detail provisions of particular significance, such as those related to retroactivity and the detention of certain aliens that the Attorney General certifies endanger national security. This memorandum also provides preliminary instructions to field offices concerning how to bring individual cases to the attention of Headquarters for consideration under the new detention provision.

The Act authorizes increased resources for immigration enforcement, amends the Immigration and Nationality Act (INA) relating to the detention and removal of aliens who engage in terrorist activities, and contains provisions to ensure that the immigration status of victims of the September 11 terrorist attacks and their families is not adversely affected as a result of the attacks. The immigration provisions are summarized below by subtitle.

Headquarters will provide additional guidance regarding the implementation of these provisions in the future.

Subtitle A, Sections 401-405:

- authorizes tripling of personnel along the northern border; waives overtime cap applicable to INS employees; authorizes appropriations for improvements in technology to monitor the northern border; requires DOJ and FBI to provide the State Department and INS information from its NCIC files; and requires a DOJ report to Congress on the feasibility of enhancing the FBI's Integrated Automated Fingerprint Identification System as well as other identification systems.

513

Subtitle B, Section 411:

- broadens the grounds of inadmissibility to include: (a) any representative of a political or social group that publicly endorses terrorist activity in the United States; (b) a person who uses his prominence to endorse terrorist activity, or persuade others to support terrorist activity; (c) spouses and children of persons engaged in terrorism; and (d) anyone the Secretary of State or Attorney General determines has been associated with a terrorist organization and who intends to engage in activities that could endanger the welfare, safety, or security of the United States;

- broadens the definition of "terrorist activity" to include the use of dangerous devices;

- adds a definition of "terrorist organization" that includes: (a) any organization designated under section 219; (b) any organization otherwise designated, upon publication in the Federal Register, by the Secretary of State (after consultation with or at the request of the Attorney General) as a terrorist organization after a finding that the organization commits or incites to commit terrorist activity, prepares or plans a terrorist activity, or gathers information on potential targets for terrorist activity, or that the organization provides material support to further terrorist activity; and (c) a group of two or more individuals, whether organized or not, that commits or incites to commit terrorist activity, prepares or plans a terrorist activity, or gathers information on potential targets for terrorist activity;

- amends the definition of "engage in terrorist activity"—which is conduct that can render an alien inadmissible (under section 212(a)(3)(B)) or deportable (under section 237(a)(4)(B))—in two principal ways: (a) by clarifying that an alien's solicitation of funds or members for a terrorist organization constitutes "engaging in a terrorist activity," even if the alien did not intend to further terrorist activity and/or did not know that the organization was a terrorist organization; and (b) by providing that an alien "engages in a terrorist activity" by committing an act that the alien knows or reasonably should know affords material support to a terrorist organization, even if the alien did not specifically intend to support terrorist activity and did not know (and should not reasonably have known) that the organization was a terrorist organization. The statute further provides, however, that an alien's solicitation of funds or members for, or provision of material support to, a terrorist organization will not be deemed "engaging in a terrorist activity" where (i) the organization is at the time of the solicitation or support a non- designated terrorist organization and (ii) the alien demonstrates that he did not know, and should not reasonably have known, that the solicitation or material support would further the organization's terrorist activity.

- adds as a bar to asylum the new ground of inadmissibility for using a position of prominence to endorse terrorist activity or persuade others to support terrorist activity;

- contains an express retroactive application clause mandating the application of these new provisions (a) to actions taken by an alien before, on, or after the date of enactment, (b) to all aliens without regard to the date of the alien's entry or attempted entry, (c) in removal proceedings on or after the date of enactment (except for proceedings in which there has been a final administrative decision before enactment), and (d) to aliens seeking admission to the United States on or after the date of enactment;

- contains an express provision requiring application of sections 212 and 237, as amended, to all aliens who are in exclusion or deportation proceedings on or after the date of enactment (except where there has been an administratively final order issued); and

- allows a waiver of the bar to admission for spouses and children if they did not know or should not reasonably have known the principal alien was engaged in terrorism or if they renounced the terrorist activity.

Subtitle B, Section 412:

- requires mandatory detention of aliens until they are removed or until removal proceedings are terminated in the alien's favor where the Attorney General issues a certification that he has "reasonable grounds to believe" the alien is described in sections 212(a)(3)(A)(i), 212(a)(3)(A)(iii), 212(a)(3)(B), 237(a)(4)(A)(i), 237(a)(4)(A)(iii), or 237(a)(4)(B), or is engaged in any other activity that endangers the national security of the United States, as long as removal or criminal charges are brought within 7 days of arrest.

Subtitle B, Sections 413-418:

- gives the Secretary of State discretion to provide visa record information on a basis of reciprocity to foreign governments to fight international terrorism or other crimes;
- requires the Attorney General to expedite the implementation of the integrated entry and exit data system authorized by Congress in 1996 and includes the Office of Homeland Security in such development;
- requires the Attorney General to fully implement and expand the foreign student monitoring program; and
- requires the Secretary of State to determine if consular shopping is a problem.

Subtitle C, Sections 421-428:

- creates a special immigrant status for people who were in the process of securing permanent residence through a family member who died, was disabled, or lost employment as a result of September 11;
- temporarily extends the derivative status of spouses and minor children of a nonimmigrant who was killed or injured on September 11 if they are in the United States;
- provides remedies for people whose eligibility was adversely affected because they could not meet certain deadlines as a result of September 11 (visa waiver, diversity lottery, immigrant visas, and advance parole);
- Extends voluntary departure periods that expired between September 11 and October 11 by an additional 30 days;
- gives relief to the spouses and children of citizens and lawful permanent residents killed on September 11 by allowing adjudication of permanent resident applications;
- provides an additional period during which a beneficiary of an immigration petition or application that was pending on September 11, and whose 21st birthday occurs in or after September, 2001, will be considered to be a "child" under the INA;
- precludes any immigration benefits under this Subtitle of the Act for anyone culpable for the terrorist attacks on September 11 or any family member of such person.

Effect of Amendments on Inadmissibility and Removal

The new legislation enhances the Government's ability to deport or deny admission and immigration benefits to alien terrorists. Under prior law, representatives (including even officers and commanders) of terrorist organizations were not inadmissible to the United States unless their organization was one of the twenty-eight terrorist organizations currently designated by the Secretary of State under section 219 of the INA. Under the new law, such persons will also be inadmissible if the Secretary of State has determined that the organization is a political, social or other similar group whose public endorsement of acts of terrorist activity undermines United States efforts to reduce or eliminate terrorist activities. Under prior law, members of section 219 designated organizations were inadmissible if the alien knew or should have known the organization was a terrorist organization. The new law makes inadmissible any member of either a section 219-designated terrorist organization or any terrorist organization that the alien knows or should know is a terrorist organization. The new law also adds as grounds for inadmissibility any alien who uses his or her position of prominence to endorse or espouse terrorist activity or to persuade others to support terrorist activity "in a way that the Secretary of State has determined undermines United States efforts to reduce or eliminate terrorist activities," and any alien who has been determined by the Secretary of State or the Attorney General (after consulting one with the other) to have been associated with a terrorist organization and intends while in the United States to engage, even incidentally, in activities that could endanger the welfare, safety, or security of the United States.

Further, under prior law, aliens who engaged in terrorist activity were inadmissible to and deportable from the United States. The term "engaged in terrorist activity" included soliciting funds or members for a terrorist organization. The law, however, did not define terrorist organization. It also did not clearly specify whether an alien's solicitation of funds or members for a terrorist organization constitutes "engaging in a terrorist activity" if the alien did not intend to further terrorist activity and/or did not know that the organization was a terrorist organization. Furthermore, the term "engaged in terrorist activity" included affording material support to a terrorist organization only "in conducting a terrorist activity."

The new law corrects these deficiencies in three ways. First, it defines terrorist organizations by providing that an organization can be established as a terrorist organization in one of three ways: (1) by Secretary of State designation under section 219; (2) by Secretary of State designation upon Federal Register publication after a finding is made that the organization (a) commits or incites to commit terrorist activity, (b) prepares or plans a terrorist activity, (c) gathers information on potential targets for terrorist activity, or (d) provides material support to further terrorist activity; or (3) by being a group (of two or more persons, whether formally organized or not) that (a) commits or incites to commit terrorist activity, (b) prepares or plans a terrorist activity, (c) gathers information on potential targets for terrorist activity, or (d) provides material support to further terrorist activity.

Second, the law clarifies that an alien's solicitation of funds or members for a terrorist organization constitutes "engaging in a terrorist activity," even if the alien did not intend to further terrorist activity and/or did not know that the organization was a terrorist organization.

Third, the law makes clear that the Government does not have to prove that an alien specifically intended to support an organization's terrorist activity in order to establish his inadmissibility or deportability on the ground that the alien provided "material support" to a terrorist organization. Regardless of his intent, if after the date of designation under section 219 or publication in the Federal Register of the

Secretary's other designation, the alien supported an organization that was designated or subject to the published finding by the Secretary of State, he is inadmissible or deportable. Regardless of his intent, if he provided the support to organizations prior to designation or publication or for which no such designation or publication has yet occurred, he is inadmissible or deportable if the Government proves that the organization which he supported was a terrorist organization, unless the alien can establish that he did not know and should not reasonably have known that his support would further the organization's terrorist activity.

Finally, by expanding the definitions of "engaged in terrorist activity" and "terrorist organization," the law acts to increase the classes of aliens ineligible for certain forms of relief or protection under the immigration laws, such as adjustment of status, release pending deportation, and withholding of removal.

Retroactivity

Sections 411(c)(1) and (2) of the Act provide expressly for retroactive application of all of the amendments in section 411. Pursuant to section 411(c)(1) the amendments expressly apply to (a) to any actions taken by an alien before, on, or after the date of enactment, (b) to all aliens without regard to the date of the alien's entry or attempted entry, (c) in removal proceedings on or after the date of enactment (except for proceedings in which there has been a final administrative decision issued before enactment), and (d) to aliens seeking admission to the United States on or after the date of enactment. This retroactivity provision is comprehensive and inclusive—it applies in all removal cases. In addition, section 411(c)(2) applies expressly to aliens in exclusion and deportation proceedings, and mandates that INA sections 212 and 237, as amended, be applied to all aliens in such proceedings, as if they were in removal proceedings, unless a final administrative order has issued.

Sections 411(c)(3) and (4), however, create a special rule in cases involving designated terrorist organizations. The provisions prevent retroactive application of the provisions making inadmissible any alien who has solicited members or funds for, or provided material support to, a designated terrorist organization where that alien's actions pre-date the designation of the organization, in cases where the alien can demonstrate that he did not know, and should not reasonably have known, that the conduct in question would further the organization's terrorist activity. The provisions further clarify, however, that where the actions in question post-date the designation of the organization, or where the alien cannot demonstrate that he did not know and should not reasonably have known that the conduct in question would further the organization's terrorist activity, then the provisions related to solicitation and material support do apply retroactively. Thus, the key to determining retroactive application in these designated terrorist organization cases will be the date of the designation and the time of the alien's actions, not the date of the enactment of these amendments.

Attorney General Certification and Detention

Section 412 of the Act adds a new section 236A to the INA relating to the detention of aliens who are certified by the Attorney General as endangering national security. Under new section 236A(a)(1) of the INA, the Attorney General shall detain any alien whom he certifies until that alien is removed, until the Attorney General determines that the alien is no longer an alien who may be certified, or until the alien is finally determined not to be removable, as long as criminal or removal charges are issued within 7 days of his arrest. In order to make such a certification under new section 236A(a)(3), the Attorney General must have "reasonable grounds to believe" that the alien is engaged in any activity that endangers the national security of the United States, or that the alien is described in any of the following INA provisions concerning security or terrorism- related grounds of removal and/or inadmissibility: INA § 212(a)(3)(A)(i) (entry to violate any law relating to espionage or sabotage), § 212(a)(3)(A)(iii) (entry to oppose, control or overthrow the government of the United States by force, violence, or other unlawful means), § 212(a)(3)(B) (inadmissibility grounds related to terrorism), § 237(a)(4)(A)(i) (has engaged in activity to violate any law relating to espionage, sabotage, or the unlawful exportation of goods, technology, or sensitive information), § 237(a)(4)(A)(iii) (has engaged in any activity to oppose, control or overthrow the government of the United States by force, violence, or other unlawful means), or § 237(a)(4)(B) (alien who has engaged in terrorist activity).

Once the Attorney General certifies that there are reasonable grounds to believe that an alien is described in any of the enumerated provisions and the alien is detained, section 236A(a)(5) requires the Attorney General, through the applicable INS district or federal criminal prosecutors, to file removal or criminal charges against the alien within seven days. If the alien is not charged under either the INA or a criminal statute within that time, the Attorney General must release the alien. Every six months while the alien is detained pursuant to the certification, the Attorney General must review the certification to determine whether it should be revoked. The alien may request each six months in writing that the Attorney General reconsider the certification and may submit documents or other evidence in support of that request. Even where there is no likelihood that the alien will be removed in the reasonably foreseeable future, so long as the Attorney General does not revoke the certification, the alien shall be detained.

Only the Attorney General or the Deputy Attorney General has the authority to make the certification. This authority cannot be delegated to any other official in the Department of Justice, EOIR, or INS. Thus, once an alien is detained pursuant to an Attorney General (or Deputy Attorney General) certification and charges have been filed within seven days of the alien's arrest, INS cannot release the alien from detention unless and until the Attorney General revokes the certification, the alien is removed, or the alien is finally determined not to be removable.

Please note that the new certification and detention provisions do not alter the recently amended regulatory requirements regarding the period of time for which an alien can otherwise be held in custody prior to a decision to issue a charging document. See 66 Fed. Reg. 48334 (Sept. 20, 2001). As amended, 8 C.F.R. § 287.3(d) requires that the INS determine whether or not to issue a notice to appear within 48 hours for anyone arrested without warrant unless an emergency or other extraordinary circumstance prevents making that determination within the 48-hour period. The seven-day provision in section 236A(a)(5), however, can extend the time allotted by the regulation in any case where the Attorney General makes the new statutory certification.

In cases where the Attorney General issues a certification, and after removal proceedings are completed, in those cases where the alien has been ordered removed but his or her removal is unlikely in the reasonably foreseeable future, the alien may be continued in detention for additional periods of up to six months, but only if the alien's release would threaten national security or the safety of the community or any person. The Attorney General must review every six months whether the certification should be revoked. If the Attorney General decides to revoke the certification, the alien may be released under appropriate conditions as determined by the Attorney General, unless release is otherwise prohibited by law. The alien may request reconsideration of the certification every six months and may submit evidence in support of his or her release. Any alien in custody as a result of the Attorney General's certification under section 236A, may seek review of his or her detention as well as review of the certification decision itself, by habeas corpus in federal court, but can appeal an adverse decision made by a district court, regardless of the district, only to the United States Court of Appeals for the District of Columbia, whose rulings will control in all federal districts nationwide.

More detailed guidance on the implementation of this new statute will follow. In the meantime, if any District or local office detains an alien who appears to be a candidate for certification under the provisions of new section 236A, they should immediately notify Executive Associate Commissioner for Field Operations, Michael A. Pearson, or his designee, through their chain of command, and should consult with their District or Sector Counsel. Any legal questions should be raised through channels to Deputy General Counsel Dea Carpenter.

APPENDIX 7-15

USCIS Guidance on Making Naturalization Process Accessible to Applicants with Disabilities

U.S. Department of Justice
Immigration and Naturalization Service

---

425 I Street NW
Washington, DC 20536

January 21, 2003

MEMORANDUM FOR ALL REGIONAL DIRECTORS
ALL DISTRICT DIRECTORS
ALL OFFICERS-IN-CHARGE
ALL SERVICE CENTER DIRECTORS

FROM: William R. Yates /S/
           Deputy Executive Associate Commissioner
           Office of Field Operations
           Immigration Services Division

SUBJECT: Guidance on Making the Naturalization Process Accessible to Applicants with
           <u>Disabilities</u>

This memorandum provides comprehensive policy guidance on how to make modifications or accommodations in the practices or procedures of the naturalization program for applicants with disabilities. Each field office must use this guidance to provide accommodations for naturalization *applicants* with disabilities. **Field offices must come into compliance with this guidance within 90 days of the date of this memorandum**.

To assist field offices in complying with this guidance, this memorandum suggests best practices that offices can implement in processing requests for, and in providing, accommodations. The memorandum also provides examples of types of accommodations that may be provided at each stage of the naturalization process. We encourage each field office to work with the local community-based organizations (CBOs) and AILA chapter as the office works to come into compliance with this guidance.

Memorandum For All Regional Directors, All District Directors   Page 2
All Officers in Charge, All Service Center Directors
Subject: Guidance on Making the Naturalization Process Accessible to Applicants with
Disabilities

I.   **Background**

Section 504 of the Rehabilitation Act provides that "[n]o otherwise qualified individual with a disability in the United States…shall, solely by reason of her or his disability, be excluded from participation in, be denied the benefits of, or be subjected to discrimination under any program or activity receiving Federal financial assistance or under any program or activity conducted by any Executive agency."[1] As a federal agency, the Immigration and Naturalization Service (INS) may not exclude qualified persons with disabilities from its programs or activities based solely on the person's disability. To ensure that persons with disabilities are not excluded from INS programs or activities because of their disabilities, the Rehabilitation Act requires the INS to provide modifications or accommodations that permit qualified persons with disabilities to have an equal opportunity to participate in its programs.[2]

The Rehabilitation Act requires INS to provide accommodations that will help the particular applicant with a disability to fully participate in the naturalization program. In the naturalization context, INS must provide accommodations for naturalization applicants who have physical and/or mental impairments that make it difficult for them to complete the naturalization process.

1.   *Difference between Accommodations and Statutory Waivers*

Accommodations are *different* from statutory waivers. If an individual receives a waiver, that individual does <u>not</u> have to meet the specific naturalization requirement for which the waiver is granted. All applicants qualifying for a waiver receive the same relief. For example, all applicants receiving an English test waiver will not have to take the English exam. Existing waivers (also called exemptions) cover the English and/or civics requirements and the oath of allegiance.

On the other hand, an accommodation is a *modification,* not an exemption from an existing practice or procedure that will allow an applicant with a disability to participate in the naturalization process. The applicant will still have to satisfy the requirement; however, the *manner* in which the applicant demonstrates meeting the requirement is changed. Accommodations are likely to vary with the individual's disability. For example, an applicant who is unable to use his or her hands should be permitted to take the civics tests orally. An applicant who is unable to speak might receive an accommodation that would allow that applicant to respond to questions on the English and/or civics test with a previously agreed upon

---

[1] 29 U.S.C. § 794(a).

[2] 28 C.F.R. §§ 39.103 & 39.149-60.

nonverbal form of assent. *The essential aspect of an accommodation is that it is <u>effective</u> in allowing the applicant to participate fully in the naturalization process.*

2.   *When INS Does Not Have to Provide Accommodations*

The Rehabilitation Act requires that the INS operate each program or activity so that the program or activity, when viewed in its entirety, is readily accessible to and usable by persons with disabilities. This does not require the INS to take any action that would result in a fundamental alteration in the nature of the naturalization program for this individual applicant or in undue financial and administrative burdens in conducting the naturalization program.[3]

Only on rare occasions will an accommodation requested by an applicant rise to the level of a fundamental alteration of the program or an undue burden for the agency. In most cases, the field office must provide either the specific accommodation requested by an applicant with a disability or an alternative accommodation that enables that applicant to participate in the naturalization process.

II.   Three Steps to Handling Requests for Accommodations

The obligation to request an accommodation for a particular program requirement is initially on the *applicant* (or someone acting on the applicant's behalf). However, once an accommodation has been requested, the obligation is then on the *field office* to provide a timely response to that request.

The duty to provide accommodations is ongoing. Certain individuals may only require one accommodation, while others may need more than one. Certain individuals may need one accommodation at a particular stage of the naturalization process, and then, at a later date, require another type of accommodation. The following three steps should be taken when processing requests for accommodations.[4]

1.   Each field office must respond to inquiries on how applicants with disabilities can request accommodations, process the requests, and provide the accommodations.

2.   Each field office must have procedures for handling all requests for accommodation, *regardless of when the request is made*. Applicants may submit a request for an

---

[3] *See* 28 C.F.R. § 39.103 (definition of qualified handicapped person) *and* § 39.150 (describing agency obligation to make programs readily accessible to persons with disabilities).

[4] See Appendix 2, Examples of Accommodations.

accommodation with the N-400, or may submit requests directly to the field office at any time during the naturalization process.

3. An office's ability to provide an accommodation on the date that it is needed will depend on when the accommodation was requested and whether the accommodation is one that requires advance planning. Some types of accommodations, such as speaking loudly and slowly to an applicant with a mild to moderate hearing impairment, or allowing an applicant to take extra time to write the answers to a civics test because of arthritis, do not require advance notification and can be immediately provided. Others, like arranging for a sign language interpreter or scheduling an applicant for a homebound interview, cannot be accommodated without advance planning.

Field offices should strive to provide __all__ *accommodation requests on the date that the applicant is originally scheduled to complete the naturalization process.* Whenever possible, field offices should avoid having to reschedule an examination or the oath because an accommodation is not available. If the accommodation cannot be made available on the scheduled date of the examination, the applicant should be notified as soon as possible that the accommodation will not be available and the examination should be rescheduled within a reasonable period of time.

> **Each field office must designate staff to handle accommodations requests.**

To assure accountability, each field office must designate *who* will be responsible for handling accommodations requests from naturalization applicants. Regardless of how many staff members are tasked to handling requests for accommodations, the office must ensure that the *entire* INS staff is aware of the procedure for handling such requests and can direct applicants to the appropriate person or persons.

> **Each field office must provide information to applicants on how to request accommodations from the field office.**

> **Each field office must ensure that an applicant may request an accommodation *after* his or her naturalization application has been filed.**

A field office may not bar requests for accommodations that come in after the applicant has filed his or her naturalization application. Many applicants may be unaware of their right to request an accommodation; others may develop a disability (or their impairments may worsen) after their applications have been filed. Field offices must allow applicants to submit accommodations requests at any time during the naturalization process.

Memorandum For All Regional Directors, All District Directors   Page 5
All Officers in Charge, All Service Center Directors
Subject: Guidance on Making the Naturalization Process Accessible to Applicants with Disabilities

> ➤ **Each field office must review accommodations requests in a timely fashion.**

Each field office must review and respond to requests for accommodations that may be received in advance or received on the day that the accommodation is needed. The office must respond to requests for accommodation *as promptly as possible*, depending on the nature of the request and the resources of the office. If an office is unable to provide a requested accommodation on a certain date, the applicant should be notified and rescheduled as soon as possible.

The office must evaluate each request and contact the applicant (and his or her attorney or accredited representative) if further information is needed before the request can be approved. While an applicant is not required to include documentation of his or her impairment with the accommodations request,[5] in some cases, documentation may be needed to determine if the applicant is eligible for an accommodation. The office must inform the applicant (and his or her attorney or accredited representative) if an *alternative* accommodation has been approved, and explain the alternative.

> ➤ **Inform applicants in the rare case when a request for accommodation is rejected.**

In the rare case where a request for accommodation is rejected by the field office, the office must provide the applicant (and his or her attorney or accredited representative) with an explanation of why the accommodation was rejected and provide an appropriate alternative accommodation. Applicants who believe that they have been unlawfully denied an accommodation may file a complaint with the Department of Justice Civil Rights Division pursuant to 28 CFR Part 39.

III.   Conclusion

INS Service Centers and field offices must make every attempt to help naturalization applicants with disabilities proceed through the naturalization process. DAOs are reminded again of the need for utmost courtesy, respect and sensitivity in dealing with applicants with physical or mental impairments who need accommodations to effectively complete the naturalization process.

---

[5] *See* Policy Memorandum No. 47 on Section 312 Disability Naturalization Adjudications, issued on April 7, 1999,**K. Reasonable Accommodations and Modifications under the Rehabilitation Act.** With accommodations or modifications, many applicants with disabilities will be able to meet the section 312 requirements. Section 504 of the Rehabilitation Act of 1973 requires all Federal agencies to make reasonable accommodations for persons with disabilities. Applicants are not required to file an N-648 or present a letter or other documentation from their doctor to request an accommodation or modification to the naturalization process because of a disability.

Memorandum For All Regional Directors, All District Directors   Page 6
All Officers in Charge, All Service Center Directors
Subject: Guidance on Making the Naturalization Process Accessible to Applicants with
Disabilities

Field offices must comply with this guidance in providing naturalization applicants with
physical or mental impairments with the accommodations they need to participate in the
naturalization process. Providing accommodations to persons with physical or mental
impairments will help many qualified applicants to successfully complete the naturalization
process. In addition, providing such accommodations enables the INS to fulfill its obligations
under Section 504 of the Rehabilitation Act.[6]

Please refer to Appendix 1 for accepted practices for training, scheduling, and processing
accommodation requests. Please refer to Appendix 2 for examples of possible accommodations.

If you have any questions about this guidance, please contact Kellie LeClair, Business
Process and Reengineering, Immigration Services Division at (202) 307-9919.

---

[6] The INS has a separate policy for providing accommodations to INS employees with disabilities. Please contact
HQEEO.

Appendix 1

Accepted Practices

A. Training

- Train *all* staff members on how to appropriately evaluate and respond to accommodation requests.

- Designate *one* staff member or a specific unit to evaluate and respond to all requests for accommodations. The field office must describe how it will ensure that accommodation requests are handled properly if the designated person is out of the office or is otherwise unable to fulfill those duties. Be sure all staff is aware of the accommodations process.

B. Informing the Public

- Create and distribute a pamphlet or flyer that clearly explains the process to applicants.

- Use an automated answering machine system to provide information regarding procedures to request accommodations (including the use of a dedicated TDD line for persons with hearing impairments[7]).

- Provide informational seminars for your local CBOs and AILA chapter.

C. Scheduling Accommodations

- Identify applicants who have submitted requests for accommodation. In some cases, an applicant will submit a request for an accommodation even before the field office has received the applicant's naturalization file from the service center. Each field office must have a process for receiving and filing such requests so that they can be matched to the applicant's file when it arrives from the service center.

- Accept requests for accommodation in any written form, from either the applicant or his or her attorney or accredited representative.

- Accept oral requests for accommodations if the request is made on the day the accommodations are needed and the accommodation can be easily provided.

D. Processing Accommodations

- Set time deadlines (or goals) for reviewing a request. For example, set a goal that all requests for accommodations be reviewed and decided in 30 days or less.

- Ensure that the applicant receives the approved accommodation. Once an applicant's request for accommodation has been approved (or an alternative accommodation has been approved), the field office must ensure that the accommodation is provided to the

---

[7] If your office does not already use such a device, Headquarters may be able to procure one for you at no cost. Please contact Kathy Lane from HQEEO at 202-514-1246.

Memorandum For All Regional Directors, All District Directors   Page 8
All Officers in Charge, All Service Center Directors
Subject: Guidance on Making the Naturalization Process Accessible to Applicants with Disabilities

applicant on the scheduled day and at the scheduled time (either on the date and time originally scheduled, or as rescheduled by the office in accordance with it rescheduling procedures).

- Notify applicants (and their attorneys or accredited representatives) by letter *before* the date of the naturalization examination if an accommodation to the examination cannot be provided at the scheduled time or on the scheduled day. Notify the applicant (and the attorney or accredited representative) of any need to reschedule by telephone (or, if the applicant is hearing impaired, by TDD) if there is insufficient time to reach the applicant by mail before the originally scheduled examination date.

- Set a deadline or goal for rescheduling any examinations that must be postponed because an accommodation could not be made available on the originally scheduled date (for example, set a goal that all examinations canceled for this reason must be rescheduled within 30 days of the original date).

Memorandum For All Regional Directors, All District Directors   Page 9
All Officers in Charge, All Service Center Directors
Subject: Guidance on Making the Naturalization Process Accessible to Applicants with
Disabilities

<u>Appendix 2</u>

<u>Examples of Accommodations</u>

Set forth below, are *examples* of possible accommodations. The list of examples is <u>not</u> intended to be an all-inclusive list. Field offices must evaluate each request for an accommodation *individually* and provide an accommodation that addresses the unique needs of the particular applicant. As discussed above, if the particular accommodation requested by the applicant cannot be provided, the field office should provide an appropriate alternative accommodation.

1.   Off-site Accommodations

If an applicant, because of the severity of his/her disability, is unable to appear in person, field offices may conduct off-site visits at the homes or residences of applicants with disabilities, or at an alternate location as determined by the agency. In addition, some applicants may have impairments that confine them to their homes or residences (such as a nursing home). Accommodations for persons who are unable to access the field office include:

> **Off-site interview**. If an applicant's illness or disability makes it medically inappropriate for the applicant to appear at the field office, an examiner should conduct the interview in the applicant's home or at an alternate site (e.g., nursing home, hospice, hospital, senior citizens center). This includes applicants who would require use of a stretcher or ambulance to appear at the field office.

> *Note:* Some applicants who may have qualified for an off-site interview will nevertheless appear at a field office for a regular interview. Examiners should make an effort to attend to such applicants expeditiously and make arrangements to naturalize the applicant in the office on that day if approvable and request supervisory review, whenever possible.

> **Off-site administration of the oath.** If an applicant's illness or disability makes it medically inappropriate for the applicant to appear at an oath ceremony, examiners should, if possible, administer the oath after the naturalization interview. If this is not possible, a second in-home visit should be scheduled to administer the oath. However, it is important to note that some applicants may complete the interview at the field office, but later be unable to attend an oath administration ceremony because of a deteriorating condition (or because they become disabled or impaired after the interview).

> **Off-site fingerprinting.** Refer to the ASC SOP regarding off-site fingerprinting.

Memorandum For All Regional Directors, All District Directors   Page 10
All Officers in Charge, All Service Center Directors
Subject: Guidance on Making the Naturalization Process Accessible to Applicants with
Disabilities

>   2.   *Accommodations for Naturalization Examination*
>
>   a.   General

The naturalization examination process can be a challenge for many applicants with
physical and/or mental impairments. Field offices can make several modifications to the
naturalization examination to provide accommodations to such applicants. Field offices should
establish procedures that increase the likelihood that applicants will be examined on their
scheduled examination day, at the designated appointment time, and that minimize the need to
reschedule examinations. The following are examples of accommodations for the examination
of the applicant's eligibility for the naturalization program.

- **Prompt examination.** Some applicants with disabilities are unable to wait in an
office for an extended period of time. Therefore, if an applicant can be examined
at the field office, but would be prevented from waiting for the examination due
to disability or medical reasons, the field office should *make every effort* to
examine the applicant *promptly* at the designated appointment time. Examples of
applicable medical reasons may include, but are not limited to, extreme fatigue,
behavioral problems, special needs related to the effects of medication and
problems sitting for long periods of time.

- **Extended examination time and breaks.** Some applicants with disabilities may
need more time than usually allotted to comprehend, process and provide
information. Therefore, examiners should provide applicants with disabilities
with additional time and should allow them to take breaks, if necessary.

- **Assistance for applicants with hearing impairments.** Field offices must ask an
applicant with a hearing impairment which method of communication the
applicant prefers and employ that method if possible. The common methods of
communication are: sign language, lip reading, note writing, telephone devices for
the deaf (TDD) or some combination of these methods. If a sign language
interpreter is requested, the field office can provide a sign language interpreter
who is linguistically matched to the applicant or allow an applicant to provide an
interpreter of the applicant's own choosing and approved by the Service.

- **Assistance for applicants with vision impairments.** Examiners should conduct
all aspects of the examination orally to accommodate applicants who are
completely or partially blind.

Memorandum For All Regional Directors, All District Directors   Page 11
All Officers in Charge, All Service Center Directors
Subject: Guidance on Making the Naturalization Process Accessible to Applicants with Disabilities

> **Assistance for nonverbal applicants.** Examiners should allow nonverbal applicants to point to answers written on a piece of paper (i.e., the DAO writes "yes" and "no" on a piece of paper, and the applicant points to "yes" or "no" in response to questions requiring merely a "yes" or "no" answer). Alternatively, an examiner should accept any other nonverbal forms of communication, such as blinking, nodding/shaking head, and tapping, that have been previously agreed to by the applicant (or his or her attorney or accredited representative) and the DAO.

> **Presence of family member, guardian, social worker or other familiar individual during the examination.** The presence of a family member or other familiar person may help applicants with disabilities remain calm and responsive during the examination. As an accommodation, the field office may allow applicants to bring such an individual with them to the examination. The applicant may need the individual to keep the applicant company or to calm the applicant. An applicant may bring this individual into the examination *in addition* to an interpreter or that person may also serve as an interpreter, depending on the field office's policies regarding interpreters. Under the direction and supervision of the examiner, the family member may *repeat* the questions posed by the examiner if this repetition is needed to facilitate a responsive answer.

b.   Accommodations Particular to Parts of the Naturalization Examination

i.   <u>English and/or Civics Exams</u>

To qualify for an N-648 waiver of the English and/or civics tests due to disability, applicants must be unable to learn or demonstrate knowledge. There are applicants, however, whose disabilities do not render them *unable* to learn or demonstrate knowledge, but which make it extremely *difficult* to learn or demonstrate knowledge. Such applicants cannot receive waivers of the English and/or civics requirements, but are eligible under the Rehabilitation Act for an accommodation that will give them an opportunity to fulfill these requirements. The following are some accommodations that may be made to the English and/or civics tests.

> **Questions in plain language.** When necessary, examiners should ask applicants questions during the English and civics tests in simplified language and should speak slowly and clearly.

> **Written tests for people who have hearing difficulties.** If an applicant cannot take either or both tests orally, he or she must be allowed to take the test in written form.

Memorandum For All Regional Directors, All District Directors   Page 12
All Officers in Charge, All Service Center Directors
Subject: Guidance on Making the Naturalization Process Accessible to Applicants with
Disabilities

> **Tests in large print or oral questions for applicants with vision impairments.**
> If an applicant cannot take either or both tests in regular written form, examiners
> should provide him or her with a version in large print (at least 14 point type).
> Alternatively, examiners can administer the tests orally.

---

*Note: In some cases, applicants with physical impairments such as vision or hearing
loss may be unable to take the English and/or civics exams (even with an
accommodation) and will have filed an N-648 form. In such cases, the DAO should
first make a determination on the N-648.* See Policy Memo 47 dated April 7, 1999:
Section 312 Disability Naturalization Adjudications

---

ii.   Examination of Applications - Third Party Testimony

Field offices conduct examinations to verify the information on the application for
naturalization and to make determinations regarding the applicant's eligibility to be admitted to
citizenship. The INS received a legal opinion concerning whether the Service can accept third
party testimony in lieu of the applicant's testimony as to her or his eligibility for naturalization.
The Service is reviewing the legal opinion and will publish regulations detailing the parameters
of this practice at a later date.

3.   *Oath of Allegiance*

A disability or medical condition may make it difficult for some applicants to take the
Oath of Allegiance at the traditional oath ceremony. If the applicant is not eligible for a waiver of
the oath, the following are some accommodations that may be made to the oath process:

> **Expedited oath.** If possible, field offices should provide an expedited
> administrative naturalization (i.e., an expedited oath) for an applicant who,
> because of a physical or mental impairment, is unable to attend the judicial oath
> ceremony.

> **Nonverbal assent.** Examiners should accept any predetermined nonverbal form
> of assent when administering the oath, including blinking, nodding and tapping.

> **Sign language interpreter.** If the court in which the oath ceremony is taking
> place does not provide a sign language interpreter, the INS should provide an
> applicant with a hearing impairment with a linguistically-matched sign language
> interpreter to sign the oath, or permit the applicant to use his or her own
> interpreter. Applicants must request such interpreter prior to the oath ceremony.

Modifications to demonstrate assent to oath. When necessary, INS should determine whether the applicant has assented to the oath by asking questions in simplified language and by speaking slowly and clearly. DAOs must determine that an applicant: (1) understands that he or she is becoming a U.S. citizen; (2) is foreswearing allegiance to his or her country of nationality; and (3) is personally and voluntarily agreeing to a change in status to that of a U.S. citizen. In determining whether assent has been given, a DAO should simplify questions to allow for "yes" or "no" answers to determine whether the applicant understands the requirements for the oath of allegiance.[8]

---

[8] See Policy Memorandum No 47 on Section 312 Disability Naturalization Adjudications, issued on April 7, 1999.

APPENDIX 7-16

USCIS Memorandum on Oath Waivers

U.S. Department of Homeland Security
Bureau of Citizenship and Immigration Services

HQISD 70/33

425 I Street NW
Washington, DC 20536

June 30, 2003

MEMORANDUM FOR REGIONAL DIRECTORS
                             DISTRICT DIRECTORS
                             OFFICERS-IN-CHARGE
                             SERVICE CENTER DIRECTORS

FROM: William R. Yates */s/ Janis Sposato*
                   Acting Associate Director
                   Bureau of Citizenship and Immigration Services

SUBJECT: Procedures for Implementing the Waiving of the Oath of Renunciation and
                   <u>Allegiance for the Naturalization of Aliens having Certain Disabilities</u>

       This memorandum provides comprehensive policy guidance on procedures for conducting examinations and waiving the oath of allegiance for naturalization applicants with disabilities.

Background

       This memorandum is issued in order to provide procedures for conducting examinations and waiving the oath of allegiance and the requirement of demonstrating attachment to the principles of the Constitution and well disposition to the good order and happiness of the United States for naturalization applicants with disabilities.

       Naturalization applicants must establish that they meet all the requirements for naturalization, including the demonstration of the applicant's residence, physical presence in the United States, good moral character, understanding of and attachment to the fundamental principles of the Constitution of the United States, ability to read, write and speak English, and other qualifications to become a naturalized citizen as required by law.

Memorandum for Regional Directors   Page 2
                District Directors
                Officers-in-Charge
                Service Center Directors

Subject: Procedures for Implementing the Waiving of the Oath of Renunciation and Allegiance
        for the Naturalization of Aliens having Certain Disabilities

        In 1994, Section 108 of the Immigration and Nationality Technical Corrections Act of
1994 (INTCA), Public Law 103-416, amended section 312 of the Immigration and Nationality
Act (Act) to provide a waiver of the English and civics requirements for applicants with
disabilities. However, the naturalization oath was required for all applicants under section 337 of
the Act. To fulfill the oath requirement, an applicant must understand that he or she is (1)
becoming a citizen of the United States, (2) foreswearing allegiance to his or her country of
nationality, and (3) personally and voluntarily agreeing to a change in status. Certain disabled
applicants were precluded from naturalization because they could not personally express intent
or voluntary assent to the oath requirement.

        To remedy this problem, Public Law 106-448, enacted on November 6, 2000, authorizes
the Attorney General to waive the attachment requirement under section 316(a) and the oath
requirement under section 337 of the Act for any individual who has a developmental or physical
disability or mental impairment that makes him or her unable to understand, or communicate an
understanding of, the meaning of the oath. Public Law 106-448 was enacted to remove any
further obstacles in the naturalization process for applicants with disabilities.

Examination of applicants

        Pursuant to section 332 of the Act, the Attorney General is authorized to prescribe the
scope and nature of the examination of naturalization applicants. Currently under 8 CFR 335.2,
all applicants for naturalization are required to appear in person and give testimony under oath as
to their eligibility for naturalization. The Bureau of Citizenship and Immigration Services
(BCIS), however, has concluded that these procedures should be modified for applicants with
severe disabilities who otherwise may be eligible for naturalization but are unable to personally
attest to their eligibility through the current examination process.

        The BCIS has determined that, in certain instances, it is appropriate to permit a
designated representative to complete the naturalization examination on behalf of a qualified
applicant, attesting orally (and through affidavits and submission of documentary evidence) to
the disabled applicant's qualifications for naturalization. Such a modified procedure will allow
the BCIS to obtain the most accurate information available regarding the applicant's eligibility
from those individuals who are most familiar with the applicant's life history and current
impairment.

Memorandum for Regional Directors   Page 3
                  District Directors
                  Officers-in-Charge
                  Service Center Directors

Subject: Procedures for Implementing the Waiving of the Oath of Renunciation and Allegiance
         for the Naturalization of Aliens having Certain Disabilities

Requirements for Oath and Attachment Waiver Under Public Law 106-448

A.   Eligibility for waiver.

        To be eligible for an oath waiver, an individual must have a developmental or physical
disability or mental impairment that prevents him or her from being able to understand the
meaning of the oath or to communicate an understanding of the oath requirement.

        The requirements for the oath waiver are distinct from the requirements for the English
and civics waiver under section 312 of the Act. While both section 312 and section 337 of the
Act, as amended, require that the applicant have a "developmental or physical disability or
mental impairment" and while the BCIS is adopting a definition of this phrase that is similar to
the one provided in current §§ 312.1(b)(3) and 312.2(b)(1), the assessment of a person's ability
to meet the oath requirement is different from the assessment of the applicant's ability to learn
English and civics.

        Currently, the BCIS tests an applicant's English language and civics knowledge during
the naturalization examination. For applicants with disabilities who are unable (even with
reasonable modifications) to pass the English and civics tests, the BCIS allows the applicant to
submit a Form N-648, Request for Medical Certification For Disability Exceptions, from a
qualified physician, describing the applicant's disability and explaining how, and to what extent,
the disability prevents the applicant from learning English and civics. If the BCIS determines
that the applicant has a disability that prevents him or her from learning English and civics even
with reasonable modifications, the BCIS grants the waiver. In many instances, however,
applicants who are granted an English and civics waiver can still fulfill the oath requirement
despite their disability.

        The BCIS assesses whether the applicant can meet the oath requirement and is willing to
take the oath in a public ceremony by asking questions during the naturalization examination.
To fulfill the oath requirement, an applicant must understand that he or she is (1) becoming a
citizen of the United States, (2) foreswearing allegiance to his or her country of nationality, and
(3) personally and voluntarily agreeing to a change in status. For disabled applicants, the BCIS
uses various methods to assess whether the applicant understands the oath requirement and can
communicate such an understanding to a BCIS officer. These methods include explaining the
requirements to family members who are acting as interpreters, permitting the applicant to
demonstrate assent by giving "yes" or "no" responses to simplified questions about the oath, and
accepting predetermined physical motions or signals that the applicant uses to communicate.

        The oath waiver also is not intended for applicants who find the naturalization process
challenging or attendance at an oath ceremony inconvenient. Nor is the oath waiver available to
applicants who object to taking the oath as written but cannot qualify for a modified oath as

Memorandum for Regional Directors   Page 4
            District Directors
            Officers-in-Charge
            Service Center Directors

Subject: Procedures for Implementing the Waiving of the Oath of Renunciation and Allegiance
for the Naturalization of Aliens having Certain Disabilities

provided under section 337(a) of the Act. The oath waiver is designed for those applicants who
are so severely disabled that they cannot, in any fashion or by any means, either demonstrate an
understanding of the oath or communicate that understanding to a BCIS officer. Any individual
whom the BCIS determines qualifies for an oath waiver also will be deemed to have met the
attachment requirement under section 316(a)(3) of the Act.

        B.   Procedures for requesting waiver.

        The BCIS decided not to create a form for the oath and attachment waiver because the
waiver applies to a very small class of individuals. The BCIS, however, will ask that applicants
either annotate Part 3, section I of the current Form N-400, Application for Naturalization or
submit a letter requesting the waiver at the time of filing the Form N-400. The BCIS is not
making this requirement mandatory because there are certain instances where an applicant may
have a disability that, through the passage of time, causes significantly impaired functioning that
may not have manifested at the time of filing the application for naturalization.

        An applicant who is eligible for an oath waiver may need a designated representative to
act on his or her behalf. Filing the waiver request with the N-400 will allow the BCIS sufficient
time to review the request prior to the initial examination and determine if any additional
documentation is necessary to establish eligibility for the waiver or to determine who is qualified
to act as a designated representative on the applicant's behalf. Nonetheless, the BCIS will accept
requests for an oath and attachment waiver at any point in the naturalization process up until the
administration of the oath ceremony.

        C.   Documentary requirements for waiver.

        Applicants who need a waiver generally will have disabilities or have a medical condition
as a result of these disabilities that makes the need for the waiver apparent upon seeing or
attempting to examine the applicant (e.g. applicants in a vegetative state or comatose, or non-
responsive due to severe mental impairments).

        The BCIS, however, will require applicants seeking a waiver (or designated
representatives acting on the applicant's behalf) to submit a written evaluation completed by
either a medical or osteopathic doctor licensed to practice medicine in the United States or a
clinical psychologist licensed to practice psychology in the United States. The BCIS also will
require that the evaluation:

        (1)   Be completed by the physician who has had the longest relationship with
           the applicant or is most familiar with the applicant's medical history;

Memorandum for Regional Directors   Page 5
    District Directors
    Officers-in-Charge
    Service Center Directors

Subject: Procedures for Implementing the Waiving of the Oath of Renunciation and Allegiance
    for the Naturalization of Aliens having Certain Disabilities

 (2)   Express the applicant's condition/disability in lay terms (except for the names and medical definitions of the disabilities) that can be easily understood by both the designated representative and the BCIS examiner;

 (3)   State why and how the applicant is unable to understand or communicate an understanding of the meaning of the oath because of the disability;

 (4)   Indicate the likelihood of the applicant being able to communicate or demonstrate an understanding of the meaning of the oath in the near future; and

 (5)   Contain the signature and state license number for the medical professional completing the written evaluation, reflecting that the professional is authorized to practice in the United States.

The BCIS will not require doctors to provide an explanation of how they reached their diagnosis, a listing of clinical or laboratory techniques used to reach the diagnosis or supporting documentation to establish the claimed disability. The BCIS, however, will require the doctor to provide a thorough explanation of how the applicant's disability impairs their functioning so severely that the applicant is unable to demonstrate an understanding of the oath requirements or communicate an understanding of its meaning. The BCIS reserves the right to request documentation if there is a question upon examination about the applicant's disability and ability to understand the oath requirement.

  D. Adjudication of waiver requests.

In adjudicating a request for an oath waiver, the BCIS will evaluate the relevant documentary evidence submitted by the applicant and his or her designated representative, including the doctor's assessment of the applicant's condition. The BCIS will also consider the applicant's physical conditions and response to questions customarily asked during the naturalization examination, as well as any statements of the designated representative regarding the applicant's capabilities.

If the BCIS determines that the applicant understands that he or she is (1) becoming a citizen of the United States, (2) foreswearing allegiance to his or her country of nationality, and (3) personally and voluntarily agreeing to a change in status, the waiver is not necessary, will not be granted, and the BCIS will schedule the applicant for participation in an oath ceremony. If the BCIS determines that the applicant cannot express intent or voluntary assent to the oath requirement, even after reasonable modifications such as simplified questioning or use of predetermined signals, the BCIS will grant the oath waiver.

Designated Representatives

A. Individuals eligible to act as designated representatives.

Memorandum for Regional Directors   Page 6
         District Directors
         Officers-in-Charge
         Service Center Directors

Subject: Procedures for Implementing the Waiving of the Oath of Renunciation and Allegiance
        for the Naturalization of Aliens having Certain Disabilities

The BCIS has defined the phrase "designated representative" to mean any individual who either has been recognized by a court of competent jurisdiction over family law matters in the state of the applicant's place of residence or appropriate state agency to exercise legal authority to act on behalf of an applicant in all matters, including filing of applications for benefits, or has a recognized familial relationship with the applicant and primary custodial care and responsibility for the applicant. This rule authorizes designated representatives to act on behalf of applicants with disabilities in every stage of the naturalization proceeding.

The designated representative may be either:

1. a legal guardian or surrogate appointed by a recognized court with jurisdiction over matters of guardianship or surrogacy or an appropriate state agency with authority to make such appointments in the jurisdiction of the applicant's place of residence in the United States; or

2. in the absence of a legal guardian or surrogate, a U.S. citizen spouse, parent, adult son or daughter, or adult brother or sister.

The designated representative may have filed the application on behalf of the applicant and, if not a legal guardian or surrogate, must have knowledge of the facts supporting the applicant's eligibility for naturalization.

    B. Documentary requirements.

A legal guardian or surrogate should submit documentary evidence from the appropriate state authority or court of competent jurisdiction in the state of the applicant's place of residence that granted legal guardianship or custody over the applicant.

A U.S. citizen spouse, parent, adult son or daughter, or adult brother or sister must submit evidence of their citizenship status as described in § 204.1(g).

A U.S. citizen spouse also must submit evidence that he or she is legally married to the applicant and must state under oath that they are still legally married. A U.S. citizen parent must submit evidence that the applicant is their child or son or daughter as required in § 204.2(d)(2).

A U.S. citizen adult son or daughter who is primary caretaker of the applicant must submit evidence required in § 204.2(d)(2) of this chapter establishing that he or she at some time met the requirements of the definition of "child" found at section 101(b)(1) of the Act. The adult son or daughter must also submit evidence that he or she has primary custodial responsibility for the applicant, e.g. tax returns reflecting that the applicant has been declared a dependent in the household or an executed power of attorney.

Subject: Procedures for Implementing the Waiving of the Oath of Renunciation and Allegiance
         for the Naturalization of Aliens having Certain Disabilities

A U.S. citizen adult brother or sister who is the primary caretaker of the applicant must
submit evidence required under § 204.2(g)(2) of this chapter establishing that he or she meets the
requirements of being a sibling of the applicant. The adult brother or sister must also submit
evidence that he or she has primary custodial responsibility for the applicant, e.g. tax returns
reflecting that the applicant has been declared a dependent in the household or an executed
power of attorney.

The BCIS will require that every qualified designated representative state, in writing and
under oath, that to the best of his or her knowledge and belief no other person has been granted
the legal guardianship or authority over the affairs of the applicant whom he or she seeks to
represent.

C. Determination of eligibility to act as designated representative.

The BCIS will review all the documentation submitted by the individual seeking to act as
a designated representative on behalf of a disabled applicant to determine if the individual is a
qualified legal guardian or surrogate, or has the required familial relationship and custodial
responsibility for the applicant.

For consistency, the BCIS will permit only one recognized designated representative to
represent the applicant at any time throughout the naturalization process. In the case of multiple
parties seeking to represent the applicant in the naturalization proceeding, the BCIS will
recognize designated representatives in the following order of priority: (1) legal guardian or
surrogate; (2) U.S. citizen spouse; (3) U.S. citizen parent; (4) U.S. citizen adult son or daughter;
and (5) the U.S. citizen adult brother or sister. If there is a priority conflict between the
individuals seeking to represent the applicant and the individuals share the same degree of
familial relationship, the BCIS will give priority to the party with seniority in age.

Procedures for handling Form N-400 for qualified waiver applicants

A.   Filing of Form N-400

A granting of the oath waiver does not relieve the applicant of establishing eligibility for
naturalization in all respects. Applicants who are eligible for an oath and attachment waiver are
still required to file the Form N-400 with all supporting documentation, including the
photographs and fees required under § 103.7(b)(1). If the applicant has not yet reached his or her
75th birthday at the time of filing, the applicant must be fingerprinted in order for the Federal
Bureau of Investigation to conduct a background check or, if eligible for a fingerprint waiver,
provide local police clearances from every jurisdiction where the applicant has resided during the
statutory period.

Memorandum for Regional Directors   Page 8
            District Directors
            Officers-in-Charge
            Service Center Directors

Subject: Procedures for Implementing the Waiving of the Oath of Renunciation and Allegiance
         for the Naturalization of Aliens having Certain Disabilities

        In most instances, individuals who will act as the designated representative will file the
application on behalf of the applicant. Individuals seeking to represent an applicant who has a
physical or developmental disability or mental impairment should provide documentation with
the applicant's Form N-400 establishing their eligibility to act on behalf of the applicant as a
designated representative. In addition, if the designated representative prepares the application,
the BCIS will require that the designated representative sign the application in the Preparer's box
of section 11 and, in cases where the applicant is physically unable to sign, in the signature box,
attesting under penalty of perjury that the information being provided is true and correct.

            a. Examination on Form N-400.

        The BCIS will still require that all applicants for naturalization appear for an
examination. However, in those cases where applicants are homebound or in medical care
facilities and cannot be transported to the BCIS office for medical reasons, the BCIS will
conduct an off-site examination at an alternate location as provided in § 334.4. The BCIS will
conduct the examination with the applicant, making reasonable accommodations as appropriate
to elicit responses to questions on the Form N-400. The BCIS will only conduct an examination
through a designated representative when it is determined that the applicant cannot respond in
any fashion, including through the use of predetermined signals or motions, to questions posed
by the BCIS officer. In such cases, a designated representative will be permitted to complete the
naturalization examination on behalf of a qualified applicant, attesting orally under oath and
through affidavits and submission of documentary evidence to the applicant's qualifications for
naturalization.

        The BCIS will require that the designated representative address every requirement for
naturalization including lawful permanent residence, duration of lawful residence, physical
presence, continuity of residence, and good moral character, and the designated representative
will bear the burden of establishing the applicant's eligibility for naturalization. The designated
representative will be required to annotate any amendments to the N-400 and at the conclusion of
the examination sign the application under penalty of perjury, attesting to the truthfulness of the
statements contained on the Form N-400 and to his or her testimony during the examination.

        If the BCIS determines that the designated representative has made false statements under
oath or willfully concealed or misrepresented material facts during the naturalization process, the
BCIS will deny the application for naturalization. In addition, if the BCIS subsequently
determines after approval of the naturalization application but before administration of the oath
that the designated representative made false statements or willfully misrepresented material
facts on the Form N-400, the BCIS will reopen the application under § 335.5 and deny the
application based on the derogatory information.

Memorandum for Regional Directors   Page 9
                  District Directors
                  Officers-in-Charge
                  Service Center Directors

Subject: Procedures for Implementing the Waiving of the Oath of Renunciation and Allegiance
           for the Naturalization of Aliens having Certain Disabilities

b. NQP Notations

On oath waiver cases, the DAO will initial and date the "Established attachment to the Constitution" line on the N-650B. In the remarks section, write "oath waived per PL 106-448" and initial and date. The notation, "oath waived per PL 106-448" and the officer's initials and date should be made on the Certificate Preparation Sheet and Oath Declaration or Part 14 of the revised N-400 depending on the version of the N-400 filed. The applicant granted an oath waiver and the designated representative are not required to sign the Oath of Allegiance on the Certificate Preparation Sheet and Oath Declaration or Part 14 of the revised N-400.

Oath ceremony

If the BCIS approves an oath and attachment waiver, the disabled applicant will not be required to appear in a public oath ceremony as required under section 337 of the Act. However, the BCIS will honor requests by applicants or their designated representatives either to participate in an oath ceremony or to receive the Certificate of Naturalization in an appropriate manner. In keeping with the spirit of § 337.2(a), the BCIS will deliver or present the Certificate of Naturalization in such a manner as to preserve the dignity and significance of the occasion while respecting the wishes of the applicant and his or her designated representative.

Pending cases

Any case that is currently pending and which would have been approved if the person(s) who assisted the applicant had met the requirements of being a Designated Representative pursuant to this memorandum should be approved.

In any case that has had an initial examination and that cannot be approved because of the applicant's lack of understanding or inability to participate in the examination, the applicant should be afforded the opportunity of having another examination at which the applicant can be represented by a person who meets the requirements of this memorandum. Before the N-400 is adjudicated, the applicant should have the opportunity of receiving the assistance of a Designated Representative, as authorized by this memorandum.

Denials

Since November 6, 2000, no N-400, Application for Naturalization, can be properly denied because of the applicant's failure to understand the oath of renunciation and allegiance.

If an applicant with a disability, with or without the assistance of a Designated Representative, fails to demonstrate required lawful admission for permanent residence, sufficient duration of residence, required continuity of residence, sufficient physical presence,

Memorandum for Regional Directors   Page 10
                    District Directors
                    Officers-in-Charge
                    Service Center Directors

Subject: Procedures for Implementing the Waiving of the Oath of Renunciation and Allegiance
              for the Naturalization of Aliens having Certain Disabilities

residence in the jurisdiction, good moral character, English literacy and knowledge of civics, if
not waived or exempted, and freedom from any statutory bar to naturalization, the N-400 should
be denied for failure to demonstrate the required eligibility or freedom from a bar, not for the
applicant's failure to understand.

Questions

The Federal Regulations are forthcoming and will be published in the Federal Register.

If you have any questions about this memorandum, please forward them through
appropriate channels.

Attachment

Memorandum for Regional Directors
          District Directors
          Officers-in-Charge
          Service Center Directors

Subject: Procedures for Implementing the Waiving of the Oath of Renunciation and Allegiance
for the Naturalization of Aliens having Certain Disabilities

Attachment 1

Public Law 106-448

An Act To amend the Immigration and Nationality Act to provide a waiver of the oath of renunciation and allegiance for naturalization of aliens having certain disabilities.

Public Law 106-448

An Act

To amend the Immigration and Nationality Act to provide a waiver of the oath of renunciation and allegiance for naturalization of aliens having certain disabilities.

Be it enacted by the Senate and House of Representatives of the United States of America in Congress assembled,

SECTION 1. WAIVER OF OATH OF RENUNCIATION AND ALLEGIANCE FOR NATURALIZATION OF ALIENS HAVING CERTAIN DISABILITIES.

Section 337(a) of the Immigration and Nationality Act (8 U.S.C. 1448(a)) is amended by adding at the end the following: `The Attorney General may waive the taking of the oath by a person if in the opinion of the Attorney General the person is unable to understand, or to communicate an understanding of, its meaning because of a physical or developmental disability or mental impairment. If the Attorney General waives the taking of the oath by a person under the preceding sentence, the person shall be considered to have met the requirements of section 316(a)(3) with respect to attachment to the principles of the Constitution and well disposition to the good order and happiness of the United States.'.

SEC. 2. EFFECTIVE DATE.

The amendment made by section 1 shall apply to persons applying for naturalization before, on, or after the date of the enactment of this Act.

APPENDIX 7-17

Memorandum Regarding Disability Waivers

U.S. Department of Homeland Security
20 Massachusetts Ave., NW
Washington, DC 20529

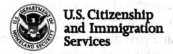

**U.S. Citizenship
and Immigration
Services**

HQRPM 70/33-P
AD06-09

Interoffice Memorandum

To: Service Center Directors
      Regional Directors
      District Directors
      Officers-in-Charge

From: Michael Aytes /s/
      Acting Associate Director
      Domestic Operations

Date: May 10, 2006

Re: Adjudication of Form N-648, Medical Certification for Disability Exceptions
      to the Immigration and Nationality Act (INA) Section 312 Naturalization Requirements

      Revisions to *Adjudicator's Field Manual (AFM)* Chapter 72.2(d)(5) and Appendix 72-13
      (*AFM* Update AD06-09)

1. Purpose

USCIS has detected patterns of fraud and misrepresentation in the submission of Form N-648, Medical Certification for Disability Exceptions. In order to address these concerns and protect the integrity of the naturalization process, USCIS is issuing this memorandum to provide comprehensive and updated policy guidance for the review of Form N-648. This memorandum supersedes the April 7, 1999 Memorandum entitled, "Section 312 Disability Naturalization Adjudications (Policy Memo # 47 and attachments)," and updates the *Adjudicator's Field Manual (AFM)*.

2. Background

Section 312(b) of the INA provides that the English and Civics requirements "shall not apply to any person who is unable because of **physical or developmental disability or mental impairment** to comply therewith." Under the regulations at 8 CFR 312.2, a medical professional must establish that the applicant has a "**medically determinable**" physical or developmental disability or mental impairment in order for the applicant to qualify for the disability exception.

Adjudication of Form N-648, Medical Certification for Disability Exceptions to Section 312 Naturalization Requirements; HQOPRD 70/33-P

Revisions to *Adjudicator's Field Manual (AFM)* Chapter 72.2(d)(5) and Appendix 72-13 (*AFM* Update AD06-09)

Page 2

"Medically determinable" means that the disability or impairment, or combination thereof "results from anatomical, physiological, or psychological abnormalities which can be shown by medically acceptable clinical or laboratory diagnostic techniques to have resulted in functioning so impaired as to render an individual unable to demonstrate an understanding" of English and/or U.S. history and government. In simple terms, the regulations require that the medical professional establish and certify that the applicant has a physical or mental abnormality that has impaired the individual's functioning *so severely* that the individual is unable to learn or demonstrate knowledge of English and/or U.S. history and government.

It is important to note that an exception from the Section 312 requirements **does not** waive any other naturalization requirements. Therefore, those applicants, whose disability exception requests have been accepted, must still establish good moral character, residence, and assent to the oath (unless waived), etc.

It is also important to note that the statutory exception requested in a Form N-648 is not the same as a request for accommodations under the Rehabilitation Act of 1973 or a request for waiver of the oath requirement.

3. Contact Information

Questions related to this memorandum should be directed to Bunnie Bryce, through appropriate supervisory channels.

4. Use

This memorandum is intended solely for the guidance of USCIS personnel in performing their duties relative to adjudications of applications. It is not intended to, does not, and may not be relied upon to create any right or benefit, substantive or procedural, enforceable at law by any individual or other party in removal proceedings, in litigation with the United States, or in any other form or manner.

5. Field Guidance *AFM* Chapter 72.2(d)(5)

Effective immediately, USCIS field offices are directed to comply with the following instructions, as set forth in revised *AFM* Chapter 72.2(d)(5):

Adjudication of Form N-648, Medical Certification for Disability Exceptions to Section 312 Naturalization Requirements; HQOPRD 70/33-P

Revisions to *Adjudicator's Field Manual (AFM)* Chapter 72.2(d)(5) and Appendix 72-13 (*AFM* Update AD06-09)

Page 3

(5) <u>Adjudication Guidelines for the Form N-648 Waiver</u>. **[Revised as of 05/10/2006]**

(A) <u>Medical Professionals Authorized to Complete the Form N-648</u>.

Under 8 CFR 312.2, the following medical professionals who are licensed to practice in the United States (including Guam, Puerto Rico, and the Virgin Islands) are eligible to sign a Form N-648 diagnosis and medical opinion on behalf of an applicant: 1) medical doctors; 2) doctors of osteopathy; and 3) clinical psychologists.

Medical professionals must certify, under penalty of perjury, that their statements are true and correct. In addition, 8 CFR 312.2(b)(2) and the Form N-648 Instructions require the certifying medical professional to have appropriate experience and qualifications that will enable him/her to diagnose and assess the claimed disability and/or impairment. For example, a certification by a general practitioner regarding a mental disability will be acceptable if the general practitioner has appropriate experience and qualifications to diagnose and assess that type of disability. A Form N-648 should be reviewed based on the standard of review outlined in section (D) below.

(B) <u>Validity and Timeliness of the Form N-648</u>.

The Form N-648 may be submitted as an attachment to the Form N-400 Application for Naturalization, as a supplement to the Form N-400 after the initial filing of the Application for Naturalization, or at the time of the interview. If the Form N-648 is submitted at the time of the interview, the examination may be continued pending the adjudication of the Form N-648.

The Form N-648 must be submitted within six months of when it was completed by the medical professional or psychologist. A properly submitted Form N-648 will remain valid indefinitely unless it is denied, or until such time as the District Adjudications Officer (DAO) determines that the disability described does not preclude the applicant from demonstrating the requisite knowledge and understanding of English and/or U.S. history and government.

(C) <u>Appropriate Role of Adjudicators in Reviewing Form N-648</u>.

DAOs are responsible for determining whether the applicant meets the requirements of Section 312 of the INA. Each district office should designate a Journeyman DAO

Adjudication of Form N-648, Medical Certification for Disability Exceptions to Section 312 Naturalization Requirements; HQOPRD 70/33-P

Revisions to *Adjudicator's Field Manual (AFM)* Chapter 72.2(d)(5) and Appendix 72-13 (*AFM* Update AD06-09)

Page 4

to be the point of contact for training and oversight of the Form N-648 adjudications. In reviewing the Form N-648, the DAO's role is to determine whether the Form N-648 contains sufficient information to establish that the applicant is eligible for a disability exception. The medical professional's role is to establish and certify the applicant's diagnosis, to explain how the anatomical, physiological, or psychological impairment diagnosis was arrived at (including which medically acceptable clinical or laboratory diagnostic tests were used to reach the diagnosis), and to explain how this condition affects the applicant's ability to learn or demonstrate knowledge of English and/or U.S. history and government.

DAOs must ensure that the Form N-648 contains an explanation of the origin, nature, and extent of the medical condition including a list of the medically acceptable clinical or laboratory diagnostic tests employed in reaching the diagnosis, a notation that the disability has lasted, or is expected to last, 12 months or longer, and a notation that the disability is not the direct effect of the illegal use of drugs.

The diagnosis of the medical professional will be presumed valid in the absence of significant discrepancies or credible doubt. However, the DAO may, pursuant to the regulations, refer the applicant to another authorized medical specialist, at the applicant's expense, for a supplemental disability determination when there are "credible doubts about the veracity of a medical certification." 8 CFR 312.2(b)(2) For this purpose, each district shall refer the applicant to the state medical board in order to locate a medical specialist in the appropriate specialty area (i.e., psychiatrist, neurologist, psychologist). See Attachments A and B.

[(b)(2) or (b)(7)(E)]

(D) Standard of Review of the Form N-648.

A DAO must first review the Form N-648 to ensure that it is properly completed. If more than one Form N-648 was submitted, the most recent Form N-648 will be considered. DAOs can, however, examine previously submitted Form N-648s for additional information or discrepancies.

The focal point of the DAO's review should be to determine if the medical professional has clearly shown how the applicant's diagnosed condition affects the applicant's ability to function, i.e., the **nexus** (connection) between the disability, impairment, or combination of impairments **and** the applicant's ability to learn or demonstrate knowledge of English and/or U.S. history and government. There are no key words, phrases, or tests that will by themselves constitute a sufficient nexus,

Adjudication of Form N-648, Medical Certification for Disability Exceptions to Section 312 Naturalization Requirements; HQOPRD 70/33-P

Revisions to *Adjudicator's Field Manual (AFM)* Chapter 72.2(d)(5) and Appendix 72-13 (*AFM* Update AD06-09)

Page 5

nor is there a list of conditions, symptoms, or complications that will always be caused by or linked to certain disabilities or impairments. Rather, DAOs must evaluate each Form N-648 individually and determine, based on all the information, whether the applicant has met the burden of showing that the anatomical, physiological, or psychological abnormality described has so impaired the applicant's functioning that he or she is unable to learn or demonstrate knowledge of English and/or U.S. history and government.

The Form N-648 must also include a sufficiently thorough explanation of how the disability or impairment was diagnosed. The medical professional should include a list of medically acceptable clinical or laboratory diagnostic tests employed to determine that the applicant has a condition that makes him or her unable to learn or demonstrate knowledge of English and/or U.S. history and government. If the Form N-648 does not provide a sufficiently thorough explanation, regulatory authority exists that allows the DAO to request a copy of the applicant's medical records to determine that the claimed diagnostic tests were performed. Prior to the DAO issuing a request for the applicant's medical records, the specific case should be referred to the Supervisory District Adjudications Officer (SDAO) for approval. The DAO may review the records to determine the veracity of the medical professional's claims on the Form N-648 regarding how he or she reached the diagnosis. DAOs are not permitted to request medical records solely to question whether there was a proper medical basis for the noted impairment. DAOs may only review medical records to determine whether the certifying medical professional has conducted the claimed medically acceptable clinical or laboratory diagnostic tests to arrive at the diagnosis noted in the Form N-648.

DAOs should review the Forms N-648 reflecting mental impairments such as depression or disabilities related to, associated with, or caused by "old age" the same way they review all other medically determinable conditions that may qualify for a Section 312 disability exception. "Old age," in and of itself, is not a medically determinable physical or developmental disability or mental impairment. However, an individual with a disease or disability that is related to, associated with, or caused by old age (e.g., Alzheimer's, Parkinson's Disease, senile dementia) can qualify for a disability exception, if the disability results in an impairment in functioning so severe that the applicant is unable to learn or demonstrate knowledge of English and/or U.S. history and government. Similarly, depression should be treated like any other disability or impairment. Post Traumatic Stress Disorder (PTSD) should be similarly evaluated under the standard of review set forth in this section.

Adjudication of Form N-648, Medical Certification for Disability Exceptions to Section 312 Naturalization Requirements; HQOPRD 70/33-P

Revisions to *Adjudicator's Field Manual (AFM)* Chapter 72.2(d)(5) and Appendix 72-13 (*AFM* Update AD06-09)

Page 6

[(b)(2) or (b)(7)(E)]

(E) <u>Procedures for Review of and Action on Form N-648</u>.

Under 8 CFR 312.2(b)(2), applicants are required to submit the Form N-648 with their Form N-400. Applicants may also submit their Form N-648 waiver as a supplement to the Form N-400 prior to the interview, or may submit the Form N-648 waiver at the time of the interview. If the Form N-648 is submitted at the time of the interview, the examination may be continued pending the adjudication of the Form N-648.

Under 8 CFR 312.5, applicants should receive two opportunities to meet the requirements of Section 312 of the INA. If the DAO finds that the Form N-648 is insufficient to establish eligibility for an exception from the English and/or U.S. history and government requirements for naturalization, the DAO must give the applicant a choice to either proceed with testing or to be rescheduled for re-examination. If the applicant fails the test, or opts for rescheduling, the DAO must issue a Form N-14 and schedule the applicant for re-examination within 45 days. The Form N-14 must include a detailed explanation of the deficiencies and inconsistencies in the Form N-648 and, if appropriate, request the applicant to obtain another evaluation from an authorized medical specialist for a supplemental determination.

If upon re-examination, the DAO determines that an applicant is not eligible for a disability exception and the applicant fails to pass the English and/or U.S. history and government tests, the Form N-400 must be denied. The Form N-648 denial may be reviewed in the context of a hearing on the denial of the Form N-400 under Section 336 of the INA (336 hearing). An applicant may submit additional documentation for review at the 336 hearing, including a new Form N-648.

Adjudication of Form N-648, Medical Certification for Disability Exceptions to Section 312 Naturalization Requirements; HQOPRD 70/33-P

Revisions to *Adjudicator's Field Manual (AFM)* Chapter 72.2(d)(5) and Appendix 72-13 (*AFM* Update AD06-09)

Page 7

(F) [(b)(2) or (b)(7)(E)]

(G) <u>Reasonable Accommodations and Modifications under the Rehabilitation Act</u>.

Section 504 of the Rehabilitation Act of 1973 requires all Federal agencies to make reasonable accommodations for persons with disabilities. As a federal agency, USCIS may not exclude qualified persons with disabilities from its programs or activities based solely on the person's disability. To ensure that persons with disabilities are not excluded from USCIS programs or activities because of their disabilities, the Rehabilitation Act requires USCIS to provide modifications or accommodations that permit qualified persons with disabilities to have an equal opportunity to participate in its programs. DAOs should refer to the January 21, 2003 policy memo, "Guidance on Making the Naturalization Process Accessible to Applicants with Disabilities," for further guidance on accommodations.

Accommodations are different from statutory waivers or exceptions. If an applicant receives a waiver, that applicant is <u>exempted</u> from meeting the specific naturalization requirement for which that waiver is granted. All applicants qualifying for a waiver receive the same relief. For example, all applicants receiving an English test waiver will not have to take the English exam. Existing waivers cover the English and/or U.S. history and government requirements and the Oath of Allegiance.

On the other hand, an accommodation is not a waiver but rather a modification of an existing practice or procedure that will enable an applicant with a disability to participate in the naturalization process. The accommodation does not exempt the applicant from the obligation to satisfy the requirement, but modifies the manner in which the applicant demonstrates that he or she meets the requirement. Accommodations are likely to vary according to the nature of the individual's disability. For example, an applicant who is unable to use his or her hands should be permitted to take the U.S. history and government tests orally. An applicant who is unable to speak might receive an accommodation that would allow that applicant to respond to questions on the English and/or U.S. history and government test with a previously agreed upon nonverbal form of assent.

Making reasonable accommodations or modifications to the entire naturalization process is our mandate under the Rehabilitation Act of 1973. DAOs are reminded of the need for the utmost courtesy, respect, and sensitivity in adjudicating cases where the applicant requests an accommodation for the Section 312 requirements.

Adjudication of Form N-648, Medical Certification for Disability Exceptions to Section 312 Naturalization Requirements; HQOPRD 70/33-P

Revisions to *Adjudicator's Field Manual (AFM)* Chapter 72.2(d)(5) and Appendix 72-13 (*AFM* Update AD06-09)

Page 8

(H) Procedures for Waiver of the Oath of Allegiance.

Under Section 337 of the INA, as amended, the Oath of Allegiance and attachment requirements may be waived for applicants having a disability or impairment that prevents them from being able to understand the meaning of the oath or to communicate an understanding of the oath requirement. The procedures for conducting examinations and waiving the oath are outlined in the June 30, 2003 Memorandum entitled, "Procedures for Implementing the Waiving of the Oath of Renunciation and Allegiance for the Naturalization of Aliens having Certain Disabilities." http://uscis.gov/graphics/lawsregs/handbook/PolMem96Pub.pdf

The requirements for the oath waiver are distinct from the requirements for the English and/or U.S. history and government waiver under Section 312 of the INA. While both Section 312 and Section 337 of the Act, as amended, require that the applicant have a "developmental or physical disability or mental impairment," the assessment of a person's ability to meet the oath requirement is different from the assessment of the applicant's ability to learn English and Civics.

6. Field Guidance *AFM* Appendix 72-13, Attachments A-C.

Effective immediately, USCIS field offices are directed to comply with the following instructions as set forth in revised *AFM* Appendix 72-13, Attachments A-C.

Adjudication of Form N-648, Medical Certification for Disability Exceptions to Section 312 Naturalization Requirements; HQOPRD 70/33-P

Revisions to *Adjudicator's Field Manual (AFM)* Chapter 72.2(d)(5) and Appendix 72-13 (*AFM* Update AD06-09)

Page 9

Appendix 72-13 Disability Naturalization Applications [Revised as of 05/10/2006]

Attachment A
State Medical Boards Contact Information

State	Telephone	Web Address
Alabama	(334) 242-4116	www.albme.org
Alaska	(907) 269-8163	www.dced.state.ak.us/occ/pmed.htm
Arizona	(480) 551-2700	www.bomex.org/middle.asp
Arkansas	(501) 296-1802	www.armedicalboard.org
California	(916) 263-2389	www.medbd.ca.gov
Colorado	(303) 894-7690	www.dora.state.co.us/medical
Connecticut	(860) 509-8000	www.dph.state.ct.us
Delaware	(302) 744-4507	www.professionallicensing.state.de.us
District of Columbia	(202) 671-5000	www.doh.dc.gov
Florida	(850) 245-4100	www.doh.state.fl.us
Georgia	(404) 656-3913	www.medicalboard.georgia.gov
Hawaii	(808) 586-3000	www.hawaii.gov/dcca/areas/pvl
Idaho	(208) 327-7000	www.bom.state.id.us
Illinois	(217) 785-0800	www.idfpr.com/dpr/default.asp
Indiana	(317) 234-2060	www.in.gov/pla/bandc/mlbi/

Adjudication of Form N-648, Medical Certification for Disability Exceptions to Section 312 Naturalization Requirements; HQOPRD 70/33-P

Revisions to *Adjudicator's Field Manual (AFM)* Chapter 72.2(d)(5) and Appendix 72-13 (*AFM* Update AD06-09)

Page 10

Iowa	(515) 281-5171	www.docboard.org/ia/ia_home.htm
Kansas	(785) 296-7413	www.ksbha.org
Kentucky	(502) 429-7150	www.state.ky.us/agencies
Louisiana	(504) 568-6820	www.lsbme.org
Maine	(207) 287-3601	www.docboard.org/me/me_home.htm
Maryland	(410) 764-4777	www.mbp.state.md.us
Massachusetts	(617) 654-9800	www.massmedboard.org/contact/shtm
Michigan	(517) 241-9427	www.michigan.gov
Minnesota	(612) 617-2130	www.state.mn.us/portal/mn/jsp/home
Mississippi	(601) 987-3079	www.msbml.state.ms.us
Missouri	(573) 751-0098	www.pr.mo.gov/healingarts.asp
Montana	(406) 841-2300 www.emedicine-resources.com/montana-board-of-medicine.htm	
Nebraska	(402) 471-3121	www.hhs.state.ne.us
Nevada	(775) 688-2559	www.medboard.nv.gov
New Hampshire	(603) 271-1203	www.nh.gov/medicine/
New Jersey	(973) 504-6200	www.state.nj.us/lps/ca/contactinfo.htm
New Mexico	505) 476-7220	www.state.nm.us/nmbme/
North Carolina	(919) 326-1100	www.ncmedboard.org
North Dakota	(701) 328-6500	www.ndbomex.com

Adjudication of Form N-648, Medical Certification for Disability Exceptions to Section 312 Naturalization Requirements; HQOPRD 70/33-P

Revisions to *Adjudicator's Field Manual (AFM)* Chapter 72.2(d)(5) and Appendix 72-13 (*AFM* Update AD06-09)

Page 11

Ohio	(614) 466-3934	www.med.ohio.gov
Oklahoma	(405) 848-6841	www.okmedicalboard.org
Oregon	(503) 229-5770	www.egov.oregon.gov/BME/
Pennsylvania	(717) 787-8503	www.dos.state.pa.us/bpoa/site/default.asp
Rhode Island	(401) 222-3855	www.health.ri.gov/hsr/bmld/
South Carolina	(803) 896-4500	www.llr.state.sc.us/pol/medical/
South Dakota	(605) 367-7781	www.state.sd.us/doh/medical/
Tennessee	(615) 532-3202	www.state.tn.us/health/
Texas	(800) 248-4062	www.tmb.state.tx.us/
Utah	(801) 530-6628	www.dopl.utah.gov/
Vermont	(802) 657-4220	www.healthyvermonters.info/bmp/bmp.shtml
Virginia	(804) 662-9900	www.dhp.virginia.gov/
Washington	(360) 236-4700	www.doh.wa.gov/contact.htm
West Virginia	(304) 558-2921	www.wvdhhr.org/wvbom/
Wisconsin	(608) 266-2112	www.drl.wi.gov/index.htm
Wyoming	(307) 778-7053	www.wyomedboard.state.wy.us/

Adjudication of Form N-648, Medical Certification for Disability Exceptions to Section 312 Naturalization Requirements; HQOPRD 70/33-P

Revisions to *Adjudicator's Field Manual (AFM)* Chapter 72.2(d)(5) and Appendix 72-13 (*AFM* Update AD06-09)

Page 12

Adjudication of Form N-648, Medical Certification for Disability Exceptions to Section 312 Naturalization Requirements; HQOPRD 70/33-P

Revisions to *Adjudicator's Field Manual (AFM)* Chapter 72.2(d)(5) and Appendix 72-13 (*AFM* Update AD06-09)

Page 13

Attachment B

Disability Diagnosis

Medical Specialist

<u>Organic Mental Disorder</u>

Psychiatrist, Psychologist, or Neurologist

Psychological or behavioral abnormalities associated with a dysfunction of the brain. Demonstration of a loss of specific cognitive abilities or affective changes and the medically documented persistence of at least one of the following: Disorientation to time and place; or Memory impairment, either short-term (inability to learn new information), intermediate, or long-term (inability to remember information that was known sometime in the past); or Perceptual or thinking disturbances (e.g., hallucinations, delusions); or Change in personality; or Disturbance in mood; or Emotional lability (e.g., explosive temper outbursts, sudden crying, etc.) and impairment in impulse control; or Loss of measured intellectual ability.

<u>Schizophrenic, Paranoid and Other Psychotic Disorders</u>

Psychiatrist, Psychologist, or Neurologist

- Delirium
- Hallucinosis
- Catatonia
- Schizophrenia
- Manic Disorder
- Bipolar Affective Disorder
- Depressive Disorder
- Mixed Affective Disorder

Characterized by the onset of psychotic features with deterioration from a previous level of functioning.

Adjudication of Form N-648, Medical Certification for Disability Exceptions to Section 312 Naturalization Requirements; HQOPRD 70/33-P

Revisions to *Adjudicator's Field Manual (AFM)* Chapter 72.2(d)(5) and Appendix 72-13 (*AFM* Update AD06-09)

Page 14

Affective Disorders   Psychiatrist, Psychologist, or Neurologist

Characterized by a disturbance of mood, accompanied by a full or partial manic or depressive syndrome. Mood refers to a prolonged emotion that colors the whole psychic life; it generally involves either depression or elation and manifests in difficulty in concentrating or thinking.

Mental Retardation   Psychiatrist, Psychologist, or Neurologist

Characterized by significantly sub-average intelligence.

Anxiety-related Disorders, e.g. Post Traumatic Stress   Psychiatrist, Psychologist, or Neurologist
Disorder (PTSD)

Characterized by significant decrease in normal functioning and intellect when placed in anxiety producing settings.

Substance Addiction Disorders   Psychiatrist, Psychologist, or Neurologist

Characterized by the manifestation of a cluster of cognitive, behavioral, and physiological symptoms that cause loss of concentration and control.

Autistic and Other Development Disorders   Psychiatrist, Psychologist, or Neurologist

Characterized by deficits in developmental verbal and non-verbal communication.

Attention Deficit Hyperactivity Disorder or Attention Deficit   Psychiatrist, Psychologist, or Neurologist
Disorder (ADHD and ADD)

Characterized by inattention, impulsivity, and hyperactivity with the inability to concentrate.

Adjudication of Form N-648, Medical Certification for Disability Exceptions to Section 312 Naturalization Requirements; HQOPRD 70/33-P

Revisions to *Adjudicator's Field Manual (AFM)* Chapter 72.2(d)(5) and Appendix 72-13
(*AFM* Update AD06-09)

Page 15

<u>Dementia</u>	Psychiatrist, Psychologist, or Neurologist

- Alzheimer's
- Vascular
- Pick's
- Creutzfeldt-Jakob
- Huntington's
- Parkinson's
- HIV

Characterized by the inability to retain or learn new language or information.

<u>Traumatic Brain Injury (TBI)</u>	Psychiatrist, Psychologist, or Neurologist

Characterized by neurological and mental impairments with a wide variety of posttraumatic symptoms and signs. Sometimes a mental impairment may appear to improve immediately following TBI and then worsen, or, conversely, it may appear much worse initially but improve after a few months. Therefore, the mental findings immediately following TBI may not reflect the actual severity of mental impairment (s). The actual severity of a mental impairment may not become apparent until 6 months post-injury.

<u>Brain Tumors – Primary or Metastatic</u>	Neurologist, Neurosurgeon, Radiologist, or Oncologist

Characterized by neurological and mental impairments.

Note: Specified disorders may be due to brain damage, dysfunction, and physical disease. Disorders must be of the severity that they prevent the applicant from learning or demonstrating knowledge of English and/or civics.

Adjudication of Form N-648, Medical Certification for Disability Exceptions to Section 312 Naturalization Requirements; HQOPRD 70/33-P

Revisions to *Adjudicator's Field Manual (AFM)* Chapter 72.2(d)(5) and Appendix 72-13 (*AFM* Update AD06-09)

Page 16

Adjudication of Form N-648, Medical Certification for Disability Exceptions to Section 312 Naturalization Requirements; HQOPRD 70/33-P

Revisions to *Adjudicator's Field Manual (AFM)* Chapter 72.2(d)(5) and Appendix 72-13 (*AFM* Update AD06-09)

Page 17

Attachment C

[(b)(2) or (b)(7)(E)]

7. *AFM* Transmittal Memoranda

The *AFM* Transmittal Memoranda button is revised by adding a new entry, in numerical order, to read:

| AD 06-09 (05/10/2006) | **Chapter 72.2(d)(5) and Appendix 72-13** | This memorandum revises **Chapter 72.2(d)(5)** and **Appendix 72-13** of the *Adjudicator's Field Manual (AFM)* regarding adjudications of N-648 medical certifications for disability exceptions |

APPENDIX 7-18

Federal Register Notice of Naturalization Test Redesign

Tuesday, December 19, 2006

AGENCY: U.S. Citizenship and Immigration Services, DHS.

ACTION: Notice.

SUMMARY

This notice announces that U.S. Citizenship and Immigration Services (USCIS) will be conducting a pilot of a redesigned naturalization test. Applicants for naturalization must, among other things, demonstrate an understanding of the English language, a knowledge and understanding of the fundamentals of the history, and the principles and form of government in the United States. Currently the naturalization testing process and test content vary in each USCIS district office. USCIS plans to revise the naturalization testing process to ensure that the naturalization testing process is uniform. Thus, a newly redesigned English reading and writing test, as well as the U.S. history and government test, will be pilot tested in the following, randomly selected sites:

Albany, New York sub-office; Boston, Massachusetts, District Office; Kansas City, Missouri, District Office; Charleston, South Carolina sub-office; El Paso, Texas District Office; San Antonio, Texas District Office; Miami, Florida District Office; Denver, Colorado District Office; Tucson, Arizona Sub-Office; and Yakima, Washington Sub-Office. Based on the evaluation of the pilot, the final test will be implemented nationally beginning in 2008.

DATES: This notice is effective January 3, 2007.

FOR FURTHER INFORMATION CONTACT: Lynn L. Thai, Department of Homeland Security, U.S. Citizenship and Immigration Services, Office of Citizenship, 20 Massachusetts Avenue, NW., Room 5200, Washington, DC, 20529, telephone (202) 272-1721.

SUPPLEMENTARY INFORMATION:

Background

Applicants for naturalization must, among other things, demonstrate an understanding of the English language including an ability to speak, read, and write, words in ordinary usage. 8 U.S.C. 1423(a)(1); 8 CFR 312.1(c)(1)- (c)(2). Another requirement is that applicants for naturalization must demonstrate a knowledge and understanding of the fundamentals of the history, and the principles and form of government in the United States. Under USCIS regulations, an applicant for naturalization may satisfy these requirements by passing a citizenship test. 8 U.S.C. 1423(a)(2); 8 CFR 312.2(c). Certain applicants who meet specific age and length of residence thresholds or who have a physical or developmental disability or mental impairment may be exempt from the English and civics requirements.

562

In 1997, the U.S. Commission on Immigration Reform (the Commission) recommended that the former Immigration and Naturalization Service (INS)[1] standardize the naturalization testing process. The Commission recommended that the naturalization tests be revised to better determine if applicants have a meaningful knowledge of U.S. history and government and can communicate in English. Also in 1997, the Department of Justice (DOJ) began to reengineer the naturalization process. With respect to naturalization testing, DOJ determined that it should develop a more uniform approach to testing, including standard and meaningful test content, standardized testing instruments and protocols, standard scoring, and standard levels of passing. The former INS began to redesign the testing process, with a goal of developing a new process that would be uniform, fair, and meaningful. The redesigned naturalization test USCIS plans to pilot is the culmination of test redesign efforts resulting from the Commission's recommendations and work in this area since that time.

Current Testing Procedures

Currently USCIS District Adjudications Officers (DAOs) examine an applicant's English language skills and knowledge of U.S. history and government during the naturalization interview. DAOs generally test an applicant's ability to understand the English language while verifying that the information on his or her application for naturalization (Form N-400) is correct. The preferred manner of testing an applicant's reading ability by asking the applicant to read up to three sentences out loud and they test the applicant's ability to write in English by dictating from one to three English sentences to the applicant and having that applicant write in English what was dictated. Test content for the reading and writing portion of the test is taken from either former INS textbooks (United States History--1600 to 1987 (former INS publication M-289) and U.S. Government Structure (former INS publication M-291)), and from sample sentences in the Guide to Naturalization (M-476), which is available on USCIS' Web site, http://www.uscis.gov.

DAOs test an applicant's knowledge of U.S. history and government by asking up to 10 fundamental civics questions. For the U.S. history and government test, DAOs ask questions from either former INS textbooks or from a list of 96 questions published on the USCIS Web site. Each office's testing method may vary in terms of how the test is prepared and administered, and how the results are collected and evaluated. Test formats also vary among offices, even among offices that use the same test methods.

USCIS Plans To Revise the Tests and Testing Procedures

USCIS has worked with community-based organizations and other stakeholders to help ensure that the new test and testing procedures are developed and implemented fairly and consistently. USCIS' redesign project revises the English and U.S. history test items, and the test administration procedures.

During the redesign process of the U.S. history and government test, USCIS considered multiple perspectives, including views of U.S. history professors and experts, USCIS officers, and community-based organizations. It also reviewed State and local history standards, adult learning standards, citizenship preparation courses, and the current government authorized textbooks and other sound civics curricula.

---

[1]On March 1, 2003, INS transferred from the Department of Justice (DOJ) to the Department of Homeland Security (DHS), pursuant to the Homeland Security Act of 2002 (Pub. L. 107-296). INS' adjudication functions transferred to USCIS

Based on this review, USCIS is planning to retain the current U.S. history and government test format of asking 10 questions. Applicants need to answer six questions correctly to pass. However USCIS intends to replace the current trivia-based content of the questions with questions that will test applicants on the fundamentals of American democracy such as the rule of law, separation of powers, and unalienable rights. Making the test more meaningful will encourage civic learning and patriotism.

While redesigning the content of the English test, USCIS considered multiple perspectives, including the views of Teachers of English to Speakers of Other Languages (TESOL), selected English experts knowledgeable on adult learning standards (principally the National Reporting System (NRS) for adult education), USCIS officers, and community-based organizations. After considering these perspectives, USCIS intends to continue the current format for English testing. Applicants are asked to read a question and write a dictated sentence. However, USCIS intends to change the content of the dictation. Applicants will no longer be tested on everyday English sentences and phrases; under the revised procedures, the content for the reading and writing questions will be structured on civics.

Pilot Test

USCIS plans to conduct a pilot test in 10 randomly selected USCIS district and sub-offices, beginning in early 2007. The pilot test will be given to approximately 5,000 applicant volunteers. During the pilot, all applicants at the 10 selected pilot sites will be asked whether they want to participate in the pilot test, which will accompany the naturalization interview. If the applicant elects to take the pilot test and passes it, the adjudications officer will note in the file that the applicant has passed the reading, writing and civics test sections, and the current test will not be administered. Failure to pass the pilot test will not affect an applicant's eligibility of admission to citizenship. If the applicant elects to take the pilot test but fails the reading, writing and/or civics test section(s), the DAO will, without prejudice, administer the corresponding current test section(s) in the same sitting. If the applicant fails a given section of the current naturalization test, the applicant will be allowed another opportunity within 60-90 days to take the failed section(s) of the current test again. USCIS expects the pilot test to take approximately 5 minutes to administer to each willing applicant. The total length of the pilot test evaluation period is estimated to last up to 4 months. USCIS plans to collect and evaluate test administration procedures, scoring rules and procedures, and training procedures. This information will be gathered through information collected on each pilot testing situation, focus groups with DAOs who administer the pilot test as well as through observations of applicants taking the revised test.

Once all the information from the pilot test is collected, evaluated, and considered, USCIS will finalize a redesigned test. USCIS will produce study guides and work with community-based organizations to prepare applicants for the redesigned naturalization tests.

Paperwork Reduction Act

Examinations designated to test the aptitude, abilities, or knowledge of the person tested, and the collection of information and identification or classification in connection with such examinations, are not considered information collections under 5 CFR 1320.3(h)(7). Dated: November 21, 2006.

Emilio T. Gonzalez,

Director, U.S. Citizenship and Immigration Services.

Chapter 8

Removability and removal proceedings

I. INTRODUCTION

§ 8:1 Removability, in general

Because the process of naturalization is commenced by filing an application with

USCIS in which the applicant must establish lawful admission to permanent residence, the applicant will be giving USCIS information that not only might result in denial of naturalization, but could subject the person to removal.[1] Thus, before filing a naturalization application, the practitioner must determine whether, for example, the client obtained residency improperly (whether through fraud or other ineligibility),[2] or whether they have committed acts since obtaining residency status—such as criminal acts, or abandonment—that make them deportable.[3] If any of these circumstances exist, the attorney should advise the client of the possible consequences of applying for naturalization, and might advise against filing an application.

Most grounds of deportability are not themselves bars to naturalization, but will often trigger the initiation of removal proceedings. Once removal proceedings have been started, the agency cannot proceed forward on the naturalization application.[4]

The first part of this chapter will address the main deportability issues that face permanent residents considering applying for citizenship. The second part will then address the effects of removal proceedings upon naturalization applications.

II. GROUNDS OF REMOVABILITY

§ 8:2 Overview of removability

This book does not attempt a comprehensive overview of all grounds of removability, but focuses on the grounds of removability most commonly encountered by potential applicants for citizenship. These are broken into four sections: (a) criminal-based removability, including aggravated felonies, firearms offenses, drug offenses, moral turpitude offenses, and family violence offenses; (b) unlawful voting and false claims to U.S. citizenship; (c) abandonment of residence; and (d) ineligibility for LPR status at time of admission, whether through fraud or through non-fraudulent ineligibility. Each will be addressed in turn.

A. CRIMINAL REMOVABILITY

1. General Rules

§ 8:3 General rules—Definition of conviction

Research References

A.L.R. Index, Immigration and Naturalization
Gallagher, Immigration Law Service 2d § 14:147

As initially enacted, the INA did not define the word "conviction." The first approach of the Board was to defer to state law as to which dispositions qualified as final convictions for immigration purposes.[1] Over time, the BIA moved toward a federal standard for whether a person had been convicted of a crime, eventually ar-

---

[Section 8:1]

[1]See, e.g., Boutilier v. I.N.S., 387 U.S. 118, 87 S.Ct. 1563, 18 L.Ed.2d 611 (1967); Chan v. I.N.S., 629 F.2d 579 (9th Cir. 1980).

[2]See §§ 8:25 to 8:26.

[3]See §§ 8:2 to 8:24.

[4]INA § 318, 8 U.S.C.A. § 1429; see § 8:29.

[Section 8:3]

[1]Matter of F—, 1 I. & N. Dec. 343 (B.I.A. 1942) (deferring to California procedure for finality of conviction; Pino v. Landon, 349 U.S. 901 (1955) (Massachusetts procedure, which permitted the

riving at the *Ozkok* standard.[2] The *Ozkok* standard—subsequently altered by statute—required that: (1) the person was found guilty or entered a plea of guilt or *nolo contendere*; (2) the judge ordered some form of punishment or restraint on the person's liberty; and (3) a judgment or adjudication of guilt may be entered without further proceedings regarding the person's guilt, if the person violates the terms imposed by the court.[3]

In 1996, Congress codified the Board's case law, specifically left out the last prong of the conviction definition.[4] Thus, the statute now states that a conviction is established if: "(i) a judge or jury has found the alien guilty or the alien has entered a plea of guilty or *nolo contendere* or has admitted sufficient facts to warrant a finding of guilt, and (ii) the judge has ordered some form of punishment, penalty, or restraint on the alien's liberty to be imposed."[5] The State Department has interpreted this to mean that a conviction will be found if: (1) there has been a plea or judicial finding of guilt, and (2) the court has imposed a term of probation or some other form of restraint on the defendant.[6]

To count as a conviction, an adjudication must be final. A conviction is not considered final until the direct appeal has been either waived or exhausted.[7] However, if the case is under collateral attack, e.g., if a writ of *coram nobis* or a *habeas corpus* motion has been filed, the conviction is still final until the motion is decided.[8] If the collateral attack is decided in the person's favor, the disposition may cure the ground of inadmissibility.[9] The requirement of finality applies whether the person was convicted in the U.S. or abroad.[10]

In spite of this change, some forms of adjudication, like the "pre-trial diversion" would still not be convictions, since the defendant did not enter any pleas in such proceedings.[11] The State of California previously used just such a system; but altered its rules in 1997 to require the entry of a plea.[12]

Unless Congress intended the ground of inadmissibility to apply only to U.S. convictions, a conviction by a foreign country may bring about the same immigra-

---

sentence to be revoked and the case to be put "on file," had not "attained such finality as to support an order of deportation").

[2]Matter of Ozkok, 19 I. & N. Dec. 546 (B.I.A. 1988).

[3]Matter of Ozkok, 19 I. & N. Dec. 546 (B.I.A. 1988).

[4]IIRAIRA § 322 adding INA § 101(a)(48), 8 U.S.C.A. § 1101(a)(48).

[5]INA § 101(a)(48)(A), 8 U.S.C.A. § 1101(a)(48)(A). What was left out of this definition is the requirement that there is no conviction unless a judgment or adjudication of guilt may be entered without availability of further proceedings regarding his or her guilt or innocence of the original charge, if the person violates the terms of his or her probation or fails to comply with the requirements of the court's order. See Matter of Ozkok, 19 I. & N. Dec. 546, 1988 WL 235459 (B.I.A. 1988).

[6]State Department Cable No. 96-State-225256 (Oct. 29, 1996) reproduced in 73 Interpreter Releases 1585 (Nov. 11, 1996).

[7]Will v. I.N.S., 447 F.2d 529, 533 (7th Cir. 1971); Matter of Ozkok, 19 I. & N. Dec. 546, 552, 1988 WL 235459 (B.I.A. 1988). Cf. Morales-Alvarado v. I.N.S., 665 F.2d 172 (9th Cir. 1989).

[8]See Matter of Cardenas Abreu, 24 I&N Dec. 795 (BIA 2009).

[9]Aguilera-Enriquez v. I.N.S., 516 F.2d 565, 570-71 (6th Cir. 1975).

[10]Marino v. I.N.S., 537 F.2d 686, 692 (2d Cir. 1976).

[11]See, e.g., California Penal Code §§ 1000, 1000.2 prior to 1996 amendment.

[12]See generally, K. Brady, et al., California Criminal Law and Immigration, § 2.1, Immigrant Legal Resources Center, 1997.

tion consequences as a conviction inside the U.S.[13] To create inadmissibility, the foreign conviction must be for conduct that would also be considered criminal in the U.S.[14] If there is a conviction, the U.S. courts will not look behind the conviction to see if the proceedings violated U.S. constitutional guarantees.[15] The conviction only needs to have been duly obtained under the laws of the foreign country.[16]

It used to be established law that the statute under which the noncitizen was convicted had, at a minimum, to require knowledge by the person committing the action.[17] If the statute could convict a person of narcotics possession even when the person was entirely unaware that a prohibited substance was in his or her possession, then the statute could not be used as the basis of inadmissibility of any noncitizen.[18] Since the Second Circuit decided *Lennon*, however, the BIA and some courts have been retreating from this position. First, it was established that if the statute allows for guilty knowledge, even when the defendant has the burden of proving *lack* of knowledge, then the statute could be used as the basis for inadmissibility of noncitizens.[19] More recently, the BIA has held that convictions under strict liability statutes relating to controlled substances will carry the same immigration consequences as statutes requiring guilty knowledge.[20]

Congress has expanded the means of proving the existence of a criminal conviction. Under the new formulation, "[i]n any proceeding under [the INA], any of the following documents or records (or a certified copy of such an official document or record) shall constitute proof of a criminal conviction: (i) An official record of judgment and conviction; (ii) An official record of plea, verdict, and sentence; (iii) A docket entry from court records that indicates the existence of the conviction; (iv) Official minutes of a court proceeding or a transcript of a court hearing in which the court takes notice of the existence of the conviction; (v) An abstract of a record of conviction prepared by the court in which the conviction was entered, or by a State official associated with the State's repository of criminal justice records, that indicates the charge or section of law violated, the disposition of the case, the existence and date of conviction, and the sentence; (vi) Any document or record prepared by, or under the direction of, the court in which the conviction was entered that indicates the existence of a conviction; or (vii) Any document or record attesting to the conviction that is maintained by an official of a State or Federal penal institution, which is the basis for that institution's authority to assume custody of the individual named in the record."[21]

In addition, a record of conviction or abstract that has been submitted in electronic form to the DHS by state or court may be used to prove a conviction if it is: (1) certified (including computer generated authentication) by a state official associated with the repository of criminal records or by a court officer from the court in which

---

[13]See Pasquini v. I.N.S., 557 F.2d 536, 538 (5th Cir. 1977).

[14]Matter of McNaughton, 16 I. & N. Dec. 569, 572 (B.I.A. 1978).

[15]Brice v. Pickett, 515 F.2d 153, 154 (9th Cir. 1975).

[16]Chiaramonte v. I.N.S., 626 F.2d 1093, 1098 (2d Cir. 1980).

[17]Lennon v. I.N.S., 527 F.2d 187, 194 (2d Cir. 1975).

[18]Lennon v. I.N.S., 527 F.2d 187, 194 (2d Cir. 1975).

[19]Pasquini v. I.N.S., 557 F.2d 536, 539 (5th Cir. 1977).

[20]Matter of Esqueda, 20 I. & N. Dec. 850 (B.I.A. 1994).

[21]INA § 240(c)(3)(B) as amended by IIRAIRA § 304(a)(3); but cf. Fequiere v. Ashcroft, 279 F.3d 1325 (11th Cir. 2002) (statutory list not the exclusive means of proving a criminal conviction; noncitizen's admission of the conviction is sufficient).

the conviction was entered; and (2) certified by the DHS official as having been received electronically from the depository of records of the state or the court.[22] In certain cases, the statute under which the individual was convicted is "divisible"; that is, the criminal statute includes several offenses some but not all of which would render the individual removable.[23] When this occurs, courts have held that the record of conviction can be examined for the limited purpose of determining whether the alien's conviction was under the branch of the statute that permits removal for having been convicted of an aggravated felony.[24] The Ninth Circuit has made clear that the record of conviction that can be examined includes only the state charging document, a signed plea agreement, jury instructions, guilty pleas, transcripts of a plea proceeding and the judgment.[25] The pre-sentence report is not part of the record of conviction and such a report is insufficient to demonstrate that an individual has been convicted of a removable offense.[26]

The BIA will not treat as a conviction a charge that a criminal court dismisses on the merits.[27] However, the Board has held that where a court vacates a conviction for reasons solely related to rehabilitation or immigration hardships, rather than due to defects in the underlying criminal proceedings, the conviction will not be eliminated for immigration purposes.[28] The Fifth Circuit, however, has found that even convictions vacated on the merits constitute convictions for purposes of the statute.[29] DHS has taken the position that it will exercise its discretion not to seek removal based on vacated convictions, in fidelity to BIA case law; but it is unclear whether USCIS would consider itself able to make good moral character determinations acting as if such vacated convictions were not convictions under the Act.[30]

§ 8:4 General rules—Juvenile dispositions

A minor facing prosecution will receive treatment under the Federal Juvenile Delinquency Act unless the minor, upon advice of counsel, expressly requests adult treatment in writing.[1] Nevertheless, not all crimes that a noncitizen commits while she or he is a minor will necessarily result in delinquency adjudications. A minor in federal proceedings faces possible prosecution as an adult if she or he committed a delinquent act between the ages of 15 and 18 that if committed by an adult would

---

[22]INA § 240(c)(3)(C) as amended by IIRAIRA § 304(a)(3).

[23]See, e.g., Dickson v. Ashcroft, 346 F.3d 44 (2d Cir. 2003).

[24]See, e.g., Dickson v. Ashcroft, 346 F.3d 44 (2d Cir. 2003).

[25]Hernandez-Martinez v. Ashcroft, 329 F.3d 1117 (9th Cir. 2003).

[26]Hernandez-Martinez v. Ashcroft, 329 F.3d 1117 (9th Cir. 2003) (considering whether driving under the influence in violation of Arizona law was a crime involving moral turpitude); see also Dickson v. Ashcroft, 346 F.3d 44 (2d Cir. 2003) (finding that the Board's reference to the narrative statement of facts in the pre-sentence report was in error).

[27]Matter of Rodriguez-Ruiz, 22 I. & N. Dec. 1378, 2000 WL 1375514 (B.I.A. 2000).

[28]In re Pickering, 23 I. & N. Dec. 621 (B.I.A. 2003).

[29]Renteria-Gonzalez v. I.N.S., 322 F.3d 804 (5th Cir. 2002).

[30]Cf. Discipio v. Ashcroft, 417 F.3d 448 (5th Cir.2005); Gaona-Romero v. Gonzales, 497 F.3d 694 (5th Cir. 2007).

[Section 8:4]

[1]18 U.S.C.A. § 5032.

be a crime of violence that is a felony or for certain designated controlled substance offenses.[2]

The general rule is that findings of delinquency by a juvenile court are not convictions for immigration purposes.[3] In state proceedings, a state will apply its own law to determine whether to try a minor as a juvenile or as an adult. The First and Ninth Circuits have held that when a state court forgoes juvenile court proceedings and tries a minor as an adult, the disposition is a conviction for immigration purposes.[4] If the a state proceeds against a defendant as an adult for conduct that the Federal Juvenile Delinquency Act would require treatment as a juvenile, a noncitizen may argue that the Federal Juvenile Delinquency Act should be the standard for determining whether an offense is a conviction for immigration purposes. Although the First Circuit rejected this view, other circuits have not ruled on this theory.[5]

In evaluating whether a foreign offense committed by a noncitizen when she or he was younger than eighteen years old is a conviction for immigration purposes, the BIA uses a federal standard.[6] The BIA will try to find a comparable offense under United States law.[7] If the defendant could face adult prosecution in the United States for a comparable offense to the foreign crime, the BIA treats the foreign offense as a conviction.[8]

§ 8:5 General rules—Term of imprisonment or sentence

Research References

A.L.R. Index, Immigration and Naturalization

Several sections of the INA make grounds of inadmissibility, deportability, waivers, and various requirements depend on the term of imprisonment imposed upon a defendant.[1] In 1996, Congress amended the INA to provide a uniform guide for all

---

[2]18 U.S.C.A. § 5032. There are other exceptions in the statute, as well. 18 U.S.C.A. § 5032.

[3]Matter of Devison, 22 I. & N. Dec. 1362 (B.I.A. 2000); Matter of C-M-, 5 I. & N. Dec. 327, 329 (B.I.A. 1953); but cf. DeLuca v. Ashcroft, 203 F. Supp. 2d 1276 (M.D. Ala. 2002) (written confession of a shoplifting charge evidenced lack of good moral character even though criminal case was never tried because defendant was adjudicated a youthful offender).

[4]Viera Garcia v. I.N.S., 239 F.3d 409 (1st Cir. 2001); Morasch v. I.N.S., 363 F.2d 30, 31 (9th Cir. 1966); see also U.S. v. Hovsepian, 359 F.3d 1144 (9th Cir. 2004) (en banc) (conviction not illegal where district court failed to anticipate that sentencing youth as an adult would subsequently render his conviction a removable offense); but see Ejelonu v. I.N.S., 355 F.3d 539 (6th Cir. 2004) (court granted a writ of *audita querela* preventing INS from using petitioner's "Youthful Trainee" status as the basis for removability, as long as petitioner completes her obligations under the Youthful Trainee Act).

[5]Viera Garcia v. I.N.S., 239 F.3d 409 (1st Cir. 2001).

[6]Matter of Ramirez-Rivero, 18 I. & N. Dec. 135, 137-38 (B.I.A. 1981) (this case uses as the basis of comparison the Federal Juvenile Delinquent Act, which has subsequently been amended several times; presumably the changes in the definition of juvenile delinquency follow the amendments of that act).

[7]Matter of De La Nues, 18 I. & N. Dec. 140, 142 (B.I.A. 1981) (the BIA in this case dealt with convictions between the ages of 16 and 18; however, the Federal Juvenile Delinquency Act, which served as the basis for the BIA decision, was subsequently amended to expand the exception to include delinquent acts committed while the minor was 15 years old).

[8]Matter of De La Nues, 18 I. & N. Dec. 140, 144 (B.I.A. 1981).

[Section 8:5]

[1]See e.g. §§ 8:15 to 8:16.

references to terms of imprisonment and sentence.[2] Under this definition, whenever the INA refers to a "term of imprisonment" or to a "sentence," the term includes any period of incarceration or confinement by a court of law.[3] Even if imposition or execution of the sentence or of the confinement was suspended, the INA will take the full term as the imprisonment or sentence.[4]

§ 8:6   General rules—Post-conviction relief—Expungements

Research References
A.L.R. Index, Immigration and Naturalization
Gallagher, Immigration Law Service 2d § 14:149

In March 1999, the BIA decided *Matter of Roldan*, which held that the Board would no longer recognize expungements as having any effect on the immigration consequences of criminal convictions.[1] This decision has been upheld by most Courts of Appeals to consider the issue.[2]

Practitioners within the Ninth Circuit should be aware that while the Ninth Circuit follows the general rule for expungements outside of the drug context,[3] a separate analysis is required for expunged drug convictions. In 2000, the Ninth Circuit held that a drug conviction expunged for rehabilitative reasons will not be considered to be a conviction for immigration purposes.[4] In the following decade, it applied its rule even to drug convictions in other countries.[5] However, every other circuit disagreed with the Ninth Circuit, and the Ninth Circuit eventually reheard the matter en banc, and deferred to the Board's approach.[6] However, the Ninth Circuit declined to apply that rule retroactively, reasoning that "aliens often have pled guilty to minor drug crimes and have completed drug treatment in order to have their convictions expunged—all in reliance on Lujan-Armendariz's promise that doing so would spare them from adverse immigration consequences."[7] Therefore,

---

[2]IIRAIRA § 322(a) adding INA § 101(a)(48)(B), 8 U.S.C.A. § 1101(a)(48)(B).

[3]INA § 101(a)(48)(B), 8 U.S.C.A. § 1101(a)(48)(B).

[4]INA § 101(a)(48)(B), 8 U.S.C.A. § 1101(a)(48)(B).

[Section 8:6]

[1]Matter of Roldan-Santoyo, 22 I. & N. Dec. 512, 1999 WL 126433 (B.I.A. 1999); see also Matter of Marroquin-Garcia, 23 I. & N. Dec. 705 (A.G. 2005) (reaffirming *Roldan* decision).

[2]See, e.g., Herrera-Inirio v. I.N.S., 208 F.3d 299, 304-05 (1st Cir. 2000); Acosta v. Ashcroft, 341 F.3d 218 (3rd Cir. 2003); Moosa v. I.N.S., 171 F.3d 994, 1005-06 (5th Cir. 1999); Madriz-Alvarado v. Ashcroft, 383 F.3d 321 (5th Cir. 2004); Uritsky v. Gonzales, 399 F.3d 728 (6th Cir. 2005); Gill v. Ashcroft, 335 F.3d 574 (7th Cir. 2003); Vasquez-Velezmoro v. U.S. I.N.S., 281 F.3d 693 (8th Cir. 2002); Ikenokwalu-White v. I.N.S., 316 F.3d 798 (8th Cir. 2003) (B.I.A. did not err in considering expunged convictions in its moral character determination); Fernandez-Bernal v. Attorney General of U.S., 257 F.3d 1304 (11th Cir. 2001); Resendiz-Alcaraz v. U.S. Atty. Gen., 383 F.3d 1262 (11th Cir. 2004).

[3]Murillo-Espinoza v. I.N.S., 261 F.3d 771 (9th Cir. 2001); see also Ramirez-Castro v. I.N.S., 287 F.3d 1172 (9th Cir. 2002) (finding that an expunged conviction for a firearms offense remained a conviction for immigration purposes); U.S. v. Hovsepian, 359 F.3d 1144 (9th Cir. 2004) (en banc) (permitting consideration of expunged convictions for good moral character purposes, reasoning that the fact that the conviction was expunged did not mean that the individual did not commit the crime or engage in the in the underlying behavior).

[4]Lujan-Armendariz v. I.N.S., 222 F.3d 728 (9th Cir. 2000).

[5]Dillingham v. I.N.S., 267 F.3d 996 (9th Cir. 2001).

[6]Nunez-Reyes v. Holder, 646 F.3d 684 (9th Cir. 2011).

[7]Nunez-Reyes v. Holder, 646 F.3d 684, 692 (9th Cir. 2011)

within the Ninth Circuit, for convictions from August 1, 2000 (the date of Lujan-Armendariz) to July 14, 2011, (the date of Nunez-Reyes), expungements will be given validity. Presumably, this rule would have significant effects for naturalization applicants within the Ninth Circuit.

The Board has never applied Lujan-Armendariz outside the Ninth Circuit.[8] Thus, individuals with convictions outside of the Ninth Circuit could not plausibly argue any reliance on Lujan-Armendariz. Several questions remain, most notably: (a) where an individual has a conviction which was expunged within the Ninth Circuit, but subsequently applies for naturalization or is placed into removal proceedings elsewhere, will the Nunez-Reyes rule apply? and (b) where individuals with expunged convictions from other circuits apply for naturalization within the Ninth Circuit, will they get the benefit of the Nunez-Reyes rule? Further elaboration of the rule is to be expected.

One question not yet reached by the Board is the issue of the Federal First Offender Act (FFOA).[9] Under the FFOA a discharge "shall not be considered a conviction for the purpose of a disqualification or a disability imposed by law upon conviction of a crime, or for any other purpose."[10] In order to qualify for relief under the FFOA, a person must (1) be "found guilty of an offense described in section 404 of the Controlled Substances Act (21 U.S.C.A. § 844)," i.e., simple possession of a controlled substance; (2) prior to the commission of such offense, never have been convicted of violating a federal or state law relating to controlled substances; and (3) never before been the subject of a disposition under FFOA.[11] Courts other than the Ninth Circuit have distinguished state expungement statutes from the FFOA, and some have suggested that an FFOA disposition would be a conviction for immigration purposes.[12]

The Fifth Circuit would go even farther than the Board, and has held that even a conviction vacated for constitutional or statutory infirmity remains a conviction for immigration purposes.[13] Since 2005, the government has decided as a matter of prosecutorial discretion to seek remand or termination, in fidelity to the Board's position in *Roldan*,[14] but the Fifth Circuit's precedent remains highly unfavorable.

§ 8:7 General rules—Executive pardons

Research References

Gallagher, Immigration Law Service 2d §§ 14:146, 14:147

---

[8]In re Salazar-Regino, 23 I. & N. Dec. 223, 2002 WL 339535 (B.I.A. 2002).

[9]18 U.S.C.A. § 3607.

[10]18 U.S.C.A. § 3607(b).

[11]18 U.S.C.A. § 3607(a); Matter of Manrique, 21 I. & N. Dec. 58, 1995 WL 314732 (B.I.A. 1995).

[12]Fernandez-Bernal v. Attorney General of U.S., 257 F.3d 1304 (11th Cir. 2001); Vasquez-Velezmoro v. U.S. I.N.S., 281 F.3d 693 (8th Cir. 2002); Gill v. Ashcroft, 335 F.3d 574 (7th Cir. 2003); see also Acosta v. Ashcroft, 341 F.3d 218 (3rd Cir. 2003) (finding that INA's definition of conviction does not implicitly incorporate the FFOA).

[13]See, Renteria-Gonzalez v. INS, 322 F.3d 804 (5th Cir.2003).

[14]See, Discipio v. Ashcroft, 417 F.3d 448 (5th Cir.2005); Gaona-Romero v. Gonzales, 497 F.3d 694 (5th Cir. 2007).

Unlike expungements, full unconditional executive pardons are specifically mentioned in the Immigration and Nationality Act.[1] The INA specifically provides that a pardon eliminates removability for the moral turpitude grounds, as well as the aggravated felony ground.[2]

The Board has held, however, that a presidential or gubernatorial pardon waives only the grounds of removal specifically set forth in INA § 237(a)(2)(A)(v), and that no implicit waivers may be read into the statute.[3] Thus, a pardon would eliminate removability for moral turpitude offenses and aggravated felonies, but not the family violence ground at INA § 237(a)(2)(E)(i),[4] or the controlled substances ground.

However, for the crimes covered by the statute, an executive pardon will erase the conviction for purposes of both the bars to good moral character based on the grounds of inadmissibility and the bar based on having been imprisoned for more than 180 days for the conviction.[5] The INS and some courts had taken the position that under the prior permanent bar to good moral character due to having committed murder, a full unconditional pardon will eliminate the bar if the pardon was granted prior to the period of required good moral character.[6] Even those courts that would not give effect to such pardons have stated in dicta that if the pardon had been granted because the person had been improperly convicted in the first trial, such pardon would be effective to erase the permanent bar to good moral character.[7] One court granted a petition based on that rationale.[8]

The regulations confirm the applicability of the former INS' position to the current permanent bar to good moral character, stating that a person is not precluded from establishing good moral character because of murder or an aggravated felony if the person is granted a full and unconditional pardon before the beginning of the relevant statutory period and demonstrates that reformation and rehabilitation occurred before the start of the period.[9] If the pardon is granted during the statutory period, the applicant will not be barred from establishing good moral character if the person can demonstrate extenuating or exonerating circumstances that would establish his or her good moral character.[10]

§ 8:8 General rules—Judicial recommendations against deportation

Judicial Recommendations Against Deportation (JRAD) were a statutory vehicle

---

[Section 8:7]

[1]INA § 237(a)(2)(A)(v), 8 U.S.C.A. § 1227(a)(2)(A)(v) ("[INA § 237(a)(2)](i), (ii), (iii), and (iv) shall not apply in the case of an alien with respect to a criminal conviction if the alien subsequent to the criminal conviction has been granted a full and unconditional pardon by the President of the United States or by the Governor of any of the several States").

[2]INA § 237(a)(2)(A)(v), 8 U.S.C.A. § 1227(a)(2)(A)(v).

[3]Matter of Suh, 23 I. & N. Dec. 626 (B.I.A. 2003).

[4]Matter of Suh, 23 I. & N. Dec. 626 (B.I.A. 2003).

[5]INS Interp. 316.1(g)(4)(i).

[6]INS Interp. 316.1(g)(4)(i).

[7]In re Siacco's Petition, 184 F.Supp. 803 (D.Md. 1960); Petition of Salani, 196 F. Supp. 513 (N.D. Cal. 1961); Petition of Salani, 196 F. Supp. 513 (N.D. Cal. 1961).

[8]*Petition of Rocca, No. CO 101.2-P (D.W.Va.)* unreported opinion cited in INS Interp. 316.1(g)(4)(i).

[9]8 CFR § 316.10(c)(2)(i).

[10]8 CFR § 316.10(c)(2)(ii).

that existed prior to the Immigration Act of 1990.[1] The JRAD provisions allowed criminal courts to issue an order recommending that the noncitizen not be deported.[2] If the proper procedures were followed, JRADs were effective in overcoming deportability, excludability, and the bars to good moral character.[3]

The INS interpreted the abolition of the JRAD provision as having only *prospective* effect.[4] JRADs are not effective against a charge of deportability if they were granted on or after November 29, 1990, or if they were granted for deportability for a drug offense under the former INA § 241(a)(11).[5] The cut-off is related to the date the JRAD was issued rather than to the date of the commission of the crime.[6]

§ 8:9   General rules—Vacating sentence

It is the final sentence that counts for immigration purposes where a motion to correct sentence has been made and granted in state court.[1] In *Matter of Song*, the criminal court vacated *nunc pro tunc* a noncitizen's original one-year prison sentence for a theft offense and revised the sentence to 360 days.[2] This was held to have effect for immigration purposes, and to render the offense no longer an aggravated felony.[3] This decision was restated by the Board four years later in *Matter of Cota-Vargas*, making clear that *Matter of Song* remains good law notwithstanding that the immigration courts give no effect to state court decisions that vacate convictions solely for immigration purposes.[4]

§ 8:10   General rules—Other forms of post-conviction relief

Neither the regulations nor the former INS interpretations discuss other forms of post-conviction relief. However, it is a well-established principle that post-conviction relief in which the court reopens or vacates a conviction ab initio is effective in removing all immigration consequences of the conviction (even in cases of drug-related offenses).[1] This is so even if the conviction was vacated on account of the failure of the state court to give required advisals as to possible immigration

---

[Section 8:8]

[1]INA § 241(b), 8 U.S.C.A. § 1251(b) abolished by IA90 § 602(b).

[2]INA § 241(b), 8 U.S.C.A. § 1251(b) abolished by IA90 § 602(b).

[3]Santarelli v. Hughes, 116 F.2d 613 (3d Cir. 1940) (deportability); U.S. v. Castro, 26 F.3d 557, 558 n.2 (5th Cir. 1994) (Excludability); Giambanco v. I.N.S., 531 F.2d 141 (3d Cir. 1976) (good moral character).

[4]McNary, Commissioner, ImmAct90 Wire No.5 (Nov. 28,1990).

[5]8 CFR § 240.10(d).

[6]See U.S. v. Koziel, 954 F.2d 831 (2d Cir. 1992); U.S. v. Bodre, 948 F.2d 28 (1st Cir.) cert. denied 112 S.Ct. 1487 (1992) (ex post facto clause does not apply to crimes committed before the abolition of JRADs, where JRAD is sought after effective date of IA90 provision).

[Section 8:9]

[1]See, e.g., Matter of Rodriguez-Ruiz, 22 I. & N. Dec. 1378, 2000 WL 1375514 (B.I.A. 2000).

[2]Matter of Song, 23 I. & N. Dec. 173 (B.I.A. 2001); see also Bayudan v. Ashcroft, 298 F.3d 799 (9th Cir. 2002) (not a crime of violence where sentence amended to be less than one year).

[3]Matter of Song, 23 I. & N. Dec. 173, 174 (B.I.A. 2001).

[4]Matter of Cota-Vargas, 23 I. & N. Dec. 849, 2005 WL 3105750 (B.I.A. 2005).

[Section 8:10]

[1]Matter of Sirhan, 13 I. & N. Dec. 592, 599-600 (B.I.A. 1975).

consequences.[2] Such actions may be based on writs of error coram nobis,[3] writs of habeas corpus,[4] writs of audita querela[5] or motions to withdraw guilty pleas,[6] among others. Immigration decisions, such as deportation orders, that took place before the conviction was vacated are still valid even if the conviction is later vacated.[7] Where a court vacates a conviction for reasons solely related to rehabilitation or immigration hardships, rather than due to defects in the underlying criminal proceedings, the conviction will not be eliminated for immigration purposes.[8]

Even though expungements, pardons, and the petty offense exemption negate certain convictions for purposes of the statutory bars to good moral character, USCIS will still consider those convictions for purposes of the residual category requiring a general determination of the moral character of the applicant.[9] It is unclear whether USCIS may consider a conviction that a court order negates *ab initio* in determination of good moral character under the residual category.[10]

It has been ruled that waivers under section 212(h) do not remove the statutory bar to good moral character based on the crimes of moral turpitude ground of inadmissibility.[11] It is unclear whether former 212(c) waiver would be effective in removing any or all the statutory bars to good moral character. The INS, however, took the position that the applicant would still be precluded from establishing good moral character even when a 212(c) waiver had been granted.[12] It is too early to know the effect of the newly introduced cancellation of removal provisions on the statutory bar to good moral character.[13]

---

[2]Matter of Adamiak, 23 I&N Dec. 878 (BIA 2006).

[3]Matter of Tucker, 15 I. & N. Dec. 337, 340 (B.I.A. 1975); Matter of C-, 8 I. & N. Dec. 611 (B.I.A. 1960).

[4]See People v. Soriano, 194 Cal. App. 3d 1470, 240 Cal. Rptr. 328 (1st Dist. 1987).

[5]See, e.g., U.S. v. Salgado, 692 F.Supp. 1265 (E.D.Wash. 1988). Several circuits have held or suggested that audita querela cannot be used to vacate a conviction for equitable reasons, U.S. v. LaPlante, 57 F.3d 252, 253 (2d Cir. 1995) (audita querela available only for legal reasons, not equitable); U.S. v. Ayala, 894 F.2d 425 (D.C.Cir. 1990) (suggesting, but not holding, same); U.S. v. Kimberlin, 675 F.2d 866 (7th Cir.), cert. denied, 456 U.S. 964, 102 S.Ct. 2044, 72 L.Ed.2d 489 (1982) (same); U.S. v. Holder, 936 F.2d 1 (1st Cir. 1991) (audita querela only available on legal, not equitable basis); but see Ejelonu v. I.N.S., Dept. of Homeland Sec., 355 F.3d 539 (6th Cir. 2004) (en banc) (finding audita querela available for equitable reasons as well as legal, granting writ).

[6]See People v. Guzman, 116 Cal. App. 3d 186, 172 Cal. Rptr. 34 (2d Dist. 1981).

[7]Ramirez-Juarez v. I.N.S., 633 F.2d 174 (9th Cir. 1980); Matter of C-, 8 I. & N. Dec. 611; WL 12129 (B.I.A. 1960).

[8]In re Pickering, 23 I. & N. Dec. 621 (B.I.A. 2003). In *Pickering*, the Board indicated that it would apply an even broader rule in the Fifth Circuit based upon that Court's ruling in Renteria-Gonzalez v. I.N.S., 322 F.3d 804 (5th Cir. 2002). In a subsequent Fifth Circuit decision, the panel deciding the case was highly critical of *Renteria-Gonzalez*, but nevertheless determined that it was bound by it. Discipio v. Ashcroft, 369 F.3d 472 (5th Cir. 2004).

[9]INS Interp. 316.1(g)(4)(iv).

[10]But see Paredes-Urrestarazu v. U.S. I.N.S., 22 F.3d 909 (9th Cir. 1994) (finding proper an inquiry into a diversion order for purposes of exercise of discretion).

[11]Miller v. I.N.S., 762 F.2d 21 (3d Cir. 1985). Since INA § 212(h) was amended specifically as it relates to lawful permanent residents, the conclusions of *Miller* may need some review. See INA § 212(h), 8 U.S.C.A. § 1182(h) as amended by IIRAIRA § 348(a).

[12]Letter, Miller, Acting Asst. Comm. Adjudications HQ 316-C (May 5, 1993) reprinted in 70 Interpreter Releases 769-70 (June 7, 1993). Section 212(c) was repealed by IIRAIRA § 304(b).

[13]See INA § 240A added by IIRAIRA § 304(a).

2. Aggravated Felonies

§ 8:11 Aggravated felonies—generally

Research References

A.L.R. Index, Immigration and Naturalization

What Constitutes "Aggravated Felony" for Which Alien Can Be Deported or Removed Under § 237(a)(2)(a)(III) of Immigration and Nationality Act (8 U.S.C.A. § 1227(a)), 168 A.L.R. Fed. 575

Gallagher, Immigration Law Service 2d §§ 14:146, 14:154

The Anti-Drug Abuse Act of 1988 introduced the concept of aggravated felony to immigration.[1] Since then, the coverage of this definition has been repeatedly expanded.[2] Indeed, this definition has become a vehicle for creating ever-expanding restrictions on the rights of immigrants by rapid and significant changes to its coverage. In addition to the statutory expansion of the term, the Board and some courts have interpreted the statute broadly. For example, both the Board and courts have found that certain misdemeanor offenses can constitute aggravated *felonies*, even in the absence of qualifying statutory language.[3] The latest major amendment to the aggravated felony definition came in the Illegal Immigration Reform and Immigrant Responsibility Act of 1996.[4]

It has been clear for some time that persons convicted of an aggravated felony after November 18, 1988, are deportable,[5] even if the crime was not an aggravated felony at the time of conviction.[6] The BIA has now extended this finding, concluding that a conviction that fits the definition of aggravated felonies makes the person deportable regardless of the date of the conviction.[7] Thus, under the Board's interpretation, convictions entered prior to November 18, 1988, also make the noncitizen deportable.[8] The Board's interpretation has been upheld in several circuits under varying reasoning, but has now been rejected in the Ninth Circuit.[9]

[Section 8:11]

[1]Anti-Drug Abuse Act of 1988 § 7342, Pub. L. No. 100-690, 102 Stat. 4181 (Nov. 18, 1988) (adding INA § 101(a)(43), "aggravated felony" definition).

[2]IIRAIRA § 321; Antiterrorism and Effective Death Penalty Act of 1996, Pub.L. 104-132, § 441(e), 110 Stat. 1214 (Apr. 24, 1996); Immigration and Nationality Technical Corrections Act of 1994, Pub. L. No. 103-416, § 222(a), 108 Stat. 4305 (Oct. 25, 1994); Miscellaneous and Technical Immigration and Naturalization Amendments of 1991, Pub. L. No. 102-232, § 306(a)(1), (7), 105 Stat. 1733 (Dec. 12, 1991) (corrected 1990 act); Immigration Act of 1990, Pub. L. No. 101-649, § 501, 104 Stat. 4978 (Nov. 29, 1990) (expanded definition).

[3]Matter of Small, 23 I. & N. Dec. 448, 2002 WL 1226862 (B.I.A. 2002) (reversing a prior interpretation and finding that misdemeanor abuse of a child was an aggravated felony); U.S. v. Marin-Navarette, 244 F.3d 1284 (11th Cir. 2001), cert. denied, 122 S. Ct. 317, 151 L. Ed. 2d 236 (U.S. 2001); U.S. v. Gonzales-Vela, 276 F.3d 763 (6th Cir. 2001).

[4]IIRAIRA § 321(a) reproduced as Appendix 8–1. The new definition is applicable to "actions taken on or after the date of the enactment" of the IIRAIRA. IIRAIRA § 321(c) reproduced as Appendix 8–1.

[5]Matter of A-A-, 20 I. & N. Dec. 492 (B.I.A. 1992).

[6]INA § 101(a)(43); see also § 8:13.

[7]Matter of Lettman, 22 I. & N. Dec. 365, 1998 WL 811588 (B.I.A. 1998).

[8]Matter of Lettman, 22 I. & N. Dec. 365, 1998 WL 811588 (B.I.A. 1998).

[9]Ledezma-Galicia v. Holder, 599 F.3d 1055 (9th Cir. 2010); compare Lettman v. Reno, 207 F.3d 1368, 1370-72 (11th Cir.2000) (deferring to Board's interpretation); Lewis v. INS, 194 F.3d 539, 545-46

§ 8:12 Aggravated felonies—Current statutory definition

Research References

A.L.R. Index, Immigration and Naturalization
What Constitutes "Aggravated Felony" for Which Alien Can Be Deported or Removed Under
§ 237(a)(2)(a)(III) of Immigration and Nationality Act (8 U.S.C.A. § 1227(a)), 168 A.L.R.
Fed. 575

The entire statutory definition of the term "aggravated felony" is reproduced in
Appendix 8-1. The most commonly encountered aggravated felonies are discussed
below.[1] Three points bear noting. First, a crime may be an aggravated felony even if
it is a misdemeanor.[2] Second, for some types of crimes, such as crimes of violence,
theft, and burglary, the length of incarceration is relevant;[3] for other crimes, such as
drug possession, it is not.[4] The aggravated felony definition, as well as the case law,
must be consulted. Third, there are many complexities in the interpretation of this
definition, particularly related to controlled substances, crimes of violence, and
theft. Given the high stakes involved with being labeled an aggravated felon, one
should be extremely careful in assessing an individual's criminal convictions.

§ 8:13 Aggravated felonies—Applicability of definition

Research References

A.L.R. Index, Immigration and Naturalization
What Constitutes "Aggravated Felony" for Which Alien Can Be Deported or Removed Under
§ 237(a)(2)(a)(III) of Immigration and Nationality Act (8 U.S.C.A. § 1227(a)), 168 A.L.R.
Fed. 575

The aggravated felony definition applies to offenses regardless of whether the
person was convicted under state, federal, or foreign law, provided that if convicted
under a foreign country's law, the term of imprisonment was completed within the
previous 15 years.[1] The aggravated felony definition as amended by the IIRAIRA
also states that "[n]otwithstanding any other provision of law (including any effective date), the term applies regardless of whether the conviction was entered before,
on, or after the date of enactment of this paragraph."[2]

§ 8:14 Aggravated felonies—Drug convictions that are aggravated felonies

Research References

A.L.R. Index, Immigration and Naturalization

Illicit trafficking in controlled substances needs further discussion. The BIA has

---

(4th Cir.1999) (same), with Bell v. Reno, 218 F.3d 86 (2d Cir.2000) (rejecting Board's analysis but
reaching same ultimate conclusion by different line of reasoning).

[Section 8:12]

   [1]See §§ 8:14 to 8:16.
   [2]See § 8:15, n.9.
   [3]INA §§ 101(a)(43)(F), 101(a)(43)(G).
   [4]INA § 101(a)(43)(B).

[Section 8:13]

   [1]INA § 101(a)(43), 8 U.S.C.A. § 1101(a)(43), reproduced at Appendix 8-1.

   [2]INA § 101(a)(43), 8 U.S.C.A. § 1101(a)(43) as amended by IIRAIRA § 321(b), reproduced at
Appendix 8-1.

taken the position that in order to determine whether a person has been convicted of illicit trafficking in controlled substances for purposes of the aggravated felony provision, it will engage in a two-step test. First, if the person is convicted of a state, federal, or qualified foreign crime that is defined as a felony and involves unlawful "trafficking"—as the term is commonly understood—in any substance defined as a controlled substance in section 102 of the Controlled Substances Act, then the person will be considered an aggravated felon.[1] No further inquiry is necessary in these cases.

However, even if the crime is not one that is normally understood as "trafficking," it is still necessary to determine whether the crime is nevertheless considered a "drug trafficking crime" within the meaning of the aggravated felony definition. This is because that definition specifically includes within its parameters a "drug trafficking crime" as defined in 18 U.S.C.A. § 924(c).[2] The drug trafficking definition there includes "any felony punishable under the Controlled Substances Act (21 U.S.C.A. §§ 801 et seq.), the Controlled Substance Import and Export Act (21 U.S.C.A. §§ 951 et seq.), or the Maritime Drug Law Enforcement Act (46 U.S.C.A. §§ 1901 et seq.)."[3] This is a very expansive definition of "drug trafficking."

The matter has now been to the Supreme Court three times. In 2006, the Supreme Court in Lopez found that a drug possession offense would not qualify as a drug trafficking crime under the CSA unless it would be punishable as a felony under the federal criminal law.[4] Thus, the fact that a state categorized possession of a particular drug as a felony would not render the conviction an aggravated felony. The Court's hypothetical approach benefitted the noncitizen, because the federal criminal law generally treats possessory offenses as misdemeanors.

Shortly thereafter, the issue in *Carachuri-Rosendo* was how the hypothetical federal felony rule would apply where an individual had been twice convicted of drug possession in state court. In the federal scheme, a second conviction may be—but need not be (and indeed, is rarely)—prosecuted as a felony.[5] The Board held that it was not enough to say that an individual could have been convicted of a federal felony, but refused to treat it as an aggravated felony "unless we are confident that the State offense corresponds in a meaningful way to the essential requirements that must be met before a felony sentence can be imposed under Federal law on the basis of recidivism."[6] Because the issue involved interpretation of the Controlled Substances Act, however, the Board deferred to the Courts of Appeals in which cases arose, and some Courts of Appeals disagreed with the Board. The Supreme Court resolved the split, agreeing with the Board. It emphasized that an individual had to be "convicted" of an aggravated felony, which focuses on the offense for which they were convicted; moreover, while Congress could define aggravated felonies counter-intuitively, the Court sought a reading which would be

---

[Section 8:14]

[1]Matter of Davis, 20 I. & N. Dec. 536, 543 (B.I.A. 1992); Matter of K-L-, 20 I. & N. Dec. 654, 658 (B.I.A. 1993).

[2]INA § 101(a)(43), 8 U.S.C.A. § 1101(a)(43).

[3]18 U.S.C.A. § 924(c)(2).

[4]Lopez v. Gonzales, 549 U.S. 47, 56, 127 S.Ct. 625, 166 L.Ed.2d 462 (2006).

[5]21 U.S.C.A. §§ 844, 851.

[6]Matter of Carachuri-Rosendo, 24 I. & N. Dec. 382, 387, 390 (2007).

more in line with the "drug trafficking" description of the ground.[7] While it is not clear precisely what procedural protections (if any) a state would have to provide to make a state recidivist drug punishment akin to the federal scheme, it is clear that any offense not prosecuted as a recidivist offense is not an aggravated felony, unless it is one of the two drugs where Congress finds felony punishment appropriate.[8]

Finally, the Supreme Court considered whether distribution of a small amount of marijuana for no remuneration is an aggravated felony. Under the federal scheme, "distributing a small amount of marihuana for no remuneration" is only a misdemeanor.[9] However, many state statutes do not mirror the federal statute, so that individuals could be convicted of drug distribution or sale even for conduct which would be a misdemeanor under federal law. The Board of Immigration Appeals held that a noncitizen bears the burden of proof on this question, and that the issue cannot be resolved on a categorical basis; therefore, held the Board, extrinsic evidence is admissible on the point.[10] The Supreme Court rejected the Board's interpretation, finding that the categorical test was the appropriate test, and that if state convictions did not categorically match a federal felony, that they are not aggravated felonies.[11]

§ 8:15 Aggravated felonies—Crimes of violence

Research References

A.L.R. Index, Immigration and Naturalization

What Constitutes "Aggravated Felony" for Which Alien Can Be Deported or Removed Under § 237(a)(2)(a)(III) of Immigration and Nationality Act (8 U.S.C.A. § 1227(a)), 168 A.L.R. Fed. 575

Another noteworthy inclusion in the aggravated felony definition are crimes of violence for which the term of imprisonment is at least one year.[1]

Crimes of violence under the INA are those that either: (1) have as an element the use, attempted use, or threatened use of physical force against the person or property of another, or (2) are felonies, the nature of the crime—as elucidated by the generic elements of the offense—is such that its commission would ordinarily present a substantial risk that physical force would be used against the person or property of another.[2]

The Supreme Court has held that a felony conviction for driving under the influ-

---

[7]Carachuri-Rosendo v. Holder, 130 S.Ct. 2577, 2585 (2010).

[8]Those drugs are crack cocaine and flunitrazepam (the "date rape drug"). 21 U.S.C.A. § 844(a).

[9]21 U.S.C.A. §§ 841(b)(4), 844.

[10]Matter of Castro Rodriguez, 25 I. & N. Dec. 698, 2012 WL 523321 (B.I.A. 2012); Matter of Aruna, 24 I. & N. Dec. 452, 2008 WL 512678 (B.I.A. 2008).

[11]Moncrieffe v. Holder, 133 S. Ct. 1678, 1690–92 (2013).

[Section 8:15]

[1]INA § 101(a)(43)(F), 8 U.S.C.A. § 1101(a)(43)(F).

[2]Matter of B-, 21 I. & N. Dec. 287, 1996 WL 170049 (B.I.A. 1996); Matter of Alcantar, 20 I. & N. Dec. 801, 1994 WL 232083 (B.I.A. 1994); see also Bovkun v. Ashcroft, 283 F.3d 166 (3d Cir. 2002) (finding the Pennsylvania crime of making terroristic threats an aggravated felony because it included as an element the threatened use of physical force); U.S. v. Rodriguez-Rodriguez, 323 F.3d 317 (5th Cir. 2003) (burglary of a building and unauthorized use of a vehicle are not crimes of violence for sentence enhancement purposes); but cf. U.S. v. Fuentes-Rivera, 323 F.3d 869 (11th Cir. 2003) (burglary of a building is a crime of violence for sentence enhancement purposes).

ence is not a crime of violence.[3] The reasoning of the Supreme Court was that with regard to 18 U.S.C.A. § 16(a), the word "use" implies a higher mental state than negligence or accidental usage.[4] Similarly, with regard to 18 U.S.C.A. § 16(b), the Court held that at least a state of recklessness would be required for a crime to be a crime of violence.[5]

Under *Leocal*, it is clear that a simple negligence crime will not be a crime of violence, even if it results in someone's injury.[6] Some cases have appeared to hold categorically that crimes with a mental state of "recklessness" categorically cannot be crimes of violence.[7] However, other case law elaborate, holding, in effect, that while reckless use of force cannot itself suffice to show a crime of violence, this does not preclude a reckless offense from being a crime of violence under 16(b), if there is a substantial likelihood that intentional force would be used in the course of committing the offense.[8]

However, it has now been held by practically every circuit in the country that misdemeanors may fall within the definition of 18 U.S.C.A. § 16(a), and that misdemeanors with a one-year sentence of imprisonment qualify as aggravated felonies.[9] Practitioners should take great care with even minor misdemeanor convictions, as these could subject an applicant to removal as an aggravated felon.

§ 8:16 Aggravated felonies—Other commonly encountered aggravated felonies

Research References

A.L.R. Index, Immigration and Naturalization
What Constitutes "Aggravated Felony" for Which Alien Can Be Deported or Removed Under
  § 237(a)(2)(a)(III) of Immigration and Nationality Act (8 U.S.C.A. § 1227(a)), 168 A.L.R.
  Fed. 575

Other common aggravated felonies include theft, burglary, and obstruction of justice offenses where the sentence imposed (regardless of any suspension of

---

[3]Leocal v. Ashcroft, 125 S.Ct. 377, 160 L.Ed.2d 271 (2004).

[4]Leocal v. Ashcroft, 125 S.Ct. 377, 382, 160 L.Ed.2d 271 (2004).

[5]Leocal v. Ashcroft, 125 S.Ct. 377, 383, 160 L.Ed.2d 271 (2004).

[6]See, U.S. v. Chapa-Garza, 243 F.3d 921, 925-27 (5th Cir. 2001); Bazan-Reyes v. I.N.S., 256 F.3d 600, 609-10 (7th Cir. 2001); U.S. v. Parson, 955 F.2d 858, 864-66 (3d Cir. 1992).

[7]Tran v. Gonzales, 414 F.3d 464 (3d Cir. 2005); Bejarano-Urrutia v. Gonzales, 413 F.3d 444 (4th Cir. 2005); Jobson v. Ashcroft, 326 F.3d 367 (2d Cir. 2003) (holding that recklessness must go to the "use" of force, such as burglary, not to injury); Jimenez-Gonzalez v. Mukasey, 548 F.3d 557 (7th Cir. 2008).

[8]See, e.g., United States v. Gomez-Leon, 545 F.3d 777, 787 (9th Cir.2008) ("the underlying offense must require proof of an intentional use of force or a substantial risk that force will be intentionally used during its commission."); Aguilar v. Attorney General of U.S., 663 F.3d 692, 701–02 (3d Cir. 2011) (distinguishing "pure reckless" crimes, explaining that sexual intercourse in reckless disregard of the lack of consent of victim carried substantial risk that force would be used if resistance were encountered).

[9]See, U.S. v. Cordoza-Estrada, 385 F.3d 56 (1st Cir. 2004) (misdemeanor assault); U.S. v. Pacheco, 225 F.3d 148 (2d Cir. 2000) (misdemeanor domestic assault, suspended sentence); Wireko v. Reno, 211 F.3d 833, 835 (4th Cir. 2000) (misdemeanor sexual battery); U.S. v. Urias-Escobar, 281 F.3d 165, 167-68 (5th Cir. 2002) (misdemeanor assault); U.S. v. Gonzalez-Tamariz, 310 F.3d 1168, 1170-71 (9th Cir. 2002) (misdemeanor battery); U.S. v. Saenz-Mendoza, 287 F.3d 1011, 1014-15 (10th Cir. 2002) (misdemeanor cruelty toward child).

sentence) is at least one year.[1] Offenses that involve fraud or deceit where the loss to the victim exceeds $10,000, and tax evasion violations where the loss to the government exceeds $10,000, are also aggravated felonies.[2] Sexual abuse of a minor and rape (even statutory rape) are aggravated felonies, regardless of sentence imposed.[3]

As with crimes of violence, most circuits have held that misdemeanor theft, burglary, obstruction of justice, and sexual abuse of a minor will be considered aggravated felonies where a one-year sentence is imposed.[4]

§ 8:17 Aggravated felonies—Categorical approach

The Supreme Court has traditionally adopted a categorical approach to defining a federal meaning for a term like "burglary," which seeks to define the generic category of a type of crime by reference to common law definitions, the Model Penal Code, and state laws.[1] The BIA has generally followed this approach in determining whether crimes fit into certain categories of crimes which are considered aggravated felonies. For instance, burglary with a one-year jail sentence is an aggravated felony;[2] the question thus arises, what constitutes burglary? The BIA held that "burglary of a vehicle" is not "burglary" for aggravated felony purposes, because that use of the term falls outside the generic definition of burglary crimes.[3] A state law's use of the term "burglary" to punish that act does not turn it into a burglary offense for

---

[Section 8:16]

[1]INA § 101(a)(43)(F), (G), 8 U.S.C.A. § 1101(a)(43)(F), (G).

[2]INA § 101(a)(43)(M), 8 U.S.C.A. § 1101(a)(43)(M); Kawashima v. Holder, __ U.S. __, 132 S.Ct. 1166, 1172 (2012); Nijhawan v. Holder, 557 U.S. 29, 129 S.Ct. 2294, 2300 (2009). See also Lee v. Ashcroft, 368 F.3d 218 (3d Cir. 2004) (conviction for tax offense under 26 U.S.C.A. § 7206 not an aggravated felony); Evangelista v. Ashcroft, 359 F.3d 145 (2d Cir. 2004) (conviction of a tax offense under 26 U.S.C.A. § 7201 is an aggravated felony). Cf. Ming Lam Sui v. I.N.S., 250 F.3d 105 (2d Cir. 2001) (mere possession of counterfeit travelers check of over $10,000 insufficient to constitute an attempt to pass these checks and cause a loss); Valansi v. Ashcroft, 278 F.3d 203 (3d Cir. 2002) (bank employee's embezzlement of over $10,000 not an aggravated felony where conviction did not involve an intent to defraud); Nugent v. Ashcroft, 367 F.3d 162 (3d Cir. 2004) ("theft by deception" was a fraud, not theft offense, and thus where loss to the victim did not exceed $10,000 it was not an aggravated felony). The Board would hold that potential or intended losses of over $10,000 would suffice to make the crime an aggravated felony; the circuits are in some disagreement over this. Matter of S-I-K, 24 I. & N. Dec. 324 (BIA 2007); Matter of Onyido, 22 I. & N. Dec. 552 (BIA 1999); Eke v. Mukasey, 512 F.3d 372, 380 (7th Cir. 2008) (potential loss can suffice); cf. Singh v. Attorney General of U.S., 677 F.3d 503 (3d Cir. 2012) (requiring actual loss of $10,000).

[3]INA § 101(a)(43)(A), 8 U.S.C.A. § 1101(a)(43)(A); U.S. v. Gonzales-Vela, 276 F.3d 763, 767-68 (6th Cir. 2001); Guerrero-Perez v. I.N.S., 242 F.3d 727, 734-37 (7th Cir. 2001); Mugalli v. Ashcroft, 258 F.3d 52 (2d Cir. 2001) (statutory rape was "sexual abuse of a minor"); Lara-Ruiz v. I.N.S., 241 F.3d 934 (7th Cir. 2001) (same).

[4]See, e.g., U.S. v. Pacheco, 225 F.3d 148 (2d Cir. 2000) or U.S. v. Graham, 169 F.3d 787 (3d Cir.), cert. denied, 120 S.Ct. 116 (1999); U.S. v. Gonzales-Vela, 276 F.3d 763, 767-68 (6th Cir. 2001); Guerrero-Perez v. I.N.S., 242 F.3d 727, 734-37 (7th Cir. 2001).

[Section 8:17]

[1]Taylor v. U.S., 495 U.S. 575, 110 S.Ct. 2143, 109 L.Ed.2d 607 (1990).

[2]INA § 101(a)(43)(G), 8 U.S.C.A. § 1101(a)(43)(G).

[3]Matter of Perez, 22 I. & N. Dec. 1325, 2000 WL 726849 (B.I.A. 2000); see also, Solorzano-Patlan v. I.N.S., 207 F.3d 869 (7th Cir. 2000).

federal purposes. Similarly, to fit into the category of "theft" aggravated felonies, the state statute must describe acts which fit within the generic definition of theft.[4]

Under the categorical approach, the first step is to define the offense, either through express federal rules or through the *Taylor* approach to a generic definition of the crime.[5] The next step is to consider whether a particular state statute is equivalent to that generic or federal definition.[6] For a state offense to be considered broader than the federal offense, there must be a "realistic possibility" that conduct not criminalized under the federal statute is criminalized by the state.[7] The third step, if state statute is divisible, and only some parts of the state statute would fit within the federal definition, is to consult the record of conviction to determine which portion of the divisible statute was applicable to a particular conviction.[8]

However, the categorical approach has been held not to be appropriate for all situations. Convictions for both fraud and income tax evasion are aggravated felonies only where the loss amount exceeds $10,000.[9] The BIA and Supreme Court rejected arguments that the Government could only show the loss amount where a state statute included amount of loss as an element.[10] Rather, the amount of loss may be proven by extrinsic evidence, meaning that it is not governed by the categorical approach.[11] The Supreme Court's decision in *Nijhawan* suggests that extrinsic evidence may be admissible with regard to several prongs of the aggravated felony definition, in addition to the fraud prong.[12]

3. Other Criminal Removability Provisions

§ 8:18 Firearms offenses

Certain firearms offenses can qualify as aggravated felonies, including possession of a firearm by a felon,[1] but most possessory offenses and offenses that relate to firearms but do not fit within the aggravated felony definition will trigger removability only under INA § 237(a)(2)(C).[2]

Where an individual has been convicted of a weapons charge, but the charge does

---

[4]See e.g., U.S. v. Corona-Sanchez, 291 F.3d 1201 (9th Cir. 2002) (California petty theft statute was broader than generic definition); Nevarez-Martinez v. I.N.S., 326 F.3d 1053 (9th Cir. 2003) (theft by means of transportation statute was not equivalent to theft statute).

[5]See e.g., Taylor v. United States, 495 U. S. 575 (1990); Shepard v. United States, 544 U. S. 13 (2005).

[6]Gonzales v. Duenas-Alvarez, 549 U.S. 183, 193 (2007).

[7]Gonzales v. Duenas-Alvarez, 549 U.S. 183, 193 (2007).

[8]Matter of Sweetser, 22 I&N Dec. 709, 714 (BIA 1999); Matter of Pichardo, 21 I&N Dec. 330, 335 (BIA1996).

[9]INA § 101(a)(43)(M)(ii); 8 U.S.C.A. § 1101(a)(43)(M).

[10]See Matter of Babaisakov, 24 I&N Dec. 306 (BIA 2007); Nijhawan v. Holder, 557 U.S. 29, 129 S. Ct. 2294, 174 L. Ed. 2d 22 (2009).

[11]Matter of Babaisakov, 24 I&N Dec. 306 (BIA 2007).

[12]See e.g., INA § 101(a)(43)(K)(ii), 8 U.S.C.A. § 1101(a)(43)(K)(ii) (prostitution offenses "if committed for commercial advantage"); INA § 101(a)(43)(P), 8 U.S.C.A. § 1101(a)(43)(P) (creating exception to forgery prong where offense committed to help immediate family members); INA § 101(a)(43)(N), 8 U.S.C.A. § 1101(a)(43)(N) (similar where smuggling committed to help immediate family members);

[Section 8:18]

[1]Matter of Vasquez-Muniz, 23 I & N Dec. 207, 2002 WL 110599 (BIA 2002); Negrete-Rodriguez v. Mukasey, 518 F.3d 497 (7th Cir. 2008).

[2]INA § 101(a)(43)(F), (G), 8 U.S.C.A. § 1101(a)(43)(F), (G).

not specify whether the weapon was a firearm, the Board has found that removability cannot be established.[3]

In the past, when an individual had their sentence "enhanced" because of use of a firearm, that could not constitute a firearms conviction, because most sentence enhancements did not require proof beyond a reasonable doubt.[4] However, recent Supreme Court decisions now require that sentence enhancements be proven beyond a reasonable doubt.[5] Thus, sentence enhancements under the new constitutional scheme may satisfy the "conviction" requirements of the firearms ground.

The firearms ground will include any offense involving a gun, including unlawful possession, unlawful use, and related offenses. It should be noted that the Supreme Court has recently struck down some state and federal gun law as violative of the Second Amendment.[6] In a 2011 case, the Fifth Circuit held that undocumented immigrants are not "persons" for purposes of the Second Amendment, and thus cannot bring a Second Amendment claim.[7] However, the matter remains open in other circuits.

§ 8:19 Drug crimes

As was noted above, most drug offenses are now considered to be aggravated felonies.[1] This includes convictions for possession of drug paraphernalia, though that is not a crime under the federal criminal code.[2] However, even in those few instances where a drug offense escapes the aggravated felony label, the crime will still render a resident removable.[3] The only exception is for a one-time possession of less than 30 grams of marijuana.[4]

Based on the Federal First Offender Act, the Ninth Circuit has held that where simple drug possession offenses are expunged, that this eliminates the ground of removability,[5] even if the crime was foreign,[6] or was expunged while the case was on appeal.[7] This approach has not been followed in other circuits.[8]

---

[3]Matter of Teixeira, 21 I. & N. Dec. 316 (B.I.A. 1996).

[4]Matter of Rodriguez-Cortes, 20 I. & N. Dec. 587, 590-91 (B.I.A. 1992); but see Matter of Lopez-Amaro, 20 I & N Dec. 668 (B.I.A. 1993), aff'd, 25 F.3d 986 (11th Cir. 1994), cert. denied, 115 S.Ct. 1093 (1995) (where enhancement requires proof beyond reasonable doubt, can be a conviction).

[5]See, Blakely v. Washington, 542 U.S. 296, 124 S.Ct. 2531, 159 L.Ed.2d 403 (2004); U.S. v. Booker, 125 S.Ct. 738, 160 L.Ed.2d 621 (2005).

[6]McDonald v. City of Chicago, 130 S.Ct. 3020 (2010).

[7]U.S. v. Portillo-Munoz, 643 F.3d 437 (5th Cir. 2011), as revised, (June 29, 2011) and cert. denied, 132 S. Ct. 1969, 182 L. Ed. 2d 821 (2012).

[Section 8:19]

[1]See § 8:14.

[2]Matter of Martinez Espinoza, 25 I&N Dec. 118 (BIA 2009); Estrada v. Holder, 560 F.3d 1039, 1042 (9th Cir. 2009); Escobar Barraza v. Mukasey, 519 F.3d 388, 389–90 (7th Cir. 2008); Luu-Le v. INS, 224 F.3d 911, 914–16 (9th Cir. 2000).

[3]See INA § 237(a)(2)(B)(i), 8 U.S.C.A. § 1227(a)(2)(B)(i).

[4]See INA § 237(a)(2)(B)(i), 8 U.S.C.A. § 1227(a)(2)(B)(i).

[5]Lujan-Armendariz v. I.N.S., 222 F.3d 728 (9th Cir. 2000).

[6]Dillingham v. I.N.S., 267 F.3d 996 (9th Cir. 2001).

[7]Cardenas-Uriarte v. I.N.S., 227 F.3d 1132 (9th Cir. 2000).

§ 8:20   Crimes involving moral turpitude

Research References

A.L.R. Index, Immigration and Naturalization

Even if a crime does not fall into the aggravated felony category, it may nonetheless render an individual removable on grounds that the crime involved moral turpitude. There are two grounds of moral turpitude removability. First, any individual who commits a felony crime involving moral turpitude within five years of entry is removable.[1] Second, any individual who commits two crimes involving moral turpitude is removable, regardless of when the crimes occurred.[2] Further, it should be noted that individuals applying for admission (for instance, returning from a trip abroad) are inadmissible even for a single crime involving moral turpitude unless the crime falls within the "petty offense exception."[3]

For decades, when analyzing whether a particular offense was for a crime involving moral turpitude, one needed to look only to the face of the statute under which the individual was convicted.[4] Under the categorical test, the BIA was precluded from looking behind the fact of conviction to the true facts at issue.[5] The BIA was obligated to ask whether the least reprehensible conduct prohibited by statute was turpitudinous,[6] though some courts referred alternately to the "general nature of the crime."[7] Where the statute defining the offense is divisible, reference was made to the record of conviction to determine which section of the statute was implicated by the conviction.[8] But under all variations, the analysis focused on the offense as defined in the statute; not the underlying facts.

A recent Attorney General decision appears to have significantly changed that approach. In *Matter of Silva-Trevino*, the Attorney General held that where the categorical approach was insufficient to determine whether an offense involves moral turpitude, the immigration judges could look to the facts underlying the conviction.[9] The *Silva-Trevino* test represents a significant break with past treat-

---

[8]Acosta v. Ashcroft, 341 F.3d 218 (3rd Cir. 2003); Vasquez-Velezmoro v. U.S. I.N.S., 281 F.3d 693 (8th Cir. 2002); Gill v. Ashcroft, 335 F.3d 574 (7th Cir. 2003); Madriz-Alvarado v. Ashcroft, 383 F.3d 321 (5th Cir. 2004); Resendiz-Alcaraz v. U.S. Atty. Gen., 383 F.3d 1262 (11th Cir. 2004).

[Section 8:20]

[1]INA § 237(a)(2)(A)(i), 8 U.S.C.A. § 1227(a)(2)(A)(i).

[2]INA § 237(a)(2)(A)(ii), 8 U.S.C.A. § 1227(a)(2)(A)(ii).

[3]INA § 212(a)(2)(A), 8 U.S.C.A. § 1182(a)(2)(A).

[4]Matter of Torres-Varela, 23 I&N Dec. 78, 84 (BIA 2001).

[5]Rodriguez-Castro v. Gonzales, 427 F.3d 316, 320–21 (5th Cir. 2005); Rodriquez-Herrera v. INS, 52 F.3d 238 (9th Cir. 1995).

[6]Amouzadeh v. Winfrey, 467 F.3d 451, 455 (5th Cir. 2006) (analyzing the "minimum criminal conduct necessary to sustain a conviction under the statute"); Partyka v. Att'y Gen., 417 F.3d 408, 411 (3d Cir. 2005) (considering whether the "least culpable conduct" covered by the criminal statute in issue would necessarily involve moral turpitude); see also, e.g., Quintero-Salazar v. Keisler, 506 F.3d 688, 692 (9th Cir. 2007) (analyzing "whether the full range of conduct encompassed by the statute" involves moral turpitude).

[7]See, e.g., Marciano v. INS, 450 F.2d 1022, 1025 (8th Cir. 1971); Nicanor-Romero v. Mukasey, 523 F.3d 992, 1004–05 (9th Cir. 2008).

[8]*Nicanor-Romero, 523 F.3d at 1007; Amouzadeh, 467 F.3d at 455.*

[9]Matter of Silva-Trevino, 24 I&N Dec. 687 (A.G. 2008).

ment of the moral turpitude ground, and is analyzed at some length in chapter 7.[10] To vastly generalize, it is still possible to say that crimes categorically involve moral turpitude, but it is now difficult to categorically exclude the possibility that particular convictions will trigger removability under the moral turpitude ground.

In evaluating whether a particular crime involves moral turpitude, the DHS does not look at the underlying conduct of the applicant, but at the language in the criminal statute.[11] Where the statute is broad or multisectional, the courts will look at the record of conviction, that is the "charge (indictment), plea, verdict, and sentence," to determine whether the crime for which the person was convicted involved moral turpitude.[12]

Crimes that have fraud as an element are considered to involve moral turpitude.[13] Crimes predicated on "possession" of an object are considered crimes of moral turpitude only when accompanied with intent to commit a crime of moral turpitude.[14] Some sexual crimes, such as prostitution, are considered crimes of moral turpitude.[15] Some crimes against property, such as arson, larceny and burglary, are also crimes of moral turpitude.[16]

In *Matter of Torres-Varela* the BIA held that aggravated driving under the influence (DUI), defined under an Arizona statue as a third conviction for simple DUI, is not a crime involving moral turpitude because a conviction for simple DUI is not a crime of moral turpitude.[17] This finding can be compared to the Board's finding in *Matter of Lopez-Meza*, which held that a conviction for DUI with the knowledge that one's license has been suspended or revoked is a crime involving moral turpitude.[18] A divided Ninth Circuit upheld the Board's approach.[19]

Crimes involving violence deserve separate discussion. In general, violent crimes

---

[10]See § 7:26.

[11]U.S. v. Neely, 18 F.2d 337 (7th Cir. 1953). Cf. Okabe v. I.N.S., 6471 F.2d 863 (5th Cir. 1982); Matter of Esfandiary, 16 I. & N. Dec. 659, 660 (BIA 1979); Matter of Short, 20 I. & N. Dec. 136 (B.I.A. 1989).

[12]Matter of Esfandiary, 16 I. & N. Dec. 659, 1979 WL 44422 (B.I.A. 1979); see also Hernandez-Martinez v. Ashcroft, 329 F.3d 1117 (9th Cir. 2003) (pre-sentence report not part of the record of conviction); Dickson v. Ashcroft, 346 F.3d 44 (2d Cir. 2003) (Board erred in considering narrative statement in pre-sentence report).

[13]Jordan v. De George, 341 U.S. 223, 227-28 (1951).

[14]Matter of Serna, 20 I. & N. Dec. 579, 584 (B.I.A. 1992) (deciding that knowing possession of an altered immigration document was not a crime of moral turpitude); cf. Beltran-Tirado v. I.N.S., 213 F.3d 1179, 1183-84, 48 Fed. R. Serv. 3d 48 (9th Cir. 2000) (using an unlawful social security number as an employment verification document did not involve moral turpitude); but cf. Omagah v. Ashcroft, 288 F.3d 254 (5th Cir. 2002) (conspiring to obtain, possess and use unlawful immigration documents is a crime involving moral turpitude); see also U.S. v. Samaei, 260 F. Supp. 2d 1223 (M.D. Fla. 2003) (shoplifting convictions found to be crimes of moral turpitude).

[15]Lane v. Tillinghast, 38 F.2d 231 (1st Cir. 1930).

[16]See Smalley v. Ashcroft, 354 F.3d 332 (5th Cir. 2003) (racketeering offense of agreeing to launder money is a crime involving moral turpitude); Chiaramonte v. Immigration and Naturalization Service, 626 F.2d 1093, 1097 (2d Cir. 1980); DeLuca v. Ashcroft, 203 F. Supp. 2d 1276 (M.D. Ala. 2002) (theft offense); Matter of De La Nues, 18 I. & N. Dec. 140 (B.I.A. 1981); Matter of S-, 3 I. & N. Dec. 617 (Central Off. 1949). For a fuller discussion of crimes of moral turpitude see Immigration Law and Crimes § 6.2; Kurzban, Kurzban's Immigration Law Sourcebook 40-48 (7th ed. 2000).

[17]Matter of Torres-Varela, 23 I. & N. Dec. 78 (B.I.A. 2001) (en banc).

[18]In Re Jose Luis Lopez-Meza, 22 I. & N. Dec. 1188, 1999 WL 1223810 (B.I.A. 1999).

[19]Cf. Marmolejo-Campos v. Holder, 558 F.3d 903 (9th Cir. 2009), cert. den. 130 S.Ct. 1011 (2009) (finding aggravated DUI to be turpitudinous); with Hernandez-Martinez v. Ashcroft, 329 F.3d 1117 (9th Cir.2003) (simple DUI not turpitudinous).

involving intent, such as murder, voluntary manslaughter, or rape also involve moral turpitude.[20] On the other hand, involuntary manslaughter is usually not a crime of moral turpitude.[21] However, if the involuntary manslaughter statute requires a conscious disregard of an unjustifiable risk, then it would be a crime of moral turpitude.[22] Whereas simple assault does not involve moral turpitude, an assault with intent to commit a felony involving moral turpitude is itself a crime of moral turpitude.[23] The Board has also recently confirmed that a conviction for battery is not a crime involving moral turpitude.[24]

Domestic violence crimes may also involve moral turpitude. For instance, stalking has been held to involve moral turpitude.[25] However, the Board has held that domestic violence assault crimes only involve moral turpitude where the offense involves the infliction of bodily injury.[26] Where bodily injury is not an element of the offense, moral turpitude is not present.[27] It should be noted that even if a domestic violence and other family violence crime does not involve moral turpitude, it may trigger removability under INA § 237(a)(2)(E), discussed below.[28] It is necessary to analyze the crime under both sections.

Appendix 8-2 reproduces the State Department's conclusions regarding crimes of moral turpitude.

In evaluating statutes for the purpose of deciding whether the behavior criminalized involves moral turpitude for purposes of the naturalization provisions, the courts must be cognizant of the constitutional requirement of establishing a uniform rule of naturalization. uniformity would be defeated by allowing some state legislatures to prevent the naturalization of persons because the legislature made behavior criminal that was offensive to the morality of a majority of the legislators of a state.[29] When the behavior is not uniformly criminalized throughout the United

---

[20]De Lucia v. Flagg, 297 F.2d 58 (7th Cir. 1962), cert. denied, 369 U.S. 837 (1962); Ng Sui Wing v. U.S., 46 F.2d 755 (7th Cir. 1931); Matter of Abi-Rached, 10 I. & N. Dec. 551 (B.I.A. 1964).

[21]Matter of Szegedi, 10 I. & N. Dec. 28 (B.I.A. 1962).

[22]Matter of Franklin, 20 I. & N. Dec. 867, 870 (B.I.A. 1994) (finding Missouri's involuntary manslaughter statute to be a crime of moral turpitude). But note that recklessness by itself it not sufficient for a finding of moral turpitude.

[23]Matter of Short, 20 I. & N. Dec. 136, 139, 1989 WL 331878 (B.I.A. 1989); In re Luaiva Tui Fualaau, 21 I. & N. Dec. 475, 1996 WL 413576 (B.I.A. 1996) (conviction for Hawaii's third degree assault is not a crime of moral turpitude because the offense is similar to simple assault); cf. Yousefi v. U.S. I.N.S., 260 F.3d 318 (4th Cir. 2001) (finding conviction for assault with a dangerous weapon a crime involving moral turpitude after discerning no appreciable difference between it and assault with a deadly weapon); see also Chanmouny v. Ashcroft, 376 F. 3d 810, 2004 WL 1586874 (8th Cir. 2004) (conviction under statute that prohibited threatening a crime of violence for the purpose of terrorizing another was a crime involving moral turpitude).

[24]In re Garcia-Hernandez, 23 I. & N. Dec. 590 (B.I.A. 2003).

[25]In re Sanudo, 23 I. & N. Dec. 968, 2006 WL 2361706 (B.I.A. 2006) (neither party disputed that stalking involved moral turpitude).

[26]Cf. Matter of Phong Nguyen Tran, 21 I & N Dec. 291, 1996 WL 170083 (B.I.A. 1996) (where bodily injury an element, offense involves moral turpitude) with In re Sanudo, 23 I. & N. Dec. 968, 2006 WL 2361706 (B.I.A. 2006) (where no bodily injury element, crime did not involve moral turpitude).

[27]In re Sanudo, 23 I. & N. Dec. 968, 2006 WL 2361706 (B.I.A. 2006).

[28]See § 8:21.

[29]See Nemetz v. Immigration and Naturalization Service, 647 F.2d 432, 436 (4th Cir. 1981).

States, only those statutes that criminalize acts harmful to the public may serve as the basis of a finding of moral turpitude.[30]

Attempts are considered to be crimes of moral turpitude if the underlying offense is itself a crime of moral turpitude.[31] The same rule applies to aiding and abetting.[32] Similarly, conspiracy follows the same rule: "[w]here the underlying, substantive offense is a crime involving moral turpitude . . . conspiracy to commit such an offense is also a crime involving moral turpitude."[33] Misprison of a felony has also been found to be a crime involving moral turpitude, on the basis that it involves dishonest or fraudulent behavior.[34]

§ 8:21   Family violence grounds of removability

The INA also provides for removability for individuals who have been convicted of various crimes of family violence, including "domestic crimes of violence" against spouses or partners, stalking, violation of orders of protection, and child abuse, abandonment, or neglect.[1]

The domestic violence ground incorporates the "crime of violence" definition of 18 U.S.C.A. § 16, but does not contain the requirement for aggravated felonies that there be a sentence of imprisonment of one year.[2] There is currently a split in the circuits at this point as to whether the domestic nature of the assault offense must be an element of the offense, or can be proven by extrinsic evidence.[3] The Board of Immigration Appeals, as well as the Fifth and Seventh Circuits, permit extrinsic evidence to show that the victim was a family member, such that an assault crime involved domestic violence.[4] The Ninth Circuit disagrees.[5] However, a recent Supreme Court case in the non-immigration context suggests that the "domestic"

---

[30]Nemetz v. Immigration and Naturalization Service, 647 F.2d 432, 436 (4th Cir. 1981). The INS adopted this test in INS Interp. 316.1(f)(7).

[31]Matter of Short, 20 I. & N. Dec. 136 (B.I.A. 1989) (If the underlying or substantive crime involves moral turpitude, then a conviction for aiding in the commission of the crime or for otherwise acting as an accessory before the fact is also a conviction for a crime involving moral turpitude).

[32]Matter of Awaijane, 14 I. & N. Dec. 117, 118-19 (B.I.A. 1972) (citing U.S. ex rel. Meyer v. Day, 54 F.2d 336 (2d Cir. 1931)).

[33]McNaughton v. I.N.S., 612 F.2d 457, 459 (9th Cir. 1980). See also Guarneri v. Kessler, 98 F.2d 580 (5th Cir.), cert. denied, 305 U.S. 648 (1938); Mercer v. Lence, 96 F.2d 122 (10th Cir.), cert. denied, 305 U.S. 611 (1938); Matter of Goldeshtein, Int. Dec. 3158 (B.I.A. 1991); Matter of G-, 7 I. & N. Dec. 114, 115 (B.I.A. 1956).

[34]Itani v. Ashcroft, 298 F.3d 1213 (11th Cir. 2002).

[Section 8:21]

[1]INA § 237(a)(2)(E), 8 U.S.C.A. § 1227(a)(2)(E).

[2]INA § 237(a)(2)(E), 8 U.S.C.A. § 1227(a)(2)(E).

[3]Cf. Tokatly v. Ashcroft, 371 F.3d 613 (9th Cir. 2004) (relationship with victim cannot be proved by fact testimony, but must appear in elements of crime, or indictment), Flores v. Ashcroft, 350 F.3d 666, 670-72 (7th Cir. 2003) (relationship with victim a "real offense" rather than "charge offense" characteristic).

[4]Matter of Velasquez, 25 I&N Dec. 278 (BIA 2010); Bianco v. Holder, 624 F.3d 265 (5th Cir. 2010); Flores v. Ashcroft, 350 F.3d 666, 670–72 (7th Cir. 2003) (relationship with victim a "real offense" rather than "charge offense" characteristic).

[5]Tokatly v. Ashcroft, 371 F.3d 613 (9th Cir. 2004) (relationship with victim cannot be proved by fact testimony, but must appear in elements of crime, or indictment).

aspect of the conviction may not need to be an element of the offense, giving support to the Board's view.[6]

B. UNLAWFUL VOTING AND FALSE CLAIMS TO CITIZENSHIP

§ 8:22 Unlawful voting

In the 1996 elections, a nonprofit organization registered naturalization applicants for voting after their approval at the interview but before the swearing in ceremony, causing a political scandal.[1] Congress responded by including a provision in the IIRAIRA that made unlawful voting in a local, state, or federal election a ground for both deportability and inadmissibility.[2]

It is unclear what intent requirement those deportation grounds will be interpreted to have.[3] The USCIS has cautioned its district offices that since voting laws change from location to location, there is no general rule as to who has voted unlawfully; in some jurisdictions, unlawful voting is only a crime if the violation is knowing or intentional.[4] Practitioners should attempt to prevail upon USCIS to exercise prosecutorial discretion and not to start removal proceedings if the person registered or voted as a result of a good faith mistake.[5] Registering to vote, but not actually voting, is discussed in the next section.[6]

There is now a very narrow exemption to both grounds of inadmissibility and deportability, which applies only if the noncitizen satisfies all of the following conditions: (1) each natural parent of the noncitizen (or, in the case of an adopted noncitizen, each adoptive parent of the noncitizen) is or was a citizen (whether by birth or naturalization); (2) the noncitizen permanently resided in the United States prior to attaining the age of 16; and (3) the noncitizen reasonably believed at the time of engaging in the relevant act that he or she was a citizen.[7]

§ 8:23 Unlawful voting—Registering to vote and false claims to citizenship

When the IIRAIRA made unlawful voting in elections grounds a ground of deportability and inadmissibility, it also created a ground of deportability and inadmis-

---

[6]United States v. Hayes, 129 S. Ct. 1079 (2009).

[Section 8:22]

[1]On December 31, 1996, INS District Director for the Los Angeles district of INS sent a letter to all community-based organization reminding them that persons are only citizens after the oath ceremony. Rogers, INS District Director, CBO Letter (Dec. 31, 1996).

[2]INA §§ 212(a)(10)(D), 237(a)(6), 8 U.S.C.A. §§ 1182(a)(10)(D), 1227(a)(6).

[3]The State Department has issued a cable to all consular posts which indicates that "[i]n the normal course of events, the consular officer can presume that an alien voting in a political election did so in violation of some law or ordinance." State Department Cable No. 96-State-219622 (Oct. 21, 1996) reproduced in 73 Interpreter Releases 1505 (Oct. 28, 1996).

[4]See Policy Memorandum No. 86, William Yates, Procedures for Handling Naturalization Applications of Aliens Who Voted Unlawfully or Falsely Represented Themselves as U.S. Citizens by Voting or Registering to Vote (March 7, 2002), reproduced as Appendix 8-4.

[5]See Appendix 8-4.

[6]See § 8:23.

[7]INA §§ 212(a)(10)(D), 237(a)(6), 8 U.S.C.A. §§ 1182(a)(10)(D), 1227(a)(6), as amended by Child Citizenship Act of 2000, Pub. L. No. 106-395, § 201(b),(c), 114 Stat. 1631 (Oct. 30, 2000).

sibility for false claims to U.S. citizenship.[1] Unfortunately, it is not uncommon for permanent residents to unwittingly register to vote at the time that they apply for a drivers license or other governmental benefits. This ground of removability applies to any false claim made to obtain any benefit under federal or state law, provided the claim was made on or after September 30, 1996.[2]

It is unclear what intent requirement those deportation grounds will be interpreted to have.[3] However, Congress has now created an "exception" which applies to very few people, but has the side effect of making it difficult to argue that Congress intended the "false claims" ground to apply only to intention false claims to citizenship.

The narrow exemption mentioned above applies only if the noncitizen satisfies all of the following conditions: (1) each natural parent of the noncitizen (or, in the case of an adopted noncitizen, each adoptive parent of the noncitizen) is or was a citizen (whether by birth or naturalization); (2) the noncitizen permanently resided in the United States prior to attaining the age of 16; and (3) the noncitizen reasonably believed at the time of engaging in the relevant act that he or she was a citizen.[4]

A memorandum from the legacy INS discussing false claims in the context of voting registration is reproduced at Appendix 8-4.[5] The USCIS appears willing to exercise prosecutorial discretion not to start removal proceedings if the person registered or voted as a result of a good faith mistake.[6] Applicants are well-advised to have prepared for their interview by taking steps to withdraw their voting registration, preparing affidavits explaining the circumstances of their false claim, and being prepared to discuss the matter at their interview.

C. ABANDONMENT OF LAWFUL PERMANENT RESIDENCE

§ 8:24 Abandonment of lawful permanent residence

Research References

A.L.R. Index, Immigration and Naturalization

Persons who abandon their lawful permanent residence by departing the United States with the intention of remaining abroad are no longer permanent residents;

[Section 8:23]

[1] INA §§ 212(a)(6)(C)(ii), (10)(D), 237(a)(3)(D), (6), 8 U.S.C.A. §§ 1182(a)(6)(C)(ii), 1227(a)(3)(D), (6).

[2] See State Department Cable No. 97-State-174342 (Sept. 17, 1997) reproduced in 74 Interpreter Releases 1483 (September 29, 1997) (discussing inadmissibility).

[3] The State Department has issued a cable to all consular posts which indicates that "[i]n the normal course of events, the consular officer can presume that an alien voting in a political election did so in violation of some law or ordinance." State Department Cable No. 96-State-219622 (Oct. 21, 1996) reproduced in 73 Interpreter Releases 1505 (Oct. 28, 1996).

[4] INA §§ 212(a)(6)(C)(ii), 237(a)(3)(D), 8 U.S.C.A. §§ 1182(a)(6)(C)(ii), 1227(a)(3)(D), as amended by the Child Citizenship Act of 2000, Pub. L. No. 106-395, § 201(b),(c), 114 Stat. 1631 (Oct. 30, 2000).

[5] Policy Memorandum No. 86, William Yates, Procedures for Handling Naturalization Applications of Aliens Who Voted Unlawfully or Falsely Represented Themselves as U.S. Citizens by Voting or Registering to Vote (March 7, 2002), reproduced as Appendix 8-4.

[6] See Appendix 8-4.

they are subject to deportation and may no longer be naturalized.[1] This is different from the interruption of the five years continuous residence required for naturalization,[2] because abandonment of permanent residence is based on intention. In removal proceedings, the government has the burden of proving by clear, unequivocal and convincing evidence that the permanent resident abandoned his or her residence.[3]

The central question in abandonment of permanent residence cases is whether the person's visit abroad was temporary.[4] The intention of the person will determine whether the trip abroad was temporary.[5] To ascertain this intention, the DHS examines such objective indicators as: (1) the location of the person's family ties, property holdings, and job; (2) whether the person intended to return to the U.S. as the place of employment or business or as an actual home; (3) whether, when the person departed the U.S., the visit abroad could have been expected to terminate within a relatively short time, and whether that termination could have been fixed by an early event.[6] Having an actual dwelling place in the U.S. is not a requirement for finding that the person has *not* abandoned his or her permanent residence.[7]

The length of the person's absence from the U.S. is obviously a significant factor in determining whether the person abandoned his or her lawful permanent residence.[8] Even extended visits abroad could be considered temporary provided that at the time of departure the visit would appear to terminate upon the occurrence of an event having a reasonable possibility of occurring within a relatively short period of time.[9] Thus, for example, if a person goes abroad to care for a sick relative who is expected to be cured or die within a reasonable amount of time, the person has not abandoned his or her lawful permanent residence.[10] But if at the time the lawful permanent resident departs the U.S., the sick relative is likely to require the person's presence for an indefinite period of time then the visit is not temporary and the person has abandoned his or her residence.[11]

Visits that depend on an event that is expected to occur within a relatively short period may end up being extended for a long time. In such cases, the person will be held not to have abandoned his or her lawful permanent residence in the U.S. if he or she had a continuous, uninterrupted intention to return to the U.S. during the

---

[Section 8:24]

[1]INA § 101(a)(20), 8 U.S.C.A. § 1101(a)(20); INS Interp. 318.4 (abandonment of residence by an immigrant constitutes a change of status under section 101(a)(20) and extinguishes the status of permanent resident). For a thorough discussion of abandonment of lawful permanent residence, see Endelman, You Can Go Home Again—How to Prevent Abandonment of Lawful Permanent Resident Status, 91-4 Immigration Briefings (April 1991).

[2]See §§ 7:4 to 7:10.

[3]Khodagholian v. Ashcroft, 335 F.3d 1003 (9th Cir. 2003).

[4]Singh v. Reno, 113 F.3d 1512 (9th Cir. 1997); Matter of Huang, 19 I. & N. Dec. 749, 752-53 (B.I.A. 1988).

[5]Matter of Huang, 19 I. & N. Dec. 749, 753, 1988 WL 235431 (B.I.A. 1988).

[6]Matter of Huang, 19 I. & N. Dec. 749, 753, 1988 WL 235431 (B.I.A. 1988).

[7]Matter of Huang, 19 I. & N. Dec. 749, 753, 1988 WL 235431 (B.I.A. 1988).

[8]Matter of Huang, 19 I. & N. Dec. 749, 755, 1988 WL 235431 (B.I.A. 1988).

[9]See Chavez-Ramirez v. I.N.S., 792 F.2d 932, 937 (9th Cir. 1986).

[10]See Chavez-Ramirez v. I.N.S., 792 F.2d 932, 935-36 (9th Cir. 1986).

[11]Angeles v. District Director, I.N.S., 729 F.Supp. 479 (D.Md. 1990).

entire visit.[12] Thus, the fact that the convalescence takes longer than expected will not affect the temporary nature of the visit abroad provided the person continues to have an uninterrupted intention to return to the U.S.[13] If during the stay abroad, however, the person settles down and evinces the intention of remaining abroad indefinitely, then the person has abandoned his or her lawful permanent residence in the U.S.[14]

On a related issue, some short trips abroad may be prolonged by events beyond the person's control, such as political upheavals or war. In such cases, the person is not considered to have abandoned his or her permanent residence provided there was always the intention to return to the United States.[15] Thus, where the Iranian government refused to allow a permanent resident to leave Iran for 11 months until an old tax bill was paid, the court determined that the government had failed to meet its burden of showing that the individual intended to abandon his permanent residence in the United States.[16] Similarly, where a woman remained in Iraq due to fears for her family and a desire to help them immigrate to this country, abandonment was held not to have occurred.[17]

An indicator of abandonment of lawful permanent residence that the DHS pays particular attention to is voluntary claim of nonresident status for tax purposes and failure to file either federal or state tax returns because he or she considers himself or herself to be a nonresident noncitizen. Persons making such claims or failing to file for such reason are presumed to have abandoned lawful permanent residence and may no longer be eligible for naturalization.[18] This presumption may be rebutted by proving that the applicant was unaware that by filing as a nonresident taxpayer, he or she was terminating his or her status as lawful permanent resident.[19] To substantiate this claim, the applicant must file a corrected tax return with the IRS for each year on which nonresident status was claimed.[20] In addition, failure to file tax returns may be considered an element in the determination of good moral character of the applicant.[21]

Another indicator of the applicant's intention when departing the United States is whether he or she obtained a reentry permit before departing the United States.[22] The reentry permit serves as an entry document for lawful permanent residents when they reenter the United States.[23] Normally, a lawful permanent resident uses the "alien" registration receipt card (green card) for this purpose, since it can be used as an entry document if the holder was absent from the United States for less

---

[12]Chavez-Ramirez v. I.N.S., 792 F.2d 932, 937 (9th Cir. 1986).

[13]Chavez-Ramirez v. I.N.S., 792 F.2d 932, 936 (9th Cir. 1986).

[14]Chavez-Ramirez v. I.N.S., 792 F.2d 932, 937 (9th Cir. 1986); see also Katebi v. Ashcroft, 396 F.3d 463 (1st Cir. 2005).

[15]In re Naturalization of Vafaei-Makhsoos, 597 F.Supp. 499 (D. Minn. 1984) (applicant prevented from returning to the U.S. by the hostage crisis in Iran).

[16]Khodagyholian v. Ashcroft, 355 F.3d 1003 (9th Cir. 2003).

[17]Hana v. Gonzales, 400 F.3d 472 (6th Cir. 2005).

[18]8 CFR § 316.5(c)(2); INS Interp. 318.4.

[19]See INS Interp. 318.4.

[20]INS Interp. 318.4.

[21]See § 7:41.

[22]INS Form I-327.

[23]8 CFR § 223.1(a).

than a year.[24] An unexpired reentry permit, however, allows the holder to enter even if the absence is longer than one year.[25] More importantly, a permanent resident in possession of a valid reentry permit is deemed not to have abandoned his or her status based solely on the duration of an absence or absences if he or she returns to the United States while the reentry permit is valid.[26] One court has held, however, that a reentry permit in and of itself does not prevent a finding that the individual has abandoned her residence. The court found that the reentry permit merely serves as evidence of intent to return which the government can refute with clear, unequivocal, and convincing evidence to the contrary.[27] Additionally, the DHS holds that the presumption of retention of permanent residence does not apply when the permanent resident obtained the reentry permit by fraud.[28]

In addition, a reentry permit will not prevent the break of continuity of residence required for naturalization.[29] Only an Application to Preserve Residence for Naturalization Purposes will preserve *continuity* of residence when the applicant has absences longer than one year.[30] It should be noted that eligibility to preserve continuity of residency is very limited,[31] but all permanent residents are eligible to request a reentry permit, so long as they file the application while still inside the United States.[32] A copy of the I-131, the form by which reentry permits are obtained, is found at Appendix 8-6.

D. FRAUD AND INADMISSIBILITY AT TIME OF ADMISSION

§ 8:25 Fraud in obtaining residency

Persons who obtained their immigrant visa or LPR status by willful misrepresentation of material facts were never lawfully admitted for permanent residence.[1] Such individuals are subject to rescission proceedings within the first five years after their admission,[2] but the BIA — unlike the Third Circuit — believes that there are is no statute of limitation on removal for past fraud.[3]

It is not uncommon for naturalization interviews to focus on whether the applicant engaged in some sort of fraud in order to obtain permanent residency status.

---

[24]8 CFR § 211.1(a)(2).

[25]8 CFR § 211.1(a)(3).

[26]8 CFR § 223.3(d)(1).

[27]Moin v. Ashcroft, 355 F.3d 415 (5th Cir. 2003).

[28]Letter, Weinig, Field Manual Project Director, INS (Apr. 17, 1997) reproduced in 74 Interpreter Releases 1275.

[29]Cf. § 7:5.

[30]See §§ 7:6 to 7:10.

[31]See § § 7:6-7:10.

[32]8 C.F.R. § 223.2(b)(1).

[Section 8:25]

[1]Fedorenko v. U. S., 449 U.S. 490, 515, 101 S. Ct. 737, 751, 66 L. Ed. 2d 686 (1981); see also In re Koloamatangi, 23 I. & N. Dec. 548 (B.I.A. 2003) (person who obtained permanent residency through fraud or misrepresentation has never been "lawfully admitted for permanent residence" and is ineligible for cancellation of removal under INA § 240A(a)).

[2]INA § 246, 8 U.S.C.A. § 1256.

[3]Matter of Belenzo, 17 I. & N. Dec. 374 (A.G. 1981) (no statute of limitations on deportations grounds, five year limit for rescission does not bar removal for excludability at time of entry; marriage fraud case); but see Bamidele v. INS, 99 F.3d 557 (3d Cir. 1996); Garcia v. Att'y Gen. of the United States, 553 F.3d 724, 728 (3d Cir. 2009).

If fraud is discovered, this may trigger not only denial of residency, but removal proceedings.

One common area of focus is the possibility of marriage fraud. Individuals who obtained their residency through a sham marriage are deportable for having been inadmissible at time of entry.[4] The INA has a special presumption of deportability for individuals who obtain lawful status through a marriage contracted less than two years before the LPR status, where there is a divorce or annulment within two years of the status being granted.[5] However, even marriages that do not end within that time frame leave an individual susceptible to a charge of fraud.[6]

A second area where USCIS commonly looks for fraud is where an individual obtained status as a single person. It has been stated that fraudulently claiming to be unmarried, where one is in fact married, is one of the most common forms of fraud.[7]

A third area where USCIS suspects fraud is in the area of legalization. While USCIS is barred from examining legalization files, even to find fraud,[8] independent information (such as through questioning of a naturalization applicant) can give USCIS an independent basis to begin rescission or removal proceedings.[9]

Finally, as USCIS's ability to do record checks has improved, it can now detect past failures to disclose arrests or convictions, or failures to disclose past removals.[10] The failure to disclose arrests or convictions can be material, even if the arrests themselves did not render the individual inadmissible at that point.[11]

Individuals who made fraudulent representations at the time of admission—but who would have been admissible despite their fraud—are eligible for a waiver under INA § 237(a)(1)(H), formerly INA 241(f). Where such a waiver is granted, the individual is eligible for naturalization, as the waiver is considered to have cured the original unlawful entry.[12] In such cases the person is considered to have been a lawful permanent resident since the initial entry.[13]

§ 8:26 Inadmissibility at time of admission

Even if the individual made no willful misrepresentation and committed no fraud

---

[4]Matter of Magana, 17 I. & N. Dec. 111 (B.I.A. 1979) (annulment of prior marriage did not erase fraud).

[5]INA § 237(a)(1)(G)(i), 8 U.S.C.A. § 1227(a)(1)(G)(i).

[6]INA § 237(a)(1)(G)(ii), 8 U.S.C.A. § 1227(a)(1)(G)(ii); INA § 237(a)(1)(A), 8 U.S.C.A. § 1227(a)(1)(A).

[7]Matter of Anabo, 18 I. & N. Dec. 87 (B.I.A. 1981) ("The great majority of cases involving a [fraud] charge as a result of material misrepresentation of marital status involve married sons or daughters of lawful permanent residents and sham marriages").

[8]Matter of Masri, 22 I. & N. Dec. 1145 (B.I.A. 1999).

[9]See, e.g., Aparicio v. Blakeway, 302 F.3d 437 (5th Cir. 2002) (class action challenging investigation of naturalization applicants suspected of fraud in their legalization applications).

[10]Matter of Li, 15 I. & N. Dec. 514 (B.I.A. 1975) (individual obtained permanent residency without obtaining permission to reapply).

[11]Kungys v. U.S., 485 U.S. 759 (1981) (test is whether misrepresentation "had a natural tendency to influence the decision").

[12]OI 318.2(d); INS Interp. 318.5. The visa fraud deportability waiver has been redesignated from INA § 241(f) to INA § 237(a)(1)(H), 8 U.S.C.A. § 1227(a)(1)(H), as redesignated by Illegal Immigration Reform and Immigrant Responsibility Act of 1996 (IIRAIRA), Pub.L. 104-208, § 305(a)(2), 110 Stat. 3009, (Sept. 30, 1996).

[13]Matter of Sosa-Hernandez, 20 I. & N. Dec. 758 (B.I.A. 1993).

at the time of their residency application, their status may be rescinded or taken away if they were in fact ineligible for the status at that time.[1] Nothing in INA § 237(a)(1)(A) limits that ground of removability to those circumstances involving fraud. Thus, for example, a woman who obtained permanent residency status through a father whose residency status was illegally obtained, was inadmissible at time of admission despite her own lack of fraud or misrepresentation.[2] The Third Circuit would apply the five year statute of limitations for LPR rescission to removal proceedings,[3] though the Third Circuit's approach does not protect applicants outside that jurisdiction, and has been rejected elsewhere.[4]

The courts have held that persons inadmissible at the time of entry will not be naturalized.[5]

III. EFFECT OF REMOVABILITY PROCEEDINGS

§ 8:27 Lawful permanent residents who become deportable— Deportability by itself not bar to naturalization

The mere fact that a permanent resident has become deportable for reasons that arose after admission to permanent residence does not per se bar them from naturalizing, if they were granted lawful permanent residence according to the provisions of the statute and such status has not been terminated.[1] Of course, a crime that renders an individual deportable may also bar them from establishing good moral

---

[Section 8:26]

[1]See, e.g., Matter of Hernandez-Puente, 20 I. & N. Dec. 335, 337 (B.I.A. 1991) (INS granted residency nunc pro tunc after individual married, later decided that it lacked authority to do so; rescission upheld); Matter of Raqueno, 17 I. & N. Dec. 10 (B.I.A. 1979) (innocent misrepresentation of marital status); Matter of Teng, 15 I. & N. Dec. 516 (B.I.A. 1975) (stepchildren in fraudulent marriage ineligible for residency despite their innocence as to the fraud); Matter of Ideis, 14 I. & N. Dec. 701 (B.I.A. 1974) (daughter obtained LPR status through apparently LPR father, then LPR father's status revoked; found excludable at time of entry).

[2]Matter of Ideis, 14 I. & N. Dec. 701 (B.I.A. 1974) (daughter obtained LPR status through apparently LPR father, then LPR father's status revoked; found excludable at time of entry); see also, Matter of Teng, 15 I. & N. Dec. 516 (B.I.A. 1975) (stepchildren in fraudulent marriage ineligible for residency despite their innocence as to the fraud).

[3]Bamidele v. INS, 99 F.3d 557 (3d Cir. 1996); Garcia v. Att'y Gen. of the United States, 553 F.3d 724, 728 (3d Cir. 2009).

[4]Kim v. Holder, 560 F.3d 833 (8th Cir. 2009) (upholding BIA's interpretation); Monet v. INS, 791 F.2d 752, 754 (9th Cir. 1986) (same); Asika v. Ashcroft, 362 F.3d 264, 270–71 (4th Cir. 2004) (same); Stolaj v. Holder, 577 F.3d 651 (6th Cir. 2009) (same).

[5]Eng v. I.N.S., 464 F.2d 1265 (2d Cir. 1972) (excludable for misrepresentation, lawful permanent residence only started on date in which he was granted registry); Brymer v. U.S., 83 F.2d 276 (9th Cir. 1936) (reentry after conviction for crime of moral turpitude); INS Interp. 318.3; 318.5.

[Section 8:27]

[1]INS Interp. 318.2(c)(1)(iii). One exception to this general rule may be when a lawful permanent resident becomes deportable for having reentered the U.S. without inspection. In such cases, the INS has historically taken the position that the reentry without inspection automatically terminated the immigrant status and the applicant was no longer eligible for naturalization. INS Interp. 318.2(c)(1) (iii). The IIRAIRA removed entry without inspection as a ground of deportation and replaced it with a ground of inadmissibility; namely, being in the United States without admission or parole. INA § 212(a)(6)(A), 8 U.S.C.A. § 1182(a)(6)(A). It is unclear whether this will affect ability to Naturalize; the INS Interpretations have not been altered.

character.[2] But for crimes that do not bar good moral character — such as offenses (other than aggravated felonies) outside the required good moral character period, and even aggravated felonies before November 29, 1990 — it is not deportability itself which precludes naturalization. It is only where actual removal proceedings are begun that naturalization (except for members and former members of the military) is generally precluded.[3]

§ 8:28   Lawful permanent residents who become deportable—The Exercise of Prosecutorial Discretion

In recent years, DHS has clarified that it maintains prosecutorial discretion to begin, or not to begin, removal proceedings. USCIS's sister agency, ICE, has issued several memoranda regarding the prosecutorial discretion issue.[1] USCIS has also issued a recent memorandum, amending the AFM and setting forth procedures for determining whether and how to exercise prosecutorial discretion.[2]

Under the new procedures, the first question is whether the case is considered an "Egregious Public Safety" (EPS) case.[3] EPS includes any case where the application is "under investigation for, has been arrested for (without disposition), or has been convicted of,"[4] any of several offenses:

1. Specified aggravated felonies, including (a) Murder, rape, or sexual abuse of a minor (INA § 101(a)(43)(A)), (b) illicit trafficking in firearms or destructive devices (INA § 101(a)(43)(C)), (c) offenses relating to explosive materials or firearms (INA § 101(a)(43)(E)); (d) "crimes of violence" for which the term of imprisonment imposed, or where the penalty for a pending case, is at least one year (INA § 101(a)(43)(F)); (e) an offense relating to a demand for ransom (INA § 101(a)(43)(H)); (f) offenses relating to child pornography (INA § 101(a)(43)(L)); (g) offenses relating to slavery and trafficking in persons (INA § 101(a)(43)(K)(iii)); and (h) offense relating to alien smuggling INA § 101(a)(43)(N));

2. Human Rights Violators, known or suspected street gang members, or Interpol hits

---

[2]8 U.S.C. § 1101(f); see generally §§ 7:18 to 7:46.

[3]For the military provisions, see §§ 12:3 to 12:12.

[Section 8:28]

[1]See Memorandum from John Morton, Assistant Secretary, ICE, "Guidance Regarding the Handling of Removal Proceedings of Aliens with Pending or Approved Applications or Petitions" (Aug. 20, 2010) http://www.ice.gov/doclib/detention-reform/pdf/aliens-pending-applications.pdf; Memorandum from John Morton, Director, ICE, "Civil Immigration Enforcement: Priorities for the Apprehension, Detention, and Removal of Aliens" (March 2, 2011) http://www.ice.gov/doclib/news/releases/2011/110302washingtondc.pdf; Memorandum from John Morton, Director, ICE, "Exercising Prosecutorial Discretion Consistent with the Civil Immigration Enforcement Priorities of the Agency for the Apprehension, Detention, and Removal of Aliens" (June 17, 2011), www.ice.gov/doclib/secure-communities/pdf/prosecutorial-discretion-memo.pdf, and Memorandum from John Morton, Director, ICE, "Prosecutorial Discretion: Certain Victims, Witnesses, and Plaintiffs" (June 17, 2011), www.ice.gov/doclib/secure-communities/pdf/domestic-violence.pdf; Unattributed memorandum, "Next Steps in the Implementation of the Prosecutorial Discretion Memorandum and the August 18th Announcement on Immigration Enforcement Priorities" (undated), www.ice.gov/doclib/about/offices/ero/pdf/pros-discretion-next-steps.pdf; Memorandum from Peter S. Vincent, Principal Legal Advisor, ICE, "Case-by-Case Review of Incoming and Certain Pending Cases" (Nov. 17, 2011) http://www.ice.gov/doclib/foia/dro__policy__memos/case-by-case-review-incoming-certain-pending-cases-memorandum.pdf.

[2]See App 8-6.

[3]App 8-6 at 7.

[4]App 8-6 at 3.

3. Re-entry after an order of exclusion, deportation or removal subsequent to conviction for a felony where a Form I-212, Application for Permission to Reapply for Admission into the U.S. after Deportation or Removal, has not been approved.[5] The last category of EPS cases is not likely implicated in naturalization applications, since one must generally be a permanent resident to qualify for naturalization. Thus, only the listed aggravated felony categories, as well as human rights violators, known or suspected gang members, and Interpol hits, should be subject to EPS treatment.

Under EPS procedures, after the EPS situation is detected, USCIS makes a Referral to ICE (RTI) and suspends its processing of the case for 60 days or until ICE makes a decision of how to proceed.[6] If ICE issues an NTA, the processing of the N-400 cannot proceed forward.[7] If ICE fails to issue an NTA or to inform USCIS of its decision within 60 days, USCIS may resume processing; but before USCIS approves the application, it must inform ICE of its intention prior to adjudication.[8] USCIS must also inform ICE of its ultimate decision in the case, whether it has been approved or denied.[9] USCIS may suspend its case processing for longer than 60 days, at ICE's request.[10]

For non-EPS cases where an offense precludes a showing of good moral character, USCIS will deny the N-400 and then refer the case to ICE for potential NTA issuance.[11] USCIS will issue an RTI, and will send ICE the A-file if it is in USCIS's possession.[12]

For non-EPS cases where the crime does not preclude approval of the NTA, USCIS is now instructed to "Make a written recommendation on the issuance of an NTA through a review of the totality of the circumstances to include factors such as: severity of crime, time since crime committed, other criminal conduct, reformation, immigration history including method of entry, length of presence in the U.S., and prior immigration violations, and contributions to society to include the pursuit of education and military service."[13] Once a recommendation is made, it is to be sent to an NTA Review Panel, which is supposed to exist in every USCIS district.[14] The NTA Review Panel is to include a local USCIS Supervisor, a local USCIS Office of Chief Counsel attorney, and a district representative; moreover, an attorney from ICE's local Office of Chief Counsel should be invited to participate and to have "an advisory role" on the panel.[15] If the NTA Review Panel reaches consensus, its decision is a final one; if there is no consensus, the case is elevated to the District Director, through the district representative.[16]

If the NTA Review Panel decides to issue an NTA, the N-400 is to be placed on

---

[5]App 8-6 at 3-4.

[6]App 8-6 at 4.

[7]See § 8:30.

[8]App 8-6 at 4-5.

[9]App 8-6 at 5.

[10]App 8-6 at 5.

[11]App 8-6 at 5-7.

[12]App 8-6 at 6.

[13]App 8-6 at 7.

[14]App 8-6 at 7.

[15]App 8-6 at 7.

[16]App 8-6 at 7.

hold pending completion of removal proceedings.[17] If the NTA Review Panel declines to issue an NTA, the naturalization application may be adjudicated (presumably favorably).[18]

A similar procedure occurs where USCIS determines that the individual was inadmissible at the time that they obtained lawful permanent resident status, except that such an individual is not eligible to have their naturalization application approved.[19]

§ 8:29 Lawful permanent residents who become deportable— Deportability-based removal proceedings bar naturalization— Origin and scope of provision

Research References

A.L.R. Index, Immigration and Naturalization

Commencement of Deportation Proceedings Under Antiterrorism and Effective Death Penalty Act (Aedpa) and Illegal Immigration Reform and Immigrant Responsibility Act (IIRIRA), 185 A.L.R. Fed. 221

Once deportation (removal) proceedings have commenced, the DHS is barred from considering an application for naturalization.[1] The logic of this provision derives from a desire of Congress to prevent a race to a final decision between the deportability and naturalization adjudicators.[2] Prior to the enactment of this provision, the practice was for both the deportation and naturalization processes to proceed along until either the court naturalized the petitioner or the service succeeded in deporting him or her, whichever happened first.[3] The intention of Congress in enacting this provision was to resolve the race by creating a "priority" provision.[4] The Attorney General was given the power to choose either to allow the naturalization to proceed or to commence deportation proceedings and stay naturalization. In other words, Congress gave the Attorney General the power to institute or to withhold the institution of deportation proceedings, in order to allow a deportable noncitizen to proceed with naturalization.[5]

This bar, however, does not apply to noncitizens who naturalize under the provisions for military naturalization.[6] They are allowed to naturalize even though

---

[17]App 8-6 at 7.

[18]App 8-6 at 7.

[19]App 8-6 at 8.

[Section 8:29]

[1]INA § 318, 8 U.S.C.A. § 1429; INS Interp. 318.2(c)(1)(iii).

[2]Shomberg v. U.S., 348 U.S. 540, 544, 75 S.Ct. 509, 511, 99 L.Ed. 624 (1955); Application of Martini, 184 F.Supp. 395, 399 (S.D.N.Y. 1960).

[3]Shomberg v. U.S., 348 U.S. 540, 543, 75 S. Ct. 509, 511, 99 L. Ed. 624 (1955).

[4]Application of Shomberg, 115 F.Supp. 336, 337 (S.D.N.Y. 1953) aff'd sub nom Shomberg v. U.S. 210 F.2d 82, cert. granted 75 S.Ct. 24, 348 U.S. 811, 99 L.Ed. 639, aff'd 75 S.Ct. 509, 348 U.S. 540, 99 L.Ed. 624.

[5]Application of Shomberg, 115 F.Supp. 336, 338 (S.D.N.Y. 1953) aff'd sub nom Shomberg v. U.S. 210 F.2d 82, cert. granted 75 S.Ct. 24, 348 U.S. 811, 99 L.Ed. 639, aff'd 75 S.Ct. 509, 348 U.S. 540, 99 L.Ed. 624.

[6]INA §§ 318, 324(c), 328, 329, 329, 8 U.S.C.A. §§ 1429, 1435(c), 1439, 1440.

deportation or removal proceedings are pending against them.[7] This same exemption appears to apply to former U.S. citizen women who lost their citizenship by marriage to a noncitizen, as their naturalization is allowed "notwithstanding any of the other provisions" of the Immigration Act.[8] Similarly, some courts have found that it does not bar district court review of naturalization denials.[9]

The IIRAIRA, in a conforming amendment, amended the bar relating to deportation proceedings, by replacing the terms "deportation proceedings" with "removal proceedings."[10] It is not clear whether Congress meant to expand the bar to include also removal proceedings based on inadmissibility. Such an expansive reading, however, is unlikely, since Congress retained intact the related bar prohibiting the naturalization of permanent residents who had outstanding final findings of deportation against them.[11]

§ 8:30 Lawful permanent residents who become deportable— Deportability-based removal proceedings bar naturalization— District courts may have power to review naturalization denials even after removal proceedings have commenced

Research References

A.L.R. Index, Immigration and Naturalization

Commencement of Deportation Proceedings Under Antiterrorism and Effective Death Penalty Act (Aedpa) and Illegal Immigration Reform and Immigrant Responsibility Act (IIRIRA), 185 A.L.R. Fed. 221

With the transfer of naturalization authority from the District Courts to the former INS in 1990, an ambiguity was created with regard to INA § 318, which provides that "no application for naturalization shall be considered by the Attorney General if there is pending against the applicant a removal proceeding."[1] That section used to refer specifically to the district courts, and was held to be a jurisdictional bar.[2] However, the statute currently applies on its face only to USCIS. Thus, applicants have plausibly sought district court intervention notwithstanding ongoing removal proceedings.

The Second, Sixth, and Ninth Circuits have held that while § 318 does not constitute a jurisdictional bar to their exercise of jurisdiction, that it precludes any effective remedy.[3]

---

[7]INA §§ 318, 328, 329, 328, 329, 8 U.S.C.A. §§ 1429, 1439, 1440. Cf. §§ 12:3 to 12:12.

[8]INA § 324(c), 8 U.S.C.A. § 1435(c). Cf. §§ 11:11 to 11:17.

[9]See §§ 8:30 to 8:31.

[10]IIRAIRA § 308(e)(1)(O).

[11]IIRAIRA § 308.

[Section 8:30]

[1]8 U.S.C.A. § 1429.

[2]See Petition for Naturalization of Terzich, 256 F.2d 197 (3d Cir.1958).

[3]Zayed v. U.S., 368 F.3d 902 (6th Cir. 2004); Bellajaro v. Schiltgen, 378 F.3d 1042, 1045 (9th Cir. 2004); Ajlani v. Chertoff, 545 F.3d 229 (2nd Cir. 2008). Several district courts have held similarly. Tellez v. U.S. I.N.S., 91 F. Supp. 2d 1356 (C.D. Cal. 2000); Mosleh v. Strapp, 992 F. Supp. 874 (N.D. Tex. 1998); Apokarina v. Ashcroft, 232 F. Supp. 2d 414 (E.D. Pa. 2002); Robertson-Dewar v. Mukasey, 599 F.Supp.2d 772 (W.D.Tex. 2009).

The Fourth Circuit, and possibly the Fifth Circuit, holds that federal courts lack jurisdiction over naturalization matters once removal proceedings have begun.[4]

The Third Circuit goes further. It finds not only that the District Courts have jurisdiction to consider naturalization applications notwithstanding ongoing removal proceedings, but that they may grant effective relief in the form of Declaratory Judgment.[5] The Third Circuit reasons that while the federal courts cannot order naturalization while removal proceedings are ongoing, that declaratory relief "strikes a balance between the petitioner's right to full judicial review . . . and the priority of removal proceedings enshrined in § 1429."[6] To find the courts closed to review in such cases would permit DHS to eliminate federal court review simply by instituting removal proceedings, but Congress intended that the agency not be the final word on naturalization eligibility.[7] Declaratory relief, considering the lawfulness of the denial of naturalization, held the Third Circuit, "permits the alien a day in court, . . . while not upsetting the priority of removal over naturalization established in § 1429 because it affects the record for—but not the priority of— removal proceedings, thereby preserving both congressionally mandated goals, a de novo review process and the elimination of the race to the courthouse."[8] The Third Circuit noted the potential effects of a declaratory judgment on potential termination of removal proceedings, but did not base its decision upon that fact.[9] The Seventh Circuit recently expressed agreement with the Third Circuit, at least where naturalization has been denied by USCIS on the merits.[10]

At least one district court has held that de novo review over the naturalization application is available even in cases where the naturalization was filed after the institution of removal proceedings.[11] At this point, the issue appears an open one, and if the circuits do not reach consensus, may be ultimately resolved by the Supreme Court.

§ 8:31 Lawful permanent residents who become deportable— Deportability-based removal proceedings bar naturalization— Administrative termination of removal proceedings to allow applicant to naturalize

Research References

A.L.R. Index, Immigration and Naturalization
Commencement of Deportation Proceedings Under Antiterrorism and Effective Death Penalty Act (Aedpa) and Illegal Immigration Reform and Immigrant Responsibility Act (IIRIRA), 185 A.L.R. Fed. 221

---

[4]Barnes v. Holder, 625 F.3d 801, 806-07 (4th Cir. 2010); see also, Saba-Bakare v. Chertoff, 507 F.3d 337, 340 (5th Cir. 2007) (finding no district court jurisdiction to review naturalization denial which had been reopened by USCIS and had no continuing effect).

[5]Gonzalez v. Secretary of Dept. of Homeland Sec., 678 F.3d 254 (3d Cir. 2012).

[6]Gonzalez v. Secretary of Dept. of Homeland Sec., 678 F.3d 254 (3d Cir. 2012).

[7]Gonzalez v. Secretary of Dept. of Homeland Sec., 678 F.3d 254 (3d Cir. 2012).

[8]Gonzalez v. Secretary of Dept. of Homeland Sec., 678 F.3d 254 (3d Cir. 2012).

[9]Gonzalez v. Secretary of Dept. of Homeland Sec., 678 F.3d 254 (3d Cir. 2012).

[10]Klene v. Napolitano, 697 F.3d 666 (7th Cir. 2012). A number of district courts have agreed. See, e.g., Ngwana v. Attorney General of U.S., 40 F. Supp. 2d 319 (D. Md. 1999); Saad v. Barrows, 2004 WL 1359165 (N.D. Tex. 2004); Grewal v. Ashcroft, 301 F. Supp. 2d 692 (N.D. Ohio 2004); Kestelboym v. Chertoff, 538 F. Supp. 2d 813 (D.N.J. 2008).

[11]Gatcliffe v. Reno, 23 F. Supp. 2d 581 (D.V.I. 1998).

To obtain administrative naturalization, removal proceedings must be terminated to allow the application to be considered by the DHS. Congress has placed the responsibility of deciding whether to allow naturalization or to proceed with deportation proceedings on the Attorney General.[1] The Attorney General has divided this responsibility between the DHS and the EOIR.

Removal proceedings are commenced by the filing of the Notice to Appear (NTA) with the Immigration Court.[2] The regulations delegate the issuance of NTAs to specific officers within ICE.[3] Assistant district directors for examinations usually sign NTAs against naturalization applicants.[4] The DHS, not the EOIR, has prosecutorial discretion whether to initiate removal proceedings.[5]

After an NTA has been issued and before it is filed with the court, ICE has exclusive jurisdiction to cancel the notice.[6] Any officer authorized to issue an NTA has the authority to cancel the notice.[7] Once ICE has filed a Notice to Appear with the court, ICE may move to dismiss proceedings on the same basis that would justify cancellation of the NTA.[8] The immigration judge, however, is not required to terminate proceedings even when ICE wishes to cancel the NTA.[9] After the filing of the NTA, discretion moves from ICE to the Immigration Court.[10] The immigration judge is thereafter required to make an independent evaluation of the factors that led ICE to move to dismiss.[11]

Even when ICE does not move to dismiss, the regulations specifically grant the immigration judge independent authority to terminate removal proceedings to allow an applicant to proceed to a final hearing on a naturalization application.[12] However, to obtain termination on this basis, the respondent must establish *prima facie* eligibility for naturalization and that the matter involves exceptionally appealing or humanitarian factors.[13]

The BIA has held that it has no authority to determine "prima facie" eligibility for naturalization.[14] Instead, the Board requires an "affirmative communication" from USCIS or ICE that the respondent is "prima facie eligible."[15] Although the Board recognizes that this gives a veto power to DHS, the Board says that it has no

---

[Section 8:31]

[1]Application of Shomberg, 115 F. Supp. 336, 337-38 (S.D. N.Y. 1953), order aff'd, 210 F.2d 82 (2d Cir. 1954), cert. granted, 348 U.S. 811, 75 S. Ct. 24, 99 L. Ed. 639 (1954) and judgment aff'd, 348 U.S. 540, 75 S. Ct. 509, 99 L. Ed. 624 (1955).

[2]8 CFR § 239.1(a).

[3]8 CFR § 239.1(a).

[4]Assistant District Directors for examinations are authorized to issue NTAs. 8 CFR § 239.1(a)(7).

[5]In re G-N-C, 22 I. & N. Dec. 281, 1998 WL 646918 (B.I.A. 1998).

[6]In re G-N-C, 22 I. & N. Dec. 281, 1998 WL 646918 (B.I.A. 1998).

[7]8 CFR § 239.2(a).

[8]8 CFR § 239.2(c).

[9]In re G-N-C, 22 I. & N. Dec. 281, 1998 WL 646918 (B.I.A. 1998).

[10]In re G-N-C, 22 I. & N. Dec. 281, 1998 WL 646918 (B.I.A. 1998).

[11]In re G-N-C, 22 I. & N. Dec. 281, 1998 WL 646918 (B.I.A. 1998).

[12]8 CFR § 239.2(f); INS Interp. 318.2(c)(ii).

[13]8 CFR § 239.2(f).

[14]Matter of Acosta Hidalgo, 24 I. & N. Dec. 103 (BIA 2007).

[15]Matter of Acosta Hidalgo, 24 I. & N. Dec. 103, 106, 107 (BIA 2007).

authority to order DHS to find prima facie eligibility, or even to make a decision as to prima facie eligibility.[16]

Under prior case law, a respondent could also obtain a finding of prima facie eligibility from a District Court.[17] However, that case law was based on the old regime where naturalization applicants sought citizenship in the District Court. Under the current scheme, both the BIA and the Ninth Circuit have held that the District Courts lack jurisdiction to issue such a finding, at least in the circumstances presented in those cases.[18] That said, the Ninth Circuit's decision was premised on the fact that the Naturalization had been denied because an NTA had been filed; where there had been a denial on the merits, or where the District Court acquired jurisdiction pursuant to § 1447(b), the scope of judicial review could be significantly broader.[19] Both the Third Circuit case of Gonzales and the Seventh Circuit case of Klene involved naturalization applications which had been denied on the merits.[20] In such cases, the ability of a court to review the agency decision may be thought more clear than in cases where the agency has made no decision at all.

To summarize, two circuits (the Fourth and Fifth) find themselves to have no jurisdiction to review naturalization denials for individuals in removal proceedings. Three circuits (the Second, Sixth, and Ninth) find jurisdiction, but hold that there is no remedy. Two circuits (the Third and Seventh) find, at least in some circumstances, both jurisdiction and a remedy.

§ 8:32 Lawful permanent residents who become deportable—Final finding of deportability bars naturalization

Persons against whom there are final findings of deportability, either in deportation or removal proceedings, may not be naturalized.[1] This bar requires that the order of deportation have been issued pursuant to a "warrant of arrest." The regulations interpret both a Notice to Appear and an Order to Show Cause as constituting a warrant of arrest.[2] At least one court has agreed with this interpretation.[3] This provision bars both administrative naturalization and judicial reviews of naturalization denials.[4]

---

[16]Matter of Acosta Hidalgo, 24 I. & N. Dec. 103, 107, 108 (BIA 2007).

[17]Matter of Cruz, 17 I. & N. Dec. 236 (BIA 1975).

[18]Matter of Acosta Hidalgo, 24 I. & N. Dec 103, 105 (BIA 2007); see also De Lara Bellajaro v. Schiltgen, 378 F.3d 1042, 1047 (9th Cir. 2004) (finding of prima facie eligibility would be "purely advisory," and thus barred); cf Gatcliffe v. Reno, 23 F. Supp. 2d 581, 582-83 (D.V.I. 1998) (finding prima facie eligibility).

[19]See, e.g., Ajay v. Gonzales, 2007 WL 1299325, *3 (D.Or. Apr 30, 2007) (unpublished) (distinguishing Gatcliffe v. Reno, 23 F.Supp.2d 581 (D.V.I.1998), Ibrahim v. Dept. of Homeland Sec., 2005 WL 2230152 (S.D. Tex 2005), and other cases, on grounds that "[i]n those cases, the agency's ultimate denial of the plaintiffs' naturalization applications were based on their merits rather than on the pendency of removal proceedings."); Farghaly v. Frazier, 404 F.Supp.2d 1125, 1127 (D.Minn.,2005) (same).

[20]Gonzalez v. Secretary of Dept. of Homeland Sec., 678 F.3d 254 (3d Cir. 2012); Klene v. Napolitano, 697 F.3d 666 (7th Cir. 2012).

[Section 8:32]

[1]INA § 318, 8 U.S.C.A. § 1429.

[2]8 C.F.R. § 318.1.

[3]In re Muniz, 151 F.Supp. 173 (W.D.Pa. 1956).

[4]Ngwana v. Attorney General, 40 F.Supp.2d 319 (D.Md. 1999).

It has also been held that a naturalization applicant is not allowed to collaterally attack the final order of deportability in judicial naturalization proceeding.[5]

The rule that bars the naturalization of noncitizens who have received final orders of deportation is not applicable to noncitizens who naturalize under the provisions for military naturalization.[6] The bar originally exempted regular military service naturalization but not naturalization based on service in time of war.[7] Before the bar was amended to include service in time of war, the courts gave a literal reading to this provision, not allowing naturalization applications based on service in time of war to proceed.[8] This resulted in an awkward procedure, forcing the applicant to attack the final order of deportation in another forum before the applicant could be naturalized.[9]

The bar to naturalization after a final finding of deportability should not apply to former U.S. citizen women who lost their citizenship by marriage to a noncitizen either.[10] These women are allowed to naturalize "notwithstanding any of the other provisions" of the INA.[11]

§ 8:33 Lawful permanent residents who become deportable—Removal proceedings bar naturalization denial as well as approval

As noted in the preceding chapters, the INA provides that "no application for naturalization shall be considered ... if there is pending against the applicant a removal proceeding."[1] By the plain text of the statute, USCIS is precluded from denying naturalization applications, as well as approving them. The Board of Immigration Appeals has found that it is "erroneous" and a "legal mistake" for USCIS to adjudicate and deny a naturalization application after removal proceedings have begun.[2]

While the Board has no power or jurisdiction to correct the USCIS's error,[3] it appears that the Board will treat the adjudication as being a nullity. In Matter of Acosta-Hidalgo, it proceeded to consider the application for termination to permit naturalization despite USCIS's denial of the N-400 application; termination for naturalization may only be considered where there is a "pending application or petition for naturalization."

The Fifth Circuit agreed with this analysis, finding that after removal proceedings began, "the USCIS has and had no statutory authority to consider [a]

---

[5]Petition of Terzich, 256 F.2d 197 (3d Cir., 1958); In re Muniz, 151 F.Supp. 173 (W.D.Pa. 1956); Petition of Kiseleff, 135 F.Supp. 314 (S.D.N.Y. 1955).

[6]INA §§ 318, 328, 329, 328, 329, 8 U.S.C.A. §§ 1429, 1439, 1440.

[7]For a discussion of the several military based naturalization provisions, see §§ 12:1 to 12:12.

[8]Duenas v. U.S., 330 F.2d 726 (9th Cir. 1964); Petition of Santos, 169 F. Supp. 115 (S.D. N.Y. 1958); Petition of Santos, 169 F. Supp. 115 (S.D. N.Y. 1958).

[9]Duenas v. U. S., 330 F.2d 726, 727–28 (9th Cir. 1964).

[10]INA § 324(c), 8 U.S.C.A. § 1435(c).

[11]INA § 324(c), 8 U.S.C.A. § 1435(c).

[Section 8:33]

[1]INA § 318 [8 U.S.C.A. § 1429].

[2]Matter of Acosta Hidalgo, 24 I. & N. Dec. 103, 107, n9 (BIA 2007).

[3]8 C.F.R. § 1239.2(f).

naturalization application."[4] It therefore found the USCIS naturalization denial to "ha[ve] no continuing legal effect."[5]

It is unclear what significance, if any, these declarations would have for individuals whose naturalization applications were denied during the pendency of removal proceedings. An individual placed into removal proceedings after applying for naturalization, who thereafter prevails in the removal proceeding, would have strong arguments to USCIS that it had a duty to reopen any naturalization denial.

At least one District Court has vacated an erroneous USCIS denial of a naturalization application.[6]

IV. CHALLENGING ALIENAGE IN REMOVAL PROCEEDINGS

§ 8:34   Challenging alienage in removal proceedings—General principles

In removal proceedings, the government bears the burden of proving alienage by clear and convincing evidence.[1] Indeed, the immigration courts have no jurisdiction over United States citizens, so the citizenship question is a jurisdictional one.[2] By contrast, when seeking a certificate of citizenship or a passport, the individual claiming citizenship bears the burden of proving their U.S. citizenship.[3]

The fact that an individual's files do not contain a certificate of citizenship, passport, or other prior official acknowledgement of citizenship does not necessarily preclude them from raising a claim in removal proceedings. As described above, individuals may acquire or derive citizenship automatically; it follows that their files may not have any application form or acknowledgement of their citizenship status.[4]

An individual claiming citizenship may decide to file an N-600 with USCIS while proceedings are ongoing.[5] If the N-600 application is approved, that would presumably resolve the case and require termination of the removal proceedings. If not, the case may proceed to trial before the Immigration Judge. While the Immigration Judge lacks the power to declare someone a citizen or to order production of a certificate of citizenship, the Immigration Judge does have the authority to terminate the proceedings on grounds that alienage has not been shown.[6]

---

[4]Saba-Bakare v. Chertoff, 507 F.3d 337, 340 (5th Cir. 2007).

[5]Saba-Bakare, 507 F.3d at 340.

[6]Robertson-Dewar v. Mukasey, 599 F.Supp.2d 772, 782-84 (W.D. Tex. 2009).

[Section 8:34]

[1]Woodby v. Immigration and Naturalization Service, 385 U.S. 276, 286, 87 S. Ct. 483, 17 L. Ed. 2d 362 (1966).

[2]See INA § 237, 8 U.S.C.A. § 1227; In re Fuentes-Martinez, 21 I. & N. Dec. 893, 898, 1997 WL 219496 (B.I.A. 1997); U.S. ex rel. Bilokumsky v. Tod, 263 U.S. 149, 153 (1923) (Brandeis, J.) ("alienage is a jurisdictional fact"); United States v. Sing Tuck, 194 U.S. 161, 167 (1904) (Holmes, J.).

[3]Patel v. Rice, 403 F. Supp. 2d 560, 562 (N.D. Tex. 2005), aff'd, 224 Fed. Appx. 414 (5th Cir. 2007); Reyes v. Neelly, 264 F.2d 673, 674–75 (5th Cir. 1959).

[4]See supra at §§ 4:1 et seq., 5:1 et seq.

[5]See, e.g., In re Rodriguez-Tejedor, 23 I. & N. Dec. 153, 154, 2001 WL 865412 (B.I.A. 2001).

[6]See, e.g., In re Fuentes-Martinez, 21 I. & N. Dec. 893, 898, 1997 WL 219496 (B.I.A. 1997).

A claim to already be in fact and law a U.S. citizen must be distinguished from a claim that one ought to be able to naturalize. The possibility of terminating proceedings to facilitate naturalization is discussed elsewhere in the chapter.[7]

§ 8:35 Challenging alienage in removal proceedings—Claims of birth in the United States

The simplest claim to U.S. citizenship is a claim that the individual was in fact born within the United States. The 14th Amendment and the INA automatically grant citizenship to anyone born within this country, with limited exceptions for children of foreign government officials.[1]

Where an individual claims birth in the United States, the government must show that this claim is false in order to prevail in the case.[2] The government bears the burden of proof by clear, convincing, and unequivocal evidence.[3] A contemporaneous birth certificate is not a per se requirement for citizenship, and many states issue delayed birth certificates, which are particularly common in births involving midwifes or not occurring in hospitals.[4] But some delayed birth certificates have been falsely issued, and may be disbelieved.[5]

One interesting circumstance is where an individual is issued multiple, inconsistent birth certificates. The Ninth Circuit upheld a removal order against a man with two birth certificates, after a judicial trial found by clear and convincing evidence that he was not born in the United States.[6]

§ 8:36 Challenging alienage in removal proceedings—Foreign birth and shifting burdens of proof

The more common scenario in a contested removal case is where an individual was born abroad, but claims to have automatically acquired or derived citizenship.[1] In that circumstance, the Board has found that foreign birth triggers a presumption of alienage.[2] Unless the individual can produce some evidence to support their

---

[7]See supra at § 8:31.

[Section 8:35]

[1]See U.S. Const. Amend. XIV, § 1; INA § 301(a), 8 U.S.C.A. § 1401(a); cf. supra at §§ 2:24 to 2:27.

[2]See Mondaca-Vega v. Holder, 718 F.3d 1075 (9th Cir. 2013); Murphy v. I.N.S., 54 F.3d 605, 609–10 (9th Cir. 1995).

[3]Woodby v. Immigration and Naturalization Service, 385 U.S. 276, 286, 87 S. Ct. 483, 17 L. Ed. 2d 362 (1966).

[4]See e.g., infra at § 13:10 (lawsuit relating to suspected fraud by midwives).

[5]See U.S. v. Lopez, 704 F.2d 1382 (5th Cir. 1983) (conviction of midwife for fraudulent delayed birth certificates); Patel v. Rice, 403 F. Supp. 2d 560, 562 (N.D. Tex. 2005), aff'd, 224 Fed. Appx. 414 (5th Cir. 2007) (discrediting evidence which supported delayed birth certificate).

[6]Mondaca-Vega v. Holder, 718 F.3d 1075 (9th Cir. 2013).

[Section 8:36]

[1]The principles for acquisition of citizenship at birth or derivation after birth are discussed above at chapters 4 and 5.

[2]See Matter of Tijerina-Villarreal, 13 I. & N. Dec. 327, 330, 1969 WL 16974 (B.I.A. 1969) (discussing burden to overcome "presumption" of alienage); Matter of Baires-Larios, 24 I. & N. Dec. 467, 468, 2008 WL 643136 (B.I.A. 2008). The First Circuit appears to defer to this approach. Leal Santos v. Mukasey, 516 F.3d 1, 4 (1st Cir. 2008).

citizenship claim, the evidence of their foreign birth will be sufficient to meet the government's burden to show alienage by clear and convincing evidence.[3]

The Board's case law seems to require that the individual produce evidence showing that it is more likely than not (i.e., a "preponderance of credible evidence") that they are citizens, before the presumption triggered by foreign birth is rebutted.[4] But the Board's case law on this point is from the early 1970s, before Congress adopted a different treatment of presumptions in the Federal Rules of Evidence (FRE). In adopting FRE 301, Congress rejected the Wigmore theory of presumptions in favor of Professor Thayer's "bursting bubble" theory, under which a presumption disappears from the equation once "more than a scintilla" of evidence has been presented on a point.[5] The Board's case law does not address FRE 301, or the Congressional policy underlying it. Case law in the Courts of Appeals has not substantially addressed this issue; though Ninth Circuit case law suggests that the Ninth Circuit might not require a preponderance of evidence to rebut the presumption of alienage; but the question has not been clearly resolved.[6]

§ 8:37 Challenging alienage in removal proceedings—Burden of production issues

Factual proof issues are often central to claims of acquired or derived citizenship. Yet it is not infrequent for an individual claiming citizenship in removal proceedings to be detained (even mandatorily detained) by DHS during the removal proceeding.[1] This has triggered questions regarding the burden of producing evidence, which are separate and distinct from burden of proof issues.

The Ninth Circuit has held that DHS must provide, upon request, the entire Alien file of an individual to the noncitizen.[2] The A file would commonly include evidence about how an individual immigrated to the United States, and would thus commonly include evidence of parental citizenship and marriage, evidence of legitimation, evidence of custody, and evidence regarding monetary support.[3] Such evidence would be commonly relevant potential citizenship claims.

---

[3]Matter of Tijerina-Villarreal, 13 I. & N. Dec. 327, 1969 WL 16974 (B.I.A. 1969).

[4]Matter of Tijerina-Villarreal, 13 I. & N. Dec. 327, 330, 1969 WL 16974 (B.I.A. 1969).

[5]See generally, Texas Dept. of Community Affairs v. Burdine, 450 U.S. 248, 255 n.8, 101 S. Ct. 1089, 67 L. Ed. 2d 207, 25 Fair Empl. Prac. Cas. (BNA) 113, 25 Empl. Prac. Dec. (CCH) P 31544, 9 Fed. R. Evid. Serv. 1 (1981); 10 Moore's Federal Practice, § 304.04[2] at III-9 (citing Thayer, A preliminary Treatise on Evidence at Common law, at § 352 (1898); see also, Charles Roth, "Burdens of Proof Issues in Removal Proceedings," in 2005 Immigration & Nationality Handbook 906–07 (2005); cf. Matter of Vivas, 16 I. & N. Dec. 68, 70, 1977 WL 39219 (B.I.A. 1977) (discussing shift of burden of production in deportation hearings).

[6]See Ayala-Villanueva v. Holder, 572 F.3d 736, 737 n.3 (9th Cir. 2009); Murphy v. I.N.S., 54 F.3d 605, 609–10 (9th Cir. 1995).

[Section 8:37]

[1]See, e.g., INA 236(c), 8 U.S.C.A. § 1226(c).

[2]Dent v. Holder, 627 F.3d 365 (9th Cir. 2010).

[3]Such evidence is often required by INA § 101(b), 8 U.S.C.A. § 1101(b), INA § 216, 8 U.S.C.A. § 1186, and other statutes.

APPENDIX 8-1

INA's Current Aggravated Felony Definition, Definition of Conviction, and Grounds of Removability

INA § 101(a)(43), (48)

(43) The term "aggravated felony" means—

(A) murder, rape, or sexual abuse of a minor;

(B) illicit trafficking in a controlled substance (as defined in section 802 of Title 21), including a drug trafficking crime (as defined in section 924(c) of Title 18);

(C) illicit trafficking in firearms or destructive devices (as defined in section 921 of Title 18) or in explosive materials (as defined in section 841(c) of that title);

(D) an offense described in section 1956 of Title 18 (relating to laundering of monetary instruments) or section 1957 of that title (relating to engaging in monetary transactions in property derived from specific unlawful activity) if the amount of the funds exceeded $10,000;

(E) an offense described in—

(i) section 842(h) or (i) of Title 18, or section 844(d), (e), (f), (g), (h), or (i) of that title (relating to explosive materials offenses);

(ii) section 922(g)(1), (2), (3), (4), or (5), (j), (n), (o), (p), or (r) or 924(b) or (h) of Title 18 (relating to firearms offenses); or

(iii) section 5861 of Title 26 (relating to firearms offenses);

(F) a crime of violence (as defined in section 16 of Title 18, but not including a purely political offense) for which the term of imprisonment at least one year;

(G) a theft offense (including receipt of stolen property) or burglary offense for which the term of imprisonment at least one year;

(H) an offense described in section 875, 876, 877, or 1202 of Title 18 (relating to the demand for or receipt of ransom);

(I) an offense described in section 2251, 2251A, or 2252 of Title 18 (relating to child pornography);

(J) an offense described in section 1962 of Title 18 (relating to racketeer influenced corrupt organizations), or an offense described in section 1084 (if it is a second or subsequent offense) or 1955 of that title (relating to gambling offenses), for which a sentence of one year imprisonment or more may be imposed;

(K) an offense that—

(i) relates to the owning, controlling, managing, or supervising of a prostitution business;

(ii) is described in section 2421, 2422, or 2423 of Title 18 (relating to transportation for the purpose of prostitution) if committed for commercial advantage; or

(iii) is described in any of sections 1581-1585 or 1588-1591 of Title 18 (relating to peonage, slavery, involuntary servitude, and trafficking in persons);

(L) an offense described in—

(i) section 793 (relating to gathering or transmitting national defense information), 798 (relating to disclosure of classified information), 2153 (relating to sabotage) or 2381 or 2382 (relating to treason) of Title 18;

(ii) section 421 of Title 50 (relating to protecting the identity of undercover intelligence agents); or

(iii) section 421 of Title 50 (relating to protecting the identity of undercover agents);

(M) an offense that—

(i) involves fraud or deceit in which the loss to the victim or victims exceeds $10,000; or

(ii) is described in section 7201 of Title 26 (relating to tax evasion) in which the revenue loss to the Government exceeds $10,000;

(N) an offense described in paragraph (1)(A) or (2) of section 1324(a) of this title (relating to alien smuggling), except in the case of a first offense for which the alien has affirmatively shown that the alien committed the offense for the purpose of assisting, abetting, or aiding only the alien's spouse, child, or parent (and no other individual) to violate a provision of this chapter

(O) an offense described in section 1325(a) or 1326 of this title committed by an alien who was previously deported on the basis of a conviction for an offense described in another subparagraph of this paragraph;

(P) an offense (i) which either is falsely making, forging, counterfeiting, mutilating, or altering a passport or instrument in violation of section 1543 of Title 18 or is described in section 1546(a) of such title (relating to document fraud) and (ii) for which the term of imprisonment is at least 12 months, except in the case of a first offense for which the alien has affirmatively shown that the alien committed the offense for the purpose of assisting, abetting, or aiding only the alien's spouse, child, or parent (and no other individual) to violate a provision of this chapter;

(Q) an offense relating to a failure to appear by a defendant for service of sentence if the underlying offense is punishable by imprisonment for a term of 5 years or more;

(R) an offense relating to commercial bribery, counterfeiting, forgery, or trafficking in vehicles the identification numbers of which have been altered for which the term of imprisonment is at least one year;

(S) an offense relating to obstruction of justice, perjury or subornation of perjury, or bribery of a witness, for which the term of imprisonment is at least one year;

(T) an offense relating to a failure to appear before a court pursuant to a court order to answer to or dispose of a charge of a felony for which a sentence of 2 years' imprisonment or more may be imposed; and

(U) an attempt or conspiracy to commit an offense described in this paragraph.

The term applies to an offense described in this paragraph whether in violation of Federal or State law and applies to such an offense in violation of the law of a foreign country for which the term of imprisonment was completed within the previous 15 years. Notwithstanding any other provision of law (including any effective date), the term applies regardless of whether the conviction was entered before, on, or after September 30, 1996.

* * *

(48)(A) The term "conviction" means, with respect to an alien, a formal judgment of guilt of the alien entered by a court or, if adjudication of guilt has been withheld, where—

(i) a judge or jury has found the alien guilty or the alien has entered a plea of guilty or nolo contendere or has admitted sufficient facts to warrant a finding of guilt, and

(ii) the judge has ordered some form of punishment, penalty, or restraint on the alien's liberty to be imposed.

(B) Any reference to a term of imprisonment or a sentence with respect to an offense is deemed to include the period of incarceration or confinement ordered by a court of law regardless of any suspension of the imposition or execution of that imprisonment or sentence in whole or in part.

INA § 237(a)(1), (a)(2), (a)(3), and (a)(5)

(a) Classes of deportable aliens

Any alien (including an alien crewman) in and admitted to the United States shall, upon the order of the Attorney General, be removed if the alien is within one or more of the following classes of deportable aliens:

(1) Inadmissible at time of entry or of adjustment of status or violates status

(A) Inadmissible aliens

Any alien who at the time of entry or adjustment of status was within one or more of the classes of aliens inadmissible by the law existing at such time is deportable.

(B) Present in violation of law

Any alien who is present in the United States in violation of this chapter or any other law of the United States, or whose nonimmigrant visa (or other documentation authorizing admission into the United States as a nonimmigrant) has been revoked under section 1201(i) of this title, is deportable.

(C) Violated nonimmigrant status or condition of entry

(i) Nonimmigrant status violators

Any alien who was admitted as a nonimmigrant and who has failed to maintain the nonimmigrant status in which the alien was admitted or to which it was changed under section 1258 of this title, or to comply with the conditions of any such status, is deportable.

(ii) Violators of conditions of entry

Any alien whom the Secretary of Health and Human Services certifies has failed to comply with terms, conditions, and controls that were imposed under section 1182(g) of this title is deportable.

(D) Termination of conditional permanent residence

(i) In general

Any alien with permanent resident status on a conditional basis under section 1186a of this title (relating to conditional permanent resident status for certain alien spouses and sons and daughters) or under section 1186b of this title (relating to conditional permanent resident status for certain alien entrepreneurs, spouses, and children) who has had such status terminated under such respective section is deportable.

(ii) Exception

Clause (i) shall not apply in the cases described in section 1186a(c)(4) of this title (relating to certain hardship waivers).

(E) Smuggling

(i) In general

Any alien who (prior to the date of entry, at the time of any entry, or within 5 years of the date of any entry) knowingly has encouraged, induced, assisted, abetted, or aided any other alien to enter or to try to enter the United States in violation of law is deportable.

(ii) Special rule in the case of family reunification

Clause (i) shall not apply in the case of alien who is an eligible immigrant (as defined in section 301(b)(1) of the Immigration Act of 1990), was physically present in the United States on May 5, 1988, and is seeking admission as an immediate relative or under section 1153(a)(2) of this title (including under section 112 of the Immigration Act of 1990) or benefits under section 301(a) of the Immigration Act of 1990 if the alien, before May 5, 1988, has encouraged, induced, assisted, abetted, or aided only the alien's spouse, parent, son, or daughter (and no other individual) to enter the United States in violation of law.

(iii) Waiver authorized

The Attorney General may, in his discretion for humanitarian purposes, to assure family unity, or when it is otherwise in the public interest, waive application of clause (i) in the case of any alien lawfully admitted for permanent residence if the alien has encouraged, induced, assisted, abetted, or aided only an individual who at the time of the offense was the alien's spouse, parent, son, or daughter (and no other individual) to enter the United States in violation of law.

(F) Repealed. Pub.L. 104-208, Div. C, Title VI, § 671(d)(1)(C), Sept. 30, 1996, 110 Stat. 3009-723

(G) Marriage fraud

An alien shall be considered to be deportable as having procured a visa or other documentation by fraud (within the meaning of section 1182(a)(6)(C)(i) of this title) and to be in the United States in violation of this chapter (within the meaning of subparagraph (B) if—

(i) the alien obtains any admission into the United States with an immigrant visa or other documentation procured on the basis of a marriage entered into less than 2 years prior to such admission of the alien and which, within 2 years subsequent to any admission of the alien in the United States, shall be judicially annulled or terminated, unless the alien establishes to the satisfaction of the Attorney General that such marriage was not contracted for the purpose of evading any provisions of the immigration laws, or

(ii) it appears to the satisfaction of the Attorney General that the alien has failed or refused to fulfill the alien's marital agreement which in the opinion of the Attorney General was made for the purpose of procuring the alien's admission as an immigrant.

(H) Waiver authorized for certain misrepresentations

The provisions of this paragraph relating to the removal of aliens within the United States on the ground that they were inadmissible at the time of admission as aliens, described in section 1182(a)(6)(C)(i) of this title, whether willful or innocent, may, in the discretion of the Attorney General, be waived for any alien (other than an alien described in paragraph (4)(D) who—

(i)(I) is the spouse, parent, son, or daughter of a citizen of the United States or of an alien lawfully admitted to the United States for permanent residence; and

(II) was in possession of an immigrant visa or equivalent document and was otherwise admissible to the United States at the time of such admission except for those grounds of inadmissibility specified under paragraphs (5)(A) and (7)(A) of section 1182(a) of this title which were a direct result of that fraud or misrepresentation.

(ii) is an alien who qualifies for classification under clause (iii) or (iv) of section 1154(a)(1)(A) of this title or clause (ii) or (iii) of section 1154(a)(1)(B) of this title.

A waiver of removal for fraud or misrepresentation granted under this subparagraph shall also operate to waive removal based on the grounds of inadmissibility directly resulting from such fraud or misrepresentation.

(2) Criminal offenses

(A) General crimes

(i) Crimes of moral turpitude

Any alien who—

(I) is convicted of a crime involving moral turpitude committed within five years (or 10 years in the case of an alien provided lawful permanent resident status under section 1255(j) of this title) after the date of admission, and

(II) is convicted of a crime for which a sentence of one year or longer may be imposed,

is deportable.

(ii) Multiple criminal convictions

Any alien who at any time after admission is convicted of two or more crimes involving moral turpitude, not arising out of a single scheme of criminal misconduct, regardless of whether confined therefor and regardless of whether the convictions were in a single trial, is deportable.

(iii) Aggravated felony

Any alien who is convicted of an aggravated felony at any time after admission is deportable.

(iv) High speed flight

Any alien who is convicted of a violation of section 758 of Title 18, (relating to high speed flight from an immigration checkpoint) is deportable.

(v) Failure to register as a sex offender

Any alien who is convicted under section 2250 of Title 18 is deportable.

(vi) Waiver authorized

Clauses (i), (ii), (iii), and (iv) shall not apply in the case of an alien with respect to a criminal conviction if the alien subsequent to the criminal conviction has been granted a full and unconditional pardon by the President of the United States or by the Governor of any of the several States.

(B) Controlled substances

(i) Conviction

Any alien who at any time after admission has been convicted of a violation of (or a conspiracy or attempt to violate) any law or regulation of a State, the United States, or a foreign country relating to a controlled substance (as defined in section 802 of Title 21), other than a single offense involving possession for one's own use of 30 grams or less of marijuana, is deportable.

(ii) Drug abusers and addicts

Any alien who is, or at any time after admission has been, a drug abuser or addict is deportable.

(C) Certain firearm offenses

Any alien who at any time after admission is convicted under any law of purchasing, selling, offering for sale, exchanging, using, owning, possessing, or carrying, or of attempting or conspiring to purchase, sell, offer for sale, exchange, use, own, possess, or carry, any weapon, part, or accessory which is a firearm or destructive device (as defined in section 921(a) of Title 18) in violation of any law is deportable.

(D) Miscellaneous crimes

Any alien who at any time has been convicted (the judgment on such conviction becoming final) of, or has been so convicted of a conspiracy or attempt to violate—

(i) any offense under chapter 37 (relating to espionage), chapter 105 (relating to sabotage), or chapter 115 (relating to treason and sedition) of Title 18, for which a term of imprisonment of five or more years may be imposed;

(ii) any offense under section 871 or 960 of Title 18;

(iii) a violation of any provision of the Military Selective Service Act (50 U.S.C.A. App. 451 et seq.) or the Trading With the Enemy Act (50 U.S.C.A. App. 1 et seq.); or

(iv) a violation of section 1185 or 1328 of this title,

is deportable.

(E) Crimes of domestic violence, stalking, or violation of protection order, crimes against children and

(i) Domestic violence, stalking, and child abuse

Any alien who at any time after admission is convicted of a crime of domestic violence, a crime of stalking, or a crime of child abuse, child neglect, or child abandonment is deportable. For purposes of this clause, the term "crime of domestic violence" means any crime of violence (as defined in section 16 of Title 18) against a person committed by a current or former spouse of the person, by an individual with whom the person shares a child in common, by an individual who is cohabiting with or has cohabited with the person as a spouse, by an individual similarly situated to a spouse of the person under the domestic or family violence laws of the jurisdiction where the offense occurs, or by any other individual against a person who is protected from that individual's acts under the domestic or family violence laws of the United States or any State, Indian tribal government, or unit of local government.

(ii) Violators of protection orders

Any alien who at any time after admission is enjoined under a protection order issued by a court and whom the court determines has engaged in conduct that violates the portion of a protection order that involves protection against credible threats of violence, repeated harassment, or bodily injury to the person or persons for whom the protection order was issued is deportable. For purposes of this clause, the term "protection order" means any injunction issued for the purpose of preventing violent or threatening acts of domestic violence, including temporary or final orders issued by civil or criminal courts (other than support or child custody orders or provisions) whether obtained by filing an independent action or as a pendente lite order in another proceeding.

(F) Trafficking

Any alien described in section 1182(a)(2)(H) of this title is deportable.

(3) Failure to register and falsification of documents

(A) Change of address

An alien who has failed to comply with the provisions of section 1305 of this title is deportable, unless the alien establishes to the satisfaction of the Attorney General that such failure was reasonably excusable or was not willful.

(B) Failure to register or falsification of documents

Any alien who at any time has been convicted—

(i) under section 1306(c) of this title or under section 36(c) of the Alien Registration Act, 1940,

(ii) of a violation of, or an attempt or a conspiracy to violate, any provision of the Foreign Agents Registration Act of 1938 (22 U.S.C.A. 611 et seq.), or

(iii) of a violation of, or an attempt or a conspiracy to violate, section 1546 of Title 18 (relating to fraud and misuse of visas, permits, and other admission documents), is deportable.

(C) Document fraud

(i) In general

An alien who is the subject of a final order for violation of section 1324c of this title is deportable.

(ii) Waiver authorized

The Attorney General may waive clause (i) in the case of an alien lawfully admitted for permanent residence if no previous civil money penalty was imposed against the alien under section 1324c of this title and the offense was incurred solely to assist, aid, or support the alien's spouse or child (and no other individual). No court shall have jurisdiction to review a decision of the Attorney General to grant or deny a waiver under this clause.

(D) Falsely claiming citizenship

(i) In general

Any alien who falsely represents, or has falsely represented, himself to be a citizen of the United States for any purpose or benefit under this chapter (including section 1324a of this title) or any Federal or State law is deportable.

(ii) Exception

In the case of an alien making a representation described in clause (i), if each natural parent of the alien (or, in the case of an adopted alien, each adoptive parent of the alien) is or was a citizen (whether by birth or naturalization), the alien permanently resided in the United States prior to attaining the age of 16, and the alien reasonably believed at the time of making such representation that he or she was a citizen, the alien shall not be considered to be deportable under any provision of this subsection based on such representation.

* * *

(5) Public charge

Any alien who, within five years after the date of entry, has become a public charge from causes not affirmatively shown to have arisen since entry is deportable.

(6) Unlawful voters

(A) In general

Any alien who has voted in violation of any Federal, State, or local constitutional provision, statute, ordinance, or regulation is deportable.

(B) Exception

In the case of an alien who voted in a Federal, State, or local election (including an initiative, recall, or referendum) in violation of a lawful restriction of voting to citizens, if each natural parent of the alien (or, in the case of an adopted alien, each adoptive parent of the alien) is or was a citizen (whether by birth or naturalization), the alien permanently resided in the United States prior to attaining the age of 16, and the alien reasonably believed at the time of such violation that he or she was a citizen, the alien shall not be considered to be deportable under any provision of this subsection based on such violation.

APPENDIX 8-2

Foreign Affairs Manual Description of Crimes of Moral Turpitude

The Foreign Affairs Manual (FAM) has a section describing its conclusions about which crimes are likely to involve moral turpitude. This guide should not be taken as final authority but only as reflecting what the State Department believes at this point in time. It must be noted that the State Department does not cite the sources for its conclusions. In addition, the reader should be careful in analyzing a statute as to the moral turpitude content of a specific provision since two very similar crimes may or may not involve moral turpitude depending on the elements of the crime in the statute. *Compare, e.g.*, Matter of Bart, 20 I. & N. Dec. 436 (B.I.A. 1992) (issuance of a bad check in violation of section 16-9-20(a) of the Georgia Code is a crime involving moral turpitude because Georgia case law clearly establishes that guilty knowledge, as evidenced by an intent to defraud, is an essential element of the offense); Matter of Balao, 20 I. & N. Dec. 440 (B.I.A. 1992) (intent to defraud is not an essential element of the crime of passing bad checks under title 18, section 4105(a)(1) of the Pennsylvania Consolidated Statutes and, therefore, a conviction under this law is not for a crime involving moral turpitude). This guide should, therefore, only be taken as a first step in attempting to elucidate whether a particular crime will be considered a crime of moral turpitude.

9 FAM 40.21(a) N2.3 Common Crimes Involving Moral Turpitude

Categorized below are some of the more common crimes, which are considered to involve moral turpitude. Each category is followed by a separate list of related crimes, which are held not to involve moral turpitude.

9 FAM 40.21(a) N2.3-1 Crimes Committed Against Property

a. Most crimes committed against property that involve moral turpitude include the element of fraud. The act of fraud involves moral turpitude whether it is aimed against individuals or government. Fraud generally involves: (1) Making false representation; (2) Knowledge of such false representation by the perpetrator; (3) Reliance on the false representation by the person defrauded; (4) An intent to defraud; and (5) The actual act of committing fraud.

b. Other crimes committed against property involving moral turpitude involve an inherently evil intent, such as the act of arson. The following list comprises crimes frequently committed against property, which may be held to involve moral turpitude for the purposes of visa issuance: (1) Arson; (2) Blackmail; (3) Burglary; (4) Embezzlement; (5) Extortion; (6) False pretenses; (7) Forgery; (8) Fraud; (9) Larceny (grand or petty); (10) Malicious destruction of property; (11) Receiving stolen goods (with guilty knowledge); (12) Robbery; (13) Theft (when it involves the intention of permanent taking); and (14) Transporting stolen property (with guilty knowledge).

c. Crimes against property which do not fall within the definition of moral turpitude include: (1) Damaging private property (where intent to damage not required); (2) Breaking and entering (requiring no specific or implicit intent to commit a crime involving moral turpitude); (3) Passing bad checks (where intent to defraud not required); (4) Possessing stolen property (if guilty knowledge is not essential); (5) Joy riding (where the intention to take permanently not required); and (6) Juvenile delinquency.

9 FAM 40.21(a) N2.3-2 Crimes Committed Against Governmental Authority

a. Crimes committed against governmental authority which fall within the definition of moral turpitude include: (1) Bribery; (2) Counterfeiting; (3) Fraud against revenue or other government functions; (4) Mail fraud; (5) Perjury; (6) Harboring a fugitive from justice (with guilty knowledge); and (7) Tax evasion (willful).

b. Crimes committed against governmental authority, which would not constitute moral turpitude for visa-issuance purposes, are, in general, violation of laws which are regulatory in character and which do not involve the element of fraud or other evil intent. The following list assumes that the statutes involved do not require the showing of an intent to defraud, or evil intent: (1) Black market violations; (2) Breach of the peace; (3) Carrying a concealed weapon; (4) Desertion from the Armed Forces; (5) Disorderly conduct; (6) Drunk or reckless driving; (7) Drunkenness; (8) Escape from prison; (9) Failure to report for military induction; (10) False statements (not amounting to perjury or involving fraud); (11) Firearms violations; (12) Gambling violations; (13) Immigration violations; (14) Liquor violations; (15) Loan sharking; (16) Lottery violations; (17) Possessing burglar tools (without intent to commit burglary); (18) Smuggling and customs violations (where intent to commit fraud is absent); (19) Tax evasion (without intent to defraud); and (20) Vagrancy.

9 FAM 40.21(a) N2.3-3 Crimes Committed Against Person, Family Relationship, and Sexual Morality

a. Crimes committed against the person, family relationship, and sexual morality, which constitute moral turpitude as it relates to visa issuance, include: (1) Abandonment of a minor child (if willful and resulting in the destitution of the child); (2) Adultery (see INA 101(f)(2) repealed by Public Law 97-116); (3) Assault (this crime is broken down into several categories, which involve moral turpitude): (a) Assault with intent to kill; (b) Assault with intent to commit rape; (c) Assault with intent to commit robbery; (d) Assault with intent to commit serious bodily harm; and (e) Assault with a dangerous or deadly weapon (some weapons may be found to be lethal as a matter of law, while others may or may not be found factually to be such, depending upon all the circumstances in the case. Such circumstances may include, but are not limited to, the size of the weapon, the manner of its use, and the nature and extent of injuries inflicted.); (4) Bigamy; (5) Contributing to the delinquency of a minor; (6) Gross indecency; (7) Incest (if the result of an improper sexual relationship); (8) Kidnapping; (9) Lewdness; (10) Manslaughter: (a) Voluntary, occurs when a person intentionally kills another person after "adequate provocation"; that is, there has been action that was sufficient to incite an "ordinary person" to "sudden and intense passion" such that s/he loses self-control. It should be noted that the time between provocation and the killing should not be long enough for the passion to have cooled off. In most states, "adequate provocation" is defined to be only situations in which there is a threat of deadly force, or in which a person finds his/her spouse in bed with another person. Verbal threats are usually not considered adequate provocation; and (b) Involuntary, where the statute requires proof of recklessness, which is defined as the awareness and conscious disregard of a substantial and unjustified risk which constitutes a gross deviation from the standard that a reasonable person would observe in the situation. A conviction for the statutory offense of vehicular homicide or other involuntary manslaughter that only requires a showing of negligence will not involve moral turpitude even if it appears the defendant in fact acted recklessly. (11) Mayhem; (12) Murder; (13) Pandering; (14) Possession of child pornography; (15) Prostitution; and (16) Rape (By statute, a person may be convicted of statutory rape even though the victim consents and provided she or he is under the statutory age at the time of the commission of the act. "Statutory rape" is also deemed to involve moral turpitude.)

b. Crimes committed against the person, family relationship, or sexual morality which do not involve moral turpitude include: (1) Assault (simple) (i.e., any assault, which does not require an evil intent or depraved motive, although it may involve the use of a weapon, which is neither dangerous nor deadly); (2) Illegitimacy (i.e., the offense of begetting an illegitimate child); (3) Creating or maintaining a nuisance (where knowledge that premises were used for prostitution is not necessary); (4) Incest (when a result of a marital status prohibited by law); (5) Involuntary manslaughter (when killing is not the result of recklessness); (6) Libel; (7) Mailing an obscene letter; (8) Mann Act violations (where coercion is not present); (9) Riot; and (10) Suicide (attempted).

9 FAM 40.21(a) N2.3-4 Intentional Distribution of Controlled Substances

The Board of Immigration Appeals has determined that a conviction for the intentional distribution of a controlled substance or a conviction for drug trafficking is now considered to a crime involving moral turpitude. A typical drug statute that would constitute a crime involving moral turpitude is "possession with intent to distribute." In order to be a crime involving moral turpitude, a conviction is required, as an ineligibility under INA 212(a)(2)(C)(1) based only on "reason to believe", and not a conviction is not a crime involving moral turpitude. The mere possession or use of a controlled substance is not a crime involving moral turpitude.

9 FAM 40.21(a) N2.4 Attempts, Aiding and Abetting, Accessories, and Conspiracy

a. The following types of crimes are held to be crimes involving moral turpitude: (1) An attempt to commit a crime deemed to involve moral turpitude; (2) Aiding and abetting in the commission of a crime deemed to involve moral turpitude; (3) Being an accessory (before or after the fact) in the commission of a crime deemed to involve moral turpitude; or (4) Taking part in a conspiracy (or attempting to take part in a conspiracy) to commit a crime involving moral turpitude.

b. Conversely, where an alien has been convicted of, or admits having committed the essential elements of, a criminal attempt, or a criminal act of aiding and abetting, accessory before or after the fact, or conspiracy, and the underlying crime is not deemed to involve moral turpitude, then INA 212(a)(2)(A)(i)(I) would not be applicable.

APPENDIX 8-3

Meissner Memorandum on Prosecutorial Discretion

U.S. Department of Justice
Immigration and Naturalization Service

HQOPP 50/4

Office of the Commissioner

425 I Street NW
Washington, DC 20536

NOV 17 2000

MEMORANDUM TO REGIONAL DIRECTORS
       DISTRICT DIRECTORS
       CHIEF PATROL AGENTS
       REGIONAL AND DISTRICT COUNSEL

FROM: Doris Meissner
     Commissioner
     Immigration and Naturalization Service

SUBJECT: Exercising Prosecutorial Discretion

    Since the 1996 amendments to the Immigration and Nationality Act (INA) which limited the authority of immigration judges to provide relief from removal in many cases, there has been increased attention to the scope and exercise of the Immigration and Naturalization Service's (INS or the Service) prosecutorial discretion. This memorandum describes the principles with which INS exercises prosecutorial discretion and the process to be followed in making and monitoring discretionary decisions. <u>Service officers are not only authorized by law but expected to exercise discretion in a judicious manner at all stages of the enforcement process–from planning investigations to enforcing final orders–subject to their chains of command and to the particular responsibilities and authority applicable to their specific position. In exercising this discretion, officers must take into account the principles described below in order to promote the efficient and effective enforcement of the immigration laws and the interests of justice.</u>

    More specific guidance geared to exercising discretion in particular program areas already exists in some instances,[1] and other program-specific guidance will follow separately.

---

[1] For example, standards and procedures for placing an alien in deferred action status are provided in the <u>Standard Operating Procedures for Enforcement Officers: Arrest, Detention, Processing, and Removal</u> (Standard Operating Procedures), Part X. This memorandum is intended to provide general principles, and does not replace any previous specific guidance provided about particular INS actions, such as "Supplemental Guidelines on the Use of Cooperating Individuals and Confidential Informants Following the Enactment of IIRIRA," dated December 29, 1997. This memorandum is not intended to address every situation in which the exercise of prosecutorial discretion may be appropriate. If INS personnel in the exercise of their duties recognize apparent conflict between any of their specific policy requirements and these general guidelines, they are encouraged to bring the matter to their supervisor's attention, and any conflict between policies should be raised through the appropriate chain of command for resolution.

Memorandum for Regional Directors, et al.   Page 2
Subject: Exercising Prosecutorial Discretion

However, INS officers should continue to exercise their prosecutorial discretion in appropriate cases during the period before more specific program guidance is issued.

A statement of principles concerning discretion serves a number of important purposes. As described in the "Principles of Federal Prosecution," [2] part of the U.S. Attorneys' manual, such principles provide convenient reference points for the process of making prosecutorial decisions; facilitate the task of training new officers in the discharge of their duties; contribute to more effective management of the Government's limited prosecutorial resources by promoting greater consistency among the prosecutorial activities of different offices and between their activities and the INS' law enforcement priorities; make possible better coordination of investigative and prosecutorial activity by enhancing the understanding between the investigative and prosecutorial components; and inform the public of the careful process by which prosecutorial decisions are made.

Legal and Policy Background

"Prosecutorial discretion" is the authority of an agency charged with enforcing a law to decide whether to enforce, or not to enforce, the law against someone. The INS, like other law enforcement agencies, has prosecutorial discretion and exercises it every day. In the immigration context, the term applies not only to the decision to issue, serve, or file a Notice to Appear (NTA), but also to a broad range of other discretionary enforcement decisions, including among others: Focusing investigative resources on particular offenses or conduct; deciding whom to stop, question, and arrest; maintaining an alien in custody; seeking expedited removal or other forms of removal by means other than a removal proceeding; settling or dismissing a proceeding; granting deferred action or staying a final order; agreeing to voluntary departure, withdrawal of an application for admission, or other action in lieu of removing the alien; pursuing an appeal; and executing a removal order.

The "favorable exercise of prosecutorial discretion" means a discretionary decision not to assert the full scope of the INS' enforcement authority as permitted under the law. Such decisions will take different forms, depending on the status of a particular matter, but include decisions such as not issuing an NTA (discussed in more detail below under "Initiating Proceedings"), not detaining an alien placed in proceedings (where discretion remains despite mandatory detention requirements), and approving deferred action.

---

[2] For this discussion, and much else in this memorandum, we have relied heavily upon the Principles of Federal Prosecution, chapter 9-27.000 in the U.S. Department of Justice's United States Attorneys' Manual (Oct. 1997). There are significant differences, of course, between the role of the U.S. Attorneys' offices in the criminal justice system, and INS responsibilities to enforce the immigration laws, but the general approach to prosecutorial discretion stated in this memorandum reflects that taken by the Principles of Federal Prosecution.

Courts recognize that prosecutorial discretion applies in the civil, administrative arena just as it does in criminal law. Moreover, the Supreme Court "has recognized on several occasions over many years that an agency's decision not to prosecute or enforce, whether through civil or criminal process, is a decision generally committed to an agency's absolute discretion." Heckler v. Chaney, 470 U.S. 821, 831 (1985). Both Congress and the Supreme Court have recently reaffirmed that the concept of prosecutorial discretion applies to INS enforcement activities, such as whether to place an individual in deportation proceedings. INA section 242(g); Reno v. American-Arab Anti-Discrimination Committee, 525 U.S. 471 (1999). The "discretion" in prosecutorial discretion means that prosecutorial decisions are not subject to judicial review or reversal, except in extremely narrow circumstances. Consequently, it is a powerful tool that must be used responsibly.

As a law enforcement agency, the INS generally has prosecutorial discretion within its area of law enforcement responsibility unless that discretion has been clearly limited by statute in a way that goes beyond standard terminology. For example, a statute directing that the INS "shall" remove removable aliens would not be construed by itself to limit prosecutorial discretion, but the specific limitation on releasing certain criminal aliens in section 236(c)(2) of the INA evidences a specific congressional intention to limit discretion not to detain certain criminal aliens in removal proceedings that would otherwise exist. Personnel who are unsure whether the INS has discretion to take a particular action should consult their supervisor and legal counsel to the extent necessary.

It is important to recognize not only what prosecutorial discretion is, but also what it is not. The doctrine of prosecutorial discretion applies to law enforcement decisions whether, and to what extent, to exercise the coercive power of the Government over liberty or property, as authorized by law in cases when individuals have violated the law. Prosecutorial discretion does not apply to affirmative acts of approval, or grants of benefits, under a statute or other applicable law that provides requirements for determining when the approval should be given. For example, the INS has prosecutorial discretion not to place a removable alien in proceedings, but it does not have prosecutorial discretion to approve a naturalization application by an alien who is ineligible for that benefit under the INA.

This distinction is not always an easy, bright-line rule to apply. In many cases, INS decisionmaking involves both a prosecutorial decision to take or not to take enforcement action, such as placing an alien in removal proceedings, and a decision whether or not the alien is substantively eligible for a benefit under the INA. In many cases, benefit decisions involve the exercise of significant discretion which in some cases is not judicially reviewable, but which is not prosecutorial discretion.

Prosecutorial discretion can extend only up to the substantive and jurisdictional limits of the law. It can never justify an action that is illegal under the substantive law pertaining to the conduct, or one that while legal in other contexts, is not within the authority of the agency or officer taking it. Prosecutorial discretion to take an enforcement action does not modify or waive any legal requirements that apply to the action itself. For example, an enforcement decision to focus on certain types of immigration violators for arrest and removal does not mean that the INS may arrest any person without probable cause to do so for an offense within its jurisdiction. Service officers who are in doubt whether a particular action complies with applicable constitutional, statutory, or case law requirements should consult with their supervisor and obtain advice from the district or sector counsel or representative of the Office of General Counsel to the extent necessary.

Finally, exercising prosecutorial discretion does not lessen the INS' commitment to enforce the immigration laws to the best of our ability. It is not an invitation to violate or ignore the law. Rather, it is a means to use the resources we have in a way that best accomplishes our mission of administering and enforcing the immigration laws of the United States.

Principles of Prosecutorial Discretion

Like all law enforcement agencies, the INS has finite resources, and it is not possible to investigate and prosecute all immigration violations. The INS historically has responded to this limitation by setting priorities in order to achieve a variety of goals. These goals include protecting public safety, promoting the integrity of the legal immigration system, and deterring violations of the immigration law.

It is an appropriate exercise of prosecutorial discretion to give priority to investigating, charging, and prosecuting those immigration violations that will have the greatest impact on achieving these goals. The INS has used this principle in the design and execution of its border enforcement strategy, its refocus on criminal smuggling networks, and its concentration on fixing benefit-granting processes to prevent fraud. An agency's focus on maximizing its impact under appropriate principles, rather than devoting resources to cases that will do less to advance these overall interests, is a crucial element in effective law enforcement management.

The Principles of Federal Prosecution governing the conduct of U.S. Attorneys use the concept of a "substantial Federal interest." A U.S. Attorney may properly decline a prosecution if *"no substantial Federal interest would be served by prosecution."* This principle provides a useful frame of reference for the INS, although applying it presents challenges that differ from those facing a U.S. Attorney. In particular, as immigration is an exclusively Federal responsibility, the option of an adequate alternative remedy under state law is not available. In an immigration case, the interest at stake will always be Federal. Therefore, we must place particular emphasis on the element of substantiality. How important is the Federal interest in the case, as compared to other cases and priorities? That is the overriding question, and answering it requires examining a number of factors that may differ according to the stage of the case.

As a general matter, INS officers may decline to prosecute a legally sufficient immigration case if the Federal immigration enforcement interest that would be served by prosecution is not substantial.[3] Except as may be provided specifically in other policy statements or directives, the responsibility for exercising prosecutorial discretion in this manner rests with the District Director (DD) or Chief Patrol Agent (CPA) based on his or her common sense and sound judgment.[4] The DD or CPA should obtain legal advice from the District or Sector Counsel to the extent that such advice may be necessary and appropriate to ensure the sound and lawful exercise of discretion, particularly with respect to cases pending before the Executive Office for Immigration Review (EOIR).[5] The DD's or CPA's authority may be delegated to the extent necessary and proper, except that decisions not to place a removable alien in removal proceedings, or decisions to move to terminate a proceeding which in the opinion of the District or Sector Counsel is legally sufficient, may not be delegated to an officer who is not authorized under 8 C.F.R. § 239.1 to issue an NTA. A DD's or CPA's exercise of prosecutorial discretion will not normally be reviewed by Regional or Headquarters authority. However, DDs and CPAs remain subject to their chains of command and may be supervised as necessary in their exercise of prosecutorial discretion.

Investigations

Priorities for deploying investigative resources are discussed in other documents, such as the interior enforcement strategy, and will not be discussed in detail in this memorandum. These previously identified priorities include identifying and removing criminal and terrorist aliens, deterring and dismantling alien smuggling, minimizing benefit fraud and document abuse, responding to community complaints about illegal immigration and building partnerships to solve local problems, and blocking and removing employers' access to undocumented workers. Even within these broad priority areas, however, the Service must make decisions about how best to expend its resources.

Managers should plan and design operations to maximize the likelihood that serious offenders will be identified. Supervisors should ensure that front-line investigators understand that it is not mandatory to issue an NTA in every case where they have reason to believe that an alien is removable, and agents should be encouraged to bring questionable cases to a supervisor's attention. Operational planning for investigations should include consideration of appropriate procedures for supervisory and legal review of individual NTA issuing decisions.

---

[3] In some cases even a substantial immigration enforcement interest in prosecuting a case could be outweighed by other interests, such as the foreign policy of the United States. Decisions that require weighing such other interests should be made at the level of responsibility within the INS or the Department of Justice that is appropriate in light of the circumstances and interests involved.

[4] This general reference to DDs and CPAs is not intended to exclude from coverage by this memorandum other INS personnel, such as Service Center directors, who may be called upon to exercise prosecutorial discretion and do not report to DDs or CPAs, or to change any INS chains of command.

[5] Exercising prosecutorial discretion with respect to cases pending before EOIR involves procedures set forth at 8 CFR 239.2 and 8 CFR Part 3, such as obtaining the court's approval of a motion to terminate proceedings.

Careful design of enforcement operations is a key element in the INS' exercise of prosecutorial discretion. Managers should consider not simply whether a particular effort is legally supportable, but whether it best advances the INS' goals, compared with other possible uses of those resources. As a general matter, investigations that are specifically focused to identify aliens who represent a high priority for removal should be favored over investigations which, by their nature, will identify a broader variety of removable aliens. Even an operation that is designed based on high-priority criteria, however, may still identify individual aliens who warrant a favorable exercise of prosecutorial discretion.[6]

Initiating and Pursuing Proceedings

Aliens who are subject to removal may come to the Service's attention in a variety of ways. For example, some aliens are identified as a result of INS investigations, while others are identified when they apply for immigration benefits or seek admission at a port-of-entry. While the context in which the INS encounters an alien may, as a practical matter, affect the Service's options, it does not change the underlying principle that the INS has discretion and should exercise that discretion appropriately given the circumstances of the case.

Even when an immigration officer has reason to believe that an alien is removable and that there is sufficient evidence to obtain a final order of removal, it may be appropriate to decline to proceed with that case. This is true even when an alien is removable based on his or her criminal history and when the alien–if served with an NTA–would be subject to mandatory detention. The INS may exercise its discretion throughout the enforcement process. Thus, the INS can choose whether to issue an NTA, whether to cancel an NTA prior to filing with the immigration court or move for dismissal in immigration court (under 8 CFR 239.2), whether to detain (for those aliens not subject to mandatory detention), whether to offer an alternative to removal such as voluntary departure or withdrawal of an application for admission, and whether to stay an order of deportation.

The decision to exercise any of these options or other alternatives in a particular case requires an individualized determination, based on the facts and the law. As a general matter, it is better to exercise favorable discretion as early in the process as possible, once the relevant facts have been determined, in order to conserve the Service's resources and in recognition of the alien's interest in avoiding unnecessary legal proceedings. However, there is often a conflict

---

[6] For example, operations in county jails are designed to identify and remove criminal aliens, a high priority for the Service. Nonetheless, an investigator working at a county jail and his or her supervisor should still consider whether the exercise of prosecutorial discretion would be appropriate in individual cases.

between making decisions as soon as possible, and making them based on evaluating as many relevant, credible facts as possible. Developing an extensive factual record prior to making a charging decision may itself consume INS resources in a way that negates any saving from forgoing a removal proceeding.

Generally, adjudicators may have a better opportunity to develop a credible factual record at an earlier stage than investigative or other enforcement personnel. It is simply not practicable to require officers at the arrest stage to develop a full investigative record on the equities of each case (particularly since the alien file may not yet be available to the charging office), and this memorandum does not require such an analysis. Rather, what is needed is knowledge that the INS is not legally required to institute proceedings in every case, openness to that possibility in appropriate cases, development of facts relevant to the factors discussed below to the extent that it is reasonably possible to do so under the circumstances and in the timeframe that decisions must be made, and implementation of any decision to exercise prosecutorial discretion.

There is no precise formula for identifying which cases warrant a favorable exercise of discretion. Factors that should be taken into account in deciding whether to exercise prosecutorial discretion include, but are not limited to, the following:

- <u>Immigration status</u>: Lawful permanent residents generally warrant greater consideration. However, other removable aliens may also warrant the favorable exercise of discretion, depending on all the relevant circumstances.
- <u>Length of residence in the United States</u>: The longer an alien has lived in the United States, particularly in legal status, the more this factor may be considered a positive equity.
- <u>Criminal history</u>: Officers should take into account the nature and severity of any criminal conduct, as well as the time elapsed since the offense occurred and evidence of rehabilitation. It is appropriate to take into account the actual sentence or fine that was imposed, as an indicator of the seriousness attributed to the conduct by the court. Other factors relevant to assessing criminal history include the alien's age at the time the crime was committed and whether or not he or she is a repeat offender.
- <u>Humanitarian concerns</u>: Relevant humanitarian concerns include, but are not limited to, family ties in the United States; medical conditions affecting the alien or the alien's family; the fact that an alien entered the United States at a very young age; ties to one's home country (<u>e.g.</u>, whether the alien speaks the language or has relatives in the home country); extreme youth or advanced age; and home country conditions.
- <u>Immigration history</u>: Aliens without a past history of violating the immigration laws (particularly violations such as reentering after removal, failing to appear at hearing, or resisting arrest that show heightened disregard for the legal process) warrant favorable consideration to a greater extent than those with such a history. The seriousness of any such violations should also be taken into account.

Memorandum for Regional Directors, et al.   Page 8
Subject: Exercising Prosecutorial Discretion

- <u>Likelihood of ultimately removing the alien</u>: Whether a removal proceeding would have a reasonable likelihood of ultimately achieving its intended effect, in light of the case circumstances such as the alien's nationality, is a factor that should be considered.
- <u>Likelihood of achieving enforcement goal by other means</u>: In many cases, the alien's departure from the United States may be achieved more expeditiously and economically by means other than removal, such as voluntary return, withdrawal of an application for admission, or voluntary departure.
- <u>Whether the alien is eligible or is likely to become eligible for other relief</u>: Although not determinative on its own, it is relevant to consider whether there is a legal avenue for the alien to regularize his or her status if not removed from the United States. The fact that the Service cannot confer complete or permanent relief, however, does not mean that discretion should not be exercised favorably if warranted by other factors.
- <u>Effect of action on future admissibility</u>: The effect an action such as removal may have on an alien can vary–for example, a time-limited as opposed to an indefinite bar to future admissibility–and these effects may be considered.
- <u>Current or past cooperation with law enforcement authorities</u>: Current or past cooperation with the INS or other law enforcement authorities, such as the U.S. Attorneys, the Department of Labor, or National Labor Relations Board, among others, weighs in favor of discretion.
- <u>Honorable U.S. military service</u>: Military service with an honorable discharge should be considered as a favorable factor. See Standard Operating Procedures Part V.D.8 (issuing an NTA against current or former member of armed forces requires advance approval of Regional Director).
- <u>Community attention</u>: Expressions of opinion, in favor of or in opposition to removal, may be considered, particularly for relevant facts or perspectives on the case that may not have been known to or considered by the INS. Public opinion or publicity (including media or congressional attention) should not, however, be used to justify a decision that cannot be supported on other grounds. Public and professional responsibility will sometimes require the choice of an unpopular course.
- <u>Resources available to the INS</u>: As in planning operations, the resources available to the INS to take enforcement action in the case, compared with other uses of the resources to fulfill national or regional priorities, are an appropriate factor to consider, but it should not be determinative. For example, when prosecutorial discretion should be favorably exercised under these factors in a particular case, that decision should prevail even if there is detention space available.

Obviously, not all of the factors will be applicable to every case, and in any particular case one factor may deserve more weight than it might in another case. There may be other factors, not on the list above, that are appropriate to consider. The decision should be based on the totality of the circumstances, not on any one factor considered in isolation. General guidance such as this cannot provide a "bright line" test that may easily be applied to determine the "right" answer in every case. In many cases, minds reasonably can differ, different factors may point in different directions, and there is no clearly "right" answer. Choosing a course of action in difficult cases must be an exercise of judgment by the responsible officer based on his or her experience, good sense, and consideration of the relevant factors to the best of his or her ability.

There are factors that may <u>not</u> be considered. Impermissible factors include:

- An individual's race, religion, sex, national origin, or political association, activities or beliefs;[7]
- The officer's own personal feelings regarding the individual; or
- The possible effect of the decision on the officer's own professional or personal circumstances.

In many cases, the procedural posture of the case, and the state of the factual record, will affect the ability of the INS to use prosecutorial discretion. For example, since the INS cannot admit an inadmissible alien to the United States unless a waiver is available, in many cases the INS' options are more limited in the admission context at a port-of-entry than in the deportation context.

Similarly, the INS may consider the range of options and information likely to be available at a later time. For example, an officer called upon to make a charging decision may reasonably determine that he or she does not have a sufficient, credible factual record upon which to base a favorable exercise of prosecutorial discretion not to put the alien in proceedings, that the record cannot be developed in the timeframe in which the decision must be made, that a more informed prosecutorial decision likely could be made at a later time during the course of proceedings, and that if the alien is not served with an NTA now, it will be difficult or impossible to do so later.

Such decisions must be made, however, with due regard for the principles of these guidelines, and in light of the other factors discussed here. For example, if there is no relief available to the alien in a removal proceeding and the alien is subject to mandatory detention if

---

[7] This general guidance on factors that should not be relied upon in making a decision whether to enforce the law against an individual is not intended to prohibit their consideration to the extent they are directly relevant to an alien's status under the immigration laws or eligibility for a benefit. For example, religion and political beliefs are often directly relevant in asylum cases and need to be assessed as part of a prosecutorial determination regarding the strength of the case, but it would be improper for an INS officer to treat aliens differently based on his personal opinion about a religion or belief. Political activities may be relevant to a ground of removal on national security or terrorism grounds. An alien's nationality often directly affects his or her eligibility for adjustment or other relief, the likelihood that he or she can be removed, or the availability of prosecutorial options such as voluntary return, and may be considered to the extent these concerns are pertinent.

placed in proceedings, that situation suggests that the exercise of prosecutorial discretion, if appropriate, would be more useful to the INS if done sooner rather than later. It would be improper for an officer to assume that someone else at some later time will always be able to make a more informed decision, and therefore never to consider exercising discretion.

Factors relevant to exercising prosecutorial discretion may come to the Service's attention in various ways. For example, aliens may make requests to the INS to exercise prosecutorial discretion by declining to pursue removal proceedings. Alternatively, there may be cases in which an alien asks to be put in proceedings (for example, to pursue a remedy such as cancellation of removal that may only be available in that forum). In either case, the INS may consider the request, but the fact that it is made should not determine the outcome, and the prosecutorial decision should be based upon the facts and circumstances of the case. Similarly, the fact that an alien has not requested prosecutorial discretion should not influence the analysis of the case. Whether, and to what extent, any request should be considered is also a matter of discretion. Although INS officers should be open to new facts and arguments, attempts to exploit prosecutorial discretion as a delay tactic, as a means merely to revisit matters that have been thoroughly considered and decided, or for other improper tactical reasons should be rejected. There is no legal right to the exercise of prosecutorial discretion, and (as stated at the close of this memorandum) this memorandum creates no right or obligation enforceable at law by any alien or any other party.

Process for Decisions

Identification of Suitable Cases

No single process of exercising discretion will fit the multiple contexts in which the need to exercise discretion may arise. Although this guidance is designed to promote consistency in the application of the immigration laws, it is not intended to produce rigid uniformity among INS officers in all areas of the country at the expense of the fair administration of the law. Different offices face different conditions and have different requirements. Service managers and supervisors, including DDs and CPAs, and Regional, District, and Sector Counsel must develop mechanisms appropriate to the various contexts and priorities, keeping in mind that it is better to exercise discretion as early in process as possible once the factual record has been identified.[8] In particular, in cases where it is clear that no statutory relief will be available at the immigration hearing and where detention will be mandatory, it best conserves the Service's resources to make a decision early.

Enforcement and benefits personnel at all levels should understand that prosecutorial discretion exists and that it is appropriate and expected that the INS will exercise this authority in appropriate cases. DDs, CPAs, and other supervisory officials (such as District and

---

[8] DDs, CPAs, and other INS personnel should also be open, however, to possible reconsideration of decisions (either for or against the exercise of discretion) based upon further development of the facts.

Sector Counsels) should encourage their personnel to bring potentially suitable cases for the favorable exercise of discretion to their attention for appropriate resolution. To assist in exercising their authority, DDs and CPAs may wish to convene a group to provide advice on difficult cases that have been identified as potential candidates for prosecutorial discretion.

It is also appropriate for DDs and CPAs to develop a list of "triggers" to help their personnel identify cases at an early stage that may be suitable for the exercise of prosecutorial discretion. These cases should then be reviewed at a supervisory level where a decision can be made as to whether to proceed in the ordinary course of business, to develop additional facts, or to recommend a favorable exercise of discretion. Such triggers could include the following facts (whether proven or alleged):

Lawful permanent residents;
Aliens with a serious health condition;
Juveniles;
Elderly aliens;
Adopted children of U.S. citizens;
U.S. military veterans;
Aliens with lengthy presence in United States (<u>i.e.</u>, 10 years or more); or
Aliens present in the United States since childhood.

Since workloads and the type of removable aliens encountered may vary significantly both within and between INS offices, this list of possible trigger factors for supervisory review is intended neither to be comprehensive nor mandatory in all situations. Nor is it intended to suggest that the presence or absence of "trigger" facts should itself determine whether prosecutorial discretion should be exercised, as compared to review of all the relevant factors as discussed elsewhere in these guidelines. Rather, development of trigger criteria is intended solely as a suggested means of facilitating identification of potential cases that may be suitable for prosecutorial review as early as possible in the process.

Documenting Decisions

When a DD or CPA decides to exercise prosecutorial discretion favorably, that decision should be clearly documented in the alien file, including the specific decision taken and its factual and legal basis. DDs and CPAs may also document decisions based on a specific set of facts <u>not</u> to exercise prosecutorial discretion favorably, but this is not required by this guidance.

The alien should also be informed in writing of a decision to exercise prosecutorial discretion favorably, such as not placing him or her in removal proceedings or not pursuing a case. This normally should be done by letter to the alien and/or his or her attorney of record, briefly stating the decision made and its consequences. It is not necessary to recite the facts of the case or the INS' evaluation of the facts in such letters. <u>Although the specifics of the letter</u>

will vary depending on the circumstances of the case and the action taken, it must make it clear to the alien that exercising prosecutorial discretion does not confer any immigration status, ability to travel to the United States (unless the alien applies for and receives advance parole), immunity from future removal proceedings, or any enforceable right or benefit upon the alien. If, however, there is a potential benefit that is linked to the action (for example, the availability of employment authorization for beneficiaries of deferred action), it is appropriate to identify it.

The obligation to notify an individual is limited to situations in which a specific, identifiable decision to refrain from action is taken in a situation in which the alien normally would expect enforcement action to proceed. For example, it is not necessary to notify aliens that the INS has refrained from focusing investigative resources on them, but a specific decision not to proceed with removal proceedings against an alien who has come into INS custody should be communicated to the alien in writing. This guideline is not intended to replace existing standard procedures or forms for deferred action, voluntary return, voluntary departure, or other currently existing and standardized processes involving prosecutorial discretion.

Future Impact

An issue of particular complexity is the future effect of prosecutorial discretion decisions in later encounters with the alien. Unlike the criminal context, in which statutes of limitation and venue requirements often preclude one U.S. Attorney's office from prosecuting an offense that another office has declined, immigration violations are continuing offenses that, as a general principle of immigration law, continue to make an alien legally removable regardless of a decision not to pursue removal on a previous occasion. An alien may come to the attention of the INS in the future through seeking admission or in other ways. An INS office should abide by a favorable prosecutorial decision taken by another office as a matter of INS policy, absent new facts or changed circumstances. However, if a removal proceeding is transferred from one INS district to another, the district assuming responsibility for the case is not bound by the charging district's decision to proceed with an NTA, if the facts and circumstances at a later stage suggest that a favorable exercise of prosecutorial discretion is appropriate.

Service offices should review alien files for information on previous exercises of prosecutorial discretion at the earliest opportunity that is practicable and reasonable and take any such information into account. In particular, the office encountering the alien must carefully assess to what extent the relevant facts and circumstances are the same or have changed either procedurally or substantively (either with respect to later developments, or more detailed knowledge of past circumstances) from the basis for the original exercise of discretion. A decision by an INS office to take enforcement action against the subject of a previous documented exercise of favorable prosecutorial discretion should be memorialized with a memorandum to the file explaining the basis for the decision, unless the charging documents on their face show a material difference in facts and circumstances (such as a different ground of deportability).

Legal Liability and Enforceability

The question of liability may arise in the implementation of this memorandum. Some INS personnel have expressed concerns that, if they exercise prosecutorial discretion favorably, they may become subject to suit and personal liability for the possible consequences of that decision. We cannot promise INS officers that they will never be sued. However, we can assure our employees that Federal law shields INS employees who act in reasonable reliance upon properly promulgated agency guidance within the agency's legal authority – such as this memorandum–from personal legal liability for those actions.

The principles set forth in this memorandum, and internal office procedures adopted hereto, are intended solely for the guidance of INS personnel in performing their duties. They are not intended to, do not, and may not be relied upon to create a right or benefit, substantive or procedural, enforceable at law by any individual or other party in removal proceedings, in litigation with the United States, or in any other form or manner.

Training and Implementation

Training on the implementation of this memorandum for DDs, CPAs, and Regional, District, and Sector Counsel will be conducted at the regional level. This training will include discussion of accountability and periodic feedback on implementation issues. In addition, following these regional sessions, separate training on prosecutorial discretion will be conducted at the district level for other staff, to be designated. The regions will report to the Office of Field Operations when this training has been completed.

APPENDIX 8-4

Procedures for Handling Naturalization Applications of Aliens Who Voted Unlawfully or Falsely Represented Themselves as U.S. Citizens by Voting or Registering to Vote

U.S. Department of Justice
Immigration and Naturalization Service

HQ 70/33

Office of the Executive Associate Commissioner	*425 I Street NW* *Washington, DC 20536*

May 7, 2002

MEMORANDUM FOR ALL REGIONAL DIRECTORS
                         DISTRICT DIRECTORS
                         SERVICE CENTER DIRECTORS
                         OFFICERS-IN-CHARGE

FROM: William R. Yates /s/
              Deputy Executive Associate Commissioner
              Office of Field Operations
              Immigration Services Division

SUBJECT: Procedures for Handling Naturalization Applications of Aliens Who Voted
                Unlawfully or Falsely Represented Themselves as U.S. Citizens by Voting or
                <u>Registering to Vote</u>

      This memorandum provides guidance on handling naturalization applications of aliens who have unlawfully voted or falsely represented themselves as U.S. citizens in association with registering to vote or by voting. This guidance supplements the May 13, 1997, Office of Naturalization Operations Policy Memorandum titled, "Voter Registration and Standardized Citizenship Testing," which instructs adjudicators to ask all naturalization applicants if they have ever registered to vote or voted in a U.S. election. This memorandum should be read in conjunction with the Commissioner's November 17, 2000 memorandum titled, "Exercising Prosecutorial Discretion," which provides more general guidance on determining when or if removal proceedings should be initiated for certain naturalization applicants. This memorandum can be found on the INS Power Port under the section entitled "INS Policy and Procedural Memoranda".

What sections of the Immigration and Nationality Act (INA) address illegal voting?

      The 1996 Illegal Immigration Reform and Immigrant Responsibility Act (IIRIRA) added sections 212(a)(10)(D)(i) and 237(a)(6)(A) to the INA to address illegal voting.[i] Title II of the Child Citizenship Act of 2000 (CCA), Pub. L. 106-395, added sections 212(a)(10)(D)(ii) and 237(a)(6)(B) to provide exceptions to the removal grounds for lawful permanent residents who resided in the United States prior to age 16 and who have U.S. citizen parents.[ii] The CCA also

emorandum for All RDs, DDs, SCDs, and OICs   Page 2
Subject: Procedures for Handling N-400s for Applicants Who Vote Illegally or Made False Claims to
                U.S. Citizenship for the Purpose of Voting or Registering to Vote

added a clause to section 101(f)[iii] to address good moral character (GMC) determinations for individuals who voted unlawfully.

Are there any criminal penalties for illegal voting?

Non-citizens who violate or who have violated these provisions may face criminal prosecution in addition to administrative removal. IIRIRA created a new section 18 U.S.C. 611,[iv] establishing criminal penalties for aliens who have voted in any federal election. An alien convicted of violating this provision of the law may be fined, imprisoned for up to one year, or both.

The CCA also added an exception to the criminal provision, 18 U.S.C. 611(c), for lawful permanent residents who resided in the United States prior to age 16, have U.S. citizen parents, and who reasonably believed at the time of voting in violation of the law that he or she was a citizen of the United States. The criminal provision exception only applies to convictions that became final on or after the date of enactment of the CCA – October 30, 2000.[v] In such cases, because the district court has made the determination that the applicant did not fall within the terms of the exception, the Service need not re-adjudicate this issue.

Even if there is no conviction for illegal voting, officers should continue to analyze the case as provided on page 4 of this memorandum.

Is a criminal conviction for illegal voting required to support a removal charge?

No. An alien who votes illegally but who has not been convicted under 18 U.S.C. 611 is still potentially removable. Removal charges can be sustained simply by proving that the alien voted in violation of the relevant law.

What sections of the INA address false claims to U.S. citizenship?

IIRIRA added sections 212(a)(6)(C)(ii)(I) and 237(a)(3)(D)(i) to the INA to address false claims to U.S. citizenship.[vi] The CCA added sections 212(a)(6)(C)(ii)(II) and 237(a)(3)(D)(ii) to provide exceptions to the removal grounds.[vii] The CCA also added a clause to section 101(f)[viii] to address GMC determinations for individuals who made a false claim to U.S. citizenship.

Are there any criminal penalties for making a false claim to U.S. citizenship?

IIRIRA added section 1015(f)[ix] to Title 18 to establish criminal penalties for any alien who makes a false claim to U.S. citizenship in order to vote or register to vote in an election. An alien convicted of violating this provision of the law may be fined or imprisoned for not more than five years, or both.

The CCA also added an exception to the criminal provision, the last clause of 18 U.S.C. 1015(f), for lawful permanent residents who resided in the United States prior to age 16, have U.S. citizen parents, and who reasonably believed that he or she was a citizen of the United States at the time of making the false claim. Like 18 U.S.C. 611(c), this criminal provision

emorandum for All RDs, DDs, SCDs, and OICs   Page 3
Subject: Procedures for Handling N-400s for Applicants Who Vote Illegally or Made False Claims to
                U.S. Citizenship for the Purpose of Voting or Registering to Vote

exception only applies to convictions that became final on or after October 30, 2000.[x] In such cases, because the district court has made the determination that the applicant did not fall within the terms of the exception, the Service need not re-adjudicate this issue.

Even if there is no conviction for making a false claim to U.S. citizenship, officers should continue to analyze the case as provided on page 4 of this memorandum.

Is a criminal conviction for making a false claim to U.S. citizen required to support a removal charge?

No. An alien who knowingly makes a false claim to U.S. citizenship for the purpose of voting or registering to vote, but who has not been convicted under 18 U.S.C. 1015(f) is still potentially removable. Removal charges can be sustained simply by proving that the alien knowingly made the false claim for purposes of voting or registering to vote.

How is making a false claim different from illegal voting?

In the voting context, an applicant can only be found to have violated the provision if his or her conduct would be deemed unlawful under the relevant Federal, state, or local election law.

For false claims to U.S. citizenship, there is no need to focus on the underlying election law that was violated. Officers need only establish that the applicant: (1) actually falsely represented himself or herself as a U.S. citizen on or after September 30, 1996[xi]; and (2) that such representation was made for the purpose of registering to vote or voting.

What are the exceptions to the provisions related to illegal voting and false claims to U.S. citizenship?

The CCA establishes exceptions to removal under sections 212(a) and 237(a), to GMC under 101(f) of the INA, and to criminal prosecution under 18 U.S.C. 611 and 1015(f), for any alien:

- whose natural or adoptive parents (both parents) are or were U.S. citizens
- who permanently resided in the U.S. prior to his or her 16th birthday, and
- who "reasonably believed" at the time of the violation or false representation that he or she was a US citizen.

As a matter of policy, the Service has determined that the applicant's parents had to be U.S. citizens at the time of the illegal voting or false claim to U.S. citizenship in order to meet the first prong of this exception.

How do I adjudicate these cases?

For every naturalization case where the applicant may have unlawfully voted or may have made a false claim to U.S. citizenship while voting or registering to vote, officers should analyze the case following the six steps outlined below (see also **Attachment A** for flowchart).

emorandum for All RDs, DDs, SCDs, and OICs   Page 4
Subject: Procedures for Handling N-400s for Applicants Who Vote Illegally or Made False Claims to
              U.S. Citizenship for the Purpose of Voting or Registering to Vote

Officers should note that in most instances there will not be a conviction under 18 U.S.C. 611 or 1015(f).

1. Determine if the applicant:

    (a)   actually voted in violation of the relevant election law; or
    (b)   made a false claim to U.S. citizenship when registering to vote or voting in any Federal, State, or local election any time on or after September 30, 1996;

2. If either "a" or "b" above happened, the applicant is removable. Now determine whether the applicant is eligible for the exceptions from removal as provided under sections 212(a) and 237(a) of the INA. If the applicant is eligible for the exceptions, the applicant is no longer removable. Proceed with adjudication of the N-400 (see Step 6).

3. If the applicant does not qualify for one of the exceptions, determine whether the applicant's case merits the exercise of prosecutorial discretion.

4. If the applicant's case does not merit the exercise of prosecutorial discretion, initiate removal proceedings and **continue** the naturalization application, pending the outcome of such proceedings.

5. If the applicant's case merits prosecutorial discretion, proceed with adjudication of the N-400 (see Step 6).

6. Assess the applicant's eligibility for naturalization. The assessment should focus on whether the applicant's conduct overall (including any other potential grounds of ineligibility) precludes a finding of good moral character. The assessment should also include a determination of whether the applicant is exempted from a finding that he or she does not have good moral character based on the exception contained in 101(f).

How do I determine if applicant voted in violation of relevant election law or made a false claim to U.S. citizenship?

(a)   **Voting in violation of election law**

Whether the alien actually violated federal, state or local law depends upon whether he or she: (1) actually voted and (2) the act of voting violated a specific election law provision. The provisions governing voting and eligibility to vote will vary by location. In addition, the penalties for voting unlawfully will vary and may include a specific intent requirement.

Information about whether an applicant actually voted can come from his or her own admission under oath or from independent sources, such as voter records. Even if the applicant actually voted, however, the act of voting, by itself, is not sufficient to establish that the applicant voted unlawfully. Officers must also determine whether the applicant's act of voting would be deemed a violation under the relevant election law.

emorandum for All RDs, DDs, SCDs, and OICs   Page 5
Subject: Procedures for Handling N-400s for Applicants Who Vote Illegally or Made False Claims to
               U.S. Citizenship for the Purpose of Voting or Registering to Vote

To make the violation decision, officers must determine in what type of election the applicant voted – Federal, State, or local – and then review the appropriate jurisdiction's election laws. Federal election laws provide that only U.S. citizens can vote. Clearly, if an applicant is convicted under 18 U.S.C. 611, which governs federal elections, the applicant has voted in violation of the law.

Some local municipalities permit lawful permanent residents and/or nonresident aliens to vote in municipal elections. Officers should review all code provisions that define who is eligible and/or qualified to vote in such elections.[xii]

If the election law penalizes the actual act of voting, the fact that an applicant has actually voted is sufficient to establish that he or she has voted unlawfully. If, however, the election law penalizes the act of voting only upon an additional finding that the individual acted "knowingly" or "willfully," adjudicating officers cannot conclude that an applicant voted unlawfully until they assess the circumstances surrounding the voting, the applicant's credibility, and the documentary evidence. In these situations, officers should determine:

(1)   how, when, and where the applicant registered to vote and/or voted;
(2)   the extent of the applicant's knowledge of the election laws;
(3)   whether the applicant received any instructions, or was questioned verbally about his or her eligibility to vote;
(4)   who provided the applicant with information about election laws or his or her eligibility to vote;
(5)   whether the election registration form and/or voting ballot:
       (a)   contains a specific question asking if the applicant is a U.S. citizen;
       (b)   requires the applicant to declare under penalty of perjury that he or she is a U.S. citizen; or
       (c)   requires the applicant to be qualified to vote and lists specifically the requirement of U.S. citizenship elsewhere on the form.

Officers should record the applicant's testimony regarding his or her voting in a sworn statement, and obtain any relevant evidence to support the illegal voting charge. Such evidence, for example, can include a copy of the alien's voter registration form with instructions and his or her voter registration card, establishing that U.S. citizenship was required in order to obtain the card.

If, after weighing all the favorable and unfavorable factors, the officer determines that the applicant voted with knowledge that such voting would be a violation, the officer can conclude that the applicant voted unlawfully.

If the applicant voted unlawfully, the applicant is removable. The officer must then proceed to the next steps of determining whether the applicant meets the exceptions to removal or merits an exercise of prosecutorial discretion.

(b)   Making a false claim to U.S. citizenship to vote or register to vote

emorandum for All RDs, DDs, SCDs, and OICs   Page 6
Subject: Procedures for Handling N-400s for Applicants Who Vote Illegally or Made False Claims to
             U.S. Citizenship for the Purpose of Voting or Registering to Vote

Clearly, if an applicant is convicted under 18 U.S.C. 1015(f), which governs making a false claim to U.S. citizenship in order to vote or register to vote, the applicant has violated the law. However, absent a conviction, information about whether an applicant actually falsely represented himself or herself as a U.S. citizen can come from his or her own admission under oath or from independent documentary evidence, such as voter registration forms.

The law requires that the applicant have "represented" himself or herself as a U.S. citizen on or after September 30, 1996. "Representation" is not limited to oral statements made in response to questioning by an officer; an applicant can make a false representation if he or she signed an employment application or voter registration card that specifically asked the question "Are you a U.S. citizen?" or declared under oath or penalty of perjury, in writing or orally, that he or she was a U.S. citizen. Officers should record the applicant's testimony regarding his or her misrepresentation in a sworn statement, and obtain any relevant evidence to support a false claim to US citizenship charge. Such evidence, for example, can include a copy of the alien's voter registration form with instructions and his or her voter registration card, establishing that U.S. citizenship was required in order to obtain the card.

If the officer determines that the applicant made a false claim to U.S. citizenship for the purpose of voting or registering to vote, the applicant is removable. The officer must then proceed to the next steps of determining whether the applicant meets the exceptions to removal or merits an exercise of favorable prosecutorial discretion.

How do I determine if the applicant qualifies for the exceptions to the removal grounds?

If an applicant has been convicted for violation of 18 U.S.C. 611 or 1015(f), and the conviction became final on or after October 30, 2000, the applicant is removable and not eligible for exceptions created by the CCA.[xiii]

If the applicant has not been convicted, or if the applicant's conviction became final prior to October 30, 2000, officers must analyze whether the applicant falls under the exceptions to the illegal voting and false claim to U.S. citizenship provisions under sections 212(a) and 237(a).

The exceptions apply to any alien:

- whose natural or adoptive parents (both parents) are or were U.S. citizens,
- who permanently resided in the U.S. prior to his or her 16th birthday, and
- who "reasonably believed" at the time of the violation or false representation that he or she was a U.S. citizen.

Officers will need to obtain evidence of the applicant's parents' citizenship status if not currently available in the applicant's A-file and use normal procedures for determining qualifying lawful permanent resident status. As a matter of policy, the Service has determined that the applicant's parents had to be U.S. citizens at the time of the illegal voting or false claim to U.S. citizenship in order to meet the first prong of this exception.

emorandum for All RDs, DDs, SCDs, and OICs   Page 7
Subject: Procedures for Handling N-400s for Applicants Who Vote Illegally or Made False Claims to
                U.S. Citizenship for the Purpose of Voting or Registering to Vote

To assess whether the applicant reasonably believed that he or she was a U.S. citizen at the time of the violation, officers must consider the totality of the circumstances in the case, weighing such factors as the length of time the applicant resided in the United States and the age when the applicant entered as a lawful permanent resident. For example, suppose an applicant acknowledges voting unlawfully, but claimed he or she believed he or she was a U.S. citizen because: (1) the applicant was born overseas and adopted as an infant by a U.S. citizen couple; (2) the applicant's parents mistakenly believed that the applicant's adoption and entry into the United States conferred citizenship upon the applicant; and (3) the applicant's parents always told him or her that he or she was a U.S. citizen. In this case, it is likely the applicant has established the "reasonable belief" necessary for an exception from the removal grounds.

An applicant who qualifies for the exceptions to removal is no longer removable. Officers should then determine whether the applicant is eligible for naturalization. If the applicant does not qualify for the exceptions to removal, officers should proceed to the next step and determine if the applicant's case merits a favorable exercise of prosecutorial discretion.

How do I determine whether the applicant's case merits prosecutorial discretion?

Officers should determine whether to initiate or decline to initiate removal proceedings on a case-by-case basis, following the procedures outlined in the Commissioner's November 17, 2000 memorandum titled "Exercising Prosecutorial Discretion."

If the applicant's case does not merit prosecutorial discretion, what do I do with the N-400?

If the adjudicating officer determines that initiation of removal proceedings is appropriate, the officer should follow local procedures for issuing a Notice to Appear (NTA).[xiv] In addition to initiating removal proceedings, the adjudicating officer should **continue** the naturalization application pending the outcome of the removal proceedings. The applicant's naturalization application should not be denied under INA § 318 either prior to placing him or her into proceedings or after proceedings are initiated. The applicant is not considered to be in removal proceedings until the NTA has been served on the Immigration Court. Once an applicant is in proceedings, his or her application <u>may not be denied</u> because § 318 prohibits the Attorney General from taking **any** action on the case (including naturalization adjudication) while removal proceedings are pending.

If the applicant's case merits prosecutorial discretion, what should I do with the N-400?

If the Service decides that the applicant's case merits a favorable exercise of prosecutorial discretion, the officer should proceed with adjudication of the N-400. Note that the alien is not ineligible to naturalize simply because he or she is still susceptible to a removal charge.[xv] The facts surrounding an alien's susceptibility to a removal charge, however, should be considered when assessing whether he or she is of good moral character for the purpose of naturalization.

How do I assess an applicant's good moral character?

emorandum for All RDs, DDs, SCDs, and OICs   Page 8
Subject: Procedures for Handling N-400s for Applicants Who Vote Illegally or Made False Claims to
              U.S. Citizenship for the Purpose of Voting or Registering to Vote

Officers should decide whether the unlawful voting or false claim to U.S. citizenship affects the applicant's eligibility to naturalize. Officers should analyze the case focusing on:

(1)   whether the applicant is precluded from establishing good moral character pursuant to section 101(f)(1) through (8),

(2)   whether the unlawful conduct warrants a discretionary denial based on lack of good moral character, after balancing the equities, and

(3)   whether the applicant qualifies for an exception to 101(f).

Per se Bars to Establishing Good Moral Character

If the applicant has been convicted of a violation of 18 U.S.C. 611 or 1015(f),[xvi] the officer must determine whether or not the conviction precludes the applicant from establishing good moral character (GMC). Of particular importance are the bars to GMC that involve applicants who have been convicted of certain classes of crime, specifically INA 101(f)(3) and (f)(7).[xvii]

Sections 101(f)(3) and 212(a)(2)(A)(i)(I) provide that individuals convicted of certain crimes involving moral turpitude (CIMT) are precluded from establishing GMC. Because it is unlikely that a conviction under 18 U.S.C. 611 is a CIMT, such conviction will not preclude the applicant from establishing GMC under these provisions. However, the Service has determined that section 18 U.S.C. 1015(f) is a CIMT. Because it is a felony, such conviction will preclude a finding of GMC, under 101(f)(3) and 212(a)(1)(A)(i), if the offense was committed within the statutory period, unless the officer determines that the applicant qualifies for the 101(f) exception for lawful permanent residents who resided in the United States prior to age 16 and have U.S. citizen parents.

Sections 101(f)(3) and 212(a)(2)(B) preclude individuals who have been convicted of multiple crimes for which the aggregate sentence imposed is greater than five years, regardless of whether the offenses involve moral turpitude, from establishing good moral character. In addition, section 101(f)(7) precludes an applicant from establishing GMC if he or she has been confined in a penal institution for 180 days or more, regardless of whether the offense for which he or she was convicted was committed in or outside the statutory period. Officers should determine whether an applicant who has been convicted under 18 U.S.C. 611 or 1015(f) was confined for 180 days or more or has multiple convictions with an aggregate sentence of more than five years during the statutory period. If, after a careful analysis, the officer concludes that the applicant's convictions fall under 101(f)(3) and 212(a)(2)(B), or 101(f)(7), then the officer must determine whether the applicant qualifies for the 101(f) exception for lawful permanent residents who resided in the United States prior to age 16 and have U.S. citizen parents.

Discretionary Good Moral Character

If the applicant's conviction does not preclude a finding of GMC under 101(f)(3) or (f)(7) or the applicant has not been convicted for violations of 18 U.S.C. 611 and 1015(f), the officer must still determine whether the applicant lacks GMC as a matter of discretion.

emorandum for All RDs, DDs, SCDs, and OICs   Page 9
Subject: Procedures for Handling N-400s for Applicants Who Vote Illegally or Made False Claims to
             U.S. Citizenship for the Purpose of Voting or Registering to Vote

When a discretionary denial is considered, officers must consider the totality of the circumstances in the case and weigh all factors, favorable and unfavorable, in determining whether naturalization should be denied as a matter of discretion. Officers must balance the facts regarding the applicant's unlawful voting or false representation as a U.S. citizen against other factors such as:

(1) family ties and background
(2) the absence or presence of other criminal history
(3) education and school records
(4) employment history
(5) other law-abiding behavior, e.g. meeting financial obligations, paying taxes, etc.
(6) community involvement
(7) credibility of the applicant
(8) length of time in United States.

For example, an officer might find that an applicant who: (1) unlawfully registered to vote in a federal election fifteen years ago; (2) signed the voter registration card without understanding that he or she was claiming to be a U.S. citizen by doing so; (3) was specifically told by a community organization that he or she was entitled to vote; (4) has been a law-abiding citizen in all other respects; and (5) has no other criminal history, can establish good moral character in spite of making a false claim to U.S. citizenship. Alternatively, an officer might find that an applicant who: (1) voted unlawfully but was not convicted; (2) has failed to pay taxes in the past 15 years; (3) has 50 unpaid traffic tickets; and (4) owes $20,000 in back child support, cannot establish good moral character even if the officer determines that the applicant is eligible for the CCA exceptions to 101(f) for long-term residents because the applicant's other bad acts cumulatively reflect that he or she lacks good moral character as a matter of discretion. Further, where an officer finds that the applicant's testimony is not credible and that he or she has no or few favorable factors to support a finding of good moral character, the officer can deny the application as a matter of discretion. In every instance, officers should clearly document in the file which factors were considered and, if the case is denied, cite those factors in the denial so that a person reviewing the file can clearly understand how the officer concluded that the applicant did not merit a finding of good moral character.

If, after a careful analysis, the officer concludes that the applicant's case warrants denial as a matter of discretion, then the officer must determine whether the applicant qualifies for the 101(f) exception for lawful permanent residents who resided in the United States prior to age 16 and have U.S. citizen parents.

<u>Exception to Section 101(f) for Long-Time Residents</u>

If an applicant has been convicted for violation of 18 U.S.C. 611 or 1015(f), and the conviction became final on or after October 30, 2000, the applicant does not fall within the 101(f) exception.[xviii]

If the applicant's conviction became final prior to October 30, 2000, or if the applicant has not been convicted, officers must analyze whether the applicant falls under the 101(f) exception. Because the 101(f) exception determination is identical to the exception for removal,

emorandum for All RDs, DDs, SCDs, and OICs Page 10
Subject: Procedures for Handling N-400s for Applicants Who Vote Illegally or Made False Claims to
U.S. Citizenship for the Purpose of Voting or Registering to Vote

the officer's determination should be consistent with the prior determination. Thus, if the officer determined that the applicant was not removable for illegal voting or making a false claim to U.S. citizenship, the applicant should also fall within the 101(f) exception. If, however, the officer determined that the applicant was removable, but proceedings were not initiated as a matter of prosecutorial discretion, the applicant should not be eligible for the 101(f) exception.

* *

Officers should consult with their local district counsel to receive updated information related to the election laws. Requests for additional information regarding this policy guidance should be directed to Lyle Boelens, Immigrations Services Division, (202) 514-8273.

---

[i] Sections 212(a)(10)(D)(i) and 237(a)(6)(A) provide that "[a]ny alien who has voted in violation of any Federal, State, or local constitutional provision, statute, ordinance, or regulation" is inadmissible and deportable.

[ii] Sections 212(a)(10)(D)(ii) and 237(a)(6)(B) provide that "[i]n the case of an alien who voted in a Federal, State, or local election (including an initiative, recall, or referendum) in violation of a lawful restriction on voting to citizens, if each natural parent of the alien (or, in the case of an adopted alien, each adoptive parent of the alien) is or was a citizen (whether by birth or naturalization), the alien permanently resided in the United States prior to attaining the age of 16, and the alien reasonably believed at the time of such violation that he or she was a citizen, the alien shall not be considered to be inadmissible [deportable] under any provision of this subsection based on such violation."

[iii] The last clause of section 101(f) provides: `[i]n the case of an alien who makes a false statement or claim of citizenship, or who registers to vote or votes in a Federal, State, or local election (including an initiative, recall, or referendum) in violation of a lawful restriction of such registration or voting to citizens, if each natural parent of the alien (or, in the case of an adopted alien, each adoptive parent of the alien) is or was a citizen (whether by birth or naturalization), the alien permanently resided in the United States prior to attaining the age of 16, and the alien reasonably believed at the time of such statement, claim, or violation that he or she was a citizen, no finding that the alien is, or was, not of good moral character may be made based on it."

[iv] Under 18 U.S.C. § 611, it is unlawful for an alien to vote in any election held "for the purpose of electing a candidate for the office of President, Vice President, Presidential elector, Member of the Senate, Member of the House of Representatives, Delegate from the District of Columbia, or Residential Commissioner...."

[v] See section 201(d)(3) of Pub. L. 106-395.

[vi] Sections 212(a)(6)(C)(ii)(I) and 237(a)(3)(D)(i) provide that "[a]ny alien who falsely represents, or has falsely represented, himself or herself to be a citizen of the United States for any purpose or benefit under this chapter (including section 1324a of this title) or any other Federal or State law" is inadmissible and deportable.

[vii] Sections 212(a)(6)(C)(ii)(II) and 237(a)(3)(D)(ii) provide that "[i]n the case of an alien making a representation described in subclause (I), if each natural parent of the alien (or, in the case of an adopted alien, each adoptive parent of the alien) is or was a citizen (whether by birth or naturalization), the alien permanently resided in the United States prior to attaining the age of 16, and the alien reasonably believed at the time of making such representation he or she was a citizen, the alien shall not be considered to be inadmissible [deportable], under any provision of this subsection based on such representation."

[viii] See endnote 3.

[ix]18 U.S.C. 1015(f) provides: "Whoever knowingly makes any false statement or claim that he is a citizen of the United States in order to register to vote or vote in any Federal, State, or local election (including an initiative, recall, or referendum)-- Shall be fined under this title or imprisoned not more than five years, or both."

[x] See endnote 5.

[xi]For an individual to be subject to the false claim provision, the representation must have occurred on or after September 30, 1996. However, for an individual to be subject to the voting provision, the unlawful voting could have occurred at anytime before, on or after September 30, 1996.

[xii]Some state statutes use different terms, such as "qualified," "eligible," "entitled," in defining who may vote in an election and sometimes have separate code provisions addressing who can vote. For example, under one New York election law provision, a person is only "qualified" to register to vote and to vote if he or she is: (1) a U.S. citizen, (2) 18 years or older, and (3) a resident of the state for at least 30 days prior to the election. See, e.g. N.Y. Elec. Code. §§ 5-100-102. By contrast, under one Texas election law, a person is only "eligible" to vote if he or she is "a qualified voter." See V.T.C.A. Elec. Code § 11.001. Whether a person is a "qualified voter" is defined under a separate provision as a person who is 18 years or older, a United States citizen, not a convicted felon, a resident of the state, etc. See V.T.C.A. Elec. Code § 11.002.

Officers must also review relevant election laws to determine: (1) what actions or conduct constitute a violation and (2) whether the associated penalties that can be imposed are based solely on the conduct itself, or require an additional finding that the individual acted "knowingly" or "willfully." For example, under New York election law, an individual can be found to have "illegally voted" if he or she simply voted or attempted to vote at an election more than once. See, e.g. N.Y. Elec. Code. § 17-132(3). New York law, however, also provides that an individual can be found to have "illegally voted" when he or she "knowingly vot[ed]... at any election, when not qualified." See, e.g. N.Y. Elec. Code. § 17-132(1).

[xiii]Both 18 U.S.C. 611 and 1015(f) have exceptions that are identical to the exceptions provided in INA 212(a) and 237(a). See footnote 2. The CCA amendments creating these exceptions only apply to convictions that became final on or after the date of enactment of the CCA – October 30, 2000. See section 201(d)(3) of Pub. L. 106-395. Because a district court has made the determination that the applicant did not fall within the terms of the exception, the Service need not re-adjudicate this issue.

[xiv]The Service has determined that 18 U.S.C. 1015(f) is a crime involving moral turpitude (CIMT). Officers therefore should note that if the applicant has been convicted for making a false claim to U.S. citizenship under 18 U.S.C. 1015(f), the applicant is removable under sections 212(a)(2)(A)(i) or 237(a)(2)(A)(i) and (ii) as an alien convicted of a CIMT. Officers should consult with the local district counsel to determine whether these additional charges are appropriate. See the discussion in the Office of the General Counsel, Advisory Memorandum: Legal Consequences of Voting by an Alien Prior to Naturalization, February 13, 1997. (Contact ISD for a copy.)

[xv]Id.

[xvi]It is possible that the applicant could be convicted under state criminal provisions. If the applicant has been convicted pursuant to State law, the officer must review the relevant state law provision to determine what, if any, effect the conviction has on the applicant's ability to establish good moral character.

[xvii]A conviction under § 611 is a misdemeanor, punishable by a fine, imprisonment up to one year, or both, and a conviction under § 1015(f) is a felony, punishable by a fine, imprisonment up to five years, or both. Neither conviction is an aggravated felony. Thus, an applicant is not precluded from establishing good moral character under INA 101(f)(8).

[xviii]See endnote 11.

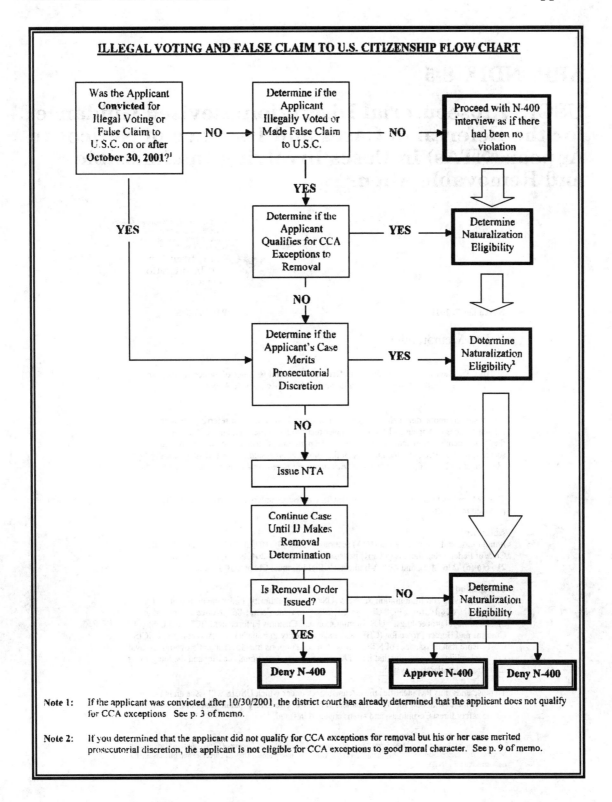

ILLEGAL VOTING AND FALSE CLAIM TO U.S. CITIZENSHIP FLOW CHART

Note 1: If the applicant was convicted after 10/30/2001, the district court has already determined that the applicant does not qualify for CCA exceptions See p. 3 of memo.

Note 2: If you determined that the applicant did not qualify for CCA exceptions for removal but his or her case merited prosecutorial discretion, the applicant is not eligible for CCA exceptions to good moral character. See p. 9 of memo.

APPENDIX 8-5

USCIS Prosecutorial Discretion: Revised Guidance for the Referral of Cases and Issuance of Notices to Appear (NTAs) in Cases Involving Inadmissible and Removable Aliens

U.S. Department of Homeland Security
U.S. Citizenship and Immigration Services
Office of the Director (MS 2000)
Washington, DC 20529-2000

**U.S. Citizenship
and Immigration
Services**

November 7, 2011   PM-602-0050

Policy Memorandum

SUBJECT: Revised Guidance for the Referral of Cases and Issuance of Notices to Appear
(NTAs) in Cases Involving Inadmissible and Removable Aliens

Purpose
This Policy Memorandum (PM) establishes new USCIS guidelines for referring cases and
issuing Notices to Appear (NTAs) in a manner that promotes the sound use of the resources of
the Department of Homeland Security and the Department of Justice to enhance national
security, public safety, and the integrity of the immigration system. This PM supersedes Policy
Memorandum No. 110, *Disposition of Cases Involving Removable Aliens*, dated July 11, 2006.

Scope
This PM applies to and is binding on all USCIS employees unless otherwise specifically
provided in this PM.

Authority
Immigration and Nationality Act (INA) sections 101(a)(43), 103(a), 239, 240 and 318; Title 8,
Code of Federal Regulations (8 CFR) parts/sections 2.1, 103, 204, 207.9, 208, 216.3(a),
216.6(a)(5), 236.14(c), and 239; Adjudicator's Field Manual Chapter 10.11(a).

Background
U.S. Citizenship and Immigration Services (USCIS) has authority, under the immigration laws,
see, e.g., INA §§ 103(a), 239; 8 CFR §§ 2.1, 239.1, to issue Form I-862, Notice to Appear, to
initiate removal proceedings.[1] U.S. Immigration and Customs Enforcement (ICE) and U.S.
Customs and Border Protection (CBP) also have authority to issue NTAs. Accordingly, USCIS
must ensure that its issuance of NTAs fits within and supports the Government's overall removal
priorities, while also ensuring that its NTA policies promote national security and the integrity of
the nation's immigration system.

To those ends, this PM identifies the circumstances under which USCIS will issue an NTA, or
will refer the case to ICE for NTA issuance, in order to effectively handle cases that involve
public safety threats, criminals, and aliens engaged in fraud.

---

[1] *Delegation by the Secretary of the Department of Homeland Security to the Bureau of Citizenship and Immigration
Services,* Delegation Number 0150.1; Paragraph 2(N). However, international District Directors and officers are not
authorized to issue NTAs.

PM-602-0050: Revised Guidance for the Referral of Cases and Issuance of NTAs in Cases
Involving Inadmissible and Removable Aliens
Page 2

Policy

I. National Security Cases

   This PM does not affect the handling of cases involving national security concerns.[2]
   Guidance from the Fraud Detection and National Security Directorate (FDNS)[3] will continue
   to govern the definition of these cases and the procedures for resolution and NTA issuance.

II. NTA Issuance Required by Statute or Regulation

   USCIS will issue an NTA in the following circumstances:[4]

   A. Termination of Conditional Permanent Resident Status and Denials of Form I-751,
      Petition to Remove the Conditions of Residence (8 CFR 216.3, 216.4, 216.5)[5]
   B. Denials of Form I-829, Petition by Entrepreneur to Remove Conditions (8 CFR 216.6)
   C. Termination of refugee status by the District Director (8 CFR 207.9)
   D. Denials of NACARA 202 and HRIFA adjustments
      1. NACARA 202 adjustment denials (8 CFR 245.13(m));
      2. HRIFA adjustment denials (8 CFR 245.15(r)(2)(i)).
   E. Asylum[6], NACARA 203, and Credible Fear cases:[7]
      1. Asylum referrals (8 CFR 208.14(c)(1));
      2. Termination of asylum or termination of withholding of removal or deportation
         (8 CFR 208.24(e));[8]
      3. Positive credible fear findings (8 CFR 208.30(f));
      4. NACARA 203 cases where suspension of deportation or cancellation of removal
         is not granted, and the applicant does not have asylum status, or lawful immigrant
         or non-immigrant status (8 CFR 240.70(d)).

   This PM does not apply to, or change, NTA or notification procedures for Temporary
   Protected Status cases.[9] Further, Form I-360, Petition for Amerasian, Widow(er), or Special
   Immigrant, processed under the Violence Against Women Act (VAWA), should continue to

---

[2] National Security Cases include cases involving Terrorist Related Grounds of Inadmissibility (TRIG) pursuant to
sections 212(a)(3)(B) and 212(a)(3)(F) of the INA.
[3] See, e.g., *Policy for Vetting and Adjudicating Cases with National Security Concerns* (April 11, 2008).
[4] If any Form I-751 or I-829 cases are also Egregious Public Safety cases, they will be referred to ICE in accordance
with Section IV.A.1 of this PM.
[5] See the October 9, 2009 internal memo, *Adjudication of Form I-751, Petition to Remove Conditions on Residence
Where the CPR Has a Final Order of Removal, Is in Removal Proceedings, or Has Filed an Unexcused Untimely
Petition or Multiple Petitions.* See also the April 3, 2009 memo, *I-751 Filed Prior to Termination of Marriage.*
[6] USCIS may issue an NTA when an asylum applicant withdraws his or her asylum application.
[7] This memo does not apply to the Asylum Division's issuance of Form I-863, Notice of Referral to Immigration
Judge, to certain stowaways, crewmembers, and VWP individuals who are requesting asylum or withholding of
removal; reasonable fear screenings and negative credible fear screenings.
[8] See also section 208(c)(3) of the INA describing removal when asylum is terminated.
[9] See the September 12, 2003 internal memo, *Service Center Issuance of Notice to Appear (Form I-862).*

PM-602-0050: Revised Guidance for the Referral of Cases and Issuance of NTAs in Cases
Involving Inadmissible and Removable Aliens
Page 3

be processed under existing protocols. If the VAWA applicant's Form I-485 is denied, this
memorandum is applicable in terms of NTA issuance.[10]

III. Fraud Cases with a Statement of Findings Substantiating Fraud

To protect the integrity of the immigration system and address fraud, USCIS will issue NTAs
when a Statement of Findings (SOF) substantiating fraud is part of the record.[11] An NTA
will be issued upon final adjudicative action on the petition and/or application or other
appropriate eligibility determination.[12] NTAs will be issued even if the petition and/or
application is denied for a ground other than fraud, such as lack of prosecution or
abandonment, is terminated based on a withdrawal by the petitioner/applicant, or where an
approval is revoked, so long as an SOF substantiating fraud is in the record.

The NTA should include the charge of fraud or misrepresentation, if possible. The
appropriate charge(s) will be determined on a case-by-case basis. Consultation with local
USCIS counsel to determine the appropriate charge(s) is recommended.

IV. Cases to be Referred to ICE for a Decision on NTA Issuance

A. Criminal Cases: Criminal aliens are a top immigration enforcement priority for the
government. The following guidance recognizes the prioritization and requires USCIS to
refer criminals to ICE for action or issue an NTA in accordance with this PM.

1. Egregious Public Safety (EPS) Cases

USCIS will refer all EPS cases, including cases with pending N-400s, to ICE
prior to adjudicating the case even if USCIS can deny the petition and/or
application on its merits. An EPS case is defined by USCIS and ICE as a case
where information indicates the alien is under investigation for, has been arrested
for (without disposition), or has been convicted of, any of the following:
a. Murder, rape, or sexual abuse of a minor as defined in
section 101(a)(43)(A) of the INA.
b. Illicit trafficking in firearms or destructive devices as defined in
section 101(a)(43)(C) of the INA.
c. Offenses relating to explosive materials or firearms as defined in
section 101(a)(43)(E) of the INA.

---

[10] When making determinations, employees must keep in mind USCIS's obligations under 8 USC § 1367, which
prohibits the release of any information, outside of DHS, relating to aliens who are seeking or have been approved
for immigration benefit(s) under the provisions for battered spouses, children, and parents in the Violence Against
Women Act.

[11] Alternatively, ICE will determine whether to issue the NTA if a criminal investigation is conducted, fraud is
found, and the investigation results in criminal prosecution.

[12] This includes, but is not limited to, aliens that were granted asylum status by USCIS, adjusted to Lawful
Permanent Resident status, presented fraud indicators, were subject to the Post Adjustment Eligibility Review
(PAER) process in an Asylum Office, and met the PAER criteria for NTA issuance.

PM-602-0050: Revised Guidance for the Referral of Cases and Issuance of NTAs in Cases Involving Inadmissible and Removable Aliens
Page 4

      d. Crimes of violence for which the term of imprisonment imposed, or where the penalty for a pending case, is at least one year as defined in section 101(a)(43)(F) of the INA.

      e. An offense relating to the demand for, or receipt of, ransom as defined in section 101(a)(43)(H) of the INA.

      f. An offense relating to child pornography as defined in section 101(a)(43)(I) of the INA.

      g. An offense relating to peonage, slavery, involuntary servitude, and trafficking in persons as defined in section 101(a)(43)(K)(iii) of the INA.

      h. An offense relating to alien smuggling as described in section 101(a)(43)(N) of the INA

      i. Human Rights Violators, known or suspected street gang members, or Interpol hits.

      j. Re-entry after an order of exclusion, deportation or removal subsequent to conviction for a felony where a Form I-212, Application for Permission to Reapply for Admission into the U.S. after Deportation or Removal, has not been approved.

All EPS cases must be referred to ICE using the procedures outlined below. The case will be referred as soon as it is identified. ICE will have an opportunity to decide if, when, and how to issue an NTA and/or detain the alien. USCIS will not issue an NTA in these cases if ICE declines to issue an NTA. If some other basis unrelated to the EPS concern becomes apparent during the course of adjudication, an NTA may be issued in accordance with this memo.

Referral Process

This referral process is utilized in order to give ICE the opportunity to determine the appropriate course of action before USCIS adjudicates the case. A decision to issue an NTA may directly affect the processing of the pending petition and/or application. Upon issuing the Referral to Immigration and Customs Enforcement (RTI), USCIS will suspend adjudication for 60 days, or until ICE provides notification of its action on the case, whichever is earlier.

In response to the RTI –

    1. ICE may issue an NTA. ICE's issuance of an NTA allows USCIS to proceed with adjudication (unless jurisdiction transfers to EOIR or the pending application is an N-400), taking into account the basis for the NTA.

    2. If ICE does not issue an NTA or otherwise provide notification of its action on the case within 60 days of the RTI, USCIS may resume its adjudication of the case, taking into account the referral grounds.

PM-602-0050: Revised Guidance for the Referral of Cases and Issuance of NTAs in Cases
Involving Inadmissible and Removable Aliens
Page 5

    a. If the case is approvable, USCIS will consult with ICE prior to
       adjudication.

    b. Once adjudicated, regardless of the decision, USCIS will notify
       ICE of the result by sending a copy of the original RTI to ICE with
       a cover memorandum advising of the outcome of the case.

EPS cases referred to ICE prior to adjudication should be called up and reviewed
no later than 60 days after referral. Normally, the case should be adjudicated by
USCIS. However, USCIS retains discretion to place the case on hold for more
than 60 days if ICE requests additional time to conduct an investigation.[13]

Office-Specific Processes

1. Cases to be adjudicated by Service Centers and the National Benefits
   Center. Adjudication will be suspended and the case will immediately be
   sent to the appropriate Service Center Background Check Unit (BCU).
   The BCU will refer the case to the ICE Benefit Fraud Unit (BFU) via an
   RTI. A hard copy of the RTI will be placed in the A-file and/or receipt
   file. The BCU will retain the file unless ICE requests it or the 60 days
   expire.

2. Cases to be adjudicated by Field Offices. The Immigration Services
   Officer (ISO) will suspend adjudication and the case will immediately be
   referred to the local ICE Special Agent in Charge (SAC) via an RTI. A
   hard copy of the RTI will be placed in the A-file and/or receipt file. A
   copy of the RTI must also be sent to the ICE BFU. USCIS will retain the
   file unless ICE requests the file for their review.

An RTI should include any relevant attachments that USCIS has at the time, such
as a copy of the RAP sheet and a copy of the petition and/or application.

2. Non-Egregious Public Safety Criminal Cases

If it appears that the alien is inadmissible or removable for a criminal offense not
included on the EPS list, USCIS will complete the adjudication and then refer the
case to ICE. This section applies to N-400 cases if the N-400 has been denied on
good moral character (GMC) grounds based on the criminal offense.[14] ICE will
decide if, and how, it will institute removal proceedings and whether or not it will
detain the alien. USCIS will not issue an NTA if ICE declines to issue an NTA.

---

[13] Pursuant to 8 CFR 274a.13(d), USCIS must complete processing of an Employment Authorization Document
(EAD) within 90 days or issue an interim EAD card valid up to 240 days. Officers should be mindful of this
regulatory timeframe when cases with a pending Form I-765, Application for Employment Authorization, are
referred to ICE.

[14] See Section V of this memo addressing N-400 cases.

PM-602-0050: Revised Guidance for the Referral of Cases and Issuance of NTAs in Cases
Involving Inadmissible and Removable Aliens
Page 6

If some other basis unrelated to the criminal offense becomes apparent upon
return of the case to USCIS, an NTA may be issued in accordance with this
memo.

Referral Process

The referral process is used to allow ICE to make a determination whether to
issue an NTA, based on the totality of circumstances and its priorities. ICE will
determine the appropriate grounds for removal if an NTA is issued.

Once adjudication is complete, USCIS will send an RTI to ICE. USCIS will
concurrently transmit a copy of the RTI to ICE Headquarters (HQ) Enforcement
and Removal Operations (ERO) Criminal Alien Division for statistical monitoring
purposes. If there is any confusion or uncertainty about classifying a case as
egregious versus non-egregious, the USCIS ISO should refer the matter as an EPS
case using the process described above.

The accompanying A-file will be referred to ICE with the RTI, if the file is in the
possession of the referring USCIS office or center. If the file is not at the
referring USCIS office or center, the RTI should include any relevant attachments
that USCIS has, such as a copy of the RAP sheet and a copy of the petition and/or
application. Where USCIS obtained certified conviction records through normal
processing of the case, USCIS will include the records with the RTI, but it will
not hold the RTI on a completed case solely to obtain disposition records. Instead
ICE will decide whether, and how, it will obtain such records as part of its
decision to issue an NTA.

Office-Specific Processes

1. Cases adjudicated by Service Centers and the National Benefits Center.
    Once adjudication is completed, if the alien is removable on a criminal
    charge, regardless of the reason for the denial, the file will be referred to
    the BCU. The BCU will refer the case, along with the A-file and/or receipt
    file, to the appropriate ERO Field Office Director (FOD) via an RTI.

2. Cases adjudicated by Field Offices. Once adjudication is completed, if the
    alien is removable on a criminal charge, regardless of the reason for the
    denial, USCIS will prepare an RTI and refer the case, along with the
    A-file and/or receipt file, to the local ERO FOD.

B. National Security Entry Exit Registration System (NSEERS) Violator Cases

USCIS will refer all cases in which an application is denied based on an NSEERS
violation to ICE for possible NTA issuance.

PM-602-0050: Revised Guidance for the Referral of Cases and Issuance of NTAs in Cases
Involving Inadmissible and Removable Aliens
Page 7

V. Cases Involving Form N-400, Application for Naturalization

The following guidance applies to the issuance of NTAs in cases in which applicants for
naturalization are removable. There are two primary situations in which NTAs may be
issued in connection with a filed Form N-400. If the N-400 case involves fraud (documented
in the SOF) the procedures found in this section must be followed, rather than the procedures
found in Section III (Fraud Cases with a Statement of Findings Substantiating Fraud).
However, the below guidance does not apply to EPS cases. EPS cases must be referred in
accordance with Section IV.A.1 (Egregious Public Safety Cases) of this memo.
Additionally, the below guidance does not apply to non-EPS criminal cases when the N-400
can be denied on GMC grounds based on the criminal act. These cases must be denied and
referred in accordance with Section IV.A.2 (Non-Egregious Public Safety Criminal Cases).

A. The first situation occurs when the applicant may be eligible to naturalize but is also
   deportable under section 237 of the INA. Examples include applicants convicted of
   aggravated felonies prior to November 29, 1990, or applicants convicted of deportable
   offenses after obtaining Lawful Permanent Resident (LPR) status that do not fall within
   the GMC period. The ISO should:

   1. Make a written recommendation on the issuance of an NTA through a review of
      the totality of the circumstances to include factors such as: severity of crime, time
      since crime committed, other criminal conduct, reformation, immigration history
      including method of entry, length of presence in the U.S., and prior immigration
      violations, and contributions to society to include the pursuit of education and
      military service.[15]

   2. Once the ISO has made a recommendation on whether or not to issue an NTA, the
      case should be forwarded to the N-400 NTA Review Panel (Review Panel), along
      with the written recommendation. A Review Panel must be formed in each Field
      Office and include a local Supervisory Immigration Services Officer (SISO), a
      local USCIS Office of Chief Counsel attorney, and a district representative. An
      attorney from ICE's local Office of Chief Counsel will be invited to participate
      and will have an advisory role on the panel. The Review Panel will make the
      final determination on NTA issuance. If consensus cannot be reached by the
      Review Panel, the case will be elevated to the District Director, through the
      district representative, for a final decision.

   3. If the Review Panel decides to issue an NTA, place the N-400 on hold until
      removal proceedings have concluded. Once proceedings have concluded, or if the
      Review Panel declines to issue an NTA, adjudicate the case appropriately.

---

[15] Additional factors to be taken under consideration can be found in the June 17, 2011 ICE memo, *Exercising
Prosecutorial Discretion Consistent with the Civil Immigration Enforcement Priorities of the Agency for the
Apprehension, Detention, and Removal of Aliens.*

PM-602-0050: Revised Guidance for the Referral of Cases and Issuance of NTAs in Cases Involving Inadmissible and Removable Aliens
Page 8

B. The second situation occurs when it is determined that the applicant was inadmissible at the time of adjustment or admission to the United States, thus deportable under section 237 of the INA and not eligible for naturalization under section 318 of the INA.[16] The ISO should:

1. Make a written recommendation on the issuance of an NTA through a review of the totality of the circumstances to include factors such as: willfulness of actions, fraud factors, length of LPR status, criminal history, and officer error at time of adjustment.

2. Once the ISO has made a recommendation on the issuance of the NTA, the case should be forwarded to the Review Panel (see Section V.A.2), along with the written recommendation. The Review Panel will make the final determination on NTA issuance. If consensus cannot be reached by the Review Panel, the case will be elevated to the District Director, through the district representative, for a final decision.

3. If the Review Panel decides to issue an NTA, place the N-400 on hold until removal proceedings have concluded. Once removal proceedings have concluded, adjudicate the case appropriately. If the Review Panel declines to issue an NTA, deny the case under section 318 of the INA.

VI. <u>Other Cases</u>

A. An alien may request NTA issuance to renew an application for adjustment or in certain cases with a denied N-400. The request must be made in writing.[17]

B. An asylum applicant issued an NTA may request NTA issuance for family members not included on the asylum application as dependents for family unification purposes. The request must be made in writing.[18]

VII. <u>Exceptions</u>

Exceptions to the guidance in this PM require concurrence from Regional or Center Directors, who will consult with ICE before issuing an NTA.

---

[16] In the Third Circuit *only* (Pennsylvania, New Jersey, Delaware, and the U.S. Virgin Islands), based on the holding in *Garcia v. Att'y Gen.*, 553 F.3d 724 (3d Cir. 2009), if the alien has been an LPR for at least five years, the alien cannot be placed in removal proceedings for fraud or willful misrepresentation of a material fact at time of adjustment, if USCIS could have learned of the fraud or misrepresentation through reasonable diligence before the five year rescission period expired. Please consult with USCIS counsel if there are questions regarding the applicability of this precedent.

[17] USCIS retains discretion to deny a request. USCIS should consider ICE actions and determinations when making an NTA issuance decision under this section.

[18] USCIS retains discretion to deny a request.

PM-602-0050: Revised Guidance for the Referral of Cases and Issuance of NTAs in Cases
Involving Inadmissible and Removable Aliens
Page 9

VIII. Coordination with ICE

According to the June 2011 ICE memo regarding the exercise of prosecutorial discretion
consistent with priorities,[19] USCIS will receive notice before an ICE attorney exercises
prosecutorial discretion and dismisses, suspends, or closes a case. The local N-400 NTA
Review Panel will work with ICE to come to a resolution if USCIS does not agree with
ICE's use of prosecutorial discretion in a particular case. If concurrence cannot be reached,
the case should be elevated to the USCIS Office of Chief Counsel in headquarters.

Implementation

Each field office must form an N-400 NTA Review Panel and create a process to complete RTIs
and refer EPS and non-EPS criminal cases to ICE. A written list enumerating the members of
the Review Panel and a document outlining the process of referral must be sent to the appropriate
district office within 30 days of the issuance of this memorandum.

Use

This PM is intended solely for the guidance of USCIS personnel in the performance of their
official duties. It is not intended to, does not, and may not be relied upon to create any right or
benefit, substantive or procedural, enforceable at law, or by any individual or other party in
removal proceedings, in litigation with the United States, or in any other form or manner.

Contact Information

Questions or suggestions regarding this PM should be addressed through appropriate channels to
the Field Operations Directorate, Service Center Operations Directorate, or the Refugee,
Asylum, and International Operations Directorate.

---

[19] *Exercising Prosecutorial Discretion Consistent with the Civil Immigration Enforcement Priorities of the Agency
for the Apprehension, Detention, and Removal of Aliens,* signed June 17, 2011.

APPENDIX 8-6

I-131 Application for Reentry Permit

OMB No. 1615-0013; Expires 03/31/2012

Department of Homeland Security
U.S. Citizenship and Immigration Services

Instructions for Form I-131,
Application for Travel Document

Instructions

Read these instructions carefully to properly complete this form. If you need more space to complete an answer, use a separate sheet of paper. Write your name and Alien Registration Number (A-Number), if any, at the top of each sheet of paper and indicate the part and number of the item to which the answer refers.

Updated Filing Address Information

The filing addresses provided on this form reflect the most current information as of the date this form was last printed. If you are filing Form I-131 more than 30 days after the latest edition date shown in the lower right corner, visit our Web site at **www.uscis.gov** before you file, and check the "FORMS" page to confirm the correct filing address and version currently in use. Check the edition date located in the lower right-hand corner of the form. If the edition date on your Form I-131 matches the edition date listed for Form I-131 on the online "FORMS" page, your version is current and will be accepted by USCIS. If the edition date on the online version is later, download a copy and use the online version. If you do not have Internet access, call the National Customer Service Center at **1-800-375-5283** to verify the current filing address and edition date. **Improperly filed forms will be rejected and the fee returned with instructions to resubmit the entire filing using the current form instructions.**

What Is the Purpose of This Form?

This form is for applying to U.S. Citizenship and Immigration Services (USCIS) for the following travel documents, and can not be used to request release from immigration custody:

1. Reentry Permit

A reentry permit allows a permanent resident or conditional resident to apply for admission to the United States upon returning from abroad during the permit's validity without the need to obtain a returning resident visa from a U.S. Embassy or consulate.

2. Refugee Travel Document

A refugee travel document is issued to a person classified as a refugee or asylee, or to a permanent resident who obtained such status as a refugee or asylee in the United States. Persons who hold asylee or refugee status and are not permanent residents must have a refugee travel document to return to the United States after temporary travel abroad.

3. Advance Parole Document

An advance parole document is issued solely to authorize the temporary parole of a person into the United States.

The document may be accepted by a transportation company in lieu of a visa as an authorization for the holder to travel to the United States. An advance parole document is not issued to serve in place of any required passport.

Advance parole is an extraordinary measure used sparingly to bring an otherwise inadmissible alien to the United States for a temporary period of time due to a compelling emergency. Advance parole cannot be used to circumvent the normal visa issuing procedures and is not a means to bypass delays in visa issuance.

NOTE: If you are in the United States and wish to travel abroad, you do not need to apply for advance parole if both conditions described below in **A** and **B** are met:

A. You are in one of the following nonimmigrant categories:

   1. An H-1, temporary worker, or H-4, spouse or child of an H-1; **or**

   2. An L-1, intracompany transferee, or L-2, spouse or child of an L-1; **or**

   3. A K-3, spouse, or K-4, child of a U.S. citizen; **or**

   4. A V-2, spouse, or V-3, child of a lawful permanent resident; **and**

B. Form I-485, Application to Register Permanent Residence or Adjust Status, was filed on your behalf and is pending with USCIS.

   However, upon returning to the United States, you must present your valid H, L, K, or V nonimmigrant visa and continue to remain eligible for that status.

Who May File Form I-131?

Each applicant must file a separate application for a travel document.

1. Reentry Permit

   A. *If you are in the United States* as a permanent resident or conditional permanent resident, you may apply for a reentry permit. After filing your application for a reentry permit, USCIS will inform you in writing when to go to your local Application Support Center (ASC) for your biometrics appointment. (See Biometrics Services Requirement.)

You must be physically present in the United States when you file the Reentry Permit application. However, a Reentry Permit may be sent to a U.S. Embassy or consulate or Department of Homeland Security (DHS) office abroad for you to pick up, if you request it when you file your application.

Departure from the United States before a decision is made on an application for a Reentry Permit usually does not affect the application. **However, if biometric collection is required and the applicant departs the United States before the biometrics are collected, the application may be denied.**

With the exception of having to obtain a returning resident visa abroad, a Reentry Permit does not relieve you of any of the requirements of U.S. immigration laws.

If you stay outside the United States for less than 1 year, you are not required to apply for a Reentry Permit. You may reenter the United States on your Permanent Resident Card (Form I-551).

If you intend to apply in the future for naturalization, absences from the United States for 1 year or more will generally break the continuity of your required continuous residence in the United States. If you intend to remain outside the United States for 1 year or more, you should file Form N-470, Application to Preserve Residence for Naturalization Purposes. For further information, contact your local USCIS office.

B. Validity of Reentry Permit

1. Generally, a Reentry Permit issued to a permanent resident is valid for 2 years from the date of issuance. However, if you have been outside the United States for more than 4 of the last 5 years since becoming a permanent resident the permit will be limited to 1 year, except that a permit with a validity of 2 years may be issued to the following:

   a. A permanent resident whose travel is on the order of the U.S. Government, other than an exclusion, deportation, removal, or rescission order;

   b. A permanent resident employed by a public international organization of which the United States is a member by treaty or statute; or

   c. A permanent resident who is a professional athlete and regularly competes in the United States and worldwide.

2. A Reentry Permit issued to a conditional resident shall be valid for 2 years from the date of issuance, or to the date the conditional resident must apply for removal of the conditions on his or her status, whichever date comes first.

3. A Reentry Permit may not be extended.

C. A Reentry Permit may not be issued to you if:

1. You have already been issued such a document, and it is still valid, unless the prior document has been returned to USCIS, or you can demonstrate that it was lost; **or**

2. A notice was published in the Federal Register that precludes the issuance of such a document for travel to the area where you intend to go.

NOTICE to permanent or conditional residents who remain outside the United States for more than 1 year: If you do not obtain a Reentry Permit and remain outside the United States for 1 year or more, we may determine that you have abandoned your permanent or conditional resident status.

2. Refugee Travel Document

A. *If you are in the United States* in valid refugee or asylee status, or if you are a permanent resident as a direct result of your refugee or asylee status in the United States, you may apply for a Refugee Travel Document. Generally, you must have a Refugee Travel Document to return to the United States after temporary travel abroad. After filing your application for a Refugee Travel Document, USCIS will inform you in writing when to go to your local USCIS ASC for your biometrics appointment.

You should apply for a refugee travel document before you leave the United States. However, a Refugee Travel Document may be sent to a U.S. Embassy or consulate or DHS office abroad for you to pick up, if you request it when you file your application. Departure from the United States before a decision is made on the application for a Refugee Travel Document usually does not affect the application. **However, if biometric collection is required and the applicant departs the United States before the biometrics are collected, the application may be denied.**

B. *If you are outside of the United States* and:

1. have valid refugee or asylee status; or

2. you are a permanent resident as a direct result of your refugee or asylee status in the United States, you may be permitted to file Form I-131 and apply for a Refugee Travel Document. The USCIS Overseas District Director with jurisdiction over your location makes this decision.

Applicants should only seek to file a Form I-131 application for a Refugee Travel Document if they are able to demonstrate that an emergent situation led them to depart the United States without first seeking the appropriate travel documents.

Travel Warning Regarding Voluntary Re-availment

WARNING to asylees who travel to the country of claimed persecution:

If you applied for asylum on or after April 1, 1997, your asylum status may be terminated if the Government determines that you have voluntarily availed yourself of the protection of your country of claimed persecution. See section 208(c)(2)(D) of the Immigration and Nationality Act, 8 U.S.C. 1158(c)(2)(D).

C. Validity of Refugee Travel Document

  1. A Refugee Travel Document is valid for 1 year.

  2. A Refugee Travel Document may not be extended.

D. A Refugee Travel Document may not be issued to you if:

  1. You have already been issued such a document and it is still valid, unless the prior document has been returned to USCIS, or you can demonstrate that it was lost; or

  2. A notice was published in the Federal Register that precludes the issuance of such a document for travel to the area where you intend to go.

  NOTICE to permanent residents who obtain permanent residence as a result of their refugee or asylee status: If you do not obtain a Reentry Permit and remain outside the United States for 1 year or more, we may determine that you have abandoned your permanent resident status.

3. Advance Parole Document

A. Travel Warning Regarding Unlawful Presence

Before you apply for an Advance Parole Document, read the following travel warning carefully:

  1. If you have been unlawfully present in the United States for more than 180 days but less than 1 year, and you leave before removal proceedings are started against you, you may be inadmissible for 3 years from the date of departure.

  2. If you have been unlawfully present in the United States for 1 year or more, you may be inadmissible for 10 years from the date of departure regardless of whether you left before, during, or after removal proceedings.

  3. Unlawful presence is defined as being in the United States without having been inspected and admitted or paroled, or after the period of authorized stay has expired.

  4. However, certain immigration benefits and time spent in the United States while certain applications are pending may place you in a period of authorized stay. These include, but are not limited to, a properly filed Form I-485, Temporary Protected Status (TPS), deferred enforced departure (DED), asylum, and withholding of removal.

  5. Although advance parole may allow you to return to the United States, your departure may trigger the 3 or 10-year bar, if you accrued more than 180 days of unlawful presence **BEFORE** the date you were considered to be in a period of authorized stay.

  6. Therefore, if you apply for adjustment of status after you return to the United States, continue with Form I-485 that was pending before you left, or return to a status that requires you to establish that you are not inadmissible, you will need to apply for and receive a waiver of inadmissibility before your Form I-485 may be approved or your status continued.

  7. Generally, only persons who can establish extreme hardship to their U.S. citizen or lawful permanent resident spouse or parent may apply for the waiver for humanitarian reasons, to assure family unity or when it is otherwise in the public interest. (See sections 209(c), 212(a)(9), and 244(c) of the Immigration and Nationality Act for more information on unlawful presence and the available waivers.)

B. If you are outside the United States and need to visit the United States temporarily for emergent humanitarian reasons:

  1. You may apply for an Advance Parole Document. However, your application must be based on the fact that you cannot obtain the necessary visa and any required waiver of inadmissibility. Parole under these conditions is granted on a case-by-case basis for temporary entry, according to conditions as prescribed.

  2. A person in the United States may file this application on your behalf. In so doing, he or she must complete **Part 1** of the form with information about him or herself.

C. If you are in the United States and seek advance parole:

  1. You may apply if Form I-485 is pending, and you seek to travel abroad for emergent personal or bona fide business reasons; **or**

  2. You may apply if you have a pending application for Temporary Protected Status (Form I-821), or have been granted Temporary Protected Status, or have been granted another immigration status that allows you to return to that status after a brief, casual, and innocent absence (as defined in 8 CFR 244.1) from the United States.

D. An Advance Parole document may not be issued to you if:

1. You held J-1 nonimmigrant status and are subject to the 2-year foreign residence requirement as a result of that status; or

2. You are in exclusion, deportation, removal, or rescission proceedings.

E. If you travel before the advance parole document is issued, your application will be considered abandoned if:

1. You depart the United States; or

2. The person seeking advance parole attempts to enter the United States before a decision is made on the application.

Note: Do not use this form if you are seeking release from immigration custody and you want to remain in the United States as a parolee. You should contact U.S. Immigration and Customs Enforcement (ICE) about your request.

General Instructions

Step 1. Fill Out Form I-131

1. Type or print legibly in black ink.

2. If extra space is needed to complete any item, attach a continuation sheet, indicate the item number, and date and sign each sheet.

3. Answer all questions fully and accurately. State that an item is not applicable with "N/A." If the answer is none, write "None."

Step 2. General Requirements

1. Initial Evidence

We may request additional information or evidence, or we may request that you appear at a USCIS office for an interview or for fingerprinting (See "Biometric Services Requirement"). You must file your application with all required evidence. Not submitting required evidence will delay the issuance of the document you are requesting.

All applications must include a **copy of an official photo identity document showing your photo, name, and date of birth.** (Example: a valid government-issued driver's license; passport identity page; Form I-551, Permanent Resident Card; or any other official identity document.) The copy must **clearly** show the photo and identity information. **Form I-94, Arrival-Departure Document, is not acceptable as a photo identity document.**

If you are applying for:

A. Reentry Permit

You **must** attach:

1. A copy of the front and back of your Form I-551; or

2. If you have not yet received your Form I-551, a copy of the biographic page(s) of your passport and a copy of the visa page showing your initial admission as a permanent resident, or other evidence that you are a permanent resident; or

3. A copy of the Form I-797, Notice of Action, approval notice of an application for replacement of your Form I-551 or temporary evidence of permanent resident status.

B. Refugee Travel Document

You **must** attach a copy of the document issued to you by USCIS showing your refugee or asylee status and the expiration date of such status.

C. Advance Parole Document

1. *If you are in the United States,* you **must** attach:

   a. A copy of any document issued to you by USCIS showing your present status in the United States; and

   b. An explanation or other evidence showing the circumstances that warrant issuance of an Advance Parole Document; or

   c. If you are an applicant for adjustment of status, a copy of a USCIS receipt as evidence that you filed the adjustment application; or

   d. If you are traveling to Canada to apply for an immigrant visa, a copy of the U.S. consular appointment letter; or

   e. If you are the surviving spouse of a U.S. citizen who died before the second anniversary of your marriage, or you are the qualified child of a surviving spouse, and you have been granted deferred action (or included in your parent's deferred action grant letter), you must file Form I-131 with a copy of the order, notice, or document placing you in deferred action. If you are a qualified child and you are requesting advance parole, you must submit a separate application.

2. *If you are applying for a person who is outside the United States,* you **must** attach:

   a. A statement of how and by whom medical care, transportation, housing, and other expenses and subsistence needs will be met; and

   b. An Affidavit of Support (Form I-134), with evidence of the sponsor's occupation and ability to provide necessary support; and

   c. A statement explaining why a U.S. visa cannot be obtained, including when and where attempts were made to obtain a visa; and

   d. A statement explaining why a waiver of inadmissibility cannot be obtained to allow issuance of a visa, including when and where attempts were made to obtain a waiver, and a copy of any DHS decision on your waiver request; and

   e. A copy of any decision on an immigrant petition filed for the person, and evidence regarding any pending immigrant petition; and

   f. A complete description of the emergent reasons explaining why advance parole should be authorized and including copies of any evidence you wish considered, and indicating the length of time for which the parole is requested; and

   g. Two completed fingerprint cards (FD-258). You must indicate your Alien Registration Number (A-Number) on the fingerprint card and ensure that the completed cards are not bent, folded, or creased. The fingerprint cards must be prepared by a U.S. Embassy or consulate, USCIS office, or U.S. military installation.

2. Photographs

   A. *If you are outside the United States and filing for a Refugee Travel Document, or if you are in the United States and filing for Advance Parole Document:*

   You **must** submit two identical color photographs of yourself taken within 30 days of the filing of this application.

   The photos must have a white to off-white background, be printed on thin paper with a glossy finish, and be unmounted and unretouched.

   NOTE: Because of the current USCIS scanning process, if a digital photo is submitted, it needs to be produced from a high-resolution camera that has at least 3.5 mega pixels of resolution.

Passport-style photos must be 2" x 2." The photos must be in color with full face, frontal view on a white to off-white background. Head height should measure 1" to 1 3/8" from top of hair to bottom of chin, and eye height is between 1 1/8" to 1 3/8" from bottom of photo. Your head must be bare unless you are wearing a headdress as required by a religious order of which you are a member. Using pencil or felt pen, lightly print your name and A-Number on the back of the photo.

   B. If the person seeking advance parole is outside the United States:

   1. If you are applying for an Advance Parole Document, and you are outside the United States, do not submit the photographs with your application. Prior to issuing the parole document, the U.S. Embassy or consulate or DHS office abroad will provide you with information regarding the photograph requirements.

   2. If you are filing this application for an Advance Parole Document for another person, submit the required photographs of the person to be paroled.

3. Biometrics Services Requirement

If you are between age 14 through 79 and you are applying for a Refugee Travel Document or Reentry Permit, you must be fingerprinted as part of USCIS biometrics services requirements. After you have filed this application, USCIS will notify you in writing of the time and location where you must go to be fingerprinted. If necessary, USCIS may also take your photograph and signature. Failure to appear to be fingerprinted or for other biometrics services may result in a denial of your application. All applicants for Reentry Permit and/or Refugee Travel Documents between the ages of 14 through 79 are required to pay the additional **$85** biometric fee. (See "**What Is the Filing Fee?**" on **Page 8**).

Invalidation of Travel Document

Any travel document obtained by making a material false representation or concealment in this application will be invalid.

A travel document will also be invalid if you are ordered removed or deported from the United States.

In addition, a Refugee Travel Document will be invalid if the United Nations Convention of July 28, 1951, shall cease to apply or shall not apply to you as provided in Articles 1C, D, E, or F of the Convention.

Copies

Unless specifically required that an original document be filed with an application or petition, an legible photocopy may be submitted. Original documents submitted when not required may remain a part of the record, and will not automatically be returned to you.

Translations

Any document containing a foreign language submitted to USCIS shall be accompanied by a full English language translation, which the translator has certified as complete and accurate, and by the translator's certification that he or she is competent to translate from the foreign language into English.

Expedite Request Instructions

To request expedited processing of applications for Re-entry Permit or Refugee Travel Document, write the word EXPEDITE in the top right corner of the application in black ink. We recommend providing e-mail addresses and a fax number with any expedite request for the Re-entry Permit or Refugee Travel Document.

Where To File?

E-Filing Form I-131

Certain Form I-131 filings may be electronically filed (e-filed) with USCIS. View our Web site at **www.uscis.gov** for a list of who is eligible to e-file this form and instructions.

Paper Filing of Form I-131

Please note that the filing locations for the paper version of this form are subject to change. Read the instructions carefully to determine where you must send your paper application.

The filing addresses provided on this form reflect the most current information as of the date this form was last printed.

If you are filing for:

1. **Applicant covered under the Haitian Refugee Immigrant Fairness Act (HRIFA):**

    If you are either the dependent spouse or child of a HRIFA principal or a HRIFA principal who has Form I-485 pending; or

    If you are a dependent spouse or a dependent child of a principal HRIFA applicant and are seeking advance parole to enter the United States to file for adjustment of status or to enter the United States to file for adjustment of status as a permanent resident, then file your application at the **USCIS Dallas Lockbox facility**.

USCIS Dallas Lockbox

For U.S. Postal Service deliveries:
USCIS
PO Box 660866
Dallas, TX 75266

For Express mail and commercial courier deliveries:
USCIS
Attn: HRIFA
2501 S. State Hwy. 121, Business
Suite 400
Lewisville, TX 75067

2. **Battered Spouse/Children:**

    If you are filing as a battered or abused spouse or child and you are filing Form I-131 concurrently with Form I-485, or, if you are requesting advance parole, based on a pending Form I-485, file all forms with the **USCIS Vermont Service Center.**

3. **T non-immigrant visa status holders and U non-immigrant visa status holders:**

    If you are a T non-immigrant visa status holder or a U non-immigrant visa status holder, and you are filing your Form I-131 **together** with Form I-485, or you are filing your Form I-131 based on a **pending** Form I-485, file Form I-131 with the **USCIS Vermont Service Center**. Include a copy of the I-797C Notice of Action, showing that your I-485 was accepted.

USCIS Vermont Service Center

USCIS Vermont Service Center
ATTN: CRU
75 Lower Welden Street
St. Albans, VT 05479-0001

4. **Advance Parole under Temporary Protected Status (TPS):**

    If you are filing for advance parole, and are filing Form I-131 together with Form I-821, Application for Temporary Protected Status, follow the filing instructions for Form I-821.

    If you are filing Form I-131 by itself, based on a **pending or approved** Form I-821, file your Form I-131 with the **USCIS Dallas Lockbox** facility. Include a copy of the I-797C Notice of Action showing that your Form I-821 application was accepted or approved.

    For U.S. Postal Service deliveries:
    USCIS
    P.O. Box 660167
    Dallas, TX 75266

For Express mail and commercial courier deliveries:

USCIS
Attn: I-131 TPS
2501 S. State Hwy. 121 Business
Suite 400
Lewisville, TX 75067

5. Advance Parole Based on Pending I-485:

You may submit Form I-131 either alone or together with Form I-485. If you are filing Form I-131 together with Form I-485, file it according to the filing instructions for the Form I-485.

If your Form I-485 is **pending** and you are now filing Form I-131, review the I-797C Notice of Action you received in the mail for your Form I-485. If your application receipt number begins with MSC or does not have three letters at the beginning of the receipt number, file your Form I-131 application at the **USCIS Chicago Lockbox** facility.

If your I-797C Receipt number begins with EAC or SRC, file your Form I-131 at the **USCIS Dallas Lockbox** facility. **NOTE: Please note specific filing instructions on Page 6 for applicants filing as "Battered Spouse/children" and "T" and "U" non-immigrant visa status holders.**

If your I-797C Receipt number begins with LIN or WAC, file your Form I-131 at the **USCIS Phoenix Lockbox** facility. See chart.

NOTE: If you are filing Form I-131 based on a **pending** Form I-485, include a copy of the I-797C, Notice of Action, which shows your Form I-485 was accepted.

If the I-797C "Notice of Action" receipt number for acceptance of the primary petition or application begins with:	Then mail your application to:
MSC or does not have a 3–letter code at the beginning of the receipt number	**USCIS Chicago Lockbox** For U.S. Postal Service deliveries: USCIS P.O Box 805887 Chicago, IL 60680-4120 For Express mail and commercial courier deliveries: USCIS Attn: FBAS 131 S. Dearborn-3rd Floor Chicago, IL 60603-5517
EAC or SRC	**USCIS Dallas Lockbox** For U.S. Postal Service deliveries: USCIS PO Box 660867 Dallas, TX 75266

	For Express Mail and commercial courier deliveries: USCIS Attn: AOS 2501 S. State Hwy. 121, Business Suite 400 Lewisville, TX 75067

NOTE: Please see filing instructions on page 6 for applicants filing as "Battered Spouse/children," and "T" and "U" non-immigrant visa status holders.

LIN or WAC	**USCIS Phoenix Lockbox** For U.S. Postal Service deliveries: USCIS P.O. Box 21281 Phoenix, AZ 85036 For Express mail and commercial courier deliveries: USCIS Attn: AOS 1820 E. Skyharbor Circle S, Suite 100 Phoenix, AZ 85034

6. Humanitarian Parole (HP):

If you are a beneficiary outside the United States making the request on humanitarian grounds, of a Private Bill, or in removal proceedings (See Form I-131, Part 2. Application Type "e" or "f"), file your applications at the **USCIS Dallas Lockbox** facility:

USCIS Dallas Lockbox
For U.S. Postal Service deliveries:
USCIS
PO Box 660865
Dallas, TX 75266

For Express mail and commercial courier deliveries:
USCIS
Attn: HP
2501 S. State Hwy. 121, Business
Suite 400
Lewisville, TX 75067

If you are seeking to file a Form I-131 at an overseas Embassy or Consulate, you must appear in person at the Embassy or Consulate to request pre-authorization. If the Overseas District Director with jurisdiction over your location determines that you may file the Form I-131, you must file the application and pay the fee at the Embassy or Consulate, either in person or by mail. You will be required to appear at the Embassy or Consulate for biometrics collection as well.

If you are currently in removal proceedings or have been previously removed from the United States, you will need to submit your request to:

Department of Homeland Security
Immigration and Customs Enforcement
Office of International Affairs
Attn: Section Chief, Law Enforcement Parole Branch
800 N. Capitol Street
Washington, DC 20536

7. **All Other Form I-131 Filings, Including Re-entry Permits:**

If you are filing Form I-131 based on a category not previously mentioned, then file your Form I-131 with either the **USCIS Phoenix Lockbox or Dallas Lockbox facility**, based on where you live. See Chart below.

NOTE: If you have already filed Form I-485, include a copy of the I-797C, Notice of Action, which shows your Form I-485 was accepted.

If you live in :	File your application at the:
Alaska, Arizona, California, Colorado, Hawaii, Idaho, Illinois, Indiana, Iowa, Kansas, Michigan, Minnesota, Missouri, Montana, Nebraska, Nevada, North Dakota, Ohio, Oregon, South Dakota, Utah, Washington, Wisconsin, Wyoming, Guam or the Commonwealth of Northern Mariana Islands	**USCIS Phoenix Lockbox** For U.S. Postal Service deliveries: USCIS PO Box 21281 Phoenix, AZ 85036 For Express mail and commercial courier deliveries: USCIS Attn: AOS 1820 E. Skyharbor Circle S, Suite 100 Phoenix, AZ 85034
Alabama, Arkansas, Connecticut, Delaware, District of Columbia, Florida, Georgia, Kentucky, Louisiana, Maine, Maryland, Massachusetts, Mississippi, New Hampshire, New Jersey, New Mexico, New York, North Carolina, Pennsylvania, Puerto Rico, Rhode Island, South Carolina, Oklahoma, Tennessee, Texas, Vermont, Virginia, U.S. Virgin Islands, or West Virginia	**USCIS Dallas Lockbox** For U.S. Postal Service deliveries: USCIS PO Box 660867 Dallas, TX 75266 For Express mail and commercial courier deliveries: USCIS Attn: AOS 2501 S. State Hwy. 121, Business Suite 400 Lewisville, TX 75067

E-Notification

If you are filing your Form I-131 at one of the USCIS Lockbox facilities, you may elect to receive an e-mail and/or text message notifying you that your application has been accepted. You must complete Form G-1145, E-Notification of Application/Petition Acceptance, and clip it to the first page of your application. To download a copy of Form G-1145, including the instructions, click on the link www.uscis.gov "FORMS."

Questions Regarding Form I-131

For additional information about Form I-131, including how to file your application or filing locations not mentioned, call the USCIS National Customer Service Center at **1-800-375-5283** or visit our Web site at www.uscis.gov.

What Is the Filing Fee?

The fee for advance parole or a Reentry Permit is **$360**. The fee for a Refugee Travel Document for an applicant age 16 or older is **$135**, and for a child under the age of 16 years, it is $105. A biometric fee of **$85** is required for a Reentry Permit and a Refugee Travel Document for applicants ages 14 through 79.

No biometric fee is required for advance parole applicants.

The fee for a humanitarian based advance parole request may be waived based upon a demonstrated inability to pay. Biometric fees may also be waived based upon a demonstrated inability to pay. Applicants should consider using Form I-912, Fee Waiver Request, to ensure such requests are supported in accordance with 8 CFR 103.7(c).

The application fee and biometrics services fee may be paid with one check.

NOTE: If you filed Form I-485 on or after July 30, 2007, and you paid the I-485 application fee required, then no fee is required to file a request for Advance Parole or for a Refugee Travel Document on Form I-131. You may file Form I-131 for advance parole or for a Refugee Travel Document together with your Form I-485, or you may submit Form I-131 for Advance Parole or a Refugee Travel Document at a later date. If you file Form I-131 for Advance Parole or a Refugee Travel Document separately, you must also submit a copy of your Form I-797, Notice of Action, receipt as evidence that you filed and paid the fee for Form I-485 required on or after July 30, 2007.

Use the following guidelines when you prepare your check or money order for the Form I-131 fee:

1. The check or money order must be drawn on a bank or other financial institution located in the United States and must be payable in U.S. currency; and

2. Make the check or money order payable to **U.S. Department of Homeland Security**.

   NOTE: Spell out U.S. Department of Homeland Security; do not use the initials "USDHS" or "DHS."

Notice to Those Making Payment by Check. If you send us a check, it will be converted into an electronic funds transfer (EFT). This means we will copy your check and use the account information on it to electronically debit your account for the amount of the check. The debit from your account will usually take 24 hours and will be shown on your regular account statement.

You will not receive your original check back. We will destroy your original check, but we will keep a copy of it. If the EFT cannot be processed for technical reasons, you authorize us to process the copy in place of your original check. If the EFT cannot be completed because of insufficient funds, we may try to make the transfer up to two times.

How to Check If the Fees Are Correct

The fees on this form are current as of the edition date appearing in the lower right corner of this page. However, because USCIS fees change periodically, you can verify if the fees are correct by following one of the steps below:

1. Visit our Web site at **www.uscis.gov**, select "FORMS," and check the appropriate fee; or

2. Telephone our National Customer Service Center at **1-800-375-5283** and ask for the fee information.

Address Changes

If you have changed your address, you must inform USCIS of your new address. For information on filing a change of address go to the USCIS Web site at **www.uscis.gov/ addresschange** or contact the National Customer Service Center at **1-800-375-5283**.

NOTE: Do not submit a change of address request to the USCIS Lockbox facilities because the USCIS Lockbox facilities do not process change of address requests.

Processing Information

Any Form I-131 that is not signed or accompanied by the correct fee(s) will be rejected with a notice that Form I-131 is deficient. You may correct the deficiency and resubmit Form I-131. An application or petition is not considered properly filed until accepted by USCIS.

Initial Processing

Once a Form I-131 has been accepted, it will be checked for completeness, including submission of the required initial evidence. If you do not completely fill out the form, or file it without required initial evidence, you will not establish a basis for eligibility, and we may deny your Form I-131.

Requests for More Information or Interview

We may request more information or evidence, or we may request that you appear at a USCIS office for an interview. We may also request that you submit the originals of any copy. We will return these originals when they are no longer required.

Decision

The decision on Form I-131 involves a determination of whether you have established eligibility for the requested benefit. You will be notified of the decision in writing.

What If You Claim Nonresident Alien Status on Your Federal Income Tax Return?

If you are an alien who has established residence in the United States after having been admitted as an immigrant or adjusted status to that of an immigrant, and are considering the filing of a nonresident alien tax return or the non-filing of a tax return on the ground that you are a nonresident alien, you should carefully review the consequences of such actions under the Immigration and Nationality Act.

If you file a nonresident alien tax return or fail to file a tax return, you may be regarded as having abandoned residence in the United States and as having lost your permanent resident status under the Act. As a consequence, you may be ineligible for a visa or other document for which permanent resident aliens are eligible.

You may also be inadmissible to the United States if you seek admission as a returning resident, and you may become ineligible for adjustment of status as a permanent resident, or naturalization on the basis of your original entry.

USCIS Forms and Information

You can get USCIS forms and immigration-related information on the USCIS Web site at **www.uscis.gov**. You may order USCIS forms by calling our toll-free number at **1-800-870-3676**. You may also obtain forms and information by telephoning our USCIS National Customer Service Center at **1-800-375-5283**.

As an alternative to waiting in line for assistance at your local USCIS office, you can now schedule an appointment through the USCIS Internet-based system, **InfoPass**. To access the system, visit USCIS Web site. Use the **InfoPass** appointment scheduler and follow the screen prompts to set up your appointment. **InfoPass** generates an electronic appointment notice that appears on the screen.

Penalties

If you knowingly and willfully falsify or conceal a material fact or submit a false document with Form I-131, we will deny Form I-131 and may deny any other immigration benefit.

In addition, you will face severe penalties provided by law and may be subject to criminal prosecution.

USCIS Privacy Act Statement

AUTHORITIES: The information requested on this form, and the associated evidence, is collected under the Immigration and Nationality Act, section 101, et seq.

PURPOSE: The primary purpose for providing the requested information on this form is to determine if you have established eligibility for the immigration benefit for which you are filing. The information you provide will be used to grant or deny the benefit sought.

DISCLOSURE: The information you provide is voluntary. However, failure to provide the requested information, and any requested evidence, may delay a final decision or result in denial of your Form I 131.

ROUTINE USES: The information you provide on this form may be shared with other Federal, State, local, and foreign government agencies and authorized organizations following approved routine uses described in the associated published system of records notices [DHS-USCIS-007 - Benefits Information System and DHS-USCIS-001 - Alien File, Index, and National File Tracking System of Records, which can be found at **www.dhs.gov/privacy**]. The information may also be made available, as appropriate, for law enforcement purposes or in the interest of national security.

Paperwork Reduction Act

An agency may not conduct or sponsor an information collection and a person is not required to respond to a collection of information unless it displays a currently valid OMB control number. The public reporting burden for this collection of information is estimated at 1 hour and 55 minutes per response, including the time for reviewing instructions, and completing and submitting the form. Send comments regarding this burden estimate or any other aspect of this collection of information, including suggestions for reducing this burden, to: U.S. Citizenship and Immigration Services, Regulatory Products Division, Office of the Executive Secretariat, 20 Massachusetts Ave., N.W., Washington, DC 20529-2020. OMB No. 1615-0013. This form expires March 31, 2012. **Do not mail your application to this address.**

FORM I-131

OMB No. 1615-0013; Expires 03/31/2012

Department of Homeland Security
U. S. Citizenship and Immigration Services

I-131, Application for Travel Document

DO NOT WRITE IN THIS BLOCK		FOR USCIS USE ONLY *(except G-28 block below)*
Document Issued	**Action Block**	**Receipt**
☐ Reentry Permit		
☐ Refugee Travel Document		
☐ Single Advance Parole		
☐ Multiple Advance Parole		
Valid to: _____		☐ Document Hand Delivered
If Reentry Permit or Refugee Travel Document, mail to:		On _____ By _____
☐ Address in Part 1		***To be completed by Attorney/Representative, if any.***
☐ U.S. Embassy/consulate at: _____		Attorney State License # _____
☐ Overseas DHS office at: _____		☐ Check box if G-28 is attached.

Part 1.   Information About You *(Type or print in black ink)*

1. A Number

2. Date of Birth *(mm/dd/yyyy)*

3. Class of Admission

4. Gender   ☐ Male ☐ Female

5. Name *(Family name in capital letters)*   *(First)*   *(Middle)*

6. Address *(Number and Street)*   Apt. Number

City   State or Province   Zip/Postal Code   Country

7. Country of Birth

8. Country of Citizenship

9. Social Security # *(if any)*

Part 2.   Application Type *(Check one)*

a. ☐ I am a permanent resident or conditional resident of the United States, and I am applying for a reentry permit.

b. ☐ I now hold U.S. refugee or asylee status, and I am applying for a Refugee Travel Document.

c. ☐ I am a permanent resident as a direct result of refugee or asylee status, and I am applying for a Refugee Travel Document.

d. ☐ I am applying for an advance parole document to allow me to return to the United States after temporary foreign travel.

e. ☐ I am outside the United States, and I am applying for an Advance Parole Document.

f. ☐ I am applying for an Advance Parole Document for a person who is outside the United States. *If you checked box "f," provide the following information about that person:*

1. Name *(Family name in capital letters)*   *(First)*   *(Middle)*

2. Date of Birth *(mm/dd/yyyy)*   **3.** Country of Birth   **4.** Country of Citizenship

5. Address *(Number and Street)*   Apt. #   Daytime Telephone # *(area/country code)*

City   State or Province   Zip/Postal Code   Country

Form I-131 (11/05/11) Y

661

Part 3. Processing Information

1. Date of Intended Departure *(mm/dd/yyyy)*   **2.** Expected Length of Trip

3. Are you, or any person included in this application, now in exclusion, deportation, removal, or rescission proceedings?   ☐ Yes ☐ No   *(Name of DHS office)*:

If you are applying for an Advance Parole Document, skip to Part 7.

4. Have you ever before been issued a reentry permit or Refugee Travel Document?
☐ No ☐ Yes   *(If "Yes," give the following information for the last document issued to you)*:

Date Issued *(mm/dd/yyyy)*:   Disposition *(attached, lost, etc.)*:

5. Where do you want this travel document sent? *(Check one)*

a. ☐ To the U.S. address shown in **Part 1** on the first page of this form.

b. ☐ To a U.S. Embassy or consulate at: City: Country:

c. ☐ To a DHS office overseas at: City: Country:

d. If you checked "b" or "c," where should the notice to pick up the travel document be sent?

☐ To the address shown in **Part 2** on the first page of this form.
☐ To the address shown below:

Address *(Number and Street)*   Apt. #   Daytime Telephone # *(area/country code)*

City   State or Province   Zip/Postal Code   Country

Part 4. Information About Your Proposed Travel

Purpose of trip. *(If you need more room, continue on a separate sheet of paper.)*	List the countries you intend to visit.

Part 5. Complete Only If Applying for a Reentry Permit

Since becoming a permanent resident of the United States (or during the past five years, whichever is less) how much total time have you spent outside the United States?

☐ less than six months   ☐ two to three years
☐ six months to one year   ☐ three to four years
☐ one to two years   ☐ more than four years

Since you became a permanent resident of the United States, have you ever filed a Federal income tax return as a nonresident or failed to file a Federal income tax return because you considered yourself to be a nonresident? *(If "Yes," give details on a separate sheet of paper.)*   ☐ Yes   ☐ No

Part 6. Complete Only If Applying for a Refugee Travel Document

1. Country from which you are a refugee or asylee:

If you answer "Yes" to any of the following questions, you must explain on a separate sheet of paper.

2. Do you plan to travel to the country named above?   ☐ Yes   ☐ No

3. Since you were accorded refugee/asylee status, have you ever:
  a. Returned to the country named above?   ☐ Yes   ☐ No
  b. Applied for and/or obtained a national passport, passport renewal, or entry permit of that country?   ☐ Yes   ☐ No
  c. Applied for and/or received any benefit from such country (for example, health insurance benefits).   ☐ Yes   ☐ No

4. Since you were accorded refugee/asylee status, have you, by any legal procedure or voluntary act:
  a. Reacquired the nationality of the country named above?   ☐ Yes   ☐ No
  b. Acquired a new nationality?   ☐ Yes   ☐ No
  c. Been granted refugee or asylee status in any other country?   ☐ Yes   ☐ No

Part 7. Complete Only If Applying for Advance Parole

On a separate sheet of paper, explain how you qualify for an Advance Parole Document, and what circumstances warrant issuance of advance parole. Include copies of any documents you wish considered. *(See instructions.)*

1. How many trips do you intend to use this document?   ☐ One Trip   ☐ More than one trip

2. If the person intended to receive an Advance Parole Document is outside the United States, provide the location (city and country) of the U.S. Embassy or consulate or the DHS overseas office that you want us to notify.

City

Country

3. If the travel document will be delivered to an overseas office, where should the notice to pick up the document be sent?:

☐   To the address shown in **Part 2** on the first page of this form.

☐   To the address shown below:

Address *(Number and Street)*   Apt. #   Daytime Telephone # *(area/country code)*

City   State or Province   Zip/Postal Code   Country

Part 8. Signature   *Read the information on penalties in the instructions before completing this section. If you are filing for a reentry permit or Refugee Travel Document, you must be in the United States to file this application.*

I certify, under penalty of perjury under the laws of the United States of America, that this application and the evidence submitted with it are all true and correct. I authorize the release of any information from my records that U.S. Citizenship and Immigration Services needs to determine eligibility for the benefit I am seeking.

Signature   **Date** *(mm/dd/yyyy)*   **Daytime Telephone Number** *(with area code)*

Note: If you do not completely fill out this form or fail to submit required documents listed in the instructions, you may not be found eligible for the requested document and this application may be denied.

Part 9. Signature of Person Preparing Form, If Other Than the Applicant *(Sign below)*

I declare that I prepared this application at the request of the applicant, and it is based on all information of which I have knowledge.

Signature   Print or Type Your Name

Firm Name and Address   Daytime Telephone Number *(with area code)*

Fax Number *(if any)*   Date *(mm/dd/yyyy)*

Chapter 9

Naturalization Procedure: Application and Examination

I. INTRODUCTION

II. INITIAL APPLICATION

A. WHAT, WHERE AND WHEN TO FILE

B. WITHDRAWAL, AMENDMENT, AND TRANSFER OF APPLICATION

III. THE N-400

A. INTRODUCTION

B. QUESTION-BY-QUESTION ANALYSIS

Research References

West's Key Number Digest

Aliens, Immigration, and Citizenship ☜715 to 728

Treatises and Practice Aids

Dizon and Wettstein, Immigration Law Service 2d (IMMLS2D)
Fragomen, Shannon, and Montalvo, Immigration Procedures Handbook, Ch 22
Steel on Immigration Law §§ 15:19 to 15:22

> **KeyCite®:** Cases and other legal materials listed in KeyCite Scope can be researched through the KeyCite service on Westlaw®. Use KeyCite to check citations for form, parallel references, prior and later history, and comprehensive citator information, including citations to other decisions and secondary materials.

I. INTRODUCTION

§ 9:1 In general

Research References

Dizon and Wettstein, Immigration Law Service 2d (IMMLS2D)

Beginning with the first naturalization act in 1790 and continuing until 1990, the courts had exclusive jurisdiction to naturalize noncitizens.[1] In 1990, Congress radically changed the naturalization process by granting exclusive power to naturalize to the U.S. Attorney General.[2] The Attorney General, in turn, delegated this power to the legacy INS.[3] Under the Homeland Security Act, the power to naturalize has now been transferred to the Secretary of the Department of Homeland Security, who, in turn, has delegated it to the USCIS.[4] The courts retain a partial ceremonial role in administering the oaths of allegiance as well as a judicial review role.[5] The courts have been granted the option of exercising exclusive authority to administer oaths if they so choose.[6] Otherwise, the USCIS may administer even the oaths.[7]

The procedure described in this and the following chapters is the sole procedure to naturalize an individual.[8] Even when the person qualifies for naturalization under a special class, he or she will have to follow the procedures described in these chapters, unless specifically stated otherwise in the sections of law governing the naturalization of that specific class.[9]

[Section 9:1]

[1]See, e.g., sec. 1, Act of March 26, 1790, 1 Stat. 103 reproduced as Appendix 4-1 to Ch 4 ("on application to any court of common law"); sec. 1, Act of January 29, 1795, 1 Stat. 414 reproduced as Appendix 4-2 to Ch 4 ("before the supreme, superior, district or circuit court of the states, or the territories northwest or south of the river Ohio, or a circuit or district court of the United States"); sec. 1, Act of April 14, 1802, 2 Stat. 153 reproduced as Appendix 4-3 to Ch 4 (same); INA § 310, 8 U.S.C.A. § 1421 as originally enacted by Act of June 27, 1952, 66 Stat. 163. ("Exclusive jurisdiction to naturalize persons as citizens of the United States is conferred upon the following specified [federal] courts . . . [and] all courts of record in any state or territory . . . "). Congress has been found to have the power to delegate naturalization power to state courts. Holmgren v. U.S., 217 U.S. 509, 516–17, 30 S.Ct. 588, 589, 54 L.Ed. 861 (1910).

[2]INA § 310(a), 8 U.S.C.A. § 1421(a), as amended by sec. 401(a), Immigration Act of 1990 (IA90), Pub.L. No. 101-649, 104 Stat. 4978 (Nov. 29, 1990). Courts retained jurisdiction if the petition for naturalization had been filed with the court prior to the October 1, 1991. IA90 § 408(a)(1), (2).

[3]8 CFR § 310.1(a), (b).

[4]See § 1:9. Note, however, that the INA continues to invest sole power to naturalize in the Attorney General. *See* 8 U.S.C.A. § 1421(a).

[5]INA § 310(b), (c), 8 U.S.C.A. § 1421(b), (c).

[6]INA § 310(b)(1)(B), 8 U.S.C.A. § 1421(b)(1)(B).

[7]INA § 310(b)(1)(A), 8 U.S.C.A. § 1421(b)(1)(A); 8 CFR § 310.1.

[8]INA § 310(d), 8 U.S.C.A. § 1421(d).

[9]See §§ 11:1 et seq. and 12:1 et seq.

II. INITIAL APPLICATION

A. WHAT, WHERE AND WHEN TO FILE

§ 9:2 Where to file

A noncitizen begins the process of naturalization by filing a naturalization application (form N-400) with the USCIS. The application must be filed by mail, sent to an address determined by the applicant's residence. Although USCIS field offices will adjudicate the N-400 application, centralized lockbox facilities and service centers handle various aspects of the naturalization process and even schedule naturalization interviews.

For individuals residing in Alaska, Arizona, California, Colorado, Hawaii, Idaho, Illinois, Indiana, Iowa, Kansas, Michigan, Minnesota, Missouri, Montana, Nebraska, Nevada, North Dakota, Ohio, Oregon, South Dakota, Utah, Washington, Wisconsin, Wyoming, Territory of Guam, and the Northern Mariana Islands, applications are sent to the USCIS Phoenix Lockbox Facility at the following address:

USCIS

P.O. Box 21251

Phoenix, AZ 85036

For Express Mail or courier deliveries, the following address is used:

USCIS

Attn: N-400

1820 E. Skyharbor Circle S

Suite 100

Phoenix, AZ 85034

For individuals residing in Alabama, Arkansas, Connecticut, Delaware, District of Columbia, Florida, Georgia, Kentucky, Louisiana, Maine, Maryland, Massachusetts, Mississippi, New Hampshire, New Jersey, New Mexico, New York, North Carolina, Oklahoma, Pennsylvania, Rhode Island, South Carolina, Tennessee, Texas, Vermont, Virginia, West Virginia, Commonwealth of Puerto Rico, and the U.S. Virgin Islands, applications are sent to the USCIS Dallas Lockbox Facility at the following address:

USCIS

P.O. 660060

Dallas, TX 75266

For Express Mail or courier deliveries, the following address is used:

USCIS

Attn: N-400

2501 S State Hwy 121

Business

Suite 400

Lewisville, TX 75067

It should be noted that special instructions, including a different address for filing, apply to individuals eligible for special filing provisions such as members of the military and spouses of individuals stationed abroad.[1]

§ 9:3　When to file

Applicants subject to residence requirements may file the N-400 up to ninety days prior to the completion of the required period of continuous residence.[1] This period varies according to the naturalization class under which the applicant applies. For general naturalization applicants, the period is five years since admission to lawful permanent residence.[2] Special classes, such as qualifying spouses of U.S. citizens, have different periods of required residence.[3] Some applicants may be naturalized without being subject to any residence requirements.[4]

The date a person became a lawful permanent resident is reflected clearly on newer permanent residence cards ("alien" registration receipt card or green card). Older versions of Form I-551 have a code on the first line of numbers in the back of the card. This code is a six-digit number representing year, month, and day of the admission to permanent residence. Thus "900216" stands for February 16, 1990 as the date of admission to permanent residence.[5]

In some cases, the date on the LPR card is different from the date of approval of the adjustment of status application. Often, this is correct. For example, the date refugees and asylees obtained permanent resident status will almost always reflect a date prior to the actual grant of their adjustment application because the date of approval for these applicants is retroactive to either the date of entry (in the case of refugees) or one year prior to the date the status of lawful permanent resident was granted (asylees).[6] The Cuban Adjustment Act requires USCIS to record a date of adjustment that is backdated 30 months for individuals adjusted under that section, a provision intended to cut the naturalization wait in half.[7] Barring clerical error on the part of USCIS, the date of admission to permanent residence reflected on the green card should guide the decision of when to seek naturalization.

Before July 8, 1997, the INS was not screening applications at filing to ensure that the applicant had the required period of lawful permanent residence before filing.[8] In many cases, the premature filing was only discovered at the naturaliza-

---

[Section 9:2]

[1]See §§ 11:7 to 11:10, 12:3 to 12:12.

[Section 9:3]

[1]INA § 334(a), 8 U.S.C.A. § 1445(a); 8 CFR §§ 310.2, 334.2(b). The INA actually says that the application may be filed up to three months prior to the date the applicant would otherwise meet the residency requirements.

[2]See §§ 7:3 to 7:17.

[3]See §§ 11:1 et seq. and 12:1 et seq.

[4]See §§ 11:6 to 11:9.

[5]Still older versions of Form I-551 simply reflect the date of admission in standard fashion as month, day and year of admission. Thus in these cards, 10-25-83 would reflect that the person became a permanent resident on October 25, 1983.

[6]See § 7:11.

[7]Matter of Carrillo-Gutierrez, 16 I&N Dec. 429 (BIA 1977); see also, Matter of Carrillo, 25 I&N Dec. 99 (BIA 2009).

[8]Yates, Deputy Exec. Assoc. Comm'r, Field Operations, Memorandum, June 29, 1999.

tion interview. This caused great hardship to applicants in districts where interviews occurred many months after the filing. To ease this hardship, the INS issued a memorandum on June 29, 1999 instructing adjudicators to offer applicants the possibility of withdrawing the originally filed application and accepting a substitute N-400, waiving the filing fee.[9] To be eligible for the policy, the application must have been filed before the date of the memorandum (June 29, 1999), must have been unintentionally filed more than ninety days before the applicant met the continuous residence requirement, and on the date of the interview, the applicant must have met the continuous residence requirement.[10] The officer will then proceed to examine the applicant based on the new application and make a decision, provided the fingerprints are current and no new criminal information has been uncovered at the interview.[11] Consult the memorandum for the appropriate procedures.

Only persons 18 years old or older may file an application for naturalization.[12] This does not mean that children may not become citizens. The provision for establishing the citizenship of a child requires the filing of Form N-600 by the U.S. citizen parent.[13] Therefore, the person filing the application will presumably be 18 years of age or older. A U.S. citizen parent applies for a certificate of citizenship for her or his child by filing INS Form N-600 rather than the N-400.[14]

Not all children need to have their parents file an application with INS in order to become U.S. citizens. Some children become U.S. citizens automatically by deriving citizenship upon the naturalization of their parents.[15] In such cases, they only need evidence of their citizenship status, which can be in the form of a certificate of citizenship or a U.S. passport.[16]

§ 9:4 What to file; forms and documentation

The application is composed of: (1) Form N-400; (2) evidence of lawful permanent residence; and (3) two photographs.[1] Form N-400 is described in detail in the next section of this chapter.[2] The regulations allow the reproduction of INS forms through photocopying or other appropriate duplicating methods.[3] Forms reproduced in this

---

[9]Yates, Deputy Exec. Assoc. Comm'r, Field Operations, Memorandum, June 29, 1999.

[10]Yates, Deputy Exec. Assoc. Comm'r, Field Operations, Memorandum, June 29, 1999.

[11]Yates, Deputy Exec. Assoc. Comm'r, Field Operations, Memorandum, June 29, 1999.

[12]INA § 334(b), 8 U.S.C.A. § 1445(b).

[13]INA § 322(a), 8 U.S.C.A. § 1433(a). Even though INA § 322(a), 8 U.S.C.A. § 1433(a), is worded in terms of applications for certificate of citizenship, the parent in reality is applying for the naturalization of the child.

[14]See §§ 11:17 to 11:25.

[15]See §§ 5:1 et seq.

[16]See §§ 13:1 et seq.

[Section 9:4]

[1]Guide to Naturalization (requiring two photographs). See also 8 CFR § 316.4(a) (requiring three photographs).

[2]See The N-400.

[3]8 CFR § 299.4(a). Forms electronically generated, as opposed to reproduced, must be approved by the director of DHS' Record Systems Division. 8 CFR § 299.4(b)(3).

fashion may be used for filing with the USCIS.[4] The N-400 is available on the USCIS website: http://uscis.gov/graphics/index.htm.[5]

Applicants must sign their applications in their own handwriting, if physically capable of writing.[6] If the applicant is not physically capable of signing, the preparer of the form must sign in the space marked "Preparer's Signature."[7] Moreover, an opinion from the Office of Legal Counsel of the Department of Justice explains that the Rehabilitation Act of 1973 requires the agency to allow a legal guardian or proxy to assist a mentally disabled applicant who is unable to file the application or participate in the interview.[8] The memorandum concludes that an individual who is unable to file an application or participate in the interview may still be "otherwise qualified" for naturalization within the meaning of the Rehabilitation Act.[9]

In addition to the N-400, the applicant must include two identical photographs[10] and a copy of the permanent residence card ("alien" registration card).[11] These requirements are described below in the section dealing with document require- ments of the N-400.[12] People seeking exemption of the naturalization exam because of inability to comply are required to also file Form N-648.[13] This form and the procedures for claiming the exemption are discussed in detail elsewhere.[14]

Under old procedures, a biographic information form used to be required with the application. This is no longer the case as the relevant information has been included in the new Form N-400. For some time, some small suboffices continued requiring the filing of Form G-325 after the rest of the districts discontinued it. With the advent of direct mailing of the naturalization application, no office requires the fil- ing of the form any more.[15] Only people who have served in the U.S. armed forces are now required to file a biographical information form (Form G-325B) with their naturalization applications.[16]

Similarly, under old procedures, a fingerprint card used to be required for ap-

---

[4]See 8 CFR § 299.4(c). The reader should be aware that the forms reproduced in this handbook have been reduced a certain percentage to allow for the printing of the handbook's header and page number.

[5]The current version of the N-400, dated July 23, 2002, can be found in Appendix 9-1. The USCIS will also accept the N-400 dated May 31, 2001. It will no longer accept any version of the N-400 that is dated earlier than May 31, 2001.

[6]INA § 334(a), 8 U.S.C.A. § 1445(a), INS Interp. 312.1(a)(2)(ii).

[7]See App 9-1, N-400 Instructions, at 8. This was previously codified at 8 C.F.R. § 334.2(a), but the regulation now simply requires applicants to comply with the form instructions.

[8]See Appendix 9-7, "Role of Legal Guardians or Proxies in Naturalization Proceedings" (March 13, 2002).

[9]See Appendix 9-7, "Role of Legal Guardians or Proxies in Naturalization Proceedings" (March 13, 2002).

[10]Guide to Naturalization. 8 CFR § 333 (includes a description of specific size and format require- ments of the photographs).

[11]Form N-400, Instructions.

[12]See Additional Documents and Forms.

[13]8 CFR § 316.4 as amended by 63 Fed. Reg. 12979 (Mar. 17, 1998).

[14]See § 7:90.

[15]Memorandum, Office of Naturalization Operations, June 15, 1998 reproduced in 75 Interpreter Releases 959 (July 13, 1998).

[16]8 CFR § 334.2(a). Special naturalization procedures for members and former members of the U.S. armed forces are discussed in Ch 12.

plicants between the ages of 14 and 75.[17] Fingerprint cards are no longer required or accepted.[18] The USCIS will schedule for fingerprinting.[19]

§ 9:5   What to file; forms and documentation—Filing fees and fee waiver

The application must also include the correct fee.[1] The current fee for an application for naturalization is $595.[2] In addition to the N-400 filing fee, applicants under the age of 79 are required to pay for the fingerprinting process. For this purpose, an additional sum of $85, must be submitted to the USCIS at the time of the N-400 filing.[3] Failure to submit the additional fingerprint fee will result in eventual rejection of the application.[4] Thus, applicants (other than applicants over age 79) must pay $680 in total for the application.

The filing fees may be waived where the applicant can substantiate inability to pay the required fee.[5] The regulations provide that the officer in charge of rendering the decision on the application may grant the fee waiver.[6]

The Department of Homeland Security has issued a "Field Guidance" regarding fee waivers, which is reproduced as Appendix 9-12 to this chapter. The guidelines encourage adjudicators to look at the following criteria and situations indicating possible inability to pay: (1) whether the applicant has received federal means-tested assistance within the 180 days preceding the application; (2) whether the applicant has demonstrated that his or her household income, on which taxes were paid the most recent year, was at or below the poverty income guidelines; (3) whether an applicant is elderly, i.e. age 65 or over; (4) whether the applicant is disabled-the guidelines require proof of a determination of disability by Social Security Administration (SSA), Health and Human Services (HHS), Veterans' Administration (VA), Department of Defense (DOD), or other relevant federal agency; (5) the age and number of dependent family members of applicant's household who are seeking derivative or concurrently applying for status; (6) humanitarian or compassionate reasons, be they temporary or permanent, which may justify granting a waiver; (7) any other factors the adjudicator believes establish the applicant's inability to pay[7]

The USCIS requires an affidavit or statement submitted under penalty of perjury,[8] but may also request documentation to support the fee waiver request. This could include: (1) proof of living arrangements (e.g., living with relatives) including dependents; (2) evidence of current employment or unemployment, (3) receipts for rent, food, clothing, utility bills, child-care expenses, tuition, transportation expenses, medical expenses, and other essential expenses; (4) proof of disability, including

---

[17]Form N-400, Instructions.

[18]Form N-400, Instructions.

[19]See § 9:46.

[Section 9:5]

[1]8 CFR § 334.2(a).

[2]8 CFR § 103.7(b)(1).

[3]8 CFR § 103.7(b)(1).

[4]8 CFR § 103.2(e)(4)(iii).

[5]8 CFR § 103.7(c).

[6]8 CFR § 103.7(c).

[7]Appendix 9-12 at 3-4.

[8]Appendix 9-12 at 2.

determinations from SSA, HHS, VA, DOD, or other agencies; (5) proof of extraordinary expenditures for dependents residing in the US; (6) proof that the individual has, within the last 6 months, qualified for and/or received a Federal "means-tested public benefit"; (7) documentation of all assets; (8) documentation showing other financial support, such as parental support; (9) documentation of debts and liabilities.[9]

The new guidance includes separate paragraphs regarding incarcerated individuals, individuals with major travel expenditures or medical expenses, and victims of domestic violence. It lists several categories where fee waivers would generally be inappropriate, including nonimmigrants, sponsored immigrants, and immigrants for whom affidavits of support have been filed.[10]

It should be noted that by regulation, USCIS no longer permits waivers for many application forms.[11] However, waivers continue to be permitted for forms N-400, N-470, N-565, N-600, N-600K, and I-290B, as well as the biometrics fee.[12]

B. WITHDRAWAL, AMENDMENT, AND TRANSFER OF APPLICATION

§ 9:6   Withdrawing application

Research References

Dizon and Wettstein, Immigration Law Service 2d § 14:327

Once an application for naturalization has been submitted, the applicant may not withdraw the application without the consent of the USCIS.[1] If the USCIS consents to the withdrawal, the application will be denied without prejudice to any future application.[2] By effectively withdrawing the application, the applicant waives his or her right to administrative review and judicial review.[3] If the USCIS does not consent to the withdrawal, the application will be decided based on the information available.[4] The applicant may still seek administrative and judicial review of the merits if the USCIS denies naturalization.[5]

§ 9:7   Amending application

Research References

Dizon and Wettstein, Immigration Law Service 2d § 14:321

The naturalization application may be amended under certain circumstances. Any applicant may request the amendment of *clerical* matters in his or her naturaliza-

---

[9]Appendix 9-12 at 4-5.

[10]Appendix 9-12 at 6.

[11]8 C.F.R. § 103.7(c)(5).

[12]8 C.F.R. § 103.7(c)(5)(i).

[Section 9:6]

[1]INA § 335(e), 8 U.S.C.A. § 1446(e); 8 CFR § 335.10.

[2]8 CFR § 335.10.

[3]8 CFR § 335.10.

[4]INA § 335(e), 8 U.S.C.A. § 1446(e); 8 CFR § 335.10.

[5]See 8 CFR § 335.10.

tion application.[1] Only clerical errors arising out of omission or oversight may be corrected through this procedure.[2] There is no time limit for this type of amendment, which may be requested even after the admission to citizenship.[3] After admission to U.S. citizenship, amendments are made through motions to reopen naturalization proceedings.[4] If the amendment is approved, the amended application is filed together with the original naturalization application.[5] The USCIS may also amend an application *sua sponte* when it receives information that clearly indicates that a clerical error has occurred.[6]

Substantive amendments that affect the jurisdiction or the decision on the merits are not allowed.[7] If, after approving an application, the USCIS receives information that indicates the application should not have been granted, the USCIS may institute proceedings to reopen the application before admission to citizenship, or, if already admitted to citizenship, may attempt to revoke the naturalization of such person.[8]

In April 2000, the INS introduced a change-of-address telephone service for naturalization applicants.[9] Instead of submitting address changes through writing with the local INS office, applicants can call 1-800-375-5283 between 8 a.m. and 6 p.m. during the applicant's local time to submit an address change or to confirm a change that was submitted prior to the establishment of this service. The automated service is available in English and Spanish.[10]

§ 9:8 Transfer of application

Research References

Dizon and Wettstein, Immigration Law Service 2d § 14:318

Naturalization applicants who move from the USCIS district where the application is pending may request the USCIS to transfer the application to any USCIS district having jurisdiction over the applicant's new place of residence.[1] These requests may be filed up to three months before the expected move or at any time after the applicant has moved.[2] These requests are made in writing to the USCIS of-

---

[Section 9:7]

[1]8 CFR § 334.5(a)(1).

[2]8 CFR § 334.5(a)(3).

[3]8 CFR § 334.5(a)(1).

[4]8 CFR § 340.1(h).

[5]8 CFR § 334.5(a)(3).

[6]8 CFR § 334.5(a)(2).

[7]8 CFR § 334.5(b).

[8]8 CFR § 334.5(b). See §§ 14:1 et seq.

[9]77 Interpreter Releases 432 (Apr. 3, 2000). The hours of service are 8-6 except for the following: Alaska 8-5; Hawaii 8-4; Puerto Rico 9-6; Virgin Islands 9-6.

[10]For more information on how to report changes of address, *see* http://uscis.gov/graphics/howdoi/address.htm.

[Section 9:8]

[1]INA § 335(f), 8 U.S.C.A. § 1446(f); 8 CFR § 335.9(a).

[2]INA § 335(f), 8 U.S.C.A. § 1446(f); 8 CFR § 335.9(a).

fice where the application is pending.[3] The request must include: (1) the applicant's name, (2) date of birth, (3) "A" number, (4) complete new address including the name of the country, (5) complete address at the time of the filing of the application, (6) reason for the transfer of the application, and (7) the date the applicant moved or intends to move to the new jurisdiction.[4]

Requests for transfer of applications are *not* automatically granted.[5] The USCIS director at the place where the application is pending is authorized to grant such transfers.[6] If the transfer is not granted, the USCIS office that retained jurisdiction over the case will adjudicate the application.[7] If the application is denied on the merits, the USCIS office must also address the reasons why it did not consent to the transfer of the application to the new jurisdiction.[8] On the other hand, if the request to transfer the application is granted, the application will continue as if it had been originally filed in the new jurisdiction.[9]

While most USCIS offices take the position that once a naturalization application is filed, the jurisdiction vests in the USCIS office, some districts are wary of the jurisdictional issue when courts are involved. These offices read the regulations as only allowing Courts to administer the oath to those who reside within their jurisdiction at the time of the oath.[10] These districts refuse to continue processing the naturalization application, making a request to transfer essential.

III. THE N-400

A. INTRODUCTION

§ 9:9   Overview

This section discusses in detail the naturalization application, Form N-400, which is the form used in standard naturalization applications and in most types of naturalization for special classes of people.

The general instructions on the form require it to be typed or printed in ink.[1] No question should be left unanswered. If the question is not applicable, the applicant is required to write "N/A" on the form.

When additional space is needed to answer a question, the applicant should attach a sheet of paper with his or her name and "alien" registration number (A#), if any, "N-400" in the top right corner of the sheet, and the number of each item being answered.[2]

The INA (as amended by the Homeland Security Act (HSA))has provided the Secretary of DHS with broad discretion in prescribing the scope and nature of the ex-

---

[3]8 CFR § 335.9(a).

[4]8 CFR § 335.9(a).

[5]INA § 335(f), 8 U.S.C.A. § 1446(f).

[6]8 CFR § 335.9(b).

[7]8 CFR § 335.9(b).

[8]8 CFR § 335.9(b).

[9]INA § 335(f), 8 U.S.C.A. § 1446(f).

[10]See 8 CFR § 310.3. See also §§ 9:56 to 9:61.

[Section 9:9]

[1]Form N-400 (Instructions).

[2]Form N-400.

amination of applicants for naturalization.[3] At the same time, the INA specifically limits such examination to an "inquiry concerning the applicant's residence; physical presence in the United States; good moral character; understanding and attachment to the fundamental principles of the Constitution of the United States; ability to read, write, and speak English; and other qualifications to become a naturalized citizen as required by law."[4]

As will be seen in the question-by-question analysis of the N-400 Form, some questions seem to go beyond the limits imposed by this provision of the INA. Even so, judicial review of the scope of the N-400 questions is limited. At least one circuit court has held that it will uphold the N-400 questions if they can be justified by facially legitimate and *bona fide* reasons.[5]

The current version of Form N-400 is available for downloading from the USCIS website at http://www.uscis.gov/files/form/N-400.pdf.

B. QUESTION-BY-QUESTION ANALYSIS

§ 9:10 In general

The INS Form N-400 is reproduced in Appendix 9-1. The reader should refer to that appendix for the entire form.[1] Specific sections of the application will be reproduced immediately preceding the analysis of that section.

This question-by-question analysis is only designed to provide a cursory explanation of the questions. After each explanation, the reader is referred to the chapter that discusses that topic in detail. The reader is urged to refer to those chapters. While the questions on the N-400 may at times appear simple, in reality they often involve very complex legal issues.

Information provided in this application may lead to removal proceedings, not only when the applicant has become deportable since acquiring lawful permanent residence, but also when the applicant was either originally ineligible for that status or committed fraud to obtain it. For example, applicants who are unable to remember the names of the spouse that filed the immigrant visa petition for them are likely to have problems in the process of naturalization. Similarly, an applicant who obtained lawful permanent residence as the son or daughter of a permanent resident will have serious problems if he or she was in fact married at the time. Form N-400 may uncover all these issues.

In some cases, applicants faced with a visa fraud issue may be able to apply for a waiver of the visa fraud in removal proceedings.[2] The applicant may also be subject to a document fraud proceeding that would result in the loss of lawful permanent residence.[3] A very limited waiver is specifically available for the document fraud ground.[4]

---

[3]INA § 332(a), 8 U.S.C.A. § 1443(a).

[4]INA § 332(a), 8 U.S.C.A. § 1443(a).

[5]Price v. U.S., 962 F.2d 836, 842-44 (9th Cir. 1992).

[Section 9:10]

[1]Readers should be aware that the form has been reduced to fit the page of this handbook. In addition, the handbook's header and page number have been added to the form.

[2]INA § 237(a)(1)(H), 8 U.S.C.A. § 1227(a)(1)(H).

[3]INA § 237(a)(3)(C)(i), 8 U.S.C.A. § 1227(a)(3)(C)(i).

[4]INA § 237(a)(3)(C)(ii), 8 U.S.C.A. § 1227(a)(3)(C)(ii).

§ 9:11   Part 1: Applicant's name

The first set of questions on the N-400 asks for the applicant's name. That part of the application is as follows.

A. Current legal name

Question A asks for the applicant's current legal name.[1]

B. Name on permanent residence card

The second question asks for the applicant's name *exactly* as it appears on the applicant's permanent residence card.[2] There are situations in which the name on the permanent residence card is different from the current legal name used by the applicant. For example, the applicant may have married and changed his or her name through marriage, or the applicant's name may have otherwise been changed through some form of legal process, or the applicant's name simply may be misspelled.

The USCIS takes the position that if the name currently used by the applicant is simply an anglicization or the English equivalent of the name on the permanent residence card, then it will not object to the naturalization application being filed under the assumed name.[3] However, if the difference goes beyond those limits, the USCIS will only accept the new name on the application if the name has been changed in compliance with the applicable state law.[4] Indeed, under the INS Interpretations, married women will only be allowed to file under their maiden name, if the state law allows the use of such name, and the woman has complied with all the requirements imposed by state law for using the maiden name.[5] In jurisdictions that allow for common law change of name without court intervention, assumed names will be accepted if they fulfill all the local common-law requirements.

C. Other names

The third question requests any other names used throughout the applicant's life.[6] The applicant is required to write *all* the names used and to use a separate sheet of paper if necessary. This information will facilitate the agency's investigation of the applicant. If the applicant has never used another name, the applicant should write "N/A" in the space for "Family Name (*Last Name*)."

D. Name change

The last question, asking whether the applicant wants to legally change his or her name, is optional.[7] If the USCIS has doubts as to the validity of an assumed name, the *INS Interpretations* recommend taking advantage of the provision of the INA

[Section 9:11]

[1] Form N-400 (Instructions).

[2] Form N-400.

[3] INS Interp. 334.1(b)(1).

[4] INS Interp. 334.1(b)(1).

[5] INS Interp. 334.1(b)(1).

[6] INS Interp. 334.1(b)(1).

[7] INS Interp. 334.1(b)(1).

that allows courts to change the applicant's legal name as part of the court's administration of the naturalization oath.[8]

If the name change relate to marriage, this information will also provide a cross-check in some cases where the applicant has been married several times. Traditionally, such cross-check will most likely only be relevant when the applicants are females. Further questions about marital history of the applicant will be asked in part 5 of the application.[9] At this point, it must be pointed out that this question may uncover possible ineligibility if the applicant is applying as a spouse of a U.S. citizen and has been married to different U.S. citizens within the last three years.[10]

§ 9:12 Part 2: Information about eligibility; generally

Part 2 requires the applicant to check one of four possible bases for eligibility.

§ 9:13 Part 2: Information about eligibility; generally—Five years of lawful permanent residence

Choice A relates to standard naturalization. The person is required to have resided in the United States for five years after lawful admission to permanent residence and to have been physically present in the United States for at least half that time. Residence is defined as having the principal dwelling place in the United States. Physical presence requires being actually physically in the United States. In addition, the applicant must have continued to be a lawful permanent resident for the entire period and must have resided in the state or USCIS district where the application is filed for three months prior to the filing of the application or, if filed early, prior to the USCIS interview. All these requirements are discussed in detail in Ch 7.[1]

Some absences, even extended absences, do not interrupt the five-year residence requirement. These absences will be discussed below.[2]

§ 9:14 Part 2: Information about eligibility; generally—Three years of lawful permanent residence

This choice relates to the special form of naturalization available to spouses of U.S. citizens. These applicants are only required to have been lawful permanent residents for three years, to reside in the United States for that period, and to have been physically present in the United States for half that time (i.e., eighteen months). For the three years preceding the application for naturalization, the applicant must have been married to a U.S. citizen and residing in "marital union" with him or her. The applicant must have been married to the same U.S. citizen throughout the entire three-year period, and that person must have been a U.S. citizen for the full three years. The marital union required during this period is more than being simply married for the entire time. Some forms of informal separations

---

[8]INA § 336(e), 8 U.S.C.A. § 1447(e), INS Interp. 334.1(b)(1).

[9]See Part 5. Information about your marital history.

[10]See §§ 11:1 et seq. (Nationality and Marriage-requirement that the applicant be married to the same U.S. citizen during the three years of required residence).

[Section 9:13]

[1]See §§ 7:3 to 7:17.

[2]See Part 3.

may break the marital union. All these topics are discussed in greater detail in Ch 11.[1]

Certain absences do not interrupt the three-year residence requirement.[2] Spouses of U.S. citizens who are engaged in qualifying employment abroad are not required to fulfill the prior residence requirement.[3]

§ 9:15   Part 2: Information about eligibility; generally—Armed services

There are several forms of naturalization based on service in the U.S. armed forces. They are discussed in Ch 12.[1] Applicants who qualify under any of those provisions must check this box. This box is *not* to be checked by former U.S. citizens who lost their U.S. citizenship by service in a foreign army.[2]

§ 9:16   Part 2: Information about eligibility; generally—Other bases for eligibility

This is the catch-all category for all the other forms of naturalization not included under the former provisions. The applicant is required to write in the section of law that applies to the specific right to naturalize. The following list should help the applicant find the specific basis and the section of law.[1]

(1) Individuals who obtained LPR status because of domestic violence or battery, either as a spouse or as a child – INA § 319(a) [8 U.S.C.A § 1430(a)]. This provision is discussed in Ch. 11.[2]

(2) Spouses of U.S. citizens stationed abroad for specific purposes-INA § 319(b), 8 U.S.C.A. § 1430(b). This provision is discussed in Ch 11.[3]

(3) Widows or widowers of U.S. citizens during a period of honorable service in an active duty status in the Armed Forces of the United States-INA § 319(d), 8 U.S.C.A. § 1430(d). Also discussed in Ch 11.[4]

(4) Former U.S. citizens who lost their citizenship by marriage to noncitizens-INA § 324, 8 U.S.C.A. § 1435. Discussed in Ch 11.[5]

(5) Employees of U.S. news media organizations-INA § 329(c), 8 U.S.C.A. § 1430(c). Discussed in Ch 11.[6]

[Section 9:14]

[1]See §§ 11:3 to 11:4.

[2]See §§ 7:5, 7:6.

[3]See §§ 11:7 to 11:10.

[Section 9:15]

[1]See § 12:12.

[2]See § 12:2.

[Section 9:16]

[1]See generally 8 CFR § 334.1.

[2]See §§ 11:6, 11:26.

[3]See §§ 11:7 to 11:10.

[4]See § 11:11.

[5]See §§ 11:12 to 11:17.

[6]See § 11:27.

(6) Former U.S. citizens whose nationality was restored by private bills-Number of the Private Bill and 8 CFR § 324.5. Discussed in Ch 11.[7]

(7) Naturalization of former U.S. citizens who lost their citizenship by service in foreign armies during World War II-INA § 327, 8 U.S.C.A. § 1438. Discussed in Ch 12.[8]

(8) Persons who make extraordinary contributions to intelligence activities-INA § 316(f), 8 U.S.C.A. § 1427(f). Discussed in Ch 12.[9]

(9) Naturalization of U.S. noncitizen nationals-INA § 325, 8 U.S.C.A. § 1436. Discussed in Ch 3.[10]

§ 9:17 Part 3: Additional information about applicant

Research References

Dizon and Wettstein, Immigration Law Service 2d § 14:325

Most of these questions are for basic identification purposes.

Practitioners should be mindful of possible use of false social security numbers. The question in this part asks for a valid social security number. It is unlikely for a naturalization applicant to use a false social security number, since most applicants have been permanent residents for some time and have had a right to obtain valid numbers. It is good policy, however, to ensure that all documents submitted with the application are valid.

Even such apparently innocuous question as a person's date of birth may bring about serious immigration consequences. One of the few immigration-related document fraud cases litigated in the administrative courts involves allegations that a naturalization applicant provided false information relating to his or her identity.[1]

Section C asks for the date the applicant became a permanent resident. This information is relevant for two reasons. First, it makes it easy to see whether the applicant satisfies the required residence after lawful admission to permanent residence for the specific form of naturalization the applicant is seeking. Thus, for example, the person reviewing this application will be able to tell at a glance whether the person has resided five years after admission to permanent residence if the person is applying under the general naturalization program, or three years if the person is applying as the spouse of a U.S, citizen.[2] Second, it helps identify the agency record relating to the applicant.

Section H asks whether the applicant is seeking a waiver from the English language and/or civics requirements using form N-648.[3] Note that this question, as

---

[7]See § 11:29.

[8]See § 12:2.

[9]See § 12:15.

[10]See §§ 3:10 to 3:12.

[Section 9:17]

[1]U.S. v. Alabado Makilan, 4 OCAHO 610 (Feb. 14, 1994).

[2]See §§ 7:1 et seq., 11:1 et seq., and 12:1 et seq. (discussing the time of residence in the United States after lawful admission to permanent residence required under the different naturalization sections).

[3]See §§ 7:87 to 7:93.

currently phrased, does not ask whether the individual is exempt from the English-language requirement on account of age.[4]

Section I will inform the USCIS that the applicant will need special accommodation during the naturalization process. One example of a special accommodation is making sure the fingerprint location is wheelchair accessible.[5]

§ 9:18   Part 4: Addresses and telephone numbers

This part is self-explanatory. If the applicant's mailing address is the same as the applicant's home address, the applicant should write "same."

It has become increasingly important for naturalization and other applicants for immigration benefits to ensure that DHS has an up-to-date address. On July 27, 2002, the agency published a proposed rule that, if promulgated, would require applicants for naturalization and other immigration benefits to sign an acknowledgment of the consequences of failing to keep the DHS informed of their current address.[1] This acknowledgment would become part of the required application, and the agency would reject any application that was not signed.[2] By signing the revised application, an applicant would acknowledge both the responsibility to keep DHS informed of his or her current address within 10 days of any change of address and the consequences of any failure to do so: that DHS would use the most recent address on file for all purposes, including service of a Notice to Appear to place an individual in removal proceedings, should that occur. Furthermore, under the proposed rule, if an applicant fails to respond to a communication sent to the most recent address, the DHS would deem the application to have been abandoned.[3]

One potential complication may arise when the applicant is transsexual, and has had a legal change of sex in the state in which they reside. After the Board of Immigration Appeals decision in *Matter of Lovo-Lara*,[4] USCIS issued field guidance on situations where a gender change has occurred. That guidance is found in the Adjudicator's Field Manual, and is reproduced as Appendix 9-13.[5] This is approximately similar to guidance issued by the State Department, though the State Department's approach appears to be more generous.[6]

§ 9:19   Part 5: Criminal records search

This information will facilitate the DHS' background check of the applicant. The Federal Bureau of Investigation will use this information to search for criminal records.

---

[4]See § 7:94.

[5]Guide to Naturalization, 9.

[Section 9:18]

[1]67 FR 48818 (July 26, 2002) (proposing a new paragraph (a)(8) to 8 CFR § 103.2). The naturalization and citizenship-related applications included in the proposed rule are Form N-300 (Application to File Declaration of Intention); Form N-410 (Motion for Amendment of Petition (application)); Form N-455 (Application for Transfer of Petition for Naturalization); Form N-470 (Application to Preserve Residence for Naturalization Purpose); Form N-600 (Application for Certificate of Citizenship); and Form N-644 (Application for Posthumous Citizenship).

[2]67 FR at 48820.

[3]67 FR at 48818.

[4]23 I&N Dec. 746 (BIA 2005).

[5]See AFM § 21.3(a)(2)(J).

[6]See 7 FAM 1300 Appendix M.

§ 9:20 Part 6: Residences and employment—Generally

This part has two sections. The first relates to the addresses where the applicant has lived; the second to his or her employment history.

§ 9:21 Part 6: Residences and employment—List of addresses

This question is self-explanatory. This information relates primarily to the statutory requirement that the USCIS conduct an investigation in the vicinities where the applicant has resided.[1]

Beyond the statutory need to conduct the investigation of the applicant, information provided here will assist in the determination of actual residence for naturalization purposes.[2] The question does ask for "addresses" so that is the information that must be furnished. Every address must be included in answering this question, including residence abroad, regardless of how short the applicant lived at that address. Separate sheets of paper can be attached to complete this section or any other section of the application. The USCIS is required by law to make neighborhood investigations.[3] The district directors, however, usually waive this requirement.[4]

Naturalization applicants who have been lawful permanent residents more than five years are required to furnish their addresses for the five years prior to the filing of the naturalization application. The question does not distinguish between the bases for the naturalization application. If the applicant has been a lawful permanent resident for more than five years, he or she must supply the addresses for the previous five years.

§ 9:22 Part 6: Residences and employment—Employment

The second section of part 6 requires the applicant to furnish the names and addresses of employment over the past five years.

The basis for requesting this information is the statutory requirement that USCIS conduct an investigation into the vicinity of the place of employment.[1] Applicants should include military service. If the applicant is self-employed, the applicant should write "self-employed."

Persons who became lawful permanent residents through employment petitions will have serious trouble, possibly leading to removal proceedings, if the answer to this question discloses that they failed to take up such employment after becoming permanent residents. Such failure will raise questions as to the whether their intentions were legitimate when they became lawful permanent residents.[2] Even though the application only requires a listing of employers over the five years preceding the naturalization application, the issue of employment after becoming permanent resident may come up in the naturalization interview.

[Section 9:21]

[1]See § 9:47.

[2]See §§ 7:3 to 7:17.

[3]See § 9:47.

[4]See § 9:47.

[Section 9:22]

[1]See § 9:47.

[2]There is no requirement that the person remain in the job for a particular amount of time after entry. Matter of Marcoux, 12 I. & N. Dec. 827 (B.I.A. 1968). But there is a requirement that when the

The public charge ground of deportability only covers individuals who became a public charge within 5 years of obtaining LPR status, and then only where the reasons for their becoming a public charge didn't arise after their admission as an LPR.[3] Thus, for most applicants, the lack of employment is not itself sufficient to lead to denial of a naturalization application. The DHS, however, takes the position that fraudulent receipt of public benefits indicates lack of good moral character.[4] Lack of employment opens the door into further questioning regarding receipt of public benefits and possible fraud in obtaining such benefits.

The list of employers over the five years preceding the naturalization application is also very relevant for persons who are naturalizing after three years of lawful permanent residence under the provisions for spouses of U.S. citizens. If the applicant was employed in the United States before becoming a lawful permanent resident, he or she may have used fraudulent documentation to obtain such employment. Such scenario may lead to possible document fraud proceedings.[5]

§ 9:23 Part 7: Time outside U.S

Under most of the naturalization provisions, applicants are required to have resided continuously in the United States for a specified period of time immediately preceding the filing of the naturalization application. For example, under the general naturalization provisions, the applicant must have resided in the United States for a period of five years. In addition, the applicant must have been physically present in this country for a total of at least two and a half years.[1]

The applicant is required to fill in, for each absence since becoming a lawful permanent resident: the date of departure, the date of return, whether the absence was six months or longer, the destination and the total days out of the United States. This table is critical to establish the person's eligibility for naturalization in terms of residence and physical presence. This table is not limited to the required period of residence but asks for *all* absences since becoming a permanent resident.

The dates of departure and return will allow the officer to determine precisely how long the absence was. Absences between six months and one year create a presumption that the continuity has been broken for purposes of the continuous residence required for naturalization. This presumption may be overcome by evidence that the applicant did not in fact intend to abandon his or her residence in the U.S.[2] Absences longer than one year will automatically break the continuity of residence unless the person has filed an application to preserve residence with the USCIS and it has been granted.[3]

The third column asks whether the applicant's absence lasted more than six months. It is designed simply to highlight that fact.

---

person entered, he or she should have had the intention to work on the job for which he or she was certified. Matter of Poulin, 13 I. & N. Dec. 264 (B.I.A. 1968).

[3]INA § 237(a)(5) [8 U.S.C.A. § 1227(a)(5)].

[4]See §§ 7:40 to 7:46.

[5]See generally Levy, A Practitioner's Guide to Section 274C: Parts 1, 94-6 Immigration Briefings (June 1994).

[Section 9:23]

[1]See §§ 7:3 to 7:10.

[2]See § 7:5.

[3]See §§ 7:6 to 7:10.

The last columns allow the officer an opportunity to determine not only whether the person has broken continuous residence for purposes of naturalization but also whether the person has abandoned lawful permanent residence in general. One of the requirements for naturalization is that the applicant continues to be a lawful permanent resident.[4] Thus, if a person travels abroad, even for a relatively short period, with the intention of remaining permanently in the other country, the person has abandoned lawful permanent residence.[5] As a general rule, absences longer than one year break the period of continuous residence required by the statute.[6] There are some statutory provisions that allow applicants to obtain a special dispensation from the USCIS so that absences longer than one year will not break the continuity of the residence for naturalization purposes.[7] In addition, absences may indicate that the applicant may have abandoned his or her lawful permanent residence at one point, which not only makes the applicant ineligible for naturalization but also deportable.[8] The applicant will most likely have to face removal proceedings based on loss of permanent residence.

§9:24 Part 8: Marital history

The following part of the N-400 relates to the marital history of the applicant.

The applicant must list the number of times he or she has been married. As was pointed out above, the marital history of the person is very relevant to determine eligibility for naturalization.[1] Persons who are applying for naturalization as spouses of U.S. citizens must establish that they have been residing in marital union with the same U.S. citizen for the three years preceding the filing of the naturalization application.[2] Similarly, persons who apply for expedited naturalization must establish that their marriage to the U.S. citizen assigned abroad is a valid one.[3] Responses to these questions may also provide information leading to a finding of good moral character if, for example, the applicant has had an adulterous affair that destroyed a marriage.[4]

If the applicant is married at present, he or she is required to provide specific information regarding the spouse in this section. Most of this information is identifying information.

Special attention should be given to naturalized U.S. citizen spouses. This section requires such information as the date of the applicant's spouse's naturalization. The applicant will only be eligible for the three years naturalization if the spouse has been a U.S. citizen for the entire three-year period.[5] If the applicant or the applicant's spouse was married previously, the applicant must fill out sections F and G. In addition, if either the applicant or the applicant's spouse has had more than

---

[4]See §7:11.

[5]See §8:24.

[6]See §7:5.

[7]See §§7:6 to 7:10.

[8]See §8:24.

[Section 9:24]

[1]See Part 3 of the N-400.

[2]See §§11:3 to 11:6.

[3]See §§11:7 to 11:10.

[4]See §7:41.

[5]See §§11:3 to 11:6.

one prior marriage, the applicant is required to furnish, on a separate piece of paper, the information requested in sections F and G for each prior marriage.

At first sight, these questions appear to go well beyond the relevant information to determine the applicant eligibility for naturalization. However, there are circumstances in which this information may be relevant. Thus, the applicant's present marriage will be valid only if all the previous marriages of both the applicant and his or her spouses have been lawfully terminated.

Failure to terminate prior marriages lawfully will obviously be relevant for those applicants who are seeking naturalization as spouses of U.S. citizens since they are required to have been lawfully married to the U.S. citizen for the previous three years.[6] In addition, the applicant's possible admissions regarding bigamy or adultery may affect the determination of the applicant's good moral character.[7] This question may also uncover other problems such as when an applicant obtained lawful permanent residence through a marriage-based petition and his or her spouse's prior marriage had not been legally terminated before marrying the applicant.

Finally, questions may be raised as to possible marriage fraud at the time the applicant or his or her spouse acquired lawful permanent residence.[8] Prior marriage fraud of the applicant is clearly relevant to a determination of the naturalization application, since if the applicant is not a lawful permanent resident, he or she may not naturalize. Prior marriage fraud of the spouse of the applicant seems to be less relevant to this determination. Of course, neither the applicant nor the applicant's spouses are protected in any way from removal based on information provided in this application.

If the naturalization application discloses immigration-related marriage fraud, the applicant will be placed in removal proceedings. Applicants should be aware that some persons placed in removal proceedings because of fraud when they became lawful permanent residents, may be eligible for section 237(a)(1)(H) waivers of deportability.[9]

§ 9:25 Part 9: Applicant's children

The naturalization application provides a table to include information about the applicant's children.

The applicant must first state the number of children he or she has and then complete specific information for each child. This information is relevant for purposes of derivative citizenship. Some children of persons who naturalize may acquire U.S. citizenship as a result of their parent's naturalization.[1] Not listing the child will create problems proving such relationship. Failure to include children will also create evidentiary issues if the parent decides to petition for permanent residence for the child at a later date.

When completing this section it is important also to include information regard-

---

[6]See § 11:3.

[7]See § 7:41.

[8]See §§ 8:25 to 8:26. Cf. Levy, The Family in Immigration and Nationality Law: Part II, 92-10 Immigration Briefings 8-12 (October 1992) (discussing exclusion and deportation issues relating to marriage fraud).

[9]Immigration Law and Defense §§ 8:42, 8:43.

[Section 9:25]

[1]See §§ 5:1 et seq.

ing adopted and illegitimate children. Not only might it be fraud not to include them, but they may be eligible to derive citizenship from the naturalizing parent.[2] However, the practitioner should be prepared to confront possible lack of good moral character issues if the applicant has failed to provide support for the children; the USCIS takes the position that failure to provide child support is a basis for a finding of lack of good moral character.[3]

§ 9:26   Part 10: Ineligibility factors; generally

Part 10 of the N-400 is divided into eight sections regarding bars and other ineligibility factors as follows: (A) General Questions; (B) Affiliations; (C) Continuous Residence; (D) Good Moral Character; (E) Removal, Exclusion, and Deportation Proceedings; (F) Military Service; (G) Selective Service Registration; and (H) Oath Requirements. Any "yes" answer must be accompanied by an attached written explanation.

§ 9:27   Part 10: Ineligibility factors; generally—General questions

This section of the N-400 poses questions to determine whether a naturalization applicant falls into a mandatory ground of ineligibility. The USCIS will examine the answers closely to determine whether an applicant cannot satisfy the requirements for naturalization.

False claims to U.S. citizenship are relevant to the determination of good moral character, if such claims involve fraud.[1] There were clearly circumstances, however, where written or oral claims to U.S. citizenship do not involve moral turpitude. Even conviction under certain criminal statutes relating to claims of U.S. citizenship may be free of moral turpitude.[2]

In addition, in the past, false claims to U.S. citizenship might uncover problems with the original grant of lawful permanent residence. Thus, false claims to U.S. citizenship made to a U.S. official in connection with a visa application or entry to the U.S. may be considered visa fraud.[3] In the past, entering the United States under a false claim to U.S. citizenship was considered entry without inspection.[4]

---

[2]See § 5:4. The INS operations instructions used to require INS examiners to ignore the illegitimate children of a male applicant when filing the petition for naturalization with the court. OI INS 334.4. However, it is important to include information regarding illegitimate children even in the case of fathers since these children may derive citizenship if legitimated before turning 16. See §§ 5:1 et seq.

[3]See § 7:41.

[Section 9:27]

[1]See e.g., Matter of B-, 7 I. & N. Dec. 342 (B.I.A. 1956) (willfully and knowingly making false statements in an application for a passport is a crime of moral turpitude).

[2]See Matter of I-, 4 I. & N. Dec. 159 (B.I.A.) approved by Att'y Gen (1950) (falsely representing himself as U.S. citizen is not a crime involving moral turpitude); Matter of K-, 3 I. & N. Dec. 69, 71 (B.I.A. 1947) (same). Cf. Matter of Serna, 20 I. & N. Dec. 579 (B.I.A. 1992) (conviction under 18 U.S.C.A. § 1546 for possession of an altered immigration document with knowledge that it was altered, but without its use or proof of any intent to use it unlawfully, is not a conviction for a crime of moral turpitude).

[3]See State Department Cable No. 97-State-174342 (Sept. 17, 1997) reproduced in 74 Interpreter Releases 1483 (September 29, 1997).

[4]Matter of E-, 6 I. & N. Dec. 275 (B.I.A. 1954).

Entry without inspection now renders a permanent resident an applicant for admission, and also inadmissible.[5]

The IIRAIRA made false claims to U.S. citizenship and unlawful voting in elections grounds for both deportability and inadmissibility.[6] False claims to U.S. citizenship made to obtain any benefit under federal or state law makes the person deportable and inadmissible, provided the claim was made on or after September 30, 1996.[7] Congress has subsequently enacted an exemption to both grounds of inadmissibility and deportability.[8] It exempts noncitizens who would otherwise be inadmissible or deportable under those grounds, if the noncitizen satisfies all of the following conditions: (1) each natural parent of the noncitizen (or, in the case of an adopted noncitizen, each adoptive parent of the noncitizen) is or was a citizen (whether by birth or naturalization); (2) the noncitizen permanently resided in the United States prior to attaining the age of sixteen; and (3) the noncitizen reasonably believed at the time of engaging in the relevant act that he or she was a citizen.[9]

Question 5 is posed because failure to file tax returns may be a factor in determining the applicant's moral character.[10]

Question 6 asks about foreign titles of nobility. Persons bearing hereditary titles and orders of nobility are required to renounce them as part of taking the naturalization oath.[11]

According to the regulations, only legal incompetence at the time of the naturalization interview or at the time of taking the oath of allegiance bars the applicant from naturalizing.[12] Question 7 asks if the applicant has ever been declared legally incompetent. If the applicant was declared legally incompetent prior to either event, he or she has the burden of proving that legal competence was timely restored.[13] Congress does now permit waiver of the competency requirement for certain individuals who are mentally or physically impaired.[14]

§ 9:28   Part 10: Ineligibility factors; generally—Affiliations

The applicant is required to list *all* the organizations the applicant has ever belonged to. This may seem somewhat overbroad, but the Ninth Circuit Court of Appeals has denied such a constitutional challenge to this question. It decided that Congress granted the Attorney General (and now the Secretary of DHS) very broad power to inquire into any fact the Attorney General (and now the Secretary of DHS)

---

[5]INA § 101(a)(13)(vi), 8 U.S.C.A. § 1101(a)(13)(vi); INA § 212(a)(6)(A)(i), 8 U.S.C.A. § 1182(a)(6)(A)(i).

[6]INA §§ 212(a)(6)(C)(ii), (10)(D), 237(a)(3)(D), (6), 8 U.S.C.A. §§ 1182(a) (6)(C)(ii), (10)(D), 1227(a) (3)(D), (6). For a more detailed discussion of the voting and false claim to U.S. citizenship grounds of deportation see §§ 8:20, 8:21.

[7]See State Department Cable No. 97-State-174342 (Sept. 17, 1997) reproduced in 74 Interpreter Releases 1483 (September 29, 1997) (discussing inadmissibility).

[8]Child Citizenship Act of 2000, Pub. L. No. 106-395, § 201(b),(c), 114 Stat. 1631 (Oct. 30, 2000) reproduced as Appendix 5-2 of Ch 5.

[9]Child Citizenship Act of 2000, § 201(b)(1), (2), (c)(1), (2) amending INA §§ 212(a)(6)(C)(ii), (10)(D), 237(a)(3)(D), (6), 8 U.S.C.A. §§ 1182(a)(6)(C)(ii), (10)(D), 1227(a) (3)(D), (6).

[10]See § 7:41.

[11]See § 9:65.

[12]8 CFR § 316.12(a).

[13]See § 7:104.

[14]See § 7:104.

may deem material to the naturalization application.[1] The USCIS has a right to ask for all the associations in which the applicant has been a member because, even if the applicant swears under penalty of perjury that he or she did not belong to an organization proscribed by the bars to naturalization, the applicant may be mistaken about whether an organization he or she belonged to was outside the prohibition.[2] Thus, the applicant is required to provide a full disclosure.

The remaining questions in this section relate to the applicant's political beliefs and activities. Questions 9(a) and 9(b) relate to Communist or totalitarian party membership and advocacy of communism or totalitarianism. The Supreme Court has held that question 9(a) is both relevant and material even when the person's membership in the Communist party did not amount to a meaningful association with the party.[3] The INA bars applicants affiliated with the Communist party or any other totalitarian organizations from citizenship.[4] These bars are discussed in detail in Ch 7.[5]

Question 9(c) asks about the applicant's association with a terrorist organization. Association with a terrorist organization can be a bar to naturalization under INA §§ 313(a)(4), (5) or (6).[6] Moreover, there is some overlap between this bar to naturalization and the grounds of inadmissibility and deportability based upon engagement in terrorist activity.[7] Thus, an individual who is a member of or affiliated with a terrorist organization could be both barred from naturalizing under INA §§ 313(a)(4), (5) or (6) (relating to political assaults and assassinations, sabotage, and the destruction of property) and also inadmissible or deportable. Congress has recently broadened the definition of a terrorist organization and also expanded the meaning of "engaging in terrorist activity" for purposes of inadmissibility and deportability.[8] As a result of these expansions, conduct that might not bar an individual from naturalizing could nevertheless be a ground of inadmissibility or deportability. Thus, it is important for naturalization applicants to consider whether their organizational memberships or associations could subject them to removal proceedings. For a more detailed discussion of the new definitions of terrorist organizations and activity, see Ch 7.[9]

Question 10 asks whether the applicant either directly or indirectly advocated the overthrow of any government by force or violence. The USCIS asks this question to identify an applicant who is ineligible for citizenship pursuant to INA § 313(a)(4) and (5).[10]

Question 11 asks whether the applicant has persecuted any person because of

---

[Section 9:28]

[1]Price v. U.S. I.N.S., 962 F.2d 836, 839–40 (9th Cir. 1991).

[2]Price v. U.S. I.N.S., 962 F.2d 836, 843 (9th Cir. 1991).

[3]Berenyi v. District Director, I.N.S., 385 U.S. 630, 638, 87 S.Ct. 666, 671, 17 L.Ed.2d 656 (1967).

[4]INA § 313(a)(1) and (2), 8 U.S.C.A. § 1424(a)(1) and (2).

[5]See §§ 7:52 to 7:76.

[6]8 U.S.C.A. § 1424(a)(4).

[7]Cf. INA § 313(a)(4), 8 U.S.C.A. § 1424(a)(4) with INA § 212(a)(3)(B), 8 U.S.C.A. § 1182(a)(3)(B) and INA § 237(a)(4)(B), 8 U.S.C.A. § 1227(a)(4)(B).

[8]Uniting and Strengthening America by Providing Appropriate Tools Required to Intercept and Obstruct Terrorism Act of 2001 (USA Patriot Act), 107 P.L. 56, § 411, 115 Stat. 272 (Oct. 26, 2001).

[9]Specifically, see § 7:72.

[10]8 U.S.C.A. § 1424(a)(4) and (5).

race, religion, national origin, membership in a particular social group or political opinion. The USCIS asks this question to identify individuals who may have procured their permanent residence by fraud.[11]

Question 12 relates to Nazi party activities between 1933 and 1945. Unlike membership in the Communist party, membership in the Nazi party or Nazi activity do not bar the applicant from being naturalized.[12] However, at different points since World War II, membership in the Nazi party and Nazi party activities have been grounds of exclusion.[13] In addition, since 1978, having been a participant in Nazi directed persecution between 1933 and 1945 has been a ground of deportation.[14] Therefore, while membership is not a statutory bar, it may uncover a ground of deportability, which would then render the applicant ineligible for naturalization.

§ 9:29   Part 10: Ineligibility factors; generally—Continuous residence

These two questions are clearly designed to uncover abandonment or loss of lawful permanent residence. This set of questions deals with taxation and false claims to U.S. citizenship. The taxation issue is two-fold. The USCIS has a *bona fide* reason to ask if after becoming a lawful permanent resident, the applicant has claimed, or considered himself or herself to be in, nonresident status. Claiming nonresident status for tax purposes or failing to file a tax return because the applicant believes himself or herself not to be a resident may amount to abandonment of lawful permanent residence.[1]

§ 9:30   Part 10: Ineligibility factors; generally—Good moral character

This section relates to the statutory bars to good moral character. The questions are directly related to those bars. These bars are discussed in Ch 7.[1] The applicant should read closely each of these questions before answering them.

A person who during the statutory period of residence required for naturalization has been convicted of crimes of moral turpitude, drug related crimes, or who has been confined for more than 180 days as a result of a conviction is barred from establishing good moral character.[2] The same rule applies to persons who admit having committed the elements of a crime of moral turpitude or of a drug related offense. Persons who are convicted of an aggravated felony are forever barred from establishing good moral character. These bars are discussed in detail in Ch 7.[3] In addition, persons who are convicted of certain crimes may be subject to removal.

Questions 15–21 are designed to uncover these bases for denial of naturalization applications. The questions overlap, and appear designed to ensure that every

---

[11]See, e.g., Kungys v. U.S., 485 U.S. 759 (1980).

[12]See § 7:70.

[13]See Levy, Exclusion Grounds under the Immigration Act of 1990: Part I, 91-8 Immigration Briefings 24.

[14]Gordon & Mailman, § 71.06[5][e].

[Section 9:29]

[1]See § 8:24.

[Section 9:30]

[1]§§ 7:18 to 7:46.

[2]See §§ 7:19 to 7:39.

[3]See §§ 7:19 to 7:39.

contact with law enforcement is required to be disclosed. Applicants who answer "yes" to any of these questions are required to provide detailed information regarding the arrest or conviction.

It must be noted that this question asks for *all* the arrests and citations the applicant was *ever* a subject of regardless of the disposition. This includes arrests that were later dismissed. It also includes traffic stops and other minor offenses. The form specifically requires the applicant to disclose arrests and conviction, even if the records were sealed or if a judge has told the applicant that he or she no longer has a criminal record.

The Supreme Court has sustained the legality of the scope of this question.[4] The case in question involved the denaturalization of a person who had answered "no" to this question when in fact the person had been arrested three times for making public speeches in a park approximately ten or eleven years before filing a petition for naturalization.[5] The applicant was required to disclose these arrests even though in one of the arrests, the charges were dismissed, in the other, judgment was suspended, and in the third, the person was fined but the fine was canceled upon review.[6]

Questions 22–24 are "yes or no" questions, and do not require that the individual actually have been arrested or that these acts have previously been disclosed. These questions all pertain to good moral character bars which do not require arrests. Smugglers (even of family members), polygamists, habitual drunkards, prostitutes, persons giving false testimony, and drug traffickers are all barred by statute from showing good moral character if related acts occurred during the period required for good moral character.[7] Individuals who answer "no" to these questions, where the answer is actually "yes," might not be detected at the time of naturalization, but would be opening themselves up to potential denaturalization by failing to give true answers to these questions.[8]

§ 9:31 Part 10: Ineligibility factors; generally—Removal, exclusion, and deportation proceedings

This section, regarding deportation proceedings, is directly relevant to the naturalization application. A person who has been ordered deported or against whom deportation proceedings have been commenced may not be naturalized.[1]

§ 9:32 Part 10: Ineligibility factors; generally—Military service

Research References

A.L.R. Index, Immigration and Naturalization
Dizon and Wettstein, Immigration Law Service 2d § 15:17

---

[4]Chaunt v. U. S., 364 U.S. 350, 353, 81 S. Ct. 147, 149, 5 L. Ed. 2d 120 (1960).

[5]Chaunt v. U. S., 364 U.S. 350, 352, 81 S. Ct. 147, 149, 5 L. Ed. 2d 120 (1960).

[6]Chaunt v. U. S., 364 U.S. 350, 352, 81 S. Ct. 147, 149, 5 L. Ed. 2d 120 (1960). Although the Court found the questions proper, defendant was not denaturalized because the misrepresentation was not considered material enough to revoke his citizenship. Chaunt v. U. S., 364 U.S. 350, 354, 81 S. Ct. 147, 5 L. Ed. 2d 120 (1960).

[7]See §§ 7:20, 7:30 to 7:35.

[8]See §§ 14:2 to 14:24.

[Section 9:31]

[1]See §§ 8:27 to 8:33.

This section relates to military-related bars to naturalization. Persons who left the United States in order to avoid being drafted, those who apply for specific noncitizenship-based exemptions from military service, and deserters are barred from obtaining U.S. citizenship. These bars are discussed in Ch 7.[1]

Question 31 is also designed to obtain information regarding conscientious objectors. Conscientious objectors are not barred from naturalizing but may be required to take a special naturalization oath.[2]

§ 9:33　Part 10: Ineligibility factors; generally—Selective service registration

Failure to register for selective service is not a specific bar to or requirement for naturalization. However, a conviction for failure to comply with selective service laws makes the person deportable.[1] Even if there is no conviction, the applicant may be prevented from naturalizing. The USCIS takes the position that failure to register for the selective service, when engaged in willfully, may lead to a determination of lack of good moral character.[2]

§ 9:34　Part 10: Ineligibility factors; generally—Oath requirements

The naturalization applicant must be attached to the U.S. Constitution and well disposed to the happiness and the good order of the U.S. In addition, the applicant must be able to take the naturalization oath without reservations. The following questions address those concerns. The first question addresses allegiance to the U.S. Constitution and form of government. What constitutes proper allegiance to the U.S. government is fully discussed in Ch 7.[1] The remaining questions in this part concern the taking of the oath and the form of the oath that will be taken. These issues are discussed in detail below.[2]

§ 9:35　Part 11: Applicant's signature

The applicant is required to sign the application. If the applicant cannot sign in English, the applicant may sign in his or her native language. If the applicant is unable to write in any language, the applicant may sign with an "X."[1]

The INA requires that applications for naturalization be "sworn [and] signed by the applicant in the applicant's own handwriting, if physically able to write."[2] If the

---

[Section 9:32]

　　[1]See §§ 7:77 to 7:83.

　　[2]See §§ 9:61 to 9:65.

[Section 9:33]

　　[1]INA § 237(a)(2)(D)(ii), 8 U.S.C.A. § 1227(a)(2)(D)(ii).

　　[2]See § 7:45.

[Section 9:34]

　　[1]See §§ 7:47 to 7:51.

　　[2]See §§ 9:56 to 9:65.

[Section 9:35]

　　[1]Form N-400 (Instructions).

　　[2]INA § 334(a), 8 U.S.C.A. § 1445(a).

person is not physically able to write, he or she is not required to sign. There is no place in the N-400 to indicate that the person is physically unable to write.[3]

§9:36 Part 12: Preparer's signature

When a person is unable to write, the preparer must sign here.[1] The regulations are silent as to other circumstances in which people who assisted in the preparation of the form must sign here. However, section 274C of the INA makes it a five-year felony to willfully fail to disclose the role as a preparer of an application, where the application was false, and where the preparer received some remuneration.[2]

§9:37 Part 13: Applicant's signature at interview

Do not complete this part. It will be filled out by the USCIS examiner and must be signed by the applicant *in front* of the USCIS examiner at the end of the USCIS examination.[1]

The USCIS officer will have the applicant subscribe this section in front of him or her; and will require the applicant to take the following oath: "I swear (affirm) and certify under penalty of perjury under the laws of the United States of America that I know that the contents of this application for naturalization subscribed by me, and the evidence submitted with it, are true and correct to the best of my knowledge and belief."[2]

If the applicant is not able to sign, adjudicating officers have been instructed to allow applicants to make some kind of mark, as a reasonable accommodation for a signature.[3] In cases where the applicant is unable to make any type of mark but has indicated assent to the requirements of naturalization, adjudicating officers have been instructed to make a notation in this section indicating that the officer has determined that the applicant has assented and responded to the questions on the N-400.[4] No actual signature is noted in those cases.[5]

§9:38 Part 14: Oath of allegiance

Research References

Dizon and Wettstein, Immigration Law Service 2d §14:356

Do not complete this part. The USCIS officer will ask the applicant to complete this part at the interview. The applicant's signature in this section indicates that the applicant has no objections to taking the Oath of Allegiance. It does not mean that the applicant has already taken the Oath.

---

[3]See Applicant's Affidavit.

[Section 9:36]

[1]8 CFR § 334.2(a).

[2]INA 274C(e), 8 U.S.C.A. § 1324c(e).

[Section 9:37]

[1]8 CFR § 335.3(d). See §§ 9:52 to 9:53.

[2]8 CFR § 335.3(d).

[3]Pearson, Exec.Assoc. Comm'r, Office of Field Operations, Memorandum No. HQ 70/33-P (Apr.7, 1999) reproduced as Appendix 7–10.

[4]Pearson, Exec.Assoc. Comm'r, Office of Field Operations, Memorandum No. HQ 70/33-P (Apr.7, 1999) reproduced as Appendix 7–10.

[5]Pearson, Exec.Assoc. Comm'r, Office of Field Operations, Memorandum No. HQ 70/33-P (Apr.7, 1999) reproduced as Appendix 7–10.

C. ADDITIONAL DOCUMENTS AND FORMS

§ 9:39 Generally

The applicant is required to file the following documents and forms together with the naturalization application: (1) evidence of lawful permanent residence, (2) two photographs, (3) if applicant served in the military, he or she must also file Form G-325B and Form N-426, and (4) any other supporting documents listed in the *Guide to Naturalization*.

§ 9:40 Evidence of lawful permanent residence

Research References

Dizon and Wettstein, Immigration Law Service 2d § 15:10

As evidence of lawful permanent residence, the applicant must file photocopies of the front and back of the permanent residence card ("alien" registration receipt card) or any other entry document.[1] At the interview, the applicant may be required to submit the originals of these documents.[2]

§ 9:41 Photographs

The *Guide to Naturalization* requires the applicant to submit *two* identical photographs.[1] In spite of the regulations stating that three photographs should be submitted,[2] virtually all USCIS offices will accept applications that include two photographs.

These photographs must: (1) have a glossy finish; (2) be in natural color; (3) have a white background; (4) have been taken within 30 days of being furnished to the USCIS; (5) be printed on thin paper; (6) *not* be mounted; (7) be a "passport-style" photograph;[3] (8) show the head of the applicant as bare unless the applicant is wearing a headdress required by a religious order of which he or she is a member; and (9) be the same size as the example in the *Guide to Naturalization*.[4]

The applicant must *lightly* print his or her name and "A" number on the back of each photograph using a pencil.[5]

At the naturalization examination, the applicant will be required to sign his or her name to each copy of the photograph unless the applicant is a child who cannot write or a person physically unable to sign his or her name.[6] The photographs will

---

[Section 9:40]

   [1]8 CFR § 316.4(a)(2).

   [2]8 CFR § 316.4(b).

[Section 9:41]

   [1]Guide to Naturalization at 33.

   [2]8 CFR §§ 316.4(a)(4), 333.1(a).

   [3]The CIS now uses passport-style photographs rather than the former "three-quarters" photographs, for all CIS applications. William Yates, Reminder of Change in Photograph Standard (August 25, 2004), found at http://uscis.gov/graphics/lawsregs/handbook/PhotoRmnd082504.pdf.

   [4]See 8 CFR § 333.1(a) or Color Photograph Specifications located in the back of the Guide for more specific guidelines.

   [5]Guide to Naturalization at 33.

   [6]8 CFR § 333.1(b), (d); Form N-400 (Instructions).

be signed on the *front* but without obscuring any of the features on the image.[7] The applicant will sign his or her full true name, and this signature must be in the English language, unless the applicant is exempt from the English language requirement, in which case the signature may be in any language.[8]

Children who cannot write will have their photographs signed by a parent or guardian.[9] The signature must read "(name of child) by (name of parent or guardian)."[10] Adults who cannot write may place a mark where the signature should be.[11] For adults who are physically unable to sign or make a mark, a guardian or the USCIS employee conducting the interview will sign the photographs.[12]

In cases where religious beliefs prohibit having one's photograph taken, the USCIS will exempt the applicant from the photograph requirement of the naturalization application.[13]

§ 9:42 Forms G-325B and N-426

Applicants who served in the military must also file Forms G-325B (Biographic Information) and N-426 (Request for Certification of Military or Naval Service) with their N-400.[1] These forms are required regardless of whether the person is applying under the general naturalization provision or under one of the military-related naturalization provisions.[2]

§ 9:43 Other supporting documents

The *Guide to Naturalization* includes a checklist of other documents the applicant may need to include.[1] The checklist, reproduced at appendix 9-7, specifies when original documents are required and when copies are acceptable.[2] The applicant should remember to keep copies of all original documents.

All districts will require applicants who have been arrested or detained by the police to present court dispositions of all criminal charges.[3] The USCIS also requests the arrest reports.[4] This may be overreaching on the part of the USCIS, since the arrest report is not part of a person's record of conviction.[5] Persons who have had

---

[7]8 CFR § 333.1(b).

[8]8 CFR § 333.1(b).

[9]8 CFR § 333.1(c)(1).

[10]8 CFR § 333.1(c)(1).

[11]8 CFR § 333.1(b).

[12]8 CFR § 333.1(c)(2).

[13]Legal Opinion, Martin, INS General Counsel, Genco Opinion 96-5 (Feb. 23, 1996).

[Section 9:42]

[1]Form N-400 (instructions). Form G-325B is reproduced as Appendix 12-3 to Ch 12. It may also be downloaded from the USCIS site at http://uscis.gov/graphics/index.htm.

[2]The military-related naturalization provisions are described in Ch 12.

[Section 9:43]

[1]Guide to Naturalization at 34.

[2]Guide to Naturalization at 34.

[3]See Appendix 9–6, List of Documents for Naturalization Interview.

[4]See Appendix 9–6, List of Documents for Naturalization Interview.

[5]Matter of Texeira, Int. Dec. 3273 (B.I.A. 1996).

arrests will be scrutinized closely by the USCIS as these arrests may not only bar a finding of good moral character but may also render them deportable.[6]

Another set of documents usually requested by the USCIS is tax returns.[7] There may be some justification to request tax returns. Such documents may be relevant to abandonment of permanent residence.[8] It may also be relevant to good moral character. However, the emphasis that some districts place on proof of means of support seems to be improper, particularly since it is well settled that poverty is not a basis for finding lack of good moral character.[9]

Similarly, the USCIS requests Selective Service Registration letter for male applicants between the ages of 18 and 31 years.[10] This relates to the finding of lack of good moral character for applicants who willfully failed to register for selective service.[11]

Additional relevant documents include proof of financial support for applicant's children who do not reside with him or her.[12] The USCIS regulations have created special areas of concern for finding lack of good moral character.[13] One such area is willfully refusing to support dependents.[14] Even though this ground is not automatic, the USCIS will require documentation relevant to this area.[15]

Finally, people who are unable to take the full oath of allegiance should provide documentary proof of the religious beliefs on which the refusal is based.[16]

§ 9:44 Other evidence required at interview

Starting in June 1999, the INS implemented a program, code named "Complete File Review" (CFR), whereby the Service Centers conduct a review of the file for possible additional documents to be required at the interview.[1] The aim of the program was to reduce rescheduling of naturalization interviews.[2] At the service center, an adjudicating officer reviews the N-400 application and immigration file of the applicant ("A" File or qualifying "T" File) to identify any additional documents needed to adjudicate the case.[3] If documents are needed, the officer will send a customized document request letter to the applicant containing a list of documents

---

[6]See §§ 8:2 to 8:26.

[7]See Appendix 9-6.

[8]See § 8:24.

[9]See § 7:43.

[10]See Appendix 9-6.

[11]See § 7:45.

[12]See Appendix 9-6.

[13]8 CFR § 316.10(b)(3).

[14]8 CFR § 316.10(b)(3)(i).

[15]For a discussion of this basis for a finding of lack of good moral character, see § 7:41.

[16]See Appendix 9-6. For a description of the exemption to the full oath, see §§ 9:61 to 9:65.

[Section 9:44]

[1]Yates, Deputy Exec. Assoc. Comm'r, Field Operations, Memorandum for Community-Based Organizations (August 13, 1999) reproduced in 4 Bender's Immigration Bulletin 944 (Sept.15, 1999).

[2]Yates, Deputy Exec. Assoc. Comm'r, Field Operations, Memorandum for Community-Based Organizations (August 13, 1999) reproduced in 4 Bender's Immigration Bulletin 944 (Sept.15, 1999).

[3]Yates, Deputy Exec. Assoc. Comm'r, Field Operations, Memorandum for Community-Based Organizations (August 13, 1999) reproduced in 4 Bender's Immigration Bulletin 944 (Sept.15, 1999).

he or she must provide to the USCIS at the time of the interview.[4] A copy of this letter will be sent to the applicant's attorney if there is a Form G-28 with the application.[5] The letter will also provide some guidance to the applicant as to where to obtain these documents.[6]

§ 9:45 Additional evidence and forms required for naturalization under special categories

Special forms of naturalization, such as applications under the special provision for spouses of U.S. citizens, require additional documentation, which must be included with the N-400 application.[1] This documentation is discussed in the chapters dealing with the specific forms of naturalization.[2]

IV. FINGERPRINTING

§ 9:46 In general

Research References

Dizon and Wettstein, Immigration Law Service 2d § 14:320

Prior to 1997, naturalization applications had to be filed with "fingerprint cards," Form FN-258. That process was completely altered by Congress,[1] and since December 3, 1997, the applicant does not obtain their own fingerprints.[2] Now, After filing the Form N-400, these naturalization applicants are notified to appear at a specially created agency office, named Application Support Centers (ASC), to be fingerprinted.[3] A sample notice to appear for fingerprinting is reproduced as Appendix 9-5.

Naturalization applications from individuals residing outside of the United States were filed with completed fingerprint cards prepared by a United States consular office at a United States embassy or consulate or a United States military installation abroad.[4]

As amended by these changes, the regulations now require the applicant to file the N-400 application without a fingerprint card.[5] It then provides that the ap-

---

[4]Yates, Deputy Exec. Assoc. Comm'r, Field Operations, Memorandum for Community-Based Organizations (August 13, 1999) reproduced in 4 Bender's Immigration Bulletin 944 (Sept.15, 1999).

[5]Yates, Deputy Exec. Assoc. Comm'r, Field Operations, Memorandum for Community-Based Organizations (August 13, 1999) reproduced in 4 Bender's Immigration Bulletin 944 (Sept.15, 1999).

[6]Yates, Deputy Exec. Assoc. Comm'r, Field Operations, Memorandum for Community-Based Organizations (August 13, 1999) reproduced in 4 Bender's Immigration Bulletin 944 (Sept.15, 1999).

[Section 9:45]

[1]8 CFR § 334.2(a).

[2]See §§ 11:1 et seq. and 12:1 et seq.

[Section 9:46]

[1]Department of Justice Appropriations Act, Pub. L. 105-119, 111 Stat. 2440 (Nov. 26, 1997).

[2]See 63 Fed. Reg. 12979 (March 17, 1998) (Supplementary Information); 74 Interpreter Releases 709 (Apr. 28, 1997).

[3]63 Fed. Reg. 12979 (March 17, 1998). A sample notice to appear for fingerprinting is reproduced as Appendix 9-5.

[4]63 Fed. Reg. 12979 (Supplementary Information).

[5]8 CFR § 316.4(a) as amended by 63 Fed. Reg. 12979.

plicant will be fingerprinted by the USCIS.[6] A fee of $85, in addition to the normal N-400 fee, has to be submitted at the time of filing of the naturalization application for fingerprinting purposes.[7]

In addition, the agency has amended the regulations to specify that the naturalization examination will not be scheduled until after the USCIS has received a definitive response from the FBI that a full criminal background check of an applicant has been completed.[8] The regulations defined this definite response as: (1) confirmation from the FBI that an applicant does not have an administrative or a criminal record; (2) confirmation from the FBI that an applicant has an administrative or a criminal record; or (3) confirmation from the FBI that two properly prepared fingerprint cards (Form FD-258) have been determined unclassifiable for the purpose of conducting a criminal background check and have been rejected.[9] In its supplementary information when introducing these changes, the INS pointed out that "[i]n the case of an applicant whose fingerprints cannot be classified, service quality assurance procedures require the applicant to submit police clearances to the service before final adjudication of the naturalization application."[10]

Traditionally, fingerprints had only been required of naturalization applicants younger than 75 years of age.[11] This same information is reproduced on the notice to appear for fingerprinting.[12] The *INS Operations Instructions* specify that only applicants between the ages of fourteen and seventy-nine should be fingerprinted.[13]

The agency issued a memorandum specifying the procedures for granting a fingerprint waiver for applicants who have disabilities that render them unable to be fingerprinted or which renders fingerprints that are illegible.[14] Only USCIS officers responsible for overseeing applicant fingerprinting are authorized to waive the fingerprinting requirement.[15] They are only authorized to waive the fingerprinting after personally seeing the applicant, attempting to fingerprint the applicant (or observing a technician attempting to do so), and determining that the applicant cannot be fingerprinted at all or cannot provide legible fingerprints.[16]

V. INVESTIGATION

§ 9:47   In general

Research References

Dizon and Wettstein, Immigration Law Service 2d § 14:330

---

[6]8 CFR § 316.4(b) as amended by 63 Fed. Reg. 12979.

[7]See § 9:5.

[8]8 CFR § 335.2(b) as amended by 63 Fed. Reg. 12979.

[9]8 CFR § 335.2(b) as amended by 63 Fed. Reg. 12979.

[10]63 Fed. Reg. 12979, 12983 (Supplementary Information).

[11]See Form N-400 (Rev. 7/17/91), Instructions. The instructions also refer to fingerprinting for children under fourteen. This is a moot point since under current law, only persons eighteen or older may file for naturalization with Form N-400. See INA § 334(b), 8 U.S.C.A. § 1445(b).

[12]See Appendix 9-5.

[13]OI 105.10(a).

[14]Yates, Deputy Executive Associate Commissioner for Field Operations (Nov. 15, 1999) reproduced in 76 Interpreter Releases 1794 (Dec. 20, 1999).

[15]Yates, Deputy Executive Associate Commissioner for Field Operations (Nov. 15, 1999) reproduced in 76 Interpreter Releases 1794 (Dec. 20, 1999).

[16]Yates, Deputy Executive Associate Commissioner for Field Operations (Nov. 15, 1999) reproduced in 76 Interpreter Releases 1794 (Dec. 20, 1999).

Once the application is filed, the USCIS will conduct an investigation that, at a minimum, will consist of a review of all pertinent records, police department checks, and, unless the District Director decides otherwise, a neighborhood investigation in the vicinities where the applicant has resided and has been employed for the five years preceding the application.[1] The law provides the Secretary of DHS the power to waive the neighborhood investigations, either on an individual basis or for classes of applicants.[2] The Secretary of DHS has delegated this power to each USCIS office.[3] These investigations have routinely been waived in the past and are likely to continue to be waived.[4]

A special investigation is also required by law to establish the loyalty of a naturalization applicant who is a native, citizen, subject, or denizen of a country with which the United States is at war.[5] These investigations may take place before or after the examination of the applicant.[6] The purpose of such investigations is to establish the applicant's loyalty to the U.S. and his or her attachment to the country, state, or sovereignty with which the U.S. is at war.[7] Unlike the general naturalization investigation, this investigation may not be waived.[8]

The USCIS conducts a different type of investigation when the applicant appears to suffer from a disease and physical impairment that precludes his or her presence at the USCIS examination or at the oath ceremony.[9] If the USCIS determines on the basis of available medical evidence that the sickness precludes the applicant's presence at the USCIS offices, the USCIS must conduct the naturalization proceedings in a location that can be reached by the applicant.[10]

VI. BACKGROUND CHECKS

§ 9:48 Background checks

Aside from the "investigation" authorized in the INA, the USCIS now runs a series of background checks on all naturalization applicants. The procedure started in 1997, after a few individuals with criminal backgrounds were naturalized; after public posturing, Congress adopted by statute a rule requiring a "full criminal background check."[1]

The agency's first interpretation of the term "criminal background check" is the traditional FBI fingerprint check, designed to discover any individual's criminal

---

[Section 9:47]

[1]INA § 335(a), 8 U.S.C.A. § 1446(a); 8 CFR § 335.1.

[2]INA § 335(a), 8 U.S.C.A. § 1446(a).

[3]8 CFR § 335.1.

[4]Gordon & Mailman, § 96.03[4][a].

[5]INA § 331, 8 U.S.C.A. § 1442; 8 CFR § 331. For a discussion of the naturalization of noncitizen enemies, see § 12:14.

[6]8 CFR § 331.3.

[7]INA § 331(a), (c), 8 U.S.C.A. § 1442(a), (c); 8 CFR § 331.3.

[8]See INA § 331, 8 U.S.C.A. § 1442; 8 CFR § 331.3.

[9]8 CFR § 334.4.

[10]8 CFR § 334.4.

[Section 9:48]

[1]Pub.L. 105-119, Title I, 111 Stat. 2448-49 (1997).

background.[2] Thus, by regulation, all applicants must have a completed FBI fingerprint check, unless the FBI is unable to perform such a test after trying at least twice.[3]

Second, the USCIS runs background checks on the "Interagency Border Inspection System," or "IBIS," both at the time of receipt of the N-400, and—if adjudication is delayed—before the oath ceremony.[4]

The third type of background check is the FBI "name check." The process is described at length at App 10-7. The FBI name check has been the source of major delays in naturalization processing,[5] giving rise to various lawsuits, both on a classwide basis and for individuals.[6]

At least one District Court has found that the sub-regulatory adoption of the "name check" requirement, together with the unreasonable delays thereby engendered, violates the Administrative Procedures Act.[7] In *Mocanu*, the District Court enjoined the use of the name check procedure as to those individual plaintiffs, unless the Government engaged in notice and comment rulemaking.[8] In the Western District of Washington, a District Court certified a district-wide class regarding this issue.[9] However, no litigation-based resolution has yet been reached. Class litigation occurred in multiple districts, and a local class was certified in *Roshandel v. Chertoff*, in the Western District of Washington.[10] The Roshandel case was settled with adjudication of all pending and delayed naturalization applications in the Western District of Washington, as was litigation in the Eastern District of New York.[11] However, neither settlement included injunctive relief for future potential class members, and no solution to the broader problem of name check delays was achieved through the various litigation attempts.

Meanwhile, the USCIS and FBI have dedicated additional resources to the resolution of outstanding background checks, and now state that background check delays will be largely eliminated by June 2009, and claim as of June 2009 to have resolved

---

[2]8 C.F.R. § 335.2(b).

[3]8 C.F.R. § 335.2(b)(3).

[4]INS Adj. Field Manual 10.3.

[5]See § 10:3.

[6]See §§ 10:2 to 10:11; App 10-7.

[7]Mocanu v. Mueller, 2008 WL 372459 (E.D. Pa. 2008), order corrected, 2008 WL 570953 (E.D. Pa. 2008).

[8]Mocanu v. Mueller, 2008 WL 372459, *15 (E.D.Pa., Feb. 8, 2008)

[9]Roshandel v. Chertoff, 2008 WL 1929894 (W.D. Wash. 2008), related reference, 2008 WL 1969646 (W.D. Wash. 2008) and amended in part, 2008 WL 2275558 (W.D. Wash. 2008); see also, Yakubova v. Chertoff, 06-CV-3203, at 6 (E.D.N.Y. Nov. 1, 2006) (unpublished) (refusing to dismiss, granting discovery, in putative class claim); but cf. Ahmadi v. Chertoff, 2007 WL 3022573 (N.D.Cal., 2007) (ruling against putative class on the merits of APA challenge, where 1447(b) possibility exists); Antonishin v. Keisler, 2007 WL 2788841 (N.D.Ill., Sept. 20, 2007) (ruling against putative class on the merits).

[10]Roshandel v. Chertoff, 554 F.Supp.2d 1194 (W.D. Wash. 2008), related reference, 2008 WL 1969646 (W.D. Wash. 2008) and amended in part, 2008 WL 2275558 (W.D. Wash. 2008); see also, *Yakubova v. Chertoff, 06-CV-3203, at 6 (E.D.N.Y. Nov. 1, 2006)* (unpublished) (refusing to dismiss, granting discovery, in putative class claim); but cf. Ahmadi v. Chertoff, 2007 WL 3022573 (N.D.Cal., 2007) (ruling against putative class on the merits of APA challenge, where 1447(b) possibility exists); Antonishin v. Keisler, 627 F. Supp. 2d 872 (N.D. Ill. 2007) (ruling against putative class on the merits).

[11]*Roshandel v. Chertoff, 2:07-cv-01739-MJP (Doc. 82) (Aug. 25, 2008)* (unpublished), full text of settlement is available at: http://www.aclu-wa.org/sites/default/files/attachments/20080813__Roshandel__Settlement.pdf; *Yakubova v. Chertoff, 06-CV-3203, Doc. 68 (July 7, 2008)* (unpublished).

the problem of name check delays.[12] However, some applicants continue to face substantial delays related to background checks or related matters.[13]

§ 9:49 Special rules applicable to SSI beneficiaries under *Kaplan*

Delays relating to background checks were particularly burdensome to refugees and other individuals who were receiving Social Security Insurance (SSI) benefits. By law, individuals may receive SSI benefits for only seven years, as aliens.[1] That law forces them to obtain U.S. citizenship, or face a cutoff of their SSI benefits.[2]

This led to class litigation, and to a nationwide class settlement, in *Kaplan v. Chertoff*.[3] In the *Kaplan* settlement, the USCIS and FBI agreed to take several steps. First, any class member may request expedited treatment of their case, which will be granted once the case has been pending for six months. Expedited treatment may be requested either by the National Customer Service Center at 1-800-375-5283; in writing at the time of the application; in-person at any USCIS office; or in writing to the address where the application was mailed.[4]

Second, the Settlement Agreement contains provisions whereby USCIS will work with the Social Security Administration to automatically expedite background checks for applicants who have lost their SSI benefits, or are about to lose their SSI benefits, by cross-checking social security numbers with USCIS applications.[5]

It appears that the Kaplan settlement has now expired, pursuant to the terms of that agreement.[6] However, as of 2012, it appears that the government continues to adhere to the terms of that agreement.

VII. EXAMINATION OF APPLICANT

§ 9:50 Overview

Unless determined to suffer from an illness that is sufficiently serious to prevent his or her personal appearance, the applicant must appear in the USCIS office for the naturalization examination.[1]

---

[12]See App. 9-11, App. 9-12.

[13]See, e.g., Memic v. Holder, 2011 WL 1361563 (E.D.Mo., Apr. 11, 2011) (unpublished) (20 month delay after filing of naturalization, not scheduled for interview); Turkmen v. Holder, 2010 WL 2607152 (E.D.Mo., June 14, 2010) (consolidated action on behalf of 11 applicants for naturalization or adjustment of status, delayed due to name check adjudication).

[Section 9:49]

[1]8 U.S.C.A. § 1612(a)(2)(A).

[2]Kaplan v. Chertoff, Slip Copy, 2008 WL 200108, (E.D.Pa. 2008).

[3]Kaplan, et al., v. Chertoff, et al., Civil Action No. 06-5304 (E.D.Pa) (found online at http://www.uscis.gov/files/article/Stipulation.pdf).

[4]Settlement Agreement at para 17. When calling the NCSC telephone number, the expedition request can be accessed via the main menu as option six.

[5]Settlement Agreement at paras. 23, 26.

[6]See App 9-10, at 21, para 54.

[Section 9:50]

[1]8 CFR § 335.2(a). See § 9:53.

Examination of the applicant is conducted by USCIS officers referred to as "immigration examiners."[2] USCIS directors may also designate other USCIS officers to conduct naturalization examinations, provided: (1) they are classified at a grade level equal to or higher than immigration examiners, and (2) they are properly trained.[3] Although rarely used, the regulations allow depositions to be taken in connection with a naturalization application.[4] No special designation is required.[5] They are also designated to administer oaths or affirmations, other than the oath of allegiance.[6]

Applicant's who fail to appear for the examination must notify the USCIS of the reasons for failure to appear within 30 days of the original date of the examination.[7] This notification must be in writing and must include a request for rescheduling the examination.[8] No specific format is required to request reopening; rather, a brief, informal note for the adjudications officer to insert into the file is sufficient.[9] If the applicant does not file a timely notification, the USCIS is authorized to administratively close the application without making a decision on the merits.[10] The applicant then has one year from the date the application was closed to request reopening the application.[11] These requests for reopening are filed without a fee.[12] For purposes of determining eligibility, the naturalization application will be deemed to have been filed on the date the request for reopening was filed.[13] If the applicant does not request reopening of an administratively closed application within one year from the date the application was closed, the USCIS will consider the application to have been abandoned and will dismiss the application without further notice to the applicant.[14]

An opinion from the Office of Legal Counsel of the Department of Justice explains that the Rehabilitation Act of 1973 requires the agency to allow a legal guardian or proxy to assist a mentally disabled applicant who is unable to file the application or participate in the interview.[15] The memorandum concludes that an individual who is unable to file an application or participate in the interview may still be "otherwise

---

[2] 8 CFR § 332.1(a), (b).

[3] 8 CFR § 332.1(a), (b).

[4] 8 CFR § 332.1(c) (the depositions may be taken by any officer or employee with a grade equal or higher to immigration examiner).

[5] 8 CFR § 332.1(c) (the regulation itself designates them to take depositions).

[6] 8 CFR § 332.1(d).

[7] 8 CFR § 335.6(a).

[8] 8 CFR § 335.6(a).

[9] 60 Fed. Reg. 6647 (Feb. 3, 1995) (supplementary information).

[10] 8 CFR § 335.6(b).

[11] 8 CFR § 335.6(b).

[12] 8 CFR § 335.6(b).

[13] 8 CFR § 335.6(b).

[14] 8 CFR § 335.6(c).

[15] See Memorandum of M. Edward Whelan III, Office of Legal Counsel, U.S. Department of Justice, to Bo Cooper, General Counsel, INS Re: "Role of Legal Guardians or Proxies in Naturalization Proceedings" (March 13, 2002) reprinted in 80 Interpreter Releases 570-571 (April 21, 2003).

qualified" for naturalization within the meaning of the Rehabilitation Act.[16] The USCIS will modify the examination procedure to allow a designated representative to complete the examination on behalf of a person with severe disabilities who otherwise may be eligible for naturalization but is unable to personally attest to eligibility through the regular procedures.[17] The representative will be allowed to attest to the applicant's eligibility.[18]

§ 9:51 Language issues and interpretation

Unless the applicant is exempt from the English language requirement, naturalization interviews will generally be conducted in English.[1] Interpreters may only be used for non-exempt applicants if the naturalization examiner needs to dwell on issues which are complex in nature and which may not be couched in simple language.[2] Use of interpreters in non-exempt cases is only allowed after the naturalization examiner has satisfied himself or herself that the applicant has the required ability to speak basic English.[3]

The USCIS or the applicant may provide interpreters.[4] The USCIS, however, may disqualify an interpreter provided by the applicant during the course of an examination if it is necessary to ensure the integrity of the examination.[5] The officer making the disqualification must make a written record of the reasons for the disqualification and make such record part of the applicant's file.[6] If the USCIS disqualifies the interpreter, the USCIS must provide another interpreter for the applicant in a timely manner so as not to delay unduly the adjudication of the application.[7] If rescheduling of the interview becomes necessary, the USCIS must set a new date as soon as practicable so as not to delay unduly the adjudication of the application.[8]

§ 9:52 Content of examination

The purpose of this examination is to elicit all material information on eligibility.[1] By law, the USCIS is required to limit the scope of the naturalization examination

---

[16]Memorandum of M. Edward Whelan III, Office of Legal Counsel, U.S. Department of Justice, to Bo Cooper, General Counsel, INS Re: "Role of Legal Guardians or Proxies in Naturalization Proceedings" (March 13, 2002)) reprinted in 80 Interpreter Releases 570-571 (April 21, 2003).

[17]See Memorandum of William Yates, Acting Assoc. Director, CIS, HQ 70/33 (June 30, 2003), entitled "Procedures for Implementing the Waiving of the Oath of Renunciation and Allegiance for the Naturalization of Aliens having Certain Disabilities," reprinted in App 7-16.

[18]See Memorandum of William Yates, Acting Assoc. Director, CIS, HQ 70/33 (June 30, 2003), entitled "Procedures for Implementing the Waiving of the Oath of Renunciation and Allegiance for the Naturalization of Aliens having Certain Disabilities," reprinted in App 7-16.

[Section 9:51]

[1]8 CFR § 312.1(c)(1).

[2]8 CFR § 312.2(c)(1)(ii); INS Interp. 312.1(a)(3).

[3]INS Interp. 312.1(a)(3).

[4]8 CFR § 312.4.

[5]8 CFR § 312.4.

[6]8 CFR § 312.4.

[7]8 CFR § 312.4.

[8]8 CFR § 312.4.

[Section 9:52]

[1]8 CFR § 335.2(a).

to an inquiry concerning the applicant's residence, physical presence in the United States, good moral character, understanding of and attachment to the fundamental principles of the Constitution, ability to read, write, and speak English, and other legal qualifications to become a naturalized citizen.[2] There is also a requirement that the all the examinations throughout the United States be uniform.[3]

The contents of Form N-400 and other forms submitted by the applicant are reviewed and may be corrected by the examiner to conform to the testimony.[4] Unless the applicant is exempted from the English requirement, the interview will be conducted in English.[5] The questions to the applicant will be repeated in a different form and elaborated, if necessary, until the officer is satisfied that either the applicant has fully understood the question or is unable to understand English.[6] Unless the applicant has satisfied the literacy and civics requirements through a standardized test, he or she will be asked history and government questions during the examination and his or her literacy will be tested.[7] Persons who have passed a standardized test within one year of the filing of the naturalization application will not be asked questions about these topics unless the USCIS officer believes the applicant's test results are fraudulent.[8]

§ 9:53 Examination procedures

The applicant will be interviewed in a setting apart from the public.[1] The applicant's attorney may be present and fully represent his or her client at the interview.[2] The applicant will be questioned under oath at the interview.[3]

The USCIS examiner is required to maintain brief notations of the examination for the record.[4] At the very least, these notes must include a record of the test administered to the applicant on the English language and civics.[5] This record may take the form of a stenographic, mechanical, electronic, videotaped transcript or an affidavit by the USCIS officer regarding the testimony of the applicant.[6] At the end of the examination, the USCIS officer will attach to the application all supplemental materials and all corrections made to the application.[7] The applicant will subscribe

---

[2]INA § 332(a), 8 U.S.C.A. § 1443(a). But see, Price v. U.S. I.N.S., 941 F.2d 878 (9th Cir. 1991).

[3]8 CFR § 335.2(a).

[4]8 CFR § 335.2(b).

[5]8 CFR § 312.1(c)(1).

[6]8 CFR § 335.2(b).

[7]See for a discussion of the English and History and Government requirements.

[8]8 CFR § 312.3(a).

[Section 9:53]

[1]8 CFR § 335.2(b).

[2]8 CFR § 335.2(a); 60 Fed. Reg. 6647 (Feb. 3, 1995) (supplementary information at 6648: "As applicants are now subject to only one examination, the rights to representation at that examination have been expanded to be consistent with all other adjudications before the Service").

[3]8 CFR § 335.2(b).

[4]8 CFR § 335.2(b).

[5]8 CFR § 335.2(b).

[6]8 CFR § 335.2(b).

[7]8 CFR § 335.2(d).

to the corrected application form with all attachments under oath.[8] The full record will include the subscribed application form with corrections and attachments, and all evidence received by the officer, including all documentary evidence.[9] If an interpreter was used during the examination, the identity of the interpreter must be included.[10] This record will be admissible as evidence at any administrative review of the denial of naturalization.[11]

Both the applicant and the USCIS have the right to present oral or documentary evidence and to conduct cross-examination of witnesses.[12] The USCIS officer has the power to take testimony in any matter relating to the admissibility of the applicant for naturalization and issue subpoenas for the attendance of witnesses and for the production of documents relevant to these issues.[13] The applicant has the right to request the USCIS to issue subpoenas for the appearance of witnesses at the naturalization hearing by making a request at the time he or she files the naturalization application.[14] These administrative subpoenas may be enforced through federal district court actions.[15] The agency has issued regulations relating to the format and the proper service of these subpoenas.[16]

§ 9:54 Continuances

Research References

Dizon and Wettstein, Immigration Law Service 2d § 14:346

If there are deficiencies in the application that arise during the examination, the USCIS officer may continue the examination at a later time, at least 60 days after the initial examination.[1] This period is granted to allow the applicant to overcome these deficiencies.[2] The USCIS officer must inform the applicant in writing of the grounds that need to be overcome or the additional evidence that needs to be submitted.[3] This information is provided on Form N-14B, which has different versions according to the deficiency to be overcome. Two versions of Form N-14B are reproduced in Appendix 9-2. The reexamination must occur within the 120 days allowed to USCIS to make a decision after the initial examination.[4] If the applicant has been unable to overcome the deficiency, the application will be denied.[5]

If the applicant does not "pass" the English literacy or history and government tests, the applicant will be afforded a second opportunity to take the test within

---

[8]8 CFR § 335.2(d).

[9]8 CFR § 335.2(d).

[10]8 CFR § 335.2(e).

[11]INA § 335(b) 8 U.S.C.A. § 1446(b). See administrative hearings of denied applications.

[12]INA § 336(c), 8 U.S.C.A. § 1447(c); 8 CFR § 335.2(b).

[13]INA § 335(b), 8 U.S.C.A. § 1446(b).

[14]INA § 336(c), 8 U.S.C.A. § 1447(c).

[15]INA § 335(b), 8 U.S.C.A. § 1446(b).

[16]8 CFR § 335.2(c).

[Section 9:54]

[1]8 CFR § 335.3(b).

[2]8 CFR § 335.3(b).

[3]8 CFR § 335.2(b).

[4]See § 9:55.

[5]8 CFR § 335.3(b).

ninety days from the initial examination.[6] If the applicant fails to appear at this new examination without good cause, the application will be deemed to have failed the test.[7] An applicant will not be allowed to request a postponement of this second examination beyond ninety days after the original examination unless the applicant agrees in writing to waive the requirement that the USCIS render a decision on the application within 120 days of the initial examination.[8] The applicant will be required to agree to allow the USCIS to render a decision within 120 days from the new interview date instead.[9]

After an applicant has appeared for the initial USCIS examination, the applicant will be considered to have failed to prosecute his or her application if, without good cause: (1) he or she fails to excuse an absence from any required subsequent appearance, or (2) fails to provide within a reasonable period any documents, information, or testimony required by the USCIS to establish his or her eligibility for naturalization.[10] The USCIS is required to provide written notice requesting these subsequent appearances or the additional documentation.[11] If the applicant fails to respond to these notices within 30 days, the USCIS will adjudicate the application on the merits and serve a notice of denial.[12] The applicant may request an administrative review from this notice of denial.[13]

§ 9:55 Decision

The USCIS must make a decision to grant or deny a naturalization application within 120 days of the interview.[1] If the USCIS fails to make a decision within that period, the applicant may request the U.S. district court to intervene either by deciding to naturalize the applicant or by ordering USCIS to make a decision on the case.[2] Procedures for such requests are discussed in Ch 10.[3]

The USCIS officer must grant the application if the applicant has complied with all the requirements for naturalization.[4] There is no discretion involved in these cases. If the application has been granted, the applicant will be notified of the date and place of the naturalization oath ceremony.[5] The Form N-445, used for these notifications, is reproduced in Appendix 9-3.

---

[6]8 CFR § 312.5(a). See § 7:103.

[7]8 CFR § 312.5(b).

[8]8 CFR § 312.5(b).

[9]8 CFR § 312.5(b).

[10]8 CFR § 335.7.

[11]8 CFR § 335.7.

[12]8 CFR § 335.7.

[13]8 CFR § 335.7. (this section specifically refers to rendering a decision under 8 CFR § 336.1, which provides for administrative review of the decision).

[Section 9:55]

[1]8 CFR § 335.3(a).

[2]INA § 336(b), 8 U.S.C.A. § 1447(b).

[3]See §§ 10:9 to 10:11.

[4]8 CFR § 335.3(a).

[5]8 CFR § 335.3(a).

If the application was denied, the applicant will be served a notice of denial within 120 days of the original naturalization interview.[6] The notice of denial must be written in narrative form and must include in clear, concise language the pertinent facts which serve as the basis for the denial, the section of law applicable to bar the applicant from admission to citizenship, and the legal conclusions for denial.[7] It must also include a statement regarding the applicant's right to seek administrative review.[8] This notice must be served in person or by certified mail at the applicant's last known address.[9] When an application is denied, the record of the examination will be transferred to the USCIS officer in charge of conducting an administrative review of denials.[10] Administrative and judicial reviews are discussed below.[11]

Applications that have been granted may be reopened by the USCIS if derogatory information is received before the taking of the oath of allegiance.[12] In such cases, the USCIS will remove the name of the applicant from any list of granted applications compiled for purposes of administering the naturalization oaths.[13] It will then notify the applicant in writing regarding the specific derogatory information it has received and allow the applicant 15 days to respond.[14] If the applicant overcomes the derogatory information, the application's grant will be reaffirmed and the applicant will be rescheduled for the naturalization oath.[15] If the applicant is unable to overcome the derogatory information, the application will be reopened and will be denied.[16] The applicant will be served a notice of denial according to the standard procedures for initial denial of applications and will have a right to administrative review of the decision.[17]

VIII. ADMISSION TO CITIZENSHIP

A. ADMINISTRATION OF THE OATH OF ALLEGIANCE

§ 9:56 Overview

Research References

Dizon and Wettstein, Immigration Law Service 2d § 14:356

If the application is granted, the applicant must still take the oath of allegiance

---

[6]8 CFR § 336.1(a). USCIS offices across the country regularly experience significant delays in adjudicating applications after the examination, in large part due to delays in processing of name checks by the FBI. Where no decision has been made on an application within 120 days after the examination, an applicant can file suit in federal district court under 8 U.S.C.A. § 1447(b). See §§ 10:2 to 10:7.

[7]8 CFR § 336.1(b).

[8]8 CFR § 336.1(b).

[9]8 CFR § 336.1(c).

[10]8 CFR § 335.4.

[11]See §§ 9:67 to 9:68 (administrative appeal); Ch 10 (judicial review).

[12]8 CFR § 335.5.

[13]8 CFR § 335.5.

[14]8 CFR § 335.5.

[15]8 CFR § 335.5.

[16]8 CFR § 335.5.

[17]8 CFR §§ 335.5, 336.1.

before he or she becomes a U.S. citizen.[1] The oath has been a requirement since the very first naturalization statute.[2] The language of the first two sections of the current oath has remained virtually unchanged since the 1795 act.[3]

Many (probably most) children who naturalize do so derivatively, automatically deriving citizenship on the naturalization of their parents, without any oath being required of them.[4] However, the law does continue to contemplate some children naturalizing upon the application of their parents.[5] Such children must take the oath, unless it is waived due to their incompetence.[6]

Similarly, applicants who, because of physical or developmental disability or mental impairment are "unable to understand, or to communicate an understanding of" the oath, may also have the requirement of the oath waived.[7]

The general rule remains, however, that one must be competent to take the oath. The competency requirement is more fully discussed in Ch 7.[8]

The courts have the authority to grant an official change of name to naturalization applicants at the time of the oath ceremony.[9] The naturalization certificate would then appear under the person's new name.[10] Applicants wishing to make such a name change should elect to have a court-administered oath ceremony.[11]

Applicants are considered U.S. citizens as of the date the naturalization oath is taken.[12] Children whose oath has been waived are considered U.S. citizens as of the date the USCIS granted the waiver of the oath.[13] If an applicant who is required to take the oath fails to appear at an oath ceremony more than once without good cause, he or she is considered to have abandoned his or her intent to be naturalized.[14] Such presumption is considered sufficient for the USCIS to reopen the grant of naturalization and to consider a denial under the provisions available for reopening when derogatory information is received before taking the oath of allegiance.[15]

In the 1996 elections, there was a political scandal based on the fact that a nonprofit organization had registered naturalization applicants for voting after their ap-

---

[Section 9:56]

[1]INA § 337(a), 8 U.S.C.A. § 1448(a).

[2]Sec. 1, Act of March 26, 1790 reproduced as Appendix 4-1 to Ch 4.

[3]Sec. 1, Act of January 29, 1795 reproduced as Appendix 4-2 to Ch 4.

[4]See §§ 5:16 to 5:19.

[5]See §§ 11:18 to 11:25, INA § 322 [8 U.S.C.A. § 1433].

[6]8 C.F.R. § 322.5.

[7]INA § 337(a), 8 U.S.C.A. § 1448(a) as amended by Act of November 6, 2000, § 1, Pub.L. 106-448 reproduced as Appendix 5-2 to Ch 5. *See also* Memorandum of William Yates, Acting Assoc. Director, CIS, HQ 70/33 (June 30, 2003), entitled "Procedures for Implementing the Waiving of the Oath of Renunciation and Allegiance for the Naturalization of Aliens having Certain Disabilities," reprinted in App. 7-16.

[8]See § 7:104.

[9]INA § 336(e), 8 U.S.C.A. § 1447(e).

[10]INA § 336(e), 8 U.S.C.A. § 1447(e).; 8 CFR §§ 337.4, 338.2.

[11]See § 9:58.

[12]8 CFR § 337.9(a).

[13]8 CFR § 337.9(b).

[14]8 CFR § 337.10.

[15]See § 9:55.

proval at the interview but before the swearing in ceremony.[16] Persons who vote or even register to vote between the time of their approval by the USCIS and their swearing in ceremony may become deportable under the new grounds of deportability.[17] It is unclear what intent requirement those deportation grounds will be interpreted to have.[18] The USCIS has cautioned its district offices that since voting laws change from location to location, there is no general rule as to who has voted unlawfully.[19] Practitioners should attempt to prevail upon the USCIS to exercise prosecutorial discretion and not to start removal proceedings if the person registered or voted as a result of a good faith mistake.[20]

§ 9:57 Overview—Jurisdiction to administer oath; generally

Research References

Dizon and Wettstein, Immigration Law Service 2d § 14:357

Traditionally the courts conducted naturalization hearings.[1] Ever since 1802, federal courts and those "court[s] of record in any individual state, having common law jurisdiction, and a seal and a clerk" could naturalize noncitizens.[2] Under the current version of the INA, these same courts are provided a ceremonial role in administering the oaths of allegiance.[3]

The INA provides two alternative procedures for administering the oaths. First, it allows any court to request exclusive jurisdiction to administer the oath of allegiance to persons residing in the jurisdiction of the court during the "exclusive jurisdiction" period.[4] This exclusive jurisdiction lasts 45 days from the date the USCIS notifies the court that the applicant qualifies for naturalization.[5] Second, even absent exclusive jurisdiction, the courts still have jurisdiction to administer the oath but so also do the USCIS and the immigration judges.[6]

Some naturalization applicants are not required to file their applications where they reside. Applicants who do not reside within the jurisdiction of the court but are only temporarily present there to apply for naturalization under one of these special

---

[16]On December 31, 1996, INS District Director for the Los Angeles district of INS sent a letter to all community -based organization reminding them that persons are only citizens after the oath ceremony. Rogers, INS District Director, CBO Letter (Dec. 31, 1996).

[17]See INA § 237(a)(3)(D), (6), 8 U.S.C.A. § 1227(a)(3)(D), (6).

[18]The State Department has issued a cable to all consular posts which indicates that "[i]n the normal course of events, the consular officer can presume that an alien voting in a political election did so in violation of some law or ordinance." State Department Cable No. 96-State-219622 (Oct. 21, 1996) reproduced in 73 Interpreter Releases 1505 (Oct. 28, 1996).

[19]INS Memorandum, May 5, 1997 reproduced in 74 Interpreter Releases (May 19, 1997).

[20]See §§ 8:22, 8:23, 8:28.

[Section 9:57]

[1]See, e.g., sec. 1, Act of March 26, 1790 reproduced as Appendix 4-1 to Ch 4.

[2]Sec. 3, Act of April 14, 1802 reproduced as Appendix 4-3 to Ch 4.

[3]INA § 310(b)(1), (5), 8 U.S.C.A. § 1421(b)(1), (5) (the term "eligible court: means—(A) a District Court of the United States in any State, or (B) any court of record in any State having a seal, a clerk, and jurisdiction in actions in law or equity, or law and equity, in which the amount in controversy is unlimited").

[4]INA § 310(b)(1)(B), 8 U.S.C.A. § 1421(b)(1)(B), 8 CFR § 310.3(c)(1).

[5]INA § 310(b)(3)(A), 8 U.S.C.A. § 1421(b)(3)(A).

[6]INA § 310(b)(1)(A), 8 U.S.C.A. § 1421(b)(1)(A); 8 CFR § 337.2(b).

provisions are not subject to the exclusive jurisdiction authority of the court and may take the oath with the USCIS.[7] Classes of applicants not required to file where they reside include: (1) spouses of U.S. citizens performing qualifying employment abroad;[8] (2) children adopted by parents performing qualifying employment abroad;[9] (3) naturalization by service in the armed forces;[10] and (4) naturalization through service in time of war.[11] The provisions governing the naturalization of these classes are discussed in detail in Chs 11 and 12.[12]

Regardless of whether the oath is administered by a court, the USCIS, or the immigration judges, the applicant will be required to fill out the questionnaire on Form N-445 before taking the oath.[13] This questionnaire is attached to the form used to notify the applicants of the date and location of the naturalization ceremony and is reproduced below as Appendix 9-3. The applicant is required to fill out the questionnaire and bring it to the oath ceremony. A USCIS officer will review the form and may question the applicant about the information contained in the form.[14] If derogatory information is uncovered, the applicant's name will be removed from the list of persons eligible to naturalize, and the oath will *not* be administered to him or her.[15]

One court has held that, once a naturalization application is approved, the agency has a non-discretionary duty to schedule the oath even if it has received derogatory information about the individual.[16] The court made clear that it was not ordering that the individual be allowed to take the oath. Rather, it reasoned that, once the oath was scheduled, INS could remove the individual's name from the list and follow the regulatory procedures for notifying the individual of the derogatory information.[17] What the INS could not do was simply refuse to schedule the individual for the oath indefinitely.[18]

§ 9:58 Overview—Jurisdiction to administer oath; generally—In absence of request by courts for exclusive jurisdiction

When local courts have not requested exclusive jurisdiction to administer the naturalization oath, the applicant will have the choice of taking the oath at a court or at an administrative public ceremony conducted either by the USCIS or an im-

---

[7]8 CFR § 310.3(b).

[8]INA § 319(b), 8 U.S.C.A. § 1430(b).

[9]INA § 322(c), 8 U.S.C.A. § 1433(c).

[10]INA § 328(a), 8 U.S.C.A. § 1439(a).

[11]INA § 329, 8 U.S.C.A. § 1440. This exemption also applied to persons naturalized under prior laws through the savings clause in INA § 405.

[12]See §§ 11:1 et seq. and 12:1 et seq.

[13]8 CFR §§ 337.2(c), 337.8(d).

[14]8 CFR §§ 337.2(c), 337.8(d).

[15]8 CFR §§ 337.2(c), 337.8(d).

[16]Patel v. I.N.S., 2000 WL 298921 (E.D. Mo. 2000).

[17]Patel v. I.N.S., 2000 WL 298921 (E.D. Mo. 2000). The regulatory procedures are found at 8 C.F.R. § 335.5.

[18]Patel v. I.N.S., 2000 WL 298921 (E.D. Mo. 2000).

migration judge.[1] The applicant may make this election either at the time of filing the application or during the examination.[2] A USCIS employee will advise the applicant of his or her right to elect, at the latest, during the examination.[3] To assist in making this election, the USCIS must advise the applicant of the dates and location of upcoming USCIS or immigration judge and court administered ceremonies.[4]

In these locations, either the USCIS local offices or the immigration judges will administer naturalization oaths at public ceremonies at least once a month.[5] The ceremony must be held within the USCIS district where the applicant filed his or her naturalization application or where it was transferred to.[6] Both administrative and judicial oath ceremonies are only held in the United States,[7] except for naturalization ceremonies conducted for active-duty military personnel.[8] The applicant must appear in person at the ceremony, unless such appearance is excused by regulation.[9] Under regular circumstances, only immigration judges and certain USCIS officers are authorized to administer the naturalization oath.[10] In exceptional cases and with prior approval by the USCIS assistant commissioner for adjudications, district directors or officers-in-charge may delegate this authority.[11]

When the applicant elects to have the ceremony at a court, the USCIS will inform the court of the applicant's eligibility to naturalize.[12] If there is no schedule of court hearings available at the time of the notification, the USCIS will advise the court that the applicant has not been scheduled for a court ceremony.[13] The USCIS will also advise the applicant that the naturalization application has been approved but that no ceremony has been scheduled.[14]

Applicants who elect to take the oath at a court ceremony may change their election and have the oath administered instead by the USCIS or the immigration judge as the case may be.[15] The USCIS may grant these requests if it finds good reason for

---

[Section 9:58]

[1] INA § 310(b)(2)(A)(i), 8 U.S.C.A. § 1421(b)(2)(A)(i), 8 CFR §§ 310.3(a), 337.7(a). The USCIS, the immigration judges, and the courts have jurisdiction to administer the oath in these situations. INA § 310(b)(1)(A), 8 U.S.C.A. § 1421(b)(1)(A); 8 CFR § 337.8.

[2] 8 CFR §§ 310.3(a), 337.8(a).

[3] 8 CFR § 337.7(a).

[4] 8 CFR § 337.7(a).

[5] 8 CFR § 337.2(a). The regulations provide that the administrative oath may be administered less often if this will not cause unreasonable delays. 8 CFR § 337.7(a).

[6] 8 CFR § 337.2(a). The regulations provide that the administrative oath may be administered less often if this will not cause unreasonable delays. 8 CFR § 337.7(a).

[7] 8 C.F.R. § 337.2(a)

[8] See App. 12-8.

[9] 8 CFR § 337.2(a). The regulations provide that the administrative oath may be administered less often if this will not cause unreasonable delays. 8 CFR § 337.7(a).

[10] 8 CFR § 337.2(b).

[11] 8 CFR § 337.2(b).

[12] 8 CFR § 337.8(b)(2). The USCIS uses Form N-646 to inform the court of the applicant's eligibility to naturalize.

[13] 8 CFR § 337.8(b)(2).

[14] 8 CFR § 337.8(b)(2).

[15] 8 CFR § 337.8(f).

the change.[16] The requests are made in writing, stating the reasons for the change of election, and are filed with the USCIS office that granted the naturalization application.[17] If the request is granted, the applicant will be notified in writing and will be scheduled for the next available administrative oath ceremony.[18]

§ 9:59 Overview—Jurisdiction to administer oath; generally—Where courts request exclusive jurisdiction

If the courts exercise their right to exclusive jurisdiction, they are required to provide USCIS with the date, time, and place of all naturalization oath ceremonies at least 60 days in advance of the ceremony and include the number of applicants that can be accommodated at the ceremony.[1] Applicants will be informed at the time of approval of the naturalization application that exclusive jurisdiction to administer the oath is with the courts and the date or dates in which the oath ceremony will take place.[2] The applicant will be notified to appear at the next available ceremony.[3] Since both state and federal courts have jurisdiction to naturalize, more than one court can request exclusive jurisdiction in the same geographical area. In these cases, the applicant has a choice of court in which to naturalize.[4] The applicant will be informed of the dates of upcoming ceremonies in each of these courts.[5] He or she must choose a court at the time of approval of the naturalization application.[6]

When courts have exclusive jurisdiction to naturalize, the USCIS is required to notify the court within ten days of the date of approval of the application that the applicant is eligible to naturalize.[7] If the schedule of court-conducted oath ceremonies does not include a ceremony within the 45 days after the date of USCIS notification of the applicant's eligibility, the court automatically relinquishes its exclusive authority to administer the oath to that applicant.[8] Furthermore, if the USCIS' certification of the eligibility of the applicant does not arrive to the court within a reasonable time before a scheduled oath ceremony, the court may decide to waive its exclusive jurisdiction to administer the oath to that person.[9] After the 45 days in which the court has exclusive jurisdiction, the USCIS may administer the oath to these applicants if the court has failed to do so.[10]

---

[16]8 CFR § 337.8(f).

[17]8 CFR § 337.8(f).

[18]8 CFR § 337.8(f).

[Section 9:59]

[1]8 CFR § 310.3(c)(2).

[2]INA § 310(b)(2)(B), 8 U.S.C.A. § 1421(b)(2)(B).

[3]8 CFR § 337.7(b).

[4]INA § 310(b)(2)(B), 8 U.S.C.A. § 1421(b)(2)(B).

[5]8 CFR § 337.7(b).

[6]INA § 310(b)(2)(B), 8 U.S.C.A. § 1421(b)(2)(B).

[7]INA § 310(b)(2)(A)(ii), 8 U.S.C.A. § 1421(b)(2)(A)(ii), 8 CFR §§ 310.3(d), 337.8(b)(1). The INS uses Form N-646 to notify courts of the applicant's eligibility.

[8]8 CFR § 310.3(d). Even if the court has exclusive jurisdiction to administer the oath, it is required to administer the oath within 45 days from the date the USCIS notifies the court that the person is eligible for naturalization. INA § 310(b)(3)(A), 8 U.S.C.A. § 1421(b)(3)(A).

[9]INA § 310(b)(3)(C), 8 U.S.C.A. § 1421(b)(3)(C), 8 CFR § 310.3(e).

[10]INA § 310(b)(3)(B), 8 U.S.C.A. § 1421(b)(3)(B).

§ 9:60 Special cases

If the applicant suffers from a serious disability or sickness that prevents him or her from appearing at the public ceremony, the USCIS may arrange for the oath to be administered in a place other than the district office.[1]

In addition, persons who have sufficient cause may be granted an expedited judicial or administrative oath administration irrespective of the jurisdictional requirements described in the previous section.[2] Courts and USCIS officials are required to consider the special circumstances of the applicant in order to determine whether to grant the expedited ceremony.[3] Among the circumstances to be considered are: (1) serious illness of the applicant or member of the applicant's immediate family; (2) permanent disability sufficiently incapacitating as to prevent the applicant's personal appearance at the scheduled ceremony; (3) developmental disability or advanced age; and (4) exigent circumstances relating to travel or employment.[4]

Requests for expedited oath administration are made to the USCIS or the court.[5] The request must be in writing and must include sufficient information to allow the USCIS or the court to make a decision on whether to grant it.[6] The USCIS or the court may seek verification of the information provided in the request.[7] If the applicant is expecting a court administered oath and the applicant submits the request to expedite to the USCIS, the USCIS will forward the court a copy of the request without reaching a conclusion on whether to grant it or not.[8]

Courts exercising exclusive jurisdiction may either hold an expedited ceremony or refer the applicant back to the USCIS for an immediate USCIS or immigration judge-administered oath ceremony, if the court finds it impracticable to effect an expedited ceremony.[9] In such cases, the court will inform the USCIS district director of its decision to grant the request for an expedited ceremony and that it has relinquished exclusive jurisdiction to administer the oath to that applicant.[10]

B. CONTENT OF OATH

§ 9:61 In general

Research References

Dizon and Wettstein, Immigration Law Service 2d § 14:179

With limited exceptions of children who cannot understand the oath, the INA requires all persons seeking to be admitted to citizenship to take an oath:

(1) to support the Constitution of the United States; (2) to renounce and abjure

---

[Section 9:60]

[1]8 CFR § 337.2.

[2]See § 9:59.

[3]INA § 337(c), 8 U.S.C.A. § 1448(c).

[4]INA § 337(c), 8 U.S.C.A. § 1448(c); 8 CFR § 337.3(a).

[5]8 CFR § 337.3(c).

[6]8 CFR § 337.3(c).

[7]8 CFR § 337.3(c).

[8]8 CFR § 337.3(c).

[9]INA § 337(c), 8 U.S.C.A. § 1448(c); 8 CFR § 337.3(b).

[10]8 CFR § 337.3(b).

absolutely and entirely all allegiance and fidelity to any foreign prince, potentate, state, or sovereign of whom or which the applicant was before a subject or citizen; (3) to support and defend the Constitution and the laws of the United States against all enemies, foreign and domestic; (4) to bear true faith and allegiance to the same; and (5)(A) to bear arms on behalf of the United States when required by the law, or (B) to perform noncombatant service in the Armed Forces of the United States when required by the law, or (C) to perform work of national importance under civilian direction when required by the law.[1]

Those excepted from the oath requirement include children who are unable to understand the oath. Additionally, any disabled individual who, in the opinion of the Secretary of DHS, is unable to understand or communicate an understanding of the meaning of the oath due to a physical or mental impairment, is also exempted from this requirement.[2] Where the oath requirement is waived in this way, the individual "shall be considered to have met the requirements of [8 U.S.C.A. § 1427(a)(3)] with respect to attachment to the principles of the Constitution and well disposition to the good order and happiness of the United States."[3] In a June 30, 2003 memorandum, the USCIS provided "comprehensive policy guidance" to supervisory personnel on procedures for conducting examinations and waiving the oath of allegiance for naturalization applicants with disabilities.[4]

In addition, by regulation, the applicant is required to swear as part of the oath that he or she "take[s] this obligation freely without any mental reservation or purpose of evasion."[5] The applicant will be required to sign a copy of the oath he or she has taken.[6]

The oath of allegiance is the third of the political allegiance requirements in naturalization. The other two involve the attachment to the U.S. Constitution and the bar to the naturalization of communists and other politically unacceptable classes of applicants. These other tests have been discussed in previous chapters.[7]

§ 9:62   State of mind at oath ceremony

Before being naturalized, an applicant is required to establish that "it is his or her intention, in good faith, to assume and discharge the obligations of the oath of allegiance, and that his or her attitude toward the Constitution and laws of the United States renders him or her capable of fulfilling the obligations of such oath."[1] Lest it be thought that this is an empty phrase, it must be pointed out that several

---

[Section 9:61]

[1]INA § 337(a), 8 U.S.C.A. § 1448(a). See 8 CFR § 337.1(a), (b) for the versions of the oath used by the regulations.

[2]8 U.S.C.A. § 1448(a).

[3]8 U.S.C.A. § 1448(a).

[4]See "Procedures for Implementing the Waiving of the Oath of Renunciation and Allegiance for the Naturalization of Aliens having Certain Disabilities" (June 30, 2003).

[5]8 CFR § 337.1(a). This statement in the oath is instrumental in establishing fraud in a denaturalization action. See Knauer v. U.S., 328 U.S. 654, 657, 66 S.Ct. 1304, 1306, 90 L.Ed. 150 reh'g denied 329 U.S. 818, 67 S.Ct. 25, 91 L.Ed. 697 (1946).

[6]8 CFR § 337.1(a).

[7]See §§ 7:47 to 7:76.

[Section 9:62]

[1]8 CFR § 337.1(c).

celebrated Supreme Court denaturalization cases involve lack of appropriate "state of mind" at the taking of the oath of allegiance.[2]

An applicant's conscious withholding of the allegiance promised is tantamount to fraud.[3] This can only occur when the person is aware of the conflict between his or her own political views and the new political allegiance he or she is assuming.[4] It is the person's intent that must be determined to establish a fraudulent oath.[5] Likewise, where the individual does not actually intend to renounce all foreign allegiances, that has been held to be a fraudulent oath.[6]

§ 9:63 Renunciation of all allegiance

As part of the current oath, as has been the case since 1795, the applicant is required to renounce all allegiance and fidelity to his or her former country.[1] The applicant is not required to forswear his or her cultural feelings and traditions.[2] The decisive question is not whether old social or cultural loyalties still exist, but "whether the new citizen still [takes] orders from, or [owes] his [or her] allegiance to a foreign chancellery."[3] Membership in a party or an organization is not by itself sufficient to prove failure to renounce allegiance, since what needs to be proven is the individual's intent.[4]

Note that many countries do not in fact give legal effect to this renunciation, leaving the applicant as a citizen of that country notwithstanding their attempted renunciation.[5] This is discussed at length below.[6]

§ 9:64 Conscientious objectors

The Supreme Court first recognized a conscientious objector's exception to the oath in 1946.[1] This exception has now been incorporated into the text of the statute.[2] Part 5 of the oath requires the applicant to promise to bear arms on behalf of the

---

[2]Knauer v. U.S., 328 U.S. 654, 66 S.Ct. 1304, 90 L.Ed. 150; Baumgartner v. U.S., 322 U.S. 665, 64 S.Ct. 1240, 88 L.Ed. 1525 (1944). Cf. Schneiderman v. U.S., 320 U.S. 118, 159–60, 63 S.Ct. 1333, 1353, 87 L.Ed. 1796 (1943) (dismissing the issue because it was not properly raised below).

[3]Baumgartner v. U.S., 322 U.S. 665, 671–72, 64 S. Ct. 1240, 1244, 88 L. Ed. 1525 (1944); Knauer v. U.S., 328 U.S. at 671, 66 S.Ct. at 1313, 90 L.Ed. 150.

[4]Baumgartner v. U.S., 322 U.S. 665, 672, 64 S. Ct. 1240, 1244, 88 L. Ed. 1525 (1944). The USCIS and some courts envision the oath as a contractual obligation, the applicant provides promises in exchange for the benefits of citizenship to be conferred upon him or her. See U.S. v. Bregler, 55 F.Supp. 837, 844 (E.D.N.Y. 1944) (in return for citizenship the noncitizen accepts full the duties and obligations of citizenship); INS Interp. 337.2(a).

[5]Knauer v. U.S., 328 U.S. at 659, 66 S.Ct. at 1307, 90 L.Ed. 150.

[6]Baumgartner v. U.S., 322 U.S. 665, 64 S.Ct. 1240 (1944); Knauer v. U.S., 328 U.S. 654, 66 S.Ct. 1304 (1946); see generally § 15:18.

[Section 9:63]

[1]See U S v. Bregler, 55 F. Supp. 837, 841 (E.D. N.Y. 1944), judgment rev'd, 155 F.2d 141 (C.C.A. 2d Cir. 1946); INS Interp. 337.1.

[2]Baumgartner v. U.S., 322 U.S. 665, 674, 64 S.Ct. 1240, 1245, 88 L.Ed. 1525.

[3]Knauer v. U. S., 328 U.S. 654, 659, 66 S. Ct. 1304, 1308, 90 L. Ed. 1500 (1946).

[4]Knauer v. U. S., 328 U.S. 654, 669, 66 S. Ct. 1304, 1312, 90 L. Ed. 1500 (1946).

[5]See §§ 15:17 to 15:19, App. 15-1.

[6]See §§ 15:17 to 15:19, App. 15-1.

[Section 9:64]

[1]Girouard v. U.S., 328 U.S. 61, 66 S.Ct. 826, 90 L.Ed. 1084 (1946).

United States whenever required by law to do so.[3] Since this is a problematic requirement for persons who qualify as conscientious objectors, the INA provides diminished requirements for such applicants. Thus, a general naturalization applicant who does not qualify as a conscientious objector is required to take the full oath including the three subsections of part (5) of the oath, namely bearing arms, performing noncombatant service, and performing work of national importance.[4] If the applicant is able to prove by clear and convincing evidence that he or she is opposed to the bearing of arms in the armed forces of the U.S. by reason of religious training or belief, the applicant is relieved from swearing to bear arms.[5] If the person's religious training and belief makes him or her opposed to any type of service in the armed forces of the U.S., then the person is also relieved from swearing to perform noncombatant service in the armed forces of the U.S.[6]

The INA defines the terms "religious training and belief" to mean "an individual's belief in a relation to a Supreme Being involving duties superior to those arising from any human relation, but does not include essentially political, sociological, or philosophical views or a merely personal moral code."[7] Contrary to what appears at first sight, this definition does not preclude a diminished oath when the objections are based on ethical grounds.

In interpreting essentially the same language in the Selective Service statute, the Supreme Court has reached the conclusion that "[i]f an individual deeply and sincerely holds beliefs that are purely ethical or moral in source and content but that nevertheless impose upon him [or her] a duty of conscience to refrain from participating in any war at any time, those beliefs" are "religious" beliefs for purposes of this statute, and the individual should be granted conscientious objector status.[8] This interpretation may at first sight seem to contradict the statutory exception relating to the inapplicability of the diminished requirements when the views of the applicant are based on "essentially political, sociological, or philosophical views or a merely personal moral code."[9] The Supreme Court, however, specifically read that language as in no way precluding a finding that if the ethical belief is strong, it is *per se* religious and should allow the person to claim conscientious objector exemption from service in the armed forces.[10]

In interpreting the requirements of the oath, the INS follows these Supreme Court decisions.[11] Thus, persons objecting to military service on the basis of deeply held moral or ethical beliefs will also be exempt from the requirement of promising to serve in the armed forces to the same extent as if the objection were based on traditional religious training and beliefs.[12]

---

[2]See INA § 337(a), 8 U.S.C.A. § 1448(a).

[3]See INA § 337(a), 8 U.S.C.A. § 1448(a).

[4]See INA § 337(a), 8 U.S.C.A. § 1448(a).

[5]See INA § 337(a), 8 U.S.C.A. § 1448(a).

[6]See INA § 337(a), 8 U.S.C.A. § 1448(a).

[7]See INA § 337(a), 8 U.S.C.A. § 1448(a).

[8]Welsh v. U.S., 398 U.S. 333, 340, 90 S.Ct. 1792, 1796, 26 L.Ed.2d 308 (1970).

[9]INA § 337(a), 8 U.S.C.A. § 1448(a).

[10]Welsh v. U. S., 398 U.S. 333, 342, 90 S. Ct. 1792, 1798, 26 L. Ed. 2d 308 (1970).

[11]INS Interp. 337.2(b)(2)(ii).

[12]See INS Interp. 337.2(b)(2)(ii), (iii) (discussing when such individual beliefs will be religious).

§ 9:65 Applicants bearing hereditary titles or orders of nobility

Persons who have hereditary titles or orders of nobility must also expressly renounce such titles or orders at the oath ceremony.[1] Such an applicant is required to make the renunciation in the following terms: "I further renounce the title of [give title or titles] which I have heretofore held" or alternatively "I further renounce the order of nobility [give the order of nobility] to which I have heretofore belonged."[2] Such renunciation will be recorded as part of the proceedings.[3]

C. CERTIFICATE OF NATURALIZATION

§ 9:66 In general

The content of the certificate of naturalization will be discussed in Ch 13.[1] Here we will discuss the delivery of the certificate to the applicant after the oath is taken. The INA provides not only that the applicant is entitled to receive the certificate of naturalization "upon admission to citizenship," but more specifically, that the certificate must be delivered at the oath ceremony.[2] Thus, the certificate, by law, must be provided at the oath ceremony.

The INS is in charge of printing and filling out the certificates regardless of whether the oath is administered by the INS or by the courts.[3] If the oath is to be administered by the courts, the INS must forward the certificate to the court sufficiently in advance of the ceremony to ensure timely delivery at the date of the ceremony.[4] The clerk of the court will then issue the certificates of naturalization to all persons upon whom he or she administers the oath of allegiance.[5] If the name was changed as part of the naturalization proceedings, the clerk of the court will also provide evidence of the change of name.[6]

The regulations generally require that the applicant turn in his residence card before receiving the naturalization certificate.[7] However, if the card has been destroyed or is otherwise unavailable, USCIS can waive that requirement.[8] In any event, it appears that under the regulation, failure to turn in the residence card ought not preclude the taking of the oath, but simply the delivery to the applicant of the naturalization certificate.[9]

[Section 9:65]

[1]INA § 337(b), 8 U.S.C.A. § 1448(b).

[2]8 CFR § 337.1(d).

[3]INA § 337(b), 8 U.S.C.A. § 1448(b).

[Section 9:66]

[1]See §§ 13:35 to 13:38.

[2]INA §§ 310(b)(4), 338, 8 U.S.C.A. §§ 1421(b)(4), 1149.

[3]8 CFR § 338.1(a).

[4]8 CFR § 338.1(a).

[5]INA § 339(a)(1), 8 U.S.C.A. § 1450(a)(1); 8 CFR § 339.1.

[6]8 CFR § 339.1.

[7]8 C.F.R. § 338.3.

[8]8 C.F.R. § 338.3.

[9]See Azize v. Bureau of Citizenship and Immigration Services, 594 F.3d 86, 90 (2d Cir. 2010).

IX. ADMINISTRATIVE DENIAL AND THE NATURALIZATION HEARING

§ 9:67 Administrative review of denied applications; scope of review

Research References

Dizon and Wettstein, Immigration Law Service 2d § 14:348
Steel on Immigration Law § 15:23

Applicants who are denied their naturalization application by an examinations officer may avail themselves of a peculiar form of administrative review. The law provides that the applicant may seek a hearing before an immigration officer.[1]

What this translates to is a review of the file and re-examination of the applicant by another USCIS officer of a classification equal or higher than the original hearing officer.[2] At a minimum, the reviewing officer will conduct some form of examination of the applicant and review the naturalization application.[3] The reviewing officer may also review any administrative record, which was created as part of the examination procedures and any DHS files and reports, and may receive new evidence and take any additional testimony as he or she deems necessary or which the applicant seeks to provide.[4] If the reviewing officer finds it necessary to review the essential naturalization requirements, he or she may, but is not required to, conduct a full *de novo* examination of the applicant, including testing the applicant on English and civics.[5] The officer has the power to affirm the findings and conclusions of the original decision, or to redetermine the original decision in whole or in part.[6]

§ 9:68 Administrative review of denied applications; scope of review— Procedures to request review

Requests for administrative reviews must be filed within 30 days after the applicant receives the notice of denial.[1] The request for administrative review must be filed with the USCIS office that denied the naturalization application. These requests for hearings are filed on Form N-336, (reproduced in Appendix 10-1), and must include a fee of $650.[2] The regulations provide that if notice to the applicant is served by mail, three days are added to the time to respond.[3] This means that if served by mail, the applicant has 33 days to respond.[4] The applicant may submit briefs, other written statements, and additional evidence with the request for a

---

[Section 9:67]

[1]INA § 336(a), 8 U.S.C.A. § 1447(a).

[2]8 CFR § 336.2(b).

[3]8 CFR § 336.2(b).

[4]8 CFR § 336.2(b).

[5]8 CFR § 336.2(b).

[6]8 CFR § 336.2(b).

[Section 9:68]

[1]8 CFR § 336.2(a).

[2]*See* Appendix 10-1 Form N-336 "Request for a Hearing on a Decision in Naturalization Proceedings Under Section 336 of the Act." The USCIS issued a new version of Form N-336 on October 26, 2005. The version dated June 24, 2005 is also accepted. Other prior versions of the form may only be used until December 31, 2005.

[3]8 CFR § 103.5a(b).

[4]This time period is reflected in the instructions to Form N-336. See Appendix 10-1.

hearing.[5] If additional time is needed for the submission of briefs, statements, or evidence, the applicant must file the requests for review and request the extension within the original 30 days.[6] Extensions may be granted for good cause.[7]

The USCIS will reject requests for review filed in an untimely fashion and will not return the filing fee.[8] Untimely requests for review will be treated as motions to reopen or reconsider if they meet the requirements of motions to reopen or reconsider. For reopening, they must: (1) state new facts to be proved at the reopened proceedings, and (2) be supported by affidavits or other documentary evidence. For reconsideration, they must: (1) state the reasons for reconsideration, and (2) be supported by pertinent precedent decisions.[9]

General immigration regulations require motions to reopen or reconsider to be filed within 30 days of the date of the decision.[10] However, these same regulations allow USCIS officers to excuse the failure to file within 30 days where the "delay was reasonable and was beyond the control of the applicant or petitioner."[11] The fact that the naturalization appeal regulations specifically contemplate requests for review to be considered as motion to reopen, if they are untimely filed, should assist the applicant in arguing the excuse of the untimely filing.[12]

Attorneys and representatives filing requests for review must include properly executed Form G-28 (reproduced as Appendix 10-2).[13] Form G-28 is also available for download from the USCIS website at http://uscis.gov/graphics/index.htm.

If the attorney or representative fails to include form G-28, the USCIS will request filing of the form within 15 days.[14] If Form G-28 is not submitted, the request for review will not be considered properly filed, but the USCIS officer may still reopen or reconsider the decision on his or her own motion and grant the application.[15] The attorney or representative will not be notified of the decision.[16]

The USCIS will reject requests for review filed by anybody other than the applicant or his or her attorney or representative and will not refund the fee.[17] If the request for review is properly filed, the USCIS will schedule the review hearing within 180 days of the filing of the request.[18]

---

[5]Form N-336 (instructions).

[6]Form N-336.

[7]Form N-336.

[8]8 CFR § 336.2(c)(2)(i).

[9]8 CFR §§ 103.5(a)(2), (3), 336.2(c)(2)(ii).

[10]8 CFR § 103.5(a)(1)(i).

[11]8 CFR § 103.5(a)(1)(i).

[12]See 8 CFR § 336.2(c)(2)(ii).

[13]INS Form N-336 (Instructions). See Appendix 10-1. This form can be accessed off the USCIS website as a "fillable." *See* http://uscis.gov/graphics/formsfee/forms/g-28.htm; *see also* 8 C.F.R. § 299.4 (explaining rules regarding electronic reproduction of forms).

[14]8 CFR § 336.2(c)(ii).

[15]8 CFR §§ 103.5(a)(5)(i), 336.2(c)(1)(ii).

[16]8 CFR § 336.2(c)(ii).

[17]8 CFR § 336.2(c)(1)(i).

[18]8 CFR § 336.2(b).

APPENDIX 9-1

Form N-400

OMB No. 1615-0052; Expires 03/31/2013

Department of Homeland Security
U.S. Citizenship and Immigration Services

Instructions for Form N-400,
Application for Naturalization

Instructions

Read these instructions carefully to properly complete this form. If you need more space to complete an answer, use a separate sheet of paper. Write your name and Alien Registration Number (USCIS A-Number), if any, at the top of each sheet of paper and indicate the part and number of the item to which the answer refers.

What Is the Purpose of This Form?

Form N-400 is an application for U.S. citizenship (naturalization). For more information about the naturalization process and eligibility requirements, read *A Guide to Naturalization* (Form M-476). If you do not already have a copy of the *Guide*, you can get a copy from:

1. USCIS Web site (**www.uscis.gov**);

2. USCIS toll-free forms line at **1-800-870-3676**; or

3. USCIS National Customer Service Center (NCSC) at **1-800-375-5283 (TTY:1-800-767-1833)**.

When Should I Use This Form?

You may apply for naturalization when you meet **all** the requirements to become a U.S. citizen. The section of the *Guide* called "Who is Eligible for Naturalization" and the Eligibility Worksheet found in the back of the *Guide* are tools to help you determine whether you are eligible to apply for naturalization. You should complete the worksheet before filling out Form N-400.

If you are applying based on five years as a lawful permanent resident or based on three years as a lawful permanent resident married to a U.S. citizen, you may apply for naturalization up to 90 days before you meet the "continuous residence" requirement. You must meet all other requirements at the time that you file your application with USCIS.

Certain applicants have different English and civics testing requirements based on their age and length of lawful permanent residence **at the time of filing**. If you are over 50 years of age and have lived in the United States as a lawful permanent resident for periods totaling at least 20 years, or if you are over 55 years of age and have lived in the United States as a lawful permanent resident for periods totaling at least 15 years, you do not have to take the English test, but you do have to take the civics test in the language of your choice.

If you are over 65 years of age and have lived in the United States as a lawful permanent resident for periods totaling at least 20 years, you do not have to take the English test, but you do have to take a simpler version of the civics test in the language of your choice.

Who May File This Form?

To use this form you must be **ONE** of the following:

1. A lawful permanent resident for at least five years and at least 18 years old; **or**

2. A lawful permanent resident for at least three years and at least 18 years old;

   AND

   You have been married to and living with the same U.S. citizen for the last three years;

   AND

   Your spouse has been a U.S. citizen for the last three years.

3. A member of one of several other groups eligible to apply for naturalization (for example, persons who are nationals but not citizens of the United States) and at least 18 years old. For more information about these groups, see the *Guide*.

4. A person who has served honorably in the U.S. Armed Forces;

   AND

   If you are at least 18 years old, a lawful permanent resident with at least one year of U.S. Armed Forces service, and you are filing your application for naturalization while still in the service or within six months after the termination of such service;

   OR

   You served honorably as a member of the Selected Reserve of the Ready Reserve or in active-duty status during a designated period of hostilities. You then may apply for naturalization without having been physically present in the United States for any specified period.

For more information, go to the USCIS Web site at
www.uscis.gov.

NOTE: If you are married to a U.S. citizen who is employed
or deployed abroad, in some circumstances you may be
eligible for expedited naturalization under section 319(b) of
the Immigration and Nationality Act (INA). For further
assistance, see the *Guide*.

Who May Not File This Form?

In certain cases, a person who was born outside of the United
States to U.S. citizen parents is already a citizen and does not
need to apply for naturalization. To find out more information
about this type of citizenship and whether you should file
Form N-600, Application for Certificate of Citizenship, read
the *Guide*.

Other permanent residents under 18 years of age may be
eligible for U.S. citizenship if their U.S. citizen parent or
parents file a Form N-600 application on their behalf. For
more information, see "Frequently Asked Questions" in the
Guide.

General Instructions

Step 1. Fill Out Form N-400

1. Type or print legibly in black ink.

2. If extra space is needed to complete any item, attach a
   continuation sheet, indicate the item number, and date and
   sign each sheet.

3. Answer all questions fully and accurately. State that an
   item is not applicable with "N/A." If the answer is none,
   write "None."

4. **Write your USCIS (or former INS) A-number on the
   top right hand corner of each page.** Use your A-number
   on your Permanent Resident Card (formerly known as the
   Alien Registration or "Green" Card). To locate your A-
   number, see the sample Permanent Resident Cards in the
   Guide. The A-number on your card consists of seven to
   nine numbers, depending on when your record was
   created. If the A-number on your card has fewer than nine
   numbers, place enough zeros before the first number to
   make a *total of nine numbers* on the application. For
   example, write card number A1234567 as A001234567,
   but write card number A12345678 as A012345678.

5. Answer all questions fully and accurately.

Step-by-Step Instructions

This form is divided into 14 parts. The information below will
help you fill out the form.

Part 1. Your Name *(the person applying for naturalization)*

A. **Your current legal name -** Your current legal name is
   the name on your birth certificate unless it has been
   changed after birth by a legal action such as a marriage
   or court order.

B. **Your name exactly as it appears on your Permanent
   Resident Card** *(if different from above)* - Write your
   name exactly as it appears on your card, even if it is
   misspelled.

C. **Other names you have used -** If you have used any
   other names, write them in this section. If you need
   more space, use a separate sheet of paper.

   If you have **never** used a different name, write "N/A" in
   the space for "Family Name *(Last Name)."*

D. **Name change** *(optional)* - A court can allow a change
   in your name when you are being naturalized. A name
   change does not become final until a court naturalizes
   you. For more information regarding a name change,
   see the *Guide*.

   If you want a court to change your name at a
   naturalization oath ceremony, check "Yes" and
   complete this section. If you do not want to change
   your name, check "No" and go to Part 2.

Part 2. Information About Your Eligibility

Check the box that shows why you are eligible to apply for
naturalization. If the basis for your eligibility is not described
in one of the first three boxes, check "Other" and briefly write
the basis for your application on the lines provided.

Part 3. Information About You

A. **U.S. Social Security Number -** Print your U.S. Social
   Security Number. If you do not have one, write "N/A"
   in the space provided.

B. **Date of birth -** Always use eight numbers to show your
   date of birth. Write the date in this order: Month, Day,
   Year. For example, write May 1, 1958, as 05/01/1958.

C. **Date you became a permanent resident -** Write the
   official date when your lawful permanent residence
   began, as shown on your Permanent Resident Card. To
   help locate the date on your card, see the sample
   Permanent Resident Cards in the *Guide*. Write the date
   in this order: Month, Day, Year. For example, write
   August 9, 1988, as 08/09/1988.

D. **Country of birth -** Write the name of the country
   where you were born. Write the name of the country
   even if it no longer exists.

E. Country of Nationality - Write the name of the country(ies) where you are currently a citizen or national.

    1. If you are stateless, write the name of the country where you were last a citizen or national.

    2. If you are a citizen or national of more than one country, write the name of the foreign country that issued your last passport.

F. Citizenship of parents - Check "Yes" if either of your parents is a U.S. citizen. If you answer "Yes," you may already be a citizen. For more information, see "Frequently Asked Questions" in the *Guide*.

G. Current marital status - Check the marital status you have on the date you are filing this application. If you are currently not married, but had a prior marriage that was annulled or otherwise legally terminated, check "Other" and explain it.

H. Request for disability waiver - If you have a medical disability or impairment that you believe qualifies you for a waiver of the tests of English and/or U.S. Government and history, check "Yes" and attach a properly completed Form N-648, Medical Certification for Disability Exceptions. If you ask for this waiver, it does not guarantee that you will be excused from the testing requirements. For more information about this waiver, see the *Guide*.

I. Request for disability accommodations - We will make every reasonable effort to help applicants with disabilities complete the naturalization process. For example, if you use a wheelchair, we will make sure that you can be fingerprinted and interviewed, and can attend a naturalization ceremony at a location that is wheelchair accessible. If you are deaf or hearing impaired and need a sign language interpreter, we will make arrangements with you to have one at your interview.

If you believe you will need us to modify or change the naturalization process for you, check the box or write in the space the kind of accommodation you need. If you need more space, use a separate sheet of paper. You do not need to send us Form N-648 to request an accommodation. You only need to send Form N-648 to request a waiver of the test of English and/or civics.

We consider requests for accommodations on a case-by-case basis. Asking for an accommodation will not affect your eligibility for citizenship.

Part 4. Information About Contacting You

A. Home address - Give the address where you now live. Do **not** put post office (P.O.) box numbers here.

B. Mailing address - If your mailing address is the same as your home address, write "Same." If your mailing address is different from your home address, write it in this part.

C. Telephone numbers - By giving us your telephone numbers and e-mail address, we can contact you about your application more quickly. If you are hearing impaired and use a TTY telephone connection, please indicate this by writing (TTY) after the telephone number.

Part 5. Information for Criminal Records Search

The Federal Bureau of Investigation (FBI) will use the information in this section, together with your fingerprints, to search for criminal records. Although the results of this search may affect your eligibility, we do **not** make naturalization decisions based on your gender, race, or physical description.

For each item, check the box or boxes that best describes you. The categories are those used by the FBI. You can select one or more.

NOTE: As part of the USCIS biometrics service requirement, you must be fingerprinted after you file this application. If necessary, USCIS may also take your photograph and signature.

Part 6. Information About Your Residence and Employment

A. Write every address where you have lived during the last five years (including in other countries).

Begin with where you live now. Include the dates you lived in those places. For example, write May 1998 to June 1999 as 05/1998 to 06/1999.

B. List where you have worked (or, if you were a student, the schools you have attended) during the last five years. Include military service. If you worked for yourself, write "Self employed." Begin with your most recent job. Also, write the dates when you worked or studied in each place.

If you need separate sheets of paper to complete section A or B or any other questions on this application, be sure to follow the instructions under **"Step 1. Fill Out Form N-400"** on **Page 2.**

Part 7. Time Outside the United States *(including trips to Canada, Mexico, and the Caribbean)*

A. Write the total number of days you spent outside of the United States (including military service) during the last five years. Count the days of every trip that lasted 24 hours or longer.

B. Write the number of trips you have taken outside the United States during the last five years. Count every trip that lasted 24 hours or longer.

C. Provide the requested information for every trip that you have taken outside the United States since you became a lawful permanent resident. Begin with your most recent trip.

Part 8. Information About Your Marital History

A. Write the number of times you have been married. Include any annulled marriages. If you were married to the same spouse more than one time, count each time as a separate marriage.

B. If you are now married, provide information about your current spouse.

C. Check the box to indicate whether your current spouse is a U.S. citizen.

D. If your spouse is a citizen through naturalization, give the date and place of naturalization. If your spouse regained U.S. citizenship, write the date and place the citizenship was regained.

E. If your spouse is not a U.S. citizen, complete this section.

F. If you were married before, give information about your former spouse or spouses. In question F.2, check the box showing the immigration status your former spouse had during your marriage. If the spouse was not a U.S. citizen or a lawful permanent resident at that time, check "Other" and explain. For question F.5, if your marriage was annulled, check "Other" and explain. If you were married to the same spouse more than one time, write about each marriage separately.

G. For any prior marriages of your current spouse, follow the instructions in section F above.

NOTE: If you or your present spouse had more than one prior marriage, provide the same information required by section F and section G about every additional marriage on a separate sheet of paper.

Part 9. Information About Your Children

A. Write the total number of sons and daughters you have had. Count **all** of your children, regardless of whether they are:

1. Alive, missing, or dead;

2. Born in other countries or in the United States;

3. Under 18 years old or adults;

4. Married or unmarried;

5. Living with you or elsewhere;

6. Stepsons or stepdaughters or legally adopted; or

7. Born when you were not married.

B. Write information about all your sons and daughters. In the last column (Location), write:

1. "With me" - if the son or daughter is currently living with you;

2. The street address and state or country where the son or daughter lives - if the son or daughter is **not** currently living with you; or

3. "Missing" or "Dead" - if that son or daughter is missing or dead.

NOTE: If you need space to list information about additional sons and daughters, attach a separate sheet of paper.

Part 10. Additional Questions

Answer each question by checking "Yes" or "No." If **any** part of a question applies to you, you must answer "Yes." For example, if you were never arrested but *were* once detained by a police officer, check "Yes" to the question "Have you ever been arrested or detained by a law enforcement officer?" and attach a written explanation.

We will use this information to determine your eligibility for citizenship. Answer every question honestly and accurately. If you do not, we may deny your application for lack of good moral character. Answering "Yes" to one of these questions does not always cause an application to be denied. For more information on eligibility, see the *Guide*.

Part 11. Your Signature

After reading the statement in Part 11, you must sign and date it. You should sign your full name without abbreviating it or using initials. The signature must be legible. Your application will be rejected if it is not signed.

If you cannot sign your name in English, sign in your native language. If you are unable to write in any language, sign your name with an "X."

NOTE: A designated representative may sign this section on behalf of an applicant who qualifies for a waiver of the Oath of Allegiance because of a developmental or physical impairment (see the *Guide* for more information). In such a case, the designated representative should write the name of the applicant and then sign his or her own name followed by the words "Designated Representative." The information attested to by the Designated Representative is subject to the same penalties discussed on **Page 8** of these instructions.

Part 12. Signature of Person Who Prepared this Application for You

If someone filled out this form for you, he or she must complete this section.

Part 13. Signature at Interview

Do not complete this part. You will be asked to complete this part at your interview.

Part 14. Oath of Allegiance

Do not complete this part. You will be asked to complete this part at your interview.

If we approve your application, you must take this Oath of Allegiance to become a citizen. In limited cases, you can take a modified oath. The oath requirement cannot be waived unless you are unable to understand its meaning because of a physical or developmental disability or mental impairment. For more information, see the *Guide*. Your signature on this form only indicates that you have no objections to taking the Oath of Allegiance. **It does not mean that you have taken the oath or that you are naturalized**. If USCIS approves your application for naturalization, you must attend an oath ceremony and take the Oath of Allegiance to the United States.

Step 2. General Requirements

Photographs. You **must** submit two identical passport-style color photographs of yourself taken within 30 days of the filing of this application. The photos must have a white to off-white background, be printed on thin paper with a glossy finish, and be unmounted and unretouched.

The photos must be 2" x 2" and must be in color with full face, frontal view on a white to off-white background. Head height should measure 1" to 1 3/8" from top of hair to bottom of chin, and eye height is between 1 1/8" to 1 3/8" from bottom of photo. Your head must be bare unless you are wearing a headdress as required by a religious order of which you are a member; however, your face must be visible. Using pencil or felt pen, lightly print your name and Alien Registration Number on the back of each photo.

NOTE: Any digital photo submitted needs to be produced from a high-resolution camera with at least 3.5 mega pixels of resolution.

Copy of Permanent Resident Card. Applicants who are lawful permanent residents of the United States must submit photocopies (front and back) of Form I-551 (Permanent Resident Card). If you have lost your Form I-551, attach a copy of any other entry document or a photocopy of a receipt showing that you have filed Form I-90, Application to Replace Permanent Resident Card.

Other Documents. Depending on the circumstances, some applicants must send certain documents with their application.

For example, if you have been arrested or convicted of a crime, you must send a certified copy of the arrest report, court disposition, sentencing, and any other relevant documents, including any countervailing evidence concerning the circumstances of your arrest or conviction that you would like USCIS to consider. Note that unless a traffic incident was alcohol or drug related, you do not need to submit documentation for traffic fines and incidents that did not involve an actual arrest if the only penalty was a fine of less than $500 or points on your driver's license.

For more information on the documents you must send with your application, see the Document Checklist in the *Guide*.

Translations. Any document containing foreign language submitted to USCIS must be accompanied by a full English language translation which the translator has certified as complete and accurate, and by the translator's certification that he or she is competent to translate from the foreign language into English.

Copies. Unless specifically required that an original document be filed with an application or petition, an ordinary legible photocopy may be submitted. Original documents submitted when not required will remain a part of the record, even if the submission was not required.

Where To File?

Mail your completed Form N-400 and accompanying documentation to the appropriate Lockbox facility.

If you reside in Alaska, Arizona, California, Colorado, Hawaii, Idaho, Illinois, Indiana, Iowa, Kansas, Michigan, Minnesota, Missouri, Montana, Nebraska, Nevada, North Dakota, Ohio, Oregon, South Dakota, Utah, Washington, Wisconsin, Wyoming, Territory of Guam, or the Commonwealth of the Northern Mariana Islands, send your Form N-400 to the **USCIS Phoenix Lockbox** facility at the following address:

USCIS
P.O. Box 21251
Phoenix, AZ 85036

For Express Mail or commercial courier deliveries, use the following address:

USCIS
Attn: N-400
1820 E. Skyharbor Circle S Ste 100
Phoenix, AZ 85034

If you reside in Alabama, Arkansas, Connecticut, Delaware, District of Columbia, Florida, Georgia, Kentucky, Louisiana, Maine, Maryland, Massachusetts, Mississippi, New Hampshire, New Jersey, New Mexico, New York, North Carolina, Oklahoma, Pennsylvania, Rhode Island, South Carolina, Tennessee, Texas, Vermont, Virginia, West Virginia, Commonwealth of Puerto Rico, or the U.S. Virgin Islands, send your Form N-400 to the **USCIS Dallas Lockbox** facility at the following address:

USCIS
P.O. 660060
Dallas, TX 75266

For Express Mail or commercial courier deliveries, use the following address:

USCIS
Attn: N-400
2501 S. State Hwy 121 Business Ste 400
Lewisville, TX 75067

Current or former members of the U.S. Armed Forces, spouses of current members of the U.S. Armed Forces, or close relatives of deceased members of the U.S. Armed Forces.

You must send all Form N-400 applications filed under the military provisions, sections 328 or 329 of the INA, to the **USCIS Nebraska Service Center** at the address below regardless of where you live and whether you are filing from within the United States or abroad.

Also, if you are the spouse of a current member of the U.S. Armed Forces, or are the close relative of a member of the U.S. Armed Forces (see section 319(d) of the INA), send your Form N-400 to the **USCIS Nebraska Service Center** at the address below regardless of where you live and whether you are filing from within the United States or abroad.

USCIS Nebraska Service Center
P.O. Box 87426
Lincoln, NE 68501-7426

For Express Mail or commercial courier deliveries, use the following address:

USCIS Nebraska Service Center
850 S Street
Lincoln, NE 68508

Section 319(b) of the INA Applicants

If you are filing under section 319(b) of the INA because you are the spouse of a U.S. citizen who is employed abroad, and the U.S. citizen spouse's employment meets the criteria for naturalization under section 319(b) of the INA, you must send your Form N-400 to the **USCIS Phoenix Lockbox** facility regardless of where you live and whether you are filing from within the United States or abroad. **However, if you are filing under 319(b) and are a spouse of a current member of the U.S. Armed Forces, file with the USCIS Nebraska Service Center as instructed above.**

USCIS
Attn: N-400
P.O. Box 21251
Phoenix, AZ 85036

For Express Mail or commercial courier deliveries, use the following address:

USCIS
Attn: N-400 319(b)
1820 E. Skyharbor Circle S Ste 100
Phoenix, AZ 85034

E-Notification

If you are filing your Form N-400 at one of the USCIS Lockbox facilities, you may elect to receive an e-mail and/or text message notifying you that your application has been accepted. You must complete Form G-1145, E-Notification of Application/Petition Acceptance, and clip it to the first page of your application. To download a copy of Form G-1145, including the instructions, visit the USCIS Web site at www.uscis.gov/G-1145.

For further information on where to file, including if you are currently overseas, read the section in the *Guide* titled "Completing Your Application and Getting Photographed" or call the NCSC at 1-800-375-5283 (TTY: 1-800-767-1833) or visit our Web site at www.uscis.gov and click on "**FORMS.**"

What Is the Filing Fee?

The filing fee for Form N-400 is **$595.**

An additional biometrics services fee of **$85** is required when filing Form N-400. After you submit Form N-400, USCIS will notify you about when and where to go for biometrics services.

Applicants 75 years of age or older are exempt from the biometrics services fee. Individuals who require fingerprinting and who reside outside of the United States at the time of filing an application or petition for immigration benefits are exempt from biometrics services fee.

NOTE: All naturalization applicants filing under the military provisions, section 328 or 329 of the INA, do not require a filing fee.

You may submit one check or money order for both the application and biometrics services fees, for a total of **$680.**

Use the following guidelines when you prepare your check or money order for Form N-400 and the biometrics services fees:

1. The check or money order must be drawn on a bank or other financial institution located in the United States and must be payable in U.S. currency; **and**

2. Make the check or money order payable to **U.S. Department of Homeland Security**.

   NOTE: Spell out U.S. Department of Homeland Security; do not use the initials "USDHS" or "DHS."

Notice to Those Making Payment by Check. If you send us a check, it will be converted into an electronic funds transfer (EFT). This means we will copy your check and use the account information on it to electronically debit your account for the amount of the check. The debit from your account will usually take 24 hours and will be shown on your regular account statement.

You will not receive your original check back. We will destroy your original check, but we will keep a copy of it. If the EFT cannot be processed for technical reasons, you authorize us to process the copy in place of your original check. If the EFT cannot be completed because of insufficient funds, we may try to make the transfer up to two times.

How to Check If the Fees Are Correct

The form and biometrics services fees on this form are current as of the edition date appearing in the lower right corner of this page. However, because USCIS fees change periodically, you can verify if the fees are correct by following one of the steps below:

1. Visit the USCIS Web site at **www.uscis.gov**, select "**FORMS,**" and check the appropriate fee;

2. Review the Fee Schedule included in your form package, if you called us to request the form; or

3. Telephone the USCIS National Customer Service Center at **1-800-375-5283** and ask for the fee information.

NOTE: If your Form N-400 requires payment of a biometrics services fee for USCIS to take your fingerprints, photograph, or signature, you can use the same procedure to obtain the correct biometrics services fee.

Processing Information

Any Form N-400 that is not signed or accompanied by the correct fee will be rejected. Any application that is not completed in accordance with these instructions, is missing pages or otherwise not executed in its entirety, or is not accompanied by the required initial evidence may also be rejected. If your Form N-400 is rejected, the form and any fees will be returned to you and you will be notified why the form is considered deficient. You may correct the deficiency and resubmit Form N-400. An application or petition is not considered properly filed until accepted by USCIS.

Requests for more information or interview. USCIS may request more information or evidence, or request that you appear at a USCIS office for an interview. USCIS may also request that you submit the originals of any copy. USCIS will return these originals when they are no longer required.

Decision. The decision on Form N-400 involves a determination of whether you have established eligibility for the requested benefit. If you do not establish a basis for eligibility, USCIS will deny your Form N-400. You will be notified of the decision in writing.

Address Changes

If you have changed your address, you must inform USCIS of your new address. For information on filing a change of address go to the USCIS Web site at **www.uscis.gov/ addresschange** or contact the USCIS National Customer Service Center at **1-800-375-5283**.

NOTE: Do not submit a change of address request to the USCIS Lockbox facilities because the Lockbox facilities do not process change of address requests.

Current Members of the U.S. Armed Forces

Contact the Military Help Line at **1-877-247-4645** if you are transferred to a new duty station after you file your Form N-400. **This includes deploying overseas or on a vessel.**

USCIS Forms and Information

You can get USCIS forms and immigration-related information on the USCIS Web site at **www.uscis.gov**. You may order USCIS forms by calling our toll-free number at **1-800-870-3676**. You may also obtain forms and information by telephoning the USCIS National Customer Service Center at **1-800-375-5283**.

As an alternative to waiting in line for assistance at your local USCIS office, you can now schedule an appointment through our Internet-based system, **InfoPass**. To access the system, visit our Web site. Use the **InfoPass** appointment scheduler and follow the screen prompts to set up your appointment. **InfoPass** generates an electronic appointment notice that appears on the screen.

NOTE: Schedule an InfoPass appointment if you do not know your USCIS A-Number or permanent resident date to obtain this information **BEFORE** you file your Form N-400.

Penalties

If you knowingly and willfully falsify or conceal a material fact or submit a false document with this Form N-400, we will deny your Form N-400 and may deny any other immigration benefit.

In addition, you will face severe penalties provided by law and may be subject to criminal prosecution.

USCIS Privacy Act Statement

AUTHORITIES: The information requested on this form request, and the associated evidence, is collected under the Immigration and Nationality Act, section 101, et seq.

PURPOSE: The primary purpose for providing the requested information on this form is to determine if you have established eligibility for the immigration benefit for which you are filing. The information you provide will be used to grant or deny the benefit sought.

DISCLOSURE: The information you provide is voluntary. However, failure to provide the requested information, and any requested evidence, may delay a final decision or result in denial of your form.

ROUTINE USES: The information you provide on this form may be shared with other Federal, State, local, and foreign government agencies and authorized organizations following approved routine uses described in the associated published system of records notices [DHS-USCIS-007 - Benefits Information System and DHS-USCIS-001 - Alien File (A-File) and Central Index System (CIS), which can be found at **www.dhs.gov/privacy**]. The information may also be made available, as appropriate, for law enforcement purposes or in the interest of national security.

Paperwork Reduction Act

An agency may not conduct or sponsor an information collection, and a person is not required to respond to a collection of information unless it displays a currently valid OMB control number. The public reporting burden for this collection of information is estimated at 6 hours and 8 minutes per response, including the time for reviewing instructions, and completing and submitting the form. Send comments regarding this burden estimate or any other aspect of this collection of information, including suggestions for reducing this burden, to: U.S. Citizenship and Immigration Services, Regulatory Products Division, Office of the Executive Secretariat, 20 Massachusetts Avenue, N.W., Washington, DC 20529-2020. OMB No. 1615-0052. **Do not mail your completed N-400 application to this address.**

OMB No. 1615-0052; Expires 03/31/2013

Department of Homeland Security
U.S Citizenship and Immigration Services

N-400 Application
for Naturalization

Print clearly or type your answers using CAPITAL letters. Failure to print clearly may delay your application. Use black ink.

Part 1. Your Name (*Person applying for naturalization*)

Write your USCIS A-Number here:

A

A. Your current legal name.

Family Name (*Last Name*)

Given Name (*First Name*)   Full Middle Name (*If applicable*)

For USCIS Use Only

Bar Code	Date Stamp
	Remarks

B. Your name **exactly** as it appears on your Permanent Resident Card.

Family Name (*Last Name*)

Given Name (*First Name*)   Full Middle Name (*If applicable*)

C. If you have ever used other names, provide them below.

Family Name (*Last Name*)	Given Name (*First Name*)	Middle Name

D. Name change (*optional*)

Read the Instructions before you decide whether to change your name.

1. Would you like to legally change your name?   ☐ Yes   ☐ No

2. If "Yes," print the new name you would like to use. Do not use initials or abbreviations when writing your new name.

Family Name (*Last Name*)

Given Name (*First Name*)   Full Middle Name

Action Block

Part 2. Information About Your Eligibility (*Check only one*)

I am at least 18 years old **AND**

A. ☐ I have been a lawful permanent resident of the United States for at least five years.

B. ☐ I have been a lawful permanent resident of the United States for at least three years, **and** I have been married to and living with the same U.S. citizen for the last three years, **and** my spouse has been a U.S. citizen for the last three years.

C. ☐ I am applying on the basis of qualifying military service.

D. ☐ Other (*Explain*) _____

Form N-400 (Rev. 03/22/12) Y

Part 3. Information About You	Write your USCIS A-Number here: A

A. U.S. Social Security Number   **B.** Date of Birth *(mm/dd/yyyy)*   **C.** Date You Became a Permanent Resident *(mm/dd/yyyy)*

D. Country of Birth   **E.** Country of Nationality

F. Are either of your parents U.S. citizens? *(If yes, see instructions)*   ☐ Yes   ☐ No

G. What is your current marital status?   ☐ Single, Never Married   ☐ Married   ☐ Divorced   ☐ Widowed

☐ Marriage Annulled or Other *(Explain)* _____

H. Are you requesting a waiver of the English and/or U.S. History and Government requirements based on a disability or impairment and attaching Form N-648 with your application?   ☐ Yes   ☐ No

I. Are you requesting an accommodation to the naturalization process because of a disability or impairment? *(See instructions for some examples of accommodations.)*   ☐ Yes   ☐ No

If you answered "Yes," check the box below that applies:

☐ I am deaf or hearing impaired and need a sign language interpreter who uses the following language: _____

☐ I use a wheelchair.

☐ I am blind or sight impaired.

☐ I will need another type of accommodation. Explain: _____

_____

_____

Part 4. Addresses and Telephone Numbers

A. Home Address - Street Number and Name *(Do **not** write a P.O. Box in this space.)*   Apartment Number

City	County	State	ZIP Code	Country

B. Care of   Mailing Address - Street Number and Name *(If different from home address)*   Apartment Number

City	State	ZIP Code	Country

C. Daytime Phone Number *(If any)*   Evening Phone Number *(If any)*   E-Mail Address *(If any)*

(   )   (   )

Part 5. Information for Criminal Records Search	Write your USCIS A-Number here: A

NOTE: The categories below are those required by the FBI. See instructions for more information.

A. Gender

☐ Male   ☐ Female

B. Height

Feet	Inches

C. Weight

Pounds

D. Are you Hispanic or Latino?   ☐ Yes   ☐ No

E. Race *(Select one or more)*

☐ White   ☐ Asian   ☐ Black or African American   ☐ American Indian or Alaskan Native   ☐ Native Hawaiian or Other Pacific Islander

F. Hair color

☐ Black   ☐ Brown   ☐ Blonde   ☐ Gray   ☐ White   ☐ Red   ☐ Sandy   ☐ Bald (No Hair)

G. Eye color

☐ Brown   ☐ Blue   ☐ Green   ☐ Hazel   ☐ Gray   ☐ Black   ☐ Pink   ☐ Maroon   ☐ Other

Part 6. Information About Your Residence and Employment

A. Where have you lived during the last five years? Begin with where you live now and then list every place you lived for the last five years. If you need more space, use a separate sheet of paper.

Street Number and Name, Apartment Number, City, State, Zip Code, and Country	Dates *(mm/dd/yyyy)*	
	From	To
Current Home Address - Same as Part 4.A		Present

B. Where have you worked (or, if you were a student, what schools did you attend) during the last five years? Include military service. Begin with your current or latest employer and then list every place you have worked or studied for the last five years. If you need more space, use a separate sheet of paper.

Employer or School Name	Employer or School Address *(Street, City, and State)*	Dates *(mm/dd/yyyy)*		Your Occupation
		From	To	

Form N-400 (Rev. 03/22/12) Y Page 3

| Part 7. Time Outside the United States | | Write your USCIS A-Number here: |
| *(Including Trips to Canada, Mexico and the Caribbean Islands)* | | A |

A. How many total days did you spend outside of the United States during the past five years? [   ] days

B. How many trips of 24 hours or more have you taken outside of the United States during the past five years? [   ] trips

C. List below all the trips of 24 hours or more that you have taken outside of the United States since becoming a lawful permanent resident. Begin with your most recent trip. If you need more space, use a separate sheet of paper.

Date You Left the United States *(mm/dd/yyyy)*	Date You Returned to the United States *(mm/dd/yyyy)*	Did Trip Last Six Months or More?	Countries to Which You Traveled	Total Days Out of the United States
		☐ Yes ☐ No		
		☐ Yes ☐ No		
		☐ Yes ☐ No		
		☐ Yes ☐ No		
		☐ Yes ☐ No		
		☐ Yes ☐ No		
		☐ Yes ☐ No		
		☐ Yes ☐ No		
		☐ Yes ☐ No		
		☐ Yes ☐ No		

| Part 8. Information About Your Marital History |

A. How many times have you been married (including annulled marriages)? [   ] If you have **never** been married, go to Part 9.

B. If you are now married, give the following information about your spouse:

1. Spouse's Family Name *(Last Name)*   Given Name *(First Name)*   Full Middle Name *(If applicable)*

2. Date of Birth *(mm/dd/yyyy)*   **3.** Date of Marriage *(mm/dd/yyyy)*   **4.** Spouse's U.S. Social Security #

5. Home Address - Street Number and Name   Apartment Number

City   State   Zip Code

Part 8. Information About Your Marital History *(Continued)*

Write your USCIS A-Number here:
A

C. Is your spouse a U.S. citizen?   ☐ Yes   ☐ No

D. If your spouse is a U.S. citizen, give the following information:

1. When did your spouse become a U.S. citizen?   ☐ At Birth   ☐ Other

   If "Other," give the following information:

2. Date your spouse became a U.S. citizen

3. Place your spouse became a U.S. citizen *(See instructions)*

City and State

E. If your spouse is **not** a U.S. citizen, give the following information :

1. Spouse's Country of Citizenship

2. Spouse's USCIS A- Number *(If applicable)*
A

3. Spouse's Immigration Status

☐ Lawful Permanent Resident   ☐ Other

F. If you were married before, provide the following information about your prior spouse. If you have more than one previous marriage, use a separate sheet of paper to provide the information requested in Questions 1-5 below.

1. Prior Spouse's Family Name *(Last Name)*   Given Name *(First Name)*   Full Middle Name *(If applicable)*

2. Prior Spouse's Immigration Status

☐ U.S. Citizen

☐ Lawful Permanent Resident

☐ Other

3. Date of Marriage *(mm/dd/yyyy)*

4. Date Marriage Ended *(mm/dd/yyyy)*

5. How Marriage Ended

☐ Divorce   ☐ Spouse Died   ☐ Other

G. How many times has your current spouse been married (including annulled marriages)?

If your spouse has **ever** been married before, give the following information about **your spouse's** prior marriage.
If your spouse has more than one previous marriage, use a separate sheet(s) of paper to provide the information requested in Questions 1 - 5 below.

1. Prior Spouse's Family Name *(Last Name)*   Given Name *(First Name)*   Full Middle Name *(If applicable)*

2. Prior Spouse's Immigration Status

☐ U.S. Citizen

☐ Lawful Permanent Resident

☐ Other

3. Date of Marriage *(mm/dd/yyyy)*

4. Date Marriage Ended *(mm/dd/yyyy)*

5. How Marriage Ended

☐ Divorce   ☐ Spouse Died   ☐ Other

Form N-400 (Rev. 03/22/12) Y Page 5

Part 9. Information About Your Children	Write your USCIS A-Number here: A

A. How many sons and daughters have you had? For more information on which sons and daughters you should include and how to complete this section, see the Instructions.

B. Provide the following information about all of your sons and daughters. If you need more space, use a separate sheet of paper.

Full Name of Son or Daughter	Date of Birth *(mm/dd/yyyy)*	USCIS A- number *(if child has one)*	Country of Birth	Current Address *(Street, City, State and Country)*
		A		
		A		
		A		
		A		
		A		
		A		
		A		
		A		

Add Children		Go to continuation page

Part 10. Additional Questions

Answer Questions 1 through 14. If you answer "Yes" to any of these questions, include a written explanation with this form. Your written explanation should (1) explain why your answer was "Yes" and (2) provide any additional information that helps to explain your answer.

A. General Questions.

1. Have you **ever** claimed to be a U.S. citizen *(in writing or any other way)*? ☐ Yes ☐ No

2. Have you **ever** registered to vote in any Federal, State, or local election in the United States? ☐ Yes ☐ No

3. Have you **ever** voted in any Federal,State, or local election in the United States? ☐ Yes ☐ No

4. Since becoming a lawful permanent resident, have you **ever** failed to file a required Federal, State, or local tax return? ☐ Yes ☐ No

5. Do you owe any Federal, State, or local taxes that are overdue? ☐ Yes ☐ No

6. Do you have any title of nobility in any foreign country? ☐ Yes ☐ No

7. Have you ever been declared legally incompetent or been confined to a mental institution within the last five years? ☐ Yes ☐ No

Part 10. Additional Questions *(Continued)*	Write your USCIS A-Number here: A

B. Affiliations.

8. a Have you **ever** been a member of or associated with any organization, association, fund foundation, party, club, society, or similar group in the United States or in any other place?   ☐ Yes   ☐ No

    b. If you answered "Yes," list the name of each group below. If you need more space, attach the names of the other group(s) on a separate sheet of paper.

Name of Group	Name of Group
1.	6.
2.	7.
3.	8.
4.	9.
5.	10.

9. Have you **ever** been a member of or in any way associated *(either directly or indirectly)* with:

    a. The Communist Party?   ☐ Yes   ☐ No

    b. Any other totalitarian party?   ☐ Yes   ☐ No

    c. A terrorist organization?   ☐ Yes   ☐ No

10. Have you **ever** advocated *(either directly or indirectly)* the overthrow of any government by force or violence?   ☐ Yes   ☐ No

11. Have you **ever** persecuted *(either directly or indirectly)* any person because of race, religion, national origin, membership in a particular social group, or political opinion?   ☐ Yes   ☐ No

12. Between March 23, 1933, and May 8, 1945, did you work for or associate in any way *(either directly or indirectly)* with:

    a. The Nazi government of Germany?   ☐ Yes   ☐ No

    b. Any government in any area (1) occupied by, (2) allied with, or (3) established with the help of the Nazi government of Germany?   ☐ Yes   ☐ No

    c. Any German, Nazi, or S.S. military unit, paramilitary unit, self-defense unit, vigilante unit, citizen unit, police unit, government agency or office, extermination camp, concentration camp, prisoner of war camp, prison, labor camp, or transit camp?   ☐ Yes   ☐ No

C. Continuous Residence.

Since becoming a lawful permanent resident of the United States:

13. Have you **ever** called yourself a "nonresident" on a Federal, State, or local tax return?   ☐ Yes   ☐ No

14. Have you **ever** failed to file a Federal, State, or local tax return because you considered yourself to be a "nonresident"?   ☐ Yes   ☐ No

Part 10. Additional Questions *(continued)*	Write your USCIS A-Number here: A

D. Good Moral Character.

For the purposes of this application, you must answer "Yes" to the following questions, if applicable, even if your records were sealed or otherwise cleared or if anyone, including a judge, law enforcement officer, or attorney, told you that you no longer have a record.

15. Have you **ever** committed a crime or offense for which you were **not** arrested? ☐ Yes ☐ No

16. Have you **ever** been arrested, cited, or detained by any law enforcement officer (including USCIS or former INS and military officers) for any reason? ☐ Yes ☐ No

17. Have you **ever** been charged with committing any crime or offense? ☐ Yes ☐ No

18. Have you **ever** been convicted of a crime or offense? ☐ Yes ☐ No

19. Have you **ever** been placed in an alternative sentencing or a rehabilitative program (for example: diversion, deferred prosecution, withheld adjudication, deferred adjudication)? ☐ Yes ☐ No

20. Have you **ever** received a suspended sentence, been placed on probation, or been paroled? ☐ Yes ☐ No

21. Have you **ever** been in jail or prison? ☐ Yes ☐ No

If you answered "Yes" to any of Questions 15 through 21, complete the following table. If you need more space, use a separate sheet of paper to give the same information.

Why were you arrested, cited, detained, or charged?	Date arrested, cited, detained, or charged? *(mm/dd/yyyy)*	Where were you arrested, cited, detained, or charged? *(City, State, Country)*	Outcome or disposition of the arrest, citation, detention, or charge *(No charges filed, charges dismissed, jail, probation, etc.)*

Answer Questions 22 through 33. If you answer "Yes" to any of these questions, attach (1) your written explanation why your answer was "Yes" and (2) any additional information or documentation that helps explain your answer.

22. Have you **ever**:

    a. Been a habitual drunkard? ☐ Yes ☐ No

    b. Been a prostitute, or procured anyone for prostitution? ☐ Yes ☐ No

    c. Sold or smuggled controlled substances, illegal drugs, or narcotics? ☐ Yes ☐ No

    d. Been married to more than one person at the same time? ☐ Yes ☐ No

    e. Helped anyone enter or try to enter the United States illegally? ☐ Yes ☐ No

    f. Gambled illegally or received income from illegal gambling? ☐ Yes ☐ No

    g. Failed to support your dependents or to pay alimony? ☐ Yes ☐ No

23. Have you **ever** given false or misleading information to any U.S. Government official while applying for any immigration benefit or to prevent deportation, exclusion, or removal? ☐ Yes ☐ No

24. Have you **ever** lied to any U.S. Government official to gain entry or admission into the United States? ☐ Yes ☐ No

Part 10. Additional Questions *(Continued)*	Write your USCIS A-Number here: A

E. Removal, Exclusion, and Deportation Proceedings.

25. Are removal, exclusion, rescission, or deportation proceedings pending against you? ☐ Yes ☐ No

26. Have you **ever** been removed, excluded, or deported from the United States? ☐ Yes ☐ No

27. Have you **ever** been ordered to be removed, excluded, or deported from the United States? ☐ Yes ☐ No

28. Have you **ever** applied for any kind of relief from removal, exclusion, or deportation? ☐ Yes ☐ No

F. Military Service.

29. Have you **ever** served in the U.S. Armed Forces? ☐ Yes ☐ No

30. Have you **ever** left the United States to avoid being drafted into the U.S. Armed Forces? ☐ Yes ☐ No

31. Have you **ever** applied for any kind of exemption from military service in the U.S. Armed Forces? ☐ Yes ☐ No

32. Have you **ever** deserted from the U.S. Armed Forces? ☐ Yes ☐ No

G. Selective Service Registration.

33. Are you a male who lived in the United States at any time between your 18th and 26th birthdays ☐ Yes ☐ No
in any status except as a lawful nonimmigrant?

If you answered "NO," go on to question 34.

If you answered "YES," provide the information below.

If you answered "YES," but you did not register with the Selective Service System and are still under 26 years of age, you must register before you apply for naturalization, so that you can complete the information below:

Date Registered (mm/dd/yyyy) [   ]   Selective Service Number [   ]

If you answered "YES," but you did not register with the Selective Service and you are now 26 years old or older, attach a statement explaining why you did not register.

H. Oath Requirements. *(See Part 14 for the text of the oath)*

Answer Questions 34 through 39. If you answer "No" to any of these questions, attach (1) your written explanation why the answer was "No" and (2) any additional information or documentation that helps to explain your answer.

34. Do you support the Constitution and form of government of the United States? ☐ Yes ☐ No

35. Do you understand the full Oath of Allegiance to the United States? ☐ Yes ☐ No

36. Are you willing to take the full Oath of Allegiance to the United States? ☐ Yes ☐ No

37. If the law requires it, are you willing to bear arms on behalf of the United States? ☐ Yes ☐ No

38. If the law requires it, are you willing to perform noncombatant services in the U.S. Armed Forces? ☐ Yes ☐ No

39. If the law requires it, are you willing to perform work of national importance under civilian direction? ☐ Yes ☐ No

Form N-400 (Rev. 03/22/12) Y Page 9

Part 11. Your Signature	Write your USCIS A-Number here: A

I certify, under penalty of perjury under the laws of the United States of America, that this application, and the evidence submitted with it, are all true and correct. I authorize the release of any information that the USCIS needs to determine my eligibility for naturalization.

Your Signature	Date *(mm/dd/yyyy)*

Part 12. Signature of Person Who Prepared This Application for You *(If applicable)*

I declare under penalty of perjury that I prepared this application at the request of the above person. The answers provided are based on information of which I have personal knowledge and/or were provided to me by the above named person in response to the *exact questions* contained on this form.

Preparer's Printed Name	Preparer's Signature

Date *(mm/dd/yyyy)*	Preparer's Firm or Organization Name *(If applicable)*	Preparer's Daytime Phone Number

Preparer's Address - Street Number and Name	City	State	Zip Code

NOTE: Do not complete Parts 13 and 14 until a USCIS Officer instructs you to do so.

Part 13. Signature at Interview

I swear (affirm) and certify under penalty of perjury under the laws of the United States of America that I know that the contents of this application for naturalization subscribed by me, including corrections numbered 1 through _____ and the evidence submitted by me numbered pages 1 through _____ , are true and correct to the best of my knowledge and belief.

Subscribed to and sworn to (affirmed) before me

	Officer's Printed Name or Stamp	Date *(mm/dd/yyyy)*
Complete Signature of Applicant	Officer's Signature	

Part 14. Oath of Allegiance

If your application is approved, you will be scheduled for a public oath ceremony at which time you will be required to take the following Oath of Allegiance immediately prior to becoming a naturalized citizen. By signing, you acknowledge your willingness and ability to take this oath:

I hereby declare, on oath, that I absolutely and entirely renounce and abjure all allegiance and fidelity to any foreign prince, potentate, state, or sovereignty, of whom or which I have heretofore been a subject or citizen;

that I will support and defend the Constitution and laws of the United States of America against all enemies, foreign and domestic;

that I will bear true faith and allegiance to the same;

that I will bear arms on behalf of the United States when required by the law;

that I will perform noncombatant service in the Armed Forces of the United States when required by the law;

that I will perform work of national importance under civilian direction when required by the law; and

that I take this obligation freely, without any mental reservation or purpose of evasion, so help me God.

Printed Name of Applicant	Complete Signature of Applicant

Form N-400 (Rev. 03/22/12) Y Page 10

APPENDIX 9-2

Form N-14B

File A#_____

Date   _____

Applicant for Naturalization

The results of your examination are checked below:

( )   Your case has been continued for a reexamination on: _____history and government, ability to _____read, _____write, _____speak, or _____understand English. You will be notified by mail regarding the date and time of your reexamination.

( )   You have passed your examination, but cannot sign your certificate until you present the document(s) requested below. You will be notified by mail within 120 days to appear with the documents. Failure to appear with the requested documents will result in denial of your application. NOTE: ALL DOCUMENT(S) MUST BE ORIGINAL/CERTIFIED COPIES.

( )   Please bring the document(s) listed below with you at the time of your reexamination.

_____ Arrest report (and)(or) court disposition for _____
_____ Birth certificate of _____
_____ Marriage certificate of _____
_____ Interlocutory and/or final divorce decree of _____
_____ Death certificate of _____
_____ Adoption decree and/or court order re: name change_____
_____ Proof of spousal and/or child support for _____

_____ Proof of Selective Service Registration (call 1-708-688-6888) _____

_____ Tax Clearance from I.R.S. for tax year(s) _____
_____ Letter from church re: religious beliefs in bearing arms.
_____ Letter from person(s) who gave affidavit of support at time of your lawful entry to the United States.
_____ Letter from Welfare Dept. and/or Social Security re: eligibility.
_____ Other:_____
_____
_____
_____

Richard K. Rogers
District Director

U.S. DEPARTMENT OF JUSTICE
IMMIGRATION & NATURALIZATION SERVICE
300 N. LOS ANGELES STREET
LOS ANGELES, CA 90012

File A _____

Date _____

Applicant for Naturalization

The results of your examination are checked below:

( ) CONGRATULATIONS! Your application is granted. You will be notified when it is time to appear for the oath taking ceremony and issuance of your naturalization certificate. Please report any changes of address. Alien registration cards lost between now and the day of the oath taking may prevent the issuance of a certificate on the day of your naturalization.

( ) You did not pass the _____ test. Since this is your second attempt, it will be necessary for you to file a new application for citizenship when you are ready to try again.

( ) Your case has been continued for: 1.___Receipt of verification of your military service or other routine clearances; 2.___Receipt of your immigration file; 3.___Reexamination on:___history and government; Ability to:___read,___write,___speak or ___understand English.

( ) A more in-depth interview is necessary in your case. It will be necessary to reschedule your examination. Please advise this office of any change of address.

( ) You will be notified by mail of further action in your case.

_____
Richard K. Rogers
District Director

Form N-14B

APPENDIX 9-3

Forms N-445 & N-445B

U.S. Department of Justice
Immigration and Naturalization Service

OMB No. 1115-0052
Notice of Naturalization Oath Ceremony

AR # _____

Date _____

You are hereby notified to appear for a Naturalization Oath Ceremony on:

at:

Please report promptly at _____ M.

SAMPLE NOT VALID FOR USE

You must being the following with you:

☒ **This letter, WITH ALL OF THE QUESTIONS ON THE OTHER SIDE ANSWERED IN INK OR ON A TYPEWRITER.**
☒ **Alien Registration Card.**
☒ **Reentry Permit, or Refugee Travel Document.**
☒ **Any Immigration documents you may have.**
☒ **If the naturalization application is on behalf of your child (children), bring your child (children).**
☐ **Other**

Proper attire should be worn.

If you cannot come to this ceremony, return this notice immediately and state why you cannot appear. In such case, you will be sent another notice of ceremony at a later date. You must appear at an oath ceremony to complete the naturalization process.

Form N-445 (Rev. 1/8/92)   **(SEE OTHER SIDE)**

In connection with your application for naturalization, please answer each of the questions by checking "Yes" or "No". You should answer these questions the day you are to appear for the citizenship oath ceremony. These questions refer to actions since the date you were first interviewed on your Application for Naturalization. They do not refer to anything that happened before that interview.

After you have answered every question, sign your name and fill in the date and place of signing, and provide your current address.

You must bring this completed questionnaire with you to the oath ceremony, as well as the documents indicated on the front, and give them to the Immigration employee at the oath ceremony. You may be questioned further on your answers at that time.

AFTER the date you were first interviewed on your Application for Naturaliztion, Form N-400:	ANSWERS
1. Have you married, or been widowed, separated, or divorced? (If "Yes" please bring documented proof of marriage, death, separation or divorce.)	1. ☐ Yes ☐ No
2. Have you traveled outside the United States?	2. ☐ Yes ☐ No
3. Have you knowingly committed any crime or offense, for which you have not been arrested; or have you been arrested, cited, charged, indicted, convicted, fined, or imprisoned for breaking or violating any law or ordinance, including traffic violations?	3. ☐ Yes ☐ No
4. Have you joined any organization, including the Communist Party, or become associated or connected therewith in any way?	4. ☐ Yes ☐ No
5. Have you claimed exemption from military service?	5. ☐ Yes ☐ No
6. Has there been any change in your willingness to bear arms on behalf of the United States; to perform non-combatant service in the armed forces of the United States; to perform work of national importance under civilian direction, if the law requires it?	6. ☐ Yes ☐ No
7. Have you practiced polygamy; received income from illegal gambling; been a prostitute, procured anyone for prostitution or been involved in any other unlawful commercialized vice; encouraged or helped any alien to enter the United States illegally; illicitly trafficked in drugs or marihuana; given any false testimony to obtain immigration benefits; or been a habitual drunkard?	7. ☐ Yes ☐ No

I certify that each of the answers shown above were made by me or at my direction, and that they are true and correct.

Signed at _____ , on _____

(City and State)   (Date)

_____   _____

(Full Signature)   (Full Address and ZIP Code)

Authority for collection of the information requested on Form N-445 is contained in Sections 101(f), 316, 332, 335 and 336 of the Immigration and Nationality Act (8 U.S.C. 1101 (f), 1427, 1443, 1446 and 1447). Submission of the information is voluntary. The principal purposes for requesting the information are to enable examiners of the Immigration and Naturalization Service to determine an applicant's eligibility for naturalization. The information requested may, as a matter of routine use, be disclosed to naturalization courts and to other federal, state, local or foreign law enforcement and regulatory agencies, the Department of Defense, including any component thereof, the Selective Service System, the Department of State, the Department of the Treasury, the Department of Transportation, Central Intelligence Agency, Interpol and individuals and organizations in the processing of any application for naturalization, or during the course of investigation to elicit further information required by the Immigration and Naturalization Service to carry out its functions. Information solicited which indicates a violation or potential violation of law, whether civil, criminal, or regulatory in nature, may be referred, as a routine use, to the appropriate agency, whether federal, state, local or foreign, charged with the responsibility of investigating, enforcing or prosecuting such violations. Failure to provide all or any of the requested information may result in a denial of the application for naturalization.

Public Reporting burden for this collection of information is estimated to average 5 minutes per response, including the time for reviewing instructions, searching existing data sources, gathering and maintaining the data needed, and completing and reviewing the collection of information. Send comments regarding this burden estimate or any other aspect of this collection of information, including suggestions for reducing this burden to: U.S. Department of Justice, Immigration and Naturalization Service, (Room 5304), Washington, DC 20536; and to the Office of Management and Budget, Paperwork Reduction Project; OMB No. 1115-0052.; Washington, DC 20503.

.S. GPO:1983-342-483/72379

U.S. DEPARTMENT OF JUSTICE
Immigration and Naturalization Service

Notice of Final
Naturalization Hearing
(Children)

OMB No. 1115-0096
Approval Expires 1/31/86

Petition No. _____

AR# _____

Date _____

Re: _____

A hearing on the petition for naturalization filed on behalf of your child(ren) will be held before a judge of the naturalization court on _____ at

Please report promptly at _____ M.

If the judge finds your child(ren) qualified for naturalization, the child(ren) will be given citizenship.

YOU MUST BRING WITH YOU THE ITEMS MARKED [X] BELOW:

[X] This letter, WITH ALL OF THE QUESTIONS ON THE OTHER SIDE ANSWERED IN INK OR ON A TYPEWRITER

[X] Alien Registration Receipt Card of the child(ren).

[X] Any immigration documents you may have for the child(ren).

[ ] Your child(ren)

[ ] Other

Proper attire should be worn in court.

If you cannot come to this hearing, return this notice immediately and state why you cannot appear. In such case, you will be sent another notice of hearing at a later date.

Form N-445B
(Rev. 4-20-82)N

(SEE OTHER SIDE)

UNITED STATES DEPARTMENT OF JUSTICE
Immigration and Naturalization Service

To Petitioner:

In connection with the hearing, please answer each of the questions below "Yes" or "No" without giving any further explanation.

The questions refer only what has happened *after the date* you appeared with your child(ren) and filed the petition for naturalization. They do not refer to anything that happened before that date.

After you have answered every question, sign your name, give your address, and fill in the date and place of signing.

You must BRING THIS COMPLETED LETTER WITH YOU to the hearing and give it to the naturalization examiner, who will question you further on your answers.

═══

After the date you filed the petition:

1. Has your child married? (If "yes" please bring marriage certificate.)   (1) Answer _____

2. Has your child been absent from the United States?   (2) Answer _____

3. Has your child knowingly committed any crime or offense, for which he or she has not been arrested; or has your child been arrested, charged, indicted, convicted, fined, or imprisoned for breaking or violating any law or ordinance, including traffic violations?   (3) Answer _____

4. Has your child joined any organization, including the Communist Party, or become associated or connected therewith in any way?   (4) Answer _____

5. Has your child claimed exemption from military service?   (5) Answer _____

6. Has there been any change in your child's willingness to bear arms on behalf of the United States; to perform non-combatant service in the armed forces of the United States; to perform work of national importance under civilian direction, if the law requires it?   (6) Answer _____

7. The law provides that, for naturalization purposes, a person shall not be regarded as of good moral character who, at any time after the filing of the petition for naturalization, has believed in polygamy or been a polygamist; received income mostly from illegal gambling; been a prostitute or procured anyone for prostitution; knowingly and for gain encouraged or helped an alien to enter the United States illegally; been an illicit trafficker in drugs or marihuana; or has been a habitual drunkard. Has your child been such a person or committed any of these acts?   (7) Answer _____

I certify that each of the answers shown above were made by me or at my direction, and that they are true and correct.

Signed at _____ on _____
              (City and State)   (Date)

_____
(Full Signature)

_____
(Street Address)

_____
(City, State, and Zip Code)

APPENDIX 9-4

N400 Processing Worksheet

Attachments 1, 4 – 18 Omitted

ATTACHMENT 2

N-400 PROCESSING WORKSHEET

A#_____

CLERICAL		Initials	Date	Remarks
Fee was paid.				
FD-258 "masthead" is complete, accurate, and legible.	Set 1			
	Set 2			
If necessary, A-number is zero filled on FD-258. (e.g., A40123456 to A040123456)	Set 1			
	Set 2			
FD-258 (fingerprints) were sent to FBI.	Set 1			
	Set 2			
All receipt data entry was completed. (NACS/CLAIMS-GUI)				
If Non-NACS site, G-325 was sent to FBI, and copy retained in file. (SCs - N/A)				
If military, G-325B and N-426 were sent, and copies retained in file.				
FD-258 Control #_____				
A-file was located in your own office.				
If not, initial A-file transfer request was made.				
If necessary, 2nd A-file transfer request was made. (30 calendar days)				
If necessary, 3rd A-file transfer request was made. (30 calendar days)				
Final status of A-file transfer request.				
A-file relates to the applicant.				

PAGE 1

Rev. May 23-97 Attachment 2

744

N-400 PROCESSING WORKSHEET (CON'T)

A# _____

OFFICER	Initials	Date	Remarks
Appeared for interview. 1)	_____	_____	_____
2)			
Was interviewed on an A-file.			
Met Section 312 English requirements at initial interview.			
If not, passed English Re-Exam.			
Met Section 312 Civics requirements at initial interview.			
If not, passed Civics Re-Exam.			
If applicable, met Section 312 disability exception.			
Established physical presence/residence.			
Established good moral character.			
Established attachment to Constitution.			
Required a modified oath. (put reason(s) in remarks)			
Met other eligibility requirements. (put reason(s) in remarks)			
Officer recommendation, if supervisory review required.			
Indicate final decision under remarks. (grant, denied, or withdrawn)			
SUPERVISORY CONCURRENCE WITH OFFICER'S RECOMMENDATION	Initials	Date	Remarks
Applicant with criminal history requiring Supervisory review.			
Applicant approved on basis of T-file.			
Applicant meeting Section 312 disability exception.			
OATH CEREMONY	Initials	Date	Remarks
No Show. 1)	_____	_____	_____
2)			

PAGE 2   Rev. 05/23/97

Reviewed and reverified_____ / _____

                       Supervisor/Officer's Signature   Date

Rev. May 23-97   Attachment 2

N-400 PROCESSING WORK SHEET

A#			
CLERICAL	Initials	Date	Remarks
Fee was paid			
FD-258 sent to FBI			
All receipt data entry completed (NACS)			
Initial A file request made (non Nacs office)			
2nd A file request made (20 days)			
3rd A file request made (20 days)			
Photos attached to application			
G-325B; N-426, if any, sent out			
OFFICER	Initials	Date	Remarks
Meets 312 English requirements			
Meets 312 civics requirements			
Residence, physical presence established			
Good Moral Character established			
Attachment to Constitution established			
Fingerprint check auto.#_____completed			
Other eligibility requirements met.			
SUPERVISOR (for review and concurrence if meets criteria listed below)	Initials	Date	Remarks
Applicants with criminal histories or other GMC determinations			
Applicant with complex statutory eligibility issues			
Applicant approved on basis of T-file			

ATTACHMENT 3

CERTIFICATE PREPARATION SHEET
and
OATH DECLARATION

A#_____

Daytime Phone#_____

NAME(changing to):_____

         FIRST   MIDDLE   LAST

DOB:_____   SEX:_____

     M/D/Y

Height: ___ ___   Marital Status:_____

     FT. IN.

Country of Former Nationality:_____

Name Change - Y or N (circle) (If yes, see attached name change form)

Oath of Allegiance

I HEREBY DECLARE, on oath, that I absolutely and entirely renounce and abjure all allegiance and fidelity to any foreign prince, potentate, state, or sovereignty of whom or which I have heretofore been a subject or citizen; that I will support and defend the Constitution and the laws of the United States of America against all enemies, foreign and domestic; that I will bear true faith and allegiance to the same; that I will bear arms on behalf of the United States when required by the law; that I will perform noncombatant service in the Armed Forces of the United States when required by the law; that I will perform work of national importance under civilian direction when required by the law; and that I take this obligation freely without any mental reservation or purpose of evasion; SO HELP ME GOD.

In acknowledgment whereof I have hereunto affixed my signature.

_____   _____

Applicant's Signature (name change)   Date

Rev. 5/23/97

APPENDIX 9-5

Sample Notice to Appear for Fingerprinting

U.S. Department of Justice
Immigration and Naturalization Service

Notice of Action

THE UNITED STATES OF AMERICA

Fingerprint Notification			NOTICE DATE November 05, 1998
CASE TYPE N400 Application For Naturalization			AREA A
APPLICATION NUMBER FPS*000*	RECEIVED DATE October 28, 1997	PRIORITY DATE October 28, 1997	PAGE 1 of 1

APPLICANT NAME AND MAILING ADDRESS

c/o
LAW OFFICES OF
          BLVD

To process your application, INS must take your fingerprints and send them to the Federal Bureau of Investigation for clearance. If you were between the ages of 14 and 75 at the time of filing your application, you must have your fingerprints taken. You are scheduled to be fingerprinted at the Designated Law Enforcement Agency (DLEA) during the time frame listed below. The DLEA fingerprint station is part of a special outreach program with limited hours and scheduling capacity, therefore, you must have this scheduled appointment. If you are unable to appear at the DLEA, you may go to the Application Support Center (ASC) listed below. PLEASE DO NOT APPEAR BEFORE YOUR SCHEDULED APPOINTMENT DATE. If you have been fingerprinted in the last 120 days, please ignore this notice. PLEASE DISREGARD THIS NOTICE IF YOU HAVE ALREADY RECEIVED YOUR NATURALIZATION CERTIFICATE. INS REGRETS THIS INCONVENIENCE.

Address

Hours of Operation
CLOSED ON FEDERAL HOLIDAYS

INS JACKSONVILLE
400 WEST BAY STREET
JACKSONVILLE FL 32202

Sun, Mon Closed
Tue, Thur 9am-8pm
Wed, Fri 9am-5pm
Sat 8am-2pm

DLEA PANAMA CITY
17110 FIRENZO ST
PANAMA CITY BEACH POLICE DEPT
PANAMA CITY BEACH FL 32413

Mon - Fri 8am - 12pm/1pm-4pm

If you cannot go to the INS Application Support Center (ASC) during your scheduled 7-day period, you may go on any Wednesday, as long as you have your fingerprints taken by 02/09/1999. If you do not have them taken within that period, your application may be considered abandoned and therefore denied. Please do not appear before your scheduled date.

When you go to have your fingerprints taken, you must bring:
1) THIS LETTER; and
2) Your Alien Registration Card (ARC). If you do not have your ARC, you must bring alternative photo identification such as a passport, valid driver's license, national ID, military ID, State-issued photo ID, or other INS-issued photo ID.

Please be reminded that you must bring this letter and proper photo identification to have your fingerprints taken, and prevent further delay in the processing of your application. Please inform the office listed below immediately of any address changes.

Please take note that the staff at the INS ASC will not be able to answer any questions about the status of your application. If you have any questions regarding this notice, or the status of your case, please contact our office at the address or customer service number listed below. You will be notified separately about any other cases you may have filed.

INS Office Address:
US IMMIGRATION AND NATURALIZATION SERVICE
PO BOX 87400
LINCOLN, NE 68501

INS Customer Service Number:
(888) 557-5398

REPRESENTATIVE COPY

Form I-797C (Rev. 09/07/93)N

APPENDIX 9-6

Sample Document List

Department of Homeland Security
U.S. Citizenship and Immigration Services

M-477

Document Checklist

All applicants must send the following 3 items with their N-400 application:

1. ☐ A photocopy of both sides of your Permanent Resident Card (formerly known as the Alien Registration Card or "Green Card"). If you have lost the card, submit a photocopy of the receipt of your Form I-90, Application to Replace Permanent Resident Card; **and**

2. ☐ 2 identical color photographs, with your name and Alien Registration Number (A-Number) written lightly in pencil on the back of each photo. For details about the photo requirements, see **Part 5** of Form M-476, A Guide to Naturalization, and the Form N-400, Application for Naturalization instructions. If your religion requires you to wear a head covering, your facial features must still be exposed in the photo for purposes of identification; **and**

3. ☐ A check or money order for the application fee and the biometrics services fee for fingerprinting, as stated in the M-479, Current Naturalization Fees, enclosure in the *Guide*. (Applicants 75 years of age or older are exempted from fingerprinting and the biometrics services fee). Write your A-Number on the back of the check or money order.

Send copies of the following documents, unless we ask for an original.

If an attorney or accredited representative is acting on your behalf, send:

☐ A completed <u>original</u> Form G-28, Notice of Entry of Appearance as Attorney or Representative.

If your current legal name is different from the name on your Permanent Resident Card, send:

☐ The document(s) that legally changed your name (marriage certificate, divorce decree, or court document).

If you are applying for naturalization on the basis of marriage to a U.S. citizen, send the following 4 items:

1. ☐ Evidence that your spouse has been a U.S. citizen for the last 3 years:
   a. Birth certificate (if your spouse never lost citizenship since birth); **or**
   b. Certificate of Naturalization; **or**
   c. Certificate of Citizenship; **or**
   d. The inside of the front cover and signature page of your spouse's current U.S. passport; **or**
   e. Form FS-240, Report of Birth Abroad of a Citizen of the United States of America; **and**
2. ☐ Your current marriage certificate; **and**
3. ☐ Proof of termination of all prior marriages of your spouse (divorce decree(s), annulment(s), or death certificate(s)); **and**
4. ☐ Documents referring to you and your spouse:
   a. Tax returns, bank accounts, leases, mortgages, or birth certificates of children; **or**
   b. Internal Revenue Service (IRS)-certified copies of the income tax forms that you both filed for the past 3 years; **or**
   c. An IRS tax return transcript for the last 3 years.

If you were married before, send:

☐ Proof that **all** earlier marriages ended (divorce decree(s), annulment(s), or death certificates(s)).

If you are currently in the U.S. military service and are seeking citizenship based on that service, send:

☐ A completed <u>original</u> Form N-426, Request for Certification of Military or Naval Service.

If you have taken any trip outside the United States that lasted 6 months or more since becoming a Lawful Permanent Resident, send evidence that you (and your family) continued to live, work and/or keep ties to the United States, such as:

☐ An IRS tax return "transcript" or an IRS-certified tax return listing tax information for the last 5 years (or for the last 3 years if you are applying on the basis of marriage to a U.S. citizen).

☐ Rent or mortgage payments and pay stubs.

If you have a dependent spouse or child(ren) who do not live with you, send:

☐ Any court or government order to provide financial support; **and**

☐ Evidence of your financial support (including evidence that you have complied with any court or government order), such as:

    a. Cancelled checks;

    b. Money and receipts;

    c. A court or agency printout of child support payments;

    d. Evidence of wage garnishments;

    e. A letter from the parent or guardian who cares for your child(ren).

If you have ever been arrested or detained by any law enforcement officer for any reason, and <u>no charges were filed</u>, send:

☐ An <u>original</u> official statement by the arresting agency or applicant court confirming that no charges were filed.

If you have ever been arrested or detained by any law enforcement officer for any reason, and <u>charges were filed</u>, send:

☐ An <u>original</u> or court-certified copy of the complete arrest record and disposition for each incident (dismissal order, conviction record or acquittal order).

If you have ever been convicted or placed in an alternative sentencing program or rehabilitative program (such as a drug treatment or community service program), send:

☐ An <u>original</u> or court-certified copy of the sentencing record for each incident; **and**

☐ Evidence that you completed your sentence:

    a. An <u>original</u> or certified copy of your probation or parole record; **or**

    b. Evidence that you completed an alternative sentencing program or rehabilitative program.

If you have ever had any arrest or conviction vacated, set aside, sealed, expunged or otherwise removed from your record, send:

☐ An <u>original</u> or court-certified copy of the court order vacating, setting aside, sealing, expunging or otherwise removing the arrest or conviction, or an <u>original</u> statement from the court that no record exists of your arrest or conviction.

    NOTE: If you have been arrested or convicted of a crime, you may send any countervailing evidence or evidence in your favor concerning the circumstances of your arrest and/or conviction that you would like U.S. Citizenship and Immigration Services to consider.

If you have ever failed to file an income tax return since you became a Lawful Permanent Resident, send:

☐ All correspondence with the IRS regarding your failure to file.

If you have any Federal, state or local taxes that are overdue, send:

☐ A signed agreement from the IRS or state or local tax office showing that you have filed a tax return and arranged to pay the taxes you owe; **and**

☐ Documentation from the IRS or state or local tax office showing the current status of your repayment program.

    NOTE: You may obtain copies of tax documents and tax information by contacting your local IRS offices, using the Blue Pages of your telephone directory, or through its Web site at **www.irs.gov**.

If you are applying for a disability exception to the testing requirement, send:

☐ An <u>original</u> Form N-648, Medical Certification for Disability Exceptions, completed less than 6 months ago by a licensed medical or osteopathic doctor or licensed clinical psychologist.

If you did not register with the Selective Service and you (1) are male, (2) are 26 years old or older, and (3) lived in the United States in a status other than as a lawful nonimmigrant between the ages of 18 and 26, send:

☐ A "Status Information Letter" from the Selective Service (Call 1-847-688-6888 for more information).

Current Naturalization Fees

The fee for filing your naturalization application is:* **$595.00**

The biometric services fee for having your fingerprints taken is:** **$ 85.00**

Total: **$680.00**

You must send the **$680.00** fee with your application. Pay the fee with a check or money order drawn on a U.S. bank payable to the **Department of Homeland Security**. Do not use the initials DHS or USDHS. **Do Not Send Cash.**

Residents of Guam should make the fee payable to the "Treasurer, Guam," and residents of the U.S. Virgin Islands should make the fee payable to the "Commissioner of Finance of the Virgin Islands."

If required, USCIS may also take your photograph and signature as part of the biometric services.

Remember that your application fee is not refundable even if you withdraw your application or if your case is denied.

* If you are applying for naturalization based on your own service in the Armed Forces of the United States, no filing fee is required.

** If you are 75 years or older, or if you are filing on the basis of your service in the Armed Forces of the United States, or if you are filing from abroad, **do not** send the biometric services fee for fingerprinting with your application.

Form M-479 (Rev. 11/23/10)N

Department of Homeland Security
U.S. Citizenship and Immigration Services

Naturalization Eligibility Worksheet Instructions

What Is the Purpose of This Worksheet?

The attached "Eligibility Worksheet" will help you decide if you are eligible to apply for naturalization. **Do not send the completed worksheet to U.S. Citizenship and Immigration Services (USCIS).**

Who Should Complete This Worksheet?

If you are 18 years of age or older and are thinking about applying for naturalization based on your years as a Permanent Resident, you should complete this worksheet.

Who Should Not Use This Worksheet?

You **should not** use this worksheet to decide your eligibilty to apply if you are:

- Under 18 years of age and want to apply for naturalization based on your parents' or adopted parents' citizenship (see Questions 25 and 26 on pages 13-15 in *A Guide to Naturalization* for information on how to obtain citizenship).

- A Permanent Resident whose spouse was a U.S. citizen who died while on active duty in the U.S. Armed Forces (see pages 18 and 19 in *A Guide to Naturalization* for information on your naturalization requirements).

- Applying for naturalization based on active duty service in the U.S. Armed Forces (see pages 18 and 19 in *A Guide to Naturalization* for information on your naturalization requirements).

- A spouse of a U.S. citizen who is (a) a member of the U.S. Armed Forces, (b) an employee or contractor of the U.S. Government, (c) an employee of an American institution of research, (d) an employee of an American owned firm, (e) an employee of a public international organization, or (f) a clergy member (see pages 20 and 21 in *A Guide to Naturalization* for more information).

Directions for the Eligibility Worksheet:

1. Answer the questions on the worksheet by checking "True" or "Not True." If you answer "Not True" to certain questions, you may be asked to answer additional questions on pages 3 and 4. Most applicants will **not** need to answer the questions on pages 3 and 4.

2. If you have completed the worksheet and believe you are eligible for naturalization, please call the USCIS Forms Line **(1-800-870-3676)** to request an application (Form N-400), or download the form from the Internet at **www.uscis.gov.**

3. If you have completed the worksheet and you still have questions regarding your eligibility, you should read *A Guide to Naturalization*. You may also wish to get advice from an immigrant assistance organization or immigration attorney.

Form M-480 (Rev. 06/15/06)N

Naturalization Eligibility Worksheet

True **Not True**

1. I am at least 18 years old. ☐ ☐ STOP → You are not eligible to apply for naturalization. **Exception:** You do not need to be at least 18 years old for military naturalization under section 329 of the INA.

2. I am a Permanent Resident of the United States, and I have been issued a Permanent Resident Card (formerly called Alien Registration Card). ☐

☐ STOP → You are not eligible to apply for naturalization.

3. I have been a Permanent Resident for:

five years or more*	**three to five years***	**less than three years**

less than three years → STOP → You are not eligible to apply for naturalization.

three to five years* → See Attachment A on Page 3

True **Not True**

4. During the last five years, I have not been out of the United States for 30 months or more. ☐ ☐ STOP → For exceptions, see Attachment B on page 3.

5. During the last five years (or the last three years if I qualify under Attachment A), I have not taken a trip out of the United States that lasted one year or more. ☐ ☐ STOP → For exceptions, see Attachment C on page 3.

6. I have resided in the district or state in which I am applying for citizenship for the last three months. ☐ ☐ STOP → You must wait until you have lived in the state or district for three months to apply.

7. I can read, write and speak basic English. ☐ ☐ STOP → For exceptions, see Attachment D on page 4.

8. I know the fundamentals of U.S. history and the form and principles of the U.S. government. ☐ ☐ STOP → For exceptions, see Attachment E on page 4.

Go to Question 9.

*Naturalization applicants may file their applications 90 days before they have satisfied the "continuous residence" requirement.

Naturalization Eligibility Worksheet

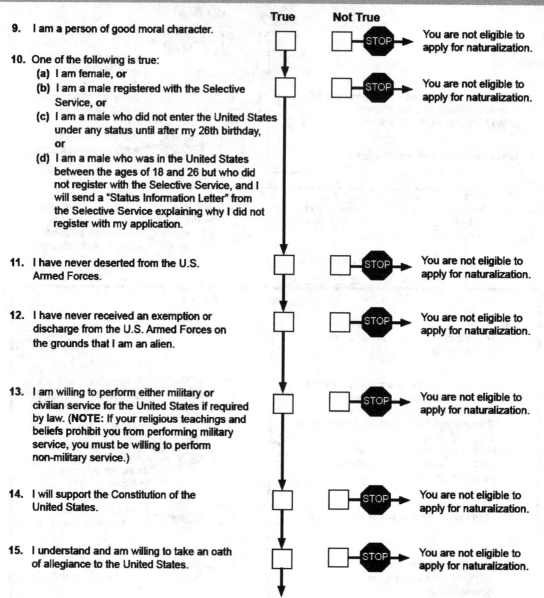

True   **Not True**

9. I am a person of good moral character.

    ☐   ☐ STOP → You are not eligible to apply for naturalization.

10. One of the following is true:
    (a) I am female, or
    (b) I am a male registered with the Selective Service, or
    (c) I am a male who did not enter the United States under any status until after my 26th birthday, or
    (d) I am a male who was in the United States between the ages of 18 and 26 but who did not register with the Selective Service, and I will send a "Status Information Letter" from the Selective Service explaining why I did not register with my application.

    ☐   ☐ STOP → You are not eligible to apply for naturalization.

11. I have never deserted from the U.S. Armed Forces.

    ☐   ☐ STOP → You are not eligible to apply for naturalization.

12. I have never received an exemption or discharge from the U.S. Armed Forces on the grounds that I am an alien.

    ☐   ☐ STOP → You are not eligible to apply for naturalization.

13. I am willing to perform either military or civilian service for the United States if required by law. (**NOTE:** If your religious teachings and beliefs prohibit you from performing military service, you must be willing to perform non-military service.)

    ☐   ☐ STOP → You are not eligible to apply for naturalization.

14. I will support the Constitution of the United States.

    ☐   ☐ STOP → You are not eligible to apply for naturalization.

15. I understand and am willing to take an oath of allegiance to the United States.

    ☐   ☐ STOP → You are not eligible to apply for naturalization.

STOP HERE: You are probably eligible to apply for naturalization. Please call the Forms Line (1-800-870-3676) for an "Application for Naturalization" (Form N-400) and be sure to read *A Guide to Naturalization.*

Form M-480 (Rev. 06/15/06)N Page 2

Attachment A - Naturalization Eligibility Worksheet

I have been a Permanent Resident for three to five years

	True	Not True	
I am married to, and living with, a U.S. citizen.	☐	☐ STOP →	You are not eligible to apply for naturalization.
I have been married to that U.S. citizen for at least the past three years.	☐	☐ STOP →	You are not eligible to apply for naturalization.
My spouse has been a U.S. citizen for at least the past three years.	☐	☐ STOP →	You are not eligible to apply for naturalization.
During the past three years, I have not been out of the country for 18 months or more.	☐	☐ STOP →	You are not eligible to apply for naturalization.

If you answered "True" to all four questions, go to Question 5 on page 1.

Attachment B

I have been out of the country for 30 months or more

	True	Not True	
I am: (a) A person who has served on board a vessel operated by or registered in the United States, or	☐	☐ STOP →	You are not eligible to apply for naturalization.

(b) An employee or an individual under contract to the U.S. Government, or

(c) A person who performs ministerial or priestly functions for a religious denomination or an interdenominational organization with a valid presence in the United States.

If you answered "True," see pages 20 and 21 in *A Guide to Naturalization* to get more information and go to Question 5 on page 1.

Attachment C

I have been out of the country for one year or more

	True	Not True	
Since becoming a Permanent Resident, I have not taken a trip out of the United States that lasted for one year or more without an approved "Application to Preserve Residence for Naturalization Purposes" (Form N-470).	☐	☐ STOP →	You are not eligible to apply for naturalization.

NOTE: Only certain persons can use Form N-470. See Pages 18-21 in *A Guide to Naturalization* for more information.

If you answered "True," go to Question 6 on page 1.

Form M-480 (Rev. 06/15/06)N Page 3

Attachment D - Naturalization Eligibility Worksheet

I cannot read, write or speak basic English

	True	Not True	
I am over 50 years old and have lived in the United States for at least 20 years since I became a Permanent Resident, or	☐	☐ STOP →	You are not eligible to apply for naturalization.
I am over 55 years old and have lived in the United States for at least 15 years since I became a Permanent Resident, or	☐	☐ STOP →	You are not eligible to apply for naturalization.
I have a disability that prevents me from fulfilling this requirement and will be filing a "Medical Certification for Disability Exceptions" (Form N-648) completed and signed by a doctor with my application.	☐	☐ STOP →	You are not eligible to apply for naturalization.

NOTE: Only certain people can use this exemption. See pages 26 and 27 in *A Guide to Naturalization* for more information.

If you answered "True" to one of these questions, go to Question 8 on page 1.

Attachment E

I have a disability that prevents me from fulfilling the civics requirement

	True	Not True	
I have a disability that prevents me from fulfilling the civics requirement, and I will be filing "Medical Certification for Disability Exceptions" (Form N-648) completed and signed by a doctor with my application.	☐	☐ STOP →	You are not eligible to apply for naturalization.

NOTE: Only certain people can use this exemption. See pages 26 and 27 in *A Guide to Naturalization* for more information.

If you answered "True" to the question, go to Question 9 on page 2.

Form M-480 (Rev. 06/15/06)N Page 4

APPENDIX 9-7

Role of Legal Guardians or Proxies in Naturalization Proceedings (March 13, 2002)

U.S. Department of Justice

Office of Legal Counsel

Office of the Principal Deputy Assistant Attorney General   *Washington, D.C. 20530*

March 13, 2002

MEMORANDUM FOR BO COOPER
GENERAL COUNSEL, IMMIGRATION AND NATURALIZATION SERVICE

Re: Role of Legal Guardians or Proxies in Naturalization Proceedings

You have asked for our opinion whether the Rehabilitation Act of 1973, as amended, 29 U.S.C. § 794 (1994 & Supp. IV 1998), requires the Immigration and Naturalization Service ("INS") as a reasonable accommodation to permit a legal guardian or other proxy to represent a mentally disabled applicant in naturalization proceedings.[1] For the reasons set forth below, we conclude that the Rehabilitation Act does require such accommodation.

I. Background

In response to earlier requests from your office, this Office issued two opinions in 1997 concluding that the oath of allegiance required under section 337 of the Immigration and Nationality Act ("INA"), 8 U.S.C. § 1448, could neither be waived by the INS nor satisfied by a guardian or proxy. We concluded that, under the statutory scheme established by Congress, the oath requirement was a fundamental and essential part of the naturalization process and that permitting a legal guardian or proxy to fulfill this central requirement thus would not constitute a reasonable accommodation under the Rehabilitation Act. *See* Letter for David A. Martin, General Counsel, Immigration and Naturalization Service, from Dawn E. Johnsen, Acting Assistant Attorney General, Office of Legal Counsel, *Re: Personal Satisfaction of Immigration and Nationality Act Oath Requirement* (Apr. 18, 1997) ("April 1997 Opinion"); Letter for David A. Martin, General Counsel, Immigration and Naturalization Service, from Dawn E. Johnsen, Acting Assistant Attorney General, Office of Legal Counsel, *Re: Waiver of Oath of Allegiance for Candidates for Naturalization* (Feb. 5, 1997).

---

[1] Memorandum for Daniel Koffsky, Acting Assistant Attorney General, Office of Legal Counsel, from Bo Cooper, General Counsel, Immigration and Naturalization Service, *Re: Request for Advisory Legal Opinion on the Role of Legal Guardians or Proxies in Naturalization Proceedings* (Aug. 6, 2001). You have asked, in the alternative, whether section 337 of the Immigration and Nationality Act, 8 U.S.C. § 1448 (2000), should be construed to enable the INS to permit a proxy to play this same role. In light of our response to your Rehabilitation Act question, we find it unnecessary to address this question.

In 2000, Congress amended section 337 to allow the Attorney General to "waive the taking of the oath by a person if in the opinion of the Attorney General the person is unable to understand, or to communicate an understanding of, its meaning because of a physical or developmental disability or mental impairment." Pub. L. No. 106-448, 114 Stat. 1939 (2000) (codified at 8 U.S.C. § 1448(a)). The amended statute further provides that "[i]f the Attorney General waives the taking of the oath by a person under the preceding sentence, the person shall be considered to have met the requirements of section 1427(a)(3) of this title with respect to attachment to the principles of the Constitution and well disposition to the good order and happiness of the United States." 8 U.S.C. § 1448(a).

II. Discussion

The 2000 amendment to section 337 removes the oath requirement as an obstacle to naturalization for certain individuals with disabilities. You ask further whether the Rehabilitation Act requires the INS to permit a legal guardian or other proxy to represent an individual with a mental disability throughout the naturalization process, from the filing of an application through the interview.

Section 504 of the Rehabilitation Act provides that "[n]o otherwise qualified individual with a disability in the United States . . . shall, solely by reason of her or his disability, be excluded from the participation in, be denied the benefits of, or be subjected to discrimination under any program or activity receiving Federal financial assistance or under any program or activity conducted by any Executive agency." 29 U.S.C. § 794(a). This Office has previously advised that all INS programs and activities, including naturalization proceedings, are covered by this prohibition. *See* April 1997 Opinion at 1; Memorandum for Maurice C. Inman, Jr., General Counsel, Immigration and Naturalization Service, from Robert B. Shanks, Deputy Assistant Attorney General, Office of Legal Counsel, *Re: Section 504 of the Rehabilitation Act of 1973* (Feb. 2, 1983).

The question, therefore, is whether a person who, as a result of a disability, is personally unable to file an application or participate in an interview may be considered "otherwise qualified" for naturalization. Department of Justice regulations implementing section 504 for federally conducted programs define a "[q]ualified handicapped person" as one "who meets the essential eligibility requirements and who can achieve the purpose of the program or activity without modifications in the program or activity that the agency can demonstrate would result in a fundamental alteration in its nature." 28 C.F.R. § 39.103 (2001). These regulations are based on, and should be construed consistent with, a series of Supreme Court decisions interpreting section 504 in the context of programs receiving federal financial assistance. The Court first interpreted section 504 in *Southeastern Community College v. Davis*, 442 U.S. 397, 406 (1979), stating that "[a]n otherwise qualified person is one who is able to meet all of a program's requirements in spite of his handicap." The Court held that an applicant with a serious hearing disability was not "otherwise qualified" under section 504 for admission to a nursing program where the ability to understand speech during the clinical phase of the program was considered essential to patient safety. The Court declined to require the college to accommodate the applicant by making "a fundamental alteration in the nature of [its] program." *Id.* at 410. The Court noted, however, that "situations may arise where a refusal to modify an existing program might become unreasonable and discriminatory." *Id.* at 412-13.

In subsequent cases, the Court has elaborated on the types of situations where modifications in a program may be required. In the employment context, the Court has advised that "[e]mployers have an affirmative obligation to make a reasonable accommodation for a handicapped employee. . . . [T]hey cannot deny an employee alternative employment opportunities reasonably available under the employer's existing policies." *School Bd. of Nassau County v. Arline*, 480 U.S. 273, 289 n.19 (1987). In *Arline*, the Court defined "an otherwise qualified person" as "one who can perform 'the essential functions' of the job," but explained that "[w]hen a handicapped person is not able to perform the essential functions of the job, the court must also consider whether any 'reasonable accommodation' by the employer would enable the handicapped person to perform those functions." *Id.* at 287 n.17 (quoting 45 C.F.R. § 84.3(k) (1985)). The Court distinguished, however, between reasonable accommodations and those that would require fundamental changes in a program. "Accommodation is not reasonable if it either imposes 'undue financial and administrative burdens' on a grantee . . . or requires 'a fundamental alteration in the nature of [the] program.'" *Arline*, 480 U.S. at 287 n.17 (citations omitted) (alteration in original); *see also Alexander v. Choate*, 469 U.S. 287, 300 (1985) ("while a grantee need not be required to make 'fundamental' or 'substantial' modifications to accommodate the handicapped, it may be required to make 'reasonable' ones"); *id.* at 299 n.19 ("the question of who is 'otherwise qualified' and what actions constitute 'discrimination' under [section 504] would seem to be two sides of a single coin; the ultimate question is the extent to which a grantee is required to make reasonable modifications in its programs for the needs of the handicapped").

Thus, in determining whether a person is "otherwise qualified" for a particular program, courts do not take an existing program as fixed. Instead, they ask whether the disabled person could meet a program's requirements if the program were revised to make reasonable accommodations for the disabled person. If permitting a legal guardian or other proxy to file an application and participate in an interview on behalf of a mentally disabled applicant does not eliminate essential requirements of, or otherwise fundamentally alter, the naturalization program, then a mentally disabled individual who meets all other requirements is "otherwise qualified" for naturalization.

We conclude that permitting a legal guardian or other proxy to play such a role on behalf of a mentally disabled applicant would not fundamentally alter the naturalization process and therefore is required by section 504. The INS may not "utilize criteria or methods of administration the purpose or effect of which would . . . [d]efeat or substantially impair accomplishment of the objectives of [the naturalization program] with respect to handicapped persons." 28 C.F.R. § 39.130(b)(3). Congress has already expressly provided that individuals with severe disabilities need not fulfill a number of significant statutory prerequisites for naturalization. By amending the INA to permit the Attorney General to waive the oath of

-3-

allegiance for persons unable to comprehend its meaning, Congress has superseded our previous conclusion that mentally disabled applicants must personally fulfill that statutory requirement. Moreover, any person who receives such a waiver is also considered to have met the requirements of section 316 of the INA with respect to being "attached to the principles of the Constitution of the United States, and well disposed to the good order and happiness of the United States." 8 U.S.C. § 1427(a)(3) (2000). In addition, Congress in 1994 amended section 312 of the INA, which requires applicants for naturalization to demonstrate understanding of the English language and the history and government of the United States, to exempt "any person who is unable because of physical or developmental disability or mental impairment to comply therewith." 8 U.S.C. § 1423(b)(1) (2000); see Pub. L. No. 103-416, §108(a)(4), 108 Stat. 4305, 4309-10 (1994).

The only significant remaining substantive prerequisites for naturalization under the INA are (1) at least five years of continuous residence in the United States after being lawfully admitted for permanent residence, and (2) "good moral character" during that period. INA § 316, 8 U.S.C. § 1427. There is no question that a mentally disabled individual can satisfy the residency requirement and establish proof of residency through documentary evidence and the testimony of others. Whether a mentally disabled individual can establish "good moral character" might be facially less obvious, especially in the case of mental disabilities so severe that they render the individual not morally responsible for his actions. We note, however, that the INA essentially defines the term "good moral character" as the absence of bad moral character, as it specifies various circumstances that preclude a finding that a person is of "good moral character." See INA §101(f), 8 U.S.C. § 1101(f) (2000) ("For the purposes of this chapter − [n]o person shall be regarded as, or found to be, a person of good moral character who, during the period for which good moral character is required to be established," has been "a habitual drunkard," has been convicted of certain crimes, has derived income principally from gambling activities or been convicted of two or more gambling offenses, has given false testimony to obtain immigration benefits, has been confined after conviction to a penal institution for 180 days or more, or has at any time been convicted of an aggravated felony.). The INS regulation states that the determination of good moral character will be based on the elements listed in the statute and "the standards of the average citizen in the community of residence." 8 C.F.R. § 316.10(a)(2) (2000). The regulation includes additional prohibitive factors beyond those contained in the statute, specifying, for example, that in the absence of extenuating circumstances an applicant will be found to lack good moral character who has "[w]illfully failed or refused to support dependents" or "[h]ad an extramarital affair which tended to destroy an existing marriage." id. § 316.10(b)(3)(i), (ii), but does not impose any positive requirements for establishing good moral character. We therefore see no barrier to a mentally disabled applicant establishing the requirement of good moral character, accord Galvez-Letona v. Kirkpatrick, 54 F. Supp. 2d 1218, 1222, 1224 (D. Utah 1999) (finding it undisputed that applicant with mental capacity of 18-month-old child met all requirements for naturalization other than ability to take oath of allegiance, including good moral character), aff'd on other grounds, 246 F.3d 680 (10th Cir. 2001) (table), and we conclude that permitting an applicant to do so through the testimony of others would not fundamentally alter the naturalization process.

-4-

We thus find nothing in the naturalization process prescribed by the INA that requires a mentally disabled applicant personally to file an application or testify at an interview. While the Supreme Court has noted that "it has been universally accepted that the burden is on the alien applicant to show his eligibility for citizenship in every respect," *INS v. Pangilinan*, 486 U.S. 875, 886 (1988) (quoting *Berenyi v. District Director, INS*, 385 U.S. 630, 637 (1967)); *see also* INA § 316(e), 8 U.S.C. § 1427(e) (directing Attorney General to determine "whether the applicant has sustained the burden of establishing good moral character and the other qualifications for citizenship"), the means of carrying that burden may vary in particular cases. Indeed, the statute and regulations already make certain accommodations for persons with disabilities. *See* INA § 334(a), 8 U.S.C. § 1445(a) (2000) ("An applicant for naturalization shall make and file with the Attorney General a sworn application in writing, signed by the applicant in the applicant's own handwriting *if physically able to write*.") (emphasis added); 8 C.F.R. § 103.2(a)(2) (2001) ("legal guardian" may sign application "for a mentally incompetent person"). *Cf.* 8 C.F.R. § 341.2(a)(2) (2001) (incompetent applicant for certificate of citizenship "must have a parent or guardian apply, appear, and testify for the applicant"). The statute expressly grants the Attorney General discretion to "make such rules and regulations as may be necessary to carry into effect the provisions of this part [dealing with naturalization]" and "to prescribe the scope and nature of the examination of applicants for naturalization as to their admissibility to citizenship." INA § 332(a), 8 U.S.C. § 1443(a) (2000).

We therefore conclude that mentally disabled individuals who cannot testify in their own behalf or fill out an application without the assistance of a legal guardian or other proxy may still be "otherwise qualified" for naturalization, and that section 504 of the Rehabilitation Act thus requires such an accommodation.[2]

M. Edward Whelan III

M. Edward Whelan III
Principal Deputy Assistant Attorney General

---

[2] Our conclusion is consistent with the legislative history of the 2000 amendment to section 337 of the INA. Proponents of that legislation expressed the view that the oath of allegiance was the sole remaining barrier to naturalization for individuals with severe mental disabilities. *See, e.g.*, 146 Cong. Rec. S6121 (daily ed. June 29, 2000) (statement of Sen. Hatch) ("such persons are able to fulfill all other requirements of naturalization, *or it is clear that the Attorney General can waive them*") (emphasis added); *id.* at S6122 (statement of Sen. Dodd) (1994 amendment "le[ft] the oath as the only barrier to citizenship for such individuals"); 146 Cong. Rec. H9546 (daily ed. Oct. 10, 2000) (statement of Rep. Smith) (bill will allow "disabled applicants who cannot understand the oath . . . to overcome this last obstruction to becoming a United States citizen").

-5-

APPENDIX 9-8

N-336: Request for a Hearing on a Decision in Naturalization Proceedings (Under Section 336 of the INA)

OMB No. 1615-0050: Expires 01/31/2016

Department of Homeland Security
U.S. Citizenship and Immigration Services

Instructions for Form N-336, Request for a Hearing on a Decision in Naturalization Proceedings (Under Section 336 of the INA)

The Purpose of Form N-336

This form is used to request a hearing before an immigration officer on the denial of your Form N-400, Application for Naturalization.

A Guide to Naturalization

To help you understand the naturalization process, U.S. Citizenship and Immigration Services (USCIS) developed A Guide to Naturalization (M-476). This publication provides information on eligibility requirements and naturalization procedures for immigrants considering U.S. citizenship. If you do not already have a copy of M-476, you can obtain a copy from the USCIS Web site at www.uscis.gov.

When You Must File

You **must** file your request for a hearing (Form N-336) within 30 calendar days of receiving the decision denying your Form N-400.

USCIS will reject (not accept) a request that is not timely filed. USCIS will not refund the filing fee if the Form N-336 is rejected because it was not timely filed. If, however, your request for a hearing is not timely filed, but it meets the requirements for a motion to reopen or motion to reconsider, USCIS will issue a decision in your case.

Document Submission

1. **Denial Notice.** You **must** submit a copy of the decision denying your Form N-400 at the time of filing your Form N-336.

2. **Supporting Documents.** You **may** submit any additional documents or briefs to support your Form N-336 at the time of filing your Form N-336 or at the time of your Form N-336 hearing.

General Instructions

1. **Type or print clearly using black ink.** Keep all information within the area provided.

If extra space is needed to answer any question, attach an additional sheet(s) of paper. You must provide the following information on the top of each sheet of paper:

  A. Your Alien Registration Number (A-Number);

  B. The date;

  C. Question number; **and**

  D. Your signature.

2. **Answer all questions fully and accurately.** Write "N/A" if an item is not applicable. Write "None" if the answer is none.

3. **Avoid highlighting, crossing out, or writing outside the area provided for a response.**

  If you must make substantial corrections to your Form N-336, USCIS recommends that you begin with a new Form N-336 rather than using correction tape or fluid to white out information. USCIS scanners may see through the white correction tape or fluid. This may lead to incorrect information being captured in USCIS systems which may cause processing delays or a rejection of your Form N-336.

  Ensure that you are using the correct edition of the Form N-336. The correct edition is available on the USCIS Web site at www.uscis.gov.

4. **Provide your A-Number on the top right corner of each page.** Your A-Number is located on your Permanent Resident Card (formerly known as the Alien Registration or "Green" Card). The A-Number on your card consists of seven to nine numbers, depending on when your record was created. If the A-Number on your card has fewer than nine numbers, place enough zeros before the first number to make a *total of nine numbers* on Form N-336. For example, write number A1234567 as A001234567, or write number A12345678 as A012345678.

Translations. You must provide a full English translation for any document written in a foreign language you submit to USCIS. The translator must certify that the translation is complete and accurate and that he or she is competent to translate from the foreign language into English.

Copies. You may submit copies of documents unless USCIS requests original documents. Original documents submitted when not required may remain a part of the record.

Specific Form Instructions

This form is divided into six parts.

Part 1. Information About You, the Naturalization Applicant

1. **Current Legal Name.** Your current legal name is the name on your birth certificate unless it has been changed after birth by a legal action such as a marriage or court order. **Do not provide a nickname.**

2. **Date of Birth.** Always use eight numbers to show your date of birth. Write the date in this order: Month, Day, Year. For example, write May 1, 1958, as 05/01/1958.

3. **Home address.** Provide the address where you now reside. If you received benefits under the Violence Against Women Act (VAWA) you may provide your safe address.

   Do **not** put a Post Office (P.O.) Box number here unless that is your **ONLY** address.

If you reside outside the United States

If you do not have a State or Province, enter the name of your city again in that box. If you do not have a ZIP or Postal Code, enter 00000 in the ZIP or Postal Code box.

4. **Mailing Address.** Provide your mailing address even if it is the same as your home address. Provide "*in care of*" name information, if applicable. You must write something in every box, except an apartment number or "C/O" if you do not have one, within "Mailing Address."

NOTE: USCIS may not be able to contact you if you do not provide a complete and valid address. Your Form N-336 may be delayed or you may not be able to seek a hearing on your Form N-400 denial. In addition, USCIS may not be able to return the fee for Form N-336 to you if you do not write a complete and valid address. If USCIS cannot return the fee, USCIS will cash your check.

5. **Telephone numbers.** Provide your current telephone numbers. If the answer is none, write "None." If you are hearing impaired and use a TTY telephone connection, indicate this by writing "TTY" after the telephone number.

6. **E-Mail address.** Provide your current e-mail address. If you do not have an e-mail address, write "None."

Part 2. Information About Form N-400 (Application for Naturalization) for Which You Are Requesting a Hearing

1. **Form N-400 Receipt Number.** Provide the Form N-400 receipt number for which you are requesting a hearing. The receipt number is located on the receipt notice you received after you filed your Form N-400 with USCIS. It appears in the upper left corner of your notice.

2. **Date of Form N-400 Denial Notice (*mm/dd/yyyy*).** Provide the date that USCIS denied your Form N-400.

3. **USCIS Office That Issued Form N-400 Denial Notice.** Provide the location of the USCIS local office that issued the denial.

Part 3. Reason You Are Requesting a Hearing

Provide the reason(s) you are requesting a hearing on your denied Form N-400. You may attach additional documents or briefs to support your Form N-336.

Part 4. Accommodations for Individuals With Disabilities and/or Impairments

USCIS is committed to providing reasonable accommodations for qualified individuals with disabilities and impairments that will help them fully participate in USCIS programs and benefits.

Reasonable accommodations vary with each disability or impairment. They may involve modifications to practices or procedures. There are various types of reasonable accommodations that may be offered. Examples include:

1. If you are unable to use your hands, you may be permitted to take the test orally rather than in writing;

2. If you are hearing impaired, you may be provided with a sign-language interpreter at an interview or other application related appointment; or

3. For those unable to travel to a designated USCIS location for an interview, you may be visited at your home or a hospital.

If you believe that you need USCIS to accommodate your disability and/or impairment, check the "Yes" box in Part 4 and then check any applicable box that describes the nature of your disability(ies) and/or impairment(s). Also, write the type(s) of accommodation(s) you are requesting on the line(s) provided. If you are requesting a sign-language interpreter, be sure to indicate for which language. If you require more space to provide additional information, please provide the information in a separate sheet(s) of paper.

NOTE: All domestic USCIS facilities meet the Accessibility Guidelines of the Americans with Disabilities Act, so you do not need to contact USCIS to request an accommodation for physical access to a domestic USCIS office. However, in Part 4 of Form N-336, you can indicate whether you use a wheelchair. This will allow USCIS to better prepare for your visit and have a wheelchair accessible interview room available for you once you enter the facility.

USCIS considers requests for reasonable accommodations on a case-by-case basis and will use its best efforts to reasonably accommodate all applicants with disabilities or impairments. Qualified individuals will not be excluded from the participation in, be denied the benefits of, USCIS's programs solely on the basis of their disability(ies) or impairment(s). Requesting and/or receiving an accommodation will not affect your eligibility for a USCIS benefit.

Part 5. Your Signature

Sign the Form N-336 as you normally sign your name. You may place an "X" mark instead of a signature if you are unable to write in any language.

NOTE: A designated representative may sign here if the applicant is unable to sign due to a physical or developmental disability or mental impairment. A designated representative who signs on behalf of an applicant attests under penalty of perjury that the information being provided in the application is true and correct. See M-476 for more information.

A designated representative that is signing on behalf of an applicant with a physical or development disability or mental impairment should write the name of the applicant and then his or her own name followed by the words "Designated Representative." If a designated representative has prepared the application, the designated representative must also sign the application in the Preparer's signature box (Part 6).

NOTE: USCIS will reject your Form N-336 if it is not signed.

Part 6. Signature of Person Who Prepared This Form N-336 for You *(if applicable)*

If you prepared Form N-336 by yourself, leave this section blank. If someone filled out this Form N-336 for you, he or she must complete this section.

Processing Information

Any Form N-336 that is not signed or accompanied by the correct fee, except those accompanied by a fee waiver request (Form I-912, Request for Fee Waiver), will be rejected. A Form N-336 that is not completed according to these instructions, is missing pages or otherwise not executed in its entirety may be rejected or delayed. If USCIS rejects your Form N-336 for any of the reasons above, the form and any fees will be returned to you if you provide a complete mailing address, and you will be notified why the form is considered deficient. You may correct the deficiency and refile a Form N-336. An application or petition is not considered properly filed until accepted by USCIS.

Requests for More Information or Hearing

You will be scheduled for an interview with USCIS within 180 days from the date upon which you properly filed your Form N-336 with USCIS. USCIS may request more information or evidence. USCIS may also request that you submit the originals of any copies you previously provided to USCIS with your Form N-336.

Decision

The decision on Form N-336 involves a determination of whether you have established eligibility for naturalization. If you do not establish a basis for eligibility, USCIS will uphold the decision to deny your Form N-400. You will be notified of the decision in writing.

What Is the Filing Fee

The fee for filing Form N-336 is **$650**.

NOTE: Members or veterans of any branch of the U.S. Armed Forces do not need to pay a fee to file Form N-336 if they have filed Form N-400 under sections 328 or 329 of the Immigration and Nationality Act (the INA) and their Form N-400 has been denied.

Use the following guidelines when you prepare your check or money order for your Form N-336 fee:

1. The check or money order must be drawn on a bank or other financial institution located in the United States and must be payable in U.S. currency; **and**

2. Make the check or money order payable to **U.S. Department of Homeland Security**.

   NOTE: Spell out U.S. Department of Homeland Security; do not use the initials "USDHS" or "DHS."

3. If you live outside the United States, contact the nearest U.S. Embassy or consulate for instructions on the method of payment.

Notice to Those Making Payment by Check

USCIS will make a copy and convert your original check into an electronic funds transfer (EFT). This means USCIS will use the account information on your check to electronically debit your account for the check amount. This debit usually takes 24 hours and should show up on your regular account statement.

USCIS will not return your original check. USCIS will destroy it and keep a copy with your file. If the EFT cannot be processed due to technical reasons, you authorize USCIS to process the copy of the check. If the EFT cannot be completed because of insufficient funds, USCIS may try the EFT up to two times.

If you receive an insufficient funds notice, USCIS will send you instructions on how to submit your penalty fee. **Do not** send a check for the penalty fee to the address where you filed your Form N-336. It will be returned to you.

How To Check If the Fees Are Correct

The fee on Form N-336 is current as of the edition date appearing in the lower right corner of this page. However, because USCIS fees change periodically, you can verify if the fees are correct by following one of the steps below:

1. Visit the USCIS Web site at **www.uscis.gov**, select **"FORMS,"** and check the appropriate fee; **or**

2. Telephone the USCIS National Customer Service Center at **1-800-375-5283** and ask for the fee information. For TDD (hearing impaired) call: **1-800-767-1833**.

Fee Waiver Request

Individuals may request a fee waiver based on an inability to pay. Form I-912 provides a standard means for submitting fee waiver requests. The instructions provide applicants with guidance on properly completing Form I-912 and submitting supporting documentation. The instructions also provide information on how USCIS makes a decision on a fee waiver request. To download a copy of Form I-912, including the instructions, click on the **"FORMS"** link on the USCIS Web site at www.uscis.gov.

Where To File

Mail your completed Form N-336 and accompanying documentation to the **USCIS Phoenix Lockbox** facility at the following address:

> **USCIS**
> **P.O. Box 20100**
> **Phoenix, AZ 85036**

For Express Mail or courier deliveries, use the following address:

> **USCIS**
> **Attn: Form N-336**
> **1820 E. Skyharbor Circle S**
> **Suite 100**
> **Phoenix, AZ 85034**

Form N-336 Requests From Current or Former Members of the Military, Spouses of Current Members of the Military, and Close Relatives of Deceased Members of the Military

You must send the Form N-336 for the naturalization application filed under the military provisions, sections 328 or 329 of the INA, to the **USCIS Nebraska Service Center** (NSC) at the address below regardless of where you live and whether you are filing from within the United States or abroad. Also, if you are the spouse of a current member of the military, or are the close relative of a member of the military (see INA section 319(d)), send your request for a hearing to the NSC at the address below regardless of where you live and whether you are filing from within the United States or abroad.

> **USCIS Nebraska Service Center**
> **P.O. Box 87426**
> **Lincoln, NE 68501-7426**

For Express Mail or courier deliveries, use the following address:

> **USCIS Nebraska Service Center**
> **850 S Street**
> **Lincoln, NE 68508**

E-Notification

If you are filing your Form N-336 at one of the USCIS Lockbox facilities, you may elect to receive an e-mail and/or text message notifying you that your Form N-336 has been accepted. You must complete Form G-1145, E-Notification of Application/Petition Acceptance, and attach it to the first page of your Form N-336. To download a copy of Form G-1145, including the instructions, click on the **"FORMS"** link on the USCIS Web site at www.uscis.gov.

Form Revision Date and Filing Addresses

The filing addresses provided on this form reflect the most current information as of the date this form was last printed. If you are filing Form N-336 more than 30 days after the latest edition date shown in the lower right corner, visit the USCIS Web site at www.uscis.gov before you file, and check the **"FORMS"** page to confirm the correct filing address and version currently in use. Check the edition date located at the lower right corner of the form. If the edition date on your **Form N-336 matches the edition date listed for Form N-336 on the online "FORMS" page, your version is current.** If the edition date on the online version is more recent, download a copy and use it. If you do not have Internet access, call the USCIS National Customer Service Center at **1-800-375-5283** to verify the current filing address and edition date. For TDD (hearing impaired) call: **1-800-767-1833**. **USCIS will reject forms with the wrong revision date and return the fee with instructions to resubmit the entire filing using the current form.**

Address Changes

If you have changed your address, you must inform USCIS of your new address. For information on filing a change of address go to the USCIS Web site at www.uscis.gov/addresschange or contact the USCIS National Customer Service Center at **1-800-375-5283**. For TDD (hearing impaired) call: **1-800-767-1833**.

NOTE: Do not submit a change of address request to the USCIS Lockbox facilities because the USCIS Lockbox facilities do not process change of address requests.

USCIS Forms and Information

To ensure you are using the latest version of this form, visit the USCIS Web site at **www.uscis.gov** where you can obtain the latest USCIS forms and immigration-related information. If you do not have internet access, you may order USCIS forms by calling our toll-free number at **1-800-870-3676**. You may also obtain forms and information by telephoning our USCIS National Customer Service Center at **1-800-375-5283**. For TDD (hearing impaired) call: **1-800-767-1833**.

You can schedule an appointment to meet with a USCIS representative at your local USCIS office through the USCIS Internet-based system, **InfoPass**. To access the system, visit the USCIS Web site. Use the **InfoPass** appointment scheduler and follow the screen prompts to set up your appointment. **InfoPass** generates an electronic appointment notice that appears on the screen.

Attorney or Accredited Representative

You may be represented, at no expense to the U.S. Government, by an attorney or other duly accredited representative. Your representative must submit Form G-28, Notice of Entry of Appearance as Attorney or Accredited Representative, with your Form N-336. Your representative may also submit the Form G-28 at the time of your interview. Form G-28 can be obtained by visiting the USCIS Web site at **www.uscis.gov**, calling the USCIS forms line number at **1-800-870-3676**, or by contacting the USCIS National Customer Service Center at **1-800-375-5283**. For TDD (hearing impaired) call: **1-800-767-1833**.

Penalties

If you knowingly and willfully falsify or conceal a material fact or submit a false document with Form N-336, USCIS will deny your Form N-336 and may deny any other immigration benefit. In addition, you may be subject to criminal prosecution and penalties provided by law.

USCIS Privacy Act Statement

AUTHORITIES: The information requested on this form, and the associated evidence, is collected under the Immigration and Nationality Act, section 101, et seq.

PURPOSE: The primary purpose for providing the requested information on this form is to determine if you have established eligibility for the immigration benefit for which you are filing. The information you provide will be used to grant or deny the benefit sought.

DISCLOSURE: The information you provide is voluntary. However, failure to provide the requested information, and any requested evidence, may delay a final decision or result in denial of your form.

ROUTINE USES: The information you provide on this form may be shared with other Federal, State, local, and foreign government agencies and authorized organizations following approved routine uses described in the associated published system of records notices [DHS-USCIS-007 - Benefits Information System and DHS-USCIS-001 - Alien File, Index, and National File Tracking System of Records), which can be found at **www.dhs.gov/privacy**]. The information may also be made available, as appropriate, for law enforcement purposes or in the interest of national security.

Paperwork Reduction Act

An agency may not conduct or sponsor information collection, and a person is not required to respond to a collection of information, unless Form N-336 displays a current valid OMB control number. The public reporting burden for this collection of information is estimated at 2 hours and 45 minutes per response. This includes the time to review the instructions, as well as complete and submit your Form N-336. Send comments regarding this burden estimate or any other aspect of this collection of information, including suggestions for reducing this burden, to: U.S. Citizenship and Immigration Services, Regulatory Coordination Division, Office of Policy and Strategy, 20 Massachusetts Avenue, N.W., Washington, DC 20529-2140; OMB No. 1615-0050. **Do not mail your completed Form N-336 to this address**.

OMB No. 1615-0050: Expires 01/31/2016

Department of Homeland Security
U.S. Citizenship and Immigration Services

**Form N-336, Request for a Hearing on a
Decision in Naturalization Proceedings
(Under Section 336 of the INA)**

Print or type all your answers fully and accurately in black ink. Write "N/A" if an item is not applicable. Write "None" if the answer is none. Failure to answer all of the questions may delay your Form N-336.

Part 1. Information About You, the Naturalization Applicant

Your A-Number:

A ____ - ____ - ____

1. **Current Legal Name** *(do not provide a nickname)*

   Family Name *(last name)*

   Given Name *(first name)*

   Middle Name *(if applicable)*

For USCIS Use Only

Bar Code	Date Stamp

Remarks

☐ **Re-Affirm
N-400 Denial**

☐ **Re-Determine
N-400 Denial**

2. **Date of Birth** *(mm/dd/yyyy)*

3. **Home Address**

   Street Number and Name *(do not provide a P.O. Box in this space unless it is your ONLY address.)*

   Apartment Number   City

   County   State

   ZIP Code   Province *(foreign address only)*

   Country *(foreign address only)*   Postal Code *(foreign address only)*

4. **Mailing Address**

   C/O *(in care of name)*

   Street Number and Name   Apartment Number

   City   State   ZIP Code

   Province *(foreign address only)*   Country *(foreign address only)*   Postal Code *(foreign address only)*

5. **Daytime Phone Number**   **Work Phone Number** *(if any)*   **Evening Phone Number**
   ( )   ( )   ( )

   Mobile Phone Number *(if any)*   6. **E-Mail Address** *(if any)*
   ( )

Form N-336 (Rev. 01/07/13) N

Part 2. Information About Form N-400 (Application for Naturalization) Denial On Which You Are Requesting a Hearing

A _____ - _____ - _____

1. **Form N-400 Receipt Number**

2. **Date of Form N-400 Denial Notice** *(mm/dd/yyyy)*

3. **USCIS Office That Issued Form N-400 Denial Notice**

Part 3. Reason You Are Requesting a Hearing

Provide the reason(s) you are requesting a hearing on your denied Form N-400. If extra space is needed to provide an explanation, attach an additional sheet(s) of paper. You must write your A-Number, the date, the question number, and sign the top of each additional sheet(s).

NOTE: Refer to Form N-336 Instructions, Page 1, Document Submission, for documents to submit with your Form N-336.

Part 4. Accommodations for Individuals With Disabilities and/or Impairments	A _____ - ____ - _____

Are you requesting an accommodation for the Form N-336 hearing because of a disability and/or impairment? (*see Part 4, Specific Form Instructions, in the Form N-336 instructions for some examples of accommodations*)   ☐ Yes   ☐ No

If you checked "Yes," check the box(es) below that apply:

☐ I am deaf or hearing impaired and need a sign language interpreter who uses the following language (e.g., American Sign Language (ASL)):

_____

☐ I use a wheelchair.

☐ I am blind or sight-impaired.

☐ I will need another type of accommodation. Explain:

_____

Part 5. Your Signature *(USCIS will reject your Form N-336 if it is not signed.)*

I certify, under penalty of perjury under the laws of the United States, that this request, and the evidence submitted with it, is all true and correct. I authorize the release of any information that U.S. Citizenship and Immigration Services needs to determine eligibility for naturalization.

Your Signature   **Date** *(mm/dd/yyyy)*

Part 6. Signature of Person Who Prepared This Form N-336 For You *(if applicable)*

I declare that I prepared Form N-336 at the request of the above person. The answers provided are based on information of which I have personal knowledge or were provided to me by the above-named person in response to the questions contained on this Form N-336.

Preparer's Printed Name   **Preparer's Signature**   **Date** *(mm/dd/yyyy)*

Preparer's Firm or Organization Name *(if applicable)*   Preparer's Daytime Phone Number
                                                                     ( )

Preparer's Address
Street Number and Name

City   State   ZIP Code

Province *(foreign address only)*   Country *(foreign address only)*   Postal Code *(foreign address only)*

Preparer's E-Mail Address *(if any)*   Preparer's Fax Number
                                                                     ( )

APPENDIX 9-9

Form G-28, Notice of Entry of Appearance as Attorney or Representative

Instructions for Notice of Entry of Appearance as Attorney or Accredited Representative

Department of Homeland Security

DHS
Form G-28
OMB No. 1615-0105
Expires 02/29/2016

What Is the Purpose of This Form?

The Department of Homeland Security (DHS) has designated Form G-28, Notice of Entry of Appearance as Attorney or Accredited Representative, as the form on which attorneys and accredited representatives provide information to establish their eligibility to appear and act on behalf of an applicant, petitioner, or respondent. An attorney or accredited representative appearing before DHS must file Form G-28 in each case. Form G-28 must be properly completed and signed by the applicant, petitioner, or respondent for the appearance of their attorney or accredited representative to be recognized by U.S. Citizenship and Immigration Services (USCIS), U.S. Customs and Border Protection (CBP), and/or U.S. Immigration and Customs Enforcement (ICE). Under 8 CFR 103.2(a)(3), a beneficiary of a petition is not a recognized party in a proceeding before USCIS. Form G-28 will be recognized by USCIS, CBP, and/or ICE until the conclusion of the matter for which it is entered. As always, an applicant, petitioner, or respondent must file a new Form G-28 with the Administrative Appeals Office when filing an appeal to that office on Form I-290B, Notice of Appeal or Motion.

Who May Use This Form?

Appearances for Immigration Matters

This form is used **only** by attorneys and accredited representatives as defined in 8 CFR 1.2 and 292.1(a)(4).

An attorney or accredited representative who appears in person at a DHS office for a limited purpose at the request of the attorney or accredited representative who has previously filed a Form G-28 in the **same** case **must** complete **Part 1. and Part 2.**, and submit Form G-28 in person at a DHS office. **In such a case, Form G-28 may not be filed through the mail or e-filed.**

A law student or law graduate who is working under the direct supervision of an attorney or accredited representative, under 8 CFR 292.1(a)(2) **must** complete **Part 1., Item Numbers 2.** and **3.** on the **same** Form G-28 filed by the supervising attorney or accredited representative. The law student or law graduate must sign the Form G-28 in **Part 4., Item Number 2.** A law student or law graduate may be required to verify that he or she is eligible as required in 8 CFR 292.1(a)(2). The appearance of a law student or law graduate requires the permission of the DHS official before whom he or she wishes to appear. The DHS official may require that the law student or law graduate be accompanied by the supervising attorney or accredited representative.

Substitution may be permitted upon the written withdrawal of the attorney or accredited representative of record or upon the filing of a new form by a new attorney or accredited representative. An attorney or accredited representative who seeks to be recognized by DHS as the new representative for an applicant, petitioner, or respondent must file a properly completed Form G-28 with the DHS office with jurisdiction over the pending matter.

Attorneys admitted to the practice of law in countries other than the United States must use Form G-28I, Notice of Entry of Appearance as Attorney In Matters Outside the Geographical Confines of the United States. Such attorneys may only represent individuals in matters filed and adjudicated in DHS offices outside the geographical confines of the United States.

Individuals seeking to appear as reputable individuals (as defined in 8 CFR 292.1(a)(3)) may not use Form G-28. They must obtain permission from DHS to appear with an applicant, petitioner, or respondent. Such reputable individuals will be required to provide the information listed in the regulations to the DHS official before whom they wish to appear.

When a person acts in a representative capacity, his or her personal appearance or signature will constitute a representation under the provisions of 8 CFR 103.2(a)(3) and 292.1(a)(1) or 292.1(a)(4) that he or she is authorized and qualified to represent the individual. DHS may require further proof of authority to act in a representative capacity.

General Instructions

If you are completing this form on a computer, the data you enter will be captured using 2D barcode technology. This capture will ensure that the data you provide is accurately entered into USCIS systems. As you complete each field, the 2D barcode field at the bottom of each page will shift as data is captured. Upon receipt of your form, USCIS will use the 2D barcode to extract the data from the form. Please **do not damage the 2D barcode** (e.g., puncture, staple, spill on, write on, etc.) as this could affect the ability of USCIS to timely process your form.

Each Form G-28 must be properly signed. A photocopy of a signed Form G-28 or a typewritten name in place of a signature is not acceptable.

Part 1. Information About Attorney or Accredited Representative

Item Numbers 1.a. - 7. - Fill in all the information and sign and date the form in black ink. Signature stamps are not permitted. Law students and law graduates must provide the name of the legal aid program, law school clinic, or non-profit organization in **Item Number 2.**, their name in **Item Number 3.**, and sign the form at **Part 4., Item Number 2.**

Attorneys must provide the State Bar Number(s) for all jurisdictions in which they are admitted to practice. Enter the State Bar Number in the space for the jurisdiction listed in **Part 2., Item Number 1.a.** If you need additional space to complete your answer, proceed to **Part 5., Additional Information**.

Part 2. Eligibility Information For Attorney or Accredited Representative

Item Numbers 1. - 1.b.1. - Attorneys admitted to practice in the United States, as defined in 8 CFR 1.2:

Check the box and fill in the required information regarding the State(s), possession(s), territory(ies), commonwealth(s) or District of Columbia bar(s) of admission. If you are subject to any order of any court suspending, enjoining, restraining, disbarring, or otherwise restricting you in the practice of law, you must disclose this information in the space provided for **Item Number 1.b.1.** If you need additional space to complete your answer proceed to **Part 5., Additional Information**. Attorneys are required to notify DHS of convictions or discipline under 8 CFR 292.3.

NOTE: Attorneys that are admitted to practice in more than one jurisdiction must enter the jurisdiction for their State Bar Number listed in **Part 1., Item Number 4**. If you need additional space to complete your answer, proceed to **Part 5., Additional Information**.

Item Numbers 2. - 2.b. - Accredited representatives of recognized organizations, as defined in 8 CFR 292.1(a)(4):

Check the box and fill in the name of the organization recognized by the Board of Immigration Appeals (BIA) under 8 CFR 292.2 and provide the expiration date of your accreditation.

A Form G-28 submitted without the required information in **Item Numbers 1. - 1.b.1.** or **2. - 2.b.** will be rejected.

Item Numbers 3. - 3.a. - Check the box and fill in the name of the attorney or accredited representative associated with the attorney or accredited representative who previously filed Form G-28 in this matter. **This type of Form G-28 may only be submitted in person at a DHS office and may not be filed through the mail or e-filed.** You must also check the box next to **Item Numbers 1.** or **2.** and provide the required information.

Item Number 4. - Law students and law graduates not yet admitted to the bar:

Check the box and complete **Part 1., Item Number 3.** and **Part 4., Item Number 2.** of the **same** Form G-28 filed by the supervising attorney or accredited representative. The appearances of law students and law graduates are subject to the requirements of 8 CFR 292.1(a)(2).

Part 3. Notice of Appearance as Attorney or Accredited Representative

Item Numbers 1. - 3.a. - Check only one box to indicate the DHS agency where the matter is filed. If USCIS, list the form number(s) filed with Form G-28. If CBP or ICE, list the specific matter in which the appearance is entered.

Item Number 4. - Check only one box to indicate applicant, petitioner, or respondent.

Item Numbers 5.a. - 5.d. - Provide the name of the applicant, petitioner, or respondent, and/or the name of the company or organization.

Item Numbers 6.a. - 6.e. - The mailing address of the applicant, petitioner, or respondent, and not the address of the attorney or accredited representative, is required in this part of the form **except when a safe mailing address is permitted on an application or petition filed with this Form G-28.**

Item Number 7. - Provide the A-Number or USCIS Receipt/Case Number, if applicable, for the applicant, petitioner, or respondent.

Item Numbers 8.a. - 8.b. - The applicant, petitioner, or respondent must sign and date the form in black ink.

Part 4. Signature of Attorney or Accredited Representative

Item Numbers 1. - 3. - The attorney or accredited representative, or law student or law graduate must sign and date the form in black ink.

Part 5. Additional Information

Please use this section to provide additional information.

Warning

Individuals appearing as attorneys or accredited representatives (including law students and law graduates permitted to appear under 8 CFR 292.1(a)(2)) are subject to the rules of Professional Conduct for Practitioners found in 8 CFR 292.3.

Freedom of Information/Privacy Act Requests

This form may not be used to request records under the Freedom of Information Act or the Privacy Act 5 U.S.C. 552 and 552a. The procedures for requesting such records are contained in 6 CFR Part 5 and may be found at www.uscis.gov.

USCIS Privacy Act Statement

AUTHORITIES: The information requested on this form, and the associated evidence, is collected under the Immigration and Nationality Act, section 101, et seq.

PURPOSE: The primary purpose for providing the requested information on this form is to determine if you have established eligibility for the immigration benefit for which you are filing. The information you provide will be used to grant or deny the benefit sought.

DISCLOSURE: The information you provide is voluntary. However, failure to provide the requested information, and any requested evidence, may delay a final decision or result in denial of your Form G-28.

ROUTINE USES: The information you provide on this form may be shared with other Federal, State, local, and foreign government agencies and authorized organizations following approved routine uses described in the associated published system of records notices [DHS-USCIS-007 - Benefits Information System and DHS-USCIS-001 - Alien File, Index, and National File Tracking System of Records, which can be found at **www.dhs.gov/privacy**]. The information may also be made available, as appropriate, for law enforcement purposes or in the interest of national security.

Paperwork Reduction Act

An agency may not conduct or sponsor an information collection, and a person is not required to respond to a collection of information, unless it displays a currently valid OMB control number. The public reporting burden for this collection of information is estimated at 20 minutes per response, including the time for reviewing instructions and completing and submitting the form. Send comments regarding this burden estimate or any other aspect of this collection of information, including suggestions for reducing this burden, to: U.S. Citizenship and Immigration Services, Regulatory Coordination Division, Office of Policy and Strategy, 20 Massachusetts Ave NW, Washington, DC 20529-2140; OMB No. 1615-0105. **Do not mail your completed Form G-28 to this address.**

Notice of Entry of Appearance
as Attorney or Accredited Representative
Department of Homeland Security

**DHS
Form G-28**
OMB No. 1615-0105
Expires 02/29/2016

Part 1. Information About Attorney or Accredited Representative

Name and Address of Attorney or Accredited Representative

1.a. Family Name
(Last Name)

1.b. Given Name
(First Name)

1.c. Middle Name

2. Name of Law Firm or Recognized Organization

3. Name of Law Student or Law Graduate

4. State Bar Number

5.a. Street Number

5.b. Street Name

5.c. Apt. ☐ Ste. ☐ Flr. ☐

5.d. City or Town

5.e. State ☐ **5.f.** Zip Code

5.g. Postal Code

5.h. Province

5.i. Country

6. Daytime Phone Number (☐☐☐) ☐☐☐ - ☐☐☐☐

7. E-Mail Address of Attorney or Accredited Representative

Part 2. Eligibility Information For Attorney or Accredited Representative

(Check applicable items(s) below)

1. ☐ I am an attorney eligible to practice law in, and a member in good standing of, the bar of the highest court(s) of the following State(s), possession(s), territory(ies), commonwealth(s), or the District of Columbia.

    1.a.

    1.b. I *(choose one)* ☐ **am not** ☐ **am** subject to any order of any court or administrative agency disbarring, suspending, enjoining, restraining, or otherwise restricting me in the practice of law. (If you are subject to any order(s), explain fully in the space below.)

    1.b.1.

2. ☐ I am an accredited representative of the following qualified nonprofit religious, charitable, social service, or similar organization established in the United States, so recognized by the Department of Justice, Board of Immigration Appeals pursuant to 8 CFR 292.2. Provide the name of the organization and the expiration date of accreditation.

    2.a. Name of Recognized Organization

    2.b. Date Accreditation expires
           (mm/dd/yyyy) ▶

3. ☐ I am associated with

    3.a.

the attorney or accredited representative of record who previously filed Form G-28 in this case, and my appearance as an attorney or accredited representative is at his or her request. If you check this item, also complete **number 1 (1.a. - 1.b.1.) or number 2 (2.a. - 2.b.)** in **Part 2** *(whichever is appropriate).*

4. ☐ I am a law student or law graduate working under the direct supervision of the attorney or accredited representative of record on this form in accordance with the requirements in 8 CFR 292.1(a)(2)(iv).

Part 3. Notice of Appearance as Attorney or Accredited Representative

This appearance relates to immigration matters before (select one):

1. ☐ USCIS - List the form number(s)

1.a. [_____]

2. ☐ ICE - List the specific matter in which appearance is entered

2.a. [_____]

3. ☐ CBP - List the specific matter in which appearance is entered

3.a. [_____]

I hereby enter my appearance as attorney or accredited representative at the request of:

4. Select only one: ☐ Applicant ☐ Petitioner
☐ Respondent (ICE, CBP)

Name of Applicant, Petitioner, or Respondent

5.a. Family Name
(Last Name) [_____]

5.b. Given Name
(First Name) [_____]

5.c. Middle Name [_____]

5.d. Name of Company or Organization, if applicable
[_____]

NOTE: Provide the mailing address of Petitioner, Applicant, or Respondent and not the address of the attorney or accredited representative, **except when a safe mailing address is permitted** on an application or petition filed with Form G-28.

6.a. Street Number
and Name [_____]

6.b. Apt. ☐ Ste. ☐ Flr. ☐ [_____]

6.c. City or Town [_____]

6.d. State [____] 6.e. Zip Code [_____]

7. Provide A-Number and/or Receipt Number

[_____]

Pursuant to the Privacy Act of 1974 and DHS policy, I hereby consent to the disclosure to the named Attorney or Accredited Representative of any record pertaining to me that appears in any system of records of USCIS, ICE, or CBP.

8.a. Signature of Applicant, Petitioner, or Respondent

[_____]

8.b. Date (mm/dd/yyyy) ▶ [_____]

Part 4. Signature of Attorney or Accredited Representative

I have read and understand the regulations and conditions contained in 8 CFR 103.2 and 292 governing appearances and representation before the Department of Homeland Security. I declare under penalty of perjury under the laws of the United States that the information I have provided on this form is true and correct.

1. Signature of Attorney or Accredited Representative

[_____]

2. Signature of Law Student or Law Graduate

[_____]

3. Date (mm/dd/yyyy) ▶ [_____]

Part 5. Additional Information

1.
_____
_____
_____
_____
_____
_____
_____
_____
_____
_____
_____

APPENDIX 9-10

Settlement Agreement in Kaplan Class Action for SSI Beneficiaries

UNITED STATES DISTRICT COURT
EASTERN DISTRICT OF PENNSYLVANIA

```
--------------------X
```
SHMUL KAPLAN, et al.,

             Plaintiffs,   Civil Action No. 06-5304

    - against -

MICHAEL CHERTOFF, et al.,

             Defendants.

```
--------------------X
```

STIPULATION AND AGREEMENT OF SETTLEMENT AND RELEASE

Plaintiffs in the above-captioned matter, on behalf of themselves, the Class and all Class Members (as defined below), and Defendants Michael Chertoff, Secretary of Homeland Security; Michael B. Mukasey, Attorney General; Emilio Gonzalez, Director of the United States Citizenship and Immigration Services ("USCIS"); Robert S. Mueller, III, Director of the Federal Bureau of Investigation ("FBI"); Michael J. Astrue, Commissioner of the Social Security Administration ("SSA"); and Donald Monica, District Director, USCIS Philadelphia District (together, "Defendants"), by and through their attorneys, hereby enter into this Stipulation and Agreement of Settlement and Release (the "Stipulation"), as of the date beneath Defendants' Counsel's signature, effective upon the approval of the Court pursuant to Rule 23 of the Federal Rules of Civil Procedure.

WHEREAS:

A.   Plaintiffs filed suit on behalf of themselves and all others similarly situated against Defendants in the United States District Court for the Eastern District of Pennsylvania on December 6, 2006, seeking class certification, designation of Class Counsel and declaratory and injunctive relief;

B.   By Order of March 29, 2007, the Court denied Defendants' Motion to Dismiss in part and granted it in part;

C.   To date, the Court has not granted class certification, designation of Class Counsel, declaratory or injunctive relief;

D.   Defendants deny all liability with respect to the Action, deny that they have engaged in any wrongdoing, deny the allegations in the Complaint and Amended Complaint, deny that they committed any violation of law, deny that they acted improperly in any way, and deny liability of any kind to the Named Plaintiffs, the Class, or the Class Members, but have agreed to the settlement and dismissal of the Action with prejudice in order to: (i) avoid the substantial expense, inconvenience, and distraction of protracted litigation; and (ii) finally put to rest and terminate the Action and any and all Settled Claims as defined in paragraph 10.

E.   Class Counsel have conducted discussions and arm's length negotiations with Defendants' Counsel with respect to a compromise and settlement of the Action with a view to settling the issues in dispute and achieving the best relief possible consistent with the interests of the Named Plaintiffs, the Class, and all Class Members.

F.   After considering the benefits that the Named Plaintiffs, the Class, and the Class Members will receive from settlement of the Action and the risks of litigation, Class Counsel have concluded that the terms and conditions of this Stipulation are fair, reasonable, and in the best interests of the Named Plaintiffs, the Class, and the Class Members; have agreed that the Released Parties should be released from the Settled Claims pursuant to the terms and provisions of this Stipulation; and have agreed to the dismissal with prejudice of all Settled Claims as defined in paragraph 10. The relief contained in this Stipulation is meant to provide relief to those Class Members actually or potentially adversely affected by 8 U.S.C. § 1612(a) prior to or during the life of the agreement.

NOW, THEREFORE, it is hereby STIPULATED AND AGREED, by and among the parties to this Stipulation, through their respective attorneys, subject to the approval of the Court pursuant to Rule 23(e) of the Federal Rules of Civil Procedure, in consideration of the benefits flowing to the parties hereto from the Settlement, that the Settled Claims as against the Released Parties shall be compromised, settled, forever released, barred, and dismissed with prejudice, upon and subject to the following terms and conditions:

I.   DEFINITIONS:

Wherever used in this Stipulation, the following terms have the meanings set forth below:

1.   "Action" means the above-captioned action pending in the United States District Court for the Eastern District of Pennsylvania (docket no. CV 06-5304).

2.   "Class" means, for purposes of this settlement only, a plaintiff class certified pursuant to Rule 23 of the Federal Rules of Civil Procedure, comprising all non-United States citizens who are receiving or have received Supplemental Security Income ("SSI") and are or may be subject to termination or suspension of SSI pursuant to 8 U.S.C. § 1612(a)(2)(A), prior to a final decision on their current or future Application for Naturalization, Form N-400, and oath ceremony to become a United States citizen. The Class ceases to exist, and all membership in the Class ends, upon the termination of this Stipulation pursuant to paragraph 54.

3.   "Class Member" means any person included in the Class.

4.   "Effective Date of Settlement" or "Effective Date" means the date upon which the Settlement provided for in this Stipulation shall become effective, as set forth in paragraph 50 below.

5.   "Plaintiff(s)" or "Named Plaintiff(s)" means Shmul Kaplan, Tasim Mandija, Feride Mandija, Rouzbeh Aliaghaei, Lidiya Burtseva, Nelli Olevskaya, Eshetu Meri, Sara Bachman, Moisey Bachman, Joe Beoplue, Sonyunor Beoplue, Glayon Bloue, Isaak Rozenblit, Semen Savaranskiy, Lyudmila Shirokaya, Igor Stepanov, and Yevheniya Strizhevskaya.

6.   "Plaintiffs' Counsel" or "Class Counsel" means Community Legal Services, Inc.; Ballard Spahr Andrews & Ingersoll, LLP; Hebrew Immigrant Aid Society and Council Migration Service of Philadelphia; and the Sargent Shriver National Center on Poverty Law. Should these entities change their names or merge with other entities, those new entities shall also qualify as Class Counsel.

7.   "Expedite" or "Expedited Processing" refers to the process by which USCIS provides priority action on applications for adjustment of status to lawful permanent residence (I-485) and on applications for naturalization (N-400), on processes within the control of USCIS. When implementing Expedited Processing hereunder, USCIS will (i) provide and/or request priority action on any pending or future security checks for the current application; (ii) provide priority action on any internal processing at USCIS; and (iii) provide the Class Member with priority for the earliest available appointment for applications requiring an appointment. Additionally, USCIS will administer or schedule the Oath of Allegiance for the Class Member at the next available opportunity.

8.   An Expedite does not mean that background checks or the adjudication of an application will be completed by a date certain, nor does Expedited Processing guarantee approval of an application.

4

9.   "Released Parties" means any and all of the Defendants, their predecessors and successors, their departments and agencies, and their past or present agents, employees, and contractors.

10.   "Settled Claims" means any and all actions, in law or equity, that were asserted or that could have been asserted by Class Members or anyone acting on behalf of or in place of a Class Member, based upon the facts alleged or that could have been alleged in the Amended Complaint relating to the subject of this action, including but not limited to the Due Process, Equal Protection, and APA claims. Only individual actions against USCIS under 8 U.S.C. § 1447(b) and individual actions against SSA under 42 U.S.C. § 405(g) are excepted from the claims settled by this action.

11.   "Settlement" means the settlement provided for in this Stipulation.

II.   RELEASE; SCOPE AND EFFECT OF RELEASE

12.   On the Effective Date, the Named Plaintiffs, the Class, and the Class Members, on behalf of themselves, their heirs, executors, administrators, representatives, attorneys, successors, assigns, agents, affiliates, and partners, and any persons they represent ("Releasing Parties"), shall be deemed to have, and by operation of the Final Judgment shall have, fully, finally, and forever released, relinquished, and discharged the Released Parties of and from any and all of the Settled Claims, and the Releasing Parties shall forever be barred and enjoined from bringing or prosecuting any Settled Claim against any of the Released Parties.

13.   This Stipulation is contingent on the preservation of the Order of the Court on Defendants' Motion to Dismiss for Lack of Jurisdiction (published at 481 F. Supp. 2d 370 (E.D. Pa. 2007)). Neither Plaintiffs' nor Defendants' concurrence with the preservation of the Order

constitutes, and shall not be deemed to imply, their agreement with the findings or decisions contained in that Order.

14.   Class Counsel, as fiduciaries to individual Class Members, agree to any and all sharing of information between USCIS and SSA required by paragraphs 22, 23, 25 and 26 of this Stipulation.

15.   In consideration for the releases contained herein, and subject to this Stipulation's conditions, USCIS will institute procedures for the Expedited Processing of all current and future Class Members' applications for adjustment to lawful permanent resident status and applications for naturalization during the existence of this Stipulation.

III.   PROCESSING OF CLASS MEMBERS' APPLICATIONS

A.   General Expedited Processing

16.   Each Class Member may request Expedited Processing of his or her pending application for adjustment of status, Form I-485, or naturalization, Form N-400, at any time. USCIS will grant Expedited Processing where such applications of Class Members have been pending without a decision for six months, unless otherwise specified in this Settlement. Requests made prior to the passage of six months shall be considered by USCIS once the six month mark is reached without further action by the individual requesting Expedited Processing.

17.   Expedited Processing may be requested (i) through the USCIS 1-800 telephone number, (ii) by appearing in person at the local USCIS District Office, (iii) by written request included with the filing of the application, or (iv) by mail to the office at which the application was filed. USCIS may verify that the individual is a Class Member by requesting the individual to produce a copy of SSA correspondence addressed to the individual.

18.   Plaintiffs agree that nothing in this Stipulation limits Defendants' authority under the law to promulgate regulations, issue policy directives and guidance, and to take other

action, as necessary, without notice to Plaintiffs, concerning the processing of such applications including, but not limited to, the substantive scope of background and security investigations conducted on aliens. However, regardless of how the processing of such applications may change, the obligation to provide Expedited Processing pursuant to this Stipulation shall be preserved so long as Expedited Processing pursuant to this Stipulation, including priority processing of FBI name checks, is consistent with the best interest of national security as determined by Defendants.

19.   Where USCIS is implementing Expedited Processing for an application and the FBI has not completed its name check, USCIS will promptly notify the FBI of the need for priority processing of the pending FBI name check separately from other priority processing requests. The FBI shall thereafter promptly undertake priority processing of the name check for the specified individual. However, nothing in this Stipulation obligates the FBI to accept more than 100 requests for priority processing from USCIS per week. USCIS reserves the right to prioritize Class members within the group of individuals receiving FBI priority name check processing pursuant to USCIS's operational needs. As USCIS is the FBI's customer agency, the FBI will prioritize requests for priority name check processing in accordance with USCIS's requests, as communicated to the FBI by USCIS. Every other week, USCIS and the FBI will conduct status checks on all pending requests for priority processing of name checks submitted pursuant to this Stipulation.

B.   Class Members Whose SSI Benefits Were Terminated Or Suspended Pursuant To 8 U.S.C. § 1612(a)(2)(A).

20.   Within 60 days of the Effective Date, Defendants, acting through SSA, shall compile a mailing list of all those Class Members whose SSI benefits were terminated or suspended pursuant to 8 U.S.C. § 1612(a)(2)(A) and whose benefits have not been restored, and

those whose SSI benefits may be terminated or suspended prior to the June following the Effective Date ("Terminated Members"). This mailing list of Terminated Members will promptly be made available to Class Counsel in paper and electronic format.

21.   Within 75 days of the Effective Date, in conjunction with Plaintiffs' Counsel pursuant to paragraph 36.a, Defendants USCIS and SSA will jointly prepare and USCIS will mail a distinctive letter to the Terminated Members. The letter shall include: a) a section encouraging all who have not yet filed applications for either naturalization or adjustment of status to do so as soon as they are statutorily eligible to file; b) notification of the availability of a fee waiver application process for naturalization (N-400) and adjustment of status (I-485) applications; c) information on the availability of Expedited Processing for those who have applications pending with USCIS; and d) a central telephone number for contacting Class Counsel.

22.   Any letters sent pursuant to paragraph 21 that are returned to sender within 90 days of the mailing will be collected and provided to USCIS. USCIS will promptly attempt to identify updated addresses for those individuals through its current address change system. Where an updated address is available, USCIS will promptly resend the letters to the updated address. At the end of the 90-day period, USCIS will provide Class Counsel with the mailing list of the individuals with updated addresses in paper and electronic format.

23.   Six months after the paragraph 21 letter has been sent, SSA will provide USCIS with identifying information for all Terminated Members who have not been restored to SSI benefits. Within three months thereafter, USCIS will attempt to match the SSA identifying information with information in USCIS' systems, in order to identify Terminated Members with pending applications. USCIS will, on its own initiative and without the need for a request,

8

Expedite the processing of all Forms I-485 and N-400 of Terminated Members where USCIS has positively identified Terminated Members through this matching process, even if the application has not been pending for more than six months.

C.   Class Members Whose SSI Benefits Will Terminate Or Be Suspended Pursuant to 8 U.S.C. § 1612(a)(2)(A) Within One Year.

24.   In or about May or June of 2008, Defendant SSA will provide individual notices to those SSI beneficiaries who face potential termination or suspension of SSI pursuant to 8 U.S.C. § 1612(a)(2)(A) in the twelve months starting July 1, 2008 ("Pending Members"). A mailing list of Pending Members will promptly be made available to Class Counsel in paper and electronic format. The notices, to be developed in conjunction with Plaintiffs' Counsel pursuant to paragraph 36.b, shall include: a) a section encouraging all who have not yet filed applications for either naturalization or adjustment of status to do so as soon as they are statutorily eligible to file; b) notification of the availability of a fee waiver application process for naturalization (N-400) and adjustment of status (I-485) applications; c) information on the availability of Expedited Processing for those who have applications pending with USCIS; and d) a central telephone number for contacting Class Counsel.

25.   Any letters sent pursuant to paragraph 24 that are returned to SSA within 90 days of the mailing will be collected by SSA and provided to USCIS. USCIS will promptly attempt to identify updated addresses for those individuals through its current address change system. Where an updated address is available, USCIS will promptly resend the letters to the updated address. At the end of the 90-day period, USCIS will provide Class Counsel with the mailing list of the individuals with updated addresses in paper and electronic format.

26.   Three months after the paragraph 24 letter has been sent by SSA, SSA will provide USCIS with identifying information for all Pending Members. Within three months

thereafter, USCIS will attempt to match the SSA identifying information with information in USCIS' systems, in order to identify Pending Members with pending applications. USCIS will, on its own initiative and without the need for a request, Expedite the processing of all Forms I-485 and N-400 of Pending Members where USCIS has positively identified Pending Members through this matching process, even if the application has not been pending for more than six months.

D.   Dissemination of Information to Class

27.   In addition to the notices mailed to individual Class Members pursuant to subsections B & C herein:

a.   Within 63 days of the Effective Date, USCIS will issue press releases regarding the availability of Expedited Processing for those non-U.S. citizens currently receiving SSI benefits and for those whose SSI benefits have been terminated or suspended pursuant to 8 U.S.C. § 1612(a)(2)(A);

b.   Within 90 days of the Effective Date, USCIS, through its Community Relations Program, will communicate the availability of Expedited Processing through USCIS' existing network of community-based and non-profit organizations who provide advice and assistance to immigrants, and to the private immigration bar, including AILA chapters through the AILA national office;

c.   Within 63 days of the Effective Date, SSA and USCIS will include information regarding Expedited Processing for Class Members on their respective websites;

d.   SSA will provide information regarding the availability of Expedited Processing, the importance of prompt filing and the availability of a fee waiver application process in all annual reminder Notices regarding the seven-year cut-off provision which SSA sends to current and future Class Members at least during the pendency of this Stipulation; and

10

e.   Within 120 days of the Effective Date, USCIS will prominently display posters in all USCIS public areas to address the availability of Expedited Processing for all N-400 and I-485 applications filed by immigrants subject to the limit on SSI benefits pursuant to 8 U.S.C. § 1612(a).

28.   All communications to Class Members shall be in English, subject to paragraph 31, and may be in other languages at the discretion of the government agency. A separate SSA "fact sheet" for non-citizen SSI recipients, with information about the importance of prompt filing, the availability of a fee waiver application process, the availability of Expedited Processing, and where to obtain additional information, will be available within 90 days of the Effective Date on the SSA "Gateway" website, which provides access to translations of documents in 15 different languages. In addition, on request by an individual applicant, SSA will endeavor to have interpreters and/or translators available to assist with inquiries.

E.   Miscellaneous Provisions

29.   Within 63 days of the Effective Date, USCIS will inform all relevant staff at USCIS District Offices and Service Centers about their responsibilities regarding Expedited Processing under this Stipulation. This communication will also include a statement that a Class Member may be applying for a fee waiver; that any application for a fee waiver will be adjudicated under the applicable fee waiver guidance; and that a Class Member will likely establish eligibility for a fee waiver. USCIS will provide Plaintiffs' counsel with a copy of the final signed guidance, solely for informational purposes, no less than three days before it is disseminated to USCIS staff. The review and comment provision of paragraph 36 will not be applicable to this guidance, but the dispute resolution provisions of paragraph 42 apply to any dispute. Plaintiffs' counsel may not disseminate nor disclose the guidance outside of Plaintiffs'

counsel unless USCIS later makes the guidance public. Defendants' counsel shall immediately inform Plaintiffs' counsel when and if the guidance is made public.

30.   Within 63 days of the Effective Date, SSA will notify all relevant staff, including those at SSA District and Field Offices, about the availability of Expedited Processing and USCIS fee waivers, by issuing an Emergency Message that will address the issues raised by this Stipulation. In the Emergency Message, SSA will encourage SSA staff to provide information to Class Members regarding the availability of Expedited Processing and USCIS fee waivers, USCIS' policies concerning expediting of naturalization (N-400) and adjustment of status (I-485) applications, and where to get more information from USCIS. Ultimately, SSA will issue a Program Operations Manual System (POMS) instruction to address the issues raised by this Stipulation.

31.   All mailings to class members by Defendant agencies pursuant to paragraphs 20 and 24 will include the following paragraph translated into the Arabic, Cambodian, Chinese, Farsi, French, Haitian-Creole, Laotian, Russian, Spanish, and Vietnamese languages: "This is a very important letter about continuing your Supplemental Security Income (SSI). Please read it carefully. If you cannot read English, please take this letter to someone who can read it to you right away."

32.   Where the sharing of information among Defendants USCIS and SSA is required by this Stipulation, Defendants shall comply with all requirements of the Privacy Act.

33.   When USCIS or SSA provide Class Counsel with personal identifying information of Class Members pursuant to paragraphs 20, 22, 24 and 25 of this Stipulation, Class Counsel shall use the information only to comply with the Stipulation's terms. Class Counsel may not duplicate or disseminate the personal identifying information except where

12

dissemination is necessary to comply with the requirements of the Stipulation, and shall destroy or return the personal identifying information within 30 days of the termination of this Stipulation pursuant to paragraph 54, except for one copy which may be retained in Class Counsel's archive of the Action until 30 days after the running of the Pennsylvania Statute of Limitations for an attorney malpractice claim accruing on or before the termination of the obligations of the parties under this Stipulation pursuant to paragraph 54 of this Stipulation. Class Counsel assume all obligations and responsibilities for the storage, retention, use and release of the data consistent with applicable law.

34.   Released Parties and Plaintiffs' Counsel will mutually approve (a) all Notices to the Class under Paragraph 47; and (b) the Notice of Final Settlement Agreement under Paragraph 49.

35.   A flow chart picturing the various provisions and deadlines shall be attached to this Stipulation as Exhibit A.

36.   Plaintiffs' Counsel will have the opportunity to review and provide written comments to Defendants on the written materials listed below:

a.   the letter to Terminated Members under Paragraph 21;

b.   the letter to Pending Members under Paragraph 24;

c.   the press releases from USCIS under Paragraph 27(a);

d.   announcements posted on USCIS's and SSA's websites under Paragraph 27(c);

e.   the revisions to the annual letter sent by SSA to Class Members under Paragraph 27(d);

f.   the USCIS posters under Paragraph 27(e);

g.   the revisions to the SSA "fact sheet" for non-citizen SSI recipients under

Paragraph 28; and

h.   the Emergency Message and POMS section from SSA under Paragraph

30.

Released Parties will provide draft copies of these materials to Plaintiffs' Counsel at least

30 days prior to their intended distribution in order to permit Plaintiffs' Counsel adequate time to

review and comment. Plaintiffs' Counsel will make comments within 10 days of receipt.

Released Parties will consider the comments of Plaintiffs' Counsel and will provide Class

Counsel with a final version prior to distribution.

IV.   DISPUTE RESOLUTION PROCEDURES; CONTINUING JURISDICTION

37.   The parties agree that this Court will retain continuing jurisdiction for the

duration of the Stipulation to supervise the implementation of this Stipulation and to enforce its

terms, and the terms of this Stipulation shall be incorporated into the Order of the Court

approving the Settlement.

38.   The parties agree that this Court will not be asked to exercise jurisdiction to

supervise the implementation of this Stipulation or to enforce its terms until exhaustion of the

dispute resolution process in paragraphs 42-43 has occurred.

39.   In or about January 2009, Defendants will provide Class Counsel with the

following reports:

a.   The number of SSI beneficiaries who have lost SSI benefits due to the

limitations in 8 U.S.C. § 1612(a) since the Effective Date;

b.   The number of SSI beneficiaries who, after losing benefits due to the

seven-year limitation, have been reinstated on SSI since the Effective Date;

14

c.   The number of SSI beneficiaries who would be expected to lose their SSI benefits between January 1, 2009 and December 31, 2011;

d.   I-485 cycle times for asylees, refugees, and regular adjustment;

e.   N-400 cycle times;

f.   The number of SSI Expedites initiated by USCIS per month as the result of a call to the USCIS 1-800 telephone number;

g.   The total number of SSI priority name check requests made by USCIS to the FBI per month;

h.   The statistical results of the data matches required by paragraphs 23 and 26;

i.   The FBI Name Check Unit's Fiscal Year Significant Activity Report.

40.   120 days after USCIS has completed the data match described in paragraph 23, USCIS will randomly select a 100-name sample from the results of the data match on the "Terminated Members". USCIS will provide a status report to Class Counsel for each application reflecting whether each application has been expedited and the last of the following actions that has been completed for the application:

I.   A request has been sent to the FBI for priority processing of the name check;

II.   The FBI has completed its name check;

III.   The case has been assigned to a USCIS adjudicator for review;

IV.   A request for additional evidence has been sent to the applicant;

V.   An interview has been scheduled;

VI.   An oath has been scheduled; or

VII.   There has been a decision made on the application.

The name, address, and alien registration number for each of the 100 cases will be forwarded to Class Counsel, in paper and electronic format.

41.   Class Counsel and counsel for Defendants shall attend a single meet and confer on April 13, 2009, or another day mutually agreeable to counsel, to discuss all issues that have arisen during the initial period of implementation of the Stipulation.

42.   The following dispute resolution process will be followed:

a.   Should Class Counsel learn of an apparent failure of USCIS to institute Expedited Processing for an individual application, Class Counsel will promptly notify the contact for Defendants, in writing, of the fact or facts that form the basis of the contention. Such notice of apparent failure to institute Expedited Processing must be substantiated with specific detailed information sufficient to enable the contact to investigate and respond, and must include verification that the applicant has contacted the USCIS 1-800 telephone number no earlier than 64 days after the Effective Date, and that the time periods of subparagraphs (1) or (2) have been met. The content of every response from USCIS must be included. If 45 days have passed since the call was made to the USCIS 1-800 telephone number and no response has been received by the applicant, Class Counsel may proceed with notifying Defendants of the alleged failure to expedite. Within 45 days after receipt of the notice from Class Counsel, contact for Defendants shall notify Class Counsel of USCIS' position and any action it has taken or intends to take in connection therewith.

(1)   If an applicant has lost his or her SSI benefits or will lose those benefits before June 30, 2009, the requisite call to the USCIS 1-800 telephone number can be

16

made no sooner than either a) 90 days after the date an applicant requested an expedite or b) 90 days after completion of the data match in paragraph 23.

(2)   If an applicant is a current SSI beneficiary and will not lose his or her benefits until after June 30, 2009, the requisite call to the USCIS 1-800 telephone number can be made after the latter of either a) 6 months after the relevant N-400 or I-485 was filed or b) 90 days after an expedite request was made.

b.   Starting from the Effective Date, upon learning of any fact or facts that constitute the basis for asserting that a party, without notice or good cause shown, has completely and materially failed to perform an affirmative act imposed by the Stipulation in paragraphs 20-31, the initiating party shall promptly notify the other party (the "responding party") in writing of the fact or facts that support the contention and request a written response with respect thereto. Such allegations of violations of this Stipulation must be substantiated with specific, detailed, and timely information about the violation sufficient to enable the responding party to investigate and respond. Within 30 days after receipt of the notice, the responding party shall notify the initiating party in writing of the responding party's position and any action it has taken or intends to take in connection therewith.

c.   Starting from the Effective Date, upon learning of any fact or facts that constitute the basis for asserting that a party, without notice or good cause shown, has engaged in a pattern or practice constituting substantial noncompliance with the terms of this Stipulation, or that any party has expressly repudiated any of its terms, the initiating party shall promptly notify the other party (the "responding party") in writing of the fact or facts that form the basis of the contention and request a written response with respect thereto. Such allegations of violations of this Stipulation must be substantiated with specific, detailed, and timely information about the violation sufficient to enable the responding party to investigate and respond. Within 90 days after receipt of the notice, the responding party shall notify the initiating party in writing of the responding party's position and any action it has taken or intends to take in connection therewith.

d.   During the 90 days following the completion of the appropriate process outlined in subparagraphs a, b, or c, the parties shall negotiate in good faith in an effort to resolve any remaining disputes. The parties agree that this negotiation period will be considered exhausted if the negotiations have reached an impasse.

43.   Should the parties be unable to resolve any issues raised between them, after exhausting all of the applicable procedures in paragraph 42, such issues must be raised before a Magistrate Judge of the Eastern District of Pennsylvania upon which all parties agree, who shall hear, mediate, and, to the fullest extent possible, obtain the agreement of both parties to resolve the issue(s) in dispute.

44.   The parties agree that the provision in paragraph 43 shall not be used to resolve any disputes regarding timeliness or form of the reports listed in paragraphs 39 and 40. The parties further agree that no claim may be made under the provisions in paragraphs 42 and 43 regarding the pace or extent of security check processing by either USCIS or the FBI. Cognizable claims regarding security check processing shall be limited to a failure to initiate or undertake Expedited or priority processing as described in paragraphs 7 and 19.

45.   The parties agree that failure to comply with the deadlines in paragraphs 27-36 of this Stipulation does not constitute a violation of this Stipulation in the case of unforeseeable circumstances.

46.   The parties agree that the mediation process shall be conducted confidentially and no public disclosure shall be made relating to the dispute before or during the mediation

18

process. All documents and information disclosed by either party during the mediation process shall be governed by rule 408 of the Federal Rules of Evidence and shall not be admissible in any judicial proceeding. All statements or conclusions of the mediator shall not be admissible in any subsequent judicial proceeding.

IV.   TERMS OF ORDER FOR NOTICE, HEARING AND FINAL JUDGMENT

47.   Concurrently with their filing of this Stipulation, Class Counsel and Defendants' Counsel shall jointly apply to the Court for Preliminary Court Approval of the Settlement provided for in this Stipulation and entry of a Preliminary Approval Order, substantially in the form appended hereto as Exhibit B. Such Preliminary Approval Order will seek approval of a Notice to the Class, as well as a finding that the following satisfies the publication requirements of Fed. R. Civ. P. 23: within five business days of the date of the Preliminary Court's Approval, (i) posting the Notice to the Class and this Stipulation in appropriate places on the USCIS and SSA public websites, and (ii) providing the Notice to the Class and this Stipulation to USCIS' Community Relations Program for distribution to the existing network of community-based and non-profit organizations who provide advice and assistance to immigrants, including AILA chapters through the AILA national office.

48.   If the Settlement contemplated by this Stipulation is approved by the Court, counsel for the parties shall request that the Court enter Final Judgment substantially in the form appended hereto as Exhibit C.

49.   Within 60 days following the Court's entry of the Final Judgment, Defendants will publish a Notice of Final Settlement Agreement employing the same methods set forth in paragraph 47. The language of the Notice of Final Settlement Agreement will be agreed upon by the parties and will constitute an updated Notice to the Class.

V.   EFFECTIVE DATE OF SETTLEMENT, WAIVER OR TERMINATION

50.   The Effective Date of this Stipulation shall be the date when all of the following shall have occurred: a) entry of the Preliminary Approval Order in all material respects in the form appended hereto as Exhibit B; b) approval by the Court of this Stipulation, following notice to the Class and a hearing, as prescribed by Rule 23 of the Federal Rules of Civil Procedure; and c) entry by the Court of Final Judgment, in all material respects in the form appended hereto as Exhibit C.

51.   In the event that the District Court's approval of the Stipulation or the Final Judgment referenced is voided on appeal, vacated, or terminated, the parties' good- faith adherence to the terms of this Stipulation prior to said voidance, vacation or termination shall not be considered unlawful.

52.   Defendants' Counsel or Class Counsel shall have the right to terminate the Settlement and this Stipulation by providing written notice of their election to do so ("Termination Notice") to all other parties hereto within thirty (30) days of (a) the District Court's declining to enter the Preliminary Approval Order or modifying that Preliminary Approval Order in any material respect; (b) the District Court's declining to approve the Settlement embodied in this Stipulation or any material part of it; (c) the District Court's declining to enter the Final Judgment or modifying the Final Judgment in any material respect; (d) the Court of Appeals or the United States Supreme Court's modifying, reversing, or vacating in any material respect the Final Judgment; or (e) the District Court, the Court of Appeals or by the United States Supreme Court's modifying, reversing, or vacating and entering an Alternative Judgment in any material respect.

20

53.   Except as otherwise provided herein, in the event the Settlement is terminated or modified in any material respect or fails to become effective for any reason, then the Settlement shall be without prejudice and none of its terms shall be effective or enforceable; the parties to this Stipulation shall be deemed to have reverted to their respective status in the Action as of the date and time immediately prior to the execution of this Stipulation; and except as otherwise expressly provided, the parties shall proceed in all respects as if this Stipulation and any related orders had not been entered. In the event the Settlement is terminated or modified in any material respect, the Defendants shall be deemed not to have waived, modified, or be estopped from asserting any additional defenses available to them.

VI.   TERMINATION OF OBLIGATIONS

54.   The obligations of this Stipulation shall terminate after two (2) years and eleven (11) months from the Effective Date without further action by the Court.

VII.   NO ADMISSION OF WRONGDOING

55.   This Stipulation, whether or not executed, and any proceedings taken pursuant to it:

a.   shall not be construed to waive, reduce or otherwise diminish the authority of the Defendants to enforce the laws of the United States against Class Members, consistent with the Constitution, laws of the United States, and applicable regulations;

b.   shall not be offered or received against the Defendants as evidence of, or construed as or deemed to be evidence of, any presumption, concession, or admission by any of the Defendants of the truth of any fact alleged by the Plaintiffs or the validity of any claim that had been or could have been asserted in the Action or in any litigation, or the deficiency of any defense that has been or could have been asserted in the Action, or of any liability, negligence, fault, or wrongdoing of the Defendants; or any admission by the Defendants of any violations of, or failure to comply with, the Constitution, laws or regulations; and

     c.   shall not be offered or received against the Defendants as evidence of a presumption, concession, or admission of any liability, negligence, fault, or wrongdoing, or in any way referred to for any other reason as against any of the parties to this Stipulation, in any other civil, criminal, or administrative action or proceeding, other than such proceedings as may be necessary to effectuate the provisions of this Stipulation; provided, however, that if this Stipulation is approved by the Court, Defendants may refer to it and rely upon it to effectuate the liability protection granted them hereunder.

VIII.   ATTORNEYS' FEES

56.   Within 120 days of entry of a final and nonappealable judgment in this case approving this Stipulation, Defendants will deliver to Class Counsel the sum of $275,000, in settlement of all claims for attorneys' fees and costs that could have been or will be claimed in this litigation. Defendants shall bear any costs incurred in connection with notifying the class of the terms and conditions of this Stipulation as provided in paragraphs 47 and 49.

IX.   ADDITIONAL PROVISIONS

57.   This Stipulation, and the obligations incurred herein, shall be in full and final disposition of the Action with prejudice, including any and all Settled Claims against Defendants. On the Effective Date, Plaintiffs shall be deemed to have fully, finally, and forever released, relinquished, and discharged the Defendants of and from any and all Settled Claims, subject to the provisions of paragraph 53.

58.   All of the exhibits attached hereto are hereby incorporated by reference as though fully set forth herein.

59.　　　This Stipulation may not be modified or amended, nor may any of its provisions be waived except by a writing signed by all parties hereto or their successors-in-interest.

60.　　　The waiver by one party of any breach of this Stipulation by any other party shall not be deemed a waiver of any other prior or subsequent breach of this Stipulation.

61.　　　This Stipulation and its exhibits constitute the entire agreement among the parties hereto concerning the Settlement of the Action, and no representations, warranties, or inducements have been made by any party hereto other than those contained and memorialized in such documents.

62.　　　This Stipulation may be executed in one or more counterparts. All executed counterparts and each of them shall be deemed to be one and the same instrument provided that counsel for the parties to this Stipulation shall exchange among themselves original signed counterparts.

63.　　　This Stipulation shall be binding upon, and inure to the benefit of, the successors and assigns of the parties hereto.

64.　　　This Stipulation shall not be construed more strictly against one party than another merely by virtue of the fact that it, or any part of it, may have been prepared by counsel for one of the parties, it being recognized by the parties that this Stipulation is the result of arm's length negotiations between the parties and that all parties have contributed substantially and materially to the preparation of this Stipulation.

65.　　　All counsel and any other person executing this Stipulation and any of the exhibits hereto, or any related settlement documents, warrant and represent that they have the full authority to do so and that they have the authority to take appropriate action required or permitted to be taken pursuant to the Stipulation to effectuate its terms.

66.   Class Counsel and Defendants' Counsel agree to cooperate fully with one another in seeking Court approval of the Preliminary Order in Connection with the Settlement Proceedings, the Stipulation and Agreement of Settlement, and to promptly agree upon and execute all such other documentation as may be reasonably required to obtain final approval by the Court of the Settlement.

THE PLAINTIFFS   THE DEFENDANTS

BY: _____   BY: _____

Dated: _____12/12/07_____   Dated: ___4 JANUARY 2008___

24

APPENDIX 9-11

USCIS News Releases on FBI Name Check Delays

USCIS and FBI Joint Plan to Eliminate Name Check Delays

Office of Communications

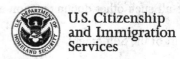

U.S. Citizenship and Immigration Services

News Release

April 2, 2008

USCIS AND FBI RELEASE JOINT PLAN TO ELIMINATE BACKLOG
OF FBI NAME CHECKS
Partnership Establishes Series of Milestones To Complete Checks

WASHINGTON – U.S. Citizenship and Immigration Services (USCIS) and the Federal Bureau of Investigation (FBI) today announced a joint plan to eliminate the backlog of name checks pending with the FBI.

USCIS and the FBI established a series of milestones prioritizing work based on the age of the pending name check. The FBI has already eliminated all name check cases pending more than four years.

"This plan of action is the product of a strong partnership between USCIS and the FBI to eliminate the backlogs and to strengthen national security," said USCIS Director Emilio Gonzalez.

By increasing staff, expanding resources, and applying new business processes, the goal is to complete 98 percent of all name checks within 30 days. USCIS and the FBI intend to resolve the remaining two percent, which represent the most difficult name checks and require additional time to complete, within 90 days or less. The goal is to achieve and sustain these processing times by June 2009.

The joint plan will focus on resolving the oldest pending FBI name checks first. USCIS has also requested that the FBI prioritize resolution of approximately 29,800 pending name checks from naturalization applicants submitted to the FBI before May 2006 where the naturalization applicant was already interviewed.

The target milestones for processing name checks are:

Completion Goal	Category
May 2008	Process all name checks pending more than three years
July 2008	Process all name checks pending more than two years
Nov. 2008	Process all name checks pending more than one year
Feb. 2009	Process all name checks pending more than 180 days
June 2009	Process 98 percent of all name checks within 30 days and process the remaining two percent within 90 days.

– USCIS –

USCIS, FBI Eliminate National Name Check Backlog

Office of Communications

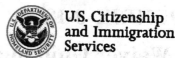

U.S. Citizenship and Immigration Services

News Release

June 22, 2009

USCIS, FBI Eliminate National Name Check Backlog

WASHINGTON—U.S. Citizenship and Immigration Services (USCIS) today announced that, in partnership with the Federal Bureau of Investigation (FBI), it has met all milestones set forth in a joint business plan announced April 2, 2008, resulting in the elimination of the FBI National Name Check Program (NNCP) backlog.

"Our close partnership with the FBI has resulted in the accomplishment of this significant achievement with national security as its foundation," said USCIS Acting Deputy Director Michael Aytes. "This continued working relationship will help to ensure that name check processing is accomplished as quickly as possible without compromising security concerns."

The final goal of the business plan was to achieve a sustainable performance level by the NNCP of completing 98 percent of name check requests submitted by USCIS within 30 days, and the remaining two percent within 90 days. This performance level will become the new standard.

These vastly improved performance levels were achieved through a variety of collaborative steps taken by USCIS and the FBI, including:

- an increase in NNCP staffing made possible by the transfer of appropriated funds from USCIS funding and additional fee revenue for name check processing;
- name check process improvements initiated by the FBI;
- refinements in the name check file search criteria which enabled the FBI to focus on files most likely to yield pertinent search results;
- training of NNCP staff on USCIS adjudication requirements and the applicability of name check search results to USCIS adjudications; and
- other cooperative measures including assignment of USCIS personnel to the NNCP.

As is the case with all security checks undertaken by USCIS, any information provided by the FBI through these checks may require further evaluation and may need additional interaction with agencies outside USCIS to obtain updated or additional information. This could result in additional delays in processing and is not governed by the processing goals contained in the joint business plan.

In the majority of instances, however, the completion of a backlogged FBI name check has resulted in a "no record response." As a result, USCIS has been able to resume normal processing of most cases which most often ends in a final determination of eligibility. Next steps in the adjudication of cases that were previously delayed as a result a pending FBI name check request may now include updating fingerprint results, scheduling interviews, requesting additional evidence and other reviews to determine whether the applicant is eligible for the requested immigration benefit.

For more information on USCIS and its programs, visit www.uscis.gov.

- USCIS -

AILA InfoNet Doc. No. 09062261. (Posted 06/22/09)

801

APPENDIX 9-12

Fee Waiver Guidance

U.S. Department of Homeland Security
U.S. Citizenship and Immigration Services

HQ70/5.5

425 I Street NW
Washington, DC 20536

March 4, 2004

MEMORANDUM FOR: SERVICE CENTER DIRECTORS, CIS
REGIONAL DIRECTORS, CIS
DISTRICT DIRECTORS, CIS

FROM: William R. Yates
Associate Director of Operations
U.S. Citizenship and Immigration Services

SUBJECT: <u>Field Guidance on Granting Fee Waivers Pursuant to 8 CFR 103.7(c)</u>

<u>PURPOSE:</u>

This memorandum replaces the October 9, 1998 fee waiver guidance and provides instructions and processing guidance for adjudication of fee waiver requests filed pursuant to 8 CFR 103.7(c). This field guidance should be followed until a final rule amending 8 CFR 103.7(c) becomes effective.

<u>DISCUSSION:</u>

Citizenship and Immigration Services (CIS) Officers retain broad discretionary authority under 8 CFR 103.7(c) in adjudicating fee waiver requests. These guidelines delineate factors CIS Officers may consider in adjudicating waiver requests, many of which are already considered in current practice. The factors noted in this memorandum are not exhaustive and CIS Officers have authority to consider other evidence in determining whether a waiver request can be approved. Each case is unique and should be considered on its own merits. All circumstances and evidence provided by the individual in support of a fee waiver request should be evaluated. A fee waiver request may be granted when it has been established to the satisfaction of the CIS Officer with jurisdiction over the request, that the individual is unable to pay the fee.

Memorandum for Regional, Service Center and District Directors   Page 2
Subject: Field Guidance on Granting Fee Waivers Pursuant to 8 CFR 103.7(c)

IMPLEMENTATION:

A.   Guideline Applicability

        As of the date of this memo, all pending and newly submitted fee waiver requests should be reviewed under these guidelines. All CIS Officers are asked to facilitate the adjudication of the fee waiver requests and the implementation of these guidelines. These guidelines apply to those applications, petitions, motions, and requests filing fees contained in 8 CFR 103.7(b). There are certain applications and petitions listed in 103.7(b), which are exempt from fee waivers or have specific fee exemptions and therefore would not fall under these fee waiver guidelines.

B.   Documentation

        Along with the affidavit or unsworn declaration pursuant to 28 U.S.C. 1746, as required by 8 CFR 103.7(c), the applicant *may* submit additional documentation to provide proof of the "inability to pay." Fee waiver requests should be decided based upon the affidavit and any additional documentation submitted in support of the fee waiver request. A fee waiver request may be approved in the absence of such additional documentation *provided* that the applicant's affidavit or unsworn declaration is sufficiently detailed to substantiate his or her inability to pay the fee. If the CIS Officer determines that the individual did not substantiate his or her inability to pay, then the fee waiver request should be denied.

C.   Submission of Both Fee and Fee Waiver Request

        When a form is submitted with both the appropriate fee for the form and a fee waiver request, the form should be processed, if otherwise acceptable, as properly filed with fee. No subsequent consideration should be given to, nor action taken on the fee waiver request.

GUIDELINES:

A.   "Inability to pay"

        An individual does not automatically qualify for a fee waiver based on any one particular situation or if he or she meets just one or more of the criteria listed below (e.g. the individual is not automatically qualified for a fee waiver if they are over 65 or if they have qualified for or received a "federal means-tested public benefit"). Each case is unique and should be considered upon it's own merits.

        A fee waiver request may be granted when it has been established to the satisfaction of the CIS Officer with jurisdiction over the request that the individual is unable to pay the fee. The CIS Officer should look at the individual's overall financial picture and take note of any evidence or documentation regarding the individual's living arrangements in the United States; the individual's extraordinary expenditures or those of his dependents residing in the United States; monetary contributions for the payment of monthly expenses received from adult children, dependents, and other people who are living in the individual's household, etc.; and other expenses for which the individual is responsible.

Memorandum for Regional, Service Center and District Directors   Page 3
Subject: Field Guidance on Granting Fee Waivers Pursuant to 8 CFR 103.7(c)

In determining whether the individual should be granted a fee waiver, the CIS Officer may consider the following situations and criteria, *in addition to the individual's overall financial picture and household situation* when adjudicating the fee waiver request:

- Whether the individual has demonstrated that within the last 180 days, he or she qualified for or received a "federal means-tested public benefit". A Federal "means-tested public benefits" is any public benefit funded in whole or in part by funds provided by the Federal Government that the Federal agency administering the Federal funds has determined to be a Federal "means-tested public benefit" under the Personal Responsibility and Work Opportunity Reconciliation Act of 1996, Public Law 104-193. This may include, but is not limited to, Food Stamps, Medicaid, Supplemental Security Income, and Temporary Assistance of Needy Families or other public benefit. Keep in mind that state and local public assistance may be based on an amount higher than the "Federal means-tested public benefits", but both should be considered as income and treated equally.

    NOTE: Each agency's public benefits are determined based on a unique set of criteria. Therefore, even though an individual has qualified for another agency's benefits, it should only be one of the factors in determining the CIS fee waiver request and should not be used as a definitive factor.

- Whether the individual has demonstrated that his or her household income, on which taxes were paid for the most recent tax year, is at or below the poverty level contained in the most recent poverty guidelines revised annually by the Secretary of Health and Human Services' "Poverty Guidelines". (See attached). A household as defined by the Census Bureau, for statistical purposes, consists of all the persons who occupy a housing unit (house or apartment), whether they are related to each other or not.

- Whether the individual is elderly (age 65 and over, at the time the fee request is submitted).

- Whether the individual is disabled. The disability should have been previously determined by the Social Security Administration (SSA), Health and Human Services (HHS), Veteran's Administration (VA), Department of Defense (DOD) or other appropriate federal agency. An applicant or petitioner may provide verification of his or her disability by submitting documentation showing that the disability has been previously determined by the SSA, HHS, VA, DOD, or other appropriate federal agency.

    NOTE: Each agency's public benefits are determined based on a unique set of criteria. Therefore, even though an individual has qualified for another agency's benefits, it should only be one of the factors in determining the CIS fee waiver request and should not be used as a definitive factor.

- The age and number of dependents in the individual's family household who are seeking derivative status or benefits concurrently with the principal applicant or beneficiary.

- Humanitarian or compassionate reasons, either temporary or permanent, which justify a granting of a fee waiver request. For example: the applicant is temporarily destitute; the applicant does not own, possess, or control assets sufficient to pay the fee without causing substantial financial hardship; or an applicant is on a fixed income and confined to a nursing home.

- Any other evidence or factors that the CIS Officer believes establishes an applicant or petitioner's inability to pay the required filing fees.

B.   Delegation of Fee Waiver Authority

The authority to grant fee waivers should not be delegated below CIS Supervisory level (i.e. SDAO, SCAO). Initial review may be performed at the Adjudication Officer level with recommendations, however the final decision must be made at the Supervisory level.

C.   Documentation

The following is a descriptive list of financial information that, if submitted, should be reviewed in order to obtain a picture of the individual's overall financial situation:

- Proof of living arrangements (i.e. living with relatives, living in the individual's own house, apartment, etc.), and evidence of whether the individual's dependents are residing in his or her household.

- Evidence of current employment or self-employment such as recent pay statements, W-2 forms, statement(s) from the individual's employer(s) on business stationary showing salary or wages paid, income tax returns (proof of filing of a tax return).

- Mortgage payment receipts, rent receipts, food and clothing receipts, utility bills (such as gas, electricity, telephone, water), child or elder care receipts, tuition bills, transportation expense receipts, medical expense receipts, and proof of other essential expenditures.

- Any other proof of essential expenditures.

- Proof that verifies the individual's disability. The individual may provide proof of his or her disability by submitting documentation showing that the disability has been previously determined by the Social Security Administration (SSA), the Department of Health and Human Services (HHS), the Department of Veterans Affairs (VA), the Department of Defense (DOD), or other appropriate federal agency.

- Proof of the individual's extraordinary expenditures or his or her dependents residing in the United States. Essential extraordinary expenses are those which do not occur on a monthly basis but which are necessary for the well being of the individual or his or her dependents.

Memorandum for Regional, Service Center and District Directors   Page 5
Subject: Field Guidance on Granting Fee Waivers Pursuant to 8 CFR 103.7(c)

- Proof that the individual has, within the last 6 months, qualified for and/or received a Federal "means-tested public benefit".

- Documentation to show all assets owned, possessed, or controlled by the individual or by his or her dependents.

- Documentation establishing other financial support or subsidies--such as parental support, alimony, child support, educational scholarships, and fellowships, pensions, Social Security or Veterans Benefits, etc. This includes monetary contributions for the payment of monthly expenses received from adult children, dependents, and other people who are living in the individual's household, etc.

- Documentation of debts and liabilities--what is owed on any outstanding loans, credit cards, etc. by the individual and his or her dependents, and any other expenses the individual is responsible for (i.e. insurance, medical/dental bills, etc.).

D.   Issues to be Considered

        In considering fee waiver requests, CIS Officers should take into consideration the following issues:

- Incarcerated Individuals Requesting a Fee Waiver – In the case of an incarcerated individual who is requesting a fee waiver, the individual will not automatically qualify for the fee waiver based solely upon his/her incarceration. CIS Officers should consider the overall financial picture of the requestor, including any outside income or assets possessed by the individual and which the individual may have access to by way of spouse or outside family member. A fee waiver request submitted by an incarcerated individual should contain a description of any and all outside income or assets possessed and include any available supporting documentation as is expected of a nonincarcerated person.

- Extraordinary Expenses – The individual requesting the fee waiver has experienced unusual or extraordinary expenses to the degree that his or her financial situation has been significantly impacted and payment of the filing fee would subject the requestor to undue hardship. Examples include: unexpected and uninsured or underinsured medical bills or situations which could not normally be expected in the regular course of life events; a medical emergency or catastrophic illness affecting the individual or the individual's dependents.

- Frequent or Prolonged Travel Expenses - If the fee waiver request states that the individual is unable to pay the filing fee because of travel expenses and the individual PROVIDES a reasonable explanation and/or supporting documentation regarding the purpose of the travel, the CIS Officer should not refer back to the associated application or petition to substantiate this statement. However, if the fee waiver request states that the individual is unable to pay the filing fee because of travel expenses and DOES NOT PROVIDE any explanation and/or supporting evidence, the associated application or

Memorandum for Regional, Service Center and District Directors   Page 6
Subject: Field Guidance on Granting Fee Waivers Pursuant to 8 CFR 103.7(c)

petition may be examined to determine the manner, amount and reason for the travel. For example: If John Smith is requesting a fee waiver because he used all his funds to travel to Australia several times for pleasure, this situation does not merit a fee waiver unless additional supporting evidence is provided to convince the CIS Officer to the contrary. However, if John states that he traveled to Australia several times in order to care for a dying relative, then travel would not be an appropriate reason to deny the fee waiver request.

- Self-Petitioning Abused/Battered Spouses and Children of Citizens or Lawful Permanent Residents applicants and adjustment of status and employment authorization applicants, under the provisions of the Violence Against Women Act (VAWA). (I-360, I-485, and I-765). Due to the sensitive nature of applications and petitions associated with this category, CIS Officers should refer to the detailed information on the treatment of this category contained in field guidance memoranda on VAWA dated 4/16/96, 5/6/97 and 5/25/01.

- Nonimmigrant Applications. Generally, nonimmigrants are required to demonstrate sufficient financial support for the duration of their stay in the United States (i.e., sufficient to overcome the public charge grounds of inadmissibility under section 212(a)(4) of the Immigration and Nationality Act (INA)). An example of a type of application for which a demonstration of financial support is required would be an application to extend or change nonimmigrant status (Form I-539). Fee waiver requests should be adjudicated in light of the level of income and support required for approval of these types of applications.

- Family-based visa petitions and applications and petitions related to classifying an orphan as an immediate relative. Petitioners for family-based visas must file an enforceable affidavit of support under section 213A of the INA, on behalf of the beneficiaries at the time the beneficiaries are applying for adjustment of status. Fee waiver requests should be adjudicated in light of the level of income and support required for approval of these types of applications or petitions. Keep in mind that multiple affidavits of support may be submitted to meet the requirement and may be from persons other than the petitioner or other relatives. In addition, the nature of applications and petitions associated with classifying an orphan as an immediate relative and applying for certificate of citizenship for adopted child (Form N-643) has the same considerations as the family-based petitions. Adoptive parents must demonstrate sufficient financial means to support the child in order to meet home study requirements. They must also file an affidavit of support on behalf of the adopted child. These applications and petitions should be treated the same as family-based visa petitions.

- Employment-based visa petitions and Employment Authorization. Generally, beneficiaries and applicants are entering the United States specifically for employment, with sponsorship from their employer, or are obtaining employment after entering. Fee waiver requests should be adjudicated in light of the level of income and support required for approval of these types of applications or petitions.

Memorandum for Regional, Service Center and District Directors   Page 7
Subject: Field Guidance on Granting Fee Waivers Pursuant to 8 CFR 103.7(c)

- <u>Travel Documents and Advance Parole.</u> A fee waiver request made in connection with this type of application should be adjudicated in light of the applicant or petitioner's representations as to the nature and purpose of travel as well as the individual's source of income for the travel requested or proposed.

- <u>Special situations concerning Adjustment of Status Applications (I-485)</u>

    <u>Public Charge Concerns.</u> The granting of a fee waiver does not necessarily subject the applicant or petitioner to public charge liability under other provisions of the INA, such as deportability under section 237(a)(5) or inadmissibility under section 212(a)(4).

    <u>Exceptions to Public Charge Requirements</u>. Refugees, Asylees, NACARA, HRIFA, Indochinese Parole Adjustment Act, Syrian Asylee Adjustment Act, Special Immigrant Juveniles and Registry applicants are exempt from the Form I-485 requirements to show evidence that they are not likely to become a public charge. Therefore, these categories may be given wider latitude in required income levels when determining fee waivers.

    <u>Self Petitioning Abused/Battered Spouses and Children of Citizens or Lawful Permanent Residents applicants and Adjustment of Status applicants under the provisions of the Violence Against Women Act (VAWA).</u> This category should be given special consideration when determining whether they should be granted a fee waiver. Due to the sensitive nature of applications and petitions associated with this category, CIS Officers should refer to the detailed information on the treatment of this category contained in field guidance memoranda on VAWA dated 4/16/96, 5/6/97 and 5/25/01.

<u>PUBLIC INFORMATION:</u>

The Office of Program and Regulations Development (OPRD) and Public Affairs have prepared an updated fact sheet which will be posted on the CIS webpage. All CBO/NGO and community groups and local Congressional Offices in your area should be re-notified about the fee waiver guidance contained in the Public Affairs Fact Sheet and the suggested documentation that should support the fee waiver requests as well as the method for facilitating the processing of fee waiver requests. The applicants and petitioners should put a large notation *"fee waiver request enclosed"* on the outside of the mailing envelope containing their application or petition and fee waiver request. In addition, a similar notation should be placed on top of the affidavit and supporting information submitted in support of their request.

<u>POINT OF CONTACT:</u>

If you have questions regarding these guidelines or their implementation, please contact Irene Hoffman in OPRD or Paul Pierre in SCOPS through appropriate channels.

Enclosure: Poverty Guidelines

APPENDIX 9-13

Adjudication of Petitions and Applications Filed By or On Behalf of Transsexuals

U.S. Department of Homeland Security
20 Massachusetts Ave., NW
Washington, D.C. 20529

U.S. Citizenship
and Immigration
Services

JAN 1 4 2009

HQOPS AD09-03
HQ 70/8

Interoffice Memorandum

To: Field Leadership

Through: Don Neufeld
            Acting Associate Director, Domestic Operations

            Lori Scialabba
            Associate Director, Refugee, Asylum and International Operations

From: Carlos Iturregui
            Chief, Office of Policy and Strategy

Re: Adjudication of Petitions and Applications Filed by or on Behalf of Transsexual
            Individuals

            Revisions to *Adjudicator's Field Manual* (AFM) Subchapter 21.3
            (AFM Update AD09-03)

1. Purpose

The purpose of this memorandum is to provide guidance to USCIS adjudicators concerning *Matter of Lovo-Lara*, 23 I&N Dec. 746 (BIA 2005) in relation to the adjudication of spousal immigrant visa petitions in which one of the claimed spouses has undergone sex reassignment surgery. Under *Matter of Lovo-Lara*, USCIS may approve a Form I-130 (or in appropriate cases, an I-360 petition) in such a case if the petitioner establishes that, under the law of the place of marriage, the surgery resulted in a *legal* change of sex, and that the marriage is recognized as a valid heterosexual marriage. This guidance also applies to adjudication of a fiancé(e) petition (Form I-129F) and to claims that one person is another person's "spouse" for purposes of the ability to accompany or follow to join a principal alien.

2. Contact Information

This guidance is effective immediately. Please direct any questions concerning these changes through appropriate supervisory channels to Anne-Marie Mulagha, Office of Policy and Strategy, via electronic mail.

www.uscis.gov

809

Adjudication of Petitions and Applications Filed by or on Behalf of Transsexual Individuals
Revisions to *Adjudicator's Field Manual* (AFM) Subchapter 21.3 (AFM Update AD09-03)

Page 2

3. Use

This guidance is created solely for the purpose of USCIS personnel in performing their duties
relative to adjudication of applications. It is not intended to, does not, and may not be relied upon
to create any right or benefit, substantial or procedural, enforceable at law by any individual or
any other party in removal proceedings, in litigation with the United States, or in any other or
form or matter.

4. Background

Previous USCIS policy disallowed recognition of a change of sex for the purpose of spousal
immigrant petitions. W. Yates, *Memorandum for Regional Directors et al, Adjudication of
Petitions and Applications Filed by or on Behalf of, or Document Requests by, Transsexual
Individuals.* (April 16, 2004). In the context of adjudicating spousal and fiancé petitions, former
USCIS policy did not recognize the marriage, or intended marriage, between two individuals
where one or both of the parties claimed to be a transsexual, regardless of whether either
individual had undergone sex reassignment surgery, or was in the process of doing so.

It is well-settled that only a legally valid and monogamous marriage between one man and one
woman can form the basis of the approval of a spousal Form I-130. 1 U.S.C. § 7; *cf. Adams v.
Howerton,* 673 F.2d 1036 (9th Cir. 1982). The basis for the USCIS position, as stated in the
Yates Memorandum, is the traditional rule of construction that, in administering 1 U.S.C. § 7, the
words "man" and "woman," as with any other words in any statute, are to be given their common
meaning in ordinary English. USCIS also noted the legislative history of 1 U.S.C. § 7, H. Rep.
104-664, at 13, in which the Committee Report specifically endorsed the traditional view that
one's sex is fixed at birth. Therefore, USCIS determined that absent specific statutory authority,
a claimed marriage between two persons of the same birth sex was not valid for immigration
purposes, even if one of them had undergone sex reassignment surgery.

In 2005, the Board of Immigration Appeals (BIA) rejected this interpretation of 1 U.S.C. § 7.
Matter of Lovo-Lara, 23 I&N Dec. 746 (BIA 2005). The Board concluded that whether sex
reassignment surgery results in a change in a person's *legal* sex, for purposes of marriage, is
determined according to the law in which the claimed marriage took place. If the petitioner
establishes that, under the law of the place of marriage, the claimed marriage is a legally valid,
monogamous, heterosexual marriage, the Form I-130 (and, as appropriate, a widow's or battered
spouse's Form I-360) may be approved.

Matter of Lovo-Lara involved a petitioner who was born in North Carolina, underwent sex
change surgery, amended her birth certificate to reflect her sex change to female, married her
husband in North Carolina and filed an I-130 petition on his behalf. The Board noted that North
Carolina law does not permit individuals of the same sex to marry each other, but permits an

Adjudication of Petitions and Applications Filed by or on Behalf of Transsexual Individuals
Revisions to *Adjudicator's Field Manual* (AFM) Subchapter 21.3 (AFM Update AD09-03)

Page 3

amendment to one's birth certificate, to reflect that one has undergone sex reassignment surgery. The petitioner submitted documentation of, among other evidence, her sex reassignment surgery and her amended birth certificate. The Board concluded that the petitioner's marriage to the beneficiary was considered valid under North Carolina law.

USCIS adjudicators will, consistently with 8 CFR 1003.1(g), take *Matter of Lovo-Lara* as establishing that if two persons of the same birth sex claim to have married in North Carolina, and establish that one of them has undergone sex reassignment surgery, then the marriage is a valid heterosexual marriage under North Carolina law.

This reasoning may not apply to other States, however, even if those States also permit changes to birth certificates. Illinois law, for example, also permits such changes after sex reassignment surgery. 410 Ill. Comp. Stat. 535/17. This change does *not* however, result in an actual legal change of sex, for purposes of marriage. *See In Re Marriage of Simmons*, 355 Ill.App. 3d 942, 825 N.W.2d 303 (Ill. App. 2005). The Texas Court of Appeals reached the same conclusion, also in a case involving a changed birth certificate. *See Littleton v. Prange*, 9 S.W.3d 223 (Tex. App. 1999).

The basic principle of *Matter of Lovo-Lara*, however, is binding on USCIS, no matter where the claimed marriage took place. A spousal Form I-130 (and, as appropriate, a widow's or battered spouse's Form I-360) may be approved, in a case involving two persons of the same birth sex, if the petitioner establishes, by a preponderance of the evidence, that:

- one of the claimed spouses has undergone sex reassignment surgery; AND
- the person who underwent sex reassignment surgery has taken whatever legal steps exist and may be required to have the legal change of sex recognized for purposes of marriage under the law of the place of marriage; AND
- the marriage is recognized under that law as a monogamous, heterosexual marriage.

5. Field Guidance and AFM Update

Accordingly, AFM chapter 21.3 (a)(2)(j) is revised in its entirety to read as follows:

☞ (J) <u>Transsexuals.</u> In the case of a spousal Form I-130 (or, as appropriate, a widow's or battered spouse's Form I-360), a claimed marriage between two persons of the same birth sex, one of whom has undergone sex reassignment surgery, is valid for immigration purposes if the petitioner establishes by a preponderance of the evidence that:

- one of the claimed spouses has, in fact, undergone sex reassignment surgery; AND

Adjudication of Petitions and Applications Filed by or on Behalf of Transsexual Individuals
Revisions to *Adjudicator's Field Manual* (AFM) Subchapter 21.3 (AFM Update AD09-03)

Page 4

- that person has taken whatever legal steps exist and may be required to have the legal change of sex recognized for purposes of marriage under the law of the place of marriage; AND
- the marriage is recognized under the law of the place of solemnization as a legally valid heterosexual marriage.

This guidance also applies to the adjudication of a Form I-129F on behalf of a K-3 spouse or fiancé(e) of a citizen. In the case of a proposed marriage between two persons of the same birth sex, one of whom has undergone sex reassignment surgery, the Form I-129F can be approved if the petitioner establishes that that person's *legal* sex has changed and the proposed marriage will be recognized under the law of the place of solemnization as a legally valid heterosexual marriage.

If the claimed marriage between two persons of the same birth sex, one of whom has undergone sex reassignment surgery, is recognized under the law of the place of solemnization as a legally valid heterosexual marriage, USCIS will recognize the partners as "spouses" for purposes of one spouse's ability to accompany or follow to join the other.

If an officer has questions about the validity of a marriage involving a person who has undergone sex reassignment surgery, the officer should contact his or her local USCIS counsel.

States that DO recognize transsexual marriages as valid heterosexual marriages:

North Carolina. North Carolina law allows amendment of a birth certificate for persons who have undergone sex reassignment surgery. N.C. Gen. Stat. § 130A-118(b)(4) (2008). In *Matter of Lovo-Lara*, 23 I&N Dec. 746 (BIA 2005), the Board held that North Carolina recognized a marriage as valid and heterosexual where one of the spouses had undergone sex reassignment surgery and her birth certificate had been amended to reflect her changed sex

New Jersey. New Jersey law recognizes as a valid heterosexual marriage a marriage solemnized between two persons of the same birth sex, one of whom has undergone sex reassignment surgery, so long as the other claimed spouse was aware of the sex change. *M.J. v. J.T.*, 140 N.J.Super. 77, 355 A.2d 204 (N.J.Super. 1976).

Maryland. Maryland law permits a change of the person's legal sex, on the basis of sex reassignment surgery. *Re: Heilig*, 372 Md. 692, 816 A.2d 68 (Md. 2003). This case did not involve the issue of the person's ability to marry a person of the same birth sex. Until such time as the Maryland courts clarify this issue, however, USCIS adjudicators will assume that Maryland law recognizes as a valid heterosexual marriage

Adjudication of Petitions and Applications Filed by or on Behalf of Transsexual Individuals
Revisions to *Adjudicator's Field Manual* (AFM) Subchapter 21.3 (AFM Update AD09-03)

Page 5

a claimed marriage between two persons of the same birth sex, one of whom has undergone sex reassignment surgery.

States that DO NOT recognize transsexual marriages as valid heterosexual marriages

As of November 2008, the following States *do not* recognize sex reassignment surgery as changing a person's legal sex, for purposes of marriage:

> **Florida** – *Kantaras v. Kantaras*, 884 So.2d 155 (Fla. App. 2004);
> **Illinois** – *Re Marriage of Simmons*, 355 Ill. App. 3d 942, 825 N.W. 2d 303 (Ill. App. 2005)
> **Kansas** – *Estate of Gardiner*, 273 Kan. 191, 42 P.3d 120 (Kan. 2002).
> **Ohio** – *Re: Ladrach*, 32 Ohio Misc. 2d 6, 513 N.E.2d 828 (Oh. Probate 1987);
> **Tennessee** – Tennessee Code 68-3-203(d)
> **Texas** – *Littleton v. Prange*, 9 S.W.3d 223 (Tex. App. 1999).

Unless a petitioner establishes that the relevant law has changed, a Form I-130 or Form I-360 may not be approved on the basis of a marriage solemnized in one of these States between two persons of the same birth sex, one of whom has undergone sex reassignment surgery. Nor may a Form I-129F be approved, if the proposed spouses intend to marry in one of these States.

Other States, and foreign countries, in which there are no precedent decisions

Several States have laws providing for the change of a person's birth record to reflect that the person has undergone sex reassignment surgery. Other countries may have similar laws.

In light of the Illinois (*Simmons*) and Texas (*Littleton*) decisions, however, it is not necessarily the case that these statutes actually provide for the change of a person's legal sex for purposes of marriage. As of November 2008, it did not appear that the highest court of any other State had addressed the issue.

A USCIS adjudicator should find that the petitioner has established the validity of the claimed marriage (or proposed marriage, for a Form I-129F case) if the petitioner establishes, based on the actual text of the relevant statute or a precedent decision from the courts of that jurisdiction (*i.e.*, State or foreign country), that sex reassignment surgery does, in fact, result in a change in the person's *legal* sex.

In a case involving a claimed marriage solemnized in a foreign country, or a claimed or proposed marriage in U.S. jurisdictions other than Florida, Illinois, Kansas, Maryland, New Jersey, North Carolina, Ohiio, Tennessee and Texas, and in which the statute is not clear and there is no binding precedent, a USCIS adjudicator may find that the

Adjudication of Petitions and Applications Filed by or on Behalf of Transsexual Individuals
Revisions to *Adjudicator's Field Manual* (AFM) Subchapter 21.3 (AFM Update AD09-03)

Page 6

petitioner has established the validity of the claimed marriage (or proposed marriage for
a Form I-129F case) if the petitioner submits a court order or a official record or
statement from an appropriate agency of the Government (such as the vital statistics
registrar or similar official) indicating that the person's having undergone sex
reassignment surgery has resulted in a change of the person's *legal* sex under the law
of the place of marriage.

Distribution List: Service Center Directors
                         National Benefits Center Directors
                         Regional Directors
                         District Directors
                         Field Office Directors

APPENDIX 9-14

Form G-1145, E-Notification of Application/Petition Acceptance

e-Notification of Application/Petition Acceptance

Department of Homeland Security
U.S. Citizenship and Immigration Services

USCIS
Form G-1145
OMB No. 1615-0109
Expires 09/30/2014

What Is the Purpose of This Form?

Use this form to request an electronic notification (e-Notification) when U.S. Citizenship and Immigration Services accepts your immigration application. This service is available for applications filed at a USCIS Lockbox facility.

General Information

Complete the information below and clip this form to the first page of your application package. You will receive one e-mail and/or text message for each form you are filing.

We will send the e-Notification within 24 hours after we accept your application. Domestic customers will receive an e-mail and/or text message; overseas customers will only receive an e-mail. Undeliverable e-Notifications cannot be resent.

The e-mail or text message will display your receipt number and tell you how to get updated case status information. It will not include any personal information. The e-Notification does not grant any type of status or benefit; rather it is provided as a convenience to customers.

USCIS will also mail you a receipt notice (I-797C), which you will receive within 10 days after your application has been accepted; use this notice as proof of your pending application or petition.

USCIS Privacy Act Statement

AUTHORITIES: The information requested on this form, and the associated evidence, is collected under the Immigration and Nationality Act, section 101, et seq.

PURPOSE: The primary purpose for providing the requested information on this form is to determine if you have established eligibility for the immigration benefit for which you are filing. The information you provide will be used to grant or deny the benefit sought.

DISCLOSURE: The information you provide is voluntary. However, failure to provide the requested information, and any requested evidence, may delay a final decision or result in denial of your form.

ROUTINE USES: The information you provide on this form may be shared with other Federal, State, local, and foreign government agencies and authorized organizations following approved routine uses described in the associated published system of records notices [DHS-USCIS-007 - Benefits Information System and DHS-USCIS-001 - Alien File, Index, and National File Tracking System of Records, which can be found at **www.dhs.gov/privacy**]. The information may also be made available, as appropriate, for law enforcement purposes or in the interest of national security.

Paperwork Reduction Act

An agency may not conduct or sponsor an information collection and a person is not required to respond to a collection of information unless it displays a currently valid OMB control number. The public reporting burden for this collection of information is estimated at 3 minutes per response, including the time for reviewing instructions and completing and submitting the form. Send comments regarding this burden estimate or any other aspect of this collection of information, including suggestions for reducing this burden, to: U.S. Citizenship and Immigration Services, Regulatory Coordination Division, Office of Policy and Strategy, 20 Massachusetts Avenue, NW, Washington, DC 20529-2140. OMB No. 1615-0109. **Do not mail your completed Form G-1145 to this address.**

Complete this form and clip it on top of the first page of your immigration form(s).		
Applicant/Petitioner Full Last Name	Applicant/Petitioner Full First Name	Applicant/Petitioner Full Middle Name
E-mail Address	Mobile Phone Number (Text Message)	

Form G-1145 02/28/13

Page 1 of 1

Chapter 10

Federal Judicial Review

Research References

West's Key Number Digest
Aliens, Immigration, and Citizenship ⟜725, 726, 728

Westlaw Databases

Steel on Immigration Law (STEEL)
Immigration Law Service (2d ed.) (IMMLS2D)

Treatises and Practice Aids

Fragomen, Shannon, and Montalvo, Immigration Procedures Handbook, Ch 22
Steel on Immigration Law §§ 15:23, 15:24

> **KeyCite®**: Cases and other legal materials listed in KeyCite Scope can be researched through the KeyCite service on Westlaw®. Use KeyCite to check citations for form, parallel references, prior and later history, and comprehensive citator information, including citations to other decisions and secondary materials.

§ 10:1 Overview of judicial review

Research References

Steel on Immigration Law § 15:23

Judicial review over a naturalization case can arise in one of three postures. First, where the USCIS conducts the initial naturalization interview, but then fails to issue a decision in the case within 120 days, the alien has a statutory right of action found at 8 U.S.C.A. § 1447(b). That permits the applicant to go into district court to seek judicial review, which can consist of either de novo review, or a remand to the agency with instructions.[1] The primary cause of USCIS delays, at present, is the "background check," which is discussed below, at § 10:3.

Second, where USCIS delays scheduling a naturalization case for an interview or a hearing, the provisions of § 1447(b) do not apply. An applicant in that circumstance could only seek relief in mandamus.[2] It is unclear how long an applicant would need to wait before seeking mandamus relief, and there is some authority questioning court jurisdiction in that circumstance.

Third, where naturalization is ultimately denied, after administrative appeal, the applicant may seek de novo judicial review over that denial, in district court.[3]

In cases not arising from naturalization—such as N-600 denials, denial of a passport, or an order of removal—other jurisdictional rules would apply. Either an N-600 denial or a denial of a passport would likely give rise to a right to seek judicial relief in district court pursuant to INA § 360. However, if removal proceedings are pending, the (alleged) citizen may need to go first to the Court of Appeals, which would then transfer the case to district court if the alleged alien has made out a prima facie case that they are in fact a citizen.[4]

I. JUDICIAL REVIEW OVER NATURALIZATION

§ 10:2 § 1447(b) Actions—Generally

Research References

West's Key Number Digest, Aliens ⚖68(6)

[Section 10:1]

[1]See §§ 10:2 to 10:7.

[2]See §§ 10:9 to 10:11.

[3]See §§ 10:12 to 10:18.

[4]Cf. §§ 10:20 to 10:23 (judicial review over N-600 denials) with §§ 10:24 to 10:25 (judicial review over citizenship claims in context of removal proceedings).

When applications are neither granted nor denied by the USCIS within 120 days after the original interview with a USCIS officer, the applicant may apply to the federal district court in the district where the applicant resides for a hearing on the naturalization application.[1] According to the statute, the district court has jurisdiction either to decide the naturalization application or remand the case to the USCIS with appropriate instructions.[2] A sample complaint is reproduced as Appendix 10-6.

The statute contains no express statute of limitations, requiring that this action be filed within any set time period. However, once the USCIS has denied the application, it is probably too late.[3]

Section 1447(b) applies on its face only where 120 days pass without "a determination under section 335" of the INA.[4] Section 335 refers to the examination process, not the oath, which is covered by INA § 337. Thus, the Second Circuit has held that § 1447(b) actions are not appropriate where the USCIS has approved the naturalization application but failed to schedule an oath ceremony.[5] It found that mandamus was a more proper vehicle in that circumstance, but that exhaustion of administrative remedies was required.[6]

§ 10:3 § 1447(b) Actions—Major causes of delays in adjudication

The primary cause of § 1447(b) actions within the past few years has been delay stemming from "background checks."[1] Due to these delays, the USCIS Ombudsman has found that tens of thousands of applicants have waited periods of one, two, and even three years for adjudication.[2]

The current background requirement began with an appropriations bill from 1998, which required that "none of the funds appropriated or otherwise made available to the Immigration and Naturalization Service shall be used to complete adjudication of an application for naturalization unless the Immigration and Naturalization Service has received confirmation from the Federal Bureau of Investigation that a full criminal background check has been completed").[3] In the face of that statutory requirement, the then-INS enacted regulations requiring an

---

[Section 10:2]

[1]INA § 336(b), 8 U.S.C.A. § 1447(b); 8 CFR § 310.5(a).

[2]INA § 336(b), 8 U.S.C.A. § 1447(b); 8 CFR § 310.5(a).

[3]See, e.g., Kia v. U.S. I.N.S., 175 F.3d 1014 (4th Cir. 1999) (unpublished) (finding that court lost jurisdiction when agency denied the application, and that applicant was then required to exhaust administrative remedies); cf. Chavez v. INS, 844 F. Supp. 1224 (N.D. Ill. 1993) (no jurisdiction to reinstate dismissed § 336(b).

[4]INA § 336(b) [8 U.S.C.A. § 1447(b)].

[5]Escaler v. USCIS, 582 F.3d 288, 291(2d Cir. 2009).

[6]Escaler v. USCIS, 582 F.3d 288, 291 (2d Cir. 2009).

[Section 10:3]

[1]U.S. Citizenship and Immigration Service Ombudsman, Annual Report 2007, at 37 (June 2007).

[2]U.S. Citizenship and Immigration Service Ombudsman, Annual Report 2007, at 38 (June 2007).

[3]Department of Justice Appropriations Act of 1998, Pub. L. No. 105-119, Title I, Nov. 26, 1997, 111 Stat. 2448, reprinted in historical and statutory notes to 8 U.S.C.A. § 1446; see also 8 U.S.C.A. § 1446(a).

FBI fingerprint check to determine whether the individual had an "administrative or a criminal record."[4]

In the wake of 9/11, however, the USCIS and FBI expanded the background checks significantly. In December 2002, USCIS and FBI reviewed their procedures, and determined that it was insufficient to check FBI "main files"; they therefore changed the procedures to include "reference files."[5] This led to an immediate need to re-run 2.7 million background checks for pending USCIS application.[6] The problem has not abated since.

Procedurally, what happens with an FBI name check is that USCIS sends a batch of names to the FBI. The FBI runs those names, and any variations on those names, against its computer system. According to the FBI, this results in an immediate elimination of about 68% of the applicants, who are then clear to proceed.[7] For names that have a "hit," the FBI then looks electronically for items such as date of birth and other ways of identifying the hits as applying to people other than the applicant. This results in the clearing of another 22% of the applicant pool.[8]

The last 10% of the applicants must be checked against the FBI's files, one-by-one. This often requires a manual search of the FBI's files.[9] Where those files actually do pertain to the applicant, and they contain derogatory information, that information is forwarded to USCIS in a summary memorandum. In less than 1% of the cases is any derogatory information found.[10]

When the FBI forwards a summary memorandum of derogatory information to the USCIS, it sends that information to a USCIS unit called the Office of Fraud Detection and National Security (FDNS). Where the "hit" pertains to potential security issues, it is referred to a unit called the National Security Adjudications Unit (NSAU), in Washington, DC. The FDNS eventually determines whether the case may or may not go forward; and then advises the local USCIS office of the contents of the investigation, if any.[11]

A recent settlement agreement required the government to take affirmative actions to prevent name check delay in cases involving recipients of Supplemental Social Security Income, though it appears that the settlement agreement has now expired.[12] Other substantive litigation relating to the background check delay issue is discussed above.[13] In response to complaints about name check delays, the USCIS and FBI recently added resources to handle more name checks, and claimed as of June 2009 to have resolved the problem of name check delays.[14]

§ 10:4   § 1447(b) Actions—Timing of when courts acquire jurisdiction

Because § 1447(b) actions are tied to the date when USCIS conducts the

---

[4]8 C.F.R. § 335.2(b).

[5]See Cannon Declaration, produced in case Yakubova v. Chertoff, reproduced at App 10-5.

[6]See Cannon Declaration, produced in case Yakubova v. Chertoff, reproduced at App 10-5.

[7]See Cannon Declaration, produced in case Yakubova v. Chertoff, reproduced at App 10-5.

[8]See Cannon Declaration, produced in case Yakubova v. Chertoff, reproduced at App 10-5.

[9]See Cannon Declaration, produced in case Yakubova v. Chertoff, reproduced at App 10-5.

[10]See Cannon Declaration, produced in case Yakubova v. Chertoff, reproduced at App 10-5.

[11]U.S. Citizenship and Immigration Service Ombudsman, Annual Report 2007, at 38 (June 2007).

[12]See App 9-10.; 9:49

[13]See § 9:48.

[14]See App. 9-11.

naturalization interview, it would seem clear that one may go into district court 120 days later, as provided in the statute. However, in the face of a conflicting Congressional requirement that naturalization cases not proceed while background checks are pending,[1] some district courts held that the "examination" is not complete until all required background checks have been completed.[2] The Fifth Circuit initially adopted this position, before reversing itself and concluding squarely to the contrary.[3] Likewise, the vast majority of district courts have rejected these jurisdictional arguments.[4] There are three main reasons. First, the language of § 1447(b) relates to "the date on which the examination is conducted." Thus, the statutory language "strongly implies that there is a single date on which the examination occurs."[5] Second, by distinguishing between examinations and investigations in § 1446, Congress has evinced an understanding that the investigation is separate from the examination.[6] Third, the regulations seem to contemplate a distinction between investigation and an examination, requiring that the investigation be completed prior to the interview,[7] and treating the term "examination" as distinct from "investigation."[8]

§ 10:5 § 1447(b) Actions—Procedural matters

Research References

West's Key Number Digest, Aliens ⟜68(6)

Actions under § 1447(b) are filed with the district court having jurisdiction over

---

[Section 10:4]

[1]See Department of Justice Appropriations Act of 1998, Pub. L. No. 105-119, Title I, Nov. 26, 1997, 111 Stat. 2448 ("During fiscal year 1998 and each fiscal year thereafter, none of the funds appropriated or otherwise made available to the Immigration and Naturalization Service shall be used to complete adjudication of an application for naturalization unless the Immigration and Naturalization Service has received confirmation from the Federal Bureau of Investigation that a full criminal background check has been completed. . . .") reprinted in historical and statutory notes to 8 U.S.C.A. § 1446; see also 8 U.S.C.A. § 1446(a).

[2]See, e.g., Danilov v. Aguirre, 370 F.Supp.2d 441, 443 (E.D.Va.2005) (finding that " 'examination' is a process, not an isolated event, which necessarily may include one or more in-person interviews, as well as other activities"); see also, Damra v. Chertoff, No. 1:05CV0929, 2006 WL 1786246 (N.D. Ohio June 23, 2006).

[3]Walji v. Gonzales, 500 F.3d 432, (5th Cir. 2007); cf. Walji v. Gonzales, 489 F.3d 738 (5th Cir. June 19, 2007) (withdrawn from publication);

[4]Khelifa v. Chertoff, 433 F.Supp.2d 836, 841 (E.D.Mich. Jun 09, 2006) (citing cases); El-Daour v. Chertoff, 417 F. Supp. 2d 679, 681 (W.D. Pa. 2005); Meyersiek v. United States Citizenship & Immigration Serv., 2006 WL 1582397 (D.R.I. June 6, 2006); Shalan v. Chertoff, 2006 WL 42143 (D. Mass. Jan. 6, 2006); Daami v. Gonzales, 2006 WL 1457862 (D.N.J. May 22, 2006); Zhang v. Chertoff, 2006 WL 4045600 (E.D. Mich. 2006); Saidi v. Jenifer, 2005 WL 5179147 (E.D. Mich. 2005); Essa v. United States Citizenship & Immigration Servs., 2005 WL 3440827 (D. Minn. Dec. 14, 2005); Al-Kudsi v. Gonzales, 2006 WL 752556 (D. Or. Mar. 22, 2006); Khan v. Chertoff, 2006 WL 2009055 (D.Ariz. Jul 14, 2006).

[5]Khan v. Chertoff, 2006 WL 2009055, *2 (D.Ariz. Jul 14, 2006); see also, El-Daour, 417 F.Supp.2d 679, 681 (W.D. Pa. 2005) (statutory language "contemplates that the examination occurs on a particular, identifiable, date. A 'process' does not occur on one particular and identifiable date.").

[6]Daami v. Gonzales, 2006 WL 1457862 at *5.

[7]8 C.F.R. § 335.2(b).

[8]8 C.F.R. § 335.2(a); Khelifa, 433 F.Supp.2d 836, 841 (E.D.Mich. Jun 09, 2006) (finding that regulations "evidence the agency's own understanding that an 'examination' is a discrete event rather than a prolonged process with multiple components").

the applicant's place of residence.[1] The Defendant in a § 1447(b) action is the United States Citizenship and Immigration Services.[2] The petitioner may also want to name the Attorney General as a defendant, as the statute confers on the Attorney General "the sole authority to naturalize persons as citizens of the United States."[3] The first step in commencing a § 1447(b) action is to file a complaint.[4] A sample complaint is reproduced as Appendix 10-6. A summons should accompany the complaint, so that the clerk of the court can issue it.[5] A sample summons is reproduced below as Appendix 10-4, but many district courts have their own forms, which should be used instead.

Once the complaint is filed and the summons is issued, they must be served on the local USCIS district director. Service upon any officer or agency of the United States is effected by delivering a copy of the summons and complaint to the U.S. Attorney for the district in which the action is brought and, in addition, by sending a copy of the summons and the complaint by registered or certified mail to the Secretary of DHS in Washington, DC, and another copy, also by registered or certified mail to the USCIS district director.[6] Service must take place within 120 days from the filing of the action and proof of service must be filed with the court.[7] The regulations also appear to require service upon the Attorney General.[8]

The government must file an answer within sixty days from the service of the summons and complaint.[9] This period is counted from the service upon the district's U.S. Attorney's office.[10]

Once the complaint and summons are filed, the U.S. Attorney's office will often contact the USCIS district office to obtain a report on the case.[11] The request will normally come to the attention of the persons in charge in the naturalization unit. If the USCIS concludes that the case has been misplaced, misdelivered, or otherwise mishandled, the USCIS may take corrective action.[12] However, the USCIS recently made public its criteria for ordering expedited treatment of the background check,

---

[Section 10:5]

[1] 8 C.F.R. § 310.5(a).

[2] Cf. 8 C.F.R. § 336.9(b) (petition for review "shall be brought against the Immigration and Naturalization Service").

[3] 8 U.S.C.A. § 1421(a).

[4] Fed.R.Civ.P. 3.

[5] Fed.R.Civ.P. 4(b).

[6] Fed.R.Civ.P. 4(i)(1), (2). In 6 C.F.R. § 542(a), DHS instructs that service of a summons and complaint in a suit against DHS is to be sent to the Office of the General Counsel, U.S. Department of Homeland Security, Washington, D.C. 20258. The postal service indicates that no such zip code exists, however, and thus this appears to be a typographical error. The DHS website lists the zip code as 20528.

[7] Fed.R.Civ.P. 4(l), (m).

[8] 8 C.F.R. § 336.9(b)

[9] Fed.R.Civ.P. 12(a)(3).

[10] Fed.R.Civ.P. 12(a)(3).

[11] Mautino, How to Move Cases in the New World of Naturalization, in 1998-99 Immigration and Nationality Law Handbook, Vol. II - Advanced Practice, 434 (Murphy, et al., ed. 1998).

[12] Mautino, How to Move Cases in the New World of Naturalization, in 1998-99 Immigration and Nationality Law Handbook, Vol. II - Advanced Practice, 434 (Murphy, et al., ed. 1998).

and determined that the filing of a mandamus should not result in expedited handling.[13]

§ 10:6   § 1447(b) Actions—District court's exclusive jurisdiction

After an applicant for naturalization files a complaint under § 1447(b), there is some question as to whether the federal courts obtain sole and exclusive jurisdiction over the naturalization action, or whether the USCIS may act on the application at that point. The USCIS (as did the legacy INS) often attempts to adjudicate naturalization applications after suit is filed under INA § 336(b). There is a substantial question as to whether it has authority to do so.

The Ninth Circuit has held that once suit is filed under INA § 336(b), the district court obtains exclusive jurisdiction over the naturalization application and the agency loses the authority to decide the case.[1] The court rejected the claim of USCIS that it retained concurrent jurisdiction over the application, and that it could proceed to adjudicate and deny the application notwithstanding the pending federal court suit.[2] Thus, in the Ninth Circuit, the USCIS will no longer be able to adjudicate and deny a naturalization application after suit is filed in district court under INA § 336(b). The Fourth and Second Circuits have joined the Ninth Circuit in that holding, and the Tenth Circuit has indicated that it finds that reasoning persuasive.[3]

In circuits other than the Ninth, Second and Fourth Circuits, the matter remains open. A number of district courts have now joined in this holding,[4] though others have rejected it or ruled to the contrary.[5] Thus far, the Ninth Circuit's opinion appears to be the majority view. The opposing view would hold that district courts and USCIS have concurrent jurisdiction.[6]

The majority view is helpful if the USCIS is inclined to deny the naturalization application. An initial denial of the N-400 would trigger an ability to file an administrative appeal on form N-336; the statute requires administrative exhaustion before any federal appeal is filed under INA § 310.[7] Thus, the government contends that in this situation, the applicant must exhaust the administrative appeal under INA § 336 before he or she can return to federal court; and in the meantime, the case is moot. This is very inconvenient for the applicant; if USCIS is

---

[13]See App 10–6.

[Section 10:6]

[1]U.S. v. Hovsepian, 359 F.3d 1144 (9th Cir. 2004) (en banc).

[2]U.S. v. Hovsepian, 359 F.3d 1144 (9th Cir. 2004) (en banc).

[3]Etape v. Chertoff, 497 F.3d 379 (4th Cir. 2007); Bustamante v. Napolitano, 582 F.3d 403 (2d Cir. 2009); Al-Maleki v. Holder, 558 F.3d 1200 (10th Cir. 2009).

[4]See, e.g., Zaranska v. U.S. Dept. of Homeland Security, 400 F.Supp.2d 500, 502 (E.D.N.Y. Nov 10, 2005); Castracani v. Chertoff, 377 F.Supp.2d 71, 73-75 (D.D.C.2005); Meyersiek v. U.S. Citizenship and Immigration Service, 2006 WL 1582397, *2 (D.R.I. Jun 06, 2006); Meraz v. Comfort, 2006 WL 861859, *2+ (N.D.Ill. Mar 09, 2006).

[5]Etape v. Chertoff, 2006 WL 2355079, *3 (D.Md. Aug 15, 2006); Farah v. Gonzales, No. 05-1944, 2006 WL 1116526, at *1-2 (D.Minn. Apr. 26, 2006); see also Kia v. U.S. Immigration & Naturalization Serv., 175 F.3d 1014, No. 98-2399, 1999 WL 172818, at *1 (4th Cir. Mar. 30, 1999) (unpublished table decision) (published before Hovsepian, coming to a different conclusion).

[6]Al-Saleh v. Gonzales, 2007 WL 990145 (D.Utah, Mar. 29, 2007) (unpublished) (after USCIS approved application, plaintiff argued that court's jurisdiction was exclusive, asked for court order and attorney's fees; court found concurrent jurisdiction and denied relief)

[7]Sidhu v. Chertoff, 2007 WL 1119690 (E.D.Cal., Apr. 16, 2007) (unpublished).

inclined to deny the application, the most efficient route is for the case to continue in federal court if the court will undertake de novo adjudication of the case.

If, however, USCIS is inclined to approve the application, it is generally in everyone's interest that this be permitted to occur. Within the Ninth Circuit, the court's clear jurisdictional rule means that USCIS must seek remand from the district court in order to approve the application. This likely constitutes a victory for purposes of the Equal Access to Justice Act, and potentially gives the applicant an ability to seek legal fees.

In other circuits, while the jurisdictional rules are unclear, an applicant would be wise to seek remand to the Agency prior to the applicant taking the oath; or alternately, a nunc pro tunc order from the district court, dismissing the case as of a point prior to the naturalization. If USCIS is indeed stripped of jurisdiction to grant naturalization while a § 1447(b) case is pending in district court, it follows that any such grant is void. This could conceivably cause significant problems for the applicant at some future point, particularly if he or she ever runs into legal problems for which they are prosecuted.

It should be noted that the provisional approval of a naturalization application by USCIS is not probably not a final agency decision, until the oath ceremony. Thus, it constitutes no final decision in the case, and the Agency can likely interview an applicant and can make a provisional decision without violating Hovsepian. Whether it is in the interests of the applicant to cooperate in such a venture may depend on the likelihood that the case will be settled.

§ 10:7   § 1447(b) Actions—Appropriate remedies

Research References

West's Key Number Digest, Aliens ⊱68(6)

The issue of background check delay has led to a focus on the type of remedy that the district courts can afford in § 1447(b) proceedings. While the statute itself permits de novo adjudication by the district court,[1] given the statutory and regulatory requirement that background checks be complete before adjudication, courts have often preferred to remand cases to the USCIS for adjudication.[2] Indeed, a number of courts have remanded without even requiring Agency action within a set period of time.[3]

Other courts have imposed a requirement on the Agency that adjudication be completed within 120 days.[4] In some cases, the government has voluntarily agreed

---

[Section 10:7]

[1] 8 U.S.C.A. § 1447(b).

[2] El-Daour v. Chertoff, 417 F. Supp. 2d 679, 681 (W.D. Pa. 2005); Daami v. Gonzales, 2006 WL 1457862 (D.N.J. May 22, 2006); Essa v. United States Citizenship & Immigration Servs., 2005 WL 3440827 (D. Minn. Dec. 14, 2005).

[3] Essa v. USCIS, 2005 WL 3440827 (D. Minn. 2005); El-Daour v. Chertoff, 2005 WL 2106572 (W.D. Pa. 2005); Sweilem v. USCIS, 2005 WL 1123582 (N.D. Ohio May 10, 2005).

[4] Khan v. Chertoff, 2006 WL 2009055 at *2 (requiring adjudication within 120 days); Al-Kudsi v. Gonzales, 2006 WL 752556, *3 (D.Or. Mar 22, 2006) (same); Alshaif v. Cherthoff, 2007 WL 1725474 (E.D.Cal., June 14, 2007) (unpub.) (adjudication within 120 days); Majid v. U.S. Dept. of Homeland Security, 2007 WL 1725272 (D.Neb., June 12, 2007) (unpublished) (60 days); Suarez v. Barrows, 2007 WL 1624358 (N.D.Tex., June 05, 2007) (unpublished) (five weeks); Alhamedi v. Gonzales, 2007 WL 1573935 (S.D.N.Y., May 30, 2007) (unpublished) (FBI check within 30 days, USCIS adjudication

to decide within a set time period.[5] Courts that impose a time period on the Agency have held that to remand the case to USCIS without instructions for timely completion of the case would be an abdication of the court's role under § 1447(b), and an expensive reminder to the Agency to do its job.

It is unclear what standards the courts use to decide which remedies are appropriate, and when. The appellate authorities do not yet address the matter.

§ 10:8 § 1447(b) Actions—Attorneys fees

The Equal Access to Justice Act (EAJA) permits a federal court to require that the government pay attorneys fees in certain cases. Generally, EAJA fees are available where the individual was a "prevailing party" in the litigation, an award would not be unjust, and the application for fees is timely.[1] If those threshold conditions are met, the government may affirmatively defend against fees by showing that its position was "substantially justified."[2]

To be timely, an EAJA fee petition must be filed "within 30 days of final judgment."[3] Generally, entry of final judgment occurs upon the expiration of time for the filing of an appeal. The parties have 60 days to appeal from a District Court decision in which the U.S. government is a plaintiff. Thus, the EAJA petition would have to be filed from 60–90 days after a victory in District Court.

In order to be a "prevailing party" under EAJA, one must establish that a federal court's actions resulted in a "material alteration of the legal relationship of the parties" and that the alteration was "judicially sanctioned."[4] It is not sufficient that the lawsuit was the "catalyst" of a voluntary change in the government's actions; there must have been a District Court decision, order, or consent decree changing the position of the parties, sufficient to constitute a "judicial imprimatur."[5]

The government's defense of "substantial justification" requires that its position was "substantially justified," at every stage of the litigation.[6] A position that is

---

within 30 days of FBI check); Abdelbagi v. U.S. Citizenship and Immigration Service, 2007 WL 1520990 (S.D.Tex., May 22, 2007) (120 days); Alhassan v. Gonzales, 2007 WL 1455841 (D.Colo., May 16, 2007) (unpublished) (120 days); Silebi De Donado v. Swacina, 486 F. Supp. 2d 1360 (S.D. Fla. 2007) (120 days); Saleh Ali v. Gonzales, 2007 WL 1288814 (W.D.N.Y., May 1, 2007) (unpublished) (120 days); Issa v. Mueller, 486 F. Supp. 2d 668 (E.D. Mich. 2007) (120 days); Syed v. Chertoff, 2007 WL 1080100 (S.D.Tex., Apr. 09, 2007) (FBI check within 120 days); Negam v. U.S., 480 F.Supp.2d 877 (N.D.Tex. ,2007) (90 days); Mahd v. Chertoff, 2007 WL 891867 (D.Colo., Mar. 22, 2007) (unpublished) (45 days).

[5]Al Saidi v. Jenifer, 2005 U.S. Dist. LEXIS 35466, at *5 (E.D.Mich. Dec. 23, 2005) (finding jurisdiction), Al Saidi v. Jenifer, No. 05-71832, Stipulation at 1 (E.D.Mich. Mar. 13, 2006) (Hood, J.) (Agency agreed to adjudicate within 80 days); Khelifa, 433 F.Supp.2d 836, 844 (E.D.Mich. Jun 09, 2006) (Agency agreed to adjudicate within 90-120 days).

[Section 10:8]

[1]28 U.S.C. § 2412(d).

[2]28 U.S.C. § 2412(d)(1)(A).

[3]28 U.S.C § 2412(d)(1)(B).

[4]See Buckhannon Bd. & Care Home, Inc. v. W.Va. Dep't of Health & Human Res., 532 U.S. 598, 604–05, 121 S.Ct. 1835, 149 L.Ed.2d 855 (2001); Perez-Arellano v. Smith, 279 F.3d 791, 794 (9th Cir.2002) (holding that the Buckhannon rule governs an application for fees under the EAJA).

[5]Buckhannon, 532 U.S. at 605, 121 S.Ct. 1835.

[6]28 U.S.C. § 2412(d); Corbin v. Apfel, 149 F.3d 1051, 1052 (9th Cir.1998).

substantially justified is one that is "justified in substance or in the main" or "justified to a degree that could satisfy a reasonable person."[7]

Petitioners who have obtained naturalization after bringing a § 1447(b) action have had variable success obtaining EAJA-based attorneys fees. Because the background checks often clear at some point during the litigation, these cases often resolve by agreement. Where the parties have jointly sought remand for the purpose of actually naturalizing the petitioner on a date certain, many courts (including the Tenth Circuit) have found that to be a material alteration making the petitioner a prevailing party.[8] However, other courts (including the First Circuit) have held that similar remand orders do not make the petitioner a prevailing party, because they simply reflected a joint decision of the parties.[9]

Another split in the case law concerns whether the government's delay in adjudicating these cases is "substantially justified." Some courts have held that the statutory prohibition on naturalization renders the agency's delay justified, or at least a reasonable interpretation of the statute.[10] Even if the government's litigation position is not unreasonable, the "substantial justification" defense also requires that the government's pre-litigation was reasonable; most courts granting EAJA fees have found unreasonableness in the government's failure to comply with statutory and regulatory deadlines, or even to explain its failure to do so.[11]

EAJA procedures also require documentation of the time expended on litigation, and impose statutory limits on fees, which may be exceeded in certain circumstances. The American Immigration Law Foundation has published a practice advisory on seeking EAJA fees, which provides a useful guide to such requests.[12]

§ 10:9 Mandamus—Delays prior to USCIS examination or hearing

Research References

West's Key Number Digest, Aliens ⬤⟶68(6)

In response to the torrent of § 1447(b) cases being filed in district court due to

---

[7]Pierce v. Underwood, 487 U.S. 552, 565 (1988).

[8]See Al-Maleki v. Holder, 558 F.3d 1200 (10th Cir. 2009); Ghanim v. Mukasey, 545 F.Supp.2d 1146, 1150 (W.D.Wash.2008) (holding that the plaintiff was a prevailing party where CIS did not voluntarily naturalize the plaintiff but was compelled to do so by court's order remanding case to CIS with explicit instructions to adjudicate the application by a date certain); Aboushaban v. Mueller, 475 F.Supp.2d 943, 946 (N.D.Cal.2007) (holding that plaintiff who obtained court order requiring CIS to adjudicate the plaintiff's application was prevailing party); Lord v. Chertoff, 526 F. Supp. 435, 438 (S.D.N.Y. 2007) (court approved consent agreement for USCIS to approve naturalization application satisfied Buckhannon standard because court retained jurisdiction to enforce the agreement if necessary); Berishev v. Chertoff, 486 F. Supp. 2d 202, 204–05 (D.Mass. 2007) (conciliatory remand order for adjudication of naturalization application satisfied Buckhannon Court's interpretation of "prevailing party"); Shalash v. Mukasey, 576 F.Supp.2d 902 (N.D.Ill. 2008).

[9]Aronov v. Napolitano, 562 F.3d 84 (1st Cir. 2009); Wagner v. Chertoff, 607 F.Supp.2d 1192 (D.Nev. 2009).

[10]Aronov v. Napolitano, 562 F.3d 84 (1st Cir. 2009); Wagner v. Chertoff, 607 F.Supp.2d 1192 (D.Nev. 2009).

[11]See, e.g., Shalash, 576 F.Supp.2d at 910; Ghanim, 545 F.Supp.2d at 1151 (holding that CIS's delay in processing the plaintiff's naturalization application was not substantially justified where defendants argued that they could not adjudicate the application until the name check was complete, but they failed to explain why the name check was delayed).

[12]"Practice Advisory: Requesting Attorney's Fees Under the Equal Access to Justice Act," found at http://www.legalactioncenter.org/sites/default/files/EAJA_Fees_04_07_06.pdf (last accessed June 27, 2011).

background checks, in 2006 the USCIS issued a memorandum reemphasizing that naturalization interviews should not even be scheduled until the background checks have been completed.[1] This had always been the official USCIS position, required by regulation;[2] but it was rarely enforced.

Where delays occur prior to the first interview, applicants will be unable to take advantage of the clear jurisdictional grant of 8 U.S.C.A. § 1447(b), because no interview will begin the 120–day clock. The only potential remedy in such a circumstance will likely be mandamus review.

Another situation where mandamus may be necessary is for applicants whose initial case has been denied, who are awaiting administrative review after filing form N-336.[3] While the regulations require that such hearings be conducted within 180 days,[4] in practice, the USCIS often takes much longer. Because jurisdiction under § 1447(b) is likely foreclosed by the denial, the only option for an applicant would be to seek relief in mandamus. It should be noted that in the latter circumstance, the deadline would likely impose a duty on the Agency, sufficient to satisfy the mandamus requirements.

§ 10:10   Mandamus—Nature of mandamus

Research References

West's Key Number Digest, Aliens ☞68(6)

Mandamus[1] actions are a long-standing form of relief that allows applicants to compel an officer or employee of the USCIS (or any other government agency) to perform a duty that is not discretionary.[2] They are typically filed, in this context, against a local USCIS official to compel them to adjudicate the application.[3]

The plaintiff in a mandamus case asks the federal court to order the USCIS official to perform his or her duty, in this case, to adjudicate the naturalization application.[4] In mandamus cases, generally, the plaintiff does not ask the court to approve or deny the underlying application, but solely to order the USCIS to

---

[Section 10:9]

[1]See Michael Ayles, "Background Checks and Naturalization Scheduling," Apr. 25, 2006, reproduced at Appendix 10-7.

[2]8 C.F.R. § 335.2(b).

[3]See §§ 9:67 to 9:68.

[4]8 C.F.R. § 336.2(b).

[Section 10:10]

[1]See generally, Mautino, How to Move Cases in the New World of Naturalization, in 1998-99 Immigration and Nationality Law Handbook, Vol. II - Advanced Practice, 433 (Murphy, et al., ed. 1998).

[2]28 U.S.C.A. § 1361.

[3]Jeffrey v. INS, 710 F.Supp. 486 (S.D.N.Y. 1989). For a general discussion of mandamus actions, see Kurzban, Immigration Law Sourcebook, 623- 24 (7th ed. 2000).

[4]Mautino, How to Move Cases in the New World of Naturalization, in 1998-99 Immigration and Nationality Law Handbook, Vol. II - Advanced Practice, 434 (Murphy, et al., ed. 1998).

adjudicate it.[5] Equal Access to Justice Act (EAJA) fees have been awarded in successful mandamus actions for inaction against the agency.[6]

While the simple filing of a mandamus complaint sometimes triggers a positive administrative resolution of the case, if the case goes forward the petitioner will require a theory for why the government owes a duty to adjudicate an individual's application within a set period of time. The government is likely to respond by citing its Congressional mandate to conduct background checks on individuals.[7]

In general, many courts find that an Agency has an obligation to act within a "reasonable" time period.[8] However, some courts have declined to find an enforceable duty to adjudicate promptly in the immigration or naturalization context.[9] Moreover, Congress has established a statutory expectation that naturalization applications be completed within six months of filing.[10] That statutory provision may be used to give specific substance to the general reasonableness requirement. As noted above, where the delay occurs between the filing of an administrative appeal and the hearing on that appeal, the petitioner can cite the regulations as setting a mandatory time period within which the hearing should occur.[11]

§ 10:11   Mandamus—Procedures

Research References

West's Key Number Digest, Aliens ⚏68(6)

Mandamus actions are filed with the district court having jurisdiction over the DHS District Director who has failed to act.[1] The defendants in a mandamus action are the individual government actors (sued in their official capacity). The petitioner may also want to name the Attorney General as a defendant, as the statute confers on the Attorney General "the sole authority to naturalize persons as citizens of the United States."[2] Moreover, where the FBI name check is the main cause of delay, it would be wise to name the FBI director, Robert Mueller, III.

---

[5]Mautino, How to Move Cases in the New World of Naturalization, in 1998-99 Immigration and Nationality Law Handbook, Vol. II - Advanced Practice, 434 (Murphy, et al., ed. 1998); Kurzban, Immigration Law Sourcebook, 623 (7th ed. 2000) citing to Patel v. Reno, 134 F.3d 929 (9th Cir. 1998) (while no jurisdiction may exist to review the correctness of the decision, the regulations require consular officers to issue a decision).

[6]Nong v. Reno, 28 F. Supp. 2d 27 (D.D.C. 1998); Harriott v. Ashcroft, 277 F. Supp. 2d 538 (E.D. Pa. 2003).

[7]Pub.L. 105-119, Title I, Nov. 26, 1997, 111 Stat. 2448.

[8]See, Telecommunications Research & Action Ctr. v. FCC, 750 F.2d 70, 80 (D.C.Cir.1984).

[9]Bian v. Clinton, 605 F.3d 249 (5th Cir. 2010), vacated on other grounds, 2010 WL 3633770 (5th Cir. 2010) (denying mandamus, finding no duty to adjudicate application for adjustment of status within a reasonable time); Saini v. Heinauer, 552 F. Supp. 2d 974 (D. Neb. 2008) (finding no duty in mandamus or APA to adjudicate naturalization application); Alzuraiki v. Heinauer, 544 F. Supp. 2d 862 (D. Neb. 2008) (same).

[10]8 U.S.C.A. § 1571(b) ("[i]t is the sense of Congress that the processing of an immigration benefit application should be completed not later than 180 days after the initial filing of the application").

[11]8 C.F.R. § 336.2(b) (requiring examination within 180 days).

[Section 10:11]

[1]Mautino, How to Move Cases in the New World of Naturalization, in 1998-99 Immigration and Nationality Law Handbook, Vol. II - Advanced Practice, 434 (Murphy, et al., ed. 1998).

[2]8 U.S.C.A. § 1421(a).

The first step in commencing a mandamus action is to file a complaint.[3] A sample complaint is reproduced as Appendix 10- 3. A summons should accompany the complaint, so that the clerk of the court can issue it.[4] A sample summons is reproduced below as Appendix 10-4, but many district courts have their own forms, which should be used instead.

Once the complaint is filed and the summons is issued, they both must be served on the local USCIS District Director. Service upon any officer or agency of the U.S. is effected by delivering a copy of the summons and complaint to the U.S. Attorney for the district in which the action is brought and, in addition, by sending a copy of the summons and the complaint by registered or certified mail to the Secretary of DHS in Washington, DC, and another copy, also by registered or certified mail to the USCIS District director.[5] Service must take place within 120 days from the filing of the action and proof of service must be filed with the court.[6]

The government must file an answer within 60 days from the service of the summons and complaint.[7] This period is counted from the service upon the district's U.S. Attorney's office.[8]

Once the complaint and summons are filed, the U.S. Attorney's office will generally contact the USCIS district office to obtain a report on the case.[9] The request will normally come to the attention of the persons in charge in the naturalization unit. If the USCIS concludes that the case has been misplaced, misdelievered, or otherwise mishandled, the USCIS may take corrective action.[10]

§ 10:12 Naturalization denials—Jurisdiction

Research References

Immigration Law Service (2d ed.) § 14:350
Steel on Immigration Law § 15:23
West's Key Number Digest, Aliens ⊜68(6)

Applicants who are denied naturalization after the administrative review procedures may seek judicial review in the federal district court where the person resides.[1] The district court review must be in accordance with 5 U.S.C.A. §§ 701 to

---

[3]Fed.R.Civ.P. 3.

[4]Fed.R.Civ.P. 4(b).

[5]Fed.R.Civ.P. 4(i)(1), (2). In 6 C.F.R. § 5:42(a), DHS instructs that service of a summons and complaint in a suit against DHS is to be sent to the Office of the General Counsel, U.S. Department of Homeland Security, Washington, D.C. 20258. The postal service indicates that no such zip code exists, however, and thus this appears to be a typographical error. The DHS website lists the zip code as 20528.

[6]Fed.R.Civ.P. 4(l), (m).

[7]Fed.R.Civ.P. 12(a)(3).

[8]Fed.R.Civ.P. 12(a)(3).

[9]Mautino, How to Move Cases in the New World of Naturalization, in 1998-99 Immigration and Nationality Law Handbook, Vol. II - Advanced Practice, 434 (Murphy, et al., ed. 1998).

[10]Mautino, How to Move Cases in the New World of Naturalization, in 1998-99 Immigration and Nationality Law Handbook, Vol. II - Advanced Practice, 434 (Murphy, et al., ed. 1998).

[Section 10:12]

[1]INA § 310(c), 8 U.S.C.A. § 1421(c), 8 CFR § 310.5(b).

706.[2] The regulations provide that this is the sole and exclusive procedure to obtain judicial review of USCIS naturalization determinations.[3]

§ 10:13   Naturalization denials—Exhaustion of administrative remedies

Research References

West's Key Number Digest, Aliens ⛭68(6)

The law and the regulations require the applicant to seek administrative review of a naturalization denial before seeking judicial review under INA § 310(c).[1]

§ 10:14   Naturalization denials—Judicial review

Research References

West's Key Number Digest, Aliens ⛭68(6)

Judicial review of a final administrative denial of naturalization is de novo, and the district court has to make its own findings of fact and conclusions of law.[1] If the petitioner so requests, the court will also conduct a hearing on the de novo application.[2]

§ 10:15   Naturalization denials—Procedures

Research References

West's Key Number Digest, Aliens ⛭68(6)

An applicant seeking judicial review of a naturalization denial must file a petition for review with the U.S. district court having jurisdiction over his or her place of residence.[1] The regulations provide that this petition must be filed no later than 120 days after the USCIS' denial of the request for review.[2] However, the Tenth Circuit has held that the INA did not grant the agency the authority to establish an appeal deadline for judicial review.[3] The court concluded that, absent such an express delegation from Congress, an administrative agency cannot "create a limitations period affecting the ability of an Article III court to review agency action."[4] Because there was no statute of limitations set by Congress, the court applied the six-year statute of limitations found in 28 U.S.C.A. § 2401, which is applicable to civil ac-

---

[2]INA § 311(c), 8 U.S.C.A. § 1421(c).

[3]8 CFR § 336.9(a).

[Section 10:13]

[1]8 U.S.C.A. § 1421(c); 8 CFR § 336.9(d). Note, however, that exhaustion of the administrative appeal is not a prerequisite for judicial review under INA § 336(b), 8 U.S.C.A. § 1447(b). See § 10:4 for a discussion of when suit can be filed under INA § 336(b).

[Section 10:14]

[1]INA § 310(c), 8 U.S.C.A. § 1421(c).

[2]INA § 310(c), 8 U.S.C.A. § 1421(c).

[Section 10:15]

[1]8 U.S.C.A. § 1421(c); 8 CFR § 336.9(b).

[2]8 CFR § 336.9(b).

[3]Nagahi v. I.N.S., 219 F.3d 1166 (10th Cir. 2000).

[4]Nagahi v. I.N.S., 219 F.3d 1166, 1167 (10th Cir. 2000).

tions against the United States under the Administrative Procedures Act.[5] The DHS and USCIS are the defendants in these petitions and the regulations require that both the Secretary of the Department of Homeland Security and the official in charge of the USCIS office that denied the administrative review be served with a copy of the petition.[6] All petitions for review must include a statement that the administrative review proceedings have been exhausted.[7]

The proceedings in district court follow the usual rules for litigation of civil actions, including the availability of summary judgment to resolve the case.[8]

§ 10:16 Naturalization denials—Reports and records

Research References

West's Key Number Digest, Aliens ⬉68(6)

The clerk of the district court is required to submit to the USCIS district director having jurisdiction over the place where the court is located a monthly report with the name of all persons who have filed petitions to review with the court.[1] The monthly report must include the petitioner's name, "alien" registration number, date of filing of the petition for a de novo review, and, once an order has been entered, the disposition of the case.[2]

§ 10:17 Naturalization denials—Remedies

Research References

Steel on Immigration Law § 15:23

The law provides that judicial review of naturalization denials must be in accordance with Chapter 7 of Title 5 of the United States Code.[1] As part of this authority, at least one court found that it had the power to order the INS (now USCIS) to schedule the taking of the oath ceremony within a specific amount of time.[2]

§ 10:18 Naturalization denials—In removal proceedings

Research References

Immigration Law Service (2d ed.) § 14:350
Steel on Immigration Law § 15:23

---

[5]Nagahi v. I.N.S., 219 F.3d 1166, 1171 (10th Cir. 2000). Of course, the court's holding is only binding in the Tenth Circuit. Thus, in all other circuits, the safest course is to file the appeal within 120 days of the USCIS denial of the request for review.

[6]8 CFR § 336.9(b).

[7]See 8 CFR § 336.9(d).

[8]See, Kariuki v. Tarango, 709 F.3d 495, 84 Fed. R. Serv. 3d 1458 (5th Cir. 2013); Chan v. Gantner, 464 F.3d 289, 295–96 (2d Cir. 2006) (per curiam); Abulkhair v. Bush, 413 Fed. Appx. 502, 507–08 n.4 (3d Cir. 2011), cert. denied, 131 S. Ct. 2884, 179 L. Ed. 2d 1197 (2011) (per curiam) (unpublished); Cernuda v. Neufeld, 307 Fed. Appx. 427, 431 n.2 (11th Cir. 2009) (per curiam) (unpublished).

[Section 10:16]

[1]8 CFR § 339.2(b).

[2]INA § 339(a)(3), 8 U.S.C.A. § 1450(a)(3); 8 CFR § 339.2(b).

[Section 10:17]

[1]INA § 310(c), 8 U.S.C.A. § 1421(c).

[2]Ali v. Smith, Case No. C99-131Z (W.D. Wash. April 21, 1999).

West's Key Number Digest, Aliens ⚷68(6)

With the transfer of naturalization authority from the District Courts to the former INS in 1990, an ambiguity was created with regard to INA § 318, which provides that "no application for naturalization shall be considered by the Attorney General if there is pending against the applicant a removal proceeding.".[1] That section used to refer specifically to the district courts, and was held to be a jurisdictional bar.[2] However, the statute currently applies on its face only to USCIS. Thus, applicants have plausibly sought district court intervention notwithstanding ongoing removal proceedings.

The Courts of Appeals are split on this issue. The Fourth and Fifth Circuits hold that federal courts lack jurisdiction over naturalization matters once removal proceedings have begun.[3] The Second, Sixth, and Ninth Circuits find federal court jurisdiction, but hold that there is no remedy which can be afforded an applicant once removal proceedings have begun.[4] However, the Third and Seventh Circuits have ruled differently.

The Third Circuit finds that it has both jurisdiction and the ability to grant relief, in the form of Declaratory Judgment.[5] The Third Circuit reasons that while the federal courts cannot order naturalization while removal proceedings are ongoing, that declaratory relief "strikes a balance between the petitioner's right to full judicial review . . . and the priority of removal proceedings enshrined in § 1429."[6] To find the courts closed to review in such cases would permit DHS to eliminate federal court review simply by instituting removal proceedings, but Congress intended that the agency not be the final word on naturalization eligibility.[7] Declaratory relief, considering the lawfulness of the denial of naturalization, held the Third Circuit, "permits the alien a day in court, . . . while not upsetting the priority of removal over naturalization established in § 1429 because it affects the record for— but not the priority of—removal proceedings, thereby preserving both congressionally mandated goals, a de novo review process and the elimination of the race to the courthouse."[8] The Third Circuit noted the potential effects of a declaratory judgment on potential termination of removal proceedings, but did not base its decision upon that fact.[9] The Seventh Circuit agrees.[10]

[Section 10:18]

[1]8 U.S.C.A. § 1429.

[2]See Petition for Naturalization of Terzich, 256 F.2d 197 (3d Cir.1958).

[3]Barnes v. Holder, 625 F.3d 801 (4th Cir.2010); Saba-Bakare v. Chertoff, 507 F.3d 337 (5th Cir. 2007).

[4]Zayed v. U.S., 368 F.3d 902, 2004 FED App. 0149P (6th Cir. 2004); De Lara Bellajaro v. Schiltgen, 378 F.3d 1042, 1045 (9th Cir. 2004), as amended, (Sept. 1, 2004); Saba-Bakare v. Chertoff, 507 F.3d 337, 341 (5th Cir. 2007); Ajlani v. Chertoff, 545 F.3d 229 (2d Cir. 2008). Several district courts have held similarly. Mosleh v. Strapp, 992 F. Supp. 874 (N.D. Tex. 1998); Apokarina v. Ashcroft, 232 F. Supp. 2d 414 (E.D. Pa. 2002); Robertson-Dewar v. Mukasey, 599 F. Supp. 2d 772 (W.D. Tex. 2009).

[5]Gonzalez v. Secretary of Dept. of Homeland Sec., 678 F.3d 254 (3d Cir. 2012).

[6]Gonzalez v. Secretary of Dept. of Homeland Sec., 678 F.3d 254, 260 (3d Cir. 2012).

[7]Gonzalez v. Secretary of Dept. of Homeland Sec., 678 F.3d 254, 260 (3d Cir. 2012).

[8]Gonzalez v. Secretary of Dept. of Homeland Sec., 678 F.3d 254, 260 (3d Cir. 2012).

[9]Gonzalez v. Secretary of Dept. of Homeland Sec., 678 F.3d 254, 260 (3d Cir. 2012).

[10]Klene v. Napolitano, 697 F.3d 666 (7th Cir. 2012).

Several district court decisions have endorsed similar reasoning.[11] At least one district court has held that de novo review over the naturalization application is available even in cases where the naturalization was filed after the institution of removal proceedings.[12]

That said, one of the main objectives for many of the petitioners in these cases was a declaration that the applicant was to support termination of removal proceedings. The regulations permit termination of removal proceedings for individuals who are "prima facie" eligible to naturalize,[13] and prior Board case law required that finding to come from either a District Court or the former INS (i.e., it barred the immigration judge from making such a finding).[14] However, the Board has now withdrawn from its prior suggestion that a district court could find someone prima facie eligible.[15] This renders District Court intervention of less potential value.

This might seem to reduce the need for District Court intervention; however, inasmuch as USCIS is often disinclined to affirmatively state a person's eligibility, District Courts may be the only possible route for many applicants. The Third Circuit has implied that the Board would also have to accept a declaratory judgment by a District Court, stating "[w]e are confident that the BIA would also accept the declaration of a district court properly exercising its jurisdiction under 8 U.S.C. § 1421(c)."[16]

§ 10:19 Termination of removal proceedings—Determination of "prima facie eligibility"

Research References

Steel on Immigration Law § 15:23
West's Key Number Digest, Aliens ⟳68(6)

Many applicants who are denied naturalization will be placed in removal proceedings. In most instances in which an applicant appears deportable to the naturalization examiner, there will not even be a formal denial. The INS Operations Instructions require examiners to refer all cases where the applicant appears deportable for issuance of an order to show cause.[1] This means that the naturalization case will then be stayed pending removal proceedings.[2] Once the DHS has filed a Notice to Appear with the court, only the immigration judge may terminate removal

---

[11]See, e.g., Ngwana v. Attorney General of U.S., 40 F. Supp. 2d 319 (D. Md. 1999); Saad v. Barrows, 2004 WL 1359165 (N.D. Tex. 2004); Grewal v. Ashcroft, 301 F. Supp. 2d 692 (N.D. Ohio 2004); Kestelboym v. Chertoff, 538 F. Supp. 2d 813 (D.N.J. 2008).

[12]Gatcliffe v. Reno, 39 V.I. 423, 23 F. Supp. 2d 581 (D.V.I. 1998).

[13]8 C.F.R. § 1239.2(f).

[14]Matter of Cruz, 17 I&N Dec. 236 (BIA 1975).

[15]Matter of Acosta Hidalgo, 24 I&N Dec. 103, 105 (BIA 2007).

[16]Gonzalez v. Secretary of Dept. of Homeland Sec., 678 F.3d 254, 260 (3d Cir. 2012).

[Section 10:19]

[1]INS OI 318.1.

[2]INA § 318, 8 U.S.C.A. § 1429 (prohibiting USCIS from considering applications for naturalization while deportation proceedings are pending).

proceedings.[3] Even if the DHS wishes to cancel the notice, the immigration judge is not required to terminate.[4]

The law contemplates the possibility of termination of removal proceedings to allow naturalization.[5] The regulations specifically provide that immigration judges are empowered to terminate removal proceedings to allow respondent to proceed to a final hearing on a naturalization application when the respondent has established prima facie eligibility for naturalization and the matter involves exceptionally appealing or humanitarian factors.[6]

The BIA has held, however, that the immigration judge cannot make an independent finding of prima facie eligibility for naturalization. In order to terminate proceedings, the immigration judge has to receive a communication from USCIS declaring that the noncitizen is prima facie eligible for naturalization but for the pendency of deportation (removal) proceedings.[7]

Prior BIA case law would also have permitted a "prima facie" finding to have been communicated from a district court, because the earlier case law arose before the USCIS took over responsibility for naturalization.[8] Thus, some applicants argued that district courts had jurisdiction to declare them prima facie eligible for naturalization, aside from the pending removal proceedings. Some courts have found this power,[9] but most have not.[10]

Petitioners in several cases have argued that IJs must have authority to find prima facie eligibility, because otherwise, DHS would have effective veto power over termination under § 1239.2(f). The circuits have thus far universally upheld the Board's interpretation, and rejected the proposition that IJs could find prima facie eligibility on their own.[11] Indeed, the Second Circuit has gone farther, interpreting § 1429 to bar USCIS from making the affirmative communication required by § 1239.2(f): "the agency could not provide an 'affirmative communication,' because § 1429 prohibited it from considering Perriello's naturalization application while removal proceedings were pending."[12] The Third Circuit agrees that USCIS would appear forbidden to make such a declaration, but has found that federal district courts may do so.[13]

---

[3]In re G-N-C, 22 I. & N. Dec. 281, 1998 WL 646918 (B.I.A. 1998).

[4]Matter of G-N-C-, 22 I. & N. Dec. 281 (B.I.A. 1998).

[5]See § 8:31.

[6]8 CFR § 1239.2(f); INS Interp. 318.2(c)(ii).

[7]Matter of Hidalgo, 24 I. & N. Dec. 103, 2007 WL 708026 (B.I.A. 2007).

[8]Matter of Cruz, 15 I. & N. Dec. 236 (BIA 1975).

[9]Gonzalez v. Secretary of Dept. of Homeland Sec., 678 F.3d 254, 260 (3d Cir. 2012); Gatcliffe v. Reno, 23 F.Supp.2d 581 (D.V.I. 1998).

[10]Saba-Bakare v. Chertoff, 507 F.3d 337 (5th Cir. 2007).

De Lara Bellajaro v. Schiltgen, 378 F.3d 1042, 1044 (9th Cir. 2004); Apokarina v. Ashcroft, 232 F.Supp. 2d 414 (E.D. Pa. 2002); Levy v. I.N.S., 6 Fed. Appx. 331 (7th Cir. 2001), cert. denied, 122 S. Ct. 138, 151 L. Ed. 2d 91 (U.S. 2001) (unpublished) (questioning Cruz because "only Congress—not an administrative agency—can confer jurisdiction on a federal court").

[11]Hernandez de Anderson v. Gonzales, 497 F.3d 927, 934 (9th Cir.2007); Ogunfuye v. Holder, 610 F.3d 303 (5th Cir. 2010); Perriello v. Napolitano, 579 F.3d 135, 142 (2d Cir.2009); Zegrean v. Att'y Gen. of United States, 602 F.3d 273, 274 to 275 (3d Cir.2010).

[12]Perriello v. Napolitano, 579 F.3d 135, 141 (2d Cir.2009).

[13]Zegrean v. Att'y Gen. of United States, 602 F.3d 273, 274 (3d Cir.2010) ("But if an application for naturalization cannot even be considered while a removal proceeding is pending, how, then, can the

II. JUDICIAL REVIEW OTHER CITIZENSHIP MATTERS

§ 10:20 Judicial declaration of citizenship—General principles

Research References

West's Key Number Digest, Citizens ☞10.1, 13, 13.1
Immigration Law Service (2d ed.) § 14:68

Persons inside the U.S. who have been denied any right or privilege enjoyed by nationals of the U.S., may file an action for a declaration of U.S. nationality.[1] These actions are only available if the right or privilege was denied by a governmental department or agency, and must be filed within five years of the final administrative denial of right or privilege.[2] They are filed in the U.S. district court for the district in which the person resides.[3]

This procedure, however, is not available either for review of removal proceedings or if the citizenship of the person is already being litigated in removal proceedings.[4] In such cases, the review of final administrative orders of exclusion must be sought as part of a habeas corpus action in district court,[5] or through a petition for review of a final order of removal.[6] Of course, where citizenship was an issue in removal proceedings which terminated favorably to the (alleged) alien, there was thus no opportunity to litigate at the Board or before the Court of Appeals, so it would be illogical for INA § 360(a) to bar a declaratory action in that situation.[7]

In addition, the provisions of INA § 360(a) facially apply only to individuals within the U.S.,[8] and it is unclear whether an individual outside the U.S. would

---

requisite 'affirmative communication regarding [an alien's] prima facie eligibility for naturalization" be provided such that an immigration judge can decide whether removal proceedings may be terminated? The obvious answer is, 'It can't.'"") (citations omitted); Gonzalez v. Secretary of Dept. of Homeland Sec., 678 F.3d 254, 260 (3d Cir. 2012) (finding that District Courts have the authority to grant declaratory judgment as to naturalization eligibility).

[Section 10:20]

[1]INA § 360(a), 8 U.S.C.A. § 1503(a).

[2]INA § 360(a), 8 U.S.C.A. § 1503(a).

[3]INA § 360(a), 8 U.S.C.A. § 1503(a).

[4]INA § 360(a), 8 U.S.C.A. § 1503(a) as amended by Illegal Immigration Reform and Immigrant Responsibility Act of 1996, Pub.L. 104-208, § 308(d)(4)(P), (Sept. 30, 1996).

Indeed, the Fifth Circuit refused to permit litigation relating to an N-600, even where prior removal proceedings had been terminated without prejudice, because the citizenship issue first "arose" in the context of removal proceedings, and did not "find[] its genesis" outside of them. Rios-Valenzuela v. Department of Homeland Sec., 506 F.3d 393, 398–99 (5th Cir. 2007). Cf. North v. Rooney, 2003 WL 21432590, at *4 (D.N.J. June 18, 2003) ("With no removal proceedings presently ongoing at this time, this action seeking judicial review by declaratory judgment does not likely 'arise out of, or in connection with' a removal proceeding.").

[5]INA § 360(c), 8 U.S.C.A. § 1503(c).

[6]See 8 U.S.C.A. § 1252(b); see also § 15:26.

[7]Ortega v. Holder, 592 F.3d 738, 744 to 745 (7th Cir. 2010) ("it would be disrespectful to impute to Congress a desire to leave someone in Ms. Ortega's situation permanently out in the cold").

[8]INA § 360(a)[8 U.S.C.A. § 1503(a)]. A number of courts have held that temporary admission into the U.S. does not permit an action under this section, Ferretti v. Dulles, 246 F.2d 544 (2d Cir. 1957); Ficano v. Dulles, 151 F. Supp. 650 (E.D. N.Y. 1954); Basma Abed Harake v. Dulles, 158 F. Supp. 413 (E.D. Mich. 1958); Rosasco v. Brownell, 163 F. Supp. 45 (E.D. N.Y. 1958), though it should be noted that these decisions all predate the subsequent Supreme Court decision in Rusk v. Cort, 369 U.S. 367 (1962).

have a right to file a declaratory action regarding their citizenship.[9] Some people alleging U.S. citizenship outside the U.S. may seek a "certificate of identity" to permit them to travel to the U.S., where they may then seek to vindicate their U.S. citizenship; that process is discussed below.[10]

A judicial declaration of citizenship would appear to be the means of appealing a denial of a U.S. passport, denial of an N-600 application for a certificate of citizenship, or a finding of loss of nationality;[11] and the author sees no reason it could not also be used in the case of denial of voting rights, denial of employment authorization, denial of a social security card, or the issuance of an immigration detainer for someone allegedly removable (but who is not placed immediately into removal proceedings).

In theory, each denial of a benefit of citizenship would give rise to a separate cause of action under INA § 360(a); but at least one court has suggested that laches might apply where the alleged citizen has delayed in vindicating his or her rights.[12]

Finally, it should be noted that the purpose of the statute is to determine citizenship, not to rule on questions of procedural regularity. If the district court determines as a matter of law that one of the requirements for citizenship is lacking, it has no discretion to find that the cancellation of the certificate of citizenship did not satisfy the requirements of INA § 342.[13]

§ 10:21 Judicial declaration of citizenship—Finality and exhaustion of administrative remedies

By statute, any federal court action to challenge a denial of a right or privilege of citizenship "may be instituted only within five years after the final administrative denial of such right or privilege."[1] This has been held by the courts to require exhaustion of available administrative remedies before instituting an action in

---

[9]In Rusk v. Cort, 369 U.S. 367 (1962), the Supreme Court interpreted the Administrative Procedures Act not to require an individual claiming citizenship to return to the United States in order to litigate the matter. Id. At 375 (rejecting the argument that "Congress intended that a native of this country living abroad must travel thousands of miles, be arrested, and go to jail in order to attack an administrative finding that he is not a citizen of the United States"). However, the Rusk Court's analysis presupposed that the Administrative Procedures Act was a grant of jurisdiction, a view rejected by the Court in Califano v. Sanders, 430 U.S. 99, 105 (1977); as such, some courts have expressed some doubts as to the continuing validity of the *Rusk* rule. See, Bensky v. Powell, 391 F.3d 894, 896 (7th Cir. 2004) (Posner, J.).

[10]See § 10:26.

[11]See, e.g., Whitehead v. Haig, 794 F.2d 115 (3d Cir. 1986) (passport denial); Maldonado-Sanchez v. Shultz, 706 F. Supp. 54 (D.D.C. 1989) (same); Heuer v. United States Secretary of State, 20 F.3d 424 (11th Cir. 1994) (certificate of loss of nationality); Garcia-Sarquiz v. Saxbe, 407 F. Supp. 789 (S.D. Fla. 1974), aff'd sub nom. Garcia-Sarquiz v. Levi, 527 F.2d 1389 (5th Cir. 1976) (per curiam) (same); Friend v. Reno, 172 F.3d 638, 647 (9th Cir. 1999), cert. denied, 528 U.S. 1163, 120 S. Ct. 1180, 145 L. Ed. 2d 1087 (2000) (cancellation of certificate of citizenship).

[12]Bensky v. Powell, 391 F.3d 894, 898 (7th Cir. 2004) (Posner, J.).

[13]Friend v. Reno, 172 F.3d 638, 647 (9th Cir. 1999), cert. denied, 528 U.S. 1163, 120 S. Ct. 1180, 145 L. Ed. 2d 1087 (2000).

[Section 10:21]

[1]INA § 360(a), 8 U.S.C.A. § 1503(a).

district court, at least to the extent of requiring any appeals made available by the agency.[2]

What constitutes a "final administrative denial" depends on the agency. For instance, denial of a certificate of citizenship by USCIS triggers the right to appeal to the Administrative Appeals Unit (AAU).[3]

By contrast, the State Department has no formal administrative appeal process for denials of passports, having abolished the Board of Appellate Review.[4] Thus, a denial of a passport, and similar Department of State actions premised on lack of citizenship, would trigger an immediate ability to sue in federal court.[5]

By regulation, an individual could seek reconsideration or reopening with the AAU.[6] Such a motion would not affect the finality of the earlier AAU decision, unless granted. However, it is an interesting question whether a motion to reopen would be required if the claimant wished to raise facts or arguments not previously raised to the agency. In other contexts, courts have required that arguments be raised in some form or other before the agency, in order to exhaust administrative remedies.[7]

As a technical matter, the statute requires a "final administrative denial"; it does not clearly require exhaustion of administrative remedies. The absence of an explicit exhaustion requirement might permit excusal of exhaustion by the courts.[8] But if exhaustion is indeed required, it might be obligatory to ensure that all arguments and relevant facts were raised to the agency.

§ 10:22 Judicial declaration of citizenship—Agency deference principles

In general, the federal courts defer to agency interpretations of ambiguous statutory provisions when the agency is given authority to interpret that statute.[1] The strongest form of deference is known as "Chevron deference," after a landmark case by that name.[2] Chevron deference applies where the agency has issued a formal, binding interpretation, either by regulation or by precedential decision of e.g., the

---

[2]See, Johnson v. Whitehead, 647 F.3d 120, 125 (4th Cir. 2011), cert. denied, 132 S. Ct. 1005, 181 L. Ed. 2d 734 (2012); U.S. v. Breyer, 41 F.3d 884, 892 (3d Cir. 1994); Whitehead v. Haig, 794 F.2d 115, 119 (3d Cir. 1986).

[3]See 8 C.F.R. §§ 103.3(a)(2)(i), 341.5(d).

[4]See, 273 Fed. Reg. 41256 to 41258 (July 18, 2008) (supplementary information).

[5]See Bensky v. Powell, 391 F.3d 894, 898, 12 A.L.R. Fed. 2d 859 (7th Cir. 2004).

[6]8 C.F.R. § 103.5.

[7]See, e.g., Puga v. Chertoff, 488 F.3d 812 (9th Cir. 2007) (a motion to reopen is not mandatory because not available "as of right," but may be required prudentially); Bonhometre v. Gonzales, 414 F.3d 442, 446 (3d Cir. 2005); Padilla v. Gonzales, 470 F.3d 1209, 1213–14 (7th Cir. 2006) (requiring motion to reopen where issue not previously argued); Ghaffar v. Mukasey, 551 F.3d 651, 655 (7th Cir. 2008) (same).

[8]Cf. "[E]xhaustion of administrative remedies is required where Congress imposes an exhaustion requirement by statute." Coit Independence Joint Venture v. Federal Sav. and Loan Ins. Corp., 489 U.S. 561, 579, 109 S. Ct. 1361, 103 L. Ed. 2d 602 (1989).

[Section 10:22]

[1]Chevron, U.S.A., Inc. v. Natural Resources Defense Council, Inc., 467 U.S. 837, 104 S. Ct. 2778, 81 L. Ed. 2d 694, 21 Env't. Rep. Cas. (BNA) 1049, 14 Envtl. L. Rep. 20507 (1984).

[2]Chevron, U.S.A., Inc. v. Natural Resources Defense Council, Inc., 467 U.S. 837, 104 S. Ct. 2778, 81 L. Ed. 2d 694, 21 Env't. Rep. Cas. (BNA) 1049, 14 Envtl. L. Rep. 20507 (1984).

Board of Immigration Appeals.[3] Where Chevron applies, it consists of two steps: (1) determining whether the statute has a plain meaning, and if so, applying that meaning; and (2) if the statute is ambiguous, deferring to a reasonable agency interpretation of those provisions.[4] The question of whether Chevron applies in the first instance is often referred to in academia as "step zero."[5] There are significant questions in the context of citizenship of whether Congress has authorized USCIS or the BIA to authoritatively interpret the provisions regarding acquisition or derivation of citizenship, and of the naturalization laws. It is often considered relevant that Congress has placed de novo review authority in the federal courts as to potential citizenship claims.[6]

The Ninth, Fifth, and Eleventh Circuits have found at "step zero" that no Chevron deference is appropriate in the context of determining whether an individual is a citizen, because the courts have been entrusted with that important task.[7] The Fourth Circuit disagrees.[8] It is worth noting that similar issues (and disagreements) exist in the naturalization context.[9]

§ 10:23   Judicial declaration of citizenship—Statute of limitations

Research References

West's Key Number Digest, Citizens ⊗10.1, 13, 13.1
Immigration Law Service (2d ed.) § 14:68

There is a five-year statute of limitations applicable to individuals bringing suit to challenge any administratively final denial of the benefits of citizenship; the courts are divided as to when the five-year statute of limitations starts to run. The Third Circuit and the District Court for the District of Columbia have held that the five-year starts to run upon the denial of a passport application.[1] On the other hand, the Eleventh Circuit and the Southern District of Florida have held that it starts to run

---

[3]Rotimi v. Gonzales, 473 F.3d 55, 57–58 (2d Cir. 2007) (per curiam); Arobelidze v. Holder, 653 F.3d 513, 519–20 (7th Cir. 2011); Garcia-Quintero v. Gonzales, 455 F.3d 1006, 1013–14 (9th Cir. 2006); Carpio v. Holder, 592 F.3d 1091, 1097 (10th Cir. 2010); Quinchia v. U.S. Atty. Gen., 552 F.3d 1255, 1258 (11th Cir. 2008); see also, U.S. v. Mead Corp., 533 U.S. 218, 121 S. Ct. 2164, 150 L. Ed. 2d 292, 23 Int'l Trade Rep. (BNA) 1129, 3 A.L.R. Fed. 2d 651 (2001).

[4]Chevron, U.S.A., Inc. v. Natural Resources Defense Council, Inc., 467 U.S. 837, 842–43, 104 S. Ct. 2778, 81 L. Ed. 2d 694, 21 Env't. Rep. Cas. (BNA) 1049, 14 Envtl. L. Rep. 20507 (1984).

[5]See, Sunstein, Chevron Step Zero, 92 Va. L. Rev. 187, 191 (2006); Merrill and Hickman, Chevron's Domain, 89 Geo. L. J. 833, 836 (2001).

[6]8 U.S.C.A. § 1252(b)(5); see also 8 U.S.C.A. § 1421(c) (granting de novo authority over naturalization appeals).

[7]See, Hughes v. Ashcroft, 255 F.3d 752 (9th Cir. 2001); Sebastian-Soler v. U.S. Atty. Gen., 409 F.3d 1280, 1283 (11th Cir. 2005) (per curiam); Alwan v. Ashcroft, 388 F.3d 507 (5th Cir. 2004); but see Marquez-Marquez v. Gonzales, 455 F.3d 548, 554 n.12 (5th Cir. 2006) (suggesting that enactment of 8 U.S.C.A. § 1252(a)(2)(D) might affect the deference question). The Tenth Circuit appears to agree with this analysis. Shepherd v. Holder, 678 F.3d 1171 (10th Cir. 2012).

[8]Fernandez v. Keisler, 502 F.3d 337, 342 (4th Cir. 2007).

[9]Cf. O'Sullivan v. U.S. Citizenship and Immigration Services, 453 F.3d 809, 811–12 (7th Cir. 2006) (granting no Chevron deference to naturalization eligibility question) with Boatswain v. Gonzales, 414 F.3d 413 (2d Cir.2005) (granting Chevron deference to same question).

[Section 10:23]

[1]Whitehead v. Haig, 794 F.2d 115 (3d Cir. 1986); Maldonado-Sanchez v. Shultz, 706 F. Supp. 54 (D.D.C. 1989).

from the issuance of the certificate of loss of nationality.[2] In the case of a loss of U.S. citizenship, the Eleventh Circuit's approach would make appeal harder, because the date triggering the statute of limitations would be much earlier.

The Seventh Circuit found that it starts to run at the time the Board of Appellate Review issued a negative decision.[3] The court also suggested in dicta that the doctrine of laches might also apply to prevent an action from being prosecuted after unreasonable delay.[4]

§ 10:24 Citizenship claims in removal proceedings

Research References

West's Key Number Digest, Citizens ⟨⟩13, 13.1

The Illegal Immigration Reform and Immigrant Responsibility Act of 1996 completely revised the procedures to remove noncitizens from the U.S..[1] It severely limited judicial review of what was formerly exclusion and deportation orders.[2] Even under the new procedures, however, there are provisions for judicial determinations of the alienage of the subject of removal proceedings.

Persons seeking admission who have been placed in expedited removal—including persons seeking entry and persons who entered without inspection—can only obtain a determination of their nationality status through habeas corpus proceedings.[3]

Persons subject to removal based on a deportability section, may dispute their removability before the immigration judge, since only non-citizens are subject to removal.[4] Birth abroad has been held to create a presumption of alienage shifting the burden to the respondent to prove citizenship.[5] However, if the respondent can prove citizenship by a preponderance of the evidence, the removal proceedings must be terminated.[6]

If a removal order is issued against an individual claiming U.S. citizenship, that person may seek judicial review of the citizenship claim in the circuit court as part of their appeal of the removal order[7] If the circuit court determines that no issues of fact regarding the nationality claim remain, then the circuit court adjudicates the

---

[2]Heuer v. United States Secretary of State, 20 F.3d 424 (11th Cir. 1994); Garcia-Sarquiz v. Saxbe, 407 F. Supp. 789 (S.D. Fla. 1974), aff'd sub nom. Garcia-Sarquiz v. Levi, 527 F.2d 1389 (5th Cir. 1976) (per curiam).

[3]Bensky v. Powell, 391 F.3d 894 (7th Cir. 2004) (Posner, J.).

[4]Bensky v. Powell, 391 F.3d 894, 898 (7th Cir. 2004).

[Section 10:24]

[1]IIRAIRA Title III-A.

[2]IIRAIRA § 306.

[3]INA § 242(e)(2), 8 U.S.C.A. § 1252(e)(2) as amended by IIRAIRA § 306(a).

[4]See INA § 237, 8 U.S.C.A. § 1227.

[5]Matter of Rodriguez-Tejedor, 23 I&N Dec. 153, 164 (BIA 2001); Matter of Tijerina-Villareal, 13 I&N Dec. 327, 330 (BIA 1969). Note that there are arguments against the Board's holding in this regard, based on Rule 301 of the Federal Rules of Evidence. See Chau v. INS, 247 F.3d 1026, 1029 n.5 (9th Cir. 2001); Charles Roth, Burden Shifting and Presumptions in Contested Alienage Cases, 6 Bender's Immigr. Bull. 256 (Mar. 1, 2001).

[6]Matter of Tijerina-Villareal, 13 I&N Dec. 327, 330 (BIA 1969).

[7]INA § 242(b)(5), 8 U.S.C.A. § 1252(b)(5) as amended by IIRAIRA § 306(a). See, e.g., Hughes v. Ashcroft, 255 F.3d 752, 755 (9th Cir. 2001); Cartagena-Paulino v. Reno, 2003 WL 21436224 (S.D. N.Y. 2003) (transferring case to the circuit court to hear the claim of derivative citizenship).

claim.[8] If there are issues of fact, the circuit court transfers the proceedings to the federal district court for the judicial district in which the petitioner resides for a new hearing on the nationality claim as if an action had been brought for declaratory relief under 28 U.S.C.A. § 2201.[9]

As a general rule, before obtaining federal judicial review at the Court of Appeals, an alien must exhaust their administrative remedies.[10] However, the Supreme Court has held that U.S. citizenship is a precious right which cannot be lost unconsciously.[11] Moreover, the statutory exhaustion rules only apply to aliens.[12] Thus, for one reason or the other, a number of Courts of Appeals have now held that administrative exhaustion is not required in order to pursue a citizenship claim on appeal from a removal order.[13] Some opinions of the Tenth Circuit have held that where the purported citizen has committed criminal offenses, that federal court jurisdiction might be limited to purely legal, statutory interpretation, claims; but the author believes that the weight of that circuit's authority permits review over the fact of citizenship as essential to determining its jurisdiction.[14]

Persons who are being criminally prosecuted based on a prior removal from the U.S. that has not been judicially reviewed in the past, may make a motion in those proceedings claiming U.S. nationality.[15] If there is no issue of material fact, the court decides the motion on the administrative record only and accepts the administrative findings as conclusion if supported by reasonable, substantial, and probative evidence on the record considered as a whole.[16] If a genuine issue of fact regarding the defendant's nationality is presented, then the court will hold a new hearing on the nationality claim and decide that claim as if an action had been brought under the declaration judgment provisions of 28 U.S.C.A. § 2201.[17]

§ 10:25 Appeal from removal order—Judicial declaration of citizenship

As noted above, an individual may contest removability by making a claim of U.S. citizenship.[1] If the individual is nonetheless ordered removed, she may file a Peti-

---

[8]INA § 242(b)(5)(A), 8 U.S.C.A. § 1252(b)(5)(A) as amended by IIRAIRA § 306(a). See, e.g., . Ashcroft, 255 F.3d 752, 755 (9th Cir. 2001).

[9]INA § 242(b)(5)(B), 8 U.S.C.A. § 1252(b)(5)(B) as amended by IIRAIRA § 306(a).

[10]8 U.S.C.A. § 1252(d)(1).

[11]Afroyim v. Rusk, 387 U.S. 253, 262, 87 S.Ct. 1660, 18 L.Ed.2d 757 (1967); Vance v. Terrazas, 444 U.S. 252, 260, 100 S.Ct. 540, 62 L.Ed.2d 461 (1980).

[12]8 U.S.C.A. § 1252(d)(1).

[13]Rivera v. Ashcroft, 394 F.3d 1129, 1136 (9th Cir.2005); Theagene v. Gonzales, 411 F.3d 1107, 1111 (9th Cir. 2005); Iasu v. Smith, 511 F.3d 881 (9th Cir. 2007); Minasyan v. Gonzales, 401 F.3d 1069, 1075 (9th Cir.2005); Poole v. Mukasey, 522 F.3d 259 (2d Cir. 2008); Omolo v. Gonzales, 452 F.3d 404, 407 (5th Cir.2006); Moussa v. INS, 302 F.3d 823 (8th Cir.2002) (noting that exhaustion rules at § 1252(d)(1) apply only to aliens); cf Taniguchi v. Schultz, 303 F.3d 950 (9th Cir.2002) (court refused to consider unexhausted, but also frivolous, citizenship claim).

[14]Abiodun v. Gonzales, 461 F.3d 1210, 1215 (10th Cir.2006); Brue v. Gonzales, 464 F.3d 1227, 1231–32 (10th Cir.2006); cf. Shepherd v. Holder, 678 F.3d 1171, 1182 (10th Cir. 2012).

[15]INA § 242(b)(7)(B), 8 U.S.C.A. § 1252(b)(7)(B) as amended by IIRAIRA § 306(a).

[16]INA § 242(b)(7)(B)(i), 8 U.S.C.A. § 1252(b)(7)(B)(i) as amended by IIRAIRA § 306(a).

[17]INA § 242(b)(7)(B)(ii), 8 U.S.C.A. § 1252(b)(7)(B)(ii) as amended by IIRAIRA § 306(a).

[Section 10:25]

[1]See §§ 8:34 to 8:36.

tion for Review to challenge the removal order.[2] Where alienage issues arise in removal proceedings, an action seeking a declaration of citizenship may not be filed in District Court.[3]

By statute, the Petition for Review must be filed in the Court of Appeals.[4] If the Court of Appeals finds no genuine issue of material fact presented by the case, the Court of Appeals resolves the matter in the first instance.[5] If a genuine issue of material fact exists as to the citizenship claim, it must be transferred to District Court for adjudication.[6] The District Court then issues a declaratory judgment to decide the matter.

It is unclear the precise nature of the transfer to District Court; the Ninth Circuit appears to find that the District Court order is not separately appealable, but rather must be transferred back to the Court of Appeals after a District Court decision.[7]

§ 10:26 Coming to United States to claim citizenship

Research References

12 A.L.R. Fed. 2d 501 ("Construction and Application of 8 U.S.C.A. § 1503(a) Providing for Proceedings for Declaration of United States Nationality")
Immigration Law Service (2d ed.) § 13:452

INA § 360 contains a special provision permitting individuals claiming citizenship, but living outside the U.S., to come to the U.S. to prosecute their claims. When any agency or department denies a person outside the U.S. a right or privilege of nationals of the U.S., the person may obtain a certificate of identity from the U.S. embassy or consulate.[1] Upon "proof to the satisfaction of such diplomatic or consular officer that such application is made in good faith and has a substantial basis," the statute requires that the consular officer "shall issue" a "certificate of identity."[2] That certificate will allow the holder to travel to the U.S., where the citizenship claim can be vindicated.[3] However, only persons who have been in the U.S. before, or persons claiming U.S. citizenship at birth abroad and who are under the age of 16 may obtain such certificates of identity.[4]

Where a certificate of identity is denied, the individual may appeal that denial to the Secretary of State.[5]

Persons holding such certificates are inspected at the border and are subject to re-

---

[2]See 8 U.S.C.A. § 1252(b)(5).

[3]See INA § 360(a), 8 U.S.C.A. § 1503(a); Rios-Valenzuela v. Department of Homeland Sec., 506 F.3d 393, 398-99 (5th Cir. 2007).

[4]See 8 U.S.C.A. § 1252(b)(2).

[5]8 U.S.C.A. § 1252(b)(5)(A).

[6]8 U.S.C.A. § 1252(b)(5)(B).

[7]Anderson v. Holder, 673 F.3d 1089, 1093–94 (9th Cir. 2012) (relying on Demirchyan v. Holder, 641 F.3d 1141, 1143 (9th Cir. 2011) ("[W]e see no meaningful distinction between transfer under 8 U.S.C. § 1252(b)(5)(B) and limited remand."), Campbell v. Blodgett, 998 F.2d 763 (9th Cir.1993) (en banc) (holding that findings and conclusions on limited remand are not separately appealable)).

[Section 10:26]

[1]INA § 360(b), 8 U.S.C.A. § 1503(b).

[2]INA § 360(b), 8 U.S.C.A. § 1503(b).

[3]INA § 360(b), 8 U.S.C.A. § 1503(b).

[4]INA § 360(b), 8 U.S.C.A. § 1503(b).

[5]INA § 360(b), 8 U.S.C.A. § 1503(b); 22 C.F.R. § 50.11(b).

moval proceedings to the same extent as noncitizens.[6] Assuming that they are placed into removal proceedings, a final determination by the BIA that such persons are inadmissible is reviewable by a U.S. district court through habeas corpus proceedings.[7] If they are not placed into removal proceedings, they would likely be able to file suit seeking a judicial declaration of their citizenship.

Although INA § 360 on its face only permits declaratory judgment actions to establish citizenship for individuals actually present within the U.S., the Supreme Court rejected this construction of the statute in 1962, in the case of *Rusk v. Cort*.[8] Looking to legislative history, the Court found that Congress had been motivated by a desire to make it more difficult for people to enter the U.S. by fraud, rather than by a desire to preclude claims by U.S. citizens, and found that individuals outside the U.S. could bring a declaratory judgment action under the Administrative Procedures Act ("APA").[9] As such, the federal courts have considered such claims.[10] However, the clarity of this holding was undercut by an unrelated development regarding the APA, when the Supreme Court found the APA to be a waiver of sovereign immunity, but not itself a grant of jurisdiction.[11] As such, some courts have suggested that the validity of Rusk may be in doubt,[12] though the existence of other jurisdictional vehicles such as 28 U.S.C.A. § 1331 would seem to afford an individual a separate means to bring suit.

---

[6]INA § 360(c), 8 U.S.C.A. § 1503(c).

[7]INA § 360(c), 8 U.S.C.A. § 1503(c); see also, 8 U.S.C.A. § 1252(e)(2), INA § 242(e)(2).

[8]Rusk v. Cort, 369 U.S. 367 (1962).

[9]Rusk v. Cort, 369 U.S. at 367, 377–80 (1962).

[10]Kahane v. Secretary of State, 700 F.Supp. 1162, 1165 n. 3 (D.D.C.1988); Icaza v. Shultz, 656 F.Supp. 819, 822 n. 5 (D.D.C.1987).

[11]Califano v. Sanders, 430 U.S. 99, 105 (1977)

[12]See, e.g., Bensky v. Powell, 391 F.3d 894, 896 (7th Cir. 2004) (Posner, J.).

APPENDIX 10-1

Mandamus Complaint[1]

DANIEL LEVY (State Bar No. 1234567)
LAW OFFICES OF DANIEL LEVY
6300 Wilshire Blvd., Suite 1020
Los Angeles, CA 90048
Telephone: (323) 951-0000
Fax Number: (323) 951-0990
Attorney for Respondent

UNITED STATES DISTRICT COURT

CENTRAL DISTRICT OF CALIFORNIA

Jane Doe, 　　　Plaintiff, 　　　　vs. Rosemary Melville, Acting District Director U.S. Im- migration and Naturaliza- tion Service 　　　Defendant.	Civ. No. COMPLAINT FOR A WRIT IN THE NATURE OF A MANDAMUS INS No. A99 999 098

Plaintiff, by her attorney, complaining of Defendant, alleges as follows:

1. Plaintiff Jane Doe is an individual and an applicant for naturalization who resides within the jurisdiction of this Court. Plaintiff's claim to relief arises under 8 U.S.C.A. §§ 1421 et seq.

2. Rosemary Melville, the Defendant herein, is the Acting District Director of the Los Angeles District of the Immigration and Naturalization Service (INS), an agency of the United States government, and she is sued herein in her official capacity.

3. The Court has jurisdiction of this action pursuant to 5 U.S.C.A. §§ 701 et seq. and 28 U.S.C.A. §§ 2201 et seq. And relief is requested pursuant to said statutes.

4. On or about October 1, 1996, Plaintiff filed her application for naturalization, under 8 U.S.C.A. §§ 1421 et seq., with Defendant. Defendant has a duty to adjudicate said application. *Id.*

5. On or about January 7, 1998, Defendant's agent told Plaintiff's counsel that

---

[1]This appendix is a slightly modified version of Robert Mautino's sample complaint, published in Mautino, How to Move Cases in the New World of Naturalization, in 1998–99 Immigration and Nationality Law Handbook, Vol. II - Advanced Practice, 439 (Murphy, et al., ed. 1998). Copyright © 1998 by the American Immigration Lawyers Association. Reprinted with permission.

his office was processing similar applications filed in January of 1997. Plaintiff's application has been filed in October of 1996.

6. Defendant is taking no action on Plaintiff's case in spite of the fact that the case has long passed Defendant's time guidelines for this type of application.

7. Plaintiff has exhausted her administrative remedies.

8. Defendant's refusal to act in this case is, as a matter of law, arbitrary and not in accordance with the law.

9. Plaintiff has been greatly damaged by the failure of Defendant to act in accord with her duties under the law.

10. The Defendant in violation of the Administrative Procedures Act, 5 U.S.C.A. §§ 701 et seq., is unlawfully withholding or unreasonably delaying action on Plaintiff's application and has failed to carry out the adjudicative functions delegated to her by law with regard to Plaintiff's case.

WHEREFORE, Plaintiff prays:

A. That the Defendant be ordered to have her agents process her case to a conclusion.

B. For reasonable attorney's fees and

C. For such other and further relief as to this Court may seem proper.

Dated: _____

_____
Daniel Levy
Attorney for Plaintiff

APPENDIX 10-2

Sample Summons

UNITED STATES DISTRICT COURT CENTRAL DISTRICT OF CALIFORNIA

LISA ROE
(INS File Number A99
999 999)
          PLAINTIFF(S),
          v.
ROSEMARY MELVILLE,
Acting District
Director, U.S. Immigra-
tion and Naturalization
Service
      DEFENDANT(S).
	CASE NUMBER
	CV- _____
	
	_____
	
	SUMMONS

TO: THE ABOVE-NAMED DEFENDANT(S):

YOU ARE HEREBY SUMMONED and required to file with this court and serve upon plaintiff's attorney _____, whose address is:

    Law Offices of Daniel Levy
    6300 Wilshire Blvd., Suite 1020
    Los Angeles, CA 90048

An answer to the complaint which is herewith served upon you within _____ days after service of this summons upon you, exclusive of the day of service. If you fail to do so, judgment by default will be taken against you for the relief demanded in the complaint.

                        CLERK, U. S. DISTRICT COURT

DATE: _____   By _____
                              Deputy Clerk
                         (SEAL OF THE COURT)

CV-1A (08/97)   SUMMONS

APPENDIX 10-3

Complaint for Failure to Adjudicate within 120 Days from Interview[1]

DANIEL LEVY (State Bar No. 1234567)
LAW OFFICES OF DANIEL LEVY
6300 Wilshire Blvd., Suite 1020
Los Angeles, CA 90048
Telephone: (323) 951-0000
Fax Number: (323) 951-0990
Attorney for Respondent

UNITED STATES DISTRICT COURT

CENTRAL DISTRICT OF CALIFORNIA

John Doe,
        Plaintiff,
            v.
 	
Rosemary Melville, Acting
District Director
U.S. Immigration and
Naturalization Service
        Defendant.
	Civ. No.
	
	COMPLAINT FOR
	DECLARATORY JUDG-
	MENT OF NATURALIZA-
	TION UNDER 8 U.S.C.A.
	§ 1447(b)
	INS No. A99 999 998

Plaintiff, by her attorney, complaining of Defendant, alleges as follows:

1. Plaintiff is an individual and resident of the United States who resides within the jurisdiction of this Court. Plaintiff's claim to naturalization arises under 8 U.S.C.A. § 1447(b).

2. Rosemary Melville, the Defendant herein, is the Acting District Director of the United States Immigration and Naturalization Service (INS) and is sued herein in her official capacity. Defendant is responsible for the grant or denial of naturalization applications filed within the Los Angeles INS district pursuant to 8 U.S.C.A. § 1421, 8 U.S.C.A. § 1427, 8 CFR § 103.1(g)(2)(ii), 8 CFR § 310.2 and 8 CFR § 316.3.

3. The Court has jurisdiction of this action pursuant to 8 U.S.C.A. § 1447(b) and 28 U.S.C.A. § 2201.

---

[1]This appendix is a modified version of Robert Mautino's sample complaint, published in Mautino, How to Move Cases in the New World of Naturalization, in 1998–99 Immigration and Nationality Law Handbook, Vol. II - Advanced Practice, 439 (Murphy, et al., ed. 1998). Copyright © 1998 by the American Immigration Lawyers Association. Reprinted with permission.

4. In or about October 1996, Plaintiff submitted an application for naturalization to the Defendant.

5. In or about December 1997, the Defendant and/or his designated agent interviewed Plaintiff on his application.

6. At his interview, Plaintiff passed all portions of the requirements for naturalization, except that Defendant's agent informed him that the only issue to be resolved was Plaintiff's application for selective service. Plaintiff was told he would be rescheduled for an interview to submit additional relating to this issue.

7. On April 20, 1998, Plaintiff appeared at the scheduled appointment and submitted the required evidence. Defendant's agent did not question Plaintiff on this issue or review the evidence. Instead, she recommended withdrawal of the application. Plaintiff did not withdraw his application.

8. More than 120 days have passed since the initial interview, and the Defendant has made no decision on Plaintiff's application.

9. The Defendant's failure to make a determination on Plaintiff's application within the 120-day statutory period allows Plaintiff to bring the matter to this Court for a hearing pursuant to 8 U.S.C.A. § 1447(b).

10. Plaintiff desires a judicial determination of her naturalization application and a declaration that she is entitled to be naturalized as a citizen of the United States.

WHEREFORE, Plaintiff prays that:

1. The Court will hear Plaintiff's case and render a declaratory judgment that she is entitled to be naturalized and

2. The Court will grant such further relief as may be just, lawful, and equitable in the premises.

Dated: _____

                                        _____
                                        Daniel Levy
                                        Attorney for Plaintiff

APPENDIX 10-4
USCIS Update

Office of Communications
U.S. Department of Homeland Security

**U.S. Citizenship
and Immigration
Services**

February 20, 2007

USCIS Update

USCIS CLARIFIES CRITERIA TO EXPEDITE FBI NAME CHECK
Federal Litigation Removed as Sole Basis to Expedite Check

WASHINGTON – U.S. Citizenship and Immigration Services (USCIS) is no longer routinely requesting the FBI to expedite a name check when the only reason for the request is that a mandamus (or other federal court petition) is filed in the case.

USCIS may continue to request an expedited FBI name check if the case meets one of the other approved criteria, including:

1. Military deployment,
2. Age-out cases not covered under the *Child Status Protection Act*, and applications affected by sunset provisions such as diversity visas,
3. Significant and compelling reasons, such as critical medical conditions, and
4. Loss of social security benefits or other subsistence at the discretion of the USCIS District Director.

The FBI name check is an invaluable part of the security screening process, ensuring that our immigration system is not used as a vehicle to harm our nation or its citizens. USCIS also requests an FBI name check to screen out people who seek immigration benefits improperly or fraudulently and ensure that only eligible applicants receive benefits.

Information about the FBI name check is available on the USCIS website at http://www.uscis.gov or by calling the USCIS National Customer Service Center toll free at 1-800-375-5283.

–USCIS –

www.uscis.gov

APPENDIX 10-5

Affidavit of Michael Cannon, Regarding FBI Name Check Procedure

1	UNITED STATES DISTRICT COURT
2	EASTERN DISTRICT OF NEW YORK

RAISA YAKUBOVA, EMMA UNGURYAN,
BELLA VESNOVSKAYA, DAVID VESNOVSKIY,
VYACHESLAV VOLOSIKOV,
SHELATA AWAD IBRAHIM

Plaintiffs,

v.

MICHAEL CHERTOFF, et al.

Defendants.

Case No:
1:06-cv-3203-ERK-RLM

SUPPLEMENTAL DECLARATION OF MICHAEL A. CANNON

I, Michael A. Cannon, declare as follows:

(1)   I am currently the Section Chief of the National Name Check Program Section ("NNCPS"), formerly part of the Record/Information Dissemination Section ("RIDS"), Records Management Division ("RMD"), at the Federal Bureau of Investigation Headquarters ("FBIHQ") in Washington, D.C. I have held this position since March 7, 2005.

(2)   In my current capacity as Section Chief, I supervise the National Name Check Units. The statements contained in this declaration are based upon my personal knowledge, upon information provided to me in my official capacity, and upon conclusions and determinations reached and made in accordance therewith.

(3)   Due to the nature of my official duties, I am familiar with the procedures followed by the FBI in responding to requests for information from its files pursuant to the policy and the procedures of the United States Citizenship and Immigration Services ("USCIS"), which was constituted from portions of the former Immigration and Naturalization Service ("INS").

(4)   I hereby incorporate by reference all the information previously provided in my Declaration dated July 20, 2006, which was submitted earlier in this case.

(5)   The purpose of this Declaration is to provide the Court and the plaintiffs further explanation regarding 1) the processing of name check requests by the NNCPS which is

1   generally completed on a first-in, first-out basis ensuring that all applicants are treated equally

2   and fairly; 2) the increasing volume of requests that must be processed with a limited budget and

3   resources; 3) the factors contributing to the delays; and 4) the specific steps taken by the NNCPS

4   to process requests more efficiently and expeditiously with its limited resources.

5   **BACKGROUND OF THE NATIONAL NAME CHECK PROGRAM**

6   (6)   The National Name Check Program ("NNCP") has the mission of

7   disseminating information from the FBI's Central Records System in response to requests

8   submitted by Federal agencies, congressional committees, the Federal judiciary, friendly foreign

9   police and intelligence agencies, and state and local criminal justice agencies. The Central

10 Records System contains the FBI's administrative, personnel, and investigative files. The NNCP

11 has its genesis in Executive Order 10450, issued during the Eisenhower Administration. This

12 executive order addresses personnel security issues and mandates National Agency Checks

13 ("NACs") as part of the pre-employment vetting and background investigation process. The FBI

14 performs the primary NAC conducted on all U.S. Government employees. From this modest

15 beginning, the NNCP has grown exponentially, with more and more customers seeking

16 background information from FBI files on individuals before bestowing a privilege – whether

17 that privilege is Government employment or an appointment, a security clearance, attendance at a

18 White House function, a Green card or naturalization, admission to the bar, or a visa for the

19 privilege of visiting our homeland. More than 70 Federal, state, and local agencies regularly

20 request FBI name searches. In addition to serving our regular governmental customers, the FBI

21 conducts numerous name searches in direct support of the FBI's counterintelligence,

22 counterterrorism, and homeland security efforts.

23   (7)   Congress enacted Public Law 105-119, Title I, 111 Stat. 2448-49 (1997)

24 which provided that the INS could not adjudicate an application for naturalization unless the

25 agency received confirmation from the FBI that a full criminal background check had been

26 completed on the applicant. Pursuant to this law, the USCIS submits name check requests to the

27 NNCPS for processing.

28

2

1   (8)   According to 8 C.F.R. Section 335.2(b), a definitive response that a full

2 criminal background check on an applicant has been completed includes: 1) Confirmation from

3 the FBI that an applicant does not have an administrative or criminal record; 2) Confirmation

4 from the FBI that an applicant has an administrative or criminal record; or 3) Confirmation from

5 the FBI that two properly prepared fingerprint cards (Form FD-258) have been determined

6 unclassifiable for the purpose of conducting a criminal background check and have been rejected.

7   (9)   A full description of the FBI's Central Records System (CRS) is contained

8 in my earlier Declaration dated July 20, 2006, and filed in this case. The earlier Declaration

9 explains, among other things, the manner in which information is "indexed" in the CRS and

10 retrievable.

11 **THE NNCPS OPERATES ON A FIRST-IN, FIRST-OUT BASIS**

12   (10)   The NNCPS generally processes all name check requests submitted by

13 USCIS on a first-in, first-out basis. The first-in, first-out process applies to the residual name

14 check requests that are still pending after the initial electronic batch check and secondary check

15 described in my earlier Declaration. This policy of first-in, first-out reflects that all applicants are

16 equally deserving and ensures that all applicants are treated fairly. However, if an applicant's

17 name check requires a review of numerous FBI records and files, even though that person came

18 in first, the name check may require additional time until all responsive records are located and

19 reviewed. An exception to the first-in, first-out policy exists when USCIS directs that a name

20 check be handled on an "expedited" basis. USCIS determines which name checks are to be

21 expedited. Once designated as an "expedite," that name check proceeds to the front of the queue,

22 in front of the others waiting to be processed. The FBI limits the number of expedites USCIS

23 can submit per week.

24   (11)   There are four stages involved in the completion of an individual name

25 check: Batch Processing, Name Searching, File Review, and Dissemination.

26   (12)   The first stage in the process, Batch Processing, involves the transfer of

27 the name check requests from USCIS to the NNCPS on magnetic tapes. Each tape can hold up to

28

3

1 10,000 names. Some requests are transmitted via facsimile. The tapes are uploaded into an FBI

2 system and the names are electronically checked against the FBI's Universal Index (UNI).

3 Approximately 68% of the name checks submitted by USCIS on the batch tapes are returned to

4 USCIS as having "No Record" within 48 hours. A "No Record" indicates that the FBI's UNI

5 database contains no identifiable information regarding a particular individual. Duplicate

6 submissions (i.e., identically spelled names with identical dates of birth and other identical

7 information submitted while the original submission is still pending) are not checked, and the

8 duplicate findings are returned to USCIS within 48 hours.

9   (13)   The second stage in the process is Name Searching. For the name check

10 requests that are still pending after the initial electronic check, additional review is required. An

11 FBI employee in the NNCPS physically enters the applicant's name into the computer database

12 searching different fields and information. This secondary manual name search completed

13 within 30 - 60 days usually identifies an additional 22% of the USCIS requests as having "No

14 Record," for a 90% overall "No Record" response rate. The results of this 22% are returned to

15 USCIS.

16   (14)   The third and fourth stages in the process are File Review and

17 Dissemination. The remaining 10% of name check requests are identified as possibly being the

18 subject of an FBI record. At this point, the FBI records in question must now be retrieved and

19 reviewed. If the record was electronically uploaded into the FBI ACS electronic record keeping

20 system, it can be reviewed quickly. If not, the relevant information must be retrieved from an

21 existing paper record. Review of this information will determine whether the information is

22 identified with the request. If the information is not identified with the request, the request is

23 closed as a "No Record," and USCIS is notified as such. Once a record is retrieved, the

24 information in the file is reviewed for possible derogatory information. Less than 1% of the

25 requests are identified with a file containing possible derogatory information. If appropriate, the

26 FBI then forwards a summary of the derogatory information to USCIS. A backlog applies to a

27 small number of overall applications for naturalization. Because of the significance and

28

4

Case 1:06-cv-02518   Document 50-6   Filed 02/20/2007   Page 6 of 10

1   permanence of the outcome, the NNCPS diligently follows the procedures established for each

2   applicant's name check.

3   (15)   After the FBI has completed the name check request for an individual, it is

4   the responsibility of USCIS to determine whether to grant or deny a pending application for

5   benefits under the Immigration and Nationality Act. The FBI is not involved in the adjudication

6   of a pending application.

7   **INCREASING VOLUME AND DEMANDS ON THE NNCPS**

8   (16)   Prior to September 11, 2001, the FBI processed approximately 2.5 million

9   name check requests per year. As a result of the government's post-9/11 counterterrorism

10   efforts, the number of FBI name checks has grown. In fiscal year 2002, the FBI processed

11   approximately 2.7 million name check requests per year; in fiscal year 2003, the FBI processed

12   approximately 5.7 million name check requests per year; in fiscal year 2004, the FBI processed

13   approximately 3.8 million name check requests per year; in fiscal year 2005, the FBI processed in

14   excess of 3.7 million name checks.

15   (17)   A significant portion of the incoming name checks submitted over the past

16   few years has been submitted by USCIS. In fiscal year 2003, 64% of the total incoming name

17   checks were submitted by USCIS; in fiscal year 2004, 46% of the total incoming name checks

18   were submitted by USCIS; in fiscal year 2005, 45% of the total incoming name checks were

19   submitted by USCIS; and in fiscal year 2006, as of August 23, 2006, 45% of the total incoming

20   name checks have been submitted by USCIS.

21   **FACTORS CONTRIBUTING TO THE DELAYS**

22   (18)   As mentioned in my previous Declaration dated July 20, 2006, which I

23   incorporated by reference in paragraph (4), in December of 2002 and January of 2003, USCIS

24   resubmitted 2.7 million name check requests to the FBI for all pending applications for benefits

25   under the Immigration and Nationality Act for which name checks were required. This was due

26   to a review of the background check procedures employed by USCIS conducted in November

27   2002. It was determined that in order to better protect the people and the interests of the United

28

5

1 States, a more detailed, in-depth clearance procedure was required. One of these procedures

2 involved the name check clearance performed by the FBI. At that time only those "main" files

3 that could be positively identified with an individual were considered responsive. The risk of

4 missing a match to possible derogatory record(s) was too great, and therefore it was agreed by the

5 FBI and USCIS that the search criteria be changed to also include access to references. *From a*

6 *process standpoint, this meant many more files were required to be reviewed for each individual,*

7 *thus adding additional time and cost to the process.*

8   (19) The 2.7 million requests were in addition to the regular submissions by

9 USCIS. The FBI has now returned an initial response for all 2.7 million requests. While many

10 initial responses unquestionably indicated that the FBI had no information relating to a specific

11 individual, approximately sixteen percent of the responses (over 440,000) indicated that the FBI

12 *may* have information relating to the subject of the inquiry. These 440,000 requests have been in

13 the process of being resolved, with over 427,000 being processed. Currently, less than 13,000 of

14 those resubmitted requests remain pending.

15   (20) The FBI's processing of the more than 440,000 residuals has delayed the

16 processing of regular submissions from USCIS. A dedicated team within NNCPS has been

17 assigned to handle only these re-submitted name check requests. To the extent that the team

18 members are working on only these applications, they are unavailable to process the normal

19 submissions which are completed on a first-in, first-out basis, unless otherwise directed by

20 USCIS.

21   (21) USCIS's name check requests outpace NNCPS's available resources. In

22 FY-05, USCIS submitted 1,512,256 or 45% of NNCPS's incoming requests. That number

23 exceeds the requests of NNCPS's next two largest customers combined. To meet the demands of

24 its customers, NNCPS currently employs 52 Research Analysts and 15 File Assistants in its

25 Dissemination Phase to process and review files for possible derogatory information, and

26 disseminate the results. Of those, 10 Research Analysts and 1 File Assistant are dedicated to

27 USCIS Resubmissions; and 15 Research Analysts and 2 File Assistants are dedicated to new

28

6

1   USCIS submissions. If a file must be retrieved from one of the 56 FBI field offices, the NNCPS

2   staff must coordinate their requests with personnel in the field.

3   (22)   The NNCPS is currently relocating to a new location, outside of

4   Washington D.C. This physical relocation has directly contributed to a loss of experienced and

5   seasoned staff. The decreased number of experienced staff has contributed to a delay in the

6   processing of a name check request.

7   (23)   The number of "hits" on a name when it is reviewed may further

8   contribute to a delay in processing a name check request. A "hit" is a possible match with a

9   name in an FBI record. The number of times the name appears in FBI records correlates to the

10   number of records which require review.

11   (24)   The processing of common names also contributes to a delay in processing

12   a name check request. The names associated with a name check request are searched in a

13   multitude of combinations, switching the order of first, last, and middle names, as well as

14   combinations with just the first and last, first and middle, and so on. Without detailed

15   information in both the file and agency submission, it is difficult to determine whether or not a

16   person with a common name is the same person mentioned in FBI records. Common names

17   often have more than 200 hits on FBI records.

18   (25)   The accessibility of the FBI record needed for review also contributes to a

19   delay in processing a name check request. If the date of the record is later than October 1995, the

20   record text may be available electronically; if the record predates October 1995, the paper record

21   has to be located, pulled, and reviewed. A record could be at one of over 265 possible locations

22   across the country. Requests often involve coordinating the retrieval and review of files from the

23   various 56 different FBI field offices. One person's name check may involve locating and

24   reviewing numerous files, all at different physical locations. Each request must be

25   communicated internally from the NNCPS to the field, and handled according to the current

26   priorities of the particular field office. Since it is a paper based process, it is time consuming and

27   labor intensive.

28

7

Case 1:06-cv-02518   Document 50-6   Filed 02/20/2007   Page 9 of 10

1   (26)   Another contributing factor which was briefly mentioned earlier in this

2   document is the expedited request. Processing an expedited case means that an employee is not

3   available to work on a normal name check request. As directed by USCIS specifically, the FBI

4   processes name check requests on a first-in, first-out basis unless USCIS directs that a name

5   check be expedited.

6

7   **THE NATIONAL NAME CHECK PROGRAM IS ADDRESSING THE FACTORS THAT
     CONTRIBUTE TO DELAYS IN PROCESSING A NAME CHECK**

8

9   (27)   NNCPS is continuing to develop the Name Check Dissemination Database

10   ("NCDD"), an electronic repository for name check results, to eliminate manual and duplicate

11   preparation of reports to other Agencies, and provide avenues for future automation of the name

12   check process.

13   (28)   NNCPS is partnering with other Agencies to provide contractors and

14   personnel to process name checks.

15   (29)   NNCPS has procured an employee development program to streamline the

16   training of new employees, thereby significantly decreasing the amount of time needed before a

17   new employee can begin to significantly impact the NNCPS workload.

18   (30)   NNCPS, through the Records Management Division's Records

19   Automation Section, is scanning the paper files required for review in order to provide machine

20   readable documents for the Dissemination Database. The scanning is also creating an Electronic

21   Records System that allows for future automation of the name check process.

22   (31)   NNCPS is working with customers to streamline incoming product and to

23   automate exchange of information.

24   (32)   NNCPS is exploring technology updates to the Name Check process.

25   **EXHIBITS**

26   (33)   Volume of Incoming Name Check Requests.

27   FY-94   1,792,874
             FY-95   2,091,426
28   FY-96   2,939,521

8

FY-97	2,850,769
FY-98	2,148,993
FY-99	2,957,525
FY-00	2,449,981
FY-01	2,771,241
FY-02	3,288,018
FY-03	6,309,346
FY-04	3,884,467
FY-05	3,346,435
FY-06*	3,267,349

(34)   Pending Name Checks at End of Fiscal Year.

FY-02	381,645
FY-03	818,397
FY-04	737,412
FY-05	368,041
FY-06*	519,539

(35)   National Name Check Program FY-05

	Total	USCIS
Pending as of 10/1/2004	737,412	236,656 (32%)
Incoming:	3,346,435	1,512,256 (45 %)
Processed:	3,715,806	1,514,340 (41 %)
Pending as of 9/30/05:	368,041	233,806 (64 %)

(36)   National Name Check Program FY-06*

	Total	USCIS
Pending as of 10/01/2005	368,041	233,806 (64%)
Incoming:	3,267,349	1,479,506 (45%)
Processed:	3,115,851	1,352,840 (43%)
Pending as of 8/23/2006:	519,539	360,472 (69%)

*FY-06 as of August 23, 2006

(38)   Pursuant to 28 U.S.C. § 1746, I declare under penalty of perjury that the foregoing is true and correct to the best of my knowledge and belief.

Executed this 31st day of August 2006.

MICHAEL A. CANNON
Section Chief
National Name Check Program Section
Records Management Division
Federal Bureau of Investigation
Washington, D.C.

9

857

Chapter 11

Naturalization of Special Classes: Spouses, Widows and Widowers, Children, and Others

APPENDIX 11-8.   USCIS Centralizes Filing for Qualifying Family of Deceased
                 Service Members

Research References

West's Key Number Digest

Aliens, Immigration, and Citizenship ☞708, 709, 711 to 714; Naturalization ☞62

Westlaw Databases

Steel on Immigration Law (STEEL)
Immigration Law Service (2d ed.) (IMMLS2D)

Treatises and Practice Aids

Dizon and Wettstein, Immigration Law Service 2d §§ 14:191 to 14:195, 14:214
Steel on Immigration Law §§ 15:16 to 15:18

> **KeyCite®:** Cases and other legal materials listed in KeyCite Scope can be researched through the KeyCite
> service on Westlaw®. Use KeyCite to check citations for form, parallel references, prior and later history,
> and comprehensive citator information, including citations to other decisions and secondary materials.

I.   INTRODUCTION

§ 11:1   Overview

Research References

West's Key Number Digest, Naturalization ☞62
A.L.R. Index, Immigration and Naturalization
Dizon and Wettstein, Immigration Law Service 2d §§ 14:195, 14:203, 14:300
Steel on Immigration Law § 15:11

This chapter discusses provisions of the INA that substantially modify the
naturalization requirements for specific persons in order to make it easier for them
to obtain U.S. citizenship. The beneficiaries of these provisions are spouses and children of U.S. citizens, certain widows and widowers of U.S. citizens, former U.S.
citizens who lost their citizenship because of marriage to noncitizens, and employees of U.S. news media organizations abroad.

Congress has made the substantive requirements and procedures for naturalization less rigorous for special classes of applicants than for general naturalization
applicants. For example, a spouse of a United States citizen may be naturalized after three years of lawful permanent residency instead of five years.[1] The INA also
provides special rules for members of the United States military,[2] spouses of U.S.
citizen employees stationed abroad by the U.S. government, a recognized research
institution, certain corporations, public international organizations, or religious
organizations,[3] lawful permanent resident employees of U.S. media corporations
stationed abroad,[4] widows and widowers of U.S. citizens who died during honorable

---

[Section 11:1]

[1]INA § 319(a), 8 U.S.C.A. § 1430(a).
[2]INA §§ 328, 329, 329A, 8 U.S.C.A. §§ 1439, 1440, 1440-1; 8 CFR §§ 328, 329.
[3]INA § 319(b), 8 U.S.C.A. § 1430(b), 8 CFR §§ 319.2, 319.5.
[4]INA § 319(c), 8 U.S.C.A. § 1430(c), 8 CFR §§ 319.4, 319.6.

service in the U.S. armed forces,[5] children of United States citizens,[6] former U.S. citizens,[7] and noncitizen nationals.[8] In addition, for members of certain professions, such as religious ministers and priests and workers in U.S. vessels, the law deems requirements of physical presence and continuous residence fulfilled by their residence abroad.[9]

Some of these issues have been discussed in other chapters. Ch 7 discusses those persons whose residence abroad is deemed as if they were in the United States for purposes of the substantive naturalization requirement of five years of continuous residence.[10] Military related nationality issues will be discussed in the next chapter.[11] Naturalization of noncitizen nationals is discussed in the chapter on rights and duties of noncitizen nationals.[12]

II. NATIONALITY AND MARRIAGE

A. IN GENERAL

§ 11:2 Overview

Research References

West's Key Number Digest, Naturalization ⟲68
Dizon and Wettstein, Immigration Law Service 2d §§ 14:191, 14:192, 14:196
Steel on Immigration Law §§ 15:10 to 15:12

This section of the chapter deals with the relationship between nationality and marriage. The nationality laws have long recognized a close link between the nationality of one person and the nationality of that person's spouse. At its most extreme, U.S. law provided that a woman who married a noncitizen would lose her U.S. citizenship.[1] As a result, a woman born in the United States would lose her U.S. citizenship by marrying a noncitizen even if she never left the United States.[2] In contrast, noncitizen women who married U.S. citizens during this period automatically acquired U.S. citizenship.[3] The principle behind these laws was the

---

[5]INA § 319(d), 8 U.S.C.A. § 1430(d), 8 CFR § 319.3.

[6]INA § 322, 8 U.S.C.A. § 1433.

[7]INA §§ 324, 327, 8 U.S.C.A. §§ 1435, 1438; 8 CFR §§ 324, 327.

[8]INA § 325, 8 U.S.C.A. § 1436, 8 CFR § 325.

[9]INA §§ 317, 330, 8 U.S.C.A. §§ 1428, 1441.

[10]See §§ 7:4 and 7:5.

[11]See §§ 12:1 et seq.

[12]See §§ 3:10 to 3:12.

[Section 11:2]

[1]Sec. 3 of Act of March 2, 1907, Pub.L. 59-193, 34 Stat. 1228 reproduced as Appendix 4-6 to Ch 4; Petition of Drysdale, 20 F.2d 957 (E.D. Mich. 1927) (holding that Act of 1907 was declaratory of preexisting common law).

[2]Mackensie v. Hare, 239 U.S. 299, 36 S.Ct. 106, 108, 60 L.Ed. 297 (1917).

[3]Sec. 2 of Act of Feb. 10, 1855, 10 Stat. 604 reproduced as Appendix 4-4 to Ch 4.

merging of the identity of the wife with that of the husband.[4] The Cable Act finally repealed both these laws in 1922.[5]

The Act of 1922 provided a relaxed procedure for the naturalization of noncitizen women who married U.S. citizen men.[6] In 1934, Congress finally made the citizenship laws more gender neutral by amending the provision to allow any "noncitizen who marries a citizen of the United States" to obtain the benefits of the relaxed procedures.[7]

At present, naturalization laws give spouses of U.S. citizens, regardless of their gender, special treatment in naturalization proceedings. First, the INA allows spouses of citizens to naturalize after a reduced period of residence and physical presence in the United States.[8] Second, the INA gives persons who became lawful permanent residents by virtue of their status as abused spouses of U.S. citizens the same treatment as spouses of U.S. citizens.[9] Third, the INA allows spouses of those U.S. citizens who have been assigned abroad for qualifying purposes to naturalize at any time they are present in the United States provided USCIS has lawfully admitted them to permanent residence and they intend to return to the United States once their citizen spouse's assignment abroad terminates.[10] A fourth provision waives the residency and physical presence requirements for widows or widowers of U.S. citizens whose spouse died while performing honorable service in the U.S. armed forces.[11]

Finally, there is a gender specific provision designed to correct the unequal treatment of women under prior law. This provision allows a woman who lost U.S. citizenship because of marriage to a noncitizen to regain U.S. citizenship without regards to any of the requirements of the naturalization law, except that it bars her from reacquiring U.S. citizenship if she was a member of the Communist or other "totalitarian" party.[12]

---

[4]See Mackenzie v. Hare, 239 U.S. 299, 311, 36 S. Ct. 106, 108, 60 L. Ed. 297 (1915) ("The identity of the husband and wife is an ancient principle of our jurisprudence").

[5]Secs. 2, 3, 6, 7 of Act of Sept. 22, 1922, Pub. L. No. 67-346, 42 Stat. 1021 reproduced as Appendix 4-8 to Ch 4.

[6]Secs. 2, Act of September 22, 1922 reproduced as Appendix 4-8 to Ch 4.

[7]Sec. 4, Act of May 24, 1934, Pub.L. 73-250, 48 Stat. 797 reproduced as Appendix 4-10 to Ch 4. It must be noted that the 1934 law also provided that children born abroad to U.S. citizen women would acquire U.S. citizenship at birth to the same extent as children born to U.S. citizen men. See §§ 4:21 to 4:30. Before the 1934 act, only children born abroad to U.S. citizen fathers could acquire U.S. citizenship at birth. See §§ 4:16 to 4:20. Even though the 1934 act provided to women the right to transmit citizenship, Congress has only now corrected the previous discriminatory practice by restoring such right retroactively. The Immigration and Nationality Technical Corrections Act of 1994 (INTCA), Pub.L.103-416, § 101, 108 Stat. 4305 (Oct. 25, 1994) reproduced as Appendix 4-21 to Ch 4. The previous practice has been held to violate the equal protection clause of the Fourteenth Amendment to the U.S. Constitution. See Wauchope v. Dept. of State, 985 F.2d 1407 (9th Cir. 1993). See generally §§ 4:12 and 4:13.

[8]INA § 319(a), 8 U.S.C.A. § 1430(a).

[9]INA § 319(a), 8 U.S.C.A. § 1430(a) as amended by Victims of Trafficking and Violence Protection Act of 2000, Pub.L. 106-386, § 1503(e), 114 Stat. 1464 (Oct. 28, 2000). This same treatment is extended to persons who became lawful permanent residents by virtue of their status as abused children of a U.S. citizen. See § 11:25.

[10]INA § 319(b), 8 U.S.C.A. § 1430(b).

[11]INA § 319(d), 8 U.S.C.A. § 1430(d).

[12]INA § 324(c), 8 U.S.C.A. § 1435(c).

B. SPOUSES OF UNITED STATES CITIZENS—GENERAL RULE

§ 11:3 Requirements

Research References

West's Key Number Digest, Naturalization ⟳62, 64
A.L.R. Index, Immigration and Naturalization
Alien's Entitlement, as Spouse of United States Citizen, to "Immediate Relative" Status
    Under §§ 201, 204, and 205 of Immigration and Nationality Act of 1952 (8 U.S.C.A. §§ 1151,
    1154, 1155), 86 A.L.R. Fed. 135
Dizon and Wettstein, Immigration Law Service 2d §§ 14:191 to 14:195
Steel on Immigration Law §§ 15:10 to 15:12

Spouses of U.S. citizens must fulfill a shorter period of continuous residence in the United States prior to naturalization—only three years, as opposed to the normal period of five years—after lawful admission to permanent residents.[1] Just as under the general rule for naturalization, they must be physically present in the U.S. for half this period; in the case of spouses of U.S. citizens, 18 months of physical presence is required.[2] In addition, applicants under this section must be living in marital union with their U.S. citizen spouses during the entire period, and the spouses must have been U.S. citizens for the full three years.[3] The three-year period must be fulfilled with the same spouse; an applicant may not add the period of residence with a prior U.S. citizen spouse to obtain the three years.[4]

The regulations define living in marital union generally as "actually residing with his or her current spouse, with certain specified exceptions."[5] The meaning of "marital union" is not equivalent to marriage.[6] Termination of the marriage through divorce or death of the U.S. citizen spouse obviously terminates the marital union.[7] In addition, however, USCIS may find that the parties were not living in marital union even when the marriage has not been legally terminated.[8] The regulations provide for an automatic end to marital union when there is a legal separation.[9] This does not include court-ordered separations envisioned as "cooling off" periods after a quarrel rather than legal separations leading to divorces.[10]

Even informal separations may break the continuity of the marital union for purposes of this section.[11] USCIS will evaluate these informal separations to determine whether they are sufficient to signify the dissolution of the marital union.[12] Case law seems to indicate that if the separation is protracted and the party leaving

---

[Section 11:3]

[1] INA § 319(a), 8 U.S.C.A. § 1430(a).

[2] INA § 319(a), 8 U.S.C.A. § 1430(a); 8 CFR § 319.1(a)(4).

[3] INA § 319(a), 8 U.S.C.A. § 1430(a).

[4] INS Interp. 319.1(d)(1).

[5] 8 CFR § 319.1(b)(1).

[6] See Petition of Kostas, 169 F. Supp. 77, 78, 79 (D. Del. 1958). Contra, In Re Petition of Olan, 257 F.Supp. 884, 890 (S.D.Cal. 1966).

[7] 8 CFR § 319.1(b)(2)(i).

[8] See Petition of Kostas, 169 F. Supp. 77, 78 (D. Del. 1958).

[9] 8 CFR § 319.1(b)(2)(ii)(A).

[10] See Omar, Petition of, 151 F. Supp. 763, 764 (S.D. N.Y. 1957).

[11] 8 CFR § 319.1(b)(2)(ii)(B).

[12] 8 CFR § 319.1(b)(2)(ii)(B).

the family home no longer regards the house as the principal residence, then the parties are no longer living in marital union.[13] One court has made clear, however, that the requirement that the applicant and spouse actually live together should not be applied as a blanket rule without first considering whether the regulatory exceptions to this rule apply.[14] Brief separations, however, do not interrupt the marital union.[15]

Similarly, involuntary separations because of circumstances beyond the spouse's control, such as military service in the U.S. armed forces, will not preclude a finding of living in marital union.[16] However, in these cases, USCIS requires that a substantial portion of the residence in marital union must be within the U.S. to count toward the three years requirement.[17] Noncitizens who have served more than three years in the U.S. armed forces, and who apply for naturalization more than six months after their release from the armed forces, may count any time served in the armed forces within the three years preceding the filing of the application for naturalization as if they had been residing and physically present in the United States.[18]

Even though the statute requires marital union prior to the filing of the application, marital union is not required at the time of the actual naturalization; only a legally valid marriage is required at that point.[19] Thus, even when the applicant's separation is significant enough to bar a finding of marital union, it will not prevent the person from naturalizing if the separation occurred after the filing of the application for naturalization.[20] This applies even when the parties separated before the filing of the application provided that such separation did not interrupt the marital union until after the filing of the application.[21]

While the statute requires the applicant to have lived in marital union with the citizen spouse for three years immediately preceding the *date of filing the naturalization application* (emphasis added), the regulations expand this requirement to include marital union for three years preceding the *date of the examination of the applicant.* (Emphasis added).[22] It is unclear what the authority of USCIS is for extending this requirement. This regulatory requirement may have developed in an attempt to accommodate the cases where the application is filed ninety days before the completion of the statutorily required period of residence.[23]

One court found this regulation to be invalid because it contradicts the plain

---

[13]In re Olan, 257 F. Supp. 884, 888–89 (S.D. Cal. 1966); INS Interp. 319.1(d)(2).

[14]U.S. v. Onabanjo, 351 F. 3d 1064 (11th Cir. 2003) (in revocation proceedings, court held that district court erred when it applied the general rule regarding marital union without considering whether the applicant's separation from his wife for employment reasons satisfied the regulatory exception to the rule).

[15]In re Olan, 257 F. Supp. 884, 889 (S.D. Cal. 1966); Omar, Petition of, 151 F. Supp. 763, 764 (S.D. N.Y. 1957).

[16]8 CFR § 319.1(b)(2)(ii)(C).

[17]INS Interp. 319.1(d)(2).

[18]INA § 328(d); 8 U.S.C.A. § 1439(d); INS Interp. 328.1(b)(6)(ii). See § 12:3.

[19]INA § 319(a), 8 U.S.C.A. § 1430(a); In re Yao Quinn Lee, 480 F.2d 673, 677 n.6 (2d Cir. 1973).

[20]In re Yao Quinn Lee, 480 F.2d 673, 677, 24 A.L.R. Fed. 331 (2d Cir. 1973) interpreting In re Petition of Olan, 257 F.Supp. 884.

[21]See In re Olan, 257 F. Supp. 884, 887, 888, 893–94 (S.D. Cal. 1966).

[22]*Cf.* INA § 319(a), 8 U.S.C.A. § 1430(a) *with* 8 CFR § 319.1(a)(3).

[23]See § 9:3.

language of the statute.[24] The statutory language requiring the person to be a spouse at the time the naturalization is granted did not authorize the agency's expansive regulation.[25]

Death of the U.S. citizen spouse terminates the right of an applicant to naturalize under this section, even when death occurs after USCIS has approved the application but before the applicant has taken the oath of allegiance.[26] Even if the applicant marries another U.S. citizen before taking the oath, this right is not preserved.[27] However, if the U.S. citizen spouse died while serving honorably in active-duty in the U.S. armed forces, the widow or widower may be entitled to naturalize under the special widow/widower provision.[28]

Just like termination of the marital union, loss of U.S. citizenship by the U.S. citizen spouse also makes the lawful permanent resident spouse ineligible for naturalization under this section.[29]

In addition to the specific requirements of this section, the applicant must comply with all other requirements of naturalization.[30] However, since the provision links the requirement of good moral character to the period of required continuous residence, applicants under this provision only need to demonstrate good moral character for the three years of continuous residence required for their naturalization and, like any other applicant, for the period between the filing of the application and the admission to U.S. citizenship.[31]

After the Supreme Court struck down the Defense of Marriage Act as unconstitutional, the Board of Immigration Appeals held in the context of a visa petition that a marriage between two same-sex partners would be recognized in law.[32] As in other contexts, the legality of the marriage is governed by the law in the state where the marriage took place.[33] The Board has yet to consider the circumstance of "civil unions," and whether this or other forms of pseudo-marriages might constitute "living in marital union" for purposes of the naturalization statute, for instance in a state which does not permit same-sex marriage.

§ 11:4 Procedures

Research References
West's Key Number Digest, Naturalization ⚷68
Dizon and Wettstein, Immigration Law Service 2d §§ 14:306 to 14:314
Steel on Immigration Law § 15:19

---

[24]Ali v. Smith, 39 F.Supp.2d 1254 (W.D. Wash., 1999).

[25]Ali v. Smith, 39 F.Supp.2d 1254 (W.D. Wash., 1999).

[26]See In re Naturalization of Noland, 185 F.Supp. 948, 952–53 (D.Neb. 1960).

[27]Petition for Naturalization of Noland, 185 F. Supp. 948, 952–53 (D. Neb. 1960).

[28]INS Interp. 319.1(d)(1). See § 11:11.

[29]8 CFR § 319.1(b)(2)(i).

[30]INA § 319(a), 8 U.S.C.A. § 1430(a).

[31]INA §§ 316(a), 319(a), 8 U.S.C.A. §§ 1427(a), 1430(a); 8 CFR § 319.1(a)(7); INS Interp. 319.1(d) (5).

[32]Matter of Zeleniak, 26 I & N Dec. 158, 160 (BIA 2013); United States v. Windsor, 133 S. Ct. 2675, 2695-96 (2013).

[33]Matter of Zeleniak, 26 I & N Dec. 158, 160 (BIA 2013).

Applications under this section are submitted on INS Form N-400 and accompanying forms, following the procedures described under the general naturalization process.[1]

§ 11:5 Conditional residence and naturalization

Where an individual obtains residence status through marriage to the U.S. citizen and within two years of that marriage, the individual may only be granted residency on a conditional basis, which expires at the end of two years.[1] Conditional residents must generally file (jointly with their spouse) form I-751 to remove the conditions in the three months prior to the second anniversary of the green card issuance.[2]

As noted above, an individual living in marital union with a U.S. citizen may seek naturalization after two years and nine months of permanent residence.[3] INA § 216(e) provides that "for purposes of naturalization" an alien in conditional status "shall be considered to have been admitted as an alien lawfully admitted for permanent residence and to be in the United States as an alien lawfully admitted to the United States for permanent residence." Because it is not unusual for it to take a year or more for USCIS to adjudicate an I-751, an individual may still be in conditional residence status at the time he or she becomes eligible to seek naturalization.

The Adjudicators Field Manual permits a conditional resident to file an N-400 without waiting for the I-751 to be adjudicated.[4] When this happens, the manual calls for the N-400 adjudicator to obtain the I-751 and to concurrently adjudicate both applications.[5] The N-400 cannot be approved prior to approval of the I-751, because naturalization requires lawful permanent residence,[6] and conditional residence is not permanent residence. Thus, a conditional resident cannot generally be naturalized, while remaining a conditional resident.[7] However, the USCIS adjudicator can approve both forms concurrently.

There are circumstances where an individual may seek naturalization before filing the I-751 form. For instance, spouses of U.S. service members and spouses of others with specified employment abroad may qualified for expedited naturalization without needing to wait for two years and nine months of resident status.[8] The USCIS has concluded that in such cases, the applicant must meet the substantive requirements implicated by removal of the conditions, even if the individual is not required or permitted to file the I-751 form.[9] Further, USCIS believes that naturalization under § 316(a) requires a higher level of evidence than a jointly filed

---

[Section 11:4]

  [1]8 CFR § 319.11(a). See §§ 9:1 and et seq. and 10:1 et seq.

[Section 11:5]

  [1]INA § 216(d)(2).

  [2]INA § 216(d)(2).

  [3]INA § 319(a).

  [4]See AFM 25.1(k) (reproduced at Appendix 12-14).

  [5]See AFM 25.1(k)(2)(A) (reproduced at Appendix 12-14).

  [6]INA § 316(a) [8 U.S.C.A. § 1427(a)].

  [7]Abghari v. Gonzales, 596 F.Supp.2d 1336 (C.D.Cal. 2008).

  [8]See generally, §§ 11:7 to 11:10.

  [9]See AFM 25.1(k)(2)(C) (reproduced at Appendix 12-14).

I-751 application.[10] At any rate, the same types of evidence presented for I-751 applications should be filed in support of the naturalization application in that context.[11] If the N-400 application is not adjudicated before the beginning of the 90 day period in which the applicant may file the I-751 form, the adjudicator will instruct the applicant to file that form prior to final adjudication or prior to taking the oath.[12] An I-751 is not required if naturalization has already occurred, and USCIS states that they will refund any fee which is accepted where the I-751 is submitted in that circumstance.[13]

Another unusual situation in which naturalization may be sought before the I-751 is filed is when the conditional resident joins the military, particularly in time of war. That subject is addressed in chapter 12 of this book.[14] Because individuals seeking naturalization through military service in time of war are not required to be lawfully admitted for permanent residence, an adjudicator adjudicating such an N-400 need not consider issues related to conditional residence.[15]

C. BATTERED SPOUSES OF U.S. CITIZENS

§ 11:6 In general

Research References

Gallagher, Immigration Law Service 2d § 7:216
Steel on Immigration Law §§ 5:12, 15:19

In the year 2000, Congress amended the Immigration and Nationality Act to allow persons who became lawful permanent residents by reason of their status as a battered spouse or child of a U.S. citizen to naturalize under the same provisions as spouses of U.S. citizens.[1] The law exempts these spouses and children from the requirement that they must have lived in marital union with the U.S. citizen spouse in the United States.[2] Moreover, this law permits a battered applicant to apply under the three-year provisions even if, within two years of applying, the citizen spouse dies or loses his or her status, the union ends in divorce, or the battered applicant remarries.[3] With these exceptions, all the requirements of the general rule applicable to spouses of U.S. citizens also apply to qualifying battered spouses and children.[4]

---

[10]See AFM 25.1(k)(2)(A)(ii) (reproduced at Appendix 12-14).

[11]See AFM 25.1(k)(2)(C) (reproduced at Appendix 12-14).

[12]See AFM 25.1(k)(2)(B) (reproduced at Appendix 12-14).

[13]See AFM 25.1(k)(2)(D) (reproduced at Appendix 12-14).

[14]See §§ 12:3 to 12:5 (military service generally), §§ 12:6-12:11 (military service in time of war).

[15]See AFM 25.1(k) (reproduced at Appendix 12-14).

[Section 11:6]

[1]INA § 319(a), 8 U.S.C.A. § 1430(a) as amended by Victims of Trafficking and Violence Protection Act of 2000, Pub.L. 106-386, § 1503(e), 114 Stat. 1464 (Oct. 28, 2000).

[2]INA § 319(a), 8 U.S.C.A. § 1430(a) as amended by Victims of Trafficking and Violence Protection Act of 2000, Pub.L. 106-386, § 1503(e), 114 Stat. 1464 (Oct. 28, 2000).

[3]INA § 319(a), 8 U.S.C.A. § 1430(a) as amended by Victims of Trafficking and Violence Protection Act of 2000, Pub.L. 106-386, § 1503(e), 114 Stat. 1464 (Oct. 28, 2000).

[4]See § 11:3.

USCIS has not yet issued regulations to implement this section, but it has issued two memoranda that are reproduced in the appendix to this chapter.[5] These memoranda make clear that this provision applies regardless of whether the battered spouse obtained residency: (a) through a self-petition under VAWA, (b) through VAWA Cancellation of Removal, or (c) through a battered-spouse waiver of the joint filing requirement for removal of conditional residency.[6]

D. SPOUSES OF U.S. CITIZENS STATIONED ABROAD FOR SPECIFIC PURPOSES

§ 11:7 Requirements

Research References

West's Key Number Digest, Naturalization ⊙⇒62
Dizon and Wettstein, Immigration Law Service 2d §§ 14:196 to 14:203

Where a lawful permanent resident ("LPR") is married to a U.S. citizen who is required to be abroad due to certain kinds of employment, the INA authorizes expedited naturalization for the LPR, even before the permanent resident has accrued the 3 years otherwise necessary to apply. The U.S. citizen's employment must fall into one of several categories: (1) with the U.S. government; (2) with an American institution of research recognized as such by the Attorney General; (3) with an American firm or corporation engaged in whole or in part in the development of foreign trade and commerce of the United States; (4) with a subsidiary of such a firm or corporation; (5) with a public international organization in which the U.S. participates by treaty or statute; (6) as a religious practitioner, provided he or she is authorized to perform the ministerial or priestly functions of a religious denomination having a *bona fide* organization within the United States; or (7) to engage solely as a missionary by a religious denomination or by an interdenominational mission organization having a *bona fide* organization within the United States.[1]

The regulations interpret the requirement that the spouse be regularly stationed abroad to mean that the spouse must proceed abroad for a period of not less than one year, pursuant to a contract or orders, and assume the duties of employment.[2] Thus, there is no requirement that the U.S. citizen spouse already be abroad before the noncitizen may apply for naturalization.[3] The noncitizen spouse may naturalize before the beginning of the employment abroad of the U.S. citizen.[4] In terms of duration of the employment abroad, the statute itself is silent.[5] The regulations, however, provide a "threshold" requirement that the employment abroad be for an

---

[5]Yates, Deputy Executive Associate Commissioner, INS, Instructions Regarding the Expanded Meaning of Section 319(a), HQISD 70/33 (Oct. 15, 2002), reproduced as App. 11-4; Yates, Associate Director of Operations, USCIS, Clarification of Classes of Applicants Eligible for Naturalization under Section 219(a) of the Immigration and Nationality Act (INA), as amended by the Victims of Trafficking and Violence Protection Act of 2000 (VTVPA), Pub. L. 106-386 (Jan. 27, 2005), reproduced as App. 11-5.

[6]See App. 11-5.

[Section 11:7]

[1]INA § 319(b), 8 U.S.C.A. § 1430(b).
[2]8 CFR § 319.2(a)(1).
[3]INS Interp. 319.2(c)(2)(i), (ii).
[4]INS Interp. 319.2(c)(2)(i), (ii).
[5]INA § 319(b), 8 U.S.C.A. § 1430(b).

intended period of at least one year.[6] The legacy INS introduced this regulatory requirement in 1991 with virtually no explanation.[7] In addition, USCIS will not grant a naturalization application until the U.S. citizen spouse shows that he or she is under contract or orders to proceed abroad and assume the duties of the employment on a fixed date in close proximity.[8]

In terms of qualifying employment abroad, this section tracks almost verbatim the sections for lawful permanent residents' preservation of residence for naturalization purposes.[9] The qualifying organizations have already been discussed in detail above.[10] The same institutions considered public international organizations in which the U.S. participates for purposes of preservation of residence serve as qualifying employment for purposes of this section.[11] Similarly, the same American institutions of research that are recognized by USCIS for preservation are recognized as qualifying employment under this section.[12] It must be emphasized, however, that USCIS recognition of an institution of research is limited to the specific component of the university or research institution that has been so recognized.[13] The U.S. citizen spouse must be conducting research for that branch of the institution for the noncitizen spouse to qualify under this section.[14] In some circumstances, USCIS will consider conducting research abroad under a grant from a recognized institution of research as qualifying employment for purposes of this section.[15]

There are three noteworthy statutory differences between the sections on preservation of residence and the present section. First, there is no statutory or regulatory requirement in § 319(a) whereby subsidiaries of American firms or corporations are required to be 50% or more owned by the U.S. firm for employment to qualify.[16] A former INS General Counsel, however, issued a legal opinion stating that in spite of the different statutory language, the 50% rule of section 316(b) also applies to section 319(b).[17] Indeed, that opinion states that exactly the same principles apply in terms of tracing the ownership of the corporation.[18]

A second, and perhaps obvious, difference is that only spouses of missionaries may take advantage of these naturalization provisions, as opposed to religious

---

[6]CFR § 319.2(a)(1).

[7]See 56 Fed. Reg. 50475, 50477 (Oct. 7, 1991) (the preliminary information states only that "[t]he section has also been revised to clarify the factors and circumstances of eligibility for expeditious naturalization by drawing definitions and standards directly from the statute and existing judicial interpretations").

[8]INS Interp. 319.2(c)(3)(ii).

[9]INA §§ 316(b), 327, 8 U.S.C.A. §§ 1427(b), 1428. Indeed, a former INS general counsel found that the same interpretation applies to both sections. Memorandum, Rees, General Counsel, File No. HQ 319-C (Feb. 23, 1993) reprinted in 72 Interpreter Releases 1178 note 1 (Aug. 28, 1995).

[10]See §§ 7:6 to 7:10. For examples of cases found to be qualifying employment under this section, see INS Interp. 319.2(e).

[11]8 CFR § 319.5.

[12]See INS Interp. 319.2(e)(5). For a list of those institutions, see Appendix 7-1 to Ch 7.

[13]INS Interp. 319.2(e)(5)(i).

[14]INS Interp. 319.2(e)(5)(i).

[15]INS Interp. 319.2(e)(5)(ii).

[16]Compare INA § 319(b), 8 U.S.C.A. § 1430(b) with INA § 316(b), 8 U.S.C.A. § 1427(b).

[17]Legal Opinion, David Martin, INS General Counsel, File No. HQ 319-P (Sept. 14, 1995) reprinted in 73 Interpreter Releases 449 (April 8, 1996).

[18]Legal Opinion, David Martin, INS General Counsel, File No. HQ 319-P (Sept. 14, 1995) reprinted in 73 Interpreter Releases 449 (April 8, 1996).

brothers, nuns, and sisters who are allowed along with missionaries to take advantage of the preservation of residence provisions.[19] The third difference is that this section does not include the restriction relating to prior employment in public international organizations that appears for preservation of residence.[20]

The provision for naturalization due to the spouse's employment abroad must also be distinguished from the general rule applicable to spouses of U.S. citizens. First, under this section, there is no required period of prior residence in the U.S.: applicants may be naturalized without regard to any of the residency or physical presence requirements of the INA, provided they have been lawfully admitted to permanent residence at the time of naturalization.[21] Second, unlike the general spousal rule, here there is no requirement that the spouses must have lived in marital union at any point.[22] Indeed, this section does not require *any* prior residence either in the United States or in marital union with the U.S. citizen spouse.[23] This means that an applicant who has recently married a U.S. citizen assigned to work abroad may be naturalized before their departure, even if the applicant has only recently become a lawful permanent resident.[24]

The regulations have added a *sui generis* requirement that would bar the naturalization of the applicant if either before or after the filing of the application, the marital union ceases to exist because of death or divorce or because the citizen spouse has expatriated.[25] Even though this may look like grafting the requirement of marital union into this provision, in reality, the regulation does no more than require that the applicant be married to a U.S. citizen at the time of naturalization. The application will be denied if the U.S. citizen spouse has died, the citizen is no longer the spouse of the applicant, or the spouse is no longer a U.S. citizen. All three of those requirements appear in the INA.[26] If the relationship with the citizen spouse terminates by death, divorce, or expatriation prior to the applicant's admission to citizenship, the right to naturalize is *not* restored even when the applicant has married another citizen before the taking of the oath.[27]

To qualify for naturalization, the applicant must be in the U.S. at the time of naturalization.[28] This is interpreted to encompass both the time of the examination on the application for naturalization and the time of taking the oath.[29] In addition, the applicant must have a *bona fide* intention to take up residence within the United States immediately upon the termination of the specific employment abroad

---

[19]Compare INA § 319(b), 8 U.S.C.A. § 1430(b) with INA § 327, 8 U.S.C.A. § 1428.

[20]Compare INA § 319(b), 8 U.S.C.A. § 1430(b) with INA § 316(b), 8 U.S.C.A. § 1427(b).

[21]INA §§ 318, 319(b), 8 U.S.C.A. §§ 1429, 1430(b); 8 CFR § 319.2(2). Not only is there a substantive exemption from the requirement, but the statute specifically bars the INS from requiring proof of prior residence and physical presence in the United States. INA § 319(b), 8 U.S.C.A. § 1430(b).

[22]Compare INA § 319(b), 8 U.S.C.A. § 1430(b) with INA § 319(a), 8 U.S.C.A. § 1430(a).

[23]INA § 319(b), 8 U.S.C.A. § 1430(b).

[24]See INS Interp. 319.2(b)(1).

[25]8 CFR § 319.2(c).

[26]INA § 319(b), 8 U.S.C.A. § 1430(b).

[27]8 CFR § 319.2(c). See § 11:3.

[28]INA § 319(b), 8 U.S.C.A. § 1430(b).

[29]8 CFR § 319.2(a)(2), (3).

of the U.S. citizen spouse.[30] Indeed, the INA requires the applicant to make a declaration that such is his or her intention.[31]

The regulations have added a requirement that at the time of naturalization, the applicant must intend to reside abroad with the citizen spouse.[32] Up to 1991, the regulations only had that added requirement.[33] The courts have affirmed this requirement as an implied requirement in the INA.[34] In 1991, the legacy INS added the following requirements to the regulations: the applicant must (1) establish that he or she will depart to join the citizen spouse within thirty to forty-five days after the date of naturalization; (2) notify the agency immediately of any delay or cancellation of the citizen spouse's assignment abroad; and (3) notify the agency immediately if the applicant is unable to reside with the citizen spouse because the citizen spouse is employed abroad in an area of hostilities where dependents may not reside.[35]

USCIS will not deny naturalization to an applicant who has the intention of going abroad with his or her spouse but is prevented from going to the spouse's place of employment by U.S. government restrictions because of the dangerous nature of the location.[36] The courts have granted naturalizations based on this exception even when the applicant would reside in a third country far away from the location of the spouse.[37] If the applicant does not intend to take up residence in a foreign country, USCIS will not grant naturalization.[38]

---

[30]INA § 319(b), 8 U.S.C.A. § 1430(b).

[31]INA § 319(b), 8 U.S.C.A. § 1430(b).

[32]8 CFR § 319.2(a)(4)(i).

[33]8 CFR § 319.2 (1990).

[34]In re Petition of Sun Cha Tom, 294 F.Supp. 791, 793 (D.Hawaii, 1968).

[35]8 CFR § 319.2(b) as amended by 56 Fed. Reg. 50475 (Oct. 7, 1991). The explanatory section is completely uninformative regarding the substantive requirements imposed into the statute by the regulations. 56 Fed. Reg. at 50477. The INS Interpretations attempt to provide a legal justification for these requirements. See INS Interp. 319.2(c)(3). In spite of lack of direct legislative history as to the matter, the legacy INS decided that the intention of Congress was for the applicant to reside abroad upon obtaining naturalization. INS Interp. 319.2(c)(3) citing to Senate Report No. 1137, Jan. 29, 1952 (to accompany S. 2250); House Report No. 1365, Feb. 14, 1952 (to accompany H.R. 5678); Conference Report No. 2096, June 9, 1952 (to accompany H.R. 5678) (to substantiate its claim that there is no direct legislative history to support its interpretation). The INS cited no cases regarding its requirement that departure of the naturalized spouse be soon after that of the spouse or shortly after naturalization. INS Interp. 319.2(c)(3)(iv), (v).

[36]INS Interp. 319.2(c)(3)(iii) citing to In re Petition of Sun Cha Tom, 294 F.Supp. 791; In re Simpson, 315 F.Supp. 584 (W.D.La. 1970).

[37]The following petitions cited in INS Interp. 319.2(c)(3)(iii) were granted even though the U.S. citizen husband was going on a tour of duty in Vietnam during the Vietnam war and the noncitizen spouse was going to a third country: Petition of Ortrud Margaret Lilly, U.S.D.C., Eastern District of Virginia, A-17277901 (1969) (unreported decision) (petitioner was to reside in Germany while husband in Vietnam); Petition of Angela Rita Bender, U.S.D.C., Southern District of Ohio, 2532-P-25940 (1968) (unreported decision) (petitioner would reside in Italy); Petition of Kim Dung Hayes, U.S.D.C., Southern District of Ohio, 2532-P-25939 (1968) (unreported decision) (petitioner to reside in Thailand); In re Petition of Sun Cha Tom, 294 F.Supp. 791 (petitioner to reside in South Korea). The following were granted when spouse was to reside in Thailand while serving in the air force: Petition of Eiko Donoho, Superior Court, Androscoggin County, Maine, 1451-P-6985 (1969) (unreported decision) (petitioner to reside in Japan); In re Simpson, 315 F.Supp. 584 (petitioner to reside in Spain).

[38]INS Interp. 319.2(c)(3)(iii).

§ 11:8 General procedures for spouses of U.S. citizens employed abroad in qualifying employment

Research References

West's Key Number Digest, Naturalization ⬥62
Dizon and Wettstein, Immigration Law Service 2d §§ 14:197, 14:198
Steel on Immigration Law § 15:19

All applicants under this section must file Form N-400 and all accompanying forms as described for the general naturalization procedures.[1] In addition, the noncitizen spouse must file a statement of intent containing the following information about the citizen spouse's employment and the applicant's intent following naturalization: (1) the name of the employer and: (a) the nature of the employer's business, or (b) the ministerial, religious, or missionary activity in which the employer is engaged; (2) whether the employing entity is owned in whole or in part by United States interests; (3) whether the employing entity is engaged in whole or in part in the development of the foreign trade and commerce of the United States; (4) the nature of the activity in which the citizen spouse is engaged; (5) the anticipated period of employment abroad (of the U.S. citizen spouse); (6) whether the noncitizen spouse intends to reside abroad with the citizen spouse; and (7) whether the noncitizen spouse intends to take up residence within the United States immediately upon termination of such employment abroad by the U.S. citizen spouse.[2]

§ 11:9 Special procedures relating to spouses of Peace Corps volunteers

Research References

West's Key Number Digest, Naturalization ⬥62
Dizon and Wettstein, Immigration Law Service 2d § 14:119
Steel on Immigration Law § 3:2

Volunteering in the Peace Corps is considered employment by the United States government for purposes of INA § 319(b).[1] However, under Peace Corps procedures, enrollment in the Peace Corps does not take place until after the applicant has completed an intensive training program overseas.[2] Therefore, the noncitizen spouse would not be entitled to file an application for naturalization until the U.S. citizen spouse has completed the training.

To circumvent this problem, USCIS and the Peace Corps have agreed to allow the noncitizen spouse of a prospective Peace Corps volunteer to submit a naturalization application together with a statement from the Peace Corps regarding the possible future enrollment of the citizen spouse.[3] USCIS will then issue a written advisory opinion regarding the naturalization eligibility of the noncitizen spouse. If found

---

[Section 11:8]

[1]8 CFR § 319.11(a). See §§ 9:1 and et seq. and 10:1 et seq.

[2]8 CFR § 319.11(a).

[Section 11:9]

[1]INS Interp. 319.2(e)(4) citing to Correspondence between Ass't Comm., Naturalization (Dec. 6, 1963) and Gen. Coun., Peace Corps (Dec. 2, 1963), file CO319.1-P.

[2]INS Interp. 319.2(e)(4).

[3]INS Interp. 319.2(e)(4).

eligible, USCIS will advise the applicant that the finding of eligibility is contingent on the U.S. citizen spouse becoming enrolled as a Peace Corps volunteer and being stationed abroad by the Peace Corps at the time of naturalization.[4]

The application with all the attachments and the advisory opinion is returned to the applicant who is instructed to resubmit the application 30 days prior to the intended return to the United States.[5] Together with the application, the applicant must submit a certification from the Peace Corps establishing the enrollment of the U.S. citizen spouse in the Peace Corps.[6] At that point, however, USCIS will make a *de novo* determination of eligibility, notwithstanding the prior advisory opinion.[7]

§ 11:10 Special procedures relating to military employment

Research References

West's Key Number Digest, Naturalization ⬤➡65
Dizon and Wettstein, Immigration Law Service 2d §§ 14:199, 14:315
Steel on Immigration Law § 15:11

Spouses of U.S. citizens traveling abroad for military employment are required to follow the general procedures provided for naturalization as spouses of U.S. citizens employed abroad in qualifying employment.[1] Instead of the declaration of intent described above, however, they are required to file specific documentation.[2]

The Department of Defense (DOD) regulations provide for the issuance of certificate of assignment abroad to spouses of U.S. citizens who will be assigned outside the U.S.[3] This "Certificate of Overseas Assignment to Support Application to File Petition for Naturalization," DD Form 1278, will be issued only if the noncitizen spouse is authorized to travel at government expense.[4] DD Form 1278 will be issued no earlier than ninety days before dependent's date of departure.[5] The *INS Interpretations* provide that if DD Form 1278 is issued more than ninety days in advance of travel, it violates DOD regulations and will not be accepted by the agency.[6]

When the military authorities pay for the transportation, compliance with all the special requirements under this section must be established from DD Form 1278 alone.[7] That form will be submitted instead of the statement of intent required for all applicants under this provision.[8] Military commanders have been instructed not

---

[4]INS Interp. 319.2(e)(4).

[5]INS Interp. 319.2(e)(4).

[6]INS Interp. 319.2(e)(4).

[7]INS Interp. 319.2(e)(4).

[Section 11:10]

[1]8 CFR § 319.11(b).

[2]8 CFR § 319.11(b).

[3]32 CFR § 94.4(c).

[4]INS Interp. 319.2(d)(2).

[5]32 CFR § 94.4(c)(1)(i), (ii), (iii).

[6]INS Interp. 319.2(d)(2).

[7]INS Interp. 319.2(d)(2).

[8]8 CFR § 319.11(b)(2). The statement of intent has been described in the subsection immediately preceding the present one. See § 11:9.

to issue letters or memoranda in lieu of that form, as USCIS will only accept DD Form 1278.[9]

DOD regulations inform applicants that they must file DD Form 1278, together with the INS Form N-400, three identical photographs, and fingerprint card (Form FD-358).[10] Applicants are urged to apply immediately for a U.S. passport upon approval of the naturalization.[11]

If the spouse travels at his or her own expense, the spouse must establish all the requirements independently from DD Form 1278 since such form will not be issued.[12] In lieu of the declaration of intent required under the general procedures for this provision, the applicant must present: (1) a copy of the U.S. citizen spouse's military travel orders; (2) a letter from the citizen spouse's commanding officer indicating that the military has no objection to the applicant traveling to and residing in the vicinity of the citizen spouse's new duty station; and (3) evidence of transportation arrangements to the new duty station.[13]

A recent statute,[14] provides that spouses and children of U.S. citizens deployed abroad, who accompany them as described above, may qualify for these protections without any separate application. Further, spouses and children abroad now qualify for overseas naturalization.[15] USCIS has begun to implement these provisions through memoranda which are attached as appendices to Ch 12.[16] These provisions apply even to individuals who are still in conditional residence status, though additional requirements apply in that circumstance.[17]

E. WIDOWS AND WIDOWERS OF U.S. VETERANS

§ 11:11 In general

Research References

West's Key Number Digest, Naturalization ⟜64
Dizon and Wettstein, Immigration Law Service 2d §§ 14:204, 14:205

The INA has a special provision that allows the naturalization of surviving spouses of a U.S. citizen who died "during a period of honorable services in an active duty status in the Armed Forces of the United States" without regards to the prior residence and physical presence requirements of section 316.[1] The surviving spouse must have been living in "marital union" with the U.S. citizen at the time of the citizen's death.[2]

---

[9]32 CFR § 94.4(c)(1).

[10]32 CFR § 94.4(c)(2). The Department of Defense regulations still include the requirement of filing biographic form. This requirement has been dropped under current naturalization procedures for all but those naturalizing through service in the armed forces. See §§ 9:1 et seq. and 12:1 et seq.

[11]32 CFR § 94.4(c).

[12]INS Interp. 319.2(d)(2).

[13]8 CFR § 319.11(b)(3). Cf. INS Interp. 319.2(d)(2).

[14]See Appendix 11–6.

[15]See Appendix 11–6, at § 674(c).

[16]See Appendix 12–9, Appendix 12–10, Appendix 12–11.

[17]See generally, § 11:5.

[Section 11:11]

[1]INA § 319(d), 8 U.S.C.A. § 1430(d).

[2]INA § 319(d), 8 U.S.C.A. § 1430(d).

For the widow or widower to obtain benefits under this section, the U.S. citizen must have been serving in active duty status in the U.S. armed forces at the time of his or her death.[3] This provision is complementary, though somewhat different, from the two provisions allowing the naturalization of certain noncitizens who served in the U.S. armed forces.[4] First, under the present provision, it is the U.S. citizen spouse who must have served in the U.S. armed forces (though citizenship may have been granted posthumously)[5], while the other two provisions provide for noncitizens who serve in the U.S. armed forces. On the one hand, there is no minimum time that the U.S. citizen must have served before his or her widow or widower may obtain the benefits of this section.[6] On the other hand, while the general naturalization provision allows for the naturalization of a noncitizen who may have served in a reserve unit, the widow/widower provision requires the U.S. citizen spouse to have been serving in active duty at the time of his or her death.[7] Finally, if compared to the provision for naturalization due to the active-duty service of the noncitizen in time of war, the widow/widower provision is broader because it is not restricted to service at time of war.[8]

The meaning of "Armed Forces of the United States" is not specifically discussed in the regulations governing this section.[9] It has been defined under both sections dealing with naturalization of noncitizen service persons to mean the U.S. Army, U.S. Navy, U.S. Marines, U.S. Coast Guard, and a National Guard unit during such time as the unit is federally recognized as a reserve component of the armed forces of the U.S.[10] Since this section requires the spouse to have died while serving in active duty, service in a national guard unit will presumably only be service in the U.S. armed forces if the unit is called for active duty.[11]

In addition to establishing that the spouse died during a period of honorable active duty service in the armed forces of the U.S., the applicant must establish that he or she was living in marital union with the citizen spouse at the time of that spouse's death.[12] Marital union under this subsection has the same general meaning as in the general rule for naturalization by marriage to a U.S. citizen.[13] That meaning is discussed above.[14] Unlike the general naturalization provision, however, the benefits of this section are available even if the widow or widower has remarried.[15]

---

[3]8 CFR § 319.3(a)(1).

[4]See §§ 12:3 to 12:9.

[5]See App 11-8.

[6]Compare INA § 319(d), 8 U.S.C.A. § 1430(d) with INA § 328, 8 U.S.C.A. § 1439 (the latter is applicable if the noncitizen served honorably a minimum of three years in the U.S. armed forces).

[7]8 CFR §§ 319.3(a)(1), 328.1.

[8]Compare INA § 319(d), 8 U.S.C.A. § 1430(d) with INA § 329, 8 U.S.C.A. § 1440.

[9]8 CFR § 319.3.

[10]8 CFR §§ 328.1, 329.1. See generally, Ch 12.

[11]See 8 CFR § 329.1.

[12]INA § 319(d), 8 U.S.C.A. § 1430(d).

[13]See 8 CFR § 319.3(a)(2).

[14]See § 11:3.

[15]8 CFR § 319.3(b).

In addition to satisfying the specific requirements of this subsection, the applicant must be otherwise eligible for naturalization.[16] This means that the applicant must also be a lawful permanent resident at the time of naturalization and must establish that he or she is a person of good moral character, attached to the principles of the U.S. Constitution, and favorably disposed towards the good order and happiness of the U.S.[17]

USCIS now instructs applicants under this section to send applications to an address at the Nebraska Service Center, to be handled by a specialized team. The address is:

Nebraska Service Center
PO Box 87426
Lincoln, NE 68501-7426

For Express Mail and Courier deliveries:

Nebraska Service Center
850 S. Street
Lincoln, NE 68508

USCIS instruction sheets are found at appendices 11-7 and 11-8 of this chapter.

F. FORMER US CITIZENS WHO LOST THEIR CITIZENSHIP BY MARRIAGE TO NONCITIZENS

§11:12 General rule

Research References

Dizon and Wettstein, Immigration Law Service 2d §§ 14:386, 14:429, 14:434
Steel on Immigration Law §§ 15:25, 15:26

Prior to 1922, some U.S. citizen women who married noncitizens were subject to automatic loss of citizenship.[1] In 1922, Congress repealed the law of expatriation of women by marriage and affirmatively provided that U.S. citizen women who married noncitizens would not lose their U.S. citizenship unless their husbands were themselves ineligible for U.S. citizenship, formally renounced their U.S. citizenship, or proceeded to reside abroad for a specific period of time and failed to establish their lack of intention to renounce U.S. citizenship.[2] Many women, however, lost their citizenship prior to 1922 under the automatic loss of citizenship provisions and after 1922 by marriage to noncitizens ineligible for citizenship. The conditions upon

---

[16]INA § 319(d), 8 U.S.C.A. § 1430(d) (only exempt the applicant from the residence requirements of section 316).

[17]8 CFR § 319.3(a)(3), (4).

[Section 11:12]

[1]Sec. 3, Act of March 2, 1907 reproduced as Appendix 4-6 to Ch 4; Mackenzie v. Hare, 239 U.S. 299, 36 S. Ct. 106, 60 L. Ed. 297 (1915); Petition of Drysdale, 20 F.2d 957 (E.D. Mich. 1927) (holding that the 1907 law was declarative of pre-existing common law). For a discussion of the conditions under which a woman's marriage to a noncitizen resulted in expatriation prior to 1922, see Ch 15.

[2]Secs. 3, 7, Act of September 22, 1922 reproduced as Appendix 4-8 to Ch 4.

which such women lost U.S. citizenship and the automatic resumption of citizenship by some women upon termination of their marriage are discussed in Ch 15.[3]

§ 11:13 General rule—Requirements and benefits

Research References

West's Key Number Digest, Naturalization ☜62
Dizon and Wettstein, Immigration Law Service 2d § 14:386
Steel on Immigration Law §§ 15:10 to 15:12

The INA provides an expedited procedure for the naturalization of women who lost their U.S. citizenship by marriage to a noncitizen.[1] These provisions apply to: (1) women who before September 22, 1922, lost their U.S. citizenship by marrying noncitizens or by marrying U.S. citizens who thereafter lost U.S. citizenship; or (2) women who lost U.S. citizenship by marrying noncitizens ineligible for citizenship after September 22, 1922.[2] Women who acquired another nationality by an affirmative act other than marrying the noncitizen person are not eligible for this section.[3]

In terms of substantive requirements, such women are exempt from the U.S. and state or USCIS district residence and physical presence requirements.[4] They are also not required to have the intention of residing in the United States after naturalization.[5] They must, however, have either resided continuously in the United States since the date of the marriage or have been lawfully admitted to permanent residence before filing their naturalization application.[6]

The applicant must also establish that she has been a person of good moral character, attached to the principles of the Constitution, and well disposed to the good order and happiness of the United States for a period of five years immediately preceding the filing of the application for naturalization and up to her admission to citizenship.[7]

After their naturalization, those women are restored to the status of native-born or naturalized citizens, depending on which status they had before expatriation through marriage.[8] However, they will not be considered U.S. citizens for the period between their expatriation and the resumption of citizenship.[9]

It should be noted that the constitutionality of these expatriation statutes is dubious at best. Chapter 15 contains a fuller discussion of the constitutional limitations on expatriation,[10] which should be consulted. At least one Court of Appeals has

---

[3]See § 15:16.

[Section 11:13]

[1]INA § 324, 8 U.S.C.A. § 1435.

[2]INA § 324(a), 8 U.S.C.A. § 1435(a); 8 CFR § 324.2(a)(2).

[3]INA § 324(a), 8 U.S.C.A. § 1435(a); 8 CFR § 324.2(a)(3).

[4]INA § 324(a)(1), 8 U.S.C.A. § 1435(a)(1).

[5]INA § 324(a)(2), 8 U.S.C.A. § 1435(a)(2)

[6]INA § 324(b), 8 U.S.C.A. § 1435(b); 8 CFR § 324.2(a)(4).

[7]INA § 324(b), 8 U.S.C.A. § 1435(b); 8 CFR § 324.2(a)(5).

[8]INA § 324(a), 8 U.S.C.A. § 1435(a). The INA declares the same rights for women who resumed citizenship under the equivalent provisions of the Nationality Act of 1940.

[9]INA § 324(a), 8 U.S.C.A. § 1435(a).

[10]See §§ 15:1, 15:16.

found these provisions unconstitutional.[11] To the extent that a woman was not expatriated by her marriage to a noncitizen, no resumption of citizenship would be required. Indeed, those arguments would likely be of extremely limited practical significance at this point in time. Any women divested of citizenship by pre-1922 marriages would now be over 100 years old, making potential resumption of citizenship of limited practical significance. However, to the extent that these women remained U.S. citizens without further action on their part, they may have conveyed U.S. citizen to their children.[12] Constitutional challenges to their alleged loss of citizenship would be more likely than attempts on their part to resume citizenship.

§ 11:14 General rule—Procedures

Research References

West's Key Number Digest, Naturalization ⊚68
Dizon and Wettstein, Immigration Law Service 2d §§ 14:306 to 14:309, 14:315, 14:319
Steel on Immigration Law § 15:19

The application is submitted on Form N-400 at the USCIS office having jurisdiction over the applicant's place of residence.[1] The procedural requirements applicable to general naturalization also apply to applicants under this section.[2] In addition, the applicant must submit with her application a statement describing her eligibility for this section as well as any documentation that tends to prove such eligibility.[3]

§ 11:15 Rule for native-born women who divorced after 1941; requirements and benefits

Research References

Dizon and Wettstein, Immigration Law Service 2d §§ 14:85, 14:341, 14:351
Steel on Immigration Law § 15:26

There is a special rule for women who were born U.S. citizens and who may have expatriated themselves by marriage to a noncitizen before September 22, 1922 or to a noncitizen ineligible for citizenship after that date and whose marriage was terminated after January 12, 1941.[1] Women are ineligible for this section if they acquire another nationality by affirmative acts other than marrying the noncitizen.[2]

To be eligible under this section, marriage must have terminated by the complete dissolution of the marital status through divorce from, or death of, the noncitizen husband.[3] USCIS takes the position that this section is inapplicable if the reason the woman is not married to a noncitizen any longer is because her husband has

---

[11]Rocha v. I.N.S., 450 F.2d 947, 948 (1st Cir. 1971).

[12]See generally, Ch 4.

[Section 11:14]

[1]8 CFR § 324.2(b).

[2]8 CFR § 324.2(b). See §§ 9:1 et seq. and 10:1 et seq.

[3]8 CFR § 324.2(b).

[Section 11:15]

[1]INA § 324(c), 8 U.S.C.A. § 1435(c); 8 CFR § 324.3(a).

[2]INA § 324(c)(1), 8 U.S.C.A. § 1435(c)(1); 8 CFR § 324.3(a)(4).

[3]INS Interp. 324.2(a)(4).

become a U.S. citizen.[4] On the other hand, it applies to termination by divorce even when the woman after 1922 once again marries the same person or another noncitizen.[5]

Such women are allowed to become U.S. citizens without filing a naturalization application.[6] In addition, they are not required to comply with any of the naturalization requirements of the INA, except that they will not be naturalized if they are barred from citizenship because of political grounds.[7]

The only formal procedure they are required to follow is taking the oath of allegiance.[8] The oath may be taken in the United States or abroad before a diplomatic or consular office of the U.S.[9] The taking of the oath is recorded and the woman, if she so requests, will be delivered a certified copy of the proceedings which serves to establish her citizenship.[10]

Upon taking of the oath, the woman is considered to be a U.S. citizen from birth.[11] However, she will not be considered to be a citizen for the period between her expatriation and her resumption of citizenship.[12]

§ 11:16 Rule for native-born women who divorced after 1941; requirements and benefits—Procedures

Research References

West's Key Number Digest, Naturalization ⊙68, 69
Dizon and Wettstein, Immigration Law Service 2d §§ 14:306, 14:315, 14:351
Steel on Immigration Law § 15:19

USCIS requires women under this section to file a Form N-400 without a fee at USCIS office having jurisdiction over their place of residence "as evidence of [their] desire to take the oath."[1] USCIS officer will review her application and advise the woman of her eligibility to take the oath.[2] The oath may be taken before a court, a USCIS officer, or a consular or diplomatic officer abroad.[3] A certified copy of the oath will be provided for a fee not to exceed $5.[4]

§ 11:17 Rule for native-born women who divorced after 1941; requirements and benefits—Oath of Allegiance under 1936 Act

Research References

West's Key Number Digest, Naturalization ⊙62, 68

---

[4]INS Interp. 324.2(a)(4).

[5]INS Interp. 324.2(a)(4).

[6]INA § 324(c)(1), 8 U.S.C.A. § 1435(c)(1).

[7]INA § 324(c)(1), 8 U.S.C.A. § 1435(c)(1); 8 CFR § 324.3(a)(5).

[8]INA § 324(c)(1), 8 U.S.C.A. § 1435(c)(1); 8 CFR § 324.1.

[9]INA § 324(c)(2), 8 U.S.C.A. § 1435(c)(2).

[10]INA § 324(c)(3), 8 U.S.C.A. § 1435(c)(3).

[11]INA § 324(c)(1), 8 U.S.C.A. § 1435(c)(1).

[12]INA § 324(c)(1), 8 U.S.C.A. § 1435(c)(1).

[Section 11:16]

[1]8 CFR § 324.3(b)(1).

[2]8 CFR § 324.3(b)(2).

[3]8 CFR § 324.3(b)(2).

[4]8 CFR § 324.3(b)(2).

Dizon and Wettstein, Immigration Law Service 2d §§ 14:21, 14:90, 14:179

Women who were restored to U.S. citizenship by the Act of 1936, as amended in 1940, were allowed to regain their citizenship rights by taking the oath of allegiance to the U.S.[1] Such an oath may still be taken.[2] However, USCIS will inquire into whether the woman intends in good faith to discharge the obligations of the oath of allegiance and whether her attitude toward the Constitution and government of the U.S. renders her capable of fulfilling the obligations of the oath.[3] If it finds the good faith intention or the attitude toward the Constitution and the government not to have been established, USCIS will object to the woman taking the oath.[4] Because of a statutory requirement, the applicant will only be charged $1 for the certified copy of the oath.[5]

III. CHILDREN OF U.S. CITIZENS

A. CITIZENSHIP UPON APPLICATION BY CITIZEN PARENT

§ 11:18   In general

Research References

West's Key Number Digest, Naturalization ⚲62
A.L.R. Index, Immigration and Naturalization
Validity, Construction, and Application of Child Citizenship Act, 194 A.L.R. Fed. 383
Dizon and Wettstein, Immigration Law Service 2d §§ 14:209, 14:211, 14:214
Steel on Immigration Law §§ 15:11, 15:16

This section only deals with the naturalization of children upon application of their U.S. citizen parent or parents. Automatic derivation of U.S. citizenship after birth is discussed in Ch 5. The acquisition of U.S. citizenship at birth abroad by children of U.S. citizens is discussed in Ch 4. This naturalization provision is designed to complement those provisions and allow children who did not automatically acquire U.S. citizenship to become citizens of this country upon the application of their U.S. citizen parents.

The provisions relating to the naturalization of children upon application of a U.S. citizen parent are contained in section 322 of the INA.[1] Congress recently substantially amended this section.[2] As amended, it now provides:[3]

A parent who is a citizen of the United States may apply for naturalization on behalf of a child born outside of the United States who has not acquired citizenship automatically

---

[Section 11:17]

[1]See § 15:16.

[2]Matter of B-, 1 I. & N. Dec. 283 (B.I.A. 1942).

[3]INS Interp. 324.2(a)(6).

[4]INS Interp. 324.2(a)(6).

[5]Act of June 25, 1936, Pub. L. No. 74-793, 49 Stat. 1917 reproduced as Appendix 4-11 to Ch 4; 8 CFR § 324.4.

[Section 11:18]

[1]8 U.S.C.A. § 1433.

[2]Child Citizenship Act of 2000, Pub. L. No. 106-395, § 102, 114 Stat. 1631 (Oct. 30, 2000), reproduced as Appendix 5-2 to Ch 5.

[3]INA § 322(a), 8 U.S.C.A. § 1433(a) as amended by the Child Citizenship Act of 2000, § 102(a) reproduced as Appendix 5-2 to Ch 5.

under section 320. The Attorney General shall issue a certificate of citizenship to such parent upon proof, to the satisfaction of the Attorney General, that the following conditions have been fulfilled:

(1) At least one parent is a citizen of the United States, whether by birth or naturalization.

(2) The United States citizen parent—

(A) has been physically present in the United States or its outlying possessions for a period or periods totaling not less than five years, at least two of which were after attaining the age of fourteen years; or

(B) has a citizen parent who has been physically present in the United States or its outlying possessions for a period or periods totaling not less than five years, at least two of which were after attaining the age of fourteen years.

(3) The child is under the age of eighteen years.

(4) The child is residing outside of the United States in the legal and physical custody of the citizen parent, is temporarily present in the United States pursuant to a lawful admission, and is maintaining such lawful status.

§ 11:19 Historical background

Research References

West's Key Number Digest, Naturalization ⌾62
Dizon and Wettstein, Immigration Law Service 2d § 14:214

Section 322 has suffered several radical amendments within the last decade. It was first completely rewritten by Congress in 1994.[1] Under that amendment, the U.S. citizen parent no longer applied for naturalization of the child. Instead, the parent filed for a certificate of citizenship.[2] This remains the practice under current law. While the statute refers to an application for a certificate of citizenship—which generally is issued to someone who is already a citizen—INA § 322 is really a naturalization procedure. The child is not a U.S. citizen until the agency adjudicates the parent's application.

In November 1996, Congress amended the INTCA to provide for a "transitional" rule.[3] The transitional rule added a special requirement for children born before November 14, 1986. Those children would not be exempt from lawful permanent residence unless their U.S. citizen parent or grandparent resided in the United States for ten years, at least five of which were after the age of 14.[4] Thus, under the 1996 amendment, children born before November 14, 1986, would benefit from the five-year/two-year rule while parents of children born after that date would be required to prove ten years of physical presence, five years of which were after age 14.

On August 8, 1997, Congress discarded the 1996 amendment and restored the INTCA to its original provisions.[5] Thus, until the year 2000 amendment, lawful permanent residence of the child was not required if the U.S. citizen parent or

---

[Section 11:19]

[1]INTCA § 102(a) reproduced as Appendix 4-21 to Ch 4.

[2]For a discussion of certificates of citizenship, see §§ 13:26 to 13:31.

[3]IIRAIRA § 671(b)(2) reproduced as Appendix 4-22 to Ch 4.

[4]IIRAIRA § 671(b)(2) reproduced as Appendix 4-22 to Ch 4.

[5]Act of August 8, 1997, Pub. L. No. 105-38 reproduced as Appendix 4-23 to Ch 4.

grandparent was physically present in the United States for five years, at least two of which were after the age of 14, regardless of the date of birth of the child.[6]

Finally, on October 30, 2000, Congress once again radically amended this section, partly in light of the amendments to sections 320 and 321 of the INA and partly restricting the scope of beneficiaries of the law.[7] The agency has issued interim regulations—effective June 13, 2001—to implement this section of the Child Citizenship Act of 2000.[8]

§ 11:20 Requirements

Research References

West's Key Number Digest, Naturalization ⚷62
A.L.R. Index, Immigration and Naturalization
Validity, Construction, and Application of Child Citizenship Act, 194 A.L.R. Fed. 383
Dizon and Wettstein, Immigration Law Service 2d §§ 14:214 to 14:219
Steel on Immigration Law §§ 15:8, 15:16

Under the current version of INA § 322 the DHS is required to issue a certificate of citizenship if the parent proves: (1) that at least one of the parents of the child is a U.S. citizen, whether by birth or naturalization; (2) that the child resides outside the United States; (3) that the child is temporarily present in the United States pursuant to lawful admission; (4) that the child is maintaining lawful status in the United States; (5) that the child is under the age of 18 years; and (6) that the child is in the legal and physical custody of the citizen parent.[1] In addition, (7) either the U.S. citizen parent or a citizen parent of the parent must have been physically present in the United States or its outlying possessions for a period totaling five years or more, at least two of which were after the parent attained the age of 14.[2]

Under a USCIS interpretation of the amendment there is no requirement that the grandparent be alive at the time of submission of the application. It is enough that he or she should have complied by the required residence.[3] This provision seems to have been modeled upon, and be a variation of, the provisions for the transmission of citizenship at birth abroad.[4] However, unlike the provisions for transmission of U.S. citizenship at birth, the prior residence of the parent or grandparent does not need to be before the child's birth.[5] Rather, such residence must be satisfied before the application is adjudicated prior to the child's 18th birthday.[6]

---

[6]INTCA § 102 reproduced as Appendix 4-21 to Ch 4.

[7]Child Citizenship Act of 2000, § 102 reproduced as Appendix 5-2 to Ch 5.

[8]8 CFR §§ 322.1 through 322.5; see also Children Born Outside the United States; Applications for Certificate of Citizenship, 66 Fed. Reg. 32,138 (2001) (adopting interim rule).

[Section 11:20]

[1]INA § 322(a), 8 U.S.C.A. § 1433(a) as amended by Child Citizenship Act of 2000, § 102 reproduced in Appendix 5-2 to Ch 5.

[2]INA § 322(a)(2), 8 U.S.C.A. § 1433(a)(2).

[3]See Appendix 11-2, "Effect of Grandparent's Death on Naturalization Under INA § 322" (April 17, 2003).

[4]See §§ 4:65 to 4:67.

[5]Letter from E.B. Duarte, Branch Chief, INS Examinations Operations Facilitation Program, to Phillip Levin (Dec. 29, 1995) reprinted in 73 Interpreter Releases 129.

[6]See Letter from E.B. Duarte, Branch Chief, INS Examinations Operations Facilitation Program, to Phillip Levin (Dec. 29, 1995) reprinted in 73 Interpreter Releases 129. Mr. Duarte's letter is some-

It is instructive to compare the pre- and post-amendment versions of this section to highlight the new restrictions of the law. The requirement of the parent being a U.S. citizen whether by birth or naturalization remains the same.[7] The requirement of the prior residence of the parent or the grandparent also remains the same.[8] The child must still be under the age of 18 years at the time of the naturalization.[9] The two laws differ greatly, however, in regards to the United States residence/presence required of the child and the availability of this benefit when neither parent nor grandparent satisfies the prior residence requirement.[10] On the one hand, the residence/presence difference is a significant limitation on the relief. On the other hand, the change in the availability of the remedy when neither parent nor grandparent satisfy the prior residence requirement is a moot point since the benefit that used to be available in those situations under prior section 322 is now subsumed under the new section 320.[11]

This is a special provision for the naturalization of children under the age of 18 upon the application of their U.S. citizen parent.[12] Under the law as it existed before 1994, since it was the parent that filed a naturalization application, when the applicant parent died before the final hearing on the application, the child could not be naturalized.[13] However, if two U.S. citizen parents filed the application, the fact that one of them died would not bar the child from becoming a U.S. citizen.[14] Even though the law now provides for the parent to file an application for a certificate of citizenship rather than a naturalization application, it seems that this principle will still govern this type of naturalization. The new law requires at least one parent to

what ambiguous as to when the residence must have been satisfied. The letter states that "the parent or grandparent may meet the physical presence requirements anytime prior to the child's 18th birthday" and that "the entire naturalization process, including the administration of the oath of allegiance, must be completed prior to that birthday."

[7]Compare INA § 322(a)(1), 8 U.S.C.A. § 1433(a)(1) as originally enacted by Pub.L. 82-414, 66 Stat. 245 (June 27, 1952), as amended by Act of Oct. 5, 1978, Pub. L. 95-417, §§ 4–6, 92 Stat. 917; Act of Dec. 29, 1981, Pub. L. 97-116, § 18(m), (n), 95 Stat. 1620; Act of Nov. 14, 1986, Pub. L. 99-653, §§ 14–16, 100 Stat. 3657; Act of Oct. 24, 1988, Pub. L. 100-525, §§ 8(l), 9 (w), 102 Stat. 2618; Act of Nov. 29, 1990, Pub.L. 101-649, Title IV, § 407(b)(2), (c)(6), (d)(5), 104 Stat. 5040 to 5042; Act of Dec. 12, 1991, Pub.L. 102-232, Title III, § 305(m)(3), 105 Stat. 1750; Act of Oct. 25, 1994, Pub.L. 103-416, Title I, § 102(a), 108 Stat. 4306; Act of Dec. 7, 1999, Pub.L. 106-139, § 1(b)(2), 113 Stat. 1697 reproduced in Appendix 5–2 to Ch 5, with INA § 322(a)(1), 8 U.S.C.A. § 1433(a)(1) reproduced in Appendix 5–3 to Ch 5.

[8]Compare INA § 322(a)(5), 8 U.S.C.A. § 1433(a)(5) pre-Child Citizenship Act of 2000 amendments reproduced in Appendix 5–2 to Ch 5, with INA § 322(a)(2), 8 U.S.C.A. § 1433(a)(2) reproduced in Appendix 5-3 to Ch 5.

[9]Compare INA § 322(a)(3), 8 U.S.C.A. § 1433(a)(3) pre-Child Citizenship Act of 2000 amendments reproduced in Appendix 5–2 to Ch 5, with INA § 322(a)(3), 8 U.S.C.A. § 1433(a)(3) reproduced in Appendix 5-3 to Ch 5.

[10]Compare INA § 322(a)(2), (3), 8 U.S.C.A. § 1433(a)(2), (3) pre-Child Citizenship Act of 2000 amendments reproduced in Appendix 5–2 to Ch 5, with INA § 322(a)(4), 8 U.S.C.A. § 1433(a)(4) reproduced in Appendix 5-3 to Ch 5.

[11]For a discussion of section 320, see § 5:16 to 5:19.

[12]INA § 322, 8 U.S.C.A. § 1433 as originally enacted by Act of June 27, 1952.

[13]INS Interp. 322.3(c).

[14]INS Interp. 322.3(c).

be a U.S. citizen in order for USCIS to issue the certificate and the law specifically states that the child does not become a U.S. citizen until he or she takes the oath.[15]

The act also requires that the child be born outside the United States.[16] However, children of foreign diplomats who were born inside the United States have been held to qualify for the provisions of this section under the legal fiction that they are deemed to have been born outside the United States.[17]

Under the law now, there is no requirement of good moral character or attachment to the Constitution.[18] This continues the rule as it existed under the 1994 amendments.[19] Before 1994, good moral character and attachment to the Constitution were required. However, mentally retarded children could still be naturalized. If the child was under the age of 14, the good moral character and attachment to the Constitution were presumed.[20] If the child was over 14 years of age, the presumption would not apply, but the parents or other witnesses could testify affirmatively that the child is of good moral character, attached to the principles of the Constitution, and not within one of the classes of people barred from admission to citizenship.[21]

§ 11:21 Requirements—Age requirement

Research References

West's Key Number Digest, Naturalization ☞62
Validity, Construction, and Application of Child Citizenship Act, 194 A.L.R. Fed. 383
Dizon and Wettstein, Immigration Law Service 2d §§ 14:211, 14:216

To qualify under this section, the child has to be under the age of 18 years.[1] The law provides that USCIS can only issue a certificate of citizenship under this section to a child who is under 18 years of age.[2] The legacy INS interpreted the identical provision in the prior law to require the application to be filed, adjudicated, approved, and the oath, if required, taken before the child reached the age of 18.[3] However, one court estopped the government from denying a certificate of citizen-

---

[15]INA § 322(a)(1), (b), 8 U.S.C.A. § 1433(a)(1), (b) as amended by Child Citizenship Act of 2000, § 102, reproduced as Appendix 5-3 to Ch 5.

[16]INA § 322(a), 8 U.S.C.A. § 1433(a) as amended by Child Citizenship Act of 2000, § 102, reproduced as Appendix 5-3 to Ch 5; see also 8 C.F.R. § 322.2(a)(4).

[17]In re Thenault, 47 F.Supp. 952, 953 (D.D.C. 1942); INS Interp. 322.1(b) (interpreting former 8 CFR § 322.1(b)).

[18]INA § 322, 8 U.S.C.A. § 1433 as amended by Child Citizenship Act of 2000, § 102, reproduced as Appendix 5-3 to Ch 5.

[19]INA § 322, 8 U.S.C.A. § 1433 pre-Child Citizenship Act of 2000 amendments reproduced in Appendix 5–2 to Ch 5.

[20]INS Interp. 322.3(b)(3) citing to Petition of behalf of Barbel Cynthia Ann Exline, File No. A-11964210 (D.Kan. 1962) (unreported).

[21]INS Interp. 322.3(b)(3) citing to Petition of behalf of John Gnacy Nowotarski, File A-7131782 (S.D.Ill. 1965) (unreported); Petition of Bertha Gomes Leite, File A-8408415 (D.C.Va. 1964) (unreported).

[Section 11:21]

[1]INA § 322(a)(3), 8 U.S.C.A. § 1433(a)(3) as amended by Child Citizenship Act of 2000, § 102, reproduced as Appendix 5-3 to Ch 5.

[2]INA § 322(a)(3), 8 U.S.C.A. § 1433(a)(3) as amended by Child Citizenship Act of 2000, § 102, reproduced as Appendix 5-3 to Ch 5.

[3]INS Form N-600, Supplement A, Instructions.

ship to a child who turned 18 while the application was pending on the basis that the legacy INS unreasonably delayed processing the application in violation of its own regulations.[4]

The requirement of being under the age of 18 applies to calendar age and not mental age.[5] Thus, under pre-1994 law, a beneficiary who had attained the calendar age of 29 was denied naturalization even though her mental age was approximately 12 years.[6] Even though this provision does not specifically state so, the child must also be unmarried since the definition of child for citizenship purposes includes such requirement.[7] In fact, the regulations explicitly adopt the definition of "child" found in INA § 101(c)(1), 8 U.S.C.A. § 1101(c)(3), for purposes of this section.[8] Interpretation of the prior law provided that marriage of the child before the final hearing disqualified the child from admission to citizenship under the predecessor section.[9]

§ 11:22 Requirements—Residence and physical presence requirements

Research References

West's Key Number Digest, Naturalization ⚷62
Dizon and Wettstein, Immigration Law Service 2d § 14:208

The new law continues the 1994 amendment's requirement that the child be present in the United States at the time of the issuance of the certificate of citizenship.[1] Under the 1994 amendment, lawful admission was enough by itself;[2] current law makes several residence and presence requirements: (1) the child must be residing abroad; (2) the child's residence abroad must be in the legal and physical custody of the U.S. citizen parent who is petitioning for the child; (3) the child must be in the United States on a temporary basis; (4) the child's presence in the United States must be pursuant to some lawful admission; and (5) the child must be maintaining his or her lawful status in the United States.[3]

The interim regulations interpret "lawful admission" as having the same meaning as provided in INA § 101(a)(13), 8 U.S.C.A. § 1101(a)(13).[4] Lawful admission is not necessarily lawful permanent residence. Indeed, if the child is a lawful permanent resident, this provision is unnecessary as the child will already be a U.S. citizen

---

[4]Harriott v. Ashcroft, 277 F. Supp. 2d 538 (E.D. Pa. 2003); cf. Robertson-Dewar v. Holder, 646 F.3d 226, 231 n.3 (5th Cir. 2011) (disagreeing with Harriott).

[5]INS Interp. 322.3(b)(5).

[6]INS Interp. 322.3(b)(5) citing to Petition of Bertha Gomes Leite, File A-8408415 (D.C.Va. 1964) (unreported decision).

[7]INA § 101(c)(1), 8 U.S.C.A. § 1101(c)(1).

[8]8 C.F.R. § 322.1.

[9]INS Interp. 322.2(i) citing to In re Marques' Petition, 172 N.E.2d 262 (1961).

[Section 11:22]

[1]INA § 322(a)(4), 8 U.S.C.A. § 1433(a)(4) as amended by Child Citizenship Act of 2000, § 102, reproduced as Appendix 5-3 to Ch 5.

[2]For the provision as it existed immediately preceding the amendments, see INA § 322(a)(2), 8 U.S.C.A. § 1433(a)(2) pre-Child Citizenship Act of 2000 amendments reproduced in Appendix 5–2 to Ch 5.

[3]INA § 322(a)(4), 8 U.S.C.A. § 1433(a)(4) as amended by Child Citizenship Act of 2000, § 102, reproduced as Appendix 5-3 to Ch 5; see also 8 CFR § 322.2.

[4]8 C.F.R. § 322.1.

derivatively.[5] Current law continues the lawful admission requirement of prior law.[6] In its implementation of the 1994 law, the State Department had issued instructions to all diplomatic and consular officials to issue B-2 visas to children who were coming to the U.S. to naturalize under this section and who were not required by law to be lawful permanent residents at the time of naturalization.[7] These instructions are probably still applicable under the new law. Indeed, current law specifies that application under this section may be filed from abroad.[8] Temporary admission would follow the application.

§ 11:23   Requirements—Physical and legal custody requirements

Research References

West's Key Number Digest, Naturalization ☞62
Dizon and Wettstein, Immigration Law Service 2d § 14:218

The current statute requires the child to be residing in the legal and physical custody of the U.S. citizen parent.[1] The interim regulations define legal custody as the responsibility for and authority over a child.[2] Absent evidence to the contrary, USCIS will presume that a U.S. citizen parent has legal custody of a child, and will recognize the parent as having lawful authority over the child, in the following three situations:

(1) where a biological child currently resides with both natural parents (who are married to each other, living in marital union, and not separated);

(2) where a biological child currently resides with a surviving natural parent (if the other parent is deceased); or

(3) where, in the case of a biological child born out-of-wedlock, the child has been legitimated and currently resides with the natural parent.[3]

The regulations allow this third presumption for children born out-of-wedlock who have been legitimated because the definition of "child" found in INA § 101(c)(1) specifically includes a child legitimated under the law of the child's residence or domicile, or under the law of the father's residence or domicile, whether in the United States or elsewhere.[4] INA § 101(c)(1) also requires that the child be legitimated before reaching the age of 16 and that the legitimation take place while the child is

---

[5]See § 5:14.

[6]INA § 322(a)(2), 8 U.S.C.A. § 1433(a)(2) pre-Child Citizenship Act of 2000 amendments reproduced in Appendix 5–2 to Ch 5.

[7]State Department Cable (No. 95-State-no number listed) (updating information contained in 7 FAM 1133.5) reproduced in 72 Interpreter Releases 350.

[8]INA § 322(b), 8 U.S.C.A. § 1433(b) as amended by Child Citizenship Act of 2000, § 102, reproduced as Appendix 5-3 to Ch 5.

[Section 11:23]

[1]INA § 322(a)(4), 8 U.S.C.A. § 1433(a)(4).

[2]8 CFR § 322.1.

[3]8 CFR § 322.1(1). These regulations do not define "living in marital union," but USCIS defines that term as it is used in INA § 319, 8 U.S.C.A. § 1430. *See* 8 CFR § 319.1(b). It is likely that USCIS will apply this definition to the term as it is used in 8 CFR § 322.1.

[4]8 U.S.C.A. § 1101(c)(1).

in the legal custody of the legitimating parent or parents.[5] In the absence of affirmative evidence to the contrary, a child is presumed to be in the custody of the legitimating parent at the time of legitimation.[6]

The BIA defines legitimation as the act of placing a child born out of wedlock in the same legal position as a child born in wedlock.[7] Unless local law provides otherwise, biological fathers have a "natural right" of custody over legitimated children that is equal to that of a biological mother.[8] Legitimation can take many forms and includes changes in the law abolishing the distinction between legitimate and out-of-wedlock children.[9] Appendix 4-26 includes a summary of BIA decisions and State Department interpretations regarding the legitimation laws of different countries and of states of the U.S.[10]

The legacy INS interpreted prior law to make out-of-wedlock children who had not been legitimated eligible for this section only if their U.S. citizen biological mother filed the application.[11] There is no specific presumption in the current regulations recognizing this situation. So long as the U.S. citizen biological mother has legal and physical custody, however, there is no reason why this situation should be treated differently than it was previously.

In the case of a child of divorced or legally separated parents, USCIS will find the U.S. citizen parent to have legal custody where there has been an award of primary care, control and maintenance of the minor child to the parent by a court or appropriate government entity pursuant to the laws of the state or country or residence.[12] USCIS will consider "joint custody" to be legal custody. "Joint custody" in the case of divorced or legally separated parents is defined as the award to both parents of equal responsibility for and authority over the care, religion, medical treatment and general welfare of a child. The award of joint custody must be by a court or appropriate government entity pursuant to the laws of the state or country of residence.[13]

The regulations additionally indicate that there may be other factual situations under which the Service will find the U.S. citizen parent to have legal custody for purposes of the Child Citizenship Act.[14] This catchall provision might include the situation—not covered in the regulations—in which the married, natural parents are living separately, though not under a legal separation, and the child is living with the U.S. citizen parent.

The regulations do not define physical custody. Under pre-1994 law, a child had to be residing permanently in the United States, with the citizen parent, pursuant to a lawful admission to permanent residence, in order to be eligible for naturalization

---

[5]8 U.S.C.A. § 1101(c)(1); see also In re Moraga, 23 I. & N. Dec. 195, 2001 WL 1513198 (B.I.A. 2001); Matter of Rivers, 17 I. & N. Dec. 419, 1980 WL 121908 (B.I.A. 1980).

[6]8 CFR § 322.1.

[7]In re Moraga, 23 I. & N. Dec. 195, 2001 WL 1513198 (B.I.A. 2001).

[8]Matter of Rivers, 17 I. & N. Dec. 419, 1980 WL 121908 (B.I.A. 1980).

[9]For an in depth discussion of legitimation, see Levy, The Family in Immigration and Nationality Law: Part I, 92-9 Immigration Briefings 10-11 (Sept. 1992).

[10]See §§ 4:1 et seq.

[11]See former 8 CFR §§ 322.2(b)(1)(iii), (2)(ii).

[12]8 CFR § 322.1.

[13]8 CFR § 322.1.

[14]8 CFR § 322.1.

benefits.[15] Judicial interpretation of this requirement had found a child to be residing with her mother even though the child was temporarily residing with the maternal grandparents until the mother and her husband could find suitable accommodations for the child.[16]

§ 11:24 Requirements—Special requirements for adopted children

Research References

West's Key Number Digest, Naturalization ☞62
Dizon and Wettstein, Immigration Law Service 2d §§ 14:210, 14:211, 14:220, 14:221

Section 322 of the INA includes specific requirements for adopted children. A parent can only confer the benefits of this section if he or she proves that the child satisfies the requirements applicable to adopted children under section 101(b)(1).[1] The general nationality definition of child has been specifically made inapplicable to INA § 322 insofar as benefits to adoptive children are concerned.[2] Instead, the law uses the adoption provisions that are applicable to immigration benefits.[3]

Under section 101(b)(1), there are two definitions applicable to "adopted" children. First, there is a general definition of adopted child which requires the child to have been adopted "while under the age of sixteen years, [to have been] in the legal custody of, and [to have] resided with, the adopting parent or parents for at least two years."[4] The second definition relates to "orphan" children who "because of the death or disappearance of, abandonment or desertion by, or separation or loss from, both parents, or for whom the sole or surviving parent is incapable of providing the proper care and has in writing irrevocably released the child for emigration and adoption."[5] This second definition is only applicable to a relationship where the adopting parent is a United States citizen.[6] The new law contemplates that children

---

[15]INA § 322(a), 8 U.S.C.A. § 1433(a) as originally enacted by Act of June 27, 1952.

[16]Petition of Donsky, 77 F. Supp. 832, 835 (S.D. N.Y. 1948).

[Section 11:24]

[1]INA § 322(c), 8 U.S.C.A. § 1433(c) as amended by Child Citizenship Act of 2000, § 102, reproduced as Appendix 5-3 to Ch 5.

[2]INA § 101(c)(1), 8 U.S.C.A. § 1101(c)(1).

[3]Before the passage of INTCA, the law did not include a requirement that the child be under the age of sixteen at the time the adoption took place. Indeed, the original provision for the naturalization of adopted children upon petition by U.S. citizen adoptive parents, as enacted in 1952, had included such a requirement. INA § 323(a)(2), 8 U.S.C.A. § 1434(a)(2) as originally enacted by Pub.L. 82-414, 66 Stat. 163. In 1978, the INA was amended and the provisions for naturalization of adopted children were transferred to the general provision for naturalization of children upon petition by their U.S. citizen parents. Secs. 6–8, Act of Oct. 5, 1978, Pub.L. 95-417, 92 Stat. 917. At the time, section 322 as amended still included the requirement that adoptive children may only be naturalized if the adoption took place while the child was under the age of 16. INA § 322(b), 8 U.S.C.A. § 1433(b), as amended by Sec. 6, Act of Oct. 5, 1978. However, in 1981, that section was once again amended to delete the requirement that the child be under the age of 16 when the adoption took place. Sec 18(m), Act of Dec. 29, 1981, Pub.L. 97-116, 95 Stat. 1621. See INS Interp. 320.1(d)(3) (conceding that the age limitation was not applicable under the old law).

[4]INA § 101(b)(1)(E)(i), 8 U.S.C.A. § 1101(b)(1)(E)(i).

[5]INA § 101(b)(1)(F)(i), 8 U.S.C.A. § 1101(b)(1)(F)(i).

[6]INA § 101(b)(1)(F)(i), 8 U.S.C.A. § 1101(b)(1)(F)(i).

adopted under either the adoption or orphan definitions will benefit from section 322.[7]

Some children who fit the general adoption or orphan definition are also able to benefit from the provisions of section 322, even when they are between the ages of 16 and 18 years. This applies to biological siblings of children who fit the adopted or orphan definitions, who themselves fit the adopted or orphan definition (except that they have been adopted while they were between 16 and 18 years of age), and who have been adopted by the same adoptive parents as their younger siblings.[8]

Under the general adoption definition, there is a requirement that the child be residing in the legal custody of the adopting parent. This requirement is only satisfied by a court award: custody begins when it is awarded by a court or other recognized governmental entity.[9] Unlike the case of legitimated children, there is no "natural" right to custody in this situation.[10] The two-year custody requirement can be satisfied before or after the adoption.[11] The two-year residence requirement can also be satisfied before or after the adoption.[12] However, the adoptive parent must have resided with the child for periods adding up to the full two years.[13]

The BIA has taken a very restrictive view of the meaning of "residence" for purposes of satisfying the general adoption definition. Under the INA, residence is defined as the principal place of abode, and the BIA has interpreted this to mean that mere visits to the child will not satisfy the requirement even when all the visits add up to more than two years.[14] In addition, if the biological parent resides in the same household as the adoptive parent and the child, the BIA will examine whether the adoptive parent or the biological parent exercises primary parental control over the child.[15] If the adoptive parent did not, in fact, exercise primary parental control during the periods that add up to the two years, then the adoptive parent will not be considered to have resided with the child.[16]

Either of the adopting parents could file for an adopted child if both were U.S. citizens.[17] If only one parent was a U.S. citizen, that parent may file for the adopted child.[18] Similarly, when a couple is adopting the child, there is no requirement that

---

[7]See H. Rep. 852, 106th Cong., 2d Sess.8 (discussing new subsection 322(c) as applying to adopted children who satisfy the requirements of either INA § 101(b)(1)(E) or (F)); Cong. Rec. H7774–78 (daily ed. Sept. 19, 2000) (virtually all examples used to support the legislation refer to children who immigrated under the orphan provisions).

[8]INA § 101(b)(1)(E)(ii), (F)(ii), 8 U.S.C.A. § 1101(b)(1)(E)(ii), (F)(ii).

[9]INS Cable CO 204.21-P (Feb. 17, 1989), reproduced in 66 Interpreter Releases 260. For a full discussion of the definition of "adopted child" for immigration purposes, see Levy, The Family in Immigration and Nationality Law: Part I, 92-9 Immigration Briefings 11-13 (Sept. 1992).

[10]See this section.

[11]See Immigration and Nationality Amendments of 1986, Pub.L. 99-653, 100 Stat. 3655 (striking out the requirement that the custody happen after the adoption).

[12]Matter of M-, 8 I. & N. Dec. 118, 121 (Att'y Gen. 1959).

[13]Matter of Repuyan, 19 I. & N. Dec. 119, 1212 (B.I.A. 1984); Matter of Lee, 11 I. & N. Dec. 911, 913 (B.I.A. 1986).

[14]Matter of Repuyan, 19 I. & N. Dec. 119, 121 (B.I.A. 1984).

[15]Matter of Marquez, 20 I. & N. Dec. 160 (B.I.A. 1990); Matter of Cuello, 20 I. & N. Dec. 94 (B.I.A. 1989).

[16]Matter of Cuello, 20 I. & N. Dec. 94, 1989 WL 331871 (B.I.A. 1989).

[17]INS Interp. 322.2(b).

[18]In re Petition of Chin Thloot Har Wong, 224 F.Supp. 155 (S.D.N.Y. 1963); INS Interp. 322.2(b).

both satisfy the two-year custody and residence requirements; it is sufficient if one of them does.[19]

Alternatively, an adopted child may obtain these citizenship benefits if he or she satisfies the definition of the orphan under the immigration laws.[20] The definition of an orphan is very technical and involves a child

who is an orphan because of death or disappearance of, abandonment or desertion by, or separation or loss from, both parents, or for whom the sole or surviving parent is incapable of providing the proper care and has in writing irrevocably released the child for emigration and adoption.[21]

In addition, to fit the definition, a U.S. parent and his or her spouse together must have adopted the child, or alternatively by one U.S. citizen parent who is at least 25 years of age.[22] To qualify under the definition, the child may be adopted abroad, provided the adoptive parent or parents personally saw the child prior to or at the adoption procedures.[23] The child may also be adopted in the United States, provided that the adoptive parent or parents comply with the pre-adoption requirements of the jurisdiction of the child's intended residence and that the child enters the United States specifically for the purpose of being adopted under the orphan provisions.[24]

§ 11:25 Procedures

Research References

West's Key Number Digest, Naturalization ⬤⁓62
Dizon and Wettstein, Immigration Law Service 2d §§ 14:222, 14:224, 14:225

On April 30, 2003, USCIS issued an updated version of the Application for Citizenship and Issuance of a Certificate Under Section 322, Form N-600K.[1] This form is to be used for the naturalization of a child who regularly resides outside of the United States. The general fee for filing this form is $600[2]. However, U.S. citizens filing on behalf of an adopted child need only pay $550.[3] This form consolidates the N-600, N-643, and N-600/N-643 Supplement A previously filed by the child's parents or grandparents. The U.S. citizen parent should submit the application with supporting documentation to USCIS office having jurisdiction over his or her place of residence, or, if living abroad, to any USCIS field office in the United States.[4] The par-

---

[19]Matter of Y- K- W-, 9 I. & N. Dec. 176 (Att'y Gen. 1961).

[20]INA § 322(a)(4), 8 U.S.C.A. § 1433(a)(4).

[21]INA § 101(b)(1)(F)(i), 8 U.S.C.A. § 1101(b)(1)(F)(i).

[22]INA § 101(b)(1)(F)(i), 8 U.S.C.A. § 1101(b)(1)(F)(i).

[23]INA § 101(b)(1)(F)(i), 8 U.S.C.A. § 1101(b)(1)(F)(i).

[24]INA § 101(b)(1)(F)(i), 8 U.S.C.A. § 1101(b)(1)(F)(i). For a general discussion of the definition of orphan, see Levy, The Family in Immigration and Nationality Law: Part 1, 92-9 Immigration Briefings, at 13–14.

[Section 11:25]

[1]See Appendix 11-1. USCIS issued a new version of Form N-600K on Oct. 26, 2005. The version dated April 30, 2004 is also accepted.

[2]The current fee became effective Oct. 26, 2005. 70 Fed. Reg. 61832 (Oct. 26, 2005).

[3]The current fee became effective Oct. 26, 2005. 70 Fed. Reg. 61832 (Oct. 26, 2005).

[4]INS, Information on Expeditious Naturalization for Certain Children under Section 322 of INA, reproduced as Appendix 11-1.

ent should also include a request noting preferred interview dates that are at least three months from the filing date.[5]

The following supporting documentation should accompany the application: (1) the child's birth certificate or birth record; (2) the parents' marriage certificate, if applicable; (3) proof of termination of any previous marriages of both parents, if applicable; (4) evidence of U.S. citizenship of parent; (5) documentation of legitimation, if applicable; (6) documentation of legal custody, if applicable; (7) documentation that the U.S. citizen parent or grandparent meets the physical presence requirements; (8) evidence that the child is present in the U.S. and maintaining lawful status; (9) if adopted, a final adoption decree showing that the child was adopted by the citizen parent before the child's sixteenth birthday; (10) for an adopted child, evidence that he or she satisfies the requirements of INA § 101(b)(1)(E) which defines "child" with regards to adoption; (11) for adopted orphans, a copy of the notice of approval of Form I-600 and supporting documentation for such a form; and (12) evidence of all legal name changes for the child, U.S. citizen parent, or U.S. citizen grandparent, if applicable.[6] Form N-600K details which documentation must be included if citizenship is claimed through either father's or mother's prior residence.[7] If USCIS requires any additional documentation, it may request such documentation under separate cover or at the time of the interview.[8]

The U.S. citizen parent and child have to appear at the scheduled interview.[9] To be admitted to citizenship, the child is required to take the oath of allegiance.[10] However, this requirement may be waived for beneficiaries under this section if the beneficiary is unable to understand its meaning.[11] In the past, the INS took the position that the inability to understand the oath justified a waiver regardless of whether it was due to the chronological age of the child or to "arrested or retarded" development.[12] Specifically, mentally retarded children could be naturalized under this section even though they could not take the oath of allegiance in any meaningful manner.[13] Upon approval, USCIS officer will administer the oath of allegiance, unless USCIS has waived the oath,[14] and issue the certificate of citizenship.[15] The child must take the oath inside the United States.[16] The child is a U.S. citizen upon completion of the application process and upon taking the naturalization oath or having it waived.[17]

If the district director denies the application, she or he will give the applicant the reasons for denial and explain the applicant's right to appeal. The applicant may file

---

[5]8 CFR § 322.3(a).

[6]8 CFR § 322.3(b)(1).

[7]Form N-600, (Rev. 10/1/00), Instructions reproduced as Appendix 13-3.

[8]8 CFR § 322.3(b)(2).

[9]8 CFR § 322.4.

[10]INA § 322(b), 8 U.S.C.A. § 1433(b) as amended by Child Citizenship Act of 2000, § 102, reproduced as Appendix 5-3.

[11]INA § 337(a), 8 U.S.C.A. § 1448(a).

[12]INS Interp. 322.3(b)(4).

[13]INS Interp. 322.3(b)(3).

[14]INA § 322(b), 8 U.S.C.A. § 1433(b). See §§ 9:56, 9:60.

[15]8 CFR § 322.5(a).

[16]INTCA § 102(a) amending INA § 322(b), 8 U.S.C.A. § 1433(b) reproduced as Appendix 4-21 to Ch 4.

[17]8 CFR § 322.5(a).

an appeal on Form I-290B to the Administrative Appeals Unit within thirty days of the denial.[18]

B. NATURALIZATION OF PERSONS WHO BECAME PERMANENT RESIDENTS AS BATTERED CHILDREN

§ 11:26 In general

Research References

West's Key Number Digest, Naturalization ⊛60.2, 62
Dizon and Wettstein, Immigration Law Service 2d § 7:216
Steel on Immigration Law §§ 5:12, 15:19

In the year 2000, Congress amended the Immigration and Nationality Act to allow persons who became lawful permanent residents by reason of their status as a battered spouse or child of a U.S. citizen to naturalize under the same provisions as spouses of U.S. citizens.[1] The law specifically exempts these spouses and children from the requirement that they must have lived in marital union in the United States with the U.S. citizen spouse.[2] Most requirements of the general rule that apply to spouses of U.S. citizens also apply to qualifying battered spouses and children.[3] USCIS has not yet issued regulations to implement this section.

IV. EMPLOYEES OF U.S. NEWS MEDIA ORGANIZATIONS

§ 11:27 In general

Research References

West's Key Number Digest, Naturalization ⊛62
Dizon and Wettstein, Immigration Law Service 2d §§ 14:285, 14:286
Steel on Immigration Law §§ 5:10, 15:18

Certain employees of U.S. news media organization have also been exempted from the residence requirements of the general naturalization provision.[1] The five-year continuous residence requirement, however, has been replaced by a requirement of continuous employment of five years by one of those organizations after lawful admission to permanent residence.[2]

To be eligible for the benefits of this section, the lawful permanent resident must be employed abroad by a "bona fide United States incorporated nonprofit organization which is principally engaged in conducting abroad through communication media the dissemination of information which significantly promotes the United

---

[18]8 CFR § 322.5(b).

[Section 11:26]

[1]INA § 319(a), 8 U.S.C.A. § 1430(a) as amended by Victims of Trafficking and Violence Protection Act of 2000, Pub.L. 106-386, § 1503(e), 114 Stat. 1464 (Oct. 28, 2000).

[2]INA § 319(a), 8 U.S.C.A. § 1430(a) as amended by Victims of Trafficking and Violence Protection Act of 2000, Pub.L. 106-386, § 1503(e), 114 Stat. 1464 (Oct. 28, 2000).

[3]See § 11:3.

[Section 11:27]

[1]INA § 329(c), 8 U.S.C.A. § 1430(c).

[2]INA § 329(c)(2), 8 U.S.C.A. § 1430(c)(2).

States interests abroad and which is recognized as such by the Attorney General."[3] Only two such organizations have been recognized by the Attorney General: Free Europe, Inc. (formerly Free Europe Committee, Inc.; National Committee for a Free Europe—including Radio Free Europe), and Radio Liberty Committee, Inc. (formerly American Committee for Liberation, Inc.; American Committee for Liberation of the Peoples of Russia, Inc.; American Committee for Liberation from Bolshevism, Inc.).[4]

The applicant may only be naturalized if he or she files the application while employed by the organization or within six months following the termination of employment.[5] There is no residence requirement, so the qualifying employment could take place abroad.[6] The applicant, however, must be in the United States at the time of naturalization and must file a declaration of intent to take up residence in the United States at the termination of such employment.[7] In addition, the applicant must have been lawfully admitted to permanent residence at the time of naturalization, be a person of good moral character, attached to the principles of the Constitution, and well disposed towards the good order and happiness of the U.S.[8] Since there is no required period of residence, the person must prove that he or she is at present a person of good moral character.[9]

The Intelligence Authorization Act for the fiscal year 1990 added the United States Army Russian Institute, located in Garmisch, Federal Republic of Germany, to this list of organizations that could serve as a basis for naturalization under this subsection.[10] It allowed periods of employment prior to the enactment of the Appropriations Act to be counted toward the five years of employment.[11] However, it limited to two persons per year the number of applicants who could be naturalized based on employment at the Russian Institute; and required that before each naturalization, the case had to be reported to the Committees on the Judiciary of the Senate and the House of Representatives and to the Select Committee on Intelligence of the Senate and the Permanent Select Committee on Intelligence of the House of Representatives.[12]

V. FORMER DANISH CITIZENS WHO INHABITED VIRGIN ISLANDS IN 1917 AND CHOSE TO RETAIN THEIR DANISH NATIONALITY

§ 11:28   In general

Research References

West's Key Number Digest, Naturalization ⊕62
Dizon and Wettstein, Immigration Law Service 2d § 14:302

When the Virgin Islands were transferred to the United States in 1917, the treaty

---

[3]INA § 319(c)(1), 8 U.S.C.A. § 1430(c)(1).

[4]8 CFR § 319.6 (stating that "an employee of a qualifying organization is eligible for benefits of section 319(c), notwithstanding that part of the five-year period of employment includes services that were performed within the United States").

[5]INA § 319(c)(3), 8 U.S.C.A. § 1430(c)(3).

[6]OI 319.2.

[7]INA § 319(c)(4), (5), 8 U.S.C.A. § 1430(c)(4), (5).

[8]8 CFR § 319.4(b), (g).

[9]See §§ 7:18 to 7:46.

[10]Intelligence Authorization Act, Fiscal Year 1990, § 506(a), Pub. L. 101-193 (Nov. 30, 1989).

[11]Intelligence Authorization Act, § 506(b).

[12]Intelligence Authorization Act, § 506(c), (d).

provided that Danish inhabitants of the islands could elect to retain their Danish citizenship by making a declaration within one year of the entry into effect of the treaty.[1] If they, in fact, made that the election, the treaty allowed them to renounce their Danish citizenship at any time thereafter and be admitted to U.S. nationality "on the same terms as may be provided according to the laws of the United States, for other inhabitants of the islands."[2] In fact, former Danish citizens who did not elect to retain their Danish citizenship became U.S. citizens on February 25, 1927.[3] Therefore, those qualifying Danish citizens who now renounce their Danish citizenship will become U.S. citizens.[4]

To qualify, the person must have resided in the Virgin Islands of the United States on January 17, 1917, and in the Virgin Islands, Puerto Rico, or the United States on February 25, 1927.[5] The meaning of the terms "residence" and "United States" on these dates and within this context is fully discussed in Ch 2.[6] In addition, they must have preserved their Danish citizenship by making a timely declaration as prescribed in the treaty of cession of the Virgin Islands.[7]

Persons who fulfill those requirements may acquire U.S. citizenship by making a declaration renouncing their Danish citizenship before any court of record in the United States regardless of their place of residence.[8] They must submit Form N-350 to USCIS in accordance with the instructions contained on the form.[9] USCIS will interview the applicant as to eligibility to renounce the Danish citizenship for these purposes and will assist the applicant in filing the renunciation with the court.[10]

The renunciation itself is made on Form N-351, which is executed under oath in duplicate and filed with the clerk of the court.[11] The fee is fixed by the court clerk and the usual procedures for naturalization do not apply.[12] The court clerk sends the local USCIS assistant district director for naturalization a copy of the court record.[13]

Once the person renounces the Danish citizenship, the person is deemed a U.S. citizen.[14] However, USCIS will not issue a certificate of naturalization or of citizenship to such person.[15]

[Section 11:28]

[1]Art. 6, Treaty of August 4, 1916, Denmark and U.S., proclaimed January 25, 1917, 39 Stat. 1715, TS 629, 3 Redmond 2558, 7 Bevans 56 reproduced as Appendix 2-6 to Ch 2.

[2]Art. 6, Treaty of August 4, 1916, reproduced as Appendix 2-6 to Ch 2.

[3]See § 2:17.

[4]8 CFR § 306.2.

[5]8 CFR § 306.1.

[6]See § 2:17.

[7]8 CFR § 306.1.

[8]8 CFR § 306.1.

[9]8 CFR § 306.11.

[10]8 CFR § 306.11.

[11]8 CFR § 306.12.

[12]8 CFR § 306.12.

[13]8 CFR § 306.12.

[14]8 CFR § 306.2.

[15]8 CFR § 306.2.

VI. FORMER U.S. CITIZENS WHOSE NATIONALITY WAS RESTORED

§ 11:29   By private bills

Research References

West's Key Number Digest, Naturalization ⊕⇒62

Construction and Application of § 245 of the Immigration and Nationality Act of 1952 (8 U.S.C.A. § 1255) Authorizing Adjustment of Status of Alien to that of Permanent Resident, 4 A.L.R. Fed. 557

Former U.S. citizens may have their nationality restored by private bills of Congress. In such cases, the former U.S. citizen must submit a Form N-400 application without a fee to USCIS.[1] The Form N-400 must be submitted in triplicate and must include a copy of the private bill.[2] After taking the oath, the applicant will receive a certified copy of the oath for a fee not to exceed $5.[3]

§ 11:30   Resumption of citizenship in general

Research References

West's Key Number Digest, Naturalization ⊕⇒62

Dizon and Wettstein, Immigration Law Service 2d § 14:86

Former U.S. citizens whose nationality was resumed under provisions of the 1940 and the 1906 nationality acts or who were naturalized under those provisions after having lost their U.S. citizenship may apply to USCIS for a certificate evidencing such citizenship.[1] Such an application is submitted on form M-580.[2] The applicant is required to appear in person at USCIS for an interrogation regarding the application.[3] If approved, a certificate of naturalization or repatriation will be issued and delivered to the applicant in person.[4] Such certificates may only be delivered in the United States and the applicant must sign a receipt for it.[5] If the application is denied, the applicant may appeal to the Administrative Appeals Unit of USCIS.[6]

§ 11:31   Restoration of citizenship lost by failure to comply with retention requirements

Research References

West's Key Number Digest, Naturalization ⊕⇒62(3), 68

[Section 11:29]

   [1]8 CFR § 324.5.

   [2]8 CFR § 324.5.

   [3]8 CFR §§ 324.3(b)(2), 324.5.

[Section 11:30]

   [1]8 CFR § 343.1.

   [2]8 CFR § 343.1.

   [3]8 CFR § 343.1.

   [4]8 CFR § 343.1.

   [5]8 CFR § 343.1.

   [6]8 CFR § 343.1.

The INTCA included a new provision for the restoration of citizenship lost by U.S. citizens through failure to comply with retention requirements.[1] Retention requirements were conditions imposed on U.S. citizens born abroad after 1934 in cases where one of their parents was a noncitizen at the time of their birth.[2] Children who failed to take up residence in the United States by a certain age lost their U.S. citizenship.

The INA now allows those persons to regain their U.S. citizenship by taking the naturalization oath, under the same procedures that govern the resumption of citizenship by women who lost their citizenship by marriage to noncitizens.[3] The only provision that would bar the resumption of citizenship would be the ideological bars to naturalization.[4]

The State Department has implemented these procedures by amending its regulations to reflect the changes in legislation.[5] The regulations restate the law, allowing former citizens who lost their citizenship by failure to comply with the retention requirements of the 1940 act and the INA.[6] The regulations only add that the person may regain his or her citizenship by applying abroad at a diplomatic or consular post in the form and manner prescribed by the State Department or in the U.S. under procedures specified by USCIS.[7] In coordination with USCIS, the State Department has also implemented a procedure to allow passport applicants to take the reacquisition oath at passport offices inside the United States.[8]

In March 1994, the State Department issued a much more detailed cable regarding these procedures.[9] The cable instructed all consular and diplomatic posts to request documentary proof to support restoration of citizenship under this section.[10] When an applicant presents such proof, the consular or diplomatic officer must prepare a statement on the consular or diplomatic post's letterhead.[11] The document will be entitled "Oath of Allegiance to the United States Under the Immigration and Nationality Act"[12] and will contain the following text:[13]

This statement is for use under section 324(d)(1) of the Immigration and Nationality Act by a person who was a citizen of the United States at birth and lost such citizenship for

---

[Section 11:31]

[1]INA § 324(d), 8 U.S.C.A. § 1435(d).

[2]See §§ 4:5, 4:6.

[3]See §§ 11:12 to 11:24.

[4]INA § 324(d), 8 U.S.C.A. § 1435(d). See §§ 7:47 to 7:76.

[5]22 CFR. § 50.30(d) added by 61 Fed. Reg. 29651 (June 12, 1996).

[6]22 CFR. § 50.30(d)(1).

[7]22 CFR. § 50.30(d)(1).

[8]Carmen DiPlacido, Dual Citizenship Panel, AILA 1997 Annual Conference.

[9]State Dept. Cable, File No. 95-State-no number listed, reproduced in 72 Interpreter Releases 350.

[10]State Dept. Cable, File No. 95-State-no number listed, reproduced in 72 Interpreter Releases 350.

[11]State Dept. Cable, File No. 95-State-no number listed, reproduced in 72 Interpreter Releases 350.

[12]State Dept. Cable, File No. 95-State-no number listed, reproduced in 72 Interpreter Releases 350.

[13]State Dept. Cable, File No. 95-State-no number listed, reproduced in 72 Interpreter Releases 350.

failure to meet the physical presence retention requirements under section 301(b) of the INA.

Name of Applicant [print name in full]

Date of birth

Place of birth

I solemnly swear that I have performed no voluntary act which would cause me to be within any of the provisions of section 313 of the Immigration and Nationality Act relating to persons opposed to government or law or who favor totalitarian forms of government. I hereby apply to take the oath of allegiance to the United States as prescribed by section 337(a) of the same Act. I understand that taking the oath restores U.S. citizenship as of the date of the oath and is not retroactive to the date of failure to retain.

Oath of Allegiance

I hereby declare, on oath, that I absolutely and entirely renounce and abjure all allegiance and fidelity to any foreign prince, potentate, state, or sovereignty, of whom or which I have heretofore been a subject or citizen; that I will support and defend the Constitution and laws of the United States of America against all enemies, foreign and domestic; that I will bear true faith and allegiance to the same; that I will bear arms on behalf of the United States when required by law; that I will perform non-combatant service in the armed forces of the United States when required by law; that I will perform work of national importance under civilian direction when required by law; and that I take this obligation freely, without any mental reservation or purpose of evasion; so help me God.

Signature of Applicant

Subscribed and sworn to before me by the above named applicant

Signed and dated by the consular officer.

The applicant is then required to fill out this document and sign it.[14] The consular officers or any other person authorized to take oaths will then administer the oath of allegiance.[15] The consular officer then signs and dates the statement.[16] At that point, the applicant will be required to fill out a passport application including two photographs, appropriate fees, and all supporting documentation.[17] The application, with the newly executed document, is forwarded to Washington, D.C., though a passport may be issued without referral to Washington, D.C.[18] If the person's name appears in a lookout list, the consular post will prepare a lookout removal request and forward it to Washington, D.C.[19]

This procedure does not restore U.S. citizenship retroactively.[20] Rather, it only allows the person to regain his or her U.S. citizenship as of the date the oath is

---

[14]State Dept. Cable, File No. 95-State-no number listed, reproduced in 72 Interpreter Releases 350.

[15]State Dept. Cable, File No. 95-State-no number listed, reproduced in 72 Interpreter Releases 350.

[16]State Dept. Cable, File No. 95-State-no number listed, reproduced in 72 Interpreter Releases 350. The statement will not bear a consular seal. State Dept. Cable, File No. 95-State-no number listed, reproduced in 72 Interpreter Releases 350.

[17]State Dept. Cable, File No. 95-State-no number listed, reproduced in 72 Interpreter Releases 350.

[18]State Dept. Cable, File No. 95-State-no number listed, reproduced in 72 Interpreter Releases 350.

[19]State Dept. Cable, File No. 95-State-no number listed, reproduced in 72 Interpreter Releases 350.

[20]61 Fed. Reg. 29651 (June 12, 1996) (Supplementary Information).

taken.[21] For this reason, this procedure does not permit the automatic transmission of citizenship to the children of its beneficiaries.[22]

The existence of this procedure, however, does not invalidate claims of constructive compliance with retention requirements due to lack of awareness of being a U.S. citizen.[23] In cases where children were born to the applicant after loss of citizenship but before restoration, it may be more advantageous to claim constructive compliance, as the children themselves may qualify as U.S. citizens born abroad.[24] Consular officers have been instructed not to preclude such claims.[25]

However, taking the oath will be considered naturalization for purposes of derivative citizenship.[26] Children under the age of 18 may be able to derive citizenship from the reacquisition of citizenship of the parent.[27]

§ 11:32 Reconsideration of loss of citizenship findings by State Department

Research References

Dizon and Wettstein, Immigration Law Service 2d §§ 14:386, 14:437

Until 1967, it was widely believed that U.S. citizens could lose their U.S. citizenship by the performance of expatriating actions. In 1967, the Supreme Court determined that the U.S. Constitution protected U.S. citizens from unwanted loss of citizenship.[1] Expatriating actions can only be given effect if they are performed with the intention of relinquishing U.S. citizenship.[2]

As a consequence of this line of decisions, the State Department adopted administrative standards in 1990 for the adjudication of loss of citizenship cases.[3] These standards provide for an administrative presumption that the person intended to retain U.S. citizenship in three situations: (1) when a U.S. citizen obtains naturalization in a foreign country; (2) when the citizen subscribes routine declarations of allegiance to a foreign state; and (3) when the citizen accepts non-policy level employment in a foreign state.[4] If the person affirmatively states that it was his or her intention to relinquish U.S. citizenship in performing those acts, then the person will lose his or her U.S. citizenship.[5] In all other loss of nationality cases, the consular officer is required to ascertain whether or not there is evidence of the

---

[21]61 Fed. Reg. 29651 (June 12, 1996).

[22]61 Fed. Reg. 29651 (June 12, 1996).

[23]61 Fed. Reg. 29651 (June 12, 1996). See § 4:48.

[24]See generally Ch 4. A requirement under all U.S. citizenship at birth abroad laws is that, at the time of the birth, at least one parent must have been a U.S. citizen.

[25]State Dept. Cable, reproduced in 72 Interpreter Releases 350.

[26]See § 5:6.

[27]See §§ 5:1 et seq.

[Section 11:32]

[1]See §§ 15:1 to 15:16.

[2]See §§ 15:1 to 15:16.

[3]61 Fed. Reg. 29651 (June 12, 1996) (Supplemental Information).

[4]22 CFR § 50.40(a) as amended by 63 Fed. Reg. 20315 (Apr. 24, 1998).

[5]22 CFR § 50.40(a).

intent to relinquish U.S. citizenship when performing the expatriating act.[6] The regulations further instruct consular and diplomatic officers to request an affidavit from persons who admit that they performed the expatriating acts with the intention of relinquishing U.S. citizenship.[7]

The State Department understands that prior adjudications made under different standards fail to pass constitutional muster. Therefore, the State Department is providing a mechanism for reviewing prior determination that persons had lost their citizenship.[8] Citizenship will be reinstated if, at the time the loss of nationality was determined, the person did not attest in writing that it was his or her intention to relinquish U.S. citizenship.[9] The Department of State's Office of Overseas Citizens Services will review all cases submitted to it, even cases which previously were before the Department of State's Board of Appellate Review.[10] An attorney need not represent claimants.[11] Individual claims may be submitted to the following address: Department of State; Bureau of Consular Affairs; Office of Policy Review and Interagency Liaison; Overseas Citizens Services; 2201 C Street, NW; Washington, DC 20520-4817.[12]

VII. POSTHUMOUS CITIZENSHIP FOR CERTAIN VICTIMS OF SEPTEMBER 11, 2001

§ 11:33   In general

Research References

Dizon and Wettstein, Immigration Law Service 2d § 14:64

Following the attacks on September 11, 2001, Congress enacted a special provision allowing for the posthumous citizenship of eligible naturalization applicants who were killed as a result of any of the four airline hijackings on that that day.[1] Under these provisions, family members or next of kin are able to complete the naturalization process for their deceased relative.[2] This Act is purely symbolic, as surviving family members cannot derive any benefits as a result of the posthumous naturalization of their relative.[3] On April 10, 2002, the legacy INS issued implementing instructions on this act.[4]

---

[6]22 CFR. § 50.40(a).

[7]22 CFR. § 50.40(b).

[8]61 Fed. Reg. 29651 (Supplemental Information).

[9]61 Fed. Reg. 29651.

[10]61 Fed. Reg. 29651.

[11]61 Fed. Reg. 29651.

[12]61 Fed. Reg. 29651.

[Section 11:33]

[1]Section 114 of the Department of Justice Appropriations Act of 2002, Pub.L. 107-77 *reproduced at the conclusion of* Appendix 11-3.

[2]Section 114(d)(2) of the Department of Justice Appropriations Act of 2002, Pub.L. 107-77 *reproduced at the conclusion of* Appendix 11-3.

[3]Section 114(g) of the Department of Justice Appropriations Act of 2002, Pub.L. 107-77 *reproduced at the conclusion of* Appendix 11-3.

[4]Implementation Instructions for Section 114 of Public Law 107-77, "Department of Commerce, Justice, State, the Judiciary, and Related Agencies Appropriations Act, 2002," 115 Stat. 748 (November 28, 2001) (hereinafter "Implementation Instructions") *reproduced at* Appendix 11-3.

§ 11:34 Requirements

Research References

Dizon and Wettstein, Immigration Law Service 2d § 14:65

To be eligible for posthumous citizenship, the non-citizen must have died as a result of an injury incurred in one of the four September 11, 2001, hijackings specified in the provision or as a result of an injury incurred while assisting in the emergency response to any of these hijackings.[1] Individuals assisting in emergency response include military personnel, police and firefighters, medical personnel, engineers and volunteers.[2] An individual who is culpable for any of these events will not be eligible under this provision.[3]

An application for naturalization must have been pending on September 11, 2001. An application will be considered to have been pending if the application was filed in accordance with the regulations prior to that date, and no final administrative action had yet been taken.[4] To be granted posthumous citizenship, the individual must have been eligible for such citizenship on their date of death and must not have been barred from citizenship by any provision of law.[5] The Act waives certain of the requirements for citizenship.[6]

§ 11:35 Procedures

Research References

Dizon and Wettstein, Immigration Law Service 2d § 14:66

The deceased's next-of-kin or representative must submit a request for posthumous citizenship to USCIS.[1] The agency has adopted the definitions of next-of-kin and representative already in place for posthumous citizenship for military personnel under INA § 329A.[2] A request for posthumous citizenship must be filed with USCIS within two years of either November 28, 2001 or the non-citizen's death, whichever is later.[3] Because a naturalization application is already on file with USCIS, there is no special form that the next-of-kin or representative must file.[4] A request can be filed at any USCIS office, though USCIS suggests that it be filed at the office with jurisdiction over the non-citizen's last residence.[5]

[Section 11:34]

[1]Implementation Instructions, § I *reproduced at* Appendix 11-3.

[2]Implementation Instructions, § I *reproduced at* Appendix 11-3.

[3]Implementation Instructions, § I *reproduced at* Appendix 11-3.

[4]Implementation Instructions, § I *reproduced at* Appendix 11-3.

[5]Implementation Instructions, § I *reproduced* Appendix 11-3.

[6]See § 11:35.

[Section 11:35]

[1]Implementation Instructions, § II *reproduced at* Appendix 11-3.

[2]Appendix 11-3; see also INA § 329A, 8 U.S.C.A. § 1440-1; 8 CFR § 392.1.

[3]Implementation Instructions, § III *reproduced at* Appendix 11-3.

[4]Implementation Instructions, § IV *reproduced at* Appendix 11-3.

[5]Implementation Instructions, § IV *reproduced at* Appendix 11-3.

All applications will be adjudicated based upon facts that existed on September 10, 2001.[6] To the maximum extent possible, USCIS will adjudicate the naturalization application based upon information it has on file about the deceased applicant. Where this information is insufficient, USCIS will consider information, documentation and testimony from the next-of-kin or representative.[7] The April 10, 2002 Implementation Instructions detail the procedures that USCIS will follow to determine whether the requirements of residence, physical presence, good moral character and attachment to the principles of the U.S. Constitution have all been established.[8] The Act specifically waives the English and history and civics requirements, as well as the taking of an oath of allegiance.[9] When an application is approved, a certificate of naturalization will be sent to the next-of-kin or representative.[10]

---

[6]Implementation Instructions, § V *reproduced at* Appendix 11-3.

[7]Implementation Instructions, § V *reproduced at* Appendix 11-3.

[8]Implementation Instructions, § V *reproduced at* Appendix 11-3.

[9]Implementation Instructions, § V *reproduced at* Appendix 11-3.

[10]Implementation Instructions, § VI *reproduced at* Appendix 11-3.

APPENDIX 11-1

Form N-600K

OMB No. 1615-0087; Expires 05/31/2015

Department of Homeland Security
U. S. Citizenship and Immigration Services

**Instructions for Form N-600K, Application for
Citizenship and Issuance of Certificate Under Section 322**

The Purpose of Form N-600K

This form is an application for U.S. citizenship (acquisition) and issuance of a Certificate of Citizenship under section 322 of the Immigration and Nationality Act (INA) for a child **who regularly resides outside of the United States.**

Who Is Eligible to File

General Requirements

You may acquire U.S. citizenship if you meet **all** the following criteria to be eligible for citizenship under section 322 of the INA:

1. Not married; **and**

2. U.S. Citizenship and Immigration Services (USCIS) must administer the Oath of Allegiance to you before you reach 18 years of age; **and**

3. Regularly reside outside the United States; **and**

4. In the legal **and** physical custody of your U.S. citizen parent; **and**

5. Have a U.S. citizen parent who has been physically present in the United States for a period or periods totaling at least 5 years, at least 2 of which were after 14 years of age. If your U.S. citizen parent does not meet this requirement, your U.S. citizen parent's own U.S. citizen parent (grandparent) has to have been physically present in the United States for a period or periods totaling at least 5 years, at least 2 of which were after 14 years of age; **and**

   In cases where your U.S. citizen parent died in the preceding 5 years, and Form N-600K has been properly filed on behalf of you by your U.S. citizen grandparent or by your U.S. citizen legal guardian, you do NOT have to be residing in the legal and physical custody of the person as long as the person who has legal and physical custody of you does not object to the Form N-600K.

6. Be temporarily present in the United States at the time of interview in lawful status pursuant to a lawful admission.

NOTE: It is the responsibility of the individual seeking your Certificate of Citizenship under section 322 of the INA to secure any visa or other document necessary for your lawful admission to the United States. USCIS cannot assist in obtaining any necessary visa or other document.

Children of Members of the U.S. Armed Forces

1. The entire process may be completed outside the United States if you are residing abroad with your U.S. citizen parent who is a member of the U.S. Armed Forces and you are authorized to accompany and reside abroad with the service member under official military orders. You do not need to demonstrate the temporary physical presence, lawful admission, and maintenance of status requirements to be eligible for naturalization under section 322 of the INA.

2. A U.S. citizen who is, or was, serving in the U.S. Armed Forces and who seeks to have you obtain a Certificate of Citizenship under section 322 of the INA may count any time spent abroad on official U.S. military orders as part of the required 5 years of physical presence in the United States or its outlying possessions as long as you are residing abroad with that service member under official military orders at the time of filing.

Section 322 For an Adopted Child

As an adopted child of a U.S. citizen, you may acquire U.S. citizenship under section 322 of the INA only if you satisfy the specific provision of the U.S. immigration laws relating to adopted children that applies to your Form N-600K.

Hague Convention Adoption Case

If your U.S. citizen parent adopted you under the Hague Intercountry Adoption Convention, then you must submit your adoption decree, a copy of the approval notice for the Form I-800, Petition to Classify Convention Adoptee, as an Immediate Relative, and the supporting evidence (other than the home study).

Orphan Case

If your U.S. citizen parent adopted you as an orphan under section 101(b)(1)(F) of the INA, then you must submit your adoption decree, a copy of the approval notice for the Form I-600, Petition to Classify Orphan as an Immediate Relative, and the supporting evidence (other than the home study).

Any Other Adoption Case

If your U.S. citizen parent did not adopt you under under the Hague Intercountry Adoption Convention or as an orphan under section 101(b)(1)(F) of the INA, you must have:

1. Been adopted before your 16th birthday (or before your 18th birthday, as specified in section 101(b)(1)(E)(ii) of the INA);

2. Been in the legal custody of your adopting U.S. citizen parent for at least 2 years; **and**

3. Resided with your adopting U.S. citizen parent for at least 2 years.

NOTE: The required 2 years of residing in the legal and physical custody of the adopting parent does not apply to an adopted orphan as described in section 101(b)(1)(F) or (G) of the INA.

Who May File

This form may be filed on behalf of you, an eligible foreign-born child, by the following individuals:

Your U.S. Citizen Parent

The U.S. citizen parent with legal **and** physical custody of you, the biological or adopted child under 18 years of age. Your U.S. citizen parent must regularly reside outside the United States and seek naturalization for you under section 322 of the INA.

OR

If your qualifying U.S. citizen parent has died, this form may be filed within 5 years of your parent's death by your U.S. citizen grandparent or U.S. citizen legal guardian.

U.S. Citizen Grandparent

A U.S. citizen parent of the U.S. citizen parent (your grandparent).

U.S. Citizen Legal Guardian

A U.S. citizen legal guardian of you, the child, who is filing Form N-600K within 5 years of the death of your qualifying citizen parent. The U.S. citizen legal guardian does not have to meet the parental physical presence requirements under section 322 of the INA. Although the physical presence requirements need not be met by the legal guardian, the requirements must have been met by either your deceased U.S. citizen parent or by your U.S. citizen grandparent prior to your U.S. citizen parent's death.

Who Should Not File This Form

This form should not be filed:

1. On behalf of you, the child, if you have already acquired citizenship **automatically** under sections 301, 309, 320 or on or before 02/27/2001 under the repealed section 321 of the INA;

2. By a U.S. citizen whose only relationship to you, the child, is as a step-parent;

3. By any person other than a U.S. citizen parent of you, the child, unless that parent has died;

4. By any person once you, the child, are over the age of 18 years of age;

5. By you if you are seeking to replace a lost or stolen certificate. Please refer to Form N-565, Application for Replacement Naturalization/Citizenship Document, for information to replace a lost or stolen certificate; **or**

6. **By you, if you previously filed a Form N-600K and received a USCIS denial. USCIS will reject (not accept) your newly filed Form N-600K. Review your Form N-600K denial notice for more information.**

Required Evidence

Unless specifically noted otherwise, you must submit each of the documents listed below for you, and your grandparent (if applicable), through whom you are claiming U.S. citizenship at the time of filing to avoid delays in processing your Form N-600K.

USCIS may require verification for any or all information provided with Form N-600K. You must bring documentation to your interview if information has been updated or has changed after filing.

NOTE: "You" and "your" in this section refers to the individual for whom a Certificate of Citizenship is sought. It is NOT the applicant's parent who may apply on the minor child's behalf.

Photographs. You **must** submit two identical passport-style color photographs of yourself. The photos must have a white to off-white background, be printed on thin paper with a glossy finish, and be unmounted and unretouched. If a digital photo is submitted, it must to be taken from a camera with at least 3.5 mega pixels of resolution.

The photos must be 2" x 2" and must be in color with full face, frontal view on a white to off-white background. Head height should measure 1" to 1 3/8" from top of hair to bottom of chin, and eye height is between 1 1/8" to 1 3/8" from bottom of photo. Your head must be bare unless you are wearing headwear as required by a religious denomination of which you are a member; however, your face must be visible. Using pencil or felt pen, lightly print your name and Alien Registration Number (A-Number) on the back of each photo.

Your Birth Certificate or Record. Issued and certified by a civil authority in the country of birth.

Birth Certificate or Record of Your U.S. Citizen Parent. If you apply, your parent must submit his or her birth certificate issued and certified by a civil authority in the country of birth. If your parent applies on your behalf, your parent must still submit his or her birth certificate issued and certified by a civil authority in the country of birth.

Marriage Certificate(s) of the U.S. Citizen Parent *(if applicable)*. Issued and certified by a civil authority in the State or country of marriage.

Documents Showing the Marriage Termination *(if applicable)*. Certified divorce decree, death certificate, or annulment document.

Proof of U.S. Citizenship of Qualifying Parent or Grandparent. Examples of this are a U.S. birth certificate; Form N-550, Certificate of Naturalization; Form N-560 Certificate of Citizenship; Form FS-240, Report of Birth Abroad of United States Citizen; or a valid unexpired U.S. passport.

NOTE: A passport must have been issued prior to your birth if it is being provided as proof of U.S. citizenship. You must provide additional documents including birth certificate or naturalization certificate as evidence that your parent was a U.S. citizen at the time of your birth if the passport was issued after your birth.

Proof or Legitimation. If you were born out of wedlock, then you must submit certified evidence establishing the proper legitimation. Documents must establish legitimation according to the laws of your residence or domicile. You must have been in the legal custody of your parent(s) at the time of legitimation.

Legal Guardianship Evidence *(if applicable)*. Certified evidence of legal guardianship issued by the legal authority of the guardian's residence or domicile.

Proof of Legal and Physical Custody. In cases of divorce, legal separation, or legal adoption, evidence that the qualifying U.S. citizen parent has legal and physical custody of someone who does not object to the application.

Evidence of Lawful Admission and Maintenance of Such Lawful Status. Form I-94, Arrival-Departure Record, is required, if available, at the time of interview for all children seeking citizenship under section 322 of the INA, except for eligible children of members of the U.S. Armed Forces.

NOTE: If U.S. Customs and Border Protection (CBP) or USCIS issued Form I-94, Arrival-Departure Record, to you, provide the I-94 admission number in the fields of this form where it is requested. This number also is known as the Departure Number on some versions of Form I-94. If you do not have an I-94 number, one of the following scenarios may apply:

1. **If CBP or USCIS issued Form I-94 to you, but it is now lost or destroyed,** you may apply for a replacement by filing Form I-102, Application for Replacement/Initial Nonimmigrant Arrival-Departure Document.

2. **If CBP or USCIS did not issue Form I-94 to you and you believe that Form I-94 should have been issued,** you may contact the agency you believe should have issued it to attempt to resolve the matter.

3. **If CBP did not issue Form I-94 to you because it captured arrival information electronically,** write "N/A" in the fields that request an I-94 Arrival-Departure Record Number. In this instance, it is important for you to provide a passport or travel document number where it is requested on the form. (See below.)

Passport and Travel Document Numbers. CBP is exploring automation of Form I-94, Arrival-Departure Record, in order to collect arrival/departure information electronically, streamlining arrival and inspection for travelers. If this occurs, CBP may scan a traveler's electronic passport (or, for travelers who do not have a passport, some other similar "travel document") instead of issuing Form I-94. In these instances, you must provide passport or travel document numbers - even if they have expired - instead of a Form I-94 number when filing Form N-600K.

Proof of Required Physical Presence in the United States. Any document that proves your U.S. citizen parent's physical presence in the United States. This pertains to grandparents if your parent does not meet the requirement. For example:

1. School, employment, or military records;

2. Deeds, mortgages, or leases showing residence;

3. U.S. Social Security Administration reports;

4. Attestations by churches, unions, or other organizations; **or**

5. Affidavits by third parties having knowledge of your residence and physical presence.

Current Status of U.S. Citizen Grandparent. Your grandparent must be a U.S. citizen, or must have been one at the time of death of your U.S. citizen parent, if your sponsoring U.S. citizen parent is using your grandparent's physical presence in the United States to meet that requirement.

NOTE: For applications filed by the grandparent or legal guardian, evidence must be submitted to prove that your grandparent was a U.S. citizen and still alive at the time of your U.S. citizen parent's death if your U.S. citizen parent has died and your grandparent's physical presence is relied upon. Evidence must also be submitted to prove that your U.S. citizen parent died within the preceeding 5 years.

Copy of Notice of Approval and Supporting Documentation, except home study *(if applicable)*. Provide the following documentation:

1. **Form I-600, Petition to Classify Orphan as an Immediate Relative;**

OR

2. Form I-800, Petition to Classify Convention Adoptee as an Immediate Relative.

NOTE: All adopted children seeking naturalization under section 322 of the INA must have had either Form I-600 or Form I-800 approved **or** have complied with the 2 years of legal custody and joint residence requirement of section 101(b)(1)(E) of the INA.

Copy of Full, Final Adoption Decree *(if applicable)*.

Evidence of All Legal Name Changes. If you legally changed your name, submit evidence of an issued and certified document by the court that authorized the legal name change(s).

What If a Document Is Unavailable?

You must provide a written explanation of the reason(s) why a required document(s) is unavailable and submit secondary evidence to establish eligibility. Secondary evidence must overcome the unavailability of the required documents. USCIS may request an original written statement from the appropriate government or other legal authority to support your claim that the documents are unavailable.

The following types of **secondary evidence** may be submitted to establish eligibility.

Baptismal Certificate. Certificate under the church seal where your baptism occurred showing your:

1. Place of birth;
2. Date of birth;
3. Baptism date;
4. Parent's names, **and**
5. Godparent(s) name(s), if known.

School Record. An official letter from school authorities pertaining to the school attended (preferably the first school) showing your:

1. Date of admission to the school;
2. Place of birth;
3. Date of birth or age at that time; **and**
4. The name(s) and residence(s) of your birth parents if shown in the school records.

Census Records. State or Federal census records showing your:

1. Name;
2. Place of birth; **and**
3. Date of birth or age.

Affidavits *(if other types of secondary evidence are not available)*. Written statements sworn to (or affirmed) by 2 people who have personal knowledge of the claimed event. Affidavits must overcome the unavailability of both required documents and secondary evidence. Examples of events you may submit an affidavit for include the following:

1. Your place and date of birth;
2. Marriage; **or**
3. Death.

The people making these statements are not required to be U.S. citizens and may be relatives. Each affidavit must contain the following information about the person making the affidavit:

1. Full legal name;
2. Address;
3. Place of birth;
4. Date of birth;
5. Relationship to you; **and**
6. Detailed information about the event to include how they came to know about its occurrence.

General Instructions

1. **Type or print clearly using black ink.** Keep all information within the area provided.

   If extra space is needed to answer any question, attach an additional sheet(s) of paper. You must provide the following information on the top of each sheet of paper:

   A. Your A-Number, if applicable;
   B. The date;
   C. Question number; **and**
   D. Your signature.

2. **Answer all questions fully and accurately.** Write "N/A" if an item is not applicable. Write "None" if the answer is none.

3. **Avoid highlighting, crossing out, or writing outside the area provided for a response.**

   Do not use highlighters on your Form N-600K as our scanners turn hightlighted areas black, making them unreadable. If you must edit your form, USCIS recommends you begin with a new Form N-600K, rather than trying to white out information. USCIS scanners may see through the white correction tape or fluid and make your form incorrect, possibly leading to processing delays or rejection.

4. **Provide your A-Number on the top right corner of each page** *(if applicable)*. Your A-Number is located on your Permanent Resident Card (formerly known as the Alien Registration or "Green" Card). The A-Number on your card consists of seven to nine numbers, depending on when your record was created. If the A-Number on your card has fewer than nine numbers, place enough zeros before the first number to make a *total of nine numbers* on Form N-600K. For example, write number A1234567 as A001234567 or write number A12345678 as A012345678.

Translations. You must provide a full English translation for any document written in a foreign language that you submit to USCIS. The translator must certify that the translation is complete and accurate and that he or she is competent to translate from the foreign language into English.

Copies. You may submit copies of documents unless USCIS requests original documents. Original documents submitted when not required may remain a part of the record and will not be automatically returned to you.

Specific Form Instructions

This form is divided into 11 parts.

Part 1. Information About Your Eligibility

Check the box that indicates why you are eligible for citizenship under section 322 of the INA.

Box 1: Check this box if you are a U.S. citizen parent applying for citizenship on behalf of your eligible biological child.

Box 2: Check this box if you are a U.S. citizen parent applying for citizenship on behalf of your eligible adopted child.

Box 3: Check this box if you are the U.S. citizen parent of the child's deceased U.S. citizen parent applying for your eligible grandchild. Also, check this box if you are the U.S. citizen legal guardian of such a child.

General Items

Current Legal Name. Provide the your legal name. This should be the name on the your birth certificate, unless it has been changed after birth by legal action such as marriage, adoption, or court order. **Do not provide a nickname.**

U.S. Social Security Number. Print the person's U.S. Social Security Number. Write "N/A" if you do not have one.

Date of Birth. Use 8 numbers to show the date of birth. For example, May 1, 1992, must be written as 05/01/1992.

Country of Birth. Provide the name of the country where the person was born. Write the name of the country even if the country's name has since changed or the country no longer exists.

Home Address. Provide the address where the person now resides. **Do not** write a Post Office (P.O.) Box number here unless it is the person's **ONLY** address.

If the person resides outside the United States. If the person does not have a State or Province, enter the name of the city again in that box. If the person does not have a ZIP or Postal Code, enter 00000 in the ZIP or Postal Code box.

Telephone Numbers. Provide the person's current telephone numbers. If the answer is none, write "None." If you are hearing impaired and use a TDD telephone connection, please indicate this by writing "TDD" after the telephone number.

E-Mail Address. Provide the person's current e-mail address. If the person does not have an e-mail address, write "None."

Part 2. Information About You, the Child

2. **Name exactly as it appears on your Permanent Resident Card** *(if applicable)*. Provide your name exactly as it appears on the card even if it is misspelled. Write "N/A" if you do not have a permanent resident card.

3. **Other names you have used since birth** *(include nicknames, if applicable)*. Provide any other name(s) you have used since birth. Attach an additional sheet(s) of paper if more space is needed.

7. **Country of Prior Citizenship/Nationality.** Provide the name of the country of your citizenship/nationality before you became a U.S. citizen.

    A. If the country no longer exists or you are stateless, provide the name of the country where you were last a citizen or national.

    B. If you are a citizen or national of more than one country, provide the name of the country that issued your latest passport.

8. **Gender.** Indicate whether you are male or female.

9. **Height.** Provide your height in feet and inches.

11. **Mailing Address.** Provide your mailing address even if it is the same as your home address. Provide "*in care of name*" information, if applicable. You must write something in every box, except an apartment number or "C/O" if you do not have one, within "Mailing Address."

    NOTE: USCIS may not be able to contact you if you do not provide a complete and valid address. If USCIS does reject your Form N-600K, USCIS may not be able to return the fee for the Form N-600K to you if you do not provide a complete and valid address. If USCIS cannot return the fee, USCIS will cash your check.

14. Marital Status. Check the marital status you have on the date you file this Form N-600K. Check "Other" if your marriage was otherwise legally terminated and explain.

15. Information About Your Admission Into the United States and Current Immigration Status.

Do not complete this part. The applicant will be asked to complete this part at the interview.

16. Previous Application for Certificate of Citizenship, or U.S. Passport. If you previously applied for a Certificate of Citizenship or a U.S. Passport (or you are a U.S. citizen parent who previously applied for a Certificate of Citizenship or U.S. Passport for your minor child), explain on an additional sheet (s) of paper what happened with that application and whether the Certificate of Citizenship or U.S. Passport was or was not issued.

17. Information on Adoption. Provide the necessary information requested.

18. Marital Status of Your Parents at Time of Birth or Adoption. Indicate whether your parents were married to each other at the time of your birth. If you were born out of wedlock, indicate "No," even if your parents subsequently married. If you were adopted, indicate whether your adoptive parents were married to each other at the time of your adoption.

Part 3. Information About Your U.S. Citizen Biological or Adoptive Parent

NOTE: Not all the questions are explained in this part because they are located in the **General Items** section of Specific Form Instructions. Please go to that section for more information.

8. U.S. Citizenship. Provide all the requested information regarding how your parent became a U.S. citizen.

9. Loss of U.S. Citizenship. Provide information on an additional sheet(s) of paper if your parent ever lost U.S. citizenship regardless of whether it has since been regained.

10. Marital History

   A. Write the number of times your qualifying U.S. citizen parent has been married, including annulled marriages. Count each marriage as separate if your parent married the same person more than one time.

   B. Check the marital status your U.S. citizen parent has on the date you file Form N-600K. Check "Other" if your parents' marriage was otherwise legally terminated and explain.

   C. If your U.S. citizen parent is now married, provide information about your parent's current spouse. Check the appropriate box to indicate the spouse's current immigration status.

   D. Indicate whether your qualifying U.S. citizen parent's current spouse is also your biological or adoptive parent. If "No," USCIS may request information about your U.S. citizen parent's previous spouse(s).

11. Member of the U.S. Armed Forces. Provide information if your U.S. citizen parent is a member of the U.S. Armed Forces.

Part 4. Information About Your Qualifying U.S. Citizen Grandparent

Complete this section only if your U.S. citizen parent **has not** been physically present in the United States for 5 years, 2 years of which were after 14 years of age. You are relying on the physical presence in the United States of the U.S citizen father or mother of your U.S citizen parent (your grandparent) to obtain your U.S. citizenship. You must provide information about the U.S. citizen parent of your U.S. citizen father or mother (your grandparent) in the sections noted.

NOTE: Not all the questions are explained in this part because they are located in the General Items section of Specific Form Instructions. Please go to that section for more information.

8. U.S. Citizenship. Provide all the requested information regarding how your grandparent became a U.S. citizen.

9. Loss of U.S. Citizenship. Provide information on an additional sheet(s) of paper if your parent ever lost U.S. citizenship regardless of whether it has since been regained.

Part 5. Physical Presence in the United States From Birth Until Filing Form N-600K

Physical Presence. Provide all the dates when your biological or adoptive U.S. citizen father, mother, or grandparent was in the United States. **Include all dates from your birth until the date you file your Form N-600K.**

NOTE: A U.S. citizen parent who is, or was, a member of the U.S. Armed Forces may count any time he or she resided abroad on official military orders towards the physical presence requirements under section 322(a)(2) of the INA as long as the applicant was residing abroad with the U.S. citizen parent per official military orders at the time of filing.

Part 6. Information About Your Legal Guardian

Complete this part **only** for Form N-600K filed by a legal guardian in lieu of a deceased U.S. citizen parent.

Part 7. Preferred Location and Date for Interview

Provide your preferences regarding when and where you would like to be interviewed. USCIS will consider your preferences.

1. USCIS office (or City, State) for your interview. If a specific USCIS office is unknown, provide the preferred city and state for your interview; **and**

2. **Date.** Your preferred interview date should be at least 90 days after you file this Form N-600K and must be before you turn 18 years of age.

NOTE: USCIS **CANNOT** immediately adjudicate your Form N-600K once you file the application. Processing of the Form N-600K must be completed within the U.S. The processing includes: interview of the applicant and qualifying relative (parent or grandparent) or guardian (if applicable); taking the Oath of Allegiance (required for 14 years of age or older); and receipt of the Certificate of Citizenship.

Part 8. Your Signature

Sign the Form N-600K as you normally sign your name. You may place an "X" mark instead of a signature if you are unable to write in any language.

A parent or legal guardian may sign for you if you are less than 14 years of age. You may also sign the Form N-600K on your own behalf without your parent's or legal guardian's signature.

NOTE: USCIS will reject your Form N-600K if it is not signed. USCIS cannot accept copies of signed application or a typewritten name in place of a signature.

Part 9. Signature of Person Who Prepared This Form for You *(if applicable)*

If you prepared this form by yourself, leave this section blank. If someone filled out this form for you, he or she must complete this section. Your parent must complete this part if your parent prepared this Form N-600K for you.

Part 10. Affidavit

Do not complete this part. You will be asked to complete this part at the interview.

Part 11. USCIS Officer Report and Recommendation

Do not complete this part as it is for USCIS use only.

Processing Information

Any Form N-600K that is not signed will be rejected. A Form N-600K that is not completed according to these instructions, is missing pages or otherwise not executed in its entirety, or is not accompanied by the required initial evidence may be rejected or delayed. If USCIS rejects your Form N-600K for any of the reasons above, the form and any fees will be returned to you if you provide a complete and valid mailing address. You will be notified why the form is considered deficient. You may correct the deficiency and refile a Form N-600K. An application or petition is not considered properly filed until accepted by USCIS.

Requests for More Information and interview

USCIS may request more information or evidence. USCIS may also request that you submit the originals of any copies you previously provided to USCIS with your Form N-600K. In addition, USCIS will request that you appear for an interview.

Decision

The decision on Form N-600K involves a determination of whether you have established eligibility for the requested benefit. If you do not establish a basis for eligibility, USCIS will deny your Form N-600K. You will be notified of the decision in writing.

When To File

In order for you, the applicant, to obtain U.S. citizenship through this Form N-600K:

1. All the required evidence must be received and verified; **and**

2. USCIS must administer the oath of allegiance to you **before you reach 18 years of age.**

You should file Form N-600K *at least* 90 days prior to the requested interview date, allowing USCIS time to review the Form N-600K as well as schedule the interview and send a timely appointment notice to the foreign address. USCIS will not schedule an interview date until it has determined that the Form N-600K is complete. **Therefore, Form N-600K processing may be further delayed if any of the required information and evidence is missing from the Form N-600K. Requests for a change in the designated local USCIS office may also delay processing.**

NOTE: USCIS advises you and the U.S. citizen applicant to wait for the appointment notice from USCIS **before** traveling to the United States with the understanding that USCIS cannot assist the applicant in obtaining a visa(s) to enter the United States.

What Is the Filing Fee

The fee for filing Form N-600K is **$600** for a biological child and **$550** for an adopted child.

The fee for the Form N-600K may be waived. Applicants should submit a Form I-912, Request for Fee Waiver, or a written request, accompanied by documentation of the applicant's financial inability to pay the fee. To download a copy of Form I-912, including the instructions, click on the "**FORMS**" link on the USCIS Web site at www.uscis.gov.

Use the following guidelines when you prepare your check or money order for your Form N-600K fee:

1. The check or money order must be drawn on a bank or other financial institution located in the Unites States and must be payable in U.S. currency; **and**

2. Make the check or money order payable to **U.S. Department of Homeland Security.**

   NOTE: Spell out U.S. Department of Homeland Security; do not use the initials "USDHS" or "DHS".

If you live outside the United States, contact the nearest U.S. Embassy or consulate for instructions on the method of payment.

Notice To Those Making Payment by Check

USCIS will make a copy and convert your original check into an electronic funds transfer (EFT). This means USCIS will use the account information on your check to electronically debit your account for the check amount. This debit usually takes 24 hours and should show up on your regular account statement.

USCIS will not return your original check. USCIS will destroy it and keep a copy with your file. If the EFT cannot be processed due to technical reasons, you authorize USCIS to process the copy of the check. If the EFT cannot be completed because of insufficient funds, USCIS may try the EFT up to two times.

If you receive an insufficient funds notice, USCIS will send you instructions on how to submit your penalty fee. **Do not** send a check for the penalty fee to the address where you filed your Form N-600K; your form will be returned to you.

How To Check If the Fees Are Correct

The filing and biometrics services fees on this form are current as of the edition date appearing in the lower right corner of this page. However, because USCIS fees change periodically, you can verify if the fees are correct by following one of the steps below:

1. Visit the USCIS Web site at **www.uscis.gov**, select "**FORMS**," and check the appropriate fee;

2. Telephone the USCIS National Customer Service Center at **1-800-375-5283** and ask for the fee information. For TDD (hearing impaired) call **1-800-767-1833**.

Where To File

See the USCIS Web site at www.uscis.gov or call the USCIS National Customer Service Center at **1-800-375-5283** for the most current information about where to file Form N-600K. For TDD (hearing impaired) call: **1-800-767-1833**.

Form Revision Date

If you are filing Form N-600K more than 30 days after the latest revision date shown in the lower right corner, please visit the USCIS Web site at **www.uscis.gov** before you file, and check the "**FORMS**" page to confirm the form version currently in use. If the revision date on your Form N-600K matches the revision date listed for Form N-600K on the online "**FORMS**" page, your version is current. If the revision date on the online version is more recent, download a copy and use it. If you do not have Internet access, call the USCIS National Customer Service Center at **1-800-375-5283** to verify the revision date. For TDD (hearing impaired): call **1-800-767-1833**.

NOTE: USCIS will reject forms with the wrong revision date and return the fee with instructions to resubmit the entire filing using the current form.

Address Changes

If you have changed your address, you must inform USCIS of your new address. For information on filing a change of address go to the USCIS Web site at **www.uscis.gov/ addresschange** or contact the USCIS National Customer Service Center at **1-800-375-5283**. For TDD (hearing impaired): call **1-800-767-1833**.

NOTE: Do not submit a change of address request to the USCIS Lockbox facilities because the USCIS Lockbox facilities do not process change of address requests.

USCIS Forms and Information

To ensure you are using the latest version of this form, visit the USCIS Web site at **www.uscis.gov** where you can obtain the latest USCIS forms and immigration-related information. If you do not have internet access, you may order USCIS forms by calling our toll-free number at **1-800-870-3676**. You may also obtain forms and information by calling the USCIS National Customer Service Center at **1-800-375-5283**. For TDD (hearing impaired) call: **1-800-767-1833**.

An alternative to waiting in line for assistance at your local USCIS office, you can schedule an appointment through the USCIS Internet-based system, **InfoPass**. To access the system, visit the USCIS Web site. Use the **InfoPass** appointment scheduler and follow the screen prompts to set up your appointment. **InfoPass** generates an electronic appointment notice that appears on the screen.

Attorney or Representative

You may be represented, at no expense to the U.S. Government, by an attorney or other duly accredited representative. Your representative must submit Form G-28, Notice of Entry of Appearance as Attorney or Representative, with your Form N-600K. Your representative may also submit the Form G-28 at the time of your interview. Form G-28 can be obtained by visiting the USCIS Web site at www.uscis.gov, calling the USCIS forms line number at 1-800-870-3676, or by contacting the USCIS National Customer Service Center at 1-800-375-5283. For TDD (hearing impaired) call 1-800-767-1833.

Penalties

If you knowingly and willfully falsify or conceal a material fact or submit a false document with this Form N-600K, USCIS will deny your Form N-600K and may deny any other immigration benefit. In addition, you may be subject to criminal prosecution and penalties provided by law.

USCIS Privacy Act Statement

AUTHORITY: Section 322 of the Immigration and Nationality Act authorizes USCIS to collect the information and associated evidence on this benefit application.

PURPOSE: The primary purpose for providing the requested information is to determine if you have established eligibility for naturalization. We will use the information you provide to grant or deny the benefit you seek. USCIS requests that the applicant and family member(s) to provide their SSN, if applicable. The SSN is used to verify the identity and residency of the applicant and family member(s) and to complete a sufficient background check.

DISCLOSURE: The information you provide is voluntary. However, failure to provide the requested information, including the SSN, and any requested evidence, may delay a final decision or result in denial of your benefit request.

ROUTINE USES: The information you provide on this benefit application may be disclosed to other federal, state, local, and foreign government agencies and authorized organizations in accordance with approved routine uses, as described in the associated published system of records notices [DHS-USCIS-007 - Benefits Information System and DHS-USCIS-001- Alien File, Index, and National File Tracking System of Records, which can be found at www.dhs.gov/privacy]. The information may also be made available, as appropriate for law enforcement purposes or in the interest of national security.

USCIS Compliance Review and Monitoring

By signing this form, you have stated under penalty of perjury (28 U.S.C. Section 1746) that all information and documentation submitted with this form is true and correct. You also have authorized the release of any information from your records that USCIS may need to determine eligibility for the benefit you are seeking and consented to USCIS verification of such information.

The Department of Homeland Security has the authority to verify any information you submit to establish eligibility for the immigration benefit you are seeking at any time. USCIS' legal authority to verify this information is in 8 U.S.C. Sections 1103, 1155, 1184, and 8 CFR parts 103, 204, 205, and 214. To ensure compliance with applicable laws and authorities, USCIS may verify information before or after your case has been decided. Agency verification methods may include, but are not limited to: review of public records and information; contact via written correspondence, the Internet, facsimile, or other electronic transmission, or telephone; unannounced physical site inspections of residences and locations of employment; and interviews. Information obtained through verification will be used to assess your compliance with the laws and to determine your eligibility for the benefit sought.

Paperwork Reduction Act

An agency may not conduct or sponsor an information collection, and a person is not required to respond to a collection of information unless it displays a currently valid OMB control number. The total public reporting burden for this collection of information is estimated at 2 hours 5 minutes per response. This total includes 1 hour and 35 minutes for the time to review the instructions and completing the form, and 30 minutes to obtain passport style photographs. Send comments regarding this burden estimate or any other aspect of this collection of information, including suggestions for reducing this burden to: U.S. Citizenship and Immigration Services, Regulatory Coordination Division, Office of Policy and Strategy, 20 Massachusetts Ave NW, Washington, DC 20529-2140; OMB No. 1615-0087. **Do not mail your completed Form N-600K to this address.**

OMB No. 1615-0087; Expires 05/31/2015

Department of Homeland Security
U. S. Citizenship and Immigration Services

Form N-600K, Application for Citizenship and Issuance of Certificate Under Section 322

Print or type your answers fully and accurately in black ink. Write "N/A" if an item is not applicable. Write "None" if the answer is none. Failure to answer all of the questions may delay your Form N-600K.

Part 1. Information About Your Eligibility *(check only one box)*

The application is being filed on your behalf. You are under 18 years of age and:

1. ☐ The BIOLOGICAL child of a qualifying U.S. citizen (USC) parent filing this form.

2. ☐ The ADOPTED child of a qualifying USC parent filing this form.

3. ☐ The grandchild of a qualifying USC grandparent or the child ward of a USC legal guardian filing this form within 5 years of the death of my USC parent.

Part 2. Information About You, the Child *(for whom this application is being filed)*

1. **Current Legal Name** *(do not provide a nickname)*

   Family Name *(last name)*

   Given Name *(first name)*   Middle Name *(if applicable)*

2. **Name exactly as it appears on your Permanent Resident Card** *(if applicable)*

   Family Name *(last name)*

   Given Name *(first name)*   Middle Name *(if applicable)*

3. **Other name(s) you have used since birth** *(if applicable. Include nicknames.)*

Family Name *(last name)*	Given Name *(first name)*	Middle Name *(if applicable)*

4. **U.S. Social Security Number** *(if applicable)*

5. **Date of Birth** *(mm/dd/yyyy)*

6. **Country of Birth**

7. **Country of Citizenship/Nationality**

8. **Gender**   ☐ Male   ☐ Female

9. **Height**   Feet ____   Inches ____

10. **Home Address**

    Street Number and Name *(do not provide a P.O. Box in this space unless it is your ONLY address.)*   Apartment Number

    City   State   ZIP Code

    Province *(foreign address only)*   Country *(foreign address only)*   Postal Code *(foreign address only)*

Your A-Number:

A _____ - _____ - _____

For USCIS Use Only

Bar Code	Date Stamp
Remarks	
Action	

Form N-600K (Rev. 05/03/13) N

Part 2. Information About You, the Child *(continued)*   A ____ - ____ - ____

11. Mailing Address

C/O *(in care of name)*

Street Number and Name   Apartment Number

City   State   ZIP Code

Province *(foreign address only)*   Country *(foreign address only)*   Postal Code *(foreign address only)*

12. Daytime Phone Number   Work Phone Number *(if any)*   **Evening Phone Number**

( )   ( )   ( )

Mobile Phone Number *(if any)*   **13. E-Mail Address** *(if any)*

( )

14. Marital Status

☐ Single, Never Married   ☐ Married   ☐ Divorced   ☐ Widowed

☐ Marriage Annulled   ☐ Other *(explain)*: _____

15. Information about your admission into the United States and current immigration status

(Do NOT complete this section. The USCIS officer will complete it with you during the interview.)

You arrived in the following manner:

Port of Entry *(City/State)*   Date of Entry *(mm/dd/yyyy)*   Current Immigration Status

Exact Name Used at Time of Entry

16. Do you know of any prior application for citizenship or for a U.S. passport?   ☐ Yes   ☐ No

17. Were you adopted?   ☐ Yes   ☐ No

Date of Adoption *(mm/dd/yyyy)*   Date Legal Custody Began *(mm/dd/yyyy)*   Date Physical Custody Began *(mm/dd/yyyy)*

18. Were your parents married to each other when you were born (or adopted)?   ☐ Yes   ☐ No

Part 3. Information About Your U.S. Citizen Biological or Adoptive Parent *(Provide information about yourself below if you are a U.S. citizen father or mother applying on behalf of your eligible child. Provide information about the child's U.S. citizen parent in the sections noted if you are the U.S. citizen grandparent or legal guardian.)*

1. Current legal name of U.S. citizen father or mother submitting this Form N-600K.

Family Name *(last name)*   Given Name *(first name)*   Middle Name *(if applicable)*

Part 3. Information About Your U.S. Citizen Biological or Adoptive Parent *(continued)*

A _____ - ____ - _____

2. Date of Birth *(mm/dd/yyyy)*

3. Country of Birth

4. U.S. Social Security Number *(if applicable)*

5. Home Address

Street Number and Name *(do **not** provide a P.O. Box in this space)*

Apartment Number

City

State

ZIP Code

Province *(foreign address only)*

Country *(foreign address only)*

Postal Code *(foreign address only)*

6. Daytime Phone Number

( )

Work Phone Number *(if any)*

( )

Evening Phone Number

( )

Mobile Phone Number *(if any)*

( )

7. E-Mail Address *(if any)*

8. Your parent is a U.S. citizen by:

☐ Birth in the United States

☐ Acquisition after birth through naturalization of alien parent(s)

☐ Birth abroad to U.S. citizen parent(s)

Certificate of Citizenship Number

A-Number *(if known)*

☐ Naturalization

Date of Naturalization *(mm/dd/yyyy)*

Place of Naturalization *(name of court and City/State or USCIS office location)*

Certificate of Naturalization Number

A-Number *(if known)*

9. Has your U.S. citizen father or mother ever lost U.S. citizenship or taken any action that would cause loss of U.S. citizenship?

☐ Yes *(provide full explanation on an additional sheet(s) of paper.)*   ☐ No

10. Marital History

   A. How many times has your U.S. citizen father or mother been married *(including annulled marriages and marriage(s) to the same person)*? _____

   B. What is your U.S. citizen father or mother's current marital status?

   ☐ Single, Never Married   ☐ Married   ☐ Separated   ☐ Divorced   ☐ Widowed

   ☐ Marriage Annulled   ☐ Other *(explain)*: _____

   C. Information about your U.S. citizen father's or mother's **current spouse:**

   Family Name *(last name)*

   Given Name *(first name)*

   Middle Name *(if applicable)*

   Date of Birth *(mm/dd/yyyy)*

   Country of Birth

   Country of Citizenship/Nationality

Form N-600K (Rev. 05/03/13) N Page 3

Part 3. Information About Your U.S. Citizen Biological or Adoptive Parent *(continued)*

A ____ - ____ - ____

Spouse's Home Address

Street Number and Name *(do **not** provide a P.O. Box in this space)*   Apartment Number

City   State   ZIP Code

Province *(foreign address only)*   Country *(foreign address only)*   Postal Code *(foreign address only)*

Date of Marriage *(mm/dd/yyyy)*   Place of Marriage *(City/State or Country)*

Spouse's Immigration Status

☐ U.S. Citizen   ☐ Permanent Resident   ☐ Other *(explain)*: _____

D. Is your U.S. citizen father's or mother's current spouse also your biological (or adopted) parent?   ☐ Yes   ☐ No

11. Member of U.S. Armed Forces

A. Is the sponsoring U.S. citizen parent a member of the U.S. Armed Forces?   ☐ Yes   ☐ No

B. If you answered yes, then are you are on official orders authorizing you to accompany and reside with your sponsoring U.S. citizen parent who is a member of the U.S. Armed Forces?   ☐ Yes   ☐ No

NOTE: If your U.S. citizen biological or adoptive parent is filing this application AND has the required physical presence in the United States, skip Part 4 and go directly to Part 5.

Part 4. Information About Your Qualifying U.S. Citizen Grandparent *(complete this part **only** if your U.S. citizen parent (or adoptive parent), grandparent, or legal guardian is applying for citizenship for you, and the U.S. citizen parent **has not** been physically present in the United States for 5 years; 2 years of which were after the age of 14.)*

1. Current legal name of U.S. citizen grandfather or grandmother submitting this Form N-600K.

Family Name *(last name)*   Given Name *(first name)*   Middle Name *(if applicable)*

2. Date of Birth *(mm/dd/yyyy)*   **3.** Country of Birth   **4.** U.S. Social Security Number *(if applicable)*

5. Home Address

Street Number and Name *(do **not** provide a P.O. Box in this space)*   Apartment Number

City   State   ZIP Code

Province *(foreign address only)*   Country *(foreign address only)*   Postal Code *(foreign address only)*

Part 4. Information About Your Qualifying U.S. Citizen Grandparent *(continued)*

A ____ - ____ - ____

6. **Daytime Phone Number**

( )

Work Phone Number *(if any)*

( )

Evening Phone Number

( )

Mobile Phone Number *(if any)*

( )

7. **E-Mail Address** *(if any)*

8. **My grandparent is a U.S. citizen by:**

☐ Birth in the United States

☐ Acquisition after birth through naturalization of alien parent(s)

☐ Birth abroad to U.S. citizen parent(s)

Certificate of Citizenship Number

A-Number *(if known)*

☐ Naturalization

Date of Naturalization *(mm/dd/yyyy)*

Place of Naturalization *(name of court and City/State or USCIS office location)*

Certificate of Naturalization Number

A-Number *(if known)*

9. **Has your grandparent ever lost U.S. citizenship or taken any action that would cause loss of U.S. citizenship?**

☐ Yes *(provide full explanation on an additional sheet(s) of paper)*   ☐ No

Part 5. Physical Presence in the United States From Birth Until Filing of Form N-600K *(Provide the dates that your U.S. citizen parent or grandparent was present in the United States. If your U.S. citizen parent has not been physically present in the United States for 5 years, 2 years of which were after the age of 14, then you must use the physical presence of your U.S. citizen grandparent.)*

Indicate whether this information relates to your U.S. citizen parent or to your qualifying grandparent

☐ U.S. Citizen Parent   ☐ U.S. Citizen Grandparent

Physical Presence in the United States *(mm/dd/yyyy)*					
From		Until		From		Until	
From		Until		From		Until	
From		Until		From		Until	
From		Until		From		Until	
From		Until		From		Until	
From		Until		From		Until	
From		Until		From		Until	
From		Until		From		Until	

NOTE: If your U.S. citizen biological/adoptive parent is filing this application, skip Part 6 and go directly to Part 7.

Part 6. **Information About Your Legal Guardian** *(complete this part only if your legal guardian is filing this application in lieu of a deceased U.S. citizen parent)*

A _____ - _____ - _____

1. **Current legal name of U.S. citizen father or mother submitting this Form N-600K.**

   Family Name *(last name)*   Given Name *(first name)*   Middle Name *(if applicable)*

2. **Date of Birth** *(mm/dd/yyyy)*   3. **Country of Birth**   4. **U.S. Social Security Number** *(if applicable)*

5. **Home Address**

   Street Number and Name *(do **not** provide a P.O. Box in this space)*   Apartment Number

   City   State   ZIP Code

   Province *(foreign address only)*   Country *(foreign address only)*   Postal Code *(foreign address only)*

6. **Daytime Phone Number**   **Work Phone Number** *(if any)*   **Evening Phone Number**

   (   )   (   )   (   )

   Mobile Phone Number *(if any)*   7. **E-Mail Address** *(if any)*

   (   )

8. **My legal guardian is a U.S. citizen by:**

   ☐ Birth in the United States
   ☐ Acquisition after birth through naturalization of alien parent(s)
   ☐ Birth abroad to U.S. citizen parent(s)

   Certificate of Citizenship Number   A-Number *(if known)*

   ☐ Naturalization

   Date of Naturalization *(mm/dd/yyyy)*   Place of Naturalization *(name of court and City/State or USCIS office location)*

   Certificate of Naturalization Number   A-Number *(if known)*

9. **Date of Legal Guardianship** *(mm/dd/yyyy)*   10. **Name of Authority that Granted Legal Guardianship**

11. **Address of Authority that Granted Legal Guardianship**

Part 7. **Preferred Location and Date for Interview**

1. **Location** *(USCIS Office, City, or State)*   2. **Preferred Date** *(mm/dd/yyyy)*

USCIS will attempt to accommodate your preferences.

NOTE: Interview date should be at least 90 days _after_ filing Form N-600K and before your (the child's) 18th birthday.

Form N-600K (Rev. 05/03/13) N Page 6

Part 8.   Your Signature *(USCIS will reject your Form N-600K if it is not signed.)*

A ____ - ___ - ____

I certify, under penalty of perjury under the laws of the United States, that this application, and the evidence submitted with it, is all true and correct. I authorize the release of any information from my records that U.S. Citizenship and Immigration Services needs to determine eligibility for the benefit I am seeking.

Your Signature

Date *(mm/dd/yyyy)*

Part 9.   Signature of Person Who Prepared This Form For You *(if applicable)*

I declare that I prepared this application at the request of the above person. The answers provided are based on information of which I have personal knowledge and/or were provided to me by the above-named person in response to the questions contained on this application.

Preparer's Printed Name

Preparer's Signature

Date *(mm/dd/yyyy)*

Preparer's Firm or Organization Name *(if applicable)*

Preparer's Daytime Phone Number

( )

Preparer's Fax Number

( )

Preparer's Email Address

Preparer's Address

Street Number and Name *(do **not** provide a P.O. Box in this space)*

City	State	ZIP Code

Province *(foreign address only)*	Country *(foreign address only)*	Postal Code *(foreign address only)*

NOTE: Do not complete the part below until the USCIS officer instructs you to do so at the interview.

Part 10.   Affidavit

I, the parent/grandparent/legal guardian, _____ do swear or affirm, under penalty of perjury under

the laws of the United States, that I know and understand the contents of this application signed by me, and the attached

supplementary pages number (____) to (____) inclusive, that the same are true and correct to the best of my knowledge, and

that corrections number (____) to (____) were made by me or at my request.

Applicant, Parent or Legal Guardian's Signature

Date *(mm/dd/yyyy)*

Subscribed and sworn or affirmed before me upon examination of the applicant and U.S. citizen parent/grandparent/legal guardian on

_____ at _____ .

Interviewing USCIS Officer's Name and Title

Interviewing USCIS Officer's Signature

Part 11. USCIS Officer Report and Recommendation

A _____ - _____ - _____

On the basis of the documents, records and the testimony of person examined, and the identification upon personal appearance of the underage beneficiary, I find that all the facts and conclusions set forth under oath in this application are:

1. ☐ true and correct;

2. ☐ The applicant derived or acquired U.S. citizenship on _____

   (mm/dd/yyyy)

3. The applicant derived or acquired U.S. citizenship through *(check the box next to the appropriate section of law or, if the section of law is not reflected, write the applicable section of law in the space next to "Other")*

   ☐ Section 322(a)(2)(A) of the INA *(Parent residence)*;

   ☐ Section 322(a)(2)(B) of the INA *(Grandparent residence)*; **or**

   ☐ Other _____

I recommend that this Form N-600K be: ☐ **Approved** ☐ **Denied**

Issue Certificate of Citizenship in the Name of

_____

USCIS Officer's Name and Title	**USCIS Officer's Signature**	**Date** *(mm/dd/yyyy)*

I do _____ do not _____ concur with the USCIS officer's recommendation of the Form N-600K.

USCIS Field Office Director's Signature | **Date** *(mm/dd/yyyy)*

Form N-600K (Rev. 05/03/13) N Page 8

APPENDIX 11-2

Effect of Grandparent's Death on Naturalization Under INA § 322

U.S. Department of Homeland Security
Bureau of Citizenship and Immigration Services

HQ 70/34.2-P

425 I Street NW
Washington, DC 20536

April 17, 2003

MEMORANDUM FOR REGIONAL DIRECTORS
                         DISTRICT DIRECTORS
                         OFFICERS-IN-CHARGE
                         SERVICE CENTER DIRECTORS

FROM: William R. Yates */s/ Janis Sposato*
               Acting Associate Director
               Bureau of Citizenship and Immigration Services

SUBJECT: <u>Effect of Grandparent's Death on Naturalization under INA Section 322</u>

       This memorandum establishes the interpretation of Section 322(a)(2)(B) of the Immigration and Nationality Act, 8 U.S.C. § 1433(a)(2)(B), that all officers of the Bureau of Citizenship and Immigration Services are to follow in adjudicating applications for citizenship under Section 322. This interpretation is to be followed in all cases that are pending on the date of this memorandum, as well as in cases filed on or after that date. For cases adjudicated before the date of this memorandum, directors should consider this memorandum to be a sufficient basis to grant an otherwise untimely motion to reopen or reconsider a previous decision.

       INA Section 322 provides for the expedited naturalization of the alien child of a citizen, if the alien child is "residing outside of the United States" and meets the relevant requirements of Section 322. One requirement is that the citizen parent must have "been physically present in the United States or its outlying possessions for a period or periods totaling not less than five years, at least two of which were after attaining the age of fourteen years." INA § 322(a)(2)(A), 8 U.S.C. § 1433(a)(2)(B). If the citizen parent cannot meet this requirement, the alien child may still qualify if the citizen parent's *own* citizen parent can meet the physical presence requirement. *Id.* § 322(a)(2)(B), 8 U.S.C. § 1433(a)(2)(B).

       The question has arisen whether the citizen parent's citizen parent must be alive in order for the alien child to qualify for naturalization under Section 322.[1] It is our understanding that some offices have held that the citizen parent's own citizen parent must be alive. The Administrative Appeals Office has reached the same result, albeit in a case not designated as a

---

[1] A recent amendment to § 322 makes clear that the alien child may qualify after the citizen parent's own death, if a citizen grandparent or citizen guardian applies for the alien child's naturalization not more than five years after the death of the citizen parent, and the person with custody does not object. 21st Century DOJ Appropriations Authorization Act, Pub. L. 107-273, Division C, § 11030B, 116 Stat. 1758, 1837 (2002).

Memorandum for Regional Directors   Page 2
            District Directors
            Officers-in-Charge
            Service Center Directors
Subject: Effect of grandparent's death on naturalization under INA Section 322

binding precedent. In contrast, at least one office has held that an alien child remains eligible after the death of the citizen parent's own citizen parent, so long as the citizen parent's own citizen parent met the physical presence requirement in Section 322(a)(2)(B) at the time of death.

Both interpretations of Section 322(a)(2)(B) are reasonable interpretations. The statute itself is ambiguous, and so does not make either interpretation inherently more reasonable. Nor does the available legislative history assist in resolving this issue.

Although both interpretations are reasonable, it is not reasonable for different officers to interpret Section 322(a)(2)(B) differently. Effective immediately, all officers of the Bureau of Citizenship and Immigration Services are to interpret Section 322(a)(2)(B) as follows:

Assuming an alien child meets all other requirements of Section 322, an alien child remains eligible after the death of the citizen parent's own citizen parent, so long as the citizen parent's own citizen parent met the physical presence requirement in Section 322(a)(2)(B) at the time of death.

cc: Official file

APPENDIX 11-3

Implementation Instructions for Section 114 of the Department of Justice Appropriations Act of 2002

U.S. Department of Justice
Immigration and Naturalization Service

HQISD 70/33

425 I Street NW
Washington, DC 20536

April 10, 2002

MEMORANDUM FOR REGIONAL DIRECTORS
        DISTRICT DIRECTORS
        OFFICERS-IN-CHARGE
        SERVICE CENTER DIRECTORS

FROM: William R. Yates */s/*
      Deputy Executive Associate Commissioner
      Office of Field Operations
      Immigration Services Division

SUBJECT: Implementation Instructions for Section 114 of Public Law 107-77, "Department
      of Commerce, Justice, State, the Judiciary, and Related Agencies Appropriations
      Act, 2002," 115 Stat. 748 (November 28, 2001)

    The budget appropriation for the Immigration and Naturalization Service (INS) for fiscal
year 2002 includes the authorization for the Attorney General to provide for the granting of
posthumous citizenship, as of September 10, 2001, to any person who died as a result of any of
the four hijackings described in subsection (e) of this section of law if an Application for
Naturalization was pending on September 11, 2001, and if the Attorney General approves an
application for such citizenship.

I. Persons Eligible for Posthumous Citizenship under Section 114 of Pub. L. 107-77

    Section 114 sets forth the criteria for the granting of posthumous citizenship or issuance
of a posthumous Certificate of Citizenship. To be eligible, an individual must:

(1) have been an alien or non-citizen national of the United States;
(2) have died either as a result of an injury incurred in one or more of the events
    described in subsection 114(c) of this act or have died as a result of an injury
    incurred while assisting in the emergency response to one of these events;

922

Memorandum for Regional Directors   Page 2
           District Directors
           Officers-in-Charge
           Service Center Directors

Subject: Implementation Instructions for Section 114 of Pub. L. 107-77, "Department of
        Commerce, Justice, State, the Judiciary, and Related Agencies Appropriations Act,
        2002," 115 Stat. 748 (November 28, 2001)

      (3)   have not been culpable for any of these events;

      (4)   have been eligible for citizenship on their date of death and not have been barred
             from citizenship by any section of law not specifically waived by Section 114;
             and

      (5)   have had pending on September 11, 2001 either an application for naturalization
             or an application for a certificate of citizenship.

For purposes of paragraph 2, individuals injured while assisting in an emergency response include military personnel, law enforcement officers, firefighters, emergency management personnel, search and rescue personnel, medical personnel, engineers and other personnel providing technical assistance, or volunteers. The Service also will require clear and convincing evidence establishing that the individual's death was a result of the September 11, 2001 events. Usually a clear statement of the events that caused death on the death certificate will suffice. However, the INS will consider other clear and convincing evidence when the death certificate is not available or does not clearly state that the death was caused by the September 11, 2001 events.

For purposes of paragraph 3, any person who has not been identified definitively by the Federal Bureau of Investigation (FBI) as a suspect or as culpable for the September 11, 2001 events will be presumed to meet the requirements of paragraph 3. If the FBI identifies an individual as a suspect, the Service will hold the posthumous naturalization request in abeyance until the issue is resolved. In addition, HQ Intelligence Liaison Projects Unit when supplied with: name, date/place of birth, social security number if available and last current address will also conduct a check to determine if any derogatory information exists relative to culpability for any of the events. The officer adjudicating the request should send a cc:Mail message, containing the information listed above and clearly identifying the request as a "Section 114" case to Colen G. Gardner. If this check identifies an individual as a suspect, the Service will hold the posthumous naturalization request in abeyance until the issue is resolved. If the response is "No record Found" the adjudication of the request should proceed.

Finally, for purposes of paragraph 5, the Service will consider an application for naturalization or certificate of citizenship as "pending" if the application was filed prior to September 11, 2001 in accordance with 8 CFR 103.2(a)(7) and as of September 11, 2001 and had not had any final administrative action taken on it.

II.   Persons Eligible to File a Written Request for Posthumous Certificate of Naturalization or Citizenship under Pub. L. 107-77

Section 114(e) and 114(h)(4) provide that a request for the granting of posthumous citizenship or issuance of a posthumous certificate of citizenship may be filed on behalf of the

Memorandum for Regional Directors   Page 3
        District Directors
        Officers-in-Charge
        Service Center Directors

Subject: Implementation Instructions for Section 114 of Pub. L. 107-77, "Department of
      Commerce, Justice, State, the Judiciary, and Related Agencies Appropriations Act,
      2002," 115 Stat. 748 (November 28, 2001)

person only by the next-of-kin (as defined by the Attorney General) or another representative (as defined by the Attorney General).

The provisions of section 114 are analogous to the provisions already in place for posthumous citizenship for military personnel under section 329A of the Immigration and Nationality Act (INA). The Service, therefore, is adopting the following definitions already published at 8 CFR § 392.1 for purposes of implementing Pub. L. 107-77:

(A)   *Decedent* means the person on whose behalf an application for a certificate of posthumous citizenship is made.

(B)   *Next-of-kin* means the closest surviving blood or legal relative of the decedent in the following order of succession:
(1) The surviving spouse;
(2) The decedent's surviving son or daughter, if the decedent has no surviving spouse;
(3) The decedent's surviving parent, if the decedent has no surviving spouse or sons or daughters; or
(4) The decedent's surviving brother or sister, if none of the persons described in paragraphs (1) through (3) of this definition survive the decedent.

(C)   *Representative* means:

(1)   The duly appointed executor or administrator of the decedent's estate, including a special administrator appointed for the purpose of seeking the decedent's naturalization;
(2)   The duly appointed guardian, conservator, or committee of the decedent's next-of-kin; or
(3)   A service organization listed in 38 U.S.C. § 3402, or chartered by Congress, or State, or other service organization recognized by the Department of Veterans Affairs.[1]

If the request is made by anyone other than the decedent's surviving spouse, the procedure described at 8 CFR § 392.3(a) shall be followed for purposes of determining who has priority to file a request:

(A)   Persons who may apply.

---

[1]The Service is retaining this reference to service organizations adopted from 8 CFR § 392.1 to cover those deceased military personnel, particularly from the Pentagon, who may have been represented by such organizations.

Memorandum for Regional Directors   Page 4
                District Directors
                Officers-in-Charge
                Service Center Directors

Subject: Implementation Instructions for Section 114 of Pub. L. 107-77, "Department of
    Commerce, Justice, State, the Judiciary, and Related Agencies Appropriations Act,
    2002," 115 Stat. 748 (November 28, 2001)

(1)   Only one person who is either the next-of-kin or another representative of
       the decedent shall be permitted to apply for posthumous citizenship on the
       decedent's behalf. A person who is a next-of-kin who wishes to apply for
       posthumous citizenship on behalf of the decedent, shall, if there is a
       surviving next-of-kin in the line of succession above him or her, be
       required to obtain authorization to make the application from all surviving
       next-of-kin in the line of succession above him or her. The authorization
       shall be in the form of an affidavit stating that the affiant authorizes the
       requester to apply for posthumous citizenship on behalf of the decedent.
       The affidavit must include the name and address of the affiant, and the
       relationship of the affiant to the decedent.

(2)   When there is a surviving next-of-kin, an application for posthumous
       citizenship shall only be accepted from a representative provided
       authorization has been obtained from all surviving next-of-kin. However,
       this requirement shall not apply to the executor or administrator of the
       decedent's estate. In the case of a service organization acting as a
       representative, authorization must also have been obtained from any
       appointed representative. A veterans' service organization must submit
       evidence of recognition by the Department of Veterans Affairs.

If the Service receives more than one request submitted by persons who share the same
degree of relationship to the decedent, the Service will process the request in the order of the
requestor's chronological seniority.

Section 114(i) provides that only the U.S. citizen parent who filed an N-600 or N-643
pursuant to section 322 of the INA on a child's behalf is eligible to file the request for the
posthumous certificate under this section of law. Thus, in the case of biological or adopted child
who was under the age of 18 and eligible for a certificate of citizenship under section 322 of the
INA on September 11, 2001, the Service will only accept requests from the U.S. citizen parent.

**III.   Deadline for Filing of Requests for Posthumous Certificates of Naturalization or
Citizenship under Pub. L. 107-77**

A request for the granting of posthumous citizenship or issuance of a posthumous
certificate of citizenship under this act must be filed not later than 2 years after the later of—

(1) November 28, 2001, or
(2) the date of the person's death.

Memorandum for Regional Directors   Page 5
           District Directors
           Officers-in-Charge
           Service Center Directors

Subject: Implementation Instructions for Section 114 of Pub. L. 107-77, "Department of
        Commerce, Justice, State, the Judiciary, and Related Agencies Appropriations Act,
        2002," 115 Stat. 748 (November 28, 2001)

IV.   Processing of Requests for Posthumous Certificates of Naturalization or Citizenship under Pub. L. 107-77

    A.   Receipt of Written Requests for Posthumous Naturalization or Issuance of <u>Posthumous Certificate of Citizenship</u>

    For purposes of implementing section 114, the Service is not creating a new form as was done with section 329A military posthumous naturalization. Unlike section 329A, the Service already has a pending application for the deceased applicant that contains most of the information the Service will need to process the certificates.

    The Service, therefore, will require that individuals interested in requesting posthumous naturalization or a posthumous certificate of citizenship under this act only file <u>a written request</u>, preferably containing sufficient identifying information (e.g., the A number, name, date of birth, and last place of residence) about the decedent in order for the Service to determine if the decedent had a pending application and which district has jurisdiction over the case.

    Any Service office can accept the written request. However, the INS website and the announcement made by the INS Office of Public Affairs will suggest that any such request be submitted to the INS office that has jurisdiction over the decedent's place of residence at the time of their death.

    Any office that receives such a request should query CIS and/or C4 in order to determine the location of the N-400, N-600 or N-643. The request should be forwarded to the office that currently has the N-400, N-600 or N-643. If the evidence of the required relationship (or status as an authorized representative) necessary to file the request does not accompany the request, the INS office that has the N-400, N-600 or N-643 should request it from the person seeking the posthumous naturalization or certificate of citizenship.

    B.   <u>Processing of Pending N-400s, N-600s or N-643s</u>

    Section 114 requires that all applications, whether for N-400, N-600 or N-643, were pending on September 11, 2001. For purposes of this act, the Service will consider an application as "pending" if the application met the filing requirements of 8 CFR § 103.2(a)(7) and no final decision was issued on the application.

    (1)   N-400s

    For purposes of an N-400, an N-400 is pending at a Field Office if the INS has not yet issued a naturalization certificate or issued a denial either at the conclusion of section 335 or 336 proceedings under section 336 of the INA.

Memorandum for Regional Directors
    District Directors
    Officers-in-Charge
    Service Center Directors

                       Page 6

Subject: Implementation Instructions for Section 114 of Pub. L. 107-77, "Department of
  Commerce, Justice, State, the Judiciary, and Related Agencies Appropriations Act,
  2002," 115 Stat. 748 (November 28, 2001)

    The following processing actions must be taken for pending N-400s <u>when the
Service receives a written request for posthumous citizenship</u>:

  (a) All pending N-400s at Service Centers should be forwarded to the Field
     Office that would have conducted an examination of the applicant.

  (b) All N-400s that were denied <u>after September 11, 2001</u> for failure to submit
     fingerprints or for failure to submit the fingerprinting fee should be
     reopened and forwarded to the Field Office that would have conducted an
     examination of the applicant.

  (c) All N-400s that had been administratively closed for failure to appear for
     an initial examination less than one year prior to September 11, 2001 or on
     or after September 11, 2001 should be reopened on a Service Motion,
     without fee, and adjudicated according to the instructions in this
     Memorandum.

  (d) All N-400s that had been denied for "Lack of Prosecution" on or after
     September 11, 2001 should be reopened on a Service Motion, without fee,
     and adjudicated according to the instructions in this Memorandum.

(2) *N-600s and N-643s*

    For purposes of an N-600 or N-643, an N-600 or N-643 is pending at a Field
Office or the Vermont Service Center if a final decision has not been issued by the
district director pursuant to 8 CFR 341.5 or by the Administrative Appeals Unit (AAU)
on review under 8 CFR 103.3.

    The following processing actions must be taken for pending N-600s or N-643s
<u>when the Service receives a written request for issuance of a posthumous certificate of
citizenship</u>:

  (a) All N-600s or N-643s that have been denied for failure to respond to
     request for evidence under 8 CFR 103.2 on or after September 11, 2001
     should be reopened on a Service Motion, without fee, and adjudicated
     according to the instructions in this Memorandum.

  (b) All N-600s that had been denied for "Lack of Prosecution" on or after
     September 11, 2001 should be reopened on a Service Motion, without fee,
     and adjudicated according to the instructions in this Memorandum.

Memorandum for Regional Directors   Page 7
            District Directors
            Officers-in-Charge
            Service Center Directors

Subject: Implementation Instructions for Section 114 of Pub. L. 107-77, "Department of
         Commerce, Justice, State, the Judiciary, and Related Agencies Appropriations Act,
         2002," 115 Stat. 748 (November 28, 2001)

C.   System Updating and NQP Requirements

CLAIMS4 has been enhanced to keep track of N-400s that are subject to a request for posthumous citizenship under section 114 of Pub. L. 107-77. A table change has been made in the database and is reflected in the Adjudication Module. On the N-400 tab, under the Basis of Eligibility, the option for "other" has been expanded to now include "Sec. 114." Upon receipt of a Section 114 request, an office must open the case in the CLAIMS 4 Adjudications Module and change the Basis of Eligibility to the "Other" option and chose "Sec. 114." Close the case and save the data changes. As sufficient information may not reside in CLAIMS4, the case will be transferred to a Manual mode for completion of processing. Notify the CLAIMS4 Help Desk to effect this action.

The NQP Processing Worksheets were designed to capture annotations relating to the processing of applications filed under any standard section of the INA. This very small group of applications may well include cases at any possible state of the processing and/or adjudication. It would be a monumental task to prescribe correct annotations for each of the possible lines of the Processing Worksheets. Therefore, for cases adjudicated pursuant to Section 114, no NQP error shall be charged for the annotations of any case that follows the guidelines in this Memorandum.

For N-600s and N-643s, when a request is received for the posthumous issuance of a certificate of citizenship, the district office which has the pending application should complete the form found in **Attachment 2** to this Memorandum and fax it to (202) 305-0108 and/or forward it as a cc:mail to "Certificates 114." When final action is taken on the application, the remaining information in **Attachment 2** should be completed and sent again to the fax and/or cc:mail address noted above.

V.   Adjudication of Requests for Posthumous Certificates of Naturalization or Citizenship under Pub. L. 107-77

A.   Guidelines for N-400, Applications for Naturalization

All N-400s pursuant to section 114 should be adjudicated based on the facts that existed on September 10, 2001. To the maximum extent possible, the N-400s should be adjudicated without requiring documents, testimony or input of any kind from the next-of-kin or other representative.

The Service should make every effort to properly adjudicate the application by relying on the information contained on the N-400, the applicant's A-file, databases available to the Service or required documents obtained by the INS without making requests of the next-of-kin or other representative.

Memorandum for Regional Directors   Page 8
             District Directors
             Officers-in-Charge
             Service Center Directors

Subject: Implementation Instructions for Section 114 of Pub. L. 107-77, "Department of
        Commerce, Justice, State, the Judiciary, and Related Agencies Appropriations Act,
        2002," 115 Stat. 748 (November 28, 2001)

      Below are guidelines for adjudicating cases of individuals who are the subject of a
request for posthumous citizenship. The guidelines address each of the naturalization
requirements that you may encounter when adjudicating these cases:

(1)   Residence/Physical Presence

      For applicants who had an initial examination:

(a)   If the residence/physical presence eligibility had been satisfactorily
       established as a result of the initial examination, this element of eligibility
       remains established.

(b)   If the residence/physical presence eligibility was not clearly established by
       Passports, Travel Documents, or other documentation at the initial
       examination, but the applicant testified under oath to facts that, if true,
       would have satisfied this requirement, the adjudicating officer can make a
       determination that this element of eligibility has been established based on
       the credible testimony of the applicant, even if requested documents or
       information has not yet been received.

(c)   If the residence/physical presence eligibility was not clearly established by
       Passports, Travel Documents, or other documentation at the initial
       examination, and the adjudicating officer determines that documentation
       or information not yet received is necessary to demonstrate this element of
       eligibility, the next of kin or representative should be given the
       opportunity to provide documentation that would establish this element of
       eligibility.

(d)   When the information provided at the initial examination or as follow-up
       to the initial examination indicates that the applicant was not eligible for
       citizenship on September 11, 2001 because of a lack of one of the required
       elements of residence/physical presence, the application should be denied.

      For applicants who did **not** have an initial examination:

(a)   When the information provided on the N-400, if accurate, indicates that
       the residence/physical presence requirements have been fulfilled, this
       should be considered to sufficiently demonstrate this element of eligibility.

Subject: Implementation Instructions for Section 114 of Pub. L. 107-77, "Department of
       Commerce, Justice, State, the Judiciary, and Related Agencies Appropriations Act,
       2002," 115 Stat. 748 (November 28, 2001)

      (b)   When the information provided on the N-400 indicates that there is a
rebuttable presumption that the applicant disrupted the required
continuous residence, i.e., an absence of more than six months but less
than one year, the next of kin or other representative should be offered the
opportunity to present credible evidence, in writing, that the absence did
not in fact disrupt the residence.

      (c)   When the information provided on the N-400 indicates one or more
absences of more than one year's duration during the statutory period, but
the nature of the applicant employment suggests that the applicant may
have been eligible for preservation of residence pursuant to an approved
Form N-470, Application to Preserve Residence for Naturalization
Purposes, the Service should make every effort to learn if such application
had been timely filed.

      (d)   When the information provided on the N-400 indicates that the applicant
was not eligible for citizenship on September 11, 2001 because of a lack
of one of the required elements of residence/physical presence, the
application should be denied.

    (2)   *Good Moral Character*

For applicants who had an initial examination:

      (a)   If the good moral character eligibility had been satisfactorily established
as a result of the initial examination, this element of eligibility remains
established.

      (b)   If the initial examination revealed that the applicant had been arrested on a
charge that falls within the categories of cases listed in Policy
Memorandum # 78, dated April 27, 2001, for which official disposition
documentation is required and the applicant has not yet submitted the
documentation, the INS should request that the next-of-kin or other
representative provide documentation from the Court or law-enforcement
agency.

      (c)   If, based on the information from the examination and/or the follow up, it
is determined that that applicant has failed to demonstrate the required
good moral character, the application should be denied.

For applicants who did **not** have an initial examination:

Memorandum for Regional Directors
        District Directors
        Officers-in-Charge
        Service Center Directors

Subject: Implementation Instructions for Section 114 of Pub. L. 107-77, "Department of Commerce, Justice, State, the Judiciary, and Related Agencies Appropriations Act, 2002," 115 Stat. 748 (November 28, 2001)

(a)   If fingerprints had been submitted to the FBI that caused a Non-ident response to be returned from the FBI, the applicant should be considered to have demonstrated good moral character unless there is other evidence that this is not the case, e.g. evidence in the A-file that the applicant had disqualifying conviction(s) in another country.

(b)   If fingerprints had been submitted, either once or twice, to the FBI and were found to be unclassifiable, the INS should request that the next-of-kin or other representative obtain the State or local police clearance from all jurisdictions in which the applicant resided during the statutory period.

(c)   If fingerprints had been submitted to the FBI that caused an Ident response to be returned from the FBI, the INS should request that the next-of-kin or other representative obtain evidence of the dispositions of all arrests that fall within the categories of cases listed in Policy Memorandum # 78, dated April 27, 2001, for which official disposition documentation is required.

(d)   If fingerprints had not yet been submitted to the FBI, the applicant's name, date of birth, country of birth and as much biometrics information as is known should be forwarded by cc:Mail to Jack L. Hartsoch at Clarksville, WV. The subject of the cc:Mail should be "Sec 114 Posthumous Citizen Applicant." Jack Hartsoch will inform the field office of the results of the background checks.

(e)   If the background checks reveal that the applicant lacked the good moral character required for naturalization, the application should be denied.

(3)   *Attachment*

For applicants who had an initial examination:

(a)   If the attachment eligibility had been satisfactorily established as a result of the initial examination, this element of eligibility remains established.

(b)   As the decedent will not be required to take the oath of renunciation and allegiance, the applicant's eligibility or lack of eligibility for admission to citizenship by means of a modified oath is not an issue. Even if this issue has not yet been resolved, the application should be granted.

Memorandum for Regional Directors   Page 11
              District Directors
              Officers-in-Charge
              Service Center Directors

Subject: Implementation Instructions for Section 114 of Pub. L. 107-77, "Department of
Commerce, Justice, State, the Judiciary, and Related Agencies Appropriations Act,
2002," 115 Stat. 748 (November 28, 2001)

(c)   If the applicant had indicated that he or she was unwilling to perform work
of national importance under civilian direction, the application should be
denied. See *Interpretations* 337.2(b)(2)(v).

For applicants who did **not** have an initial examination:

(a)   Barring any other evidence to the contrary, the process of filing an
application for naturalization that includes satisfactory responses to the
questions relating to attachment should be accepted in these cases as
sufficient evidence that the applicant had demonstrated the requisite
attachment.

(b)   As the decedent will not be required to take the oath of renunciation and
allegiance, the applicant's eligibility or lack of eligibility for admission to
citizenship by means of a modified oath is not an issue. Even if this issue
has not been resolved, the application should be granted.

(c)   If the applicant had indicated that he or she was unwilling to perform work
of national importance under civilian direction, the application should be
denied. See *Interpretations* 337.2(b)(2)(v).

(4)   English and Civics Requirements

Section 114(d)(2) specifically states that no demonstration of any part of the
requirements of Section 312 of the INA shall be required for the granting of posthumous
citizenship. This applies to all cases without regard to whether or not there has been an
initial examination and without regard as to whether or not the applicant demonstrated
the INA 312 requirements at a first or second examination.

(5)   Oath Requirement

Section 114(d)(3) specifically states that no oath of renunciation or allegiance
shall be required for the granting of posthumous citizenship. The next of kin or other
representative should not be required to take the oath of renunciation or allegiance for the
applicant. The next of kin or other representative should not be required to participate in
any public or private ceremony for the issuance of the Certificate of Naturalization.
However, in keeping with the spirit of 8 CFR § 337.2(a), the Certificate of Naturalization
should be delivered or presented in such a manner as to preserve the dignity and
significance of the occasion while respecting the wishes of the recipient.

Memorandum for Regional Directors   Page 12
    District Directors
    Officers-in-Charge
    Service Center Directors

Subject: Implementation Instructions for Section 114 of Pub. L. 107-77, "Department of
   Commerce, Justice, State, the Judiciary, and Related Agencies Appropriations Act,
   2002," 115 Stat. 748 (November 28, 2001)

  B. Guidelines for N-600s and N-643s filed under Section 341

   All approvable applications filed pursuant to INA 341 are adjudicated on behalf of
persons who claim to have already acquired U.S. citizenship under the relevant provision of law
governing his or her case. This section of law provides benefits only to those persons who had
an N-600, Application for Certificate of Citizenship or an N-643, Application for Certificate of
Citizenship on Behalf of an Adopted Child, pending on September 11, 2001. All pending N-600s
and N-643s shall be adjudicated according to the section of law that was in effect at the time that
the person was born or, for those individuals who acquired citizenship automatically after birth,
at the time the last condition was fulfilled in order for the person to become a citizen of the
United States.

   Whenever it is possible to adjudicate an N-600 or N-643 pursuant to this section of law
without the next of kin or representative being required to present additional documentation not
submitted with the application or available in INS file(s), no additional requests or requirements
shall be made of the next of kin or other representative.

  B. Guidelines for N-600s and N-643s for Parents Filed on Behalf of Biological and
    Adopted Child under Section 322

   As provided in Part I of this Memorandum, the child must have had an N-600 or N-643,
filed by his or her U.S. citizen parent pursuant to Section 320 of the INA, pending on September
11, 2001. The N-600 or N-643 must have been approvable if it had been adjudicated on
September 11, 2001.

   In the usual processing of applications filed under INA 322, pursuant to 8 CFR § 322.4,
the U.S. citizen parent and the child shall appear in person before a Service officer for
examination on the application for a certificate of citizenship. In those cases in which the
application is clearly approvable without the appearance or additional testimony of the U.S.
citizen parent, the parent should not be required to appear for an interview under this section.

VI. Issuance and Delivery of Posthumous Certificates of Naturalization or Citizenship

  A. Certificates of Naturalization

   When an application is approved under this section of law, the document to be sent shall
be a standard Form N-550, Certificate of Naturalization. Immediately after "conducted by the
Immigration & Naturalization Service" the annotation "Certificate issued posthumously; oath
waived" shall be added. The date of naturalization shall be September 10, 2001 for all
Certificates issued pursuant to this section of law.

Memorandum for Regional Directors   Page 13
                District Directors
                Officers-in-Charge
                Service Center Directors

Subject: Implementation Instructions for Section 114 of Pub. L. 107-77, "Department of
    Commerce, Justice, State, the Judiciary, and Related Agencies Appropriations Act,
    2002," 115 Stat. 748 (November 28, 2001)

>   B.   Certificates of Citizenship for Individuals Who Filed N-600s or N-643s Under
>   Section 341

>   (1)   Date of Citizenship

All approvable N-600s and N-643s adjudicated under this law were filed
by or on behalf of persons who are already citizens of the United States. The date
shown on the certificate shall be the date on which the person acquired or derived
citizenship under whatever section of law the person became a citizen.

>   (2)   Type of Certificate To Be Issued

All N-600s approved under this section of law should result in the
issuance of a standard N-560, Certificate of Citizenship. The N-560 should be
issued as an AA or AB Certificate if the person was born a citizen of the United
States. The N-560 should be issued as an A Certificate if the person became a
citizen by action of law at some date later than the date of birth.

>   (3)   Annotation of Certificate

Immediately following the date of issuance, the annotation "Issued
posthumously" should be added to the N-560.

>   (4)   Delivery of Certificate

Section 114(h)(3) specifically states that the usual requirements relating to
the taking of the oath and presence within the United States shall not apply. The
next of kin or representative shall not be required to appear at any INS office or to
participate in any public or private ceremony in order to be issued the certificate.
However, in keeping with the spirit of 8 CFR § 341.7, the Certificate of
Certificate should be delivered or presented in such a manner as to preserve the
dignity and significance of the occasion while respecting the wishes of the
recipient.

>   C.   Certificates of Citizenship for U.S. Citizen Parents Filing on Behalf of Biological
>   or Adopted Child Under Section 322

>   (1)   Date of Citizenship

The date of citizenship on all certificates issued under this law for
applications filed pursuant to INA 322 shall be September 11, 2001.

Memorandum for Regional Directors
     District Directors
     Officers-in-Charge
     Service Center Directors

Page 14

Subject: Implementation Instructions for Section 114 of Pub. L. 107-77, "Department of Commerce, Justice, State, the Judiciary, and Related Agencies Appropriations Act, 2002," 115 Stat. 748 (November 28, 2001)

  (2) *Type of Certificate To Be Issued*

    All N-600s and N-643s approved under this section of law should result in the issuance of a standard N-560, Certificate of Citizenship as an A Certificate.

  (3) *Annotation of Certificate*

    Immediately following the date of issuance, the annotation "Issued posthumously" should be added to the N-560.

  (4) *Delivery of Certificate*

    Section 114(h)(3) specifically states that the usual requirements relating to the taking of the oath and presence within the United States shall not apply. The next of kin or representative shall not be required to appear at any INS office or to participate in any public or private ceremony in order to be issued the certificate.

VII. No Derivative Benefits

  Section 114(g) provides that no derivative immigration benefits under the INA are available to any spouse, son, daughter, or other relative of a person granted posthumous citizenship under this section.

  Because section 114(h) only authorizes the posthumous issuing of Certificates to persons who were already citizens before September 11, 2001, the prohibition against any benefits under the Immigration and Nationality Act for any spouse, son, daughter, or other relative of a person granted posthumous citizenship that is found in section 114(g) does not apply in the case of persons whose citizenship is posthumously documented pursuant to section 114(h).

Attachment

APPENDIX 11-4

Memorandum Regarding VAWA Spouses and Children

U.S. Department of Justice
Immigration and Naturalization Service

HQISD 70/33

425 I Street NW
Washington, DC 20536

October 15, 2002

POLICY MEMO #89

MEMORANDUM FOR REGIONAL DIRECTORS
DISTRICT DIRECTORS
OFFICERS-IN-CHARGE
SERVICE CENTER DIRECTORS

FROM: William R. Yates */s/*
             Deputy Executive Associate Commissioner
             Office of Field Operations
             Immigration Services Division

SUBJECT: Instructions Regarding the Expanded Meaning of Section 319(a)

       Public Law 106-386 amended section 319(a) of the Immigration and Nationality Act
(INA) (8 U.S.C. 1430(a)) by extending the benefit of this section of law to persons who obtained
status as a lawful permanent resident by reason of being a spouse or child who was subjected to
battering or extreme cruelty by a United States citizen. This Memorandum is issued in order to
provide guidance in the adjudication of applications filed pursuant to the expanded language.
Section 319(a) of the INA now reads:

     Sec. 319. [8 U.S.C. 1430]

    (a) Any person whose spouse is a citizen of the United States, *or any person who*
       obtained status as a lawful permanent resident by reason of his or her status as a
       spouse or child of a United States citizen who battered him or her or subjected him or
       her to extreme cruelty (added text), may be naturalized upon compliance with all the
       requirements of this title except the provisions of paragraph (1) of section 316(a) if
       such person immediately preceding the date of filing his application for naturalization
       has resided continuously, after being lawfully admitted for permanent residence,
       within the United States for at least three years, and during the three years
       immediately preceding the date of filing his application has been living in marital

Memorandum for Regional Directors
                    District Directors
                    Officers-in-Charge
                    Service Center Directors

Subject: Instructions Regarding the Expanded Meaning of Section 319(a)

union with the citizen spouse *(except in the case of a person who has been battered or subjected to extreme cruelty by a United States citizen spouse or parent)* (added text), who has been a United States citizen during all of such period, and has been physically present in the United States for periods totaling at least half of that time and has resided within the State or the district of the Service in the United States in which the applicant filed his application for at least three months.

I.   Qualified Applicants

In order to be eligible for Section 319(a) benefits as a battered spouse or as a battered child, the applicant must have obtained lawful permanent residence status based on either an approved Form I-360, Petition for Amerasian, Widow(er), or Special Immigrant in a case in which an abusive spouse or parent was a U.S. citizen or through cancellation of removal and adjustment of status pursuant to INA 240A(b)(2)(A)(i)(I). If the applicant obtained lawful permanent resident status based on an approved Form I-360 as the self-petitioning battered or abused spouse or child of a U.S. citizen or pursuant to INA 240A(b)(2)(A)(i)(I), the special requirements of demonstrating eligibility as a battered spouse or child pursuant to Section 319(a) shall be considered as having been met.

Any applicant who claims eligibility for benefits under Section 319(a) of the INA as a battered spouse or child must comply with all of the requirements of 8 C.F.R. § 319.1(a), except clause (3).

II.   Benefits Available

The amendments made to section 319(a) of the INA by Pub. L. 106-386 do not change the usual requirements for section 319(a) applicants who acquired lawful permanent resident status on any basis and are currently married to U. S. citizens. Any applicant who would have been eligible to file an application under section 319(a) of the INA before it was amended is still eligible to file under the amended law. A qualifying spouse must meet all of the general requirements for naturalization except that the five years after lawful admission for permanent residence requirement is reduced to three years after lawful admission for permanent residence.

Any person who obtained status as a lawful permanent resident by reason of the approval of an I-360 based on being a spouse of a United States citizen who battered the applicant or subjected the applicant to extreme cruelty or pursuant to INA 240A(b)(2)(A)(i)(I) is excused the requirement of residing together with the citizen spouse. The ongoing validity or the termination of the marriage to the U.S. citizen will not be determinative of eligibility under Section 319(a) of a battered spouse or child. Once the applicant has established that he or she was properly granted status as a lawful permanent resident based on an approved I-360 or pursuant to INA 240A(b)(2)(A)(i)(I), length or continuity of cohabitation with the United States citizen spouse is not an issue in determining the applicant's eligibility for naturalization. Also it is not required

Memorandum for Regional Directors
        District Directors
        Officers-in-Charge
        Service Center Directors

Subject: Instructions Regarding the Expanded Meaning of Section 319(a)

that the United States citizen spouse still be alive or be a United States citizen at the time the applicant who obtained status as a lawful permanent resident by reason of an approved I-360 or pursuant to INA 240A(b)(2)(A)(i)(I) files an application for naturalization.

An application also can be filed under section 319(a) as amended by an applicant who obtained lawful permanent resident status through the approval of a Form I-360 or cancellation of removal and adjustment of status pursuant to INA 240A(b)(2)(A)(i)(I) as a child of a U.S. citizen who battered the child or subjected the child to extreme cruelty. It is not required that the U.S. citizen parent still be alive or be a U.S. citizen at the time the applicant files an application for naturalization (Form N-400). Also, at the time of lawful admission for permanent residence, whether through immigration or adjustment of status, the applicant would have to have met the requirements of being a child of a U.S. citizen parent pursuant to section 101(b)(1) of the INA. The applicant therefore is not required to meet the definition of child pursuant to sections 101(b)(1) or (c)(1) at the time of filing the N-400.

All applicants under section 319(a) as amended are excused from the usual requirement of residing in the United States for five years after being lawfully admitted for permanent residence and are eligible to file an N-400 once they are within three months of completing the three years of continuous residence after being lawfully admitted for permanent residence required by section 319(a) of the INA.

The amendments made to section 319(a) of the INA by Pub. L. 106-386 do not waive the requirement of section 334(b) of the INA that no person shall file a valid application for naturalization unless he shall have attained the age of eighteen years.

APPENDIX 11-5

Memorandum Regarding Expansion of VAWA-based Naturalization

U.S. Department of Homeland Security
20 Massachusetts Ave., NW
Washington, D.C. 20529

**U.S. Citizenship
and Immigration
Services**

HQOPRD 70/33.1

Interoffice Memorandum

To: Regional Directors
       District Directors
       Officers-in-Charge
       Administrative Appeals Office Director

From: William R. Yates /S/
       Associate Director of Operations

Date: January 27, 2005

Re: Clarification of Classes of Applicants Eligible for Naturalization under Section 319(a) of the
       Immigration and Nationality Act (INA), as amended by the Victims of Trafficking and
       Violence Protection Act of 2000 (VTVPA), Pub. L. 106-386

Purpose

This memorandum modifies the October 15, 2002, policy memorandum entitled,
"Instructions Regarding the Expanded Meaning of Section 319(a)" (INS Policy Memo #89), to
incorporate one additional class of qualified applicants who may claim eligibility for naturalization
under section 319(a) of the INA, as amended. This memorandum clarifies that individuals who
obtained lawful permanent residence by reason of an approved waiver of the joint filing requirement
under section 216(c)(4)(C) of the INA are also eligible to apply for naturalization under section
319(a).

Background

Section 316(a) of the INA lists the general eligibility requirements for naturalization. Under
that section, a lawful permanent resident (LPR) must be a resident continuously for a period of five
years subsequent to obtaining LPR status before he or she may apply for naturalization. However,
section 319(a) of the INA provides that if the LPR is married to a U.S. citizen (USC), the LPR may
naturalize after only three years if the LPR has lived in marital union with his or her USC spouse
during the three years immediately preceding the date of filing of the naturalization application. The
VTVPA amended INA section 319(a) by expanding this provision to include spouses, former
spouses, intended spouses, and children of USCs who obtained lawful permanent residence by
reason of having been battered or subjected to extreme cruelty by their USC spouse or parent.

www.uscis.gov

939

Clarification of Classes of Applicants Eligible for Naturalization under Section 319(a) of the Immigration and Nationality Act (INA), as amended by the Victims of Trafficking and Violence Protection Act of 2000 (VTVPA), Pub. L. 106-386
HQOPRD 70/33.1
Page 2

Guidance

The following three categories of individuals became eligible to apply for naturalization under section 319(a) by the enactment of the VTVPA:

(1)   Aliens who obtained lawful permanent residence by reason of an approved Form I-360, Petition for Amerasian, Widow(er), or Special Immigrant under section 204(a)(1)(A)(iii) or (iv) of the INA, or under section 204(a)(1)(B)(ii) or (iii), if the abusive spouse or parent naturalizes after the Form I-360 has been approved.;

(2)   Aliens who obtained lawful permanent residence by reason of cancellation of removal under section 240A(b)(2)(A)(i)(I), or 240A(b)(2)(A)(i)(III) of the INA where the applicant was the intended spouse of a USC; or

(3)   Aliens who obtained lawful permanent residence by reason of an approved waiver of the joint filing requirement under section 216(c)(4)(C) of the INA.

Motions to Reopen

A naturalization applicant whose application was denied on or after October 28, 2000, on the sole ground that s/he was not entitled to benefit under section 319(a) of the INA based upon an approved waiver of the joint-filing requirement under section 216(c)(4)(C), may seek reconsideration of the denial by filing a motion to reopen with the appropriate USCIS office with the appropriate fee or fee waiver request.

Further information

The preceding clarification of INS Policy Memo #89 is effective immediately and applies to all naturalization applications filed by the above listed categories of applicants pending on or filed on or after October 28, 2000. Personnel with questions regarding this memorandum or other VAWA-related issues, please contact Laura Dawkins, Office of Program and Regulations Development by electronic mail.

APPENDIX 11-6

National Defense Authorization Act for Fiscal Year 2008

Pub. L. 110-181

National Defense Authorization Act for Fiscal Year 2008

110th Congress

January 28, 2008

122 Stat. 3

H.R.4986

§ 674. OVERSEAS NATURALIZATION FOR MILITARY SPOUSES AND CHILDREN.

(a) Spouses- Section 319 of the Immigration and Nationality Act (8 U.S.C. 1430) is amended by adding at the end the following new subsection:

(e) (1) In the case of a person lawfully admitted for permanent residence in the United States who is the spouse of a member of the Armed Forces of the United States, is authorized to accompany such member and reside abroad with the member pursuant to the member's official orders, and is so accompanying and residing with the member in marital union, such residence and physical presence abroad shall be treated, for purposes of subsection (a) and section 316(a), as residence and physical presence in--

(A) the United States; and

(B) any State or district of the Department of Homeland Security in the United States.

(2) Notwithstanding any other provision of law, a spouse described in paragraph (1) shall be eligible for naturalization proceedings overseas pursuant to section 1701(d) of the National Defense Authorization Act for Fiscal Year 2004 (Public Law 108-136; 8 U.S.C. 1443a).

(b) Children- Section 322 of the Immigration and Nationality Act (8 U.S.C. 1433) is amended by adding at the end the following new subsection:

(d) In the case of a child of a member of the Armed Forces of the United States who is authorized to accompany such member and reside abroad with the member pursuant to the member's official orders, and is so accompanying and residing with the member--

(1) any period of time during which the member of the Armed Forces is residing abroad pursuant to official orders shall be treated, for purposes of subsection (a)(2)(A), as physical presence in the United States;

(2) subsection (a)(5) shall not apply; and

(3) the oath of allegiance described in subsection (b) may be subscribed to abroad pursuant to section 1701(d) of the National Defense Authorization Act for Fiscal Year 2004 (Public Law 108-136; 8 U.S.C. 1443a).

(c) Overseas Naturalization Authority- Section 1701(d) of the National Defense

Authorization Act for Fiscal Year 2004 (Public Law 108-136; 8 U.S.C. 1443a) is amended--

(1) in the subsection heading, by inserting 'and Their Spouses and Children' after 'Forces'; and

(2) by inserting ', and persons made eligible for naturalization by section 319(e) or 322(d) of such Act,' after 'Armed Forces'.

(d) Effective Date- The amendments made by this section shall take effect on the date of enactment of this Act and apply to any application for naturalization or issuance of a certificate of citizenship pending on or after such date.

APPENDIX 11-7

Survivor Benefits for Non-Citizen Relatives of Military Personnel

Once posthumous citizenship is granted, the surviving spouse, parent, or child may qualify for immigration benefits under section 1703.

If the deceased service member was a Lawful Permanent Resident (LPR) who had filed a Petition for Alien Relative (Form I-130) for you as his or her spouse or child under section 203(a)(2)(A) of the INA before death, and the Form I-130 was approved, then once he or she has been granted posthumous citizenship you will be considered an "immediate relative" for purposes of immigration. This means that an immigration visa will be immediately available.

If the deceased service member had not filed Form I-130 for you, you may file Form I-360, Petition for Amerasian, Widow(er), or Special Immigrant within two years of the date the deceased service member is granted posthumous citizenship.

Adjustment of Status to Permanent Residence (Form I-485)

If you filed an Application to Register Permanent Residence or Adjust Status (Form I-485) as the spouse, child, or parent of a service member prior to his or her death, USCIS will adjudicate that application as if the service member had not died if:

- The deceased service member served honorably in an active-duty status in the U.S. Armed Forces;

- The service member died as a result of injury or disease incurred in or aggravated by that service;

- The deceased service member was a citizen at the time of death or was granted posthumous citizenship under INA section 329A; and

- You write a letter to the USCIS office having jurisdiction over your case, or you indicate at the time of your adjustment interview that you are eligible for adjustment under Section 1703 of Public Law 108-136 and provide proof of eligibility.

Naturalization For Certain Relatives

Section 319(d) of the INA allows you to apply for naturalization without demonstrating residence or physical presence in the United States if you are the spouse, child, or parent of a deceased service member who was a citizen (including someone granted posthumous citizenship) and who was serving honorably on active duty in the U.S. Armed Forces at the time of death. You must meet all other naturalization requirements, such as being a Lawful Permanent Resident.

If you are a surviving spouse seeking naturalization under section 319(d), you must have been living in marital union with your spouse at the time of your spouse's death. However, you remain eligible for naturalization under this section even if you remarry after your spouse's death.

NOTE: When filing Form N-400, it is important to check box D. "Other" in Part 2 of the form and write "319(d)."

USCIS Resources

If you would like to learn more, please visit www.uscis.gov/military. You can download forms by clicking on "Forms" at the top of the page.

USCIS Military Help Line

You may also contact the toll-free USCIS Military Help Line, 1-877-CIS-4MIL (1-877-247-4645) to request forms or more information. USCIS customer service specialists are available to answer calls Monday through Friday from 8 a.m. until 4:30 p.m. (CST), except federal holidays. You may also send an e-mail to militaryinfo.nsc@dhs.gov. See the USCIS pamphlet, "USCIS Military Help Line" (M-671), for more information.

Survivor Benefits for Non-Citizen Relatives of Military Personnel

Information and Customer Service Division

U.S. Citizenship and Immigration Services

M-601 (rev. 12/09)

In his Second Inaugural Address, Abraham Lincoln spoke of the Nation's obligation to care for those who had borne the battle, and for their widows and orphans. In that spirit, U.S. immigration law provides special immigration benefits to the widow(ers), children and parents of U.S. citizens who serve honorably in the Armed Forces, and die as a result of injury or disease incurred in or aggravated by combat.

This special provision is found in section 1703 of Public Law 108-136, National Defense Authorization Act for Fiscal Year 2004, which amended the Immigration and Nationality Act (INA). It extends immigration benefits to the survivors of those who have served on active duty in the U.S. Armed Forces. Thus, the benefit is available to the survivors of those who have served on active duty in the Army, Navy, Marine Corps, Air Force, and Coast Guard. It also includes certain service in the National Guard and Selected Reserve of the Ready Reserve.

If the U.S. Armed Forces Member Was a U.S. Citizen

If you are the spouse, parent, or child of a U.S. citizen who served on active duty and whose death was combat related, you may qualify to immigrate as an immediate relative despite his or her death. To qualify, you must file a visa petition (Form I-360, Petition for Amerasian, Widow(er), or Special Immigrant) no later than two years after the date of his or her death.

The Surviving Spouse:

You will be considered an immediate relative for immigration purposes if all of the requirements below are met:

- You were married to a U.S. citizen who served honorably on active duty

and you were not legally separated at the time of his or her death;

- Your deceased spouse died as a result of injury or disease incurred in or aggravated by that military service;

- You file Form I-360, Petition for Amerasian, Widow(er), or Special Immigrant within two years of the death of the deceased spouse;

- You do not remarry prior to obtaining lawful permanent residence based on your relationship to the deceased citizen.

NOTE: *When filing Form I-360, it is important to check box M. "Other" in Part 2 of the form and write "PUBLIC LAW 108-136."*

The Surviving Children and Parents:

USCIS will consider a child (unmarried and under 21 at the time of the parent's death) or parent of a U.S. citizen service member an immediate relative for immigration purposes if:

- The service member's death was combat related;

- The service member served honorably in an active-duty status in the U.S. Armed Forces;

- The service member died as a result of injury or disease incurred in or aggravated by combat; and

- The child or parent files Form I-360 within two years of the service member's death.

NOTE: *Ordinarily, a citizen has to be at least 21 to file a visa petition for his or her parent. If you are the parent of a deceased service member who was a citizen and whose death was combat related, you may file Form I-360 even if your son or daughter was not yet 21 at the time of death.*

For a child of a deceased service member, you may remain eligible even if you married or reached the age of 21 after your parent died.

If the U.S. Armed Forces Member Was Not a U.S. Citizen at Death

Section 1703 can also benefit the spouse, children, and parents of active duty service members who were not citizens, but who served honorably on active duty and whose deaths were combat related.

The first step is to obtain posthumous citizenship on behalf of the deceased service member by filing an Application for Posthumous Citizenship, Form N-644. The deceased service member may be naturalized after death if:

- Application for Posthumous Citizenship, Form N-644 is filed no later than two years after the death of the service member; and

- The military certifies that the service member served honorably in an active duty status during a qualifying period of armed conflict and died as a result of injury or disease incurred in or aggravated by that service.

If USCIS approves the Application for Posthumous Citizenship, USCIS will send a certificate of citizenship to the next-of-kin. The deceased service member will be considered to have been a U.S. citizen at the time of death.

APPENDIX 11-8

USCIS Centralizes Filing for Qualifying Family of Deceased Service Members

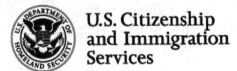

U.S. Citizenship and Immigration Services

Home >
NEWS >
Public Releases by Topic >
Military

USCIS Centralizes Filing for Qualifying Family of Deceased Service Members

WASHINGTON - U.S. Citizenship and Immigration Services (USCIS) is now accepting applications for naturalization from qualifying family members of deceased service members at the Nebraska Service Center (NSC). Eligible applications received at the NSC will be handled by a specialized team dedicated to processing applications for members of the U.S. armed forces and their families.

If you are the spouse, child, or parent of a deceased service member who was:

1. A citizen (including someone granted posthumous citizenship) and
2. Was serving honorably on active duty in the U.S. armed forces at the time of death,

you may now file your Application for Naturalization (Form N-400) under section 319(d) of the Immigration and Nationality Act (INA) at the NSC, regardless of your geographic location. The correct address is:

For U.S. Postal Service deliveries:

Nebraska Service Center
PO Box 87426
Lincoln, NE 68501-7426

For Express Mail and Courier deliveries:

Nebraska Service Center
850 S. Street
Lincoln, NE 68508

Members of the military community applying for naturalization, including service members and military spouses, also should submit their N-400 applications to this address. All other applicants should continue to file Form N-400 at the designated facility based on the location of their residence.

The N-400 form instructions have been updated to reflect the new filing location. Therefore, this filing address change takes effect immediately. Family members of deceased service members who file their Form N-400 with a Lockbox facility may face a delay in processing while USCIS forwards the incorrectly filed application to the NSC.

For more information on USCIS programs for the military, visit www.uscis.gov/military, or call the USCIS toll-free Military Help Line, 1-877-247-4645.

Last updated:05/19/2010

Chapter 12

Military and National Security Naturalization Issues

Research References

West's Key Number Digest

Aliens, Immigration, and Citizenship ⚲710

Westlaw Databases

Steel on Immigration Law (STEEL)
Immigration Law Service (2d ed.) (IMMLS2D)

Treatises and Practice Aids

Steel on Immigration Law § 15:17

KeyCite®: Cases and other legal materials listed in KeyCite Scope can be researched through the KeyCite service on Westlaw®. Use KeyCite to check citations for form, parallel references, prior and later history, and comprehensive citator information, including citations to other decisions and secondary materials.

I. INTRODUCTION

§ 12:1 Overview

Research References

A.L.R. Index, Immigration and Naturalization
Construction and Application of 8 U.S.C.A. § 1440 Permitting Naturalization Through Active Duty Service in Armed Forces During Certain Periods of Military Hostilities, 196 A.L.R. Fed. 365
Dizon and Wettstein, Immigration Law Service 2d § 14:253
Steel on Immigration Law § 15:17

There can be little doubt that in the last two centuries there has been a close link between wars and nationality. This link has been reflected in the U.S. nationality law for more than a century. Even though, the provisions relating to treatment of noncitizen enemies during conflict go back to the beginning of the republic, it was not until the U.S. Civil War that the issues of war and citizenship came to the fore.[1] Beginning in 1862, Congress has passed statutory provisions expediting the naturalization of noncitizens who served honorably in the U.S. army.[2] These provisions were closely followed with provisions forbidding the naturalization of deserters and draft evaders.[3] At the same time, the first statutory provisions for the expatriation of military deserters were passed.[4]

This chapter deals with the current provisions assisting in naturalization proceedings for those noncitizens who have served in the military. In addition, this chapter includes other naturalization-related provisions, such as treatment of noncitizen enemies and naturalization of certain persons who contribute to U.S. intelligence endeavors. The naturalization of noncitizen widows of U.S. citizens who died while in active duty service in the U.S. armed forces is discussed in Ch 11. Provisions relating to bars to naturalization because of military service are discussed in Ch 8. Special provisions on conscientious objectors are discussed in the section on Admission to Citizenship in Ch 9. Loss of citizenship in relation to military service and war is discussed in Ch 15. In addition, the practitioner should be aware of the existence of specific provisions relating to preservation of residence in the U.S. while a lawful permanent resident is serving in the U.S. army.[5]

The modern statutory provisions specifically geared to service in armed forces and to wartime naturalization are contained in sections 327 through 329, and 331 of the INA.[6] In addition the Immigration Act of 1990 included a special provision for the naturalization of Filipinos who served in the armed forces of the U.S. during World War II.[7]

II. NATURALIZATION OF FORMER U.S. CITIZENS WHO LOST THEIR CITIZENSHIP BY SERVICE IN FOREIGN ARMIES DURING WORLD WAR II

§ 12:2 In general

Research References

Dizon and Wettstein, Immigration Law Service 2d §§ 14:238 to 14:241

Many U.S. citizens lost their citizenship by serving in the armed forces of allied countries.[1] In response to their plight, Congress passed a special provision in 1942,

---

[Section 12:1]

[1]Act of July 6, 1798, 1 Stat. 577 reproduced as Appendix 12-1A; INS Interp. 331.1(a)(1).

[2]Act of July 17, 1862, 12 Stat. 594; reproduced as Appendix 12-1B; U.S. v. Sison, 272 F.2d 366, 368 (9th Cir. 1959); INS Interp. 328.1(a).

[3]Act of March 3, 1865, 13 Stat. 487 reproduced as Appendix 12-1C, incorporated as sec. 1998, Revised Statutes of the United States, 1878 reproduced as Appendix 4-5 to Ch 4; INS Interp. 314.1.

[4]Act of March 3, 1865 reproduced as Appendix 12-1C.

[5]See § 7:5.

[6]INA §§ 327 to 329, 331, 8 U.S.C.A. §§ 1438 to 1440, 1442

[7]Sec. 405 of the Immigration Act of 1990 ("IA90"), Act of Nov. 29, 1990, Pub. L. 101-649, 104 Stat. 4978.

[Section 12:2]

[1]See § 15:9.

which was later incorporated into the INA.[2] According to this provision, persons who lost U.S. citizenship because they served in the armed forces of a country, which was fighting a common enemy of the U.S. during World War II, could reacquire U.S. citizenship without regard to the residence and physical presence requirements of the INA.[3] The applicant, however, is required to have been lawfully admitted to permanent residence and to have been a person of good moral character and attached to the principles of the Constitution for the five years preceding the application for naturalization.[4] This section is *not* applicable to persons who during World War II served in the armed forces of a country with which the U.S. was at war.[5]

The application for naturalization is submitted on Form N-400 following the other naturalization procedures applicable to general naturalization applicants.[6] A statement describing eligibility under this section must accompany the application.[7] That statement must include facts that establish:[8]

(1) that the applicant, on or after September 1, 1939 and on or before September 2, 1945, either

    (a) served in the armed forces of any country at war with a country with which the U.S. was at war after December 7, 1941 and before September 2, 1945, or

    (b) took an oath of allegiance or obligation for purposes of entering or serving in the armed forces of such a country;

(2) the applicant was a U.S. citizen at the time of performing such military service or taking such oath; and

(3) the applicant lost U.S. citizenship as a result of such actions.

USCIS deems citizenship granted under this section to have been reacquired. Thus if the person was a naturalized U.S. citizen prior to the loss of the citizenship because of service in the armed forces, then the person is considered a U.S. naturalized citizen, and if the person was a native-born citizen, the person is again considered a native-born citizen.[9] However, the statute is not retroactive in that it does not make the person a U.S. citizen for the period after the person lost his or her U.S. citizenship and before such citizenship was reacquired.[10]

III. NATURALIZATION THROUGH SERVICE IN ARMED FORCES OF U.S.

§ 12:3   Naturalization under current provisions

Research References

A.L.R. Index, Immigration and Naturalization

---

[2]See generally, Gordon & Mailman, § 97.07[3][a].

[3]INA § 327(a), 8 U.S.C.A. § 1438(a).

[4]INA § 327(b), 8 U.S.C.A. § 1438(b).

[5]INA § 327(e), 8 U.S.C.A. § 1439(e).

[6]8 CFR § 327.2(a). For a description of those procedures, see Ch 9.

[7]8 CFR § 327.2(a).

[8]8 CFR §§ 327.1(a), (b), (c), 327.2(a).

[9]INA § 327(c), 8 U.S.C.A. § 1438(c).

[10]INA § 327(c), 8 U.S.C.A. § 1438(c).

Construction and Application of 8 U.S.C.A. § 1440 Permitting Naturalization Through
  Active Duty Service in Armed Forces During Certain Periods of Military Hostilities, 196
  A.L.R. Fed. 365
Dizon and Wettstein, Immigration Law Service 2d § 14:253
Steel on Immigration Law § 15:17

Section 328 of the INA provides the general naturalization provision related to
military service in the U.S.[1] In 2003, Congress amended this provision by eliminating the fee for naturalization for anyone applying under this section. This amendment is effective October 1, 2004.[2] This provision is specifically geared for noncitizens
who file for naturalization either while they are serving in the U.S. armed forces or
within six months from the termination of such service. It applies to any noncitizen
who has served honorably in the U.S. armed forces for periods aggregating to at
least on year.[3]

For purposes of this section service in the armed forces of the U.S. means active
or reserve service in the U.S. Army, U.S. Navy, U.S. Marines, U.S. Air Force, or
U.S. Coast Guard.[4] Service in a National Guard unit during such time as the unit is
federally recognized as a reserve component of the Armed Forces of the U.S. will
also count for purposes of this section.[5] Service in the Philippine Scouts before the
independence of the Philippines is also considered service in the U.S. armed forces
for purposes of this provision.[6]

The provision exonerates the applicant from the basic continuous residence and
physical presence requirements of naturalization provided the person has served for
a period of at least one year in the aggregate and if he or she has been separated
from service, it has been under honorable conditions.[7] The applicant is also
completely relieved of the requirement of residence in a state or USCIS district for
three months prior to the filing of the application.[8]

The one year of service may be fulfilled by a combination of active duty and inac-
tive duty in a reserve status.[9] In addition, applicants who are on temporary disability retired list are still considered to be in the armed forces and are not considered
to have been separated from the armed forces.[10]

If the one year of service was not continuous, the applicant is required to comply
with the residency, physical presence, good moral character, and attachment to the
constitution requirements of section 316 between periods of armed service within

---

[Section 12:3]

[1]INA § 328, 8 U.S.C.A. § 1439.

[2]Pub. L. 108-136, Div. A, Title XVII, §§ 1701(b)(1)(B), 1705(b), Nov. 24, 2003, 117 Stat. 1691,
1696.

[3]INA § 328, 8 U.S.C.A. § 1439, as amended by Section 1701(a) of the National Defense Authorization Act for Fiscal Year 2004, Pub. L. No. 108-136, November 24, 2003, 117 Stat 613.

[4]8 CFR § 328.1(1); 32 CFR § 94.3(b); INS Interp. 328.1(4)(ii).

[5]8 CFR § 328.1(2).

[6]INS Interp. 328.1(b)(4). See INS Interp. 329.1(c)(4)(i) for a historical description of the Philippine Scouts. Cf. In re Roble, 207 F.Supp. 384, 385–88 (N.D.Cal. 1962) (for eligibility of service in the
Philippine Scouts under the Nationality Act of 1940).

[7]INA § 328(a), 8 U.S.C.A. § 1439(a).

[8]INA § 328(b)(1), 8 U.S.C.A. § 1439(b)(1).

[9]32 CFR § 94.4(a)(2).

[10]INS Interp. 328.1(b)(5).

the five years immediately preceding the naturalization application.[11] This includes the three months residency requirement in the state or USCIS district where the application is filed.[12] There is no requirement that such residence be after lawful admission for permanent residence.[13]

In order to naturalize under section 328, the applicant is required to have been admitted to lawful permanent residence by the time of filing of the application for naturalization.[14] This lawful admission for permanent residence may occur before, during, or after the qualifying military service.[15] This provision may have become less significant in recent years since in 1961 the codes relating to enlistment in the army and air force were amended to require that only U.S. citizens and lawful permanent residents could be enlisted in times of peace.[16]

Applicants who apply after six months of separation from the armed forces are required to comply with the full residency and physical presence requirements after admission to lawful permanent residence, as well as with all the other requirements contained in section 316 of the INA.[17] For the purpose of the naturalization requirements, however, any service in the armed forces within the five years preceding the naturalization application will be considered both residence and physical presence in the United States.[18]

The applicant may be naturalized immediately even though there may be a final order of deportation or pending removal proceedings against him or her, provided that the applicant is currently serving in the armed forces of the U.S. and is examined by a USCIS officer prior to the naturalization.[19] The bar to naturalization while a final deportation order is outstanding or while removal proceedings are pending,[20] is not applicable to noncitizens seeking naturalization under this section.

USCIS requires the applicant to provide a certified statement from the proper executive department stating that for each period of his or her service, the applicant's service was honorable, and that in his or her whole history of service in the armed forces of the U.S. there have been no discharges from services that were less than honorable.[21] The definition of honorable service is that used by the executive department in which the applicant served.[22] The applicant is presumed to be a person of good moral character and attached to the principles of the constitution for all the

---

[11]INA § 328(c), 8 U.S.C.A. § 1439(c).

[12]INA § 328(c), 8 U.S.C.A. § 1439(c).

[13]See 8 CFR § 328.2(e)(1); INS Interp. 328.1(b)(3).

[14]8 CFR § 328.2(c); INS Interp. 328.1(b)(3). Cf. INA § 328(b)(2), 8 U.S.C.A. § 1439(b)(2) (exonerating the applicant from section 318 prohibition of naturalization while deportation proceedings are pending, but silent towards the requirement of lawful admission to permanent residence contained in that same section).

[15]INS Interp. 328.1(b)(3).

[16]Act of August 17, 1961, 75 Stat. 364 amending 10 U.S.C.A. §§ 3253, 8253.

[17]INA § 328(d), 8 U.S.C.A. § 1439(d).

[18]INA § 328(d), 8 U.S.C.A. § 1439(d).

[19]INA §§ 318, 328(b)(2), 8 U.S.C.A. §§ 1429, 1439(b)(2); INS Interp. 318.2(c).

[20]INA § 318, 8 U.S.C.A. § 1429.

[21]INA § 328(b)(3), 8 U.S.C.A. § 1439(b)(3).

[22]8 CFR § 328.1. For the Department of Defense's definitions regarding separation, see 32 CFR § 41, appendix A.

periods in which the person served honorably in the armed forces.[23] The applicant must prove those requirements for the relevant periods in which he or she was not serving: the period from the date of discharge to the date of admission to citizenship; and, if the service was discontinuous, the periods in which he or she was not serving.[24]

USCIS has streamlined the process to make it easier to apply under this provision. Effective October 1, 2004, the naturalization process will be made available overseas at U.S. embassies, consulates, and, where practical, U.S. military installations abroad.[25] Every military installation is to have a designated point person who will certify the Form N-426 and assist with filing the application.[26]

§ 12:4 Under Nationality Act of 1940

Even though the general rule is that only current naturalization provisions apply, some of the naturalization provisions of 1940 survived the enactment of the INA. Section 405 of the INA preserved in some cases the right to apply for naturalization under prior naturalization provisions.[1] This right was terminated on September 26, 1961 when Congress amended the INA to provide that all naturalizations had to be determined in accordance with the INA.[2]

Those noncitizens who at the time the INA was enacted were eligible to apply under section 324 of the Nationality Act of 1940 and those who at the date of enactment of the INA were serving in the U.S. armed forces and completed the required service after the date of enactment, continued to be eligible to apply under the 1940 Act provided they filed the petition while serving in the military or within six months after termination of such service, and provided the petition was filed before September 26, 1961.[3] The importance of the preservation of that right is that section 324 of the Nationality Act of 1940 provided the same benefits and had the same requirements as the current law, except that there was no requirement for the applicant to be a lawful permanent resident in order to naturalize.[4]

In addition, in 1940, Congress passed another naturalization provision regarding service in the U.S. army.[5] This law provided not only that the applicant did not need to be a lawful permanent resident but that the period of military service should be considered to have been performed immediately preceding the filing of the application, thus curing the requirement of filing within six months after the termination

---

[23]8 CFR § 328.2(d)(1).

[24]8 CFR § 328.2(d)(2), (3).

[25]*See* "Naturalization Information for Military Personnel," http://uscis.gov/graphics/services/natz/MilitaryBrochurev7.htm.

[26]*See* "Naturalization Information for Military Personnel," http://uscis.gov/graphics/services/natz/MilitaryBrochurev7.htm.

[Section 12:4]

[1]INA § 405, 8 U.S.C.A. § 1101, note.

[2]Former INA § 310(e), 8 U.S.C.A. § 1421(e) (1980) ("Notwithstanding the provisions of section 405(a), any petition for naturalization filed on or after the enactment of this subsection shall be heard and determined in accordance with the requirements of this title"); INS Interp. 328.1(b)(1). Cf. current INA § 310(d), 8 U.S.C.A. § 1421(d) (providing that all naturalizations must be done "in the manner and under the conditions" prescribed in the INA).

[3]INS Interp. 328.1(b)(1).

[4]INS Interp. 328.1(b)(1).

[5]Act of August 16, 1940.

of the service.[6] When combining the Act of August 16, 1940 and section 204 of the Nationality Act of 1940, a person could file for naturalization more than six months after termination of military service provided that the time spent in the military at any point of time added to five years.[7] Just like section 204 of the Nationality Act of 1940, the Act of August 16, 1940 was also preserved by section 405 of the INA.[8] The savings clause continued in effect until September 26, 1961 when the INA was amended to be the only procedure for naturalization.[9]

§ 12:5   Procedural considerations

An application for benefits under this section is filed on Form N-400 following the procedures applicable to general naturalization applicants.[1] The application must be accompanied by proof of honorable service. This has traditionally been accomplished by submitting Form N-426, Certificate of Military or Naval Service.[2] That document is likely dispositive of the issue of honorable service.[3] For individuals who have been discharged, USCIS recently promulgated new procedures whereby a military form—DD Form 214, Certificate of Release or Discharge from Active Duty—may be accepted in place of the N-426.[4] The applicant must also submit Form G-325B, Biographic Form.[5] These forms are reproduced as appendices, but updated USCIS forms may also be downloaded from the USCIS Web site.[6] Beginning October 1, 2004, there will be no fee charged for a naturalization application under this section.[7]

Effective December 1, 1999, all active duty applicants are required to file their applications with the Nebraska Service Center at the following address: Nebraska Service Center, Attention: N-400 Naturalization Facilitation Unit, P.O. Box 87426, Lincoln, Nebraska 68501-7426.[8] For Express Mail or courier deliveries, the address is Nebraska Service Center, 850 S. Street, Lincoln, NE 68508. Applications filed within six months after discharge from service should be filed with any USCIS office in the United States regardless of the place of residence of the applicant.[9] Applications filed more than six months after discharge are filed with the USCIS office having jurisdiction over the applicant's state or USCIS district of residence, according to the general naturalization filing procedures.[10]

---

[6]In Re Roble, 207 F.Supp. 384, 389 (N.D.Cal. 1962).

[7]U. S. v. Sison, 272 F.2d 366, 370–71 (9th Cir. 1959).

[8]In In re Roble, 207 F. Supp. 384, 390–91 (N.D. Cal. 1962).

[9]INS Interp. 328.1(b)(1) citing to former INA § 310(e).

[Section 12:5]

[1]8 CFR § 328.4.

[2]See Appendix 12-2.

[3]See Appendix 12-13.

[4]See Appendix 12-12.

[5]See Appendix 12-3.

[6]See www.uscis.gov.

[7]Pub. L. 108-136, Div. A, Title XVII, §§ 1701(b)(1)(B), 1705(b), Nov. 24, 2003, 117 Stat. 1691, 1696.

[8]64 Fed. Reg. 67323 (Dec. 1, 1999) (notice).

[9]8 CFR § 328.3.

[10]8 CFR § 328.3.

The applicant submits Form N-426 to USCIS.[11] USCIS in turn will use this form to obtain the military record from the relevant armed forces authority. Operations Instructions 328 details the process USCIS follows in order to obtain this record, including the addresses used to request particular records. Some applicants may wish to request their record prior to submitting the application to USCIS. Operations Instructions 328 is reproduced in full as Appendix 12-5.

IV. NATURALIZATION THROUGH SERVICE IN TIME OF WAR

Research References

A.L.R. Library

A.L.R. Index, Immigration and Naturalization

Construction and Application of 8 U.S.C.A. § 1440 Permitting Naturalization Through Active Duty Service in Armed Forces During Certain Periods of Military Hostilities, 196 A.L.R. Fed. 365

Treatises and Practice Aids

Dizon and Wettstein, Immigration Law Service 2d § 14:253
Steel on Immigration Law § 15:17

§ 12:6 Service in time of war—Qualifying hostilities

Beyond the general provision for naturalization of noncitizens who served in the U.S. armed forces, the INA includes a different provision for naturalization of noncitizens who served in the U.S. armed forces during specific hostilities.[1] Similar provisions have existed since World War I.[2] Rights under provisions prior to the INA were preserved by the savings clause of the INA.[3] However, with the September 26, 1961 amendment of the INA such rights were terminated.[4] In 1990 Congress passed special legislation to assist with naturalization of Filipinos who had served in the U.S. armed forces during World War II.[5] This legislation will be discussed separately below. Here we will discuss the general provision of the INA for naturalization of noncitizens who served in time of war.

Section 329 of the INA allows for the naturalization of noncitizens who served in the U.S. armed forces during designated periods of hostilities.[6] The INA itself designates four periods of hostilities to which this section applies:[7]

(1) during World War I (between April 6, 1917 and November 11, 1918);

(2) between September 1, 1939 and December 31, 1946 (World War II);

(3) between June 25, 1950 and July 1, 1955 (Korean War);

(4) and beginning February 28, 1961 and ending October 15, 1978 (Vietnam War).

---

[11]CFR § 328.4; INS Form N-426 (rev. 5/12/77) (instructions) reproduced as Appendix 12-2.

[Section 12:6]

[1]INA § 329, 8 U.S.C.A. § 1440.

[2]INS Interp. 329.1(a)(1) citing to Act of May 9, 1918.

[3]INA § 405, 8 U.S.C.A. § 1101, note.

[4]See discussion of Naturalization through service in the armed forces under the Nationality Act of 1940.

[5]IA90 § 405.

[6]INA § 329, 8 U.S.C.A. § 1440.

[7]INA § 329(a), 8 U.S.C.A. § 1440(a); Executive order 12081, 43 Fed. Reg. 42237 (1978); 8 CFR § 329.2; INS Interp. 329.1(c)(1).

(7) USCIS has taken the position that if active-duty service in the armed forces *began* before the end of the day on October 15, 1978, it qualifies for section 329.[8]

The INA also provides that after the end of the Vietnam War, this section will apply to any other period "which the President by Executive order shall designate as a period in which Armed Forces of the United States are or were engaged in military operations involving armed conflict with a hostile foreign force."[9] President Reagan designated the Grenada invasion as active duty for the purposes of this section, but only for active service between October 25, 1983 and November 2, 1983 conducted (1) on the islands of Grenada, Carriacou, Green Hog, and those islands adjacent to Grenada in the Atlantic seaboard where such service was in direct support of the military operations in Grenada; or (2) in the air space of Grenada; or (3) in the seas adjacent to Grenada where military operations were conducted; or (4) at the Grantly Adams International Airport in Barbados.[10] This designation was held to be an invalid exercise of executive power because of the geographical limitations that President Reagan imposed on the grant.[11] The court held the whole designation ineffective, rather than extend it to all the persons serving in the army at that time.[12]

On November 22, 1994, President Clinton designated the period of Persian Gulf Conflict as a period in which the armed forces of the U.S. were engaged in armed conflict with a hostile army for purposes of section 329 of the INA.[13] The designated period started on August 2, 1990 and ended on April 11, 1991.[14] Based on this designation, persons who served honorably in the U.S. armed forces during this period are eligible for naturalization in accordance with INA § 329.[15]

On July 3, 2002, President Bush designated the period of the "war against terrorists of global reach" as a period in which the armed forces of the United States were engaged in armed conflict with a hostile foreign force for purposes of INA § 329.[16] The designated period began on September 11, 2001 and "will be deemed to terminate on a date designated by future Executive Order."[17] Based on this designation, those persons who served or are serving honorably in active duty status in the Armed Forces during the period beginning September 11, 2001 and ending on the future date designated by Executive Order are eligible for naturalization under INA § 329.

§ 12:7   Service in time of war—Substantive requirements

To qualify for section 329 active duty, service must have been in the U.S. Army,

---

[8]INS Interp. 329.1(c)(1).

[9]INA § 329(a), 8 U.S.C.A. § 1440(a).

[10]8 CFR § 329.2(a)(5).

[11]Matter of Reyes, 910 F.2d 611, 613 (9th Cir. 1990).

[12]Matter of Reyes, 910 F.2d 611, 613–14 (9th Cir. 1990).

[13]Executive Order 12939 of November 22, 1994, 59 Fed. Reg. 61231 (Nov. 29, 1994).

[14]Executive Order 12939 of November 22, 1994, 59 Fed. Reg. 61231 (Nov. 29, 1994).

[15]Executive Order 12939 of November 22, 1994, 59 Fed. Reg. 61231 (Nov. 29, 1994).

[16]Expedited Naturalization of Aliens and Noncitizen Nationals Serving in An Active-Duty Status During the War on Terrorism, Executive Order (July 3, 2002), 2002 WL 1436412 (White House), Appendix 12-6.

[17]Expedited Naturalization of Aliens and Noncitizen Nationals Serving in An Active-Duty Status During the War on Terrorism, Executive Order (July 3, 2002), 2002 WL 1436412 (White House), Appendix 12-6.

U.S. Navy, U.S. Marines, U.S. Air Force, or U.S. Coast Guard.[1] Service in a National Guard unit during such time as the unit was federally recognized as a reserve component of the Armed Forces of the U.S. and that unit was called for active duty also serves as the basis for benefits under this section.[2] Service in the Philippine Scouts, Philippine Army, and recognized guerrilla units of the Philippines during World War II, were also service in the U.S. army for purposes of this section.[3]

Naturalization is available to noncitizens who served honorably in active-duty status during the periods described in § 12:6 and, if separated from the service, were separated under honorable conditions.[4] Determination of whether the service was honorably in active duty is left completely to the relevant executive department.[5] However, the departments are barred from finding the person to have served honorably if the person (1) was separated from the service on account of alienage; (2) was a conscientious objector who performed no military, air, or naval duty whatever; or (3) refused to wear the uniform.[6] Separation on account of alienage will only bar benefits under this section if it occurred at the request of the applicant rather than because of administrative convenience.[7] Furthermore, a noncitizen honorably discharged from service performed during and in a qualifying period and area is eligible for naturalization under this section even though he or she was discharged on account of alienage from a subsequent unrelated and separate period of service.[8]

Active duty includes full-time duty in active military service.[9] It also includes (1) full-time training duty; (2) annual training duty; (3) attendance, while in the active military service, at a service school, designated by the military authorities; and (4) active duty in a noncombatant capacity.[10] However, service in the standby reserve does not qualify the applicant for the benefits of section 329.[11]

If the induction of that person occurred in the United States, the Canal Zone of Panama, American Samoa, the Midway Island (prior to August 21, 1959), or the Swains Island, or in the ports, harbors, bays, enclosed sea areas, or territorial waters of these land areas, the applicant may naturalize even though the person was never admitted to lawful permanent residence.[12] Excludable noncitizens who were paroled into the United States and then were inducted into the armed forces are considered to have been in the United States at the time of induction for

---

[Section 12:7]

[1]8 CFR § 329.1.

[2]8 CFR § 329.1.

[3]INS Interp. 329.1(c)(4)(i), (ii). See also § 12:10.

[4]INA § 329(a), 8 U.S.C.A. § 1440(a).

[5]INA § 329(a), 8 U.S.C.A. § 1440(a), 8 CFR § 329.1.

[6]INA § 329(a), 8 U.S.C.A. § 1440(a), 8 CFR § 329.1(1), (2), (3).

[7]INS Interp. 329.1(d)(1) following In re Petition for Naturalization of Lennox Watson, 502 F.Supp. 145 (1980).

[8]INS Interp. 329.1(d)(2).

[9]INS Interp. 329.1(c)(4)(iv).

[10]INS Interp. 329.1(c)(4)(iv) citing to 10 U.S.C.A. 101(22); In re Kinloch, 53 F.Supp. 521 (W.D.Wash. 1944); In re Sawyer, 59 F.Supp. 428 (D.Del. 1945); see also, App. 12-13.

[11]INS Interp. 329.1(c)(4)(v) citing to 10 U.S.C.A. 273(a); Petition of Yiu Nam Donn, 512 F.2d 808 (3d Cir. 1975).

[12]INA § 329(a)(1), 8 U.S.C.A. § 1440(a)(1), 8 CFR § 329.2(c)(2); INS Interp. 329.1(c)(3)(ii). For a discussion of the meaning of the United States, see §§ 2:8 to 2:14.

purposes of this section.[13] Enlistment in the Philippine Islands has specifically been found not to be enlistment in the United States for purposes of this section even when the Philippine Islands were a possession of the U.S.[14]

The rule exempting applicants from the requirement of lawful permanent residence applies even when the qualifying service occurred after an intervening enlistment or induction in a nonqualifying area, and had no connection with the previous enlistment or induction in the United States or other qualifying area.[15] Similarly, lawful permanent residence is not required when, *following* service performed during a qualifying period but pursuant to an enlistment in a nonqualifying geographical area, reenlistment or a new enlistment occurs in a qualifying area.[16] Even an actual extension of an expired reenlistment or enlistment period while the service person is within a qualifying geographical area brings the person within the benefit of this rule, regardless of how short the extension had been.[17] Furthermore, recall to temporary active-duty will serve the same function as reenlistment for disposing of the lawful permanent residence requirement when the recall occurred within a qualifying area.[18] An advance agreement to reenlist will not bring the person within the exemption to the requirement of lawful permanent residence unless the actual commencement of the reenlistment occurred within the geographical qualifying areas.[19] Barring all these exceptions, if the induction or enlistment occurred outside the geographically qualifying areas, the noncitizen must have become a lawful permanent resident at any time after the induction or enlistment for this section to apply.[20]

Thus, an individual with conditional permanent resident status who seeks naturalization based on military service during a time of war need not prove that his conditional residence status was lawfully granted.[21] This may be compared with INA § 319(b), which permits spouses of military members to naturalize abroad and in an expedited manner. That section does not omit the requirement to prove a lawful admission to permanent residence, meaning that even where naturalization is sought before a Form I-751 may be filed, the spouse must prove the bona fides of the marriage.[22] By contrast, since § 329 does not require proof of lawful permanent residence, such queries ought be unnecessary for an individual naturalizing as a service member during time of war.

Just as in the provision that applies to peacetime service in the armed forces, the U.S. and state or USCIS district residence and physical presence requirements to

---

[13]INS Interp. 329.1(c)(3)(iv) citing to Petition of Martinez, 202 F. Supp. 153 (N.D. Ill. 1962).

[14]INS Interp. 329.1(c)(3)(ii) citing to Dela Cena v. U.S., 249 F.2d 341 (9th Cir. 1962); Petition of Mata, 196 F. Supp. 523 (N.D. Cal. 1961); Petition of Garces, 192 F. Supp. 439, 400 (N.D. Cal. 1961). This position is coherent with the legal status of the Philippine Islands while they were under U.S. rule. See §§ 2:1 et seq.

[15]INS Interp. 329.1(c)(3)(i) citing to Villarin v. U.S., 307 F.2d 774 (9th Cir. 1962).

[16]INS Interp. 329.1(c)(3)(i) citing to In re Petition of Zamora, 232 F.Supp. 1017 (S.D.Cal. 1964); In re Convento, 210 F. Supp. 265 (D. D.C. 1962), judgment aff'd, 336 F.2d 954 (D.C. Cir. 1964).

[17]INS Interp. 329.1(c)(3)(i) citing to In re Petition of Alon, 342 F.Supp. 596 (E.D.La. 1972); In re Petition of Roque, 339 F.Supp. 339 (S.D.Miss. 1971); In re Gabriel, 319 F.Supp. 1312 (D.P.R. 1970).

[18]INS Interp. 329.1(c)(3)(i) citing to Villarin v. U.S. 307 F.2d 774.

[19]INS Interp. 329.1(c)(3)(i) citing to In re Fechalin Ladrido, 307 F.Supp. 799 (D.R.I. 1969).

[20]INA § 329(a)(2), 8 U.S.C.A. § 1440(a)(2).

[21]See AFM 25.1(k) (reproduced at Appendix 12-14).

[22]See Appendix 12-14.

naturalize are waived.[23] Beginning October 1, 2004, there also will be no fee charged for a naturalization application under this section.[24] Similarly, the noncitizen may be naturalized even though there are removal proceedings pending, against him or her.[25] Unlike the peacetime service provision, however, the naturalization requirements relating to minimum age and the special provisions relating to noncitizen enemies do not apply to these applicants.[26]

The regulations have added a requirement that the person must have been of good moral character and attached to the principles of the Constitution, and require that this be established for a year preceding the application under this section.[27] Veterans have argued that there is no good moral character requirement in the statute, but this argument has been uniformly rejected by the courts.[28] A secondary argument raised is that where the statute is silent as to duration of requirement of good moral character, the general rule has been that only good moral character for a reasonable period must be established; the INS Interpretations follow that general rule.[29] However, the Second, Seventh, and Ninth Circuits have upheld the one-year regulatory period as being a valid interpretation of the law and, as such, as having the force of law.[30]

§ 12:8 Service in time of war—Conditions subsequent

A person may not use a period of service in the U.S. armed forces to naturalize under this section if the person has already been naturalized previously on the basis of that same period.[1] This provision is not applicable to noncitizens who served in World War I, who expatriated themselves before the enactment of the INA, and who

---

[23]Compare INA § 329(b)(2), 8 U.S.C.A. § 1440(b)(2) with INA § 328(b)(1), 8 U.S.C.A. § 1439(b)(1). We will refer to section 328 as the peace-time provision even though it may also be used for persons who served in the military during time of war.

[24]Pub. L. 108-136, Div. A, Title XVII, §§ 1701(b)(1)(B), 1705(b), Nov. 24, 2003, 117 Stat. 1691, 1696.

[25]INA § 329(b)(1), 8 U.S.C.A. § 1440(b)(1), 8 CFR § 329.2(e). The regulations appear to exclude a final order from this exception. This interpretation would be counter to the plain language of the statute and the INS Interpretations state unequivocally that even when there is a final order of deportation, the person still qualifies for naturalization under section 329. INA § 318, 8 U.S.C.A. § 1429; INS Interp. 318.2(c).

[26]INA § 329(b)(1), 8 U.S.C.A. § 1440(b)(1).

[27]8 C.F.R. § 329.2(d).

[28]Santamaria-Ames v. I.N.S., 104 F.3d 1127 (9th Cir. 1996); Castiglia v. I.N.S., 108 F.3d 1101, 1102 (9th Cir. 1997); Nolan v. Holmes, 334 F.3d 189, 196 A.L.R. Fed. 755 (2d Cir. 2003); Boatswain v. Gonzales, 414 F.3d 413 (2d Cir. 2005), cert. denied, 126 S. Ct. 445, 163 L. Ed. 2d 338 (U.S. 2005); Lopez v. Henley, 416 F.3d 455 (5th Cir.2005); O'Sullivan v. U.S. Citizenship and Immigration Services, 453 F.3d 809 (7th Cir. 2006).

[29]See § 7:18; INS Interp. 329.1(c)(6); Matter of Sanchez-Linn, 20 I & N Dec. 362, 364-65 (BIA 1991).

[30]Santamaria-Ames v. I.N.S., 104 F.3d 1127 (9th Cir. 1996); Castiglia v. I.N.S., 108 F.3d 1101, 1102 (9th Cir. 1997); Nolan v. Holmes, 334 F.3d 189, 196 A.L.R. Fed. 755 (2d Cir. 2003); O'Sullivan v. U.S. Citizenship and Immigration Services, 453 F.3d 809 (7th Cir. 2006). It was argued in some of those cases that because no particular time period for good moral character was required, the provisions of INA § 101(f), particularly INA § 101(f)(8), were not triggered. These arguments have also been rejected. Boatswain v. Gonzales, 414 F.3d 413, 418 (2d Cir. 2005), cert. denied, 126 S. Ct. 445, 163 L. Ed. 2d 338 (U.S. 2005); Castiglia v. I.N.S., 108 F.3d 1101, 1103 (9th Cir. 1997); O'Sullivan v. U.S. Citizenship and Immigration Services, 453 F.3d 809, 816-817 (7th Cir. 2006).

[Section 12:8]

[1]INA § 329(a), 8 U.S.C.A. § 1440(a).

filed their naturalization applications before September 26, 1961, as those noncitizens retained their right to naturalize under the prior law until the savings clause of the INA was made ineffective to naturalization proceedings.[2] In addition, it is USCIS' position that persons who were U.S. citizens during the relevant periods of service in the armed forces cannot take advantage of section 329 to naturalize after they expatriate themselves because section 329 requires that the service must have been performed while the person was a noncitizen or a noncitizen national.[3]

Citizenship granted under this section may be revoked if the armed service provides a duly authenticated certification that after the person was naturalized under this section, he or she was separated from the service under other than honorable conditions.[4] Normal denaturalization procedures must be followed in those circumstances.[5] Of course, the person may also be denaturalized on any of the other bases for denaturalization.[6]

§ 12:9 Service in time of war—Procedural requirements

Applications under this section may be filed in any USCIS office regardless of the place of residence of the applicant.[1] The applicant must file Form N-400 as with the regular naturalization process.[2] The application must be accompanied by proof of honorable service. This has traditionally been accomplished by submitting Form N-426, Certificate of Military or Naval Service, in triplicate.[3] For individuals who have been honorably discharged, USCIS recently promulgated new procedures whereby a military form—DD Form 214, Certificate of Release or Discharge from Active Duty—may be accepted in place of the N-426.[4] The applicant must also submit Form G-325B, Biographic Form.[5] These forms are reproduced as appendices, but updated USCIS forms may also be downloaded from the USCIS Web site.[6] Form N-426 provides statutory proof that the person performed honorable active-duty service and, if separated from the service, was honorably separated.[7] Corrections as to, for example, place of enlistment will not be accepted unless they are established by a duly authenticated certification from the executive department under which the applicant served.[8]

---

[2]INS Interp. 329.1(c)(2) citing to Petition of Strati, 131 F. Supp. 786 (E.D. Pa. 1954), order aff'd, 223 F.2d 470 (3d Cir. 1955).

[3]INS Interp. 329.1(c)(2).

[4]INA § 329(c), 8 U.S.C.A. § 1440(c).

[5]INA § 329(c), 8 U.S.C.A. § 1440(c).

[6]See §§ 14:2 to 14:28.

[Section 12:9]

[1]8 CFR § 329.3.

[2]8 CFR § 329.4(a). For a discussion of the general naturalization procedures, see Ch 9.

[3]See Appendix 12-2.

[4]See Appendix 12-12.

[5]See Appendix 12-3.

[6]See www.uscis.gov.

[7]See INA § 329(b)(3), 8 U.S.C.A. § 1440(b)(3) (requiring honorable active-duty service and honorable separation be proven by a duly authenticated certification from the executive department of the force the alien served in). See also, Appendix 12-13.

[8]INS Interp. 329.1(c)(iii).

The applicant submits Form N-426 to USCIS.[9] USCIS in turn will use this form to obtain the military record from the relevant armed forces authority. INS Operations Instructions 328 details the process USCIS follows in order to obtain this record, including the addresses used to request particular records. This is reproduced in full as Appendix 12-5. The same address is used for current military personnel as for former members of the military.[10] For U.S. mail deliveries, the address is: Nebraska Service Center, P.O. Box 87426, Lincoln, NE 68501-7426. For Express Mail or courier deliveries, the physical address is: Nebraska Service Center, 850 S. Street, Lincoln, NE 68508.

USCIS has now promulgated procedures whereby active-duty military personnel may have their naturalization processing done abroad.[11] Since those procedures were implemented, over 9000 service members have been naturalized abroad.[12]

§ 12:10 Naturalization for spouses and children of servicemembers deployed abroad

In 2008, Congress added INA § 319(e), which aids spouses of members of the military deployed abroad. Under the new law, such spouses may either obtain expedited naturalization in the United States, or may be naturalized while residing with their spouses abroad. This is discussed more fully at § 11:10.

§ 12:11 Active-duty service by natives of Philippines during World War II

Research References

Dizon and Wettstein, Immigration Law Service 2d §§ 14:257, 14:258

In response to what Congress felt was unfair treatment of natives of the Philippines who had served in the U.S. armed forces during World War II, it added a provision in the IA90 which waives for them certain requirements of section 329 of the INA.[1] This unfair treatment relates to an episode at the end of World War II in which the legacy INS consciously prevented the naturalization of thousands of Filipino war veterans.

In March 1942, Congress passed a provision facilitating the naturalization of foreigners who served in the U.S. armed forces, provided that the applications for naturalization were filed within a certain period after the end of the war, which in effect was December 31, 1946.[2] The law authorized the INS commissioner to designate representatives to receive naturalization petitions pursuant to this provision.[3] After the Philippines was liberated from the Japanese, in August 1945, the INS commissioner designated the American vice consul in Manila, George Ennis, to

---

[9]8 CFR § 329.4(a); INS Form N-426 (rev. 5/12/77) (instructions) reproduced as Appendix 12-2. The current version of Form N-426 is dated May 28, 2004. Prior versions can be used until September 30, 2004.

[10]See § 12:5.

[11]See Appendix 12-8, Appendix 12-11.

[12]See Appendix 12-8.

[Section 12:11]

[1]IA90 § 405.

[2]INS v. Pangilinan, 486 U.S. 875, 877–78, 108 S.Ct. 2210, 2213, 100 L.Ed.2d 882 reh'g denied 487 U.S. 1264, 109 S.Ct. 27 (1988); INS Interp. 329.1(b).

[3]I.N.S. v. Pangilinan, 486 U.S. 875, 878, 108 S. Ct. 2210, 2213, 100 L. Ed. 2d 882 (1988).

receive the naturalization petitions pursuant to this law.[4] On October 26, 1945, after an apparent informal agreement with the government of the Philippines, the U.S. Attorney General revoked Vice Consul Ennis's authority to receive naturalization petitions.[5] Since the Philippine Islands were outside the jurisdiction of any naturalization court in the U.S., the revocation was aimed at effectively preventing the naturalization pursuant to this law of all nationals of the Philippines who served in the U.S. armed forces and who were at the time living in the Philippines.[6] No official was designated in the Philippines to receive naturalization petitions until four months prior to the deadline to file petitions under this provision of law.[7]

This episode resulted in a stream of litigation in the U.S. courts by Filipino veterans who were prevented from naturalizing by this maneuver.[8] The cases ended up in the Supreme Court where a unanimous court expressed the view that U.S. district courts have no authority to naturalize except as provided by statute, and that, in exercising its authority as it did, the INS had not violated the due process or equal protection rights of the Philippine servicepeople.[9]

Those veterans then turned to Congress, which in 1990 passed a law providing relief to them.[10] Under the provisions of that law, persons born in the Philippines, who were residing in the Philippines before enlisting in (1) active-duty service under the command of the U.S. armed forces in the Far East, or (2) at any time between September 1, 1939 and December 31, 1946 enlisted within the Philippine Army, the Philippine Scouts, or recognized guerrilla unit, were exempt from the requirement of being lawful permanent residents before applying for naturalization under the provisions of INA § 329.[11] In addition, once they became citizens, they could remain abroad and the presumption of lack of intent to remain in the U.S. would not apply to them.[12] These veterans were given until November 29, 1992 to file the applications.[13] This deadline was later extended to October 6, 1994, and then to February 3, 1995.[14] The deadline then expired. In 1997, Congress once again extended the deadline until February 3, 2001.[15] Applications for naturalization were

---

[4]I.N.S. v. Pangilinan, 486 U.S. 875, 879, 108 S. Ct. 2210, 2214, 100 L. Ed. 2d 882 (1988).

[5]I.N.S. v. Pangilinan, 486 U.S. 875, 879, 108 S. Ct. 2210, 2214, 100 L. Ed. 2d 882 (1988).

[6]Memorandum to Attorney General Clark from INS Commissioner Carussi, dated September 13, 1945 quoted in I.N.S. v. Pangilinan, 486 U.S. 875, 879, 108 S. Ct. 2210, 2214, 100 L. Ed. 2d 882 (1988).

[7]I.N.S. v. Pangilinan, 486 U.S. 875, 880, 108 S. Ct. 2210, 2214, 100 L. Ed. 2d 882 (1988). INS had taken the position that the law allowed but not required it to designate an official to receive naturalization petitions.

[8]I.N.S. v. Pangilinan, 486 U.S. 875, 879, 108 S. Ct. 2210, 2214, 100 L. Ed. 2d 882 (1988).

[9]I.N.S. v. Pangilinan, 486 U.S. 875, 883–86, 108 S. Ct. 2210, 2215–17, 100 L. Ed. 2d 882 (1988), I.N.S. v. Pangilinan, 486 U.S. 875, 108 S. Ct. 2210, 100 L. Ed. 2d 882 (1988).

[10]IA90 § 405.

[11]IA90 § 405. This requirement was applicable to them because they were not enlisted in the United States, the Canal Zone, American Samoa, or Swains Island.

[12]IA90 § 405(b).

[13]IA90 § 405(a)(1)(D).

[14]Departments of Commerce, Justice, and State, the Judiciary, and Related Agencies Appropriations Act, 1993, Act of Oct. 6, 1992, Pub. L. No. 102-395, § 113, 106 Stat. 1828; 60 Fed. Reg. 45658 (Sept. 1, 1995).

[15]Departments of Commerce, Justice, State, and the Judiciary, Appropriations Act, 1998, Pub. L. No. 105-119, § 112(d)(2), effective December 3, 1997.

allowed to be filed and processed in the Philippines as well as in the U.S.[16] Under the original fee schedules if the application is filed in the Philippines the filing fee was $120 rather than the normal fee of $95 which is applicable if filing naturalization in the U.S.[17] When the INS proposed a fee increase in January 1998, it had specifically proposed including a higher fee for the N-400 if the interview was to take place in the Philippines.[18] The final rule, however, contained no separate filing fee for naturalizations to be held in the Philippines.[19] Procedures for naturalization under this section were specified in the INS regulations.[20]

Litigation did not stop with Congress' passage of this corrective measure. Filipino war veterans had to sue the INS in order to be allowed to present official Philippine government records instead of U.S. Army records to prove naturalization.[21] The INS implemented the Almero decision by advising INS offices that applicants under the special Philippine Armed Forces service will be allowed to prove qualifying military service "with documents verified from Philippine government records kept by the general headquarters of the Armed Forces of the Philippines at Camp General Emilio Aguinaldo (Camp Aguinaldo) and through their Veterans Affairs Office."[22] The INS offices, however, were instructed to still engage in primary verification through the U.S. Armed Forces on Form N-426.[23] The cable advises INS to segregate these cases and hold them in abeyance until further instructions.[24]

Because of unacceptable delays in processing these claims, a class action on behalf of Filipino veterans was filed in federal district court in Los Angeles.[25] In September 1994, the judge set up a timetable for INS' processing of these naturalization applications.[26] The timetable was modified in January 1995, after the INS failed to evaluate a single application in the four-month period.[27] In July 1995, the judge found the INS in contempt of court, after discovering that, in 1995, the INS had only adjudicated two applications under the special Philippine service legislation.[28] The court ruled that if the INS failed to adjudicate the applications according to a new timetable, the court would adjudicate the applications *de novo* and would bar the INS from objecting to the authenticity or the validity of the evidence or documentation presented to the court to support the plaintiffs' applications.[29]

In 1998, Congress not only extended the deadline for filing these applications, but also amended the substantive requirements. Under the new provisions, in order to qualify, the applicant must: "(i) [be] listed on the final roster prepared by the Recovered Personnel Division of the United States Army of those who served in an

[16]Sec. 113(a)(1), (2), Act of Oct. 6, 1992.

[17]8 CFR § 103.7; as amended by 60 Fed. Reg. 9774 (Feb. 22, 1995).

[18]63 Fed. Reg. 1775 (Jan. 12, 1998) (proposed rule).

[19]8 CFR § 103.7; as amended by 63 Fed. Reg. 43604 (Aug. 14, 1998).

[20]8 CFR § 329.5.

[21]Almero v. I.N.S., 18 F.3d 757 (9th Cir. 1994). See also Serquina v. U.S., 19 F.3d 29 (9th Cir. 1994) (table - unpublished, same holding).

[22]INS Cable, File No. HQ 329.5-C (Nov. 9, 1994).

[23]INS Cable, File No. HQ 329.5-C (Nov. 9, 1994).

[24]INS Cable, File No. HQ 329.5-C (Nov. 9, 1994).

[25]Serquina v. United States, CV93-129-SVW (JRx) reported in LA Daily Journal, July 13, 1995.

[26]Serquina v. United States, CV93-129-SVW (JRx) reported in LA Daily Journal, July 13, 1995.

[27]Serquina v. United States, CV93-129-SVW (JRx) reported in LA Daily Journal, July 13, 1995.

[28]Serquina v. United States, CV93-129-SVW (JRx) reported in LA Daily Journal, July 13, 1995.

[29]Serquina v. United States, CV93-129-SVW (JRx) reported in LA Daily Journal, July 13, 1995.

active duty status within the Philippine Army during the World War II occupation and liberation of the Philippines; (ii) [be] listed on the final roster prepared by the Guerrilla Affairs Division of the United States Army of those who received recognition as having served honorably in an active duty status within a recognized guerrilla unit during World War II occupation and liberation of the Philippines; or (iii) served honorably in an active duty status within the Philippine Scouts or within any other component of the United States Armed Forces in the Far East (other than a component described in clause (i) or (ii)) at any time during the period beginning September 1, 1939 and ending December 31, 1946."[30] At least one court has found that the 1998 amendment to the statute implicitly overruled the Almero decision with respect to individuals who served within a guerrilla unit of the Philippine Army.[31]

§ 12:12   Hmong veterans' legislation

In the year 2000, Congress passed legislation specifically designed to address the plight of Hmong Veterans who served "with a special guerrilla unit, or irregular forces, operating from a base in Laos in support of the United States military at any time during the period beginning February 28, 1961, and ending September 18, 1978," their spouses and their widows/widowers.[1] This legislation is not based on the provisions of INA § 328 or 329. Instead, Hmong veterans, their spouses and widows are required to satisfy all the regular naturalization requirements, except that they are exempt from the English language requirements and receive "special consideration" in the civics testing.[2]

V. POSTHUMOUS CITIZENSHIP THROUGH DEATH WHILE IN ACTIVE DUTY IN PERIODS OF HOSTILITY

§ 12:13   In general

Research References

Dizon and Wettstein, Immigration Law Service 2d § 14:63

In 1989 Congress added a provision to the INA allowing for the posthumous conferring of U.S. citizenship to noncitizens and noncitizens nationals who died as a result of injuries incurred while serving in periods of hostilities recognized for purposes of section 329 of the INA.[1] The only other provision allowing for posthu-

---

[30]Departments of Commerce, Justice, State, and the Judiciary, Appropriations Act, 1998, § 112(b).

[31]Jacob v. U.S., 128 F. Supp. 2d 638 (D. Haw. 2000); see also Cano v. Reno, 210 F.3d 381 (9th Cir. 2000) (unpublished decision) (same).

[Section 12:12]

[1]Hmong Veterans' Naturalization Act of 2000, Pub.L. 106-207, 114 Stat. 316 (May 26, 2000) amended by Act of November 1, 2000, Pub.L. 106-415 reproduced as Appendix 7-12 to Ch 7.

[2]For a detailed discussion of this legislation, see § 7:95.

[Section 12:13]

[1]INA § 329A, 8 U.S.C.A. § 1440-1, added by § 2 of the Posthumous Citizenship for Active Duty Service Act of 1989, Pub. L. 101-249, 104 Stat. 94 (Mar. 6, 1990).

mous naturalization is for certain victims of the September 11, 2001 terrorist attacks.[2]

To qualify the person must have (1) been a noncitizen or noncitizen national at the time of service; (2) served in an active duty status in the armed forces of the U.S. during a period recognized for purposes of section 329; (3) died as a result of injury or disease incurred in or aggravated by that service; and (4) either have been enlisted in the United States or other qualifying areas for purposes of section 329, or been a lawful permanent resident.[3] Benefits under this section may be obtained by application filed by surviving next of kin.[4] Procedural and substantive requirements are detailed in the regulations.[5] Applications for posthumous citizenship are filed on Form N-644 which is reproduced below as Appendix 12-4. Form N-644 is also available for download from the USCIS Web site at http://uscis.gov/graphics/for msfee/forms/index.htm. The filing fee for this application is $80. USCIS issued a new edition of Form N-644 on February 25, 2003, with the correct filing fee included. The May 31, 1991 version of the form may still be used, but the correct fee must be included with the application.

Historically, posthumous naturalization of service members has been of purely symbolic significance. However, the 2004 legislation, reproduced at Appendix 12-7, contains explicit benefits to surviving spouses and children.[6] USCIS appears to have now accepted that posthumous naturalization of service members does provide benefits to surviving family members, permitting them to be treated as children or spouses of a U.S. citizen for purposes of naturalization, adjustment of status, and other benefits.[7]

VI. SPECIAL PROVISIONS FOR NONCITIZEN ENEMIES

§ 12:14 In general

Research References

Dizon and Wettstein, Immigration Law Service 2d §§ 14:297, 14:298

Statutes prohibiting the naturalization of noncitizen enemies go back to the beginning of the republic.[1] By 1813, the first statute was amended to allow for the naturalization of noncitizen enemies who by the date of the beginning of the hostilities were already eligible for naturalization.[2] That amendment also stipulated that

---

[2]Department of Justice Appropriations Act of 2002, P.L. 107-77, title I, section 114, *reproduced as* Appendix 11-2; *cf.* Wiedersperg v. I.N.S., 189 F.3d 476 (9th Cir. 1999) (unpublished decision) (noting that at that time there were no other provisions for posthumous naturalization).

[3]INA § 329A(b), 8 U.S.C.A. § 1440-1(b).

[4]INA § 329A(c), 8 U.S.C.A. § 1440-1(c).

[5]8 C.F.R. § 392.

[6]See Appendix 12-7 at § 1703.

[7]See Appendix 12-8 at 3.

[Section 12:14]

[1]Act of April 14, 1802, 2 Stat. 153 reproduced as Appendix 4-3 to Ch 4. See also Act of July 6, 1798 reproduced as Appendix 12-1A (providing for the restraint, regulation, and removal of "alien" enemies).

[2]Act of July 30, 1813, incorporated as sec. 2171, Revised Statutes of the United States, 1878 reproduced as Appendix 4-5 to Ch 4.

its provisions did not prevent the apprehension and removal of a noncitizen enemy according to law.[3]

The modern version of these provisions can be found in INA § 331.[4] There is no filing fee for this application.

The status of noncitizen enemy ceases to exist at the moment the president of the U.S. proclaims, or Congress passes a concurrent resolution, declaring that the hostilities between the U.S. and that country have ended.[5]

If the naturalization application was pending at the beginning of the war, the DHS will determine if the noncitizen is a noncitizen enemy.[6] The DHS will notify the applicant of such determination and thereafter the time limitations applicable under normal naturalization procedures will not apply.[7] It will also conduct a full investigation of the noncitizen to establish the applicant's loyalty to the U.S. and his or her attachment to the country, state, or sovereignty with which the U.S. is at war.[8] If the DHS concludes that the applicant's loyalty and attachment to the U.S. have been fully established, the naturalization application may be granted.[9]

If the application was not pending at the onset of hostilities, the noncitizen may only be naturalized if the DHS upon investigation fully establishes the loyalty of the applicant, and allows the applicant to apply for naturalization by classifying him or her as not being a noncitizen enemy.[10]

Just like the statutes pertaining to the early nineteenth century, the INA includes a provision that "nothing contained [in this section] shall be taken or construed to interfere with or prevent the apprehension and removal, consistent with law, of any noncitizen enemy at any time prior to the actual naturalization of such noncitizen."[11]

VII. PERSONS WHO MAKE EXTRAORDINARY CONTRIBUTIONS TO INTELLIGENCE ACTIVITIES

§ 12:15   In general

Research References

Dizon and Wettstein, Immigration Law Service 2d § 14:304

Section 316(f) of the INA provides for the naturalization of persons who have made an extraordinary contribution to the national security of the U.S. or to the conduct of the U.S. intelligence gathering activities.[1] This section is only applicable to those persons who are determined by the director of the Central Intelligence

---

[3]Act of July 30, 1813, incorporated as sec. 2171, Revised Statutes of the United States, 1878 reproduced as Appendix 4-5 to Ch 4. See generally INS Interp. 331.1(a)(1).

[4]8 U.S.C.A. § 1442.

[5]INA § 331(d), 8 U.S.C.A. § 1442(d); 8 CFR § 331.1.

[6]8 CFR § 331.4.

[7]8 CFR § 331.4(a). The INA provides that the DHS must receive at least ninety days notice of the pendency of a naturalization application and may object to its adjudication, in which case, the application will be continued as long as the DHS may require. INA § 331(a), (b), 8 U.S.C.A. § 1442(a), (b).

[8]8 CFR § 331.3.

[9]8 CFR § 331.4(b).

[10]INA § 331(c), 8 U.S.C.A. § 1442(c).

[11]INA § 331(e), 8 U.S.C.A. § 1442(e).

[Section 12:15]

[1]INA § 316(f)(1), 8 U.S.C.A. § 1427(f)(1).

Agency (CIA), the Attorney General, and the commissioner of the INA to have made such a contribution.[2] The Attorney General has delegated its authority to make these determinations to the criminal division and the deputy assistant attorneys general, criminal division.[3]

Only five persons are allowed to apply under this section each year and the director of the CIA must inform the Select Committee on Intelligence and the Committee on the Judiciary of the Senate and the Permanent Select Committee on Intelligence and the Select Committee of the Judiciary of the House of Representatives within a reasonable time prior to filing any of those applications.[4]

The applicant is required to be otherwise eligible for naturalization except that the residency and physical presence requirements and the prohibition against naturalization of members of the Communist party and other subversives do not apply.[5] The applicant is, however, required to have resided continuously in the United States for a period of one year prior to naturalization in order to qualify for this provision.[6] In addition, persecutors of others, persons who have committed serious nonpolitical crimes outside the United States, persons who have been convicted of particularly serious crimes in the United States, and noncitizens who are a danger to the security of the U.S. are barred from naturalizing under this section, and are inadmissible under the terrorist ground of inadmissibility.[7]

---

[2]INA § 316(f)(1), 8 U.S.C.A. § 1427(f)(1).

[3]28 CFR § 0.63(b).

[4]INA § 316(f)(3), 8 U.S.C.A. § 1427(f)(3).

[5]INA § 316(f)(1), 8 U.S.C.A. § 1427(f)(1).

[6]INA § 316(f)(1), 8 U.S.C.A. § 1427(f)(1).

[7]INA §§ 208(b)(2)(A), 316(f)(1), 8 U.S.C.A. §§ 1158(b)(2)(A), 1427(f)(1).

APPENDIX 12-1

Naturalization-Related Military Statutes

A. ACT OF JULY 6, 1789, 1 STAT. 577

An Act Respecting Alien Enemies

Section 1. *Be it enacted by the Senate and House of Representatives of the United States of America in Congress assembled,* That whenever there shall be a declared war between the United States and any foreign nation or government, or any invasion or predatory incursion shall be perpetrated, attempted, or threatened against the territory of the United States, by any foreign nation or government, and the President of the United States shall make public proclamation of the event, all natives, citizens, denizens, or subjects of the hostile nation or government, being males of the age of fourteen years and upwards, who shall be within the United States, and not actually naturalized, shall be liable to be apprehended, restrained, secured and removed, as noncitizen enemies. And the President of the United States shall be, and is hereby authorized, in any event, as aforesaid, by his proclamation thereof, or other public act, to direct the conduct to be observed, on the part of the United States, towards the aliens who shall become liable, as aforesaid; the manner and degree of the restraint to which they shall be subject, and in what cases, and upon what security their residence shall be permitted, and to provide for the removal of those, who, not being permitted to reside within the United States, shall refuse or neglect to depart therefrom; and to establish any other regulations which shall be found necessary in the premises and for the public safety: *Provided,* that aliens resident within the United States, who shall become liable as enemies, in the manner aforesaid, and who shall not be chargeable with actual hostility, or other crime against the public safety, shall be allowed, for the recovery, disposal, and removal of their goods and effects, and for their departure, the full time which is, or shall be stipulated by the hostile nation or government, of which they shall be natives, citizens, denizens or subjects: and where no such treaty shall have existed, the President of the United States may ascertain and declare such reasonable time as may be consistent with the public safety, and according to the dictates of humanity and national hospitality.

. . .

B. ACT OF JULY 17, 1862, 12 STAT. 594.

Be it enacted by the Senate and House of Representatives of the United States of America in Congress assembled, That . . .

. . .

Sec. 21. *And be it further enacted,* That any alien, of the age of twenty-one years and upwards, who has enlisted or shall enlist in the armies of the United States, either the regular or the volunteer forces, and has been or shall be hereafter honorably discharged, may be admitted to become a citizen of the United States, upon his petition, without any previous declaration of his intention to become a citizen of the

United States and that he shall not be required to prove more than one year's residence within the United States previous to his application to become such citizen; and that the court admitting such alien shall, in addition to such proof of residence and good moral character as is now provided by law, be satisfied by competent proof of such person having been honorably discharged from the service of the United States as aforesaid.

. . .

C. ACT OF MARCH 3, 1865, 13 STAT. 487

An Act to amend several Acts heretofore passed to provide for the Enrolling and Calling out the national Forces, and for other Purposes

Be it enacted by the Senate and House of Representatives of the United States of America in Congress assembled, That . . .

. . .

Sec. 21. *And be it further enacted,* That, in addition to the other lawful penalties of the crime of desertion from the military or naval service, all persons who have deserted the military or naval service of the United States, who shall not return to said service, or report themselves to a provost-marshal within sixty days after the proclamation hereinafter mentioned, shall be deemed and taken to have voluntarily relinquished and forfeited their rights of citizenship and their rights to become citizens; and such deserters shall be forever incapable of holding any office of trust or profit under the United States, or of exercising their rights of citizens thereof; and all persons who shall hereafter desert the military or naval service, and all persons who, being duly enrolled, shall depart the jurisdiction of the district in which he is enrolled, or go beyond the limits of the United States, with intent to avoid any draft into the military or naval service, duly ordered, shall be liable to the penalties of this section. And the President is hereby authorized and required forthwith, on the passage of this act, to issue his proclamation setting forth the provisions of this section, in which proclamation the President is requested to notify all deserters returning within sixty days as aforesaid that they shall be pardoned on condition of returning to their regiments and companies or to such other organizations as they may be assigned to, until they shall have served for a period of time equal to their original term of enlistment.

APPENDIX 12-2

Form N-426

OMB No. 1615-0053; Expires 02/28/2013

Department of Homeland Security
U.S. Citizenship and Immigration Services

Instructions for Form N-426, Request for Certification of Military or Naval Service

Instructions

NOTE: Type or print clearly with black ink. Be sure this form and the complete return address are legible. Do not leave any questions unanswered. When appropriate, insert "None," "Not Applicable," or "N/A." For further assistance, contact the Military Help Line, 1-877-CIS-4MIL (1-877-247-4645) or visit **www.uscis.gov/military**.

What Is the Purpose of This Form?

This form is for current or former members of the U.S. Armed Forces who are applying for naturalization under the Immigration and Nationality Act. Completion and certification of this form by the applicant and certifying official will serve as an authenticated certification of military service.

Failure to provide the information requested, with the exception of your U.S. Social Security Number (SSN), may delay a final decision or result in denial of your Form N-400, Application for Naturalization. Your application will not be denied for failure to provide your SSN; however, it may prove difficult to verify your military service if you do not provide it since military records are indexed by SSN.

How to File

If you are applying for naturalization under section 328 or 329 of the Immigration and Nationality Act, submit this form along with:

1. Form N-400, Application for Naturalization; and
2. Copy of Form DD-214, Certificate of Release or Discharge from Active Duty, or NGB Form 22, National Guard Report of Separation and Record of Service.

Refer to "Where to File?" of the filing instructions for Form N-400.

Authority for Collecting This Information

Our authority for collecting the information requested on this form is contained in sections 328 and 329 of the Immigration and Nationality Act (8 U.S.C. 1439 and 1440).

Information solicited that indicates a violation or potential violation of law, whether civil, criminal, or regulatory in nature, may be referred as a routine use to the appropriate agency, whether Federal, State, local, or foreign, charged with the responsibility of investigating, enforcing, or prosecuting such violations.

All or part of the information solicited may as a matter of routine use be disclosed to courts exercising naturalization jurisdiction and to other Federal, State, local, and foreign law enforcement and regulatory agencies, the Department of Defense, including any component thereof, Selective Service System, Department of State, Department of the Treasury, Central Intelligence Agency, Interpol, and individuals and organizations that process the application for naturalization, or during the courses of investigations, to elicit further information required by USCIS to carry out its functions.

Failure to provide any or all of the solicited information may delay the naturalization process or result in a failure to locate military records or prove qualifying military service.

USCIS Privacy Act Statement

AUTHORITIES: The information requested on this form, and the associated evidence, is collected under the Immigration and Nationality Act, section 101, et seq.

PURPOSE: The primary purpose for providing the requested information on this form is to determine if you have established eligibility for the immigration benefit for which you are filing. The information you provide will be used to grant or deny the benefit sought.

DISCLOSURE: The information you provide is voluntary. However, failure to provide the requested information, and any requested evidence, may delay a final decision or result in denial of your form.

ROUTINE USES: The information you provide on this form may be shared with other Federal, State, local, and foreign government agencies and authorized organizations following approved routine uses described in the associated published system of records notices **[DHS-USCIS-007 - Benefits Information System and DHS-USCIS-001 - Alien File, Index, and National File Tracking System of Records,** which can be found at **www.dhs.gov/privacy].** The information may also be made available, as appropriate, for law enforcement purposes or in the interest of national security.

Paperwork Reduction Act

An agency may not conduct or sponsor an information collection and a person is not required to respond to a collection of information unless it displays a currently valid OMB control number. The public reporting burden for this collection of information is estimated at 20 minutes per response, including the time for reviewing instructions and completing and submitting the form. Send comments regarding this burden estimate or any other aspect of this collection of information, including suggestions for reducing this burden, to: U.S. Citizenship and Immigration Services, Regulatory Products Division, Office of the Executive Secretariat, 20 Massachusetts Avenue, N.W., Washington, DC 20529-2020, OMB No. 1615-0053. **Do not mail your application to this address.**

OMB No. 1615-0053 ; Expires 02/28/2013

Department of Homeland Security
U.S. Citizenship and Immigration Services

Form N-426, Request for
Certification of Military or Naval Service

Persons who are serving or have served under specified conditions in the Armed Forces of the United States are granted certain exemptions from the general requirements for naturalization. To establish eligibility, the law requires the department with custody of the service record to certify whether the service member served honorably, and whether each separation from the service was under honorable conditions. Certification of the service member's military service listed on this form is required. **Submit this form with Form N-400, Application for Naturalization.** For further assistance, contact the Military Help Line, 1-877-CIS-4MIL (1-877-247-4645) or visit www.uscis.gov/military.

For USCIS Use Only

Date Returned:
To:
Initials:
Comments:

Alien Registration Number	Military Service Number	Date of Request
A		

Name Used During Military Service *(Last, First, Middle)*	U.S. Social Security Number	Date of Birth	Place of Birth *(Country and City)*

Present Address:

Phone Number(s):   E-Mail Address(es):

Military Service
List all periods of service. (attach an additional sheet(s) if you need to provide more information.)

TO BE COMPLETED BY APPLICANT OR CERTIFYING OFFICIAL				TO BE COMPLETED BY CERTIFYING OFFICIAL
Branch of Service	Date Service Began	Date Service Ended	Type of Service *(includes all active, reserve, and National Guard Service)*	Applicant served honorably or is currently serving honorably?
			☐ Active Duty ☐ Selected Reserve of the Ready Reserve*	☐ Yes ☐ No (give details in Remarks)
			☐ Active Duty ☐ Selected Reserve of the Ready Reserve*	☐ Yes ☐ No (give details in Remarks)
			☐ Active Duty ☐ Selected Reserve of the Ready Reserve*	☐ Yes ☐ No (give details in Remarks)

*Selected Reserve of the Ready Reserve members: (1) participate in at least 48 scheduled drills or training periods during each year and serve on active duty for training at least 14 days each year; or (2) participate in training at encampments, maneuvers, outdoor target practice, or other exercises at least 15 days each year. (10 U.S.C. 10143)

Where did the applicant enlist (Country, State, and City where the applicant entered service)?

Has the applicant reenlisted?   ☐ Yes ☐ No   Where did the applicant reenlist?

Signature of Applicant

Separation Information

Is the applicant separated?	☐ Yes	☐ No
If separated, select discharge type:	☐ Honorable	☐ Other (give details in Remarks section)
Was the applicant discharged on account of alienage?	☐ Yes	☐ No (if "Yes," give details in Remarks section)

Remarks

Use for continuation of any of the above items. You should also list in the space below any **derogatory information** in your records relating to the service member's character, loyalty to the United States, disciplinary actions, convictions, or other matters concerning his or her fitness for citizenship. **(Use a blank sheet if more space is needed.)**

Certification
TO BE COMPLETED BY CERTIFYING OFFICIAL

I am authorized to certify that the information given here concerning the service of the person named on this form is correct according to the records of the

_____   Official Signature _____
Name of Department

[SEAL, *if available*]
(No State-issued notary
Public seals accepted.)   Date _____, _____

Name and Title _____

Phone Number and E-Mail Address _____

Form N-426 (02/09/12) Y

APPENDIX 12-3

Form G-325B, Biographic Information

OMB No. 1615-0008; Expires 02/28/2015

Department of Homeland Security
U.S. Citizenship and Immigration Services

Form G-325B, Biographic Information

Family Name	First Name	Middle Name	☐ Male ☐ Female	Date of Birth *(mm/dd/yyyy)*	Citizenship/Nationality	File Number A

All Other Names Used (include names by previous marriages)	City and Country of Birth	U.S. Social Security No. *(if any)*

	Family Name	First Name	Date of Birth *(mm/dd/yyyy)*	City and Country of Birth *(if known)*	City and Country of Residence
Father					
Mother (Maiden Name)					

Current Husband or Wife (If none, so state) Family Name (For wife, give maiden name)	First Name	Date of Birth *(mm/dd/yyyy)*	City and Country of Birth	Date of Marriage *(mm/dd/yyyy)*	Place of Marriage

Former Husbands or Wives (If none, so state) Family Name (For wife, give maiden name)	First Name	Date of Birth *(mm/dd/yyyy)*	Date of Marriage *(mm/dd/yyyy)*	Place of Marriage	Date *(mm/dd/yyyy)* and Place of Termination of Marriage

Applicant's residence last 5 years. List present address first.

				From		To	
Street Name and Number	City	Province or State	Country	Month	Year	Month	Year
						Present Time	

Applicant's last address outside the United States of more than 1 year.

				From		To	
Street Name and Number	City	Province or State	Country	Month	Year	Month	Year

Applicant's employment last 5 years. (If none, so state.) List present employment first.

		From		To	
Full Name and Address of Employer	Occupation *(specify)*	Month	Year	Month	Year
				Present Time	

Last occupation abroad if not listed above. (Include all information requested above.)

This form is submitted in connection with an application for:

☐ Naturalization   ☐ Other (Specify): _____

☐ Status as Permanent Resident

If serving or ever served in the Armed Forces of the United States, complete the following:

Branch of Service	Rank	Service Number

To Other Agency: Furnish on Page 2 of this form, or by attachment hereto, any derogatory information that may be contained in your records concerning the above person for use in connection with consideration of above application and return to U.S. Citizenship and Immigration Services.

FOR USCIS USE ONLY (Office of Origin)

Office Code _____

Type of Case _____

Date _____

(Other Agency)

(All Defense Checks)

MIL PERS	AIR RESERVE
USAF PERS	ARMY PERS
SEE O.I. 328.1 FOR MAILING ADDRESS	

☐ OSI (USAF)   ☐ ONI (USN)

☐ MID G-2   ☐ PROV. MAR.

FOR STATE DEPARTMENT USE

☐ SY
☐ RSC
☐ RMR
☐ C:Visa
☐ R:Visa
☐ ORM

STATE (P.P.)	STATE (S.Y.)	OTHER

SEE O.I. 105.4 FOR MAILING ADDRESS

Form G-325B (Rev. 02/07/13) Y

Date:
Date of entry into service:
Date of separation:
Service number:

The records of this Department show the following with respect to the subject of your inquiry:
All organizations, clubs, or societies in the United States, or in any other country, of which subject was a member at any time, and dates thereof. (If none, write "None.")

All arrests, convictions, disciplinary actions, court martial proceedings, and illegal or immoral conduct in which subject involved, including dates and results thereof. (If none, write "None.")

Details of any oral or written statements, conduct, behavior, or associations of the subject that may indicate belief in, advocacy of or preference or sympathy for Communism, or any other foreign ideology inconsistent with loyalty to the United States, or the form of Government of the United States or attachment to the principles of the U.S. Constitution. (If none, write "None.")

Additional information or references.

I certify that the information here given concerning the person named is correct according to the records of the:

Name of Department or Organization: _____

Printed Name of Official: _____

Signature of Official: _____

By: _____

Form G-325B (Rev. 02/07/13) Y Page 2

Instructions

What Is the Purpose of This Form?

USCIS will use the information you provide on this form to process your application or petition.

Complete this biographical information form and include it with the application or petition you are submitting to U.S. Citizenship and Immigration Services (USCIS).

If you have any questions on how to complete the form, call our National Customer Service Center at **1-800-375-5283**. For TDD (hearing impaired) call: **1-800-767-1833**.

Privacy Act Notice

We ask for the information on this form, and associated evidence, to determine if you have established eligibility for the immigration benefit for which you are filing. Our legal right to ask for this information can be found in the Immigration and Nationality Act, as amended. We may provide this information to other government agencies. Failure to provide this information, and any requested evidence, may delay a final decision or result in denial of your immigration benefit.

Paperwork Reduction Act

An agency may not conduct or sponsor an information collection and a person is not required to respond to a collection of information unless it displays a currently valid OMB control number. The public reporting burden for this collection of information is estimated at 25 minutes per response, including the time for reviewing instructions and completing and submitting the form. Send comments regarding this burden estimate or any other aspect of this collection of information, including suggestions for reducing this burden, to: U.S. Citizenship and Immigration Services, Regulatory Coordination Division, Office of Policy and Strategy, 20 Massachusetts Avenue, NW, Washington, DC 20529-2140, OMB No. 1615-0008. **Do not mail your completed Form G-325B to this address.**

APPENDIX 12-4

Form N-644, Application for Posthumous Citizenship

OMB No. 1615-0059; Expires 12/31/2015

Department of Homeland Security
U.S. Citizenship and Immigration Services

Instructions for N-644, Application for Posthumous Citizenship

What Is the Purpose of This Form?

Public Law 101-249, as amended, provides that an alien or non-citizen national of the United States who dies as a result of injury or disease incurred by active duty with the U.S. Armed Forces during specified periods of military hostilities may be granted U.S. citizenship.

If the application is approved, a Certificate of Citizenship will be issued in the name of the deceased veteran.

The certificate establishes that the decedent is considered a citizen of the United States as of the date of his or her death. Posthumous citizenship is an honorary status commemorating the bravery and sacrifices of the veteran. The certificate allows certain qualifying family members to apply for benefits under section 319(d) of the INA or remain classified as immediate relatives for obtaining lawful permanent residence.

When Should I Use Form N-644?

The application must be filed no later than two years after the date of the decedent's death.

Who May File Form N-644?

1. You may file this form only if your relationship to the decedent was:

   A. Spouse;

   B. Father/Mother;

   C. Son/Daughter;

   D. Brother/Sister.

   OR

2. You are the decedent's representative, defined as:

   A. Executor or administrator of decedent's estate;

   B. Guardian, conservator, or committee of decedent's next-of-kin;

   C. Service organization recognized by the Department of Veterans Affairs; or

   D. The Secretary of Defense or the Secretary's designee with USCIS after request by the next-of-kin.

NOTE: After a Certificate of Citizenship has been issued for a veteran, U.S. Citizenship and Immigration Services (USCIS) will **not** approve any later application on his or her behalf, except in the case of an application to replace a certificate that was lost, mutilated, or destroyed.

General Instructions

Step 1. Fill Out Form N-644

1. Type or print legibly in black ink.

2. If extra space is needed to complete any item, attach a continuation sheet, indicate the item number, and date and sign each sheet.

3. Answer all questions fully and accurately. State that an item is not applicable with "N/A." If the answer is none, write "none."

4. **Complete only Part I** of this application. **Do not write in Parts II, III, or IV**, which are reserved for the use of the executive departments.

Step 2. General Requirements

To qualify for posthumous citizenship, the decedent must have been an alien or non-citizen national of the United States who:

1. Served honorably in an active-duty status in the military, air, or naval forces of the United States during:

   A. 04/06/1917 - 11/11/1918 (World War I);

   B. 09/01/1939 - 12/31/1946 (World War II);

   C. 06/25/1950 - 07/01/1955 (Korean Hostilities);

   D. 02/28/1961 - 10/15/1978 (Vietnam Hostilities);

   E. 08/02/1990 - 04/11/1991 (Persian Gulf Conflict);

   F. From 09/11/2001 until terminated by Executive Order of the President (Iraq Hostilities);

   G. Any other period of military hostilities designated by Executive Order of the President for the purpose of naturalization benefits; or

   H. A period of at least five years following enlistment or reenlistment in the U.S. Army under the Lodge Act of June 30, 1950, and who:

2. Died because of injury or disease incurred in or aggravated by that service; and

3. Met one of the following enlistment requirements:

   A. Was enlisted, reenlisted, or inducted in the United States, Panama Canal Zone, American Samoa, or Swain's Island;

   B. Was admitted to the United States as a lawful permanent resident at any time; or

   C. If a person described in (1)(F), entered the United States, Panama Canal Zone, American Samoa, or Swain's Island pursuant to military orders at some time during such service.

Evidence

Authorization documents

1. Unless you are the spouse of the decedent or the executor or administrator of the decedent's estate, you must obtain authorization from all living next-of-kin above you in the order of succession.

2. For example, if you are the decedent's brother, you would have to obtain authorization from all living relatives in classes (a), (b), and (c) in the **"Who May File Form N-644?"** section on **Page 1** of these instructions.

   The authorization must be in the form of an affidavit stating the affiant's name, address, and relationship to the decedent and authorizing you to apply for posthumous U. S. Citizenship on behalf of the decedent. If the affidavit is in a language other than English, it must be accompanied by a certified English translator.

3. If you are in category (e) or (f) of the section **"Who May File Form N-644?"** you must submit a certified copy of your letter of appointment as the executor or administrator of the decedent's estate, or as the guardian, conservator, or committee of the decedent's next-of-kin.

4. If you are in group (g) of the section **"Who May File Form N-644?"** you must submit evidence of recognition of your organization by the Department of Veterans Affairs.

Documentation of the decedent's service and death

To facilitate certification of the decedent's military service and service-connected death by the executive departments, you should submit a legible copy of each of the following documents, if available:

1. Form DD214, Certificate of Release or Discharge from Active Duty;

2. Form DD 1300, Report of Casualty/Military Death Certificate; or

3. Any other military or state issued certificate of the decedent's death.

Failure to submit any of these documents may not automatically result in the denial of your application, but will delay the certification process.

Translations

Any document containing a foreign language submitted to USCIS shall be accompanied by a full English language translation which the translator has certified as complete and accurate, and by the translator's certification that he or she is competent to translate from the foreign language into English.

Copies

Unless specifically required that an original document be filed with an application or petition, an ordinary legible photocopy may be submitted. Original documents submitted when not required will remain a part of the record, even if the submission was not required.

Where To File?

Submit your Form N-644 to the following address:

   USCIS California Service Center
   P.O. Box 10360
   Laguna Niguel, CA 92607

What Is the Filing Fee?

No fee is collected for this application.

Address Changes

If you have changed your address, you must inform USCIS of your new address. For information on filing a change of address go to the USCIS Web site at **www.uscis.gov/ addresschange** or contact the National Customer Service Center at **1-800-375-528**.

NOTE: Do not submit a change of address request to the USCIS Lockbox facilities because the USCIS Lockbox facilities do not process change of address requests.

Processing Information

Any Form N-644 that is not signed will be rejected with a notice that your Form N-644 is deficient. You may correct the deficiency and resubmit Form N-644. An application or petition is not considered properly filed until accepted by USCIS.

Initial processing

Once Form N-644 has been accepted, it will be checked for completeness, including submission of the required initial evidence. If you do not completely fill out the form, or file it without required initial evidence, you will not establish a basis for eligibility, and we may deny your Form N-644.

Will You Have to Appear for an Interview?

No. However, if the application is approved and you reside outside the United States, you will be required to appear at the nearest U.S. Embassy or consulate to sign for the Certificate of Citizenship.

Decision

The decision on Form N-644 involves a determination of whether you have established eligibility for the requested benefit. You will be notified of the decision in writing.

USCIS Forms and Information

To order USCIS forms, call our toll-free number at **1-800-870-3676**. You can also get USCIS forms and information on immigration laws, regulations, and procedures by telephoning our National Customer Service Center at **1-800-375-5283** or visiting our Internet website at **www.uscis.gov**.

As an alternative to waiting in line for assistance at your local USCIS office, you can now schedule an appointment through our Internet-based system, **InfoPass**. To access the system, visit our website. Use the **InfoPass** appointment scheduler and follow the screen prompts to set up your appointment. **InfoPass** generates an electronic appointment notice that appears on the screen.

Penalties

If you knowingly and willfully falsify or conceal a material fact or submit a false document with this Form N-644, we will deny your Form N-644 and may deny any other immigration benefit.

In addition, you will face severe penalties provided by law and may be subject to criminal prosecution.

Privacy Act Notice

We ask for the information on this form, and associated evidence, to determine if you have established eligibility for the immigration benefit for which you are filing. Our legal right to ask for this information can be found in the Immigration and Nationality Act, as amended. We may provide this information to other government agencies. Failure to provide this information, and any requested evidence, may delay a final decision or result in denial of your Form N-644.

Paperwork Reduction Act

An agency may not conduct or sponsor an information collection and a person is not required to respond to a collection of information unless it displays a currently valid OMB control number. The public reporting burden for this collection of information is estimated at 1 hour and 50 minutes per response, including the time for reviewing instructions, and completing and submitting the form. Send comments regarding this burden estimate or any other aspect of this collection of information, including suggestions for reducing this burden, to: U.S. Citizenship and Immigration Services, Regulatory Coordination Division, Office of Policy and Strategy, 20 Massachusetts Ave NW, Washington, DC 20529-2140. OMB No. 1615-0059. **Do not mail your completed Form N-644 to this address.**

OMB No. 1615-0059; Expires 12/31/2015

N-644, Application for Posthumous Citizenship

Department of Homeland Security
U.S. Citizenship and Immigration Services

For USCIS Only
Fee Stamp

Part I.   Information About the Applicant and Decedent *(To be completed by the applicant only)*

A.   Information About the Applicant

1. Name (Last/First/Middle)

_____

2. Address (Street Name and Number)

_____

(Town/City, State/Country, Zip/Postal Code)

_____

3. If Abroad, City/Country of Nearest U.S. Embassy or Consulate

_____

4. Date of Birth	5. A-Number, if applicable

6. Total Number of Authorization Affidavits Attached (See instructions)

_____

7. Telephone Number (Include Area/Country Code)

(___) _____

8. Your Relationship to Decedent at Time of His/Her Death (Check one)

Next-of-Kin

A. ☐ Spouse

B. ☐ Parent

C. ☐ Son/Daughter

D. ☐ Brother/Sister

Representative

E. ☐ Executor or Administrator of Decedent's Estate

F. ☐ Guardian, Conservator, or Committee of Decedent's Next-of-Kin

G. ☐ VA Recognized Service Organization (Name below)

(Name of Service Organization)

_____

9. E-mail Address

_____

B.   Information About the Decedent

1. Name Used During Active Service (Last/First/Middle)

_____

2. Other Names Used

_____

3. Date of Birth (mm/dd/yyyy)	4. Place of Birth (City/State/Country)
5. Date of Death (mm/dd/yyyy)	6. Place of Death (City/State/Country)

7. Immigration Status at Time of Death (Permanent Resident, Student, Visitor, etc.)

_____

_____

8. A-Number or Other USCIS File Number

_____

9. U.S. Social Security Number (If any)

_____

B. Information About the Decedent *(Continued)*

10. Father's Full Name

_____

☐ Living
☐ Deceased

B. ☐ Living   ☐ Deceased

Name (Last/First/Middle)   Date of Birth
(mm/dd/yyyy)

_____   _____

11. Mother's Maiden Name

_____

☐ Living
☐ Deceased

C. ☐ Living   ☐ Deceased

Name (Last/First/Middle)   Date of Birth
(mm/dd/yyyy)

_____   _____

12. Marital Status at Time of Death

☐ a. Married   ☐ c. Widowed

☐ b. Divorced   ☐ d. Single

D. ☐ Living   ☐ Deceased

Name (Last/First/Middle)   Date of Birth
(mm/dd/yyyy)

_____   _____

13. Military Service Serial Number *(If different from Social Security Number)*

_____

E. ☐ Living   ☐ Deceased

Name (Last/First/Middle)   Date of Birth
(mm/dd/yyyy)

_____   _____

14. Date Entered Active Duty Service (mm/dd/yyyy)

_____

15. Place Entered Active Duty Service (City/State/Country)

_____

16. Date Released From Active Duty Service (mm/dd/yyyy)

_____

24. Total Number of Brothers and Sisters (If none, write "None")

_____

17. Branch of Service	**18.** Type of Discharge
19. Military Rank at Time of Discharge	**20.** Retired From Military? ☐ Yes ☐ No

25. Complete the Following for Each Brother and Sister

A. ☐ Living   ☐ Deceased

Name (Last/First/Middle)   Date of Birth
(mm/dd/yyyy)

_____   _____

21. VA Claim Number (If any)

_____

B. ☐ Living   ☐ Deceased

Name (Last/First/Middle)   Date of Birth
(mm/dd/yyyy)

_____   _____

22. Total Number of Children (If none, write "None")

_____

C. ☐ Living   ☐ Deceased

Name (Last/First/Middle)   Date of Birth
(mm/dd/yyyy)

_____   _____

23. Complete the Following for Each Child

A. ☐ Living   ☐ Deceased

Name (Last/First/Middle)   Date of Birth
(mm/dd/yyyy)

_____   _____

D. ☐ Living   ☐ Deceased

Name (Last/First/Middle)   Date of Birth
(mm/dd/yyyy)

_____   _____

Form N-644   12/02/12   Y   Page 2

B. Information About the Decedent *(Continued)*

E. ☐ Living   ☐ Deceased

Name (Last/First/Middle)   Date of Birth
(mm/dd/yyyy)

_____   _____

F. ☐ Living   ☐ Deceased

Name (Last/First/Middle)   Date of Birth
(mm/dd/yyyy)

_____   _____

G. ☐ Living   ☐ Deceased

Name (Last/First/Middle)   Date of Birth
(mm/dd/yyyy)

_____   _____

Certificate of Applicant

I certify, under penalty of perjury under the laws of the United States of America, that the information in **Part I** is true and correct.

Signature   Date *(mm/dd/yyyy)*

_____   _____

Name (Print or Type)

_____

Address (Street Number and Name, City/Town, State/Province, Country, Zip-Postal Code

_____

_____

Part II.   To Be Completed by the Department of Defense Official for Appropriate Branch of Military Service

1. ☐ No Active Duty Records Found for This Individual

2. ☐ No Casualty Records Found for This Individual

3. ☐ Name of Decedent Correctly Shown

4. ☐ Name of Decedent Different in Records
   (List name shown in records)

   _____

5. ☐ Active Duty Service Records Found (Complete **A** through **F**)

   A. Branch of Service

   _____

   B. Date Entered Active Duty *(mm/dd/yyyy)*

   _____

   C. Place Entered Active Duty Service (City/State/Country)

   _____

   D. Service Number

   _____

   E. Date Released From Service *(mm/dd/yyyy)*

   _____

   F. Honorable Service During a Period of Hostilities (If no is checked, please provide an explanation.)
      ☐ Yes

      ☐ No _____

6. Individual Entered Service Under the Lodge Act?
   ☐ Yes   ☐ No   ☐ Unable to Determine

7. ☐ Record of Death Found (Complete **a** and **b**)
   a. Date of Death (mm/dd/yyyy)

   _____

   b. Death resulted from injury or disease incurred in or aggravated by active duty service during a period of military hostilities specified by law?

   ☐ Yes   ☐ No   ☐ Unable to Determine

8. **Certification**
   I certify the information given here concerning the *(Check one or both, as appropriate)* ☐ Service   ☐ Death

   of the individual named on this form is correct according to the records of the (name below).

   (Department of Defense Military Branch)

   _____

   Signature   Date *(mm/dd/yyyy)*

   _____   _____

   Title   Phone Number

   _____   _____

   E-mail Address

   _____

Part III.   To Be Completed by the Department of Defense Official for Appropriate Branch of Military Service

A. Certification

Based on the information received from the Department of Veterans Affairs concerning the death of the individual named on this form, I certify that the individual died on (Date *(mm/dd/yyyy)*) _____ as a result of injury or disease incurred in or aggravated by service during a period of hostilities specified by law.

Signature   Date *(mm/dd/yyyy)*

_____   _____

Title

_____

B. Unable to Certify

Based on the information received from the Department of Veterans Affairs concerning the death of the individual named on this form, I am unable to certify that the individual died as a result of injury or disease incurred in or aggravated by service during a period of hostilities specified by law.

Signature   Date *(mm/dd/yyyy)*

_____   _____

Title

_____

NOTE: Space below (Part IV) for use by U.S. Citizenship and Immigration Services Only

Part IV.   To be Completed by U.S. Citizenship and Immigration Services

☐ Applicant Authorized Next-of-Kin or Representative

☐ Positive Certification Military Service

☐ Positive Certification Service Connected Death

☐ Place of Enlistment Qualifies Under INA Section 329 (a)(1)

☐ Decedent Admitted for Lawful Permanent Residence

Action Block

Cert. #	Date Mailed						
A #	Reg. Mail #	Initial Receipt	Resubmitted	Relocated		Completed	
				Rec'd	Sent	App'd	Denied	Ret'd

APPENDIX 12-5

INS Operations Instructions Relating to Military Records

OI 328.1 Authenticated copies of military service records.

Form N-426 shall be used to obtain duly authenticated copies of certifications of military service required by sections 328 and 329 of the Act. When received, the authenticated certification shall not form a part of the petition or be attached thereto but shall be retained in the file. Form N-426, in duplicate, shall be sent to the appropriate office listed below:

IMPORTANT: If the applicant has two or more periods of service within the same branch of service, send the request to the office having the records for the latest period.

BRANCH OF SERVICE	CATEGORY OF MILITARY PERSONNEL RECORDS	OFFICE OF RECORD
AIR FORCE	All reserve members (including National Guard released from active duty and transferred to reserve) All retired reservists in a non-pay status All active duty personnel (including National Guard on active duty in Air Force) Personnel on Temporary Disability Retired List	Air Reserve Personnel Center, 3800 York Street Denver, Colorado 80205
ARMY	Officers separated before July 1, 1917 Enlisted personnel separated before November 1, 1912	USAF Military Personnel Center Military Personnel Records Division Randolph AFB Texas 78148
	All reserve members All retired personnel (except general officers)	National Records Administration National Archives Building 7th & Pennsylvania Ave., NW Washington, DC 20408
	Personnel on Temporary Disability Retired List	Commanding Officer U.S. Army Administration Center TAGO 9700 Page Boulevard St. Louis, Missouri 63132
	All officers on active duty (including National Guard on active duty in U.S. Army)	Commander, U.S. Army Military Personnel Center Attn: DAPC-MRS-S 200 Stovall Street Alexandria, Virginia 22332

BRANCH OF SERVICE	CATEGORY OF MILITARY PERSONNEL RECORDS	OFFICE OF RECORD
	Enlisted personnel on active duty	Commanding Officer U.S. Army Enlisted Personnel Support Center Fort Benjamin Harrison, Indiana 46249
	Current National Guard Enlisted members	Adjutant General of Appropriate State National Guard (See addresses)
COAST GUARD	All personnel separated less than six months All active Coast Guard personnel and members of the reserve Enlisted personnel temporarily retired less than five years	Commandant, G-PE-3/TP/45 U.S. Coast Guard 2100 2nd Street, S.W Washington, DC 20593
MARINE CORPS	All personnel on active duty Reserve Officers Class II enlisted reserve Officer and enlisted personnel separated less than four months Personnel on Temporary Disability Retired List	Commandant of the Marine Corps Headquarters U.S. Marine Corps Washington, DC 20380
	Individual Ready Reserve (formerly class II reservists - inactive)	Commanding Officer Marine Corps Reserve Support Center 10950 El Monte Shawnee Mission Overland Park, Missouri 66211
NAVY	Officers on active duty and those separated less than one year Enlisted personnel on active duty and those separated less than six months Members of enlisted reserve in drill status Members of the enlisted reserve status pool who will not be eligible for discharge for more than 18 months. Reserve officers and members on Temporary Disability Retired List	Department of the Navy Commander Naval Military Personnel Command Washington, DC 20370-5000
ALL	If your request does not pertain to any of the categories listed above, address your inquiry to:	National Personnel Records Center (Military Personnel Records) 9700 Page Boulevard St. Louis, Missouri 63132

DEPARTMENTS OF THE ARMY AND THE AIR FORCE NATIONAL GUARD BUREAU Washington, DC 20310 STATE ADJUTANTS GENERAL

STATE	ADDRESS
Alabama	P.O. Box 3711, Montgomery, AL 36193-4701
Alaska	3601 C Street, Suite 620, Anchorage, AK 99503-5989

STATE	ADDRESS
Arizona	5636 E. McDowell Road, Phoenix, AZ 85008-3495
Arkansas	Camp Robinson, N. Little Rock, AR 72118-2200
California	2829 Watt Avenue, Sacramento, CA 95821-4405
Colorado	300 Logan Street, Denver, CO 80203-4072
Connecticut	360 Broad Street, Hartford, CT 06105-3795
Delaware	First Regiment Road, Wilmington, DE 19808-219
Florida	State Arsenal, St. Augustine, FL 32084-1008
Georgia	Dept. of Defense, Mil. Div., P.O. Box 17965, Atlanta, GA 30316-0965
Hawaii	3949 Diamond Head Road, Honolulu, HI 96816-4495
Idaho	P.O. Box 45, Boise, ID 83707-0045
Illinois	1301 N. MacArthur Blvd., Springfield, IL 62702-2399
Indiana	Mil. Dept. of Indiana, P.O. Box 41326, Indianapolis, IN 46241-0326
Iowa	Camp Dodge, 7700 Northwest Beaver Drive, Johnston, IA 50131-1902
Kansas	P.O. Box C-300, Topeka, KS 66601-0300
Kentucky	Boone National Guard Center, Frankfort, KY 40601-6168
Louisiana	HQ Bldg., Jackson Barracks, New Orleans, LA 70146-0330
Maine	Camp Keyes, Augusta, ME 04333-0033
Maryland	Military Dept, 5th Regiment Armory, Baltimore, MD 21201-2288
Massachusetts	905 Commonwealth Avenue, Boston, MA 02215-1399
Michigan	2500 S. Washington Avenue, Lansing, MI 48913-5101
Minnesota	Veterans Service Bldg., St. Paul, MN 55155-2098
Mississippi	P.O. Box 5027, Jackson, MS 39216-1027

STATE	ADDRESS
Missouri	1717 Industrial Drive, Jefferson City, MO 65101-1468
Montana	P.O. Box 4789, Helena, MT 59604-4789
Nebraska	1300 Military Road, Lincoln, NE 68508-1090
Nevada	2525 S. Carson Street, Carson City, NV 89701-5502
New Hampshire	State Mil Res, #1 Airport Road, Concord, NH 03301-5353
New Jersey	Eggert Crossing Road, CN 340, Trenton, NJ 08625-0340
New Mexico	P.O. Box 4277, Santa Fe, NM 87502-4277
New York	330 Old Niskayuna Road, Latham, NY 12110-2224
North Carolina	4105 Reedy Creek Road, Raleigh, NC 27607-6410
North Dakota	Fraine Barracks, P.O. Box 5511, Bismarck, ND 58502-5511
Ohio	2825 W. Granville Road, Worthington, OH 43085-2712
Oklahoma	3501 Military Circle, NE, Oklahoma City, OK 73111-4398
Oregon	2150 Fairgrounds Road, NE, Salem, OR 97303-3241
Pennsylvania	Department of Military Affairs, Annville, PA 17003-5002
Rhode Island	1051 N. Main Street, Providence, RI 02904-5717
South Carolina	The Rembert C. Dennis Bldg., 1000 Assembly St., Columbia, SC 29201-3117
South Dakota	2823 West Main, Rapid City, SD 57702-8196
Tennessee	Houston Barracks, P.O. Box 41502, Nashville, TN 37204-1501
Texas	P.O. Box 5218, Austin, TX 78763-5218
Utah	P.O. Box 8000, Salt Lake City, UT 84108-0900
Vermont	Bldg., #1, Camp Johnson, Winooski, VT 05404-1697
Virginia	501 East Franklin Street, Richmond, VA 23219-2317
Washington	Camp Murray, Tacoma, WA 98430-5000

STATE	ADDRESS
West Virginia	1703 Coonskin Drive, Charleston, WV 25311-1085
Wisconsin	P.O. Box 8111, Madison, WI 53708-8111
Wyoming	P.O. Box 1709, Cheyenne, WY 82003-1709
Other:	
Dist. of Col. 2001 E. Capitol Street,	NG Armory, Washington, DC 20003-1719
Guam	622 E. Harmon Industrial Park Road, Bldg. 31, Fort Juna Muna, Tamuning, Guam 96911-4421
Puerto Rico	P.O. Box 3786, San Juan, PR 00904-3786
Virgin Islands	P.O. Box 1150, Christiansted, St. Croix, U.S. VI 00820-1150

OI 328.2 Verification of National Guard service as qualifying service.

(This section inapplicable to certification of active service for section 329. See OI 328.1.) A request on form N-426 for verification of a period of ready reserve service in the Army or Air National Guard shall be addressed to the Office of the Adjutant General of the specific State National Guard involved. Since a State National Guard Adjutant General has no authority to certify that a State National Guard was Federally recognized as a reserve component of the Armed Forces of the United States during a period of verified service, the State National Guard Adjutant General involved shall be requested, by cover letter, to certify the period or periods of honorable reserve service on the form and then forward it directly to the Chief, National Guard Bureau, Department of the Army and the Air Force, Washington, D.C. 20310, so that the further required certification can be made. The cover letter should request that the form be returned directly to the originating Service field office by the National Guard Bureau.

The above instructions apply only to verification of periods of active or reserve service for petitioners under section 328. Verification of active duty periods of National Guardsmen for section 329 purposes (such as initial active duty for training or a Federal mobilization call to active duty) need not be forwarded to the National Guard Bureau for endorsement. Such active duty periods are, by their nature, Federally-recognized service, and may be certified by the State Adjutant General alone. The N-426 will then be returned directly to the originating office.

OI 328.3 Outside investigation when eligibility based on reserve service.

When reserve service forms a substantial part of the requisite three year period of service, an outside investigation shall be conducted to develop proof of the petitioner's qualifications for naturalization during the period of reserve serviced. The outside investigation or testimony shall be in addition to the military certifications required by the statute.

OI 328.4 Types of discharges.

32 CFR, Part 41, sets forth the types of discharges from military service, the basis therefor, and the procedures for effecting discharges.

OI 328.5 Verification when official records have been destroyed.

U.S. Army records for the years preceding 1960 have been destroyed, and verification of service cannot be obtained from St. Louis. A petitioner, claiming military service before 1960, shall submit original DD Form 214, with his Form N-426. The latter will not be forwarded to St. Louis, but shall be retained in the "A" file. In addition, the petitioner shall be called upon to submit his discharge certificate and any other available documentation relating to the claimed period of service, in support of the claim. The petitioner's signature must be carefully compared to signatures appearing on documents relating to military service, and the petitioner, at the time of filing the petition, and without advance warning, shall be required to present documentation establishing his identity as the person named in the DD Form 214, such as drivers license, alien registration receipt card, possible lease of apartment or home. In addition, a personal investigation at the claimed place of residence or employment shall be conducted, the investigator being fortified with a photo of the petitioner, to determine the claimed identity of the petitioner as the veteran named in the DD Form 214. Upon the ultimate conclusion that the claim is authentic, the DD Form 214 may be accepted as secondary evidence and presented, on that issue, grant, facts to court.

Where verification of U.S. Army service after 1959, on Form N-426 cannot be verified after two requested at least two months apart, and the lapse of six months, the procedure outlined hereinafter for the use of DD Form 214 as secondary evidence shall be followed.

No secondary evidence shall be acceptable in any case, unless supported by a DD Form 214, and proof of identity in the manner indicated.

Records of the U.S. Air Force, for names starting with the letters Hu and continuing through the alphabet through the letter Z are not available for the periods prior to 1965. The procedure outlined above shall be followed respecting the use of secondary evidence.

Records of service for the Navy, Marines and Coast Guard are available and regular Form N-426 procedures shall be followed until verification cannot be obtained under procedures herein, at which point secondary evidence (DD Form 214) procedures will be followed.

APPENDIX 12-6

Executive Order on Expedited Naturalization of Aliens and Noncitizen Nationals Serving in Active-Duty Status During the War on Terrorism

the
White House
President George W. Bush

For Immediate Release
Office of the Press Secretary
July 3, 2002

Executive Order Expedited Naturalization of Aliens and Noncitizen Nationals Serving in An Active-Duty Status During the War on Terrorism

By the authority vested in me as President by the Constitution and the laws of the United States of America, including section 329 of the Immigration and Nationality Act (8 U.S.C. 1440) (the "Act"), and solely in order to provide expedited naturalization for aliens and noncitizen nationals serving in an active-duty status in the Armed Forces of the United States during the period of the war against terrorists of global reach, it is hereby ordered as follows:

For the purpose of determining qualification for the exception from the usual requirements for naturalization, I designate as a period in which the Armed Forces of the United States were engaged in armed conflict with a hostile foreign force the period beginning on September 11, 2001. Such period will be deemed to terminate on a date designated by future Executive Order. Those persons serving honorably in active-duty status in the Armed Forces of the United States, during the period beginning on September 11, 2001, and terminating on the date to be so designated, are eligible for naturalization in accordance with the statutory exception to the naturalization requirements, as provided in section 329 of the Act. Nothing contained in this order is intended to affect, nor does it affect, any other power, right, or obligation of the United States, its agencies, officers, employees, or any other person under Federal law or the law of nations.

GEORGE W. BUSH
THE WHITE HOUSE,
July 3, 2002.

# # #

APPENDIX 12-7

National Defense Authorization Act for Fiscal Year 2004

Pub. L. 108-136

National Defense Authorization Act for Fiscal Year 2004

108th Congress

November 24, 2003

116 Stat.

H.R.1588

SEC. 1701. REQUIREMENTS FOR NATURALIZATION THROUGH SERVICE IN THE ARMED FORCES OF THE UNITED STATES

(a) REDUCTION OF PERIOD FOR REQUIRED SERVICE- Section 328(a) of the Immigration and Nationality Act (8 U.S.C. 1439(a)) is amended by striking 'three years,' and inserting 'one year,'.

(b) PROHIBITION ON IMPOSITION OF FEES RELATING TO NATURALIZATION- Title III of the Immigration and Nationality Act (8 U.S.C. 1401 et seq.) is amended--

(1) in section 328(b)--

(A) in paragraph (3)--

(i) by striking 'honorable. The' and inserting 'honorable (the'; and

(ii) by striking 'discharge.' and inserting 'discharge); and'; and

(B) by adding at the end the following:

`(4) notwithstanding any other provision of law, no fee shall be charged or collected from the applicant for filing the application, or for the issuance of a certificate of naturalization upon being granted citizenship, and no clerk of any State court shall charge or collect any fee for such services unless the laws of the State require such charge to be made, in which case nothing more than the portion of the fee required to be paid to the State shall be charged or collected.'; and

(2) in section 329(b)--

(A) in paragraph (2), by striking 'and' at the end;

(B) in paragraph (3), by striking the period at the end and inserting '; and'; and

(C) by adding at the end the following:

`(4) notwithstanding any other provision of law, no fee shall be charged or collected from the applicant for filing a petition for naturalization or for the issuance of a certificate of naturalization upon citizenship being granted to the applicant, and no clerk of any State court shall charge or collect any fee for such services unless the laws of the State require such charge to be made, in which case nothing more than the portion of the fee required to be paid to the State shall be charged or collected.'.

(c) REVOCATION OF CITIZENSHIP FOR SEPARATION FROM MILITARY SERVICE UNDER OTHER THAN HONORABLE CONDITIONS-

990

(1) IN GENERAL- Title III of the Immigration and Nationality Act (8 U.S.C. 1401 et seq.) is amended--

(A) by adding at the end of section 328 the following:

`(f) Citizenship granted pursuant to this section may be revoked in accordance with section 340 if the person is separated from the Armed Forces under other than honorable conditions before the person has served honorably for a period or periods aggregating five years. Such ground for revocation shall be in addition to any other provided by law, including the grounds described in section 340. The fact that the naturalized person was separated from the service under other than honorable conditions shal l be proved by a duly authenticated certification from the executive department under which the person was serving at the time of separation. Any period or periods of service shall be proved by duly authenticated copies of the records of the executive departments having custody of the records of such service.'; and

(B) by amending section 329(c) to read as follows:

`(c) Citizenship granted pursuant to this section may be revoked in accordance with section 340 if the person is separated from the Armed Forces under other than honorable conditions before the person has served honorably for a period or periods aggregating five years. Such ground for revocation shall be in addition to any other provided by law, including the grounds described in section 340. The fact that the naturalized person was separated from the service under other than honorable conditions shall be proved by a duly authenticated certification from the executive department under which the person was serving at the time of separation. Any period or periods of service shall be proved by duly authenticated copies of the records of the executive departments having custody of the records of such service.'.

(2) EFFECTIVE DATE- The amendments made by paragraph (1) shall apply to citizenship granted on or after the date of the enactment of this Act.

(d) NATURALIZATION PROCEEDINGS OVERSEAS FOR MEMBERS OF THE ARMED FORCES- Notwithstanding any other provision of law, the Secretary of Homeland Security, the Secretary of State, and the Secretary of Defense shall ensure that any applications, interviews, filings, oaths, ceremonies, or other proceedings under title III of the Immigration and Nationality Act (8 U.S.C. 1401 et seq.) relating to naturalization of members of the Armed Forces are available through United States embassies, consulates, and as practicable, United States military installations overseas.

(e) FINALIZATION OF NATURALIZATION PROCEEDINGS FOR MEMBERS OF THE ARMED FORCES- Not later than 90 days after the date of the enactment of this Act, the Secretary of Defense shall prescribe a policy that facilitates the opportunity for a member of the Armed Forces to finalize naturalization for which the member has applied. The policy shall include, for such purpose, the following:

(1) A high priority for grant of emergency leave.

(2) A high priority for transportation on aircraft of, or chartered by, the Armed Forces.

(f) TECHNICAL AND CONFORMING AMENDMENT- Section 328(b)(3) of the Immigration and Nationality Act (8 U.S.C. 1439(b)(3)) is amended by striking 'Attorney General' and inserting 'Secretary of Homeland Security'.

SEC. 1702. NATURALIZATION BENEFITS FOR MEMBERS OF THE SELECTED RESERVE OF THE READY RESERVE.

Section 329(a) of the Immigration and Nationality Act (8 U.S.C. 1440(a)) is amended by inserting ' as a member of the Selected Reserve of the Ready Reserve or' after 'has served honorably'.

SEC. 1703. EXTENSION OF POSTHUMOUS BENEFITS TO SURVIVING SPOUSES, CHILDREN, AND PARENTS.

(a) TREATMENT AS IMMEDIATE RELATIVES-

(1) SPOUSES- Notwithstanding the second sentence of section 201(b)(2)(A)(i) of the Immigration and Nationality Act (8 U.S.C. 1151(b)(2)(A)(i)), in the case of an alien who was the spouse of a citizen of the United States at the time of the citizen's death and was not legally separated from the citizen at the time of the citizen's death, if the citizen served honorably in an active duty status in the military, air, or naval forces of the United States and died as a result of injury or disease incur red in or aggravated by combat, the alien (and each child of the alien) shall be considered, for purposes of section 201(b) of such Act, to remain an immediate relative after the date of the citizen's death, but only if the alien files a petition under section 204(a)(1)(A)(ii) of such Act within 2 years after such date and only until the date the alien remarries. For purposes of such section 204(a)(1)(A)(ii), an alien granted relief under the preceding sentence shall be considered an alien spouse described in the second sentence of section 201(b)(2)(A)(i) of such Act.

(2) CHILDREN-

(A) IN GENERAL- In the case of an alien who was the child of a citizen of the United States at the time of the citizen's death, if the citizen served honorably in an active duty status in the military, air, or naval forces of the United States and died as a result of injury or disease incurred in or aggravated by combat, the alien shall be considered, for purposes of section 201(b) of the Immigration and Nationality Act (8 U.S.C. 1151(b)), to remain an immediate relative after t he date of the citizen's death (regardless of changes in age or marital status thereafter), but only if the alien files a petition under subparagraph (B) within 2 years after such date.

(B) PETITIONS- An alien described in subparagraph (A) may file a petition with the Secretary of Homeland Security for classification of the alien under section 201(b)(2)(A)(i) of the Immigration and Nationality Act (8 U.S.C. 1151(b)(2)(A)(i)). For purposes of such Act, such a petition shall be considered a petition filed under section 204(a)(1)(A) of such Act (8 U.S.C. 1154(a)(1)(A)).

(3) PARENTS-

(A) IN GENERAL- In the case of an alien who was the parent of a citizen of the United States at the time of the citizen's death, if the citizen served honorably in an active duty status in the military, air, or naval forces of the United States and died as a result of injury or disease incurred in or aggravated by combat, the alien shall be considered, for purposes of section 201(b) of the Immigration and Nationality Act (8 U.S.C. 1151(b)), to remain an immediate relative after the date of th e citizen's death (regardless of changes in age or marital status thereafter), but only if the alien files a petition under subparagraph (B) within 2 years after such date.

(B) PETITIONS- An alien described in subparagraph (A) may file a petition with the Secretary of Homeland Security for classification of the alien under section 201(b)(2)(A)(i) of the Immigration and Nationality Act (8 U.S.C. 1151(b)(2)(A)(i)). For purposes of such Act, such a petition shall be considered a petition filed under section 204(a)(1)(A) of such Act (8 U.S.C. 1154(a)(1)(A)).

(C) EXCEPTION- Notwithstanding section 201(b)(2)(A)(i) of the Immigration and Nationality Act (8 U.S.C. 1151(b)(2)(A)(i)), for purposes of this paragraph, a citizen described in subparagraph (A) does not have to be 21 years of age for a parent to benefit under this paragraph.

(b) APPLICATIONS FOR ADJUSTMENT OF STATUS BY SURVIVING SPOUSES, CHILDREN, AND PARENTS-

(1) IN GENERAL- Notwithstanding subsections (a) and (c) of section 245 of the Immigration and Nationality Act (8 U.S.C. 1255), any alien who was the spouse, child, or parent of an alien described in paragraph (2), and who applied for adjustment of status prior to the death described in paragraph (2)(B), may have such application adjudicated as if such death had not occurred.

(2) ALIEN DESCRIBED-

(A) An alien is described in this paragraph if the alien-- (A) served honorably in an active duty status in the military, air, or naval forces of the United States;

(B) died as a result of injury or disease incurred in or aggravated by combat; and

(C) was granted posthumous citizenship under section 329A of the Immigration and Nationality Act (8 U.S.C. 1440-1).

(c) SPOUSES AND CHILDREN OF LAWFUL PERMANENT RESIDENT ALIENS-

(1) TREATMENT AS IMMEDIATE RELATIVES-

(A) IN GENERAL- A spouse or child of an alien described in paragraph (3) who is included in a petition for classification as a family-sponsored immigrant under section 203(a)(2) of the Immigration and Nationality Act (8 U.S.C. 1153(a)(2)) that was filed by such alien, shall be considered (if the spouse or child has not been admitted or approved for lawful permanent residence by such date) a valid petitioner for immediate relative status under section 201(b)(2)(A)(i) of the Immigration and Nationality Act (8 U.S.C. 1151(b)(2)(A)(i)). Such spouse or child shall be eligible for deferred action, advance parole, and work authorization.

(B) PETITIONS- An alien spouse or child described in subparagraph (A) may file a petition with the Secretary of Homeland Security for classification of the alien under section 201(b)(2)(A)(i) of the Immigration and Nationality Act (8 U.S.C. 1151(b)(2)(A)(i)). For purposes of such Act, such a petition shall be considered a petition filed under section 204(a)(1)(A) of such Act (8 U.S.C. 1154(a)(1)(A)).

(2) SELF-PETITIONS- Any spouse or child of an alien described in paragraph (3) who is not a beneficiary of a petition for classification as a family-sponsored immigrant may file a petition for such classification under section 201(b)(2)(A)(i) of the Immigration and Nationality Act (8 U.S.C. 1151(b)(2)(A)(i)) with the Secretary of Homeland Security, but only if the spouse or child files a petition within 2 years after such date. Such spouse or child shall be eligible for deferred action, advance parole, and work authorization.

(3) ALIEN DESCRIBED- An alien is described in this paragraph if the alien--

(A) served honorably in an active duty status in the military, air, or naval forces of the United States;

(B) died as a result of injury or disease incurred in or aggravated by combat; and

(C) was granted posthumous citizenship under section 329A of the Immigration and Nationality Act (8 U.S.C. 1440-1).

(d) PARENTS OF LAWFUL PERMANENT RESIDENT ALIENS-

(1) SELF-PETITIONS- Any parent of an alien described in paragraph (2) may file a petition for classification under section 201(b)(2)(A)(i) of the Immigration and Nationality Act (8 U.S.C. 1151(b)(2)(A)(i)), but only if the parent files a petition within 2 years after such date. For purposes of such Act, such petition shall be considered a petition filed under section 204(a)(1)(A) of such Act (8 U.S.C. 1154(a)(1)(A)). Such parent shall be eligible for deferred action, advance parole, and work authorization.

(2) ALIEN DESCRIBED- An alien is described in this paragraph if the alien--

(A) served honorably in an active duty status in the military, air, or naval forces of the United States;

(B) died as a result of injury or disease incurred in or aggravated by combat; and

(C) was granted posthumous citizenship under section 329A of the Immigration and Nationality Act (8 U.S.C. 1440-1).

(e) WAIVER OF GROUND FOR INADMISSIBILITY- In determining the admissibility of any alien accorded an immigration benefit under this section for purposes of the Immigration and Nationality Act, the ground for inadmissibility specified in section 212(a)(4) of such Act (8 U.S.C. 1182(a)(4)) shall not apply.

(f) NATURALIZATION FOR SURVIVING SPOUSES-

(1) IN GENERAL- Section 319(d) of the Immigration and Nationality Act (8 U.S.C. 1430(d)) is amended by adding at the end the following: 'For purposes of this subsection, the terms 'United States citizen' and 'citizen spouse' include a person granted posthumous citizenship under section 329A.'.

(2) EFFECTIVE DATE- The amendment made by paragraph (1) shall apply with respect to persons granted posthumous citizenship under section 329A of the Immigration and Nationality Act (8 U.S.C. 1440-1) due to death on or after September 11, 2001.

(g) BENEFITS TO SURVIVORS; TECHNICAL AMENDMENT- Section 329A of the Immigration and Nationality Act (8 U.S.C. 1440-1) is amended--

(1) by striking subsection (e); and

(2) by striking 'Attorney General' each place that term appears and inserting 'Secretary of Homeland Security'.

(h) TECHNICAL AND CONFORMING AMENDMENTS- Section 319(d) of the Immigration and Nationality Act (8 U.S.C. 1430(d)) is amended--

(1) by inserting ', child, or parent' after 'surviving spouse';

(2) by inserting ', parent, or child' after 'whose citizen spouse'; and

(3) by striking 'who was living' and inserting 'who, in the case of a surviving spouse, was living'.

SEC. 1704.   EXPEDITED PROCESS FOR GRANTING POSTHUMOUS CITIZENSHIP TO MEMBERS OF THE ARMED FORCES.

Section 329A of the Immigration and Nationality Act (8 U.S.C. 1440-1) is amended-- (1) by striking subsection (c) and inserting the following:

(c) REQUESTS FOR POSTHUMOUS CITIZENSHIP-

(1) IN GENERAL- A request for the granting of posthumous citizenship to a person described in subsection (b) may be filed on behalf of that person--

(A) upon locating the next-of-kin, and if so requested by the next-of-kin, by the Secretary of Defense or the Secretary's designee with the Bureau of

Citizenship and Immigration Services in the Department of Homeland Security immediately upon the death of that person; or

(B) by the next-of-kin.

(2) APPROVAL- The Director of the Bureau of Citizenship and Immigration Services shall approve a request for posthumous citizenship filed by the next-of-kin in accordance with paragraph (1)(B) if--

(A) the request is filed not later than 2 years after--

(i) the date of enactment of this section; or

(ii) the date of the person's death;

whichever date is later;

(B) the request is accompanied by a duly authenticated certificate from the executive department under which the person served which states that the person satisfied the requirements of paragraphs (1) and (2) of subsection (b); and

(C) the Director finds that the person satisfied the requirement of subsection (b)(3).'; and

(2) by striking subsection (d) and inserting the following:

(d) DOCUMENTATION OF POSTHUMOUS CITIZENSHIP- If the Director of the Bureau of Citizenship and Immigration Services approves the request referred to in subsection (c), the Director shall send to the next-of-kin of the person who is granted citizenship, a suitable document which states that the United States considers the person to have been a citizen of the United States at the time of the person's death.'.

SEC. 1705. EFFECTIVE DATE.

(a) IN GENERAL- Except as provided in subsection (b), this title and the amendments made by this title shall take effect as if enacted on September 11, 2001.

(b) EXCEPTION- The amendments made by sections 1701(b) (relating to naturalization fees) and 1701(d) (relating to naturalization proceedings overseas) shall take effect on October 1, 2004.

Speaker of the House of Representatives.

Vice President of the United States and

President of the Senate.

APPENDIX 12-8

USCIS Fact Sheet: Naturalization Process for the Military

Home >
Military

Military

Members of the Military and their Families

This section of the USCIS Web site contains immigration information and links to resources geared specifically for members of the military and their families.

USCIS is continuously working with the Department of Defense to ensure the military community has accurate and up-to-date information about immigration services and benefits.

If you are a U.S. armed forces member seeking to petition for your family member for permanent residence (green card), see the "Family" link to the right.

Citizenship for Military Members & Dependents

Members and veterans of the U.S. armed forces, and their dependents may be eligible for citizenship under special provisions of law. For more information, see the "Citizenship for Military Personnel & Family Members" link to the left.

Family Based Survivor Benefits (for Relatives)

Immediate relatives of U.S. armed forces members who die as a result of combat while in an active duty status may be eligible for certain "survivor" immigration benefits, including citizenship. For more information, see the "Family Based Survivor Benefits" link to the left.

Military Help Line

USCIS has established a toll-free "Military Help Line" exclusively for members of the military and their families: 1-877-CIS-4MIL (1-877-247-4645). For more information, see the "Military Help Line" link to the left.

This page can be found at: http://www.uscis.gov/military

Last updated: 02/17/2011

APPENDIX 12-9

USCIS Fact Sheet: Requirements for Naturalization Abroad by Spouses of Members of the U.S. Armed Forces

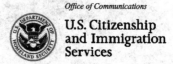

Office of Communications

U.S. Citizenship and Immigration Services

Fact Sheet

Oct. 2, 2008

REQUIREMENTS FOR NATURALIZATION ABROAD BY SPOUSES OF MEMBERS OF THE U.S. ARMED FORCES

On January 28, 2008, President Bush signed the National Defense Authorization Act for Fiscal Year 2008 (H.R.4986 / Public Law 110-181) into law. Part of that law is a new section 319(e) of the Immigration and Nationality Act (INA) which allows certain eligible spouses of members of the U.S. armed forces to naturalize abroad without traveling to the United States for any part of the naturalization process.

To be eligible for naturalization abroad, lawful permanent resident spouses of members of the U.S. armed forces, who live abroad on official military orders, must meet the requirements of either section 316(a) or 319(a) of the INA at the time of filing.

- Section 319(a) applies to individuals who have been lawful permanent residents for three years as the current spouse of a U.S. citizen, and continue to be married that U.S. citizen spouse.
- Section 316(a) applies to spouses who have been lawful permanent residents for five years.

For naturalization purposes, the time eligible spouses have spent abroad on official military orders may count for both continuous residency and physical presence in the United States.

Individuals applying for naturalization abroad as the spouse of a member of the armed forces must live in marital union with that member of the armed forces. However, involuntary separations due to circumstances beyond their control, such as military deployments, do not prevent naturalization.

A spouse of a member of the armed forces must have official military orders authorizing them to accompany their spouse abroad, and must accompany or live with that member of the armed forces as provided in those orders.

Note that only those eligible spouses who prefer naturalization abroad should apply for that option. Those who prefer to apply for naturalization in the United States may still elect to do so. Eligible spouses who live abroad and want to naturalize abroad should follow these instructions:

Submit a completed and signed *Application for Naturalization* **(Form N-400)** – In Part 2 (*Information About Your Eligibility*), please note whether the eligibility is under INA Section 316(a) or 319(a) and mark Section D (Other). Write in: "319(e) Overseas Naturalization." Include the following information:

Cover Letter – USCIS encourages applicants to place a brief cover letter on top of the application package with the heading "319(e): Deliver to Military N-400 Point of Contact" explaining their desire to naturalize abroad. The cover letter should include the applicant's current address of residence abroad and indicate whether they qualify for naturalization under either Section 316(a) or 319(a) of the INA. Applicants should print their name and overseas address (both local and APO/FPO) and include the location of the USCIS office overseas most convenient to conduct the interview (for example, "the U.S. Consulate in Frankfurt").

Form DD-1278 – Include a signed and completed Form DD-1278, "Certificate of Overseas Assignment to Support Application to File Petition for Naturalization" from the military official certifying the applicant has "concurrent travel orders" and is authorized to join their spouse military service member abroad.

Fingerprint Cards – Include two completed fingerprint cards (FD-258). Those applying overseas must have their fingerprints taken at a U.S. military base, an overseas USCIS field office, or an American Embassy/Consulate. Individuals applying in the United States must have their fingerprints taken at a USCIS Application Support Center.

Marriage Certificate – Provide proof of the current marriage and, if applicable, the legal end of all prior marriages for both the applicant and the spouse (photocopies of marriage or death/divorce certificates).

Proof of U.S. Citizenship – The applicant must show proof the military spouse is a U.S. citizen if applying under INA Section 319(a). Acceptable forms of evidence include copies of a valid U.S. passport, a U.S. birth certificate, certificate of naturalization, certificate of citizenship (A or AA), or the Registration of Birth Abroad, (Form FS-240).

Photos – Two identical passport-style photos (See instruction sheet).

Proof of LPR Status – Submit a photocopy of the applicant's Permanent Resident Card (both front and back) or I-551 stamp to show proof the applicant is a Lawful Permanent Resident of the U.S.

Evidence of Marital Relationship – This includes, but is not limited to: birth certificates for children born to you and your spouse, joint bank accounts, joint tax returns, etc.

Fees – Include the correct fee. The amount depends on from where the application is filed:

- Applicants who file from outside the United States and had their fingerprints taken overseas (see above), should submit a check or money order for $595(USD) with the application.
- Applicants filing from within the United States should submit a single check or money order of $675(USD) with the application (the N-400 fee of $595 and biometrics fee of $80 combined).
- Make the check or money order payable to the "Department of Homeland Security" or "U.S. Citizenship and Immigration Services." Note: for payment overseas, please check local payment procedures.

Mailing Address – USCIS recommends that applicants submit all 319(e) naturalization applications to the USCIS overseas office having jurisdiction over the spouse's overseas residence, or to USCIS at the following address:

Nebraska Service Center
P.O. Box 87426
Lincoln, NE 68501-7426

For private courier deliveries, send to:
Nebraska Service Center
850 S Street
Lincoln, NE 68508

Processing Time – Once the USCIS Nebraska Service Center receives the application, it will generally take between 120 to 180 days to complete its processing, provided all of the required background checks have been completed and the applicant has submitted all required documentation. Applicants should save all receipts and notices of action, and always refer to the "A" number or N-400 receipt number when contacting USCIS or when checking the status of their application at www.uscis.gov.

– USCIS –

APPENDIX 12-10

USCIS Fact Sheet: Overseas Naturalization Eligibility for Certain Children of U.S. Armed Forces Members

Office of Communications

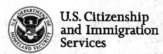

U.S. Citizenship and Immigration Services

Fact Sheet

Oct. 2, 2008

OVERSEAS NATURALIZATION ELIGIBILITY FOR CERTAIN CHILDREN OF U.S. ARMED FORCES MEMBERS

On January 28, 2008, President Bush signed into law the National Defense Authorization Act for Fiscal Year 2008 (H.R.4986 / Public Law 110-181). This law amended Section 322 of the Immigration and Nationality Act (INA) to allow certain eligible children of members of the armed forces to become naturalized U.S. citizens without having to travel to the United States for any part of the naturalization process.

Section 322 provides for the naturalization of minor children of U.S. citizens residing abroad. The general conditions are that at least one parent is a U.S. citizen, that the child is younger than age 18 and resides abroad in the physical and legal custody of that parent, and that parent has been physically present in the United States for a certain period of time. Section 322 requires that in general, the child must be temporarily present in the United States pursuant to a lawful admission in order to complete the naturalization.

The amendments to Section 322 benefit children of U.S. citizen members of the military who are accompanying their parent abroad on official orders. Specifically, Section 322(d) provides that:

- such children are not required to have a lawful admission or be present in the U.S.; and
- the U.S. citizen-parent member of the armed forces may count any period of time they have resided abroad on official orders as physical presence in the United States.

Accordingly, a qualified child of a member of the armed forces, who is on official orders authorizing him or her to accompany and reside with that parent-service member, can file for naturalization from overseas and can proceed with the entire process overseas without being required to travel to the United States.

Section 322(d) benefits are available only to biological and adopted children of U.S. citizen members of the U.S. armed forces; they are not available to step-children of the U.S. citizen parent.

A biological child of the U.S. citizen parent member of the armed forces must meet the requirements in Section 101(c)(1) of the INA. An adopted child must meet the requirements of Section 101(b)(1)(E), (F), or (G) of the INA.

To apply for citizenship for eligible children who live abroad and meet the requirements under Section 322, follow these instructions:

Application – Submit a completed Form N-600K, *Application for Citizenship and Issuance of Certificate Under Section 322*, with the following items:

Cover Letter – USCIS encourages applicants to include a brief cover letter on top of the application package with the heading "322(d): Child of Military Member Overseas" explaining that the child currently lives overseas and qualifies to naturalize under Section 322(d) of the INA. Also print the full name of the child and their parent(s) and list the current overseas address (both local and APO/FPO). Include the location of the USCIS office overseas most convenient to conduct the interview (for example, "the U.S. Consulate in Frankfurt").

Birth Certificate – Include a photocopy of the child's birth certificate, showing the relationship to the U.S. citizen parent. If the parent-child relationship is through adoption, then copies of the adoption documents should also be submitted.

Proof of U.S. Citizenship – The parent member of the U.S. armed forces must show proof they are a U.S. citizen. Acceptable forms of evidence include a copy of a valid U.S. passport, U.S. birth certificate, Certificate of Naturalization, Certificate of Citizenship (A or AA), or Registration of Birth Abroad (Form FS-240).

Photos – Two identical passport-style photos (See instruction sheet).

Evidence of Residence Abroad – Show that the child resides abroad on official orders with the U.S. citizen-parent member of the armed forces by submitting a copy of the Permanent Change of Station (PCS) orders that include the child's name. If the PCS orders do not specifically name the applicant beyond reference to "child" or "dependent," then also include a copy of the service member's Form DD-1172 (DEERS Enrollment), naming the child. Other supporting documents reflecting residence abroad may include school transcripts and medical or dental records.

Fees – Include the correct fee with the application. Application fees depend upon the following factors:

- For a biological child younger than age 18, submit a check or money order for $460.
- For an adopted child younger than age 18, submit a check or money order for $420.
- Make the check or money order made payable to the Department of Homeland Security or U.S. Citizenship and Immigration Services. Note: please check local payment procedures.

Mailing Address –USCIS recommends that applicants submit all 322(d) N-600K applications for citizenship to the USCIS overseas office having jurisdiction over the child's overseas residence, or to the USCIS Nebraska Service Center at the following address:

Nebraska Service Center	For private courier deliveries, send to:
P.O. Box 87426	Nebraska Service Center
Lincoln, NE 68501-7426	850 S Street
	Lincoln, NE 68508

Processing Time – Once the USCIS Nebraska Service Center receives the application, it will generally take between 120 to 180 days to complete its processing, provided all the required background checks have been completed and the applicant has submitted all required documentation. Applicants should save all receipts and notices of action, and always refer to the "A" number or N-600K receipt number when contacting USCIS or when checking the status of their application at www.uscis.gov.

– USCIS –

APPENDIX 12-11

USCIS FAQ: Immigration Information for Members of the U.S. Armed Forces and Their Families

Office of Communications

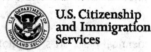

U.S. Citizenship and Immigration Services

Frequently Asked Questions   Dec. 9, 2008

IMMIGRATION INFORMATION FOR MEMBERS OF THE U.S. ARMED FORCES AND THEIR FAMILIES

U.S. Citizenship and Immigration Services (USCIS) offers immigration services and resources specifically for members of the U.S. Armed Forces and their family stationed in the United States and abroad. Below is a list of answers to frequently asked questions received by our military assistance team. USCIS established this team to ensure that the military community receives quick and secure access to accurate information.

MEMBERS OF THE U.S. ARMED FORCES

Q.   **I am in the military and have official Permanent Change of Station (PCS) orders reassigning me to an overseas duty station. Will the move impact my naturalization application? Do I qualify for expedited processing of my application?**

A.   Your reassignment overseas should not impact your naturalization application. USCIS will continue to process your *Application for Naturalization* (Form N-400). Currently, a dedicated team at the USCIS Nebraska Service Center (NSC) processes all Form N-400s filed by members of the U.S. military. After the military assistance team completes their processing, they transfer the file to the appropriate overseas USCIS office, which schedules an interview and the naturalization oath ceremony overseas. You may ask to expedite handling of your application because of these special circumstances by:

- Calling the toll-free USCIS Military Help Line at, 1-877-CIS-4MIL (1-877-247-4645). Operator assistance is available from 8 a.m. to 4:30 p.m. Central Time, Monday through Friday, excluding federal holidays, or
- E-mailing USCIS' military assistance team at: militaryinfo.nsc@dhs.gov, or
- Contacting your military installation's designated USCIS liaison, who should request USCIS expedite your application.

Q.   **I am stationed abroad serving on active duty in the U.S. Armed Forces, how can I notify USCIS of my new military address?**

A.   Members of the military stationed abroad should notify USCIS of their new address by contacting the Military Help Line by e-mail: militaryinfo.nsc@dhs.gov, or telephone: 1-877-247-4645. We are working to add APO and FPO address changes to the on-line change of address tool and anticipate a solution soon. It is important to notify USCIS of your address change to receive so that you and your family may continue to receive information and correspondence about immigration benefits and services.

Q.   **I am scheduled for an appointment at a USCIS office in the United States, but I am now at an overseas duty station. What do I do?**

A.   If you have an appointment, an interview or are scheduled for an oath ceremony, and you have transferred overseas, contact USCIS and request we transfer your case to the nearest USCIS overseas office. Either you or your military installation's liaison to USCIS can do this by e-mail: militaryinfo.nsc@dhs.gov, or telephone: 1-877-247-4645.

USCIS' military assistant team at the Nebraska Service Center is available to the military and their family members through a dedicated toll-free number, 1-877-CIS-4MIL (1-877-247-4645) or by e-mail: militaryinfo.nsc@dhs.gov

SPOUSES OF MEMBERS OF THE U.S. ARMED FORCES

Q.   I am in the military and have PCS orders to an overseas duty station; does my spouse qualify for expedited processing of the *Petition to Remove the Conditions of Residence* (Form I-751)?

A.   If you or your spouse has official military orders to PCS overseas, you may ask USCIS to expedite the I-751 petition. Call USCIS at 1-877-4645 <u>before you leave the United States.</u>

Q.   My spouse left the United States, traveling on official PCS orders to join me overseas at our new duty station, but did not receive her/his permanent resident (green) card, after we filed the I-751 petition. What do we do?

A.   If you filed the Form I-751 in United States, e-mail or telephone the USCIS military assistance team and let us know your spouse did not receive a permanent resident (green) card. We will review your case and determine if your spouse's card was produced and if USCIS can forward the card to your new APO/FPO address.

Q.   How can I expedite my *Petition for Alien Relative* (Form I-130) to bring my spouse to the United States? Is there any way she/he can enter the United States while the petition is being processed?

A.   Citizens of the United States, who are serving in the military and have a pending *Petition for Alien Relative* (Form I-130) on behalf of their spouse, may e-mail or telephone the USCIS military assistance team and ask for expedited processing of that petition. During that time, your spouse may enter the United States on a K-3 nonimmigrant visa. To get a K-3 visa, you must file a *Petition for Alien Fiancé(é)* (Form I-129F) on behalf of your spouse. An approved Form I-129F will allow your spouse to enter the United States. If USCIS approves the I-130 petition while your spouse is in the United States on a K-3 visa, she/he can file an *Application to Register Permanent Residence or Adjust Status* (Form I-485) to become a legal permanent resident.

Q.   I am a U.S. citizen and serving in the military, who in my family is considered as my immediate relative so that I may file a *Petition for Alien Relative* (Form I-130) on their behalf?

A.   In general, spouses, unmarried children younger than age 21 and parents of U.S. citizens are considered 'immediate relatives' to file a *Petition for Alien Relative* (Form I-130). This means they will not have to wait long to receive an immigrant visa or adjust status in the United States, because a visa number is immediately available.

If you recently became a U.S. citizen and have Form I-130 pending with USCIS you can call the USCIS Military Help Line to request USCIS upgrade your relative's visa category to 'immediate relative' status.

Q.   I am a legal permanent resident and serving in the U.S. Armed Forces, who in my family is considered as my immediate relative so that I may file a Form I-130 petition on their behalf?

A.   Spouses and unmarried children younger than age 21, of permanent residents are not considered 'immediate relatives' to file a Form I-130. Therefore, relatives of permanent residents may have to wait several years before immigrating because of the combination of high demand and the limits set by law on the number of persons who can immigrate each year.

USCIS' military assistant team at the Nebraska Service Center is available to the military and their family members through a dedicated toll-free number, 1-877-CIS-4MIL (1-877-247-4645) or by e-mail: <u>militaryinfo.nsc@dhs.gov</u>

If you are a legal permanent resident, and have a pending Form I-130 petition on your spouse's behalf, your spouse may be eligible to file for a V-1 nonimmigrant visa at a U.S. consulate overseas by concurrently filing the U.S Department of State Forms DS-3052 and DS-156 nonimmigrant visa applications.

An application for the visa does not guarantee your spouse will qualify for the V-1 visa. If approved, the V-1 visa, like the K-3 visa, will permit your spouse to lawfully enter the United States and then adjust his or her status to lawful permanent resident when his or her immigrant visa number becomes available.

For specific information about the K-3 and V-1 visas, please see the U.S. Department of State Web page, www.unitedstatesvisas.gov.

FIANCÉ(E)S OF MEMBERS OF THE U.S. ARMED FORCES

Q.   I am in the military and am engaged to marry a non-citizen. I filed a *Petition for Alien Fiance(é)* (Form I-129F) to bring my fiancé(e) into the United States. Do we qualify for expedited processing of the petition?

A.   If you are a U.S. citizen and have Form I-129F, *Petition for Alien Fiance(é),* pending on your spouse's behalf, you may ask USCIS to expedite the processing of Form I-129F by calling the Military Help Line. If you are a U.S. citizen and do not plan to marry your fiancé(e) before he or she enters the United States, you may file the Form I-129F petition on his or her behalf. If you are outside the United States, you can mail the forms to the appropriate USCIS Service Center listed on the Form I-129F instructions. (Unlike a U.S. citizen, a lawful permanent resident cannot file a Form I129F.)

After USCIS approves the Form I-129F, your fiancé(e) may file an application for a K-1 nonimmigrant visa at a U.S. Consulate overseas. A K-1 visa allows your fiancé(e) to enter the United States to marry you, and for no other purpose. If you and your fiancé(e) do not marry within 90 days of his or her admission to the United States, the K-1 visa will expire. If you marry your fiancé(e) within those 90 days, your spouse may file to become a lawful permanent resident by filing an *Application to Register Permanent Residence or Adjust Status,* (Form I-485).

For more information, please review the Department of State Web page: unitedstatesvisas.gov.

OVERSEAS APPLICATION PROCESS

Q.   How does overseas processing work?

A.   Overseas processing of immigration benefits depends on the type of application or petition. For example, USCIS can process an *Application for Naturalization,* (Form N-400) filed by members of the military who are stationed overseas. The service member must work with the installation's designated USCIS liaison to coordinate the request for processing with the appropriate USCIS office overseas. If the service member is already overseas, contact the overseas USCIS office at the following e-mail address:

- For inquiries from the Rome District, including Iraq: email Rome.Natz@dhs.gov
- For inquiries from Germany, email USCIS.frankfurt@dhs.gov
- For inquiries from Japan or South Korea, email CIS-Seoul.Natz@dhs.gov
- For inquiries from Afghanistan, email USCIS.Afghanistan@dhs.gov

The service member may also telephone or e-mail the USCIS military assistance team to request overseas processing. Currently, a dedicated team at the USCIS Nebraska Service Center (NSC) processes all Form

---

USCIS' military assistant team at the Nebraska Service Center is available to the military and their family members through a dedicated toll-free number, 1-877-CIS-4MIL (1-877-247-4645) or by e-mail: militaryinfo.nsc@dhs.gov

N-400s filed by members of the U.S. Armed Forces. After the military assistance team completes their processing, they transfer the file to the appropriate overseas USCIS office, which schedules an interview and the naturalization oath ceremony overseas.

Q. Can USCIS process my spouse or children's application overseas?

A. It depends on the type of application and where you and your children are stationed overseas. Please see the following for guidance:

- Form I-130, *Petition for Alien Relative*: If you are a military member stationed abroad, you can file the Form I-130 either at a USCIS Office overseas or U.S. consulate. Please go to www.uscis.gov and click on "Services & Benefits" then look under "Immigration Overseas Offices" to determine the USCIS office overseas with jurisdiction over your location. If you do not live near an overseas USCIS office, then you may file the Form I-130 with the State Department through the U.S. Consulate with jurisdiction over your location.

- Form N-400, *Application for Naturalization*: A spouse of a service member may proceed with his or her naturalization application overseas if the spouse is residing abroad on official U.S. military orders. Please refer to the fact sheet: *"Requirements for Naturalization Abroad By Spouses of Members of the U.S. Armed Forces"* on www.uscis.gov/military for filing instructions and additional information.

- Form I-485, *Application to Register Permanent Residence or Adjust Status*: Form I485 may only be filed by applicants who are inside the United States seeking lawful permanent residence. If the person is overseas, they must apply for a visa with the U.S. Embassy or consulate overseas. Please see above for more information about visa processing through the U.S. Embassy or consulate overseas. The service member (petitioner) should work directly with the U.S. Embassy or consulate to determine if the U.S. Department of State can expedite issuing the relative's (beneficiary's) visa. For more information regarding visas, please see the Department of State webpage at www.unitedstatesvisas.gov.

- N-600K, *Application for Citizenship and Issuance of Certificate under Section 322*: Eligible children of members of the military may also benefit from overseas processing of their applications for citizenship under section 322 of the Immigration and Nationality Act, if those children live abroad with the military member on official orders. Please refer to the fact sheet: *"Overseas Naturalization Eligibility for Certain Children of U.S. Armed Forces Members"* located on www.uscis.gov/military for filing instructions and additional information.

- Form I-751, *Petition to Remove Conditions on Residence*: You may file a Form I-751 while you and your spouse are overseas on official government orders. You should mail Form I751 to the USCIS Service Center having jurisdiction over your residence of record in the United States if you are overseas on official government orders. Please refer to the form's instructions (www.uscis.gov/files/form/I-751instr.pdf) for specific filing requirements.

– USCIS –

USCIS' military assistant team at the Nebraska Service Center is available to the military and their family members through a dedicated toll-free number, 1-877-CIS-4MIL (1-877-247-4645) or by e-mail: militaryinfo.nsc@dhs.gov

APPENDIX 12-12

USCIS Memorandum: Acceptance of DD Form 214 as Certification of Military or Naval Service for Veterans of the U.S. Armed Forces

U.S. Department of Homeland Security
U.S. Citizenship and Immigration Services
Domestic Operations Directorate
Washington, DC 20529-2010

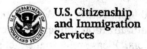

**U.S. Citizenship
and Immigration
Services**

HQ 70/34.5
HQ 70/34.6
AD09-24

April 29, 2009
Memorandum

TO: Field Leadership

FROM: Donald Neufeld /s/
         Acting Associate Director

SUBJECT: Acceptance of DD Form 214 as Certification of Military or Naval Service for Veterans
of the U.S. Armed Forces

Revisions to *Adjudicator's Field Manual* Chapter 72 (AFM Update AD09-24)

1. Purpose

This memorandum provides field guidance and the Adjudicator's Field Manual (AFM) update on the
acceptance of DD Form 214, Certificate of Release or Discharge from Active Duty,[1] and Form
N-426, Certificate of Military or Naval Service, to certify service in the Armed Forces for purposes
of naturalization under section 328 or 329 of the Immigration and Nationality Act (INA).

2. Background

Members of the Armed Forces applying for naturalization pursuant to section 328 or 329 of the INA
are required to submit a certified statement from the executive department under which the applicant
served, or is serving, in order to establish eligibility for naturalization. To comply with the
certification requirements, USCIS requires the applicant to submit Form N-426, Certification of
Military or Naval Service, along with the Form N-400, Application for Naturalization.[2] Form N-426
is only required when service members apply to naturalize under section 328 or 329 of the INA;
Form N-426 is not necessary if someone who served in the Armed Forces is applying under another
provision of law.

Form N-426 is generally certified locally by the military installation where the applicant is serving.
However, applicants who are discharged from the Armed Forces (hereafter "veteran applicants")
cannot obtain a locally certified Form N-426 because service records of veterans are transferred to
the military personnel records center of each branch upon separation and are not accessible to

---

[1] Department of Defense form issued to members of the Armed Forces upon completion of active duty service.
[2] See 8 CFR 328.4 and 329.4.

Certification Exemption for Form N-426, Request for Certification of Military or Naval Service
Revisions to *Adjudicator's Field Manual* Chapter 72 (AFM Update AD09-24)
Page 2

individual military installations. Therefore, veteran applicants have the following options to obtain
certification of Form N-426: 1) send the completed Form N-426 to the military personnel records
center for certification; or 2) submit an uncertified completed Form N-426 to the Nebraska Service
Center (NSC) and the NSC will send it to the military personnel records center for certification.
These options are burdensome to veteran applicants and USCIS, and have resulted in excessive
delays in processing of Form N-400.

Veteran applicants, however, do receive certification of their military service upon discharge. The
DD Form 214 is a report of separation that captures the dates and character of service (type of
discharge) of the service member. The Department of Defense issues DD Form 214 to each veteran
upon his or her separation from the Armed Forces. DD Form 214 is already certified by the
respective Armed Forces branch and therefore meets the military service certification requirements
set forth in section 328 and 329 of the INA.

3. Field Guidance and Adjudicator's Field Manual Update

All USCIS offices are directed to comply with this guidance.[3] To assist veteran applicants, USCIS
will begin accepting N-400 packets that include uncertified copies of Form N-426 provided that they
are accompanied by DD Form 214. If the applicant was issued more than one DD Form 214, the
applicant must submit a copy of each DD Form 214, showing all periods of service. Upon receipt,
the NSC will ensure that all periods of service listed on Form N-426 are covered on the DD Form
214 form(s).

Effective immediately, all USCIS offices will accept an uncertified Form N-426 from veteran
applicants for purposes of naturalization if all of the following conditions have been met:

1. The applicant is separated from the Armed Forces at the time of filing Form N-400;
2. The applicant submitted a completed but uncertified Form N-426;
3. The applicant submitted a photocopy of his or her DD Form 214 (or photocopies of
   multiple DD Form 214s) for all periods of service captured on Form N-426; **and**
4. The DD Form 214 lists information on the type of separation and character of service
   (such information is found on page "Member-4").

When all four conditions are met, the NSC will process Form N-400 applications accompanied by an
uncertified Form N-426. USCIS may request additional verification if needed to verify military
service.

---

[3] USCIS overseas offices should be aware of these requirements but will not see DD Form 214s with uncertified Form
N-426s because only active duty service members are naturalized overseas.

Certification Exemption for Form N-426, Request for Certification of Military or Naval Service
Revisions to *Adjudicator's Field Manual* Chapter 72 (AFM Update AD09-24)
Page 3

The *Adjudicator's Field Manual* (AFM) is updated as follows:

1. Subchapter 72.2(d)(3) is revised to read as follows:

72.2 Examination Preparation.

(d) <u>Important Forms to Review in Preparation for the Examination</u>.

* * * * *

(3) <u>G-325B and N-426 Military Forms</u>. All applicants who have served or are now
serving in the Armed Forces of the United States are required to submit Form G-325B
(which is used in connection with the Defense Clearance and Investigative Index (DCII)
check) when the application is filed. In addition to the G-325B, applicants who are filing
under section 328 or 329 must also submit Form N-426 (which is used to certify military
service) when the application is filed. The completed packet is then sent to the
Nebraska Service Center (NSC) for processing. See 8 CFR 328.4 and 329.4.

Note that applicants filing for naturalization under any other provision than section 328
or 329 (such as section 316 or 319) who have served in the Armed Forces are also
required to submit Form G-325B, but their N-400s should be submitted to the lockbox
having jurisdiction over their place of residence or as otherwise directed by the
instructions on Form N-400. See 8 CFR 316.5(b)(1) and the memoranda *Facilitated
Military Member Naturalization,* dated February 3, 2000, located in Appendix 72-19;
Scheduling Military N-400 Cases, dated April 7, 2000, located in Appendix 72-20; and
Military G-325B Processing, dated April 7, 2000, located in Appendix 72-21.

- <u>G-325B: Biographic Information</u>.

* * *

- <u>N-426: Request for Certification of Military or Naval Service</u>. An applicant who is
  filing under section 328 or 329 of the Act must submit Form N-426, Request for
  Certification of Military or Naval Service. Form N-426 confirms whether the applicant
  served in an active duty status honorably or otherwise, and whether he or she has
  ever been excused or released from military service based on a claim of alienage.
  The military will complete Form N-426 by certifying military service from official
  records and sending it to the Nebraska Service Center (NSC) for processing. Note
  that the NSC will accept a completed but uncertified Form N-426 submitted by an
  applicant filing for naturalization under section 328 or 329 who has separated from
  the Armed Forces so long as all of the following conditions have been met:

    (1) The applicant is separated from the Armed Forces at the time of filing Form
        N-400;

Certification Exemption for Form N-426, Request for Certification of Military or Naval Service
Revisions to *Adjudicator's Field Manual* Chapter 72 (AFM Update AD09-24)
Page 4

(2) The applicant submitted a completed but uncertified Form N-426;

(3) The applicant submitted a photocopy of his or her DD Form 214, Certificate of Release or Discharge from Active Duty, (or photocopies of multiple DD Form 214s) for all periods of service captured on Form N-426; **and**

(4) The DD Form 214 lists information on the type of separation and character of service (such information is found on page "Member-4").

The NSC may request additional verification if needed to verify military service. See Policy Memorandum *Acceptance of DD Form 214 as Certification of Military or Naval Service for Veterans of the Armed Forces* dated April XX, 2009.]

* * * * *

2. The *AFM* **Transmittal Memoranda** button is revised by adding, in numerical order, a new entry to read as follows:

AD09-24 [Enter Date]	**Chapter 72.2(d)(3)**	This memorandum revises the *Adjudicator's Field Manual* (*AFM*) Chapter 72.2 to clarify when Form N-426 is required with naturalization applications.

4. Use

This memorandum is intended solely for the instruction and guidance of USCIS personnel in performing their duties relative to adjudications. It is not intended to, does not, and may not be relied upon to create any right or benefit, substantive or procedural, enforceable by law or by any individual or other party in removal proceedings, in litigation with the United States, or in any other form or manner.

5. Contact Information

Questions regarding the operational guidance in this memorandum may be directed through appropriate channels to the Field Operations and Service Center Operations Divisions.

Distribution List: Regional Directors
District and Field Office Directors
Service Center Directors
National Benefits Center Director

APPENDIX 12-13

Legal Opinion of Navy Regarding Definition of "Active Duty"

DEPARTMENT OF THE NAVY
OFFICE OF THE JUDGE ADVOCATE GENERAL
WASHINGTON NAVY YARD
1322 PATTERSON AVENUE SE SUITE 3000
WASHINGTON DC 20374-5066

IN REPLY REFER TO

5000.2
Ser 13/MS11026.09
January 6, 2009

Ms. Debra A. Rogers, Division Chief
Information and Customer Service
U.S. Citizenship and Immigration Service (USCIS)
111 Massachusetts Avenue, NW, Suite 6000
Washington, D.C. 20529

Dear Ms. Rogers:

My office has been requested to provide a legal opinion
regarding the definition of "active duty" as used in Title 8,
United States Code, Section 1440, and whether attendance at the
U.S. Naval Academy constitutes "active duty" service. In
addition, my office has been requested to opine on the issue of
whether Service certification of "active status" is conclusive
evidence of such service.

"Active duty" is defined in Title 10, as "full-time duty in the
active military service of the United States." This includes
"full-time training duty, annual training duty, and attendance,
while in the active military service, at a school designated as
a service school by law or by the Secretary of the military
department concerned." *See* 10 U.S.C. § 101(d)(1). Although
Title 8 does not specifically define "active duty" or "active
status," USCIS has interpreted "active duty" as "full-time duty
in active military service, and includes full-time duty, which
constitutes qualifying service under current 8 U.S.C. § 1440.
It includes also annual training duty and attendance, while in
the active military service, at a service school designated by
the military authorities. Active duty in a noncombatant
capacity is qualifying service." *See* UCCIS Interpretation 329.1
(adopting the Title 10 definition). Accordingly, attendance at
the U.S. Naval Academy constitutes "active duty" service as
contemplated under Title 8.

In addition, it is the legal opinion of this office that the N-
426 certification of "active duty" status is conclusive evidence
of such service. In looking to the statutory language provided
in Section 328 of the INA (8 U.S.C. § 1439) the "certificate or
certificates . . . provided [by the executive department] . . .
shall be conclusive evidence of such service and discharge."

Although not specifically provided in INA Section 329, "it is clear that this was intended and that the executive certification is the exclusive method of proving the nature of the service." *See* 7-97 Immigration Law and Procedure § 97.05 [3] [b] (*citing* INS Interpretation 329.1(c)(5)(additional citations omitted)).

If you have any questions regarding this legal opinion, the point of contact in my office is LCDR Christine L. Luster, JAGC, USN. She can be reached at (202) 685-5995.

Sincerely,

C. N. MORIN
Captain, JAGC, U.S. Navy
Deputy Assistant Judge Advocate
General (Administrative Law)

2

APPENDIX 12-14

Conditional Permanent Residents and Naturalization under Section 319(b) of the Act

U.S. Department of Homeland Security
U.S. Citizenship and Immigration Services
Washington, DC 20529

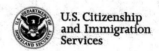

U.S. Citizenship and Immigration Services

HQ 70/6.1.8
HQ 70/34.1
AD 09-28

Date: August 4, 2009

Memorandum

TO: Field Leadership

FROM: Donald Neufeld /s/
           Acting Associate Director, Domestic Operations

           Lori Scialabba /s/
           Associate Director, Refugee, Asylum & International Operations

           Pearl Chang /s/
           Acting Chief, Office of Policy & Strategy

SUBJECT: Conditional Permanent Residents and Naturalization under Section 319(b) of the Act

           Revision to *Adjudicator's Field Manual* Chapter 25 (AFM Update AD09-28)

1. Purpose

This memorandum provides field guidance and updates the Adjudicator's Field Manual (AFM) to address circumstances under which an alien who was admitted as a lawful permanent resident on a conditional basis ("conditional permanent resident" or "CPR") pursuant to section 216 of the Immigration and Nationality Act (the Act) may be naturalized under section 319(b) of the Act prior to the removal of the conditions.

This memorandum supplements the guidance provided by the memorandum entitled "Removal of Conditional Resident Status Prior to, or Concurrently with, Adjudication of Form N-400" issued on February 4, 2004.

This memorandum does not apply to CPRs admitted pursuant to section 216 of the Act who are naturalizing under any provision of law other than section 319(b), and does not apply to CPRs admitted pursuant to section 216A of the Act (EB-5 alien entrepreneurs). Although such CPRs may *apply* for naturalization, their applications may not be approved until the conditions on their residence have been removed.

Conditional Permanent Residents and Naturalization under Section 319(b) of the Act (AD09-28)
HQ 70/6.1.8; HQ 70/34.1
Page 2

2. Background

Generally, applicants for naturalization are required to establish a certain period of residence and physical presence in the United States.[1] However, Congress recognized that spouses of certain U.S. citizens who are regularly employed abroad, to include spouses of U.S. Armed Forces personnel or other U.S. Government employees stationed abroad, could be precluded from naturalization based on their residence abroad.

Accordingly, as part of the Immigration and Nationality Act of 1952, Congress enacted section 319(b) to protect the interests of such spouses in becoming U.S. citizens. Section 319(b) of the Act permits the spouses of certain U.S. citizens who are regularly stationed abroad to naturalize without having to demonstrate any specific period of residence or physical presence in the United States. Therefore, section 319(b) permits aliens admitted for lawful permanent residence to naturalize immediately after obtaining lawful permanent resident (LPR) status in the United States.

In 1986, Congress enacted the Immigration Marriage Fraud Amendments (IMFA) to combat marriage fraud for purposes of obtaining immigration benefits. Section 216 of the Act, added by IMFA, combats marriage fraud by placing conditions on the permanent residence of any alien spouse or child who obtains (LPR) status by virtue of a marriage to a U.S. citizen or LPR that is less than two years old at the time of admission or adjustment of status.[2]

In order to remove the conditions on their LPR status, CPRs must jointly file with their petitioning spouse a Form I-751, Petition to Remove Conditions on Residence, during the 90-day period immediately preceding the second anniversary of their admission as CPRs, or as otherwise provided in section 216, to establish that the marriage was not entered into for purposes of evading U.S. immigration laws.[3] Failure to establish the bona fides of the marriage, or failure to timely file the petition or otherwise comply with section 216, results in the termination of the alien's LPR status.[4]

Although section 319(b) ensures that eligible spouses of qualifying U.S. citizen employees are not precluded from eligibility for naturalization because of their residence abroad, section 319(b) otherwise requires "compliance with all the requirements of the naturalization laws." This includes the requirement that naturalization applicants demonstrate they have been lawfully admitted for permanent residence "in accordance with all applicable provisions" of the Act as stipulated in section 318 of the Act.

CPRs admitted pursuant to section 216 of the Act who apply for naturalization under section 319(b) must, therefore, comply with the requirements of section 216. Section 216(e) of the Act, which provides that for purposes of naturalization an alien in conditional status "shall be considered to have been admitted as an alien lawfully admitted for permanent residence and to be in the United States as an alien lawfully admitted to the United States for permanent residence," does not relieve a conditional permanent resident applying for naturalization from the requirements of section 216.

---

[1] For example, see sections 316(a) and 319(a) of the Act.
[2] See section 216(g)(1) of the Act.
[3] See section 216(c) and 216(d) of the Act. Also see 8 CFR 216.4.
[4] See section 216(c)(2) and 216(c)(3)(C) of the Act.

Conditional Permanent Residents and Naturalization under Section 319(b) of the Act (AD09-28)
HQ 70/6.1.8; HQ 70/34.1
Page 3

Section 216(e) merely ensures that the time spent in the United States as a conditional resident may, after the conditions have been removed, be considered for purposes of establishing the residence and physical presence requirements of the naturalization laws, such as those required by sections 316(a) and 319(a) of the Act.

Therefore, CPRs admitted pursuant to section 216 who seek naturalization under section 319(b) must comply with the requirements of section 216, though such CPRs who naturalize under section 319(b) prior to the 90-day Form I-751 filing period are not required to file Form I-751 for those purposes because they would not be within the designated filing period. However, such applicants must nevertheless establish that the qualifying marriage (1) was entered into in accordance with the laws of the place where the marriage occurred, (2) has not been judicially annulled or terminated, (3) was not entered into for the purpose of procuring an alien's admission as an immigrant, and (4) that no fee or other consideration was given (other than attorney's fees) for filing the immigrant or fiancé(e) visa petition that forms the basis for their admission to the United States.[5]

3. Field Guidance and Adjudicator's Field Manual Update

All USCIS offices are directed to comply with the following guidance. The Adjudicator's Field Manual (AFM) Chapter 25.1 entitled "Immigration Marriage Fraud Amendments of 1986" is amended by revising the subchapter 25.1(k) in its entirety. The revisions read as follows:

25.1   Immigration Marriage Fraud Amendments of 1986

(k) Naturalization Issues Relating to Conditional Residence.

Generally, before approving a naturalization application filed by a conditional permanent resident, the adjudicator should ensure that the applicant has met all of the applicable requirements of section 216 of the Act as evidenced by an approved Form I-751.

Note: There are special circumstances to consider in cases involving conditional permanent residents applying for naturalization under section 319(b) of the Act. See guidance provided in paragraph (2) of subchapter 25.1(k) of this manual.

Additionally, any conditional permanent resident who is otherwise eligible for naturalization under section 329 of the Act (based on military service), **and** who is not required to be lawfully admitted to the United States for permanent residence as provided for in section 329 of the Act, is exempt from all of the requirements of section 216. This is because section 329 does not require certain otherwise eligible applicants to have a lawful admission for permanent residence in order to qualify. See section 329 of the Act. Therefore, these applicants are not required to have an approved Form I-751 before their N-400s are approved.

(1) Treatment of Period under Conditional Status for Purposes of Naturalization.

---

[5] See sections 216(b)(1) and 216(d)(1)(A) of the Act.

Section 216(e) of the Act provides that for purposes of naturalization an alien in conditional status "shall be considered to have been admitted as an alien lawfully admitted for permanent residence and to be in the United States as an alien lawfully admitted to the United States for permanent residence."

While this provision ensures that the time spent in the United States as a conditional permanent resident may, after the conditions have been removed, be considered for purposes of establishing the residence and physical presence requirements for naturalization (such as those in section 316(a) and 319(a) of the Act), it does not relieve a conditional permanent resident applying for naturalization from the requirements of section 216. See sections 216(c), 216(d), and 216(e) of the Act. Also see H.R. REP. 99-906, 1986 U.S.C.C.A.N. 5978.

Note: There are special circumstances to consider in cases involving conditional permanent residents applying for naturalization under section 319(b) of the Act. See guidance provided below in paragraph (2) of subchapter 25.1(k) of this manual.

(2) Form I-751 and Form N-400 Issues.

(A) Concurrent Adjudication of Pending Form I-751 and Form N-400.

Because of differences in the adjudication processing times for Form I-751 and Form N-400 and because conditional permanent residents are eligible to *apply* for naturalization (if otherwise eligible) pursuant to 8 CFR 216.1, there may be instances when a conditional permanent resident admitted pursuant to section 216 will apply for naturalization while their Form I-751 is pending.

Unless otherwise provided by the Act, the adjudicator should ensure that the Form I-751 filed by the conditional permanent resident applying for naturalization is adjudicated in accordance with section 216 prior to, or concurrently with, the adjudication of Form N-400. In all cases where a final decision on Form I-751 has been reached, the adjudicator should update MFAS accordingly.

Note: There are special circumstances to consider in cases involving conditional permanent residents who have both a pending Form I-751 and Form N-400 filed under section 329 of the Act. See guidance provided in the introductory paragraphs of subchapter 25.1(k) of this manual.

(i) Form N-400 with Pending Form I-751 at Different USCIS Office.

Generally, a Form N-400 should not be continued to await the final adjudication of a Form I-751 that is pending at a different USCIS office. The adjudicator should conduct the Form N-400 examination as scheduled and should request the pending Form I-751 from the other USCIS office. Once the adjudicator

App. 12-14 U.S. CITIZENSHIP AND NATURALIZATION HANDBOOK

Conditional Permanent Residents and Naturalization under Section 319(b) of the Act (AD09-28)
HQ 70/6.1.8; HQ 70/34.1
Page 5

receives the Form I-751, the adjudicator may adjudicate to completion both the Form N-400 and Form I-751 in accordance with all applicable provisions.

However, while the adjudication of a conditional permanent resident's naturalization application should not be delayed solely because of USCIS processing delays of Form I-751, a pending Form N-400 should not be approved under any circumstances prior to the adjudication of a pending Form I-751, unless otherwise provided by the Act. In all cases where a final decision on Form I-751 has been reached, the adjudicator should update MFAS accordingly.

(ii) Form N-400 Filed under Section 319(a) or 319(b).

In almost all cases, a Form N-400 that is filed while a Form I-751 is pending will have been filed pursuant to section 319(a) or 319(b) of the Act. These provisions require a higher level of evidence of marital union and joint residence than is required for the approval of Form I-751 filed jointly.

If a Form I-751 is pending at the time of the conditional permanent resident's Form N-400 examination, the adjudicator should conduct the examination for naturalization. The adjudicator should ensure that the applicant has established that they are the spouse of the qualifying U.S. citizen and that they are in a bona fide marriage prior to the favorable adjudication of their Form N-400.

If the Form I-751 is in the applicant's A-file and the applicant establishes their eligibility for naturalization under section 319(a) or 319(b), and also established that they have met the requirements under sections 216(b)(1) and 216(d)(1)(A) of the Act (as evidenced by such documentation listed in 8 CFR 216.4(a)(5)), the adjudicator may approve the applicant's Form I-751 and Form N-400 concurrently. See paragraph (2)(A) of subchapter 25.1(k) and subchapter 25.1(e) of this manual.

If the Form I-751 is not in the applicant's A-file, the adjudicator should proceed with the naturalization examination and request the pending Form I-751 from the USCIS office with custody of the petition. However, the applicant's Form N-400 should not be approved until the pending Form I-751 is reviewed and approved based on a determination that the applicant meets the requirements of section 216 of the Act. See paragraph (2)(A)(i) of subchapter 25.1(k) of this manual.

(iii) Form N-400 Filed under Provision Not Requiring Marital Union.

Regardless of whether a Form N-400 is filed under a provision of law that does not require marital union (in contrast to section 319(a) or 319(b)) the adjudicator should request any applicable Form I-751 that is pending prior to the final adjudication of Form N-400. After receipt of the Form I-751, both the Form I-751

CONDITIONAL PERMANENT RESIDENTS

Conditional Permanent Residents and Naturalization under Section 319(b) of the Act (AD09-28)
HQ 70/6.1.8; HQ 70/34.1
Page 6

and Form N-400 may be concurrently adjudicated to completion as inst
paragraph (2)(A)(i) of subchapter 25.1(k) of this manual.

(B) Reaching Form I-751 Filing Period while Form N-400 is Pending.

Unless otherwise provided by the Act, any conditional permanent resident admitted
pursuant to section 216 who files for naturalization, to include those filing under
section 319(b), who reaches the 90-day period for filing Form I-751 prior to the final
adjudication of their naturalization application or prior to taking the Oath of
Allegiance for naturalization should be instructed to file Form I-751 in accordance
with section 216(d)(2) of the Act.

After the conditional permanent resident has properly filed Form I-751, the
adjudicator should proceed with the adjudication of the naturalization application in
accordance with the guidance provided in paragraph (2)(A) of subchapter 25.1(k) of
this manual.

(C) Naturalization under Section 319(b) Prior to Form I-751 Filing Period.

Conditional permanent residents admitted pursuant to section 216 are permitted to
naturalize under section 319(b) of the Act, if otherwise eligible for naturalization
under section 319(b), prior to filing Form I-751 so long as they have been conditional
permanent residents for less than one year and nine months, and have therefore not
reached the Form I-751 filing period at the time of the final adjudication of their
naturalization application **and** at the time of taking the Oath of Allegiance for
naturalization.

Note that applicants for naturalization pursuant to section 319(b) of the Act are not
required to establish any specific period of residence or physical presence in the
United States. See 8 CFR 319.2 and Chapter 73 of this manual. Therefore, in many
cases, a conditional permanent resident who applies for naturalization under section
319(b) of the Act may not yet have reached the Form I-751 filing period when they
file their application for naturalization.

Such conditional permanent residents (who seek naturalization under section 319(b)
and who have not reached the Form I-751 filing period) must, however, comply with
the applicable requirements of section 216 because section 319(b) otherwise
requires "compliance with all the requirements of the naturalization laws." This
includes the requirement that naturalization applicants establish they have been
lawfully admitted for permanent residence "in accordance with all applicable
provisions" of the Act as stipulated in section 318 of the Act.

Accordingly, conditional permanent residents admitted pursuant to section 216 who
apply for naturalization under section 319(b) must, therefore, comply with the
requirements of section 216, though such applicants who have not reached the 90-
day Form I-751 filing period described in section 216(d)(2) of the Act at the time of

App. 12-14   U.S. CITIZENSHIP AND NATURALIZATION HANDBOOK

Conditional Permanent Residents and Naturalization under Section 319(b) of the Act (AD09-28)
HQ 70/6.1.8; HQ 70/34.1
Page 7

their naturalization under section 319(b) should not file Form I-751 because they would not be within the designated filing period.

However, such conditional permanent residents admitted pursuant to section 216 who seek naturalization under section 319(b) prior to the Form I-751 filing period must nevertheless establish, before they may be naturalized under section 319(b), that the qualifying marriage (1) was entered into in accordance with the laws of the place where the marriage occurred; (2) has not been judicially annulled or terminated; (3) was not entered into for the purpose of procuring an alien's admission as an immigrant; and (4) that no fee or other consideration was given (other than attorney's fees) for filing the immigrant or fiancé(e) visa petition that forms the basis for their admission to the United States.

The adjudicator should pay particular attention to issues surrounding the bona fides of the qualifying relationship in such cases and should review the record for documentary evidence of the type required to support an I-751 petition, in addition to the eligibility criteria for naturalization, though the applicant is not required to file Form I-751. See sections 216(b)(1) and 216(d)(1)(A) of the Act. Also see 8 CFR 216.4(a)(5) and subchapter 25.1(e) of this manual.

Under no circumstances can an application for naturalization be approved under section 319(b) of the Act unless the applicant meets their burden of proof of demonstrating compliance with the requirements of section 216 of the Act or as otherwise provided by the guidance in subchapter 25.1(k) of this manual.

Note: If the documentary evidence suggests that there are legitimate concerns that can be properly articulated about the bona fides of the qualifying marital relationship, the adjudicator is reminded that they are authorized to request for further evidence or for the attendance of witnesses, to include the U.S. citizen spouse, as part of the naturalization examination. See section 335(b) of the Act and 8 CFR 335.2(d).

(D) Form I-751 Filed by a Naturalized Citizen.

The requirement to apply for the removal of conditions through the filing of Form I-751 does not apply to conditional permanent residents who were admitted pursuant to section 216 of the Act and who have already naturalized under section 319(b) of the Act (or under section 329 in accordance with the guidance provided in the introductory paragraphs of subchapter 25.1(k) of this manual, or as otherwise provided by the Act) prior to the Form I-751 filing period described in section 216(d)(2) of the Act.

If a naturalized U.S. citizen files Form I-751 either jointly with their petitioning spouse or individually as a waiver under section 216(c)(4) of the Act, the adjudicator should advise the naturalized U.S. citizen in writing that, as a citizen of the United States, the removal of conditions provisions do not apply.

Conditional Permanent Residents and Naturalization under Section 319(b) of the Act (AD09-28)
HQ 70/6.1.8; HQ 70/34.1
Page 8

Moreover, the Form I-751 filing fee should be refunded in cases where the U.S. citizen filed a Form I-751 because of USCIS error (for example, if the U.S. citizen received a computer-generated notice advising they should file). In such cases, the Form I-751 should be counted as a statistical denial.

Note: If the naturalized citizen is the parent of a child who was admitted as a conditional permanent resident based on the parent's marriage, and that child did not also become a citizen, the child is required to file Form I-751 for removal of conditions in accordance with section 216 of the Act and 8 CFR 216.4(a)(2).

AD09-28 August 4, 2009	**Chapter 25.1(k)**	This memorandum revises AFM 25.1(k) to provide guidance on conditional permanent residents and naturalization under section 319(b) of the Act.

4. Use

This memorandum is intended solely for the training and guidance of USCIS personnel in performing their duties relative to the adjudication of applications. It is not intended to, does not, and may not be relied upon to create any right or benefit, substantive or procedural, enforceable at law or by any individual or other party in removal proceedings, in litigation with the United States, or in any other form or manner.

5. Contact Information

Policy questions regarding this memorandum should be directed through appropriate supervisory channels to the Residence & Naturalization Division of the Office of Policy & Strategy or the Office of Policy & Regulations Mgmt (DOMO). Operational questions on processing should be directed to the Citizenship Branch of the Office of Field Operations; Adjustment and Naturalization Branch of Service Center Operations; or the Programs Branch of International Operations (RAIO).

Distribution List: Regional Directors
                      District and Field Office Directors (including overseas)
                      Service Center Directors
                      National Benefits Center Director

Chapter 13

Proof of Citizenship

§ 13:31   Certificate of citizenship for children of U.S. citizens

VI.   SPECIAL PROVISIONS FOR PERSONS BORN BEFORE MAY 24, 1934, TO U.S. CITIZEN MOTHERS

VII.   U.S. CITIZENSHIP CARD FOR AMERICAN INDIANS AND MEMBERS OF COMMONWEALTH OF NORTHERN MARIANA

VIII.   CERTIFICATE OF NATURALIZATION

IX.   AMENDING AND REPLACING CITIZENSHIP-RELATED DOCUMENTS

X.   CANCELLATION OF DHS DOCUMENTS

XI.   OTHER RECORDS

APPENDIX 13-11.   Statement of Consent or Special Circumstances: Issuance of a
                  Passport to a Minor Under Age 16
APPENDIX 13-12.   7 FAM 1300, Appendix M: Gender Change

Research References

West's Key Number Digest
Aliens, Immigration, and Citizenship ⊙672, 674

Westlaw Databases
Steel on Immigration Law (STEEL)
Immigration Law Service (2d ed.) (IMMLS2D)

Treatises and Practice Aids
Steel on Immigration Law §§ 15:5, 15:6

KeyCite®: Cases and other legal materials listed in KeyCite Scope can be researched through the KeyCite
service on Westlaw®. Use KeyCite to check citations for form, parallel references, prior and later history,
and comprehensive citator information, including citations to other decisions and secondary materials.

I. INTRODUCTION

§ 13:1 Overview

Research References
Steel on Immigration Law §§ 15:1, 15:5

Persons who are born citizens or who become citizens derivatively are automatically U.S. citizens once the prescribed conditions are fulfilled. Therefore, there is no
official action they need to take to acquire citizenship. They do not need to file an
application, request a court order, or take an oath of allegiance. However, at times
U.S. citizens need to prove their citizenship status. For example, since passage of
the Immigration Reform and Control Act of 1986, proof of employment eligibility is
required for any person who wants to work legally in the United States. To prove
that a person born in Wyoming, for example, is a citizen, his or her birth certificate
is sufficient. U.S. citizens born abroad may need various documents to prove their
U.S. citizenship, including papers evidencing U.S. citizenship and residence of the
parents, as well as proof of the birth and possible residence of the child. All of these
documents together prove citizenship. However, it is easier to meet documentation
requirements by using a single official document to prove citizenship.

As part of its efforts to implement the 1996 welfare reform legislation,[1] the INS
proposed the following documentation as primary evidence of U.S. Nationality: (1)
birth certificate showing birth in one of the 50 states, the District of Columbia,
Puerto Rico (on or after January 13, 1941), Guam, the U.S. Virgin Islands (on or after November 4, 1986, Northern Mariana Islands Local Time) (unless born to a
foreign diplomat residing in that location); (2) U.S. Passport; (3) Report of Birth
Abroad (FS-240) issued by the U.S. Department of State to U.S. Citizens; (4) Certificate of Report of Birth (Form FS-545) or Certification of Report of Birth (Form DS-

---

[Section 13:1]

[1]Personal Responsibility and Work Opportunity Reconciliation Act of 1996, Pub. L. 104-193
(1996), as amended by IIRIRA § 504, Pub. L. 104-208 (1996) and section 5572 of the Balanced Budget
Act of 1997, Pub. L. No. 105-33 (1977), 8 U.S.C.A. § 1642.

1350); (5) Certificate of Naturalization; (6) Certificate of Citizenship; (7) United States Citizen Identification Cards; (8) Northern Mariana Cards (issued before November 3, 1986); (9) Certification of Consular Official that Individual Derived Citizenship Upon Naturalization of his or her Parent; (10) American Indian Card with classification "KIC" identifying the bearer as member of the Texas band of Kickapoo Indians.[2] Incomplete as this primary list is, it provides an idea of the variety of documents that can prove U.S. citizenship. What follows describes the most commonly used documentary proof of citizenship.

Procedurally, the means by which an individual born abroad may obtain proof of U.S. citizenship depends on whether they are inside or outside of the U.S.. Inside the U.S., the individual may either file an N-600 with the USCIS, or a passport application with the U.S. State Department.[3] In removal proceedings, an individual can defend against removal by claiming citizenship, but because the burden of proof as to alienage is on the government, termination of removal proceedings does not constitute an affirmative finding of citizenship. Outside the United States, an individual under 18 years of age may obtain a Consular Report of Birth by application of the child's parents.[4] An individual over 18 may obtain a U.S. passport through the consulate; or alternatively, may obtain a special visa in order to come to the United States to litigate their claim to citizenship.[5]

II. BIRTH CERTIFICATE

§ 13:2   Generally

Research References

Steel on Immigration Law § 15:5

The primary document proving U.S. citizenship is a birth certificate showing birth in the United States. To be considered valid proof of citizenship, it is often required that copies of birth certificates be certified by the records clerk in the state or county where the original birth certificate is filed. Appendix 13-1 lists the addresses and fee structure for obtaining birth (as well as death, marriage, and divorce) certificates in all the states of the United States.[1] Birth, death, marriage and divorce certificates may also be obtained through the Internet. Vital records for the United States may be ordered online at http://www.vitalchek.com (no "c" after the "e").

For persons born in the United States for whom a birth certificate does not exist, baptismal records and affidavits from persons with knowledge of the birth may be used to prove birth in the United States.

For purposes of filling out an I-9 form for employment, proof of identity will be required in addition to a birth certificate.

In 2004, Congress passed the "Intelligence Reform Act," which requires, among other things, that the Department of Health and Human Services (HHS) publish

---

[2]63 Fed. Reg. 41662 (Aug. 4, 1998) (proposing regulation 8 CFR § 104.23). The proposed regulations dealt with most collective naturalization issues under the secondary evidence category.

[3]See §§ 13:26 to 13:31 (N-600); §§ 13:3 to 13:14 (passport).

[4]See §§ 13:15 to 13:25.

[5]See § 13:5 (passport); § 10:26.

[Section 13:2]

[1]This list is available through the National Center for Health Statistics website at http://www.cdc.gov/nchs/howto/w2w/w2welcom.htm.

regulations establishing minimum standards for the issuance of birth certificates.[2] Those standards will minimally require the use of safety paper and other means of preventing fraudulent replication of documents and standards for deciding when to issue birth certificates.[3] That Act also directed grants to the states to begin computerizing their birth and death records,[4] and some observers expect the final HHS rules to require electronic data entry of all birth certificates from 1935-present, as well as a centralized data registry for each state.[5] Congress required HHS to have published regulations implementing these rules by 2005,[6] but HHS has not yet done so.

The government of Puerto Rico recently enacted legislation (Law 191 of 2009) that basically invalidates all birth certificates issued before July 1, 2010, as of September 30, 2010.[7] Thus, individuals with pre-2010 Puerto Rican birth certificates will have to apply for a new birth certificate, particularly before traveling to the mainland U.S. or obtaining a U.S. passport, though the State Department has indicated that until Puerto Rican birth certificates are invalidated, they may still be used to obtain passports.[8] The new birth certificates issued by Puerto Rico will be more secure than the previous certificates, which were reputedly subject to identity theft.[9]

III. U.S. PASSPORT

§ 13:3 Generally

Research References

Steel on Immigration Law § 15:5

In addition to a birth certificate, a valid U.S. passport issued for the maximum period allowed by law is legal evidence of U.S. citizenship.[1] It is, unless void on its face, "conclusive proof of citizenship."[2] Passports are issued by the U.S. State Department.

§ 13:4 Where to apply for U.S. passport—Within U.S

Research References

Dizon and Wettstein, Immigration Law Service 2d § 1:1217
Steel on Immigration Law §§ 2:19, 15:5

Within the United States, individuals can apply for a passport at passport offices,

---

[2]Intelligence Reform Act, Pub. L. No. 108-458, § 7211(b)(3), 118 Stat. 3754, 3825-27 (2004).

[3]Intelligence Reform Act, Pub. L. No. 108-458, § 7211(b)(3), 118 Stat. 3754, 3825-27 (2004).

[4]Intelligence Reform Act, Pub. L. No. 108-458, § 7211(b)(3), 118 Stat. 3754 at § 7211(c)(2).

[5]See, e.g., "Vital Records System Automation Project," Wisconsin Legislative Fiscal Bureau, LFB 2007-09, found at http://www.legis.state.wi.us/lfb/2007-09budget/Budget%20Papers/411.pdf. (last accessed June 27, 2007).

[6]Intelligence Reform Act, Pub. L. No. 108-458, § 7211(b)(3).

[7]See http://www.prfaa.com/birthcertificates/.

[8]See http://www.travel.state.gov/passport/passport__4807.html.

[9]See "Frequently Asked Questions," found at http://www.prfaa.com/docs/prfaafactsheetfaq.pdf.

[Section 13:3]

[1]22 U.S.C.A. § 2705(1).

[2]Matter of Villanueva, 19 I. & N. Dec. 101 (BIA 1984); see also, 22 U.S.C.A. § 2705.

at specifically designated post offices, with clerks of federal and state courts, and with specially designated Department of Defense employees at military installations within the United States.[1] Passport offices encourage applicants to use alternative reception points such as designated post offices and clerks of courts. Passport acceptance facilities can be located online at http://iafdb.travel.state.gov/. The passport offices now require appointments and only issue them to applicants who need passports on an emergency basis due to planned travel in the near future, and tend to have long lines during the busiest months. Most passport offices instruct applicants not to schedule an appointment unless a scheduled date for international travel is less than two weeks away, or the applicant needs a passport within four weeks to obtain a foreign visa. As of the press date, the Arkansas, Buffalo, Colorado, Detroit, El Paso, Honolulu, Minneapolis, San Diego, Seattle, and Vermont offices do not restrict appointments to emergency travel needs; nor does the Special Passport Agency, though that agency is restricted to governmental employees and referrals.

An "Expedited Service fee" of $60 is charged for anyone applying for a passport at one of the passport agencies or centers.

The 24 regional passport agencies within the United States are listed below.[2] These passport agencies and offices now have a unified, automated appointment system at 1-877-487-2778.

Arkansas Passport Center
191 Office Park Drive
Hot Springs, AR 71913
Appointments Available 8:00 a.m. — 1:00 p.m. Mondays, and Wednesdays through Fridays 10:00 a.m. — 1:00 p.m. Tuesdays
Travel plans not required.

Atlanta Passport Agency
230 Peachtree St N.W.,
Suite 1000
Atlanta, GA 30303
Hours: 8:00 a.m. — 3:00 p.m., local time, M-F, excluding Federal holidays

Boston Passport Agency
10 Causeway Street,
Suite 247
Boston, MA 02222-1094
This Agency issues the US Passport Card on-site!
Hours: 8:30 a.m. — 4:30 p.m., local time, M-F, excluding Federal holidays

Buffalo Passport Agency
Genesee Gateway Building
111 Genesee Street,

[Section 13:4]

[1]22 C.F.R. § 51.21(b). There are 6000 passport application facilities throughout the country. The locations of these can be found by checking http://travel.state.gov/passport/index.html.

[2]Passport agencies, hours, and other material is available at http://www.travel.state.gov/passport/npic/agencies/agencies_913.html.

Suite 101
Buffalo, NY 14203
This Agency issues the US Passport Card on-site!
Hours: 9:00 a.m. — 3:00 p.m., M,T,Th,F; 10:00 a.m. — 3:00 p.m. Wednesday, local time, excluding Federal holidays
Travel plans not required.

Chicago Passport Agency
Kluczynski Federal Building
230 S. Dearborn Street,
18th Floor
Chicago, IL 60604-1564
This Agency issues the US Passport Card on-site!
Appointments available 8:30 a.m. — 3:30 p.m., M-F, excluding federal holidays

Colorado Passport Agency
Cherry Creek III
3151 South Vaughn Way,
Suite 600
Aurora, CO 80014
Hours: 8:00 a.m. — 3:00 p.m., M,T,W,F, 9:00 a.m. — 3:00 p.m. Thursday, local time, excluding Federal holidays
Travel plans not required.

Connecticut Passport Agency
850 Canal Street
Stamford, CT 06902
Hours: 8:30 a.m. to 3:30 p.m., M-W, F, 10:30 a.m. to 3:30 p.m., Thursdays (Excluding Federal Holidays).

Dallas Passport Agency
Earle Cabell Federal Building
1100 Commerce St,
Suite 1120
Dallas, TX 75242
This Agency issues the US Passport Card on-site!
Hours: 8:00 a.m.- 3:00 p.m., Local Time, M-F, excluding Federal holidays.

Detroit Passport Agency
211 West Fort Street,
2nd floor
Detroit, MI 48226-3269
This Agency issues the US Passport Card on-site!
Hours: 8:30 a.m. to 3:00 p.m., M-Tues, 9:30 a.m. to 3:00 p.m. W-F, excluding federal holidays
Travel plans not required.

El Paso Passport Agency
303 N. Oregon St
El Paso, TX 79901
This Agency issues the US Passport Card on-site!
Hours: 7:30 a.m.- 3:00 p.m., Local Time, M-F, excluding Federal holidays
Travel plans not required.

Honolulu Passport Agency
Prince Kuhio Federal Building
300 Ala Moana Blvd.,
Suite 1-330
Honolulu, HI 96850
Hours: 8:30 a.m. — 3:00 p.m., local time, M-F, excluding Federal holidays
Travel plans not required.

Houston Passport Agency
Mickey Leland Federal Building
1919 Smith Street,
4th Floor
Houston, TX 77002-8049
This Agency issues the US Passport Card on-site!
Hours: 8:00 a.m. — 3:30 p.m., local time, M-F, excluding Federal holidays

Los Angeles Passport Agency
Federal Building
11000 Wilshire Blvd.,
Suite 1000
Los Angeles, CA 90024-3615
This Agency issues the US Passport Card on-site!
Hours: 7:00 a.m. — 3:00 p.m., local time, M-F, excluding Federal holidays

Miami Passport Agency
Omni Center
1501 Biscayne Boulevard,
Suite 210
Miami, FL 33132
This Agency issues the US Passport Card on-site!
Hours: 8:00 a.m. — 3:00 p.m., local time, M-F, excluding Federal holidays

Minneapolis Passport Agency
212 3rd Ave S
Minneapolis, MN 55401
This Agency issues the US Passport Card on-site!
Hours: 8:00 a.m. to 3:00 p.m, M, T,Th, F; 9:00 a.m. to 3:00 p.m. Wednesday, local time,
Travel plans not required.

National Passport Center
207 International Drive
Portsmouth, NH 03801
Hours: 9:00 a.m. — 4:00 p.m., local time, M-F, excluding Federal holidays

New Orleans Passport Agency
One Canal Place
365 Canal Street,
Suite 1300
New Orleans, LA 70130-6508
Hours: 8:00 a.m. — 12 p.m., local time, M-F, excluding Federal holidays

New York Passport Agency
Great New York Federal Building
376 Hudson Street
New York, NY 10014
This Agency issues the US Passport Card on-site!
Hours: 7:30 a.m. — 3:00 p.m., local time, M-F, excluding Federal holidays

Philadelphia Passport Agency
U.S. Custom House
200 Chestnut Street,
Room 103
Philadelphia, PA 19106-2970
Hours: 8:00 a.m. — 3:00 p.m., local time, M-F, excluding Federal holidays

San Diego Passport Agency
401 West A St.,
10th Floor
San Diego, CA 92101
This Agency issues the US Passport Card on-site!
8:00 a.m. — 4:00 p.m. M-F excluding Federal Holidays
Travel plans not required.

San Francisco Passport Agency
95 Hawthorne Street,
5th Floor
San Francisco, CA 94105-3901
Hours: 9:00 a.m. — 4:00 p.m., local time, M-F, excluding Federal holidays

Seattle Passport Agency
Fifth and Yesler Building
300 5th Avenue, Suite 600
Seattle, WA 98104
This Agency issues the US Passport Card on-site!
Hours: 8:00 a.m. — 3:00 p.m., local time, M-F, excluding Federal holidays

Travel plans not required.

Vermont Passport Agency
50 South Main Street,
Suite 101
St. Albans, VT 05478
This Agency issues the US Passport Card on-site!
8:30 a.m. to 1:30 p.m. M-F, excluding Federal Holidays
Travel plans not required.

Washington Passport Agency
1111 19th Street, N.W.,
First Floor, Sidewalk Level
Washington, D.C. 20036
8:00 a.m. — 3:00 p.m. M-Tues, Thu-F; 9:00 a.m. — 3:00 p.m., Wed., excluding
Federal Holidays

Western Passport Center
7373 East Rosewood Street
Tucson, AZ 85710
This Agency issues the US Passport Card on-site!
Hours: M, T, W, F — 8:30 a.m. to 3:00 p.m., Thurs. 9:00 a.m. to 3:00 p.m., local
time, excluding Federal holidays

Special Issuance Agency
1111 19th Street, N.W.,
Suite 200
Washington, D.C. 20036
Hours: 9:00 a.m. to 4:00 p.m., M-F, excluding Federal holidays
Applications for Diplomatic, Official, No-Fee and Congressional referrals only

§ 13:5　Where to apply for U.S. passport—Outside U.S

Research References
Dizon and Wettstein, Immigration Law Service 2d § 1:1217
Steel on Immigration Law §§ 2:19, 15:5

Outside the U.S., passport applications may be filed at U.S. consular or diplomatic
posts.[1] However, due to rules requiring added security,[2] regular passports are now
produced only at the National Passport Center in New Hampshire, then sent to the

---

[Section 13:5]

[1]22 C.F.R. § 51.21(a), (b)(6). *See also* http://travel.state.gov/passport/index.html.

[2]See Section 7209 of the Intelligence Reform and Terrorism Prevention Act of 2004, Public Law
108–458, 118 Stat. 3638, 3823 (Dec. 17, 2004).

consulate abroad;[3] which is to say, it will take at least several weeks to obtain a regular passport abroad. Individuals needing emergency passport issuance will therefore be issued a passport for only one year, in order to permit them to return to the U.S. and apply for a new passport there.[4] This does not preclude individuals residing abroad from renewing their expiring passports by mail, and receiving new regular passports.[5]

§13:6 Procedures; generally

Research References

Dizon and Wettstein, Immigration Law Service 2d §14:93
Steel on Immigration Law §15:5

A first-time passport applicant must appear in person and submit Form DSP-11 with the appropriate fee, proof of citizenship, proof of identity, and two photos. A copy of the passport application is reproduced below as Appendix 13-10. The State Department regulations allow for the issuance of a passport to U.S. citizens born abroad upon showing of citizenship of the parent or parents at birth of the child and compliance with the prior residence requirements by the parent.[1] Similarly, derivative citizens may be issued a U.S. passport upon presenting evidence of naturalization of the parent or parents and the appropriate lawful residence in the U.S. during minority of the applicant.[2]

The State Department may, and usually does, require additional evidence to establish a claim to citizenship.[3] The issuing officer will generally return the evidence submitted in relation to the passport application.[4] However, in some cases the officer may retain the evidence.[5] Still, given the DHS adjudication delays, it may be more convenient to prove citizenship to the State Department than to the DHS.

Passports for applicants 16 years and older are normally issued for a ten-year period of validity.[6] Passports to applicants under the age of 16 are normally issued for a five-year period of validity.[7]

The fee for a regular passport is $110 for an applicant 16 years or older, and $80 for an applicant under 16 years of age.[8] There is an additional fee of $25 for any individual applying in person at either a "Passport Acceptance Facility" like a Post Office, or a Regional Passport Agency.[9] Several categories of applicants must apply in-person at either a Passport Acceptance Facility or a Passport Agency, including

---

[3]See 7 FAM 1311(i).

[4]See 7 FAM 1311(j).

[5]See 22 C.F.R. §51.21(c); see also, "Form DS-82: Application for a U.S. Passport by Mail," found at http://travel.state.gov/passport/forms/ds82/ds82__843.html (last accessed July 3, 2009).

[Section 13:6]

[1]22 CFR §51.44(b)(2).

[2]22 CFR §51.44(c)(2).

[3]22 CFR §51.54.

[4]22 CFR §51.55.

[5]22 CFR §51.55.

[6]22 CFR §51.4(b) as amended by 63 Fed. Reg. 7385 (Feb 13, 1998).

[7]22 CFR §51.4(b) as amended by 63 Fed. Reg. 7385 (Feb 13, 1998).

[8]22 CFR §22.1.

[9]22 CFR §22.1.

First-time applicants, individuals under age 16, individuals whose earlier passport was issued when they were under 16, individuals whose prior passport was lost, stolen, or damaged, individuals whose last passport was issued more than 15 years prior to the current application, and individuals unable to document a name change.[10] Individuals able to renew their passport by mail need not pay the $25 execution fee.

There are various other fees which may apply in particular cases. There is an Expedite service fee of $60, and applicants may also wish to pay for express mail return of the passport.[11] Moreover, the Government charges an additional $60 fee for "search and verification" of U.S. citizenship when a person has not presented evidence of citizenship.[12]

The State Department now issues a more limited "Passport Card," which is valid only for land and sea travel to Mexico, Canada, and many Caribbean islands.[13] That card costs only $30 (plus a $25 execution fee) for individuals aged 16 and older, and $15 (plus a $25 execution fee) for individuals under 16 years of age.[14]

§ 13:7 Procedures; generally—Proof of citizenship

Research References

Dizon and Wettstein, Immigration Law Service 2d § 14:96
Steel on Immigration Law § 15:5

A person born in the United States in a place where official records of birth were kept at the time of his or her birth must submit a birth certificate under the seal of the official custodian of birth records as proof of citizenship.[1] To be acceptable, a certificate must show the full name of the applicant, the place and date of birth, and that the record thereof was recorded at the time of birth or shortly thereafter.[2] The DSP-11 application instructs that if the birth was recorded more than one year after occurring, the person must submit secondary evidence along with this "delayed" birth certificate.[3]

If primary evidence cannot be submitted, the applicant must submit the best obtainable secondary evidence.[4] If a person was born at a place in the United States when birth records were filed, he or she must submit a "no record" certification from the official custodian of such birth records before secondary evidence may be considered.[5] The passport issuing office will consider, as secondary evidence, baptismal certificates, certificates of circumcision, or other documentary evidence

---

[10]See "Passport Fees," found at http://travel.state.gov/passport/get/fees/fees_837.html (last accessed July 3, 2009).

[11]See "Passport Fees," found at http://travel.state.gov/passport/get/fees/fees_837.html (last accessed July 3, 2009).

[12]22 CFR § 22.1.

[13]22 C.F.R. 51.3(d).

[14]22 CFR § 22.1.

[Section 13:7]

[1]22 CFR § 51.43(a); 7 FAM 1116.

[2]22 CFR § 51.43(a). The FAM provides that it should have been recorded within one year of the birth. 7 FAM 116(b)(2).

[3]Form DSP-11 (rev. 12/87), instructions.

[4]22 CFR § 51.43(b).

[5]22 CFR § 51.43(b).

created shortly after birth but not more than five years after birth, and/or affidavits of persons having personal knowledge of the facts of the birth.[6]

However, provisions in the Intelligence Reform and Terrorism Prevention Act of 2004 will require state and federal standardization of birth certificate issuance, as well as encouraging the development of computerized birth and death records.[7] These standards are to be established by the federal government by late 2006, and implemented by the states by 2007.[8]

A person naturalized in his or her own right as a U.S. citizen must submit his or her certificate of naturalization as proof of nationality.[9]

U.S. citizens at birth abroad may prove their citizenship by presenting their own certificate of citizenship.[10] Alternatively, they may submit evidence of their parents' citizenship at the time of the applicant's birth, and evidence of the applicant's and his or her parent(s)' residence and physical presence in the United States.[11] The type of evidence that may be used to establish citizenship and prior residence or physical presence of the parents is discussed in greater detail below.[12] The passport issuing office may require the applicant to establish the marriage of his or her parents and/or grandparents and his or her relationship to them.[13]

An applicant who derived citizenship through his or her parent's or parents' naturalization may submit his or her own certificate of citizenship as proof of nationality.[14] Alternatively, the applicant may submit the naturalization certificate of the parent or parents through whom he or she claims U.S. citizenship.[15] In this case, he or she must also show that he or she resided in the United States during minority as required by the law under which he or she claims citizenship.[16] An applicant who claims citizenship through a mother who resumed citizenship or a parent who was repatriated must submit evidence of the resumption or repatriation as the case may be.[17] The applicant must establish also that he or she resided in the United States for the period prescribed by law.[18]

The State Department regulations also detail evidence to prove citizenship for very specific cases including women who lost their U.S. citizenship by marriage to noncitizens,[19] former citizens of Spain and Denmark,[20] citizenship through birth in

---

[6]22 CFR § 51.43(b).

[7]Intelligence Reform and Terrorism Prevention Act of 2004, Pub. L. 108-458, 118 Stat 3638, 3825-26, § 7211(b), § 7211(c)(2)(A) (Dec. 17, 2004).

[8]Intelligence Reform and Terrorism Prevention Act of 2004, Pub. L. 108-458, 118 Stat 3638, 3826, § 7211(b)(3), § 7211(b)(1), § 7211(c)(2)(A) (Dec. 17, 2004).

[9]22 CFR § 51.44(a).

[10]22 CFR § 51.44(b)(1).

[11]22 CFR § 51.44(b)(2).

[12]See §§ 13:17 to 13:21.

[13]22 CFR § 51.44(b)(2).

[14]22 CFR § 51.44(c)(1).

[15]22 CFR § 51.44(c)(2).

[16]22 CFR § 51.44(c)(2).

[17]22 CFR § 51.44(c)(3).

[18]22 CFR § 51.44(c)(3).

[19]22 CFR §§ 51.45–51.50.

[20]22 CFR § 51.51.

territories under the jurisdiction of the U.S.,[21] and former citizens who resumed U.S. citizenship.[22]

§ 13:8 Procedures; generally—Proof of identity

Research References

Steel on Immigration Law § 15:5

Proof of identity is required as part of the passport application. An applicant who is personally known to the official receiving the application needs not prove identity.[1] If the official does not personally know the applicant, the applicant may submit a previous passport, other identifying documents, or affidavits of witnesses as proof of identity.[2] Persons who have received or expect to receive a fee in connection with obtaining the passport may not serve as witnesses.[3] Persons who are applying inside the United States and who have been issued a passport within the previous 12 years must submit the previous passport as proof of identity.[4] Regardless of the evidence presented, additional proof of identity may be required if the official deems it necessary.[5]

The State Department regulations emphasize the requirement that the name used in the passport be the same full name used in the documentary evidence of citizenship and in the proof of identity.[6] The passport office will require documentary proof of any discrepancy between the name used in the passport application and that used in supporting documents.[7] Naturalized citizens must be careful to include their full name as it appears in the naturalization certificate when filling out a passport application.

Another issue which may arise is where the applicant has had a sex-change operation, or is in the midst of a process which will lead to such an operation. The State Department has now promulgated detailed guidance on this situation, which is reproduced at Appendix 13-12.[8] Under the new State Department rules, actual sex-reassignment surgery is not required in order for an applicant to obtain a passport denoting him or her as being a particular gender.[9] In that circumstance, the applicant must present a sworn statement by a licensed physician — on office letterhead — which states that the doctor "has treated the applicant or has reviewed and evaluated the medical history of the applicant and that he/she has a doctor/patient relationship with the applicant" and that "the applicant has had appropriate

---

[21]22 CFR § 51.52.

[22]22 CFR § 51.53.

[Section 13:8]

[1]22 CFR § 51.28(a).

[2]22 CFR §§ 51.28(a), 51.31.

[3]22 CFR § 51.30.

[4]22 CFR § 51.28(b).

[5]22 CFR § 51.28(c).

[6]22 CFR § 51.23.

[7]22 CFR § 51.23.

[8]See 7 FAM 1300 Appendix M.

[9]7 FAM 1310 Appendix M para. (d).

clinical treatment for gender transition to the new gender of either male or female."[10] Where such a certification is made, a two-year passport reflecting the new gender may be issued.[11] A full validity passport is issued at no additional charge, upon application; it does not appear that the FAM actually requires sex reassignment surgery to obtain a full validity passport.[12]

Under the State Department rules, a passport reflecting a gender change may be issued regardless of the laws of the state in which the applicant resides.[13]

§13:9 Procedures; generally—Minors and incapacitated

Research References

Steel on Immigration Law §15:5

Children age 14 and over execute their own passport application, unless, in the judgment of the person accepting the application, the person believes that it is not desirable for the minor to execute his or her own application.[1] If that is the case, the application must be executed by the parent, guardian, or person *in loco parentis*.[2] A person applying on behalf of a child under the age of 14 must demonstrate that both parents consent to the issuance of a passport to the child or that the applying parent or guardian has sole custody.[3] A copy of the State Department's form DS-3053 is found at App 13-11.

DOS adopted an interim final regulation, effective March 26, 2004, that requires all passport applicants, including minors under age 14, to personally appear when applying for a passport.[4] The only exceptions to this are for those who are eligible to apply by mail, or where a senior passport officer or senior consular officer has waived the personal appearance requirement due to compelling circumstances. Agents at non-DOS acceptance facilities have no authority to waive the personal appearance requirement.[5] Guidance on waivers is still to be issued by the Department of State. Where a waiver is granted, the person executing the application on behalf of the minor must appear in person and verify the application by oath or affirmation. In overseas cases, a senior consular officer can waive the requirement that the individual executing the passport appear personally.[6] Prior to adoption of this interim regulation, minors under 14 were generally exempted from the personal appearance requirement.

The passport issuing office may require a minor under the age of 18 years to obtain and submit the written consent of a parent, a legal guardian, or a person *in*

---

[10] 7 FAM 1320 Appendix M para. (b)(1)(F), (G).

[11] 7 FAM 1320 Appendix M para. (b)(2).

[12] 7 FAM 1320 Appendix M para. (c).

[13] 7 FAM 1320 Appendix M para. (a)(1), (2).

[Section 13:9]

[1] 22 CFR §51.27(b)(1).

[2] 22 CFR §51.27(b)(1).

[3] 22 CFR §51.27(b)(2).

[4] *See* 69 Fed. Reg. 15669 (Mar. 26, 2004) amending 22 C.F.R. §§ 15.21(a) and 15.27(b)(2).

[5] *See* 69 Fed. Reg. 15669 (Mar. 26, 2004) amending 22 C.F.R. § 15.27(b)(2).

[6] *See* 69 Fed. Reg. 15669 (Mar. 26, 2004) amending 22 C.F.R. § 15.27(b)(2).

loco parentis to the issuance of the passport.[7] A passport may be denied when a person having legal control over the minor objects to the issuance of the passport.[8] Either parent may obtain information regarding the application for and issuance of a passport to a minor unless the inquiring parent's parental rights have been terminated by a court order, which has been registered with the appropriate office at the State Department.[9] The State Department, however, may deny such information to the parent if it determines that the minor is of sufficient maturity to assert a privacy interest in his or her own right.[10] In such cases, the written consent of the minor is required before providing the information to the parent.[11]

The State Department may also deny a passport in custody dispute situations. First, the State Department may require that conflicts regarding custody orders, whether domestic or foreign, be settled by the appropriate court before a passport may be issued.[12] Second, when there is a custody dispute over a minor under age 18, a passport may be denied if the Department has on file, or is provided in the course of a passport application executed on behalf of a minor, a copy of a court order from a court of competent jurisdiction in the U.S. or abroad.[13] In order to consider denial in such situations, the court order must do one of the following: (1) grant sole custody to the objecting parent; (2) establish joint legal custody; (3) prohibit the child's travel without the permission of both parents or the court; or (4) require the permission of both parents or the court for important decisions, unless permission is granted in writing as provided therein.[14] A court order providing joint custody is interpreted as requiring the permission of both parents to issue the passport.[15] The State Department considers U.S. state courts and foreign courts located in the child's home state or place of habitual residence to be courts of competent jurisdiction.[16] Even when such an order has been registered, a passport may be issued without such notification or permission, if there are compelling humanitarian or emergent reasons relating to the welfare of the child.[17]

Applications for passports for persons declared incompetent must also be executed by a parent, a legal guardian, or a person *in loco parentis*.[18]

§ 13:10 Procedures; generally—Special issues; suspected fraud

Research References

Dizon and Wettstein, Immigration Law Service 2d §§ 14:95, 14:98
Steel on Immigration Law § 15:5

The Foreign Affairs Manual (FAM) provides detailed instructions to U.S. consular

---

[7]22 CFR § 51.27(b)(3).

[8]22 CFR § 51.27(c).

[9]22 CFR § 51.27(d)(2).

[10]22 CFR § 51.27(d)(2).

[11]22 CFR § 51.27(d)(2).

[12]22 CFR § 51.27(d)(3).

[13]22 CFR § 51.27(d)(1)(i).

[14]22 CFR § 51.27(d)(1)(i).

[15]22 CFR § 51.27(d)(1)(ii).

[16]22 CFR § 51.27(d)(1)(ii).

[17]22 CFR § 51.27(d)(1)(ii).

[18]22 CFR § 51.26.

officers regarding suspected fraudulent claims of U.S. citizenship by birth abroad to a U.S. citizen parent.[1] The State Department identifies the following circumstances as likely to raise the possibility of fraud: (1) conception or birth of a child when either of the alleged natural parents was married to another; (2) naming on the birth certificate, as father, mother, or both, persons other than the alleged natural parents; (3) establishment that supposed father lacked physical access to the mother at the time of conception.[2] Other circumstances giving rise to suspicion of paternity fraud are described in other sections of the Foreign Affairs Manual.[3]

The Foreign Affairs Manual provides that if the child was conceived or born when the mother was married to someone other than the man claiming paternity, it is usually necessary for the parents to submit: (1) a statement from the man to whom she was married disavowing paternity; (2) a divorce or custody decree mentioning certain of her children but omitting or specifically excluding the child in question; or (3) credible statements from neighbors or friends having knowledge of the circumstances leading up to the birth.[4]

To ascertain the true circumstances surrounding the child's conception, the Foreign Affairs Manual advises consular officers to: (1) obtain available records showing periods of time when the alleged father was within the consular district; (2) interview the parents separately to determine any differences in their respective stories as to when and where the child was conceived; (3) interview neighbors and friends to determine the facts as understood within the local community; (4) if the couple continues to pursue the claim even though the facts as developed seem to disprove it, communicate with the department to determine whether blood testing is advisable.[5] If the consular post disapproves the application on these grounds, it is required to forward the case to the department.[6]

Another common set of facts, according to the State Department is for adoptive parents to claim an infant child as their biological child.[7] The Foreign Affairs Manual recommends the consular officer to make a further inquiry to establish that a pregnancy actually existed, which may include requesting prenatal records from the United States.[8]

As a final recourse in paternity cases, the consular officer may request blood tests.[9] The State Department admonishes that such a step should not be requested without the concurrence of the Department. If the applicant submits blood tests on

---

[Section 13:10]

[1]7 FAM 1131.4(a).

[2]7 FAM 1131.4(b).

[3]7 FAM 1131.5-3(a) (these include: (1) the child was conceived or born out of wedlock; (2) the child was conceived at a time when the father had no physical access to the mother; (3) the mother admits that, or there are other indications that, she had physical relationships with other men around the time of conception; (4) the child allegedly was born prematurely, but its weight at birth appears to indicate that it was a full-term baby; (5) the physical characteristics of the child and of the alleged parents do not seem compatible; (6) the consular district has a large number of American military or Department of Defense civilian personnel).

[4]7 FAM 1131.4(c).

[5]7 FAM 1131.5-3(b).

[6]7 FAM 1131.5-3(b).

[7]7 FAM 1131.5-4(a).

[8]7 FAM 1131.5-4(b).

[9]7 FAM 1131.5-4(c).

his or her own volition, the evidence will be accepted. However, the alleged parents will be advised that compatible results will not necessarily mean that the Department will approve a Report of Birth or issue a passport.[10]

Finally, the State Department suspects fraud in the case of individuals born to some midwives. This led to widespread problems with passport applicants being sent letters informing them that their applications had been "closed," "abandoned," or "filed without further action."[11] After a class action lawsuit was filed, the State Department has entered into a settlement agreement, promising to actually make a timely decision in any midwife cases, rather than engaging in this type of delay.[12] The Settlement Agreement permits people whose passport applications were closed or abandoned to obtain a new adjudication, without cost, by resubmitting their applications.[13] For children of midwives who actually have their passports denied on the basis that they are not citizens, a district court appeal is possible.[14]

In the *Castelano* litigation, counsel for the Plaintiff class submitted a list of midwives suspected of fraud by the former INS.[15] Most of the individuals on the list have not been convicted or otherwise shown to have engaged in fraud; but birth certificates signed by these individuals appear to be viewed suspiciously by the government. It should be noted that the State Department is alleged to have another, longer list of suspected midwives; but that list has not yet become public at this point.[16]

§ 13:11 Denial of passport

Research References

Steel on Immigration Law § 15:5

The regulations contain a list of both mandatory and permissible grounds for denying a passport.[1] A passport will not be issued when the Secretary determines, or is informed by a competent authority, that, for example, any of the following partial list of grounds exist: the applicant is subject to an outstanding felony warrant; the applicant is subject to criminal court restrictions on travel outside of the U.S.; the applicant is subject to an extradition request which has been presented to a foreign government; the applicant has not repaid certain loans from the U.S.; and the applicant has been certified by the Secretary of the Health and Human Services

---

[10]7 FAM 1131.5-4(c).

[11]See, Castelano v. Clinton, No 7:08-cv-00057 (S.D.Tex.). The settlement agreement is available at: http://www.aclu.org/files/pdfs/racialjustice/castelanovclinton_agreement.pdf.

[12]See, Castelano v. Clinton, No 7:08-cv-00057 (S.D.Tex.). The settlement agreement is available at: http://www.aclu.org/files/pdfs/racialjustice/castelanovclinton_agreement.pdf.

[13]See, Castelano v. Clinton, No 7:08-cv-00057 (S.D.Tex.). The settlement agreement is available at: http://www.aclu.org/files/pdfs/racialjustice/castelanovclinton_agreement.pdf.

[14]See §§ 10:20 to 10:23.

[15]The list of midwifes involved is available from the District Court's website, Castelano v. Clinton, No 7:08-cv-00057 (S.D.Tex.), docket entry 36-2. The settlement agreement is available at: http://www.aclu.org/files/pdfs/racialjustice/castelanovclinton_agreement.pdf.

[16]See, Castelano v. Clinton, No 7:08-cv-00057 (S.D.Tex.), Second Amended Complaint at 15, ¶ 46.

[Section 13:11]

[1]22 CFR § 51.70.

to be in arrears in child support of more than $5000.[2] At least two courts have found that a passport denial based upon a child support arrearage does not violate the Constitution.[3] Passports also will be denied to certain convicted drug traffickers.[4]

The regulations also contain a number of grounds that permit, though do not mandate, the denial of a passport. For example, an individual who has been legally declared incompetent can be denied a passport unless accompanied in the travel abroad by a guardian or other person responsible for the individual's care.[5] Similarly, a passport can be denied to an individual under 18 years of age in certain circumstances.[6]

§13:12 Revocation of passport

Research References

Steel on Immigration Law §15:5

In 1994, Congress added a section to the Immigration and Nationality Act authorizing the Secretary of State to cancel passports and reports of birth if it appeared that they were obtained illegally, fraudulently, or erroneously.[1] The State Department has implemented this provision by providing for the revocation of a U.S. passport if: (1) the national would not be entitled to issuance of a new passport under the passport issuance provisions; (2) the passport has been obtained illegally, by fraud, or has been fraudulently altered, or has been fraudulently misused, or has been issued in error; or (3) the Department of State is notified that a certificate of naturalization issued to the applicant for or bearer of the passport has been canceled by a federal court.[2] One court has held that the revocation of a passport does not deprive an individual of citizenship, since a passport is simply proof of citizenship.[3]

USCIS adopted an interim final regulation, effective March 26, 2004, that clarifies that any passport that has been revoked or has been reported lost or stolen is invalid.[4] The purpose of this interim regulation is to forestall the use of revoked, lost or stolen passports for illegal entry into the United States. As a result of the regulation change, however, a U.S. citizen who reports that a passport has been lost or stolen will not be able to use the passport if it is subsequently found.

---

[2]22 CFR §51.70(a)(1), (2), (4), (6) and (8). *See* 22 CFR §51.70(a) for a complete list of mandatory grounds for denial of a passport application.

[3]Weinstein v. Albright, 261 F.3d 127 (2d Cir. 2001) (no procedural due process or equal protection violation); Eunique v. Powell, 302 F.3d 971 (9th Cir. 2002) (no violation of the constitutional right to international travel); *but see* Eunique v. Powell, 302 F.3d 971 (9th Cir. 2002) (Kleinfeld, J., *dissenting*) (opining that the right to international travel was too important to let the government take it away as punishment to advance a government policy, just because the policy is important).

[4]22 CFR §51.71.

[5]22 CFR §51.70(b)(2).

[6]22 CFR §51.70(b)(3). *See* 22 CFR §51.70(b) for a complete list of permissible, though not mandatory, grounds for denial of a passport.

[Section 13:12]

[1]Act of Oct. 25, 1994, Pub.L. 103-416, Title I, §107(a), 108 Stat. 4309, adding INA §361, 8 U.S.C.A. §1504.

[2]22 CFR §51.72 (as amended by 64 Fed. Reg. 19713 (April 22, 1999)).

[3]Atem v. Ashcroft, 312 F. Supp. 2d 792 (E.D. Va. 2004).

[4]*See* 69 Fed. Reg. 15669 (Mar. 26, 2004) amending 22 C.F.R. §51.4 by adding a new paragraph (h).

§ 13:13 Appeal or denial or revocation of a passport

Research References

Gallagher, Immigration Law Service 2d §§ 1:1219, 1:221

There is no longer any administrative appeal from denial or cancellation of a Passport.[1] Prior to 2008, the State Department maintained an appellate body for these appeals, called the Board of Appellate Review (BAR); however, the State Department eliminated the BAR in 2008, because it received very few appeals.[2] It will, however, entertain motions to reconsider.[3]

§ 13:14 How to obtain evidence of issuance of old U.S. passport

Persons who need to establish U.S. citizenship or prior U.S. residence of a parent or grandparent may find it useful to submit a Freedom of Information Act Request to the U.S. passport agency. Records of passport applications dated October 27, 1795, through December 31, 1924, are kept at the National Archives at College Park, Textual Reference Branch (NNR2), 8601 Adelphi Road; College Park, Maryland 20740-6001. This archive also holds the records of emergency applications submitted abroad between 1877 and 1924, and applications for special (diplomatic) passports from 1829 to 1897.[1]

Passport records dated after 1924 remain in the custody of the Department of State's Passport Services Office, Research and Liaison Branch; 1111 19th Street, NW, Suite 200; Washington, DC 20522-1705.[2]

To request a search, the applicant must provide a notarized statement containing (1) full name, date and place of birth, current address, and reason for request; (2) the full name, date and place of birth subject filed, and the date of possible application for a U.S. passport; and (3) the notarized consent of the file subject to release information, or convincing proof that the file subject is deceased.[3] There is a $15 fee per file search for each subject.[4] Copies certified by the Department of State Seal, cost an additional $10 fee.[5] Checks should be made payable to Department of State.[6]

[Section 13:13]

   [1]22 C.F.R. § 50.51.

   [2]73 Fed. Reg. 41256 to 41258 (July 18, 2008) (supplementary information).

   [3]73 Fed. Reg. 41256 to 41258 (July 18, 2008) (supplementary information).

[Section 13:14]

   [1]Clarence F. Lyons, Chief, Archives II Textual Reference Branch, Letter to Donald Sheridian (June 11, 1996).

   [2]Clarence F. Lyons, Chief, Archives II Textual Reference Branch, Letter to Donald Sheridian (June 11, 1996).

   [3]Clarence F. Lyons, Chief, Archives II Textual Reference Branch, Letter to Donald Sheridian (June 11, 1996).

   [4]Clarence F. Lyons, Chief, Archives II Textual Reference Branch, Letter to Donald Sheridian (June 11, 1996).

   [5]Clarence F. Lyons, Chief, Archives II Textual Reference Branch, Letter to Donald Sheridian (June 11, 1996).

   [6]Clarence F. Lyons, Chief, Archives II Textual Reference Branch, Letter to Donald Sheridian (June 11, 1996).

IV. CONSULAR REPORT OF BIRTH

§ 13:15   Requirements

Research References
Dizon and Wettstein, Immigration Law Service 2d § 14:93
Steel on Immigration Law § 15:4

The Consular Report of Birth Abroad of a Citizen of the United States has the same force and effect as proof of U.S. citizenship as a U.S. passport, a certificate of naturalization, or a certificate of citizenship issued by the Attorney General or by a court having naturalization jurisdiction.[1] The consular officer issues the report on Form FS-240.[2] Since it is an official document certifying citizenship, it is issued on a controlled, prenumbered form.[3] The purpose of issuing the consular report is to provide an accurate record, which has been fully documented, of the acquisition of U.S. citizenship by a child born in a foreign state that can be used by that citizen throughout life.[4] This document is only available to children who acquire U.S. citizenship at birth abroad, and not to those who derive citizenship upon naturalization of their parents.[5]

In 2011, the State Department began issuing a redesigned FS-240. The new documents come with a variety of new security features, and are now printed only in Passport Agencies in Portsmouth, New Hampshire and New Orleans, Louisiana.[6]

§ 13:16   Application procedures

Research References
Dizon and Wettstein, Immigration Law Service 2d § 14:96
Steel on Immigration Law § 15:4

A consular officer may issue the consular report of birth upon application made by the parents or their authorized representative at any time before the child's 18th birthday.[1] The fee for this application is $100.[2] Under current policy, only the parent or legal guardian may apply for this report; no other person is authorized to apply on a child's behalf.[3] The child's parent or legal guardian must fill out an Application for Consular Report of Birth Abroad of a Citizen of the United States, Form DS-

---

[Section 13:15]

[1] 22 U.S.C.A. § 2705.

[2] 7 FAM 1441.1(a).

[3] 7 FAM 1441.1(b), 1446.2-1(a).

[4] 7 FAM 1441.1(d).

[5] 7 FAM 1445.5-1.

[6] 7 FAM 1441.1(b).

[Section 13:16]

[1] 22 CFR § 50.5; 7 FAM 1443(a), 1445.2(a) (policy effective after November 1990).

[2] 8 CFR § 22.1, Schedule of Fees, Item #7.

[3] 7 FAM 1443(d).

2029.[4] This is a combined Consular Report of Birth/Social Security Number Card application.[5] A copy of the form is reproduced at App 13-11.

The personal appearance of the child on whose behalf the report of birth is requested may be required at the consular officer's discretion (for example, when the consular officer suspects that the child is deceased, is living in the United States, or that the child's true identity is not being reported).[6] Minors of age 13 or above are generally required to appear with the requesting parent or guardian.[7]

An application for a consular report of birth is normally made in the consular district in which the birth occurred.[8] Although it is permissible for a birth that occurred in one consular district to be reported in another, reports may not be issued for a child who is physically present in the United States.[9] Special rules apply to reporting a birth in a consulate other than where the birth occurred.[10]

Normally, the application will be made at the consulate or embassy, but under special circumstances, it may be made in the form of a *jurat* administered by a person other than the consular officer who will then forward it to the consulate for further processing.[11] In addition, when a birth takes place in a country in which the United States has no diplomatic or consular representative, but maintains an Interests Section in the embassy of a third country, the report is accepted by the Interests Section and forwarded to the post in the third country for approval, if appropriate.[12]

Parents or legal guardians must apply for a report of birth on Form DS-2029.[13] The first page of the form is the application for a report of birth. The second page of the form is the application for a social security number card. The application for a social security number is to be completed only for children under the age of five when the child's natural, adoptive or stepparent, or legal guardian applies for a report of birth.[14] If no social security number is necessary or if the child is over five years of age, only the first page is filled out.[15]

§ 13:17 Evidentiary issues; generally

Research References

Dizon and Wettstein, Immigration Law Service 2d § 14:96
Steel on Immigration Law § 15:4

---

[4]7 FAM 1443(b).

[5]7 FAM 1443(b).

[6]7 FAM 1445.1.

[7]7 FAM 1445.1.

[8]7 FAM 1445.3-1(a).

[9]7 FAM 1445.3-1(a), (b). If the child has already been determined to be a U.S. citizen, either through a certificate of citizenship or through the issuance of a U.S. passport, the parents may file to register the child at the consulate of birth, even when the child is physically present in the United States. 7 FAM 1445.3-1(c).

[10]For detailed discussion of these rules, see 7 FAM 1445.3-2, 1445.4-4.

[11]7 FAM 1445.3(d).

[12]7 FAM 1445.4-4(b).

[13]7 FAM 1445.4-1(a)(1).

[14]7 FAM 1445.4-1(a)(3).

[15]7 FAM 1445.4-1(b).

The proof requirement is the same as that to obtain a passport.[1] When a child has been documented previously with a full validity U.S. passport or certificate of citizenship, the application need only be accompanied by proof of the child's birth and citizenship.[2] If the actual full validity passport or certificate of citizenship is not presented, the parent must provide sufficient information to allow the Department to verify the issuance of either of those documents.[3]

When the child has never been documented as a U.S. citizen before, then the parent must present specific proof of the child's U.S. citizenship at birth. This proof must include evidence of the child's birth, of the parent's U.S. citizenship and identity, of the parent's prior physical presence in United States, and of the parent's marriage.[4]

§ 13:18 Evidentiary issues; generally—Child's birth

Research References

Dizon and Wettstein, Immigration Law Service 2d § 14:96
Steel on Immigration Law § 15:4

The Foreign Affairs Manual requires the submission of "satisfactory proof of the child's birth."[1] Primary evidence of birth is a certified copy of a birth registration issued by local authorities.[2] Secondary evidence of birth includes a baptismal certificate, a local or military hospital birth certificate, a certification of the birth by the physician attending the birth, or an affidavit executed by another person attending the birth, setting forth the facts and circumstances of the birth.[3] The consular officer will insist on submission of primary evidence of birth, especially in the case of a child older than five years.[4]

If primary evidence is not obtainable, the applicant must submit an affidavit explaining why such proof is not obtainable and setting forth the facts relating to the birth.[5] In every case the consular officer must be satisfied that the evidence submitted is sufficient to establish the facts of birth, particularly when an adoptive parent or legal guardian, rather than the natural parent, reports the facts of the child's birth.[6]

When a child is born out of wedlock to a citizen father and a noncitizen mother, the consular officer will usually require an affidavit from the father acknowledging that he is the biological father of the child.[7] An affidavit will always be required when the consular officer has reason to doubt that the alleged father is, in fact, the

---

[Section 13:17]

[1] 7 FAM 1443(d).
[2] 7 FAM 1445.5-1.
[3] 7 FAM 1445.5-1.
[4] 7 FAM 1445.5-2.

[Section 13:18]

[1] 7 FAM 1445.5-3(a).
[2] 7 FAM 1445.5-3(a).
[3] 7 FAM 1445.5-3(a).
[4] 7 FAM 1445.5-3(a).
[5] 7 FAM 1445.5-3(b).
[6] 7 FAM 1445.5-3(b).
[7] 7 FAM 1445.5-3(c).

father of the child.[8] A statement of support must be included in the affidavit in those cases where the child's acquisition of U.S. citizenship is determined by the provisions of the INA as amended by the Act of November 14, 1986.[9]

If the current name of the child is different from the one appearing on the birth certificate, the applicant must submit appropriate evidence of name change.[10]

§ 13:19 Evidentiary issues; generally—Evidence of parent's U.S. citizenship and identity

Research References

Dizon and Wettstein, Immigration Law Service 2d § 14:96

The parents may submit as evidence of citizenship any of the types of evidence ordinarily acceptable for passport purposes.[1] This includes an original or certified copy of a birth certificate or, if not available, a U.S. passport, a previously approved consular report of birth, a certificate of citizenship or naturalization, or other acceptable secondary evidence of birth, such as a baptismal certificate.[2] The procedures for obtaining old passport records are discussed above.[3]

If both parents are U.S. citizens but only one parent presents evidence of citizenship, the consular officer should inform the parents that the child will be considered to have acquired citizenship under the provisions governing birth abroad to the child of one citizen and one noncitizen parent.[4] The report will be issued if the parent who presented the evidence complied with all the conditions for the transmission of U.S. citizenship to the child.[5]

§ 13:20 Evidentiary issues; generally—Evidence of parent's prior physical presence in U.S

Research References

Dizon and Wettstein, Immigration Law Service 2d § 14:96
Steel on Immigration Law § 15:4

Under the current statute, if both parents are U.S. citizens at the time of the child's birth, U.S. citizenship is transmitted if either of them was ever present in the United States.[1] In all other cases, however, the U.S. citizen parent must demonstrate a longer period of physical presence in the United States.[2]

Unless both parents are U.S. citizens, the application for a consular report of

---

[8]7 FAM 1445.5-3(c).

[9]7 FAM 1445.5-3(c). See § 4:65.

[10]7 FAM 1445.5-4 (explaining what evidence must be submitted).

[Section 13:19]

[1]7 FAM 1445.5-5(b).

[2]7 FAM 1445.5-5(b).

[3]See § 13:14.

[4]7 FAM 1445.5-5(d).

[5]For current rules on acquisition of citizenship, see § 4:65.

[Section 13:20]

[1]See § 4:64.

[2]7 FAM 1445.5-6(a).

birth must show that the U.S. citizen parent had the necessary periods of physical presence in the United States or its outlying possessions to transmit U.S. citizenship to the child.[3] In addition, some qualifying presence abroad, such as service abroad with the U.S. armed forces, satisfies the physical presence requirement.[4]

When doubt exists that the parent's physical presence in the United States meets the requirements necessary to establish the child's U.S. citizenship, documentary evidence of the citizen parent's physical presence in the United States for the periods claimed is required to be submitted with the application.[5] Evidentiary proof usually accepted includes proof of registration in U.S. public or private schools, deeds, court records, military records, or other legal documents as valid evidence of physical presence for the periods of time required by the citizen parent to transmit citizenship.[6]

Other sources of official documents useful in establishing physical presence include census bureau records, old passport records, military service records, and social security earnings records. The census bureau keeps records about individuals. An explanation of the type of records kept and the procedures for obtaining them is detailed below.[7] Old passport records may also assist the person in proving physical presence. Procedures for obtaining old passport records are discussed above.[8] Military service records are another source of documentation regarding physical presence in the Unites States. Social Security Administration makes available a statement detailing the history of earnings for each individual. Form SSA-7004 is used to request these statements by mail. This form is attached as Appendix 13-9. This form is attached as Appendix 13-8. It may also be accessed through the Internet. The address is: http://www.ssa.gov/online/ssa-7004.html.

In addition, it may be useful to check the availability of other official documentation. Most U.S. agencies have websites that provide forms and information electronically. The most useful to obtain official records are (1) Social Security Administration at http://www.ssa.gov/; (2) U.S. Census Bureau at http://www.census.gov/; (3) U.S. Passport Office at http://travel.state.gov/passport__services.html. For a comprehensive listing of U.S. federal agency websites see http://www.usa.gov/Agencies/Federal/All__Agencies/index.shtml. Official state documents are also useful in proving physical presence.

In the absence of such primary evidence and upon presentation of satisfactory proof of the inability to obtain such evidence, consuls may accept the sworn statements of at least two U.S. citizens having personal knowledge of the parent's periods of physical presence in the United States as sufficient evidence to establish the claim.[9] Evidentiary proof of the parent's qualifying presence abroad is discussed in the Foreign Affairs Manual.[10] A model affidavit of physical presence is found at App 13-11.

---

[3]7 FAM 1445.5-6(a).

[4]See §§ 4:55, 4:56.

[5]7 FAM 1445.5-6(b).

[6]7 FAM 1445.5-6(c).

[7]U.S. Census Bureau, Factfinder for the Nation, Availability of Census Records About Individuals, April 1997 reproduced as Appendix 13-8.

[8]See § 13:14.

[9]See Appendix 12-5 to Ch 12.

[10]7 FAM 1445.5-7.

§ 13:21 Evidentiary issues; generally—Evidence of parent's marriage

The marital status of the parents can be the determining factor in whether a child has a claim to U.S. citizenship.[1] The consular does not accept a U.S. passport in the mother's married name as sufficient evidence of marriage because a woman is generally not required to present proof of her marriage when she applies for a passport using her married name.[2] If the parents cannot obtain a marriage certificate, they are required to submit other evidence of their marriage, such as extracts from church records, affidavits from persons in a position to know when and where they were married, and any other pertinent evidence.[3]

If either of the parents was married previously, and the child's claim to U.S. citizenship is dependent upon the marriage of the parents, evidence of the termination of the previous marriage or marriages must be presented.[4] A divorce or annulment decree or a death certificate is sufficient evidence.[5] Certified true copies of the original documents should be attached to the application file copy.[6]

When the child's citizenship is not dependent upon the existence of the parents' marriage or termination of a previous marriage, it is not necessary to delay issuance of a consular report of birth and/or a passport if the parents cannot present evidence of those events.[7] The parent may present these documents at a later date if he or she wishes to complete the file.[8]

§ 13:22 Decision

Research References

Dizon and Wettstein, Immigration Law Service 2d § 14:96

The consular officer at the post in whose jurisdiction the birth occurred is authorized to complete and approve the application and issue the consular report of birth, without specific authorization.[1] In most cases, upon determining that the child acquired U.S. citizenship, and if the child's name clears the Department's passport name check system, the application will be approved and the consular officer will issue and sign the consular report of birth.[2]

State Department authorization before approval is required when: (1) there is a "hold" on the registrant's name entered into the CLASS system or a lookout card in the registrant's name; (2) there is a question about the blood relationship between the citizen parent and the child; (3) a possibility of fraud exists; (4) there is a pos-

---

[Section 13:21]

[1]7 FAM 1445.5-8(a).
[2]7 FAM 1445.5-8(b).
[3]7 FAM 1445.5-8(c).
[4]7 FAM 1445.5-8(d).
[5]7 FAM 1445.5-8(d).
[6]7 FAM 1445.5-8(d).
[7]7 FAM 1445.5-8(e).
[8]7 FAM 1445.5-8(e).

[Section 13:22]

[1]7 FAM 1445.4(a).
[2]7 FAM 1445.4(a).

sibility that the child may have committed an expatriating act; (5) the child's 18th birthday is reached before application is made.[3]

When a referral to the State Department is necessary, the consular posts are advised to email their counterpart in CA/OCS/ACS, and either fax or scan copies of the original documents presented.[4] Where the consular post suspects that submitted evidence is counterfeit or appears to have been altered, the post is instructed to send the original evidence to the Consular Affairs Office of Fraud Prevention Programs (CA/FPP), attached to the application.[5] The post may also forward original documentation in cases where fraud is not suspected, but where review of the original documentation appears appropriate.[6]

When the available evidence supports a determination of acquisition of U.S. citizenship, the posts are not allowed to keep the application in suspense.[7] The applications will be approved under any applicable section that the documentation supports.[8] The documents in support of a consular report of birth will be filed in the State Department with the report of birth (Form FS-240) file copy and the application.[9]

Consular posts are authorized to hold an application in suspense for 90 days if awaiting receipt of documentary evidence, such as the parent's citizenship or marriage evidence, or department authorization to approve the application.[10] Where the application contains insufficient evidence to approve the application, and no further evidence has been supplied after 90 days, the post is instructed to deny the application for insufficient evidence.[11] A notation that it was denied for insufficient evidence is entered into the CLASS database, and the applicant must thereafter file a new FS-240, with new fees, before additional evidence will be considered.[12]

If the application is denied on the grounds that the applicant simply is not a citizen, a different code is entered into the database.[13] The State Department professes itself willing to reconsider denials at any time, noting that new evidence may arise.[14]

In case of denial, it is not completely clear whether a federal appeal would lie. There are good arguments that a declaratory judgment action could be filed in

---

[3]7 FAM 1445.4(b)(1). Consular posts have been specifically authorized to approve certain types of cases relating to children born out of wedlock to U.S. citizen parents. If the case fits that pattern, the consular official may approve the report without prior State Department authorization. 7 FAM 1445.4(a).

[4]7 FAM 1445.4(b)(2).

[5]7 FAM 1445.7-2(b).

[6]7 FAM 1445.7-2(c).

[7]7 FAM 1445.4(c)(2).

[8]7 FAM 1445.4(c)(3).

[9]7 FAM 1445.4(c)(4).

[10]7 FAM 1445.4(c)(1).

[11]7 FAM 1445.8(c).

[12]7 FAM 1445.8(d), (e).

[13]7 FAM 1445.9(a)

[14]7 FAM 1445.9(b)

federal district court,[15] but there are also counter-arguments that only individuals within the United States can file suit, pursuant to the statute.[16]

§ 13:23   Amendment of consular report of birth

Research References

Dizon and Wettstein, Immigration Law Service 2d § 14:96

The consular report of birth now, in certain circumstances, may be amended or replaced.[1] Amendments usually are made to correct an error of information shown on the face of the document.[2] Amendments may also be made to record a change of name by an adoption or other legal proceeding.[3]

After a consular report of birth has been issued and the application filed in the State Department, the document can be amended by the Department Passport Services, Correspondence Branch.[4] That office prepares a new report of birth showing the amended data, upon request by the parent, legal guardian, or the registrant (person in whose name it was issued).[5] After the registrant's 18th birthday, only the registrant may request an amendment.[6]

Persons wishing to request an amendment may write to: U.S. Department of State Passport Services Correspondence Branch (CA/PPT/PS/PC); 1425 K Street, N.W.; Washington, D.C. 20524.[7] Requesters must include appropriate supporting documents (such as an adoption decree or court decree showing legal change of name).[8] The previously issued consular report of birth must be included, or, if unavailable, an affidavit explaining the unavailability of this document.[9] The appropriate fee, i.e., the same as for the originally issued consular report, must be included with the request.[10] The fee will be refunded when it is determined that the need for amendment is due to State Department error.[11]

§ 13:24   Replacement of consular report of birth

Research References

Dizon and Wettstein, Immigration Law Service 2d § 14:96

When a consular report of birth is lost, stolen, mutilated, or accidentally destroyed, a person may obtain a replacement from the Department upon writing to: Vital Re-

---

[15]*See, e.g.*, Rusk v. Cort, 369 U.S. 367 (1962); § 10:24.

[16]INA § 360(a), 8 U.S.C.A. § 1503(a).

[Section 13:23]

[1]7 FAM 1443(f).

[2]7 FAM 1447.1.

[3]7 FAM 1447.1.

[4]7 FAM 1447.2 (Ref. CA/PPT/PS/PC).

[5]7 FAM 1447.2.

[6]7 FAM 1447.2.

[7]7 FAM 1447.3-1.

[8]7 FAM 1447.3-2.

[9]7 FAM 1447.3-2.

[10]7 FAM 1447.3-2.

[11]7 FAM 1447.3-2.

cords Section, Passport Services, 1111 19th Street, NW, Suite 510, Washington, D.C. 20522-1705.[1]

The written request must include: (1) full name of child at birth (plus any adoptive names); (2) date and place of birth; (3) names of parents; (4) serial number, if known, of the FS-240 (on those issued after November 1, 1990) if known; (5) any available passport information; (6) signature of requester and; (7) notarized affidavit for a replacement FS-240 (if applicable).[2] The affidavit should set forth the circumstances surrounding the loss, theft, or mutilation.[3] The request should include a copy of valid photo identification of the requester. The appropriate fee, currently $30, must be submitted.[4] That fee is currently $30.

The replacement FS-240 will be issued with the same identifying number, except that it will end in a dash and a number (as in –1), to indicate that it is a replacement.[5]

A "Certification of Report of Birth" (DS-1350) may also be requested, in multiple copies. This form is also legal evidence of citizenship, and may be issued in multiple copies, within the United States.[6]

§13:25 Cancellation of consular report of birth

Research References

Dizon and Wettstein, Immigration Law Service 2d §§ 14:96, 14:98

In 1994, Congress added a section to the Immigration and Nationality Act authorizing the Secretary of State to cancel passports and reports of birth if it appeared that they were obtained illegally, fraudulently, or erroneously.[1] According to the regulations, a consular report of birth, or a certification thereof, may be canceled if it appears that such document was illegally, fraudulently, or erroneously obtained, or was created through illegality or fraud.[2] The cancellation of such a document affects only the document and not the citizenship status of the person in whose name the document was issued.[3] Written notice of this action is provided to the person in whose name the report of birth was made.[4] The notice is sent to the person's last known address.[5] The notice must include specific reasons why the action was taken and must include explanation of the procedures for review.[6] The procedures for

---

[Section 13:24]

[1] 7 FAM 1448.1-1.

[2] 7 FAM 1448.1-2; see also, http://travel.state.gov/law/family__issues/birth/birth__593.html.

[3] 7 FAM 1448.1-3.

[4] 22 C.F.R. § 22.1.

[5] 7 FAM 1448.2.

[6] See http://travel.state.gov/law/family__issues/birth/birth__593.html.

[Section 13:25]

[1] Act of Oct. 25, 1994, Pub.L. 103-416, Title I, § 107(a), 108 Stat. 4309 adding INA § 361, 8 U.S.C.A. § 1504.

[2] 8 CFR § 50.7(d)(as amended by 64 Fed. Reg.19713 (April 22, 1999)).

[3] 8 CFR § 50.7(d)(as amended by 64 Fed. Reg.19713 (April 22, 1999)).

[4] 8 CFR § 50.7(d)(as amended by 64 Fed. Reg.19713 (April 22, 1999)).

[5] 8 CFR § 50.7(d)(as amended by 64 Fed. Reg.19713 (April 22, 1999)).

[6] 8 CFR § 50.7(d)(as amended by 64 Fed. Reg.19713 (April 22, 1999)).

seeking review are detailed in the regulations.[7] It must be pointed out that the affected party only has 60 days to request review of the cancellation.[8]

V. CERTIFICATE OF CITIZENSHIP

§ 13:26 Who has right to certificate of citizenship

Research References
Steel on Immigration Law §§ 15:1, 15:4, 15:5

A certificate of citizenship is available for people upon whom U.S. citizenship vested by any means other than birth inside the United States.[1] The certificate is specifically available to:[2] (1) U.S. citizens born abroad;[3] (2) U.S. citizens born in an outlying possession of the United States;[4] (3) U.S. citizens born in Panama;[5] (4) persons who derive citizenship upon the naturalization of one or both of their parents;[6] and (5) women who derived citizenship through their spouses[7] under former law. A special provision also exists for the issuance of certificates of citizenship to adopted children of U.S. citizens.[8] The law does not make certificates of citizenship available to people who acquired U.S. citizenship through collective naturalization upon the acquisition of a territory by the U.S.[9] A copy of the certificate of citizenship is reproduced as Appendix 13-2.

§ 13:27 Filing for certificate after citizenship vests

Research References
Steel on Immigration Law §§ 15:1, 15:4, 15:5

Persons wishing to obtain a certificate of citizenship must submit an application on Form N-600 to the local USCIS office, together with the requisite filing fee.[1] The filing fee is $460.[2] Form N-600 is attached to this chapter as Appendix 13-3.[3] Documentary evidence establishing the basis for the citizenship claim should be

---

[7]22 CFR §§ 51.80–51.89.

[8]22 CFR § 51.81.

[Section 13:26]

[1]INA § 341(a), 8 U.S.C.A. § 1452(a).

[2]INA § 341(a), 8 U.S.C.A. § 1452(a).

[3]See §§ 4:1 et seq.

[4]See §§ 3:7 to 3:8.

[5]See §§ 4:67, 4:68.

[6]See §§ 5:1 et seq.

[7]See § 11:2.

[8]INA § 341(c), 8 U.S.C.A. § 1452(c).

[9]See §§ 2:15 to 2:23.

[Section 13:27]

[1]8 CFR § 341.1(a).

[2]8 CFR § 103.7.

[3]It is also available for download from the USCIS website at http://uscis.gov/graphics/index.htm. The current edition of Form N-600 is dated November 15, 2002. Earlier editions are no longer acceptable.

included.[4] If the applicant is 14 years of age or older, he or she must sign the application; otherwise it can be signed by the child's parent or guardian.[5] Also required are three photographs of the applicant. Photographs must be unglazed, taken within 30 days of the date of application, and must be two inches by two inches in size.[6]

The USCIS will require the certificate of citizenship applicant, or the parent acting on the child's behalf, to appear for examination under oath. The in-person examination is waived if the application is substantiated by a Report of Birth Abroad of a Citizen of the United States (State Form FS-240), an unexpired U.S. passport issued for the maximum period allowed by law, or the applicant's parent's or parents' naturalization certificate.[7] At the examination, the applicant may be represented by counsel and present evidence and cross-examine witnesses.[8] If essential witnesses are not available in the United States but can be located abroad, provisions allow for depositions in the form of written interrogatories before a DHS officer or United States consular official.[9] After the examination, the DHS officer makes a report and recommendation to the district director, upon which basis the application must be approved or denied.[10]

If the application for the certificate of citizenship is approved, the applicant must be in the United States or its outlying possessions and must take an oath of allegiance.[11] The certificate will be issued even when the person lacks mental capacity to understand the oath.[12] The certificate is delivered personally or may be forwarded by certified mail.[13] The certificate will not be delivered outside the United States.[14]

By statute, a State Department Consular Report of Birth Abroad or a full U.S. passport, valid for the maximum period authorized by law, "have the same force and effect as proof of United States citizenship as certificates of naturalization or of citizenship."[15] Thus, the Board of Immigration Appeals has found a passport to constitute "conclusive proof" of citizenship, unless void on its face.[16] Applicants in possession of either document ought not face stringent examination as to citizenship; however, it appears that USCIS is often not treating these documents as "conclusive" in the way that the case law might suggest.

§ 13:28 Denial of Certificate of Citizenship

If an application for a Certificate of Citizenship is denied, the applicant receives written notice of the grounds for denial. The decision of the district director may be

---

[4]8 CFR § 341.1(a).

[5]Form N-600 (Rev. 04/11/91), Instructions.

[6]8 CFR § 333.1. The requirements for these photographs are fully discussed in §§ 9:43 to 9:49.

[7]8 CFR § 341.2(a).

[8]8 CFR § 341.2(f).

[9]8 CFR § 341.3.

[10]8 CFR § 341.5.

[11]INA § 341, 8 U.S.C.A. § 1452; 8 CFR § 341.7.

[12]INS Interp. 341.2(a)(4).

[13]8 CFR § 341.7.

[14]INS Interp. 341.2(a)(7).

[15]22 U.S.C.A. § 2705.

[16]Matter of Villanueva, 19 I. & N. Dec. 101 (BIA 1984).

appealed to the Administrative Appeals Unit within 30 days of notice of denial.[1] An appeal may be filed on Form I-290B, along with the requisite filing fee and must be submitted to the office that made the original decision.[2] (It is important for the applicant not to send it directly to the Administrative Appeals Unit). Requests for submission of written briefs and oral argument may be included in the notice of appeal.[3] Upon receipt of the appeal, the USCIS District Office which denied the decision originally may treat the appeal as a motion to reopen or reconsider and grant the case, if so inclined.[4]

The possibility of appeal to the federal courts is discussed earlier in this book.[5] An appeal to the AAU has been found required prior to a federal court appeal of a denial of a Certificate of Citizenship.[6]

§ 13:29 Multiple applications prohibited

Oddly, multiple N-600 applications are barred by regulation.[1] Rather, the regulations instruct that "[a]fter an application for a certificate of citizenship has been denied and the time for appeal has expired, USCIS will reject a subsequent application submitted by the same individual and the applicant will be instructed to submit a motion to reopen or reconsider in accordance with 8 CFR 103.5. The motion must be accompanied by the rejected application and the fee specified in 8 CFR 103.7."[2]

This requirement does not appear to be based in the statute, which provides simply that an individual claiming citizenship "may apply to the Attorney General for a certificate of citizenship."[3] The statute contains no bar to multiple applications.

The deadline for any motion to reopen under 8 C.F.R. § 103.5 would be 30 days, the same as the deadline for any appeal; so almost definitionally, the motions required under this section would be untimely.[4] USCIS has broad authority to waive untimeliness in motions to reopen,[5] but the regulation in a sense puts an individual claiming citizenship into a posture where only a discretionary decision to excuse untimeliness would permit consideration of the renewed claim to citizenship.

The N-600 application fee is currently $600, while the fee for a motion to reopen is $630.[6]

It appears, given the requirement to attach the earlier application and decision,

---

[Section 13:28]

   [1]8 CFR §§ 103.3(a)(2)(i), 341.6.

   [2]8 CFR §§ 103.3(a)(2)(i), 341.5(d).

   [3]Form I-290B is reproduced as Appendix 7-4 to Ch 7.

   [4]8 CFR § 103.5(a)(8).

   [5]See §§ 10:20 to 10:22.

   [6]See § 10:21.

[Section 13:29]

   [1]8 C.F.R. § 341.5(e).

   [2]8 C.F.R. § 341.5(e).

   [3]Cf. INA § 341(a), 8 U.S.C.A. § 1452(a).

   [4]8 C.F.R. § 103.5(a)(1)(i) (30 days for reopening).

   [5]See 8 C.F.R. § 103.5(a)(1)(i) ("[F]ailure to file before this period expires, may be excused in the discretion of the Service where it is demonstrated that the delay was reasonable and was beyond the control of the applicant or petitioner."); see also, 8 C.F.R. § 103.5(a)(5) (USCIS sua sponte reopening authority).

   [6]Cf. Appendix 13-3 (N-600) with Appendix 7-4 (I-290B).

that the rationale for the rule is to ensure that any subsequent adjudicator has possession of the earlier N-600 application before ruling on a second application.[7] It would seem that modern technology and USCIS file handling rules would address these concerns without need for the blanket prohibition on new filings, particularly given the legal rights at issue and the occasional difficulties in providing the elements of a citizenship claim.

§ 13:30 Certificate and removal proceedings

An individual is not prohibited from filing an N-600 while removal proceedings are pending.[1] To the contrary, it is commonly a way to obtain resolution of the case short of a trial on the merits. It should be noted, however, that any federal court action related to the N-600 would likely be precluded on grounds that the citizenship issue arose in connection with the removal proceeding.[2]

§ 13:31 Certificate of citizenship for children of U.S. citizens

Research References

Dizon and Wettstein, Immigration Law Service 2d §§ 14:214 to 14:226
Steel on Immigration Law §§ 15:4, 15:5

U.S. citizen parents may file for a certificate of citizenship for their children under 18 years of age, even when citizenship has not vested automatically. A child issued a certificate of citizenship through this procedure is not a U.S. citizen already. In spite of its name, this is a naturalization procedure. The child is naturalized and becomes a citizen upon taking the oath of allegiance.[1]

The requirements for the child to be issued the certificate are: (1) at least one parent is a citizen of the United States, whether by birth or naturalization; (2) the child is under the age of 18 years; (3) the child is residing outside of the United States in the legal and physical custody of the citizen parent, is temporarily present in the United States pursuant to a lawful admission, and is maintaining such lawful status; and (4) (a) the U.S. citizen parent of the child must have been physically present in the United States or its outlying possessions for a period or periods totaling at least five years, at least two of which were after the parent reached 14 years of age, or (b) the U.S. citizen parent of the U.S. citizen parent (i.e. the child's grandparent), must meet the 5 years/two years physical presence requirement.[2]

If the child is adoptive, he or she must satisfy the definition of adopted child for immigration purposes.[3]

The application for the certificate may be filed while the child is abroad,[4] in which case the U.S. used to issue a tourist visa for the child to enter the United States to

---

[7]8 C.F.R. § 341.5(e).

[Section 13:30]

[1]Cf. INA § 341(a), 8 U.S.C.A. § 1452(a) (permitting anyone within the United States to obtain a certificate of citizenship).

[2]See §§ 10:20 to 10:22.

[Section 13:31]

[1]INA § 322(b), 8 U.S.C.A. § 1433(b).

[2]INA § 322(a), 8 U.S.C.A. § 1433(a).

[3]INA § 322(c), 8 U.S.C.A. § 1433(c).

[4]INA § 322(b), 8 U.S.C.A. § 1433(b).

be sworn in as a citizen.[5] A child who is in the United States may only be issued a certificate of citizenship if he or she entered lawfully and is currently in lawful status.[6] Both the requirements and procedures have been discussed in detail in the chapter dealing with special immigration procedures.[7]

The law before 1994 provided for a certificate of citizenship for certain adopted children of U.S. citizens. The procedures to obtain a certificate of citizenship for adoptive children were the same procedures used to obtain a certificate of citizenship after the citizenship has vested.[8] However, the child was required to file form N-643 together with the filing fee and the documentation described in the instructions of the form. The USCIS has done away with Form N-643 and replaced it with Form N-600K, Application for Citizenship and Issuance of a Certificate Under Section 322.[9] This form is to be used for the naturalization of a child who regularly resides outside of the Untied States. The general fee for filing this form is $460. However, U.S. citizens filing on behalf of an adopted child need only pay $420. This form consolidates the N-600, N-643, and N-600/N-643 Supplement A previously filed by the child's parents or grandparents.

VI. SPECIAL PROVISIONS FOR PERSONS BORN BEFORE MAY 24, 1934, TO U.S. CITIZEN MOTHERS

§ 13:32 The 1994 law

Research References

Dizon and Wettstein, Immigration Law Service 2d §§ 14:31, 14:32

Under the laws in effect before May 24, 1934, as interpreted at the time, only children born to U.S. citizen fathers acquired U.S. citizenship abroad.[1] This provision was successfully challenged as violating equal protection of U.S. citizen mothers.[2] Shortly after this challenge, Congress passed a law retroactively granting citizenship to those people.[3]

The October 7, 1994 law grants U.S. citizenship retroactively to birth to children born abroad to a noncitizen father and a U.S. citizen mother before May 24, 1934.[4] To qualify for citizenship under this provision, the U.S. citizen mother must have resided in the United States before the birth of the child.[5] The grant of citizenship is

---

[5]State Department Cable, File No. 95-State-no number listed) (updating information contained in 7 FAM 1133.5) reproduced in 72 Interpreter Releases 350 (Mar. 13, 1995).

[6]INA § 322(a)(4), 8 U.S.C.A. § 1433(a)(4).

[7]See §§ 11:18 to 11:25.

[8]See § 13:27.

[9]See Appendix 11-1; see also the USCIS website at http://uscis.gov/graphics/index.htm.

[Section 13:32]

[1]See § 4:18.

[2]See §§ 4:13 to 4:14.

[3]See § 4:18.

[4]INTCA § 101(a)(2) adding INA § 301(h), 8 U.S.C.A. § 1401(h) reproduced as Appendix 4-21, to Ch 4.

[5]INA § 301(h), 8 U.S.C.A. § 1401(h).

automatic.[6] It vests by operation of law, and it is retroactive to birth.[7] Persons who participated in persecution under the direction of the Nazi government or who have engaged in genocide are barred from obtaining the benefits of this section.[8]

Persons who become citizens retroactively under the 1994 law are not subject to any retention requirements.[9] However, the legislation will not cure lack of prior residence requirements for the transmission of citizenship.[10] In other words, persons born to a U.S. citizen mother before May 24, 1934, will only be U.S. citizens if the U.S. mother was present in the United States prior to their birth.[11] Similarly, for these sons and daughters to transmit U.S. citizenship to their own children born abroad, they themselves must have complied with the prior resident requirements in effect at the time of their children's birth.[12]

The actual nature of this legislation is difficult to gauge. Because at least two of the constitutional challenges to the pre-1934 statutes were successful,[13] there is a strong argument that this law simply implements a constitutional mandate. Therefore, it only recognizes statutorily a reality that existed before its passage: the beneficiaries were already U.S. citizens.

If that is the case, the provisions purporting to exclude Nazi government officials and perpetrators of genocide from the benefits of this law are not effective, unless these people lost their U.S. citizenship after birth.[14]

On the other hand, if the provisions are considered as vesting citizenship upon those people, it works in the manner of the statutory collective naturalizations of subjects of other countries when their territories are acquired by the United States.[15] The new provision of the INA simply defines all those people as citizens of the United States.[16]

§13:33 Procedures

Research References

Dizon and Wettstein, Immigration Law Service 2d §§ 14:31, 14:32

The legacy INS issued a final rule implementing procedures for the retroactive

---

[6]INA § 301, 8 U.S.C.A. § 1401 ("The following shall be nationals and citizens of the United States at birth").

[7]INTCA § 101(c)(1) reproduced as Appendix 4-21, to Ch 4.

[8]INTCA § 101(c)(2) reproduced as Appendix 4-21, to Ch 4.

[9]INTCA § 101(b) reproduced as Appendix 4-21, to Ch 4; 62 Fed. Reg. 39926 (July 25, 1997) (Supplementary Information).

[10]INTCA § 101(d) as amended by IIRAIRA § 671(b)(1) reproduced in footnote 357 to Appendix 4-21, to Ch 4. For a discussion of conditions subsequent and their applicability, see §§ 4:5, 4:6.

[11]INA § 301(h), 8 U.S.C.A. § 1401(h).

[12]See INTCA § 101(c)(1) reproduced as Appendix 4-21, to Ch 4 ("the immigration and nationality laws of the United States shall be applied (to persons born before, on, or after the date of the enactment of this Act) as though the amendment made by subsection (a), and subsection (b), had been in effect as of the date of their birth"); 62 Fed. Reg. 39926 (July 25, 1997) (Supplementary Information).

[13]See § 4:18.

[14]See §§ 15:1 et seq. (discussing loss of citizenship).

[15]See §§ 2:8 to 2:23.

[16]INA § 301(h), 8 U.S.C.A. § 1401(h) as added by INTCA § 101(a)(2) reproduced as Appendix 4-21 to Ch 4 ("a person born before noon (Eastern Standard Time) May 24, 1934, outside the limits and jurisdiction of the United States of an alien father and a mother who is a citizen of the United States who, prior to the birth of such person, had resided in the United States").

grant of citizenship, effective August 25, 1997. These procedures do not grant U.S. citizenship upon the applicant, since the statute automatically bestowed U.S. citizenship upon him or her.[1]

Persons residing in the United States, who wish to be documented as citizens under this provision, may file an N-600 with the USCIS or apply for a passport at a U.S. passport agency.[2] Persons residing abroad make a claim to their citizenship at a U.S. embassy or consulate.[3]

Form N-600 is filed with the USCIS office having jurisdiction over the applicant's place of residence or with any other office designated for that purpose by the DHS.[4] Applications must be submitted according to the requirements for such applications when the citizenship has vested automatically.[5] The application must be accompanied by the $240 fee required for those applications and by the documentation necessary to establish the claim to citizenship, such as birth, adoption, marriage, death, and divorce certificates.[6] A USCIS officer will then call the applicant for an examination.[7] If the USCIS officer determines that the person is a U.S. citizen under section 301(h) of the INA, the USCIS will require the person to take the naturalization oath.[8] The person will be issued a certificate of citizenship and will be considered a citizen as of the date of his or her birth.[9] The legacy INS previously issued an advisory to all field offices stating that persons who cannot take the oath because of lack of capacity should not be required to do so.[10] The text of the advisory is not very clear but, presumably, persons who cannot take the oath will still be issued certificates of citizenship. The general procedures applicable to N-600 applications are discussed above.[11]

Persons desiring to obtain a U.S. passport instead are not required to take an oath of allegiance.[12] Procedures for obtaining U.S. passports are described above.[13]

[Section 13:33]

[1]8 CFR § 301.1.

[2]8 CFR § 301.1(a)(1). For procedures to obtain U.S. passports see § 13:3.

[3]8 CFR. § 301.1(a)(2) added by 61 Fed. Reg. 35111.

[4]8 CFR. § 301.1(a)(1). Form N-600 is reproduced as Appendix 13-3.

[5]See § 13:27.

[6]8 CFR. § 301.1(a)(1).

[7]8 CFR. § 301.1(a)(1).

[8]8 CFR. § 301.1(b).

[9]8 CFR. § 301.1(b).

[10]INS Advisory Cable, No File Number (July 9, 1996) reprinted in 73 Interpreter Releases 1291 (Sept. 30, 1996); *see also* Memorandum of William Yates, Acting Assoc. Director, CIS, HQ 70/33 (June 30, 2003), entitled "Procedures for Implementing the Waiving of the Oath of Renunciation and Allegiance for the Naturalization of Aliens having Certain Disabilities," *posted on* AILA InfoNet at Doc. No. 03071544.

[11]See § 13:27.

[12]The original INS interim regulation required persons applying for a U.S. passport to take an oath of allegiance. 61 Fed. Reg. 35111 (July 5, 1996) creating 8 CFR. § 301.1(b)(2). After the INS was informed by the State Department that it does not require an oath of allegiance to issue a passport to a U.S. citizen, the INS was forced to amend its interim regulation. See 61 Fed. Reg. 43948 (Aug. 27, 1996) (Supplementary Information).

[13]See §§ 13:3 to 13:14.

VII. U.S. CITIZENSHIP CARD FOR AMERICAN INDIANS AND MEMBERS OF COMMONWEALTH OF NORTHERN MARIANA

§ 13:34 Generally

Research References

Dizon and Wettstein, Immigration Law Service 2d § 2:8
Steel on Immigration Law § 15:3

The DHS issues identification cards for U.S. Citizens from the commonwealth of Northern Mariana and for certain American Indians.[1] The Northern Mariana Card is issued to the following persons and their children under 18 years of age, who were born on or before November 3, 1986, and were not citizens or nationals of the United States, and did not owe allegiance to any foreign state on that date: (1) a person in the Northern Mariana Islands (NMI), who, as of November 2, 1986, was a citizen of the Trust Territory of the Pacific Islands and was domiciled as of that date in the Commonwealth of the Northern Mariana Islands (CNMI) or the United States, or any territory or possession of the United States; or (2) a citizen of the Trust Territory of the Pacific Islands on November 2, 1986, who had been domiciled continuously in the NMI for the preceding five years and who, unless under age, registered to vote in elections for the NMI district legislature or for any municipal election in the NMI prior to January 1, 1975; or (3) a person domiciled in the NMI on November 2, 1986, who although not a citizen of the Trust Territory of the Pacific Islands on that date, had been continuously domiciled in the NMI beginning prior to January 1, 1974.[2] Procedures for obtaining the Northern Mariana Card are detailed in the regulations.[3] A new Northern Mariana Card designated as INS Form I-873 has replaced the original card.[4] However, the old cards remain valid.[5] The procedures for obtaining the cards also remain the same.[6]

In 2004, the Ninth Circuit overruled the USCIS's interpretation of the law of citizenship with regard to individuals born in the Northern Marianas Islands between November 4, 1986, and January 9, 1978.[7] The Ninth Circuit held that during this time, the commonwealth was part of the U.S. for purposes of birthright citizenship under the Fourteenth Amendment.[8] The State Department has now acquiesced in the Ninth Circuit's interpretation.[9]

On the August 20, 1997, a legacy INS final regulation also introduced a new card attesting to the U.S. citizenship of members of the Texas Band of the Kickapoo

---

[Section 13:34]

[1] 8 CFR § 235.12,

[2] 8 CFR § 235.12(a).

[3] 8 CFR § 235.12(b).

[4] 62 Fed. Reg. 44292 (August 20, 1997).

[5] 62 Fed. Reg. 44292 (August 20, 1997).

[6] 62 Fed. Reg. 44292 (August 20, 1997).

[7] Sabangan v. Powell, 375 F.3d 818 (9th Cir. 2004).

[8] Sabangan v. Powell, 375 F.3d 818, 819-20 (9th Cir. 2004).

[9] 7 FAM 1126.3(c)(5) ("Although the Department (CA and L/CA) believed the decision was clearly erroneous, the Solicitor General's office did not seek Supreme Court review, and it is now final. In order to maintain a uniform application of the nationality laws and for operations reasons, the Department (CA) decided to apply the decision worldwide.").

Indian Tribe.[10] The new card will be INS Form I-872.[11] The old cards issued to the members of this tribe remain valid.[12]

VIII.   CERTIFICATE OF NATURALIZATION

§ 13:35   Delivery of certificate

Research References

Dizon and Wettstein, Immigration Law Service 2d § 14:363
Steel on Immigration Law § 15:5

A Certificate of Naturalization (Form N-550) is issued by the USCIS once the naturalization applicant has taken the oath of allegiance.[1] It is delivered at the oath taking ceremony.[2] If the oath is administered by the court, the clerk of the court will be the one to issue to the applicant the certificate of naturalization provided to the court by the USCIS.[3] The applicant is required to surrender his or her "alien" registration receipt card (green card) at the time of delivery of the naturalization certificate.[4] If the green card has been lost, destroyed or is otherwise unavailable, the USCIS will waive the requirement to deliver the green card before receiving the certificate of naturalization.[5]

Before the 1990 changes in the naturalization laws, the clerks of the court issued certificates.[6] A duplicate copy of the certificate was filed with the former INS.[7] Certificates of naturalization or citizenship issued by the USCIS have the same legal effect as certificates of naturalization or citizenship issued by the courts.[8]

§ 13:36   Contents of certificate

Research References

Dizon and Wettstein, Immigration Law Service 2d § 14:364

By law, the certificate of naturalization must include the following information: (1) the number of the application for naturalization; (2) the number of the certificate of naturalization; (3) date of naturalization; (4) signature, place of residence, autographed photograph, and personal description of the naturalized person, including age, sex, marital status, and country of former nationality; (5) location of the USCIS district office in which the application was filed, and the title, authority, and location of the USCIS office or court administering the oath of allegiance; (6) a statement by the DHS finding that the applicant: (a) intends to reside in the United

---

[10]62 Fed. Reg. 44292 (August 20, 1997).

[11]62 Fed. Reg. 44292 (August 20, 1997).

[12]62 Fed. Reg. 44292 (August 20, 1997).

[Section 13:35]

[1]INA § 338, 8 U.S.C.A. § 1449; 8 CFR § 338.1.

[2]See § 9:66.

[3]8 CFR § 339.1.

[4]8 CFR § 338.3.

[5]8 CFR § 338.3.

[6]8 CFR § 338.11(a).

[7]8 CFR § 338.11(c).

[8]INA § 332(e), 8 U.S.C.A. § 1443(e).

States (unless exempted from this intention); (b) has complied in all respects with all the applicable requirements for naturalization; (c) is entitled to admission to citizenship; and (d) thereupon ordering the applicant be admitted to U.S. citizenship; (7) an attestation by a USCIS officer; and (8) seal of the DHS.[1] A copy of the certificate issued by the former INS is attached as Appendix 13-5.

The certificate will be issued to the applicant in his or her true, full, and correct name, as it exists at the time of the administration of the oath.[2] When the court as part of admission has changed the name of the applicant to citizenship, the certificate will be issued in the new name.[3] The clerk of the court issuing the naturalization certificate to the applicant will also issue a certificate of the name change.[4]

The certificate will show the applicant's last country of citizenship, even when the applicant is stateless at the time of admission to U.S. citizenship.[5]

The certificate must be signed by the applicant.[6] If the person being admitted to citizenship is a child who cannot sign his or her name, the citizen parent who submitted the application for naturalization must sign the certificate.[7] In such cases the signature should read "(name of naturalized child) by (name of U.S. citizen parent)."[8] If the applicant has a disability, which prevents the signature of the document, USCIS adjudicating officers have been instructed to note on the signature line "Person's Disability Prevents Signature."[9] In such cases, legal guardians are not permitted to sign the certificate.[10] Since the USCIS regulations allow certain applicants to sign the naturalization applications in a foreign language, if the person signed the application in the foreign language, the certificate of naturalization may also be signed in a foreign language.[11]

§ 13:37 Correction of certificate

Research References

Dizon and Wettstein, Immigration Law Service 2d §§ 14:367, 14:371

The certificate of naturalization will be corrected if the information on the certificate does not correspond to the information provided in the naturalization applica-

---

[Section 13:36]

[1]INA § 338, 8 U.S.C.A. § 1449.

[2]8 CFR § 338.1(b).

[3]8 CFR § 338.2. The clerk of the court is required to have forwarded a copy of the order changing the name to the INS. 8 CFR § 338.1(b).

[4]8 CFR § 339.1.

[5]8 CFR § 338.1(b).

[6]8 CFR § 338.1(b).

[7]8 CFR § 338.4.

[8]8 CFR § 338.4.

[9]Pearson, Exec. Assoc. Comm'r, Office of Field Operations, Memorandum No. HQ 70/33-P (Apr.7, 1999) reproduced as App. 7-10.

[10]Pearson, Exec. Assoc. Comm'r, Office of Field Operations, Memorandum No. HQ 70/33-P (Apr.7, 1999) reproduced as App. 7-10.

[11]8 CFR § 338.4. See §§ 9:35, 9:37.

tion, or if some other clerical error was made in the preparation of the certificate.[1] The certificate will not be corrected if the naturalized person alleges that the name or date of birth on the naturalization application were in fact incorrect at the time of the naturalization.[2]

To correct the certificate, the naturalized citizen files INS Form N-565, reproduced in Appendix 13-6, without a fee, with the USCIS office having jurisdiction over his or her place of residence.[3] This form is filed with USCIS even if a court issued the certificate and even if issued under prior laws.[4] The USCIS will then authorize the court to make the necessary corrections to the naturalization certificate.[5]

If the certificate itself can be corrected without mutilation, the corrected certificate will be delivered to the applicant, and a copy of the USCIS form authorizing the correction will be included in the citizen's naturalization file.[6] Otherwise, a replacement certificate will be issued on Form N-570 and delivered to the applicant.[7] The USCIS will then destroy the original certificate.[8]

Even though the certificate may not be corrected if erroneous information was submitted in the naturalization application, there is a procedure to reopen naturalization proceedings after admission to citizenship to correct these errors.[9] This procedure may only be used to correct *clerical* errors in the application.

§ 13:38 Special certificates to prove naturalization to foreign authorities

Research References

Dizon and Wettstein, Immigration Law Service 2d §§ 14:366, 14:368
Steel on Immigration Law § 15:5

The DHS is authorized to issue a special certificate on behalf of any naturalized citizen.[1] This certificate, INS form N-578, is furnished directly to the U.S. Department of State for transmission to a foreign authority.[2] The sole purpose of this certificate is for the person to obtain recognition abroad as a citizen of the U.S.[3] When

---

[Section 13:37]

[1]8 CFR § 338.5(a).

[2]8 CFR § 338.5(e).

[3]8 CFR § 338.5(a). The current version of Form N-565 is dated April 30, 2004. Prior versions can only be used until September 30, 2004. *See* http://uscis.gov/graphics/index.htm. This form is also used to replace naturalization citizenship documents. The fee associated with this is $210.

[4]8 CFR § 338.5(b).

[5]8 CFR § 338.5(b).

[6]8 CFR § 338.5(b), (c). If the court makes the correction, the USCIS file of the applicant will include a copy of the form N-459 with a notation indicating the date and nature of the correction. 8 CFR § 338.5(b). If the USCIS makes the correction, the Form N-565 which the person used to request the correction will be annotated as to the correction made and placed on the citizen's file. 8 CFR § 338.5(c).

[7]8 CFR § 338.5(d).

[8]8 CFR § 338.5(e).

[9]8 CFR § 340.1(h).

[Section 13:38]

[1]INA § 343(b), 8 U.S.C.A. § 1454(b).

[2]INA § 343(b), 8 U.S.C.A. § 1454(b); 8 CFR § 343b.11(a).

[3]INA § 343(b), 8 U.S.C.A. § 1454(b).

the certificate is forwarded to the State Department, the applicant will be notified of the issuance of this certificate.[4] Form N-578 is reproduced in Appendix 13-7.

The naturalized citizen files applications for these certificates on Form N-565.[5] Form N-565 is reproduced as Appendix 13-6 and is also available for downloading from the USCIS website at http://uscis.gov/graphics/index.htm. The person must file a separate application for each foreign official that needs to be served with an official certificate of naturalization.[6] Separate applications must be filed even when the officials are in the same country.[7]

The applicant must appear in person and will be interrogated by a USCIS officer.[8] If the application presents a *prima facie* case, it may be transmitted to the district director for issuance of the certification without the interrogation.[9] If the applicant files the application in person, he or she may be interrogated at that time.[10] Otherwise, the applicant may be interrogated at any time before the transmission of the certificate to the State Department.[11]

If a DHS officer abroad receives the application, the applicant should be interrogated before the application is forwarded to the USCIS district director in the United States, if this is practicable.[12] An applicant abroad may also submit the application directly to the USCIS district director in the United States.[13] In such cases, and in other cases in which interview of the applicant before forwarding the application is not practicable, the USCIS may issue a certificate conditioned on the applicant being interviewed by a State Department official.[14]

When applications are denied, the applicant will receive notice of the reasons for the denial.[15] The applicant may appeal a denial to the Administrative Appellate Unit (AAU).[16]

IX. AMENDING AND REPLACING CITIZENSHIP-RELATED DOCUMENTS

§ 13:39 Lost, mutilated, and destroyed documents

Research References

Dizon and Wettstein, Immigration Law Service 2d § 14:368
Steel on Immigration Law § 15:5

If a person's certificate of naturalization or citizenship or his or her declaration of intent has been lost, mutilated or destroyed, that person is entitled to receive a new

---

[4] 8 CFR § 343b.11(a) (the applicant will be sent notification on Form N-568).

[5] 8 CFR § 343b.1.

[6] 8 CFR § 343b.2.

[7] 8 CFR § 343b.2.

[8] 8 CFR § 343b.1.

[9] 8 CFR § 343b.3.

[10] 8 CFR § 343b.3.

[11] 8 CFR § 343b.3.

[12] 8 CFR § 343b.4.

[13] 8 CFR § 343b.4.

[14] 8 CFR § 343b.4.

[15] 8 CFR § 343b.11(b).

[16] 8 CFR § 343b.11(b).

certificate or declaration.[1] The citizen applies for this new certificate by filing Form N-565 with the USCIS.[2] The citizen will only be required to appear in person if the USCIS determines that such interview is necessary to properly adjudicate the request.[3]

If the USCIS determines that the document was in fact lost, mutilated, or destroyed, the USCIS must issue a new certificate or declaration.[4] The new certificate will be delivered to the applicant by personally handing the certificate to the applicant, or his or her attorney, or by mailing it certified or registered mail to the applicant's last known address.[5] Denials of these applications may be appealed to the AAU.[6]

If the certificate or declaration has been mutilated, it must be surrendered to the USCIS before the new certificate will be issued.[7] If the certificate has been lost, it must be surrendered to the USCIS if the applicant or any other person finds it.[8]

§ 13:40   Name change after naturalization

Research References

Dizon and Wettstein, Immigration Law Service 2d § 14:365
Steel on Immigration Law § 15:5

If a person officially changes names after naturalization, he or she will receive a new certificate of naturalization.[1] This document will only be issued if the name change was accomplished either by order of a competent court or by marriage.[2] If the USCIS finds that the name has been officially changed as claimed, the USCIS must issue the new certificate and must notify the naturalization court that the new certificate was issued.[3] Applications for new certificate under a changed name are filed with the USCIS on Form N-565.[4]

X.   CANCELLATION OF DHS DOCUMENTS

§ 13:41   Generally

Research References

Dizon and Wettstein, Immigration Law Service 2d § 14:428
Steel on Immigration Law § 15:5

[Section 13:39]

[1] INA § 343(a), 8 U.S.C.A. § 1454(a); 8 CFR § 343a.1(a).

[2] INA § 343(a), 8 U.S.C.A. § 1454(a). Form N-565 is reproduced as Appendix 13-6.

[3] 8 CFR § 343a.1(c).

[4] INA § 343(a), 8 U.S.C.A. § 1454(a).

[5] 8 CFR § 343a.1(c).

[6] 8 CFR § 343a.1(c).

[7] INA § 343(a), 8 U.S.C.A. § 1454(a).

[8] INA § 343(a), 8 U.S.C.A. § 1454(a).

[Section 13:40]

[1] INA § 343(c), 8 U.S.C.A. § 1454(c).

[2] INA § 343(c), 8 U.S.C.A. § 1454(c).

[3] INA § 343(c), 8 U.S.C.A. § 1454(c).

[4] 8 CFR § 343a.1(b). Form N-565 is reproduced as Appendix 13-6.

The USCIS is authorized by statute to cancel naturalization and citizenship-related documents issued by the USCIS.[1] Such cancellation, however, does not affect the citizenship status of the person whose name appears on the document.[2] In order to revoke a person's naturalization, the USCIS must follow the procedures described in Ch 14.[3] Expatriation determinations are discussed in Ch 15.[4]

Cancellation may only be achieved upon notice to the affected party.[5] The notice must contain the allegations regarding why the USCIS plans to cancel the document and must advise the person of his or her right to submit an answer within 60 days of the service of the notice.[6] This notice must be served upon the respondent either personally or by registered mail.[7]

If the respondent requests a hearing, the regulations provide for a hearing in front of a naturalization examiner, in which the respondent has the right to be represented by counsel, to examine or object to evidence against him or her, to present evidence on his or her own behalf, and to cross-examine witnesses presented by the government.[8] The naturalization examiner issues a report to the district director after the hearing.[9] The USCIS district director determines whether the proceedings should be terminated or the certificate should be canceled.[10] If the district director decides to cancel the certificate, the citizen has a right to appeal to the AAU.[11]

The citizen is required to surrender the document to the USCIS. The district director in the district in which the citizen resides will serve upon the citizen a notice to surrender the certificate.[12] Failure to surrender the document within 60 days of the notice is a felony punishable by up to five years in prison and $5,000 in fines.[13]

XI. OTHER RECORDS

§ 13:42 Court records

Research References

Dizon and Wettstein, Immigration Law Service 2d § 14:308

[Section 13:41]

[1]INA § 342, 8 U.S.C.A. § 1453.
[2]INA § 342, 8 U.S.C.A. § 1453.
[3]§§ 14:20 to 14:24.
[4]§§ 15:1 to 15:16.
[5]8 CFR § 342.1.
[6]8 CFR § 342.1.
[7]8 CFR § 342.2(a).
[8]8 CFR §§ 342.4, 342.5.
[9]8 CFR § 342.7.
[10]8 CFR § 342.7.
[11]8 CFR § 342.8.
[12]8 CFR § 342.9.
[13]18 U.S.C.A. § 1428.

Courts authorized to naturalize noncitizens have been required since 1790 to keep a record of the naturalization proceedings.[1] Court records may also be used to establish the naturalization of the person. In order to obtain certification of any naturalization records, the clerk of the court must receive a specific order of the court.[2] However, many clerks of the court will inform you informally whether such record exists. The DHS also has the power to certify any part of a court record relating to naturalization.[3]

Since 1990, courts have been divested of their authority to naturalize. Until 1990, the naturalization regulations required the courts to forward a copy of the certificate of naturalization and the attached complementary record to the legacy INS.[4] The court would retain the original complementary record, which had been signed by the naturalized citizen, containing among other information, the number of the naturalization certificate issued to the citizen.[5] Information regarding naturalization may, therefore, be found in both the naturalizing court and in the DHS records.

Naturalization-related court records are required to be kept in bound volumes under the custody of the clerk of the court.[6] Recently, courts have been allowed to maintain their records in electronic form.[7] After a court relinquishes its naturalization jurisdiction, the USCIS district office having jurisdiction over the geographical area where the court is located will be notified and will send a representative to inspect the naturalization records in the office of the clerk of the court. The USCIS will bind and lock them.[8]

§ 13:43 DHS certifications

Research References

Dizon and Wettstein, Immigration Law Service 2d § 14:308

The DHS is authorized by statute to issue "certifications" of any part of the naturalization record of any court, or of any certificate of naturalization or citizenship, if such certifications are required by any state or federal statute, or in any judicial proceedings.[1] The regulations provide that these certifications should be requested on Form G-641, which apparently no longer exists.[2]

§ 13:44 Judicial declaration of citizenship

Research References

Dizon and Wettstein, Immigration Law Service 2d § 14:68

[Section 13:42]

[1] See, sec. 1, Act of March 26, 1790, 1 Stat. 103 reproduced as Appendix 4-1 to Ch 4.

[2] INA § 343(c), 8 U.S.C.A. § 1454(c).

[3] INA § 343(c), 8 U.S.C.A. § 1454(c). See § 13:43.

[4] 8 CFR § 338.11(c).

[5] 8 CFR § 338.11.

[6] 8 CFR § 339.4.

[7] 8 CFR § 339.5.

[8] 8 CFR § 339.3.

[Section 13:43]

[1] INA § 343(c), 8 U.S.C.A. § 1454(c).

[2] 8 CFR § 343c.1. That form is not listed among current forms in the regulations. 8 CFR §§ 299.1, 299.4, 499.1. The LA District Office of INS informed me that this form no longer exists.

Persons inside the United States, who have been denied any right or privilege enjoyed by nationals of the U.S., may file an action for a declaration of U.S. nationality.[1] These actions are only available if the right or privilege was denied by a governmental department or agency, and must be filed within five years of the final administrative denial of right or privilege.[2] They are filed in the U.S. district court for the district in which the person resides.[3] This procedure is described in more detail in Chapter 10.[4]

A district court has jurisdiction under INA § 360 to review a cancellation of a certificate of citizenship under INA § 342, 8 U.S.C.A. § 1453.[5] However, if the district court determines as a matter of law that one of the requirements for citizenship is lacking, it has no discretion to find that the cancellation of the certificate of citizenship did not satisfy the requirements of INA § 342.[6]

§ 13:45 Coming to the United States to claim citizenship

Research References

Immigration Law Service § 13:452

The statute contains a special provision permitting individuals outside the United States to come to the U.S. in order to vindicate their citizenship rights. When any agency or department denies a person outside the United States a right or privilege of nationals of the U.S., then the person may obtain a certificate of identity from the U.S. embassy or consulate.[1] Upon "proof to the satisfaction of such diplomatic or consular officer that such application is made in good faith and has a substantial basis," the statute requires that the consular officer "shall issue" a "certificate of identity."[2] If a certificate of identity is denied, the individual may appeal that denial to the Secretary of State.[3]

The certificate of identity will allow the holder to travel to the United States, where the citizenship claim can be vindicated.[4] However, only persons who have been in the United States before, or persons claiming U.S. citizenship at birth abroad and who are under the age of sixteen may obtain a certificate of identity.[5]

Persons holding such certificates are inspected at the border and are subject to removal proceedings to the same extent as noncitizens.[6] A final determination by the

---

[Section 13:44]

[1] INA § 360(a), 8 U.S.C.A. § 1503(a).

[2] INA § 360(a), 8 U.S.C.A. § 1503(a).

[3] INA § 360(a), 8 U.S.C.A. § 1503(a).

[4] See §§ 10:20 to 10:25.

[5] Friend v. Reno, 172 F.3d 638, 639 (9th Cir. 1999). *See generally,* § 13:41, for a discussion of INA § 342.

[6] Friend v. Reno, 172 F.3d 638, 647 (9th Cir. 1999).

[Section 13:45]

[1] INA § 360(b), 8 U.S.C.A. § 1503(b).

[2] INA § 360(b), 8 U.S.C.A. § 1503(b).

[3] INA § 360(b), 8 U.S.C.A. § 1503(b); 20 C.F.R. § 50.11(b).

[4] INA § 360(b), 8 U.S.C.A. § 1503(b).

[5] INA § 360(b), 8 U.S.C.A. § 1503(b).

[6] INA § 360(c), 8 U.S.C.A. § 1503(c).

Board of Immigration Appeals (BIA) that such persons are inadmissible is only reviewable by a U.S. district court through habeas corpus proceedings.[7]

Application and adjudication procedures are found in the Foreign Affairs Manual.[8] The FAM requires that the consulate give 60 days advance notice to various other U.S. governmental agencies before issuing the certificate.[9] The document may be issued only after the applicant has specific, confirmed travel plans; it appears that these certificates are valid only as to one particular port of entry.[10]

The statute requires that the request for the certificate "is made in good faith and has a substantial basis."[11] The State Department interprets the term "substantial basis" to exclude situations where the claim was already considered: "[a] substantial basis does **not** exist if a court in the United States has already ruled that the applicant is not a U.S. national. The same is true if a previous ruling to this effect has been made by a department, agency, or executive official of the United States."[12] This categorical rule appears inconsistent with § 1503(b); it seems odd to deny the certificate on the grounds of the denial of nationality rights, where the certificate is sought precisely when someone has been denied some right on the grounds of non-citizenship. Moreover, the second sentence appears to go well beyond the normal rules of *res judicata*, which applies to agency-level decisions only where several factors are met.[13] It is unlikely that adjudication before USCIS or the Passport Office could constitute *res judicata*; yet such an adjudication appears to bar an applicant from showing a "substantial basis" under the FAM. Indeed, even where an individual was denied citizenship at some point in the past, if they have additional facts or arguments to present, it is unlikely that normal exhaustion rules would apply to bar the attempt.[14] The agency's rules would be more defensible if they created a presumption that the application is non-substantial, but the categorical rule of the FAM appears legally erroneous.

The FAM notes that individuals seeking a certificate of identity would have other options: (1) reapplication for a passport; (2) application or reapplication for a Consular Report of Birth Abroad of a Citizen of the United States of America; or (3) legal action in federal court.[15]

---

[7]INA § 360(c), 8 U.S.C.A. § 1503(c); see also, INA § 242(e)(2), 8 U.S.C.A. § 1252(e)(2).

[8]See 7 FAM 1150 Appendix H.

[9]See 7 FAM 1150 Appendix H.

[10]See 7 FAM 1150 Appendix H para. (l).

[11]INA § 360(b), 8 U.S.C.A. § 1503(b).

[12]See 7 FAM 1150 Appendix H para. (j) (emphasis in original).

[13]See Meyer v. Rigdon, 36 F.3d 1375, 1379–80 (7th Cir. 1994)("Administrative agency decisions will only be given preclusive effect under the collateral estoppel doctrine if (1) the original action was properly before the agency, (2) the same disputed issues of fact are before the court as were before the agency, (3) the agency acted in a judicial capacity, and (4) the parties had an adequate opportunity to litigate the issue before the agency."). "An agency acts in a judicial capacity when it provides the following safeguards: (1) representation by counsel, (2) pretrial discovery, (3) the opportunity to present memoranda of law, (4) examinations and cross-examinations at the hearing, (5) the opportunity to introduce exhibits, (6) the chance to object to evidence at the hearing, and (7) final findings of fact and conclusions of law." Reed v. AMAX Coal Co., 971 F.2d 1295, 1300 (7th Cir. 1992).

[14]See generally, Rivera v. Ashcroft, 394 F.3d 1129, 1136 (9th Cir.2005); Theagene v. Gonzales, 411 F.3d 1107, 1111 (9th Cir. 2005); Iasu v. Smith, 511 F.3d 881 (9th Cir. 2007); Minasyan v. Gonzales, 401 F.3d 1069, 1075 (9th Cir.2005); Poole v. Mukasey, 522 F.3d 259 (2d Cir. 2008); Omolo v. Gonzales, 452 F.3d 404, 407 (5th Cir.2006); Moussa v. INS, 302 F.3d 823 (8th Cir.2002).

[15]See 7 FAM 1150 Appendix H para. (d).

§ 13:46   Judicial determination of nationality in context of removal proceedings

Research References

Dizon and Wettstein, Immigration Law Service 2d § 13:452

The Illegal Immigration Reform and Immigrant Responsibility Act of 1996, completely revised the procedures to remove noncitizens from the United States.[1] It severely limited judicial review of what was formerly exclusion and deportation orders.[2] Even under the new procedures, however, there are provisions for judicial determinations of whether the subject of removal proceedings is a U.S. national. These procedures are described in detail below.[3]

§ 13:47   Voter registration card is not proof of citizenship

The anti-terrorism law specifically provides that:

Notwithstanding any other provision of law, a Federal, State, or local government agency may not use a voter registration card (or other related document) that evidences registration for an election for Federal office, as evidence to prove United States citizenship.[1]

[Section 13:46]

   [1]IIRAIRA Title III-A.
   [2]IIRAIRA § 306.
   [3]See §§ 10:24 to 10:25.

[Section 13:47]

   [1]Antiterrorism and Effective Death Penalty Act of 1996, Pub.L. 104-132, 100 Stat. 1214 (Apr. 24, 1996).

APPENDIX 13-1

U.S. Department of Health and Human Services Where to Write for Vital Records: Births, Deaths, Marriages and Divorces

WHERE TO WRITE FOR VITAL RECORDS

(UPDATED OCTOBER 2012)

National Center for Health Statistics

Edward J. Sondik, *Ph.D., Director*

Jennifer H. Madans, Ph.D., *Acting Co-Deputy Director*

Michael H. Sadagursky, *Acting Co-Deputy Director*

Jennifer H. Madans, Ph.D., *Associate Director for Science and Acting Associate Director for Planning, Budget, and Legislation*

Michael H. Sadagursky, *Associate Director for Management and Operations*

Division of Vital Statistics

Charles J. Rothwell, *Director*

Delton Atkinson, *Deputy Director*

Office of Information Services

Linda Torian, *Acting Director*

Introduction

As part of its mission to provide access to data and information relating to the health of the Nation, the National Center for Health Statistics produces a number of publications containing reference and statistical materials. The purpose of this publication is solely to provide information about individual vital records maintained only on file in State or local vital statistics offices.

An official certificate of every birth, death, marriage, and divorce should be on file in the locality where the event occurred. The Federal Government does not maintain files or indexes of these records. These records are filed permanently either in a State vital statistics office or in a city, county, or other local office.

To obtain a certified copy of any of the certificates, write or go to the vital statistics office in the State or area where the event occurred. Addresses and fees are given for each event in the State or area concerned.

To ensure that you receive an accurate record for your request and that your request is filled expeditiously, please follow the steps outlined below for the information in which you are interested:

- Write to the appropriate office to have your request filled.
- Under the appropriate office, information has been included for birth and death records concerning whether the State will accept checks or money orders and to whom they should be made payable. This same information would apply when marriage and divorce records are available from the State office. However, it is impossible for us to list fees and addresses for all county offices where marriage and divorce records may be obtained.
- For all certified copies requested, make check or money order payable for the correct amount for the number of copies you want to obtain. Cash is not recommended because the office cannot refund cash lost in transit.
- Because all fees are subject to change, a telephone number has been included in the information for each State for use in verifying the current fee.
- States have provided their home page address for obtaining current information.
- Type or print all names and addresses in the letter.
- Give the following facts when writing for birth or death records:

    1. Full name of person whose record is being requested.
    2. Sex.
    3. Parents' names, including maiden name of mother.
    4. Month, day, and year of birth or death.

    5. Place of birth or death (city or town, county, and State; and name of hospital, if known).
    6. Purpose for which copy is needed.
    7. Relationship to person whose record is being requested.

- Give the following facts when writing for marriage records:

    1. Full names of bride and groom.
    2. Month, day, and year of marriage.
    3. Place of marriage (city or town, county, and State).
    4. Purpose for which copy is needed.
    5. Relationship to persons whose record is being requested.

- Give the following facts when writing for divorce records:

    1. Full names of husband and wife.
    2. Date of divorce or annulment.
    3. Place of divorce or annulment.
    4. Type of final decree.
    5. Purpose for which copy is needed.
    6. Relationship to persons whose record is being requested.

Alabama

Place of event	Cost of copy	Address	Remarks
Birth or Death	$15.00	Alabama Center for Health Statistics Alabama Department of Public Health P.O. Box 5625 Montgomery, AL 36103-5625	State office has records since January 1908. Additional copies of the same record ordered at the same time are $6.00 each. Personal check or money order should be made payable to **State Board of Health**. To verify current fees, the telephone number is (334) 206-5418. This is a recorded message. Information on how to obtain certified copies is also available via the Internet at http://adph.org/vitalrecords. A signature of the applicant is required.
Marriage	$15.00	Same as Birth or Death	State office has records since August 1936. Additional copies ordered at the same time are $6.00 each. Personal check or money order should be made payable to **State Board of Health**. To verify current fees, the telephone number is (334) 206-5418. This is a recorded message. Information on how to obtain certified copies is also available via the Internet at http://adph.org/vitalrecords. A signature of the applicant is required.
	Varies	See remarks	For marriages prior to August 1936, contact Probate Court in county where license was issued.
Divorce	$15.00	Same as Birth or Death	State office has records since January 1950. Additional copies ordered at the same time are $6.00 each. Personal check or money order should be made payable to **State Board of Health**. To verify current fees, the telephone number is (334) 206-5418. This is a recorded message. Information on how to obtain certified copies is also available via the Internet at http://adph.org/vitalrecords. A signature of the applicant is required.
	Varies	See remarks	For divorces prior to 1950, contact Clerk of Circuit Court in county where divorce was granted.

Alaska

Place of event	Cost of copy	Address	Remarks
Birth or Death	$25.00	Bureau of Vital Statistics Department of Health and Social Services 5441 Commercial Boulevard Juneau, AK 99801	State office has records since the 1890's; however, many events before 1930 were never registered with the Bureau. Personal check or money order should be made payable to **Bureau of Vital Statistics**. To verify current fees, the telephone number is (907) 465-3391. This is a recorded message. Information on how to obtain certified copies is also available via the Internet at http://www.hss.state.ak.us/dph/bvs/. **ALL REQUESTS MUST INCLUDE A COPY OF A PICTURE ID OF THE APPLICANT.** Enlarge the copy and lighten it as much as possible to be sure that it is clear and readable when sent to the Bureau. Signature under the copied ID is also required.
Heirloom Birth	$50.00	Same as Birth or Death	Two different heirloom birth certificates by Alaskan artists are available. Friends and relatives may order gift certificates for persons entitled to order the record. The heirloom certificates as well as instructions and order forms may be viewed via the Internet at http:www.hss.state.ak.us/dph/bvs/.
Marriage	$25.00	Same as Birth or Death	State office has records since the 1890's; however, many events before 1930 were never registered with the Bureau.
Heirloom Marriage	$60.00	Same as Birth or Death	Three different heirloom marriage certificates are available. Friends and relatives may order gift certificates for persons entitled to order the record. The heirloom certificates as well as instructions and order forms may be viewed via the Internet at http:www.hss.state.ak.us/dph/bvs/.
Divorce	$25.00	Same as Birth or Death	State office has records since 1950.
	Varies	See remarks	Clerk of Superior Court in judicial district where divorce was granted. Juneau and Ketchikan (First District), Nome (Second District), Anchorage (Third District), Fairbanks (Fourth District).

American Samoa

Place of event	Cost of copy	Address	Remarks
Birth or Death	$5.00	American Samoa Government	Registrar has birth records since 1890 and death
Amendments	$7.00	Department of Homeland	records since 1900. Money order should be made
		Security	payable to the **Office of Vital Statistics/ASG.**
		Office of Vital Statistics	Personal checks are not accepted. To verify current
		P.O. Box 6894	fees, the telephone numbers are: (684) 633-
		Pago Pago, AS 96799	1405/1406. For Health Information Office, Health
			and Vital Statistics call (684) 633-4606/2262.
			Personal identification is required for verification
			and a notarized letter before record will be sent.
Marriage	$5.00	Same as Birth or Death	
Marriage License	$20.00		
Divorce	$5.00	High Court of American Samoa	
		American Samoa Government	
		Pago Pago, AS 96799	

Arizona

Place of event	Cost of copy	Address	Remarks
Birth	Varies	Office of Vital Records	State office has records since July 1909 and abstracts of records filed in counties before then.
Death	Varies	Arizona Department of Health Services P.O. Box 3887 Phoenix, AZ 85030-3887	Some county offices in Arizona are able to provide certified copies of birth and death certificates. Please go to http://www.azdhs.gov for a listing of county offices.
			The State Office of Vital Records does not accept personal checks. A money order or cashiers check should be made payable to **Office of Vital Records**. To verify current fees, the telephone number is (602) 364-1300. This is a recorded message. Information on how to obtain certified copies is also available via the Internet at http://www/azdhs.gov.
			Applicants must submit a copy of picture identification or have their request notarized.
Marriage	Varies	See remarks	Clerk of Superior Court in county where license was issued.
Divorce	Varies	See remarks	Clerk of Superior Court in county where divorce was granted.

Arkansas

Place of event	Cost of copy	Address	Remarks
Birth	$12.00	Arkansas Dept. of Health	State office has records since February 1914 and some original Little Rock and Fort Smith records from 1881. Additional copies of the same birth record, when requested at the same time, are $10.00 each. Additional copies of the same death record, when requested at the same time, are $8.00 each.
Death	$10.00	Vital Records Section Slot 44 4815 West Markham St. Little Rock, AR 72205	
			Personal check or money order should be made payable to **Arkansas Department of Health**. To verify current fees, the telephone number is (501) 661-2336. This is a recorded message. Information on how to obtain certified copies is also available via the Internet at http://www.healthyarkansas.com.
			A photo ID of the person requesting the record is required with each application.
Marriage	$10.00	Same as Birth or Death	Coupons since 1917. Additional copies of the same marriage record, when requested at the same time, are $10.00 each.
Marriage (County)	Varies	Same as Birth or Death	Full certified copy may be obtained from County Clerk in county where license was issued.
			A certified copy of a marriage coupon may be obtained from the state.
Divorce	$10.00	Same as Birth or Death	State office has coupons since 1923. Additional copies of the same marriage record, when requested at the same time, are $10.00 each.
	Varies	See remarks	Full certified copy may be obtained from Circuit or Chancery Clerk in county where divorce was granted.
			A certified copy of a divorce coupon may be obtained from the state.

California

Place of event	Cost of copy	Address
Birth	$18.00	CA Dept. of Public Health -
Death	$14.00	Vital Records
Fetal Death	$11.00	MS: 5103
		P.O. Box 997410
		Sacramento, CA 95899-7410

Remarks

The State office has records since July 1905. For earlier records, contact the County Recorder in the county where the event occurred.

A personal check or money order should be made payable to **CDPH Vital Records**. Please do not send cash. To verify current fees, the telephone number is (916) 445-2684. This is a recorded message. Information on how to obtain certified copies is also available via the California Department of Public Health website at: http://www.cdph.ca.gov/certlic/birthdeathmar/Pages/default.aspx.

BIRTH AND DEATH RECORDS:
In order to obtain a Certified Copy, you **MUST** complete the sworn statement included with the certificate application form, sign the statement under penalty of perjury, and your sworn statement must be notarized. If your request indicates that you want a Certified **Informational** Copy but does include a notarized statement sworn under penalty of perjury, the request will be rejected as incomplete and returned to you without being processed.

If you request a Certified **Informational** Copy of the record, a notarized sworn statement is not required. Please refer to the CDPH website for further information about Informational copies

Place of event	Cost of copy	Address
Marriage (State)	$14.00	Same as Birth or Death

State office only has indexes for public marriage certificates that occurred from 1949-1986 and 1998-1999. For all other years, contact the County Recorder in the county where the event occurred; for confidential marriages, contact the County Clerk where the marriage license was issued.

Information on how to obtain a marriage certificate, as well as information about current processing times, is available via the California Department of Public Health website at: http://www.cdph.ca.gov/certlic/birthdeathmar/Pages/default.aspx.

In order to obtain a Certified Copy, you MUST complete the sworn statement included with the marriage certificate application form, sign the

CALIFORNIA

Place of event	Cost of Copy	Address	Remarks
			statement under penalty of perjury, and your sworn statement must be notarized. If your request indicates that want a Certified Copy but does not include a notarized statement sworn under penalty of perjury, the request will be rejected as incomplete and returned to you without being processed.
			If you request a Certified **Informational** Copy of the record, a notarized sworn statement is not required. Please refer to the CDPH website for further information about Informational copies.
Marriage (County)	Varies	See remarks	Contact the County Recorder (for public marriages) or County Clerk (for confidential marriages) in the county where the license was issued. Contact information is available via the California Department of Public Health website at: http://www.cdph.ca.gov/certlic/birthdeathmar/Pages/CountyRecorderOffice.aspx.
Divorce (State) Certificates of Record only	$13.00	Same as Birth or Death	A Certificate of Record includes only the names of the parties to the divorce, the county where the divorce was filed, and the court case number – It is not a certified copy of the divorce decree and does not indicate whether the divorce was finalized in court. The Office of Vital Records only as information for divorces that were filed with the court between 1962 and June 1984, and the processing times may exceed six months. For all other years or for a copy of the decree, contact the Superior Court in the county where the event occurred. Information on how to obtain a divorce record, as well as current processing times, is available via the California Department of Public Health website: http://www.cdph.ca.gov/certlic/birthdeathmar/Pages/CertifiedCopiesof MarriageandDivorceRecords.aspx.
Divorce (County) Decrees	Varies	See remarks	Contact the Clerk of Superior Court in county where the divorce was granted. Contact information is available via the Department of Public Health website at: http://www.cdph.ca.gov/certlic/birthdeathmar/Pages/CertifiedCopiesofMarriageandDivorceRecords. aspx.

Canal Zone
(Effective
December 1, 1999)

Place of event	Cost of copy	Address	Remarks
Birth or Death	$30.00	Vital Records Section Passport Services U.S. Department of State 1111 19th Street NW Suite 510 Washington, DC 20522-1705	Records available from May 1904 to September 1979. Additional copies of the same record requested at the same time are $20.00 each. Personal check or money order must be signed, dated and made payable to **U.S. Department of State**. Remittance must be payable in U.S. dollars through a U.S. Bank. No credit cards or cash accepted. Telephone or facsimile requests are not accepted. To verify current fees, the telephone number is (202) 955-0307. A signed and notarized written request must be submitted along with a copy of the requester's valid photo identification.
Marriage	$30.00	Same as Birth or Death	Records available from May 1904 to September 1979.

Colorado

Place of event	Cost of copy	Address	Remarks
Birth	$17.75	Vital Records Section CO Department of Public Health and Environment 4300 Cherry Creek Drive South HSVRD-VS-A1 Denver, CO 80246-1530	State office has birth records since 1910 and death records since 1900. Additional copies of the same birth record ordered at the same time are $10.00 each. Additional copies of the same death record ordered at the same time are $13.00 each.
Death	$20.00		
			Personal check or money order should be made payable to **Vital Records Section**. To verify current fees, the telephone number is (303) 692-2200. This is a recorded message. Information on how to obtain certified copies is also available via the Internet at http:www.cdphe.state.co.us/certs/index.html.
			A request for a birth or death record must be accompanied by a photo copy of the requestor's identification before processing.
Marriage	See remarks	Same as Birth or Death	Certified copies are not available from State Health Department. Fee for verification is $17.00.
	Varies	See remarks	Copies available from County Clerk in county where license was issued.
Divorce	See remarks	Same as Birth or Death	Certified copies are not available from State Health Department. Fee for verification is $17.00.
	Varies	See remarks	Copies available from Clerk of District Court in county where divorce was granted.

Connecticut

Place of event	Cost of copy	Address	Remarks
State issued:			
Birth	$30.00	CT Dept. of Public Health 410 Capitol Ave, MS #11 VRS Hartford, CT 06134	Requests for certified copies of birth should be submitted to the vital records office in the city/town where the person was born, or where the
Death	$20.00	Same as Birth	mother lived at the time of the birth. Requests for certified copies of birth and death certificates may also be submitted to the State Vital Records
Marriage	$20.00	Same as Birth	Office.
Civil Union	$20.00	Same as Birth	A copy of a valid, government issued photographic identification such as a driver's license, must be
City/Town issued:			submitted with any request for a birth certificate.
Birth	$20.00	See remarks	If a photo ID is not available, photocopies of two alternative forms of identification may be
Death	$20.00	See remarks	accepted.
Marriage	$20.00	See remarks	For additional details about ordering vital records from CT, please refer to the CT Department of
Civil Union	$20.00	See remarks	Public Health (DPH) website at http://www.ct.gov/dph "Vital Records" or contact a Customer Service Representative at (806) 509-7897 between 12:00 and 4:00 pm EST.

Payment for requests sent to the town of the vital event must be in the form of a check or money order made payable to the respective town or city. Requests sent to the State Vital Records Office require a postal money order made payable to the **Treasurer, State of Connecticut.**

Refer to the CT DPH website above for town contact information via a link to a listing of the CT Town Clerk and Registrar Directory.

Requests for certified copies of a marriage or civil union certificate may be submitted to the city/town where the marriage or civil union ceremony took place, to the town in which either of the parties resided at the time of the marriage or civil union, or to the State Vital Records Office.

Place of event	Cost of copy	Address	Remarks
Dissolution of Marriage or Civil Union		See remarks	Applicant must contact the Clerk of Superior Court where the dissolution of marriage/civil union was granted. The State Office of Vital Records does not have dissolution decrees and cannot issue certified copies.

Delaware

Place of event	Cost of copy	Address	Remarks
Birth	$25.00	Office of Vital Statistics Division of Public Health	State office has birth records since 1938. For previous years, write to Archives Hall of Records, Dover, DE 19901.
Death	$25.00	417 Federal Street Dover, DE 19901	
			A photo identification is **REQUIRED** for all transactions. If submitting by mail, a copy of **ID IS REQUIRED**.
			Personal check or money order should be made payable to **Office of Vital Statistics**. To verify current fees, the telephone number is (302) 744-4549. Information on how to obtain certified copies is also available via the Internet at http://www.dhss.delaware.gov/dhss/dph/ss/vitalstats.html.
Marriage	$25.00	Same as Birth or Death	Records since 1969.
Divorce	$25.00	Same as Birth or Death	Records since 1935. Inquiries will be forwarded to appropriate office. Certified copies are not available from the Office of Vital Statistics.
		See remarks	Prothonotary in county where divorce was granted up to 1975. For divorces granted after 1975, the parties concerned should contact Family Court in county where divorce was granted. Certified copies are not available from the State office.

District of Columbia

Place of event	Cost of copy	Address	Remarks
Birth Death	$23.00 $18.00	Vital Records Division 899 North Capitol Street NE 1st Floor Washington, DC 20002	Office has birth and death records since August 1874. Personal check or money order should be made payable to **DC Treasurer**. A copy of a government issued picture identification must accompany each request. To verify current fees and obtain general information, the telephone number (202) 671-5000. This is a recorded message. Information on how to obtain certified copies is also available via the Internet at http://www.dchealth.dc.gov.
Marriage	$10.00	DC Superior Court 500 Indiana Avenue, NW Room 4485 Washington, DC 20001	Marriage information telephone number: 202-879-4840.
Divorce	$6.50	DC Superior Court 500 Indiana Avenue, NW Room 4335 Washington, DC 20001	Records since September 16, 1956. Divorce information telephone number: 202-879-1261.
Divorce	Varies	Clerk, U.S. District Court for the District of Columbia Washington, DC 20001	Records before September 16, 1956.

Florida

Place of event	Cost of copy	Address	Remarks
Birth	$9.00	Department of Health	State office has some birth records dating back to April 1865. The majority of records date from January 1917. (If the exact date is unknown, the fee is $9.00 (births) or $5.00 (deaths) for the first year searched and $2.00 for each additional year up to a maximum of $50.00. Fee includes one certification of record if found or statement stating record not on file.) Additional copies are $4.00 each when requested at the same time.
Death	$5.00	Bureau of Vital Statistics P.O. Box 210 1217 Pearl Street (Zip 32202) Jacksonville, FL 32231-0042	

Personal check or money order should be made payable to **Bureau of Vital Statistics**. To verify current fees, please visit our website at http://www.floridavitalstatisticsonline.com or call our telephone number (904) 359-6900. This is a recorded message.

All letters or applications for birth and death must include the signature and relationship/eligibility stated, and a copy of a valid **PICTURE ID** (Driver's License, Passport, Military ID, or State Identification card) of the applicant.

If requesting cause of death, you must also include a copy of a valid **PICTURE ID** (Driver's License, Passport, Military ID, or State Identification card) of the applicant.

Birth records and cause-of-death information in Florida are confidential by law. Please visit our website for information on eligibility.

A self-addressed stamped envelope is appreciated.

Place of event	Cost of copy	Address	Remarks
Marriage	$5.00	Same as Birth or Death	Records since June 6, 1927. (If the exact date is unknown, the fee is $5.00 for the first year searched and $2.00 for each additional year up to a maximum of $50.00. Fee includes one copy of record if found or certified statement stating record not on file.) Additional copies are $4.00 each when requested at the same time.
Divorce	$5.00	Same as Birth or Death	Records since June 6, 1927. If the exact date is unknown, the fee is $5.00 for the first year searched and $2.00 for each additional year up to a maximum of $50.00. Fee includes one copy of record if found or certified statement stating record not on file.) Additional copies are $4.00 each when requested at the same time.

Georgia

Place of event	Cost of copy	Address	Remarks
Birth or Death	$25.00	GA Dept. of Public Health Vital Records 2600 Skyland Drive, NE Atlanta, GA 30319-3640	State office has records since January 1919. For earlier birth records in Atlanta or Savannah or other cities or counties, write to the Vital Records Office in the county where the event occurred. For earlier death records write to the Vital Records Office in the county where the event occurred.
			Additional copies of the same record ordered at the same time are $5.00.
			A certified check or money order should be made payable to **George Department of Public Health**. To verify current fees, the telephone number is (404) 679-4702. This is a recorded message. Information on how to obtain certified copies is also available via the Internet at http://health.state.ga.us/programs/vitalrecords/.
			The requestor must provide a copy of a valid government- issued photo ID.
Marriage	$10.00	Same as Birth or Death	Centralized State records since June 9, 1952. Certified copies of marriage from June 9, 1952 to 1996 are issued at the State office. All other years contact the Probate Judge in the county where the license was issued.
			See "County Directories" at http://sos.georgia.gov/cgi-bin/OfficialDirectoryIndex.asp for information about how to contact probate courts.
Divorce (State)	$10.00 for verification letter which verifies date and county of divorce.	See remarks	Certified copies of divorce records are not issued at the State office. Contact the Clerk of Superior Court where the divorce was granted for certified copies.
			See "County Directories" at http://sos.georgia.gov/cgi-bin/OfficialDirectoryIndex.asp for information about how to contact clerks of Superior Court.

Guam

Place of event	Cost of copy	Address	Remarks
Birth or Death	$5.00	Office of Vital Statistics P.O. Box 2816 Hagatna, Guam 96932	Office has records since October 16, 1901. Money order should be made payable to **Treasurer of Guam**. Personal checks are not accepted. To verify current fees, the telephone number is 671-735-7292.
Marriage	$5.00	Same as Birth or Death	
Divorce	Varies	Clerk, Superior Court of Guam Guam Judicial Center 120 West O'Brian Drive Hagatna, Guam 96910	

Hawaii

Place of event	Cost of copy	Address	Remarks
Birth or Death	$10.00	State Department of Health Office of Health Status Monitoring Issurance/Vital Statistics Section P.O. Box 3378 Honolulu, HI 96801	State office has some records as early as 1853. Additional copies ordered at the same time are $4.00 each. Cashiers check, certified check, or money order should be made payable to **State Department of Health.** Personal checks are not accepted. To verify current fees, the telephone number is (808) 586-4533. This is a recorded message. Information on how to obtain certified copies is also available via the Internet at http://hawaii.gov/health/vital-records/vital-records.
Marriage	$10.00	Same as Birth or Death	
Divorce	$10.00	Same as Birth or Death	Records since July 1951-December 2002. From January 2003, divorce records are available only through the county circuit court.
	Varies	See remarks	Circuit Court in county where divorce was granted.

Idaho

Place of event	Cost of copy	Address	Remarks
Birth Death	$13.00 $14.00 Computer generated	Vital Records Unit Bureau of Vital Records and Health Statistics P.O. Box 83720 Boise, ID 83720-0036	The state office has records since July 1911. Also, some birth records before 1911. For records from 1907 to 1911, write to the County Recorder in the county where the event occurred. Birth records at the state office are legally confidential for 100 years and death records are legally confidential for 50 years.
Birth Death	$18.00 $19.00 Photostatic copy		
			Personal check or money order should be made payable to **Idaho Vital Records**. To verify current fees, the telephone number is (208) 334-5988. This is a recorded message. Information on how to obtain certified copies is also available via the Internet at http://www.healthandwelfare.idaho.gov.
			Applicants must provide a government-issued photo identification with a signature. If this is not available, the applicant must provide a copy of two forms of identification with one having a signature.
Marriage	$13.00 Computer generated $18.00 Photostatic copy	Same as Birth or Death	The state office has records since May 1947. Earlier records are with the County Recorder in the county where the license was issued. Records at the state office are legally confidential for 50 years.
			Personal check or money order should be made payable to **Idaho Vital Records**. To verify current fees, the telephone number is (208) 334-5988. This is a recorded message. Information on how to obtain certified copies is also available via the Internet at http://www.healthandwelfare.idaho.gov.
			Applicants must provide a government issued photo identification with a signature. If this is not available, the applicant must provide a copy of two other forms of identification with one having a signature
	Varies	See remarks	County Recorder in county where license was issued.

IDAHO

Place of event	Cost of copy	Address	Remarks
Divorce (Computer generated)	$13.00	Same as Birth or Death	The state office has records since May 1947. Only a Certificate of Divorce is available from 1950 to present. Records prior to May 1947 are with the Clerk of the Court in the county where the divorce was granted. Records at the state office are legally confidential for 50 years.
(Photostatic copy)	$18.00		
			Personal check or money order should be made payable to **Idaho Vital Records**. To verify current fees, the telephone number is (208) 334-5988. This is a recorded message. Information on how to obtain certified copies is also available via the Internet at http://www.healthandwelfare.idaho.gov.
			Applicants must provide a clear and readable copy of both sides of their current driver's license or other current government issued identification with signature. If this is not available, the applicant must either provide a clear and readable copy of both sides of two other forms of current identification with a signature or have their request notarized
	Varies	See remarks	A full certified copy of the divorce decree is available from the Clerk of the Court in the county where the divorce was granted.

Illinois

Place of event	Cost of copy	Address	Remarks
Birth	$15.00 certified copy $10.00 certification	Division of Vital Records Illinois Department of Public Health 925 E Ridgely Avenue Springfield, IL 62702	State office has records since January 1916. For earlier records and for copies of State records since January 1916, write to County Clerk in county where event occurred (county fees vary). Genealogical (uncertified) copies are available from the State for death records 20 years or older for $10.00. Additional certified copies of the same birth record ordered at the same time are $2.00 each. Additional genealogical copies of the same record ordered at the same time are $2.00 each. Additional certified copies of the same death record ordered at the same time are $4.00 each.
Death	$19.00 certified copy $10.00 genealogical copy		Personal check or money orders should be made payable to **Illinois Department of Public Health**. To verify current fees, the telephone number is (217) 782-6553. This is a recorded message. Information on how to obtain certified copies is also available via the Internet at http://www.idph.state.il.us.
Marriage	$5.00	Same as Birth or Death	Marriage Index since January 1962. Selected items may be verified (fee $5.00). Certified copies are NOT available from State office. For certified copies, write to the County Clerk in county where license was issued.
Divorce	$5.00	Same as Birth or Death	Divorce Index since January 1962. Selected items may be verified (fee $5.00). Certified copies are NOT available from State office. For certified copies, write to the Clerk of Circuit Court in county where divorce was granted.

Indiana

Place of event	Cost of copy	Address	Remarks
Birth	$10.00	Vital Records	State office birth records begin in October 1907
Death	$8.00	Indiana State Department of Health P.O. Box 7125 Indianapolis, IN 46206-7125	and death records since January 1900. Additional copies of the same birth or death record ordered at the same time are $4.00 each. For earlier records, write to Health Officer in city or county where event occurred.
			Personal check or money order should be made payable to **Indiana State Department of Health**. To verify current fees, the telephone number is (317) 233-2700. Information on how to obtain certified copies is also available via the Internet at http://www.in.gov/isdh/index.htm.
			Applicant must provide a photocopy of a valid identification with picture and signature along with the application. Proof of relationship may be required.
Marriage (State)	$8.00	Same as Birth or Death	State office retain index for marriages since 1958. Certified copies of Record of Marriage are available from the state. However, certified copies of Marriage Certificates are only a vailable from county Clerk of Circuit Court or Clerk of Superior Court in the county where event occurred.
	Varies	See remarks	Clerk of Circuit Court or Clerk of Superior Court in county where license was issued.
Divorce	Varies	See remarks	County Clerk in county where divorce was granted.

Iowa

Place of event	Cost of copy	Address	Remarks
Birth or Death	$15.00	Iowa Department of Public Health Bureau of Vital Records Lucas Office Building 1st Floor 321 East 12th Street Des Moines, IA 50319-0075	State office has records since July 1880. Personal check or money order should be made payable to **Iowa Department of Public Health**. To verify current fees, the telephone number is (515) 281-4944. This is a recorded message. Information on how to obtain certified copies is also available via the Internet at http://www.idph.state.ia.us/. Applicants for all records must provide a photo identification when applying in person. Written applications must include a clear photo copy of a current government issued ID and applicant's notarized signature.
Marriage	$15.00	Same as Birth or Death	State office has records since July 1880.
Divorce	See remarks	Same as Birth or Death	Brief statistical record only since 1906. Inquiries will be forwarded to appropriate office. Certified copies are not available from State Health Department.
	$6.00	See remarks	Clerk of District Court in county where divorce was granted.

Kansas

Place of event	Cost of copy	Address	Remarks
Birth	$15.00	Office of Vital Statistics	State office has records since July 1911. For earlier records, write to County Clerk in county where event occurred. Additional copies of the same record ordered at the same time are $15.00 each.
Death	$15.00	Curtis State Office Building	
		1000 SW Jackson Street	
		Suite 120	
		Topeka, Kansas 66612-2221	
			Personal check or money order should be made payable to **Vital Statistics**. To verify current fees, the telephone number is (785) 296-1400. This is a recorded message with the option to speak with a Customer Service Representative. Information on how to obtain certified copies is also available via the Internet at http://www.kdheks.gov/vital.
			The applicant **MUST** include a copy of a photo ID and a handwritten signature with the request.
Marriage	$15.00	Same as Birth or Death	State office has records since May 1913. Additional copies of the same record ordered at the same time are $7.00 each.
	Varies	See remarks	Write to: District Judge in county where license was issued.
Divorce	$15.00	Same as Birth or Death	State office has records since July 1951. Additional copies of the same record ordered at the same time are $7.00 each.
	Varies	See remarks	Write to: Clerk of District Court in county where divorce was granted.

Kentucky

Place of event	Cost of copy	Address	Remarks
Birth	$10.00	Office of Vital Statistics	State office has records since January 1911.
Death	$6.00	Department for Public Health	
		Cabinet for Health and Family Services	Personal check or money order should be made payable to **Kentucky State Treasurer**. To verify current fees, the telephone number is (502) 564-4212. Information on how to obtain certified copies is also available via the Internet at http://chfs.ky.gov/dph/vital/.
		275 East Main Street 1E-A Frankfort, KY 40621-0001	
Stillbirth	$6.00	Same as Birth or Death	State office has records since January 1911.
			Personal check or money order should be made payable to **Kentucky State Treasurer**. To verify current fees, the telephone number is (502) 564-4212. Information on how to obtain certified copies is also available via the Internet at http://chfs.ky.gov/dph/vital/.
Marriage	$6.00	Same as Birth and Death	Records since June 1958.
	Varies	See remarks	Clerk of County Court in county where license was issued.
Divorce	$6.00	Same as Birth or Death	Records since June 1958.
	Varies	See remarks	Clerk of Circuit Court in county where decree was issued.

Louisiana

Place of event	Cost of copy	Address	Remarks
Birth (long form)	$15.50	Office of Public Health	State office has birth records for 100 years past date of birth and deaths records for 50 years past the date of death. To obtain current information on who may obtain a record, how to submit a request and an official request form, click on at http://vitalrecords.dhh.la.gov/.
Birth (short form)	$9.50	Vital Records Registry P.O. Box 60630	
Death	$7.50	New Orleans, LA 70160	
			Older records are available through the Louisiana State Archives, P.O. Box 94125, Baton Rouge, LA 70804.
Marriage Orleans Parish Only	$5.50	Same as Birth or Death	To obtain current information on how to submit a request for a certified copy of Orleans Parish marriage record less than 50 years old and a request form, click on http://vitalrecords.dhh.la.gov/.
			Certified copies for other parishes are issued by Clerk of Court in the parish were the marriage license was issued.
			Marriage records over 50 years are stored by the Louisiana State Archives, P.O. Box 94125, Baton Rouge, LA 70804.
Other Parishes	Varies	See remarks	Certified copies are issued by Clerk of Court in the parish were the marriage license was issued.
Divorce All Parishes	Varies	See remarks	Certified copies are issued by Clerk of Court in the parish where the divorce was granted.

Maine

Place of event	Cost of copy	Address	Remarks
Birth or Death	Certified $15.00 Non-Certified $10.00	Maine CDC vital records office Department of Health and Human Services 244 Water Street #11 State House Station Augusta, ME 04333-0011	State office has records since 1923. Records for 1892 to1922 are available at the Maine State Archives (207) 287-5795. For earlier records, write to the municipality where the event occurred. Additional copies of same record ordered at same time are $6.00 each.

To purchase a certified copy, the request must include proof of identification (valid photo IDs such as a driver's license, passport, or other government-issued photo identification) and proof of lineage, if possible.

Personal check or money order should be made payable to **Treasurer, State of Maine**. To verify current fees, the telephone number is (207) 287-3181, or toll-free at 1-888-664-9491. This is a recorded message. Information on how to obtain certified copies is also available via the Internet at http://www.state.me.us. |
Marriage	$15.00	Same as Birth or Death	Same as Birth or Death.
Divorce	$15.00	Same as Birth or Death	Same as Birth or Death.
Divorce	Varies	See remarks	Clerk of District Court in judicial division where divorce was granted.

Maryland

Place of event	Cost of copy	Address	Remarks
Birth	$24.00	Division of Vital Records Department of Health and Mental Hygiene 6550 Reisterstown Road P.O. Box 68760 Baltimore, MD 21215-0036	State office has records since August 1898. Records for City of Baltimore are available from January 1875. Fee for Commemorative Birth Certificate is $30.00.
Death	$12.00		For genealogical studies, you must apply through the Maryland State Archives, 350 Rowe Blvd., Annapolis, MD 21401, (410) 260-6400.
			Personal check or money order should be made payable to **Division of Vital Records**. To verify current fees, the telephone number to contact is (410) 764-3038. This is a recorded message. Information on how to obtain certified copies is also available via the Internet at http://www.vsa.state.md.us
Marriage (State, county)	$12.00	Same as Birth or Death	Records since January 1990. Clerk of Circuit Court in county where license was issued or Clerk of Court of Common Pleas of Baltimore City (for licenses issued in City of Baltimore).
Divorce (State, county) Verification only	12.00	Same as Birth or Death	Records since January 1992. Certified divorce decrees may be obtained through the Clerk of Circuit Court in the city/county where the divorce was granted. Some items may be verified.

Massachusetts

Place of event	Cost of copy	Address	Remarks
Birth or Death	$18.00 (In person) $28.00 (Mail request) $3.00 (State Archives)	Registry of Vital Records and Statistics 150 Mount Vernon Street 1st Floor Dorchester, MA 02125-3105	State office has no records previous to 1916. For earlier records, write to The Massachusetts Archives at Columbia Point, 220 Morrissey Boulevard, Boston, MA 02125 (617) 727-2816. Personal check or money order should be made payable to **Commonwealth of Massachusetts**. To verify current fees, the telephone number is (617) 740-2600. This is a recorded message. Information on how to obtain certified copies is also available via the Internet at http://www.state.ma.us/dph/bhsre/rvr/vrcopies.htm
Marriage	Same as Birth or Death	Same as Birth or Death	Records since 1916.
Divorce	No Fee	Same as Birth or Death	Index only since 1952. Inquirer will be directed where to send request. Certified copies are not available from State office.
Divorce	Varies	See remarks	Registrar of Probate Court in county where divorce was granted.

Michigan

Place of event	Cost of copy	Address	Remarks
Birth or Death	$26.00	Vital Records Request P.O. Box 30721 Lansing, MI 48909	State office has records of births and deaths that occurred and were filed with the state since 1867. Some of the records (especially pre-1906 births and pre-1897 deaths) were not filed with the state. Personal check or money order should be made payable to **State of Michigan**. Fees are $26.00 for the search and first certified copy of any birth, death, marriage, divorce or Affidavit of Parentage. Exception is Senior Citizen ($7.00) requesting their own birth record. Additional copies of any record are $12.00 each. To verify current fees, the telephone number is (517) 335-8656. This is a recorded message. To speak to a customer service representative, the telephone number is (517) 335-8666. Information on how to obtain certified copies is also available via the Internet at http://www.michigan.gov/mdch. Michigan birth records are restricted documents and are available only to eligible individuals. A photocopy of an eligible individual's photo identification (state driver's license, state personal ID card, Military ID, etc.) is required to be sent in, along with the signed application and appropriate fee. Copies of records may also be obtained from the County Clerk in county where event occurred. Fees vary from county to county. Records of Detroit births occurring since 1893 and deaths since 1897 may be obtained from the city of Detroit Health Department.
Marriage	$26.00	Same as Birth or Death	Records since 1867. Some marriages (especially pre-1926) were not filed with the state.
	Varies	See remarks	County Clerk in county where license was issued.
Divorce	$26.00	Same as Birth or Death	Records since 1897. Some divorces (especially pre-1924) were not filed with the state.
	Varies	See remarks	County Clerk in county where divorce was granted.

Minnesota

Place of event	Cost of copy	Address	Remarks
Birth	$26.00	MN Department of Health	Office of the State Registrar has birth records on file from January 1900 to current and death records on file from January 1908 to current. Copies of earlier records may be obtained from Local Registrar in county where event occurred.
Death	$13.00	Central Cashiering – Vital Records P.O. Box 64499 St. Paul, MN 55164	
			Personal check or money order should be made payable to **Minnesota Department of Health**. To verify current fees, the telephone number is (651) 201-5970. This is a recorded message. Information on how to obtain certified copies is also available via the Internet at http://www.health.state.mn.us. Any questions in regards to obtaining a certified copy, the telephone number is (651) 201-5980. An application and credit card information and also be faxed to (651) 201-5980.
Marriage	See remarks		Marriage records are not recorded at the state level.
	$9.00	See remarks	Local Registrar in county where license was issued. Additional copies of the marriage record when ordered at the same time are $2.00 each.
Divorce	See remarks		Divorce records are not recorded at the state level.
	$10.00	See remarks	Court Administrator in county where divorce was granted.

Mississippi

Place of event	Cost of copy	Address	Remarks
Birth and Death	$15..00	Mississippi Vital Records State Department of Health P.O. Box 1700 Jackson, MS 39215-1700	State office has records since November 1, 1912. Additional copies of same record ordered at the same time are $5.00 each. Personal check , bank or postal money order or bank cashier's check are accepted and should be made payable to **Mississippi State Department of Health.**
			A copy of a valid photo ID for the applicant is required.
			To verify current fees, the telephone number is (601) 576-7981. A recorded message may be reached on (601) 576-7450. Information on how to obtain certified copies is also available via the Internet at http://www.msdh.state.ms.us.
Marriage	$15.00	Same as Birth or Death	Statistical records only from January 1, 1926 to July 1, 1938, and since January 1942.
			Additional copies of the same record ordered at the same time are $5.00.
Marriage (County)	Varies	See remarks	Circuit Clerk in county where license was issued.
Divorce	See remarks	Same as Birth or Death	Records since January 1926. Certified copies are not available from State office. Index search only available at $15.00 for each 5-year increment. Book and page number for county record provided.
Divorce	Varies	See remarks	Chancery Clerk in county where divorce was granted.

Missouri

Place of event	Cost of copy	Address	Remarks
Birth	$15.00	Missouri Department of Health and Senior Services Bureau of Vital Records 930 Wildwood P.O. Box 570 Jefferson City, MO 65102-0570	State office has records since January 1910. Certified copies of most Missouri birth and death records are also available from local county health department or the St. Louis City or Kansas City Health Departments. For details, please contact these offices directly. If event occurred in St. Louis (City), St. Louis County, or Kansas City before 1910, write to the City or County Health Department. Copies of these records are $13.00 each.
Death	$13.00		

Additional copies of the same death record ordered at the same time are $10.00 each.

Personal check or money order should be made payable to **Missouri Department of Health and Senior Services**. Please include a legal size self-addressed stamped envelope. To verify current fees on birth and death records, the telephone number is (573) 751-6387. This is a recorded message. Information on how to obtain certified copies is also available via the Internet at http://www.dhss.mo.gov.

A valid photo ID is required for walk-in applicants. A signature is required. Notarized requests are required for mail-in orders.

Place of event	Cost of copy	Address	Remarks
Marriage	$15.00	See remarks	Reports of marriage records are on file from July 1948 to the present. Recorder of Deeds in county where license was issued.

Certified copies of Missouri marriage records are also available from the county recorder of deeds in which the marriage occurred. For details, please contact these offices directly.

Personal check or money order should be made payable to **Missouri Department of Health and Senior Services**. Please include a self-addressed stamped envelope. To verify current fees on marriage records, the telephone number is (573) 751-6387. Information on how to obtain certified copies is also available via the Missouri Department of Health and Senior Services, Vital Records website.

A valid photo ID is required for walk-in applicants. A signature is required. Notarized requests are required for mail-in orders

Divorce	$15.00	See remarks	

Reports of divorce records are on file from July 1948 to the present.

Certified copies of Missouri divorce records are also available from the Clerk of the Circuit Court in the county were the divorce was granted. For details, please contact these offices directly. Certified copies of reports of divorce records are $15.00 each.

Personal check or money order should be made payable to **Missouri Department of Health and Senior Services**. Please include a self-addressed stamped envelope. To verify current fees on divorce records, the telephone number is (573) 751-6387. Information on how to obtain certified copies is also available via the Missouri Department of Health and Senior Services, Vital Records website.

A valid photo ID is required for walk-in applicants. A signature is required. Notarized requests are required for mail-in orders

Montana

Place of event	Cost of copy	Address	Remarks
Birth or Death	$12.00	Office of Vital Statistics MT Dept of Public Health and Human Services 111 N Sanders, Rm. 209 P.O. Box 4210 Helena, MT 59604	State office has records since late 1907. Additional copies of the same record requested at the same time are $5.00. Applicants **MUST** provide a clear and readable copy of both sides of their current driver's license or other current government issued identification with signature. If this is not available, the applicant must either provide a clear and readable copy of two other forms of current identification with one having a signature or have their request notarized. Personal check or money order should be made payable to **Montana Vital Records**. To verify current fees, the telephone number is 1-(406) 444-2685. Information on how to obtain certified copies is also available via the Internet at http://www.dphhs.mt.gov.
Marriage	See remarks	Same as Birth or Death	Indexes to locate marriage license since July 1943. Certified copies are not available from State Office. Fee for search and verification of essential facts of marriage is $10.00. Apply to Clerk of District Court were marriage license was purchased if known.
	Varies	See remarks	Clerk of District Court in county where marriage license was purchased.
Divorce	See remarks	Same as Birth or Death	Indexes to locate divorce decrees since July 1943. Certified copies are not available from State Office. Fee for search and verification of essential facts of divorce is $10.00. Apply to Clerk of District Court where divorce was granted if known.
	Varies	See remarks	Clerk of District Court in county where divorce was granted.

Nebraska

Place of event	Cost of copy	Address	Remarks
Birth	$12.00	Vital Records Office	State office has records since late 1904. If birth or death occurred before then, write the State office for information.
Death	$11.00	1033 O Street, Suite 130 P.O. Box 95065 Lincoln, NE 68509-5065	
			Personal check or money order should be made payable to **Vital Records Office**. To verify current fees, the telephone number is (402) 471-2871. This is a recorded message. Information on how to obtain certified copies is also available via the Internet at http://www.dhhs.ne.gov/publichealth/pages/vitalrecords.aspx.
			All requests must include a photocopy of the requestor's valid government- issued photo identification, i.e., valid driver's license, valid State ID card, valid passport or visa.
Marriage	$11.00	Same as Birth or Death	Records since January 1909.
	Varies	See remarks	County Court in county where license was issued.
Divorce	$11.00	Same as Birth or Death	Records since January 1909.
	Varies	See remarks	Clerk of District Court in county where divorce was granted.

Nevada

Place of event	Cost of copy	Address	Remarks
Birth or Death	$20.00	Office of Vital Records 4150 Technology Way Suite 104 Carson City, NV 89706	State office has records since July 1911. For earlier records, write to County Recorder in county where event occurred. Personal check or money order should be made payable to **Office of Vital Records**. To verify current fees, the telephone number is (775) 684-4242. This is a recorded message. Information on how to obtain certified copies is also available via the Internet at http://health.nv.gov/VS.htm. The applicant **MUST** include a copy of a photo ID with the request.
Marriage	See remarks	Same as Birth or Death	Indexes since January 1968. Certified copies are not available from State Health Division. Inquiries will be forwarded to appropriate office.
	Varies	See remarks	County Recorder in county where license was issued.
Divorce	See remarks	Same as Birth or Death	Indexes since January 1968. Certified copies are not available from State Health Division. Inquiries will be forwarded to appropriate office.
	Varies	See remarks	County Clerk in county where divorce was granted.

New Hampshire

Place of event	Cost of copy	Address	Remarks
Birth or Death	$15.00	Division of Vital Records Administration Archives Building 71 South Fruit Street Concord, NH 03301-2410	State office has records since 1640. Copies of records may be obtained from State office or from City or Town Clerk in place where event occurred or the license was registered. Recent records (birth since 1983, death since 1990, and marriage since 1989) may be obtained from ANY City or Town running the Vital Records Automated software called NHVRIN.

Additional copies ordered at the same time are $10.00 each.

Applicant must submit a written request and a photo ID with signature of the requestor or notarized assignment of access from registrant authorizing non-direct or tangibly related individual access and a self-addressed stamped envelope.

Personal check or money order should be made payable to **Treasurer, State of New Hampshire**. To verify current fees, the telephone number is (603) 271-4654. This is a recorded message. Information on how to obtain certified copies is also available via the Internet at http://www.sos.nh.gov/vitalrecords. |
Marriage	$15.00	Same as Birth or Death	State Office has records since 1640.
	$15.00	See remarks	Town Clerk in town where license was issued.
Divorce	$15.00	Same as Birth or Death	Records since 1808.
	Varies	See remarks	Clerk of Superior/Family Division Court in the county where divorce was granted.

New Jersey

Place of event	Cost of copy	Address
Birth, Death, Marriage, Civil Union or Domestic Partnership (State)	$25.00	See remarks
Genealogical Birth, Marriage, or Death	$10.00	New Jersey State Archives 225 West State Street P.O. Box 307 Trenton, NJ 08625-0307

Remarks

The State Office of Vital Statistics and Registry maintains records from 1901 to present. For older records, please see information for the State Archives at the bottom of the page.

All requests must include a copy of the requestor's valid identification, payment of the appropriate fee and proof of relationship to the individual listed on the vital record, if ordering a certified copy.

The State or local Registrar may issue a certified copy of a vital record only to persons who establish themselves as the subject of the vital record, the subject's parent, legal guardian or legal representative, spouse, child, grandchild or sibling, if of legal age, to a State or Federal agency for official purposes, pursuant to court order or under other emergent circumstances as determined by the Commissioner. All other applicants will be issued a Certification that state the document is not for identification or legal purposes.

Additional copies of the same record ordered at the same time are $2.00 each.

Please visit the New Jersey Vital Statistics website for the most up to date information regarding ordering options and information. The website address is www.state.nj.us/health/vital or call toll-free at 1-866-649-8726.

The New Jersey State Archives holds original birth, marriage, and death records from the period May 1, 1848 to December 31, 1900.

The New Jersey Archives also holds microfilm copies of: birth records 1878-1929; marriage records 1878-1940; and death records 1878-1940. These materials are available for in-person use only.

Personal check or money order should be made payable to **New Jersey General Treasury**. The general information telephone number is (609) 292-6260.

New Jersey

Place of event	Cost of copy	Address	Remarks
Divorce	$10.00	Clerk of the Superior Court Superior Court of NJ Public Information Center 171 Jersey Street P.O. Box 967 Trenton, NJ 08625-0967	The fee is for a certified Blue Seal copy. Make check payable to **Clerk of the Superior Court**.

New Mexico

Place of event	Cost of copy	Address	Remarks
Birth	$10.00	NM Vital Records	State office has records since 1920 and delayed
Death	$5.00	P.O. Box 25767	records since 1880.
		Santa Fe, NM 87125	
			Personal check or money order should be made payable to **NM Vital Records**. To verify current fees, the telephone number is 1-866-534-0051. This is a recorded message. Information on how to obtain certified copies is also available via the Internet at http://www.VitalRecordsNM.org
Marriage	Varies	See remarks	County Clerk in county where license was issued.
Divorce	Varies	See remarks	Clerk of Court where divorce was granted.

New York

(except New York
City)

Place of event	Cost of copy	Address	Remarks
Birth or Death	$30.00	Certification Unit Vital Records Section 2nd Floor 800 North Pearl Street Menands, NY 12204	State office has records since 1880. For records before 1914 in Albany, Buffalo, and Yonkers, or before 1880 in any other city, write to Registrar of Vital Statistics in city where event occurred. For the rest of the State, except New York City, write to State office. Personal check or money order should be made payable to **New York State Department of Health**. Payment of mail order copies submitted from foreign countries must be made by a check drawn on a United States bank or by an international money order. To verify current fees, the telephone number is (518) 474-3075. This is a recorded message. Information on how to obtain certified copies is also available via the Internet at http://www.health.state.ny.us. For all types of State and local issued copies, the applicant is required to provide government issued photo identification.
Marriage	$30.00	Same as Birth or Death	Records from 1881 to present.
	$10.00	See remarks	For records from 1880-1907 and licenses issued in the cities of Albany, Buffalo, or Yonkers, apply to Albany: City Clerk, City Hall, Albany, NY 12207; Buffalo: City Clerk, City Hall, Buffalo, NY 14202; Yonkers: Registrar of Vital Statistics, Health Center Building, Yonkers, NY 10701.
Divorce	$30.00	Same as Birth or Death	Records since January 1963.
	Varies	See remarks	County Clerk in county where divorce was granted.

New York City

Place of event	Cost of copy	Address	Remarks
Birth or Death	$15.00	NYC Health Department Office of Vital Records 125 Worth St., CN4, Rm. 133 New York, NY 10013	The Office has birth and death records for people who were born and/or died in the five boroughs of New York City: Brooklyn, the Bronx, Manhattan, Queens, or Staten Island. Birth records issued before 1910 and death records issued before 1949 must be ordered through the Municipal Archives. For more information please visit http://www.nyc.gov/html/records/html/vitalrecords/home.shtml or write to Department of Records and Information Services, 31 Chambers Street, New York, NY 10007. Additional information on ordering and correcting NYC birth and death records can be found by visiting http://www.nyc.gov/vitalrecords or calling 311(or 212-639-9675 outside New York City).
Marriage Manhattan Borough	$15.00	Office of the City Clerk 141 Worth Street New York, NY 10013	Marriage Record Requests in Person: Marriage records from 1996 to present can be obtained in person from any office of the New York City Clerk. Marriage records from 1930 to 1955 can be obtained solely in the Manhattan Office. For additional information go to http://nycmarriagebureau.com/MarriageBureau/index.htm?RecordRoom.htm. Additional copies of the same record ordered at the same time are $10.00 each.
Bronx Borough	$15.00	Office of the City Clerk Supreme Court Building 851 Grand Concourse Room B131 Bronx, NY 10451	
Brooklyn Borough	$15.00	Office of the City Clerk Brooklyn Municipal Building 210 Joralemon Street, Room 205 Brooklyn, NY 11201	Marriage Record Requests by Mail: To obtain a Marriage Record by mail, please call the main office at (212) 669-8090 to request a form or to download the Marriage Record mail request form go to http://nycmarriagebureau.com/MarriageBureau/MailRequestForm.htm

New York
City

Place of event	Cost of copy	Address	Remarks
Queens Borough	$15.00	Office of the City Clerk Borough Hall Building 120-55 Queens Boulevard Ground Floor, Room X001 Kew Gardens, NY 11424	Please mail all Marriage Record Requests to the following address: Office of the City Clerk Municipal Building 1 Centre Street, Room 252 South New York, New York 10007
Staten Island Borough (no longer called Richmond)	$15.00	Office of the City Clerk Borough Hall Building 10 Richmond Terrace Room 311 Staten Island, NY 10301	
Divorce			Go to the New York State page on this website at http://www.cdc/gov/nchs/howto/w2w/newyork.htm.

North Carolina

Place of event	Cost of copy	Address	Remarks
Birth or Death	$24.00	NC Vital Records 1903 Mail Service Center Raleigh, NC 27699-1903	The State office has birth records beginning with October 1913 and death records beginning with January 1, 1930. Business or certified check or money order should be made payable to **NC Vital Records**. To verify current fees and access additional information on how to obtain copies of vital records, the telephone number is (919) 733-3000 or visit the North Carolina Vital Records website. The cost of each additional copy of the same record ordered at the same time is $15.00. A copy of a valid photo ID with a signature is required of the applicant for in-person requests. The Register of Deeds in the county where the birth or death occurred can provide copies of birth and death certificates upon request.
Marriage (County)	$24.00	NC Vital Records 1903 Mail Service Center Raleigh, NC 27699-1903	For records beginning with 1962, contact either the Register of Deeds in the county where the marriage license was obtained or the NC State Office of Vital Records in Raleigh. For records before 1962, contact the county Register of Deeds. To verify current fees and access additional information on how to obtain copies of vital records, the telephone number is (919) 733-3000 or visit the North Carolina Vital Records website. The cost of each additional copy of the same record ordered at the same time is $15.00.
Divorce	$24.00	NC Vital Records 1903 Mail Service Center Raleigh, NC 27699-1903	For records beginning with January 1958, contact either the NC State Office of Vital Records in Raleigh or the Clerk of Court in the county where the divorce occurred. For records before 1958, contact the Clerk of Court in the county where the divorce occurred. To verify current fees and access additional information on how to obtain copies of vital records, the telephone number is (919) 733-3000 or visit the North Carolina Vital Records website. The cost of each additional copy of the same record ordered at the same time is $15.00.

North Dakota

Place of event	Cost of copy	Address	Remarks
Birth Death	$7.00 $5.00	ND Dept. of Health Division of Vital Records 600 East Boulevard Avenue Dept. 301 Bismarck, ND 58505-0200	State office has some birth records since 1870 and some death records since July 1893. Birth years from 1870 to 1920 are incomplete. Death years from 1894 to 1920 are incomplete. Additional copies of birth records are $4.00 each and death records are $2.00 each. Copies are generally processed in 5-7 working days after request is received. Personal check or money order should be made payable to **ND Department of Health**. To verify current fees, the telephone number is (701) 328-2360. This is an automated attendant with a recorded message. Information on how to obtain certified copies is also available via the Internet at http://www.ndhealth.gov/vital/birth.htm. The applicant must submit a photocopy of a government issued ID with their request.
Marriage	Varies	The following link provides county contact information regarding certified copies of marriage records: http://www.ndhealth.gov/vital/marriage.htm	As of January 1, 2008, the ND Department of Health no longer issues certified copies of marriage records.
Divorce	Varies	The following link provides county contact information regarding certified copies of marriage records: http://www.ndhealth.gov/vital/divorce.htm	Certified copies are not available from the ND Department of Health.

Northern Mariana Islands

Place of event	Cost of copy	Address	Remarks
Birth	$20.00	Commonwealth Healthcare Corporation Vital Statistics Office P.O. Box 500409 Saipan, MP 96950	Office has records for birth and death since 1946. Records from 1946 to 1950 are incomplete.
Death	$15.00		Money order or bank cashiers check should be made payable to **Commonwealth Healthcare Corporation**. To verify current fees, call (670) 236-8717 or (670) 236-8702. E-mail address is info@vs-cnmi.org.
Marriage	$10.00	Commonwealth Recorder Superior Court Vital Records Section P.O. Box 307 Saipan, MP 96950	Money order or bank cashiers check should be made payable to **Commonwealth Healthcare Corporation**. To verify current fees, call (670) 236-9830 or fax (670) 236-9831.
Divorce	$0.50 per page for Divorce Decree plus $2.50 for certification	Commonwealth Recorder Superior Court Vital Records Section P.O. Box 307 Saipan, MP 96950	Office has records for divorce since 1960.

Ohio

Place of event	Cost of copy	Address	Remarks
Birth or Death	$21.50	Vital Statistics Ohio Department of Health P.O. Box 15098 Columbus, OH 43215-0098	State office has birth records since December 20, 1908 and death records since January 1, 1954. For earlier birth and death records, write to the Probate Court in the county where the event occurred. Death records that occurred December 20, 1908–December 31, 1954, can be obtained from the Ohio Historical Society, Archives Library Division, 1982 Velma Avenue, Columbus, OH 43211-2497. A searchable index to records from 1913 to 1944 is also available via the Internet at http://www.ohiohistory.org. Personal check or money order should be made payable to **Treasury, State of Ohio**. To verify current fees, the telephone number is (614) 466-2531. This is a recorded message. Information on how to obtain certified copies is also available via the Internet at http://www.odh.ohio.gov/vitalstatistics/vitalstats.aspx.
Marriage	See remarks	Same as Birth or Death	Copies of marriage records are not available from the State Health Department. For certified copies of marriage records, please write to the Probate Court in the in the county where the event occurred. Information on how to obtain certified copies is also available via the Internet at http://www.odh.ohio.gov/vitalstatistics/mrgdiv.aspx.
	Varies	See remarks	
Divorce	See remarks	Same as Birth or Death	Certified copies are not available from the State Health Department. For certified copies of divorces, please write to Clerk of Court of where the divorce was granted divorce was granted . Information on how to obtain certified copies is also available via the Internet at http://www.odh.ohio.gov/vitalstatistics/mrgdiv.aspx
	Varies	See remarks	

Oklahoma

Place of event	Cost of copy	Address	Remarks
Birth or Death	$15.00	Vital Records Service State Department of Health 1000 Northeast 10th Street Oklahoma City, OK 73117	State office has records since October 1908. Personal check or money order should be made payable to **Vital Records Service**. To verify current fees, the telephone number is (405) 271-4040. This is a recorded message. Information on how to obtain certified copies, eligibility requirements, and a list of acceptable IDs are also available via the Internet at http://vr.health.ok.gov/. A copy of a current legal photo ID from the applicant is required, as well as a completed application and appropriate fees. Commemorative heirloom certificates are also available: cost $35.oo and includes one (1) certified copy. Detailed description of the heirloom certificate is available at http://vr.health.ok.gov/.
Marriage	Varies	See remarks	Clerk of Court in county where license was issued.
Divorce	Varies	See remarks	Clerk of Court in county where divorce was granted.

Oregon

Place of event	Cost of copy	Address	Remarks
Birth or Death	$20.00	Oregon Vital Records P.O. Box 14050 Portland, OR 97293-0050	State vital records office has birth and death records starting from 1903. Oregon State Archives has birth records for the City of Portland from 1864 to 1902 and statewide delayed birth records from 1845 to 1902; City of Portland death records from 1862 to 1902 and statewide death records from 1903 to 1955. Additional copies of the same record ordered at the same time are $15.00 each. Personal check or money order should be made payable to **OHA/Vital Records**. To verify current fees, the telephone number is (971) 673-1190. This is a recorded message. Information on how to obtain certified copies is also available via the Internet at http://healthoregon.org/chs.
		Oregon State Archives 800 Summer Street, NE Salem, OR 97310	The telephone number for the Oregon State Archives is (503) 373-0701 and the fax number is (503) 373-0953. Information on how to obtain copies is also available via the internet at http://arcweb.sos.state.or.us/reference html
Heirloom Birth	$45.00	Same as Birth or Death	Presentation-style calligraphy certificate suitable for framing.
Marriage	$20.00	Same as Birth or Death	State vital records office has marriage records starting from 1911. Oregon State Archives has some county records from the 1800s and statewide records for 1906-1910.
	Varies	See remarks	County Clerk in county where license was issued. County Clerks also have some records before 1906. Some older county records have been transferred to the Oregon State Archives, 800 Summer Street NE, Salem, OR 97310
Divorce	$20.00	Same as Birth or Death	State vital records office has divorce records starting from 1925.
(Certificates Only)	Varies	See remarks	County Circuit Court Clerk in county where divorce was granted. County Clerks also have some records before 1925.

Pennsylvania

Place of event	Cost of copy	Address	Remarks
Birth	$10.00	Division of Vital Records ATTN: Birth Unit 101 South Mercer Street Room 401 P.O. Box 1528 New Castle, PA 16103	State office has records since January 1906.

All requests must be submitted on an application form, which requires the signature of the individual requesting the certificate and a legible copy of his/her valid government issued photo ID that verifies name and mailing address of the individual requesting the certificate. Application forms, eligibility requirements, fees, and additional information, including how to apply online or by fax with a credit card are available via the Internet http://www.health.state.pa.us/vitalrecords. The telephone number is (724) 656-3100. This is a recorded message. |
| Death | $9.00 | Division of Vital Records ATTN: Death Unit 101 South Mercer Street Room 401 P.O. Box 1528 New Castle, PA 16103 | Personal check or money order should be made payable to **Vital Records**.

Pennsylvania birth or death certificates prior to 1906 can be accessed through the courthouse in the county were the person was born or died. A list of court houses is available via the Internet at http://www.health.state.pa.us/vitalrecords. |
| Marriage | Varies | | Make application to the Marriage License Clerks, County Court House, in county where license was issued. A list of court houses is available via the Internet at http://www.portal.state.pa.us/portal/server.pt/community/marriage_and_divorce_certificates/14126. |
| Divorce | Varies | | Make application to the Prothonotary, Court House, in county seat of county where divorce was granted. A list of court houses is available via the Internet athttp://www.portal.state.pa.us/portal/server.pt/community/marriage_and_divorce_certificates/14126. |

Puerto Rico

Place of event	Cost of copy	Address	Remarks
Birth or Death	$5.00	Department of Health Demographic Registry P.O. Box 11854 Fernández Juncos Station San Juan, PR 00910	Central office has records since June 21, 1931. Copies of earlier records may be obtained by writing to local Registrar (Registrador Demografico) in municipality where event occurred. Additional copies ordered at the same time by the same person are $4.00 each. Information on how to obtain certified copies is also available via the Internet at http://www.prfaa.com/services.asp?id=44.
			Money order should be made payable to **Secretary of the Treasury**. Personal checks are not accepted. To verify current fees, the telephone number is (787) 767-9120.
Marriage	$5.00	Same as Birth or Death	All applications must be accompanied by a photocopy of a recent, valid IDENTIFICATION OF APPLICANT.
Divorce	$2.00	Same as Birth or Death	
		See remarks	Superior Court where divorce was granted.

Rhode Island

Place of event	Cost of copy	Address	Remarks
Birth or Death	$20.00	RI Department of Health Office of Vital Records Room 101 3 Capitol Hill Providence, RI 02908-5097	State office keeps birth and marriage records for 100 years and keeps death records for 50 years. In general, copies can be obtained from the State office, the city/town clerk where the event occurred or the city of residence at the time of the occurrence. Additional copies of the same record ordered at the same time are $15.00 each. Information for city/town addresses are available via the Internet at: http://www.health.ri.gov/chic/vital/clerks.php. For earlier records, write to the city/town clerk where the event occurred or to the Rhode Island State Archives, 337 Westminster Street, Providence, RI 02903. Personal check or money order should be made payable to **Rhode Island General Treasurer**. To verify current fees after office hours, the telephone number is (401) 222-2811. To verify current fees and general information during office hours, please call the Health Hot Line at (401) 222-5960. Information on how to obtain certified copies is also available via the Internet at http://www.health.ri.gov. All requests must be accompanied by a photocopy of the applicant's valid government-issued picture identification, e.g., driver's license. In lieu of a valid government-issued picture identification, two pieces of mail are accepted showing the correct name and address of the individual requesting the record.
Pre-Adoption Non-Certified Birth	$20.00	Same as Birth or Death	In June, 2011 the State of Rhode Island passed a law allowing adult adoptees born in Rhode Island access to a non-certified copy of their unaltered, original birth certificate. If you are an adoptee who was born in Rhode Island and you are age 25 or older, you can request a non-certified copy of your original, pre-adoption birth record from the State Office of Vital Records. According to state law, we can only release your record to you, the adoptee. Relatives cannot request copies of your record on your behalf. Please visit the web-site at www.health.ri.gov under Adult Adoptees for

further information on applications, ID requirements and access.

Personal check or money order should be made payable to **General Treasurer, State of Rhode Island.**

All requests must be accompanied by a photocopy of the applicant's valid government-issued picture identification, e.g., driver's license. In lieu of valid government-issued picture identification, two pieces of mail are accepted showing the correct name and address of the individual requesting the record.

Marriage	$20.00	Same as Birth or Death
Divorce	$3.00	Clerk of Family Court 1 Dorrance Plaza Providence, RI 02903

South Carolina

Place of event	Cost of copy	Address	Remarks
Birth or Death	$12.00	Office of Vital Records SCDHEC 2600 Bull Street Columbia, SC 29201	State office has records since January 1915. City of Charleston births from 1877 and deaths from 1821 are on file at Charleston County Health Department. Ledger entries of Florence City births and deaths from 1895 to 1914 are on file at Florence County Health Department. Ledger entries of Newberry City births and deaths from the late 1800's are on file at Newberry County Health Department. These are the only early records obtainable. Additional copies of the same birth records ordered at the same time of certification are $3.00. Anyone requesting a vital record must submit a photocopy of their valid identification. Acceptable method of payment is a money order or cashier's check made payable to **SCDHEC**. To verify current fees, the telephone number is (803) 898-3630. Information on how to obtain certified copies is also available via the Internet at http://www.scdhec.net/vr.
Marriage	$12.00	Same as Birth or Death	Records since July 1950.
	Varies	See remarks	Records prior to July 1950. Probate Judge in county where license was issued.
Divorce	$12.00	Same as Birth or Death	Records since July 1962.
	Varies	See remarks	Records since April 1949. Clerk of Court in county where petition was filed.

South Dakota

Place of event	Cost of copy	Address	Remarks
Birth or Death	$15.00	Vital Records State Department of Health 207 E Missouri Ave, Ste 1-A Pierre, SD 57501	State office has records filed after July 1905. Anyone requesting a vital record must submit a photocopy of their identification. Personal check or money order should be made payable to **South Dakota Department of Health**. To verify current fees, the telephone number is (605) 773-4961. Information on how to obtain certified copies is also available via the Internet at http://vitalrecords.sd.gov. Mail-in applicants must send in a clear copy of a government- issued photo ID OR have their signature notarized.
Marriage	$15.00	Same as Birth or Death	Records since July 1905. Marriages can also be obtained from the County Register of Deeds where the marriage occurred.
Divorce	$15.00	Same as Birth or Death	Records since July 1905. Divorces can also be obtained from the Clerk of Courts in the county where the divorce was granted.

Tennessee

Place of event	Cost of copy	Address	Remarks
Birth (long form)	$15.00	Tennessee Vital Records	State office has birth records for entire State since January 1914, for Nashville since June 1881, for Knoxville since July 1881, and for Chattanooga since January 1882. Birth enumeration records by school district are available for July 1908 through June 1912. Birth records more than 100 years old are maintained by Tennessee Library and Archives, Archives Division, Nashville, Tennessee 37243-0312. Additional copies of the same birth, marriage, or divorce record requested at the same time are $5.00 each.
Birth (short form)	$8.00	Central Services Building	
Death	$7.00	4215th Avenue, North Nashville, TN 37243	

If the birth has been amended by adding the father with a Voluntary Acknowledgement Of Paternity (VAOP), a certified copy of the VAOP may be ordered if a $15 long form birth certificate is ordered at the same time. The cost of the certified VAOP is an additional $5.00.

Vital Records office keeps death records for 50 years; older records are maintained by Tennessee Library and Archives, Archives Division, Nashville, Tennessee 37243-0312.

Personal check or money order should be made payable to **Tennessee Vital Records**. To verify current fees, the telephone number is (615) 741-1763. Information on how to obtain certified copies is also available via the Internet at http://health.state.tn.us/vr/.

A photocopy of a valid government-issued form of identification which includes the requestor's signature, usually a driver's license, must accompany the request.

Place of event	Cost of copy	Address	Remarks
Marriage	$15.00	Same as Birth or Death	Vital Records Office keeps marriage records for 50 years. Older records are maintained by Tennessee Library and Archives, Archives Division, Nashville, TN 37243-0312.
	Varies	See remarks	County Clerk in county where license was issued.
Divorce	$15.00	Same as Birth or Death	Vital Records Office keeps divorce records for 50 years. Older records are maintained by Tennessee Library and Archives, Archives Division, Nashville, TN 37243-0312.
	Varies	See remarks	Clerk of Court in county where divorce was granted.

1124

Texas

Place of event	Cost of copy	Address	Remarks
Birth	$22.00	Texas Vital Records	State office has birth and death records since 1903. Additional copies of the birth record ordered at same time are $22.00 each. Additional copies of the death record ordered at the same time are $3.00 each.
Death	$20.00	Department of State Health Services P.O. Box 12040 Austin, TX 78711-2040	

Request for certified copies of birth and death certificates can be made via the internet, with a credit card, through Texas.gov. An Expedited Application for Birth and Death Record (see Form VS142.21.pdf) can also be completed and sent by an overnight service or by USPS Express Mail, with a check or money order, to the address on the application. Most Texas.gov and Expedited mail requests will be processed within 10 to 15 business days.

Mail-in requests must be made by personal check or money order made payable to **DSHS**. To verify current fees, the telephone number is (512) 776-7111. This is a recorded message. Information on how to obtain certified copies is also available via the Internet at http://www.dshs.state.tx.us/vs.

Place of event	Cost of copy	Address	Remarks
Marriage (State)	See remarks		Records since January 1966. Certified copies are not available from State office. Fee for search and verification of essential facts of marriage is $20.00 each.

Request for marriage verification can be made via the internet, with a credit card, through Texas.gov.

Marriage verification requests may also be sent via mail and paid with a check or money order by completing the Mail Application for Marriage and Divorce Verification (http://www.dshs.state.tx.us/vs/reqproc/forms.shtm#birthdeath). Personal checks or money orders should be made payable to **DSHS**.

Place of event	Cost of copy	Address	Remarks
Marriage (County)	Varies	See remarks	County Clerk in county where license was issued. Texas County contact information can be found at the Texas Department of State Health Services website.

Texas

Place of event	Cost of copy	Address	Remarks
Divorce (State)	See remarks		Records since January 1968. Certified copies are not available from State office. Fee for search and verification of essential facts of divorce is $20.00 each.

Request for divorce verification can be made via the internet, with a credit card, through Texas.gov.

Divorce verification requests may also be sent via mail and paid with a check or money order by completing the Mail Application for Marriage and Divorce Verification (http://www.dshs.state.tx.us/vs/reqproc/forms.shtm #birthdeath). Personal checks or money orders should be made payable to **DSHS**. |
| Divorce (County) | Varies | See remarks | Clerk of District Court in county where divorce was granted. Texas District Clerk contact information can be found at http://localoffices.texasvsu.org. |

Utah

Place of event	Cost of copy	Address	Remarks
Birth	$18.00	Office of Vital Records and Statistics Utah Department of Health 288 North 1460 West P.O. Box 141012 Salt Lake City, UT 84114-1012	State office has records since 1905. Identification is now required for the purchase of a Utah Birth Certificate. Mailed request must include an enlarged and easily identifiable photocopy of the back and front of your identification. If no proofs are enclosed, your application will be returned. For a list of acceptable identification see our website at http://www.health.utah.gov/vitalrecords. Additional copies, when requested at the same time, are $8.00 each.
Death	$16.00		
			Personal check or money order should be made payable to **Vital Records**. To verify current fees, the telephone number is (801) 538-6105. This is a recorded message. Information on how to obtain certified copies is also available via the Internet at http://www.health.utah.gov/vitalrecords.
Marriage	$16.00	Same as Birth or Death	State office has records since 1978. Only short form certified copies are available.
	Varies	See remarks	County Clerk in county where license was issued.
	$16.00	Same as Birth or Death	State office has records since 1978. Only short form certified copies are available.
Divorce			
	Varies	See remarks	County Clerk in county where divorce was granted.

Vermont

Place of event	Cost of copy	Address	Remarks
Birth or Death	$10.00	VT Department of Health Vital Records Section P. O. Box 70 108 Cherry Street Burlington, VT 05402-0070	State office has records for the most recent five years. Personal check or money order should be made payable to **Vermont Department of Health**. To verify current fees, the telephone number is (802) 863-7275. This is a recorded message. Information on how to obtain certified copies is also available via the Internet at http://www.healthvermont.gov/research/records/obtain_record.aspx.
Birth, Death, Marriage or Divorce	$10.00	VT State Archives and Records Administration Office of the Secretary 1078 US Route 2, Middlesex Montpelier, VT 05633-7701	Records more than five years old (as early as 1909). Personal check or money order should be made payable to **Vermont Secretary of State**. To verify current fees, the telephone number is (802) 828-3286. Information on how to obtain certified copies is also available via the Internet at http://vermont-archives.org/certifications/.
Birth or Death	$10.00	See remarks	Town or City Clerk of town/city where birth or death occurred.
Marriage	$10.00	Same as Birth or Death	State office has records for the most recent 5 years.
	$10.00	See remarks	Town or City Clerk in town/city where license was issued.
Divorce	$10.00	Same as Birth or Death	State office has records for the most recent 5 years.
	$10.00	See remarks	Family court in county where divorce was granted.

Virginia

Place of event	Cost of copy	Address	Remarks
Birth or Death	$12.00	Division of Vital Records P.O. Box 1000 Richmond, VA 23218-1000	State office has records from January 1853 to December 1896 and since June 14, 1912. Personal check or money order should be made payable to **State Health Department**. To verify current fees, the telephone number is (804) 662-6200. This is a recorded message. Information on how to obtain certified copies is also available via the Internet at http://www.vdh.virginia.gov/. Anyone requesting a vital record must submit a photocopy of their identification.
Marriage	$12.00	Same as Birth or Death	Records since January 1853.
	Varies	See remarks	Clerk of Court in county or city where license was issued.
Divorce	$12.00	Same as Birth or Death	Records since January 1918.
	Varies	See remarks	Clerk of Court in county or city where divorce was granted.

Virgin Islands

Place of event	Cost of copy	Address	Remarks
Birth or Death St. Croix	$15.00 (Mail request) $12.00 (In person)	Department of Health Vital Statistics Charles Harwood Memorial Hospital St. Croix, VI 00820	Registrar has birth and death records on file since 1840.
St. Thomas and St. John	$15.00 (Mail request) $12.00 (In person)	Department of Health Vital Statistics Knud Hansen Complex St. Thomas, VI 00802	Registrar has birth records on file since July 1906 and death records since January 1906. Money order for birth and death records should be made payable to **Department of Health**. Personal checks are not accepted. To verify current fees, the telephone number is (340) 774-9000 ext. 4685 or 4686.
Marriage	See remarks	Bureau of Vital Records and Statistical Services Virgin Islands Department of Health Charlotte Amalie St. Thomas, VI 00801	Certified copies are not available. Inquiries will be forwarded to the appropriate office.
St. Croix	$2.00	Chief Deputy Clerk Family Division Territorial Court of the Virgin Islands P.O. Box 929 Christiansted St. Croix, VI 00820	
St. Thomas and St. John	$2.00	Clerk of the Territorial Court of the Virgin Islands Family Division P.O. Box 70 Charlotte Amalie St. Thomas, VI 00801	
Divorce	See remarks	Same as Marriage	Certified copies are not available. Inquiries will be forwarded to appropriate office.
St. Croix	$5.00	Same as Marriage	Money order for marriage and divorce records should be made payable to Territorial Court of the Virgin Islands. Personal checks are not accepted.
St. Thomas and St. John	$5.00	Same as Marriage	

Washington

Place of event	Cost of copy	Address	Remarks
Birth or Death	$20.00	Department of Health Center for Health Statistics P.O. Box 47814 Olympia, WA 98504-7814	Must have exact information for births. State office has birth records since July 1907 to present. For King, Pierce, and Spokane counties copies may also be obtained from county health departments. County Auditor of county of birth has registered births prior to July 1907. State office has death records from July 1, 1907 to 2 months before present date. Personal check or money order should be made payable to **Department of Health**. To verify current fees, the telephone number is (360) 236-4300. Information on how to obtain certified copies is also available via the Internet at http://www.doh.wa.gov.
Heirloom Birth	$40.00	Same as Birth or Death	
Marriage	$20.00		State office has records since January 1968.
	Varies	See remarks	County Auditor in county where license was issued.
Divorce	$20.00	Same as Birth or Death	State office has records since January 1968.
	Varies	See remarks	County Clerk in county where divorce was granted.

West Virginia

Place of event	Cost of copy	Address	Remarks
Birth or Death	$12.00	Vital Registration Office Room 165 350 Capitol Street Charleston, WV 25301-3701	State office has records since January 1917. For earlier records, write to Clerk of County Court in county where event occurred. Personal check or money order should be made payable to **Vital Registration**. To verify current fees, the telephone number is (304) 558-2931. Information on how to obtain certified copies is also available via the Internet at http://www.wvdhhr.org.
Marriage	$12.00	Same as Birth or Death	Records since 1921. Certified copies available from 1964.
	Varies	See remarks	County Clerk in county where license was issued.
Divorce	See remarks	Same as Birth or Death	Index since 1968. Some items may be verified (fee $5.00). Certified copies are not available from State office.
	Varies	See remarks	Clerk of Circuit Court, Chancery Side, in county where divorce was granted.

Wisconsin

Place of event	Cost of copy	Address	Remarks
Birth or Death	$20.00	WI Vital Records Office 1 West Wilson Street P.O. Box 309 Madison, WI 53701-0309	State Office has scattered records earlier than 1857. Records before October 1, 1907, are very incomplete. Additional copies of the same record ordered at the same time are $3.00 each. Customers should use a state birth or death certificate application form to apply. A copy of a valid photo ID and a signature is required of the applicant. Personal check or money order should be made payable to **State of Wisconsin Vital Records**. A stamped, self-addressed business size (#10) envelope should be included with the request. Information on how to obtain certified copies including application forms is available via the Internet at http://www.dhfs.state.wi.us/vitalrecords.
Marriage	$20.00	Same as Birth or Death	Records since April 1857. Records before October 1, 1907 are very incomplete. Additional copies of the same record ordered at the same time are $3.00 each. Customers should use a state marriage certificate application form to apply. A copy of a valid photo ID and a signature is required of the applicant.
Divorce	$20.00	Same as Birth or Death	Records since October 1857. Records before October 1, 190, are very incomplete. Additional copies of the same record ordered at the same time are $3.00 each. Customers should use a state divorce certificate application form to apply. A copy of a valid photo ID and a signature is required of the applicant.

Wyoming

Place of event	Cost of copy	Address	Remarks
Birth	$13.00	Vital Statistics Services	State office has birth records since 1909.
Death	$10.00	Hathaway Building Cheyenne, WY 82002	Death records more than 50 years old should be obtained from the Wyoming State Archives at (307) 777-7826 or WyArchive@state.wy.us.
			Personal check or money order should be made payable to **Vital Records Services**. A personal check is accepted only if personalized with the name of current address of individual signing the request. To verify current fees, the telephone number is (307) 777-7591. Information on how to obtain certified copies is also available via the Internet at http://www.health.wyo.gov.
			A legible photocopy of a current state issued ID or passport is required which bears the signature of the applicant. ID with no expiration date is not accepted unless recently issued and additional proof of identification may be requested.
Marriage	$13.00	Same as Birth or Death	Marriage records more than 50 years old should be obtained from the Wyoming State Archives at (307) 777-7826 or WyArchive@state.wy.us.
	Varies	See remarks	County Clerk in county where license was issued.
Divorce	$13.00	Same as Birth or Death	Divorce records more than 50 years old should be obtained from the Wyoming State Archives at (307) 777-7826 or WyArchive@state.wy.us.
	Varies	See remarks	Clerk of District Court where divorce took place.

Foreign, high-seas, or Panama Canal Zone births and deaths and certificates of citizenship

Birth records of persons born in foreign countries who are U.S. citizens at birth

The birth of a child abroad to U.S. citizen parent(s) should be reported to the nearest U.S. Consulate or Embassy as soon after the birth as possible. To do this, the child's parent or legal guardian should file an Application for Consular Report of Birth Abroad of a Citizen of the United States of America (Form FS-240). This form may also be used to apply for a Social Security Number for the child. A $100.00 fee is charged for reporting the birth.

The application must be supported by evidence to establish the child's U.S. citizenship. Usually, the following documents are needed:

1. the child's foreign birth certificate;
2. evidence of the U.S. citizenship of the parent(s) such as a certified copy of a birth certificate, U.S. passport, or Certificate of Naturalization or Citizenship;
3. evidence of the parents' marriage, if applicable; and
4. affidavit(s) of the physical presence of the parent(s) in the United States.

Each document should be certified as a true copy of the original by the registrar of the office that issued the document. Other documents may be needed in some cases. Contact the nearest U.S. Embassy or Consulate for details on what evidence is needed.

When the application is approved, a Consular Report of Birth Abroad of a Citizen of the United States of America (Form FS-240) is given to the applicant. This document, known as the Consular Report of Birth, has the same value as proof of citizenship as the Certificate of Citizenship issued by the Immigration and Naturalization Service.

A Consular Report of Birth can be prepared only at a U.S. Embassy or Consulate overseas, and only if the person who is the subject of the report is under 18 years of age when the application is made. A person ӏ who is now 18 years of age or ɑ claim to U.S. citizenship h documented, should contact t Embassy or Consulate foɪ registering as a U.S. citizen.

The Department began issuing a new Consular Report of Birth on January 3, 2011. You may request multiple copies of this document at any time. As of December 31, 2010 the Certificate of Report of Birth Abroad (DS-1350) is no longer issued. All previously issued FS-240 and DS-1350 documents are still valid for proof of identity, citizenship and other legal purposes. Documents are issued only to the subject of the Consular Report of Birth, the subject's parents or legal guardian. Effective September 1, 2003, all requests must be notarized to include a picture ID.

To request multiple copies of the FS-240, write to Passport Services, Vital Records Section, U.S. Department of State, 1111 19th Street NW, Suite 510, Washington, DC 20036. Please include the following items:

1. the full name of the child at birth (and any adoptive name);
2. the date and place of birth;
3. the names of the parents;
4. the serial number of the FS-240 (if the FS-240 was issued after November 1, 1990);
5. any available passport information;
6. the signature of the requestor and the requestor's relationship to the subject;
7. a check or money order for $50.00 for the FS-240, made payable to the U.S. Department of State. Remittance must be payable in U.S. dollars through a U.S. Bank. Do Not Send Cash.

To obtain a Consular Report of Birth in a new name, send a written request and fees as noted above, the original (or replacement) Consular Report of Birth, or if not available, a notarized affidavit about its whereabouts. Also, send a certified copy of the court order or final adoption decree which identifies the child and shows the change of name with the request. If the name has been changed informally, submit public records and affidavits that show the change of name.

Birth records of alien children adopted by U.S. citizens

Birth certifications for alien children adopted by U.S. citizens and lawfully admitted to the United States may be obtained from the Immigration and Naturalization Service (INS) if the birth information is on file. (Address can be found in a telephone directory.) To obtain the birth data, it is necessary to provide the Immigration Office with proof of adoption or legitimation.

Certificate of citizenship

Persons who were born abroad and later naturalized as U.S. citizens or who were born in a foreign country to a U.S. citizen (parent or parents) may apply for a Certificate of Citizenship pursuant to the provisions of Section 341 of the Immigration and Nationality Act. Application can be made for this document in the United States at the nearest office of the Bureau of Citizenship and Immigration Services in the Department of Homeland Security. Upon approval, a Certification of Citizenship will be issued for the person if proof of citizenship is submitted and the person is within the United States. The decision whether to apply for a Certificate of Citizenship is optional; its possession is not mandatory because a valid U.S. passport or a Form FS-240 has the same evidentiary status.

Death and marriage records of U.S. citizens that occurred in a foreign country

The death of a U.S. citizen in a foreign country may be reported to the nearest U.S. consular office. If reported, and a copy of the local death certificate and evidence of U.S. citizenship are presented, the consul prepares the official *Report of the Death of an American Citizen Abroad'* (Form DS-2060, formerly OF-180). A copy of the Report of Death is then filed permanently in the U.S. Department of State (see exceptions below).

To obtain a copy of a report filed in 1975 or after, write to Passport Services, Vital Records Section, U.S. Department of State, 1111 19th

Street NW, Suite 510, Washington, DC 20036. The fee for a copy is $50.00 per document. Please include a notarized request to include picture ID. Fee may be subject to change.

Reports of Death filed before 1975 are maintained by the National Archives and Records Service, Diplomatic Records Branch, Washington, DC 20408. Requests for such records should be sent directly to that office.

Reports of deaths of persons serving in the Armed Forces of the United States (Army, Navy, Marines, Air Force, or Coast Guard) or civilian employees of the Department of Defense are not maintained by the U.S. Department of State. In these cases, requests for copies of records should be sent to the National Personnel Records Center (Military Personnel Records), 9700 Page Ave., St. Louis, Missouri 63132-5100.

To obtain a copy of a Certificate of Witness to Marriage (FS-87), you may write to the address above, the fee is $50.00 per document. As of November 9, 1989 a Consular Officer no longer served as a witness to marriages performed abroad. Persons married abroad after 1989 may contact the embassy or consulate of the country where the marriage was performed for a certified copy. Foreign marriage documents are not maintained by the Department.

Records of birth and death occurring on vessels or aircraft on the high seas

When a birth or death occurs on the high seas, whether in an aircraft or on a vessel, the record is usually filed at the next port of call.

1. If the vessel or aircraft docked or landed at a foreign port, requests for copies of the record may be made to the U.S. Department of State, Washington, DC 20036.

2. If the first port of entry was in the United States, write to the registration authority in the city where the vessel or aircraft docked or landed in the United States.

3. If the vessel was of U.S. registry, contact the local authorities at the port of entry and/or search the vessel logs at the U.S. Coast Guard Facility at the vessel's final port of call for that voyage.

Records maintained by foreign Countries

Most, but not all, foreign countries record births and deaths. It is not possible to list in this publication all foreign vital records offices, the charges they make for copies of records, or the information they may require to locate a record. However, most foreign countries will provide certifications of births and deaths occurring within their boundaries.

Persons who need a copy of a foreign birth or death record should contact the Embassy or the nearest Consulate in the U.S. of the country in which the death occurred. Addresses and telephone numbers for these offices are listed in the U.S. Department of State Publication 7846, *Foreign Consular Offices in the United States,* which is available in many local libraries. Copies of this publication may also be purchased from the U.S. Government Printing Office, Washington, DC 20402.

If the Embassy or Consulate is unable to provide assistance, U.S. citizens may obtain assistance by writing to the Office of Overseas Citizens Services, U.S. Department of State, Washington, DC 20520–4818. Aliens residing in the United States may be able to obtain assistance through the Embassy or Consulate of their country of nationality.

Records of birth, death, or marriage in the Panama Canal Zone for U.S. citizens and foreign nationals

From 1904 until September 30, 1979, the Canal Zone Government registered all civil acts of birth, death and marriage in the Canal Zone for U.S. citizens and foreign nationals. Since 1979, the Panama Canal Commission has issued certified copies of these documents in response to requests from the public. On December 31, 1999, the Panama Canal Commission ceased to exist. On December 1, 1999, those records were transferred to Passport Services in the U.S. Department of State, which will provide the certification service just as it does for similar records issued by U.S. Embassies and Consulates abroad.

To request copies, write to Vital Records Section, Passport Services, U.S. Department of State, 1111 19th Street NW, Suite 510,

Washington, DC 20036. Please include a notarized request to include a picture ID the following items for birth and death:

1. the full name of subject at the time of event;
2. month, day and year of event;
3. place of event (city and country);
4. parents' names, date and place of birth, and nationality for birth record;
5. any available U.S. passport information;
6. signature of the requestor, parent or guardian, or legal representative;
7. requestor address and telephone number;
8. a check or money order for $50.00 for each copy made payable to U.S. Department of State. Remittance must be payable in U.S. dollars through a U.S. bank. Do not send cash;
9. Marriage records from the Canal Zone issued 1904 -1979 were forwarded to the National Archives and Records Administration (NARA) instead. You may submit a request to Civilian Records (NWCTC), Textual Archives Services Division, 8601 Adelphi Road, College Park, MD 20740-6001 for a copy. Do not send any money with your request. If any fees are required, you will be contacted by NARA.

APPENDIX 13-2
Certificate of Citizenship

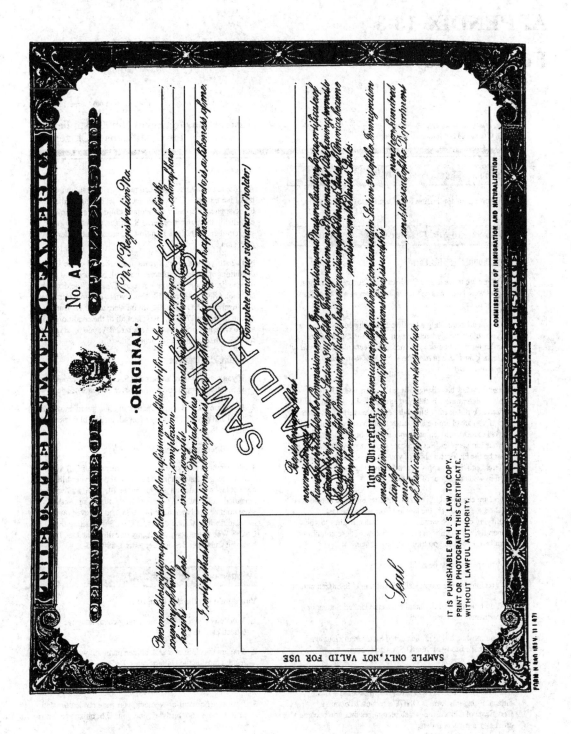

APPENDIX 13-3

Form N-600

OMB No. 1615-0057; Expires 12/31/2014

Department of Homeland Security
U.S. Citizenship and Immigration Services

Instructions for Form N-600, Application for Certificate of Citizenship

Purpose of Form N-600

This form is an application for a Certificate of Citizenship.

Who Should File This Form

You Should File This Form

1. If you are requesting a Certificate of Citizenship because you were born outside the United States to a U.S. citizen parent; **or**

2. If you are requesting a Certificate of Citizenship because you automatically became a citizen of the United States after birth, but before you turned 18 years old. (*A parent or legal guardian can also file Form N-600 on behalf of a minor child.*)

Citizenship law has changed over the years and different laws apply to determine whether you automatically became a U.S. citizen at birth, or after birth but before you turned 18 years of age. If you are claiming U.S. citizenship based on your birth abroad to a U.S. citizen parent(s), the law in effect on the date of your birth applies. For purposes of these provisions, you must be the biological child of your U.S. citizen parent, and different provisions apply depending on whether you were born in wedlock or out of wedlock.

If you are claiming U.S. citizenship after birth but before you reached the age of 18, the law in effect when the last qualifying condition was met is the law that applies to you. Generally, the conditions are listed below. These conditions must be met before you turn 18 years of age.

1. Your parent must be a U.S. citizen;

2. You must be the biological child of that U.S. citizen parent;

3. You must be lawfully admitted to the United States for permanent residence; **and**

4. You must be living in the United States in the legal and physical custody of your U.S. citizen parent.

You can file Form N-600 at any time if you became a U.S. citizen at birth, or after birth, but before you turned 18 years old. Filing this form is **NOT** a request to become a U.S. citizen. Filing this form is **ONLY** a request to obtain a Certificate of Citizenship which recognizes that you became a citizen on a particular date.

Adopted Child

An adopted child may also acquire U.S. citizenship through his or her adoptive U.S. citizen parent depending on the law being applied. Currently, an adopted child can acquire U.S. citizenship through his or her U.S. citizen parent. However, step children **CANNOT** acquire U.S. citizenship under this provision.

NOTE: If you are now 18 years of age, but all of the above conditions apply to you before your 18th birthday **and** you were under the age of 18 on February 27, 2001 (the date the law took affect), you may file this form to obtain a Certificate of Citizenship. **HOWEVER**, if you were under 18 years of age on February 27, 2001, **BUT** not all of the conditions noted above were met prior to your 18th birthday, you must qualify for U.S. citizenship in your own right.

You May File This Form

1. If you claim to have acquired U.S. citizenship through a U.S. citizen parent and are now over 18 years of age.

2. If you are the U.S. citizen parent or legal guardian who has legal and physical custody of an adopted or biological child (under 18 years of age).

Law In Effect at the Time of Your Birth

To determine if you were born a U.S. citizen, USCIS must look at the law that was in effect at the time of your birth. The current law was enacted on November 14, 1986, **and** was last amended on February 27, 2001 (Child Citizenship Act). If you were born before November 14, 1986, and believe you may be a U.S. citizen, you should contact USCIS by visiting the USCIS Web site at **www.uscis.gov** or calling the USCIS National Customer Service Center at **1-800-365-5283**.

Who Should Not File This Form

You should not file this form if:

1. You do not have at least one biological or adoptive U.S. citizen parent;

2. You are the child of a U.S. citizen parent(s) who regularly resides outside the United States. Refer to Form N-600K, Application for Citizenship and Issuance of Certificate Under Section 322;

3. You were born out-of-wedlock, you were not legitimated prior to your 16th birthday, and your U.S. citizen parent is your father.

NOTE: This does not affect you if you were born abroad to an eligible U.S. citizen mother. You may also be eligible for citizenship through the naturalization of your mother.

4. You are seeking to replace a lost or stolen certificate. Please refer to Form N-565, Application for Replacement Naturalization/Citizenship Document, for information to replace a lost or stolen certificate; or

5. **You already filed a Form N-600 and received a decision from USCIS on that previously filed Form N-600. USCIS will reject (not accept) any subsequently filed Form N-600. Please review your Form N-600 denial notice for more information.**

Required Evidence

Unless specifically noted otherwise, you must submit each of the documents listed below for you and your U.S. citizen parent through whom you are claiming U.S. citizenship at the time of filing to avoid delays in processing your Form N-600. USCIS may require verification for any or all information provided with Form N-600. Additionally, if you are scheduled for an interview with USCIS, you must bring in documentation if information has been updated or has changed after filing.

NOTE: "You" and "your" in this section refers to the individual for whom a Certificate of Citizenship is sought. It is NOT the applicant's parent or legal guardian who may apply on the minor child's behalf.

Photographs. You **must** submit two identical passport-style color photographs of yourself taken within 30 days of filing Form N-600. The photos must have a white to off-white background, be printed on thin paper with a glossy finish, and be unmounted and unretouched. If a digital photo is submitted, it must to be taken from a camera with at least 3.5 mega pixels of resolution.

The photos must be 2" x 2" and must be in color with full face, frontal view on a white to off-white background. Head height should measure 1" to 1 3/8" from top of hair to bottom of chin, and eye height is between 1 1/8" to 1 3/8" from bottom of photo. Your head must be bare unless you are wearing a headdress as required by a religious denomination of which you are a member; however, your face must be visible. Using pencil or felt pen, lightly print your name and Alien Registration Number (A-Number) on the back of each photo.

Your Birth Certificate or Record. Submit a birth certificate or record issued and certified by a civil authority in the country of birth.

Birth Certificate or Record of Your U.S. Citizen Parent. Submit a birth certificate or record issued and certified by a civil authority in the country of birth.

If your U.S. citizen parent applies, your U.S. citizen parent must submit his or her birth certificate or record issued and certified by a civil authority in the country of birth.

Marriage Certificate(s) of Your U.S. Citizen Parent. Issued and certified by a civil authority in the State or country of marriage.

Documents Showing the Marriage Termination (*if applicable*). Certified divorce decree, death certificate, or annulment document.

Proof of U.S. Citizenship. Examples of this are birth certificates showing birth in the United States; a Form N-550, Certificate of Naturalization; a Form N-560, Certificate of Citizenship; a Form FS-240, Report of Birth Abroad of United States Citizen; or a valid unexpired U.S. passport.

Proof of Status as U.S. National (*only required if you are claiming U.S. citizenship through a U.S. national, such as a person born in American Samoa or Swains Island*).

If you were born outside the United States or its outlying possessions, you are born a U.S. citizen if your parents met the following conditions:

1. Your U.S. citizen parent was physically present in the United States or one of its outlying possessions for a continuous period of 1 year prior to your birth; **and**

2. Your other parent was a national but not a U.S. citizen.

NOTE: If you have a U.S. citizen parent and a noncitizen parent who is an alien but not a national, your U.S. citizen parent must have met the physical presence requirements prior to your birth.

Proof of Legitimation (*only required if you who were born out-of-wedlock*). Provide legitimation documentation from the country or State in which you legitimated. Legitimation can also be established according to the laws of your father's residence or your residence.

Proof of Legal Custody - (*only required for applicants whose U.S. citizen parent(s) divorced and/or separated and for applicants who are adopted or legitimated.*)

Copy of Permanent Resident Card or Other Evidence of Permanent Resident Status (*only required if you are claiming U.S. citizenship after birth through a U.S. citizen parent*).

Proof of Required Residence or Physical Presence In the United States. Any document that proves the U.S citizen parent's residence or physical presence in the United States.

This proof may include but is not limited to the following:

1. School, employment, military records;

2. Deeds, mortgages, leases showing residence;

3. Attestations by churches, unions, or other organizations;

4. U.S. Social Security quarterly reports; **and**

5. Affidavits of third parties having knowledge of the residence and physical presence.

Copy of Full, Final Adoption Decree *(only required for adopted applicants).*

Re-adoption in the United States. If you had to be re-adopted in the United States, submit evidence of a full and final foreign adoption if the appropriate authority in the applicant's current location of residence recognizes its validity.

Evidence of All Legal Name Change(s). If you legally changed your name, submit evidence of an issued and certified document by the court that authorized the legal name change(s).

What if a Document Is Unavailable?

You must provide a written explanation of the reason(s) a required document(s) is unavailable and submit secondary evidence to establish eligibility. Secondary evidence must overcome the unavailability of the required documents. USCIS may request an original written statement from the appropriate government or other legal authority to support your claim that the documents are unavailable.

The following types of **secondary evidence** may be submitted to establish eligibility.

Baptismal Certificate. Certificate under the church seal where your baptism occurred showing your:

1. Place of birth;

2. Date of birth;

3. Baptism date;

4. Parents names; **and**

5. Godparent(s) name(s), if known.

School Record. An official letter from school authorities for the school attended (preferably the first school) showing your:

1. Date of admission to the school;

2. Place of birth;

3. Date of birth or age at that time; **and**

4. The name(s) and residence(s) of your birth parents, if shown in the school records.

Census Records. State or Federal census records showing your:

1. Name;

2. Place of birth; **and**

3. Date of birth or age.

Affidavits *(if other types of secondary evidence are not available).* Written statements sworn to (or affirmed) by 2 people who have personal knowledge of the claimed event. Affidavits must overcome the unavailability of both required documents and secondary evidence. Examples of events you may submit an affidavit for include the following:

1. Your place and date of birth;

2. Marriage; **or**

3. Death.

The people making these statements are not required to be U.S. citizens and may be relatives. Each affidavit must contain the following information about the person making the affidavit:

1. Full legal name;

2. Address;

3. Place of birth;

4. Date of birth;

5. Relationship to you; **and**

6. Detailed information about the event to include how they came to know about its occurrence.

General Instructions

1. **Type or print clearly using black ink.** Keep all information within the area provided.

   If extra space is needed to answer any question, attach an additional sheet(s) of paper. You must provide the following information on the top of each sheet of paper:

   A. Your A-Number, if applicable;

B. The date;

C. Question number; **and**

D. Your signature.

2. **Answer all questions fully and accurately.** Write "N/A" if an item is not applicable. Write "None" if the answer is none.

3. **Avoid highlighting, crossing out, or writing outside the area provided for a response.**

   If you must make substantial corrections to your Form N-600, USCIS recommends that you begin with a new Form N-600 rather than using correction tape or fluid to white out information. USCIS scanners may see through the white correction tape or fluid. This may lead to incorrect information being captured in USCIS systems which may cause processing delays or a rejection of your Form N-600.

   Ensure that you are using the correct edition of the Form N-600. The correct edition is available on the USCIS Web site at **www.uscis.gov**.

4. **Provide your A-Number on the top right corner of each page** (*if applicable*). Your A-Number is located on your Permanent Resident Card (formerly known as the Alien Registration or "Green" Card). The A-Number on your card consists of seven to nine numbers, depending on when your record was created. If the A-Number on your card has fewer than nine numbers, place enough zeros before the first number to make a *total of nine numbers* on Form N-600. For example, write number A1234567 as A001234567 or write number A12345678 as A012345678.

Translations. You must provide a full English translation for any document written in a foreign language you submit to USCIS. The translator must certify that the translation is complete and accurate and that he or she is competent to translate from the foreign language into English.

Copies. You may submit copies of documents unless USCIS requests original documents. Original documents submitted when not required may remain a part of the record.

Specific Form Instructions

This form is divided into 10 parts.

General Items (*all of the following items pertain to Part, 1, Part 2, AND Part 3 in the form*)

Current Legal Name. Provide the person's legal name. This should be the name on the person's birth certificate unless it has been changed after birth by legal action such as marriage, adoption, or court order. **Do not provide a nickname.**

U.S. Social Security Number. Print the person's U.S. Social Security Number. Write "N/A" if the person does not have one.

Date of Birth. Use eight numbers to show the date of birth. For example, May 1, 1992, must be written as 05/01/1992.

Country of Birth. Provide the name of the country where the person was born. Write the name of the country even if country's name has since changed or the country no longer exists.

Home Address. Provide the address where the person now resides. Do **not** provide a Post Office (P.O.) Box number unless it is the person's **ONLY** address.

Telephone Numbers. Provide the person's current telephone numbers. If the answer is none, write "None." If the person is hearing impaired and uses a TTY telephone connection, please indicate this by writing "TTY" after the telephone number.

E-Mail Address. Provide the person's current e-mail address. If the person does not have an e-mail address, write "None."

Part 1. Information About Your Eligibility (*Check only one box. USCIS will reject your Form N-600 if you check more than one box.*)

Check the box in number **1 OR 2** that best indicates why you are eligible for a Certificate of Citizenship.

Check the box in number **3** (Other) if the basis for your eligibility is not described in any of the previous categories and briefly write the basis for your application on the lines provided.

Part 2. Information About You

Complete information must be provided about the person seeking a Certificate of Citizenship. **If you are the U.S. citizen parent** applying for a Certificate of Citizenship on behalf of your minor biological or adopted child, submit information relating to **your minor child**.

NOTE: Not all of the questions are explained in this part because they are located in the **General Items** section of Specific Form Instructions. Please go to that section for more information.

2. **Name Exactly as it Appears on Your Permanent Resident Card** (*if different from above*). Write your name exactly as it appears on your card, even if it is misspelled. Write N/A if you do not have a permanent resident card.

3. **Other Names Used Since Birth** (*if applicable. Include nicknames*). Write any other name(s) you have used since birth. Attach an additional sheet(s) of paper if more space is needed.

7. **Country of Prior Citizenship/Nationality.** Provide the name of the country of your citizenship/nationality before you became a U.S. citizen.

   A. If the country no longer exists or you are stateless, provide the name of the foreign country where you were last a citizen or national.

   B. If you are a citizen or national of more than one country, provide the name of the foreign country that issued your latest passport.

8. **Gender.** Indicate whether you are male or female.

9. **Height.** Provide your height in feet and inches.

11. **Mailing Address.** Provide your mailing address even if it is the same as your home address. Provide "*in care of name*" information, if applicable. You must write something in every box, except an apartment number or "C/O" if you do not have one, within "Mailing Address."

   NOTE: USCIS may not be able to contact you if you do not provide a complete and valid address. If USCIS rejects your application, USCIS may not be able to return the fee for the Form N-600 to you if you do not provide a complete and valid address. If USCIS cannot return the fee USCIS will cash your check.

14. **Marital Status.** Check the marital status you have on the date you file this Form N-600. Check "Other" if your marriage was otherwise legally terminated and explain.

15. **U.S. Armed Forces.** Indicate if you are a member or veteran of any branch of the U.S. Armed Forces.

16. **Information About Your Admission Into the United States and Current Immigration Status.**

   A. Provide information about where you entered the United States and what name you used when you entered.

   B. Provide information about what documents you presented to enter the United States. Provide your passport number and date of issuance, if known.

   C. Provide information about your current immigration status in the United States.

   D. Provide information if you adjusted to permanent resident status while in the United States including the date, USCIS office, and location where USCIS granted your status or location where you were admitted as a permanent resident.

17. **Previous Application for Certificate of Citizenship or U.S. Passport.** If you previously applied for a Certificate of Citizenship or a U.S. Passport (or you are a U.S. citizen parent who previously applied for a Certificate of Citizenship or U.S. Passport for your minor child), explain on a sheet of paper what happened with that application and whether the Certificate of Citizenship or U.S. Passport was or was not issued.

18. **Permanent Resident Status Abandonment.** Indicate if you have ever abandoned your permanent residence.

19. **Information on Adoption.** If you were adopted, provide information as to the date and place of the adoption and the dates that legal and physical custody began.

20. **Re-Adoption in the United States.** Indicate if you have been re-adopted in the United States. (See **Required Evidence** for more information.)

21. **Marital Status of Your Parents At Time of Birth (or Adoption).** Indicate whether your parents were married to each other at the time of your birth. If you were born out-of-wedlock, indicate "No" even if your parents subsequently married. If you were adopted, indicate whether your adoptive parents were married to each other at the time of your adoption.

   NOTE: If you are a U.S. citizen parent applying on behalf of a minor biological or adopted child, indicate whether you were married to his or her parent at the time of your minor child's birth (or adoption). If your minor child was born out-of-wedlock, indicate "No," even if you subsequently married your child's biological parent.

22. **Marital Status of Your Parents After Birth.** Indicate whether your parents married after your birth.

23. **Legal and Physical Custody.** Indicate whether you are in the physical and legal custody of your U.S. citizen parent.

24. **Absences from the United States.** Provide the requested information for every trip that you have taken since you first arrived in the United States. Begin with the most recent trip. This information is needed only for persons born before October 10, 1952, who are claiming U.S. citizenship at the time of birth.

Part 3. Information About Your U.S. Citizen Biological Father (or Adoptive Father)

Complete this section if you are claiming citizenship through a U.S. citizen biological father (or adoptive father). Complete Part 4 if you are claiming citizenship solely through a U.S. citizen biological mother (or adoptive mother).

Provide information about yourself if you are a U.S. citizen biological father (or adoptive father) applying for a Certificate of Citizenship on behalf of your minor child, where information is requested about the U.S. citizen father.

NOTE: Not all of the questions are explained in this part because some are located in the **General Items** section of **Specific Form Instructions.** Please go to that section for more information.

4. **Country of Citizenship/Nationality.** Provide the name of the country of your U.S. citizen father's citizenship/nationality.

   If the country no longer exists or your U.S. citizen father is stateless, provide the name of the country where your U.S. citizen father was last a citizen or national.

   If your U.S. citizen father is a citizen or national of more than one country, provide the name of the country that issued your U.S. citizen father's latest passport.

6. **U.S. Citizenship.** Provide all requested information regarding how your father became a U.S. citizen.

7. **Loss of U.S. Citizenship.** Provide information on an additional sheet(s) of paper if your father ever lost U.S. citizenship regardless of whether it has since been regained.

8. **Marital History**

   A. Provide the number of times your U.S. citizen father has been married. Include any annulled marriages. Count each marriage as separate if your parent married the same spouse more than one time.

   B. Check the marital status your U.S. citizen father has on the date you file Form N-600. Check "Other" if his marriage was otherwise legally terminated and explain.

   C. If your U.S. citizen father is now married, provide information about his current spouse. Check the appropriate box to indicate his spouse's current immigration status.

   D. Indicate whether your U.S. citizen father's current spouse is also your biological (or adopted) mother. If "No", USCIS may ask you to provide additional information about your father's previous spouse(s).

Part 4. Information About Your U.S. Citizen Biological Mother (or Adoptive Mother)

Complete this section if you are claiming citizenship through a U.S. citizen biological mother (or adoptive mother). Complete Part 3 if you are claiming citizenship solely through a U.S. citizen biological father (or adoptive father).

Provide information about yourself if you are a U.S. citizen biological mother (or adoptive mother) applying for a Certificate of Citizenship on behalf of your minor child, where information is requested about the U.S. citizen mother.

NOTE: Not all of the questions are explained in this part because some are located in the **General Items** section of **Specific Form Instructions.** Please go to that section for more information.

4. **Country of Citizenship/Nationality.** Provide the name of the country of your U.S. citizen mother's citizenship/nationality.

   If the country no longer exists or the U.S. citizen mother is stateless, provide the name of the country where your U.S. citizen mother was last a citizen or national.

   If your U.S. citizen mother is a citizen or national of more than one country, provide the name of the country that issued your U.S. citizen mother's latest passport.

6. **U.S. Citizenship.** Provide all the requested information regarding how your mother became a U.S. citizen.

7. **Loss of U.S. Citizenship.** Provide information on an additional sheet(s) of paper if your mother ever lost U.S. citizenship regardless of whether it has since been regained.

8. **Marital History**

   A. Provide the number of times your U.S. citizen mother has been married. Include any annulled marriages. If she was married more than one time to the same spouse, count each time as a separate marriage.

   B. Check the marital status your U.S. citizen mother has on the date you file Form N-600. Check "Other" if her marriage was otherwise legally terminated and explain.

   C. If your U.S. citizen mother is now married, provide information about her current spouse. Check the appropriate box to indicate her spouse's immigration status.

   D. Indicate whether your U.S. citizen mother's current spouse is also your biological (or adopted) father. If "No," USCIS may ask you to provide additional information about your mother's previous spouse(s).

Part 5. Physical Presence in the United States From Birth Until Filing of Form N-600

Physical Presence. If you were born outside the United States and claim to have been born a U.S. citizen, you are required to provide all the dates when your U.S. citizen biological father or U.S. citizen biological mother resided in the United States. **Include all dates from your birth until the date you file your Form N-600.**

Children of Members of the U.S. Armed Forces or U.S. Government Employees temporarily stationed abroad are generally considered to be "residing in the United States" for purposes of acquisition of citizenship at birth.

Part 6. Information About Military Service of U.S. Citizen Parent *(Applicable only for applications filed under section 301(g))*

Provide the requested information if either U.S. citizen parent served in the U.S. Armed Forces. Also indicate whether he or she was honorably discharged from service.

Part 7. Your Signature

Sign the Form N-600 as you normally sign your name. You may place an "X" mark instead of a signature if you are unable to write in any language.

A parent or legal guardian may sign for a child who is under 14 years of age. A child under 14 years of age may also sign the Form N-600 on their own behalf without their parent's or legal guardian's signature.

NOTE: USCIS will reject your Form N-600 if it is not signed.

Part 8. Signature of Person Who Prepared this Form N-600 For You *(if applicable)*

If you prepared this form by yourself, leave this section blank. If someone filled out this form for you, he or she must complete this section. Your parent must complete this part if your parent prepared this Form N-600 for you.

Part 9. Affidavit

Do **NOT** complete this part unless instructed to do so **AT THE INTERVIEW.**

Part 10. Officer Report and Recommendation On Application for Certificate of Citizenship

For USCIS use **ONLY**.

Processing Information

Any Form N-600 that is not signed or accompanied by the correct fee, except those accompanied by a fee waiver request (Form I-912, Request for Fee Waiver), will be rejected. A Form N-600 that is not completed according to these instructions, is missing pages or otherwise not executed in its entirety, or is not accompanied by the required initial evidence may be rejected or delayed. If USCIS rejects your Form N-600 for any of the reasons above, the form and any fees will be returned to you if you provided a complete and valid mailing address. You will be notified why the form is considered deficient. You may correct the deficiency and refile Form N-600. An application or petition is not considered properly filed until accepted by USCIS.

Requests for More Information or Interview

USCIS may request more information or evidence. USCIS may also request that you submit the originals of any copies that you previously provided to USCIS with your Form N-600. USCIS may request that you appear for an interview.

Decision

The decision on Form N-600 involves a determination of whether you have established eligibility for the requested benefit. If you do not establish a basis for eligibility, USCIS will deny your Form N-600. You will be notified of the decision in writing.

What Is the Filing Fee

The fee for filing Form N-600 is **$600** except for U.S. citizen parents requesting a Certificate of Citizenship for an adopted child.

For U.S. citizen parents filing on behalf of an adopted minor child under section 320 of the INA (checking **Part 1, Box 3 on the Form**), the fee for Form N-600 is **$550**.

NOTE: There is no filing fee for Form N-600 if you are a member or veteran of any branch of the U.S. Armed Forces filing on your own behalf. You must attach proof of U.S. military service; otherwise USCIS will charge a fee to file the Form N-600. Children of members or veterans of the Armed Forces ARE required to pay the filing fee for Form N-600.

Use the following guidelines when you prepare your check or money order for your Form N-600 fee:

1. The check or money order must be drawn on a bank or other financial institution located in the Unites States and must be payable in U.S. currency; **and**

2. **Make the check or money order payable to U.S. Department of Homeland Security.**

NOTE: Spell out U.S. Department of Homeland Security; do not use the initials "USDHS" or "DHS."

USCIS will reject your Form N-600 if you submit the incorrect fee. In such a case, USCIS will return any filing fee you submitted with your Form N-600.

Notice To Those Making Payment by Check

USCIS will make a copy and convert your original check into an electronic funds transfer (EFT). This means USCIS will use the account information on your check to electronically debit your account for the check amount. This debit usually takes 24 hours and should show up on your regular account statement.

USCIS will not return your original check. USCIS will destroy it and keep a copy with your file. If the EFT cannot be processed due to technical reasons, you authorize USCIS to process the copy of the check. If the EFT cannot be completed because of insufficient funds, USCIS may try the EFT up to two times.

If you receive an insufficient funds notice, USCIS will send you instructions on how to submit your penalty fee. **Do not** send a check for the penalty fee to the address where you filed your Form N-600. It will be returned to you.

How to Check If the Fees Are Correct

The fee on Form N-600 is current as of the edition date appearing in the lower right corner of this page. However, because USCIS fees change periodically, you can verify if the fees are correct by following one of the steps below:

1. Visit the USCIS Web Site at **www.uscis.gov**, select "FORMS," and check the "filing fee" column for the form you are filing;

2. Telephone the USCIS National Customer Service Center at **1-800-375-5283** and ask for the fee information.

Fee Waiver Request

Individuals may request a fee waiver based on an inability to pay. Form I-912 provides a standard means for submitting fee waiver requests. The instructions provide applicants with guidance on properly completing Form I-912 and submitting

supporting documentation. The instructions also give information on how USCIS makes a decision on a fee waiver request. To download a copy of Form I-912, including the instructions, click on the "**FORMS**" link on the USCIS Web site at **www.uscis.gov**.

Where To File

Mail your completed Form N-600 and accompanying documentation to the USCIS Phoenix Lockbox facility at the following address:

> **USCIS**
> **P.O. Box 20100**
> **Phoenix, AZ 85036**

For Express Mail or courier deliveries, use the following address:

> **USCIS**
> **Attn: N-600**
> **1820 E. Skyharbor Circle S**
> **Suite 100**
> **Phoenix, AZ 85034**

E-Notification

If you are filing your Form N-600 at one of the USCIS Lockbox facilities, you may elect to receive an e-mail and/or text message notifying you that your Form N-600 has been accepted. You must complete Form G-1145, E-Notification of Application/Petition Acceptance, and attach it to the first page your of Form N-600. To download a copy of Form G-1145, including the instructions, click on the "**FORMS**" link on the USCIS Web Site at **www.uscis.gov**.

Form Revision Date and Filing Addresses

The filing addresses provided on this form reflect the most current information as of the date this form was last printed. If you are filing Form N-600 more than 30 days after the latest edition date shown in the lower right corner, visit the USCIS Web site at **www.uscis.gov** before you file, and check the "**FORMS**" page to confirm the correct filing address and version currently in use. Check the edition date located at the lower right corner of the form. If the edition date on your Form N-600 matches the edition date listed for Form N-600 on the online "**FORMS**" page, your version is current. If the edition date on the online version is more recent, download a copy and use it. If you do not have Internet access, call the USCIS National Customer Service Center at **1-800-375-5283** to verify the current filing address and edition date. **USCIS will reject forms with the wrong revision date and return the fee with instructions to resubmit the entire filing using the current form.**

Address Changes

If you have changed your address, you must inform USCIS of your new address. For information on filing a change of address go to the USCIS Web site at **www.uscis.gov/ addresschange** or by calling the USCIS National Customer Service Center at **1-800-375-5283.**

NOTE: Do not submit a change of address request to the USCIS Lockbox facilities because the USCIS Lockbox facilities do not process change of address requests.

USCIS Forms and Information

You can get USCIS forms and immigration-related information on the USCIS Web site at **www.uscis.gov**. You may order USCIS forms by calling the USCIS toll-free number at **1-800-870-3676**. You may also obtain forms and information by calling the USCIS National Customer Service Center at **1-800-375-5283**.

You can schedule an appointment to meet with a USCIS representative at your local USCIS office through the USCIS Internet-based system, **InfoPass**. To access the system, visit the USCIS Web site. Use the **InfoPass** appointment scheduler and follow the screen prompts to set up your appointment. **InfoPass** generates an electronic appointment notice that appears on the screen.

Attorney or Representative

You may be represented, at no expense to the U.S. Government, by an attorney or other duly accredited representative. Your representative must submit Form G-28, Notice of Entry of Appearance as Attorney or Representative, with your Form N-600. If USCIS requests you to appear for an interview, your representative may also submit the Form G-28 at that time. Form G-28 can be obtained by visiting the USCIS Web site at **www.uscis.gov**, calling the USCIS forms line number at **1-800-870-3676**, or by calling the USCIS National Customer Service Center at **1-800-375-5283**.

Penalties

If you knowingly and willfully falsify or conceal a material fact or submit a false document with this Form N-600, USCIS will deny your Form N-600 and may deny any other immigration benefit. In addition, you may be subject to criminal prosecution and penalties provided by law.

USCIS Privacy Act Statement

AUTHORITIES: The information requested on this form, and the associated evidence, is collected under the Immigration and Nationality Act, section 101, et seq.

PURPOSE: The primary purpose for providing the requested information on this form is to determine if you have established eligibility for the immigration benefit for which you are filing. The information you provide will be used to grant or deny the benefit sought.

DISCLOSURE: The information you provide is voluntary. However, failure to provide the requested information, and any requested evidence, may delay a final decision or result in denial of your form.

ROUTINE USES: The information you provide on this form may be shared with other Federal, State, local, and foreign government agencies and authorized organizations following approved routine uses described in the associated published system of records notices [DHS-USCIS-007 - Benefits Information System and DHS-USCIS-001 - Alien File, Index, and National Filed Tracking System of Records, which can be found at **www.dhs.gov/privacy**]. The information may also be made available, as appropriate, for law enforcement purposes or in the interest of national security.

Paperwork Reduction Act

An agency may not conduct or sponsor an information collection, and a person is not required to respond to a collection of information unless it displays a currently valid OMB control number. The public reporting burden for this collection of information is estimated at 1 hour 35 minutes per response, including the time for reviewing instructions and completing and submitting the form. Send comments regarding this burden estimate or any other aspect of this collection of information, including suggestions for reducing this burden to: U.S. Citizenship and Immigration Services, Regulatory Products Division, Office of the Executive Secretariat, 20 Massachusetts Avenue, N.W., Washington, DC 20529-2020; OMB No 1615-0057. Form expires January 31, 2012. **Do not mail your completed Form N-600 to this address.**

OMB No. 1615-0057; Expires 12/31/2014

Department of Homeland Security
U. S. Citizenship and Immigration Services

**Form N-600, Application for
Certificate of Citizenship**

Print or type all your answers fully and accurately in black ink. Write or type "N/A" if an item is not applicable. Write or type "None" if the answer is none. Failure to answer all of the questions may delay processing your Form N-600.

Part 1. Information About Your Eligibility *(Check only one box. USCIS will reject your Form N-600 if you check more than one box.)*

This application is being filed based on the fact that:

1. ☐ I am a BIOLOGICAL child of a U.S. citizen parent(s).

2. ☐ I am an ADOPTED child of a U.S. citizen parent(s).

3. ☐ Other *(explain fully)*:

_____

_____

_____

_____

_____

Part 2. Information About You *(Provide information about yourself if you are a person applying for the Certificate of Citizenship.* **Provide information about your child** *if you are a U.S. citizen parent applying for a Certificate of Citizenship for your minor child.)*

1. **Current Legal Name** *(do **not** provide a nickname)*

Family Name *(last name)*

[   ]

Given Name *(first name)*

[   ]

Middle Name *(if applicable)*

[   ]

2. **Your name exactly as it appears on your Permanent Resident Card** *(if different from above)*

Family Name *(last name)*

[   ]

Given Name *(first name)*

[   ]

Middle Name *(if applicable)*

[   ]

3. **Other name(s) you have used since birth** *(if applicable. Include nicknames)*

Family Name *(last name)*	Given Name *(first name)*	Middle Name *(if applicable)*

4. **U.S. Social Security Number** *(if applicable)* 5. **Date of Birth** *(mm/dd/yyyy)* 6. **Country of Birth**

Your A-Number *if any*:

A ____ - ____ - ____

Bar Code	Date Stamp

Remarks

Action

Form N-600 (Rev. 12/16/12) N

Part 2. Information About You *(Continued)*   A _____ - _____ - _____

7. Country of Prior Citizenship/Nationality

8. Gender   ☐ Male   ☐ Female

9. Height   Feet [   ]   Inches [   ]

10. Home Address

Street Number and Name *(do **not** provide a P.O. Box in this space unless it is your **ONLY** address)*   Apartment Number

City   State   Zip Code

Province *(foreign address only)*   Country *(foreign address only)*   Postal Code *(foreign address only)*

11. Mailing Address

C/O *(in care of name, if applicable)*

Street Number and Name   Apartment Number

City   State   Zip Code

Province *(foreign address only)*   Country *(foreign address only)*   Postal Code *(foreign address only)*

12. Daytime Phone Number   ( )   **Work Phone Number** *(if any)* ( )   **Evening Phone Number** ( )

Mobile Phone Number *(if any)* ( )   **13. E-Mail Address** *(if any)*

14. Current Marital Status

☐ Single, Never Married   ☐ Married   ☐ Divorced   ☐ Widowed

☐ Marriage Annulled   ☐ Other *(explain)*:

15. Are you a member or veteran of any branch of the U.S. Armed Forces?   ☐ Yes   ☐ No

16. Information about admission into the United States and current immigration status

A. I arrived in the following manner

Port of Entry *(City/State)*   Date of Entry *(mm/dd/yyyy)*   Exact Name Used at Time of Entry:

B. I used the following travel document to be admitted to the United States

☐ Passport   Passport Number   Passport Issuing Country   Date Passport Issued *(mm/dd/yyyy)*

☐ Other *(specify document name and issuance date(s))*

Part 2. Information About You *(Continued)*	A ____ - ____ - ____

C. I am

☐ A Permanent Resident

☐ A Nonimmigrant

☐ A Refugee/Asylee

☐ Other *(explain)* _____

D. I obtained permanent resident status through adjustment of status in the United States or admission as a permanent resident *(if applicable)*

Date I became a permanent resident *(mm/dd/yyyy)*	USCIS office that granted my permanent resident status or location where I was admitted

17. Have you previously applied for a Certificate of Citizenship or U.S. passport?   ☐ Yes *(attach explanation)*   ☐ No

18. Have you ever abandoned or lost your permanent resident status?   ☐ Yes *(attach explanation)*   ☐ No

19. Were you adopted?   ☐ Yes *(complete the following information)*   ☐ No

Date of Adoption *(mm/dd/yyyy)*	Place of Final Adoption *(City/State or Country)*

Date Legal Custody Began *(mm/dd/yyyy)*	Date Physical Custody Began *(mm/dd/yyyy)*

20. Did you have to be re-adopted in the United States?   ☐ Yes *(complete the following information)*   ☐ No

Date of Final Adoption *(mm/dd/yyyy)*	Place of Final Adoption *(City/State)*

Date Legal Custody Began *(mm/dd/yyyy)*	Date Physical Custody Began *(mm/dd/yyyy)*

21. Were your parents married to each other when you were born (or adopted)?   ☐ Yes   ☐ No

22. Did your parents marry after you were born?   ☐ Yes   ☐ No

23. Do you regularly reside in the United States in the legal and physical custody of your U.S. citizen parent(s)?   ☐ Yes   ☐ No

24. Have you been absent from the United States since you first arrived?   ☐ Yes   ☐ No

*(complete the following information **only** if you are claiming U.S. citizenship at the time of birth if you were born before October 10, 1952)*

Date You Left the United States *(mm/dd/yyyy)*	Date You Returned to the United States *(mm/dd/yyyy)*	Place of Entry Upon Return to the United States *(City, State)*

Part 3. Information About Your U.S. Citizen Biological Father (or Adoptive Father) (*Complete this section if you are claiming citizenship through a U.S. citizen biological father (or adoptive father).* ***Provide information about yourself*** *if you are a U.S. citizen father applying for a Certificate of Citizenship on behalf of your minor biological or adopted child.*)

A ____-____-____

1. Current legal name of U.S. citizen father

Family Name *(last name)*

Given Name *(first name)*

Middle Name *(if applicable)*

2. Date of Birth *(mm/dd/yyyy)*

3. Country of Birth

4. Country of Citizenship/Nationality

5. Home Address

Street Number and Name *(write "Deceased" and date of death if your father has passed away)*

Apartment Number

City

State

Zip Code

Province *(foreign address only)*

Country *(foreign address only)*

Postal Code *(foreign address only)*

6. My father is a U.S. citizen by

☐ Birth in the United States
☐ Acquisition after birth through naturalization of alien parent(s)
☐ Birth abroad to U.S. citizen parent(s)

Certificate of Citizenship Number

A-Number *(if known)*

☐ Naturalization

Date of Naturalization *(mm/dd/yyyy)*

Place of Naturalization *(name of court and City/State or USCIS office location)*

Certificate of Naturalization Number

A-Number *(if known)*

7. Has your father ever lost U.S. citizenship or taken any action that would cause loss of U.S. citizenship?

☐ Yes *(provide full explanation on an additional sheet(s) of paper)*   ☐ No

8. Marital History

   A. How many times has your U.S. citizen father been married *(including annulled marriages and marriage(s) to the same person)*? _____

   B. What is your U.S. citizen father's current marital status?

   ☐ Single, Never Married   ☐ Married   ☐ Separated   ☐ Divorced   ☐ Widowed
   ☐ Marriage Annulled   ☐ Other *(explain)*: _____

Part 3. Information About Your U.S. Citizen Biological Father (or Adoptive Father) *(Continued)*

A _____ - _____ - _____

C. Information about U.S. citizen father's current spouse

Family Name *(last name)*

Given Name *(first name)*

Middle Name *(if applicable)*

Date of Birth *(mm/dd/yyyy)*

Country of Birth

Country of Citizenship/Nationality

Spouse's Home Address

Street Number and Name

Apartment Number

City

State

Zip Code

Province *(foreign address only)*

Country *(foreign address only)*

Postal Code *(foreign address only)*

Date of Marriage *(mm/dd/yyyy)*

Place of Marriage *(City/State or Country)*

Spouse's Immigration Status

☐ U.S. Citizen   ☐ Permanent Resident   ☐ Other *(explain)*: _____

D. Is your U.S. citizen father's current spouse also your biological (or adopted) mother?   ☐ Yes   ☐ No

Part 4. Information About Your U.S. Citizen Biological Mother (or Adoptive Mother) *(Complete this section if you are claiming citizenship through a U.S. citizen biological mother (or adoptive mother). Provide information about yourself if you are a U.S. citizen mother applying for a Certificate of Citizenship on behalf of your minor biological or adopted child.)*

1. Current legal name of U.S. citizen mother

Family Name *(last name)*

Given Name *(first name)*

Middle Name *(if applicable)*

2. Date of Birth *(mm/dd/yyyy)*

3. Country of Birth

4. Country of Citizenship/Nationality

5. Home Address

Street Number and Name *(write "Deceased" and date of death if your mother has passed away)*

Apartment Number

City

State

Zip Code

Province *(foreign address only)*

Country *(foreign address only)*

Postal Code *(foreign address only)*

Part 4. Information About Your U.S. Citizen Biological Mother (or Adoptive Mother) *(Continued)*	A _____ - ____ - _____

6. My mother is a U.S. citizen by

☐ Birth in the United States

☐ Acquisition after birth through naturalization of alien parent(s)

☐ Birth abroad to U.S. citizen parent(s)

Certificate of Citizenship Number	A-Number *(if known)*

☐ Naturalization

Date of Naturalization *(mm/dd/yyyy)*	Place of Naturalization *(name of court and City/State or USCIS office location)*

Certificate of Naturalization Number	A-Number *(if known)*

7. Has your mother ever lost U.S. citizenship or taken any action that would cause loss of U.S. citizenship?

☐ Yes *(provide full explanation on an additional sheet(s) of paper)*   ☐ No

8. Marital History

A. How many times has your U.S. citizen mother been married *(including annulled marriages and marriage(s) to the same person)*? _____

B. What is your U.S. citizen mother's current marital status?

☐ Single, Never Married   ☐ Married   ☐ Separated   ☐ Divorced   ☐ Widowed

☐ Marriage Annulled   ☐ Other *(explain)*: _____

C. Information about U.S. citizen mother's current spouse

Family Name *(last name)*	Given Name *(first name)*	Middle Name *(if applicable)*

Date of Birth *(mm/dd/yyyy)*	Country of Birth	Country of Citizenship/Nationality

Spouse's Home Address

Street Number and Name	Apartment Number

City	State	Zip Code

Province *(foreign address only)*	Country *(foreign address only)*	Postal Code *(foreign address only)*

Date of Marriage *(mm/dd/yyyy)*	Place of Marriage *(City/State or Country)*

Spouse's Immigration Status

☐ U.S. Citizen   ☐ Permanent Resident   ☐ Other *(explain)*: _____

D. Is your U.S. citizen mother's current spouse also your biological (or adopted) father?   ☐ Yes   ☐ No

Form N-600 (Rev. 12/16/12) N Page 6

| Part 5. | Physical Presence in the United States From Birth Until Filing of Form N-600 *(Only applicants born outside the United States claiming to have been born U.S. citizens are required to provide all the dates when your U.S. citizen biological father or U.S. citizen biological mother resided in the United States. **Include all dates from your birth until the date you file your Form N-600.**)* | A ____ - ____ - ____ |

Indicate whether this information relates to your U.S. citizen (USC) father or mother   ☐ USC Father   ☐ USC Mother

Physical Presence in the United States *(mm/dd/yyyy)*					
From		Until		From		Until	
From		Until		From		Until	
From		Until		From		Until	
From		Until		From		Until	

| Part 6. | Information About Military Service of U. S. Citizen Parent(s) *(Complete this only if you are an applicant claiming U.S. citizenship at time of birth abroad.)* |

1. Has your U.S. citizen parent(s) served in the U.S. Armed Forces?   ☐ Yes   ☐ No

2. If "Yes," which parent?   ☐ U.S. Citizen Father   ☐ U.S. Citizen Mother

3. Dates of Service *(if time of service fulfills any of required physical presence, submit evidence of service)*

From *(mm/dd/yyyy)*   To *(mm/dd/yyyy)*   From *(mm/dd/yyyy)*   To *(mm/dd/yyyy)*

4. Type of discharge   ☐ Honorable   ☐ Other than Honorable   ☐ Dishonorable

| Part 7. | Your Signature *(USCIS will reject your Form N-600 if it is not signed.)* |

I certify, under penalty of perjury under the laws of the United States, that this application and the evidence submitted with it is all true and correct. I authorize the release of any information from my records, or my minor child's records, that U.S. Citizenship and Immigration Services needs to determine eligibility for the benefit I am seeking.

Your Signature *(parent may sign on behalf of a minor child)*   **Date** *(mm/dd/yyyy)*

| Part 8. | Signature of Person Who Prepared This Form N-600 For You *(if applicable)* |

I declare that I prepared this application at the request of the above person. The answers provided are based on information of which I have personal knowledge and/or were provided to me by the above-named person in response to the questions contained on this form.

Preparer's Printed Name   **Preparer's Signature**   **Date** *(mm/dd/yyyy)*

Part 8. Signature of Person Who Prepared This Form N-600 For You *(if applicable)*

A ☐☐☐ - ☐☐☐ - ☐☐☐☐

Preparer's Firm or Organization Name *(if applicable)*

Preparer's Daytime Phone Number

( )

Preparer's Address

Street Number and Name

City

State

Zip Code

Province *(foreign address only)*

Country *(foreign address only)*

Postal Code *(foreign address only)*

Preparer's E-Mail Address

Preparer's Fax Number

( )

NOTE: Do not complete the next part unless the USCIS officer instructs you to do so at the interview.

Part 9. Affidavit (do *NOT* complete this part unless instructed to do so *AT THE INTERVIEW*)

A _____ - _____ - _____

I, the (applicant, parent, or legal guardian) _____ do swear or affirm, under penalty of perjury under the laws of the United States, that I know and understand the contents of this application signed by me, and the attached supplementary pages number (___) to (___) inclusive, that the same are true and correct to the best of my knowledge, and that corrections number (___) to (___) were made by me or at my request.

Applicant's, Parent's, or Legal Guardian's Signature

Date (mm/dd/yyyy)

Subscribed and sworn or affirmed before me upon examination of the applicant (parent, legal guardian) on _____ at

_____ .
                    (Location)

(mm/dd/yyyy)

USCIS Officer's Name and Title

USCIS Officer's Signature

Part 10. Officer Report and Recommendation on Application for Certificate of Citizenship *(for USCIS use ONLY)*

On the basis of the documents, records, the testimony of person(s) examined, and the identification upon personal appearance of the underage beneficiary, I find that all the facts and conclusions set forth under oath in this application are:

1. ☐ True and correct

2. ☐ The applicant derived or acquired U.S. citizenship on _____
                                                            (mm/dd/yyyy)

3. ☐ The applicant derived or acquired U.S. citizenship through *(mark "X" next to the appropriate section of law, or if the section of law is not reflected, write the applicable section of law in the space next to "Other")*

☐ *Section 301 of the INA*
☐ *Section 309 of the INA*
☐ *Section 320 of the INA*
☐ *Section 321 of the INA*
☐ *Other:* _____

4. ☐ The applicant has not been expatriated since that time

I recommend that this Form N-600 application be   ☐ **Approved**   ☐ **Denied**

Issue Certificate of Citizenship in the name of

Last Name

First Name

Middle Name

USCIS Officer's Name and Title

USCIS Officer's Signature

Date (mm/dd/yyyy)

I do _____ do not _____ concur with the USCIS Officer's recommendation of the Form N-600.

USCIS District Director's or Field Office Director's Signature

Date (mm/dd/yyyy)

Form N-600 (Rev. 12/16/12) N Page 9

APPENDIX 13-4

Certificate of Naturalization

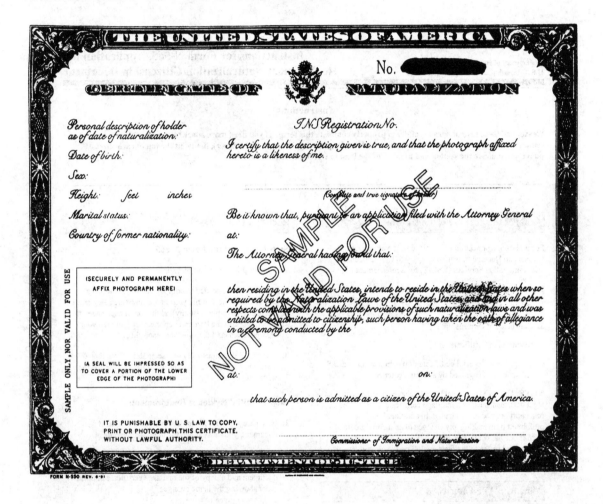

APPENDIX 13-5

Form N-565

OMB No. 1615-0091 Expires 02/28/2015

Department of Homeland Security
U.S. Citizenship and Immigration Services

Instructions for Form N-565, Application for Replacement Naturalization/Citizenship Document

Instructions

Please read these instructions carefully to properly complete this form. If you need more space to complete an answer, use a separate sheet of paper. Write your name and Alien Registration Number (A-Number), if any, at the top of each sheet of paper and indicate the section and number of the item to which the answer refers.

What Is the Purpose of This Form?

Form N-565, Application for Replacement Naturalization/ Citizenship Document, is used to apply to U.S. Citizenship and Immigration Services (USCIS) for a replacement of a:

1. Declaration of Intention;

2. Certificate of Naturalization;

3. Certificate of Citizenship;

4. Repatriation Certificate; or

5. To apply for a special certificate of naturalization as a U.S. citizen to be recognized by a foreign country.

NOTE: USCIS has no legal basis to change a name absent a legal document such as a marriage certificate, divorce decree, or a court ordered name change. In addition, USCIS is prohibited from making any changes to an incorrect date of birth if one has completed the naturalization/citizenship process and sworn to the facts, including the wrong date of birth.

Who May File Form N-565?

You may apply for a replacement:

1. If you have been issued a Certificate of Naturalization, Certificate of Citizenship, Declaration of Intention or Repatriation Certificate which has been lost, mutilated, or destroyed;

2. If your name has been changed by marriage or by court order after the document was issued and you seek a document in the new name; or

3. If you are a naturalized citizen desiring to obtain recognition as a citizen of the United States by a foreign country, you may apply for a special certificate for that purpose.

General Instructions

Step 1. Fill Out the Form N-565.

1. Type or print legibly in black ink.

2. If extra space is needed to complete any item, attach a continuation sheet, write your name and Alien Registration Number (A-Number) (if any), at the top of each sheet of paper, indicate the Part and item number to which your answer refers, and date and sign each sheet.

3. Answer all questions fully and accurately. State that an item is not applicable with "N/A." If the answer is none, write "none."

Step 2. Initial Evidence Requirements.

1. If you are applying for replacement of a mutilated document, you must attach the mutilated document.

2. If you are applying for a new document because your name has been changed, you must submit the original USCIS document and a copy of the marriage certificate or court order showing the name change.

3. If you are applying for a special certificate of naturalization, you must attach a copy of your naturalization certificate.

Copies. Unless specifically required that an original document be filed with an application, a legible photocopy may be submitted. Original documents submitted when not required may remain a part of the record, and will not be automatically returned to you.

Translations. Any document containing a foreign language submitted to USCIS shall be accompanied by a full English language translation which the translator has certified as complete and accurate, and by the translator's certification that he or she is competent to translate from the foreign language into English.

Photographs

You **must** submit two identical color photographs of yourself taken within 30 days of the filing of this application. The photos must have a white to off-white background, be printed on thin paper with a glossy finish, and be unmounted and unretouched.

Passport-style photos must be 2" x 2." The photos must be in color with full face, frontal view on a white to off-white background. Head height should measure 1" to 1 3/8" from top of hair to bottom of chin, and eye height is between 1 1/8" to 1 3/8" from bottom of photo. Your head must be bare unless you are wearing a headdress as required by a religious denomination of which you are a member. However, your face must be visible. Using pencil or felt pen, lightly print your name and Alien Registration Number on the back of the photo.

Where to File?

If you reside in **AL, AR, CT, DE, DC, FL, GA, KY, LA, MS, ME, MD, MA, NH, NJ, NM, NY, NC, SC, OK, PA, PR, RI, TN, TX, VA, VI, VT, WV**

Submit your N-565 to the USCIS Texas Service Center at:

DHS/USCIS
Texas Service Center
PO Box 851182
Mesquite, TX 75185-1182

If you reside in **AK, AZ, CA, CO, GU, HI, ID, IL, IN, IA, KS, MI, MN, MO, MT, NE, NV, ND, OH, OR, SD, UT, WA, WI, WY**

Submit your N-565 to the USCIS Nebraska Service Center at:

DHS/USCIS
Nebraska Service Center
PO Box 87565
Lincoln, NE 68501-7565

What Is the Filing Fee?

The filing fee Form N-565 is **$345**, except there is no fee if you check **block 2 (d)** of **Part 2** of the form.

You may submit one check or money order for the application and other documents for which you are applying.

Use the following guidelines when you prepare your check or money order for the Form N-565 fee:

1. The check or money order must be drawn on a bank or other financial institution located in the United States and must be payable in U.S. currency; **and**

2. Make the check or money order payable to **U.S. Department of Homeland Security**.

NOTE: Please spell out U.S. Department of Homeland Security; do not use the initials "USDHS" or "DHS."

How to Check If the Fees Are Correct

Form N-565 fees and biometrics services fees are current as of edition date in the lower right corner of this page. However, because USCIS fees change periodically, you can verify if the fees are correct by following one of the steps below.

1. Visit the USCIS Web site at **www.uscis.gov**, select "FORMS," and check the appropriate fee; or

2. Telephone the USCIS National Customer Service Center at **1-800-375-5283** and ask for fee information. For TDD (hearing impaired) call: **1-800-767-1833**.

NOTE: If your Form N-565 requires payment of a biometrics services fee for USCIS to take your fingerprints, photograph or signature, you can use the same procedure to obtain the correct biometrics fee.

Processing Information

Rejection. Any application that is not signed or not accompanied by the correct fee will be rejected with a notice that the application is deficient. You may correct the deficiency and resubmit the application. However, an application is not considered properly filed until accepted by USCIS.

Initial processing. Once the application has been accepted, it will be checked for completeness, including submission of the required initial evidence. If you do not completely fill out the form, or file it without required initial evidence, you will not establish a basis for eligibility and we may deny your application.

Requests for more information or interview. We may request more information or evidence or we may request that you appear at a USCIS office for an interview. We may also request that you submit the originals of any document. We will return these originals when they are no longer required.

Decision. If you establish eligibility for the document, your application will be approved and the document issued. Where appropriate, a special certificate of naturalization will be forwarded to the U.S. Department of State for delivery to a foreign government official. If your application is denied, you will be notified in writing of the reasons for the denial.

USCIS Forms and Information

To ensure you are using the latest version of this form, visit the USCIS Web site at **www.uscis.gov** where you can obtain the latest USCIS forms and immigration-related information. If you do not have internet access, you may order USCIS forms by calling our toll-free number at **1-800-870-3676**. You may also obtain forms and information by telephoning our USCIS National Customer Service Center at **1-800-375-5283**. For TDD (hearing impaired) call: **1-800-767-1833**.

As an alternative to waiting in line for assistance at your local USCIS office, you can now schedule an appointment through the USCIS Internet-based system, **InfoPass**. To access the system, visit the USCIS Web site. Use the **InfoPass** appointment scheduler and follow the screen prompts to set up your appointment. **InfoPass** generates an electronic appointment notice that appears on the screen.

Penalties

If you knowingly and willfully falsify or conceal a material fact or submit a false document with this request, we will deny the benefit you are filing for, and may deny any other immigration benefit.

In addition, you will face severe penalties provided by law, and may be subject to criminal prosecution.

USCIS Privacy Act Statement

AUTHORITIES: The information requested on this form, and the associated evidence, is collected under the Immigration and Nationality Act, section 101, et seq.

PURPOSE: The primary purpose for providing the requested information on this form is to determine if you have established eligibility for the immigration benefit for which you are filing. The information you provide will be used to grant or deny the benefit sought.

DISCLOSURE: The information you provide is voluntary. However, failure to provide the requested information, and any requested evidence, may delay a final decision or result in denial of your form.

ROUTINE USES: The information you provide on this form may be shared with other Federal, State, local, and foreign government agencies and authorized organizations following approved routine uses described in the associated published system of records notices [DHS-USCIS-007 - Benefits Information System and DHS-USCIS-001 - Alien File (A-File) and Central Index System (CIS), which can be found at **www.dhs.gov/privacy**]. The information may also be made available, as appropriate, for law enforcement purposes or in the interest of national security.

Paperwork Reduction Act

An agency may not conduct or sponsor an information collection and a person is not required to respond to a collection of information unless it displays a currently valid OMB control number. The public reporting burden for this collection of information is estimated at 55 minutes per response, including the time for reviewing instructions, completing and submitting the form. Send comments regarding this burden estimate or any other aspect of this collection of information, including suggestions for reducing this burden, to: U.S. Citizenship and Immigration Services, Regulatory Coordination Division, Office of Policy & Strategy, 20 Massachusetts Avenue, NW, Washington, DC 20529-2140. OMB No. 1615-0091. **Do not mail your completed Form N-565 to this address.**

OMB No. 1615-0091; Expires 02/28/2015

Department of Homeland Security
U.S. Citizenship and Immigration Services

**Form N-565, Application for Replacement
Naturalization/Citizenship Document**

START HERE - Please type or print in black ink

	For USCIS Use Only	

Part 1.   Information about you.

Family Name	Given Name	Middle Name

Address - In care of:

Street Number and Name	Apt. Number

City or Town	State or Province

Country	Zip or Postal Code

Date of Birth *(mm/dd/yyyy)*	Country of Birth

Certificate Number	A-Number

Telephone Number *(with area/country codes)*	E-Mail Address *(if any)*

For USCIS Use Only

Returned
_____

Resubmitted
_____

Reloc Sent
_____

Reloc Rec'd
_____

☐ Applicant
Interviewed

☐ Declaration of Intention verified by
_____

☐ Citizenship verified by
_____

Remarks

Part 2. Type of application

1. I hereby apply for: *(check one)*

a. ☐ New Certificate of Citizenship
b. ☐ New Certificate of Naturalization
c. ☐ New Certificate of Repatriation
d. ☐ New Declaration of Intention
e. ☐ Special Certificate of Naturalization to obtain recognition of my U.S. citizenship by a foreign country. *(Skip Number 2 and go to Part 3)*

2. Basis for application: *(Refer to the instructions for additional information.)*

a. ☐ My certificate is/was lost, stolen or destroyed *(attach a copy of the certificate if you have one)*. Explain when, where and how.

_____

b. ☐ My certificate is mutilated *(attach the certificate)*.
c. ☐ My name has been changed *(attach the certificate)*.
d. ☐ My certificate or declaration is incorrect *(attach the document(s))*.

Part 3. Processing information

Gender	☐ Male	Height	Marital Status	☐ Single	☐ Widowed
	☐ Female			☐ Married	☐ Divorced

My last certificate or Declaration of Intention was issued to me by:

USCIS Office or Name of Court:	Date *(mm/dd/yyyy):*

Name in which the document was issued:

Other names I have used *(if none, so indicate):*

Since becoming a citizen, have you lost your citizenship in any manner?

☐ No   ☐ Yes *(attach an explanation)*

Action Block

Part 4. Complete if applying for a new document because of a name change

Name changed to present name by: *(check one)*

☐ Marriage or divorce on *(mm/dd/yyyy)*
   (Attach a copy of marriage or divorce certificate) _____

☐ Court Decree *(mm/dd/yyyy)*
   (Attach a copy of the court decree) _____

To Be Completed by
Attorney or Representative, if any.

☐ Fill in box if Form G-28 is attached to represent the applicant.

VOLAG No.

ATTY State License Number

Form N-565 (Rev. 02/28/13) Y

Part 5.   Complete if applying to correct your document

If you are applying for a new certificate or Declaration of Intention because your current one is incorrect, explain why it is incorrect and attach copies of the documents supporting your request.

_____

_____

_____

_____

_____

Part 6.   Complete if applying for a special certificate of recognition as a citizen of the U.S. by the government of a foreign country

Name of Foreign Country _____

Information about official of the country who has requested this certificate *(if known)*

Name	Official Title

Government Agency:

Address: Street Number and Name		Suite Number
City	State/Province	
Country	Zip or Postal Code	

Part 7.   Signature   *Read the information on penalties in the instructions before completing this part. If you are going to file this application at a USCIS office in the United States sign below. If you are going to file this application at a USCIS office abroad, sign it in front of a USCIS or Consular Official.*

I certify, or if outside the United States, I swear or affirm, under penalty of perjury under the laws of the United States of America, that this application and the evidence submitted with it is all true and correct. I authorize the release of any information from my records which U.S. Citizenship and Immigration Services needs to determine eligibility for the benefit I am seeking.

Signature	**Date** *(mm/dd/yyyy)*

Signature of USCIS or Consular Official	Print Your Name	Date *(mm/dd/yyyy)*

NOTE: *If you do not completely fill out this form or fail to submit required documents listed in the instructions, you may not be found eligible for a certificate and this application may be denied.*

Part 8.   Signature of person preparing form, if other than the applicant

I declare that I prepared this application at the request of the applicant and it is based on all information of which I have knowledge.

Signature	**Print Your Name**	**Date** *(mm/dd/yyyy)*

Firm Name and Address	Telephone Number *(with area code)*
	E-Mail Address *(if any)*

Form N-565 (Rev. 02/28/13) Y Page 2

APPENDIX 13-6

Form N-578

[prescribed edition date: 10/03/62 (8 CFR § 499.1, *as amended by* 59 Fed. Reg. 25561 (May 17, 1994)]

APPENDIX 13-7

U.S. Census Bureau, Factfinder for the Nation, Availability of Census Records About Individuals, April 1997

Availability of Census Records About Individuals

Introduction

The United States population census records contain a wealth of information about people. They are useful in learning about one's family and local social and economic conditions at various times in history. For more recent years especially, they are official documents for persons who need to prove their age (in the absence of a birth certificate), relationship, citizenship, residence, and other facts in order to qualify for pensions; get jobs, naturalization papers, passports, or insurance policies; establish an inheritance; or trace ancestry. There was a population census taken in 1790 and every tenth year after that. (Page 3 lists the items covered in the existing censuses for each year.) The U.S. Census Bureau publication, *Measuring America: The Decennial Censuses From 1790 to 2000* (Washington, DC, 2002) provides a history of each census and reproduces the questionnaires and instructions given to enumerators for taking each census. You can download this publication at <www.census.gov/prod/www/abs/ma.html>.

This Factfinder explains what census materials are available and how to obtain them and also lists the sources for some other useful records about individuals.

Census Schedules Available to the Public

Individual records from the federal population censuses are confidential for 72 years, by law (Title 44, U.S. Code). Thus, April 2012 is the scheduled date for the National Archives to open the 1940 records to public use.

Microfilm copies of the original population schedules, from 1790 through 1930 (virtually all of the 1890 records were destroyed as a result of a 1921 fire), are available at the National Archives in Washington (www.archives.gov) and its 13 regional archives (see page 4), and

many libraries in various parts of the United States. Most have facilities for making paper copies from the microfilm. The National Archives also rents and sells the microfilm rolls (see below). The Reference Branch at National Archives headquarters (see listing on page 4) will accept photocopy orders by mail or through orders online, given exact page numbers; it will not do research.

There are Soundex (that is, by the sound of the surname rather than its spelling) indexes on microfilm for the 1880, 1900, and 1920 censuses for each state, and for 1910 for 21 states, principally in the South. Ten southern states, plus a few counties in West Virginia and Kentucky were soundexed for 1930. Alphabetic indexes to the 1790–1860 and most of the 1870 censuses are available in genealogical libraries. Most states began keeping a more accurate birth registration in the early 1920s.

Researchers may find two Census Bureau publications useful; most major libraries have copies. *Heads of Families at the First Census of the United States Taken in the Year 1790* (12 vols., Washington, DC, 1907–1908, reprinted 1965–75), contains specific names. *A Century of Population Growth—1790–1900* (Washington, DC, 1909, reprinted 1967–1970), includes the incidence of surnames in 1790, and a variety of summary tables from colonial censuses from 1790 to 1900.

A number of state and territorial censuses were taken in the intradecennial years, particularly in the 19th century. See Henry J. Dubester, *An Annotated Bibliography of Censuses Taken After the Year 1790, by States and Territories of the United States* (Washington, DC, 1948, reprinted 1969 and 1975) and *State Census Records*, Ann S. Lainhart (Baltimore, MD, 1992). An appendix to the Dubester book tells where the existing records (some including names) were located; copies of many can be obtained commercially on microfiche.

Some 19th century industrial, agricultural, and mortality census schedules have survived, mainly in state archives, although the National Archives has film for some states. These nonpopulation schedules generally are available on microfilm. These records frequently can be related to individuals listed in the population censuses.

Microfilm Rental and Sales

Rental. The National Archives rents microfilm copies of historical records to libraries and individuals. These copies are of federal population census schedules 1790–1930; Soundex indexes, 1880–1930; Revolutionary War–compiled military service records; and pension and bounty-land-warrant application files, and Freedman's Bureau records. For details, contact the National Archives Microfilm Rental Program, P.O. Box 30, Annapolis Junction, MD 20701-0030, 301-604-3699.

Sales. Microfilmed copies of census schedules, 1790–1930, and Soundex indexes, 1880–1930, can be purchased from the Customer Service Center (NWCC2), College Park, MD 20740; 301-837-2000 or 1-866-272-6272. The office has catalogs, prices, and ordering information.

Access to Closed Records

The Census Bureau can release details from recent files in the form of official transcripts, but only to the named persons, their heirs, or legal representatives. There is a congressionally mandated fee for this service. Since by law, this census information is confidential and collected only for statistical purposes, it is exempt from the disclosure provisions of the Freedom of Information Act (FOIA) and the Privacy Act. This means that no one can gain access to confidential census records or avoid the search fees through these acts. Transcript application forms

USCENSUSBUREAU
Helping You Make Informed Decisions

U.S. Department of Commerce
Economics and Statistics Administration
U.S. CENSUS BUREAU

1166

(BC-600) may be obtained from
<www.census.gov/genealogy/www
/agesearch.html> or from the following:

- Personal Census Search Unit
  U.S. Census Bureau
  P.O. Box 1545
  Jeffersonville, IN 47131
  812-218-3046
  Fax: 812-288-3371

- History Staff
  U.S. Census Bureau
  Washington, DC 20233
  301-763-1167
  www.census.gov/history/

- Census Bureau regional offices:
  Atlanta, GA 404-730-3832 or
  1-800-424-6974 Fax: 404-730-3835
  TDD: 404-730-3963 E-mail:
  atlanta.regional.office@census.gov

  Boston, MA 617-424-4501 or
  1-800-562-5721 Fax: 617-424-0547
  TDD: 617-424-0565 E-mail:
  boston.regional.office@census.gov

  Charlotte, NC 704-424-6400 or
  1-800-331-7360 Fax: 704-424-6944
  TDD: 704-424-6963 E-mail:
  charlotte.regional.office@census.gov

  Chicago, IL 630-288-9200 or
  1-800-865-6384 Fax: 630-288-9288
  TDD: 708-562-1791 E-mail:
  chicago.regional.office@census.gov

  Dallas, TX 214-253-4400 or
  1-800-835-9752 Fax: 214-655-5362
  TDD: 214-655-5363 E-mail:
  dallas.regional.office@census.gov

  Denver, CO 303-264-0202 or
  1-800-852-6159 Fax: 303-969-6777
  TDD: 303-969-6767 E-mail:
  denver.regional.office@census.gov

  Detroit, MI 313-259-0056 or
  1-800-432-1495 Fax: 313-259-5045
  TDD: 313-259-5169 E-mail:
  detroit.regional.office@census.gov

  Kansas City, MO 913-551-6728 or
  1-800-728-4748 Fax: 913-551-6789
  TDD: 913-551-5839 E-mail:
  KC.regional.office@census.gov

  Los Angeles, CA 818-267-1700 or
  1-800-992-3530 Fax: 818-267-1711
  TDD: 818-904-6429 E-mail:
  LA.regional.office@census.gov

  New York, NY 212-584-3400
  or 1-800-991-2520 Fax: 212-478-4800
  TDD: 212-478-4783 E-mail:
  new.york.regional.office@census.gov

  Philadelphia, PA 215-717-1800 or
  1-800-262-4236 Fax: 215-717-0755
  TDD: 215-717-0894 E-mail:
  Philadelphia.Regional.Office@census.gov

  Seattle, WA 206-381-6200 or
  1-800-233-3308 Fax: 206-381-6310
  TDD: 206-381-6318 E-mail:
  seattle.regional.office@census.gov

Other Sources

Some of the major types of information not found in census records, and their sources, are the following:

Information	Source
Birth, death, marriage, and divorce records, U.S. and outlying areas	U.S. Department of Health and Human Services "Where to Write for Vital Records" 1-800-232-4636 <www.cdc.gov/nchs>
Birth and death records, Americans overseas	Passport Services—Vital Records Section 1111 19th Street, NW, Suite 510 Washington, DC 20522-1705
Birth, death, marriage, and divorce records, foreign	American citizens: Passport Services—Vital Records Section 1111 19th Street, NW, Suite 510 Washington, DC 20522-1705 Aliens: Nearest consular office of the country in question
Immigration or naturalization records, 1906 to present (earlier records are held by local courts) Birth records of aliens, children adopted by U.S. citizens	Department of Homeland Security Bureau of Citizenship and Immigration Services 1-800-375-5283 TTY 1-800-767-1833
Death records of members of U.S. Army, Navy, Air Force, or Coast Guard	National Personnel Records Center (Military Personnel Records) 9700 Page Avenue St. Louis, MO 63132-5100 314-801-0800 Fax 314-801-9195 <www.archives.gov/veterans>
Military records from World War I and later (those prior to World War I are in the National Archives)	Military Records Division National Personnel Records Center 9700 Page Avenue St. Louis, MO 63132-5100 314-801-0800 Fax 314-801-9195
Selective Service records Men born on or after Jan 1, 1960	Selective Service System National Headquarters Arlington, VA 22209-2425 847-688-6888 <www.sss.gov/records.htm>
Selective Service Records Men born pre-1960	NARA—Archival Programs P.O. Box 28989 St. Louis, MO 63132-0989
U.S. Government civilian personnel whose service ended after 1909	National Personnel Records Center Civilian Personnel Records 111 Winnebago Street St. Louis, MO 63118-4126 314-801-9269 Fax 314-801-9269 <www.archives.gov/st-louis/civilian-person-nel/index.html>
Historical map records, family and local histories, and other historical records	Library of Congress History & Genealogy Division 101 Independence Ave., SE Thomas Jefferson Bldg., LJ G42 Washington, DC 20540-4660 202-707-5537 <www.loc.gov/rr/askalib/>
Homestead applications, ships' passenger lists, American Indian tribal census rolls	National Archives & Records Administration 700 Pennsylvania Avenue, NW Washington, DC 20408-0001 1-866-325-7208 <www.archives.gov>

Detailed information on Archives' holdings of the above and other useful materials about individuals can be found in "Using Civilian Records for Genealogical Research in the National Archives," Reference Information Paper 110; "Guide to Genealogical Research in the National Archives" (Third Edition; for sale), and other NARA family history research tools available from Archives Customer Services Center (see page 4).

Besides these federal sources, persons interested in researching their families or communities also should consider some of the following: local and state historical societies, local and state libraries, the American Association for State and Local History in Nashville, TN (www.aaslh.org), and various other associations, bookstores, and publishers.

Population Census Items 1790–2000

(Includes only those supplemental schedules still in existence; excludes questions asked on a sample basis only—the long-form questionnaire.)

1790
Name of family head; free white males of 16 years and up; free white males under 16; free white females; slaves; other free persons.

1800
Names of family head; if white, age and sex; race; slaves.

1810
Name of family head; if white, age and sex; race; slaves.

1820
Name of family head; age; sex; race; foreigners not naturalized; slaves; industry (agriculture, commerce, and manufactures).

1830
Name of family head; age; sex; race; foreigners not naturalized; slaves; industry.

1840
Name of family head; age; sex; race; slaves; number of deaf and dumb; number of blind; number of insane and idiotic and whether in public or private charge; number of persons in each family employed in each of six classes of industry and one of occupation; literacy; pensioners for Revolutionary or military service.

1850
Name; age; sex; race; whether deaf and dumb, blind, insane, or idiotic; value of real estate; occupation; birthplace; whether married within the year; school attendance; literacy; whether a pauper or convict.

Supplemental schedules for slaves, and persons who died during the year.

1860
Name; age; sex; race; value of real estate; value of personal estate; occupation; birthplace; whether married within the year; school attendance; literacy; whether deaf and dumb, blind, insane, idiotic, pauper, or convict.

Supplemental schedules for slaves, and persons who died during the year.

1870
Name; age; race; occupation; value of real estate; value of personal estate; birthplace; whether parents were foreign born; month of birth if born within the year; month of marriage if married within the year; school attendance; literacy; whether deaf and dumb, blind, insane, or idiotic; male citizens 21 and over, and number of such persons denied the right to vote for other than rebellion.

Supplemental schedule for persons who died during the year.

1880
Address; name, relationship to family head; sex; race; age; marital status; month of birth if born within the census year; occupation; months unemployed during the year; sickness or temporary disability; whether blind, deaf and dumb, idiotic, insane, maimed, crippled, bedridden, or otherwise disabled; school attendance; literacy; birthplace of person and parents.

Supplemental schedules for persons who died during the year.

1890
General schedules—destroyed.

Supplemental schedules for Union veterans of the Civil War and their widows.

1900
Address; name; relationship to family head; sex; race; age; marital status; number of years married; for women, number of children born and number now living; birthplace of person and parents; if foreign born, year of immigration and whether naturalized; occupation; months not employed; school attendance; literacy; ability to speak English; whether on a farm; home owned or rented and if owned, whether mortgaged.

1910
Address; name; relationship to family head; sex; race; age; marital status; number of years of present marriage for women, number of children born and number now living; birthplace and mother tongue of person and parents; if foreign born, year of immigration, whether naturalized, and whether able to speak English, or if not, language spoken; occupation, industry, and class of worker; if an employee, whether out of work during year; literacy; school attendance; home owned or rented; if owned, whether mortgaged; whether farm or house; whether a survivor of Union or Confederate Army or Navy; whether blind or deaf and dumb.

1920
Address; name; relationship to family head; sex; race; age; marital status; if foreign born, year of immigration to the U.S., whether naturalized, and year of naturalization; school attendance; literacy; birthplace of person and parents; mother tongue of foreign born; ability to speak English; occupation, industry, and class of worker; home owned or rented; if owned, whether free or mortgaged.

1930
Address; name; relationship to family head; home owned or rented; value or monthly rental; radio set; whether on a farm; sex; race; age; marital status; age at first marriage; school attendance; literacy; birthplace of person and parents; if foreign-born language spoken in home before coming to U.S., year of immigration, whether naturalized, and ability to speak English; occupation, industry, and class of worker; whether at work previous day (or last regular working day); veteran status; for Indians, whether of full or mixed blood, and tribal affiliation.

1940
Address; home owned or rented; value or monthly rental; whether on a farm; name; relationship to household head; sex; race; age; marital status; school attendance; educational attainment; birthplace; citizenship of foreign born; location of residence 5 years ago and whether on a farm; employment status; if at work, whether in private or nonemergency government work, or in public emergency work (WPA, CCC, NYA, etc.); if in private work, hours worked in week; if seeking work or on public emergency work, duration of unemployment; occupation, industry, and class of worker; weeks worked last year, income last year.

1950
Address; whether house is on farm; name; relationship to household head; race; sex; age; marital status; birthplace if foreign born, whether naturalized; employment status; hours worked in week; occupation, industry, and class of worker.

1960-1970
Address; name; relationship to household head; sex; race; age; marital status.

1980-1990
Address; name; household relationship; sex; race; age; marital status; Spanish/Hispanic origin or descent.

2000
Address; home owned or rented; name; household relationship; sex; age; birth date; race; Spanish/Hispanic/Latino origin or descent.

- National Archives and regional branches (see page 4)

- Many social security and post offices have blank forms

Transcripts ordinarily show age (not birth date) at the time of the census, gender, relationship to the householder, and—where requested—race. If obtained in the particular census, state or country of birth (but not place), citizenship, or occupation can be listed as well. A "full schedule" showing all of the information

collected for one individual in a given census (see above for questions) can be ordered at extra cost.

The records are organized geographically, rather than by name, so except for those censuses that have indexes (see page 1), addresses are necessary to find them. Thus, the Census Bureau's files cannot be used to locate missing persons, obtain addresses (prohibited by law in any case), or even discover how many people have the same surname. The Census Bureau publication,

Age Search Information (Washington, DC, 2000), has details about this service and also discusses other possible sources of data about individuals. You can download this publication at <www.census .gov/prod/www/abs/gen-ref.html>.

Factfinder for the Nation

Inquiries about census data.
The Census Bureau publishes data summarized for various geographic units (as distinguished from information about

U.S. Census Bureau

CFF-2 3

individuals) in considerable detail in printed reports (paper or microfiche), compact discs, DVDs, and online through the Census Bureau's data dissemination and inquiry system, American Fact-Finder®, which can be accessed from the agency's Internet site <www.census .gov>. PDFs of the latest publications can be downloaded from the Census Bureau Web site or the publications can be purchased directly from the agency. They are described in the Census Bureau's annual *Census Catalog and Guide*; a separate catalog available in many libraries lists reports covering the period 1790 to 1972. There are over 1,500 federal and Census Bureau depository libraries in the United States that have reference

collections of these materials. The Census Bureau's regional offices and state data centers and the International Trade Administration's district offices make census data available in a variety of formats.

Questions about these and other Census Bureau products may be directed to:
Customer Services Center
Customer Liaison and Marketing
Services Office
U.S. Census Bureau
Washington, DC 20233
1-800-923-8282 or 301-763-4636
Fax: 301-763-4636

For more information. CFF-4, "History and Organization," another Factfinder in this series, explains the history of the Census Bureau and its programs. A PDF file of the publication can be obtained from the following page on the Census Bureau Web site <www.census.gov /prod/www/abs/gen-ref.html>.

Questions, comments, or suggestions about any of the Census Bureau's activities are welcomed and may be addressed to:

Director
U.S. Census Bureau
Washington, DC 20233

NATIONAL ARCHIVES AND RECORDS ADMINISTRATION HEADQUARTERS AND REGIONAL BRANCHES
(Business hours: 9 a.m.–4:30 p.m., M-F. Contact each office to find out about extended hours.)

Washington, DC Headquarters
800 & Pennsylvania Ave., NW
Washington, DC 20408
202-357-5400 or 1-866-325-7208
www.archives.gov
E-mail: inquire@nara.gov

Reference Branch
202-357-5400
Customer Services Center
800-234-8861
Fax: 301-837-0483

NARA—College Park, MD
8601 Adelphi Rd.
College Park, MD 20740
301-837-2000 or 1-866-272-6272
www.archives.gov
E-mail: inquire@nara.gov

Regional Archives

**NARA—Pacific Alaska Region
(Anchorage)**
654 West Third Ave.
Anchorage, AK 99501-2145
907-261-7800
www.archives.gov/pacific-alaska
/anchorage/
E-mail: alaska.archives@nara.gov
Serves Alaska

**NARA—Pacific Region
(Laguna Niguel)**
24000 Avila Rd.
Laguna Niguel, CA 92677-3497
949-360-2641
www.archives.gov/pacific/laguna
E-mail: laguna.archives@nara.gov
Serves AZ, Southern CA, and Clark County, NV

**NARA—Pacific Region
(San Francisco)**
1000 Commodore Dr.
San Bruno, CA 94066-2350
650-238-3501
www.archives.gov/pacific/san-fransisco

E-mail: sanbruno.archives@nara.gov
Serves northern and central CA, NV (except Clark County), HI, American Samoa, and the Trust Territory of the Pacific Islands.

NARA—Rocky Mountain Region
Denver Federal Center, Building 48
West 6th Ave. and Kipling St.
P.O. Box 25307
Denver, CO 80225-0307
303-407-5740
www.archives.gov/rocky-mountain
E-mail: denver.archives@nara.gov
Serves CO, MT, NM, ND, SD, UT, WY

NARA—Southeast Region
5780 Jonesboro Rd.
Morrow, GA 30260-3806
770-968-2100
www.archives.gov/southeast/
E-mail: atlanta.archives@nara.gov
Serves AL, FL, GA, KY, MS, NC, SC, TN

**NARA—Central Plains Region
(Kansas City)**
2312 East Bannister Rd.
Kansas City, MO 64131-3011
816-268-8012
www.archives.gov/central plains
/kansas city
E-mail: kansascity.archives@nara.gov
Serves AL, FL, GA, KY, MS, NC, SC, TN

NARA—Great Lakes Region
7358 South Pulaski Rd.
Chicago, IL 60629-5898
773-948-9001
www.archives.gov/great-lakes/chicago
E-mail: chicago.archives@nara.gov
Serves IL, IN, MI, MN, OH, WI

NARA—Northeast Region (Boston)
380 Trapelo Rd.
Waltham, MA 02452-6399
866-406-2379
www.archives.gov/northeast/waltham/
E-mail: waltham.archives@nara.gov
Serves CT, ME, MA, NH, RI, VT

NARA—Northeast Region (Pittsfield)
10 Conte Dr.
Pittsfield, MA 01201-8230
413-236-3600
www.archives.gov/northeast/pittsfield/
E-mail: pittsfield.archives@nara.gov
(Microfilm only)

**NARA—Northeast Region
(New York City)**
201 Varick St., 12th Floor
New York, NY 10014-4811
866-840-1752
www.archives.gov/northeast/nyc
E-mail: newyork.archives@nara.gov
Serves NJ, NY, Puerto Rico, and the U.S. Virgin Islands

**NARA—Mid Atlantic Region
(Center City Philadelphia)**
900 Market St.
Philadelphia, PA 19107-4292
215-606-0100
www.archives.gov/midatlantic/
E-mail: philadelphia.archives@nara.gov
Serves DE, MD, PA, VA, WV

NARA—Southwest Region
501 West Felix St.
P.O. Box 6216
Ft. Worth, TX 76115-0212
817-831-5620
www.archives.gov/southwest/
E-mail: ftworth.archives@nara.gov
Serves AR, LA, OK, TX

NARA—Pacific Alaska Region (Seattle)
6125 Sand Point Way, NE
Seattle, WA 98115-7999
206-336-5115
www.archives.gov/pacific-alaska/seattle
E-mail: seattle.archives@nara.gov
Serves ID, OR, WA

4 CFF-2

U.S. Census Bureau

APPENDIX 13-8

Form SSA-7004 (Request of Earnings and Benefit Estimate Statement)

Request for *Social Security Statement*

☐ Please check this box if you want to get your *Statement* in Spanish instead of English.

Please print or type your answers. When you have completed the form, fold it and mail it to us. If you prefer to send your request using the Internet, go to *www.socialsecurity.gov.*

1. Name shown on your Social Security card:

   _____   _____
   First Name   Middle Initial

   _____
   Last Name Only

2. Your Social Security number as shown on your card:

   ☐☐☐-☐☐-☐☐☐☐

3. Your date of birth (Mo.-Day-Yr.)

   ☐☐-☐☐-☐☐☐☐

4. Other Social Security numbers you have used:

   ☐☐☐-☐☐-☐☐☐☐
   ☐☐☐-☐☐-☐☐☐☐

5. Your Sex: ☐ Male   ☐ Female

For items 6 and 8, show only earnings covered by Social Security. Do NOT include wages from state, local or federal government employment that are NOT covered by Social Security or that are covered ONLY by Medicare.

6. Show your actual earnings (wages and/or net self-employment income) for last year and your estimated earnings for this year.

   A. Last year's actual earnings: *(Dollars Only)*

   $ ☐☐☐,☐☐☐.☐☐

   B. This year's estimated earnings: *(Dollars Only)*

   $ ☐☐☐,☐☐☐.☐☐

7. Show the age at which you plan to stop working:

   ☐☐ *(Show only one age)*

8. Below, show the average yearly amount (not your total future lifetime earnings) that you think you will earn between now and when you plan to stop working. Include performance or scheduled pay increases or bonuses, but not cost-of-living increases.

   If you expect to earn significantly more or less in the future due to promotions, job changes, part-time work or an absence from the work force, enter the amount that most closely reflects your future average yearly earnings.

   If you don't expect any significant changes, show the same amount you are earning now (the amount in 6B).

   Future average yearly earnings: *(Dollars Only)*

   $ ☐☐☐,☐☐☐.☐☐

9. Do you want us to send the *Statement:*
   • To you? Enter your name and mailing address.
   • To someone else (your accountant, pension plan, etc.)? Enter your name with "c/o" and the name and address of that person or organization.

   _____
   "C/O" or Street Address (Include Apt. No., P.O. Box, Rural Route)

   _____
   Street Address

   _____
   Street Address (If Foreign Address, enter City, Province, Postal Code)

   _____
   U.S. City, State, ZIP code (If Foreign Address, enter Name of Country only)

   NOTICE:
   I am asking for information about my own Social Security record or the record of a person I am authorized to represent. I declare under penalty of perjury that I have examined all the information on this form, and on any accompanying statements or forms, and it is true and correct to the best of my knowledge. I authorize you to use a contractor to send the *Social Security Statement* to the person and address in item 9.

   ▶ _____
   Please sign your name (Do Not Print)

   _____
   Date   (Area Code) Daytime Telephone No.

Form SSA-7004-SM (06-2008) EF (06-2008)
10-2006 edition may be used

♻ Printed on recycled paper

About The Privacy Act

Social Security is allowed to collect the facts on this form under section 205 of the Social Security Act. We need them to quickly identify your record and prepare the *Statement* you asked us for. Giving us these facts is voluntary. However, without them we may not be able to give you a *Statement*. Neither the Social Security Administration nor its contractor will use the information for any other purpose.

Paperwork Reduction Act Notice

This information collection meets the requirements of 44 U. S. C. §3507, as amended by Section 2 of the Paperwork Reduction Act of 1995. You do not need to answer these questions unless we display a valid Office of Management and Budget control number. We estimate that it will take about 5 minutes to read the instructions, gather the facts and answer the questions. *You may send comments on our time estimate above to: SSA, 6401 Security Blvd., Baltimore, MD 21235-6401. Send only comments relating to our time estimate to this address, not the completed form.*

Request for *Social Security Statement*

Within four to six weeks after you return this form, we will send you:
- a record of your earnings history;
- an estimate of how much you have paid in Social Security taxes; and
- estimates of benefits you (and your family) may be eligible for now and in the future.

Please note: If you have been receiving a *Social Security Statement* each year about three months before your birthday, this request will stop your next scheduled mailing. You will not receive a scheduled *Statement* until the following year.

We hope you will find the *Statement* useful in planning your financial future. Remember, Social Security is more than a program for retired people. It helps people of all ages in many ways. For example, it can help support your family in the event of your death and pay you benefits if you become severely disabled.

If you have questions about Social Security or this form, please call our toll-free number, **1-800-772-1213.**

MAIL TO:
SOCIAL SECURITY ADMINISTRATION
WILKES BARRE DATA OPERATIONS CENTER
PO BOX 7004
WILKES BARRE PA 18767-7004

APPENDIX 13-9

U.S. Passport Application

APPLICATION FOR A U.S. PASSPORT

PLEASE DETACH AND RETAIN THIS INSTRUCTION SHEET FOR YOUR RECORDS

I applied: Place: _____

            Date: _____

FOR INFORMATION, QUESTIONS, AND INQUIRIES:

Please visit our website at **travel.state.gov**. In addition, you may contact the National Passport Information Center (NPIC) toll-free at 1-877-487-2778 (TDD: 1-888-874-7793) or by email at **NPIC@state.gov**. Customer Service Representatives are available Monday-Friday 8:00a.m.-10:00p.m. Eastern Time (excluding federal holidays.) Automated information is available 24/7.

U.S. PASSPORTS, EITHER IN BOOK OR CARD FORMAT, ARE ISSUED ONLY TO U.S. CITIZENS OR NON-CITIZEN NATIONALS. EACH PERSON MUST OBTAIN HIS OR HER OWN PASSPORT BOOK OR PASSPORT CARD. THE PASSPORT CARD IS A U.S. PASSPORT ISSUED IN CARD FORMAT. LIKE THE TRADITIONAL PASSPORT BOOK, IT REFLECTS THE BEARER'S ORIGIN, IDENTITY, AND NATIONALITY AND IS SUBJECT TO EXISTING PASSPORT LAWS AND REGULATIONS. UNLIKE THE PASSPORT BOOK, THE PASSPORT CARD IS VALID ONLY FOR ENTRY TO THE UNITED STATES AT LAND BORDER CROSSINGS AND SEA PORTS OF ENTRY WHEN TRAVELING FROM CANADA, MEXICO, THE CARIBBEAN, AND BERMUDA. THE U.S. PASSPORT CARD IS NOT VALID FOR INTERNATIONAL AIR TRAVEL.

APPLICANTS WHO HAVE HAD A PREVIOUS U.S. PASSPORT BOOK AND/OR U.S. PASSPORT CARD

If your most recent passport book and/or passport card was issued less than 15 years ago and you were over 16 years old at the time of issuance, you may be eligible to use Form DS-82. To determine your eligibility, please visit **travel.state.gov**, or contact NPIC. Address any requests for the addition of visa pages to a passport agency or a U.S. consulate or embassy abroad. In advance of your departure, check for any visa requirements with consular officials of the countries you will be visiting.

SPECIAL REQUIREMENTS FOR CHILDREN

● AS DIRECTED BY PUBLIC LAW 106-113 AND 22 CFR 51.28:

To submit an application for a child under age 16 both parents or the child's legal guardian(s) must appear and present the following:
- Evidence of the child's U.S. citizenship
- Evidence of the child's relationship to parents/guardian(s), AND
- Parental/guardian identification.

IF ONLY ONE PARENT APPEARS, YOU MUST ALSO SUBMIT ONE OF THE FOLLOWING:
- Second parent's notarized written statement. or DS-3053 (including the child's full name and date of birth) consenting to the passport issuance for the child. Statement can not be more than 3 months old and must come with a photocopy of the front and back side of the second parent's identification, OR
- Second parent's death certificate if second parent is deceased, OR
- Primary evidence of sole authority to apply, OR
- A written statement or DS-3053 (made under penalty of perjury) explaining in detail the second parent's unavailability.

● AS DIRECTED BY REGULATION 22 CFR 51.21 AND 51.28:
- Each minor child applying for a passport book and/or passport card must appear in person.

FAILURE TO PROVIDE INFORMATION REQUESTED ON THIS FORM, INCLUDING YOUR SOCIAL SECURITY NUMBER, MAY RESULT IN SIGNIFICANT PROCESSING DELAYS AND/OR THE DENIAL OF YOUR APPLICATION.

WHAT TO SUBMIT WITH THIS FORM:

1. **PROOF OF U.S. CITIZENSHIP** (Evidence of U.S. citizenship that is not damaged, altered, or forged will be returned to you.)
2. **PROOF OF IDENTITY** (You must present your original identification **AND** submit a photocopy of the front and back side with your passport application.)
3. **RECENT COLOR PHOTOGRAPH** (Photograph must meet passport requirements – full front view of the face and 2x2 inches in size.)
4. **FEES** (Please visit our website at **travel.state.gov** for current fees.)

See page 2 of the instructions for detailed information on the completion and submission of this form.

WHERE TO SUBMIT THIS FORM:

Please complete and submit this application in person to one of the following acceptance agents: a clerk of a federal or state court of record or a judge or clerk of a probate court accepting applications; a designated municipal or county official; a designated postal employee at an authorized post office; an agent at a passport agency (by appointment only); or a U.S. consulate official at a U.S. embassy or consulate, if abroad. To find your nearest acceptance facility, visit **travel.state.gov** or contact the National Passport Information Center.

WARNING: False statements made knowingly and willfully in passport applications, including affidavits or other documents submitted to support this application, are punishable by fine and/or imprisonment under U.S. law including the provisions of 18 USC 1001, 18 USC 1542, and/or 18 USC 1621. Alteration or mutilation of a passport issued pursuant to this application is punishable by fine and/or imprisonment under the provisions of 18 USC 1543. The use of a passport in violation of the restrictions contained herein or of the passport regulations is punishable by fine and/or imprisonment under 18 USC 1544. All statements and documents are subject to verification.

DS-11 12-2010

Instruction Page 1 of 4

1. PROOF OF U.S. CITIZENSHIP

APPLICANTS BORN IN THE UNITED STATES. Submit a previous U.S. passport or **certified** birth certificate. Passports that are limited in validity will need to be supplemented by other evidence. A birth certificate must include your full name, date and place of birth, sex, date the birth record was filed, the seal or other certification of the official custodian of such records (state, country, or city/town office), and the full names of your parent(s).

- If the birth certificate was filed more than 1 year after the birth: It must be supported by evidence described in the next paragraph.
- If no birth record exists: Submit a registrar's notice to that effect. Also, submit a combination of the following evidence: an early baptismal or circumcision certificate, hospital birth record, early census, school, medical, or family Bible records, or newspapers or insurance files. Notarized affidavits of persons having knowledge of your birth may be submitted in addition to some of the records listed above. Evidence should include your given name and surname, date and/or place of birth, and the seal or other certification of the office (if customary) and the signature of the issuing official. Visit travel.state.gov for details.

APPLICANTS BORN OUTSIDE THE UNITED STATES: Submit a previous U.S. passport, Certificate of Naturalization, Certificate of Citizenship, Report of Birth Abroad, or evidence described below:

- If you Claim Citizenship through Naturalization of Parent(s): Submit the Certificate(s) of Naturalization of your parent(s), your foreign birth certificate (and official translation if the document is not in English), **and** proof of your admission to the United States for permanent residence.
- If you Claim Citizenship through Birth Abroad to One U.S. Citizen Parent: Submit a Consular Report of Birth (Form FS-240), Certification of Birth (Form DS-1350 or FS-545), **or** your foreign birth certificate (and official translation if the document is not in English), proof of citizenship of your parent, your parents' marriage certificate, **and** an affidavit showing all of your U.S. citizen parents' periods and places of residence/physical presence in the United States and abroad before your birth.
- If you Claim Citizenship through Birth Abroad to Two U.S. Citizen Parents: Submit a Consular Report of Birth (Form FS-240), Certification of Birth (Form DS-1350 or FS-545), **or** your foreign birth certificate (and official translation if the document is not in English), parents' marriage certificate, proof of your parents' citizenship, **and** an affidavit showing all of your U.S. citizen parents' periods and places of residence/physical presence in the United States and abroad before your birth.
- If you Claim Citizenship through Adoption by a U.S. Citizen Parent(s): Submit evidence of your permanent residence status, full and final adoption **and** your U.S. citizen parent(s) evidence of legal and physical custody. (**NOTE**: Acquisition of U.S. citizenship for persons born abroad and adopted only applies if the applicant was born on or after 02/28/1983.)

ADDITIONAL EVIDENCE: You must establish your citizenship to the satisfaction of the acceptance agent and Passport Services. We may ask you to provide additional evidence to establish your claim to U.S. citizenship.

NOTE: You may receive your newly issued document and your returned citizenship evidence in two separate mailings. If you are applying for both a passport book and passport card, you may receive three separate mailings; one with your returned citizenship evidence; one with your newly issued passport book, and one with your newly issued passport card.

2. PROOF OF IDENTITY

You may submit items such as the following containing your signature AND a photograph that is a good likeness of you: previous or current U.S. passport book; previous or current U.S. passport card; driver's license (not temporary or learner's license); Certificate of Naturalization; Certificate of Citizenship; military identification; or federal, state, or municipal government employee identification card. Temporary or altered documents are not acceptable.

You must establish your identity to the satisfaction of the acceptance agent and Passport Services. We may ask you to provide additional evidence to establish your identity. If you have changed your name, please see travel.state.gov for instructions.

IF YOU CANNOT PROVIDE DOCUMENTARY EVIDENCE OF IDENTITY as stated above, you must appear with an IDENTIFYING WITNESS who is a U.S. citizen, non-citizen U.S. national, or permanent resident alien who has known you for at least 2 years. Your witness must prove his or her identity and complete and sign an Affidavit of Identifying Witness (Form DS-71) before the acceptance agent. You must also submit some identification of your own.

3. RECENT COLOR PHOTOGRAPH

Submit a color photograph of you alone, sufficiently recent to be a good likeness of you (taken within the last six months), and 2x2 inches in size. The image size measured from the bottom of your chin to the top of your head (including hair) should not be less than 1 inch and not more than 1 3/8 inches. The photograph must be color, clear, with a full front view of your face, and printed on thin paper with a plain light (white or off-white) background. The photograph must be taken in normal street attire, without a hat, head covering, or dark glasses unless a signed statement is submitted by the applicant verifying the item is worn daily for religious purposes or a signed doctor's statement is submitted verifying the item is used daily for medical purposes. Headphones, "bluetooth", or similar devices must **not** be worn in passport photographs. Any photographs retouched so that your appearance is changed are unacceptable. Snapshots, most vending machine prints, and magazine or full-length photographs are unacceptable. Digitized photos must meet the previously stated qualifications and will be accepted for use at the discretion of Passport Services. Visit our website at travel.state.gov for details and information.

4. FEES

- **If you are sixteen years of age or older:** Your passport will be valid for 10 years from the date of issue except where limited by the Secretary of State to a shorter period. (See information below about the additional cost for expedited service.)

- **If you are under sixteen years of age:** Your passport will be valid for 5 years from the date of issue except where limited by the Secretary of State to a shorter period. (see information below about the additional cost for expedited service.)

  BY LAW, THE PASSPORT FEES ARE NON-REFUNDABLE. PLEASE VISIT OUR WEBSITE AT TRAVEL.STATE.GOV FOR CURRENT FEES.

- **The passport processing, execution, and security fees may be paid in any of the following forms:** Checks (personal, certified, or traveler's) with the applicant's full name and date of birth printed on the front; major credit card (Visa, Master Card, American Express, and Discover); bank draft or cashier's check; money order (U.S. Postal, international, currency exchange), or if abroad, the foreign currency equivalent, or a check drawn on a U.S. bank. All fees should be payable to the "Department of State" or if abroad, the appropriate U.S. embassy or U.S. consulate. When applying at a designated acceptance facility, the execution fee will be paid separately and should be made payable to the acceptance facility. **NOTE:** Some designated acceptance facilities do not accept credit cards as a form of payment.

- **For faster processing,** you may request expedited service. Please include the expedite fee in your payment. Our website contains updated information regarding fees and processing times for expedited service. Expedited service is available only in the United States.

- **If you desire OVERNIGHT DELIVERY SERVICE** for the return of your passport please include the appropriate fee with your payment.

- An additional fee will be charged when, upon your request, the U.S. Department of State verifies issuance of a previous U.S. passport or Consular Report of Birth Abroad because you are unable to submit evidence of U.S. citizenship.

- **For applicants with U.S. government or military authorization for no-fee passports,** no fees are charged except the execution fee when applying at a designated acceptance facility.

NOTE REGARDING MAILING ADDRESSES: Passport Services will not mail a passport to a private address outside the United States. If you do not live at the address listed in the "mailing address" then you must put the name of the person and mark it as "In Care Of." If your mailing address changes prior to receipt of your new passport, please contact the National Passport Information Center.

If you choose to provide your email address in Item #6 on this application, Passport Services will use that information to contact you in the event there is a problem with your application or if you need to provide information to us.

DS-11 12-2010   Instruction Page 2 of 4

FEDERAL TAX LAW

Section 6039E of the Internal Revenue Code (26 USC 6039E) requires you to provide your Social Security Number (SSN), if you have one, when you apply for a U.S. passport or renewal of a U.S. passport. If you have not been issued a SSN, enter zeros in box #5 of this form. If you are residing abroad, you must also provide the name of the foreign country in which you are residing. The Department of State must provide your SSN and foreign residence information to the Department of Treasury. If you fail to provide the information, you are subject to a $500 penalty enforced by the IRS. All questions on this matter should be directed to the nearest IRS office.

NOTICE TO CUSTOMERS APPLYING OUTSIDE A STATE DEPARTMENT FACILITY

If you send us a check, it will be converted into an electronic funds transfer (EFT). This means we will copy your check and use the account information on it to electronically debit your account for the amount of the check. The debit from your account will usually occur within 24 hours and will be shown on your regular account statement.

You will not receive your original check back. We will destroy your original check, but we will keep the copy of it. If the EFT cannot be processed for technical reasons, you authorize us to process the copy in place of your original check. If the EFT cannot be completed because of insufficient funds, we may try to make the transfer up to two times and we will charge you a one-time fee of $25, which we will also collect by EFT.

REMITTANCE OF FEES

Passport service fees are established by law and regulation (see 22 USC 214, 22 CFR 22.1, and 22 CFR 51.50-56) and are collected at the time you apply for the passport service. If the Department fails to receive full payment of the applicable fees because, for example, your check is returned for any reason or you dispute a passport fee charge to your credit card, the Department of State will take action to collect the delinquent fees from you under 22 CFR Part 34 and the Federal Claims Collection Standards (see 31 CFR Parts 900-904). In accordance with the Debt Collection Improvement Act (Pub.L. 104-134), if the fees remain unpaid after 180 days and no repayment arrangements have been made, the Department will refer the debt to the Department of Treasury for collection. Debt collection procedures used by Treasury may include referral of the debt to private collection agencies, reporting of the debt to credit bureaus, garnishment of private wages and administrative offset of the debt by reducing or withholding eligible federal payments (e.g. tax refunds, social security payments, federal retirement, etc.) by the amount of your debt, including any interest penalties or other costs incurred. In addition, non-payment of passport fees may result in the invalidation of your passport. An invalidated passport cannot be used for travel.

OTHER USES OF SOCIAL SECURITY NUMBERS

Your Social Security Number will be provided to Treasury, used in connection with debt collection and checked against lists of persons ineligible or potentially ineligible to receive a U.S. passport, among other authorized uses.

PAPERWORK REDUCTION STATEMENT

Public reporting burden for this collection of information is estimated to average 85 minutes per response, including the time required for searching existing data sources, gathering the necessary data, providing the information and/or documents required, and reviewing the final collection. You do not have to supply this information unless this collection displays a currently valid OMB control number. If you have comments on the accuracy of this burden estimate and/or recommendations for reducing it, please send them to: A/GIS/DIR, Room 2400 SA-22, U.S. Department of State, Washington, DC 20520-2202.

IMPORTANT NOTICE TO APPLICANTS WHO HAVE LOST OR HAD A PREVIOUS PASSPORT BOOK AND/OR PASSPORT CARD STOLEN

A United States citizen may not normally bear more than one valid or potentially valid U.S. passport book or more than one valid or potentially valid U.S. passport card at a time. Therefore, when a valid or potentially valid U.S. passport book or U.S. passport card cannot be presented with a new application, it is necessary to submit a Form DS-64, Statement Regarding a Lost or Stolen Passport. Your statement must detail why the previous U.S. passport book or U.S. passport card cannot be presented.

The information you provide regarding your lost or stolen U.S. passport book or passport card will be placed into our Consular Lost or Stolen Passport System. This system is designed to prevent the misuse of your lost or stolen U.S. passport book or passport card. Anyone using the passport book or passport card reported as lost or stolen may be detained upon entry into the United States. Should you locate the U.S. passport book or passport card reported lost or stolen at a later time, report it as found and submit it for cancellation. It has been invalidated. You may not use that passport book or passport card for travel.

PROTECT YOURSELF AGAINST IDENTITY THEFT!
REPORT YOUR LOST OR STOLEN PASSPORT BOOK OR PASSPORT CARD!

For more information or to report your lost or stolen passport book or passport card by phone, call NPIC or visit our website at **travel.state.gov**.

ACTS OR CONDITIONS

(If any of the below-mentioned acts or conditions have been performed by or apply to the applicant, the portion which applies should be lined out, and a supplementary explanatory statement under oath (or affirmation) by the applicant should be attached and made a part of this application.) I have not, since acquiring United States citizenship/nationality, been naturalized as a citizen of a foreign state; taken an oath or made an affirmation or other formal declaration of allegiance to a foreign state; entered or served in the armed forces of a foreign state; accepted or performed the duties of any office, post, or employment under the government of a foreign state or political subdivision thereof; made a formal renunciation of nationality either in the United States, or before a diplomatic or consular officer of the United States in a foreign state; or been convicted by a court or court martial of competent jurisdiction of committing any act of treason against, or attempting by force to overthrow, or bearing arms against, the United States, or conspiring to overthrow, put down, or to destroy by force, the government of the United States.

Furthermore, I have not been convicted for a federal or state drug offense or convicted for "sex tourism" crimes statute and I am not the subject of an outstanding federal, state or local warrant of arrest for a felony; a criminal court order forbidding my departure from the United States; a subpoena received from the United States in a matter involving federal prosecution for, or grand jury investigation of, a felony.

PRIVACY ACT STATEMENT

AUTHORITIES: Collection of the information solicited on this form is authorized by Titles 8, 22, and 26 of the United States Code, and other applicable laws and regulations, including 22 USC 211a et seq.; 8 USC 1104; 26 USC 6039E, Section 236 of the Admiral James W. Nance and Meg Donovan Foreign Relations Authorization Act, Fiscal Years 2000 and 2001; Executive Order 11295 (August 5, 1966); and 22 CFR parts 50 and 51.

PURPOSE: The primary purpose for soliciting the information is to establish citizenship, identity, and entitlement to issuance of a U.S. passport.

ROUTINE USES: The information solicited on this form may be made available as a routine use to other government agencies and private contractors to assist the U.S. Department of State in adjudicating passport applications and requests for related services, and for law enforcement, fraud prevention, border security, counterterrorism, litigation activities, and administrative purposes. The information may be made available to foreign government agencies to fulfill passport control and immigration duties. The information may also be provided to foreign government agencies, international organizations and, in limited cases, private persons and organizations to investigate, prosecute, or otherwise address potential violations of law or to further the Secretary's responsibility for the protection of U.S. citizens and non-citizen nationals abroad. The information may be made available to the Department of Homeland Security and private employers for employment verification purposes. For a more detailed listing of the routine uses to which this information may be put see the Department of State's Prefatory Statement of Routine Uses relative to the Privacy Act (Public Notice 6290 of July 15, 2008) and the listing of routine users set forth in the System of Records Notices for Overseas Citizen Services Records (State-05) and Passport Records (State-26) published in the Federal Register.

Your social security numbers will be provided to the U.S. Department of Treasury and failure to provide it may subject you to a penalty, as described in the Federal Tax Law provision. It also may be used for identification verification for passport adjudication and in connection with debt collection, among other purposes as authorized and generally described in this section. Providing your social security number and other information requested on this form otherwise is voluntary, but failure to provide the information requested on this form may result in processing delays or the denial of your U.S. passport application.

CONSEQUENCES OF FAILURE TO PROVIDE INFORMATION: Failure to provide the information requested on this form may result in Passport Services' refusal to accept your application or result in the denial of a U.S. passport.

ELECTRONIC PASSPORT STATEMENT

The Department of State now issues a type of passport book containing an embedded electronic chip and called an "Electronic Passport". The electronic passport book continues to be proof of the bearer's United States citizenship/nationality and identity, and looks and functions in the same way as a passport without a chip. The addition of an electronic chip in the back cover enables the passport book to carry a duplicate electronic copy of all information from the data page. The electronic passport book is usable at all ports-of-entry, including those that do not yet have electronic chip readers.

Use of the electronic format provides the traveler the additional security protections inherent in chip technology. Moreover, when used at ports-of-entry equipped with electronic chip readers, the electronic passport book provides for faster clearance through some of the port-of-entry processes.

The electronic passport book does not require special handling or treatment, but like previous versions should be protected from extreme heat, bending, and from immersion in water. The electronic chip must be read using specially formatted readers, which protects the data on the chip from unauthorized reading.

The cover of the electronic passport book is printed with a special symbol representing the embedded chip. The symbol will appear in port-of-entry areas where the electronic passport book can be read.

NOTICE TO APPLICANTS FOR OFFICIAL, DIPLOMATIC, OR NO-FEE PASSPORTS

You may use this application if you meet all of the provisions listed on Instruction Page 2, however you must CONSULT YOUR SPONSORING AGENCY FOR INSTRUCTIONS ON PROPER ROUTING PROCEDURES BEFORE FORWARDING THIS APPLICATION. Your completed passport will be released to your sponsoring agency for forwarding to you.

APPLICATION FOR A U.S. PASSPORT
Please Print Legibly Using Black Ink Only

OMB APPROVAL NO. 1405-0004
EXPIRATION DATE: 12-31-2013
ESTIMATED BURDEN: 85 MIN

Attention: Read WARNING on page 1 of instructions
Please select the document(s) for which you are applying:

☐ **U.S. Passport Book**   ☐ **U.S. Passport Card**   ☐ **Both**

The U.S. passport card is **not** valid for international air travel. For more information see page 1 of instructions.

☐ 28 Page Book (Standard)   ☐ 52 Page Book (Non-Standard)

Note: The 52 page option is for those who frequently travel abroad during the passport validity period and is recommended for applicants who have previously required the addition of visa pages.

1. Name Last

☐ D   ☐ O   ☐ DP   DOTS Code _____

End. # _____   Exp. _____

First   Middle

2. Date of Birth *(mm/dd/yyyy)*   **3. Sex** M F   **4. Place of Birth** *(City & State if in the U.S., or City & Country as it is presently known.)*

5. Social Security Number   **6. Email Address** *(e.g. my_email@domain.com)*   @   **7. Primary Contact Phone Number**

8. Mailing Address: Line 1: Street/RFD#, P.O. Box, or URB.

Address Line 2: **Clearly label** Apartment, Company, Suite, Unit, Building, Floor, In Care Of or Attention if applicable. *(e.g. In Care Of - Jane Doe, Apt # 100)*

City   State   Zip Code   Country, if outside the United States

9. List all other names you have used. *(Examples: Birth Name, Maiden, Previous Marriage, Legal Name Change. Attach additional pages if needed)*

A.   B.

10. Parental Information
Mother/Father/Parent - First & Middle Name   Last Name *(at Parent's Birth)*

Date of Birth *(mm/dd/yyyy)*   Place of Birth   Sex   U.S. Citizen?
☐ Male   ☐ Yes
☐ Female   ☐ No

Mother/Father/Parent - First & Middle Name   Last Name *(at Parent's Birth)*

Date of Birth *(mm/dd/yyyy)*   Place of Birth   Sex   U.S. Citizen?
☐ Male   ☐ Yes
☐ Female   ☐ No

STAPLE   2" x 2"   FROM 1" TO 1⅜"   2" x 2"   STAPLE

STAPLE   STAPLE

Submit a recent color photograph

➤ **CONTINUE TO PAGE 2** ➤

DO NOT SIGN APPLICATION UNTIL REQUESTED TO DO SO BY AUTHORIZED AGENT

I declare under penalty of perjury all of the following: 1) I am a citizen or non-citizen national of the United States and have not, since acquiring U.S. citizenship or nationality, performed any of the acts listed under "Acts or Conditions" on the reverse side of this application (unless explanatory statement is attached); 2) the statements made on the application are true and correct; 3) I have not knowingly and willfully made false statements or included false documents in support of this application; 4) the photograph submitted with this application is a genuine, current photograph of me; and 5) I have read and understood the warning on page one of the instructions to the application form.

x _____
Applicant's Legal Signature - age 16 and older

x _____
Mother/Father/Parent/Legal Guardian's Signature (if identifying minor)

x _____
Mother/Father/Parent/Legal Guardian's Signature (if identifying minor)

☐ Acceptance Agent   ☐ (Vice) Consul USA   ☐ Passport Staff Agent

(Seal)

_____
Facility Name/Location

_____
Signature of person authorized to accept applications   Date

Identifying Documents - Applicant or Mother/Father/Parent on Second Signature Line (If identifying minor)
☐ Driver's License   Issue Date _____   Exp. Date _____   Place of Issue _____
☐ Passport
☐ Military   Name _____
☐ Other _____   ID No _____

Identifying Documents - Applicant or Mother/Father/Parent on Third Signature Line (If identifying minor)
☐ Driver's License   Issue Date _____   Exp. Date _____   Place of Issue _____
☐ Passport
☐ Military   Name _____
☐ Other _____   ID No _____

Facility ID Number   Agent ID Number

For Issuing Office Only ➤ Bk _____ Card _____ Execution _____ EF _____ Postage _____ Other _____

DS 11 C 12 2010 1

DS-11 12-2010   Page 1 of 2

Name of Applicant *(Last, First & Middle)*

Date of Birth *(mm/dd/yyyy)*

11. Height   **12. Hair Color**   **13. Eye Color**   **14. Occupation** *(if age 16 or older)*   **15. Employer or School** *(if applicable)*

16. Additional Contact Phone Numbers

☐ Home   ☐ Cell
☐ Work

☐ Home   ☐ Cell
☐ Work

17. Permanent Address - *If P.O. Box is listed under Mailing Address **or** if residence is different from Mailing Address.*

Street/RFD # or URB *(No P.O. Box)*

Apartment/Unit

City

State   Zip Code

18. Emergency Contact - *Provide the information of a person not traveling with you to be contacted in the event of an emergency.*

Name   Address: Street/RFD # or P.O. Box   Apartment/Unit

City   State   Zip Code   Phone Number   Relationship

19. Travel Plans

Date of Trip *(mm/dd/yyyy)*   Duration of Trip   Countries to be Visited

20. Have you ever been married?   ☐ Yes   ☐ No   *If yes, complete the remaining items in #20.*

Full Name of Current Spouse or Most Recent Spouse   Date of Birth (mm/dd/yyyy)   Place of Birth   U.S. Citizen?
☐ Yes   ☐ No

Date of Marriage
(mm/dd/yyyy)   Have you ever been widowed or divorced?   ☐ Yes   Date *(mm/dd/yyyy)*
                                                                       ☐ No

21. Have you ever applied for or been issued a <u>U.S. Passport Book</u>?   ☐ Yes   ☐ No   *If yes, complete the remaining items in #21*

Name as printed on your most recent passport book   Most recent passport book number

Status of your most recent passport book
☐ Submitting with application   ☐ Stolen   ☐ Lost   ☐ In my possession *(if expired)*   Date most recent passport book was issued
or approximate date you applied *(mm/dd/yyyy)*

22. Have you ever applied for or been issued a <u>U.S. Passport Card</u>?   ☐ Yes   ☐ No   *If yes, complete the remaining items in #22*

Name as printed on your most recent passport card   Most recent passport card number

Status of your most recent passport card
☐ Submitting with application   ☐ Stolen   ☐ Lost   ☐ In my possession *(if expired)*   Date most recent passport card was issued
or approximate date you applied *(mm/dd/yyyy)*

PLEASE DO NOT WRITE BELOW THIS LINE

FOR ISSUING OFFICE ONLY

☐ Sole Parent

Name as it appears on citizenship evidence _____

☐ Birth Certificate   SR   CR   City   Filed: Issued:

☐ Report of Birth   240   545   1350   Filed/City:

☐ Nat. / Citz. Cert.   Date/Place Acquired: A#

☐ Passport   C/R   S/R   Per PIERS   #/DOI:

☐ Other:

☐ Attached:

☐ P/C of ID   ☐ DS-3053   ☐ DS-64   ☐ Bio Quest   ☐ Citz W/S   ☐ DS-10   ☐ DS-86   ☐ DS-71   ☐ DS-60

* DS 11 C 12 2010 2 *

DS-11 12-2010   Page 2 of 2

APPENDIX 13-10

Application for Consular Report of Birth Abroad and Sample Affidavit Form DS-2029

U.S. Department of State

INSTRUCTIONS

APPLICATION FOR CONSULAR REPORT OF BIRTH ABROAD
OF A CITIZEN OF THE UNITED STATES OF AMERICA

A Consular Report of Birth Abroad may be issued for any U.S. citizen child under the age of 18 who was born abroad and who acquired U.S. citizenship at birth. Only the child's parent(s), legal guardian, person acting in loco parentis or the child may apply on the child's behalf. The application generally must be signed before a U.S. consular officer, a consular agent, or, in the case of children born in U.S. military hospitals, a designated military official. A Consular Report of Birth Abroad is proof of U.S. citizenship; however, **it is not a travel document** and does not take the place of a passport for travel purposes.

IMPORTANT: You **MUST** provide the required evidence listed below before we can process the application. Please follow the instructions below.

STEP 1: Read the instructions before completing and submitting this application. The instructions contain important information about completing the application and list what documents can be submitted as evidence to support the application.

STEP 2: Complete the application.

STEP 3: Make an appointment with the U.S. embassy or consulate online or contact the U.S. consular agency or designated U.S. military official.

STEP 4: Assemble the required documentary evidence. Take the application and supporting documents with you to your appointment at the U.S. embassy, consulate, consular agency, or with a military acceptance agent. NOTE: Do not sign the application until you are before a designated U.S. consular official or military acceptance agent.

STEP 5: Once the citizenship claim has been approved, the Consular Report of Birth Abroad will be printed in the United States and sent to the address you designate in the United States or the address you designate abroad in countries where the mailing of U.S. citizenship documents is permitted unless you indicate that you will pick it up at the U.S. embassy, consulate or consular agency.

ABOUT YOUR DOCUMENTS

• You must submit **ORIGINAL** documents or **copies certified by the custodian of the record**. Generally, we will return your documents after we have seen them.
• **We cannot accept photocopies or notarized copies of documents.**

DOCUMENTS WE NEED TO SEE

When applying for a Consular Report of Birth Abroad for a child who has never been documented as a U.S. citizen, the documentary evidence listed below should be presented. In certain instances, additional evidence may be required. Unless otherwise provided, all documentation submitted must be originals or certified copies of the originals bearing the seal of the issuing vital records office, court, or other authority.

1. Child's birth certificate.
2. Evidence of the parent(s)' U.S. citizenship and identity. This may consist of a U.S. passport, U.S. passport card, Consular Report of Birth Abroad, Naturalization Certificate, Certificate of Citizenship or timely filed U.S. birth certificate. For other forms of acceptable U.S. citizenship evidence, contact the U.S. consul. A passport or government issued Photo ID must be presented as proof of identity.
3. Evidence of the U.S. citizen parent(s)' physical presence or residence in the United States prior to the birth of the child. Such evidence may include, but is not limited to affidavits, school, employment, tax, bank, and medical records, utility bills, rent receipts, or other official public documents. Evidence of time spent abroad working for the U.S. government, U.S. Armed Forces or qualifying international organization, or as a dependent child of a person working abroad for such entities prior to the birth of the child is also acceptable in some cases.
4. Parents' marriage certificate, if applicable.
5. Evidence of the termination of any previous marriages of the parents (divorce decree, annulment decree, or death certificate).
6. If a person other than a parent or the child is applying for the Consular Report of Birth Abroad, the person must present a certified copy of legal guardianship or notarized affidavit from the parent(s) authorizing the person to make the application.

HOW TO COMPLETE THIS APPLICATION

Most of the items on the form are self-explanatory with the exception of the items discussed below. The numbers match the numbered items on the form.

1. **Name of Child in Full:** Enter the name of the child as it is recorded on the local birth certificate. If a different name is shown on the birth certificate, an explanatory affidavit from the parent or legal guardian must be presented regarding the correct name. When a child's name has been legally changed by adoption or certain other legal action amending the child's name from birth, the new name may be recorded on the application if supported by documentary evidence.

2. **Sex:** Check (X) box to indicate whether male or female.

3. **Date of Birth:** Write the month before the date and year. (Example: 10/2/2009).
(month)(day)(year)

4. **Place of Birth:** Enter the name of the city and country.

Mother/Father/Parent. NOTE: If the U.S. citizen parent transmitting citizenship to the child is not present, he or she may complete State Department Form DS 5507 Affidavit of Parentage Physical Presence and Support and submit separately. The parent completing this application should provide as much information on the parent completing the Form DS 5507 as he or she has.)

INFORMATION ABOUT MOTHER/FATHER/PARENT

5 and 11. **Full Name:** Enter Mother/Father/Parent's name as it appears on the passport and/or government issued identity document.

6 and 12. **All Previous Legal Names:** Enter all legal names ever used by father, including name at birth.

7 and 13. **Sex:** Check (X) box to indicate whether male or female.

8 and 14. **Date of Birth:** Write the month before the day and year. (Example: 10/2/2009).
(month)(day)(year)

9 and 15. **Place of Birth:** Enter the name of the city, state/province (if applicable) and country.

10 and 16. **Current Physical Address (Do not list a P.O. Box) (You may list an A.P.O. Address):** Enter the address in the foreign country where the application is completed.

17. Enter Mailing Address

18 and 19. **Citizenship:** Please place an "X" in the "yes" box or the "no" box to indicate whether you are a U.S. citizen.

20. Enter yes or no if you and U.S. citizen parent of child were/was married to the child's other biological parent when the child was born.

21. List Date and Place of marriage and check current status of that marriage, adding date of death or divorce if applicable.

22 and 23. **Marriage(s):** Please list any other marriages as follows: Date of marriage; end date, if any; and manner ended, if applicable. If you have never been married, enter "none."

24 and 25. **Time spent in the United States:** List all dates you have been present in the United States.

26 and 27. Time spent abroad in U.S. Armed Forces, in other U.S. Government employment, with qualifying international organization, or as a dependent child of a person so employed: Official documentation of relevant periods of service from the appropriate governmental department or international organization must be presented. For names of qualifying organizations, consult the U.S. embassy or consulate.

28. Do not sign until you are appearing before the person administering the oath/affirmation.

29. Do not sign until you are appearing before the person administering the oath/affirmation.

30. The U.S. embassy or consulate official approving the issuance of the Consular Report of Birth Abroad will enter the serial number of the Consular Report of Birth Abroad and the date and place of issuance before signing this section.

U.S. Department of State

APPLICATION FOR CONSULAR REPORT OF BIRTH ABROAD
OF A CITIZEN OF THE UNITED STATES OF AMERICA

OMB NO. 1405-0011
EXPIRES: 02/29/2016
Estimated Burden: 20 minutes

Registration Number _____

A. THIS SECTION TO BE COMPLETED BY THE CHILD'S PARENT(S) OR GUARDIAN(S) OR THE CHILD *(USE SECTION D CONTINUATION SHEET)*

INFORMATION ABOUT THE CHILD

1. Name of Child in Full

_____   _____   _____
(Last/Surname)   *(First)*   *(Middle)*

2. Sex   3. Date of Birth   4. Place of Birth

☐M ☐F   ___/___/___   _____   _____
(month) (day) (year)   *(City)*   *(Country)*

NOTE: *(If the U.S. citizen parent transmitting citizenship to the child is not present, he or she may complete State Department Form DS 5507 Affidavit of Parentage Physical Presence and Support and submit it separately. The parent completing this application should provide as much information on the parent completing the Form DS 5507 as he or she has.)*

INFORMATION ON MOTHER/FATHER/PARENT	INFORMATION ON MOTHER/FATHER/PARENT
5. Full Name	11. Full Name
_____ _____ _____ *(Last/Surname)* *(First)* *(Middle)*	_____ _____ _____ *(Last/Surname)* *(First)* *(Middle)*
6. All Previous Legal Names Used	12. All Previous Legal Names Used
_____ _____ _____ *(Last/Surname)* *(First)* *(Middle)*	_____ _____ _____ *(Last/Surname)* *(First)* *(Middle)*
_____ _____ _____ *(Last/Surname)* *(First)* *(Middle)*	_____ _____ _____ *(Last/Surname)* *(First)* *(Middle)*
7. Sex 8. Date of Birth ☐M ☐F ___/___/___ *(month) (day) (year)*	13. Sex 14. Date of Birth ☐M ☐F ___/___/___ *(month) (day) (year)*
9. Place of Birth _____ _____ _____ *(City)* *(State/Province)* *(Country)*	15. Place of Birth _____ _____ _____ *(City)* *(State/Province)* *(Country)*
10. Current Physical Address *(Do not list P.O. Box)* *(A.P.O. Address Permitted)* _____ *(Address Line 1)* _____ *(City, State/Province, Country, Postal Code)* _____ *(Phone Number(s))* _____ *(Email Address)*	16. Current Physical Address *(Do not list P.O. Box)* *(A.P.O. Address Permitted)* _____ *(Address Line 1)* _____ *(City, State/Province, Country, Postal Code)* _____ *(Phone Number(s))* _____ *(Email Address)*
Use this address if Consular Report of Birth will be mailed? ☐Yes ☐No	Use this address if Consular Report of Birth will be mailed? ☐Yes ☐No

17. Mailing Address *(if different from Current Physical Address) (Do not list a P.O. Box.)*
(You may list an A.P.O. address)

_____   _____
(Address Line 1)   *(City, State/Province, Country and Postal Code)*

DS-2029
04-2013

Page 1 of 7

(Continued) **INFORMATION ON MOTHER/FATHER/PARENT**	*(Continued)* **INFORMATION ON MOTHER/FATHER/PARENT**
18. Citizenship Are you a U.S. Citizen or U.S. Non-Citizen National? ☐ Yes ☐ No	19. Citizenship Are you a U.S. Citizen or U.S. Non-Citizen National? ☐ Yes ☐ No

MARITAL STATUS OF THE PARENTS

20. Were you married to the child's other biological parent when the child was born? ☐ Yes ☐ No

21. Date and Place of Marriage to the child's other biological parent and current status

___ / ___ / _____   _____   _____   _____
(month) (day) (year)   (City)   (State/Province)   (Country)

☐ Still Married   ☐ Divorced ___ / ___ / _____   ☐ Death ___ / ___ / _____
                              (month)(day)(year)   (month)(day)(year)

(Continued) **INFORMATION ON MOTHER/FATHER/PARENT**	*(Continued)* **INFORMATION ON MOTHER/FATHER/PARENT**
22. Please list any other marriages *(Show Name(s) of Spouse(s), Dates and Current Status)* if applicable *(Death, Divorce, Still Married)*. If you have never been married, enter "None." *(If additional space is needed, please use the Section D Continuation Sheet)*	23. Please list any other marriages *(Show Name(s) of Spouse(s), Dates and Current Status)* if applicable *(Death, Divorce, Still Married)*. If you have never been married, enter "None." *(If additional space is needed, please use the Section D Continuation Sheet)*

24. Precise Periods of Time in United States
(if additional space is needed, please use the Section D Continuation Sheet)

Place *(City, State)*	Date *(month-day-year)*	Date *(month-day-year)*
	From	To
	From	To
	From	To
	From	To
	From	To
	From	To
	From	To
	From	To
	From	To
	From	To

25. Precise Periods of Time in United States
(if additional space is needed, please use the Section D Continuation Sheet)

Place *(City, State)*	Date *(month-day-year)*	Date *(month-day-year)*
	From	To
	From	To
	From	To
	From	To
	From	To
	From	To
	From	To
	From	To
	From	To
	From	To

(Continued)		
INFORMATION ON MOTHER/FATHER/PARENT		

26. Precise Periods Abroad in U.S. Armed Forces, in other U.S. Government Employment, with Qualifying International Organization, or as a dependent child of a person so employed *(Specify)* *(if additional space is needed please use the Section D Continuation Sheet)*

Branch/Agency/Org.	Date (month-day-year)	Date (month-day-year)
	From	To
	From	To
	From	To
	From	To
	From	To
	From	To
	From	To
	From	To
	From	To
	From	To

(Continued)		
INFORMATION ON MOTHER/FATHER/PARENT		

27. Precise Periods Abroad in U.S. Armed Forces, in other U.S. Government Employment, with Qualifying International Organization, or as a dependent child of a person so employed *(Specify)* *(if additional space is needed please use the Section D Continuation Sheet)*

Branch/Agency/Org.	Date (month-day-year)	Date (month-day-year)
	From	To
	From	To
	From	To
	From	To
	From	To
	From	To
	From	To
	From	To
	From	To
	From	To

B.   THIS SECTION TO BE COMPLETED BEFORE/BY CONSULAR OFFICER, NOTARY PUBLIC, OR OTHER PERSON QUALIFIED TO ADMINISTER OATH

NOTE: If a U.S. citizen parent transmitting citizenship to the child born out of wedlock is not present, he or she may complete State Department Form DS 5507 Affidavit of Parentage Physical Presence and Support and submit separately. Only the U.S. citizen father of a child born abroad out of wedlock must complete the acknowledgement of paternity and agreement to provide financial support.

28. I _____ do solemnly swear *(or affirm)* *(check all that apply)*

(Name)

☐ I am a U.S. citizen or non-citizen national.   ☐ I am the father of _____ ,

(Name of Child)

who was born on _____ in _____ .   ☐ My child was born out of wedlock, and I am the

(Date of Birth)   *(Place of Birth)*

the father through whom he/she is claiming U.S. citizenship.   ☐ I agree to provide financial support for this child until he/she reaches the age of eighteen

_____

(Signature of Affiant)

SUBSCRIBED AND SWORN TO *(AFFIRMED)* before me this _____ day of _____ , _____

_____

(Signature and Title of Administering Officer)

(SEAL)

(Continued)
THIS SECTION TO BE COMPLETED BEFORE/BY CONSULAR OFFICER, NOTARY PUBLIC, OR OTHER PERSON QUALIFIED TO ADMINISTER OATHS

29. Affirmation: I SOLEMNLY SWEAR (OR AFFIRM) THAT THE STATEMENTS MADE ON THIS APPLICATION ARE TRUE TO THE BEST OF MY KNOWLEDGE AND BELIEF.

Name of Person(s) Providing Information   Relationship to the Child
(Parent, Legal Guardian, Other (Specify))   Signature of Person(s) Providing Information

_____   _____   _____

Type Name and Title of Official   Signature of Official   City   Date

_____   _____   _____   ___ / ___ / ___
                                                                (month) (day)   (year)

Subscribed to: *(SEAL)*

---

30. Approval of Consular Report of Birth

_____   _____
(Printed Name of Consular Officer)   *(Signature of Consular Officer)*

_____   ___ / ___ / ___   _____
(Approving Post)   *(month) (day)   (year)*   *(Registration Number)*
                        (Date of Approval)

C. THIS SECTION TO BE COMPLETED BY CONSULAR OFFICER

31. Documents Presented - Please mark accordingly and provide date of document. (If more space is required, list on separate page)

☐ Child's Birth Certificate ___/___/___ _____ _____ _____
                   (month) (day) (year)   (City)   (Province)   (Country)

☐ Marriage Certificate ___/___/___ ___/___/___ _____ _____
              (month)(day) (year) (month)(day) (year)   (City)   (State)
              (File Date)   (Date of Issuance)

            _____ _____
               (Province)   (Country)

☐ Divorce Decree(s) (a) ___/___/___ ___/___/___ _____ _____
              (month)(day) (year) (month)(day) (year)   (City)   (State)
              (File Date)   (Date of Issuance)

            _____ _____
               (Province)   (Country)

        (b) ___/___/___ ___/___/___ _____ _____
              (month)(day) (year) (month)(day) (year)   (City)   (State)
              (File Date)   (Date of Issuance)

            _____ _____
               (Province)   (Country)

        (c) ___/___/___ ___/___/___ _____ _____
              (month)(day) (year) (month)(day) (year)   (City)   (State)
              (File Date)   (Date of Issuance)

            _____ _____
               (Province)   (Country)

☐ Death Certificate(s) (a) ___/___/___ _____ _____
              (month) (day) (year)   (City)   (State)

         (b) ___/___/___ _____ _____
              (month) (day) (year)   (City)   (State)

☐ Mother/Father/Parent's Passport _____ ___/___/___ _____
                   (Passport Number) (month) (day) (year)   (Nationality)
                                     (Date of Issuance)

☐ Mother/Father/Parent's Passport _____ ___/___/___ _____
                   (Passport Number) (month) (day) (year)   (Nationality)
                                       (Date of Issuance)

☐ Other Identity Document of Mother/Father/Parent (e.g. Naturalization Certificate) _____ _____ ___/___/___
                                      (Name of the Citizenship Document) (Document Number) (month) (day) (year)
                                                          (Date of Issuance)

☐ Other Identity Document of Mother/Father/Parent (e.g. Naturalization Certificate) _____ _____ ___/___/___
                                      (Name of the Citizenship Document) (Document Number) (month) (day) (year)
                                                          (Date of Issuance)

☐ Other Identity Document of Mother/Father/Parent (e.g. Driver's License) _____ _____ ___/___/___
                                        (Name of the Identity Document) (Document Number) (month) (day) (year)
                                                            (Date of Issuance)

☐ Other Identity Document of Mother/Father/Parent (e.g. Driver's License) _____ _____ ___/___/___
                                        (Name of the Identity Document) (Document Number) (month) (day) (year)
                                                            (Date of Issuance)

☐ Other (Legal Guardianship; Power of Attorney, etc.) _____ _____ ___/___/___
                                        (Name of the Document) (Document Number) (month) (day) (year)
                                                           (Date of Issuance)

D.	CONTINUATION SHEET *(USE THIS SPACE FOR ADDITIONAL INFORMATION)*

PRIVACY ACT STATEMENT

AUTHORITY: The information solicited on this form is requested pursuant to provisions in Titles 8 and 22 of the United States Code (U.S.C.), whether or not codified, including specifically 22 U.S.C. 2705 and predecessor statutes, and by regulations issued pursuant to E.O. 11295 (August 5, 1966), including Part 50, Title 22 Code of Federal Regulations (CFR).

PURPOSE: The primary purpose for soliciting the information is to establish citizenship, identity, and entitlement to issuance of a Consular Report of Birth and to properly administer and enforce the laws pertaining thereto. The information may also be used in connection with issuing other evidence of citizenship, and in furtherance of the Secretary's responsibility for the protection of U.S. nationals abroad.

ROUTINE USES: The information solicited on this form may be made available as a routine use to other government agencies, to assist the U.S. Department of State in adjudicating passport applications and requests for related services, and for law enforcement and administrative purposes. It may also be disclosed pursuant to court order. The information may be made available to foreign government agencies to fulfill passport control and immigration duties. The information may also be provided to foreign government agencies, international organizations and, in limited cases, private persons and organizations to investigate, prosecute, or otherwise address possible violations of law or to further the Secretary's responsibility for the protection of U.S. nationals abroad. The information may be made available to private U.S. citizen 'wardens' designated by the U.S. embassies and consulates. More information on the Routine Uses for the form can be found in the System of Records Notice, Public Notice 6209 for May 2, 2008. The title of this notice is Overseas Citizens Services Records.

DISCLOSURE: Providing the information requested on this form is voluntary. Failure to provide the information requested on this form may result in the denial of a Consular Report of Birth, related document or service to the individual seeking such report, document or service.

PAPERWORK REDUCTION ACT (PRA) STATEMENT

Public reporting burden for this collection of information is estimated to average 20 minutes per response, including time required for searching existing data sources, gathering the necessary documentation, providing the information and/or documents required, and reviewing the final collection. You do not have to supply this information unless this collection displays a currently valid OMB control number. If you have comments on the accuracy of this burden estimate and/or recommendations for reducing it, please send them to: CA/OCS/L, SA-29, 4th Floor, U.S. Department of State, Washington, DC 20037-3202.

DS-2029   Page 7 of 7

APPENDIX 13-11

Statement of Consent or Special Circumstances: Issuance of a Passport to a Minor Under Age 16

STATEMENT OF CONSENT OR SPECIAL CIRCUMSTANCES: ISSUANCE OF A PASSPORT TO A MINOR UNDER AGE 16

HOW DO I USE THIS FORM?

FORM INSTRUCTIONS
1. **Complete items 1, 2, and 3.**
2. **Complete item 4a**, Statement of Consent, **only** if you are a non-applying parent or guardian consenting to the issuance of a passport for your minor child. **NOTE: Your signature must be witnessed and notarized in item 4b.**
3. The written consent from the non-applying parent that accompanies an application for a new passport must **not** be **more than 3 months old.** A photocopy of the front and back side of the non-applying parent's identification is **required** with the written consent.
4. **Complete item 5**, Statement of Special Circumstances, **only** if you are an applying parent or guardian and the written consent of the non-applying parent or guardian cannot be obtained. The statement must explain **in detail** the non-applying parent's unavailability and recent efforts made to contact the non-applying parent.

> **WARNING:** **False statements made knowingly and willfully on passport applications, including affidavits or other supporting documents submitted therewith, may be punishable by fine and/or imprisonment under U.S. law, including the provisions of 18 U.S.C. 1001, 18 U.S.C. 1542, and/or 18 U.S.C. 1621.**

FOR INFORMATION, QUESTIONS, AND INQUIRIES

Please visit our website at **travel.state.gov**. In addition, contact the National Passport Information Center (NPIC) toll-free at 1-877-487-2778 (TDD 1-888-874-7793) or by e-mail at **NPIC@state.gov**. Customer Service Representatives are available Monday-Friday, 8:00a.m.-10:00p.m. Eastern Time (excluding federal holidays). Automated information is available 24/7.

PRIVACY ACT STATEMENT

AUTHORITIES: Collection of the information solicited on this form is authorized by Titles 8, 22, and 26 of the United States Code, and other applicable laws and regulations, including 22 USC 211a et seq.; 8 USC 1104; 26 USC 6039E, Section 236 of the Admiral James W. Nance and Meg Donovan Foreign Relations Authorization Act, Fiscal Years 2000 and 2001; Executive Order 11295 (August 5, 1966); and 22 CFR parts 50 and 51.

PURPOSE: The primary purpose for soliciting the information is to establish citizenship, identity, and entitlement to issuance of a U.S. passport.

ROUTINE USES: The information solicited on this form may be made available as a routine use to other government agencies and private contractors to assist the U.S. Department of State in adjudicating passport applications and requests for related services, and for law enforcement, fraud prevention, border security, counterterrorism, litigation activities, and administrative purposes. The information may be made available to foreign government agencies to fulfill passport control and immigration duties. The information may also be provided to foreign government agencies, international organizations and, in limited cases, private persons and organizations to investigate, prosecute, or otherwise address potential violations of law or to further the Secretary's responsibility for the protection of U.S. citizens and non-citizen nationals abroad. The information may be made available to the Department of Homeland Security and private employers for employment verification purposes. For a more detailed listing of the routine uses to which this information may be put see the Department of State's Prefatory Statement of Routine Uses relative to the Privacy Act (Public Notice 6290 of July 15, 2008) and the listing of routine users set forth in the System of Records Notices for Overseas Citizen Services Records (State-05) and Passport Records (State-26) published in the Federal Register.

CONSEQUENCES OF FAILURE TO PROVIDE INFORMATION: Failure to provide the information requested on this form may result in Passport Services' refusal to accept your application or result in the denial of a U.S. passport.

PAPERWORK REDUCTION ACT STATEMENT

Public reporting burden for this collection of information is estimated to average 60 minutes per response, including the time required for searching existing data sources, gathering the necessary data, providing the information and/or documentation required, and reviewing the final collection. You do not have to supply this information unless this collection displays a currently valid OMB control number. If you have comments on the accuracy of this burden estimate and/or recommendations for reducing it, please send them to: A/GIS/DIR, Room 2400 SA-22, U.S. Department of State, Washington, DC 20520-2202.

DS-3053 12-2010

Page 1 of 2

**STATEMENT OF CONSENT OR SPECIAL CIRCUMSTANCES:
ISSUANCE OF A PASSPORT TO A MINOR UNDER AGE 16**
Attention: Read WARNING and FORM INSTRUCTIONS on page 1

OMB APPROVAL NO: 1405-0129
EXPIRATION DATE: 12-31-2013
ESTIMATED BURDEN: 60 Minutes

1. MINOR'S NAME

Last		First		Middle	

2. MINOR'S DATE OF BIRTH (mm/dd/yyyy)

3. YOUR RELATIONSHIP TO MINOR

4a. STATEMENT OF CONSENT To be completed by the non-applying parent or guardian when he or she will not be present at the time the applying parent or guardian submits the minor's application. Statement must **not** be more than 3 months old.

I, _____ , give my consent to the issuance of a United States passport to
                    Print Your Name

my minor child named on this application.

OATH: I declare under penalty of perjury that all statements made in this supporting document are true and correct.

_____   _____
Signature of Parent or Guardian   Date (mm/dd/yyyy)

4b. STATEMENT OF CONSENT NOTARIZATION

Name of Notary   _____
                              Print Name

Location   _____
                        City, State

Commission Expires   _____
                                    Date (mm/dd/yyyy)

Signature of Notary   _____

NOTARY
SEAL

Date of
Notarization _____   Identification Presented
                    Date (mm/dd/yyyy)   by Non-Applying Parent or
                                          Guardian:

☐ Driver's License   ☐ Passport   ☐ Military Identification

☐ Other (specify) _____

Place of Issue: _____   Issue Date: _____

ID Number: _____

5. STATEMENT OF SPECIAL CIRCUMSTANCES To be completed by applying parent or guardian when the written consent of the non-applying parent or guardian cannot be obtained. The statement must explain **in detail** the non-applying parent's unavailability and recent efforts made to contact the non-applying parent. **Attach additional pages if needed.**

OATH: I declare under penalty of perjury that all statements made in this supporting document are true and correct.

_____   _____
Signature of Parent or Guardian   Date (mm/dd/yyyy)

DS-3053 12-2010

Page 2 of 2

1189

APPENDIX 13-12

7 FAM 1300, Appendix M: Gender Change

U.S. Department of State Foreign Affairs Manual – Volume 7 Consular Affairs

7 FAM 1300 APPENDIX M
GENDER CHANGE

(CT:CON-351; 01-20-2011)
(Office of Origin: CA/OCS/PRI)

7 FAM 1310 APPENDIX M SUMMARY

(CT:CON-351; 01-20-2011)

a. This appendix provides policy and procedures that passport specialists and consular officers must follow in cases in which an applicant requests a gender on the passport application different from the one reflected on some or all of the submitted citizenship and/or identity evidence, including a prior passport.

b. This policy explains the need for medical certification from a *licensed* physician *who has treated the applicant or reviewed and evaluated the medical history of the applicant* regarding the change in gender, as well as the need for accurate identification and a photograph reflecting the applicant's current appearance. It is based on standards and recommendations of the World Professional Association for Transgender Health (WPATH), recognized as the authority in this field by the American Medical Association.

c. A passport is defined by INA 101(a)(30) (Immigration and Nationality Act) (8 U.S.C. 1101(a)(30)) as "any travel document issued by competent authority showing the bearer's origin, identity, and nationality if any, which is valid for the entry of the bearer into a foreign country." An individual's gender is an integral part of that person's identity.

d. Sexual reassignment surgery is not a prerequisite for passport issuance.

e. Medical certification of gender transition from a *licensed* physician as described in 7 FAM 1320 Appendix M is the only documentation of gender change required. Other medical records are not to be requested. If a passport *specialist* or consular officer has questions about this guidance or a particular case, see 7 FAM *1370* Appendix M.

7 FAM 1320 APPENDIX M DOCUMENTS TO BE SUBMITTED WITH PASSPORT APPLICATION

(CT:CON-351; 01-20-2011)

U.S. Department of State Foreign Affairs Manual – Volume 7 Consular Affairs

a. Requirements for all elements of the passport application aside from gender still apply, including:

    (1) **Evidence of U.S. citizenship/nationality.** The applicant must submit acceptable evidence of U.S. citizenship or nationality. (See 7 FAM 1100 Acquisition and Retention of U.S. Citizenship and Nationality.) It is not necessary, however, for the applicant to obtain an amended birth record reflecting the change of gender. State law in the United States and the laws of other countries vary on whether an amended birth certificate may be issued reflecting a gender change;

    (2) **Evidence of identity.** The applicant must be asked to submit acceptable evidence of identity in the new gender, if available, and must submit evidence of the new name, if changed. (See 7 FAM 1320.) State law and foreign laws vary as to whether a driver's license or other State government form of identity document may be issued reflecting a gender change. If evidence of change of gender in the identity documents is not obtainable because of state or local requirements, the passport may still be issued in the new gender based on the medical certification outlined below in paragraph b(1)(f).;

    (3) **Photograph.** A recent photograph that reflects a good likeness of, and satisfactorily identifies the applicant must be submitted. The photograph must agree with the submitted identification evidence and reflect the applicant's current and true appearance. (See also 7 FAM 1300 Appendix E Passport Photographs.)

    (4) **Passport Fee.** All necessary passport fees must be submitted. (See 7 FAM 1300 Appendix G Passport Fees.)

    (5) **Name Change.** If the applicant's name has been changed, he/she must present satisfactory evidence of a legal name change. Adjudication of the name change must be handled as a routine request and conform to the requirements of 7 FAM 1300 Appendix C, Names to Be Used in Passports.

b. **Medical Certification *Accepted for Gender Change/Transition.***

    (1) A full validity U.S. passport will be issued reflecting a new gender upon presentation of a signed original statement, **on office letterhead**, from *a licensed* physician *who has treated the applicant for his/her gender-related care or reviewed and evaluated the gender-related medical history of the applicant.*

> **Note:**
> *Such licensed physicians include Medical Doctors (M.D.) and Doctors of Osteopathy (D.O.). The physicians may specialize in*

7 FAM 1300 Appendix M Page 2 of 10

U.S. Department of State Foreign Affairs Manual – Volume 7 Consular Affairs

> *various medical fields, including, but not limited to, internists, endocrinologists, gynecologists, urologists, surgeons, psychiatrists, pediatricians, and family practitioners.*
>
> *Statements from persons who are not licensed physicians, such as psychologists, nurse practitioners, health practitioners, chiropractors, are not acceptable.*

The statement **must** include the following information (See 7 FAM 1320 Appendix M Exhibit B):

(a)   Physician's full name;

(b)   Medical license or certificate number;

(c)   Issuing state, *country*, or other jurisdiction of medical license/certificate;

(d)   Drug Enforcement Administration (DEA) registration number assigned to the *doctor or comparable foreign registration number, if applicable;*

   (i)   *If the U.S.-based licensed physician does not provide a DEA number, you must request that this be provided in a new statement. If the statement with the DEA number is not provided after an appropriate period of time (generally 90 days), the application must be denied.*

   (ii)   *Licensed physicians in foreign countries might not have a DEA number, but might have a comparable foreign registration number. Domestic passport agencies/centers must scan copies of the application and attach all submitted documents to the Adjudication Policy Division (CA/PPT/A/AP) at CA-PPT-AdjQ@state.gov. CA/PPT/A/AP will work with the Directorate of Overseas Citizens Services' Office of Policy Review and Inter Agency Liaison (CA/OCS/PRI) to verify the bona fides of the foreign physician with the applicable post abroad.*

   (iii)   *Posts must verify their own foreign-based licensed physicians or, if the statement is from a physician in another country, contact the post which covers that country for verification.*

(e)   Address and telephone number of the physician;

(f)   Language stating that he/she *has treated* the applicant *or has reviewed and evaluated the medical history of the applicant* and that he/she has a doctor/patient relationship with the applicant;

7 FAM 1300 Appendix M Page 3 of 10

U.S. Department of State Foreign Affairs Manual – Volume 7 Consular Affairs

(g) Language stating the applicant has had appropriate clinical treatment for gender transition to the new gender *of either* male or female; *and*

(h) Language stating "I declare under penalty of perjury under the laws of the United States that the forgoing is true and correct."

(2) A two year limited validity passport reflecting the new gender will be issued upon presentation of the following:

(a) Information listed in paragraph 1(a)-(*f*) above;

(b) Language stating the applicant is in the process of gender transition to the new gender *of either* male or female; and

(c) *Language stating "I declare under penalty of perjury under the laws of the United States that the forgoing is true and correct."*

c. ***Adjudication Actions.***

(1) The passport specialist or consular officer will annotate the application "gender change" to record the reason for issuing the full validity passport in the new gender.

> ***NOTE:*** *Passport specialists and consular officers must not ask for additional specific clinical details regarding the gender change from the applicant.*

(2) The passport specialist or consular officer will annotate the application "gender transition" to record the reason for issuing the limited validity passport in the new gender. When limited passports are issued in these cases:

(a) Use endorsement code 46 for domestic and Overseas Photodigitized Passports (OPDP) issuance. Annotate the application "gender transition" to record the reason for the limited validity book in the new gender.

> *Endorsement Code 46: THIS PASSPORT EXPIRES ON (MON DAY, YEAR). IT CANNOT BE REPLACED WITHOUT THE EXPRESS AUTHORIZATION OF THE DEPARTMENT OF STATE.*

(b) Use endorsement code 109 in Emergency Photodigitized Passports (EPDPs) for urgent overseas cases where the applicant must travel immediately. Limit the EPDP to three months.

> ***Endorsement Code 109: THIS PASSPORT EXPIRES ON (mon day, year). IT CANNOT BE REPLACED WITHOUT THE***

U.S. Department of State Foreign Affairs Manual – Volume 7 Consular Affairs

> **EXPRESS AUTHORIZATION OF THE DEPARTMENT OF STATE.**

(3) An applicant will receive a passport for the remaining full validity period without further fee (except for expedited service), if:

    (a) He/she applies for the new passport within two years of issuance using Form DS-5504, Application for a U.S. Passport (Name Change, Data Correction, and Limited Passport Book Replacement); and

    (b) Meets the requirements of 7 FAM 1320 Appendix M paragraph a and 7 FAM 1320 Appendix M paragraph b(1).

    (c) Use endorsement code 3 and list the expiration date as five (for minors) or ten years from the issuance date of the original, limited validity passport book, minus one day.

> **Example (for an adult):**
>
> The issuance date of the limited passport is "July 31, 2010."
>
> The issuance date in the new full validity passport will be automatically assigned by TDIS.
>
> However, the issuance date is placed in endorsement code must be that of the original, limited passport "July 31, 2010."
>
> The expiration date listed in the endorsement must be five (for minors) or ten years from the issuance date of the original, limited validity passport book, minus one day.
>
> **Endorsement Code 3: THIS PASSPORT REPLACES (REGULAR/OFFICIAL/ DIPLOMATIC) PASSPORT NUMBER (NUMBER) ISSUED ON (MON DAY, YEAR). IT IS VALID UNTIL (MON DAY, YEAR).**

(4) If the applicant has not submitted the requested medical certification, use the appropriate Information Request Letter (IRL)

in corresponding with the passport applicant. (See also 7 FAM 1320 Appendix M Exhibit A, Example Letter Regarding Gender Change.) (See 7 FAM 1300 Appendix T for general guidance about IRLs.)

(5) *If, after two years, the applicant applies for a new passport and gender transition has not been completed, the applicant must submit a new physician's statement reflecting that the applicant still is in the process of gender transition. Another two-year validity passport will be issued.*

(6) *If an applicant is renewing his/her passport, but is applying for the renewal in a new gender, the applicant must use Form DS-11, and submit medical certification, including all elements previously stated in listed in 7 FAM 1320 Appendix M paragraph b, or birth documentation in the new gender.*

(7) *If an applicant who has been issued a passport in a new gender requests issuance of a passport in the birth gender, a certification under penalty of perjury from a licensed physician who has treated the applicant or reviewed and evaluated the medical history of applicant is required. The statement must include all the elements previously stated in 7 FAM 1320 Appendix M paragraph b.*

7 FAM 1330 APPENDIX M CONVERSATIONS WITH PASSPORT APPLICANTS SEEKING TO DOCUMENT GENDER TRANSITION

(CT:CON-334;   06-10-2010)

a. As with all passport applicants, you must be sensitive and respectful at all times.

b. Refer to the applicant by the pronoun appropriate to his/her new gender.

c. Ask only appropriate questions regarding information necessary to determine citizenship and identity of the applicant.

7 FAM 1340 APPENDIX M AMENDING GENDER IN REPORTS OF BIRTH

(CT:CON-351;   01-20-2011)

The Form FS-240, Consular Report of Birth Abroad of Citizen of the United States of America, can be amended by the Vital Records Section of Passport Services (CA/PPT/TO/RS/VR) to reflect the change in gender. The same documentary requirements specified above for passport services would pertain to amending gender in a Form FS-240. (See 7 FAM 1440, Consular Report of Birth Abroad of a Citizen/*Non-Citizen National* of the United States of America.) Inquirers should be directed to Passport Vital Records.

```
+--------------------------------------------+
|              Contact ...                   |
|                                            |
| U.S. Department of State                   |
| Passport Services                          |
| Vital Records Section                      |
| 1111 19th Street, NW, Suite 510            |
| Washington, DC 20522-1705                  |
| (202) 955-0307                             |
+--------------------------------------------+
```

7 FAM 1350 APPENDIX M INTERSEX CONDITIONS (DISORDERS OF SEX DEVELOPMENT)

(CT:CON-351;   01-20-2011)

a. *"Intersex" is a condition in which a person is born with a reproductive or sexual anatomy and/or chromosomal pattern that does not fit typical definitions of male or female.*

b. *Birth documentation is often not updated to reflect corrected gender. The applicant must provide a statement from a licensed physician who has treated the applicant for his/her gender-related care or reviewed and evaluated the gender-related medical history of the applicant. The statement must include all the information required in 7 FAM 1320 Appendix M paragraph b(1), adjusting the language to reflect the intersex condition and specify the gender correction to either male or female.*

c. *Unless the applicant provides the statement described above, the gender listed on his/her birth documentation will determine the gender to be listed in the passport.*

7 FAM 1360 APPENDIX M GENDER ERRORS IN ORIGINAL BIRTH CERTIFICATE

(CT:CON-351;   01-20-2011)

If an applicant advises that the gender on his/her birth document mistakenly lists the wrong gender due to typographical error, refer the applicant to the appropriate issuing vital records office *to have the error corrected.*

7 FAM 1370 APPENDIX M QUESTIONS

(CT:CON-334;   06-10-2010)

a. Passport agencies and centers should contact CA-PPT-ADJQ@state.gov for specific guidance.

b. U.S. embassies and consulates should contact ASKPRI@state.gov for specific guidance.

7 FAM 1380 THROUGH 1390 APPENDIX M UNASSIGNED

7 FAM 1320 APPENDIX M EXHIBIT A INFORMATION REQUEST LETTER TO APPLICANTS REGARDING GENDER CHANGE

(CT:CON-351;   01-20-2011)

Dear [Name of subject]:

Thank you for your recent passport application. We need your help in order to continue processing your request for the issuance of a passport reflecting a gender different from the one reflected on some or all of the submitted citizenship and/or identity evidence.

A full validity passport reflecting the new gender will be issued to you upon submission of a signed original statement, on office letterhead, from your *licensed* physician. The statement, signed under penalty of perjury, must include *all of* the following information:

   (a)   Physician's full name;

   (b)   Medical license or certificate number;

   (c)   Issuing state of medical license/certificate;

   (d)   Drug Enforcement Administration (DEA) registration number assigned to the physician *or comparable foreign designation, if applicable;*

   (e)   Address and telephone number of the physician;

   (f)   Language stating that he/she *has treated the applicant or reviewed and evaluated the medical history of* the applicant. He/she *also* has a doctor/patient relationship with the applicant;

   (g)   Language stating that the applicant has had appropriate clinical treatment for gender transition to the new gender (*specifying* male or female); *and*

(h) Language stating *"I declare under penalty of perjury under the laws of the United States that the foregoing is true and correct."*

If your gender transition process is ongoing, a two year limited validity passport reflecting the new gender will be issued upon submission of the items above and a statement from your *licensed* physician that you are in the process of gender transition.

If we do not receive the requested information within ninety (90) days or the information you submit is insufficient to establish your gender transition, your passport will be issued in your birth gender. If you prefer you may withdraw your application. By law, passport fees are not refundable. Any special return postage will be returned or refunded.

Sincerely,

[Signature]

[Name]

[Title]

[Name of Passport Issuing Office]

7 FAM 1320 APPENDIX M EXHIBIT B MODEL LETTER FOR LICENSED PHYSICIAN CERTIFYING TO THE APPLICANT'S GENDER CHANGE

(CT:CON-351; 01-20-2011)

Licensed Physician's Letterhead
(Physician's Address and Telephone Number)

I, (physician's full name), (physician's medical license or certificate number), (issuing *U.S.* State/*Foreign Country* of medical license/certificate), (DEA Registration number *or comparable foreign designation*), am the physician of (name of patient), with whom I have a doctor/patient relationship *and whom I have treated (or with whom I have a doctor/patient relationship and whose medical history I have reviewed and evaluated).*

(Name of patient) has had appropriate clinical treatment for gender transition to the new gender (specify new gender male or female).

U.S. Department of State Foreign Affairs Manual – Volume 7 Consular Affairs

    Or

(Name of patient) is in the process of gender transition to the new gender (specify new gender male or female).

I declare under penalty of perjury under the laws of the United States that the forgoing is true and correct.

Signature of Physician

Typed Name of Physician

Date

Chapter 14

Revocation of Naturalization

Research References

West's Key Number Digest
Aliens, Immigration, and Citizenship ⟥729 to 751

Westlaw Databases
Steel on Immigration Law (STEEL)
Immigration Law Service (2d ed.) (IMMLS2D)

Treatises and Practice Aids
Steel on Immigration Law §§ 15:25, 15:27

KeyCite®: Cases and other legal materials listed in KeyCite Scope can be researched through the KeyCite service on Westlaw®. Use KeyCite to check citations for form, parallel references, prior and later history, and comprehensive citator information, including citations to other decisions and secondary materials.

I.   INTRODUCTION

§ 14:1   Overview

Research References

A.L.R. Index, Immigration and Naturalization
Dizon and Wettstein, Immigration Law Service 2d §§ 14:386, 14:387
Steel on Immigration Law § 15:27

The Immigration and Nationality Act contains two provisions for denaturalization.[1] One creates a civil denaturalization procedure to revoke admissions to citizenship and cancel certificates of naturalization obtained by fraud or misrepresentation, or otherwise obtained contrary to law.[2] The other allows the setting aside of admission to citizenship where there has been a criminal conviction for

---

[Section 14:1]

[1] INA § 340(a), (e), 8 U.S.C.A. § 1451(a), (e).

[2] INA § 340(a), 8 U.S.C.A. § 1451(a).

procuring naturalization by fraud.[3] Both of these procedures will be discussed in this chapter. Finally, naturalized citizens may be subject to loss of citizenship under the same provisions that apply to native-born citizens. These provisions are discussed in the next chapter.[4]

The judicial denaturalization procedures discussed in this chapter are used to revoke naturalization whether it was obtained under the present act or under any prior law.[5] Indeed, these have been held to be the only provisions under which the U.S. Attorney may bring denaturalization proceedings on the grounds of fraud or illegality.[6] There is no statute of limitations, and revocation proceedings may be brought many years after the original naturalization.[7] These judicial proceedings are also used to revoke citizenship obtained through administrative proceedings, and even to revoke U.S. citizenship resumed by taking the oath of allegiance before a U.S. consular officer abroad.[8]

When naturalization was transformed into mainly an administrative proceeding in 1990, the INA was also amended to transfer to the Attorney General the power previously held by the courts to reopen their own naturalization decisions.[9] The legacy INS started a campaign to extensively use these procedures. In preparation for this campaign, the INS published a final rule on administrative denaturalization,[10] and also issued additional guidance to its district offices.[11] However, on February 14, 2001, a district court issued a permanent injunction prohibiting the government

---

[3]INA § 340(e), 8 U.S.C.A. § 1451(e). See § 14:29.

[4]See §§ 15:1 et seq.

[5]INA § 340(h), 8 U.S.C.A. § 1451(h).

[6]Bindczyck v. Finucane, 342 U.S. 76, 79, 72 S.Ct. 130, 132, 96 L.Ed. 100 (1951); Simons v. U.S., 452 F.2d 1110, 1115 (2d Cir. 1971) (J. Friendly); Petition of De Roma, 603 F.Supp. 127, 131 (D.N.J. 1985). In U.S. v. Zucca, 351 U.S. 91, 99, 76 S.Ct. 671, 676, 100 L.Ed. 964 (1956), the Supreme Court used an even more sweeping statement to the effect that section 340(a) is the only section under which the Attorney General can institute denaturalization proceedings. Under a previous version of the statute, courts interpreted this statement as being limited to plenary actions by the Attorney General, since former section 340(j) allowed the Attorney General to proceed with denaturalization by a motion under the Federal Rules of Civil Procedure Rule 60(b). Simons v. U.S., 452 F.2d 1110, 1115 n. 6 (2d Cir. 1971). See also, Petition of Tabilos, 637 F.Supp. 969, 971 (N.D.Cal. 1986) (discussing conflicting holdings of district courts regarding the scope of the predecessor to section 340(h)). In 1990, Congress deleted former section 340(j) and inserted the current savings clause found in INA § 340(h), 8 U.S.C.A. § 1451(h). See Gorbach v. Reno, 219 F.3d 1087, 1096-98 (9th Cir. 2000) (explaining history and relying, *inter alia*, on Bindczvk and Zucca to hold that current INA § 340(h) does not grant the Attorney General the power to denaturalize citizens). See § 14:30.

[7]Costello v. U.S., 365 U.S. 265, 281–84, 81 S.Ct. 534, 542–44, 5 L.Ed.2d 551 (1961); INS Interp. 340.1(d). See generally Gordon & Mailman, § 100.02[1][e]. Little or no authority would support the existence of other equitable defenses such as estoppels and laches, but the case law does not seem to preclude such arguments at this point. See, e.g., U.S. v. Rebelo, 358 F.Supp.2d 400, 412-13 (D.N.J. 2005).

[8]See U.S. v. Rojas-Vasquez, 97 F.Supp. 550 (W.D.Tex. 1951).

[9]See § 14:30.

[10]61 Fed. Reg. 55550 (Oct. 28, 1996) adding 8 CFR § 340.1.

[11]INS Implementation Guidelines: INA § 340(h), 8 CFR § 340.1 reproduced in 74 Interpreter Releases 555 (March 28, 1997).

from invoking the administrative denaturalization power of the Attorney General.[12] Administrative denaturalization proceedings are described in detail below.[13]

II. BASES FOR DENATURALIZATION

A. IN GENERAL

§ 14:2 Generally

Research References

A.L.R. Index, Immigration and Naturalization
Dizon and Wettstein, Immigration Law Service 2d § 14:387
Steel on Immigration Law § 15:27

Denaturalization proceedings are instituted

for the purpose of revoking and setting aside the order admitting such person to citizenship and canceling the certificate of naturalization on the ground that such order and such certificate of naturalization were illegally procured or were procured by concealment of a material fact or by willful misrepresentation . . . .[1]

As the law clearly states, the purpose of the proceedings is to revoke the order admitting the person to citizenship and to cancel the certificate of naturalization.[2] This revocation, however, can only occur if the order and certificate were "illegally procured" or procured by "concealment of a material fact or by willful misrepresentation."[3]

If one of the bases for denaturalization is proven, the courts must denaturalize the defendant.[4] The court has no equitable discretion to consider mitigating factors and to refuse to denaturalize the defendant.[5] On this basis, one court rejected an argument that it refrain from denaturalizing an individual because he was incompetent.[6]

B. FRAUD, CONCEALMENT AND WILLFUL MISREPRESENTATION

§ 14:3 Generally

Research References

A.L.R. Index, Immigration and Naturalization
Dizon and Wettstein, Immigration Law Service 2d § 14:388
Steel on Immigration Law § 15:27

---

[12]Gorbach v. Reno, 2001 WL 34145464 (W.D. Wash. Feb. 14, 2001) (implementing decision of the Ninth Circuit in Gorbach v. Reno, 219 F.3d 1087 (9th Cir. 2000)).

[13]See § 14:30.

[Section 14:2]

[1]INA § 340(a), 8 U.S.C.A. § 1451(a).

[2]INA § 340(a), 8 U.S.C.A. § 1451(a).

[3]INA § 340(a), 8 U.S.C.A. § 1451(a).

[4]Fedorenko v. U.S., 449 U.S. 490, 517, 101 S.Ct. 737, 752–53, 66 L.Ed.2d 689 (1981).

[5]Fedorenko, 449 U.S. at 517, 101 S.Ct. at 517, 66 L.Ed.2d. 689.

[6]U.S. v. Mandycz, 199 F. Supp. 2d 671 (E.D. Mich. 2002) (rejecting both a comparison to criminal trials and a due process claim).

Before enactment of the INA, denaturalization was permitted only for "fraud or illegality.[1] The current statute was reworded to require "concealment of a material fact" or "willful misrepresentation" instead of fraud.[2] The change from "fraud" to "concealment of a material fact" and "willful misrepresentation" was apparently made in response to prior lower court decisions which found naturalization fraud only actionable if it involved external actions, such as concealing witnesses from the court, but not if it involved perjured testimony.[3] Under current law, courts consistently equate "concealment of a material fact or willful misrepresentation" with fraud.[4] As the Supreme Court pointed out, in making this change, "there appears to be no congressional purpose to lay down a looser definitional standard for 'willful misrepresentation' or laxer requirements of proof than had previously been applied by the courts."[5]

Courts have not required proof of intent to deceive as one of the elements of this "fraud."[6] It is sufficient that the applicant must have willfully concealed or misrepresented a material fact to establish the required "fraud."[7]

§ 14:4 Materiality and willfulness required

Research References

A.L.R. Index, Immigration and Naturalization
Dizon and Wettstein, Immigration Law Service 2d § 14:389
Steel on Immigration Law § 15:27

In spite of the statutory language which allows revocation if the original naturalization was obtained either through concealment of a material fact or through willful misrepresentation, the courts have required that concealment of a material fact may not be actionable in denaturalization proceedings unless it is willful, and willful misrepresentation of a fact may not serve as a basis for denaturalization unless the fact is material.[1] Following this approach, courts have required that the government prove four separate issues: (1) that the naturalized citizen con-

---

[Section 14:3]

[1]Sec. 338(a), Nationality Act of 1940, Pub.L. 76-853, 54 Sat. 1137 (Oct. 14, 1940) ("It shall be the duty of the United States district attorneys for the respective districts, upon affidavit showing good cause therefore, to institute proceedings in any court specified in subsection (a) of section 301 in the judicial district in which the naturalized citizen may reside at the time of bringing suit, for the purpose of revoking and setting aside the order admitting such person to citizenship and canceling the certificate of naturalization on the ground of fraud or on the ground that such order and certificate were illegally procured").

[2]INA § 340(a), 8 U.S.C.A. § 1451(a).

[3]Costello v. U. S., 365 U.S. 265, 281, 81 S. Ct. 534, 538, 5 L. Ed. 2d 551 (1961).

[4]Stacher v. U.S., 258 F.2d 112, 123 (9th Cir. 1958), cert. denied, 358 U.S. 989 (1958); U.S. v. Title, 132 F.Supp. 185, 187 (S.D.Cal. 1955) ("Government alleges that the naturalization was procured by concealment and willful misrepresentation, i.e., fraud"); U.S. v. Jerome, 115 F.Supp. 818, 821 (S.D.N.Y. 1953).

[5]Costello v. U. S., 365 U.S. 265, 287, 81 S. Ct. 534, 538, 5 L. Ed. 2d 551 (1961).

[6]See U. S. v. Title, 132 F. Supp. 185, 195–96 (S.D. Cal. 1955).

[7]See U. S. v. Title, 132 F. Supp. 185, 190–91, 195–96 (S.D. Cal. 1955).

[Section 14:4]

[1]Kungys v. U.S., 485 U.S. 759, 767, 108 S.Ct. 1537, 1544, 99 L.Ed.2d 839 (1988) (plurality opinion); Fedorenko v. U. S., 449 U.S. 490, 507, 101 S. Ct. 737, 748, 66 L. Ed. 2d 686 (1981) (plurality opinion); Fedorenko v. U. S., 449 U.S. 490, 507, 101 S. Ct. 737, 748, 66 L. Ed. 2d 686 (1981).

cealed or misrepresented a fact; (2) that the misrepresentation or concealment was willful; (3) that the fact was material; and (4) that the naturalized citizen procured citizenship as a result of the misrepresentation or concealment.[2]

§ 14:5 Meaning of concealment

Research References

Evidence Warranting Refusal of Admission, Removal, or Denaturalization for Nazi-Related Conduct, 180 A.L.R. Fed. 243
Dizon and Wettstein, Immigration Law Service 2d § 14:388
Steel on Immigration Law § 15:27

Concealment of a material fact encompasses swearing under oath that the person lacks a record of misconduct, or has never done certain actions.[1] Thus, when an applicant with a criminal record states that he or she has no criminal record, the applicant is engaging in concealment.[2] Concealment also includes misstatements tending to cover up information that the applicant does not wish the court to find out.[3] Thus, the statement that a person was employed as a tailor in order to conceal real employment as a guard under Nazi supervision amounted to concealment.[4] The same applied to a defendant who misrepresented his illegal employment by stating in his naturalization application that he was a real estate broker.[5] Even though this form of concealment could also be interpreted as misrepresentation, the Supreme Court treated it as concealment of a material fact.[6]

Concealment usually arises out of incomplete or false answers.[7] The importance of the actual question asked the defendant is emphasized by the dissent in *Costello*, where the defendant stated that his occupation was "real estate" instead of the illegal activities that constituted his main source of income. The dissent found that the defendant should only have been denaturalized if he had been asked to list all his occupations.[8] The naturalization application that Costello filled out only asked him to state his occupation and there was some plausible argument that the defendant was in the "real estate" business.[9] The majority, on the other hand, found that the

---

[2]Kungys v. U.S., 485 U.S. 759, 767, 108 S. Ct. 1537, 1544–45, 99 L. Ed. 2d 839 (1988).

[Section 14:5]

[1]See U.S. v. Oddo, 314 F.2d 115, 116 (2d Cir. 1963) cert. denied, 375 U.S. 833 (1963).

[2]U. S. v. Oddo, 314 F.2d 115, 116 (2d Cir. 1963).

[3]U.S v. Kowalchuk, 773 F.2d 488, 492 (3d Cir. 1985) (en banc), cert. denied, 475 U.S. 1012 reh'g denied 475 U.S. 1132 (1985) (concealment in prior application for lawful permanent residence).

[4]U.S. v. Kowalchuk, 773 F.2d 488, 492 (3d Cir. 1985).

[5]Costello v. U. S., 365 U.S. 265, 268, 81 S. Ct. 534, 536, 5 L. Ed. 2d 551 (1961).

[6]See Costello v. U. S., 365 U.S. 265, 271–72, 81 S. Ct. 534, 538, 5 L. Ed. 2d 551 (1961). The lower court had apparently based its decision on the fact that defendant had willfully misrepresented his occupation in the naturalization application. Costello v. U. S., 365 U.S. 265, 268, 81 S. Ct. 534, 536, 5 L. Ed. 2d 551 (1961).

[7]See, e.g., U.S. v. Accardo, 113 F.Supp. 783, 784 (D.N.J. 1953) aff'd per curiam 208 F.2d 632 (3d Cir. 1953), cert. denied, 347 U.S. 952 (1954) (defendant disclosed only part of his criminal record claiming that was the complete record).

[8]Costello v. U. S., 365 U.S. 265, 289, 81 S. Ct. 534, 547, 5 L. Ed. 2d 551 (1961) (J. Douglas, dissenting).

[9]Costello v. U. S., 365 U.S. 265, 288–89, 81 S. Ct. 534, 546–47, 5 L. Ed. 2d 551 (1961) ("The fact that this real estate business was secondary . . . did not make it any less his 'occupation' ").

real estate business was no more than a cover up for his real occupation that was boot legging.[10]

This same point was also emphasized by the Court's decision in *Nowak v. U.S.*[11] The Court held that the defendant could not be found to have failed to disclose membership in the Communist party since the question asked in the naturalization application could have been interpreted as requiring only a disclosure of affiliations to anarchist organizations.[12] When the question is so ambiguous, it cannot be the basis for denaturalization based on fraudulent procurement of naturalization.[13]

At least one court has found, however, that a defendant had an affirmative duty to disclose the fact that he was under criminal proceedings at the time of his naturalization hearing.[14] This duty appears to derive from the fact that at the time of the defendant's filing of the application, the applicant fulfilled all the requirements of naturalization, but by the time of the final hearing, he did not fulfill them any longer.[15]

§ 14:6 Willful misrepresentation

Research References

Dizon and Wettstein, Immigration Law Service 2d § 14:388
Steel on Immigration Law § 15:27

Willful misrepresentation and concealment are not substantially different in coverage. Indeed, the Supreme Court has pointed out that, even though the denaturalization statute speaks of "concealment of a material fact" and "willful misrepresentation," misrepresentation must be of a material fact and concealment must be willful.[1]

§ 14:7 Material fact; generally

Research References

A.L.R. Index, Immigration and Naturalization
Dizon and Wettstein, Immigration Law Service 2d § 14:390
Steel on Immigration Law § 15:27

Concealment or misrepresentation may only be the basis for revocation proceedings if they related to a *material* fact. In 1988, Justice Scalia set out to clarify the concept of "materiality" in denaturalization proceedings. Justice Scalia's objective

---

[10]Costello v. U. S., 365 U.S. 265, 276, 81 S. Ct. 534, 540, 5 L. Ed. 2d 551 (1961).

[11]Nowak v. U.S., 356 U.S. 660, 78 S.Ct. 955, 2 L.Ed.2d 1048 (1958).

[12]Nowak v. U.S., 356 U.S. 660, 663–64, 78 S. Ct. 955, 957–58, 2 L. Ed. 2d 1048 (1958).

[13]Nowak v. U.S., 356 U.S. 660, 665, 78 S. Ct. 955, 958, 2 L. Ed. 2d 1048 (1958).

[14]U.S. v. Palmeri, 52 F.Supp. 226, 227 (E.D.N.Y. 1943) ("[t]he failure to disclose the arrest was the failure to perform a duty which the applicant owed the court").

[15]See US v. Palmeri, 52 F. Supp. 226, 227 (E.D. N.Y. 1943).

[Section 14:6]

[1]Fedorenko v. U. S., 449 U.S. 490, 507, 101 S. Ct. 737, 748, 66 L. Ed. 2d 686 (1981).

was to correct the confusion that prior Supreme Court pronouncements had generated on this issue.[1] It is remarkable how unsuccessful Justice Scalia was.

Kungys has been referred to as "an uncertain guide to the Court's future action."[2] Part of the problem with the case is that there was no majority opinion. Five different opinions were written. Justice Scalia's is considered the plurality opinion. However, only two other justices, Justice Brennan and Chief Justice Rehnquist, fully joined that opinion.[3] In addition, Justice Brennan wrote a separate concurrent opinion to qualify his support of Justice Scalia.[4] Indeed, the Ninth Circuit has taken the position that Justice Brennan's view of materiality controls, as his opinion was the one that concurred on the narrowest grounds with the plurality.[5] Justice O'Connor concurred with the reasoning of the plurality opinion but disagreed with the application of the reasoning to the facts of the case.[6] Justices Marshall, Stevens, and Blackmun, concurred in judgment based on the *Chaunt* test—the prior interpretation of materiality formulated by the Court in 1960.[7] Finally, Justice White dissented.[8] This split in the Supreme Court was not based on political considerations, as can be seen from the fact that the only justices joining Justice Scalia's plurality opinion were Rehnquist and Brennan.[9]

Since the decision has left this area of law in disarray, the plurality test, J. Brennan's opinion, and the *Chaunt* test will all be discussed here.

§ 14:8   Material fact; generally—*Kungys* test; materiality element

In formulating his test of materiality, Justice Scalia ignored more than half a century of administrative and judicial efforts to clarify this concept in the immigration and nationality context.[1] Instead, he based the interpretation of "materiality" on that found in the criminal context.[2] He believed that to be material, the statement only needed to "be predictably capable of affecting" or have "a natural ten-

---

[Section 14:7]

[1]See Kungys v. U.S., 485 U.S. 759, 772, 108 S. Ct. 1537, 1547, 99 L. Ed. 2d 839 (1988).

[2]Gordon & Mailman, § 100.02[2].

[3]Kungys v. U.S., 485 U.S. 759, 762, 108 S. Ct. 1537, 1542, 99 L. Ed. 2d 839 (1988).

[4]Kungys v. U.S., 485 U.S. 759, 783, 108 S. Ct. 1537, 1553, 99 L. Ed. 2d 839 (1988).

[5]Forbes v. I.N.S., 48 F.3d 439 (9th Cir. 1995); U.S. v. Puerta, 982 F.2d 1297, 1303–04 (9th Cir. 1992).

[6]Kungys v. U.S., 485 U.S. 759, 801, 108 S. Ct. 1537, 1562, 99 L. Ed. 2d 839 (1988) (Justice O'Connor, concurring in part, dissenting in part).

[7]Kungys v. U.S., 485 U.S. 759, 784, 108 S. Ct. 1537, 1562, 99 L. Ed. 2d 839 (1988).

[8]Kungys v. U.S., 485 U.S. 759, 801, 108 S. Ct. 1537, 1562, 99 L. Ed. 2d 839 (1988). Justice Kennedy took no part in the consideration of the case. Kungys v. U.S., 485 U.S. 759, 783, 108 S. Ct. 1537, 1552, 99 L. Ed. 2d 839 (1988).

[9]Kungys v. U.S., 485 U.S. 759, 762, 108 S. Ct. 1537, 1542, 99 L. Ed. 2d 839 (1988).

[Section 14:8]

[1]See, e.g., U.S. ex rel. Leibowitz v. Schlotfeldt, 94 F.2d 263 (7th Cir. 1938) (holding that use of applicant's brother's name and date of birth was not relevant to immigration proceedings since person qualified for a visa under his own name).

[2]Kungys v. U.S., 485 U.S. 759, 769–70, 108 S. Ct. 1537, 1546, 99 L. Ed. 2d 839 (1988). Indeed, his formulation has a long tradition in the context of 18 U.S.C.A. § 1001, the general statute penalizing fraud in applications to U.S. agencies and departments. U.S. v. Naserkhaki, 722 F.Supp. 242, 247 (E.D.Va. 1989).

dency to influence" the decisions of the agency.[3] Having a natural tendency to influence a decision, under his formulation, would be more than being simply relevant evidence.[4]

§ 14:9 Material fact; generally—*Kungys* test; materiality element— Procurement element

If it is established that the misrepresentation or concealment was material, the court would have to determine whether the applicant procured naturalization by means of those misrepresentations or concealments.[1] A minimum requirement for this determination is that the person obtained naturalization as a result of the application in which the misrepresentation or concealment occurred.[2] A finding that the material concealment or misrepresentation occurred in the appropriate proceedings would raise a *rebuttable* presumption that the applicant was disqualified for naturalization.[3] The person would be able to rebut this presumption by showing that the requirement affected by the misrepresentation or concealment was in fact met.[4] The standard of proof to establish that he or she met the requirement is the preponderance of the evidence standard.[5]

§ 14:10 Material fact; generally—*Kungys* test; materiality element— Justice Brennan's concurrence in *Kungys*

In his concurrence, Justice Brennan agreed with the procedure set out by Justice Scalia, which he described as requiring three steps: (1) a misrepresentation or concealment is material if it has "a natural tendency to produce the conclusion that the applicant was qualified for citizenship"; (2) a misrepresentation or concealment has that "tendency" if honest representations would predictably have disclosed other facts relevant to the applicant's qualifications; and (3) proof by clear, unequivocal, and convincing evidence that the misrepresentation had this tendency raises a presumption of ineligibility, which the naturalized citizen is called upon to rebut.[1]

However, Justice Brennan understands this test to require the government to "produce evidence sufficient to raise a fair inference that a statutory disqualifying

---

[3]Kungys v. U.S., 485 U.S. 759, 771, 772, 108 S. Ct. 1537, 1547, 99 L. Ed. 2d 839 (1988). See also U.S. v. Tarango-Pena, 173 F. Supp. 2d 588 (E.D. Tex. 2001) (applying this test and finding that a misrepresentation about the U.S. citizenship of applicant's wife was material).

[4]U.S. v. Gaudin, 28 F.3d 943, 948 (9th Cir. 1994), cert. granted, 513 U.S. 1071, 115 S. Ct. 713, 130 L. Ed. 2d 621 (1995) and judgment aff'd, 515 U.S. 506, 115 S. Ct. 2310, 132 L. Ed. 2d 444 (1995) ("relevance determines what evidence the jury could have considered, while materiality determines what would have tended to influence its verdict").

[Section 14:9]

[1]Kungys v. U.S., 485 U.S. 759, 108 S. Ct. 1537, 99 L. Ed. 2d 839 (1988).

[2]Kungys v. U.S., 485 U.S. 759, 776, 108 S. Ct. 1537, 1549, 99 L. Ed. 2d 839 (1988).

[3]Kungys v. U.S., 485 U.S. 759, 777, 108 S. Ct. 1537, 1549–50, 99 L. Ed. 2d 839 (1988).

[4]Kungys v. U.S., 485 U.S. 759, 777, 108 S. Ct. 1537, 1550, 99 L. Ed. 2d 839 (1988). See also U.S. v. Tarango-Pena, 173 F. Supp. 2d 588 (E.D. Tex. 2001) (where defendant failed to submit evidence, rebuttable presumption was not overcome).

[5]Kungys v. U.S., 485 U.S. 759, 777, 108 S. Ct. 1537, 99 L. Ed. 2d 839 (1988).

[Section 14:10]

[1]Kungys v. U.S., 485 U.S. 759, 783, 108 S. Ct. 1537, 99 L. Ed. 2d 839 (1988).

fact actually existed."[2] If the evidence only raises the *possibility* that a disqualifying fact may have existed, then the government is not entitled to the benefit of the presumption that the citizen was ineligible.[3] Justice Brennan joined the plurality because he did not find the plurality opinion inconsistent with his formulation.[4] Read in this manner, *Kungys* is more consistent with prior applications of the materiality test.[5]

§ 14:11 Material fact; generally—*Chaunt* test

Until superseded by *Kungys*, the *Chaunt* decision was the authoritative Supreme Court statement on materiality in denaturalization proceedings.[1] Under this test, a concealment or misrepresentation is material if either (1) on the true facts the applicant would have been ineligible for naturalization, or (2) the true facts might have been useful in an investigation possibly leading to the discovery of other facts warranting denial of citizenship.[2]

§ 14:12 Material fact; generally—Post-*Kungys* Courts of Appeals decisions

The Ninth Circuit has embraced Justice Brennan's reading of the *Kungys* decision, on the basis that "[w]hen a fragmented Court decides a case and no single rationale explaining the result enjoys the assent of five Justices, the holding of the Court may be viewed as that position taken by those Members who concurred in the judgments on the narrowest grounds."[1]

Thus, the Ninth Circuit, in both criminal denaturalization and deportation proceedings, has found that even when misrepresentation is willful, it will not be material unless the government can link the misrepresentation to some statutory ground of ineligibility.[2] The government needs to present evidence that the statu-

---

[2]Kungys v. U.S., 485 U.S. 759, 783, 108 S. Ct. 1537, 99 L. Ed. 2d 839 (1988).

[3]Kungys v. U.S., 485 U.S. 759, 783, 108 S. Ct. 1537, 99 L. Ed. 2d 839 (1988).

[4]Kungys v. U.S., 485 U.S. 759, 784, 108 S. Ct. 1537, 99 L. Ed. 2d 839 (1988).

[5]See § 14:11. Justice Stevens disagrees with Justice Brennan's formulation because he finds that creating a presumption the respondent must rebut is inconsistent with "the previous recognition of the special burden the Government must bear when it seeks to denaturalize an American citizen." Kungys v. U.S., 485 U.S. 759, 794, 108 S. Ct. 1537, 1558, 99 L. Ed. 2d 839 (1988) (J. Stevens, concurring in the judgment).

[Section 14:11]

[1]Chaunt v. U.S., 364 U.S. 350, 81 S.Ct. 147, 5 L.Ed.2d 120 (1960).

[2]Chaunt v. U.S., 364 U.S. 350, 355, 81 S. Ct. 147, 151, 5 L. Ed. 2d 120 (1960). Attorney General Reno adopted a similar test of materiality in the context of visa fraud. It requires a finding of materiality if "the misrepresentation tends to shut off a line of inquiry which is relevant to the noncitizen's eligibility and which might well have resulted in a proper determination that he be excluded." Matter of S- and B-C-, 9 I. & N. Dec. 436, 447 (B.I.A. 1960).

[Section 14:12]

[1]U.S. v. Puerta, 982 F.2d 1297, 1304 (9th Cir. 1992) quoting Marks v. U.S., 430 U.S. 188, 193, 97 S.Ct. 990, 993, 51 L.Ed.2d 260 (1977).

[2]Forbes v. I.N.S., 48 F.3d 439, 443 (9th Cir. 1995) (deportation proceedings); U.S. v. Puerta, 982 F.2d 1297, 1304 (9th Cir. 1992) (deportation proceedings); U.S. v. Puerta, 982 F.2d 1297, 1304 (9th Cir. 1992) (criminal denaturalization proceedings).

tory disqualification in fact actually existed at the time the original decision was made.[3]

For example, lying about an arrest for failure to appear at a court hearing where the charges were dismissed, is not material to a visa application.[4] Similarly, lying in a naturalization application about past use of aliases and about a short absence, was found not to be material when the legacy INS did not produce any evidence that the person had a criminal record, or that his or her absences would have disqualified him or her from naturalizing.[5]

§ 14:13 Material fact; generally—Prior applications of materiality tests

Under any test of materiality, if the applicant would be ineligible to naturalize on true facts, the concealment or misrepresentation is material.[1] The disagreement in approach between these courts is as to how to word the relevance of the concealment or misrepresentation when its disclosure did not make the person ineligible for naturalization.[2]

Chaunt itself did not deal with the *procurement* issue that *Kungys* raised, i.e. how to establish if the naturalization was procured through the misrepresentation or concealment. As *Kungys* points out, under the *Chaunt* test both the materiality and the procurement issues appear to have been consolidated into one.[3] In the context of determining ineligibility due to visa fraud, however, the Attorney General used *Chaunt* as the basis for establishing a shifting burden of proof—similar to that developed by Justice Scalia in *Kungys*—to determine the materiality of a misrepresentation. Thus, in proceedings relating to visa fraud, once the DHS establishes that the misrepresentation tended to cut off a relevant avenue of inquiry, the burden shifts to the noncitizen to show that the inquiry would not have resulted in a proper denial of the visa.[4]

Even though the materiality of each misrepresentation will depend on the facts of each case, some general patterns can be discerned.[5] The courts have usually held that willful misrepresentations regarding marital status at the time of the naturalization application are material.[6] Similarly, willful failure to disclose a rec-

---

[3]Forbes v. I.N.S., 48 F.3d 439, 443 (9th Cir. 1995).

[4]Forbes v. I.N.S., 48 F.3d 439 (9th Cir. 1995).

[5]U.S. v. Puerta, 982 F.2d 1297 (9th Cir. 1992).

[Section 14:13]

[1]Solis-Muela v. I.N.S., 13 F.3d 372, 377 (10th Cir. 1993) (misrepresentation material because on true facts applicant was excludable).

[2]For a discussion of how different lower courts have evaluated the materiality of specific instances of concealment and misrepresentation in naturalization proceedings as they related to criminal record, subversive activities, marital status, residences, identity, and other instances of false information, see Gordon & Mailman, § 100.02[3][b][iv]. For a discussion of the application of the materiality test in exclusion and deportation proceedings, see Levy, Exclusion Grounds Under the Immigration Act of 1990: Part II, 91-9 Immigration Briefings 3–5 (September 1991).

[3]Kungys v. U.S., 485 U.S. 759, 768, 108 S. Ct. 1537, 1545, 99 L. Ed. 2d 839 (1988).

[4]Matter of S-- and B-- C--, 9 I. & N. Dec. 436, 449, 1960 WL 12154 (B.I.A. 1960).

[5]U.S. v. Gaudin, 28 F.3d 943, 948 (9th Cir. 1994) ("a factual inquiry would nearly always be necessary" in order to determine materiality).

[6]See U.S. v. Alameh, 341 F.3d 167 (2d Cir. 2003); U.S. v. D'Agostino, 338 F.2d 490, 491 (2d Cir. 1964).

ord of arrests immediately preceding the naturalization application has also usually been held to be concealment of a material fact.[7]

Failure to disclose participation in Nazi persecution rises to the level of a separate genre in denaturalization proceedings. Much of the denaturalization activity in the last two decades turns on this issue.[8] Indeed, between 1979 and 1998, 61 Nazi persecutors were stripped of their U.S. citizenship,[9] and since then even more have lost their citizenship.[10] The majority of these cases, however, appear to have been framed as involving illicit procurement based on the misrepresentations that occurred in gaining admission to the United States rather than in the naturalization application.[11] This probably derives from the difficulty of establishing the materiality of the misrepresentation for nationality purposes. Unlike Communists and anarchists, Nazis are not *per se* barred from becoming citizens.[12] Therefore, the DHS would have to prove that concealment of Nazi activities might have otherwise led to a finding of ineligibility for naturalization, possibly based on lack of attachment to the principles of the U.S. Constitution. Proving this lack of attachment, however, is particularly difficult, as membership in the party is not sufficient—it must be proven that the applicant in question subscribed to the specific opinions that were hostile to the constitution.[13]

§ 14:14   Object of fraud

It is clear that if a petitioner committed fraud on the naturalization court, denaturalization proceedings are possible.[1] They are also possible when the petitioner's fraud was committed on the immigration examiner rather than on the court, and as a consequence of the fraud the government did not oppose

---

[7]See U. S. v. Oddo, 314 F.2d 115, 116 (2d Cir. 1963); U.S. v. Reve, 241 F.Supp. 2d 470 (D.N.J. 2003).

[8]See, e.g., Kungys v. U.S., 485 U.S. 759, 108 S. Ct. 1537, 99 L. Ed. 2d 839 (1988); Fedorenko v. U. S., 449 U.S. 490, 101 S. Ct. 737, 66 L. Ed. 2d 686 (1981); U.S. v. Dailide, 227 F.3d 385, 55 Fed. R. Evid. Serv. 740, 2000 FED App. 299P (6th Cir. 2000); U.S. v. Negele, 222 F.3d 443 (8th Cir. 2000), cert. denied, 531 U.S. 1153, 121 S. Ct. 1100, 148 L. Ed. 2d 972 (2001). U.S. v. Sokolov, 814 F.2d 864 (2d Cir. 1987), cert. denied, 108 S.Ct. 1728 (1988); U.S. v. Kowalchuk, 773 F.2d 488 (3d Cir. 1985); U.S. v. Palciauskas, 734 F.2d 625 (11th Cir. 1984); U.S. v. Schellong, 717 F.2d 329 (7th Cir. 1983), cert. denied, 465 U.S. 1007 (1984).

[9]75 Interpreter Releases 1597 (Nov. 16, 1998).

[10]*See, e.g.,* U.S. v. Reimer, 356 F.3d 456 (2d Cir. 2004); U.S. v. Demjanjuk, 367 F.3d 623 (6th Cir. 2004).

[11]See, e.g., Fedorenko v. U. S., 449 U.S. 490, 101 S. Ct. 737, 66 L. Ed. 2d 686 (1981); U.S. v. Dailide, 316 F.3d 611, 618 (6th Cir. 2003) (finding that the determination of whether citizenship was illegally procured "necessarily requires an examination of the original visa process"); U.S. v. Demjanjuk, 367 F.3d 623 (6th Cir. 2004) (individual's knowing misrepresentation of his war record on the immigration visa application was material, rendering entry into U.S. unlawful and naturalization illegal). Cf. § 14:16.

[12]With the INA, Congress expressly made the naturalization bar inapplicable to Nazis. See §§ 7:83 to 7:87.

[13]See §§ 7:47 to 7:51.

[Section 14:14]

[1]See Knauer v. U.S., 328 U.S. 654, 66 S.Ct. 1304, 90 L.Ed. 150 reh'g denied 329 U.S. 818, 67 S.Ct. 25, 91 L.Ed. 697 (1946).

naturalization.² Denaturalization is also available for the revocation of repatriation obtained by fraudulently taking the oath in consular proceedings.³

§14:15 Fraud and res judicata

Several defendants in denaturalization proceedings have argued that denaturalization should be barred because the same issues were already litigated by the same parties in the naturalization hearing and should not be relitigated.¹ Fraud in the application, however, means that naturalization was obtained through a deceit on the court that granted it, and courts have equitable power to set aside decrees obtained by fraud.² The facts raised in these proceedings were never before litigated.³ In addition, congressional power to require revocation of a naturalization decree obtained through fraud has been upheld as constitutionally sound.⁴

C. ILLEGAL PROCUREMENT

§14:16 Generally

Research References

Steel on Immigration Law §15:27

The INA provides that an order admitting a person to citizenship may be revoked and a certificate of naturalization may be canceled if it was "illegally procured."¹ This language could be read not to require any concealment or misrepresentation, but might be read even to include unwitting ineligibility for naturalization. In *Fedorenko*, the Supreme Court interpreted this language as allowing denaturalization proceedings when the applicant did not strictly comply with all the conditions precedent to naturalization.² This case may signal a change of approach by the courts. Formerly, courts uniformly refused to denaturalize citizens based on naturalization defects that were not considered sufficiently substantial.³

Further, the text of the statute may not require any misrepresentation in the

---

²U.S. v. Saracino, 43 F.2d 76 (3d Cir. 1930).

³U.S. v. Rojas-Vasquez, 97 F. Supp. 550 (W.D. Tex. 1951).

[Section 14:15]

¹See Knauer v. U. S., 328 U.S. 654, 670, 66 S. Ct. 1304, 1312–13, 90 L. Ed. 1500 (1946).

²Knauer v. U. S., 328 U.S. 654, 671, 66 S. Ct. 1304, 1313, 90 L. Ed. 1500 (1946); U.S. v. Candella, 131 F.Supp. 249, 250 (S.D.N.Y. 1954); U S v. Jerome, 115 F. Supp. 818, 821, (S.D. N.Y. 1953); U S v. Jerome, 115 F. Supp. 818, 821, (S.D. N.Y. 1953).

³The fact that naturalization now is granted by the USCIS instead of the courts adds a new variable to the issue of res judicata in denaturalization proceedings. Moreover, there is quite a bit of disagreement among the courts as to the effectiveness of the defense of res judicata when denaturalization is based on grounds of illegality. See INS Interp. 340.2(a)(3)(iii).

⁴Knauer v. U. S., 328 U.S. 654, 673, 66 S. Ct. 1304, 1314, 90 L. Ed. 1500 (1946).

[Section 14:16]

¹INA §340(a), 8 U.S.C.A. §1451(a).

²Fedorenko v. U. S., 449 U.S. 490, 506, 101 S. Ct. 737, 747, 66 L. Ed. 2d 686 (1981); see also U.S. v. Kiang, 175 F. Supp. 2d 942 (E.D. Mich. 2001) (naturalization revoked for lack of good moral character where individual was convicted of a crime involving moral turpitude between filing his naturalization application and being sworn in and where he was on probation at the time of his swearing in); U.S. v. Samaei, 260 F.Supp 2d 1223 (M.D. Fla. 2003) (naturalization revoked for lack of good moral character where individual convicted of a second shoplifting offense prior to his swearing in).

³INS Interp. 340.2(a)(3)(iv).

actual application process, buy may include ineligibility for naturalization. Three recent Court of Appeals cases have permitted denaturalization of an individual without any showing of fraud or misrepresentation, where it was found that the individual was statutorily ineligible for naturalization due to a criminal conviction.[4]

§ 14:17   Fraud in obtaining permanent residence

Research References
Steel on Immigration Law § 15:27

Ineligibility for permanent residence or fraud in obtaining permanent residence is probably the single most important basis for denaturalization due to "illegal procurement."[1] Most of the naturalization provisions require that applicants be lawfully admitted to permanent residence, as a prerequisite to naturalization.[2] This, in turn, requires that the person must have had a valid visa at the time that he or she was admitted to permanent residence.[3] Thus, at least two circuit courts found that where an individual was ineligible for a visa at the time it was granted, any subsequent naturalization based upon this visa could be revoked as having been illegally procured, regardless of whether fraud was involved in securing the visa.[4] Moreover, in evaluating the legitimacy of the original visa, the court in one case made clear that INA § 340 "not only permits the federal judiciary to substitute its judgment, but requires it."[5]

More often, however, fraud in securing the visa is an issue. In *Fedorenko*, the Supreme Court held that visas obtained through material misrepresentations are not valid visas and would render illegal any subsequent naturalization derived from those visas.[6] Subsequently, the plurality opinion in *Kungys*, confronting a similar

---

[4]United States v. Jean-Baptiste, 395 F.3d 1190, 1191 (11th Cir.2005); U.S. v. Dang, 488 F.3d 1135 (9th Cir. 2007); U.S. v. Suarez, 664 F.3d 655 (7th Cir. 2011).

[Section 14:17]

[1]Two circuit courts have recently rejected a claim that a district court lacks jurisdiction to review a visa eligibility question and on that basis vacate an order of naturalization. U.S. v. Tittjung, 235 F.3d 330, 337 (7th Cir. 2000), cert. denied, 533 U.S. 931, 121 S. Ct. 2554, 150 L. Ed. 2d 721 (2001) (stating "unequivocally" that Article III courts have jurisdiction to vacate an order of naturalization when it is based on an illegally obtained visa); U.S. v. Negele, 222 F.3d 443 (8th Cir. 2000), cert. denied, 531 U.S. 1153, 121 S. Ct. 1100, 148 L. Ed. 2d 972 (2001).

[2]See §§ 7:1 et seq., 11:1 et seq., and 12:1 et seq.

[3]Fedorenko v. U. S., 449 U.S. 490, 514–15, 101 S. Ct. 737, 751, 66 L. Ed. 2d 686 (1981). See also, Kalejs v. I.N.S., 10 F.3d 441, 446–47 (7th Cir. 1993) (disclosure of Nazi persecution activities would have been material to exclusion under INA § 212(a)(27) in 1958); U.S. v. Dailide, 227 F.3d 385, 55 Fed. R. Evid. Serv. 740, 2000 FED App. 299P (6th Cir. 2000) (same); U.S. v. Negele, 222 F.3d 443 (8th Cir. 2000), cert. denied, 531 U.S. 1153, 121 S. Ct. 1100, 148 L. Ed. 2d 972 (2001) (same).

[4]U.S. v. Szehinskyj, 277 F.3d 331 (3d Cir. 2002) (holding that where the visa was obtained under the Displaced Person's Act of 1948—which included an ineligibility ground based on assistance in persecution—proof of assistance in persecution "is an independent ground of [visa ineligibility] that does not include a fraud element: once a determination is made on this ground, there is no need to look for and find a material misrepresentation"); U.S. v. Dailide, 316 F.3d 611, 620 (6th Cir. 2003) (INA § 340 "makes no mention of a 'falsity' requirement, but only requires an inquiry into whether citizenship was illegally procured").

[5]U.S. v. Dailide, 316 F.3d 611, 618 (6th Cir. 2003).

[6]Fedorenko v. U. S., 449 U.S. 490, 515, 101 S. Ct. 737, 751, 66 L. Ed. 2d 686 (1981). See also U.S. v. Tarango-Pena, 173 F. Supp. 2d 588 (E.D. Tex. 2001) (permanent residence was illegally procured

set of facts, failed to consider this rationale.[7] Instead it held that misrepresentations in procuring lawful permanent residence may form the basis of denaturalization, on the ground that providing "false testimony" at the immigrant visa proceedings would bar the person from establishing good moral character and, if that misrepresentation occurred during the statutory period of required good moral character, the applicant would not have qualified for naturalization because of this lack of good moral character.[8] As a result, the naturalization would have been illegally procured.[9] The plurality opinion distinguished this basis for denaturalization from the concealment of a material fact or willful misrepresentation basis of denaturalization because the misrepresentation did not occur in the naturalization proceedings.[10]

The difference of approach between *Kungys* and *Fedorenko* is not merely academic. Based on *Kungys*, misrepresentations would, as a practical matter, have to have occurred within five years of the naturalization application to serve as the basis of denaturalization.[11] In addition, only *oral* testimony is covered under that good moral character bar.[12] Thus written applications would not be so considered.[13] On the other hand, *Kungys* does not require the misrepresentation to have been material, as would be required if the court were to determine that the visa was invalid.[14] The *Kungys* approach, however, must be read as an additional basis on which to find illegality: it does not replace the grounds in *Fedorenko*, but supplements them. In fact, courts have continued to rely on *Fedorenko*, denaturalizing citizens based upon material misrepresentations in the visa process.[15]

§ 14:18 Fraud in obtaining naturalization

Research References

Dizon and Wettstein, Immigration Law Service 2d § 14:399
Steel on Immigration Law § 15:27

A more troubling aspect of the plurality opinion in *Kungys* is that it allows nonmaterial misrepresentations at the naturalization proceedings to result in denaturalization on the basis of illegal procurement. The mechanism for this "il-

---

where defendant knowingly submitted false information regarding his wife's citizenship in order to adjust status).

[7]Kungys v. U.S., 485 U.S. 759, 773, 808, 108 S. Ct. 1537, 1547–48, 1565–66, 99 L. Ed. 2d 839 (1988).

[8]Kungys v. U.S., 485 U.S. 759, 779, 108 S. Ct. 1537, 1551, 99 L. Ed. 2d 839 (1988).

[9]Kungys v. U.S., 485 U.S. 759, 779, 108 S. Ct. 1537, 99 L. Ed. 2d 839 (1988).

[10]Kungys v. U.S., 485 U.S. 759, 773–74, 108 S. Ct. 1537, 1548, 99 L. Ed. 2d 839 (1988).

[11]The false testimony ground only bars a finding of good moral character if it occurs within the period of required good moral character. Prior misbehavior may be considered, but mainly as a guide to interpret behavior within the statutory period. See § 7:37.

[12]See § 7:37.

[13]Written applications, as well as, misrepresentations that occurred more than five years prior to the naturalization application would be relevant under the general "residual" category to determine good moral character. See §§ 7:40 to 7:46.

[14]See Kungys v. U.S., 485 U.S. 759, 797, 108 S. Ct. 1537, 1560, 99 L. Ed. 2d 839 (1988) (J. Stevens, concurring in judgment).

[15]*See, e.g.,* U.S. v. Demjanjuk, 367 F.3d 623 (6th Cir. 2004) (individual's knowing misrepresentation of his war record on the immigration visa application was material, rendering entry into U.S. unlawful and naturalization illegal).

legality" would be that the applicant was barred from establishing good moral character because of false testimony given at the naturalization hearing itself.[1]

This approach undermines all the protections established by the materiality requirement, since denaturalization could be based on "illegal procurement" rather than on the "concealment" or "misrepresentation" ground of denaturalization. The only requirements imposed by *Kungys* for a finding of illegality based on lack of good moral character are (1) that the applicant would have given false testimony under oath, and (2) that the misrepresentation must have been made "with the subjective intent of obtaining immigration benefits."[2]

The requirement that the misrepresentation occur in testimony would restrict the coverage of this basis of illegality to oral statements made under oath.[3] In addition, that bar would only apply to misrepresentations and not to concealment.[4]

However, the lack of materiality would greatly broaden the basis of denaturalization. It is irrelevant whether the misrepresentation could properly have led to a denial of naturalization.[5] Under this approach, a ground for denaturalization based on illegal procurement can be established if the DHS can show by clear, unequivocal and convincing evidence that in giving the false testimony, the applicant had the subjective intent of obtaining those benefits.[6]

The lower courts are divided as to the import of this aspect of *Kungys*. In the context of criminal denaturalization proceedings, the Ninth Circuit has read a materiality requirement into misrepresentations that lead to denaturalization.[7] In the same context, the Southern District of New York took the opposite view, holding that a false statement made in order to procure naturalization was contrary to law, even when the statement was not material.[8]

§ 14:19 Non-fraudulent illegal procurement

Research References
Immigration Law Service (2d ed.) § 14:399
Steel on Immigration Law § 15:27

The denaturalization statute permits denaturalization where the naturalization was "illegally procured or were procured by concealment of a material fact or by

---

[Section 14:18]

[1]Kungys v. U.S., 485 U.S. 759, 779, 108 S. Ct. 1537, 99 L. Ed. 2d 839 (1988) ("the alleged ground of 'illegal procurement' is that [the individual] lacked the requisite good moral character . . . at the time of his naturalization, because he had given false testimony for the purpose of obtaining benefits in both the visa and naturalization proceedings").

[2]Kungys v. U.S., 485 U.S. 759, 780, 108 S. Ct. 1537, 99 L. Ed. 2d 839 (1988).

[3]Kungys v. U.S., 485 U.S. 759, 780, 108 S. Ct. 1537, 99 L. Ed. 2d 839 (1988).

[4]Kungys v. U.S., 485 U.S. 759, 781, 108 S. Ct. 1537, 99 L. Ed. 2d 839 (1988).

[5]Kungys v. U.S., 485 U.S. 759, 780, 108 S. Ct. 1537, 99 L. Ed. 2d 839 (1988) (there is no requirement of materiality for purposes of the good moral character bar).

[6]Kungys v. U.S., 485 U.S. 759, 780–81, 108 S. Ct. 1537, 99 L. Ed. 2d 839 (1988).

[7]U.S. v. Puerta, 982 F.2d 1297, 1301 (9th Cir. 1992).

[8]U.S. v. Rogers, 898 F.Supp. 219 (S.D.N.Y. 1995).

willful misrepresentation."[1] This phraseology may suggest that concealment or misrepresentation is not necessary for the procurement to be illegal.[2]

In the *Fedorenko* decision, the Supreme Court bracketed its consideration of a denaturalization case by stating that "strict compliance with all the congressionally imposed prerequisites to the acquisition of citizenship" was required for naturalization.[3] This, together with the holding in that case, implied that the materiality of a misrepresentation in the course of obtaining naturalization was irrelevant to denaturalization proceedings.

A recent Eleventh Circuit case took this argument one step further. In *U.S. v. Jean-Baptiste*, the Eleventh Circuit permitted denaturalization in the absence of any proof of concealment or misrepresentation, where the Court found that a criminal act rendered the applicant ineligible to naturalize as a matter of law.[4]

The holding in *Jean-Baptiste* is a troubling one, as it would seem to lead inexorably to the conclusion that unwitting ineligibility for permanent residency or citizenship could be used as a basis for denaturalization years after the fact.

The Ninth Circuit recently joined the Eleventh Circuit in finding that commission of illegal activity during the statutory period barred an individual from naturalization. The Ninth Circuit upheld 8 C.F.R. § 316.10(b)(3)(iii) against various challenges, finding it a valid exercise of delegated authority.[5] It went on to uphold a grant of summary judgment in the denaturalization context where an individual had committed an act of which she was later convicted, without requiring evidence that she made any intentionally false or fraudulent statements, because her daughter had completed the misleading form just before her mother took her oath.[6]

III. PROCEDURES IN JUDICIAL DENATURALIZATION PROCEEDINGS

§ 14:20 DHS reports

Whenever any DHS official believes that a certificate of naturalization has been illegally obtained or obtained by concealment of a material fact or by willful misrepresentation, the DHS official will report the fact to the DHS director having jurisdiction over the person's last known place of residence in the U.S.[1] The DHS office

---

[Section 14:19]

    [1]INA § 240(a), 8 C.F.R. § 1451(a).

    [2]Such a reading has its flaws, however. The doctrine of "noscitur a sociis" holds that the meaning of a phrase may be gathered in part by reference to the text surrounding the phrase. The placement of the "illegal procurement" phrase together with provisions regarding concealment or misrepresentation—together with the jointure with the term "procurement" with "illegal"—suggests that Congress saw the illegality as relating to the procurement of the citizenship itself in ways similar to misrepresentation. Under this approach, illegality may be read as going not to unwitting statutory ineligibility, but to willfully obtaining citizenship in an illegal manner, in ways akin to misrepresentation or concealment.

    [3]Fedorenko v. U.S., 449 U.S. 490, 506, 101 S.Ct. 737, 747, 66 L.Ed.2d 686 (1981).

    [4]U.S. v. Jean-Baptiste, 395 F.3d 1190, 1193-96 (11th Cir. 2005).

    [5]U.S. v. Dang, 488 F.3d 1135, 1140–42 (9th Cir. 2007).

    [6]U.S. v. Dang, 488 F.3d 1135, 1137–38 (9th Cir. 2007).

[Section 14:20]

    [1]8 CFR § 340.2(a) as amended and redesignated by 62 Fed. Reg. 55550 (Oct. 28, 1996).

originating this information will thereafter be kept abreast of developments in the investigation.[2]

If the district director is satisfied that a *prima facie* case for revocation is made, he or she will in turn make a report to the DHS regional commissioner with a recommendation as to whether a revocation proceeding should be instituted.[3] In addition, if it appears that the naturalization was obtained in violation of the criminal law penalizing naturalization fraud, the district director may also apprise the appropriate U.S. attorney of the relevant facts for possible criminal prosecution.[4]

The *INS Interpretations* recommend using a 1909 Department of Justice circular letter to evaluate whether to institute denaturalization proceedings.[5] The circular emphasizes that naturalization proceedings should only be instituted if betterment of the citizenship of this country would result, as the purpose of denaturalization proceedings is remedial and denaturalization causes a serious disturbance of personal and property rights.[6] It admonishes officials not to institute denaturalization proceedings merely to correct errors or irregularities, which would properly have been the subject of consideration at the hearing or correction on appeal.[7] Mere consent by the holder to the cancellation of his or her certificate of naturalization because of some defect or irregularity should not be regarded as in itself sufficient to justify denaturalization proceedings.[8] In cases of willful and deliberate fraud at the original naturalization proceedings, the following elements should be considered before deciding to institute denaturalization proceedings: (1) length of time since the judgment of naturalization; (2) whether the party has conducted himself or herself as a good citizen since naturalization; and (3) whether the party possesses the necessary qualifications for citizenship.[9]

In January 2000, a memorandum of understanding was executed between the INS, the Office of Immigration Litigation of the Civil Division of the Department of Justice (OIL), the Executive Office for the U.S. Attorneys (USAO), and the Chair of the Attorney General's Advisory Committee.[10] This move appears to be in response to their failure to institute a "quick and dirty" procedure for revoking naturalization through administrative proceedings.[11] The memorandum details the procedures used by the INS before and after the issuance of the report (including the procedures for the issuance of the report itself). It also affects the procedures employed by the U.S. attorneys in the institution of actions to revoke naturalization. The memorandum is described in detail below.[12]

---

[2]8 CFR § 340.2(c).

[3]8 CFR § 340.2(a).

[4]8 CFR § 340.2(b).

[5]INS Interp. 340.1(f) quoting Department of Justice Circular Letter No. 107 (Sept. 20, 1909).

[6]Department of Justice Circular Letter No. 107 (Sept. 20, 1909) quoted in INS Interp. 340.1(f).

[7]Department of Justice Circular Letter No. 107 (Sept. 20, 1909) quoted in INS Interp. 340.1(f).

[8]Department of Justice Circular Letter No. 107 (Sept. 20, 1909) quoted in INS Interp. 340.1(f).

[9]Department of Justice Circular Letter No. 107 (Sept. 20, 1909) quoted in INS Interp. 340.1(f).

[10]Memorandum of Understanding Between INS, OIL, and U.S. Attorney, January 22, 2000 reproduced as Appendix 14-1.

[11]See § 14:30.

[12]See § 14:22. The complete memorandum is reproduced as Appendix 14-1.

§ 14:21 Institution of proceedings

The U.S. attorneys for the district where naturalization took place institute denaturalization proceedings.[1]

The USAO has signed memoranda of understanding with the INS and the OIL, involving its assistance in instituting and conducting denaturalization proceedings in certain circumstances.[2] In addition, Attorney General's Order No. 851-79 (9/4/79) confers upon the Criminal Division's Office of Special Investigations (OSI) the authority to prepare, initiate, and conduct denaturalization proceedings in all federal districts against individuals who, prior to and during World War II, participated in persecution in association with the Nazi government or its allies.[3]

The *U.S. Attorneys Manual* forbids the institution of any civil judicial denaturalization proceedings without prior consultation with the Office of Immigration Litigation of the Civil Division of the Department of Justice.[4] The only exception to this requirement is for cases under the OSI to be initiated without consulting with the Office of Immigration Litigation.[5]

Under the act, the institution of the proceedings by the USAO must be based upon affidavits showing good cause.[6] The USAO is required to file these affidavits with the district court as a procedural prerequisite for maintaining the denaturalization action.[7] Failure to file the required affidavit will result in the complaint being dismissed.[8] This dismissal, however, is without prejudice to later filing denaturalization proceedings on the same grounds.[9]

This affidavit must set forth evidentiary matters showing good cause for cancellation of citizenship.[10] Allegation of ultimate facts is insufficient to satisfy this standard.[11] On the other hand, the DHS official signing the affidavit is not required to have personal knowledge of the events, but may use DHS records as basis.[12] The rationale for the affidavit requirement is that the mere filing of a denaturalization proceeding brings about serious consequences for the defendants; even when their citizenship is not canceled, their reputation will be tarnished and their standing in the community damaged.[13]

These proceedings are instituted in the U.S. district court for the district where

---

[Section 14:21]

[1]INA § 340(a), 8 U.S.C.A. § 1451(a).

[2]See § 14:22.

[3]U.S. Attorneys Manual, § 9-73.801 (October 1997).

[4]U.S. Attorneys Manual, § 9-73.801 (October 1997).

[5]U.S. Attorneys Manual, § 9-73.801 (October 1997).

[6]INA § 340(a) [8 U.S.C.A. § 1451(a)].

[7]U.S. v. Zucca, 351 U.S. 91, 99, 76 S.Ct. 671, 676, 100 L.Ed. 964 (1956).

[8]U.S. v. Zucca, 351 U.S. 91, 100, 76 S.Ct. 671, 677, 100 L.Ed. 964 (1956); Matles v. U.S., 356 U.S. 256, 78 S.Ct. 712, 2 L.Ed.2d 741 (1958); Lucchese v. U.S., 356 U.S. 256, 78 S.Ct. 713, 2 L.Ed.2d 741 (1958); Costello v. U.S., 356 U.S. 256, 78 S.Ct. 714, 2 L.Ed.2d 741 (1958). Cf. Title v. U.S., 263 F.2d 28 (9th Cir. 1959) (refusing to reopen a final denaturalization order rendered in absence of such affidavit when the original order was not appealed) cert. denied, 359 U.S. 989 reh'g denied 360 U.S. 914 (1959).

[9]Costello v. U.S., 365 U.S. at 287, 81 S.Ct. at 546, 5 L.Ed.2d 551.

[10]U.S. v. Zucca, 351 U.S. 91, 99, 76 S.Ct. 671, 676, 100 L.Ed. 964 (1956).

[11]U.S. v. Zucca, 351 U.S. 91, 98–99, 76 S.Ct. 671, 676, 100 L.Ed. 964 (1956).

[12]Nowak v. I.N.S., 356 U.S. 660, 78 S.Ct. 995, 2 L.Ed.2d 1048 (1958).

[13]U.S. v. Zucca, 351 U.S. 91, 100, 76 S.Ct. 671, 677, 100 L.Ed. 964 (1956).

the naturalized citizen resides.[14] If the person does not reside in any judicial district of the U.S., the proceedings may be instituted in the U.S. district court for the District of Columbia, or in the U.S. district where the person last resided in the U.S.[15]

The naturalized citizen must be served by personal notice.[16] If the person is absent from the U.S. or from the district in which the person last resided, he or she may either be served by personal notice or by publication in the manner provided for the service of summons by publication or upon absentees by the laws of the state or the place where such suit is brought.[17] An *in absentia* denaturalization order which was entered in 1935 was vacated because the 1935 court failed to strictly comply with the local service of notice requirements.[18]

The party has 60 days from the date of service in which to answer the denaturalization petition.[19]

§ 14:22   Memorandum of understanding between INS, OIL, and U.S. Attorneys

In January 2000, apparently as a consequence of the failure of its administrative denaturalization procedures, the INS signed a memorandum of understanding with the Office of Immigration Litigation of the Civil Division of the Department of Justice, the Executive Office for United States Attorneys, and the U.S. Attorney for the Western District of North Carolina, acting as Chair of the Attorney General's Advisory Committee.[1] The memorandum details the steps to be followed by the DHS, the OIL and the USAO in instituting and litigating revocation of naturalization for a set of cases identified by the DHS' Central Revocation Unit.[2] The memorandum also delineates mutual responsibilities for consideration and possible institution of criminal proceedings in appropriate cases.[3] Finally, the memorandum discusses a different procedure for when the DHS intends to have the cases prosecuted criminally and seek revocation under the criminal section provisions.[4]

As part of the agreement, the DHS delegates DHS trial attorneys to OIL to assist in the litigation of revocation suits.[5] These attorneys will assist OIL in litigation in the most heavily affected areas, which are specifically named: Central District of

---

[14]INA § 340(a), 8 U.S.C.A. § 1451(a).

[15]INA § 340(a), 8 U.S.C.A. § 1451(a).

[16]INA § 340(b), 8 U.S.C.A. § 1451(b).

[17]INA § 340(b), 8 U.S.C.A. § 1451(b).

[18]U.S. v. Studak Not Reported in F.Supp., 1994 WL 16779120 E.D.Mich.,1994, reported in 71 Interpreter Releases 1183 (Sept. 1, 1994).

[19]INA § 340(b), 8 U.S.C.A. § 1451(b).

[Section 14:22]

[1]Memorandum of Understanding Between INS, OIL and US Attorneys, January 22, 2000 reproduced as Appendix 14-1.

[2]Memorandum of Understanding Between INS, OIL and US Attorneys, January 22, 2000 reproduced as Appendix 14-1.

[3]Memorandum of Understanding Between INS, OIL and US Attorneys, January 22, 2000 reproduced as Appendix 14-1.

[4]Memorandum of Understanding Between INS, OIL and US Attorneys, January 22, 2000 reproduced as Appendix 14-1. For a description of criminal procedures, see § 14:29.

[5]Memorandum of Understanding Between INS, OIL and US Attorneys, January 22, 2000 reproduced as Appendix 14-1. For a description of criminal procedures, see § 14:29.

California, Northern District of California, Southern District of Florida, Eastern District of New York, Southern District of New York, Northern District of Illinois, District of New Jersey, Eastern District of Virginia, Southern District of Texas, and Western District of Texas.[6] The DHS will also provide support staff for the DHS attorneys.[7]

Beyond the delegated attorneys, the DHS will still continue to provide litigation support to OIL, including obtaining official documentation, locating and interviewing witnesses and defendants, and serving the complaint and summons when service by mail is not appropriate or possible.[8]

The memorandum gives the DHS Central Revocation Unit the responsibility of preparing a referral packet and referring to OIL for its approval civil denaturalization proceedings.[9] The referral packet should include an executed Affidavit of Good Cause and an DHS point of contact to assist in the litigation of these actions.[10] DHS attorneys delegated to OIL may be called upon to continue preparing referral packages.[11]

The memorandum gives OIL the primary responsibility for litigating these revocation actions, except where USAO elects to assume either primary or exclusive responsibility for the litigation.[12] Under the memorandum, delegation of authority is sufficient for OIL to prosecute denaturalization proceedings without further case authorization.[13] When no delegation of authority has been provided by USAO, USAO case authorization is necessary before the initiation of revocation actions.[14]

OIL will continue to review all the actions seeking to revoke naturalization (with the exception of those within the jurisdiction of OSI).[15] OIL is responsible for providing the US Attorneys with a "Suit Authorization Memorandum" which provides the factual and legal basis for the revocation action, proposed litigation responsibilities, and the names of the OIL/DHS attorneys responsible for the action.[16]

---

[6]Memorandum of Understanding Between INS, OIL and US Attorneys, January 22, 2000 reproduced as Appendix 14-1. For a description of criminal procedures, see § 14:29.

[7]Memorandum of Understanding Between INS, OIL and US Attorneys, January 22, 2000 reproduced as Appendix 14-1. For a description of criminal procedures, see § 14:29.

[8]Memorandum of Understanding Between INS, OIL and US Attorneys, January 22, 2000 reproduced as Appendix 14-1. For a description of criminal procedures, see § 14:29.

[9]Memorandum of Understanding Between INS, OIL and US Attorneys, January 22, 2000 reproduced as Appendix 14-1. For a description of criminal procedures, see § 14:29.

[10]Memorandum of Understanding Between INS, OIL and US Attorneys, January 22, 2000 reproduced as Appendix 14-1. For a description of criminal procedures, see § 14:29.

[11]Memorandum of Understanding Between INS, OIL and US Attorneys, January 22, 2000 reproduced as Appendix 14-1. For a description of criminal procedures, see § 14:29.

[12]Memorandum of Understanding Between INS, OIL and US Attorneys, January 22, 2000 reproduced as Appendix 14-1. For a description of criminal procedures, see § 14:29.

[13]Memorandum of Understanding Between INS, OIL and US Attorneys, January 22, 2000 reproduced as Appendix 14-1. For a description of criminal procedures, see § 14:29.

[14]Memorandum of Understanding Between INS, OIL and US Attorneys, January 22, 2000 reproduced as Appendix 14-1. For a description of criminal procedures, see § 14:29.

[15]Memorandum of Understanding Between INS, OIL and US Attorneys, January 22, 2000 reproduced as Appendix 14-1. For a description of criminal procedures, see § 14:29. For the authority of the Office of Special Investigations, see § 14:21.

[16]Memorandum of Understanding, reproduced as Appendix 14-1.

Except in cases where USAO elects to assume primary responsibility, OIL is required to keep the DHS point of contact appraised of the status of the litigation and to coordinate litigation efforts with the DHS contact.[17]

The memorandum provides for a broad mechanism to delegate authority to OIL for the litigation of revocation actions.[18] USAO has the authority to decline the prosecution of the action.[19] Even when OIL/INS assume primary responsibility for an action, USAO will have the option of handling any part or all of the litigation within its district.[20]

The memorandum provides that if there is authorization for OIL/DHS to initiate and litigate revocation actions, the OIL/DHS attorney may use the U.S. attorney's name, address, and a point of contact in all pleadings, motions, and memoranda consistent with local rules and practice and in accordance with the individual U.S. attorney.[21] The U.S. attorney will provide a point of contact in all these actions, and his or her name will appear in all relevant pleadings.[22] This point of contact provides only assistance in filing and guidance in local practice.[23] Unless specifically agreed by USAO, the point of contact does not provide substantive litigation assistance, such as preparing pleadings and memoranda, or making court appearances.[24] In those cases where the U.S. attorney retains primary responsibility for the litigation, it provides OIL and the DHS with the name and phone number of the attorney in charge of the case.[25] The U.S. attorneys in those cases acquiesce to being contacted by the OIL and DHS regarding this litigation, and are required to coordinate litigation efforts with the DHS point of contact.[26]

The memorandum contemplates three types of authorization by USAO.[27] In some districts the U.S. attorney can agree to authorize denaturalization suits by "delegation and acquiescence."[28] According to the memorandum, under this modality, the U.S. attorney would give OIL/DHS a free hand to file suit and litigate denaturalization proceedings in that district.[29] Prior to commencing such a case, OIL would file with the U.S. attorney a "Suit Authorization Memorandum", setting out the legal and factual basis for revocation and specifying the proposed attorneys assigned to the litigation and the primary litigation unit.[30] If the U.S. attorney fails to respond to this memorandum within 30 days, the suit would be deemed approved and OIL/DHS would prosecute the case.[31] The U.S. attorney could also respond to the memorandum by assuming primary responsibility for the litigation, authorizing the litiga-

---

[17]Memorandum of Understanding, reproduced as Appendix 14-1.

[18]Memorandum of Understanding, reproduced as Appendix 14-1.

[19]Memorandum of Understanding, reproduced as Appendix 14-1.

[20]Memorandum of Understanding, reproduced as Appendix 14-1.

[21]Memorandum of Understanding, reproduced as Appendix 14-1.

[22]Memorandum of Understanding, reproduced as Appendix 14-1.

[23]Memorandum of Understanding, reproduced as Appendix 14-1.

[24]Memorandum of Understanding, reproduced as Appendix 14-1.

[25]Memorandum of Understanding, reproduced as Appendix 14-1.

[26]Memorandum of Understanding, reproduced as Appendix 14-1.

[27]Memorandum of Understanding, reproduced as Appendix 14-1.

[28]Memorandum of Understanding, reproduced as Appendix 14-1.

[29]Memorandum of Understanding, reproduced as Appendix 14-1.

[30]Memorandum of Understanding, reproduced as Appendix 14-1.

[31]Memorandum of Understanding, reproduced as Appendix 14-1.

tion as set forth on the memorandum, or declining to authorize the filing of the lawsuit.[32]

The second modality of authorization is for districts where the U.S. attorney has failed to sign the blanket "delegation and acquiescence" agreement.[33] Under this second modality, OIL also files with the U.S. attorney a "Suit Authorization Memorandum."[34] However, unlike the prior option, the suit does not get approved by the U.S. attorney's inaction. OIL/DHS can only conduct the litigation if the U.S. attorney specifically signs an authorization.[35] The U.S. attorney may also exercise the other two options: assume primary responsibility for the litigation, or decline to authorize the litigation altogether.[36]

Some districts have plainly refused to delegate to OIL/DHS the prosecution of these cases. In those districts, the U.S. attorney retains primary responsibility for filing and litigating revocation cases.[37]

Overall, the U.S. attorney retains the authority to decline to authorize the initiation or continuation of any revocation suit.[38]

§ 14:23 Burden of proof

The DHS must prove by "clear, unequivocal, and convincing" evidence that the applicant sought to obtain naturalization illegally and that issue may not be left in doubt.[1] Facts should be construed in favor of the citizen, in so far as it is reasonably possible.[2] This standard of proof is very strict.[3] The government carries a heavy burden of proof in proceedings to divest a naturalized citizen of his or her citizenship.[4] Despite this heavy burden, the facts of a case may be such that revocation can occur by summary judgment.[5]

On appeal, the U.S. Supreme Court will not accept the concurrent findings of fact of two lower courts, but will reexamine the facts to determine whether the U.S. has met its burden of proof.[6] Courts of appeals are also required to draw their own conclusions from the facts, and cannot accept the lower courts findings as conclusive.[7]

The strict character of this test is based on the consequences of denaturalization:

---

[32]Memorandum of Understanding, reproduced as Appendix 14-1.

[33]Memorandum of Understanding, reproduced as Appendix 14-1.

[34]Memorandum of Understanding, reproduced as Appendix 14-1.

[35]Memorandum of Understanding, reproduced as Appendix 14-1.

[36]Memorandum of Understanding, reproduced as Appendix 14-1.

[37]Memorandum of Understanding, reproduced as Appendix 14-1.

[38]Memorandum of Understanding, reproduced as Appendix 14-1.

[Section 14:23]

[1]Fedorenko v. U. S., 449 U.S. 490, 505, 101 S. Ct. 737, 746–47, 66 L. Ed. 2d 686 (1981); Knauer v. U. S., 328 U.S. 654, 657–58, 66 S. Ct. 1304, 1307, 90 L. Ed. 1500 (1946); Schneiderman v. U.S., 320 U.S. 118, 123, 63 S.Ct. 1333, 1335, 87 L.Ed. 1796 (1943).

[2]Schneiderman v. U.S., 320 U.S. 118, 122, 63 S. Ct. 1333, 1335, 87 L. Ed. 1796 (1943).

[3]Knauer v. U. S., 328 U.S. 654, 657, 66 S. Ct. 1304, 1306, 90 L. Ed. 2d 1500 (1946).

[4]Costello v. U. S., 365 U.S. 265, 269, 81 S. Ct. 534, 536, 5 L. Ed. 2d 551 (1961).

[5]U.S. v. Dailide, 227 F.3d 385, 55 Fed. R. Evid. Serv. 740, 2000 FED App. 299P (6th Cir. 2000); see also U.S. v. Kiang, 175 F. Supp. 2d 942 (E.D. Mich. 2001).

[6]Knauer v. U. S., 328 U.S. 654, 657, 66 S. Ct. 1304, 1306–07, 90 L. Ed. 1500 (1946).

[7]Stacher v. U. S., 258 F.2d 112, 120 (9th Cir. 1958); but cf. U.S. v. Demjanjuk, 367 F.3d 623 (6th Cir. 2004) (applying a plain error standard of review).

denaturalization involves not only tremendously high stakes for the person but also can call into play fundamental principles of the U.S. political system designed to protect minorities and majorities alike.[8]

Courts have found the DHS to have met its burden when it can demonstrate through circumstantial and redundant evidence that the person knew the falsity of the answer and repeatedly asserted its veracity.[9] Prior contrary statements and admissions by the defendant[10] and documentary evidence to establish that true facts were contrary to what the applicant claimed have been used to meet this burden.[11] Willfulness has been established by showing repeated concealment or misrepresentation under oath[12] and cumulative evidence leading to the conclusion that no one in defendant's position would have reasonably thought answers were true.[13] In addition, courts have emphasized that the defendant's failure to introduce any mitigating or explanatory evidence for the concealment or misrepresentation makes the evidence introduced by the government uncontroverted, thus strengthening its case.[14] The Supreme Court in *Costello* failed to reach the issue of whether an inference may constitutionally be drawn in denaturalization proceedings from defendant's failure to take the stand.[15] Finally, one court has held that, where the government met its burden of proof and the defendant failed to rebut it, the court would not consider the defendant's affirmative defenses because the court lacks the equitable discretion to excuse the defendant's conduct in illegally procuring citizenship.[16]

§ 14:24 Appeals and reopening

Appeals from district court orders are taken to the circuit courts and may reach the U.S. Supreme Court via certiorari.[1] Either side may take an appeal from a

---

[8]Knauer v. U. S., 328 U.S. 654, 659, 66 S. Ct. 1304, 1307, 90 L. Ed. 1500 (1946).

[9]See Costello v. U. S., 365 U.S. 265, 273–77, 81 S. Ct. 534, 538–40, 5 L. Ed. 2d 551 (1961); U. S. v. D'Agostino, 338 F.2d 490, 491–92 (2d Cir. 1964); U. S. v. Oddo, 314 F.2d 115, 116–17 (2d Cir. 1963).

[10]Costello v. U. S., 365 U.S. 265, 273–74, 81 S. Ct. 534, 538, 5 L. Ed. 2d 551 (1961) (admissions in federal and state inquiries); U. S. v. D'Agostino, 338 F.2d 490, 491–92 (2d Cir. 1964) (declaration when landing in the U.S. that he was married, statement to the same effect in a declaration of intent to become citizen, also a statement in an application to replace the naturalization certificate after the naturalization but before the revocation proceedings).

[11]Costello v. U. S., 365 U.S. 265, 81 S. Ct. 534, 5 L. Ed. 2d 551 (1961) (corporate records from Registries of Deeds showing that purported business had done no significant transactions during the period in question); U. S. v. D'Agostino, 338 F.2d 490, 491–92 (2d Cir. 1964) (certificate of the registrar of Vital Statistics in Calabbria certifying person was married and marriage had not been terminated, declarations and other documents filed by defendant; U. S. v. Oddo, 314 F.2d 115, 116–17 (2d Cir. 1963) (record of arrests, certificates completed and signed by defendant); U.S. v. Demjanjuk, 367 F.3d 623 (6th Cir. 2004) (relying on service pass and expert testimony).

[12]U. S. v. D'Agostino, 338 F.2d 490 (2d Cir. 1964); U. S. v. Oddo, 314 F.2d 115, 117 (2d Cir. 1963); U.S. v. Demjanjuk, 367 F.3d 623 (6th Cir. 2004) (relying on service pass and expert testimony).

[13]Costello v. U. S., 365 U.S. 265, 277, 81 S. Ct. 534, 540–41, 5 L. Ed. 2d 551 (1961).

[14]U. S. v. D'Agostino, 338 F.2d 490, 493 (2d Cir. 1964); U. S. v. Oddo, 314 F.2d 115, 117 (2d Cir. 1963).

[15]Costello v. U. S., 365 U.S. 265, 278, 81 S. Ct. 534, 541, 5 L. Ed. 2d 551 (1961).

[16]U.S. v. Reve, 241 F.Supp. 2d 470, 478 (D.N.J. 2003) (relying on I.N.S. v. Pangilinan, 486 U.S. 875, 108 S. Ct. 2210 (1988) and Fedorenko v. U.S., 449 U.S. 490, 517, 101 S. Ct. 737 (1981), the court refused to hear the equitable defenses of waiver, estoppel, or laches).

[Section 14:24]

[1]See, Knauer v. U. S., 328 U.S. 654, 657, 66 S. Ct. 1304, 1306, 90 L. Ed. 1500 (1946).

denaturalization judgment. On appeal, the appellate court is required to make its own findings of fact.[2]

It is advisable that defendants take the necessary appeals, as the courts do not look favorably on motions to reopen after the denaturalization orders have become final.[3] In some unusual cases, however, even courts of appeal have themselves revisited their own decisions when possible misconduct by the U.S. government has been uncovered.[4]

IV. PRESUMPTIONS AND SPECIAL CASES

§ 14:25 Failure to testify before Congressional committee

The statute specifically provides that refusal to testify before a Congressional committee concerning the person's subversive activities constitutes a ground of revocation based on concealment of a material fact or willful misrepresentation, provided the person was convicted of contempt for the failure to testify.[1] No such presumption exists if the person naturalized over 10 years before the refusal to testify.[2]

§ 14:26 Joining Communist Party

Persons who naturalized after December 24, 1952 are subject to a presumption of lack of attachment to the U.S. Constitution if within five years after such naturalization they became "members of or affiliated with any organization, membership in or affiliation with which at the time of naturalization would have been precluded under the provisions of section 313 [of the INA, barring naturalization of members of the Communist and other subversive organizations]."[1] That bar is discussed in detail in Ch 7.[2]

This presumption sets up a very special burden of proof. Membership in such organization is considered *prima facie* evidence that the person was not attached to the principles of the Constitution and was not well disposed to the good order and happiness of the U.S. at the time of naturalization.[3] Such a presumption may be overcome by producing countervailing evidence.[4] Failure to produce such countervailing evidence makes this presumption sufficient to establish the fact presumed.[5] The naturalization will then have been properly revoked provided the proceeding has been proper, the order admitting the person to citizenship will be set aside, and the

---

[2]Knauer v. U. S., 328 U.S. 654, 657, 66 S. Ct. 1304, 1306–07, 90 L. Ed. 1500 (1946). See § 14:22.

[3]Polites v. U.S., 364 U.S. 426, 81 S.Ct. 202, 5 L.Ed.2d 173 (1960); Ackerman v. U.S., 340 U.S. 193, 71 S.Ct. 209, 95 L.Ed. 207 (1950).

[4]See Justice Department Refiles Nazi Denaturalization Case, 76 Interpreter Releases 856 (May 28, 1999).

[Section 14:25]

[1]INA § 340(a), 8 U.S.C.A. § 1451(a).

[2]INA § 340(a), 8 U.S.C.A. § 1451(a).

[Section 14:26]

[1]INA § 340(c), 8 U.S.C.A. § 1451(c).

[2]See §§ 7:68 to 7:90.

[3]INA § 340(c), 8 U.S.C.A. § 1451(c).

[4]INA § 340(c), 8 U.S.C.A. § 1451(c).

[5]INA § 340(c), 8 U.S.C.A. § 1451(c).

certificate of naturalization will be canceled.[6] Such revocations and cancellations are retroactive to the original dates of admission to citizenship and of issuance of the certificate.[7]

§ 14:27 Taking up residence in another country

Until the passage of the INTCA, persons who within one year after naturalization took up permanent residence in any foreign country, including their country of nativity, were subject to a presumption of lack of intent on their part to reside permanently in the United States at the time of their admission to citizenship.[1] This presumption used to establish *prima facie* evidence of having obtained naturalization through concealment of a material fact or by willful misrepresentation, and in the absence of countervailing evidence, was sufficient to form the basis for revocation of the naturalization, retroactively setting aside the admission of citizenship and canceling the certificate of naturalization.[2]

Not all naturalization applicants were required to have the intention of residing permanently in the United States. As part of the remedial legislation to allow the naturalization of Filipino service people who fought in the U.S. armed forces in World War II, Congress specifically provided that the presumption of lack of intent to reside in the United States would not apply to those service people.[3]

The diplomatic and consular officers of the U.S. in foreign countries were required to furnish the Department of Justice with the names of persons within their jurisdictions who had been naturalized and had taken up residence in those countries.[4] When duly certified, those statements were admissible into evidence in all court proceedings to revoke naturalization.[5]

The INTCA repealed the provision establishing the presumption of fraud if the naturalized citizen takes up residence abroad within one year of admission to citizenship.[6] Accordingly, State Department personnel are no longer required to furnish the names of persons who took up residence abroad.[7]

The State Department has advised consular and diplomatic officers to cease all action on cases under the prior law.[8] If a case was in suspense, the consular officers have been instructed to notify the subject that all further actions on the case will be

---

[6]INA § 340(c), 8 U.S.C.A. § 1451(c).

[7]INA § 340(c), 8 U.S.C.A. § 1451(c).

[Section 14:27]

[1]INA § 340(d), 8 U.S.C.A. § 1451(d) as amended by sec. 17, Pub. L. No. 99-653, 100 Stat. 3655 (Nov. 14, 1986).

[2]INA § 340(d), 8 U.S.C.A. § 1451(d) as amended by sec. 17, Pub. L. No. 99-653, 100 Stat. 3655 (Nov. 14, 1986).

[3]See § 12:11.

[4]INA § 340(d), 8 U.S.C.A. § 1451(d) as amended by sec. 17, Pub. L. No. 99-653, 100 Stat. 3655 (Nov. 14, 1986).

[5]INA § 340(d), 8 U.S.C.A. § 1451(d) as amended by sec. 17, Pub. L. No. 99-653, 100 Stat. 3655 (Nov. 14, 1986).

[6]INTCA § 104(b) reproduced as Appendix 4-21 to Ch 4.

[7]INTCA § 104(b) reproduced as Appendix 4-21 to Ch 4.

[8]State Dept. Cable, File No. 95-State-no number listed, reproduced in 72 Interpreter Releases 350 (Mar. 13, 1995).

terminated.[9] Indeed, the State Department has repealed its regulations regarding the collection of information about naturalized citizens who return to their country of origin within one year of admission to citizenship.[10] The State Department, however, has no authority to reinstate citizenship to those who were judicially denaturalized because of consular reports of taking up residence in another country.[11]

§ 14:28 Revocation of naturalization based on active-duty service in time of war

Any person who has been naturalized under the provisions allowing such naturalization for service rendered in the U.S. armed forces during time of war is subject to denaturalization proceedings if at any time subsequent to naturalization the person is separated from the military under other than honorable conditions.[1] Naturalization of persons through service in the U.S. armed forces in time of war is discussed in detail in Ch 12.[2]

Unlike the other presumptions in this section, this is a special form of denaturalization and *not* a presumption of fraud at the time of admission to citizenship. The proceedings used to revoke naturalization in these cases are the same as for general denaturalization.[3] However, the fact of separation from the service under other than honorable conditions must be proven by a duly authenticated certification from the executive department under which the person was serving at the time of separation.[4]

V. DENATURALIZATION ANCILLARY TO CRIMINAL CONVICTION FOR NATURALIZATION FRAUD

§ 14:29 Generally

Whenever a naturalized citizen is convicted criminally of knowingly procuring naturalization in violation of law, under the provisions of 18 U.S.C.A. § 1425, the court will also set aside the order admitting the person to citizenship and declare the certificate of naturalization canceled.[1] The criminal provision in question punishes any person who:

(a) . . . knowingly procures or attempts to procure, contrary to law, the naturalization of any person, or documentary or other evidence of naturalization or of citizenship; or

(b) . . . whether for himself [or herself] or another person not entitled thereto, knowingly issues, procures or obtains or applies for or otherwise attempts to procure or obtain naturalization, or citizenship, or a declaration of intention to become a citizen

---

[9]State Dept. Cable, File No. 95-State-no number listed, reproduced in 72 Interpreter Releases 350 (Mar. 13, 1995).

[10]61 Fed. Reg. 29651 (June 12, 1996).

[11]State Dept. Cable, File No. 95-State-no number listed.

[Section 14:28]

[1]INA § 329(c), 8 U.S.C.A. § 1440(c).

[2]See §§ 12:6 to 12:9.

[3]INA § 329(c), 8 U.S.C.A. § 1440(c).

[4]INA § 329(c), 8 U.S.C.A. § 1440(c).

[Section 14:29]

[1]INA § 340(e), 8 U.S.C.A. § 1451(e).

. . . or evidence of naturalization or citizenship, documentary or otherwise, or duplicates of any of the foregoing.[2]

Courts that possess jurisdiction to try these criminal provisions have also specifically been conferred jurisdiction to "revoke, set aside, and declare void the final order admitting such person to citizenship" and to "declare the certificate of naturalization of such person to be canceled."[3] Upon a conviction under this criminal provision, the judge is required to set aside the order admitting to citizenship and to cancel the naturalization certificate.[4] However, conviction under other criminal sections, such as the general immigration fraud provision, does not bring about the automatic setting aside of the order admitting to citizenship.[5]

An acquittal on a criminal prosecution does not necessarily preclude a civil denaturalization proceeding.[6] Even though the naturalization may be revoked incident to the criminal prosecution, dismissal in the criminal trial, especially if based on the statute of limitations, will not bar civil denaturalization proceedings.[7] On the other hand, if a court in a *civil* denaturalization proceeding finds that the defendant did not commit the act he or she was charged with, a criminal court may consider that fact established based on the principle of *res judicata*.[8]

The courts are divided as to whether there is a requirement of materiality. Even though the statute does not specifically require it, the Ninth Circuit has read a

---

[2]18 U.S.C.A. § 1425.

[3]INA § 340(e), 8 U.S.C.A. § 1451(e).

[4]INA § 340(e), 8 U.S.C.A. § 1451(e).

[5]See INA § 340(e), 8 U.S.C.A. § 1451(e). See also, Memorandum of Understanding Between INS, OIL and US Attorneys, January 22, 2000 reproduced as Appendix 14-1.

[6]INS Interp. 340.1(e).

[7]Sourino v. U.S., 86 F.2d 309 (5th Cir. 1936).

[8]See U.S. v. Bridges, 123 F.Supp. 705, 708 (N.D.Cal. 1954) (holding civil proceedings not barred by prior acquittal in criminal proceedings). This decision was part of an extraordinarily tenacious effort by the U.S. government to deport Harry Bridges, a labor organizer of Australian origin. Deportation proceedings were originally started against him in 1939 on the grounds that he was a member of an organization that advocated violent overthrow of the U.S. government. A finding in favor of Bridges was entered by the administrative officer, which was affirmed by the Secretary of Labor. After the law was amended, another administrative hearing was held in 1941. The administrative hearing officer found that Bridges belonged to an organization affiliated with the Communist Party and therefore was a member of the Communist Party. The BIA reversed this decision, but was, in turn, reversed by the Attorney General. Mr. Bridges was taken into custody and sought relief through a habeas corpus petition which was denied by the district court. Ex Parte Bridges, 49 F.Supp. 292 (N.D.Cal. 1943) aff'd 144 F.2d 927 (9th Cir. 1944). The Supreme Court reversed in Bridges v. Wixon, 326 U.S. 135, 65 S.Ct. 1443, 89 L.Ed. 2103 (1945). See §§ 7:68 to 7:76. Shortly thereafter, on September 17, 1945, Bridges sought and received a decree of naturalization. In 1949, both civil denaturalization proceedings against him and criminal proceedings for naturalization fraud against him and two of his witnesses at the naturalization hearing were instituted. U.S. v. Bridges, 86 F.Supp. 922 (denying motion to dismiss criminal indictment as barred by statute of limitations), 86 F.Supp. 931 (N.D.Cal. 1949) (staying denaturalization proceedings). Bridges was convicted in his criminal trial and ordered denaturalized, both rulings being affirmed by the Ninth Circuit. Bridges v. U.S. 199 F.2d 811 (affirming conviction), 199 F.2d 845 (affirming denaturalization) reh'g en banc denied 201 F.2d 254 (9th Cir. 1952) (per curiam). The Supreme Court once more reversed, on the grounds that prosecution was barred by the statute of limitations. Bridges v. U.S., 345 U.S. 979, 73 S.Ct. 1130, 97 L.Ed.2d 1393 (denaturalization judgment), 346 U.S. 209, 73 S.Ct. 1055, 97 L.Ed. 1557 (1953) (conviction judgment). The civil denaturalization proceeding which had been started before the criminal trial was then reactivated, leading to the present decision. On the merits, the trial court finally found for Mr. Bridges on the ground that the government's evidence was insufficient to denaturalize him. U.S. v. Bridges, 133 F.Supp. 638 (N.D.Cal. 1955). See also, Roberts, The Bridges Cases, 76 Interpreter Releases 1385 (Sept. 20, 1999).

materiality requirement in order for misrepresentations to be contrary to law in the context of a criminal conviction under this section.[9] The Southern District of New York has taken the opposite view.[10]

In addition, courts have also read a requirement of intent for a conviction under this section.[11] The fact that the naturalization was obtained contrary to law is not sufficient for a conviction, as this is not a strict liability statute.[12]

In 2000, the INS, the Office of Immigration Litigation of the Department of Justice (OIL), and the Office of U.S. Attorneys signed an agreement mainly relating to the prosecution of civil revocation litigation.[13] However, the memorandum also specifies the procedures to be followed when the DHS decides to criminally prosecute cases within the specific set of cases contemplated by the agreement.[14] Under the agreement, the DHS has primary responsibility for referring cases for prosecution under 18 U.S.C.A. § 1425 and concurrent revocation under 8 U.S.C.A. § 1451(e).[15] The DHS is required to promptly notify OIL of its intention.[16] The DHS official then prepares the case and refers it to USAO.[17] The memorandum urges the U.S. attorney to prosecute these cases under 18 U.S.C.A. § 1425, as this section brings about the setting aside of the admission to citizenship.[18] If the U.S. attorney decides to negotiate a plea, he or she has to notify DHS and OIL promptly.[19] Similar prompt notification is required if the U.S. attorney decides not to prosecute the case criminally or to proceed with a civil denaturalization proceeding.[20]

VI. ADMINISTRATIVE DENATURALIZATION

§ 14:30 Generally

Research References

Gopal, From Judicial to Administrative Denaturalization: For Better or For Worse?, 72 U. Colo. L. Rev. 779 (Summer, 2001)

---

[9]U.S. v. Puerta, 982 F.2d 1297, 1301 (9th Cir. 1992).

[10]U.S. v. Rogers, 898 F.Supp. 219 (S.D.N.Y. 1995) (refusing to dismiss an indictment and holding that section 1425(a) does not require an allegation that the false statement was material). For a discussion of the materiality requirement, see § 14:7.

[11]U.S. v. Pasillas-Gaytan, 192 F.3d 864 (9th Cir. 1999); U.S. v. Moses, 94 F.3d 182 (5th Cir. 1996); U.S. v. Alameh, 341 F.3d 167 (2d Cir. 2003).

[12]U.S. v. Pasillas-Gaytan, 192 F.3d 864 (9th Cir. 1999); U.S. v. Moses, 94 F.3d 182 (5th Cir. 1996); U.S. v. Alameh, 341 F.3d 167 (2d Cir. 2003).

[13]Memorandum of Understanding Between INS, OIL, and USAO, January 22, 2000 reproduced as Appendix 14-1.

[14]Memorandum of Understanding Between INS, OIL, and USAO, January 22, 2000 reproduced as Appendix 14-1.

[15]Memorandum of Understanding Between INS, OIL, and USAO, January 22, 2000 reproduced as Appendix 14-1.

[16]Memorandum of Understanding Between INS, OIL, and USAO, January 22, 2000 reproduced as Appendix 14-1.

[17]Memorandum of Understanding Between INS, OIL, and USAO, January 22, 2000 reproduced as Appendix 14-1.

[18]Memorandum of Understanding Between INS, OIL, and USAO, January 22, 2000 reproduced as Appendix 14-1.

[19]Memorandum of Understanding Between INS, OIL, and USAO, January 22, 2000 reproduced as Appendix 14-1.

[20]Memorandum of Understanding Between INS, OIL, and USAO, January 22, 2000 reproduced as Appendix 14-1.

The INA provides that in addition to judicial denaturalization, the Attorney General (now Secretary of the Department of Homeland Security (DHS)) retains the power to correct, reopen, alter, modify, or vacate his or her naturalization orders.[1] This provision derives from a similar one allowing naturalization courts to modify or vacate their own orders.[2] When the INA was amended in 1990 to replace judicial naturalization with administrative naturalization, this "residual" clause was also amended transferring that power to the Attorney General who was now in charge of granting naturalizations.[3]

On July 9, 1998, a District Court preliminarily enjoined the INS from continuing with administrative denaturalization proceedings.[4] The preliminary injunction was appealed to the Ninth Circuit, where a panel originally overturned the District Court decision.[5] This decision, however, was later withdrawn by the full court, which granted rehearing en banc.[6] The Court then, unanimously, upheld the district court decision.[7] The Court held that the regulations were void because they had no statutory authority.[8]

As the Court pointed out, Congress never granted the legacy INS the authority to denaturalize U.S. citizens.[9] Indeed, it found that Congress had been unambiguous in *not* granting this power to the INS.[10] The INS attempt to appropriate to itself such authority by issuing regulations has been struck down. The regulations codified in 8 CFR § 340 cannot be employed by the INS to revoke the citizenship of any person.[11] On February 13, 2001, the court issued a permanent injunction enjoining the INS (and now the DHS) from using its administrative denaturalization procedures.[12]

At this point, the only valid administrative reopening of naturalization proceedings occurs *prior* to the swearing in ceremony.[13] After the applicant has taken the

---

[Section 14:30]

[1]INA § 340(h), 8 U.S.C.A. § 1451(h).

[2]INA § 340(j), 8 U.S.C.A. § 1451(j) as originally enacted by Act of June 27, 1952, 66 Stat. 163, redesignated as INA § 340(i), 8 U.S.C.A. § 1451(i) by Pub.L. 100-525, § 9 (dd)(3) redesignated as INA § 340(h), 8 U.S.C.A. § 1451(h) by INTCA § 104(c)(1) reproduced as Appendix 4-21, to Ch 4.

[3]Sec. 407(d)(18)(D), Immigration Act of 1990, Pub.L. 101-649, 104 Stat. 4978 (Nov. 29, 1990).

[4]Gorbach v. Reno, Case No. C98-278R (W.D. Wash., July 9, 1998) (preliminary injunction).

[5]Gorbach v. Reno, 179 F.3d 1111 (9th Cir. 1999).

[6]Gorbach v. Reno, 192 F.3d 1329 (9th Cir. 1999) (granting rehearing en banc and withdrawing the three-judge panel opinion, Gorbach v. Reno, 179 F.3d 1111 (9th Cir. 1999)).

[7]Gorbach v. Reno, 219 F.3d 1087 (9th Cir. 2000).

[8]Gorbach v. Reno, 219 F.3d 1087 (9th Cir. 2000).

[9]Gorbach v. Reno, 219 F.3d 1087 (9th Cir. 2000).

[10]Gorbach v. Reno, 219 F.3d 1087 (9th Cir. 2000).

[11]For a detailed description of the regulatory scheme and the court decisions issued under prior law, see Levy, Administrative Denaturalization: Practical Issues Under New Standards, 74 Interpreter Releases 1701 (Nov. 7, 1997).

[12]Gorbach v. Reno, 2001 WL 34145464 (W.D. Wash. Feb. 14, 2001).

[13]See § 14:20.

naturalization oath, he or she may only be denaturalized through judicial proceedings.[14]

Between the years 1998 and 1999, the INS initiated a number of administrative denaturalization proceedings. It even issued some orders reopening the proceedings and revoking the person's naturalization. These orders are obviously invalid since the INS did not have the authority to issue such orders. The District Court ultimately entered a permanent injunction (1) enjoining the government "from denying to any individual the rights or benefits of United States citizenship as the result of such proceedings," and (2) ordering the government to "reinstate and return all certificates of naturalization heretofore revoked as a result of proceedings conducted pursuant to 8 C.F.R. § 340.1."[15]

VII. CONSEQUENCES OF DENATURALIZATION

§ 14:31 Retroactivity of revocation

Research References

Dizon and Wettstein, Immigration Law Service 2d § 14:426

The judicial canceling of the naturalization certificate and the order admitting to citizenship under the general revocation provisions is effective retroactively to the date the certificate and the order were issued.[1] This retroactivity has been upheld against constitutional challenges that it violated separation of powers and the prohibition against *ex post facto* laws.[2]

The effect of cancellation of naturalization *ab initio* is to render the original order of naturalization and certificate of naturalization completely null and void for purposes of derivation of citizenship benefits from such naturalization.[3] However, this "relation back" concept does not apply to deportation: actions committed by the person while a naturalized citizen are not actions of a noncitizen for purposes of deportation statutes.[4]

§ 14:32 Removal proceedings

Research References

Dizon and Wettstein, Immigration Law Service 2d § 14:426

Whenever a court sets aside an order admitting a person to citizenship, or cancels a certificate of naturalization, the court is required to notify the DHS that it has

---

[14]For a detailed description of the regulatory scheme and the court decisions issued under prior law, see Levy, Administrative Denaturalization: Practical Issues Under New Standards, 74 Interpreter Releases 1701 (Nov. 7, 1997).

[15]Gorbach v. Reno, 2001 WL 34145464, *1 (W.D.Wash., Feb. 14, 2001) (unpublished).

[Section 14:31]

[1]INA § 340(a), 8 U.S.C.A. § 1451(a).

[2]Johannessen v. U.S., 225 U.S. 227, 32 S.Ct. 613, 56 L.Ed. 1066 (1912).

[3]Rosenberg v. U.S., 60 F.2d 475, 476 (3d Cir. 1932); Antonacci v. Bronwell, 133 F.Supp. 201, 203 (S.D.Ill. 1955).

[4]Costello v. I.N.S., 376 U.S. 120, 128–29, 84 S.Ct. 580, 585–86, 11 L.Ed.2d 559 (1964). Cf. § 14:32.

taken such action, by sending it a certified copy of the order.[1] Upon notification of the court or the DHS, a holder of a canceled certificate of naturalization must surrender the certificate to the DHS.[2] Failure to surrender that document is a felony punishable by up to 5 years in prison and $5,000 in fines.[3]

On the one hand, the DHS will institute removal proceedings if the person becomes deportable through denaturalization.[4] Not all persons become deportable when they are denaturalized.[5] Denaturalization does not relate back to its inception for purposes of deportation.[6] Acts done while a citizen will only render a person deportable if the statute did not require the person to have been a noncitizen at the time of taking such action.

Thus, the Supreme Court interpreting the deportation provisions of the Act of May 10, 1920 found two former citizens deportable for acts committed while citizens.[7] That act made deportable "[a]ll aliens who since August 1, 1914 have been or may hereafter be convicted" of violating the Espionage Act of 1917.[8] The Court found that the words plainly required that the persons be "aliens" at the time of the deportation and that they must have been convicted of a violation contained in the Espionage Act of 1917.[9] Nothing in that deportation provision required that the person must have been a noncitizen *when convicted* of the criminal violation.[10]

On the other hand, if the deportation provision requires the person to be a noncitizen *at the time* of the commission of the act making him or her deportable, then persons who were citizens at the time but were later denaturalized are not deportable. Thus, in interpreting the provision relating to deportability for two or more crimes of moral turpitude committed after entry the Court found that if the person was a citizen at the time, he or she did not become deportable.[11] That provision then read: "[a]ny alien [who] at any time after entry is convicted of two crimes involving moral turpitude" shall be deported.[12] The court found that this section required the person to be an "alien" at the time of conviction, and therefore was not

---

[Section 14:32]

[1]INA § 340(f), 8 U.S.C.A. § 1451(f).

[2]INA § 340(f), 8 U.S.C.A. § 1451(f).

[3]18 U.S.C.A. § 1428. Cf. § 13:41.

[4]*See, e.g.,* Negele v. Ashcroft, 368 F.3d 981 (8th Cir. 2004) (upholding removal order of BIA in proceeding instituted after individual was denaturalized).

[5]Costello v. Immigration and Naturalization Service, 376 U.S. 120, 130–31, 84 S. Ct. 580, 586–87, 11 L. Ed. 2d 559 (1964).

[6]Costello v. Immigration and Naturalization Service, 376 U.S. 120, 128–29, 84 S. Ct. 580, 585–86, 11 L. Ed. 2d 559 (1964).

[7]U.S. Ex rel. Eichenlaub v. Shaughnessy, 338 U.S. 521, 70 S.Ct. 329, 94 L.Ed. 397 (1950).

[8]United States ex rel. Eichenlaub v. Shaughnessy, 338 U.S. 521, 527, 70 S. Ct. 329, 332, 64 L. Ed. 307, 94 L. Ed. 307 (1950).

[9]United States ex rel. Eichenlaub v. Shaughnessy, 338 U.S. 521, 529–30, 70 S. Ct. 329, 333, 64 L. Ed. 307, 94 L. Ed. 307 (1950).

[10]United States ex rel. Eichenlaub v. Shaughnessy, 338 U.S. 521, 530, 70 S.Ct. 329, 333, 64 L.Ed.2d 307, 94 L.Ed.2d 307 (1950).

[11]Costello v. I.N.S., 376 U.S. 120, 84 S.Ct. 580, 11 L.Ed.2d 559.

[12]INA § 241(a)(4), 8 U.S.C.A. § 1251(a)(4) as originally enacted by Act of June 27, 1952, 66 Stat. 163.

applicable if the person was a naturalized citizen at the time.[13] The same result should be expected for the equivalent provision under the present deportation statute since it is identical in all relevant respects.[14]

Similarly, it has been held that deportation based on provisions requiring the person to have committed a specific act within a certain period after "entry" refer to entry into the United States as a noncitizen.[15] Before the 1996 amendments, the word "entry" was defined as "any coming of an *alien* into the United States."[16] Thus, a court has found that the provision mandating deportation of a noncitizen who is convicted of a crime of moral turpitude within five years after entry did not apply to a person whose conviction occurred more than five years after the person had entered as a noncitizen but within five years of having reentered as a U.S. citizen.[17]

The Board has distinguished Costello subsequently, upholding removability on account of convictions occurring after (a subsequently revoked) naturalization.[18] The Board characterized Costello as turning on the unavailability of a "Judicial Recommendation Against Deportation" (JRAD) for a person who thought they were a citizen.[19] A 1990 statute made JRADs prospectively unavailable to noncitizens convicted of crimes.[20] Thus, to the extent that Costello was premised on the existence of JRADs, the elimination of the JRAD possibility would seem to render Costello inapplicable to any post-1990 convictions.[21] However, the Supreme Court was also construing statutory language in Costello, language Congress has not seen fit to alter. The Eleventh Circuit, the only Court of Appeals to address this issue, rejected the Board's reinterpretation of the statute in an unpublished decision, reasoning that lenity, Congressional acquiescence, and the unchanged statutory text led to a conclusion contrary to the Board's.[22]

§ 14:33 Derivative revocation

Research References
Dizon and Wettstein, Immigration Law Service 2d § 14:427

Persons who claimed U.S. citizenship through the U.S. citizenship of a spouse or parent whose naturalization was revoked because of concealment or misrepresentation will also automatically lose their U.S. citizenship as of the time of the order set-

---

[13]Costello v. I.N.S., 376 U.S. 120, 84 S.Ct. 580, 11 L.Ed.2d 559.

[14]See INA § 237(a)(2)(A)(ii), 8 U.S.C.A. § 1227(a)(2)(A)(ii).

[15]U.S. ex rel. Brancato v. Lehman, 239 F.2d 663, 666 (6th Cir. 1956).

[16]INA § 101(a)(13), 8 U.S.C.A. § 1101(a)(13) prior to IIRAIRA Amendments.

[17]U. S. ex rel. Brancato v. Lehmann, 239 F.2d 663 (6th Cir. 1956).

[18]See e.g., Matter of Rossi, 11 I. & N. Dec. 514 (BIA 1966); Matter of Gonzalez-Muro, 24 I. & N. Dec. 472 (BIA 2008).

[19]Matter of Rossi, 111 I. & N. Dec. at 515-16 (describing Costello as "primarily predicated on the provisions of section 241(b) [of the Immigration and Nationality Act, 8 U.S.C. § 1251(b)] and the fact that Costello, being a naturalized citizen at the time of his convictions, was deprived of any opportunity of requesting the sentencing court to recommend against his deportation."); see also Gonzalez-Muro, 24 I. & N. Dec. at 473.

[20]Immigration Act of 1990 ("IMMACT"), Pub. L. No. 101-649, § 505, 104 Stat. 4978, 5050.

[21]See Gonzalez-Muro, 24 I. & N. Dec. at 473-74.

[22]Adams v. U.S. Atty. Gen., 472 Fed. Appx. 898 (11th Cir. 2012) (unpublished).

ting aside the principal's citizenship.[1] The rationale behind this law is that since the admission to citizenship was canceled *ab initio*, no rights derived from such admission.[2] However, if the denaturalization is based on "illegality" rather then fraud, the derivative will *not* lose his or her citizenship.[3]

Furthermore, the INA distinguishes between revocation for fraud and for presumptive fraud. If the spouse or parent was revoked naturalization under the general proceedings for revocation because of concealment of a material fact or willful misrepresentation, the relative loses his or her citizenship regardless of whether at the time of the revocation the relative was living in the United States.[4]

The situation is different if the principal was denaturalized under one of the presumptions in the INA. In such case, if the relative is residing in the United States at the time of denaturalization of the principal, the relative will *not* lose his or her citizenship if the principal's denaturalization is based on the presumptions derived from (1) having joined the Communist or other subversive party within five years after admission to citizenship, or (2) having taken up residence in a foreign country within one year of admission to citizenship, or (3) under the special provision for denaturalization of servicemen separated from the U.S. armed forces under less-than-honorable conditions, provided this latter denaturalization was not based on procurement of naturalization through concealment of a material fact or willful misrepresentation.[5]

At the statutory level, the INA has a special provision that shelters abused spouses and children of United States citizens from loss of their immediate relative classification if the abusive citizen spouse is denaturalized or otherwise loses or renounces his or her U.S. citizenship.[6]

[Section 14:33]

[1]INA § 340(d), 8 U.S.C.A. § 1451(d).

[2]Rosenberg v. U S, 60 F.2d 475, 476 (C.C.A. 3d Cir. 1932); Antonacci v. Brownell, 133 F. Supp. 201, 203–04 (S.D. Ill. 1955).

[3]INA § 340(d), 8 U.S.C.A. § 1451(d); INS Interp. 340.3(a)(3)(i).

[4]INA § 340(d), 8 U.S.C.A. § 1451(d).

[5]INA § 340(d), 8 U.S.C.A. § 1451(d).

[6]Victims of Trafficking and Violence Protection Act of 2000, Pub.L. 106-386, § 1507(a)(1), (3), 114 Stat. 1464 (Oct. 28, 2000) amending INA §§ 201(b)(2)(A)(i), 204(a)(1)(A), 8 U.S.C.A. §§ 1151(b)(2)(A)(i), 1154(a)(1)(A).

APPENDIX 14-1

Memorandum of Understanding Between INS, OIL, and USAO

U.S. Department of Justice

Washington, DC 20530

MEMORANDUM OF UNDERSTANDING

Between the United States Attorneys Offices, the Immigration and Naturalization Service, and the Civil Division - Office of Immigration Litigation Regarding Actions to Revoke Naturalization.

This memorandum sets forth the agreement between the United States Attorneys Offices (USAOs), the Immigration and Naturalization Service (the INS) and the Civil Division - Office of Immigration Litigation (OIL) with respect to the mutual responsibilities for action seeking to revoke naturalization under 8 U.S.C. § 1451(a), and as relevant, actions brought under 18 U.S.C. §§ 1015, 1425, 1001 as they affect illegal or fraudulent procurement of naturalization. This memorandum, however, only applies to cases appropriately designated as part of this special population by the INS's Central Revocation Unit. Except as set forth in this memorandum, actions to revoke naturalization shall be prepared, presented, and litigated as set forth in the United States Attorneys Manual, as well as any applicable memoranda of understanding, Attorney General directives, statutes and regulations. Nothing contained in this memorandum is intended to provide substantive, procedural or other rights to individuals or groups outside the Department of Justice.

I.   LITIGATION RESPONSIBILITIES

A.   Civil Actions, pursuant to 8 U.S.C. § 1451(a)

1.   INS Responsibilities:

a. The INS's Central Revocation Unit is responsible for preparing a referral packet and referring to OIL for its approval, all actions seeking revocation of naturalization pursuant to 8 U.S.C. § 1451(a). The referral packet shall include, among other documentation, an executed Affidavit of Good Cause and an INS point of contact to assist in the litigation of these actions.

b. The INS shall detail to OIL no less than fifteen attorneys to assist in litigating revocation actions for which OIL is the primary litigating unit. Although these attorneys will be detailed to OIL to litigate revocation actions, the detailed attorneys' duties may continue to include assistance in preparing the initial referral packets, depending upon availability and necessity. These INS attorneys shall be primarily responsible for assisting OIL to litigate revocation actions in the most heavily affected districts. Those districts include, but are not limited to, the following: C.D. Cal.; N.D. Cal.; S.D. Fl.; E.D.N.Y.; S.D.N.Y.; N.D. Ill.; D.N.J.; E.D. Va.; S.D. Tx.; W.D. Tx.

1235

-2-

c. The INS shall provide the necessary investigations and litigation support for the proper prosecution of these revocation actions. This support includes, but is not necessarily limited to, obtaining official documentation, locating and interviewing witnesses and defendants, as well as serving the complaint and summons where service by mail is not otherwise appropriate or possible. Further, the INS shall be responsible for providing adequate support staff to assist those INS attorneys detailed to OIL. *See also I.A.3.h. below* —

2.   **OIL Responsibilities:**

a. OIL will be primarily responsible for litigating civil revocation actions with the assistance of the INS attorneys, as provided in I.A.1.b. above, except in those cases for which the USAO elects to assume either primary or exclusive responsibility (*see II.A. and II.B. below*).

b. As is already the procedure, the Director of OIL will review all actions seeking to revoke naturalization with the exception of those involving alleged Nazi collaborators for which the Criminal Division, Office of Special Investigations retains exclusive authority.

c. OIL, where applicable, will prepare and provide to the relevant United States Attorney a Suit Authorization Memorandum. *See II.A. below.* The Suit Authorization Memorandum shall provide the factual and legal basis for the revocation action, as well as the proposed litigation responsibilities and the name of the OIL/INS attorney primarily responsible for the action.

d. Except in those cases for which the USAO elects to assume responsibility, OIL shall make every effort to keep the INS point of contact apprised of the status of the litigation, as well as coordinate litigation efforts with the INS point of contact.

3.   **USAO Responsibilities/Authority:**

a. No revocation action shall be initiated by OIL/INS without the authorization of the relevant United States Attorney either in the form of delegation and acquiescence or specific case authorization. *See II.B. below.*

b. The United States Attorney for the relevant district shall have the option to exercise his or her declination authority over a revocation action. *See II.C. below.*

c. Authorization for OIL/INS to initiate and litigate any revocation action includes the use of the United States Attorney's name, address, and a point of contact on all pleadings, motions, and memoranda in a location and manner consistent with local practice and/or rules, and in a manner to be determined by the individual United States Attorney.

d. Notwithstanding OIL and INS's primary responsibilities, USAOs will have the option of handling any portion or all of the litigation in their districts. *See also II.A. and II.B. below.*

e. USAOs shall promptly provide a point of contact in all actions in which OIL/INS will be primarily responsible for the litigation. The point of contact's name and phone number shall be included in all relevant pleadings. As necessary to the proper prosecution of these actions, the point of contact shall provide assistance to the OIL/INS attorney(s) primarily responsible for the action. This assistance shall include, but not be limited to, local support in filing pleadings and guidance on local practices. Unless specifically permitted or offered by the relevant USAO, however, this assistance does not include substantive litigation such as preparing pleadings or memoranda, as well as making any appearances in court.

f. In those districts for which authorization is granted on a case by case basis, II.B.2. below, the USAOs shall provide OIL and the INS with a point of contact as soon as possible in order to determine how the United States Attorney would like to proceed with the action.

g. In those districts or cases in which the United States Attorney elects to retain primary or exclusive responsibility for the litigation, the USAO shall promptly notify the INS and OIL points of contacts of the name and phone number of the attorney assigned to handle each case. The designated USAO attorney shall make every effort to keep the INS and OIL points of contact apprised of the status of the litigation and may be contacted by the INS and/or OIL regarding the litigation. The designated USAO attorney shall also make every effort to coordinate litigation efforts with the INS point of contact.

h. The USAOs are to supply available local support as needed to visiting OIL/INS attorneys who are responsible for litigation of these revocation actions. This support shall include, but not necessarily be limited to, providing available office space for visiting OIL/INS attorneys, clerical assistance, office supplies, and copying or faxing, etc.

B.   **Criminal Prosecutions under 18 U.S.C. § 1425, as well as for False Statements Made under 18 U.S.C. §§ 1015, 1001, etc.**

1.   **INS Responsibilities:**

a. The INS shall be responsible for promptly notifying OIL of its intention to refer a case for criminal prosecution under 18 U.S.C. § 1425 and seek revocation under 8 U.S.C. § 1451(e). This notification shall include a litigation packet for the Director of OIL for review. Any case in which INS intends to refer specifically for criminal prosecution, should be clearly labeled - **"CRIMINAL REFERRAL UNDER 18 U.S.C. § 1425"**.

-4-

b. Following notification to OIL, the case shall be referred to the appropriate INS official for preparation and referral to the United States Attorney.

2.   **OIL Responsibilities:**

a. Promptly after notification of the INS's intention to refer a case for—criminal prosecution under 18 U.S.C. § 1425 and revocation under 18 U.S.C. § 1451(e), OIL shall appoint a point of contact within the office to provide any necessary guidance and support to the USAO and/or the INS in the prosecution of these actions. *See I.B.2. above.*

3.   **USAO Responsibilities:**

a. The USAO shall be responsible for the prosecution of criminal cases for illegal procurement of naturalization under 18 U.S.C. § 1425. Successful prosecution under 18 U.S.C. § 1425 carries with it the penalty of civil revocation, as well as any fine or imprisonment included within the sentence. 8 U.S.C. § 1451(e). Although other statutes, such as 18 U.S.C. §§ 1015, 1001, provide criminal sanctions for false statements and fraud in procurement of immigration benefits, including naturalization, only 18 U.S.C. § 1425 carries the penalty of revocation of naturalization. As a result, the United States Attorney should consider prosecution under 18 U.S.C. § 1425. If, however, the United States Attorney wishes to negotiate a plea to a different offense, he or she will promptly notify INS and OIL.

b. The United States Attorney shall notify the INS, as soon as practicable, whether he or she intends to prosecute the action criminally, under 18 U.S.C. § 1425. If the United States Attorney declines to prosecute the action or intends to proceed with a civil revocation, rather than a criminal prosecution, INS and OIL should be notified promptly in order to take appropriate action.

c. The United States Attorney shall promptly notify the INS and the OIL point of contact of the name and phone number of the attorney assigned to handle each criminal case. This designated USAO attorney may be contacted by the INS and/or OIL regarding the status of the action.

-5-

II.   AUTHORIZATION

A.   Suit Authorization Memorandum

1. In all revocation actions for which OIL is primarily responsible, OIL will seek authorization by the preparation of a Suit Authorization Memorandum for the relevant United States Attorney prior to filing any complaint under 8 U.S.C. § 1451(a).

2. The Suit Authorization Memorandum shall set forth the legal and factual basis for revocation, as well as the proposed attorney assignment and the primary litigating unit.

3. The United States Attorney shall have the following options: (1) authorize the filing of the complaint and litigation of the case, as set forth in the memorandum; (2) exercise his or her option to assume primary responsibility for the litigation; or (3) to exercise his or her declination authority to the filing of the complaint and the litigation of the action by OIL/INS.

B.   Categories of Districts Authorization

1.   Districts Authorizing Suit Through Delegation and Acquiescence

a. The United States Attorney can agree to authorize suit by delegation and acquiescence.

b. By their signatures, the United States Attorneys for the districts listed in attachment (A) to this memorandum authorize OIL/INS to file suit and litigate actions seeking to revoke naturalization, pursuant to 8 U.S.C. § 1451(a), in each and every case that, under the terms of this memorandum, is presented to the United States Attorney and such United States Attorney elects not to exercise, within 30 days of the date of the Suit Authorization Memorandum, any of the options listed in II.A.3. above. [1]

2.   Districts Authorizing Suit on a Case by Case Basis

a. In those districts for which OIL/INS will be the primary litigating unit but the United States Attorney has not agreed to authorization by delegation and acquiescence, as set forth in II.B.1. above, authorization can only be obtained on a case by case basis from the United States Attorney.

b. To grant such authorization, the United States Attorney (or his or her official designee) must sign the individual Suit Authorization Memorandum, specifically

---

[1] See attachment (A) for a list of those districts that are authorizing suit through delegation and acquiescence as described in section II.B.1. of this memorandum.

-6-

authorizing OIL/INS's filing suit on behalf of the United States Attorney.[2]

        c. The United States Attorney retains all the same options set forth in II.A. above.

        3.   **Districts In Which The USAOs Will Retain Primary Responsibility**

By their signatures, the United States Attorneys for the districts listed in attachment (C) elect to retain primary litigation responsibility for filing and litigation of the cases referred by the INS and OIL, pursuant to 8 U.S.C. § 1451(a).[3]

    C.   **Exercise of Declination Authority**

        1. The United States Attorney shall have declination authority over the initiation or continuation of any revocation action within his or her district.

        2. In order to exercise this declination authority, the United States Attorney shall provide the INS and OIL with a written statement that he or she declines to authorize the initiation or continuation of the revocation suit, accompanied by a brief statement of the reason(s).

III.   SETTLEMENT AND ALTERNATIVE DISPUTE RESOLUTION

Settlement and Alternative Dispute Resolution should be considered and employed whenever the factual or legal circumstances warrant.

---

[2] See attachment (B) for a list of those districts that are authorizing suit on a case by case basis as described in section II.B.2. of this memorandum.

[3] See attachment (C) for a list of those districts that will retain primary litigation responsibility for filing and litigation of the cases referred by the INS and OIL as described in section II.B.3. of this memorandum.

_____,   Signed the ____ of November, 1999.
Mary H. Murguia, Director
Executive Office for United States Attorneys

_____,   Signed the _10th_ of November, 1992.
Mark T. Calloway, United States Attorney
Western District of North Carolina and
Chair of the Attorney General's Advisory
Committee

_____,   Signed the _6th_ of November, 1999.
Thomas W. Hussey, Acting Director
Office of Immigration Litigation
Civil Division

JAN 22 2000
_____,   Signed the _____ of November, 1999.
Doris M. Meissner, Commissioner
Immigration and Naturalization Service

Chapter 15

Relinquishment of Citizenship: Expatriation Statutes

Research References

West's Key Number Digest
Aliens, Immigration, and Citizenship ☞680 to 685

Westlaw Databases
Steel on Immigration Law (STEEL)
Immigration Law Service (2d ed.) (IMMLS2D)

A.L.R. Library
A.L.R. Index, Immigration and Naturalization

Treatises and Practice Aids
Dizon and Wettstein, Immigration Law Service 2d §§ 14:429, 14:430, 14:434
Steel on Immigration Law § 15:26

I. GENERAL PRINCIPLES

§ 15:1 Is past loss of citizenship effective?

Research References

Dizon and Wettstein, Immigration Law Service 2d § 14:434

Expatriation refers to actions a citizen takes which result in his or her loss of U.S. citizenship. There have been expatriating statutes since 1865 when Congress passed a law declaring deserters as having abandoned their U.S. citizenship.[1] In spite of the 1865 statute, most courts consider congressional legislation relating to expatriation to have begun in 1868, when Congress declared the right of U.S. citizens to expatriate themselves.[2] It was not until 1907 that Congress set out the actions that would effect this expatriation.[3] In 1994, Congress amended the INA to replace the references to "expatriation" with the phrase "loss of nationality".[4]

Generally all statutes repealing a prior expatriation law have specifically provided that citizenship lost under the repealed statute would not be restored by its repeal.[5] Therefore, in order to determine whether a finding of a person's loss of his or her citizenship had been lawfully adjudicated, the law in effect at the time the person committed the expatriating act must be applied.[6]

However, in 1967, the Supreme Court held that no person could lose his or her U.S. citizenship unless that person relinquished it voluntarily.[7] The Court found that the Constitution did not grant Congress an affirmative power to expatriate any citizen.[8] On the contrary, the Fourteenth Amendment was specifically designed to protect the individual from any possible governmental abridgment of his or her citizenship rights.[9] Therefore, loss of citizenship statutes, regardless of when passed by Congress, may only be given effect if they apply to voluntary relinquishment of citizenship.[10] Thus, regardless of when it was made, a determination that a person has lost U.S. citizenship can only survive now, if it comports with the constitutional

---

[Section 15:1]

[1]Sec. 21, Act of March 3, 1865, 13 Stat. 487 reproduced as Appendix 12-1C to Ch 12.

[2]See Afroyim v. Rusk, 387 U.S. 253, 263–66, 87 S.Ct. 1660, 1665–67, 18 L.Ed.2d 753 (1967).

[3]Act of March 2, 1907, Pub.L. 59-193, 34 Stat. 1228 reproduced as Appendix 4-6 to Ch 4.

[4]INTCA § 105 reproduced as Appendix 4-21 to Ch 4.

[5]See, e.g., sec. 7, Act of September 22, 1922, Pub.L. 67-346, 42 Stat. 1021 reproduced as Appendix 4-8 to Ch 4 (repealing section 3 of the Expatriation Act of 1907; "[s]uch repeal shall not restore citizenship lost under such section nor terminate citizenship resumed under such section").

[6]INS Interp. 349.1(A).

[7]Afroyim v. Rusk, 387 U.S. 253, 87 S. Ct. 1660, 18 L. Ed. 2d 757 (1967).

[8]Afroyim v. Rusk, 387 U.S. 253, 257, 87 S. Ct. 1660, 1662, 18 L. Ed. 2d 757 (1967).

[9]Afroyim v. Rusk, 387 U.S. 253, 261–62, 87 S. Ct. 1660, 1665, 18 L. Ed. 2d 757 (1967).

[10]See Afroyim v. Rusk, 387 U.S. 253, 268, 87 S. Ct. 1660, 1668, 18 L. Ed. 2d 757 (1967) ("the Fourteenth Amendment was designed to, and does, protect every citizen of this Nation against congressional forcible destruction of his citizenship").

requirements as currently interpreted.[11] This protection applies whether the person is a citizen by birth or by naturalization.[12]

In 1986, the expatriation sections of the INA were completely revised, adding the requirement that expatriation could only be effected if the expatriating acts were performed with the intention to relinquish U.S. citizenship.[13] The amendment also changed the wording of the expatriating actions to make them comport with constitutional requirements.[14] Such amendments were made retroactive so that current determinations of whether a person expatriated himself or herself by acts committed before 1986 must be based on the current statute.[15]

If the acts are done voluntarily and with the intention of relinquishing citizenship, expatriation is automatic.[16] The citizenship status is divested, in the same sense that U.S. citizenship vests upon a child through naturalization under the Child Citizenship Act.[17] Judicial and administrative proceedings that may be brought do not take away citizenship from the person but are a mechanism to prove that citizenship had been lost in the past by actions taken by the former U.S. citizen.[18] Both the State Department and the Secretary of the Department of Homeland Security have jurisdiction to determine whether a person has in fact lost his or her U.S. citizenship.[19]

Many determinations that a person has expatriated himself or herself, particularly those that preceded the *Afroyim* decision, are unconstitutional and can be challenged. Children of persons so expatriated may at present be U.S. citizens on

---

[11]Rocha v. I.N.S., 450 F.2d 947 (1st Cir. 1971) (per curiam).

[12]Afroyim v. Rusk, 387 U.S. 253, 87 S. Ct. 1660, 18 L. Ed. 2d 757 (1967) (Afroyim was a naturalized citizen). There may be an argument that U.S. citizens born abroad do not have the full protection of the Fourteenth Amendment. See Rogers v. Bellei, 401 U.S. 815, 827, 91 S.Ct. 1060, 1067, 28 L.Ed.2d 499 (1971) (the Fourteenth Amendment does not apply to U.S. citizens born abroad because they were neither born or naturalized in the United States); U.S. v. Cervantes-Nava, 281 F.3d 501, 503 n.1 (5th Cir. 2002), cert. denied, 122 S. Ct. 2379, 153 L. Ed. 2d 197 (U.S. 2002). Cf. §§ 4:2 to 4:14.

[13]Sec. 18(a), Immigration and Nationality Act Amendments of 1986, Pub.L. 99-653, 100 Stat. 3655 (Nov. 14, 1986) punctuation amended by Sec. 8(m), Immigration Technical Corrections Act of 1988, Pub.L. 100-525, 102 Stat. 2609 (Oct. 24, 1988).

[14]Sec. 18, Immigration and Nationality Act Amendments of 1986 punctuation amended by Sec. 8(m), Immigration Technical Corrections Act of 1988.

[15]Sec. 23(g), Immigration and Nationality Act Amendments of 1986 added by sec. 8(r), Immigration Technical Corrections Act of 1988.

[16]See INA § 358, 8 U.S.C.A. § 1501 ("Whenever a diplomatic or consular officer of the United States has reason to believe that a person while in a foreign state has lost his [or her] United States nationality . . . he [or she] shall certify the facts upon which such belief is based to the Department of State," emphasis added).

[17]See § 5:16.

[18]See, e.g., Afroyim v. Rusk, 387 U.S. 253, 254, 87 S. Ct. 1661, 18 L. Ed. 2d 757 (1967). Expatriation takes place on the date of the expatriating act and not on the date of the administrative determination of loss of citizenship. Endelman, How to Prevent Loss of Citizenship: 89-11 Immigration Briefings, Pt I 12 (November 1989); DiPlacido, Naturalization: Problem Clients, Dual Citizenship, Expatriation and Repatriation, 1994 AILA Annual Convention, Tape 14.

[19]INA §§ 103(a), 104(a)(3), 358, 8 U.S.C.A. §§ 1103(a), 1104(a)(3), 1501. See generally, 89-11 Immigration Briefings 3-7. Note that under the Homeland Security Act, the Attorney General may also retain some authority to make these decisions through the immigration courts and the Board of Immigration Appeals. See § 1:9.

the basis that their parents were still U.S. citizens at the time of their birth since the determination that they have expatriated themselves was not lawful.[20]

§ 15:2 Loss of citizenship and U.S. taxation

Research References

Cantley, Taxation Expatriation: Will the Fast Act Stop Wealthy Americans from Leaving the United States?, 36 Akron Law Review 221 (2003)

Voluntary expatriation may have tax advantages.[1] Because of this, Congress passed a law in 1996 penalizing persons who voluntarily relinquished citizenship in order to obtain tax advantages.[2] According to this provision, "[a] former citizen of the United States who officially renounces United States citizenship and who is determined by the Secretary of the Department of Homeland Security to have renounced United States citizenship for the purpose of avoiding taxation by the United States" may not be admitted to the United States.[3] This rule applies to all former citizens who renounce their U.S. citizenship on or after September 30, 1996.[4]

In addition, under current tax laws, persons who renounce their citizenship in order to avoid taxation suffer serious adverse tax consequences.[5] In order to avoid such consequences, they must establish that their renunciation did not have for one of its principal purposes the avoidance of U.S. taxes.[6] On April 30, 1997, the IRS published its first quarterly listing of people about whom the Department of the Treasury has received information that they have lost their United States citizenship to avoid taxation.[7]

II. STRUCTURE OF CURRENT LOSS OF CITIZENSHIP PROVISIONS

§ 15:3 Generally

At present, the Immigration and Nationality Act has four sections dealing with loss of citizenship.[1] Section 349 provides the grounds upon which nationality may be lost.[2] Section 351 deals with geographic and age restrictions on expatriation.[3] Sections 356 and 357 are meant to be read together. Section 356 provides that the only basis for expatriation is the performance of the acts or fulfillment of the conditions speci-

---

[20]See §§ 4:11 to 4:12.

[Section 15:2]

[1]See § 15:24.

[2]IIRAIRA § 352(a) adding INA § 212(a)(10)(E).

[3]INA § 212(a)(10)(E), 8 U.S.C.A. § 1182(a)(10)(E).

[4]IIRAIRA § 352(b).

[5]IRS Notice 97-19, Guidance for Expatriates Under Sections 877, 2501, 2107 and 6039F, (March 10, 1997) reproduced in 74 Interpreter Releases (May 23, 1997).

[6]IRS Notice 97-19, Guidance for Expatriates Under Sections 877, 2501, 2107 and 6039F, (March 10, 1997) reproduced in 74 Interpreter Releases (May 23, 1997).

[7]62 Fed. Reg. 23532 (April 30, 1997) (notice).

[Section 15:3]

[1]INA §§ 349, 351, 356, 357, 8 U.S.C.A. §§ 1481, 1483, 1488, 1489.

[2]INA § 349, 8 U.S.C.A. § 1481.

[3]INA § 351, 8 U.S.C.A. § 1483.

fied in INA § 349.[4] Section 357 provides that the INA is not controlling if when it was enacted, there was a pre-existing conflictive ratified treaty.[5] In the Nineteenth Century, several treaties were negotiated between the U.S. and other powers providing for expatriation of dual citizens under certain circumstances.[6] However, even in presence of such a treaty, no woman will be held to have lost her U.S. citizenship solely because of marriage to a noncitizen.[7]

In addition, the 1986 amendments to section 349 govern loss of citizenship whether the expatriating acts occurred before or after 1986.[8] Therefore, the following are the only grounds upon which a person may lose citizenship, regardless of when the expatriating acts occurred. A brief description of prior expatriating statutes is also included in this chapter because if a person was determined to have lost citizenship under a prior statute and the loss comported with the constitutional requirement that the action must have been performed with the intent of relinquishing citizenship, then citizenship was not restored by the 1986 amendments.[9]

§ 15:4 Loss of citizenship under INA

The INA provides seven grounds upon the performance of which a person may lose his or her U.S. citizenship.[1] However, for loss of U.S. citizenship to occur under these grounds, the required actions must be performed "with the intention of relinquishing United States nationality."[2] The seven expatriating acts are:[3]

(1) obtaining naturalization in a foreign state upon his [or her] own application, or upon an application filed by a duly authorized agent, after having attained the age of eighteen years;

(2) taking an oath or making an affirmation or other formal declaration of allegiance to a foreign state or a political subdivision thereof after having attained the age of eighteen years;

(3) entering, or serving in, the armed forces of a foreign state if (A) such armed forces are engaged in hostilities against the United States, or (B) such persons serve as a commissioned or noncommissioned officer;

(4)

(A) accepting, serving in, or performing the duties of any office, post, or employment under the government of a foreign state or a political subdivision thereof after attaining the age of eighteen years, if he [or she] has or acquires the nationality of such foreign state; or

---

[4]INA § 356, 8 U.S.C.A. § 1488.

[5]INA § 357, 8 U.S.C.A. § 1489.

[6]See e.g., Perkins v. Elg, 307 U.S. 325, 335–36, 59 S.Ct. 884, 890, 83 L.Ed. 1320 (1939).

[7]INA § 357, 8 U.S.C.A. § 1489. For a discussion of resumption of citizenship by those women who lost it by marriage to noncitizens, see §§ 11:12 to 11:17.

[8]Sec. 23(g), Immigration and Nationality Act Amendments of 1986 added by sec. 8(r), Immigration Technical Corrections Act of 1988.

[9]Actually, the 1986 amendments as amended by the technical corrections of 1988 are silent as to restoration of citizenship lost under prior laws. Sec. 23(g), Immigration and Nationality Act Amendments of 1986 added by sec. 8(r), Immigration Technical Corrections Act of 1988. However, those amendments did not amend section 405 of the INA which provides that "[e]xcept as otherwise specifically provided in this Act, the repeal of any statute by this Act shall not . . . restore nationality heretofore lost under any law of the United States." INA § 405(c), 8 U.S.C.A. § 1101, note.

[Section 15:4]

[1]INA § 349(a), 8 U.S.C.A. § 1481(a).

[2]INA § 349(a), 8 U.S.C.A. § 1481(a).

[3]INA § 349(a), 8 U.S.C.A. § 1481(a).

(B) accepting, serving in, or performing the duties of any office, post, or employment under the government of a foreign state or a political subdivision thereof after attaining the age of eighteen years, for which office, post, or employment an oath, affirmation, or declaration of allegiance is required;

(5) making a formal renunciation of nationality before a diplomatic or consular officer of the United States in a foreign state, in such form as may be prescribed by the Secretary of State;

(6) making in the United States a formal written renunciation of nationality in such form as may be prescribed by, and before such officer as may be designated by, the Attorney General, whenever the United States shall be in a state of war and the Attorney General shall approve that renunciation as not contrary to the national defense; or

(7) committing any act of treason against, or attempting by force to overthrow, or bearing arms against, the United States, violating or conspiring to violate any of the provisions of section 2383 of Title 18, or willfully performing any act in violation of section 2385 of Title 18, or violating section 2384 of Title 18 by engaging in a conspiracy to overthrow, put down, or to destroy by force the Government of the United States, or to levy war against them, if and when he [or she] is convicted thereof by a court martial or by a court of competent jurisdiction.

Except for the acts described in subsections 6 and 7, expatriating acts committed inside the United States or its outlying possessions do not effect the expatriation of the person until the person takes up residence outside the United States and its outlying possessions.[4]

A U.S. citizen does not expatriate himself or herself even if he or she committed an act described in subsections 3 and 5, if at the time, he or she was under the age of 18, provided that within six months after attaining that age, the citizen asserts his or her claim to United States citizenship with the appropriate consular or diplomatic officer.[5]

§ 15:5 Burden of proof

Research References

Dizon and Wettstein, Immigration Law Service 2d §§ 14:451, 14:458

The INA provides that whenever loss of citizenship is put at issue, the person claiming that loss of citizenship has occurred has the burden of proving that such loss has occurred.[1] This burden may be met by establishing by the preponderance of the evidence that such loss has occurred.[2]

The INA has an evidentiary presumption establishing that a person who has performed any expatriating acts described in the INA, has done so voluntarily.[3] This presumption may be rebutted upon showing, by the preponderance of the evidence, that the act or acts committed or performed were not done voluntarily.[4] In other words, proving that the person has committed one of the enumerated expatriating acts is sufficient to prove that he or she has done so voluntarily. The citizen then

---

[4]INA § 351(a), 8 U.S.C.A. § 1483(a).

[5]INA § 351(b), 8 U.S.C.A. § 1483(b).

[Section 15:5]

[1]INA § 349(b), 8 U.S.C.A. § 1481(b).

[2]INA § 349(b), 8 U.S.C.A. § 1481(b).

[3]INA § 351(b), 8 U.S.C.A. § 1483(b); Vance v. Terrazas, 444 U.S. 252, 267, 100 S.Ct. 540, 549, 62 L.Ed.2d 461(1980) (holding this presumption constitutional).

[4]INA § 349(b), 8 U.S.C.A. § 1481(b).

has the burden of proving that he or she committed that act under duress.[5] Both the commission of the act and the duress must be proven by the preponderance of the evidence.[6]

In addition to proving that the person committed the acts voluntarily, the party claiming loss of citizenship must establish that the person had the intention of relinquishing his or her U.S. citizenship when such action was committed.[7] This is a constitutional requirement and Congress is powerless to legislate against it.[8] As explained by the Supreme Court, "the trier of fact must in the end conclude that the citizen not only voluntarily committed the expatriating act prescribed in the statute, but also intended to relinquish his [or her] citizenship."[9]

The intention to relinquish U.S. citizenship, like the performance of expatriating acts, must be proven by a preponderance of the evidence.[10] Even though proof of intention to relinquish citizenship is constitutionally required, neither the citizenship clause, nor the due process clause of the Fourteenth Amendment requires an evidentiary standard higher than preponderance of the evidence to establish loss of citizenship.[11]

The statutory requirements of the INA relating to burden of proof and presumption of voluntariness apply to present day proceedings whether the person's loss of citizenship is claimed under the INA or under any prior law.[12]

In 1990, the State Department created an administrative presumption that most U.S. citizens who commit acts of expatriation, i.e. those enumerated under INA § 349, do so with an intent to *retain* citizenship.[13] This presumption has now been enshrined into the regulations.[14] The regulations now provide that in adjudicating potentially expatriating acts, the State Department presumes that the person intended to retain U.S. citizenship in three situations: (1) when a U.S. citizen obtains naturalization in a foreign country; (2) when the citizen subscribes routine declarations of allegiance to a foreign state; and (3) when the citizen accepts non-policy level employment in a foreign state.[15] If the person affirmatively states that it was his or her intention to relinquish U.S. citizenship in performing those acts, then

[5]See Vance v. Terrazas, 444 U.S. 252, 268–70, 100 S. Ct. 540, 549–50, 62 L. Ed. 2d 461, 5 Fed. R. Evid. Serv. 273 (1980).

[6]INA § 349(b), 8 U.S.C.A. § 1481(b); Vance v. Terrazas, 444 U.S. 252, 270, 100 S. Ct. 540, 550, 62 L. Ed. 2d 461, 5 Fed. R. Evid. Serv. 273 (1980).

[7]Vance v. Terrazas, 444 U.S. 252, 259, 100 S. Ct. 540, 544–45, 549, 62 L. Ed. 2d 461, 5 Fed. R. Evid. Serv. 273 (1980).

[8]Vance v. Terrazas, 444 U.S. 252, 260, 100 S. Ct. 540, 545, 62 L. Ed. 2d 461, 5 Fed. R. Evid. Serv. 273 (1980) ("In the last analysis, expatriation depends on the will of the citizen rather than on the will of Congress and its assessment of his conduct").

[9]Vance v. Terrazas, 444 U.S. 252, 261, 100 S. Ct. 540, 546, 62 L. Ed. 2d 461, 5 Fed. R. Evid. Serv. 273 (1980).

[10]Vance v. Terrazas, 444 U.S. 252, 267, 100 S. Ct. 540, 548, 62 L. Ed. 2d 461, 5 Fed. R. Evid. Serv. 273 (1980).

[11]Vance v. Terrazas, 444 U.S. 252, 266–67, 100 S. Ct. 540, 548, 62 L. Ed. 2d 461, 5 Fed. R. Evid. Serv. 273 (1980).

[12]INA § 349(b), 8 U.S.C.A. § 1481(b).

[13]61 Fed. Reg. 29651 (June 12, 1996) (Supplementary Information); Carmen DiPlacido, Naturalization: Problem Clients, Dual Citizenship, Expatriation and Repatriation, 1994 AILA Annual Convention, Tape 14.

[14]22 CFR. § 50.40(a) as amended by 61 Fed. Reg. 29651.

[15]22 CFR § 50.40(a) as amended by 63 Fed. Reg. 20315 (Apr. 24, 1998).

the person will lose his or her U.S. citizenship.[16] In all other loss of nationality cases, the consular officer is required to ascertain whether or not there is evidence of the intent to relinquish U.S. citizenship when performing the expatriating act.[17] The regulations instruct consular and diplomatic officers to request an affidavit from persons who admit that they performed the expatriating acts with intention to relinquish U.S. citizenship.[18] These affidavits can only be executed with the consent of the person.[19] The presumptions regarding intent in performing expatriating acts are applied retroactively, so that if the person was certified as having lost citizenship, the person may request a review of that certificate under the new standard adopted by the State Department.[20]

III. LOSS OF CITIZENSHIP GROUNDS

A. NATURALIZING IN FOREIGN COUNTRY

§15:6 Expatriation under prior statutes

Research References

Dizon and Wettstein, Immigration Law Service 2d §14:437
Steel on Immigration Law §15:26

The Act of 1907 introduced the first statutory pronouncement that naturalizing in a foreign country could effect expatriation.[1] Prior to 1907, it had been the administrative position that an individual could expatriate himself or herself if he or she naturalized in a foreign country, provided the individual took up permanent residence in that country.[2]

Beginning in 1907, voluntarily naturalizing in another country statutorily effected the expatriation of the U.S. citizen.[3] An administrative position also developed that naturalization of a person in a foreign country by automatic effect of law could be the basis of expatriation if the person thereafter evinced acceptance of the foreign nationality through words or action.[4]

Between 1907 and 1922, women who married U.S. citizens who naturalized in another country lost their U.S. citizenship because women were considered to acquire the nationality of their husbands.[5] Thus they expatriated themselves under the section of the 1907 act which provided for expatriation upon acquisition of a foreign nationality.[6] In order for this expatriation to occur, however, the woman must have established residence abroad with her naturalized husband prior to September 22, 1922, and must have acquired the nationality of the foreign country in which he had

---

[16]22 CFR. §50.40(a).

[17]22 CFR. §50.40(a).

[18]22 CFR. §50.40(b).

[19]22 CFR. §50.40(b).

[20]See §11:32.

[Section 15:6]

[1]Sec. 2, Act of March 2, 1907 reproduced as Appendix 4-6 to Ch 4.

[2]INS Interp. 349.2(a)(1).

[3]INS Interp. 349.2(a)(2).

[4]INS Interp. 349.2(a)(3)(i).

[5]See §15:16.

[6]Sec. 2, Act of March 2, 1907 reproduced as Appendix 4-6 to Ch 4.

naturalized.[7] Taking the oath of allegiance to a foreign country was not sufficient for the woman to lose her U.S. citizenship: the husband must have acquired the foreign nationality.[8] Thus, even when a male U.S. citizen expatriated himself by taking an oath of allegiance to a foreign country, if he did not acquire the nationality of that country through the oath, the wife did not expatriate herself.[9]

Expatriation under the 1907 statute could occur even when the naturalization into a foreign country occurred while the person was in the United States.[10] Minority age at the time the naturalization took place, on the other hand, prevented loss of U.S. citizenship unless when the person became an adult, he or she voluntarily performed acts evincing a continued acceptance of the foreign nationality.[11] The act itself provided that no expatriation should occur while the U.S. was at war.[12]

The 1940 Act provided for the loss of citizenship when a person naturalized upon his or her own application, or when the person became naturalized upon the naturalization of his or her parent having custody of such person.[13] The INA as originally enacted included exactly the same provision, but added that the person could also expatriate himself or herself upon an application filed on their behalf by a parent, guardian, or duly authorized agent.[14]

In 1986, the expatriation sections of the INA were completely revised, adding the requirement that expatriation could only be effected if the acts were done with the intention to relinquish U.S. citizenship.[15] Expatriation through naturalization abroad was revised to allow such expatriation only when the naturalization is performed upon application of the person or of a duly authorized agent, and only when the person was over 18 years of age at the time such application was made.[16] Such amendments were made to apply to determinations of loss of citizenship regardless of when the expatriating act occurred.[17]

§ 15:7 Current statute

The current statute requires the person to perform the following actions with the intention of relinquishing U.S. citizenship: (1) (a) applying for naturalization in a foreign country; or (b) having an authorized representative apply for naturalization

---

[7]INS Interp. 324.1(a)(2); Matter of K-, 4 I. & N. Dec. 154, 156, 1950 WL 6634 (B.I.A. 1950) (to expatriate herself under section 2, the wife must do some affirmative action to show adoption of, concurrence with, or acquiescence with her husband's naturalization in the foreign country).

[8]Matter of B-, 1 I. & N. Dec. 429, 431, 1943 WL 6306 (B.I.A. 1943) (holding that the basis for expatriation under this section was section 3 of the 1907 act which worked the expatriation of women through marriage to a foreigner).

[9]INS Interp. 324.1(a)(2) citing to 30 Op. Atty. Gen. 412 (1915); Matter of B-, 1 I. & N. Dec. 429, 431, 1943 WL 6306 (B.I.A. 1943).

[10]INS Interp. 349.2(a)(4)(i).

[11]INS Interp. 349.2(a)(4)(ii).

[12]Sec. 2, Act of March 2, 1907 reproduced as Appendix 4-6 to Ch 4.

[13]Sec. 401(a), Nationality Act of 1940, Pub.L. 76-853, 54 Sat. 1137 (October 14, 1940).

[14]INA § 349(a)(1), 8 U.S.C.A. § 1481(a)(1) as originally enacted by Act of June 27, 1952, 66 Stat. 163.

[15]Sec. 18(a), Immigration and Nationality Act Amendments of 1986, Pub.L. 99-653, 100 Stat. 3655 (Nov. 14, 1986) punctuation amended by Sec. 8(m)(1), Immigration Technical Corrections Act of 1988, Pub.L. 100-525, 102 Stat. 2609 (Oct. 24, 1988).

[16]Sec. 18(b), Immigration and Nationality Act Amendments of 1986.

[17]See § 15:1.

in a foreign country; (2) making the application after the age of 18; and (3) being naturalized in the foreign country.[1] In addition, like most other forms of loss of citizenship, these acts are only expatriating either if performed abroad or after the person takes up residence abroad.[2]

The first requirement is that naturalization must be achieved through "application." This means that naturalization effected through workings of law is not effective to produce loss of citizenship.[3] Such type of naturalization occurs, for example, when a person acquires a foreign nationality by marriage to a national of that country.[4] However, a subsequent voluntary acceptance may be effective.

Within this context, it has been considered that there was highly persuasive proof of intent to relinquish U.S. citizenship, when the applicant for foreign naturalization knowingly and voluntarily swore an oath expressly renouncing allegiance to the U.S.[5] On the other hand, when a person before taking that same oath consulted with the U.S. consul who assured the person that the Canadian naturalization oath would have no effect on the person's U.S. citizenship, and as a result the person took the oath, then the government needs to produce more evidence that the applicant intended to relinquish his or her U.S. citizenship when the person naturalized.[6] Furthermore, some foreign naturalization proceedings *do not* require the applicant to renounce allegiance to the former country of citizenship.[7] In such cases, the government would be hard put to establish that the applicant had the intention of relinquishing U.S. citizenship when naturalizing in such countries.[8]

It is clear that naturalization cannot be voluntary if it is done under duress.[9] Economic advantages of taking up a foreign nationality are not sufficient to establish "duress" for purposes of the intent to relinquish U.S. citizenship when there is a

---

[Section 15:7]

[1] INA § 349(a)(1), 8 U.S.C.A. § 1481(a)(1).

[2] INA § 351(a), 8 U.S.C.A. § 1483(a).

[3] Matter of Picone, 10 I. & N. Dec. 139, 146, 1962 WL 12936 (B.I.A. 1962) (prior to the 1940 Act, voluntary active acceptance of naturalization by operation of law effected expatriation); 39 Op. Att'y Gen. 411 (1940); 7 FAM § 1261(a)(1). See generally, Gordon & Mailman, § 100.03[4][c][iii].

[4] See § 15:16.

[5] Richards v. Secretary of State, Dep't of State, 752 F.2d 1413, 1421 (9th Cir. 1985); Matter of Wayne, 16 I. & N. Dec. 248, 251, 1977 WL 39263 (B.I.A. 1977) (overruled in part by, Matter of Kekich, 19 I. & N. Dec. 198, 1984 WL 48607 (B.I.A. 1984)); Matter of Wayne, 16 I. & N. Dec. 248, 251, 1977 WL 39263 (B.I.A. 1977) (overruled in part by, Matter of Kekich, 19 I. & N. Dec. 198, 1984 WL 48607 (B.I.A. 1984)) (holding that the government must prove expatriation by a preponderance of the evidence and not by clear, convincing, and unequivocal evidence as held in *Wayne*). The voluntary commission of an expatriating act is not by itself sufficient to prove intent to relinquish U.S. citizenship, but may be highly persuasive proof of this intent. Vance v. Terrazas, 444 U.S. 252, 258–59, 100 S. Ct. 540, 544–46, 62 L. Ed. 2d 461, 5 Fed. R. Evid. Serv. 273 (1980).

[6] Matter of Wayne, 16 I. & N. Dec. 248, 249, 252, 1977 WL 39263 (B.I.A. 1977) (overruled in part by, Matter of Kekich, 19 I. & N. Dec. 198, 1984 WL 48607 (B.I.A. 1984)).

[7] See 89-11 Immigration Briefings 15 (After May 7, 1973, Canada no longer requires renunciation of allegiance to the former country of citizenship as part of the naturalization process. England and France do not require renunciation either). See generally, Endelman's discussion of when an oath is considered renunciatory by the State Department. Matter of Wayne, 16 I. & N. Dec. 248, 249, 252, 1977 WL 39263 (B.I.A. 1977) (overruled in part by, Matter of Kekich, 19 I. & N. Dec. 198, 1984 WL 48607 (B.I.A. 1984)).

[8] 89-11 Immigration Briefings 15.

[9] See § 15:5.

knowing and voluntary renunciation of U.S. citizenship.[10] The courts distinguish between motive and duress: the facts that the alternatives are painful, or the motive is commendable does not transform an otherwise free choice into an involuntary action.[11] Absent duress, mistake, or incapacity, the motivation for the choice is irrelevant and relinquishment of U.S. citizenship will be given effect.[12]

B. TAKING OATH OF ALLEGIANCE TO FOREIGN STATE

§ 15:8 Generally

Research References

A.L.R. Index, Immigration and Naturalization
Dizon and Wettstein, Immigration Law Service 2d §§ 14:438 to 14:440
Steel on Immigration Law § 15:26

Since the expatriation act of 1907, all expatriation acts have considered taking an oath of allegiance to a foreign country to be a cause of expatriation.[1] The current version of the INA provides that to be expatriating, the oath must satisfy the following elements in addition to being taken with the intention of relinquishing U.S. citizenship: (1)(a) an oath of allegiance, or (b) an affirmation of allegiance, or (c) a formal declaration of allegiance, must be taken or made; (2) the allegiance must be to a foreign state or a political subdivision thereof; and (3) it must be made after attaining the age of 18.[2]

Usually the taking of an oath of allegiance is required by foreign countries in connection with military service.[3] It is also required for certain types of governmental, government-related, or public work in general.[4] Other circumstances include an oath of allegiance in order to marry a foreign functionary or as part of an application for a passport by a dual citizen.[5]

Just like any other basis for expatriation, the taking of the oath must evince an intention to renounce U.S. citizenship. Thus, it has been held that a dual national's exercising of his or her routine prerogatives as a citizen of the other country, such as obtaining a passport, cannot be construed as an intention to relinquish U.S. citizenship.[6] The same applies to a routine taking of the oath of allegiance as part of

---

[10]Richards v. Secretary of State, Dept. of State, 752 F.2d 1413, 1421 (9th Cir. 1985).

[11]Matter of Kekich, 19 I. & N. Dec. 198, 200, 1984 WL 48607 (B.I.A. 1984).

[12]Richards v. Secretary of State, Dept. of State, 752 F.2d 1413, 1421–22 (D.C.Cir. 1950); Matter of Kekich, 19 I. & N. Dec. 198, 200, 1984 WL 48607 (B.I.A. 1984).

[Section 15:8]

[1]Sec. 2, Act of March 2, 1907 reproduced as Appendix 4-6 to Ch 4; sec. 401(b), Nationality Act of 1940; INA § 349(a)(2), 8 U.S.C.A. § 1481(a)(2) as originally enacted by Act of June 27, 1952, 66 Stat. 163.

[2]INA § 349(a)(2), 8 U.S.C.A. § 1481(a)(2).

[3]See Coumas v. Bronwell, 222 F.2d 331, 332 (9th Cir. 1955); Dulles v. Richter, 246 F.2d 709, 711 (D.C.Cir. 1957).

[4]See Gilliars v. U.S., 182 F.2d 962, 982 (D.C.Cir. 1950) (required to continue work with Nazi propaganda radio in Germany); Baker v. Rusk, 296 F.Supp. 1244 (C.D.Cal. 1969) (oath of allegiance as part of admission to the bar in Canada).

[5]Jalbuena v. Dulles, 254 F.2d 379 (3d Cir. 1958) (application for passport); Revedin v. Acheson, 194 F.2d 482 (2d Cir. 1952) (marriage to a foreign diplomat).

[6]Jalbuena v. Dulles, 254 F.2d 379, 381 (3d Cir. 1958). Cf. Kawakita v. U.S., 343 U.S. 717, 726–27, 72 S.Ct. 950, 957, 96 L.Ed.2d 1249 (1952) (if petitioner's entry of petitioner's name into

a ceremony of admission to the bar.[7] In general, the State Department now takes the view that, unless there is evidence to the contrary, persons who take an oath of allegiance to a foreign country do so without the intention of relinquishing U.S. citizenship.[8]

C. SERVING IN FOREIGN ARMED FORCES

§15:9 Generally

Research References

Dizon and Wettstein, Immigration Law Service 2d §§14:441 to 14:443
Steel on Immigration Law §15:26

Before 1941, armed services in a foreign army *per se* did not effect expatriation.[1] The 1940 act included a provision for expatriation but only if performed by one who had acquired the nationality of the other state, unless the service was expressly authorized by the laws of the U.S.[2] The INA, as originally enacted, went farther than the 1940 act providing that unless specifically authorized by the Secretary of State and the Secretary of Defense, any service in the armed forces of another country would result in expatriation.[3] The only exception to this rule was for persons who entered service in a foreign armed forces prior to their 18th birthday and either there was no option to secure release from the service, or if there was, the person exercised that option upon attaining the age of 18.[4]

The current INA provision makes service in foreign armed forces, an expatriating act if, with the intention of relinquishing U.S. citizenship: (1) the person enters or serves in the armed forces of a foreign state; and (2)(a) such armed forces are engaged in hostilities against the U.S., or (b) the person serves as a commissioned or noncommissioned officer.[5]

---

petitioner's uncle's Family Census Register and petitioner's registration with the police and at the university as Japanese were not done with the intent of renouncing U.S. citizenship, then they amounted to no more than a public declaration of an established and preexisting fact, i.e. petitioner's Japanese nationality.)

[7]Baker v. Rusk, 296 F. Supp. 1244, 1246 (C.D. Cal. 1969).

[8]DiPlacido, 1994 AILA Annual Convention, Tape 14; Gordon & Mailman, §100.03[4][d].

[Section 15:9]

[1]INS Interp. 349.4(a)(1).

[2]Gordon & Mailman, §100.03[4][f]; *see also* Breyer v. Ashcroft, 350 F.3d 327 (3d Cir. 2003) (finding that under the 1940 statute, continued service in the SS Waffen was not voluntary for expatriation purposes where person believed penalty for desertion would be execution).

[3]INA §349(a)(3), 8 U.S.C.A. §1481(a)(3) as originally enacted by Act of June 27, 1952, 66 Stat. 163.

[4]INA §349(a)(3), 8 U.S.C.A. §1481(a)(3) as originally enacted by Act of June 27, 1952, 66 Stat. 163.

[5]INA §349(a)(3), 8 U.S.C.A. §1481(a)(3). For a broad exposition of expatriation law, as it relates to service in hostile armed forces, see John C. Yoo, Survey of the Law of Expatriation, Memorandum Opinion for the Solicitor General (June 12, 2002), available at http://www.usdoj.gov/olc/expatriation.htm (last accessed June 21, 2008).

Prior to *Terrazas* and the 1986 amendment, the Supreme Court held that the government bears the burden of proving that services in the armed forces was engaged in voluntarily.[6]

An issue likely to be raised in this type of expatriation is whether service was in the *armed forces* of the foreign country. Thus the BIA has held that service in the Canadian Officer's Training Corps was not service in the armed forces of a foreign country for purposes of expatriation because members of that corps were not liable for military service unless there was "*levée en masse*" and then members of that corps could only be placed on active duty upon enlistment in the Canadian armed forces or upon induction according to the Canadian Selective Service Act.[7] The same was true for the University Air Training Corps of Canada.[8]

Similarly, in another case, the BIA held that service in the An Forsa (defense forces) of Ireland was considered service in the armed forces of Ireland only when the unit was called out on permanent service.[9] In that case, during the time the citizen served in the An Forsa, it was not called out on permanent service.[10]

A separate issue is whether the forces the citizen serves in are in fact the forces of a foreign *country*. This issue becomes clearly defined in relation to revolutionary forces. Thus, service in an insurgent armed forces is not service in the armed forces of a foreign country.[11] However, if upon taking over power the insurgent army becomes officially recognized, as was the case with the Rebel Army of Cuba, then service in that army after the take over becomes service in the armed forces of a foreign country.[12]

Service in a munitions factory during World War II has been held not to have been service in the armed forces of a foreign country for purposes of expatriation.[13] In that case, the U.S. citizen worked as an interpreter in a private munitions factory which was closely controlled by the government. Employees of the factory were not allowed to quit their employment without the consent of the government, and the company's mine and factory were partly manned with prisoners of war, who lived in an army controlled camp.[14] However, since the citizen was not a soldier in the armed forces, he was considered not to have expatriated himself.[15]

D. EMPLOYMENT BY FOREIGN GOVERNMENT

§ 15:10   Generally

Research References

Dizon and Wettstein, Immigration Law Service 2d §§ 14:444, 14:445
Steel on Immigration Law § 15:26

---

[6]Nishikawa v. Dulles, 356 U.S. 129, 78 S.Ct. 612, 2 L.Ed.2d 659 (1958). The constitutionality of pre-1986 version of this section has been upheld by an equally divided Supreme Court. Marks v. Esperdy, 377 U.S. 214 (1964).

[7]Matter of Z-, 2 I. & N. Dec. 346, 349–50, 1945 WL 5568 (B.I.A. 1945).

[8]Matter of L- F-, 2 I. & N. Dec. 455, 1946 WL 6037 (B.I.A. 1946).

[9]Matter of S-, 8 I. & N. Dec. 340, 342, 1959 WL 11578 (B.I.A. 1959).

[10]Matter of S-, 8 I. & N. Dec. 340, 342, 1959 WL 11578 (B.I.A. 1959).

[11]Matter of M-, 9 I. & N. Dec. 452, 455, 1961 WL 12188 (B.I.A. 1961).

[12]Matter of M-, 9 I. & N. Dec. 452, 455–57, 1961 WL 12188 (B.I.A. 1961).

[13]Tomoya Kawakita v. U. S., 343 U.S. 717, 727–28, 72 S. Ct. 950, 958, 96 L. Ed. 1249 (1952).

[14]Tomoya Kawakita v. U. S., 343 U.S. 717, 727, 72 S. Ct. 950, 957, 96 L. Ed. 1249 (1952).

[15]Tomoya Kawakita v. U. S., 343 U.S. 717, 727, 72 S. Ct. 950, 957, 96 L. Ed. 1249 (1952).

Employment by a foreign government first became an expatriation ground in 1940.[1] Under the 1940 act, a person expatriated himself or herself if he or she accepted a government post "for which only nationals of such state were eligible."[2] The INA, as originally enacted, went much further, requiring expatriation if the person worked in a government post, provided the person was a national of that country, or if the position required an oath of allegiance to that country.[3] No longer was there a requirement that the position should be only available to nationals of that country. The 1986 amendments left the INA provision almost intact, the only change being that the person must have been over the age of 18 at the time of having such job.[4]

The employment must be "under the government of a foreign state."[5] Employment by an international organization is not the basis for expatriation since international organizations are not foreign states.[6] In addition to employment "under the government" of a foreign state, the employment must create the relationship that public employees have with their government, or with bureaus or corporations that are government owned and controlled.[7] Private companies that are controlled and supervised by a government do not satisfy this requirement, even when the government supplies the labor force for such companies.[8]

The oath of allegiance requirement under the current act is also restrictively interpreted. Only employment which requires oaths that would completely subject the person to the foreign state are considered the basis for expatriation.[9] Oaths that require the applicant to do what every resident of a country must do, i.e. obey the laws, do not constitute the basis for an expatriation act.[10] However, if the oath is required for the post, it is irrelevant that the person in question did not actually take the oath.[11]

Usually only acceptance of "important political" posts in a foreign government has been considered as highly persuasive of a desire to relinquish U.S. citizenship.[12] The USCIS considers the following as "important political" posts that would trigger the

---

[Section 15:10]

[1]INS Interp. 349.5(a)(1).

[2]INS Interp. 349.5(a)(1).

[3]INA § 349(a)(4), 8 U.S.C.A. § 1481(a)(4) as originally enacted by Act of June 27, 1952, 66 Stat. 163.

[4]INA § 349(a)(4), 8 U.S.C.A. § 1481(a)(4).

[5]INA § 349(a)(4), 8 U.S.C.A. § 1481(a)(4).

[6]Endelman, 89-11 Interpreter Releases 14 citing to 7 FAM 1264(a)(2).

[7]Tomoya Kawakita v. U. S., 343 U.S. 717, 729, 72 S. Ct. 950, 958, 96 L. Ed. 1249 (1952).

[8]Tomoya Kawakita v. U. S., 343 U.S. 717, 728, 72 S. Ct. 950, 958, 96 L. Ed. 1249 (1952).

[9]Matter of Acosta, 10 I. & N. Dec. 675, 677, 1964 WL 12112 (B.I.A. 1964).

[10]INS Interp. 349.5(a)(3) citing to Fletes-Mora v. Rogers, 160 F.Supp. 215 (1950).

[11]Matter of Acosta, 10 I. & N. Dec. 675, 676, 1964 WL 12112 (B.I.A. 1964).

[12]INS Interp. 349.5(b)(1). Cf. Matter of Becher, 12 I. & N. Dec. 380, 1965 WL 12337 (B.I.A. 1965) (nothing in the record evinced the intention to relinquish citizenship when dual citizen took up public school teaching in Canada); INS Interp. 349.5(b)(3)(ii), (iii), (iv) (the following employments have been consider as lacking the political importance to evidence intent to relinquish U.S. citizenship: lower echelon police officers, post office clerks, minor judicial clerks, consular office clerks, clerk in the Census and Statistics Bureau of Australia; clerk in the British war Department in Malta; clerk in the Canadian Department of National Revenue; sanitary officer of an Italian commune [the position required performance of physician's duties]; psychiatric aide in a Canadian hospital; chemist in an Israeli Ministry for Trade and Industry; social worker in the municipality of Jerusalem; translator for the German Ministry of Defense; cashier for the Municipal Government of Mexicali; assistant curator for

evidentiary presumption of intention to abandon U.S. citizenship: chief of a foreign state or a significant geographical subdivision; cabinet minister or high-level official of an executive department of a foreign state; a mayor or chief executive officer of a city; a member of the national, provincial, or municipal legislature, and the military or civilian chief of the armed forces of a foreign state.[13] Of course, employment in lower level positions in a foreign government may also be the basis of expatriation if the person admits that by entering in such employment, he or she intended to relinquish his or her U.S. citizenship.[14] The USCIS considers employment in communist countries on a case-by-case basis.[15]

E. FORMAL RENUNCIATION OF U.S. NATIONALITY

§ 15:11   Generally

Research References

Dizon and Wettstein, Immigration Law Service 2d §§ 14:446, 14:447, 14:462
Steel on Immigration Law § 15:26

This is by far the most effective method of achieving expatriation. It is the only method that expressly carries within its terms the required intent to relinquish U.S. citizenship.[1] For this reason, this form of expatriation is the basic one in which the State Department will presume that the person intended to relinquish his or her citizenship when such declaration was made.[2]

This was the logical form to obtain expatriation after the 1868 congressional declaration that expatriation was a right of U.S. citizens.[3] It is not surprising that even in the absence of a precise statutory procedure, expatriation by formal relinquishment of U.S. citizenship has been considered effective.[4] The first statute to specifically include formal renunciation as a procedure for relinquishing U.S. citizenship was the Nationality Act of 1940.[5] It provided for renunciation before a diplomatic or consular officer of the U.S. abroad. A loss of citizenship has recently been sustained based upon a renunciation under the Nationality Act of 1940.[6] In 1944, the act was amended to allow, in addition, renunciation of U.S. citizenship within the United

---

the National Museum of Dublin; telephone operator for a Canadian Government Telephone company; translator and deputy head of foreign language department of Hungarian Radio.).

[13]INS Interp. 349.5(b)(1).

[14]INS Interp. 349.5(b)(1).

[15]INS Interp. 349/5(b)(2).

[Section 15:11]

[1]Kahane v. Secretary of State, 700 F.Supp. 1162, 1166 (D.D.C. 1988) (voluntarily renouncing citizenship under the act effects both the expatriating act and provides evidence of intent to relinquish U.S. citizenship).

[2]DiPlacido, 1994 AILA Annual Convention, Tape 14.

[3]See § 15:1.

[4]Gordon & Mailman, § 100.03[4][b][i] citing to 14 Op. Atty. Gen. 295 (1873); Bouchard, Diplomatic Protection of Citizens Abroad 522, 681.

[5]Sec. 401(f), Nationality Act of 1940.

[6]Kuper v. Mulrean, 209 F. Supp. 2d 1079 (S.D. Cal. 2002).

States during times of war.[7] The current statute reproduces both forms of renunciation.[8]

§ 15:12 Renunciation outside U.S

Research References

Steel on Immigration Law § 15:26

The current statute provides that a person expatriates himself or herself, if with the intention of relinquishing U.S. citizenship, the person: (1) makes a formal renunciation of U.S. nationality; (2) before a (a) diplomatic, or (b) consular officer of the U.S.; (3) in a foreign state; and (4) this renunciation is done in the manner prescribed by the Secretary of State.[1]

The requirements imposed by the State Department regulations are very simple: the person must present himself or herself in front of a diplomatic or consular officer of the U.S. in a foreign country and renounce the U.S. citizenship "in the manner and form prescribed by the [State] Department."[2] The diplomatic or consular official forwards the oath of renunciation together with a certificate of loss of nationality to the State Department for approval.[3] The State Department must approve the officer's report for the issuance of the certificate of loss of citizenship.[4]

A central issue in renunciation of citizenship is whether the person understood the implications of that renunciation. Usually the validity of these renunciations is questioned when seeking a reexamination of the certificate of loss of nationality.[5] In one case, the State Department overruled a finding of loss of citizenship because it believed that the individual had not understood the full ramifications of the renunciation of citizenship.[6] The case involved six individuals, members of a group who believed in the return of Jews to the Holy Land.[7] When they emigrated to Israel, they were refused permanent residence.[8] However, since Israeli law did not allow deportation of stateless persons, these six individuals renounced their citizenship at the U.S. embassy.[9] Considering that the decision to abandon U.S. citizenship was made under "severe economic deprivation and personal duress leading them to a perceptible fear of family division," the State Department overturned its determination of loss of citizenship.[10]

State Department policy does not allow persons who are under 18 years of age to renounce U.S. citizenship. In some cases such renunciations were approved after the person turned 18. A State Department determination has found one such certif-

---

[7]Sec. 401(i), Nationality Act of 1940 added by Act of July 1, 1944, 58 Stat. 677.

[8]INA § 349(a)(5), (6), 8 U.S.C.A. § 1481(a)(5), (6).

[Section 15:12]

[1]INA § 349(a)(5), 8 U.S.C.A. § 1481(a)(5).

[2]22 CFR § 50.50(a) as amended by 61 Fed. Reg. 29651 (June 12, 1996).

[3]22 CFR § 50.50(b).

[4]22 CFR § 50.50(b).

[5]See §§ 15:21, 15:23.

[6]See 70 Interpreter Releases (March 8, 1993).

[7]See 70 Interpreter Releases (March 8, 1993).

[8]See 70 Interpreter Releases (March 8, 1993).

[9]See 70 Interpreter Releases (March 8, 1993).

[10]See 70 Interpreter Releases (March 8, 1993).

icate of loss of citizenship to be improperly issued, because neither the child, nor the child's parents were ever informed that the child could have changed the child's mind about renouncing U.S. citizenship after reaching the age of 18.[11]

The State Department has emphasized the issue of voluntariness in the renunciation of U.S. citizenship. Carmen DiPlacido, former director of the Office of Policy Review and Interagency Liaison, outlined current procedures regarding renunciation of citizenship.[12] Mr. DiPlacido pointed out that at the time of renunciations, the consular officer would interview the renunciant to ascertain the issue of voluntariness.[13] The renunciant is free to present a written statement, if he or she so desires.[14] However, if either the oral statements or the written declaration contain language that indicates that the renunciant does not have the intent to renounce or that the act itself is not voluntary, the renunciation will not be approved, until the State Department is satisfied with those issues.[15] Apparently, the intention required is to renounce from all the benefits of U.S. citizenship.[16]

The statute requires a formal renunciation in front of a U.S. diplomatic or consular official.[17] This takes the form of the renunciant reading, understanding and signing a Statement of Understanding and Oath of Renunciation.[18] The Foreign Affairs Manual contains relatively detailed descriptions of the process and policies of renunciation.[19] The individual desiring renunciation will be asked to read DS-4081, which explains the consequences of renunciation, though executing DS-4081 is not *per se* required to effectuate renunciation.[20] The renunciant must take the oath of renunciation specifically as provided for by statute and regulation; form DS-4080 is reproduced at Appendix 15-2. The renunciant may make a separate affidavit explaining their reasons for renouncing citizenship, a statement which should be witnessed if in a foreign language.[21]

Renunciation of U.S. citizenship in other settings, e.g. as part of the proceedings to obtain a nationality certificate from another country, will not by itself effect expatriation.[22] Those forms of renunciation, however, may provide the necessary evidence of an intention to relinquish U.S. citizenship, to give effect to another

---

[11]70 Interpreter Releases (July 2, 1993).

[12]DiPlacido, Letter to Gary Endelman, reproduced in 73 Interpreter Releases 735 (May 24, 1996). The Office of Policy Review and Interagency Liaison is in charge of the administrative review of prior determinations of loss of nationality. See § 15:24.

[13]DiPlacido, Letter to Gary Endelman, reproduced in 73 Interpreter Releases 735 (May 24, 1996). The Office of Policy Review and Interagency Liaison is in charge of the administrative review of prior determinations of loss of nationality. See § 15:24.

[14]DiPlacido, Letter to Gary Endelman, reproduced in 73 Interpreter Releases 735 (May 24, 1996). The Office of Policy Review and Interagency Liaison is in charge of the administrative review of prior determinations of loss of nationality. See § 15:24.

[15]DiPlacido, Letter to Gary Endelman, reproduced in 73 Interpreter Releases 735 (May 24, 1996). The Office of Policy Review and Interagency Liaison is in charge of the administrative review of prior determinations of loss of nationality. See § 15:24.

[16]See Lozada Colon v. U.S. Dept. of State, 2 F. Supp. 2d 43 (D.D.C. 1998).

[17]INA § 349(a)(5), 8 U.S.C.A. § 1481(a)(5).

[18]DiPlacido, Letter to Gary Endelman.

[19]See 7 FAM 1261-1268.

[20]7 FAM 1262.4. The form is reproduced as Appendix 15-3.

[21]7 FAM 1262.4(g).

[22]In Terrazas, the person swore an oath of allegiance to Mexico and, in conjunction with it, renounced allegiance to the U.S. The sole expatriation act the court considered that he might have

expatriating act, such as naturalizing in a foreign country.[23] However, recently, the State Department has adopted a presumption that subscription of routine declarations of allegiance to a foreign state does not evince intent to abandon U.S. citizenship.[24]

§ 15:13 Renunciation inside U.S

Research References

Steel on Immigration Law § 15:26

In times of war, the INA authorizes renunciation of U.S. citizenship within the United States.[1] To be effective, that renunciation must be (1) a formal written renunciation of U.S. nationality; (2) in such form as is prescribed by the Attorney General; (3) in front of such officer as is designated by the Attorney General; (4) at a time when the U.S. is in a state of war; and (5) the Attorney General must approve the renunciation as not contrary to the interest of the national defense.[2]

It is unclear whether this section is presently operative, i.e., whether the "global war on terror," and associated Congressional authorizations,[3] is the functional equivalent of a war declaration.[4] If it is, the Attorney General or DHS probably has to adjudicate renunciation requests within the United States.[5] The renunciation procedures were used during World War II to exact renunciation of U.S. citizenship by Japanese-Americans.[6] Many of these renunciations appear to have been found invalid because they were obtained under duress.[7]

F. TREASON, SUBVERSION, AND DESERTION

§ 15:14 Generally

Research References

Dizon and Wettstein, Immigration Law Service 2d § 14:448
Steel on Immigration Law § 15:26

---

performed was the swearing of the oath to Mexico. Vance v. Terrazas, 444 U.S. 252, 254, 100 S. Ct. 540, 542, 62 L. Ed. 2d 461, 5 Fed. R. Evid. Serv. 273 (1980). Cf. Matter of H--, 9 I. & N. Dec. 411, 1961 WL 12182 (B.I.A. 1961) (renouncing U.S. nationality in front of a Canadian notary public did not effect expatriation).

[23]Richards v. Secretary of State, Dept. of State, 752 F.2d 1413, 1421 (9th Cir. 1985). See also, 89-11 Immigration Briefings 15 ("the express renunciation of U.S. citizenship in the context of swearing an oath of allegiance to a foreign country is compelling evidence of an intent to relinquish U.S. citizenship") citing to Kahane v. Secretary of State, 700 F. Supp. 1162, 1166 (D.D.C. 1988); David v. District Director, 481 F.Supp. 1178, 1181 (D.D.C. 1979).

[24]See § 15:21.

[Section 15:13]

[1]INA § 349(a)(6), 8 U.S.C.A. § 1481(a)(6).

[2]INA § 349(a)(6), 8 U.S.C.A. § 1481(a)(6).

[3]Authorization for Use of Military Force Against Iraq Resolution of 2002, Pub. L. No. 107-243, 116 Stat. 1498 (2002) (Iraq); Authorization for Use of Military Force (2001 AUMF), Pub. L. No. 107-40, 115 Stat. 224 (2001)(Afghanistan).

[4]See generally, Hamdi v. Rumsfeld, 542 U.S. 507 (2004).

[5]See generally, Kaufman v. Mukasey, 524 F.3d 1334, 1340 (D.C.Cir. 2008).

[6]Gordon & Mailman, § 100.03[4][b][iii].

[7]Gordon & Mailman, § 100.03[4][b][iii]. citing to Acheson v. Murakami, 176 F.2d 953 (9th Cir. 1949); McGrath v. Abo, 186 F.2d 766 (9th Cir. 1951); Kiyama v. Rusk, 291 F.2d 10 (9th Cir.), cert. denied, 368 U.S. 866 (1961).

The very first expatriation provision in the history of the U.S. relates to desertion from the armed forces.[1] Such provisions were also found in the acts of 1940 and the original INA.[2] The Supreme Court has held that such punitive expatriation was unconstitutional as beyond the war powers of Congress.[3] In 1978, Congress repealed that basis for expatriation.[4]

A similar fate befell the provision dealing with expatriation for draft evaders.[5] The Supreme Court found it unconstitutional in *Kennedy v. Mendoza-Martinez*.[6] That basis for expatriation was repealed from the statute in 1976.[7]

The treason provision, on the other hand, has not been repealed.[8] The Supreme Court has never ruled on the constitutionality of this provision. One commentator has pointed out, however, that unlike desertion and draft evasion, treason touches on an element of choice of allegiance and expatriation by treason could conceivably be held constitutional under certain circumstances.[9]

G. VOTING IN FOREIGN ELECTIONS, RESIDING IN FOREIGN COUNTRIES, AND EXPATRIATION OF DUAL CITIZENS

§ 15:15   Generally

Both the 1940 act and the INA as originally enacted provided for the expatriation of U.S. citizens who voted in foreign political elections.[1] The Supreme Court found this provision unconstitutional in *Afroyim v. Rusk*,[2] and Congress repealed that provision in 1978.[3]

As originally enacted, the INA had a special provision that provided for loss of citizenship by naturalized citizens who resided for a specific amount of time abroad.[4]

[Section 15:14]

[1]Sec. 21, Act of March 3, 1865, 13 Stat. 487 reproduced as Appendix 12-1C to Ch 12.

[2]INA § 349(a)(8), 8 U.S.C.A. § 1481(a)(8) as originally enacted by Act of June 27, 1952, 66 Stat. 163; sec. 401(g), Nationality Act of 1940.

[3]Trop v. Dulles, 356 U.S. 86, 78 S.Ct. 590, 2 L.Ed.2d 630 (1958).

[4]Sec. 2, Act of Oct. 10, 1978, Pub.L. 95-432, 92 Stat. 1046 reproduced as Appendix 4-18 to Ch 4.

[5]INA § 349(a)(10), 8 U.S.C.A. § 1481(a)(10) as originally enacted by Act of June 27, 1952, 66 Stat. 163.

[6]Kennedy v. Mendoza-Martinez, 372 U.S. 144, 83 S.Ct. 554, 92 L.Ed.2d 644 (1963).

[7]Sec. 501(a)(2), National Emergencies Act, Pub.L. 94-412, 90 Stat. 1255 (Sept. 14, 1976).

[8]INA § 349 (a)(7), 8 U.S.C.A. § 1481(a)(7).

[9]Gordon & Mailman, § 100.03[4][k].

[Section 15:15]

[1]Sec. 401(3), Nationality Act of 1940; INA § 349(a)(5), 8 U.S.C.A. § 1481(a)(5) as originally enacted by Act of June 27, 1952, 66 Stat. 163.

[2]Afroyim v. Rusk, 387 U.S. 253, 87 S.Ct. 1660, 18 L.Ed.2d 753.

[3]Sec. 2, Act of Oct. 10, 1978 reproduced as Appendix 4-18 to Ch 4.

[4]INA § 353(a), 8 U.S.C.A. § 1484(a) as originally enacted by Act of June 27, 1952, 66 Stat. 163 (if returned to country of prior nationality residence of three years was required, otherwise five years were required).

The Supreme Court found this provision unconstitutional as discriminating against naturalized citizens.[5] This section and related sections were repealed in 1978.[6]

Under former versions of the INA, certain acts by dual nationals expatriated them.[7] Congress has repealed all these provisions.[8] There is little likelihood that such provisions would have been found to be constitutional.[9]

H. EXPATRIATION OF WOMEN BY MARRIAGE TO NONCITIZENS

§ 15:16 Generally

At present this form of expatriation does not exist. However, it continues to have more than historical importance because the laws governing expatriation by marriage may affect citizenship by descent for certain persons. In addition, there is still a small pool of women who may have expatriated themselves under these provisions and who would be eligible to resume citizenship under the special provisions for resumption of citizen by women who lost citizenship through marriage of noncitizens.[1]

For a long period of U.S. history, U.S. citizen women lost their citizenship by marriage to noncitizens. The Act of 1907, gave clear expression to this principle when it required that "any American woman who marries a foreigner shall take the nationality of her husband."[2] That act was repealed by the Act of 1922, which still, however, allowed for expatriation by marriage to a noncitizen ineligible for citizenship.[3] The Act of 1931, finally repealed the provision for expatriation for U.S. citizen women who married noncitizens ineligible for citizenship, and put an end to all statutes based on expatriation through marriage.[4]

Prior to 1907, the courts were divided as to whether women lost their U.S. citizenship by marrying noncitizens.[5] Originally, the legacy INS took the position that U.S. citizen women that married noncitizens would expatriate themselves if, prior to

---

[5]Schneider v. Rusk, 377 U.S. 163, 84 S.Ct. 1187, 12 L.Ed.2d 218 (1964) (Congress's power to prescribe a uniform rule of naturalization does not authorize it to restrict citizenship acquired through that power).

[6]Sec. 2, Act of Oct. 10, 1978 reproduced as Appendix 4-18 to Ch 4 (repealing also INA §§ 353, 354, 8 U.S.C.A. §§ 1185, 1186 which provided specific conditions for the applicability of INA § 352, 8 U.S.C.A. § 1184).

[7]INA §§ 349(a)(1), 350, 352, 355, 8 U.S.C.A. §§ 1481(a)(1), 1482, 1484, 1487 as originally enacted by Act of June 27, 1952, 66 Stat. 163.

[8]Secs. 1, 2, Act of Oct. 10, 1978 reproduced as Appendix 4-18 to Ch 4; sec. 18, Act of Nov. 14, 1986, Pub.L. 99-653, 100 Stat. 3655.

[9]See Gordon & Mailman, § 100.03[4][l].

[Section 15:16]

[1]See §§ 11:12 to 11:17.

[2]Sec. 3, Act of March 2, 1907 reproduced as Appendix 4-6 to Ch 4.

[3]Secs. 3, 7, Act of September 22, 1922 reproduced as Appendix 4-8 to Ch 4.

[4]Sec. 3(a), Act of March 3, 1931, Pub.L. No. 71-829, 46 Stat. 1511 reproduced as Appendix 4-9 to Ch 4; INS Interp. 324.1(a)(4).

[5]See INS Interp. 324.1(a)(1) citing to In re Wohlgemuth, 35 F.2d 1007, 1008 (W.D.Mich. 1929) (common-law doctrine of the U.S. prior to 1907 was that U.S. women who married foreigners lost their citizenship); In re Krausmann, 28 F.2d 1004 (E.D.Mich. 1928) (statute of 1907 was merely declaratory of preexisting common law); In re Lynch, 31 F.2d 762 (S.D.Cal. 1929) (to expatriate herself the U.S. citizen woman must marry a noncitizen, and must change domicile to the country of her husband); In re Fritzroy, 4 F.2d 541 (D.Mass. 1925) (marriage to noncitizen and removal to another country is required for expatriation); In re Wright, 19 F.Supp. 224 (E.D.Penn. 1937) (marriage to a foreigner

September 22, 1922, the woman emigrated to the country of her husband's nationality, acquired citizenship thereof under its laws, and such country was a signatory of a treaty with the U.S. by virtue of which each country would recognize its own nationals as citizens of the other upon naturalization in the other country pursuant to the laws thereof.[6] Such a standard would allow for loss of nationality even when the other nationality is acquired by operation of law without any intent on the part of the woman. The Attorney General, however, in a decision dealing with the Trading with the Enemy Act set a higher standard. To expatriate herself by marriage prior to 1907, a U.S. citizen woman must have intended to renounce her U.S. citizenship; moving to her husband's country, acquiring the foreign nationality by workings of the law, and U.S recognition of such nationality are insufficient to find a clear intent of the woman to renounce her U.S. citizenship.[7] This interpretation seems more in line with the later ruling of *Afroyim v. Rusk,* which provides the basis for interpreting abandonment of U.S. citizenship during any period of U.S. history.[8] The only caveat is that under that ruling, it is the DHS' burden to establish an intention to abandon U.S. citizenship.[9]

From March 2, 1907 until September 21, 1922 there was a clear statutory provision which required the U.S. woman's expatriation upon marriage to a noncitizen.[10] During this period, marriage itself effected the loss of nationality of the U.S. citizen woman, regardless of the place of residence of the woman after marriage, the minority of the woman at marriage, the manner in which she had acquired citizenship, and even if she acquired the citizenship of the husband's country.[11] In addition, a woman married to a U.S. citizen who naturalized himself in a foreign country may have lost her U.S. citizenship through her own acquisition of the foreign nationality.[12]

Section 2 of the 1907 act specifically provided that "no American citizen shall be allowed to expatriate himself [or herself] when this country is at war."[13] This provision applies to women who otherwise would have expatriated themselves by marriage to a foreigner.[14] Thus women who married noncitizens during World War I did not lose their citizenship because of their marriage.[15] However, if the woman continued to be married to the noncitizen after the formal termination of the war on

---

before 1907 gave U.S. woman an election whether she wanted to retain U.S. citizenship; by moving to her husband's country of nationality and remaining there for a substantial amount of time, woman evinced her election against retaining her U.S. citizenship); Watkins v. Morgenthau, 56 F.Supp. 529 (E.D.Penn. 1944) (same result). Cf. Shanks v. Dupont, 28 U.S. (3 Pet.) 242, 245, 7 L.Ed. 666, 667 (1830) (marriage to a noncitizen, even when woman moves to the country of origin of the husband, does not work to deprive of citizenship under common law).

[6]INS Interp. 324.1 (a)(1).

[7]INS Interp. 324.1 (a)(1) citing to Matter of Fanny Cristy v da. de Hepp, Office of Noncitizen Property, Dep't of Justice, Claim No. 60469, Docket No. 59 T 13 (1963) (Copy in file CO 324-P).

[8]See § 15:1.

[9]See INS Interp. 324.1(b)(3).

[10]Sec. 3, Act of March 2, 1907 reproduced as Appendix 4-6 to Ch 4, repealed by Sec. 7, Act of September 22, 1922 reproduced as Appendix 4-8 to Ch 4.

[11]Mackenzie v. Hare, 239 U.S. 299, 36 S.Ct. 106 (1915) (resided all her life in California); U.S. v. Dang Mew Wan, 88 F.2d 88 (9th Cir. 1937) (acquired U.S. citizenship through collective naturalization of citizens of Hawaii); In re Wittus, 47 F.2d 652 (E.D.Mich. 1931) (acquired U.S. citizenship derivatively through father's naturalization and married a noncitizen at the age of 19).

[12]See § 15:6.

[13]Sec. 2, Act of March 2, 1907 reproduced as Appendix 4-6 to Ch 4

[14]In re Varat, 1 F.Supp. 898 (E.D.N.Y. 1932).

[15]INS Interp. 324.1(a)(3).

July 21, 1921, then the woman would expatriate herself at that point in time.[16] To expatriate herself, the woman must have continued to reside abroad with her noncitizen husband after the end of the war.[17] Of course, if the husband became a naturalized U.S. citizen during the war, the wife never expatriated herself.[18]

The Act of September 22, 1922 repealed prospectively the Act of 1907.[19] In addition, it affirmatively stated that no woman would cease to be a U.S. citizen by virtue of her marriage of a noncitizen, unless she (1) renounced her U.S. citizenship in a naturalization court, or (2) married a noncitizen ineligible for citizenship.[20] Marriage to a noncitizen ineligible for citizenship included marriage to a noncitizen who was *racially* ineligible for citizenship.[21] Marriage to a noncitizen ineligible for citizenship ceased to be a ground of expatriation on March 2, 1931.[22]

The Act of 1922 also made women who married noncitizens subject to a presumption of abandonment of her U.S. citizenship. If the woman resided two years in the country of nationality of her husband, or five years in any other foreign country, she was presumed to have expatriated herself.[23] This is the same presumption that applied to naturalized citizens who proceeded to reside abroad.[24] The 1931 amendments, also repealed the expatriation by residence abroad of a U.S. citizen woman married to a noncitizen.[25]

Neither the Act of 1922, nor the amendments of 1931, provided for the automatic restoration of citizenship to women who had lost it because of marriage to a noncitizen.[26] Instead they allowed former U.S. citizens who had expatriated themselves by marriage to take advantage of the expedited provisions available to noncitizen women who married U.S. citizens.[27]

The automatic loss of citizenship provided by the 1907 and 1922 acts would not pass muster under the requirements of *Afroyim v. Rusk*.[28] Under those rules, the person expatriating herself must evince the desire to abandon U.S. citizenship. Marriage to a noncitizen is not sufficient to evince that intention.[29] Procedurally, the DHS would have the burden of establishing that the woman intended to expatriate herself through marriage.[30] At least one court of appeals has found the loss of

---

[16]In re Varat, 1 F. Supp. 898 (E.D. N.Y. 1932).

[17]Petition of Peterson, 33 F.Supp. 615 (E.D.Wash. 1940) (dating the end of World War I on September 2, 1921).

[18]Matter of M-, 4 I. & N. Dec. 398 (B.I.A. 1951).

[19]Sec. 7, Act of September 22, 1922 reproduced as Appendix 4-8 to Ch 4.

[20]Sec. 3, Act of September 22, 1922 reproduced as Appendix 4-8 to Ch 4.

[21]Ex Parte Hing, 22 F.2d 554, 556 (W.D.Wash. 1927). Cf Matter of W-, 2 I. & N. Dec. 778 (1947) (noncitizen national who married noncitizen ineligible for citizenship did not lose her noncitizen nationality under the 1922 Act).

[22]Sec. 4, Act of March 3, 1931 reproduced as Appendix 4-9 to Ch 4.

[23]Sec. 3, Act of September 22, 1922 reproduced as Appendix 4-8 to Ch 4.

[24]See Sec. 2, Act of March 2, 1907 reproduced as Appendix 4-6 to Ch 4.

[25]Sec. 4, Act of March 3, 1931 reproduced as Appendix 4-9 to Ch 4.

[26]Sec. 7, Act of September 22, 1922 reproduced as Appendix 4-8 to Ch 4; Sec. 4, Act of March 3, 1931 reproduced as Appendix 4-9 to Ch 4.

[27]Sec. 4, Act of September 22, 1922 reproduced as Appendix 4-8 to Ch 4.

[28]See Afroyim v. Rusk, 387 U.S. 253, 87 S.Ct. 1660, 18 L.Ed.2d 753 (1967) discussed in § 15:1.

[29]INS Interp. 324.1(b)(3)(i).

[30]INS Interp. 324.1(b)(3)(i).

citizenship provisions of the 1907 act unconstitutional.[31] The DHS, however, continues to hold the position that expatriation under that act, as well as under the 1922 act, may be constitutional under certain circumstances.[32]

Women who lost their citizenship by marriage to a noncitizen have always been allowed to resume U.S. citizenship upon termination of the marriage. If termination occurred prior to September 22, 1922 and they were residing in the United States, resumption of U.S. citizenship occurred automatically upon termination of the marriage.[33] If they were residing abroad, resumption of U.S. citizenship occurred upon return to the United States, provided they returned to the United States for permanent residence prior to September 22, 1922, or, after March 1, 1907, upon registration before a consular official of the U.S. within one year of termination of the marriage.[34]

In the Act of 1922, Congress repealed the resumption provisions of the 1907 act.[35] Even though it reaffirmed the citizenship status acquired by the women who resumed citizenship under those provision, it did not enact a similar provision for women who had expatriated themselves before 1922 and whose marriage terminated after 1922.[36] Instead those women had to rely on the general provision for naturalization of women who lost their U.S. citizenship by marriage to noncitizens before 1922 and who continued to be married thereafter.[37] This procedure required one year of residence as lawful permanent residents in the United States before those women could be naturalized.[38]

To remedy this oversight, Congress passed an act in 1936 deeming U.S. citizens all native-born U.S. citizen women who had lost, or may have lost citizenship, by marriage to a noncitizen prior to September 22, 1922 and whose marriage had either terminated or they had resided continuously in the U.S. since the marriage.[39] This statute applies to women who had acquired U.S. citizenship at birth either within or without the United States.[40] The women whose marriage had terminated before June 25, 1926 were automatically reinvested with U.S. citizenship at the date of enactment.[41] Women whose marriage terminated after that date were reinvested with U.S. citizenship upon the termination of the marriage, provided it terminated before January 13, 1941.[42] Women who had resided continuously in the U.S. since their marriage were reinvested with U.S. citizenship on July 2, 1940.[43] Even though, under this statute as amended, citizenship vested automatically,

---

[31]Rocha v. I.N.S., 450 F.2d 947, 948 (1st Cir. 1971).

[32]INS Interp. 324.1(b)(3).

[33]After March 1, 1907, a short time of residence in the United States after termination of marriage was required. See INS Interp. 324.2(a)(1).

[34]After March 1, 1907, a short time of residence in the United States after termination of marriage was required. See INS Interp. 324.2(a)(1).

[35]Sec. 7, Act of September 22, 1922 reproduced as Appendix 4-8 to Ch 4.

[36]Sec. 7, Act of September 22, 1922 reproduced as Appendix 4-8 to Ch 4.

[37]Sec. 4, Act of September 22, 1922 reproduced as Appendix 4-8 to Ch 4.

[38]See Sec. 2, Act of September 22, 1922 reproduced as Appendix 4-8 to Ch 4.

[39]Act of June 25, 1936, Pub. L. No. 74-793, 49 Stat. 1917, as amended by Act of July 2, 1940, 54 Stat. 715.

[40]INS Interp. 324.2(a)(2)(i).

[41]INS Interp. 324.2(a)(2)(i).

[42]INS Interp. 324.2(a)(2)(i).

[43]INS Interp. 324.2(a)(2)(i).

those women could not exercise any of the rights of U.S. citizenship vested upon them until they took the oath of allegiance.[44] However, the vesting of citizenship, even without the oath, was considered a sufficient act of naturalization for the children of those women to derive citizenship under the derivative citizenship provisions.[45]

The Nationality Act of 1940, and the INA have almost identical provisions allowing for the naturalization of women who had expatriated themselves.[46] The provisions of the INA are fully discussed in Ch 11.[47] At this point, however, it must be emphasized that both the 1940 act and the INA provisions apply when a marriage terminated after January 12, 1941.[48] However, unlike the Nationality Act of 1940, the INA allows women who expatriated themselves through marriage to noncitizens ineligible for citizenship after 1922 to resume U.S. citizenship under those same provisions.[49] Unlike the 1936 act, both provisions date the resumption of U.S. citizenship to the date of taking the oath of allegiance.[50] Also unlike prior acts, the INA prohibits the resumption of U.S. citizenship by women who are barred from citizenship by their political opinion.[51]

IV. DUAL CITIZENSHIP

§ 15:17   Dual citizenship; General principles

Research References

Steel on Immigration Law 2d § 15:7

Dual citizenship exists because the laws of the country granting nationality control nationality.[1] International law imposes very few limitations on countries regarding whom they decide to make a citizen of their country. There are, of course, some limitations. For example, short of annexing that country, the United States

---

[44]INS Interp. 324.2(a)(2)(ii); Matter of P-, 1 I. & N. Dec. 127, 130–31 (B.I.A.) approved (Att'y Gen. 1941) (Congress intended to confer the status of citizenship as of June 25, 1936, but to make possession of rights of citizenship contingent upon the taking of the oath of allegiance)

[45]Matter of P-, 1 I. & N. Dec. 127, 133, 1941 WL 7928 (B.I.A. 1941) (although the mother, prior to taking the oath, held the bare status of citizenship without any rights, the derivative citizenship statute confers rights to the son through the status of the mother rather than conferring rights to the mother; the derivative citizenship of the son does not constitute an exercise of rights by the mother).

[46]Compare sec. 317, Nationality Act of 1940 reproduced as Appendix 4-12 to Ch 4 with INA § 324, 8 U.S.C.A. § 1435.

[47]See §§ 11:12 to 11:17.

[48]Sec. 317(b), Nationality Act of 1940 reproduced as Appendix 4-12 to Ch 4; INA § 324(c), 8 U.S.C.A. § 1435(c).

[49]Compare INA § 324(c), 8 U.S.C.A. § 1435(c) with sec. 317(b), Nationality Act of 1940 reproduced as Appendix 4-12 to Ch 4.

[50]Sec. 317(b), Nationality Act of 1940 reproduced as Appendix 4-12 to Ch 4; INA § 324(c), 8 U.S.C.A. § 1435(c); INS Interp. 324.2(a)(3)(ii).

[51]INA § 324(c), 8 U.S.C.A. § 1435(c). The DHS takes the position that a similar bar also applied under the provisions of the Nationality Act of 1940. INS Interp. 324.2(a)(3)(iii).

[Section 15:17]

[1]Convention on Certain Questions Relating to the Conflict of Nationality Laws (hereinafter The Hague Codification Conference of 1930), April 12, 1930, 179 L.N.T.S. 89, 5 Hudson, Int'l Legislation 359, art. 1.

could not properly make all persons born in Canada citizens of the United States.[2] The treaties or conventions to which the country is a party may impose similar restrictions.[3] There is also an internationally recognized "minimum contacts" type of jurisdictional requirement before one country will recognize the naturalization of a person by another country.[4] However, given these limitations, all questions regarding the nationality of a person are determined in accordance with the laws of the country of claimed nationality.[5] If a person has two or more nationalities because of this form of determination, the person is considered a dual national, i.e. a national of each of these states.[6]

Most countries subscribe to the principles of nationality by descent (jus sanguinis), i.e. by being the child of a national, nationality by birth within a certain territory (jus soli), or a combination of these two principles.[7] Therefore, it is not uncommon for a person to derive citizenship in one country because he or she was born there (jus soli) while deriving citizenship of another country under the principle of jus sanguinis, as the child of a citizen of that country. Thus, a child born in the United States to Italian parents will be a U.S. citizen and perhaps a citizen of Italy.[8] Most children born abroad to U.S. citizen parents could be both U.S. citizens and citizens of the foreign country, depending upon the laws of that country.[9]

Absent a specific statutory requirement, dual citizens in the United States are not required to choose one or the other nationality.[10] Some U.S. nationality statutes have imposed retention requirements for U.S. citizens born abroad.[11] These retention requirements are valid and work as an election in cases where dual nationals fail to return to the United States within the required time frame.[12] Retention requirements, however, may be fulfilled constructively, thus nullifying their function as "election" mechanisms.[13]

Persons who naturalize in the U.S. may also acquire dual citizenship, in spite of the U.S. law requirement that they take an oath renouncing all foreign allegiances.[14] Many countries do not allow their citizens to renounce their nationality, and some of the countries that allow renunciation require such renunciation to be performed

---

[2]See German Government's comments at the Convention, League of Nations Docs. 1929, V.1, at 13.

[3]The Hague Codification Conference of 1930, art. 1.

[4]See The Nottebohm Case (Liechtenstein v. Guatemala), 1955 I.C.J. 4, 1955 WL 1 (ICJ 1955) (International Court of Justice).

[5]The Hague Codification Conference of 1930, art. 2.

[6]The Hague Codification Conference of 1930, art. 3.

[7]For a collection of laws concerning nationality, see U.N. Secretariat, Laws Concerning Nationality, U.N. Doc. ST/LEG/SER.B/4 (1954), supplemented by ST/LEG/SER.B/9 (1959).

[8]See Mandoli v. Acheson, 344 U.S. 133, 73 S. Ct. 135, 97 L. Ed. 146 (1952); Tomoya Kawakita v. U. S., 343 U.S. 717, 72 S. Ct. 950, 96 L. Ed. 1249 (1952).

[9]See Rogers v. Bellei, 401 U.S. 815, 91 S. Ct. 1060, 28 L. Ed. 2d 499 (1971).

[10]Mandoli v. Acheson, 344 U.S. 133, 73 S. Ct. 135, 97 L. Ed. 146 (1952); Tomoya Kawakita v. U. S., 343 U.S. 717, 72 S. Ct. 950, 96 L. Ed. 1249 (1952).

[11]See §§ 4:1 et seq.

[12]Rogers v. Bellei, 401 U.S. 815, 91 S. Ct. 1060, 28 L. Ed. 2d 499 (1971).

[13]See §§ 4:38, 4:47.

[14]8 C.F.R. § 337.

before a diplomatic or consular official of the country.[15] Therefore, persons who naturalize as U.S. citizens may continue to be citizens of the country of prior citizenship. Similarly, in some cases, U.S. citizens who naturalize in a foreign country may not lose their U.S. citizenship, thus also becoming dual citizens.[16] Appendix 15-1 details the effects of U.S. naturalization upon nationality of origin.

§15:18 Dual citizenship—Different models of maintaining foreign citizenship after naturalization

Research References

Steel on Immigration Law 2d §15:7

Over the past decades, many foreign countries have liberalized their laws regarding retention of citizenship. This permits nationals of those countries to become U.S. citizens, while not losing citizenship in their native lands. This, in turn, often encourages continued ties to the native land, permits continued land ownership in that country, facilitates free travel, and aids in some business transactions. There are four main models whereby individuals may obtain dual nationality: (1) refusal on the part of the country to permit individuals to renounce their citizenship; (2) permitting individuals to apply, in advance of naturalization, to maintain citizenship while acquiring U.S. citizenship, (3) permitting individuals to apply to regain or retain citizenship after naturalizing in the U.S.; and (4) granting something called citizenship, but which is somewhat less than full citizenship. It is the author's assessment that the second model may be problematic under U.S. citizenship laws, and that in some cases, there are dangers in the third model as well.

Australia is an example of the first model. Under a 2002 law, an Australian no longer loses his or her citizenship when he or she naturalizes in the United States.[1] Thus, the Australian takes the prescribed oath of citizenship, renouncing Australian citizenship, but it simply has no effect. Thus, there is no inherent inconsistency in the applicant's frame of mind between the oath of allegiance and continued Australian citizenship. Subsequent acts by the individual, taking advantage of their dual citizenship, do not deprive the individual of U.S. citizenship because they would not involve "voluntary relinquishment" of U.S. citizenship.[2] Other examples of the first model include the Dominican Republic, Ecuador, Pakistan, Nicaragua, the Philippines, and Mexico.[3] A less common version of the first model is that an individual can lose citizenship only upon completion of specified steps, often at a consulate, prior to naturalization abroad. Dominica is an example of this approach. This is a de facto refusal to accept renunciation, and it has approximately the same effect.

It should be noted that even under these "safer" models, an individual who seeks a new passport or other benefit of their old citizenship in particularly close temporal proximity to the oath of allegiance might run some additional risks. While there is no inconsistency between the oath and continued citizenship in that country, it is

---

[15]The U.S. imposes such a requirement on renunciation of citizenship. See §15:11.

[16]See §15:6.

[Section 15:18]

[1]See Embassy of Australia website, "Resumption of Citizenship," found at http://www.australian visasdc.com/citizenship/resumption.html.

[2]See, Afroyim v. Rusk, 387 U.S. 253, 87 S.Ct. 1660, 18 L.Ed.2d 757 (1967).

[3]See App.15-1.

still the case that the applicant must have taken the oath in the proper frame of mind.[4] "[W]hen an alien takes the oath with reservations or does not in good faith forswear loyalty and allegiance to the old country, the decree of naturalization is obtained by deceit. The proceeding itself is then founded on fraud."[5] The Supreme Court has looked to "evidence prior to . . . naturalization, that which clusters around that date, and that which follows in the next few years" in assessing the legitimacy of an oath.[6] An action taken just before or just after the oath ceremony, premised on continued citizenship elsewhere, might be evidence suggesting that the applicant had not truly foresworn loyalty and allegiance. While the government would bear a substantial burden, modern technology makes it possible to trace back numerous actions; any denaturalization would be unlikely in the absence of unusual circumstances, but it is a possibility which ought to be considered by individuals who remain dual nationals despite an oath of renunciation.

Germany is an example of the second model. For Germans, naturalization in the U.S. will result in loss of German citizenship unless the individual — before he or she naturalizes — files an application for a special permit with the German embassy. The special permit, called a "Beibehaltungsgenehmigung," permits maintenance of German nationality.[7] South Africa and Sri Lanka have similar mechanisms, although those countries apparently also permit the application to be filed after the naturalization ceremony.[8] The problem with the German approach is that filing the special permit before naturalizing is significant evidence that the individual does not actually intend to renounce all foreign allegiances. That is to say, when the individual takes the oath, "renounce[ing] and abjur[ing] absolutely and entirely all allegiance and fidelity to any foreign state,"[9] they do not actually mean it. But conscious withholding of allegiance is tantamount to fraud.[10] This would support denaturalization.[11] If the individual subsequently finds themselves in legal trouble, it is not unlikely that this flaw in their U.S. citizenship may be discovered.

The third model is for the individual to request that their original citizenship be regained or retained at some point after the taking of the oath. Egypt is an example of the third model. Egyptians who have become naturalized in the U.S. may subsequently apply to the Government of Egypt for permission to retain their Egyptian citizenship.[12] This application cannot be filed until the individual is in possession of the other nation's nationality. This model is used, with some variation, by South Africa, Sri Lanka, Ethiopia, and Brazil. Again, the question would seem to be whether the individual took the oath with the proper frame of mind. If the individual applies one day after the oath ceremony to retain their citizenship abroad, this could be evidence that their purported renunciation of foreign allegiance was

---

[4]See generally, 9:62.

[5]See, Knauer v. U.S., 328 U.S. 654, 66 S.Ct. 1304, 90 L.Ed. 1500 (1946).

[6]*Id.* at 668, 66 S.Ct. at 1312.

[7]See German Consulates United States, "General Information on German citizenship - FAQs," found at http://www.germany.info/relaunch/info/consular__services/citizenship/generalinformation.html.

[8]See App. 15-1.

[9]INA § 337(a), 8 U.S.C.A § 1448(a).

[10]Baumgartner v. U.S., 322 U.S. 665, 64 S. Ct. 1240, 88 L. Ed. 1525 (1944); Knauer v. U.S., 328 U.S. 654, 66 S. Ct. 1304, 90 L. Ed. 1500 (1946); see generally §§ 9:61 to 9:63.

[11]See generally §§ 14:3 to 14:15.

[12]Consulate General of Egypt in New York, "Apply for a Permit from the Egyptian Authorities for a Dual Citizenship Approval," found at http://www.egyptnyc.net/english/dual__citizenship.asp.

fraudulent.[13] On the other hand, this resumption of citizenship does not require the taking of a new oath (which might be a willing renunciation of U.S. citizenship).[14] Thus, if the individual makes an application years later after obtaining U.S. citizenship, so that the fraud aspect is minimized, it seems safe to resume citizenship abroad. This seems particularly true where a country has changed its laws to permit resumption of citizenship. For instance, Australians no longer lose their citizenship due to naturalizations in other countries, but any Australian who lost citizenship may now apply to resume their citizenship.[15] This seems relatively safe, particularly in that no oath of allegiance is required.[16]

The fourth model is not true citizenship at all, even if it is called citizenship. India is an example of this model. The Indian Constitution bars dual citizenship, so the Indian Parliament created a scheme which is called Overseas Citizenship, but does not include all of the rights of citizenship (such as voting).[17] This seems fairly safe from the standpoint of U.S. immigration law, precisely because it has the name of citizenship, but it does not involve full allegiance.

§ 15:19 Effects of Dual Citizenship

Where a person is a dual citizen, they "may have and exercise rights of nationality in two countries and be subject to the responsibilities of both."[1] Dual citizenship has many benefits, such as the ability to travel freely in both countries (staying as long as desired) and the ability to engage freely in employment opportunities; it also has some extra costs, such as potential double-taxation and the potential of military obligations in both countries.[2]

U.S. citizens — including dual citizens — are generally obligated by law and regulation to exit and enter the United States using a U.S. passport.[3]

The State Department is technically not able to issue nonimmigrant visas to U.S. citizens.[4] However, if an individual cannot fully prove his or her citizenship and does not want to seek documentation to prove that claim, the consulate may presume their alienage for purposes of issuance of the nonimmigrant visa, and issue the visa before a final determination as to the potential citizenship claim.[5]

---

[13]See Baumgartner v. U.S., 322 U.S. 665, 64 S. Ct. 1240, 88 L. Ed. 1525 (1944); Knauer v. U.S., 328 U.S. 654, 66 S. Ct. 1304, 90 L. Ed. 1500 (1946); see generally §§ 9:61 to 9:63.

[14]See § 15:8.

[15]Australian Citizenship Act 2007 (No. 20 as amended) [Australia], Act No. 20 of 2007 as amended., 1 November 2010, available at: http://www.refworld.org/docid/4cf3ac052.html [accessed 13 May 2013].

[16]See Application to Resume Australian Citizenship, found at http://www.immi.gov.au/allforms/pdf/132.pdf (last accessed May 12, 2013).

[17]Embassy of India in Washington, D.C., "Overseas Citizenship of India Scheme," found at http://www.indianembassy.org/New_Template/oci.asp.

[Section 15:19]

[1]Kawakita v. United States, 343 U.S. 717 (1952).

[2]See 7 FAM 081(b).

[3]8 U.S.C.A. 1185(b); 22 C.F.R. § 53.1. For limited exceptions, see 22 C.F.R. § 53.2.

[4]See 7 FAM 085(b).

[5]See 7 FAM 085(b), (c).

V. PROCEDURES TO DETERMINE LOSS OF CITIZENSHIP

A. STATE DEPARTMENT'S DETERMINATIONS

§ 15:20   Generally

Research References

Dizon and Wettstein, Immigration Law Service 2d § 14:460

The INA provides that,[1]

[w]henever a diplomatic or consular officer of the United States has reason to believe that a person while in a foreign state has lost his [or her] United States nationality under any [of the loss of citizenship provisions of the INA], or under any provision of chapter IV of the Nationality Act of 1940, as amended, he [or she] shall certify the facts upon which such belief is based to the Department of State, in writing, under regulations prescribed by the Secretary of State. If the report of the diplomatic or consular officer is approved by the Secretary of State, a copy of the certificate shall be forwarded to the Attorney General, for his information, and the diplomatic or consular office in which the report was made shall be directed to forward a copy of the certificate to the person to whom it relates. Approval by the Secretary of State of a certificate under this section shall constitute a final administrative determination of loss of United States nationality under [the INA], subject to such procedures for administrative appeal as the Secretary may prescribe by regulation, and also shall constitute a denial of a right or privilege of United States nationality for purposes of [INA §] 360.

§ 15:21   Initial determination by consular or diplomatic officials

Research References

Dizon and Wettstein, Immigration Law Service 2d § 14:461

The INA has delegated the determination of loss of nationality in the first instance to consular and diplomatic officials abroad.[1] Consular and diplomatic officers are also authorized to accept voluntary renunciation of U.S. citizenship.[2]

Closely following the statute, the State Department regulations provide that whenever diplomatic or consular officials have reason to believe that the person has lost his or her U.S. nationality, they must prepare a certificate of loss of nationality containing the facts which support this believe and forward the certificate to the State Department.[3] All relevant documents will be attached to the certificate, unless the official believes it should not be attached in which case, the relevant information is summarized.[4] When a person consents to execute an affidavit admitting the relevant acts of expatriation, the official will either recite it in the certificate or attach it to the certificate.[5] In addition, if the person admits that the act was performed with the intention of relinquishing U.S. citizenship and admits to the execution of an af-

---

[Section 15:20]

[1]INA § 358, 8 U.S.C.A. § 1501.

[Section 15:21]

[1]INA § 358, 8 U.S.C.A. § 1501. Prior regulations specified that determinations of loss of citizenship were only made when a person applied for a U.S. passport. These regulations have been deleted. 61 Fed. Reg. 29651 removing 22 CFR. § 50.42.

[2]22 CFR § 50.50(a).

[3]INA § 358, 8 U.S.C.A. § 1501; 22 CFR § 50.40(c).

[4]22 CFR § 50.40(d).

[5]22 CFR § 50.40(e).

fidavit to that respect, the affidavit will also be affixed to the certificate of loss of nationality prepared by the consular or diplomatic officer.[6]

However, consular and diplomatic determinations are now governed by a presumption that the following actions are performed with the intention of *retaining* U.S. citizenship, and, without further proof, should *not* be a basis for losing U.S. citizenship: (1) obtaining naturalization in a foreign country; (2) subscribing routine declarations of allegiance to a foreign state; and (3) accepting non-policy level employment in a foreign state.[7] Indeed, a State Department cable sent to the U.S. embassies in London, Seoul, Islamabad, Guatemala, and Nairobi, instructs consular and diplomatic officers to handle these purportedly expatriating acts by placing in the person's file, a signed certification by the consular officer indicating that the act was performed but that it did not result in loss of nationality.[8] The cable explains that there is still a legal requirement to make a determination of whether an expatriating act has been committed and that it is in both the State Department and the citizen's interest to have a documentation of the non-loss of U.S. citizenship, for future reference.[9] The cable allows consular officers to give a copy of this determination to the citizen, if the citizen so desires.[10]

In spite of this presumption, when a person affirmatively asserts to a consular or diplomatic officer that he or she performed the expatriating act with the intention of abandoning U.S. citizenship, the person will lose his or her U.S. nationality.[11] The regulations provide that whenever a person admits that he or she had the intent to relinquish citizenship by the voluntary and intentional performance of one of the acts specified in Section 349(a) of the Immigration and Nationality Act, and the person consents to the execution of an affidavit to that effect, the diplomatic or consular officer must attach such affidavit to the certificate of loss of nationality.[12]

Finally, the presumption does not apply at all to the following acts: (1) serving in official positions in a foreign country, and (2) formal renunciation of U.S. nationality at a U.S. consular or diplomatic post abroad. Regarding service in official positions in foreign countries, the State Department has instructed some consular and diplomatic posts to attempt to determine on a case by case basis whether service in a foreign government was performed with the intention of relinquishing U.S. citizenship.[13] To make this determination, the posts were instructed to make sure they obtained the following information in developing their cases: (1) name of the person; (2) data and place of birth; (3) how U.S. citizenship was acquired; (4) whether the person has the nationality of the foreign State, and, if so, how and when this nationality was acquired; (5) the position of the person in the foreign government; (6) whether the person was elected or appointed to this position; and (7) any state-

---

[6]8 CFR. § 50.40(b).

[7]61 Fed. Reg. 29651 (Supplementary Information).

[8]State Department Cable, No. 95-State-034797 (Feb. 10, 1995) reproduced in 72 Interpreter Releases 1618 (December 4, 1995).

[9]State Department Cable, No. 95-State-034797 (Feb. 10, 1995) reproduced in 72 Interpreter Releases 1618 (December 4, 1995).

[10]State Department Cable, No. 95-State-034797 (Feb. 10, 1995) reproduced in 72 Interpreter Releases 1618 (December 4, 1995).

[11]22 CFR. § 50.40(a).

[12]22 CFR. § 50.40(b).

[13]State Department Cable, No. 95-State-034797.

ments regarding the intent to retain or relinquish U.S. citizenship.[14] If the position the person accepted was *not* a policy level position, the State Department will presume that the employment with the foreign government was done with the intention of retaining U.S. citizenship, and therefore will normally not lead to loss of U.S. nationality.[15]

In cases of voluntary renunciation of U.S. nationality at the consulate, the diplomatic or consular officer will also forward to the State Department for approval the oath of renunciation together with a certificate of loss of nationality.[16]

§ 15:22 Issuance of certificate by State Department

Consular and diplomatic officials only prepare a report.[1] It is then forwarded to the State Department for a determination of whether loss of nationality actually occurred.[2] If the certificate of loss of nationality is approved by the State Department, a copy of it is forwarded to the DHS, and another is sent to the person or his or her representative through the consular or diplomatic official that originally prepared the certificate.[3]

§ 15:23 Reconsideration by Office of Policy Review and Interagency liaison

Research References

Dizon and Wettstein, Immigration Law Service 2d § 14:438, 439

There is no prescribed administrative appeal from issuance of a Certificate of Loss of Nationality, and thus no mandatory administrative review procedure prior to the availability of judicial review under INA § 360 [8 U.S.C.A. 1503].[1] Prior to 2008, the State Department maintained an appellate body for these appeals, called the Board of Appellate Review (BAR). However, the State Department eliminated the BAR in 2008, preferring the "less cumbersome and more timely" procedure of discretionary requests for reconsideration.[2]

The State Department's discretionary ability to revisit findings of loss of nationality has now been formally recognized in regulation.[3] Under the new regulations, the "primary reasons" for reconsideration include: (1) that the law under which the finding of loss was made has been held unconstitutional; (2) a major change in the interpretation of the law of expatriation is made as a result of a U.S. Supreme Court decision; (3) a major change in the interpretation of the law of expatriation is made by the Department, or is made by a court or another agency and adopted by the Department; and (4) the person presents substantial new evidence, not previously

---

[14]State Department Cable, No. 95-State-034797.

[15]61 Fed. Reg. 29651 (Supplementary Information).

[16]22 CFR. § 50.50(b).

[Section 15:22]

[1]INA § 358, 8 U.S.C.A. § 1501.

[2]INA § 358, 8 U.S.C.A. § 1501.

[3]INA § 358, 8 U.S.C.A. § 1501.; 22 CFR §§ 50.40(f), 50.50(b).

[Section 15:23]

[1]22 C.F.R. § 50.51.

[2]73 Fed. Reg. 41256-58 (July 18, 2008) (supplementary information).

[3]See 22 C.F.R. § 50.51(b).

considered, of involuntariness or absence of intent at the time of the expatriating act.[4]

Those requesting reconsideration under this section do not need to be represented by an attorney, and such requests may be submitted to: Department of State; Bureau of Consular Affairs; Office of Policy Review and Interagency Liaison; Overseas Citizens Services; 2201 C Street, NW; Washington, DC 20520-4817.[5]

§ 15:24 Tax consequences of reconsideration of loss of nationality certificates

Reconsideration of a certificate of loss of nationality may have some tax consequences. Because of the highly complex and evolving nature of tax law, the client should be referred to a tax attorney. As an example of possible consequences, we summarize a 1992 revenue ruling.[1] This ruling is only reviewed as a way of illustration and should not be considered the definitive answer to the questions posed. It must be pointed out that other rulings have taken a less generous approach to tax liability.[2]

The 1992 Revenue Ruling reviewed the tax consequences of the State Department's review of a certificate of loss of nationality.[3] The ruling posed four hypothetical questions.[4] All four questions were predicated upon the consideration that if the person performed an expatriating act, such an act did not have as one of its principal purposes the avoidance of federal income, estate, or gift taxes.[5]

The first question asked the tax liability of U.S. citizens who had been determined by the State Department to have lost their U.S. citizenship and later had it retroactively restored by the State Department.[6] It found that in cases of individuals who lost their United States citizenship and had it retroactively restored before January 1, 1993, they would not be held liable for federal income taxes as United States citizens between the date they lost their United States citizenship and the beginning of the taxable year when their citizenship was restored, and they would not be held liable for federal gift taxes as United States citizens between the date they lost their United States citizenship and January 1 of the calendar year when their citizenship was restored.[7]

The second hypothetical related to the federal tax consequences of former citizens who are eligible to have their United States citizenship retroactively restored but who have not applied to do so [or who applied after January 1, 1993].[8] According to the revenue ruling, former citizens who have not sought administrative review of

---

[4]See 22 C.F.R. § 50.51(b).

[5]61 Fed. Reg. 29651, June 12, 1996.

[Section 15:24]

[1]Rev. Rul. 92-109, 1992-52 IRB 5.

[2]See Rev. Rul. 75-357, 1975-2 CB 5 (holding that a U.S. citizen who had lost her citizenship under a statute later found to be unconstitutional had, for tax purposes, continued to be U.S. citizen during the whole period).

[3]Rev. Rul. 92-109, 1992-52 IRB 5.

[4]Rev. Rul. 92-109, 1992-52 IRB 5.

[5]Rev. Rul. 92-109, 1992-52 IRB 5.

[6]Rev. Rul. 92-109, 1992-52 IRB 5 (issue 1).

[7]Rev. Rul. 92-109, 1992-52 IRB 5 (Analysis and Holdings: Situation 1).

[8]Rev. Rul. 92-109, 1992-52 IRB 5 (issue 2).

the determination of loss of nationality, are not taxable as U.S. citizens since the date they lost their U.S. citizenship.[9] Under the tax code, they would be considered noncitizens—either nonresident or resident noncitizens depending on the circumstances of each case.[10] However, if their certificate of loss of nationality is reviewed by the State Department and their U.S. citizenship is retroactively restored after January 1, 1993, they would be liable for federal taxes stating on January 1, 1993, regardless of the date their citizenship is restored.[11]

The third hypothetical related to the tax liability of those who performed expatriating acts but were never found by the State Department to have lost their U.S. citizenship.[12] Absent a State Department determination, those persons are considered to have continued being U.S. citizens for tax purposes even after the purportedly expatriating act.[13] The Internal Revenue Service has designated for special consideration individuals who did not file federal income and gift tax returns as U.S. citizens because they had a reasonable good faith belief that they had lost their U.S. citizenship.[14] Not only was there never a determination that they had lost their U.S. citizenship, but those individuals never intended to relinquish their U.S. citizenship when they performed those acts.[15] Pursuant to IRS policy, the assistant commissioner (international) and district directors may grant relief to these individuals similar to that available to persons who had their citizenship restored by the State Department.[16] In making these decisions, the IRS will consider the circumstances of each case, including whether the individuals acted in a manner consistent with a good faith belief they had lost their U.S. citizenship by, among others, not affirmatively exercising any rights of U.S. citizenship in the period when they did not file federal tax returns as U.S. citizens.[17]

Regarding U.S. citizens residing abroad who never perform expatriating acts and who were never determined to have lost their U.S. citizenship, the ruling plainly holds that they are liable for income and gift and estate taxes for the entire period.[18] Their liability depends on other tax law considerations.[19]

B. BOARD OF IMMIGRATION APPEALS (B.I.A.)

§ 15:25 Generally

Even though the INA provides that consular or diplomatic officials are required to make a determination of loss of citizenship abroad, it does not preclude other agencies from making similar determinations.[1] Indeed, the INA provides that the Attorney General's determinations of the law are controlling over those of the State

---

[9]Rev. Rul. 92-109, 1992-52 IRB 5 (Analysis and Holdings: Situation 2).

[10]Rev. Rul. 92-109, 1992-52 IRB 5.

[11]Rev. Rul. 92-109, 1992-52 IRB 5.

[12]Rev. Rul. 92-109, 1992-52 IRB 5 (issue 3).

[13]Rev. Rul. 92-109, 1992-52 IRB 5 (Analysis and Holdings: Situation 3).

[14]Rev. Rul. 92-109, 1992-52 IRB 5.

[15]Rev. Rul. 92-109, 1992-52 IRB 5.

[16]Rev. Rul. 92-109, 1992-52 IRB 5.

[17]Rev. Rul. 92-109, 1992-52 IRB 5.

[18]Rev. Rul. 92-109, 1992-52 IRB 5 (issue 4; Analysis and Holdings: Situation 4).

[19]Rev. Rul. 92-109, 1992-52 IRB 5 (Analysis and Holdings: Situation 4).

[Section 15:25]

[1]INA § 358, 8 U.S.C.A. § 1501.

Department.[2] However, by statute, if the State Department has made a determination of loss of nationality, such determination is binding on the DHS.[3]

The DHS finds itself making determinations regarding loss of nationality in a host of different situations. Most commonly, those determinations are made in relation to visa petitions filed by a person believed to have lost his or her citizenship, or in the context of exclusion proceedings in which the citizenship of the person seeking to enter the U.S. is at issue. A determination of loss of citizenship in these contexts may be appealed through the normal avenues of appeal for each type of proceeding. Thus, for example, determinations of excludability may be appealed to the Board of Immigration Appeals.

C. JUDICIAL PROCEEDINGS

§ 15:26 Judicial declaration of U.S. citizenship

The INA confers a mechanism for judicial declaration of U.S. citizenship.[1] If the person is inside the United States and governmental department or agency has denied him or her of any right or privilege enjoyed by nationals of the U.S., then he or she may file an action for a declaration of U.S. nationality.[2] These actions must be filed within five years of the final administrative denial of right or privilege and must be filed in the U.S. district court for the district in which the person resides.[3] This procedure, however, is not available either for review of removal proceedings or if the citizenship of the person is already being litigated in removal proceedings.[4] In such cases, the review of final administrative orders of exclusion must be sought as part of a *habeas corpus* action in district court,[5] or through a petition for review of a final order of removal.[6]

The courts are divided as to when the five-year statute of limitations starts to run. The Third Circuit and the District Court for the District of Columbia have held that the five-year starts to run upon the denial of a passport application.[7] On the other hand, the Eleventh Circuit and the Southern District of Florida have held that it starts to run from the issuance of the certificate of loss of nationality.[8] This would make it much earlier than the denial of the passport.

---

[2]INA § 103(a)(1) [8 U.S.C.A. § 1103(a)(1)].

[3]INA § 358, 8 U.S.C.A. § 1501; Legal Opinion, Aleinikoff, General Counsel INS, File Nos. HQ 349-P, HQ 359-P (Dec. 14, 1994) reprinted in 72 Interpreter Releases 361 (Mar. 13, 1995).

[Section 15:26]

[1]INA § 360, 8 U.S.C.A. § 1503.

[2]INA § 360(a), 8 U.S.C.A. § 1503(a).

[3]INA § 360(a), 8 U.S.C.A. § 1503(a).

[4]INA § 360(a), 8 U.S.C.A. § 1503(a) as amended by Illegal Immigration Reform and Immigrant Responsibility Act of 1996, Pub. L. 104-208, § 308(d)(4), 110 Stat. 3009 (Sept. 30, 1996).

[5]INA § 360(c), 8 U.S.C.A. § 1503(c).

[6]See 8 U.S.C.A. § 1252(b); see also § 15:28.

[7]Whitehead v. Haig, 794 F.2d 115 (3d Cir. 1986); Maldonado-Sanchez v. Shultz, 706 F. Supp. 54 (D.D.C. 1989).

[8]Heuer v. U.S. Secretary of State, 20 F.3d 424 (11th Cir. 1994); Garcia-Sarquiz v. Saxbe, 407 F. Supp. 789 (S.D. Fla. 1974), aff'd sub nom. Garcia-Sarquiz v. Levi, 527 F.2d 1389 (5th Cir. 1976) (per curiam).

The Seventh Circuit found that it starts to run at the time the Board of Appellate Review issued a negative decision.[9] The Court also suggested in dicta that the doctrine of laches might also apply to prevent an action from being prosecuted after unreasonable delay.[10]

When any agency or department denies a person outside the United States a right or privilege of nationals of the U.S., the person may obtain a certificate of identity from the U.S. embassy or consulate.[11] That certificate will allow the holder to travel to the United States.[12] However, only persons who have been in the United States before, or persons claiming U.S. citizenship at birth abroad and who are under the age of 16 may obtain such certificates of identity.[13]

Persons holding such certificates are inspected at the border and are subject to exclusion proceedings to the same extent as noncitizens.[14] A final determination by the BIA that such persons are excludable is only reviewable by a U.S. district court through *habeas corpus* proceedings.[15]

§ 15:27 Declaration in relation to removal proceedings

The Illegal Immigration Reform and Immigrant Responsibility Act of 1996, completely revised the procedures to remove noncitizens from the United States.[1] It severely limited judicial review of what was formerly exclusion and deportation orders.[2] Even under the new procedures, however, there are provisions for judicial determinations of the *alienage* of the subject of removal proceedings.

Persons seeking admission who have been placed in expedited removal—including persons seeking entry and persons who entered without inspection—can only obtain a determination of their nationality status through *habeas corpus* proceedings.[3]

Persons subject to removal based on a deportability section, may seek judicial review of the citizenship claim in the circuit court as part of their appeal of the removal order.[4] If the circuit court determines that no issues of fact regarding the nationality claim remain, then the circuit court adjudicates the claim.[5] If there are issues of fact, the circuit court transfers the proceedings to the federal district court for the judicial district in which the petitioner resides for a new hearing on the

---

[9]Bensky v. Powell, 391 F.3d 894 (7th Cir. 2004) (Posner, J.).

[10]Bensky v. Powell, 391 F.3d 894, 898 (7th Cir. 2004).

[11]INA § 360(b), 8 U.S.C.A. § 1503(b).

[12]INA § 360(b), 8 U.S.C.A. § 1503(b).

[13]INA § 360(b), 8 U.S.C.A. § 1503(b).

[14]INA § 360(c), 8 U.S.C.A. § 1503(c).

[15]INA § 360(c), 8 U.S.C.A. § 1503(c).

[Section 15:27]

[1]IIRAIRA Title III-A.

[2]IIRAIRA § 306.

[3]INA § 242(e)(2), 8 U.S.C.A. § 1252(e)(2) as amended by IIRAIRA § 306(a).

[4]INA § 242(b)(5), 8 U.S.C.A. § 1252(b)(5) as amended by IIRAIRA § 306(a). *See, e.g.,* Hughes v. Ashcroft, 255 F.3d 752, 755 (9th Cir. 2001); Cartagena-Paulino v. Reno, 2003 WL 21436224 (S.D.N.Y. 2003) (transferring case to the circuit court to hear the claim of derivative citizenship).

[5]INA § 242(b)(5)(A), 8 U.S.C.A. § 1252(b)(5)(A) as amended by IIRAIRA § 306(a). *See, e.g.,* Hughes v. Ashcroft, 255 F.3d 752, 755 (9th Cir. 2001).

nationality claim as if an action had been brought for declaratory relief under 28 U.S.C.A. § 2201.[6]

Although aliens seeking federal judicial review at the Court of Appeals by statute must exhaust their administrative remedies,[7] those exhaustion rules may not apply to potential citizens. The Supreme Court's case law precluding involuntary loss of citizenship,[8] as well as the statute's reference only to aliens,[9] have led a number of Courts of Appeals to find administrative exhaustion not required before a citizenship claim can be pursued on appeal from a removal order.[10]

Persons who are being criminally prosecuted based on a prior removal from the United States which has not been judicially reviewed in the past, may make a motion in those proceedings claiming U.S. nationality.[11] If there is no issue of material fact, the court decides the motion on the administrative record only and accepts the administrative findings as conclusion if supported by reasonable, substantial, and probative evidence on the record considered as a whole.[12] If a genuine issue of fact regarding the defendant's nationality is presented, then the court will hold a new hearing on the nationality claim and decide that claim as if an action had been brought under the declaration judgment provisions of 28 U.S.C.A. § 2201.[13]

---

[6]INA § 242(b)(5)(B), 8 U.S.C.A. § 1252(b)(5)(B) as amended by IIRAIRA § 306(a).

[7]8 U.S.C.A. § 1252(d)(1).

[8]Afroyim v. Rusk, 387 U.S. 253, 262, 87 S.Ct. 1660, 18 L.Ed.2d 757 (1967); Vance v. Terrazas, 444 U.S. 252, 260, 100 S.Ct. 540, 62 L.Ed.2d 461, 5 Fed. R. Evid. Serv. 273 (1980).

[9]8 U.S.C.A. § 1252(d)(1).

[10]Rivera v. Ashcroft, 394 F.3d 1129, 1136 (9th Cir.2005); Theagene v. Gonzales, 411 F.3d 1107, 1111 (9th Cir. 2005); Iasu v. Smith, 511 F.3d 881 (9th Cir. 2007); Minasyan v. Gonzales, 401 F.3d 1069, 1075 (9th Cir.2005); Poole v. Mukasey, 522 F.3d 259 (2d Cir. 2008); Omolo v. Gonzales, 452 F.3d 404, 407 (5th Cir.2006); Moussa v. INS, 302 F.3d 823 (8th Cir.2002) (noting that exhaustion rules at § 1252(d)(1) apply only to aliens); cf Taniguchi v. Schultz, 303 F.3d 950 (9th Cir.2002) (court refused to consider unexhausted, but also frivolous, citizenship claim).

[11]INA § 242(b)(7)(B), 8 U.S.C.A. § 1252(b)(7)(B) as amended by IIRAIRA § 306(a).

[12]INA § 242(b)(7)(B)(i), 8 U.S.C.A. § 1252(b)(7)(B)(i) as amended by IIRAIRA § 306(a).

[13]INA § 242(b)(7)(B)(ii), 8 U.S.C.A. § 1252(b)(7)(B)(ii) as amended by IIRAIRA § 306(a).

APPENDIX 15-1

Countries recognizing dual citizenship[1]

The following is a list indicating which countries recognize dual citizenship, where the individual has become a United States citizen. The list is based primarily on Citizenship Laws of the World (March 2001, Office of Personnel Management (OPM)), found at http://www.opm.gov/extra/investigate/IS-01.pdf, a survey of every country in the world.

In the list below, "Retain" means that the individual does not lose his or her prior citizenship upon naturalizing in the United States. "Lose" means that the individual does lose his or her prior citizenship. Where possible, the list is annotated to provide additional relevant information.

For some listed countries, the information comes not from the OPS survey, but from one of two sources:(1) Cohen, Bowyer, Garcia, Ong Hing, Lydon, Steadman and Silverman, "Naturalization: A Guide for Legal Practitioners and Other Community Advocates," Appendix 2-D, Immigrant Legal Resources Center (1995) (updated 1998), or (2) Belchak, "Dual Citizenship in the European Union," Nationality and Citizenship Handbook, 37 (Mautino and Endelman, eds., AILA 1996). Other sources are listed in footnotes. Each URL was last accessed on August 22, 2006.

- AFGHANISTAN — **Unclear**[2]
- ALBANIA — Retain
- ALGERIA — Lose
- ANDORRA — Lose
- ANGOLA — Retain
- ANTIGUA and BARBUDA — Retain
- ARGENTINA — Lose[3]
- ARMENIA — Lose

---

[1]A version of this appendix appeared at Charles Roth, Wolrdwide Liberalization of Dual Citizenship Rules and Potential Side Effects on US Citizenship, 83 Interpreter Releases 2529 to 2531 (Nov. 26, 2006). Reprinted with permission.

[2]The 2000 citizenship law (adopted by the Taliban) forbids dual citizenship. However, Article 4 of the 2004 Constitution provides that "[n]o individual shall be deprived of citizenship. The citizenship and asylum related matters shall be regulated by law." Immigration and Refugee Board of Canada, Afghanistan: Citizenship, including legislation and whether dual citizenship is permitted (2008-2013), 5 February 2013, available at: http://www.refworld.org/docid/51345c1a2.html [accessed 14 May 2013]. There is also some indication that Afghanistan is using citizenship legislation which was passed in 1315 of the Afghan calendar (1936). Immigration and Refugee Board of Canada, Afghanistan: Information on citizenship since the fall of the Taliban government (1996-2001), 8 January 2008, AFG102673.E, available at: http://www.refworld.org/docid/47ce6d7b22.html [accessed 14 May 2013]. The OPM's assessment is based on 1992 legislation, under the former communist government. New legislation is apparently being prepared.

[3]According to Cohen, et al., an individual does not lose Argentine citizenship upon naturalization; but other sources are to the contrary. See, e.g., United States (US). March 2001. Office of Personnel

1280

- AUSTRALIA   Retain (after April 4, 2002)[4]
- AUSTRIA   Lose (except in very specific circumstances)
- AZERBAIJIAN   Lose
- BAHAMAS   Lose (if U.S.oath is taken after July 9, 1973)
- BAHRAIN   Lose
- BANGLADESH   Lose
- BARBADOS   Retain (unless renounce by specific procedure)
- BELARUS   Lose
- BELGIUM   Lose
- BELIZE   Retain
- BENIN   Retain
- BHUTAN   Lose
- BOLIVIA   Lose
- BOSNIA and   Retain (pursuant to a bilateral agreement with
  HERZEGOVINA   the U.S. that permits dual citizenship)[5]
- BOTSWANNA   Lose
- BRAZIL   Retain (if the individual declares acquisition of
                     U.S. citizenship at a Brazilian mission or consul-
                     ate and a finding is made that acquisition is
                     required in order to reside permanently with full
                     civil rights)[6]
- BRUNEI   Lose
- BULGARIA   Retain
- BURKINA FASO   Retain
- BURUNDI   Lose (after court proceedings)
- CAMBODIA   Lose
- CAMEROON   Lose
- CANADA   Retain
- CAPE VERDE   Retain
- CENTRAL AFRICAN   Retain
  REPUBLIC
- CHAD   Retain
- CHILE   Lose

Management (OPM). "Argentina." Citizenship Laws of the World.; Immigration and Refugee Board of Canada: Argentina: Update to ARG34787.E of 20 July 2000 regarding whether the acquisition of a foreign nationality would result in the loss of Argentinean citizenship; if so, steps necessary to recover lost citizenship (July 2000-May 2005) - May 2005, found at www.unhcr.org/cgi-bin/texis/vtx/rsd/rsddocv iew.html?tbl=RSDCOI&id=42df609b28.

[4]Under the Australian Citizenship Legislation Amendment Act 2002, an individual who naturalizes after April 4, 2002, no longer loses their Australian citizenship. See http://www.australianvisasdc. com/citizenship/resumption.html; http://www.citizenship.gov.au/australians-os/dual-citz.htm.

[5]Cohen, Bowyer, Garcia, Ong Hing, Lydon, Steadman and Silverman, "Naturalization: A Guide for Legal Practitioners and Other Community Advocates," Appendix 2-D, Immigrant Legal Resources Center (1995) (updated 1998).

[6]Cohen, Bowyer, Garcia, Ong Hing, Lydon, Steadman and Silverman, "Naturalization: A Guide for Legal Practitioners and Other Community Advocates," Appendix 2-D, Immigrant Legal Resources Center (1995) (updated 1998).

- CHINA (PRC)   Lose
- COLOMBIA   Retain
- COMOROS   Unknown
- CONGO (DRC)   Lose
- CONGO (RC)   Lose
- COSTA RICA   Retain (effective June 27, 1995, but must maintain Costa Rican documents)
- CROATIA   Retain
- CUBA   Lose
- CYPRUS   Retain
- CYPRUS (NORTH)   Retain[7]
- CZECH REPUBLIC   Lose (except if individual became a U.S. citizen between September 17, 1938, and May 7, 1957)
- DENMARK   Lose
- DJIBOUTI   Lose
- DOMINICA   Retain (unless renounces by specific procedure)[8]
- DOMINICAN REPUB-LIC   Retain (since 1994)[9]
- ECUADOR   Retain[10]
- EGYPT   Retain upon application[11]
- EL SALVADOR   Retain
- EQUITORIAL GUINEA   Lose
- ERITREA   Unclear[12]

---

[7]Cohen, Bowyer, Garcia, Ong Hing, Lydon, Steadman and Silverman, "Naturalization: A Guide for Legal Practitioners and Other Community Advocates," Appendix 2-D, Immigrant Legal Resources Center (1995) (updated 1998).

[8]Cohen, Bowyer, Garcia, Ong Hing, Lydon, Steadman and Silverman, "Naturalization: A Guide for Legal Practitioners and Other Community Advocates," Appendix 2-D, Immigrant Legal Resources Center (1995) (updated 1998).

[9]Both the 1994 and 2002 constitutions prevent the loss of citizenship by naturalization abroad. See, http://pdba.georgetown.edu/Constitutions/DomRep/dominicanrepublic.html; Cohen, Bowyer, Garcia, Ong Hing, Lydon, Steadman and Silverman, "Naturalization: A Guide for Legal Practitioners and Other Community Advocates," Appendix 2-D, Immigrant Legal Resources Center (1995) (updated 1998). The "Citizenship Laws of the World" publication states that such individuals lose Dominican citizenship upon naturalization, but this appears to be incorrect.

[10]The OPM publication states that naturalization may result in loss of Ecuadorian citizenship, but Article 11 of the 1998 Ecuadorian Constitution provides that "Ecuadorians by birth, who are naturalized or will become naturalized in another country, will maintain their Ecuadorian citizenship status." Found at http://www.ecuador.org/ecuador/miscellaneous.htm. The Ecuadorian consulate suggests requesting a copy of the birth records to determine whether citizenship status has been maintained. Id.

[11]The OPM publication states that naturalization may result in loss of Egyptian citizenship, the Egyptian consular website states that dual citizenship is permitted upon application. Consulate General of Egypt, New York, "Apply for a Permit from the Egyptian Authorities for a Dual Citizenship Approval," found at http://www.egyptnyc.net/english/dual_citizenship.asp; see also, Cohen, et al., supra.

[12]Eritrea became independent in 1992, and its nationality law remains somewhat unclear. While the OPM publication states that voluntary acquisition of another country's citizenship involuntarily terminates citizenship, OPM at 73, the State Department reports for Eritrea, travel.state.gov/travel/ci

- ESTONIA   Retain (1940 to 1992, a formal release was required); Lose (1992 to present)[13]
- ETHIOPIA   Lose[14]
- FIJI   Lose
- FINLAND   Retain[15]
- FRANCE   Retain
- GABON   Lose
- GAMBIA   Unclear[16]
- GEORGIA   Lose[17]
- GERMANY   Lose, but may apply to retain citizenship[18]
- GHANA   Retain
- GREECE   Lose
- GRENADA   Retain
- GUATEMALA   Lose
- GUINEA   Lose
- GUINEA-BISSAU   Lose
- GUYANA   Lose
- HAITI   Lose (can reacquire after living in Haiti for 5 years)
- HONDURAS   Lose
- HUNGARY   Retain

---

s__pa__tw/cis/cis__1111.html, report that "Eritrea has complicated citizenship laws and does not recognize renunciation of Eritrean citizenship. Dual nationals who enter the country on Eritrean documents are treated as Eritrean citizens, regardless of their other citizenship." The 1992 Eritrean Nationality Proclamation (Proclamation No. 21/1992) provided Eritrean citizenship to all people born in Eritrea or to Eritrean parents; but implicitly provided that naturalization abroad could preclude Eritrean citizenship. Article 5(e) ("[a]ny person who is Eritrean by birth, resides abroad and possesses foreign nationality shall apply to the Department of Internal Affairs if he wishes to officially renounce his foreign nationality and acquire Eritrean nationality or wishes, after providing adequate justification, to have his Eritrean nationality accepted while maintaining his foreign nationality") (quoted at Human Rights Watch, The Horn of Africa War: Mass Expulsions and the Nationality Issue (June 1998 - April 2002), Vol. 15, No. 3 (A) at 15 (New York January 2003).

[13]While Estonian statutes prohibit dual citizenship and provide that naturalization deprives someone of Estonian citizenship, Article 8 of the Estonian Constitution provides that no individual who acquired citizenship at birth may be deprived of it. http://www.coe.int/t/e/legal__affairs/legal__co-o peration/foreigners__and__citizens/nationality/documents/bulletin/Estonia%20E%202004.pdf. Thus, the answer is somewhat unclear.

[14]Human Rights Watch, The Horn of Africa War: Mass Expulsions and the Nationality Issue (June 1998 - April 2002), Vol. 15, No. 3 (A) at 20 (New York January 2003).

[15]Since the publication of the OPM, Finland has amended its citizenship laws to permit dual citizenship. http://www.finland.org/doc/en/consular/nationality.html.

[16]According to the 2001 OPM publication, Gambia was considering changes to permit dual nationality, and the State Department's 2006 Consular Information Sheet does indicate that Gambia recognizes dual citizenship; however, the author was unable to locate any authority for this proposition, or to confirm whether this would apply after naturalization.

[17]Cohen, et al., supra.

[18]See German Consulates United States, "General Information on German citizenship - FAQs," found at http://www.germany.info/relaunch/info/consular__services/citizenship/generalinformation.h tml.

- ICELAND — Retain, but Lost before July 1, 2003 (can regain by application)[19]
- INDIA — May Retain[20]
- INDONESIA — Loses (unless with government permission and without voting)
- IRAN — Retain
- IRELAND — Retain
- ISRAEL — Lose
- ITALY — Lose (prior to August 15,1992); Retain (August 15,1992 to present)
- IVORY COAST — Retain
- JAMAICA — Retain
- JAPAN — Lose
- JORDAN — Retain
- KAZAKSTAN — Lose
- KENYA — Lose
- KIRIBATI — Lose
- N. KOREA (PRK) — Retain
- KOREA (REPUBLIC OF) — Lose
- KUWAIT — Unclear, probably retain
- KYRGYZ REP. — Lose
- LAOS — Lose
- LATVIA — Permitted for individuals fleeing Nazi or Communist control
- LEBANON — Retain
- LESOTHO — Lose
- LIBERIA — Lose
- LIBYA — Lose (unless Government permission to naturalize)
- LIECHTENSTEIN — Retain (but will have diminished rights and protections)
- LITHUANIA — Lose (must notify local authorities within 30 days of oath)
- LUXEMBOURG — Lose
- MACEDONIA — Retain
- MADAGASCAR — Lose
- MALAWI — Lose
- MALAYSIA — Lose

---

[19] At the time of the 2001 OPM publication, citizens of Iceland automatically lost citizenship at time of naturalization. Since then, Iceland passed a new law permitting retention of citizenship. http://www.dkm.is/laws-and-regulations/nr/31.

[20] At the time of the 2001 OPM publication, Indian law did not permit dual nationality. Indian law has subsequently been revised to permit "Overseas Citizenship of India," which does not permit voting, but does permit unlimited travel and other civil rights. Embassy of India, Washington, D.C., "Overseas Citizenship of India Scheme," found at http://www.indianembassy.org/New__Template/oci.asp.

- MALDIVES Retain
- MALI Retain
- MALTA Lose
- MARSHALL ISLANDS Lose
- MAURITANIA Lose
- MAURITIUS Retain
- MEXICO Retain
- MICRONESIA Lose
- MOLDOVA Lose
- MONACO Lose
- MONGOLIA Retain
- MOROCCO Lose
- MOZAMBIQUE Lose
- MYANMAR Lose
- NAMIBIA Lose
- NAURU Lose
- NEPAL Lose
- NETHERLANDS Lose, with exceptions[21]
- NEW ZEALAND Retain
- NICARAGUA Retain[22]
- NIGER Lose
- NIGERIA Retain
- NORWAY Lose
- OMAN Retain
- PAKISTAN Retain[23]
- PALAU Lose
- PANAMA Lose
- PAPUA NEW GUINEA Lose
- PARAGUAY Lose
- PERU Retain

[21]Under a 2003 law, a Dutch citizen loses citizenship upon naturalization in the U.S. unless, as pertinent here, (a) the Dutch citizen had a principal residence in the U.S. before turning 18, for an uninterrupted period of 5 years; or (b) the Dutch citizen is married to a U.S. citizen. See Loss of Dutch Nationality, located at http://www.government.nl/issues/nationality/loss-of-dutch-nationality (accessed May 13, 2013). Dutch citizens who lost citizenship before 2003 may regain it by application; that process appears to require the taking of an oath of allegiance, but does not always require an oath of renunciation.

[22]Prior to 2000, Nicaraguans lost their citizenship upon naturalization. However, the law was amended on January 19, 2000, to provide that "Nicaraguan nationality shall not be lost upon acquisition of another nationality." Article 20, Nicaraguan Constituion (as reported in REPORT N₀ 25/01, CASE 12.144, ALVARO JOSÉ ROBELO GONZÁLEZ v. NICARAGUA, Inter-American Commission on Human Rights (March 5, 2001).

[23]As of August 29, 2002, Pakistan now permits its citizens to naturalize without losing their Pakistani citizenship. Pakistani Communication, S.R.O. 581 (1)/2002 (Aug. 29, 2002).

- PHILIPPINES   Retain[24]
- POLAND   Retain
- PORTUGAL   Retain
- QATAR   Lose
- ROMANIA   Retain
- RUSSIA   Retain
- RWANDA   Lose
- ST.KITTS and NEVIS   Retain
- ST.LUCIA   Retain
- ST.VINCENT   Retain (but lost if person lives abroad for 5 years)
- SAMOA   Lose
- SAO TOME AND PRINCIPE Lose
- SAUDI ARABIA   Lose
- SENEGAL   Retain
- SEYCHELLES   Lose
- SIERRA LEONE   Retain
- SINGAPORE   Lose
- SLOVAK REP.   Retain
- SLOVENIA   Retain
- SOLOMAN ISLANDS   Lose after two years
- SOMALIA   Unknown, no real government
- SOUTH AFRICA   Lose (however, citizenship may be retained upon request prior to becoming a U.S. citizen, or may be reobtained by subsequent application)[25]
- SPAIN   Lose
- SRI LANKA   Lose (unless application to retain citizenship)[26]
- SUDAN   Lose
- SURINAM   Lose[27]
- SWAZILAND   Retain
- SWEDEN   Retain[28]
- SWITZERLAND   Retain
- SYRIA   Retain
- TAIWAN (ROC)   Lose

---

[24]As of Sept. 17, 2003, the Citizenship Retention and Re-acquisition Act of 2003 (Republic Act No. 9225), prevents the loss of Filipino citizenship upon naturalization in another country. It also retroactively restores Filipino citizenship which had been lost. Found at http://www.gov.ph/faqs/dualcitizenship.asp.

[25]South African Citizenship Act, 1995, § 6 (Act 88 of 1995).

[26]Application may be made prior to naturalization, or may be made subsequently. http://www.slembassyusa.org/consular/dual_citizenship.html.

[27]Cohen, et al., supra.

[28]As of February 21, 2001, Sweden now permits dual citizenship, such that Swedes do not lose their Swedish citizenship upon naturalization. See, http://eudo-citizenship.eu/docs/CountryReports/Sweden.pdf.

- TAJIKISTAN   Unknown
- TANZANIA   Lose
- THAILAND   Lose
- TOGO   Retain
- TONGA   Lose
- TRINIDAD and   Lose
  TOBAGO
- TUNISIA   Retain
- TURKEY   Retain
- UGANDA   Lose
- TURKMENISTAN   Unknown
- TUVALU   Retain
- UGANDA   Lose
- UKRAINE   Lose
- UAE   Lose
- UNITED KINGDOM   Retain
- URUGUAY   Lose
- UZBEKISTAN   Lose
- VANUATU   Lose
- VENEZUELA   Lose
- VIETNAM   Retain
- YEMEN   Lose
- YUGOSLAVIA   Unknown
- ZAMBIA   Lose
- ZIMBABWE   Lose

APPENDIX 15-2

Form DS-4080: Oath/Affirmation of Renunciation of Nationality of United States

U. S. Department of State

BUREAU OF CONSULAR AFFAIRS

OATH/AFFIRMATION OF RENUNCIATION OF NATIONALITY OF UNITED STATES

_____ at _____

(Embassy/Consulate)

_____ ss:

(Country)

I, _____, a national of the United States,

Name (Print Full Name)

solemnly swear/affirm that I was born at _____,

(City or Town)

_____ , _____ , on _____

(Province or County)   (State or Country)   Date (mm-dd-yyyy)

That I formerly resided in the United States at:

_____

(Street Address)

_____

(City, State and ZIP Code)

That I am a national of the United States by virtue of:

☐ Birth in United States or Abroad to U.S. Parent(s)

☐ Naturalization   Date of Naturalization _____

Date (mm-dd-yyyy)

(If naturalized, give the name and place of the court in the United States before which naturalization was granted.)

_____

(Name of Court)

_____

(Street Address)

_____

(City, State and ZIP Code)

I desire and hereby make a formal renunciation of my U.S. nationality, as provided by section 349(a)(5) of the Immigration and Nationality Act of 1952, as amended, and pursuant thereto, I hereby absolutely and entirely renounce my United States nationality together with all rights and privileges and all duties and allegiance and fidelity thereunto pertaining. I make this renunciation intentionally, voluntarily, and of my own free will, free of any duress or undue influence.

_____ ,

(Signature)

Subscribed and sworn/affirmed to before me this _____ day of _____ , _____

at the _____ _____

(Embassy/Consulate)   (Place)

_____

(Signature of Officer)

SEAL   _____

(Typed Name of Officer)

_____

(Title of Officer)

Note: A renunciation of United States nationality/citizenship is effective only upon approval by the U.S. Department of State but, when approved, the loss of nationality/citizenship occurs as of the date the above Oath/Affirmation was taken.

DS-4080
01-2013

Page 1 of 1

1288

APPENDIX 15-3

Form DS-4081: Statement of Understanding Concerning the Consequences and Ramifications of Relinquishment or Renunciation of U.S. Citizenship

U. S. Department of State
Bureau of Consular Affairs

STATEMENT OF UNDERSTANDING CONCERNING THE CONSEQUENCES AND RAMIFICATIONS OF RENUNCIATION OR RELINQUISHMENT OF U.S. CITIZENSHIP

I, _____ , understand that:

1. I have the right to renounce/relinquish my United States citizenship.

2. I have the intention of relinquishing my United States citizenship.

3. I am exercising my right of renunciation/relinquishment freely and voluntarily without force, compulsion or undue influence placed upon me by any person.

4. Upon renouncing/relinquishing my U.S. citizenship, I will become an alien with respect to the United States, subject to all laws and procedures of the United States regarding entry and control of aliens.

5. If I do not possess the nationality/citizenship of any country other than the United States, upon my renunciation/relinquishment I will become a stateless person and may face extreme difficulties traveling internationally and entering most countries and maintaining a place to reside.

6. If I am found to be deportable by a foreign country, my renunciation/relinquishment may not prevent my involuntary return to the United States.

7. My renunciation/relinquishment may not affect my military or selective service status, if any. I understand that any problems in this area must be resolved with the appropriate agencies.

8. My renunciation/relinquishment may not affect my liability, if any, to prosecution for any crimes which I may have committed or may commit in the future which violate United States law.

9. My renunciation/relinquishment may not affect my liability for extradition to the United States.

10. My renunciation/relinquishment may not exempt me from United States income taxation. With regard to United States taxation consequences, I understand that I must contact the United States Internal Revenue Service. Further, I understand that if my renunciation of United States citizenship is determined by the United States Attorney General to be motivated by tax avoidance purposes, I will be found excludable from the United States under Immigration and Nationality Act, as amended.

11. Upon renouncing/relinquishing my U.S. citizenship, I will no longer be able to transmit U.S. citizenship to my children born subsequent to this act.

12. The extremely serious and irrevocable nature of the act of renunciation/relinquishment has been explained to me by the *(Vice)* consul _____ at the American Embassy/Consulate General at _____ . I fully understand its consequences.

I: ☐ do ☐ do not choose to make a separate written explanation of my reasons for renouncing/relinquishing my United States citizenship. I: ☐ swear ☐ affirm that I have: ☐ read ☐ had read to me this statement in the _____ language and fully understand its contents.

Name *(Typed)* _____

Signature _____

CONSULAR OFFICER'S ATTESTATION

_____ appeared personally and: ☐ read   ☐ had read to him/her

this statement after my explanation of its meaning and the consequences of renunciation/relinquishment of United States

citizenship and signed this statement: ☐ under oath   ☐ by affirmation   before me this _____ day of

(Day)

_____ , _____
(Month)   (Year)

SEAL

_____
Consul of the United States of America

DS-4081   Page 2 of 2

APPENDIX 15-4

Form DS-4079: Request for Determination of Possible Loss of United States Citizenship

U. S. Department of State

BUREAU OF CONSULAR AFFAIRS

OMB NO. 1405-0178
EXPIRES: 12/31/2013
Estimated Burden -15 minutes

**REQUEST FOR DETERMINATION OF POSSIBLE LOSS OF
UNITED STATES CITIZENSHIP**

The following information is needed to determine your present citizenship status and possible loss of U.S. citizenship. You cannot lose U.S. citizenship unless you VOLUNTARILY perform an act designated by U.S. statute and do so with the intent to relinquish U.S. citizenship. You are advised to consult an attorney before completing this form. If you have any questions about the form, you should discuss them with a member of our consular staff before completing the form. You are requested to complete this form carefully. Use extra paper as needed and attach any supporting documents to this form.

PART I		
1. Name *(Last, First, MI)*	2. Date of Birth *(mm-dd-yyyy)*	3. Place of Birth
4. (a) Last U.S. Passport Number	(b) Issued at *(Place)*	(c) Issued on *(Date)* *(mm-dd-yyyy)*

5. If not born in the United States, did you acquire citizenship by birth outside the United States to U.S. citizen parent(s): ☐ Yes ☐ No;

or Naturalization? *(Naturalization petitions prior to 11/29/1990 were submitted to and adjudicated by a court. After that date they were submitted to and adjudicated by INS/USCIS.)* ☐ Yes ☐ No

(a) Name of Naturalizing Court/Office _____ (b) Date of Naturalization *(mm-dd-yyyy)* _____

Dates and Countries of Residence Outside the United States Since Birth

Date *(From) (mm-dd-yyyy)*	Date *(To) (mm-dd-yyyy)*	Country

6. When did you first become aware that you might be a United States citizen *(Give Approximate Date)*?

7. How did you find out that you are a citizen of the United States? *(For example, did you always know you were a U.S. citizen? If not, when did you learn about your citizenship? Did someone tell you that you are a U.S. citizen?)*

8. Are you a national or citizen of any other country other than the United States? ☐ Yes ☐ No

(a) If yes, of what country? _____

(b) If yes, did you acquire that citizenship in the foreign country by:

(i) Birth? ☐ Yes ☐ No

(ii) Marriage? ☐ Yes ☐ No

(iii) Naturalization or registration; if yes, please provide a date *(mm-dd-yyyy)* _____ ☐ Yes ☐ No

DS-4079 *(Formerly FS-581)*
12-2011

(If more space is needed, use additional paper)

Page 1 of 5

1291

(c) If other, explain.

(d) If you checked YES to question 8 (B) part (iii) by what means, or in what kind of proceeding, were you naturalized as a citizen of a foreign state?

9. Have you taken an oath or made an affirmation or other formal declaration of allegiance to a foreign state? ☐ Yes ☐ No

   If yes, please provide a date *(mm-dd-yyyy)* and country _____ _____

  (a) If you checked YES to question 8 or 9 or both, what was the nature of the oath you took? What were the words used? If you have a copy of the oath please attach it.

10. Have you served in the armed forces of a foreign state? ☐ Yes ☐ No

  (a) If so, what country? _____

  (b) In which branch of the armed forces did you serve? _____

  (c) Dates of Service *(mm-dd-yyyy)* _____ _____

  (d) What ranks did you hold? _____

  (e) What was your highest rank? _____

  (f) What responsibilities did you have and what functions and activities were you engaged in?

  (g) Did you take an oath? If so, describe the oath. ☐ Yes ☐ No

11. Have you accepted, served in, or performed the duties of any office, post or employment with the government of a foreign state? ☐ Yes ☐ No

  (a) If yes, please provide dates of service, country and the job title

_____ _____ _____

_____ _____ _____

_____ _____ _____

_____ _____ _____

  (b) What were your duties and responsibilities for each of the foreign government jobs you held?

(c) Did you take an oath, affirmation, declaration or allegiance in connection with the job? If yes, describe the oath,   ☐ Yes   ☐ No
    affirmation, declaration or allegiance.

12. What ties did you have to the country where you performed the act or acts indicated in Questions 8-11? For example:

(a) Did you maintain a residence? If yes, please explain.   ☐ Yes   ☐ No

(b) Did you own property? If yes, please explain.   ☐ Yes   ☐ No

(c) Do you have family or social ties? If yes, please explain.   ☐ Yes   ☐ No

(d) Do you vote? If yes, please explain.   ☐ Yes   ☐ No

(e) What other ties did you have to the country where you performed the act or acts indicated in Questions 8-11?

13. What ties do you retain with the United States? For example:

(a) Do you maintain a residence? If yes, please explain.   ☐ Yes   ☐ No

(b) Do you own property? If yes, please explain.   ☐ Yes   ☐ No

(c) Do you have family or social ties? If yes, please explain.   ☐ Yes   ☐ No

(d) Do you vote? If yes, please explain.   ☐ Yes   ☐ No

(e) Do you file U.S. income or other tax returns? If yes, please explain.   ☐ Yes   ☐ No

(f) Do you maintain a profession, occupation, or license in the United States? If yes, please explain.   ☐ Yes ☐ No

(g) Have you registered your children as citizens of the United States?   ☐ Yes ☐ No

14. What passport do you use to travel to and from the United States?

15. What passport do you use to travel to and from other countries?

16. Have you renounced your U.S. nationality at a U.S. Consulate or Embassy? If yes, provide a date and place.   ☐ Yes ☐ No

_____   _____

17. Describe in detail the circumstances under which you performed the act or acts indicated in Questions 8-16.

18. Did you perform the act or acts voluntarily?   ☐ Yes ☐ No

(a) If not, in what sense was your performance of the act or acts involuntary?

(b) Did you perform the acts with the intent to relinquish U.S. citizenship? If so, please explain your answer.   ☐ Yes ☐ No

19. Did you know that by performing the act described in Questions 8-18 you might lose U.S. citizenship? Please explain your answer.

20. Your answers on this form will become part of the official record in your case. Before signing this form, you are advised to consider consulting with an attorney, and to read over your answers to make certain that they are as complete and accurate as possible. If you would like to provide additional information you believe relevant to a determination of your citizenship status, and in particular to your intention or lack of intention to relinquish U.S. citizenship, you may attach separate sheets with that information.

If your answer to each of the questions above is "No," please sign below before a Consular Officer at a U.S. Embassy or Consulate. If you answered "Yes", to one or more of questions 8(b)(iii)-11 and your action was completely VOLUNTARY, please continue with PART II.

Subscribed and Sworn

[SEAL]   _____
                          Signature

                _____
                Signature of Consular Officer

DS-4079   (If more space is needed, use additional paper)   Page 4 of 5

21. **You should be aware that under United States law, a citizen may lose U.S. citizenship if he/she voluntarily performs any of the acts specified above in questions 8(b)(iii)-11 with the intent of relinquishing United States citizenship. If you voluntarily performed an act stated above with the intent to relinquish United States citizenship, you may sign Part II of this statement before a Consular Officer at a U.S. Embassy or Consulate. The U.S. Consulate or Embassy will prepare the forms necessary to document your loss of U.S. citizenship.**

PART II

STATEMENT OF VOLUNTARY RELINQUISHMENT OF U.S. CITIZENSHIP

Subscribed and Sworn

I, _____ , performed the act of expatriation indicated in Questions 8-19,

voluntarily and with the intent to relinquish my U.S. citizenship.

[SEAL]

| _____ | _____ |
| Signature | Date *(mm-dd-yyyy)* |

| _____ | _____ |
| Signature of Consular Officer | Date *(mm-dd-yyyy)* |

PRIVACY ACT STATEMENT

AUTHORITIES: The information on this form is requested under the authority of 8 U.S.C. 1104, 1481, 1483, 1488, and 1501, and 22 U.S.C. 212. Although furnishing the information is voluntary, applicants may not be eligible for a U.S. passport or for relinquishment or renunciation of U.S. nationality if they do not provide the required information.

PURPOSE: The principal purpose of gathering this information is to determine if the individual performed a potentially expatriating act as defined in 8 U.S.C. 1481 voluntarily and with the intention of relinquishing U.S. nationality.

ROUTINE USES: The information solicited on this form may be made available to foreign government agencies to fulfill passport control and immigration duties, to investigate or prosecute violations of law, or when a request for information is made pursuant to customary international practice. In the event a finding of loss of nationality is made, the information solicited on this form may be made available to other federal entities with law enforcement responsibilities relating to or affected by nationality, including but not limited to the U.S. Citizenship and Immigration Service, the Internal Revenue Service, and the Federal Bureau of Investigation. The information provided also may be released to federal, state or local agencies for law enforcement, counter-terrorism and homeland security purposes; to Congress and courts within their sphere of jurisdiction; and to other federal agencies for certain personnel and records management matters.

Paperwork Reduction Act (PRA) Statement

Public reporting burden for this collection of information is estimated to average 15 minutes per response, including time required for searching existing data sources, gathering the necessary documentation, providing the information and/or documents required, and reviewing the final collection. You do not have to supply this information unless this collection displays a currently valid OMB control number. If you have comments on the accuracy of this burden estimate and/or recommendations for reducing it, please send them to: A/GIS/DIR, Room 2400 SA-22, U.S. Department of State, Washington, DC 20522-2202.

Table of Laws and Rules

UNITED STATES CONSTITUTION

ANTI-DRUG ABUSE ACT OF 1988

CHILD CITIZENSHIP ACT OF 2000

CONTROLLED SUBSTANCES ACT

HOMELAND SECURITY ACT OF 2002

ILLEGAL IMMIGRATION REFORM AND IMMIGRANT RESPONSIBILITY ACT OF 1996

IMMIGRATION AND NATIONALITY ACT

IMMIGRATION AND NATIONALITY ACT—Continued

IMMIGRATION AND NATIONALITY ACT—Continued

IMMIGRATION AND NATIONALITY ACT—Continued

IMMIGRATION AND NATIONALITY ACT—Continued

IMMIGRATION AND NATIONALITY TECHNICAL CORRECTIONS ACT OF 1994

IMMIGRATION ACT OF 1990

IMMIGRATION AND NATIONALITY ACT AMENDMENTS OF 1986

IMMIGRATION REFORM AND CONTROL ACT

IMMIGRATION TECHNICAL CORRECTIONS ACT OF 1988

MICELLANEOUS AND TECHNICAL IMMIGRATION AND NATURALIZATION AMENDMENTS OF 1991

UNITED STATES CODE ANNOTATED

UNITED STATES CODE ANNOTATED—Continued

UNITED STATES CODE ANNOTATED—Continued

UNITED STATES CODE ANNOTATED—Continued

UNITED STATES CODE ANNOTATED—Continued

UNITED STATES CODE ANNOTATED—Continued

UNITED STATES PUBLIC LAWS

UNITED STATES PUBLIC LAWS—Continued

UNITED STATES PUBLIC LAWS—Continued

UNITED STATES STATUTES AT LARGE

CODE OF FEDERAL REGULATIONS

CODE OF FEDERAL REGULATIONS—Continued

CODE OF FEDERAL REGULATIONS—Continued

CODE OF FEDERAL REGULATIONS—Continued

CODE OF FEDERAL REGULATIONS—Continued

CODE OF FEDERAL REGULATIONS—Continued

FEDERAL RULES OF CIVIL PROCEDURE

FEDERAL RULES OF EVIDENCE

DEPARTMENT OF STATE FOREIGN AFFAIRS MANUAL

DEPARTMENT OF STATE FOREIGN AFFAIRS MANUAL—Continued

DEPARTMENT OF STATE FOREIGN AFFAIRS MANUAL—Continued

IMMIGRATION AND NATURALIZATION SERVICE INTERPRETATIONS

IMMIGRATION AND NATURALIZATION SERVICE
INTERPRETATIONS—Continued

IMMIGRATION AND NATURALIZATION SERVICE
INTERPRETATIONS—Continued

IMMIGRATION AND NATURALIZATION SERVICE OPERATIONS INSTRUCTIONS

INTERNAL REVENUE SERVICE NOTICE

INTERNAL REVENUE SERVICE REVENUE RULINGS

FEDERAL REGISTER

FEDERAL REGISTER—Continued

UNIFORM PROBATE CODE

Index

THOMSON REUTERS IMMIGRATION LAW LIBRARY

Available from Thomson Reuters
Opperman Drive, St. Paul, MN 55164
(800) 344-5009 or your Thomson Reuters representative

ISBN 978-0-314-611

9 780314 611703